INGENIX.
*e*solutions

Electronic coding, billing and reimbursement products.

Ingenix provides a robust suite of eSolutions to solve a wide variety of coding, billing and reimbursement issues. As the industry moves to electronic products, you can rely on Ingenix to help support you through the transition.

← Web-based applications for all markets

← Dedicated support

← Environmentally responsible

Key Features and Benefits

Using eSolutions is a step in the right direction when it comes to streamlining your coding, billing and reimbursement practices. Ingenix eSolutions can help you save time and increase your efficiency with accurate and on-time content.

SAVE UP TO 20%
with source code FB11B

 Visit **www.shopingenix.com** and enter the source code to save 20%.

 Call toll-free **1.800.INGENIX** (464.3649), option 1 and save 15%.

- **Simplify ICD-10 transition.** ICD-10 mapping tools provide crosswalks between ICD-9-CM and ICD-10 codes quickly and easily

- **Save time and money.** Ingenix eSolutions combine the content of over 37 code books and data files

- **Increase accuracy.** Electronic solutions are updated regularly so you know you're always working with the most current content available

- **Get the training and support you need.** Convenient, monthly webinars and customized training programs are available to meet your specific needs

- **Rely on a leader in health care.** Ingenix has been producing quality coding products for over 26 years. All of the expert content that goes into our books goes into our electronic resources

- **Get Started.** Visit shopingenix.com/ eSolutions for product listing

D1569978

100% Money Back Guarantee If our merchandise ever fails to meet your expectations, please contact our Customer Service Department toll-free at 1.800.INGENIX (464.3649), option 1, for an immediate response. Software: Credit will be granted for unopened packages only.

Also available from your medical bookstore or distributor.

FB11B

INGENIX®

2011 Essential Coding Resources

ICD-9-CM Resources
Available: Sept 2010

CPT® Coding Resources
Available: Dec 2010

HCPCS Resources
Available: Dec 2010

SAVE UP TO 20%

with source code FB11D

 Visit **www.shopingenix.com** and enter the source code to save 20%.

 Call toll-free **1.800.INGENIX** (464.3649), option 1 and save 15%.

2011 Essential Coding Resources

Looks can be deceiving. Competitors attempt to imitate Ingenix code books because interpreting coding and reimbursement rules correctly and understanding the professional workflow is what we've helped coding professionals do successfully for over 25 years. Count on Ingenix to deliver accurate information, familiar features, industry-leading content, and innovative additions that help you improve coding practices, comply with HIPAA code set regulations, and realize proper reimbursement.

← A professional team's expertise

← Trusted and proven ICD-9-CM, CPT® and HCPCS coding resources

← Industry-leading content

← More value, competitive prices

Key Features and Benefits

Select from a range of formats for your ICD-9-CM, CPT,® and HCPCS coding resources to fit your individual preferences, skill level, business needs, and budget—you can trust your resource to be accurate and complimentary to your daily work when it's under an Ingenix cover.

2011 ICD-9-CM

Physician, Hospital, Home Health, and Skilled Nursing (with Inpatient Rehabilitation and Hospices) editions available

- New Look! Modified font and more vibrant colors increase readability
- New! Highlighted coding informational notes
- New! Snap-in tab dividers (*Expert* spiral editions only)
- More official coding tips and ICD-10 Spotlight codes
- Hallmark additional digit required symbols, intuitive color-coded symbols and alerts, QuickFlip™ color bleed tabs, dictionary headers, and symbol keys

2011 Current Procedural Coding Expert

- Code "Resequencing" identification
- Interventional radiology guidance section
- Reimbursement and mid-year changes information not found in the American Medical Association's CPT® code books
- Easy-to-navigate design
- Comprehensive and up-to-date listings with an extensive, user-friendly index
- PQRI icons and appendix

2011 HCPCS Level II Expert

- Comprehensive code updates for accurate reporting of supplies and services in physician, hospital outpatient, and ASC settings
- User-friendly format and expanded index to ease code look-up
- Important coding indicators and icons, PQRI icons, detailed illustrations, glossary of terms, and special MUEs

---

Ingenix | Information is the Lifeblood of Health Care | Call toll-free 1.800.INGENIX (464.3649), option 1.

100% Money Back Guarantee If our merchandise ever fails to meet your expectations, please contact our Customer Service Department toll-free at 1.800.INGENIX (464.3649), option 1, for an immediate response. Software: Credit will be granted for unopened packages only.

Also available from your medical bookstore or distributor. CPT is a registered trademark of the American Medical Association.   FB11D

INGENIX®

Coders' Desk Reference
for ICD-9-CM
Procedures

2011

Ingenix Notice

Coders' Desk Reference for ICD-9-CM Procedures was conceived to be an accurate and authoritative source of information about coding and reimbursement issues. Every effort has been made to verify accuracy and information is believed reliable at the time of publication. Absolute accuracy cannot be guaranteed, however. This publication is made available with the understanding that the publisher is not engaged in rendering legal or other services requiring a professional license. Please address questions regarding this product to the Ingenix customer service department at:

1.800.INGENIX (464.3649), option 1
or email us at customerservice@ingenix.com.

Acknowledgments

The following staff contributed to the development and/or production of this book:

Anita C. Hart, RHIA, CCS, CCS-P, *Product Manager*
Karen Schmidt, BSN, *Technical Director*
Stacy Perry, *Desktop Publishing Manager*
Lisa Singley, *Project Manager*
Beth Ford, RHIT, CCS, *Clinical/Technical Editor*
Temeka Lewis, MBS, CCS, *Clinical/Technical Editor*
Tracy Betzler, *Desktop Publishing Specialist*
Hope M. Dunn, *Desktop Publishing Specialist*
Toni Stewart, *Desktop Publishing Specialist*
Kate Holden, *Editor*
Kimberli Turner, *Editor*

All rights reserved. No part of this publication may be reproduced or transmitted in any form or by any means, electronic or mechanical, including photocopy, recording, or storage in a database or retrieval system, without the prior written permission of the publisher. Printed in the United States of America.

© Ingenix 2010

Made in the USA

ISBN 978-1-60151-405-9

About the Technical Editors

Beth Ford, RHIT, CCS

Ms. Ford is a clinical/technical editor for Ingenix. She has extensive background in both physician and facility ICD-9-CM and CPT/HCPCS coding. Ms. Ford has served as a coding specialist, coding manager, coding trainer/educator, and coding consultant, as well as a health information management director. She is an active member of the American Health Information Management Association (AHIMA).

Temeka Lewis, MBA, CCS

Ms. Lewis is a clinical/technical editor for Ingenix with expertise in hospital and physician coding. Her areas of expertise include ICD-9-CM, CPT, and HCPCS coding. Ms Lewis's past experience includes conducting coding audits and physician education, teaching ICD-9-CM and CPT coding, participating in a revenue cycle team, chargemaster maintenance, and writing compliance newsletters. Most recently she was responsible for coding and compliance in a specialty hospital. She is an active member of the American Health Information Management Association (AHIMA).

Our Commitment to Accuracy

Ingenix is committed to producing accurate and reliable materials.

To report corrections, please visit www.ingenixonline.com/accuracy or email accuracy@ingenix.com. You can also reach customer service by calling 1.800.INGENIX (464.3649), option 1.

Contents

© 2010 Ingenix

Volume 3 Procedure Codes: 2011 Highlights

Annual changes were made to ICD-9-CM Volume 3 procedures for 2011. Twenty-two new codes were added effective October 1, 2010. Of these procedures, code 39.8 was expanded to the subcategory level, creating nine new codes, eight of which classify carotid sinus stimulation device procedures. New procedure codes are distributed as follows throughout the procedure classification. The following list highlights some of the changes for 2011:

- 00 Procedures and Interventions, Not elsewhere classified—One new drug-eluting stent code
- 01-05 Operations on the Nervous System—Two new cranial neurostimulator procedure codes
- 17 Other Miscellaneous Diagnostic and Therapeutic Procedures—One new code to classify noncoronary intraoperative fluorescence vascular angiography
- 30-34 Operations on the Respiratory System—One new bronchoscopic bronchial thermoplasty code
- 35-39 Operations on the Cardiovascular System—Twelve new codes, eight of which classify carotid sinus stimulation device procedures
- 76-84 Operations on the Musculoskeletal System—Two new codes to classify reverse total shoulder replacement, and insertion of sternal fixation device
- 85-86 Operations of the Integumentary System—Three new fat graft procedure codes

Volume 3 revisions include 22 revised code titles, the majority of which occur in subcategories 81.0 Spinal fusion and 81.3 Refusion of spine to specify anatomic site as well as the approach. Instructional notes were added to these subcategories to clarify technique specific to anatomic site of procedure. Multiple includes and excludes note changes were made to subcategory 37.3 Pericardiectomy and excision of lesion of heart, to appropriately designate operative approach. Exclusion terms were added to category 85 Operations on the breast to facilitate appropriate classification of fat grafts and category 86 Operations on the skin and subcutaneous tissue to direct the coder to code 01.20 for cranial neurostimulator procedures.

- **Superficial femoral artery drug-eluting stent**

  A new code was added to subcategory 00.6 Procedures on blood vessels to provide a unique classification code for the insertion of a drug-eluting stent in the superficial femoral artery used to treat severe, obstructive atherosclerotic lesions. This code describes the deployment of a thin, specialized self-durable metal stent that targets delivery of a drug (paclitaxel) directly to the arterial lesion to restore blood flow. Additional codes are assigned as appropriate, including angioplasty (39.50) and number of stents inserted (00.45-00.48).

- **Cranial neurostimulator**

  Two new codes were added to subcategory 01.2 Craniotomy and craniectomy to report the implantation, replacement, or removal of a responsive neurostimulator system (RNS). These devices are specifically designed to treat adults with medically refractory localization-related (focal) (partial) epilepsy. Lead implantation is separately reported (02.93).

- **Noncoronary intraoperative fluorescence vascular angiography [IFVA]**

  A new code was added to subcategory 17.7 Other diagnostic and therapeutic procedures to report noncoronary IFVA. This technology is used during bypass surgery to assess function of venous and arterial vessels and blood perfusion in tissues and organs. Code 88.59 was previously assigned for both coronary and noncoronary surgical procedures. New code 17.71 has been created to specifically identify IFVA of noncoronary sites.

- **Bronchoscopic bronchial thermoplasty**

  New code 32.27 reports a bronchoscopic procedure in which radiofrequency (RF)-based technology is applied to the smooth muscle of the tracheobronchial tree and lungs for the treatment of severe asthma. Previously, this procedure was reported with code 32.26 Other and unspecified ablation of lung lesion or tissue, which did not clearly describe the procedure.

- **Percutaneous mitral valve repair with implant**

  New code 35.97 specifically reports a minimally invasive transcatheter approach for intracardiac mitral valve repair. It is performed by interventional cardiologists in the cardiac catheterization laboratory or operating room as an alternative to the open heart surgical approach. Any transesophageal echocardiography (TEE) performed during the operative episode (88.72) is reported separately.

- **Thoracoscopic cardiac ablation (maze) procedure**

  New code 37.37 reports an ablation procedure performed via thoracoscope to treat atrial fibrillation. This procedure creates lesions in the tissue of the left and right atrium of the heart that interrupt the abnormal electrical currents of atrial fibrillation to restore normal sinus rhythm. Code 37.37 includes a modified maze procedure by thoracoscopic approach.

- **Central venous catheter (CVC) placement with guidance**

  New code 38.97 reports CVC placement by guidance, including electrocardiogram, fluoroscopy, and ultrasound. CVC placement without guidance is excluded from this new code and reported with code 38.93.

- **Carotid sinus stimulation**

  Code 39.8 has been expanded to the fourth-digit level to include new codes 39.81–39.88, which report baroreflex activation device procedures. These procedures report implantable medical device procedures designed to electrically activate the baroreflex; the system helps regulate cardiovascular function to treat primary hypertension and hypertensive heart failure recalcitrant to medical therapy. Other procedures previously classified to code 39.8 are now classified to new code 39.89.

- **Reverse total shoulder replacement**

  New code 81.88 reports a surgical alternative to conventional total shoulder replacement, mainly for patients who suffer rotator cuff arthropathy. This procedure does not report conversion of prior (failed) total shoulder replacement (arthroplasty), which is classified to code 81.97.

- **Sternal fixation device with rigid plates**

  New code 84.94 reports a rigid plate sternal fixation system consisting of implanted plates and screws that can significantly reduce the incidence of sternal wound dehiscence and subsequent deep sternal wound infections

(DSWI) in certain cardiothoracic surgery patients. This procedure was previously classified to code 78.51.

- **Fat graft procedures**

  Three new codes have been added to describe certain fat graft procedures. Previously, ICD-9-CM did not provide specific codes for harvesting or placing fat grafts used in reconstructive surgery. New code 85.55 reports extraction of fat for autologous graft, fat transplantation, or transfer, micro-fat grafting, injection of fat graft of breast whereas new code 86.87 reports fat grafting procedures of skin and subcutaneous tissues of other anatomic sites. New code 86.90 specifically identifies extraction of fat for graft or banking.

New 2011 Volume 3 Procedure Codes:

The following are new valid Volume 3 procedure codes for 2011:

00.60	Insertion of drug-eluting stent(s) of superficial femoral artery
01.20	Cranial implantation or replacement of neurostimulator pulse generator
01.29	Removal of cranial neurostimulator pulse generator
17.71	Non-coronary intra-operative fluorescence vascular angiography [IFVA]
32.27	Bronchoscopic bronchial thermoplasty, ablation of airway smooth muscle
35.97	Percutaneous mitral valve repair with implant
37.37	Excision or destruction or other lesion or tissue of heart, thoracoscopic approach
38.97	Central venous catheter placement with guidance
39.81	Implantation or replacement of carotid sinus stimulation device, total system
39.82	Implantation or replacement of carotid sinus stimulation lead(s) only
39.83	Implantation or replacement of carotid sinus stimulation pulse generator only
39.84	Revision of carotid sinus stimulation lead(s) only
39.85	Revision of carotid sinus stimulation pulse generator
39.86	Removal of carotid sinus stimulation device, total system
39.87	Removal of carotid sinus stimulation lead(s) only
39.88	Removal of carotid sinus stimulation pulse generator only
39.89	Other operations on carotid body, carotid sinus and other vascular bodies
81.88	Reverse total shoulder replacement

© 2010 Ingenix

84.94	Insertion of sternal fixation device with rigid plates
85.55	Fat graft to breast

86.87	Fat graft of skin and subcutaneous tissue
86.90	Extraction of fat for graft or banking

- **Percutaneous mitral valve repair with implant**

  New code 35.97 specifically reports a minimally invasive transcatheter approach for intracardiac mitral valve repair. It is performed by interventional cardiologists in the cardiac catheterization laboratory or operating room as an alternative to the open heart surgical approach. Any transesophageal echocardiography (TEE) performed during the operative episode (88.72) is reported separately.

- **Thoracoscopic cardiac ablation (maze) procedure**

  New code 37.37 reports an ablation procedure performed via thoracoscope to treat atrial fibrillation. This procedure creates lesions in the tissue of the left and right atrium of the heart that interrupt the abnormal electrical currents of atrial fibrillation to restore normal sinus rhythm. Code 37.37 includes a modified maze procedure by thoracoscopic approach.

- **Central venous catheter (CVC) placement with guidance**

  New code 38.97 reports CVC placement by guidance, including electrocardiogram, fluoroscopy, and ultrasound. CVC placement without guidance is excluded from this new code and reported with code 38.93.

- **Carotid sinus stimulation**

  Code 39.8 has been expanded to the fourth-digit level to include new codes 39.81–39.88, which report baroreflex activation device procedures. These procedures report implantable medical device procedures designed to electrically activate the baroreflex; the system helps regulate cardiovascular function to treat primary hypertension and hypertensive heart failure recalcitrant to medical therapy. Other procedures previously classified to code 39.8 are now classified to new code 39.89.

- **Reverse total shoulder replacement**

  New code 81.88 reports a surgical alternative to conventional total shoulder replacement, mainly for patients who suffer rotator cuff arthropathy. This procedure does not report conversion of prior (failed) total shoulder replacement (arthroplasty), which is classified to code 81.97.

- **Sternal fixation device with rigid plates**

  New code 84.94 reports a rigid plate sternal fixation system consisting of implanted plates and screws that can significantly reduce the incidence of sternal wound dehiscence and subsequent deep sternal wound infections

(DSWI) in certain cardiothoracic surgery patients. This procedure was previously classified to code 78.51.

- **Fat graft procedures**

  Three new codes have been added to describe certain fat graft procedures. Previously, ICD-9-CM did not provide specific codes for harvesting or placing fat grafts used in reconstructive surgery. New code 85.55 reports extraction of fat for autologous graft, fat transplantation, or transfer, micro-fat grafting, injection of fat graft of breast whereas new code 86.87 reports fat grafting procedures of skin and subcutaneous tissues of other anatomic sites. New code 86.90 specifically identifies extraction of fat for graft or banking.

New 2011 Volume 3 Procedure Codes:

The following are new valid Volume 3 procedure codes for 2011:

00.60	Insertion of drug-eluting stent(s) of superficial femoral artery
01.20	Cranial implantation or replacement of neurostimulator pulse generator
01.29	Removal of cranial neurostimulator pulse generator
17.71	Non-coronary intra-operative fluorescence vascular angiography [IFVA]
32.27	Bronchoscopic bronchial thermoplasty, ablation of airway smooth muscle
35.97	Percutaneous mitral valve repair with implant
37.37	Excision or destruction or other lesion or tissue of heart, thoracoscopic approach
38.97	Central venous catheter placement with guidance
39.81	Implantation or replacement of carotid sinus stimulation device, total system
39.82	Implantation or replacement of carotid sinus stimulation lead(s) only
39.83	Implantation or replacement of carotid sinus stimulation pulse generator only
39.84	Revision of carotid sinus stimulation lead(s) only
39.85	Revision of carotid sinus stimulation pulse generator
39.86	Removal of carotid sinus stimulation device, total system
39.87	Removal of carotid sinus stimulation lead(s) only
39.88	Removal of carotid sinus stimulation pulse generator only
39.89	Other operations on carotid body, carotid sinus and other vascular bodies
81.88	Reverse total shoulder replacement

© 2010 Ingenix

84.94 Insertion of sternal fixation device with rigid plates

85.55 Fat graft to breast

86.87 Fat graft of skin and subcutaneous tissue

86.90 Extraction of fat for graft or banking

Introduction

Coding is a complicated business and it's not enough to have a current copy of an ICD-9-CM book. Medical coders also need dictionaries and specialty references if they are to accurately translate operative reports into procedure codes. Experienced coders have been frustrated by limited guidance accompanying ICD-9-CM procedure codes and beginning coders need direction on proper usage of Volume 3 procedure codes. Ingenix developed *Coders' Desk Reference for ICD-9-CM Procedures* to provide a resource with answers to ICD-9-CM Volume 3 procedure coding questions.

Coders' Desk Reference for ICD-9-CM Procedures provides coders, coding managers, medical staff and health care professionals, payers, educators, and students with a comprehensive and informative guide to the ICD-9-CM procedure code set. The goal is to enrich the user's understanding of the conventions of ICD-9-CM Volume 3 procedures. The result is improved coding confidence, so code selection becomes more accurate and efficient.

Coders' Desk Reference for ICD-9-CM Procedures includes numeric codes contained in Volume 3 of ICD-9-CM with code-specific information and issues affecting code selection. The correct application of codes is demonstrated using coding scenarios that teach specific ICD-9-CM procedure codes. Detailed descriptions using terminology coders see in medical documents, together with coding clarification and guidance, coding scenarios, and important instruction regarding ICD-9-CM conventions for Volume 3, make *Coders' Desk Reference for ICD-9-CM Procedures* an unparalleled guidebook to code selection.

Coders' Desk Reference for ICD-9-CM Procedures completes the *Coders' Desk Reference* product line to cover all core segments of coding. This product is similar in function and design to the *Coders' Desk Reference for Diagnoses*; both are comprehensive resources that work hand in hand with the ICD-9-CM code book. When more coding or clinical information concerning a diagnosis or procedure is needed than the classification system instructional notes and the official coding guidelines provide, the pertinent *Coders' Desk Reference* will answer the question.

Changes reflecting the dynamic world of coding are ongoing, and Ingenix encourages input for inclusion in future editions of the book.

Format

Coders' Desk Reference for ICD-9-CM Procedures is divided into convenient sections for easy use, with each section organized in numeric order. The basic format of the book provides clinical coding support with illustrations, narrative, and other resources that will help the user work from the medical record. The book begins with special chapters that provide detailed information on coding guidelines and conventions regarding ICD-9-CM Volume 3 procedure coding, as well as surgical terms, eponyms, and common abbreviations, acronyms, and symbols found in the medical record. It then follows the organization of ICD-9-CM, looking at procedures and their codes in numeric order.

ICD-9-CM Volume 3 Conventions

For the new coder, and even for the veteran, this chapter provides an overview of the ICD-9-CM book and detailed instructions on ICD-9-CM coding guidelines and conventions for Volume 3 procedure coding.

Abbreviations, Acronyms, and Symbols

The medical profession has its own shorthand for documentation. Here, acronyms, abbreviations, and symbols commonly seen on operative reports or medical charts are listed for easy reference.

Surgical Terms

Operative reports contain words and phrases that not only communicate the importance and urgency of surgery, but they communicate the techniques as well. *Coders' Desk Reference for ICD-9-CM Procedures'* glossary of surgical terms includes the terms most commonly used in operative reports to describe techniques and tools.

Procedural Eponyms

In the medical record, procedures are often documented by their common name or eponym. Eponyms honor the developer of a procedure or test, but do little to clarify what the procedure is. Editors have researched the procedural eponyms found in the Volume 3 index of the ICD-9-CM book and identified the associated procedure codes. This quick reference list is a convenient guide to the correct code selection.

Codes and Descriptions

Using common terminology found in the medical record, narrative describing ICD-9-CM procedure codes helps the user select the appropriate ICD-9-CM procedure code. For example:

35.01   Closed heart valvotomy, aortic valve

Description
Cardiopulmonary bypass is initiated. A purse string is placed in the left ventricular apex. The purse string is reinforced with small patches of Teflon felt. An incision is made in the center of the purse string. Blunt dilators are passed through the hole and across the aortic valve. Progressively larger dilators are inserted until the valve is wide open. The dilators break the scar tissues that are cut in an open aortic valvuloplasty. The valve leaflets are frequently damaged to the point that the valve must be replaced. After the valve is fully dilated, the purse string is tied off. Cardiopulmonary bypass is discontinued when heart function returns.

The brief descriptors help differentiate the codes and determine which code is best suited for a particular clinical situation.

Coding Clarification
These assist the user in clarifying coding problems and issues that may come up. For example:

> **Coding Clarification**
> Codes from subcategory 35.0 are inappropriate for reporting percutaneous (balloon) valvuloplasty, which is correctly reported with 35.96.

Documentation Tips
This section indicates specific documentation issues that may arise while coding. For example:

> **Documentation Tip**
> The use of this code would be inappropriate for reporting an inpatient procedure since it is considered a nonspecific code selection. If the operative report contains insufficient information for identification of the involved valve, the physician should be queried.

Coding Scenarios
The correct application of codes is demonstrated using coding scenarios that help improve overall coding accuracy and teach proper usage of specific ICD-9-CM procedure codes. For example:

Coding Scenario:
A 56-year-old female patient was admitted for mitral valvotomy. Previous cardiac work-up identified moderate mitral valve stenosis. The left chest was opened and the pericardium entered. A gloved finger was used to invert the left atrial appendage into the left atrium. The finger was placed across the mitral valve. Blunt tearing was used to open the areas between the leaflets that have been obliterated by scar tissue and inflammation. The finger was removed and the chest was closed.

Code assignment:
394.2   Mitral stenosis with insufficiency
35.02   Closed heart valvotomy, mitral valve
The coding scenarios will assist the user in understanding how to code in particular situations.

Coding Guidance
Listed with the ICD-9-CM codes is AHA's (American Hospital Association) *Coding Clinic for ICD-9-CM* references that help the user master correct coding practices. These identify diagnostic coding issues and answers on how to code for them properly, based on a patient situation. For example:

> **Coding Guidance**
> **AHA:** 1Q, '97, 13

1Q indicates 1st quarter, followed by the year, and 13 is the page number in AHA's *Coding Clinic for ICD-9-CM*.

Illustrations
Illustrations provide users a better understanding of the anatomical nuances associated with specific codes. Using clinically oriented illustrations also reinforces appropriate code selection. The illustrations usually include a labeled anatomical view, and may include narrative that discusses specific procedures or anatomic sites. The illustrations are almost always simplified schematic representations. In many instances, some detail is eliminated in order to make a clear point about the anatomic site that is the focus of the depiction.

    © 2010 Ingenix

ICD-9-CM Volume 3 Conventions

ICD-9-CM Overview

The ICD-9-CM system contains two classifications: one for diseases and the other for procedures. Volume 1 of ICD-9-CM is a tabular listing of diseases and injuries divided into 17 sections, generally along anatomic sites. Two supplementary classifications contain alphanumeric codes to report factors influencing health status and other contact with health services (V codes) and causes of injury and poisoning (E codes). Appendixes to Volume 1 provide additional information and references. Volume 2 is an alphabetic index of codes contained in Volume 1. An index to external causes of injury (E codes) is included, as well as three tables to assist in the selection of codes for hypertension, neoplasms, and drugs and chemicals.

Volume 3 also contains an alphabetic index and a tabular list. It is used to report procedures performed on hospital inpatients, although some payers require outpatient procedures be reported using the ICD-9-CM procedure classification system.

The procedure classification, like the diagnosis classification, is organized by body systems rather than surgical specialty. In general, most surgical procedures on a single body system appear together (e.g., operations on the nervous system are classified in categories 01–05, operations on the digestive system are classified in categories 42–54, etc.). One major exception is the last chapter, "Miscellaneous Diagnostic and Therapeutic Procedures," which lists nonsurgical procedures on all body systems. Similarly, the first chapter, 00 Procedures and Interventions, Not Elsewhere Classified, lists certain diagnostic and therapeutic procedures and interventions that are not included in specific body system chapters. These procedures often represent new and emerging technologies.

The ICD-9-CM procedure classification is numeric only, no alphabetic characters are used. The procedure classification is based on a two-digit category, which is subdivided to three- and four-digit codes for each chapter.

Alphabetic Index to Procedures

The procedure alphabetic index contains only one section, so all procedures—surgical, therapeutic, or diagnostic—are included in the single index. The index is referenced first when coding.

Main terms, which describe the type of procedure performed and not the anatomic site, are in boldface type. Main terms may be procedures, eponyms, or adjectives.

Examples:

Procedures—Biopsy, Bronchoplasty, Bypass

Eponyms—Bischoff operation, Brock operation, Burch procedure

Adjectives—Balloon, Blood, Bone

Anatomical sites are not used as main terms. For example, eyelid reconstruction would be found under the term for the procedure, "reconstruction," not under the term for the anatomical site, "eyelid."

Modifiers are listed with the main term providing the coder with additional information that may or may not be used in code selection. The Alphabetic Index places certain modifiers relevant to classifying the procedure in parentheses or indents them under the main term. When words are indented, they are also known as **subterms.** Indentation in the Alphabetic Index follows the same specific rules as the Alphabetic Index to Disease (i.e., each new level of terms is indented one standard indent space, or two character spaces).

The terms "as," "by," and "with" immediately follow the main term to which they refer. In the case where multiple prepositional references are present, they are listed in alphabetic sequence. Other prepositions, such as "for" and "through," which indicate a relationship between the main term and subterms, are treated according to standard alphabetizing rules.

The Alphabetic Index supplements the Tabular List because it contains many procedure terms that do not appear in the Tabular List. Terms listed in the categories of the Tabular List are not meant to be exhaustive; they serve as examples of the content of the category. In such cases, the instruction given in the Procedure Index is to be followed.

Example:

The procedure Alphabetic Index contains the entry "Estes operation (ovary) 65.72," but the Tabular List does not include "Estes operation" under 65.72. The coder should follow the instruction of the index and assign 65.72.

Procedure Tabular List

The Tabular List contains codes and their narrative descriptions. Unlike the Tabular List to Diseases, which is divided into three sections, the Tabular List to Procedures contains only one. All procedures, both surgical and diagnostic, are included in one list.

The procedure Tabular List contains 17 chapters with the majority dedicated to a major body system or anatomic site. The two exceptions are chapter 13, which identifies obstetrical procedures, and chapter 16, which includes therapeutic or diagnostic procedures not considered surgical. The procedure classification contains only numeric codes, from 00.01–99.99.

Each of the chapters in the ICD-9-CM Classification of Procedures is divided into two-digit categories based on anatomical site. The two-digit categories are subdivided with a decimal point followed by a third digit and in some cases a fourth.

Category (two digits): Each chapter begins with a two-digit category. For the code to be valid at least one additional digit must be assigned.

Subcategory (three digits): All two-digit categories have been further subdivided with the addition of a decimal point followed by another digit. The third digit provides more specificity with regard to the type of operative procedure or site.

Subclassification (four digits): Greater clinical detail with regard to surgical technique or diagnosis has been added with the expansion to four-digit subclassifications. Four-digit codes are the most precise subdivisions in the procedure classification.

In many cases, terminology used in a medical record cannot be found in the procedure index. The coder must look for synonyms in order to classify the procedure. When a term cannot be found in the procedure index, try locating synonyms in the index. Then, look up the code listed after the synonym in the procedure tabular. Scan all codes in the category to see if any apply and choose the most appropriate code.

For those procedures that have not been assigned a specific code, the procedure classification provides an "other" listing. This code usually is found at the end of a group of codes for specific procedures.

ICD-9-CM Conventions for Procedure Coding

The ICD-9-CM coding conventions used in the procedure classification system are similar to those used in the diagnosis classification including modifiers, abbreviations, instructional notes, and cross-references. Two conventions are shared by the Alphabetic Index and Tabular List of Procedures: typefaces and the abbreviation NEC.

The two typefaces used in ICD-9-CM are bold and italic. Bold typeface is used for all codes and titles in the Tabular List and all main terms in the Alphabetic Index. Italicized typeface is used for the second code in a synchronous procedure situation,

notes in the Alphabetic Index, and "excludes" notes in the Tabular List.

The abbreviation NEC, not elsewhere classifiable, is used with ill-defined terms as a warning that specified forms of the procedures are classified differently. The NEC code only should be used when further information regarding the procedure is available but the classification does not provide a specific code for the procedure.

Alphabetic Index Conventions

Modifiers: The physician's procedural statement may contain one or more procedural terms. The term describing the procedure is the main term and any nouns or adjectives listed with it are called modifiers. The two types of modifiers are essential and nonessential.

- **Essential modifiers** are descriptors that have an effect on the selection of the code. These modifiers describe essential differences in the site or surgical technique. When a main term has only one modifier and that modifier is essential, the modifier appears on the same line as the main term, separated from it by a comma. Essential modifiers are referred to as subterms when a main term has more than one essential modifier.

- **A nonessential modifier** is found in parentheses following main terms and subterms. When this parenthetical term is in the procedure description it has no effect on the selection of the code listed for the main term.

For example, to locate a code for ascending aortic endarterectomy in the Alphabetic Index, select "Endarterectomy" as the main term, with "ascending" and "aortic" as the modifiers.

> Endarterectomy (gas) (with patch graft) 38.10
> abdominal 38.16
> aorta (arch) (ascending) (descending) 38.14

In the above example, 38.10 is used for endarterectomy. However aortic endarterectomy, ascending aortic endarterectomy or descending aortic endarterectomy is coded 38.14. The essential modifier or subterm "aorta" affects the code choice and the nonessential modifier "ascending" does not.

Eponyms: Surgical procedures may be identified by eponyms, or the name of their originator. Eponyms may not be listed as main terms in the Alphabetic Index under the eponym itself, but rather under the main term "operation" or "procedure." Look under the main term that describes the procedure if the eponym is not listed in the Alphabetic Index.

© 2010 Ingenix

Example:

Operation

Cox-maze procedure (ablation or destruction of heart tissue)—see Operation, maze procedure

Operation

maze procedure (ablation or destruction of heart tissue)
by incision (open) 37.33
by median sternotomy 37.33
by peripherally inserted catheter 37.34
by thoracotomy without thoracoscope 37.33
endovascular approach 37.34

Ablation

lesion
heart
maze procedure (Cox-maze)
endovascular approach 37.34
open (trans-thoracic) approach 37.33
thoracoscopic approach 37.37
thoracoscopic approach 37.37

Cross-references: A cross-reference provides the coder with possible modifiers for a term or its synonyms. Just as in the disease classification, there are three types: see, see also, and see category.

- The **see** cross-reference is an explicit direction to look elsewhere. It is used with terms that do not define the type of procedure performed.

- The **see also** cross-reference directs the coder to look under another main term if all the information sought cannot be located under the first main term entry.

- The **see category** guides the coder to the Tabular List for further information or specific site references.

Omit code: Terms that identify an operative approach or closure are followed by the instruction "omit code." A code is not assigned because these processes are an integral part of the procedure.

Example:

Thoracotomy (with drainage) 34.09
as operative approach—omit code

This instruction indicates that no code is assigned, usually for an exploratory part of a procedure, operative approach, typical lysis of adhesions, or the closure of the procedure.

Slanted brackets: For some operative procedures, it is necessary to record the individual components of the procedure. In these instances, the Alphabetic Index will list both codes, one of which appears between slanted brackets [ ]. Record these codes in the same sequence as they appear in the Alphabetic

Index. Slanted brackets are also used in the Tabular List.

Example:

Reconstruction (plastic) (see also Construction and Repair, by site)
bladder 57.87
with
ileum 57.87 *[45.51]*
sigmoid 57.87 *[45.52]*

Code 57.87 describes the reconstruction of the urinary bladder and 45.51 identifies the intestinal resection necessary to create the ileal bladder.

Instructional notes: Notes are used to list fourth-digit subclassifications for those categories that use the same fourth-digit subdivisions. In these cases, only the three-digit code is given for the individual entry; the user must refer to the note following the main term to obtain the appropriate fourth-digit subclassification.

Conventions of the Tabular List of Procedures
Abbreviation: The abbreviation NOS, not otherwise specified, is the equivalent of "unspecified." The NOS code should only be used when further information regarding the procedure is not available.

Punctuation: The Tabular List contains four kinds of punctuation: brackets "[ ]," parentheses "( )," the colon ":," and the brace "}."

[ ] Brackets are used to enclose synonyms, alternative wordings, or explanatory phrases.

( ) Parentheses are used to enclose supplementary words that may be present or absent in the statement of a procedure without affecting the code to which it is assigned.

: A colon is used in the Tabular List after an incomplete term that needs one or more of the modifiers that follow in order to make it assignable to a given category.

} A brace is used to enclose a series of terms, each of which is modified by the statement appearing to the right of the brace.

Symbols: The section mark symbol "§" preceding a subcategory code denotes the placement of a footnote at the bottom of the page, which is applicable to all subdivisions in that code.

Instructional notes: There are four types of notes in the Tabular List of Procedures. They are "Includes," "Excludes," "Code also," and "Note."

The **Includes** note appears immediately under a two- or three-digit code title to further define, or give examples of, the contents.

Conventions

The **Excludes** note is listed to prevent a code from being used incorrectly. Terms that follow the word "Excludes" are to be coded elsewhere as indicated in each case.

The **Code also** instruction is used in the Tabular List for two purposes:

1. As an instruction to code each component of a procedure when they are accomplished at the same time. For example: Code also any synchronous insertion of pseudophakos (13.71).

2. As an instruction to code the use of special adjunctive procedures or equipment. For example: Code also cardiopulmonary bypass (39.61).

The term **Note** designates important information to be considered prior to reporting a procedure or other intervention. These notes provide instruction regarding their proper coding, reporting, sequencing, and other use. They may appear listed at the beginning of a category, subcategory, or immediately following a code title.

Example:

00.44   Procedure on vessel bifurcation

Note: This code is to be used to identify the presence of a vessel bifurcation; it does not describe a specific bifurcation stent. Use this code only once per operative episode, irrespective of the number of bifurcations in vessels.

00.50   Implantation of cardiac resynchronization pacemaker without mention of defibrillation, total system [CRT-P]

Note: Device testing during procedure—*omit code*

Coding and Reporting Guidelines

Coding guidelines can be found within the procedure classification itself and published in the AHA's *Coding Clinic for ICD-9-CM*. Additional reporting guidelines are found in the Uniform Hospital Discharge Data Set (UHDDS).

UHDDS Reporting of Procedure Codes

The UHDDS published in the *Federal Register,* Volume 50, Number 147, July 31, 1985, provides the reporting instructions for diagnoses and significant procedures. An understanding of the definitions of a significant procedure is necessary to decide the appropriate sequence of the procedure codes. Procedures not considered significant are coded and reported according to hospital policy.

Significant procedure: Four criteria are listed in the *Federal Register* for a procedure to be considered significant. They include a procedure that is:

1. Surgical in nature (i.e., incision, excision, amputation, introduction, endoscopy, repair, destruction, suture, and manipulation).

2. Carries a procedural risk.

3. Carries an anesthetic risk.

4. Requires specialized training.

Codes for significant procedures are found in all chapters of the procedure classification.

Other significant procedures: All secondary procedures that meet the definition of "significant" as stated above should also be reported.

Principal procedure: The definition in the UHDDS for a principal procedure is the procedure "that was performed for definitive treatment rather than for diagnostic or exploratory purposes or for treatment of a complication." If the patient has more than one procedure that meets the definition of a principal procedure, select the one most related to the principal diagnosis as the principal procedure. The most resource intensive or complex is chosen when more than one procedure is related to the principal diagnosis.

Bilateral Procedure

The ICD-9-CM procedure classification may provide a single code to describe a bilateral procedure, in which case, only a single code is necessary. However, there are instances when the classification does not does not differentiate between unilateral and bilateral procedure. When this occurs and significant resources are used to achieve the bilateral procedure, record the procedure code twice.

Operative Approaches

As stated previously, terms that identify an operative approach or closure are not assigned a code because these processes are an integral part of the procedure. However, there are some exceptions to know and understand. If after opening a body cavity, only a diagnostic procedure such as a biopsy is carried out, then the operative approach is coded and sequenced first.

Laparoscopy and thoracoscopy: Laparoscopic and thoracoscopic approaches to certain surgeries are replacing the open technique. Requiring only a small incision, removal of tissue or organs may be done through the scope resulting in many advantages over the traditional approach. However, when a surgeon converts from a laparoscopic or thoracoscopic approach to an open technique, only the open procedure is coded. Do not assign a code for the laparoscopic or thoracoscopic approach. Diagnosis code V64.4 Laparoscopic surgical

© 2010 Ingenix

procedure converted to open procedure, should be reported as appropriate.

Other endoscopy: Two guidelines apply for other endoscopies. First, unless the Alphabetic Index states otherwise or the code descriptor includes the endoscopy, the endoscopic approach is coded. Second, when an endoscope is passed through more than one cavity, choose the code for the endoscopy that identifies the furthest site viewed.

Biopsies

Biopsies, the removal of tissue for diagnostic purposes, may be performed in two ways. The technique used to obtain tissue for study determines the type of biopsy to code.

Open biopsy: An open biopsy involves an incision. There are numerous guidelines for coding open biopsies, including:

- If after opening a body cavity, a biopsy is carried out, then the operative approach is coded and sequenced first followed by the code for the biopsy.

- In those instances where the biopsy is incidental to the removal of other tissue, code both removal and biopsy.

Closed biopsy: There are multiple methods for performing a closed biopsy: percutaneously through the use of a needle, endoscopically, or by brush or aspiration. The procedure classification provides a limited number of codes to indicate a brush or aspiration biopsy. When no code exists, code the biopsy as closed. If during an open surgical procedure a needle biopsy is performed, the biopsy is coded as closed as the technique used to obtain tissue for study determines the type of biopsy to code.

There are two methods of coding a biopsy that is done in the course of an endoscopic examination depending on whether the classification has a combination code or not. If the classification provides a code that identifies endoscopic biopsies, only a single code is necessary. If there is no code that includes both procedures, each procedure is coded separately.

Diagnostic endoscopy with biopsy is assigned a code describing the endoscopy followed by the code for the biopsy. A biopsy may be performed and afterwards further surgery may be necessary. In this circumstance, code the more extensive surgery followed by the code for the biopsy.

Canceled Procedures

For those procedures that are cancelled before they begin, no procedure code is assigned. Instead, use a diagnosis code from category V64 Persons

encountering health services for specific procedures, not carried out.

Incomplete Procedures

Sometimes a procedure that was begun may need to be terminated prior to completion. When this occurs, it will be necessary to carefully review the operative report to determine the extent of the procedure in order to determine the correct code assignment. Apply the following guidelines based on the documentation in the medical record:

- Assign a code for the exploratory procedure for the site if the cavity or space was entered.

- Assign a code for an incision if one was made.

- Assign a code for the endoscopy in the situation where the scope was not able to be advanced to the planned location.

- Do not assign a procedure code if the incomplete procedure does not involve an incision (e.g., attempted reduction of a fracture). Instead, use V64.3 Procedure not carried out because of other reasons.

Failed Procedures

A "failed" procedure is not the same as a complication of the procedure. If completed but the procedure did not achieve the therapeutic objective, the procedure is coded as performed.

ICD-9-CM Procedure Coding Steps

Coding a procedure involves reading and interpreting an operative report. A good understanding of the procedure classification conventions, coding guidelines, and clinical aspects of the specific procedure performed is necessary to identify the correct code. To assist in this process, follow these steps:

1. Identify the main term (i.e. the type of procedure performed).

2. Use the Alphabetic Index to find the main term selected.

3. Note any modifiers of the chosen main term.

4. Locate any essential modifiers (i.e., subterms).

5. Read any notes and follow any cross-references.

6. Choose a tentative code from the Alphabetic Index.

7. Look up the selected code in the Tabular List.

8. Review any notes found.

9. Select the final code from the Tabular List.

Abbreviations, Acronyms, and Symbols

The abbreviations, acronyms, and symbols used by health care providers speed communications. The following list includes the most often seen abbreviations, acronyms, and symbols. In some cases, abbreviations have more than one meaning. Abbreviations of Latin phrases are punctuated.

@	at
<	less than
>	greater than
A	1) assessment 2) blood type
a (ante)	before
AAC	apical-aortic conduit
a fib	atrial fibrillation
a flutter	atrial flutter
A&P	auscultation and percussion
a.a.	of each
a.c.	before eating
a.d.	1) right ear 2) to, up to
a.m.	morning
a.s.	left ear
a.u.	each ear, both ears
A/G	albumin-globulin ratio
A2	aortic second sound
AA	Alcoholics Anonymous
AAA	abnormal aortic aneurysm
AAHP	American Association of Health Plans
AAL	anterior axillary line
AAMT	American Association for Medical Transcription
AAPCC	adjusted average per capita cost
AAPPO	American Association of Preferred Provider Organizations
AAROM	active assistive range of motion
ab	abortion
AB	blood type
abd	abdomen
ABE	acute bacterial endocarditis
ABG	arterial blood gas
abn.	abnormal
ABO	referring to ABO incompatibility
abs. fev.	without fever
ACD	absolute cardiac dullness

ACE	1) adrenal cortical extract 2) angiotensin converting enzyme
ACL	anterior cruciate ligament
ACLS	advanced cardiac life support
ACP	acid phosphatase
acq.	acquired
ACR	adjusted community rating
ACSW	Academy of Certified Social Workers
ACTH	adrenocorticotropic hormone
ACVD	acute cardiovascular disease
ad lib	as desired, at pleasure
ad part. dolent.	to the aching parts
ad. hib.	to be administered
ad. lib.	as desired
ad. us. ext.	for external use
ADA	1) American Dental Association 2) Americans with Disabilities Act
ADH	antidiuretic hormone
ADL	activities of daily living
adm	admission, admit
ADM	alcohol, drug, or mental disorder
ADP	adenosine diphosphate
ADS	alternative delivery system
adst. feb.	when fever is present
AE	above the elbow
AF	atrial fibrillation
AESOP®	Automated Endoscopic System for Optimal Positioning
AFB	acid fast bacilli
ag. feb.	when the fever increases
AGA	appropriate (average) for gestational age
AgNO3	silver nitrate
AHA	American Hospital Association
AHC	alternative health care
AHIMA	American Health Information Management Association
AHP	accountable health plan
AI	aortic insufficiency
AICD	automatic implant cardioverter defibrillator
AID	1) acute infectious disease 2) artificial insemination donor

Abbreviations

AIDS	acquired immunodeficiency syndrome	AROM	1) active range of motion
AIH	artificial insemination by husband		2) artificial rupture of membranes
AK	above the knee	art.	artery, arterial
AKA	above knee amputation	AS	1) aortic stenosis
ALA	aminolevulinic acid		2) arteriosclerosis
alb. (albus)	white	ASAP	as soon as possible
alk. phos.	alkaline phosphatase	ASC	ambulatory surgery center
ALL	acute lymphocytic leukemia	ASCVD	arteriosclerotic cardiovascular disease
ALOS	average length of stay	ASCX12N	American Standard Committee standard for claims and reimbursement
ALP	alkaline phosphatase		
ALS	advanced life support	ASD	atrial septal defect
ALT	alanine aminotransferase	ASHD	arteriosclerotic heart disease
alt. dieb.	every other day	ASO	administrative services only
alt. hor.	every other hour	ASR	age/sex rate
alt. noc.	every other night	Asst	assistance (min= minimal; mod= moderate)
ama	against medical advice		
AMA	American Medical Association	AST	aspartate aminotransferase
amb	ambulate	ATP	adenosine triphosphate
AMCRA	American Managed Care and Review Association	AUR	ambulatory utilization review
		AV	atrioventricular
AMGA	American Medical Group Association	A-V	arteriovenous
AMI	acute myocardial infarction	AVF	arteriovenous fistula
AML	acute myelogenous leukemia	AVM	arteriovenous malformation
AMML	acute myelomonocytic leukemia	AWP	average wholesale price
AMP	1) adenosine monophosphate	ax	auxiliary
	2) ampule	AxiaLIF	axial lumbar interbody fusion
ANA	1) American Nursing Association	AZT	azidothymidine
	2) antinuclear antibodies	B&B	bowel and bladder
ANS	autonomic nervous system	b.i.d.	two times a day
ANSI	American National Standards Institute	b.i.n.	twice a night
ANSI/HISB	ANSI Health Information Standards Board	b.i.s.	twice
		Ba	barium
ant	anterior	bal.	bath
AO	aqueous oxygen therapy	BAL	bronchoalveolar lavage
AOD	arterial occlusive disease	BB	blow bottles
AODM	adult onset diabetes mellitus	BBA	Balanced Budget Act of 1997
AP	1) antepartum	BBB	bundle branch block
	2) anterior-posterior	BCC	basal cell carcinoma
Ap	apical	BCP	birth control pill
A-P	anterior posterior	BE	1) barium enema
APC	ambulatory payment classification		2) below the elbow
APM	arterial pressure monitoring	BI	biopsy
approx	approximately	bib.	drink
appy.	appendectomy	BICROS	bilateral routing of signals
APT	admissions per thousand	BIS	bispectral index monitoring
aq.	water (aqua)	BK	below the knee
ARC	AIDS-related complex	BKA	below knee amputation
ARD	acute respiratory disease	BLS	basic life support
ARDS	adult respiratory distress syndrome	BM	bowel movement
ARF	1) acute renal failure	BMR	basal metabolic rate
	2) acute respiratory failure		

© 2010 Ingenix

BMT bone marrow transplant
BO body order
BOW bag of water
BP blood pressure
BPC bare platinum coils
BPD bronchopulmonary dysplasia
BPH benign prostatic hypertrophy
Br breastfeeding
BrC breast care
BRM biological response modifier
BRP 1) bathroom, private
2) bathroom privileges
BS 1) bachelor of surgery
2) bowel sounds
3) breath sounds
BSA body surface area
BSC bedside commode
BSD bedside drainage
BUN blood urea nitrogen
BUR back-up rate (ventilator)
BUS Bartholin urethra skenes
bx biopsy
C 1) centigrade
2) cervical vertebrae
3) complements
c with
C&S culture and sensitivity
c.m. tomorrow morning
c.n. tomorrow night
c/m counts per minute
c/o complaints of
C/S cesarean section
Ca 1) calcium
2) cancer
CA cancer
CABG coronary artery bypass graft
CAC certified alcoholism counselor
CAD coronary artery disease
Cap capitation
CAPD continuous ambulatory peritoneal dialysis
caps. (capsula) capsule
CAS computer assisted surgery
CAT computerized axial tomography
cath catheterize
CBC complete blood count
CBR complete bedrest
cc chief complaint
C-collar cervical collar
CCM cardiac contractility modulation

CCPD continuous cycling peritoneal dialysis
CCU coronary care unit
CDC Centers for Disease Control and Prevention
CDH congenital dislocation of hip
CE cardiac enlargement
CEA carcinoembryonic antigen
CF cystic fibrosis
CH, Chol cholesterol
CHAMPUS Civilian Health and Medical Program of the Uniformed Services
CHD 1) congenital heart disease
2) congestive heart disease
CHF congestive heart failure
chgd changed
chr. chronic
CI 1) chloride
2) confidence interval
CIS carcinoma in situ
cl liqs clear liquids
CLC creative living center
CLD 1) chronic liver disease
2) chronic lung disease
CLL chronic lymphatic leukemia
CLO clofarabine
cm centimeter
cm2 square centimeters
CMC carpometacarpal
CMG cystometrogram
CMHC community mental health center
CML chronic myelogenous leukemia
CMP competitive medical plan
CMRI cardiac magnetic resonance imaging
CMS 1) Centers for Medicare and Medicaid Services
2) circulation motion sensation
CMS-1500 universal billing form developed by CMS
CMV cytomegalovirus
cn cranial nerves
CNM certified nurse midwife
CNP continuous negative airway pressure
CNS central nervous system
co cardiac output
CO2 carbon dioxide
COA certificate of authority
COB coordination of benefits
COBRA Consolidated Omnibus Budget Reconciliation Act
COC certificate of coverage
COLD chronic obstructive lung disease

Abbreviations

CON	certificate of need	D	1) day
conc.	concentration		2) diopter
cont.	continue	D&C	dilation and curettage
COPD	chronic obstructive pulmonary disease	D/C	1) discharge
CP	cerebral palsy		2) discontinue
CPAP	continuous positive airway pressure	D/R	dayroom
CPB	cardiopulmonary bypass	D/W	dextrose in water
CPD	cephalopelvic disproportion	DAW	dispense as written
CPHA	Commission on Professional and Hospital Activities	dc	1) discontinue
			2) doctor of chiropractic medicine
CPK	creatine phosphokinase	DC	1) doctor of chiropractic medicine
CPM	continuous passive motion		2) dual choice
CPR	1) cardiopulmonary resuscitation	DCA	deferred compensation administrator
	2) computer-based patient record	DCI	duplicate coverage inquiry
CPT	1) chest physical therapy	DCíd	1) discharged
	2) Physicians' Current Procedural Terminology		2) discontinued
		DCR	dacryocystorhinostomy
CQI	continuous quality improvement	DD	down drain
CR	1) carrier replacement	DDST	Denver developmental screening test
	2) creatine	DE	dose equivalent
CRC	community rating by class	decem	ten
CRF	chronic renal failure	decub.	1) decubitus ulcer
CRH	corticotropic releasing hormone		2) lying down
crit.	hematocrit	def.	deficient, deficiency
CROS	contralateral routing of signals	del	delivery
CRP	C-reactive protein	dep.	dependent
CS	central service	DES	drug-eluting stent
CSF	cerebrospinal fluid	det.	let it be given
CSS	carotid sinus stimulation	DEXA	dual energy x-ray absorptiometry
CT	1) carpal tunnel syndrome	dexter	right
	2) computerized tomography	dextra	right
	3) corneal thickness	DHEA	dehydroepiandrosterone
CTLSO	cervical-thoracic-lumbar-sacral-orthosis	DHHS	Department of Health and Human Services
CTZ	chemoreceptor trigger zone	DHT	dihydrotestosterone
cu	cubic	DIC	disseminated intravascular coagulopathy
CV	cardiovascular		
CVA	1) cerebral vascular accident	DIEP	deep inferior epigastric artery perforator
	2) cerebrovascular accident		
	3) costovertebral angle	DIF	direct immunofluorescence
CVD	1) cardiovascular disease	dim.	divide in half
	2) cerebrovascular disease	disp	disposition
CVI	chronic venous insufficiency	DJD	degenerative joint disease
CVL	central venous line	DKA	diabetic ketoacidosis
CVMS	clean voided midstream urine	DLIF	direct lateral interbody fusion
CVP	central venous pressure	DM	diabetes mellitus
CVU	cerebrovascular unit	DMD	Duchenne muscular dystrophy
CW	closed ward	DME	durable medical equipment
CXR	chest x-ray	DNA	deoxyribonucleic acid
CXy	chest x-ray	DNP	do not publish
cysto	cystoscopy	DNR	do not resuscitate

© 2010 Ingenix

DNS	do not show		ED	1) effective dose
DO	doctor of osteopathy			2) emergency department
DOA	dead on arrival		EDC	1) estimated date of confinement
DOB	date of birth			2) expected date of confinement
doc.	doctor		EDI	electronic data interchange
DOE	dyspnea on exertion		EEG	electroencephalogram
DOH	Department of Health		EENT	eye, ear, nose, and throat
DOS	date of service		EGA	estimated gestational age
DPR	drug price review		EGD	esophagus, stomach, and duodenum
DPT	1) days per thousand		EKG	electrocardiogram
	2) diphtheria-pertussis-tetanus		EMG	electromyogram
DR	delivery room		en	1) clyster
Dr	doctor			2) enema
dr.	dram		en bloc	in total
DRG	diagnosis-related group		ENG	electronystagmogram
Dsg	dressing		eng.	engorged
DSM-IV	Diagnostic and Statistical Manual of the American Psychiatric Association's Task Force on Terminology, Fourth Edition		ENT	ear, nose, and throat
			EO	elbow orthosis
			EOB	explanation of benefits
			EOG	electrooculography
DSS	dioctyl sulfosuccinate		EOI	evidence of insurability
DT	desitination therapy		EOM	1) end of month
DTRs	deep tendon reflexes			2) extraocular motion
DTs	delirium tremens			3) extraocular muscles
DUE	drug use evaluation		EOMB	explanation of Medicare benefits
duo	two		EOMI	extraocular motion intact
duodecim.	twelve		EOP	external occipital protuberance
DUR	drug utilization review		EOY	end of year
dur. dolor.	while pain lasts		Epis.	episiotomy
DVT	deep vein thrombosis		EPO	1) epoetin alfa
dx	diagnosis			2) exclusive provider organization
DX	diagnosis code		EPS	electrophysiologic stimulation
dz	disease		EPSDT	early periodic screening, diagnosis and treatment
e.m.p.	as directed			
E/M	evaluation and management		ER	emergency room
ead.	the same		ERC	endoscopic retrograde cholangiography
EAP	employee assistance program			
EBL	estimated blood loss		ERCP	endoscopic retrograde cholangiopancreatography
EBV	Epstein-Barr virus			
ECCE	extracapsular cataract extraction		ERG	electroretinogram
ECF	1) extended care facility		ERISA	Employee Retirement Income Security Act of 1974
	2) extracellular fluid			
ECG	electrocardiogram		ESR	erythrocyte sedimentation rate
ECHO	1) echocardiogram		ESRD	end stage renal disease
	2) enterocytopathogenic human orphan virus		EST	electroshock therapy
			ESWL	extracorporeal shockwave lithotripsy
ECMO	extracorporeal membrane oxygenation		et	and
ECT	1) electro-convulsive therapy		ET	endotracheal
	2) emission computerized tomography		ETG	episode treatment group
			ETOH	alcohol
ectopic	ectopic pregnancy (OB)		EVR	evoked visual response

Ex	examination
exc	excise
ext.	extremity
extr.	extract
F	*1)* Fahrenheit
	2) female
F (on OB)	firm
f.m.	make a mixture
F/U	follow-up
FAS	fetal alcohol syndrome
FB	foreign body
FB (fb)	fingerbreadths
FBR	foreign body removal
FBS	fasting blood sugar
FDP	fibrin degradation products
Fe	*1)* female
	2) iron
FEV	forced expiratory volume
FFP	fresh frozen plasma
FFR	fractional flow reserve
FFS	*1)* fee for service equivalency
	2) fee for service reimbursement
FH	family history
FHR	fetal heart rate
FHT	fetal heart tone
FI	firm one finger down from umbilicus
fl	fluid
f-LITT	focused laser interstitial thermal therapy
FLK	funny looking kid
fluro	fluoroscopy
FM	face mask
FME	full-mouth extraction
FMG	fine mesh gauze
FNP	family nurse practitioner
FOD	free of disease
fort.	strong (fortis)
FP	*1)* family planning
	2) family practitioner
FR	*1)* family relationship
	2) *Federal Register*
FRAT	free radical assay test
FSA	flexible spending account
FSE	fetal scalp electrode
FSH	follicle stimulating hormone
FTND	full term normal delivery
FTSG	full thickness skin graft
FTT	failure to thrive
FUO	fever of unknown origin
FVC	forced vital capacity
fx	fracture

fxBB	fracture, both bones
G	gram
GA	gastric analysis
GAP	gluteal artery perforator
gav.	gavage
GB	gallbladder
GDM	gestational diabetes mellitus
GFR	glomerular filtration rate
GH	growth hormone
GHAA	Group Health Association of America
GI	gastrointestinal
GIFT	gamete intrafallopian transfer
GLC	gas liquid chromatography
Gly. supp.	glycerin suppository
GMP	guanosine monophosphate
GNID	gram-negative intracellular diplocci
GnRH	gonadotropin-releasing hormone
GP	general practitioner
gr.	grain
grav	number of pregnancies
GS	general surgeon
GSR	galvanic skin response
gsw	gunshot wound
gt.	drop
gtt.	drops
GU	genitourinary
Gu	guaiac
GxT	graded exercise test
gyn	gynecology
H	Hertel measurement
h (hora)	hour
H&P	history and physical
h.d.	at bedtime
H.O.	house officer
h.s.	at bedtime
H2O	water
H2O2	hydrogen peroxide
HA	*1)* headache
	2) hearing aide
HAA	hepatitis antigen B
HAAb	hepatitis antibody A
HaAg	hepatitis antigen A
HAI	hemaglutination test
HAV	hepatitis A virus
HB	*1)* headbox
	2) hepatitis B
HBcAg	hepatitis antigen B
HBD	hydroxybutyric dehydrogenase
Hbg	hemoglobin
HBO	hyperbaric oxygen

© 2010 Ingenix

HbO2	oxyhemoglobin	HR	1) Harrington rod
HBP	high blood pressure		2) heart rate
HBsAb	hepatitis surface antibody B		3) hour
HBsAg	hepatitis antigen B	HRT	hormone replacement therapy
HBV	hepatitis B vaccine	hrt.	heart
HCG	human chorionic gonadotropin	HS	heelstick
HCl	hydrochloric acid	HSA	health service agreement
HCPCS	Healthcare Common Procedural Coding System	HSBG	heelstick blood gas
		HSG	hysterosalpingogram
HCPP	health care prepayment plan	HSP	health service plan
Hct	hematocrit	HSV	herpes simplex virus
Hctz	hydrochlorothiazide	ht.	height
HCVD	hypertensive cardiovascular disease	HTLV/III	human T-cell lymphotropic virus/three
HD	hip disarticulation	HTN	hypertension
HDL	high-density lipoproteins	HVA	homovanillic acid
HEDIS	Health Plan Employer Data and Information Set	Hx	history
		hypo	hypodermic injection
HEENT	head, eyes, ears, nose, and throat	I& D	incision and drainage
Hg	hemoglobin	I& O	intake and output
Hgb	hemoglobin	IA	intra-arterial
HGH	human growth hormone	IAB	intra-aortic balloon
HH	hard of hearing	IABC	intra-aortic balloon counterpulsation
HHA	home health agency	IABP	1) intra-arterial blood pressure
HHS	Department of Health and Human Services		2) intra-aortic balloon pump
		IAEMT	intraoperative anesthetic effect monitoring and titration
HIAA	1) Health Insurance Association of America	IBNR	incurred but not reported
	2) hydroxyindoleacetic acid	IBS	irritable bowel syndrome
Hib	hemophilus influenzae vaccine	IBW	ideal body weight
HIPAA	Health Insurance Portability and Accountability Act of 1996	IC	infant care
		ICAT	indirect Coombs test
HIPC	health insurance purchasing cooperative	ICCE	intracapsular cataract extraction
		ICD-10	International Classification of Diseases, Tenth Revision
HIV	human immunodeficiency virus	ICD-10-PCS	International Classification of Diseases, Tenth Revision, Procedural Coding System
HLV	herpes-like virus		
HMD	hyaline membrane disease		
HMO	health maintenance organization	ICD-9-CM	International Classification of Diseases, Ninth Revision, Clinical Modification
HMS	hepatosplenomegaly		
HNAD	hyperosmolar nonacidotic diabetes		
HOB	head of bed	ICF	1) International Classification of Functioning, Disability, and Health
hor. decub.	at bedtime		
HORF	high output renal failure		2) Intermediate care facility
HPF	high power field	ICH	intracranial/cerebral hemorrhage
HPG	human pituitary gonadotropin	ICP	intracranial pressure
HPI	history of present illness	ICS	intercostal space
HPL	human placental lactogen	ICSH	interstitial cell stimulating hormone
HPs	1) Hanta virus pulmonary syndrome 2) hot packs	ICU	intensive care unit
		ID	infective dose
HPV	human papilloma virus	Id31	radioactive iodine
		IDDM	insulin dependent diabetes mellitus

IDH	isocitric dehydrogenase
IDM	infant of diabetic mother
IFVA	intraoperative fluorescence vascular angiography
Ig	immunoglobulin, gamma
IH	infectious hepatitis
II	icteric index
IM	1) infectious mononucleosis 2) internal medicine 3) intramuscular
IMC	intermediate care
IME	independent medical evaluation
IMO	integrated multiple option
IMV	intermittent mandatory ventilation
inc.	incision
indep	independent
INF	1) inferior 2) infusion
INH	inhalation solution
INJ	injection
instill	instillation
IOL	intraocular lens
IOP	intraocular pressure
IP	1) interphalangeal 2) intraperitoneal
IPA	individual practice association
IPD	intermittent peritoneal dialysis
IPPB	intermittent positive pressure breathing
IPPV	invasive positive pressure ventilation
IQ	intelligence quotient
IRDS	idiopathic respiratory distress syndrome
ISC	infant servo-control
ISG	immune serum globulin
ISN	integrated service network
IT	intrathecal administration
ITP	idiopathic thrombocytopenia purpura
IU	international units
IUD	intrauterine device
IV	intravenous
IVAD™	implantable ventricular assist device (Thoratec®)
IVC	1) inferior vena cava 2) intravenous cholangiogram
IVF	in vitro fertilization
IVH	intraventricular hemorrhage
IVIg	intravenous immunoglobulin
IVP	intravenous pyelogram
IVUS	intravascular ultrasound

JCAHO	Joint Commission on Accreditation of Healthcare Organizations
JODM	juvenile onset diabetes mellitus
JVD	jugular venous distention
JVP	jugular venous pressure
K	potassium
Kcal	kilocalorie
KCL	potassium chloride
kg	kilogram
KJ	knee jerk
KO	1) keep open 2) knee orthosis
KUB	kidneys, ureters, bladder
KVO	keep vein open
L	1) left vertebrae 2) lumbar vertebrae
L&A	light and accommodation
L&W	living and well
LA	left atrium
LAA	left atrial appendage
LAD	left anterior descending
LAP	leucine aminopeptidase
lap.	1) laparoscopy 2) laparotomy
LAT	lateral
LAV	lymphadenopathy associated virus
LAVH	laparoscopic assisted vaginal hysterectomy
LB	legbag
LBB	left bundle branch
LBBB	left bundle branch block
LBP	lower back pain
LCP	licensed clinical psychologist
LCSW	licensed clinical social worker
LD	lethal dose
LDH	lactate dehydrogenase
LDL	low-density lipoproteins
LE	1) lower extremity 2) lupus erythematosus
LEEP	loop electrocautery excision procedure
LGA	large for gestational age
LH	luteinizing hormone
LHF	left heart failure
LHR	leukocyte histamine release
Li	lithium
lido	lidocaine
liq.	solution (liquor)
LITT	laser interstitial thermal therapy
LKS	liver, kidneys, spleen
LLETZ	large loop excision of transformation zone of cervix of uterus

© 2010 Ingenix

LLL	left lower lobe	**MCHC**	mean corpuscular hemoglobin concentration
LLQ	left lower quadrant		
LMD	local medical doctor	**MCL**	midclavicular line
LML	left medio-lateral position	**MCP**	metacarpophalangeal
LMN	lower motor neuron	**MCR**	modified community rating
LMP	last menstrual period	**MCT**	mediastinal chest tube
LMS	left mentum anterior position (chin)	**MCV**	mean corpuscular volume
LMT	left mentum transverse position	**MD**	1) manic depression
LOA	leave of absence		2) medical doctor
LOC	1) level of consciousness		3) muscular dystrophy
	2) loss of consciousness		4) myocardial disease
LOM	limitation of motion	**MDC**	major diagnostic category
LOP	left occiput posterior position	**MDD**	manic-depressive disorder
LOS	length of stay	**Mec**	meconium
LOT	left occiput transverse position	**MED**	minimal effective dose
LP	lumbar puncture	**med/surg**	medical, surgical
LPC	licensed professional counselor	**Medigap**	Medicare supplemental insurance
LPM	liters per minute	**meds**	medications
LR	1) lactated Ringer's	**Medsupp**	Medicare supplemental insurance
	2) log roll	**mEq**	milliequivalent
LS fusion	lumbar sacral fusion	**mEq/1**	milliequivalent per liter
LSA	left sacrum anterior position	**MFD**	minimum fatal dose
LSB	left sternal border	**MFT**	muscle function test
LSO	lumbar sacral orthosis	**Mg**	magnesium
LT	left	**mg**	milligram
LTC	long term care	**MH/CD**	mental health/chemical dependency
lul	left upper lobe	**MH/SA**	mental health/substance abuse
luq	left upper quadrant	**MHC**	mental health clinic
LV	left ventricle	**MI**	myocardial infarction
LVAS	left ventricle assist system	**min**	minimum, minimal, minute
lymphs	lymphocytes	**misce.**	miscellaneous
lytes	electrolytes	**ML**	midline
M	1) male	**ml**	milliliter
	2) manifest refraction	**MLC**	midline catheter
M1	mitral first sound	**mm**	millimeter
M2	mitral second sound	**mmHg**	millimeters of mercury
MA1	volume respirator	**MMPI**	Minnesota Multiphasic Personality Inventory
MAC	1) maximum allowable charge		
	2) monitored anesthesia care	**MMRV**	measles, mumps, rubella vaccine
MAD	monoamine oxidase (inhibitor)	**MOM**	milk of magnesia
man. prim.	first thing in the morning	**mono**	1) monocyte
MAP	mean arterial pressure		2) mononucleosis
MASER	microwave amplification by stimulated emission of radiation	**mor. dict.**	in the manner directed
		MPD	maximum permissible dose
MAST	military antishock trousers	**MR**	mitral regurgitation
MBC	1) maximum breathing capacity	**MRA**	magnetic resonance angiography
	2) minimum bactericidal concentration	**MRI**	magnetic resonance imaging
		mRNA	messenger RNA
MBD	minimal brain dysfunction	**MS**	1) morphine sulfate
mcg	microgram		2) multiple sclerosis
MCH	mean corpuscular hemoglobin	**MSHJ**	medical staff hospital joint venture

Abbreviations

Abbreviations

MSLT	multiple sleep latency testing
MSO	management service organization
MSS	medical social services
MSW	master's in social work
MTD	right eardrum
MTM	Metamucil
MTP	metatarsophalangeal
MTS	left eardrum
multip.	multipara
MVP	mitral valve prolapse
MWS	Mickey-Wilson syndrome
N	nitrogen
N&V	nausea and vomiting
n.p.o.	nothing by mouth
N2O	nitrous oxide
Na	sodium
NaCl	sodium chloride (salt)
NAD	no appreciable disease
NAEHCA	National Association of Employers on Health Care Action
NAHMOR	National Association of HMO Regulators
NAIC	National Association of Insurance Commissioners
NAT	nonaccidental trauma
NB	newborn
NBICU	newborn intensive care unit
NBT	nitroblue tetrazolium
NCA	neurocirculatory asthenia
NCHS	National Center for Health Statistics
NCPDP	National Council of Prescription Drug Programs
NCPR	no cardiopulmonary resuscitation
NCQA	National Committee on Quality Assurance
NCR	no cardiac resuscitation
NCV	nerve conduction velocity
NCVHS	National Committee on Vital Health Statistics
NDC	national drug code
NEC	1) necrotizing enterocolitis 2) not elsewhere classified
neg.	negative
NF	national formulary
NG	nasogastric
NGU	nongonococcal urethritis
NIDDM	non-insulin dependent diabetes mellitus
NIPPV	non-invasive positive pressure ventilation
NIR	near infrared

NJ	nasojejunal
NKA	no known allergies
NKMA	no known medical allergies
NNR	new and nonofficial remedies
noc.	night
Non-par	non-participating provider
NOS	not otherwise specified
novem.	nine
NP	1) neuropsychiatry 2) nurse practitioner
NPA	1) national prescription audit 2) non-par approved
NP-CPAP	nasopharyngeal continuous positive airway pressure
NPN	1) non-par not approved 2) nonprotein nitrogen
NPRM	notice of proposed rule making
npt	normal pressure and temperature
NS	1) normal saline 2) not significant
NSAID	nonsteroidal anti-inflammatory drug
NSD	nominal standard dose
NSR	normal sinus rhythm
NST	nonstress test
NSVB	normal spontaneous vaginal bleeding
NSVD	normal spontaneous vaginal delivery
NT	1) nasotracheal 2) nontender
NTE	neutral thermal environment
NTP	normal temperature and pressure
NUBC	National Uniform Billing Committee
nyd	not yet diagnosed
O	1) blood type 2) oxygen
o	no information
O&P	ova and parasites
o.d.	right eye
o.m.	1) every morning 2) otitis media
o.n.	every night
o.s.	left eye
o.u.	each eye, both eyes
O2	oxygen
OA	1) open access 2) osteoarthritis
OAG	open angle glaucoma
OB	obstetrician
OB-GYN	obstetrics and gynecology
OC	1) office call 2) open crib 3) oral contraceptive

© 2010 Ingenix

OCT	1) ornithine carbamyl transferase 2) oxytocin challenge test 3) optical coherence tomography	**PA**	1) physician assistant 2) posteroanterior 3) pulmonary artery
octo.	eight	**PAB**	premature atrial beats
OFC	occipitofrontal circumference	**PAC**	1) pre-admission certification
oint	ointment		2) premature atrial contraction
OJ	orange juice	**PACU**	post anesthesia care unit
omn. hor.	every hour	**PAD**	pulmonary artery diastolic
OMS	oromaxillary surgery	**PAH**	para-aminohippurate
OMT	osteopathic manipulation therapy	**PAP**	1) Papanicolaou test or smear
ONH	optic nerve head		2) pulmonary artery pressure
OOA	out-of-area	**Par**	participating provider
OOB	out of bed	**PAR**	1) parenteral
OOPs	out-of-pocket costs/expenses		2) post anesthesia recovery
OPD	outpatient department	**para**	1) along side of
OPG	oculoplethysmography		2) number of pregnancies, as para 1,
ophth	ophthalmology		2, 3, etc.
OPV	oral polio vaccine	**PARR**	post anesthesia recovery room
OR	operating room	**part. vic.**	in divided doses
ORIF	open reduction internal fixation	**PAT**	paroxysmal atrial tachycardia
oris	mouth	**path**	1) pathology
ortho.	orthopedics		2) physicians at teaching hospitals
os	mouth	**PBI**	protein-bound iodine
OSA	obstructive sleep apnea	**PC**	packed cells
OSHA	Occupational Safety and Health Administration	**PCA**	patient controlled analgesia
		PCD	polycystic disease
OST	oxytocin stress test	**PCG**	phonocardiogram
OT	occupational therapy	**PCN**	1) penicillin
OTC	over-the-counter		2) primary care network
OTD	organ tolerance dose	**PCP**	primary care physician
OTH	other routes of administration	**PCPM**	per contract per month
ov.	1) office visit 2) ovum	**PCR**	1) physician contingency reserve 2) polymerase chain reaction
OW	open ward	**PCTA**	percutaneous transluminal angioplasty
oz.	ounce	**PCV**	packed cell volume
P	1) after 2) phosphorus 3) plan 4) pulse	**PCW**	pulmonary capillary wedge
		PD	1) Parkinson's disease 2) postural drainage
P& A	percussion and auscultation	**PDA**	patent ductus arteriosus
P&T	pharmacy and therapeutics	**PDT**	percutaneous dilatational tracheostomy
p.c.	after eating		
p.m.	after noon	**PE**	1) physical examination 2) practice expense 3) pulmonary edema 4) pulmonary embolism
p.p.	near point of visual accommodation		
p.r.	1) pulsefar point of visual accommodation 2) through the rectum		
		PEC	pre-existing condition
p.r.n.	as needed for	**Peds**	pediatrics
p/o	by mouth	**PEEP**	positive end expiratory pressure
P+PD	percussion & postural drainage	**PEG**	pneumoencephalogram
P2	pulmonic 2nd sound	**PEGJJ**	percutaneous endoscopic gastrojejunostomy

PEN	parenteral and enteral nutrition		PRBC	packed red blood cells
PENS	percutaneous electrical nerve stimulation		preg	pregnant
			PREs	progressive resistive exercises
PERRLA	pupils equal, regular, reactive to light and accommodation		previa	placenta previa
			primip	primipara
PET	positron emission tomography		PRO	peer review organization
PFC	persistent fetal circulation		PROM	premature rupture of membranes
PFT	pulmonary function test		ProPAC	prospective payment assessment commission
PG	prostaglandin			
PGA	polyglycolic acid		PSA	prostate specific antigen
PH	past history		PSP	phenolsulfonphthalein
pH	potential of hydrogen		PsyD	doctor of psychology
PharmD	doctor of pharmacy		Pt	1) patient
PHO	physician-hospital organization			2) prothrombin time
PI	present illness		PT	1) physical therapy
PICC	peripherally inserted central catheter			2) prothrombin time
PID	pelvic inflammatory disease		PTA	1) percutaneous transluminal angioplasty
pk.	pack			2) prior to admission
PKU	phenylketonuria		PTB	patellar tendon bearing (cast)
PMG	primary medical group		PTCA	percutaneous transluminal coronary angioplasty
PMHx	past medical history			
PMI	point of maximum intensity		PTH	parathyroid hormone
PMN	polymorphonuclear neutrophil leukocytes		PTT	partial thromboplastin time
			PUD	peptic ulcer disease
PMPM	per member per month		pulv.	powder
PMPY	per member per year		pVAD	percutaneous ventricular assist device
PMS	premenstrual syndrome		PVC	premature ventricular contraction
PNC	premature nodal contraction		PVD	premature ventricular depolarization
PND	1) paroxysmal nocturnal dyspnea 2) post nasal drip		PVL	paraventricular leukomalacia
			Px	prognosis
PNS	peripheral nervous system		PZI	protamine zinc insulin
PO	1) (per os) by mouth 2) postoperative		q.	every
			q.2h	every two hours
POD	postoperative day		q.a.m.	every morning
polys	polymorphonuclear neutrophil leukocytes		q.d.	every day
			q.h.	every hour
POR	problem oriented record		q.h.s.	every night
POS	1) place of service 2) point of sale 3) point of service		q.i.d.	four times daily
			q.n.	every night
			q.o.d.	every other day
pos.	positive		q.q.h.	every four hours
post or PM	postmortem exam or autopsy		QA	quality assurance
post. cib.	after meals		QM	quality management
PP	postprandial		QMB	qualified Medicare beneficiary
PPD	1) percussion and postural drainage 2) purified protein derivative		qns	quantity not sufficient
			qs	quantity sufficient
PPH	postpartum hemorrhage		quattour	four
PPO	preferred provider organization		quicdecem	fifteen
PPP	protamine paracoagulation		quinque	five
PPRC	physician payment review commission		quotid	daily
pr	per return			

© 2010 Ingenix

Abbreviations

R	1) respiration
	2) right atrium
r	roentgen units (x-rays)
R&C	reasonable and customary
R,R,& E	round, regular, and equal
R/O	rule out
RA	rheumatoid arthritis
RATx	radiation therapy
RBB	right bundle branch
RBBB	right bundle branch block
RBC	red blood cell
RBOW	ruptured bag of water
RBRVS	resource based relative value scale
RCD	relative cardiac dullness
RDS	respiratory distress syndrome
REM	rapid eye movement
RESA	radial cryosurgical ablation
resp	respiration, respiratory
Retro	retrospective rate derivation
rev.	revise, revision
RFP	request for proposal
Rh	Rhesus
Rh neg	Rhesus factor negative
RHD	rheumatic heart disease
RHF	right heart failure
RIA	radioimmunoassay
RL	Ringer's lactate
RLE	right lower extremity
RLF	retrolental fibroplasia
RLL	right lower lobe
rlq	right lower quadrant
RMA	right mentum anterior position
RMC	rating method code
RML	right middle lobe
RMP	right mentum posterior position
RMT	right mentum transverse position
RN	registered nurse
RNA	ribonucleic acid
ROA	right occiput anterior position
ROM	range of motion
ROP	right occiput posterior position
ROS	review of systems
RPG	retrograde pyelogram
RPR	venereal disease report
RR	recovery room
RRA	registered record administrator
RRR	regular rate and rhythm
RS	reducing substances
RSV	respiratory syncytial virus
RT	1) recreational therapist
	2) respiratory therapist
	3) resting tracing
	4) right
RTC	return to clinic
RUL	right upper lobe
ruq	right upper quadrant
RV	right ventricle
Rx	take (prescription; treatment)
RxN	reaction
s	without
S& A	sugar and acetone
s.c.	subcutaneous
s.l.	under the tongue, sublingual
S.O.S.	if necessary (si opus sit)
S/P	status post
SAH	subarachnoid hemorrhage
SALT	serum alanine aminotransferase
SAST	serum aspartate aminotransferase
SB	sinus bradycardia
SBFT	small bowel follow through
S-C disease	sickle cell hemoglobin-c disease
SCI	spinal cord injury
SCR	standard class rate
sed rate	sedimentation rate of erythrocytes
SEM	systolic ejection murmur
Seno supp	Senokot suppository
septem	seven
sex	six
SFA	superficial femoral artery
SG	Swan-Ganz
SGA	small for gestational age
SGOT	serum glutamic oxaloacetic acid
SH	social history
SHBG	sex hormone binding globulin
SIADH	syndrome of inappropriate antidiuretic hormone
SIC	standard industry code
SIDS	sudden infant death syndrome
SIEA	superficial inferior epigastric artery
Sig.	write on label (Rx) or let it be labeled
Sig. S. (Signa)	mark or write
sine	without
SISI	short increment sensitivity index
SLE	systemic lupus erythematosus
SMI	supplementary medical insurance program
SMO	slip made out
SNF	skilled nursing facility
SNS	sympathetic nervous system

Abbreviations

SOAP	subjective objective assessment plan		TBA	to be arranged
SOB	shortness of breath		TBG	1) thyroid binding globulin
sol.	solution			2) thyroxine
SOP	standard operation procedure		TBI	total body irradiation
SPD	summary plan description		TBNA	transbronchoscopic needle aspiration
SpGr	specific gravity		TBSA	total body surface area
SPIN	standard prescriber identification number		TC&DB	turn, cough, and deep breathe
			Td	tetanus
SQ	1) status quo		TEE	transesophageal echocardiography
	2) subcutaneous		TEFRA	Tax Equity and Fiscal Responsibility Act
SROM	spontaneous rupture of membranes			
ss	half		temp	temperature
SSE	soap suds enema		TENS	transcutaneous electrical nerve stimulation
SSO2	supersaturated oxygen therapy			
ST	sinus tachycardia		TEVAP	transurethral electrovaporization of prostate
staph	staphylococcus			
stat	immediately		TFT	transfer factor test
STD	sexually transmitted disease		TGS	Tactile Guidance System™
STH	somatotrophic hormone		THA	total hip arthroplasty
strep	streptococcus		Thal	Thalassemia
STS	serology test for syphilis		THC	tetrahydrocannabinol
STSG	split thickness skin graft		TI	tricuspid insufficiency
STU	skin test unit		TIA	transient ischemic attack
subcu	subcutaneous		TIBC	total iron binding capacity
subind.	immediately after		tinct	tincture
supp	suppository		TKA	total knee arthroplasty
Sv	scalp vein		TM	tympanic membrane
SVC	service		TMJ	temporomandibular joint
SVCS	superior vena cava syndrome		TNS	transcutaneous nerve stimulator or stimulation
Sx	1) sign			
	2) symptom		TO	telephone order
T	1) temperature		TOA	tubo-ovarian abscess
	2) tender		TORCH	Toxoplasmosis, Other (includes syphilis), Rubella, Cytomegalovirus, and Herpes virus
	3) thoracic vertebrae			
T&A	tonsils and adenoids			
T&C	type and crossmatch		TP	total protein
t.d.s.	three times a day		TPA	1) third party administrator
t.i.d.	three times daily			2) trading partner agreement
T3	triiodothyronine		TPAL	term pregnancies, premature infants, abortions, living children
T4	thyroxine			
TA	1) tension by applanation		TPN	total parenteral nutrition
	2) transactional analysis		TPR	temperature, pulse, respiration
tab.	tablet (tabella)		Tr	1) tinctura, tincture
TAH	total abdominal hysterectomy			2) trace
TAH-t	total temporary artificial heart (CardioWest™)		TRAM	transverse rectus abdominos musculocutaneous
Tap/H2O/E	tap water enema		trans	transverse
TAT	1) tetanus antitoxin		tres	three
	2) turnaround time		TRF	thyrotropin releasing factor
TB	tuberculosis		TRH	thyrotropin releasing hormone
Tb	tubercule bacillus		tRNA	transfer ribonucleic acid
			Ts	tension by Schiotz

© 2010 Ingenix

TSA	tumor specific antigen		**VAD**	ventricular assist device system
TSD	Tay-Sachs disease		**VBAC**	vaginal birth after cesarean
TSE	testicular self-exam		**VC**	vena cava
TSH	thyroid stimulating hormone		**VCG**	vectorcardiogram
TSS	toxic shock syndrome		**VD**	venereal disease
TTN	transient tachypnea of newborn		**VDH**	valvular disease of the heart
TULIP	transurethral ultrasound guided laser induced prostate		**VDRL**	venereal disease report
			VE	voluntary effort
TUR	transurethral resection		**VEP**	visual evoked potential
TURP	transurethral resection of prostate		**VF**	*1)* ventricular fibrillation
TWE	tap water enema			*2)* visual field
Tx	treatment		**VHA**	Volunteer Hospital Association
U	unit		**VH-IVUS**	virtual histology intravascular ultrasound
U&C	usual and customary			
U/A	urinalysis		**VIP**	vasoactive intestinal peptide
UAC	umbilical artery catheter or catheterization		**Vit**	vitamin (followed by specific letter)
			VO	verbal order
UB-92	Uniform Billing Code of 1992		**VO2**	maximum oxygen consumption
UC	unit clerk		**VP**	*1)* vasopressin
UCHD	usual childhood diseases			*2)* voiding pressure
UCR	usual, customary, and reasonable		**VPC**	ventricular premature contraction
UE	upper extremity		**VPRC**	volume of packed red cells
UFR	uroflowmetry		**VS**	*1)* vesicular sound
UGI	upper gastrointestinal			*2)* vital signs
UM	*1)* unit manager		**VSD**	ventricular septal defect
	2) utilization management		**vv**	veins
UMN	upper motor neuron		**w/HSBH**	warmed heelstick blood gas
ung.	ointment		**WAK**	wearable artificial kidney
unus.	one		**WB**	whole blood
UPIN	universal physician identification number		**WBC**	white blood count
			WC	wheelchair
UPP	urethra pressure profile		**WCC**	well child care
UR	utilization review		**WD**	well developed
ur.	urine		**W-D**	wet to dry (dressings)
UR/QA	utilization review/quality assurance		**WEDI**	workgroup for electronic data interchange
URAC	utilization review accreditation commission			
			WHO	World Health Organization
URI	upper respiratory infection		**WLS**	wet lung syndrome
URN	utilization review nurse		**WN**	well nourished
US	*1)* ultrasound		**WNL**	within normal limits
	2) unstable spine		**Wt**	weight
ut dict.	as directed		**x**	except
UTI	urinary tract infection		**XLIF**	extreme lateral interbody fusion
UV	ultraviolet light		**XM**	cross match
UVC	umbilical vein catheter		**Y-O**	year-old
V Fib	ventricular fibrillation		**YTD**	year-to-date
V tach	ventricular tachycardia		**ZIFT**	zygote intrafallopian transfer
VA	Veterans Administration			
Va	visual acuity			

Abbreviations

Procedural Eponyms

An eponym is the name of a person who has given rise to the name of a particular place, tribe, discovery, or other item. In the medical profession, a disease or procedure may be known by the name of a person thought to have identified the disease or developed a surgical technique. This custom of identifying a procedure by the originator's name may prove to be problematic for the coder. The following list includes most of the procedures described by eponym in Volume 3 of ICD-9-CM.

Abbe
> construction of vagina 70.61
>> with graft or prosthesis 70.63

AbioCor® total replacement heart 37.52

Aburel (intra-amniotic injection for abortion) 75.0

Adams
> advancement of round ligament 69.22
> crushing of nasal septum 21.88
> excision of palmar fascia 82.35

AESOP® (Automated Endoscopic System for Optimal Positioning)-see category 17.4

Albee
> bone peg, femoral neck 78.05
> graft for slipping patella 78.06
> sliding inlay graft, tibia 78.07

Albert (arthrodesis, knee) 81.22

Aldridge (-Studdiford) (urethral sling) 59.5

Alexander
> prostatectomy
>> perineal 60.62
>> suprapubic 60.3
> shortening of round ligaments of uterus 69.22

Alexander-Adams (shortening of round ligaments of uterus) 69.22

Almoor (extrapetrosal drainage) 20.22

Altemeier (perineal rectal pull-through) 48.49

Ammon (dacryocystotomy) 09.53

Anderson (tibial lengthening) 78.37

Anel (dilation of lacrimal duct) 09.42

Arslan (fenestration of inner ear) 20.61

Asai (larynx) 31.75

Baffes (interatrial transposition of venous return) 35.91

Baldy-Webster (uterine suspension) 69.22

Ball
> herniorrhaphy (inguinal)
>> bilateral
>>> direct w/o graft 53.11
>>>> with graft 53.14
>>> comb direct/indirect w/o graft 53.13
>>>> with graft 53.16
>>> indirect w/o graft 53.12
>>>> with graft 53.15
>>> NOS w/o graft 53.10
>>>> with graft 53.17
>> unilateral
>>> direct w/o graft 53.01
>>>> with graft 53.03
>>> indirect w/o graft 53.02
>>>> with graft 53.04
>>> NOS w/o graft 53.00
>>>> with graft 53.05
> undercutting 49.02

Bankhart (capsular repair into glenoid, for shoulder dislocation) 81.82

Bardenheurer (ligation of innominate artery) 38.85

Barkan (goniotomy) 12.52
> with goniopuncture 12.53

Barr (transfer of tibialis posterior tendon) 83.75

Barsky (closure of cleft hand) 82.82

Bassett (vulvectomy with inguinal lymph node dissection) 71.5, [40.3]

Bassini
> herniorrhaphy (inguinal)
>> bilateral
>>> direct w/o graft 53.11
>>>> with graft 53.14
>>> comb direct/indirect w/o graft 53.13
>>>> with graft 53.16
>>> indirect w/o graft 53.12
>>>> with graft 53.15
>>> NOS w/o graft 53.10
>>>> with graft 53.17
>> unilateral
>>> direct w/o graft 53.01
>>>> with graft 53.03
>>> indirect w/o graft 53.02
>>>> with graft 53.04
>>> NOS w/o graft 53.00
>>>> with graft 53.05
> undercutting 49.02

Batch-Spittler-McFaddin (knee disarticulation) 84.16

Batista (partial ventriculectomy) (ventricular reduction) (ventricular remodeling) 37.35

Beck I (epicardial poudrage) 36.39

Beck II (aorta-coronary sinus shunt) 36.39

Beck-Jianu (permanent gastrostomy) 43.19

Bell-Beuttner (subtotal abdominal hysterectomy) 68.39

Belsey (esophagogastric sphincter) 44.65

Benenenti (rotation of bulbous urethra) 58.49

Berke (levator resection eyelid) 08.33

Biesenberger (size reduction of breast, bilateral) 85.32
    unilateral 85.31

Bigelow (litholapaxy) 57.0

Billroth I (partial gastrectomy with gastroduodenostomy) 43.6

Billroth II (partial gastrectomy with gastrojejunostomy) 43.7

Binnie (hepatopexy) 50.69

Bischoff (ureteroneocystostomy) 56.74

Bisection hysterectomy 68.39 (laparoscopic 68.31)

Bishoff (spinal myelotomy) 03.29

Blalock (systemic-pulmonary anastomosis) 39.0

Blalock-Hanlon (creation of atrial septal defect) 35.42

Blalock-Taussig (subclavian-pulmonary anastomosis) 39.0

Blascovic (resection and advancement of levator palpebrae superioris) 08.33

Blount
    by epiphyseal stapling 78.25
    femoral shortening (with blade plate) 78.25

Boari (bladder flap) 56.74

Bobb (cholelithotomy) 51.04

Bonney (abdominal hysterectomy) 68.49
    laparoscopic 68.41

Borthen (iridotasis) 12.63

Bost
    plantar dissection 80.48
    radiocarpal fusion 81.26

Bosworth
    arthroplasty for acromioclavicular separation 81.83
    fusion of posterior lumbar spine 81.08
        for pseudarthrosis 81.38
    resection of radial head ligaments (for tennis elbow) 80.92
    shelf procedure, hip 81.40

Bottle (repair of hydrocele of tunica vaginalis) 61.2

Boyd (hip disarticulation) 84.18

Brauer (cardiolysis) 37.10

Bricker (ileoureterostomy) 56.51

Bristow (repair of shoulder dislocation) 81.82

Brock (pulmonary valvulotomy) 35.03

Brockman (soft tissue release for clubfoot) 83.84

Browne (-Denis) (hypospadias repair) 58.45

Brunschwig (temporary gastrostomy) 43.19

Bunnell (tendon transfer) 82.56

Burch procedure (retropubic urethral suspension for urinary stress incontinence) 59.5

Burgess (amputation of ankle) 84.14

Caldwell (sulcus extension) 24.91

Caldwell-Luc (maxillary sinusotomy) 22.39
    with removal of membrane lining 22.31

Callander (knee disarticulation) 84.16

Campbell
    bone block, ankle 81.11
    fasciotomy (iliac crest) 83.14
    reconstruction of anterior cruciate ligaments 81.45

Carroll and Taber (arthroplasty proximal interphalangeal joint) 81.72

Cattell (herniorrhaphy) 53.51

Cecil (urethral reconstruction) 58.46

CentriMag® acute circulatory support device 37.62

Chamberlain procedure (mediastinotomy) 34.1

Chandler (hip fusion) 81.21

Charles (correction of lymphedema) 40.9

Charnley (compression arthrodesis)
    ankle 81.11
    hip 81.21
    knee 81.22

Cheatle-Henry
    femoral (unilateral) 53.29
        with prosthesis or graft 53.21
        bilateral 53.39
            with prosthesis or graft 53.31

Chevalier-Jackson (partial laryngectomy) 30.29

Child (radical subtotal pancreatectomy) 52.53

Chopart (midtarsal amputation) 84.12

Clagett (closure of chest wall following open flap drainage) 34.72

Clayton (resection of metatarsal heads and bases of phalanges) 77.88

Cocked hat (metacarpal lengthening and transfer of local flap) 82.69

Cockett (varicose vein)
lower limb 38.59
upper limb 38.53

Cody tack (perforation of footplate) 19.0

Coffey (uterine suspension) (Meigs' modification) 69.22

Cole (anterior tarsal wedge osteotomy) 77.28

Collis-Nissen (hiatal hernia repair) 53.80

Colonna
adductor tenotomy (first stage) 83.12
hip arthroplasty (second stage) 81.40
reconstruction of hip (second stage) 81.40

Coventry (tibial wedge osteotomy) 77.27

Cox-maze procedure (ablation or destruction of heart tissue)
endovascular approach 37.34
open (trans-thoracic) approach 37.33
thoracoscopic approach 37.37

Crawford (tarso-frontalis sling of eyelid) 08.32

Culp-Deweerd (spiral flap pyeloplasty) 55.87

Culp-Scardino (ureteral flap pyeloplasty) 55.87

Curtis (interphalangeal joint arthroplasty) 81.72

D'Ombrain (excision of pterygium with corneal graft) 11.32

Dahlman (excision of esophageal diverticulum) 42.31

Dana (posterior rhizotomy) 03.1

Danforth (fetal) 73.8

Darrach (ulnar resection) 77.83

Davis (intubated ureterotomy) 56.2

de Grandmont (tarsectomy) 08.35

Delorme
pericardiectomy 37.31
proctopexy 48.76
repair of prolapsed rectum 48.76
thoracoplasty 33.34

Denker (radical maxillary antrotomy) 22.31

Dennis-Varco (herniorrhaphy)
femoral (unilateral) 53.29
with prosthesis or graft 53.21
bilateral 53.39
with prosthesis or graft 53.31

Denonvillier (limited rhinoplasty) 21.86

Derlacki (tympanoplasty) 19.4

Dickson (fascial transplant) 83.82

Dickson-Diveley (tendon transfer and arthrodesis to correct claw toe) 77.57

Dieffenbach (hip disarticulation) 84.18

Doléris (shortening of round ligaments) 69.22

Dorrance (push-back operation for cleft palate) 27.62

Dotter (transluminal angioplasty) 39.59

Douglas (suture of tongue to lip for micrognathia) 25.59

Downstream® System (AO therapy) (aqueous oxygen) 00.49

Doyle (paracervical uterine denervation) 69.3

Duhamel (abdominoperineal pull-through) 48.65

Dunn (triple arthrodesis) 81.12

Dupuytren
fasciectomy 82.35
fasciotomy 82.12
with excision 82.35
shoulder disarticulation 84.08

Durham (-Caldwell) (transfer of biceps femoris tendon) 83.75

DuToit and Roux (staple capsulorrhaphy of shoulder) 81.82

DuVries (tenoplasty) 83.88

Dwyer
fasciotomy 83.14
soft tissue release NEC 83.84
wedge osteotomy, calcaneus 77.28

Dührssen (vaginofixation of uterus) 69.22

Eagleton (extrapetrosal drainage) 20.22

Eden-Hybinette (glenoid bone block) 78.01

Effler (heart) 36.2

Eggers
tendon release (patellar retinacula) 83.13
tendon transfer (biceps femoris tendon) (hamstring tendon) 83.75

Elliot (scleral trephination with iridectomy) 12.61

Ellis Jones (repair of peroneal tendon) 83.88

Ellison (reinforcement of collateral ligament) 81.44

Elmslie-Cholmeley (tarsal wedge osteotomy) 77.28

Eloesser
> thoracoplasty 33.34
> thoracostomy 34.09

Emmet (cervix) 67.61

Estes (ovary) 65.72
> laparoscopic 65.75

Estlander (thoracoplasty) 33.34

Evans (release of clubfoot) 83.84

Farabeuf (ischiopubiotomy) 77.39

Fasanella-Servatt (blepharoptosis repair) 08.35

Ferguson (hernia repair) 53.00

Fick (perforation of footplate) 19.0

Finney (pyloroplasty) 44.29

Foley (pyeloplasty) 55.87

Fontan (creation of conduit between right atrium and pulmonary artery) 35.94

Fothergill (-Donald) (uterine suspension) 69.22

Fowler
> arthroplasty of metacarpophalangeal joint 81.72
> release (mallet finger repair) 82.84
> tenodesis (hand) 82.85
> thoracoplasty 33.34

Fox (entropion repair with wedge resection) 08.43

Franco (suprapubic cystotomy) 57.18

Frank (permanent gastrostomy) 43.19

Frazier (-Spiller) (subtemporal trigeminal rhizotomy) 04.02

Fredet-Ramstedt (pyloromyotomy) (with wedge resection) 43.3

Frenckner (intrapetrosal drainage) 20.22

Frickman (abdominal proctopexy) 48.75

Frommel (shortening of uterosacral ligaments) 69.22

Gabriel (abdominoperineal resection of rectum) NOS 48.50
> laparoscopic 48.51
> open 48.52
> other 48.59

Gant (wedge osteotomy of trochanter) 77.25

Garceau (tibial tendon transfer) 83.75

Gardner (spinal meningocele repair) 03.51

Gelman (release of clubfoot) 83.84

Ghormley (hip fusion) 81.21

Gifford
> destruction of lacrimal sac 09.6
> keratotomy (delimiting) 11.1

Gill
> arthrodesis of shoulder 81.23
> laminectomy 03.09

Gilliam (uterine suspension) 69.22

Gill-Stein (carporadial arthrodesis) 81.25

Girdlestone
> laminectomy with spinal fusion 81.00
> muscle transfer for claw toe 77.57
> resection of femoral head and neck (without insertion of joint prosthesis) 77.85
> resection of hip prosthesis 80.05

Girdlestone-Taylor (muscle transfer for claw toe repair) 77.57

Glenn (anastomosis of superior vena cava to right pulmonary artery) 39.21

Goebel-Frangenheim-Stoeckel (urethrovesical suspension) 59.4

Goldner (clubfoot release) 80.48

Goldthwait
> ankle stabilization 81.11
> patella stabilization 81.44
> tendon transfer for patella dislocation 81.44

Goodall-Power (vagina) 70.4

Gordon-Taylor (hindquarter amputation) 84.19

Graber-Duvernay (drilling femoral head) 77.15

Green (scapulopexy) 78.41

Grice (subtalar arthrodesis) 81.13

Gritti-Stokes (knee disarticulation) 84.16

Gross (herniorrhaphy) 53.49
> laparoscopic 53.43
>> with graft or prosthesis 53.42
> other and open with graft or prosthesis 53.41
> other open 53.49

Guyon (amputation of ankle) 84.13

Hagner (epididymotomy) 63.92

Halsted
> herniorrhaphy (inguinal)
>> bilateral
>>> direct w/o graft 53.11
>>>> with graft 53.14
>>> comb direct/indirect w/o graft 53.13
>>>> with graft 53.16
>>> indirect w/o graft 53.12
>>>> with graft 53.15
>>> NOS w/o graft 53.10
>>>> with graft 53.17

© 2010 Ingenix

Eponyms

Halsted–*continued*
    unilateral
        direct w/o graft 53.01
            with graft 53.03
        indirect w/o graft 53.02
            with graft 53.04
        NOS w/o graft 53.00
            with graft 53.05
    undercutting 49.02

Hampton (anastomosis small intestine to rectal stump) 45.92

Hanging hip (muscle release) 83.19

Harelip 27.54

Harrison-Richardson (vaginal suspension) 70.77
    with graft or prosthesis 70.78

Hartmann - colectomy left (Hartmann) (lower) (radical) 45.75
    laparoscopic 17.35
    open or other 45.75

Hauser
    achillotenotomy 83.11
    bunionectomy with adductor tendon transfer 77.53
    stabilization of patella 81.44

Heaney (vaginal hysterectomy) 68.59
    laparoscopically assisted (LAVH) 68.51

HeartMate (implantable heart assist system) 37.66

HeartMate II (left ventricular assist system) 37.66

Hegar (perineorrhaphy) 71.79

Heine (cyclodialysis) 12.55

Heineke-Mikulicz (pyloroplasty) 44.29

Heller (esophagomyotomy) 42.7

Hellström (transplantation of aberrant renal vessel) 39.55

Henley (jejunal transposition) 43.81

Hey (amputation of foot) 84.12

Hey-Groves (reconstruction of anterior cruciate ligament) 81.45

Heyman (soft tissue release for clubfoot) 83.84

Heyman-Herndon (-Strong) (correction of metatarsus varus) 80.48

Hibbs (lumbar spinal fusion) lumbar, lumbosacral NEC 81.08

Higgins
    femoral (unilateral) 53.29
        with prosthesis or graft 53.21
        bilateral 53.39
            with prosthesis or graft 53.31

Hill-Allison (hiatal hernia repair, transpleural approach) 53.80

Hitchcock (anchoring tendon of biceps) 83.88

Hofmeister (gastrectomy) 43.7

Hoke
    midtarsal fusion 81.14
    triple arthrodesis 81.12

Holth
    iridencleisis 12.63
    sclerectomy 12.65

Homan (correction of lymphedema) 40.9

Hutch (ureteroneocystostomy) 56.74

Hybinette-eden (glenoid bone block) 78.01

Impella® (percutaneous external heart assist device) 37.68

Interleukin-2 (infusion); high-dose 00.15, low-dose 99.28

Irving (tubal ligation) 66.32

Irwin 77.30

Jaboulay's (gastroduodenostomy) 44.39
    laparoscopic 44.38

Janeway (permanent gastrostomy) 43.19

Jatene (arterial switch) 35.84

Johanson (urethral reconstruction) 58.46

Jones
    claw toe (transfer of extensor hallucis longus tendon) 77.57
        modified (with arthrodesis) 77.57
        dacryocystorhinostomy 09.81
        hammer toe (interphalangeal fusion) 77.56
    modified (tendon transfer with arthrodesis) 77.57
    repair of peroneal tendon 83.88

Joplin (exostectomy with tendon transfer) 77.53

Kader (temporary gastrostomy) 43.19

Kaufman (for urinary stress incontinence) 59.79

Kazanjiian (buccal vestibular sulcus extension) 24.91

Kehr (hepatopexy) 50.69

Keller (bunionectomy) 77.59

Kelly (-Kennedy) (urethrovesical plication) 59.3

Kelly-Stoeckel (urethrovesical plication) 59.3

Kerr (cesarean section) 74.1

Kessler (arthroplasty, carpometacarpal joint) 81.74

Kidner (excision of accessory navicular bone) (with tendon transfer) 77.98

Killian (frontal sinusotomy) 22.41

King-Steelquist (hindquarter amputation) 84.19

Kirk (amputation through thigh) 84.17

Kock pouch
bowel anastomosis - omit code
continent ileostomy 46.22
cutaneous uretero-ileostomy 56.51
ESWL (electrocorporeal shockwave lithotripsy)
98.51
removal, calculus 57.19
revision, cutaneous uretero-ileostomy 56.52
urinary diversion procedure 56.51

Kondoleon (correction of lymphedema) 40.9

Krause (sympathetic denervation) 05.29

Kroener (partial salpingectomy) 66.69

Kroenlein (lateral orbitotomy) 16.01

Krukenberg (reconstruction of below-elbow amputation) 82.89

Krönig (low cervical cesarean section) 74.1

Kuhnt-Szymanowski (ectropion repair with lid reconstruction) 08.44

Labbe (gastrotomy) 43.0

Ladd (mobilization of intestine) 54.95

Lagrange (iridosclerectomy) 12.65

Lambrinudi (triple arthrodesis) 81.12

Langenbeck (cleft palate repair) 27.62

Lapidus (bunionectomy with metatarsal osteotomy) 77.51

Larry (shoulder disarticulation) 84.08

Lash
internal cervical os repair 67.59
laparoscopic supracervical hysterectomy 68.31

Latzko
cesarean section, extraperitoneal 74.2
colpocleisis 70.8

Le Fort (colpocleisis) 70.8

Leadbetter (urethral reconstruction) 58.46

Leadbetter-Politano (ureteroneocystostomy) 56.74

LeMesurier (cleft lip repair) 27.54

Leriche (periarterial sympathectomy) 05.25

Lindholm (repair of ruptured tendon) 83.88

Linton (varicose vein) 38.59

Lisfranc
foot amputation 84.12
shoulder disarticulation 84.08

Littlewood (forequarter amputation) 84.09
liver NEC 50.99
Lloyd-Davies (abdominoperineal resection), NOS
48.50
laparoscopic 48.51
open 48.52
other 48.59

Lloyd-Davies (abdominoperineal resection)
laparoscopic 48.51
open 48.52
unspecified 48.50

Longmire (bile duct anastomosis) 51.39

Lord
dilation of anal canal for hemorrhoids 49.49
hemorrhoidectomy 49.49
orchidopexy 62.5

Lucas and Murray (knee arthrodesis with plate) 81.22

Madlener (tubal ligation) 66.31

Magnuson (-Stack) (arthroplasty for recurrent shoulder dislocation) 81.82

Manchester (-Donald) (-Fothergill) (uterine suspension) 69.22

Marckwald operation (cervical os repair) 67.59

Marshall-Marchetti (-Krantz) (retropubic urethral suspension) 59.5

Matas (aneurysmorrhaphy) 39.52

Mayo
bunionectomy 77.59
herniorrhaphy
laparoscopic 53.43
with graft or prosthesis 53.42
other and open with graft or prosthesis 53.41
other open 53.49
vaginal hysterectomy 68.59
laparoscopically assisted (LAVH) 68.51

Maze procedure (ablation or destruction of heart tissue)
Cox-maze, open 37.33
maze, modified, endovascular 37.34
maze, modified, open 37.33

Mazet (knee disarticulation) 84.16

McBride (bunionectomy with soft tissue correction) 77.53

McBurney
herniorrhaphy (inguinal)
bilateral
direct w/o graft 53.11
with graft 53.14
comb direct/indirect w/o graft 53.13

 © 2010 Ingenix

Eponyms

McBurney–*continued*
    with graft 53.16
    indirect w/o graft 53.12
    with graft 53.15
    NOS w/o graft 53.10
    with graft 53.17
  unilateral
    direct w/o graft 53.01
    with graft 53.03
    indirect w/o graft 53.02
    with graft 53.04
    NOS w/o graft 53.00
    with graft 53.05
  undercutting 49.02

McCall (enterocele repair) 70.92
  with graft or prosthesis 70.93

McCauley (release of clubfoot) 83.84

McDonald (encirclement suture, cervix) 67.59

McIndoe (vaginal construction) 70.61
  with graft or prosthesis 70.63

McKeever (fusion of first metatarsophalangeal joint for hallux valgus repair) 77.52

McKissock (breast reduction) 85.33

McReynolds (transposition of pterygium) 11.31

McVay (hernia repair)
  femoral (unilateral) 53.29
    with prosthesis or graft 53.21
    bilateral 53.39
      with prosthesis or graft 53.31
  inguinal (unilateral) 53.00
    with prosthesis or graft 53.05
    bilateral 53.10
      with prosthesis or graft 53.17
    direct 53.11
      with prosthesis or graft 53.14
    direct and indirect 53.13
      with prosthesis or graft 53.16
    indirect 53.12
      with prosthesis or graft 53.15
    direct (unilateral) 53.01
      with prosthesis or graft 53.03
    and indirect (unilateral) 53.01
      with prosthesis or graft 53.03
    bilateral 53.13
      with prosthesis or graft 53.16
    bilateral 53.11
      with prosthesis or graft 53.14

Mikulicz (exteriorization of intestine) (first stage) 46.03
  second stage 46.04

Miles (complete proctectomy), NOS 48.50
  laparoscopic 48.51
  open 48.52
  other 48.59

Millard (cheiloplasty) 27.54

Miller
  midtarsal arthrodesis 81.14
  urethrovesical suspension 59.4

Millin-Read (urethrovesical suspension) 59.4

Mitchell (hallux valgus repair) 77.51

Mohs (chemosurgical excision of skin) 86.24

Moore (arthroplasty) 81.52

Moschowitz
  enterocele repair 70.92
    with graft or prosthesis 70.93
  herniorrhaphy
    femoral (unilateral) 53.29
      with prosthesis or graft 53.21
      bilateral 53.39
        with prosthesis or graft 53.31
  sigmoidopexy 46.63

Muller (banding of pulmonary artery) 38.85

Mumford (partial claviculectomy) 77.81

Mustard (interatrial transposition of venous return) 35.91

Nicola (tenodesis for recurrent dislocation of shoulder) 81.82

Nissen (fundoplication of stomach) 44.66
  laparoscopic 44.67

Noble (plication of small intestine) 46.62

Norman Miller (vaginopexy) 70.77
  with graft or prosthesis 70.78

Norton (extraperitoneal cesarean operation) 74.2

O'Donoghue (triad knee repair) 81.43

Ober (-Yount) (gluteal-iliotibial fasciotomy) 83.14

Olshausen (uterine suspension) 69.22

Oscar Miller (midtarsal arthrodesis) 81.14

Osmond-Clark (soft tissue release with peroneus brevis tendon transfer) 83.75

Oxford (for urinary incontinence) 59.4

Panas (linear proctotomy) 48.0

Pancoast (division of trigeminal nerve at foramen ovale) 04.02

Pantaloon (revision of gastric anastomosis) 44.5

Paquin (ureteroneocystostomy) 56.74

Partsch (marsupialization of dental cyst) 24.4

Pattee (auditory canal) 18.6

Peet (splanchnic resection) 05.29

Pemberton
  osteotomy of ilium 77.39

Eponyms

Eponyms

Pemberton–*continued*
rectum (mobilization and fixation for prolapse repair) 48.76

Pereyra (paraurethral suspension) 59.6

Pinsker (obliteration of nasoseptal telangiectasia) 21.07

Piper (forceps) 72.6

Pirogoff (ankle amputation through malleoli of tibia and fibula) 84.14

Politano-Leadbetter (ureteroneocystostomy) 56.74

Pollicization (with nerves and blood supply) 82.61

Polya (gastrectomy) 43.7

Pomeroy (ligation and division of fallopian tubes) 66.32

Poncet
lengthening of Achilles tendon 83.85
urethrostomy, perineal 58.0

Porro (cesarean section) 74.99

Potts-Smith (descending aorta-left pulmonary artery anastomosis) 39.0

Printen and Mason (high gastric bypass) 44.31

Pterygium 11.39
with corneal graft 11.32

Puestow (pancreaticojejunostomy) 52.96

Pull-through NEC 48.49
laparoscopic 48.42
not otherwise specified 48.40
open 48.43

Push-back (cleft palate repair) 27.62

Putti-Platt (capsulorrhaphy of shoulder for recurrent dislocation) 81.82

Rabbit ear (anterior urethropexy) (Tudor) 59.79

Ramadier (intrapetrosal drainage) 20.22

Ramstedt (pyloromyotomy) (with wedge resection) 43.3

Rankin
exteriorization of intestine 46.03
proctectomy (complete), NOS 48.50
laparoscopic 48.51
open 48.52
other 48.59

Rashkind (balloon septostomy) 35.41

Rastelli (creation of conduit between right ventricle and pulmonary artery) 35.92
in repair of
pulmonary artery atresia 35.92
transposition of great vessels 35.92
truncus arteriosus 35.83

Raz-Pereyra procedure (bladder neck suspension) 59.79

Ripstein (repair of rectal prolapse) 48.75

Rodney Smith (radical subtotal pancreatectomy) 52.53

Roux-en-Y
bile duct 51.36
cholecystojejunostomy 51.32
esophagus (intrathoracic) 42.54
gastroenterostomy 44.39
laparoscopic 44.38
gastrojejunostomy 44.39
laparoscopic 44.38
pancreaticojejunostomy 52.96

Roux-Goldthwait (repair of patellar dislocation) 81.44

Roux-Herzen-Judine (jejunal loop interposition) 42.63

Ruiz-Mora (proximal phalangectomy for hammer toe) 77.99

Russe (bone graft of scaphoid) 78.04

S.P. Rogers (knee disarticulation) 84.16

Saemisch (corneal section) 11.1

Salter (innominate osteotomy) 77.39

Sauer-Bacon (abdominoperineal resection) 48.50
laparoscopic 48.51
open 48.52
other 48.59

Schanz (femoral osteotomy) 77.35

Schauta (-Amreich) (radical vaginal hysterectomy) 68.79
laparoscopic 68.71

Schede (thoracoplasty) 33.34

Scheie
cautery of sclera 12.62
sclerostomy 12.62

Schlatter (total gastrectomy) 43.99

Schroeder (endocervical excision) 67.39

Schuchardt (nonobstetrical episiotomy) 71.09

Schwartze (simple mastoidectomy) 20.41

Scott
intestinal bypass for obesity 45.93
jejunocolostomy (bypass) 45.93

Seddon-Brooks (transfer of pectoralis major tendon) 83.75

Semb (apicolysis of lung) 33.39

Senning (correction of transposition of great vessels) 35.91

© 2010 Ingenix

Sever (division of soft tissue of arm) 83.19

Sewell (heart) 36.2

Sharrard (iliopsoas muscle transfer) 83.77

Shelf (hip arthroplasty) 81.40

Shirodkar (encirclement suture, cervix) 67.59

Silver (bunionectomy) 77.59

Sistrunk (excision of thyroglossal cyst) 06.7

Skene's gland NEC 71.8

SKyphoplasty 81.66

Sling
    eyelid
        fascia lata, palpebral 08.36
        frontalis fascial 08.32
        levator muscle 08.33
        orbicularis muscle 08.36
        palpebral ligament, fascia lata 08.36
        tarsus muscle 08.35
    fascial (fascia lata)
        eye 08.32
        for facial weakness (trigeminal nerve
        paralysis) 86.81
        palpebral ligament 08.36
        tongue 25.59
    tongue (fascial) 25.59
    urethra (suprapubic) 59.4
        retropubic 59.5
    urethrovesical 59.5

Slocum (pes anserinus transfer) 81.47

Sluder (tonsillectomy) 28.2

Smith (open osteotomy of mandible) 76.62

Smith-Peterson (radiocarpal arthrodesis) 81.25

Smithwick (sympathectomy) 05.29

Soave (endorectal pull-through) 48.41
    combined abdominal, NOS 48.50
        laparoscopic 48.51
        open 48.52
        other 48.59

Sonneberg (inferior maxillary neurectomy) 04.07

Sorondo-Ferré (hindquarter amputation) 84.19

Soutter (iliac crest fasciotomy) 83.14

Spalding-Richardson (uterine suspension) 69.22

Spinelli (correction of inverted uterus) 75.93

Spivack (permanent gastrostomy) 43.19

Ssabanejew-Frank (permanent gastrostomy) 43.19

Stacke (simple mastoidectomy) 20.41

Stallard (conjunctivocystorhinostomy) 09.82
    with insertion of tube or stent 09.83

Stamm (-Kader) (temporary gastrostomy) 43.19

Steinberg 44.5

Steindler
    fascia stripping (for cavus deformity) 83.14
    flexorplasty (elbow) 83.77
    muscle transfer 83.77

Stewart (renal plication with pyeloplasty) 55.87

Stone (anoplasty) 49.79

Strassman (metroplasty) 69.49
    metroplasty (Jones modification) 69.49
    uterus 68.22

Strayer (gastrocnemius recession) 83.72

Stromeyer-Little (hepatotomy) 50.0

Strong (unbridling of celiac artery axis) 39.91

Sturmdorf (conization of cervix) 67.2

Summerskill (dacryocystorhinostomy by intubation) 09.81

Surmay (jejunostomy) 46.39

Swenson
    bladder reconstruction 57.87
    laparoscopic 48.42
    not otherwise specified 48.40
    open 48.43
    proctectomy, NEC 48.49

Swinney (urethral reconstruction) 58.46

Syme
    ankle amputation through malleoli of tibia and
    fibula 84.14
    urethrotomy, external 58.0

Taarnhoj (trigeminal nerve root decompression) 04.41

Tack (sacculotomy) 20.79

Talma-Morison (omentopexy) 54.74

TandemHeart 37.68

Tanner (devascularization of stomach) 44.99

TAPVC (total anomalous pulmonary venous connection) 35.82

Tetralogy of Fallot, total repair (one-stage) 35.81

Thal (repair of esophageal stricture) 42.85

Thiersch
    anus 49.79
    skin graft 86.69
        hand 86.62

Eponyms

Thompson
   cleft lip repair 27.54
   correction of lymphedema 40.9
   quadricepsplasty 83.86
   thumb apposition with bone graft 82.69

Thoratec implantable ventricular assist device (IVAD) 37.66

Thoratec ventricular assist device (VAD) 37.66

Thorek (partial cholecystectomy) 51.21

Three-snip, punctum 09.51

TKP (thermokeratoplasty) 11.74

Tomkins (metroplasty) 69.49

Torek (-Bevan) (orchidopexy) (first stage) (second stage) 62.5

Torkildsen (ventriculocisternal shunt) 02.2

Torpin (cul-de-sac resection) 70.92

Toti (dacryocystorhinostomy) 09.81

Touchas 86.83

Touroff (ligation of subclavian artery) 38.85

Trabeculae corneae cordis (heart) NEC 35.35

Transbronchoscopic needle aspiration (TBNA) 33.24

Trauner (lingual sulcus extension) 24.91

Truncus arteriosus NEC 35.83

Tsuge (macrodactyly repair) 82.83

Tudor rabbit ear (anterior urethropexy) 59.79

Tuffier
   apicolysis of lung 33.39
   vaginal hysterectomy 68.59
      laparoscopically assisted (LAVH) 68.51

Tunica vaginalis NEC 61.99

Turco (release of joint capsules in clubfoot) 80.48

Uchida (tubal ligation with or without fimbriectomy) 66.32

Urban (mastectomy) (unilateral) 85.47
   bilateral 85.48

Vectra vascular access graft 86.07

Vicq d'Azyr (larynx) 31.1

Vidal (varicocele ligation) 63.1

Vineberg (implantation of mammary artery into ventricle) 36.2

von Kraske (proctectomy) 48.64

Voss (hanging hip operation) 83.19

Vulpius (-Compere) (lengthening of gastrocnemius muscle) 83.85

Wang needle aspiration biopsy (transbronchoscopic) 33.24
   lung 33.27

Wardill (cleft palate) 27.62

Ward-Mayo (vaginal hysterectomy) 68.59
   laparoscopically assisted (LAVH) 68.51

Waters (extraperitoneal cesarean section) 74.2

Waterston (aorta-right pulmonary artery anastomosis) 39.0

Watkins (-Wertheim) (uterus interposition) 69.21

Watson-Jones
   hip arthrodesis 81.21
   reconstruction of lateral ligaments, ankle 81.49
   shoulder arthrodesis (extra-articular) 81.23
   tenoplasty 83.88

Weir
   appendicostomy 47.91
   correction of nostrils 21.86

Wertheim (radical hysterectomy) 68.69
   laparoscopic 68.61

West (dacryocystorhinostomy) 09.81

Wheeler
   entropion repair 08.44
   halving procedure (eyelid) 08.24

Whipple (radical pancreaticoduodenectomy) 52.7
   Child modification (radical subtotal pancreatectomy) 52.53
   Rodney Smith modification (radical subtotal pancreatectomy) 52.53

White (lengthening of tendo calcaneus by incomplete tenotomy) 83.11

Whitehead
   glossectomy, radical 25.4
   hemorrhoidectomy 49.46

Whitman
   foot stabilization (talectomy) 77.98
   hip reconstruction 81.40
   repair of serratus anterior muscle 83.87
   talectomy 77.98
   trochanter wedge osteotomy 77.25

Wier (entropion repair) 08.44

Williams-Richardson (vaginal construction) 70.61
   with graft or prosthesis 70.63

Wilms (thoracoplasty) 33.34

Wilson (angulation osteotomy for hallux valgus) 77.51

Eponyms

© 2010 Ingenix

Window

    aorticopulmonary 39.59

    bone cortex 77.10

        facial 76.09

    pericardium 37.12

    pleural 34.09

Winiwarter (cholecystoenterostomy) 51.32

Witzel (temporary gastrostomy) 43.19

Woodward (release of high riding scapula) 81.83

Young

    epispadias repair 58.45

    tendon transfer (anterior tibialis) (repair of flat foot) 83.75

Yount (division of iliotibial band) 83.14

Zancolli

    capsuloplasty 81.72

    tendon transfer (biceps) 82.56

Zenith® Renu™ AAA graft 39.71

Ziegler (iridectomy) 12.14

Eponyms

Surgical Terms

A special language is spoken in the surgical suite and written in the medical charts documenting procedures. The following list includes many of the medical terms heard most often in the operating room.

ablation. Surgical removal of a part.

abrasion. Removal of layers of skin.

achalasia. Failure of the smooth muscles within the gastrointestinal tract to relax at points of junction; most commonly referring to the esophagogastric sphincter's failure to relax when swallowing.

acromioplasty. Repair of the part of the shoulder blade that connects to the deltoid muscles and clavicle.

advance. To move away from the starting point.

allograft. Transplanted tissue from the same species.

amputation. Removal of a limb or part of a limb.

analysis. Study of a body section or parts.

anastomosis. Surgically created connection between ducts, blood vessels, or bowel segments to allow flow from one to the other.

aneurysm. Circumscribed dilation or outpouching of an artery wall, often containing blood clots connecting directly with the lumen of the artery.

angioplasty. Reconstruction of a blood vessel.

antibody. Immunoglobulin or protective protein encoded within its building block sequence to interact only with its specific antigen.

antigen. Substance inducing sensitivity or triggering an immune response and the production of antibodies.

antrum. Chamber or cavity, typically with a small opening.

appliance. Device providing function to a body part.

arthrocentesis. Aspiration of fluid from a joint with needle.

arthrodesis. Surgical fixation of a joint.

arthroplasty. Restoration of a joint.

arthroscopy. Endoscopic examination of a joint.

arthrotomy. Surgical incision into a joint.

articulate. Comprised of separate segments joined together, allowing for movement of each part on the other.

aspiration. Drawing in or out by suction.

assay. Test of purity.

astragalectomy. Surgical excision of the talus (ankle) bone.

augmentation. Add to or increase the substance of a body site, usually performed as plastic reconstructive measures. Augmentation may involve the use of an implant or prosthesis, especially within soft tissue or grafting procedures, such as bone tissue.

autograft. Any tissue harvested from one anatomical site of a person and grafted to another anatomical site of the same person. Most commonly, blood vessels, skin, tendons, fascia, and bone are used as autografts.

avulse. Tear away from.

benign. Mild or nonmalignant in nature.

biofeedback. Technique allowing the patient to control body function.

biometry. Statistical analysis of biological data.

biopsy. Tissue or fluid removed for diagnostic purposes through analysis of the cells in the biopsy material.

blood type. Classification of blood by group.

bougie. Probe used to dilate or calibrate a body part.

brachytherapy. Radiotherapy proximate to the organ being treated.

bridge. Connection between two parts of an organ.

brush. Tool used to gather cell samples or clean body part.

burr. Drill used to cut and shape bone.

bursa. Cavity or sac containing fluid that occurs between articulating surfaces and serves to reduce friction from moving parts.

bypass. Auxiliary flow.

calculus. Concretion of calcium, cholesterol, salts, or other substances that forms in any part of the body.

cannula. Tube inserted to facilitate passage.

capsulorrhaphy. Suturing or repair of a joint capsule, most frequently done on the glenohumeral joint.

capsulotomy. Incision made into a capsule, such as the lens of the eye, the kidney, or a joint.

c-arm. Portable x-ray machine for surgery.

cast. Rigid encasement for therapeutic purposes.

catheter. Any of a number of tubes inserted in body parts.

cauterize. Heat or chemicals used to burn or cut.

celiotomy. Incision into the abdomen.

cement. Prosthesis glued to bone.

centesis. Puncture.

cephalad. Toward the head.

cerclage. Looping or encircling an organ or tissue with wire or ligature for positional support.

chemodenervation. Chemical destruction of nerves.

chemosurgery. Application of chemical agents to destroy tissue, originally referring to the in situ chemical fixation of premalignant or malignant lesions to facilitate surgical excision.

chemotherapy. Treatment of disease, especially cancerous conditions, using chemical agents.

chisel. Instrument for cutting or planing bone.

chondral. Cartilage.

chromotubation. Medication injection into the uterus and tubes.

cicatricial. Concerning a scar.

ciliary. Pertaining to the eyelid.

circumcise. Circular cutting around a body part.

clamp. Tool used to grip, compress, join, or fasten body parts.

clipping. Occlusion or completely closing the orifice or lumen.

closure. Suturing of an incision.

clysis. Fluids injected into the body.

coctolabile. Capable of being destroyed or altered when boiled.

comminuted. Fracture type in which the bone is splintered or crushed.

commissure. Juncture where two corresponding parts come together, especially referring to the union site of adjacent heart valve cusps.

complex. Composite of anatomical parts or surgical procedures.

condyle. Rounded end of a bone that forms an articulation.

conization. Excision of a cone-shaped piece of tissue.

constriction. Therapeutic binding of a body part.

contour. Act of shaping along desired lines.

corpectomy. Removal of the body of a bone, such as a vertebra.

correct. Body part modification.

craterization. Formation of a depression in body tissue.

cross match. Test used to match the compatibility of a donor's blood or organ to the recipient.

crus. 1) Any body part resembling a leg. 2) Lower part of the leg.

cryotherapy. Any surgical procedure that uses intense cold for treatment.

culture. Growth of microorganisms in a medium conducive to their development.

curettage. Removal of tissue by scraping.

cutaneous. Relating to the skin.

cystotomy. Incision into the gallbladder or urinary bladder.

debridement. Removal of dead or contaminated tissue and foreign matter from a wound.

decompress. Relieve pressure.

decubitus. 1) Ulcer often spawned by bedrest. 2) Patient's position in bed.

dehiscence. Rupture or bursting open.

deligation. Closure by tying up; sutures, ligatures.

denervation. Destruction or deprivation of nerve connection, either by excision, incision or injection.

depressor. Tool used to push body tissue out of the way.

dermabrasion. Cosmetic procedure that smooths out flaws and disfigured skin and promotes the growth of a new layer of skin cells by removing the outer layer of skin by mechanical or chemical means such as fine sandpaper, wire brushes, and caustic substances.

destruction. Tissue elimination.

detection. Search for presence of a tissue or material.

diagnostic. Aid in diagnosis.

dialysis. Diffusion of body fluids to restore normal balance.

diaphysis. Central shaft of a long bone.

diathermy. Therapeutic use of heat in a part of the body.

dilation. Expansion or stretching an opening.

dilution. Concentration reduction of a mixture or solution by adding more fluid.

disarticulation. Amputation through a joint.

© 2010 Ingenix

Terms

diskectomy. Removal of an intervertebral disk.

dislocation. Displacement of a body part.

dissection. Expose during surgery.

distension. Stretched or dilated.

diversion. Rechanneling of body fluid through another conduit.

diverticulum. Pouch or sac in the walls of an organ or canal.

division. Separating into two or more parts.

donor. Person from whom tissues or organs are removed for transplantation.

dorsum. Back side or back part of the body or individual anatomical structure.

dosimetry. Component in the administration of radiation oncology therapy in which a radiation dose is calculated to a specific site, including implant or beam orientation and exposure, isodose strengths, tissue inhomogeneities, and volume.

drain. Drawing of fluid from a cavity or site.

drill. Making a hole in a bone or hard tissue.

dynamic. Motion in response to forces.

echography. Ultrasonography.

ectopic. Abnormal position.

edentulous. Toothless.

electrocautery. Division or cutting of tissue using high-frequency electrical current to produce heat, which destroys cells.

elevator. Tool for lifting tissues or bone.

elution. Separation of one solid from another, usually by washing.

embolism. Obstruction of a blood vessel resulting from a clot or foreign substance.

endoscopy. Visual inspection of the body using a fiberoptic scope.

enterostomy. Artificial anus in the abdominal wall.

epiphyses. Ends of a long bone.

epithelize. Formation of epithelial cells over a surface.

escharotomy. Surgical incision into the scab or crust resulting from a severe burn in order to relieve constriction and allow blood flow to the distal unburned tissue.

esophagoscopy. Internal visual inspection of the esophagus through the use of an endoscope placed down the throat.

evacuation. Removal of waste material.

evisceration. Removal of contents of a cavity.

examination. Comprehensive visual and tactile screening and specific testing leading to diagnosis or, as appropriate, to a referral to another practitioner.

exchange. Substitution of one thing for another.

excise. Remove or cut out.

exclusion. Closure by any method.

exenteration. Surgical removal of the entire contents of a body cavity, such as the pelvis or orbit.

exfoliate. Skin falling off in layers.

exploration. Examination for diagnostic purposes.

exposure. Displaying, revealing, or making accessible.

expression. Squeezing out of tissue.

exteriorize. Expose an organ temporarily for observation.

external fixation. Rods and pins connected in a lattice to secure bone.

extract. Condensed medication.

fascia. Fibrous sheet or band of tissue that envelops organs, muscles, and groupings of muscles.

fasciotomy. Cutting through fascia.

fenestration. Openings in tissue or bandage.

fibrosis. Formation of fibrous tissue as part of the restorative process.

filiform. Probe with woven-thread end.

fissure. Deep furrow or groove in tissue structures.

fistula. Tube-like passage between two cavities.

fistulization. Creation of a fistula for therapeutic reasons.

fit. Attack of acute symptoms.

fixate. Hold, secure, or fasten in position.

fixation. Attach tissue or material.

flap. Mass of flesh moved for grafting.

fluoroscopy. Radiology technique that allows visual examination of part of the body or a function of an organ using a device that projects an x-ray image on a fluorescent screen.

follow-up. Visits or treatment following a procedure.

forceps. Tool for grasping or compressing tissue.

fossa. Indentation or shallow depression.

fragment. Division into pieces.

free graft. Unattached tissue moved to another part of the body.

frozen section. Thin slice of frozen tissue removed for microscopic study with a special cutting

Terms

instrument, often used to confirm the nature of tissue during a procedure.

fulgurate. Destruction by electric current.

furuncle. Inflamed, painful cyst or nodule on the skin caused by bacteria, often staphylococcus, entering along the hair follicle.

fusion. Union of tissues, especially bone.

Gigli saw. Saw made of thin, flexible wire with teeth along the edge used for cutting bones (e.g., craniotomy).

glomectomy (carotid). Removal of the carotid body framework.

graft. Tissue implant from another part of the body or another person.

guillotine. Instrument for severing tonsil.

halo. Tool for stabilizing the head and spine.

harvest. Removal of cells or tissue from their native site to be used as a graft or transplant to another part of the donor's body or placed into another person.

hematoma. Tumor-like collection of blood in some part of the body caused by a break in a blood vessel wall, usually as a result of trauma.

hemilaminectomy. Excision of a portion of the vertebral lamina.

hemiphalangectomy. Excision of part of the phalanx.

hemostasis. Interruption of blood flow or the cessation or arrest of bleeding.

hemostat. Tool for clamping vessels and arresting hemorrhaging.

hernia. Protrusion of a body structure through tissue.

hidradenitis. Infection or inflammation of a sweat gland.

homograft. Transplanted tissue from one member of species to another.

hyperthermia. Therapeutic raising of body temperature.

hypertrophic. Description of body part that has grown larger.

hypophysectomy. Destruction of the pituitary gland.

hypothermia. Therapeutic lack of heat.

identification. Recognition of body part or tissue.

imaging. X-ray, ultrasound, or magnetic resonance imagery.

imbrication. Overlapping of tissues during closure.

immunotherapy. Therapeutic use of serum or gamma globulin.

implant. Insertion of a material.

impression. Mark made by one organ on another.

in situ. One position.

incise. To cut open or into.

incubation. Culture cultivation under controlled conditions.

infusion. Introduction of substance into blood.

inguinal. Groin region.

inject. Introduction into body tissues.

innervate. Supplying a stimulus or energy to nerve fibers connected to a part.

inseminate. Injection of semen.

insert. To put into.

instillation. Administering a liquid slowly over time, drop by drop.

instrumentation. Use of tool or implement for therapeutic reasons.

insufflation. Blowing air or gas into a body cavity.

interpretation. Professional health care provider's review of data with a written or verbal opinion.

interstitial. Within the small spaces or gaps occurring in tissue or organs.

intracavitary. Within a body cavity.

intubate. Insertion of a tube into a body canal or organ.

inversion. Turn inward, inside out, or upside down.

irrigate. Washing out, lavage.

kinetics. Motion or movement.

laminectomy. Removal or excision of the posterior arch of a vertebra to provide additional space for the nerves and widen the spinal canal.

lance. Incision with a lancet.

lancet. Pointed surgical knife.

laparoscopy. Endoscopic examination of the abdomen.

laparotomy. Opening of the abdomen for therapy or diagnosis.

laryngoscopy. Examination of the larynx with an endoscope.

laser. Concentrated light used to cut or seal tissue.

lateral. To the side.

lavage. Washing out of a body cavity.

lesion. Any discontinuity of tissue.

© 2010 Ingenix

ligation. Tying off a blood vessel or duct with a suture or a soft, thin wire.

limited. Bounded.

lingual. Relating to the tongue.

lithotripsy. Destruction of calcified substance in the gallbladder, urethra, or bladder (also litholapaxy).

localization. Limitation to area.

lysis. Destruction, breakdown, dissolution, or decomposition of cells or substances by a specific catalyzing agent.

manipulate. Treatment by hand.

manometric. Measurement of pressure or tension in gas or a liquid.

marsupialization. Creation of a pouch in surgical treatment of a cyst in which one wall is resected and the remaining cut edges are sutured to adjacent tissue creating an open pouch of the previously enclosed cyst.

mastectomy. Surgical removal of one or both breasts.

mastotomy. Incision of breast.

meatus. Opening or passage into the body.

metatarsectomy. Excision of metatarsus.

microdissection. Dissection of tissue using a microscope.

microrepair. Repair of tissue at a level that requires using a microscope.

modification. Changing of tissues.

monitor. Recording of events.

motility. Capability of independent, spontaneous movement.

myotomy. Division of muscle.

necropsy. Autopsy.

necrosis. Death of cells or tissue within a living organ or structure.

nephrotic. Degeneration of renal epithelium.

neurectomy. Excision of a nerve.

neurotomy. Dissection of a nerve.

obliterate. Get rid or do away with completely.

observation. Perception of events.

obturate. Occlude an opening.

obturator. Prosthesis used to close an acquired or congenital opening in the palate that aids in speech and chewing.

occlusion. Constriction, closure, or blockage of a passage.

open fracture. Exposed fracture.

orchiectomy. Surgical removal of one or both testicles via a scrotal or groin incision, indicated in cases of cancer, traumatic injury, and sex reassignment surgery. A prosthetic testis may be inserted in the scrotum at the time of surgical removal.

osteomyelitis. Inflammation of bone and bone marrow.

osteophytes. Bony outgrowth.

osteoplasty. Plastic repair of bone.

osteoporotic. Porous condition of bones.

osteotome. Tool used for cutting bone.

osteotomy. Bone incision.

oversewing. Suturing over an edge to form a closure.

packing. Material placed into a cavity or wound, such as gels, gauze, pads, and sponges.

palpate. Examination by feeling with the hand.

paring. Cutting away an edge or a surface.

paronychia. Infection of nail structures.

pedicle. Stem-like, narrow base or stalk attached to a new growth.

peduncle. Connecting structures of the brain.

penetrate. Pierce.

percutaneous. Through the skin.

periosteum. Double-layered connective membrane on the outer surface of bone.

photocoagulation. Application of an intense laser beam of light to disrupt tissue and condense protein material to a residual mass, used especially for treating ocular conditions.

pilonidal. Growth of hair under skin or in cyst.

pinning. Bone fastening.

plethysmography. Measurement of changes in organ volume.

pleurodesis. Injection of a sclerosing agent into the pleural space for creating adhesions between the parietal and the visceral pleura to treat a collapsed lung caused by air trapped in the pleural cavity, or severe cases of pleural effusion.

plication. Surgical technique involving folding, tucking, or pleating to reduce the size of a hollow structure or organ.

portable. Movable.

probing. Exploration using a slender, often flexible rod.

Terms

procedure. Conduct of operation.

process. Anatomical projection or prominence on a bone.

prone. Lying face downward.

prophylaxis. Intervention or protective therapy intended to prevent a disease.

prosthesis. Man-made substitute for a missing body part.

prostrate. Recline on one's front.

pump. Forcing gas or liquid from body part.

puncture. Creating a hole.

pyelotomy. Incision or opening made into the renal pelvis. Pyelotomies are performed to accomplish other procedures such as exploration, drainage, removal of a kidney stone, instill medications, or perform ureteropyelography or renal endoscopy.

radical. Extensive surgery.

radiograph. Image made by an x-ray.

radiopaque dye. Medium injected into the body that is impenetrable by x-rays.

ream. Shape or enlarge a hole.

recess. Small empty cavity in a body part.

reconstruct. Tissue rebuilding.

reduce. Restoration to normal position or alignment.

reduction. Correction of a fracture, dislocation, or hernia to the correct place and alignment, manually or by surgery.

refer. Recommendation to another source.

regulation. Authoritative ruling or law put forth by an executive authority of the law.

reimplant. Reinsert or reattach tissue.

reinforce. Enhancement of strength.

reinnervation. Restoration of nerve function.

release. Disconnection of a tendon or ligament.

reoperation. Repeat performance of operation.

repair. Correction of situation.

replacement. Insertion of new tissue or material in place of old one.

reposition. Bring into position.

resect. Cutting out or removing a portion or all of a bone, organ, or other structure.

reservoir. Space or body cavity for storage of liquid.

response. Reaction to stimulus.

retraction. Act of holding tissue or a structure back away from its normal position or the field of interest.

revascularize. Restoring blood flow or blood supply to a body part.

revision. Re-ordering of tissue.

rod. Straight, slim, cylindrical metal instrument for therapeutics.

rongeur. Sharp-edged instrument with a scoop-tip used to cut through tissue and bone.

routine. Normal activity.

sclerose. To become hard or firm.

section. Process of cutting a division or segment out of a part.

selective. Separation.

sequestrectomy. Excision of non-viable bone.

seton. Wire or gauze used to create fistula in tissues.

sever. Separate completely.

shunt. Surgically created passage between blood vessels or other natural passages, such as an arteriovenous anastomosis, to divert or bypass blood flow from the normal channel. Abnormal shunting may occur in the body when fistulas form or congenital anomalies are present that cause blood flow to be rerouted from the normal circulatory path.

sialolith. Salivary calculus.

sigmoidoscopy. Endoscopic examination of the entire rectum and sigmoid colon, often including a portion of the descending colon and usually performed with a flexible fiberoptic scope in conjunction with a surgical procedure.

smear. Specimen for study that is spread out across a glass slide.

snare. Wire used as a loop to excise a polyp or lesion.

sound. Long, slender tool with a type of curved, flat probe at the end for dilating strictures or detecting foreign bodies.

spatulate. Cut the open end of a tubular structure with a lengthwise incision and open the end out further for greater opening size in an anastomosis.

spectroscopy. Endoscopic measurement of emission and absorption of different wavelengths (spectra) of visible and non-visible light. Intravascular spectroscopy characterize the composition of coronary artery plaques to determine appropriate treatment.

speculum. Tool used to enlarge the opening of any canal or cavity.

spiculum. Small, needle-like body or spike.

steal. Diversion of blood to another channel.

 © 2010 Ingenix

stenosis. Narrowing or constriction of a passage.

stent. Tube to provide support in a body cavity or lumen.

stereotaxis. Three-dimensional method for precisely locating structures in the brain.

stoma. Opening created in the abdominal wall from an internal organ or structure for diversion of waste elimination, drainage, and access.

strapping. Overlapping strips of plaster.

stricture. Narrowing of a hollow structure.

subluxation. Partial or complete dislocation.

suction. Vacuum evacuation of fluid or tissue.

supine. Lying on the back.

suppression. Holding back, putting in check, or inhibiting an act, function, thought, or desire.

suppurative. Forming pus.

survival. Continued life.

suspension. 1) Fixation of an organ for support. 2) Temporary state of cessation of an activity, process, or experience.

suture. Numerous stitching techniques employed in wound closure.

symphysis. Joint that unifies two opposed bones by a junction of bony surfaces to a plate of fibrocartilage.

synchondrosis. Two bones joined by hyaline cartilage or fibrocartilage.

synovia. Clear fluid lubricant of joints, bursae, and tendon sheaths, secreted by the synovial membrane.

talectomy. Excision of the ankle bone.

tap. Withdraw fluid through a needle or trocar.

technique. Manner of performance.

teletherapy. External beam radiotherapy or other treatment applied from a source maintained at a distance away from the body.

tenodesis. Stabilization of a joint by anchoring tendons.

tenolysis. Release of a tendon from adhesions.

therapeutic. Treatment of disease.

thermoplasty. The therapeutic application of a controlled heat source to repair tissue.

thoracentesis. Surgical puncture of the chest cavity with a specialized needle or hollow tubing to aspirate fluid from within the pleural space for diagnostic or therapeutic reasons.

thoracotomy. Incision in the chest wall.

thrombectomy. Removal of venous occlusion (clot).

tomograph. Method of precise x-ray.

tracheostomy. Creation of an opening into the trachea.

traction. Drawing out or holding tension on an area by applying a direct therapeutic pulling force.

tractor. Instrument for pulling an organ.

transcatheter. Procedure or treatment performed via a catheter.

transection. 1) Transverse dissection. 2) Cut across a long axis. 3) Cross section.

transfer. Removal or moving body tissue.

transplant. Insertion of an organ or tissue from one person or site into another.

transposition. 1) Removal or exchange from one side to another. 2) Change of position from one place to another.

treatment. Management of patient.

trephine. 1) Specialized round saw for cutting circular holes in bone, especially the skull. 2) Instrument that removes small disc-shaped buttons of corneal tissue for transplanting.

tube. Hollow cylinder or pipe.

ultrasound. Imaging using ultra-high sound frequency.

undiversion. Restoration of continuity, flow, or passage through the normal channel.

urachus. Embryonic tube connecting the urinary bladder to the umbilicus during development of the fetus that normally closes before birth, generally in the fourth or fifth month of gestation.

ureostomy. Connection of the ureter to a stoma on the abdominal skin.

ureterocele. Saccular formation of the lower part of the ureter, protruding into the bladder..

ureteropyelogram. X-ray study of the ureter and bladder.

valve. Prosthesis to replace an existing valve or to shunt body fluids.

varices. Enlarge, dilated, or tortured veins.

vasectomy. Surgical procedure involving the removal of all or part of the vas deferens, usually performed for sterilization or in conjunction with a prostatectomy.

vestigal. Remains of a structure occurring in a fetus.

vomer. Flat bone that forms the lower, posterior portion of the nasal septum.

xenograft. Graft taken from non-human animal.

Terms

00

Procedures and Interventions, Not Elsewhere Classified

2011 Changes

Category 00 changes for 2011 include a revised code title for code 00.55 Insertion of drug-eluting stent(s) of other peripheral vessel(s), with the addition and revision of exclusion notes. Code 00.55 was revised to exclude insertion of superficial femoral artery stents (00.60) and stent insertions for other endovascular procedure (39.71–39.79). A new code was added to subcategory 00.60 Insertion of drug-eluting stent(s) of superficial femoral artery to provide a unique classification code for the insertion of a drug-eluting stent in the superficial femoral artery used to treat severe, obstructive atherosclerotic lesions.

This section of ICD-9-CM includes diagnostic and therapeutic procedures and interventions that are not elsewhere classified in Volume 3, as well as new and emerging technologies. The ICD-9-CM classification system for these procedures and interventions is divided into the following groups:

- Therapeutic Ultrasound (00.0)
- Pharmaceuticals (00.1)
- Intravascular Imaging of Blood Vessels (00.2)
- Computer-assisted Surgery (00.3)
- Adjunct Vascular System Procedures (00.4)
- Other Cardiovascular Procedures (00.5)
- Procedures on Blood Vessels (00.6)
- Other Hip Procedures (00.7)
- Other Knee and Hip Procedures (00.8)
- Other Procedures and Interventions (00.9)

Every subcategory in this chapter requires fourth-digit subclassification to further specify the type and/or site of intervention or procedure performed. Documentation in the medical record must support code assignment.

00.0   Therapeutic Ultrasound

Description
Therapeutic ultrasound, or intravascular sonotherapy, is an interventional treatment modality that utilizes lower frequency and higher-intensity levels of ultrasound energy than those employed in diagnostic ultrasound. Utilizing non-ablative energy to reduce intimal hyperplasia or restenosis associated with atherosclerotic vascular disease, therapeutic ultrasound permits healing of the vessels following stent implantation. It may also be used to treat recurring stenotic disease at a lesion in which a stent is already in place.

Coding Clarification
This code range is not appropriate for reporting diagnostic ultrasound, intracardiac echocardiography, or adjunctive intravascular imaging.

Documentation Tip
This treatment modality may be referred to in the operative note as anti-restenotic ultrasound or intravascular non-ablative ultrasound.

Coding Guidance
AHA: 4Q, '02, 90

00.01   Therapeutic ultrasound of vessels of head and neck

Description
A needle is inserted percutaneously into a blood vessel of the head and neck. A guidewire is threaded through the needle into the blood vessel and the needle is removed. An intravascular ultrasound catheter is placed over the guidewire. The ultrasound catheter is utilized as non-ablative energy to reduce intimal hyperplasia or restenosis associated with atherosclerotic vascular disease. The catheter and guidewire are removed and pressure is applied over the puncture site to stop bleeding.

Coding Clarification
This code is used to report therapeutic ultrasound, not diagnostic ultrasound procedures.

Report ultrasonic embolectomy/thrombectomy of intracranial vessels or other head and neck vessels with 38.01 or 38.02.

For ultrasonic endarterectomy of intracranial vessels, report 38.11; for other head and neck vessels, report 38.12.

Ultrasonic angioplasty of head and neck vessels is reported with 39.50.

00.02   Therapeutic ultrasound of heart

Description
A needle is inserted percutaneously into a blood vessel of the groin and threaded through the vessel to the heart. A guidewire is threaded through the needle into the blood vessel and the needle is removed. An intravascular ultrasound catheter is placed over the guidewire. The ultrasound catheter is used as non-ablative treatment from inside the vessel to assess the area and extent of disease prior to interventional therapy, as well as adequacy of therapy after interventional therapy. The catheter and guidewire are removed and pressure is applied over the puncture site to stop bleeding.

Coding Clarification
This code is used to report therapeutic ultrasound, not diagnostic ultrasound procedures.

This code is not used to report ultrasonic angioplasty of coronary vessels; report with 00.66 or 36.09.

00.03   Therapeutic ultrasound of peripheral vascular vessels

Description
A needle is inserted percutaneously into a peripheral blood vessel. A guidewire is threaded through the needle into the blood vessel and the needle is removed. An intravascular ultrasound catheter is placed over the guidewire. The ultrasound catheter is used to obtain images from inside the vessel to assess area and extent of disease prior to interventional therapy, as well as adequacy of therapy after interventional therapy. The catheter and guidewire are removed and pressure is applied over the puncture site to stop bleeding.

Coding Clarification
Report ultrasonic angioplasty of peripheral vascular vessels with 39.50.

Diagnostic ultrasound of the peripheral vascular system is reported with 88.77.

00.09   Other therapeutic ultrasound

Coding Clarification
This code is used to report therapeutic ultrasound, not diagnostic ultrasound procedures. It should not

be used to report the following ultrasonic procedures and therapeutic interventions:

- Fragmentation of urinary stones (59.95)
- Percutaneous nephrostomy with fragmentation (55.04)
- Physical therapy (93.35)
- Transurethral guided laser-induced prostatectomy (60.21)

Coding Guidance
   AHA: 4Q, '04, 43

00.1 Pharmaceuticals

Description
Subcategory 00.1 addresses the implantation, infusion, injection, and/or administration of specified pharmaceutical agents or substances that are not captured elsewhere in Volume 3.

00.10   Implantation of chemotherapeutic agent

Description
Code 00.10 reports the implantation of chemotherapy wafers in the brain, as well as other chemotherapeutic agents that are implanted via interstitial or intracavitary means.

Chemotherapy wafers are used in the treatment of recurrent glioblastoma multiforme (GBM), as well as in the treatment of malignancies of the liver, bladder, and other sites. A wafer containing an antineoplastic agent is implanted as an adjunct to surgery. Placed closely together into the cavity created by the tumor resection in order to assure optimal coverage of the cavity walls, the wafer delivers chemotherapy directly to the site of tumor removal. The number of wafers utilized varies depending upon the size and location of the tumor cavity. Upon achieving full coverage of the tumor cavity, a topical absorbable hemostatic agent is applied to hold the wafers in place.

Coding Clarification
This code excludes the injection or infusion of cancer chemotherapeutic substances, which is correctly reported with 99.25.

Assign this code in addition to the code for the primary procedure.

Documentation Tip
This procedure may also be referred to in the operative note as interstitial or intracavitary chemotherapy.

Coding Scenario
A 45-year-old female was admitted for resection of recurrent glioblastoma multiforme of the temporal lobe and concomitant implantation of brain wafer chemotherapeutic agents. Following excision of the

● New Code   ▲ Revised Code   ▶◀ Revised Text   © 2010 Ingenix

brain tumor, wafers were placed closely together along the tumor cavity wall using forceps. Care was taken to avoid the ventricles and large vascular structures. Once full coverage of the cavity was ensured, Surgicel was placed over the wafers to secure them in place against the surface of the cavity. The cavity was irrigated and the dura was closed.

Code Assignment:

191.2	Malignant neoplasm of temporal lobe
01.59	Other excision or destruction of lesion or tissue of brain
00.10	Implantation of chemotherapeutic agent

Coding Guidance
AHA: 4Q, '02, 93

00.11   Infusion of drotrecogin alfa (activated)

Description
Drotrecogin alfa (activated) is a genetically engineered form of naturally occurring Activated Protein C (APC), which is necessary to control inflammation and clotting in blood vessels. This biological agent is used to treat severely septic patients, who are unable to convert Protein C to its activated form in adequate amounts. By reestablishing balance to inflammation and blood clotting, blood flow is restored to the organs.

A physician or an assistant under direct physician supervision administers this therapeutic substance through an intravenous catheter inserted by needle into a patient's vein or by injection or infusion through an existing indwelling intravascular access catheter or port.

Documentation Tip
This agent is also known as recombinant protein, Xigris, or DrotAA.

Index entries are found under main terms Administration (of) and Infusion.

Coding Scenario
A 30-year-old male with severe staph aureus sepsis and acute renal failure was admitted for infusion of drotrecogin alfa (activated). Utilizing sterile technique, Xigris was administered via a dedicated intravenous line at a rate of 24 mcg/kg/hr over a period of 96 hours.

Code Assignment:

038.11	Methicillin susceptible Staphylococcus aureus septicemia
995.92	Severe sepsis
584.9	Acute renal failure, unspecified
00.11	Infusion of drotrecogin alfa (activated)

Coding Guidance
AHA: 4Q, '02, 93

00.12   Administration of inhaled nitric oxides

Description
An inhalation-administered vasodilator used to treat pulmonary hypertension in patients with respiratory failure and hypoxia, nitric oxide is normally administered over a four-day period, dilating the pulmonary blood vessels of the lungs so that they carry more oxygen. Redistribution of blood flow away from the areas of the lungs having low ventilation/perfusion ratios to those areas with normal ratios results in improved oxygenation. In term and near-term newborns with persistent pulmonary hypertension, inhaled nitric oxide may be used in conjunction with ventilator support and other agents to improve oxygenation and lessen the need for extracorporeal membrane oxygenation (ECMO).

Documentation Tip
This therapeutic intervention may also be referred to in the medical record as nitric oxide therapy, iNO, or INOmax therapy.

Coding Guidance
AHA: 4Q, '02, 94

00.13   Injection or infusion of nesiritide

Description
Recombinant human B-type natriuretic peptide is used to treat acutely decompensated congestive heart failure that presents with shortness of breath at rest or with minimal activity. Nesiritide, the generic name, is administered via intravenous infusion or bolus. Hypotension is the most often reported adverse effect of this therapeutic intervention.

The physician or an assistant under direct physician supervision injects or infuses nesiritide via an intravenous route. Infusions are administered through an intravenous catheter inserted by needle into a patient's vein or by injection or infusion through an existing indwelling intravascular access catheter or port.

Documentation Tip
Human B-type natriuretic peptide may also be documented in the medical record as hBNP.

Coding Scenario
A 70-year-old male with acutely decompensated NYHA Class III congestive heart failure was admitted for infusion of nesiritide. A 2 mcg/kg bolus was administered intravenously over 60 seconds. Immediately following administration of the bolus, nesiritide was infused at a flow rate of 0.1 mL/kg/hr over a period of 24 hours.

Code Assignment:

428.0	Congestive heart failure, unspecified
00.13	Injection or infusion of nesiritide

00

Coding Guidance
    AHA: 4Q, '02, 94

00.14   Injection or infusion of oxazolidinone class of antibiotics

Description
This class of antibiotics is selectively utilized in the treatment of gram-positive bacteria, particularly resistant strains. One of the few classes of antibiotics that can effectively treat serious infections that are resistant to most antibiotics, oxazolidinones are generally used only in the treatment of life-threatening, medically significant infections such as septicemia caused by resistant pathogens, hospital-acquired pneumonia, or ventilator-associated pneumonia in high-risk patients or those who have a substantiated resistant gram-positive infection. Other indications include postoperative and traumatic wounds, and certain cases of resistant gram-positive cellulitis infections.

The physician or an assistant under direct physician supervision injects or infuses an oxazolidinone antibiotic via an intravenous route. Infusions are administered through an intravenous catheter inserted by needle into a patient's vein or by injection or infusion through an existing indwelling intravascular access catheter or port.

Documentation Tip
May also be documented in the medical record as linezolid or Zyvox (brand name).

Coding Guidance
    AHA: 4Q, '02, 95

00.15   High-dose infusion interleukin-2 [IL-2]

Description
A genetically engineered form of human cytokine, a protein that is released by cells of the immune system and plays a role in immune response generation, interleukin-2 is generally administered in specialized inpatient treatment settings such as the ICU or bone marrow transplant unit. Rather than directly inhibiting cancer cells, interleukin-2 assists in activating the body's immune system to destroy these cells. Due to the severity of the toxicities associated with this antineoplastic immunotherapeutic regimen, close monitoring by highly-specialized oncology professionals is required.

The physician or supervised assistant prepares and administers high-dose interleukin-2 to combat malignant neoplasms. This code describes infusions through catheter tubing placed in a vein. Unlike conventional chemotherapy, which is typically administered during a series of short inpatient stays or on an outpatient basis, high-dose interleukin-2 therapy is given in two cycles. The first is administered every eight hours over a five-day

period, after which the patient is discharged home to recover for a number of days. The patient is then readmitted for the second cycle, which repeats the same regimen and dosing as the first. If a response to this therapy is noted, the regimen may be repeated at eight to twelve-week intervals. A five-course maximum is standard.

Coding Clarification
This code specifically reports infusion of high-dose IL-2; low-dose infusion of interleukin-2 is correctly reported with 99.28.

Documentation Tip
High-dose interleukin-2 infusion may also be documented in the medical record as IL-2, aldesleukin, or by brand name Proleukin.

Coding Scenario
A patient with advanced renal cell cancer of the ureteropelvic junction was admitted for the first cycle of high-dose interleukin-2 therapy. Proleukin 600,000 IU/kg was administered every eight hours by 15-minute IV infusions for a maximum of 14 doses. The patient will be discharged for nine days of rest, after which he will return for the second cycle.

    Code Assignment:

    V58.12   Encounter for antineoplastic immunotherapy
    189.1   Malignant neoplasm of the renal pelvis
    00.15   High-dose infusion interleukin-2 [IL-2]

Coding Guidance
    AHA: 4Q, '03, 92

00.16   Pressurized treatment of venous bypass graft [conduit] with pharmaceutical substance

Description
Vein graft failure is a common occurrence for the more than 400,000 coronary and 100,000 lower extremity bypass procedures performed annually in the United States. The statistical data show that 50 percent of all vein grafts fail within 10 to 15 years after coronary bypass surgery. Peripheral bypass surgery outcomes are less optimistic, with a 50 percent failure rate after only five years.

Intimal hyperplasia is the reason for the vein graft failure. The process of proliferation of abnormal cells, or neointimal hyperplasia, is not well understood. It can be diffuse or localized at the site of anastomosis of the graft. The intimal hyperplasia is thought to be a smooth-muscle cell inflammatory response. The intimal hyperplasia eventually results in accelerated atherosclerosis and graft failure.

One approach to preventing cell proliferation and thickening of the vessel walls is a combination of gene therapy, or decoy targeting, and device technology. Using small nucleic acid molecules, called oligonucleotides, that block protein transcription factors essential for the expression of

● New Code   ▲ Revised Code   ►◄ Revised Text   © 2010 Ingenix

genes that control the cell cycle for proliferating cells, cell division of the smooth-muscle cells of the graft is essentially shut down. This genetic manipulation of the graft tissue can be accomplished before reimplantation of the autogenous graft.

Once the graft material has been harvested, the vein graft section, or conduit, is placed onto a trough and connected to a cannula inside a hyperbaric chamber. Delivery of the drug solution through the cannula under nondistending pressure for six to 10 minutes facilitates the infusion of the drug into the tissue. Once the drug has been infused into the graft tissue, the graft is flushed with heparin and is ready. This is an effective, efficient, and safe method of gene therapy.

Coding Clarification
Since this is an additional step in the coronary or peripheral artery bypass procedure, assign this code in addition to the code(s) for the primary procedure.

Documentation Tip
This therapeutic intervention is also known as ex-vivo treatment of the vessel or hyperbaric pressurized graft or conduit.

Coding Scenario
A 72-year-old male patient with severe coronary arteriosclerotic disease and no prior surgical history was admitted for coronary artery bypass (CABG). A section of the saphenous vein was harvested. The vein graft section was placed onto a trough and connected to a cannula inside a Corgentech Pressure-mediated Delivery System (CPDS). E2F Decoy was delivered through the cannula under nondistending pressure for six to 10 minutes to facilitate the infusion of the drug into the tissue. Once the E2F Decoy was infused into the graft tissue, the graft was flushed with heparin. A saphenous vein graft was used to connect the aorta to the obtuse marginal branch of the circumflex artery and to the diagonal coronary artery. The left internal mammary artery was taken down to the left anterior descending artery. An intraoperative pacemaker was used during the procedure. Extracorporeal auxiliary circulation was also performed during the procedure.

Code Assignment:

414.01 Coronary atherosclerosis of native coronary artery
36.12 (Aorto) coronary bypass of two coronary arteries
36.15 Single internal mammary-coronary artery bypass
39.61 Extracorporeal circulation auxiliary to open heart surgery
00.16 Pressurized treatment of venous bypass graft [conduit] with pharmaceutical substance

Coding Guidance
AHA: 4Q, '04, 108

00.17 Infusion of vasopressor agent

Description
The use of vasopressor infusion therapy for the treatment of shock is reserved for cases that do not respond to conventional medical treatment protocol. These patients are gravely ill and the treatment outcomes are significantly affected by the higher level of patient acuity.

Shock is defined as a state in which blood flow to and perfusion of peripheral tissue or organs is restricted due to inadequate cardiac output or inadequate systemic blood flow. There are several types of shock, including hypovolemic, vasogenic, septic, and cardiogenic. Shock cases that are unresponsive to general medical management protocol are at high risk for progressing along the continuum of illness to multiple organ dysfunction syndrome (MODS) and ultimately death.

Medical treatment options include restoration of normal intravascular blood volume and treatment of the underlying cause or condition. For patients who do not respond to initial treatment of IV fluids, vasopressor drugs are administered to improve systemic blood pressure. Inotropic catecholamines, such as dopamine, norepinephrine, and dobutamine, act to increase vasoconstriction or decrease peripheral vascular resistance, stimulate myocardial contractility and stroke volume, and reduce ventricular filling to increase cardiac output.

A physician or an assistant under direct physician supervision injects or infuses a vasopressor agent via an intravenous route. Infusions are administered through an intravenous catheter inserted by needle into a patient's vein or by injection or infusion through an existing indwelling intravascular access catheter or port.

Documentation Tip
Examples of generic vasopressor drugs include dobutamine, dopamine, ephedrine, epinephrine, isoproterenol, methoxamine, norepinephrine, phenylephrine, and vasopressin.

Coding Guidance
AHA: 4Q, '04, 109

00.18 Infusion of immunosuppressive antibody therapy

Description
Organ rejection continues to pose serious problems for transplant patients. This complication occurs when the immune system reacts to the foreign tissue with an immune response. Immunosuppressive antibody therapies are used to intervene and prevent

the immune system from attacking transplanted tissue. This therapy can be employed in the induction phase (prior to, during, or immediately post-surgery) or any time thereafter. Post-induction phase therapy can be used in a maintenance capacity or to thwart an ongoing (chronic) rejection. Regardless of the phase of therapy, antibodies bind to antigens located in the T-cells that produce the rejection mechanism, thus incapacitating the offending T-cells. These drugs are commonly administered intravenously during the induction phase; however, for maintenance therapy patients, fixed or consistent doses are required over longer periods of time.

Clinical studies have shown as much as a 65 percent to 88 percent reduction in rejection rates associated with selected immunosuppressive agents used during the induction phase or as a means to reverse rejection in patients post-transplant.

A physician or an assistant under direct physician supervision infuses an immunosuppressive antibody therapeutic agent via an intravenous route during the induction phase of solid organ transplantation. Infusions are administered through an intravenous catheter inserted by needle into a patient's vein (typically a peripheral or central vein) or by infusion through an existing indwelling intravascular access catheter or port.

Documentation Tip
The induction phase may occur prior to, during, or immediately following surgical transplantation.

The two types of therapies currently utilized during the induction phase include monoclonal antibody therapy and polyclonal antibody therapy.

Generic versions of currently existing monoclonal and polyclonal antibody therapies include antithymocyte globulin, basiliximab, daclizumab, and muromonab CD3.

Coding Scenario
A 57-year-old female with chronic, longstanding, end-stage malignant, hypertensive kidney disease is admitted for a live, related donor kidney transplant. The patient receives adjuvant immunosuppressive therapy immediately post-procedure.

Code Assignment:

403.01	Malignant hypertensive chronic kidney disease with chronic kidney disease stage V or end stage renal disease
585.6	End stage renal disease
55.69	Other kidney transplantation
00.91	Transplant from live related donor
00.18	Infusion of immunosuppressive antibody therapy during induction phase of solid organ transplantation

Coding Guidance
AHA: 4Q, '05, 101

00.19 Disruption of blood brain barrier via infusion [BBBD]

Description
The blood brain barrier is a protective mechanism that protects the brain from toxins. Unlike peripheral capillaries that allow a somewhat free exchange of substances across and between the cells, the vascular system in the brain does not function in the same way. The blood brain barrier strictly limits the transport of materials into the brain, while still allowing the passage of necessary nutrients. This is a vital function for protection of the brain but poses a challenge in the treatment of brain tumors in chemotherapy patients, for which the majority of the chemotherapy drug does not reach the tumor in the traditional treatment regimen. The ability to open the blood brain barrier for a short time while the chemotherapy is infused represents a major step in eradicating the primary and secondary effects of brain tumors. The treatment is most successful for tumors that are chemo-sensitive, such as CNS lymphoma and metastatic brain tumors from breast or testicular primaries.

This procedure involves the patient being taken to surgery or interventional radiology and a solution of a substance is infused into an artery (typically the carotid or vertebral artery) directly supplying the brain. Most often Mannitol is used in current treatment regimens. This solution opens the blood brain barrier, which eliminates a substantial impediment to effective chemotherapy. Shortly after the Mannitol or other solution is infused, chemotherapy is infused into the same artery, typically delivering 10 to 100 times the concentration of the drug than is usually possible with traditional chemotherapy. Within a few hours, the blood brain barrier (BBB) closes again.

Coding Clarification
Assign 00.19 to report disruption of blood brain barrier, infusion of substance to disrupt blood brain barrier, and Mannitol infusion.

A code for chemotherapy (99.25) should also be assigned.

Code 00.19 excludes other perfusion, which is correctly reported with 39.97.

Coding Guidance
AHA: 4Q, 07, 103-104

00.2 Intravascular imaging of blood vessels

Description
Intravascular ultrasound (IVUS) is three-dimensional visualization of the interior arterial walls from the inside of the artery. Conventional invasive angiographic techniques are two-dimensional external visualizations of vessels after injection of contrast material. IVUS is also significantly different from noninvasive ultrasound angiography. Both invasive radiographic and noninvasive ultrasonographic angiography produce two-dimensional images of vessels from outside the body. IVUS produces detailed, three-dimensional images of the interior walls of vessels that allow the physician to make real-time decisions about treatment options. After intervention, IVUS is performed to assess the efficacy of the treatment.

The images produced with conventional radiographic angiography have several limitations. First, the images are only two-dimensional and do not afford real-time decision-making. Second, there is an absence of information concerning the actual condition of the interior walls of the vessel. Third, there is insensitivity to severity of plaque build-up in remodeled vessel wall, and the inability to detect any vessel wall disruption during angioplasty.

The IVUS technique is similar to conventional balloon angioplasty. A 6 to 8 French access sheath and guiding catheter are used to introduce a conventional angioplasty guidewire to distal artery sites. The intravascular ultrasound catheter, available as over-the-wire or monorail configuration, is introduced after administration of intracoronary nitroglycerin to avoid vessel spasm, as well as the administration of an anticoagulant such as heparin.

There are two types of IVUS transducers: the mechanical rotating transducer and the electronically switched multi-element array system. A high-resolution image is produced consisting of three layers around the lumen. These images are used for determining measurements of severity of plaque build-up, plaque composition, stability of the plaque, and blood flow adequacy. After the therapeutic procedure such as balloon angioplasty is performed, IVUS can be used to determine blood flow adequacy of the lumen in remodeled vessels. The completeness of the opposition of a stent against the vessel wall after a stent insertion can be determined as well. If a stent is inserted and the stent is not up against the vessel walls, the risk of restenosis is increased. Once a stent is in place, IVUS can be used to determine whether the lumen opening has been made large enough to allow adequate blood flow.

Other applications of IVUS include assessment of vasculopathy after transplant surgery, regression/progression of lumen patency after antilipemic therapy, non-coronary artery disease, interventional target lesion, restenosis vein graft disease, serial stent studies for mechanism of restenosis process, and assessment of restenosis after brachytherapy.

Coding Clarification
Codes should also be assigned for any synchronous diagnostic or therapeutic procedures.

Codes from this subcategory are inappropriate for reporting diagnostic procedures on blood vessels, diagnostic ultrasound of the peripheral vascular system, therapeutic ultrasound, or magnetic resonance imaging.

Documentation Tip
The medical record may also refer to this imaging technique using the following terminology:

- Endovascular ultrasonography
- Intravascular imaging of blood vessels
- Real-time imaging of lumen of blood vessels using sound waves

Coding Guidance
AHA: 4Q, '04, 109-111

00.21 Intravascular imaging of extracranial cerebral vessels

Description
Intravascular ultrasound may be used during diagnostic evaluation of extracranial cerebral vessels. It may also be used both before and after a therapeutic intervention to assess patency and integrity of the vessel. A needle is inserted through the skin and into an extracranial cerebral vessel. A guidewire is threaded through the needle into a vessel and the needle is then removed. An intravascular ultrasound catheter is placed over the guidewire. The ultrasound catheter is used to obtain images from inside the vessel to assess the area and extent of disease prior to interventional therapy, as well as adequacy of therapy after interventional therapy. The catheter and guidewire are removed and pressure is applied over the puncture site to stop bleeding.

Coding Clarification
Use this code to report intravascular imaging of the common carotid vessels and branches.

Diagnostic ultrasound of the head and neck is correctly reported with 88.71.

Documentation Tip
Intravascular imaging of the extracranial cerebral vessels may also be referred to in the medical record as IVUS of extracranial cerebral vessels.

00.22   Intravascular imaging of intrathoracic vessels

Description
Intravascular ultrasound may be used during diagnostic evaluation of intrathoracic vessels. It may also be used both before and after a therapeutic intervention to assess patency and integrity of the vessel. A needle is inserted through the skin and into an intrathoracic vessel. A guidewire is threaded through the needle into the vessel and the needle is then removed. An intravascular ultrasound catheter is placed over the guidewire. The ultrasound catheter is used to obtain images from inside the vessel to assess the area and extent of disease prior to interventional therapy, as well as adequacy of therapy after interventional therapy. The catheter and guidewire are removed and pressure is applied over the puncture site to stop bleeding.

Coding Clarification
Use this code to report intravascular imaging of the aorta and aortic arch, and for the inferior and superior vena cava.

Report diagnostic ultrasound of other sites of the thorax with 88.73.

Documentation Tip
Intravascular imaging of intrathoracic vessels may also be referred to in the medical record as IVUS of intrathoracic vessels.

00.23   Intravascular imaging of peripheral vessels

Description
Intravascular ultrasound may be used during diagnostic evaluation of peripheral vessels. It may also be used both before and after a therapeutic intervention to assess patency and integrity of the vessel. A needle is inserted through the skin and into a peripheral vessel. A guidewire is threaded through the needle into the vessel and the needle is then removed. An intravascular ultrasound catheter is placed over the guidewire. The ultrasound catheter is used to obtain images from inside the vessel to assess the area and extent of disease prior to interventional therapy, as well as adequacy of therapy after interventional therapy. The catheter and guidewire are removed and pressure is applied over the puncture site to stop bleeding.

Coding Clarification
Use this code to report intravascular imaging of the vessels of the arms and legs.

Report diagnostic ultrasound of the peripheral vascular system with 88.77.

Documentation Tip
Intravascular imaging of peripheral nerves may also be referred to in the medical record as IVUS of peripheral vessels.

00.24   Intravascular imaging of coronary vessels

Description
Intravascular ultrasound may be used during diagnostic evaluation of a coronary vessel or graft. It may also be used both before and after a therapeutic intervention upon a coronary vessel or graft to assess its patency and integrity. A needle is inserted through the skin and into a blood vessel. A guidewire is threaded through the needle into a coronary blood vessel or graft and the needle is then removed. An intravascular ultrasound catheter is placed over the guidewire. The ultrasound probe is used to obtain images from inside the vessel to assess the area and extent of disease prior to interventional therapy, as well as adequacy of therapy after interventional therapy. The ultrasound probe provides a two-dimensional, cross-sectional view of the vessel or graft as the probe is advanced and withdrawn along the area of interest. When the ultrasound examination is complete, the catheter and guidewire are removed and pressure is applied over the puncture site to stop bleeding.

Coding Clarification
Report 00.24 for virtual histology intravascular ultrasound (VH-IVUS). VH-IVUS is a technology used in cardiac catheterizations to perform real-time assessment of atherosclerotic plaques in coronary arteries.

Report diagnostic ultrasound of the heart with 88.72.

Report intracardiac echocardiography (ICE) with 37.28.

Documentation Tip
Intravascular ultrasound of the coronary vessels may also be referred to in the medical record as IVUS of the coronary vessels or as VH-IVUS.

Coding Scenario
A 63-year-old man was admitted to the hospital with a history of eight hours of chest pain associated with nausea, diaphoresis, and dyspnea. He has no history of previous MI. His electrocardiogram revealed 4 to 5 mm ST-segment elevation in the inferior leads with reciprocal ST-depression consistent with acute anterolateral myocardial infarction. Oxygen, aspirin, and morphine were administered. Fifty mg TPA was administered per the Global Utilization of Streptokinase and Tissue Plasminogen Activator for Occluded Coronary Arteries (GUSTO) trial protocol and eptifibatide was also initiated. The patient was intubated, stabilized, and brought to the operating room for PTCA with drug-eluting stent insertion. The right femoral artery was used for coronary angiography. Endovascular ultrasound was used to visualize the left anterior descending branch of the left main coronary artery, which was identified as the vessel with major obstruction. PTCA with

● New Code   ▲ Revised Code   ▶◀ Revised Text   © 2010 Ingenix

drug-eluting stent insertion was performed. IVUS was used to visualize the lumen of the descending branch and to determine the patency of the vessel prior to insertion of the stent. After stent placement, IVUS was used to determine if the stent was positioned fully against the wall of the artery.

Code Assignment:

410.11	Acute myocardial infarction of other anterior wall, initial episode of care
00.66	Percutaneous transluminal coronary angioplasty [PTCA] or coronary atherectomy
36.07	Insertion of drug-eluting coronary artery stent(s)
00.45	Insertion of one vascular stent
00.40	Procedure on single vessel
99.10	Injection or infusion of thrombolytic agent
00.24	Intravascular imaging of coronary vessels

Coding Guidance
AHA: 3Q, '06, 9

00.25   Intravascular imaging of renal vessels

Description
Intravascular ultrasound may be used during diagnostic evaluation of renal vessels. It may also be used both before and after a therapeutic intervention to assess patency and integrity of the vessel. A needle is inserted through the skin and into a renal vessel. A guidewire is threaded through the needle into the vessel and the needle is then removed. An intravascular ultrasound catheter is placed over the guidewire. The ultrasound catheter is used to obtain images from inside the vessel to assess the area and extent of disease prior to interventional therapy, as well as adequacy of therapy after interventional therapy. The catheter and guidewire are removed and pressure is applied over the puncture site to stop bleeding.

Coding Clarification
Use this code to report intravascular imaging of the renal vessels, including the renal artery.

Report diagnostic ultrasound of the urinary system with 88.75.

Documentation Tip
Intravascular ultrasound of the renal vessels may also be referred to in the medical record as IVUS of renal vessels.

00.28   Intravascular imaging, other specified vessel(s)

Description
Intravascular ultrasound may be used during diagnostic evaluation of specified vessels not included in the choices above. It may also be used both before and after a therapeutic intervention to assess patency and integrity of the vessel. A needle is inserted through the skin and into a specified

vessel. A guidewire is threaded through the needle into the vessel and the needle is then removed. An intravascular ultrasound catheter is placed over the guidewire. The ultrasound catheter is used to obtain images from inside the vessel to assess the area and extent of disease prior to interventional therapy, as well as adequacy of therapy after interventional therapy. The catheter and guidewire are removed and pressure is applied over the puncture site to stop bleeding.

Coding Clarification
Use this code to report intravascular imaging of specified vessels other than extracranial cerebral, intrathoracic, peripheral, coronary, or renal vessels.

This code should not be used to report diagnostic ultrasound.

Documentation Tip
May also be referred to in the medical record as IVUS of a specified vessel.

00.29   Intravascular imaging, unspecified vessel(s)

Description
Intravascular ultrasound may be used during diagnostic evaluation of vessels; it may also be used both before and after a therapeutic intervention to assess patency and integrity of the vessel. A needle is inserted through the skin and into the vessel. A guidewire is threaded through the needle into the vessel and the needle is then removed. An intravascular ultrasound catheter is placed over the guidewire. The ultrasound catheter is used to obtain images from inside the vessel to assess the area and extent of disease prior to interventional therapy, as well as adequacy of therapy after interventional therapy. The catheter and guidewire are removed and pressure is applied over the puncture site to stop bleeding.

Coding Clarification
This code is inappropriate for inpatient use. If the site of the vessel is not adequately documented within the medical record, the physician should be queried.

This code should not be used to report diagnostic ultrasound.

Documentation Tip
Intravascular ultrasound is also known as IVUS.

00.3 Computer-assisted surgery [CAS]

Description
Computer-assisted surgery is different from robotic surgery. Robotic-assisted surgery is used by physicians in performing complex laparoscopic procedures and provides increased range of motion, dexterity, and precision. Computer-assisted surgery

on the other hand, is used in intracranial, ENT, orthopedic and spinal surgeries, and involves image-guided navigation, markers, reference frames, and intraoperative sensing.

Planning, registration, and navigation are the key activities of computer-assisted surgery. The planning part is based on imaging. Preoperative 3D images may be taken, as well as intraoperative images using magnetic resonance imaging, computed tomography, and fluoroscopy in different combinations. Graphic models are linked into the surgery, and images can be merged with other data, such as electrophysiological recordings, for locating a seizure focus in the brain.

Registration occurs at the start of the procedure to set up spatial relationships between the points on the images taken and those same corresponding points on a patient's actual anatomy. Landmarks are the key to properly aligning image to actual anatomy. A landmark is a particular point on the anatomy that can be readily identified both in the actual surgical field and within the image. The landmark must be completely stationary with respect to the surrounding anatomy so that the relative position does not change. Natural anatomical structures or artificial markers, like a pin within bone, may be used.

To maintain the spatial relationship throughout the computer-assisted surgery, dynamic referencing is used. Dynamic referencing utilizes a reference frame fixed to the anatomy that allows infrared, electromagnetic, or radiowave sensors to detect and follow movement of the patient, for which the computer measures and compensates.

Navigation is the intraoperative tracking of tools and instruments, together with the surgical field in real time with display of this movement shown laid over the images and 3D models of the anatomy. This gives safe progression of invasive surgical procedures with increased precision and accuracy.

These types of computer-assisted surgery, also called image-guided surgery (IGS) or image-guided navigation (IGN), are used for intracranial and ENT procedures, as well as for orthopaedic procedures such as hip replacements, where angle calculations are critical. Spinal procedure usage is also being developed. CAS is an important adjunct to complicated surgery or surgery performed where normal anatomic reference points have been destroyed by disease or previous surgeries.

Coding Clarification
Assign this code in addition to a code for any diagnostic or therapeutic procedure performed.

Excludes robotic-assisted surgery which may or may not include a computerized image component.

Do not report this code for application of a stereotactic frame only; report 93.59.

Documentation Tip
The medical record documentation that accompanies CAS usually includes notations regarding reference frames, registration, landmarks, and guided instruments. Also noted in the medical record are measurements in mm regarding accuracy and error.

Computer-assisted surgery may be referred to in the medical record using a variety of terms, including:

- CT-free navigation
- 3-D computer surgery
- Image-guided navigation or IGN
- Image-guided surgery or IGS
- Imageless navigation
- Surgical simulation

Coding Guidance
AHA: 4Q, '04, 111-113

00.31   Computer-assisted surgery with CT/CTA

Description
Preoperative CT/CTA images of patient-specific bone geometry are obtained for the surgical plan. The patient-specific surgical plan and images of the individual's anatomy are used during surgery to help guide the surgeon by combining these with intraoperative navigation capabilities. Optical targets, or trackers, such as digitizing or LED-equipped probes, are attached to points on the bone anatomy or to surgical tools. An optical camera tracks the position of these for accurate navigation and measurement in relation to any bone or instrument movement as the surgery is performed. The software in these navigational systems matches or "registers" the position of the patient on the operating table to the geometric description of the bony surface derived from the CT/CTA images already used to plan the surgery. Multiple images are simultaneously displayed on the monitor. The "virtual" tool trajectory that corresponds to the tracked tool movements is displayed over the previously saved views in real-time as the surgeon operates.

Coding Clarification
Use this code in addition to the procedure code when the physician uses a computer to assist with coordinate determination established with CT/CTA.

Coding Scenario
A 60-year-old male patient with primary localized osteoarthritis of the knees was admitted for a minimally invasive total knee replacement utilizing computer-assisted surgery. The software application recorded and matched the CT scan performed

preoperatively to the patient's position on the operating table so that the surgeon was accurately oriented to the area of implant without full visualization of the bony landmarks.

Code Assignment:

715.16 Primary localized osteoarthrosis, lower leg
81.54   Total knee replacement
00.31   Computer-assisted surgery with CT/CTA

Coding Guidance
AHA: 4Q, '04, 113

00.32   Computer-assisted surgery with MR/MRA

Description
Preoperative MR/MRA images of patient-specific bone geometry are first obtained for the surgical plan. The patient-specific surgical plan and images of the individual's anatomy are used during surgery to help guide the surgeon by combining these with intraoperative navigation capabilities. Optical targets, or trackers, such as digitizing or LED-equipped probes, are attached to points on the bone anatomy or to surgical tools. An optical camera tracks the position of these for accurate navigation and measurement in relation to any bone or instrument movement as the surgery is performed. The software in these navigational systems matches or "registers" the position of the patient on the operating table to the geometric description of the bony surface derived from the MR/MRA images already used to plan the surgery. Multiple images are simultaneously displayed on the monitor. The "virtual" tool trajectory that corresponds to the tracked tool movements is displayed over the previously saved views in real-time as the surgeon operates.

Coding Clarification
Use this code in addition to the procedure code when the physician uses a computer to assist with coordinate determination established with MR/MRA.

Coding Guidance
AHA: 4Q, '04, 113

00.33   Computer assisted surgery with fluoroscopy

Description
Preoperative fluoroscopic images of patient-specific bone geometry are obtained for the surgical plan. The patient-specific surgical plan and images of the individual's anatomy are used during surgery to help guide the surgeon by combining these with intraoperative navigation capabilities. Optical targets, or trackers, such as digitizing or LED-equipped probes, are attached to points on the bone anatomy or to surgical tools. An optical camera tracks the position of these for accurate navigation and measurement in relation to any bone or

instrument movement as the surgery is performed. The software in these navigational systems matches or "registers" the position of the patient on the operating table to the geometric description of the bony surface derived from the fluoroscopic images already used to plan the surgery. Multiple images are simultaneously displayed on the monitor. The "virtual" tool trajectory that corresponds to the tracked tool movements is displayed over the previously saved views in real-time as the surgeon operates.

Coding Clarification
Use this code in addition to the procedure code when the physician uses a computer to assist with coordinate determination established with fluoroscopy.

00.34   Imageless computer assisted surgery

Description
By using direct imageless applications, landmarks are established on a "universal" limb model. This application requires touch-pointing the anatomic landmarks, which are then registered on the computer for use in accurate navigation and measurement in relation to any bone or instrument movement as the surgery is performed. This application provides a method for establishing coordinates as an aid for precisely locating anatomical structures in open or percutaneous procedures without the use of pre-operative or intra-operative images.

Coding Clarification
Use this code in addition to the procedure code when the physician uses an imageless system to assist with coordinate determination.

00.35   Computer assisted surgery with multiple datasets

Description
Preoperative images utilizing multiple datasets of patient-specific bone geometry are obtained for the surgical plan. The patient-specific surgical plan and images of the individual's anatomy are used during surgery to help guide the surgeon by combining these with intraoperative navigation capabilities. Optical targets, or trackers, such as digitizing or LED-equipped probes, are attached to points on the bone anatomy or to surgical tools. An optical camera tracks the position of these for accurate navigation and measurement in relation to any bone or instrument movement as the surgery is performed. The software in these navigational systems matches or "registers" the position of the patient on the operating table to the geometric description of the bony surface derived from the images already used to plan the surgery. Multiple images are simultaneously displayed on the monitor. The

00

"virtual" tool trajectory that corresponds to the tracked tool movements is displayed over the previously saved views in real-time as the surgeon operates.

Coding Clarification
Use this code in addition to the procedure code when the operative note specifies that multiple data sets were utilized to assist with coordinate determination.

00.39   Other computer assisted surgery

Description
Preoperative images of patient-specific bone geometry are obtained for the surgical plan. The patient-specific surgical plan and images of the individual's anatomy are used during surgery to help guide the surgeon by combining these with intraoperative navigation capabilities. Optical targets, or trackers, such as digitizing or LED-equipped probes, are attached to points on the bone anatomy or to surgical tools. An optical camera tracks the position of these for accurate navigation and measurement in relation to any bone or instrument movement as the surgery is performed. The software in these navigational systems matches or "registers" the position of the patient on the operating table to the geometric description of the bony surface derived from the images already used to plan the surgery. Multiple images are simultaneously displayed on the monitor. The "virtual" tool trajectory that corresponds to the tracked tool movements is displayed over the previously saved views in real-time as the surgeon operates.

Coding Clarification
Use this code in addition to the procedure code when the computer assisted surgery is not more precisely described by 00.31-00.35.

00.4   Adjunct vascular system procedures

Description
The intention of this subcategory of codes is to more adequately identify the entire scope of vascular procedures through the use of adjunct codes. These data represent major factors that require data collection. The numbers of vessels treated are identified by codes specifying one, two, three, or four or more vessels requiring intervention during a procedural episode. Similarly, the numbers of stents inserted during a procedure are accounted for by specifying one, two, three, or four or more stents inserted during a single procedural intervention. An inclusion term at code 00.45 states that this code may be used in default when the number of stents inserted during a procedure is not specified. As well, there is a specific code to identify that an

interventional procedure has been performed on a bifurcated vessel. This code will accompany other codes needed to fully describe the procedure, including number of vessels treated and number and type of stents inserted, as appropriate. An instructional note under subcategory 00.4 Adjunct vascular system procedures, informs coders that the codes within this range are to be used in conjunction with other interventional procedures. These codes are not intended to stand alone, but provide additional information only and apply to both coronary and peripheral vessels.

These codes do not represent procedures or services, but provide supplementary information such as the number of vessels or the number of stents. These codes must always be reported in addition to the primary procedure. Other examples of adjunct codes are the 00.91-00.93 codes that indicate the sources of an organ transplant. "Code also" notes are found throughout volume 3 of ICD-9-CM at vascular procedures to prompt the coder to assign these additional codes when interventions are performed on the vascular system.

Coding Clarification
Use of codes from this subcategory is not limited to coronary vessels.

These codes are to be used together with other therapeutic procedure codes in order to provide additional information regarding the number of vessels treated, the number of stents inserted, and/or the presence of a bifurcated vessel.

If appropriate, assign a code from range 00.40-00.43 to identify the number of vessels treated, a code from range 00.45-00.48 to identify the number of stents inserted, and 00.44 to identify the presence of a bifurcated vessel.

Also assign codes for any of the following procedures performed concurrently:

*   Angioplasty/atherectomy (00.61-00.62, 00.66, 39.50)
*   Endarterectomy (38.10-38.18)
*   Other removal of coronary obstruction (36.09)
*   Vascular stent insertion (00.55, 00.63-00.65, 36.06-36.07, 39.90)

Coding Guidance
   AHA: 4Q, '05, 101-106

00.40   Procedure on single vessel

Description
This code does not represent a procedure or service, but provides supplementary information regarding number of vessels treated. This code should be assigned in addition to the code for the primary procedure to identify that one coronary or peripheral

vessel was treated. It is also used if the number of vessels treated is unspecified.

Coding Clarification
Code 00.40 is used as the default code if the number of vessels treated is not specified; do not assume that two vessels were treated simply because more than one stent was inserted.

This code must always be reported in addition to the primary procedure; it may not be reported alone.

Do not assign this code when reporting aortocoronary bypass (36.10-36.19), as the bypass codes specify the number of vessels treated.

This code excludes intravascular imaging of blood vessels (00.21-00.29).

This code may be applied to coronary or noncoronary (precerebral, intracranial, or peripheral) vessels.

Also assign codes for any of the following procedures performed concurrently:

- Angioplasty/atherectomy (00.61-00.62, 00.66, 39.50)
- Endarterectomy (38.10-38.18)
- Other removal of coronary obstruction (36.09)
- Vascular stent insertion (00.55, 00.63-00.65, 36.06-36.07, 39.90)

Coding Scenario
A patient with progressive atherosclerotic coronary vascular disease and unstable angina was stabilized in the emergency department and subsequently admitted. Based on recent diagnostic catheterization studies, the decision was made to relieve the offending single vessel obstruction in the native vessel with PTCA and insertion of a drug-eluting coronary stent in the left anterior descending coronary artery via femoral access.

Code Assignment:

414.01 Coronary atherosclerosis of native coronary artery
411.1 Intermediate coronary syndrome
00.66 Percutaneous transluminal coronary angioplasty (PTCA) or coronary atherectomy
36.07 Insertion of drug-eluting coronary artery stent
00.40 Procedure on single vessel
00.45 Insertion of one vascular stent

Coding Guidance
AHA: 4Q, '05, 71, 106; 3Q, '06, 8; 2Q, '09, 12; ▶3Q, '09, 13; 2Q, '10, 9◀

00.41   Procedure on two vessels

Description
This code does not represent a procedure or service, but provides supplementary information regarding

number of vessels treated. This code should be assigned in addition to the code for the primary procedure to identify that two coronary or peripheral vessels were treated.

Coding Clarification
This code must always be reported in addition to the primary procedure; it may not be reported alone.

Do not assign this code when reporting aortocoronary bypass (36.10-36.19), as the bypass codes specify the number of vessels treated.

This code excludes intravascular imaging of blood vessels (00.21-00.29).

This code may be applied to coronary or noncoronary (precerebral, intracranial, or peripheral) vessels.

Also assign codes for any of the following procedures performed concurrently:

- Angioplasty/atherectomy (00.61-00.62, 00.66, 39.50)
- Endarterectomy (38.10-38.18)
- Other removal of coronary obstruction (36.09)
- Vascular stent insertion (00.55, 00.63-00.65, 36.06-36.07, 39.90)

Coding Guidance
AHA: 4Q, '05, 105; 4Q, '06, 119

00.42   Procedure on three vessels

Description
This code does not represent a procedure or service, but provides supplementary information regarding number of vessels treated. This code should be assigned in addition to the code for the primary procedure to identify that three coronary or peripheral vessels were treated.

Coding Clarification
This code must always be reported in addition to the primary procedure; it may not be reported alone.

Do not assign this code when reporting aortocoronary bypass (36.10-36.19), as the bypass codes specify the number of vessels treated.

This code is also excluded from intravascular imaging of blood vessels (00.21-00.29).

This code may be applied to coronary or noncoronary (precerebral, intracranial, or peripheral) vessels.

Also assign codes for any of the following procedures performed concurrently:

- Angioplasty/atherectomy (00.61-00.62, 00.66, 39.50)
- Endarterectomy (38.10-38.18)
- Other removal of coronary obstruction (36.09)

- Vascular stent insertion (00.55, 00.63-00.65, 36.06-36.07, 39.90)

00.43   Procedure on four or more vessels

Description
This code does not represent a procedure or service, but provides supplementary information regarding number of vessels treated. This code should be assigned in addition to the code for the primary procedure to identify that four or more coronary or peripheral vessels were treated.

Coding Clarification
This code must always be reported in addition to the primary procedure; it may not be reported alone.

Do not assign this code when reporting aortocoronary bypass (36.10-36.19), as the bypass codes specify the number of vessels treated.

This code excludes intravascular imaging of blood vessels (00.21-00.29).

This code may be applied to coronary or noncoronary (precerebral, intracranial, or peripheral) vessels.

Also assign codes for any of the following procedures performed concurrently:

- Angioplasty/atherectomy (00.61-00.62, 00.66, 39.50)
- Endarterectomy (38.10-38.18)
- Other removal of coronary obstruction (36.09)
- Vascular stent insertion (00.55, 00.63-00.65, 36.06-36.07, 39.90)

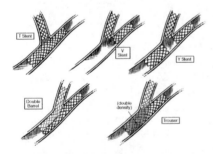

00.44 Procedure on vessel bifurcation

Description
Bifurcated vessels are "parent" vessels that branch or divide into two "child" vessels. Procedures on these vessels often require specialized surgical techniques, since they often present as complicated arteriosclerotic lesions in particularly delicate vasculature. This code does not represent a procedure or service, but provides supplementary information regarding the presence of a bifurcated vessel, and should be assigned in addition to the code for the primary procedure.

Coding Clarification
This code must always be reported in addition to the primary procedure; it may not be reported alone.

This code is used only to identify the presence of a vessel bifurcation; it does not describe a specific bifurcation stent.

Use this code only once per operative episode, regardless of the number of bifurcations in vessels.

Also assign codes for any of the following procedures performed concurrently:

- Angioplasty/atherectomy (00.61-00.62, 00.66, 39.50)
- Endarterectomy (38.10-38.18)
- Other removal of coronary obstruction (36.09)
- Vascular stent insertion (00.55, 00.63-00.65, 36.06-36.07, 39.90)

00.45   Insertion of one vascular stent

Description
This code does not represent a procedure or service, but provides supplementary information regarding the number of stents inserted. This code should be assigned in addition to the code for the primary procedure to identify that one stent was inserted. This code is also reported if the number of stents is unspecified.

Coding Clarification
Code 00.45 is used as the default code if the number of stents inserted is not specified.

This code must always be reported in addition to the primary procedure; it may not be reported alone.

This code may be applied to coronary or peripheral vessels.

Also assign codes for any of the following procedures performed concurrently:

- Angioplasty/atherectomy (00.61-00.62, 00.66, 39.50)
- Endarterectomy (38.10-38.18)
- Other removal of coronary obstruction (36.09)
- Vascular stent insertion (00.55, 00.63-00.65, 36.06-36.07, 39.90)

Coding Guidance
   AHA: 4Q, '05, 71; ►3Q, '09, 13◄

00.46   Insertion of two vascular stents

Description
This code does not represent a procedure or service, but provides supplementary information regarding the number of stents inserted. This code should be

● New Code   ▲ Revised Code   ►◄ Revised Text   © 2010 Ingenix

assigned in addition to the code for the primary procedure to identify that two vascular stents were inserted.

Coding Clarification
This code must always be reported in addition to the primary procedure; it may not be reported alone.

This code may be applied to coronary or peripheral vessels.

Also assign codes for any of the following procedures performed concurrently:

- Angioplasty/atherectomy (00.61-00.62, 00.66, 39.50)
- Endarterectomy (38.10-38.18)
- Other removal of coronary obstruction (36.09)
- Vascular stent insertion (00.55, 00.63-00.65, 36.06-36.07, 39.90)

Coding Guidance
AHA: 4Q, '05, 105-106; 2Q, '09, 12

00.47 Insertion of three vascular stents

Description
This code does not represent a procedure or service, but provides supplementary information regarding the number of stents inserted. This code should be assigned in addition to the code for the primary procedure to identify that three vascular stents were inserted.

Coding Clarification
This code must always be reported in addition to the primary procedure; it may not be reported alone.

This code may be applied to coronary or peripheral vessels.

Also assign codes for any of the following procedures performed concurrently:

- Angioplasty/atherectomy (00.61-00.62, 00.66, 39.50)
- Endarterectomy (38.10-38.18)
- Other removal of coronary obstruction (36.09)
- Vascular stent insertion (00.55, 00.63-00.65, 36.06-36.07, 39.90)

Coding Guidance
AHA: 4Q, '06, 119

00.48 Insertion of four or more vascular stents

Description
This code does not represent a procedure or service, but provides supplementary information regarding the number of stents inserted. This code should be assigned in addition to the code for the primary procedure to identify that four or more vascular stents were inserted.

Coding Clarification
This code must always be reported in addition to the primary procedure; it may not be reported alone.

This code may be applied to coronary or peripheral vessels.

Also assign codes for any of the following procedures performed concurrently:

- Angioplasty/atherectomy (00.61-00.62, 00.66, 39.50)
- Endarterectomy (38.10-38.18)
- Other removal of coronary obstruction (36.09)
- Vascular stent insertion (00.55, 00.63-00.65, 36.06-36.07, 39.90)

00.49 SuperSaturated oxygen therapy

Description
Super saturated oxygenation therapy involves the creation of super-oxygenated arterial blood, which is infused directly to oxygen-deprived myocardial tissue in acute myocardial infarction patients. Infusion of supersaturated oxygen into the infarct area results in a significant reduction in infarct size and preserves myocardial tissue. Super saturated oxygenation therapy is used as an adjunct to other procedures that restore coronary artery blood flow such as percutaneous transluminal coronary angioplasty (PTCA) or coronary atherectomy and coronary artery stent insertion.

Documentation Tip
This therapy may also be documented as SuperOxygenation, SuperOxygenation infusion therapy, SSO_2, or Aqueous oxygen (AO) therapy.

Cardiac catheterization procedures are performed using a variety of approaches and surgical techniques including introduction, positioning and repositioning of catheter. To ensure accurate code assignment, it will be necessary to review the medical record documentation for specific information regarding each procedure performed prior to final code selection.

Coding Clarification
Report separately any percutaneous coronary intervention performed such as percutaneous transluminal coronary angioplasty (PTCA) or coronary atherectomy (00.66), insertion of coronary artery stents (36.06, 36.07), intracoronary artery thrombolytic infusion (36.04), injection or infusion of thrombolytic agent (99.10), open chest coronary artery angioplasty (36.03) or other removal of coronary obstruction (36.09), and procedures on vessel bifurcation (00.44). Also report the number of vascular stents inserted (00.45-00.48) and the number of vessels treated (00.40-00.43).

SSO$_2$ should not be confused with other oxygen therapy (93.96) which is a respiratory therapy procedure or vascular perfusion (39.97) which is the infusion of other substances into the vessel.

Coding Scenario
In the cardiac catheterization suite following percutaneous coronary angioplasty, the physician uses an automated cartridge-based system to withdraw arterial blood and mix it with super oxygenated saline. Using an infusion catheter, the physician infuses the resulting highly oxygen-enriched blood into the specific areas of myocardial tissue.

Code Assignment:

00.66	Percutaneous transluminal coronary angioplasty [PTCA] or coronary atherectomy
00.40	Procedure on single vessel
00.49	SuperSaturated oxygen therapy

Coding Guidance
AHA: 4Q, '08, 162

00.5   Other cardiovascular procedures

Description
Subcategory 00.5 addresses other cardiovascular procedures, including implantation and replacement of cardiac resynchronization pacemakers, defibrillators, leads, and pulse generators. Also covered under this subcategory is insertion of drug-eluting peripheral vessel stents and implantation or replacement of subcutaneous devices and leads for intracardiac hemodynamic monitoring. All codes within this subcategory require fourth-digit subclassification for further specificity with regard to the type of procedure performed. Documentation in the medical record and operative note must support code assignment.

Coding Guidance
AHA: 4Q, '02, 95-99

00.50   Implantation of cardiac resynchronization pacemaker without mention of defibrillation, total system (CRT-P)

Description
Used to provide electrical stimulation therapy to patients with ventricular dysfunction, the cardiac resynchronization pacemaker (CRT-P) is indicated for those patients who do not require an automatic cardioverter-defibrillator (AICD).

Access to the central caval veins is obtained through the subclavian vein or jugular vein. The vein is penetrated with a large needle and a wire is passed through it. A fluoroscope is used to guide the wire into the right atrium and right ventricle. A pocket for the pacemaker generator is created and the wire is

tested and connected to the generator. Since biventricular pacing is required, an additional electrode is placed in the left ventricle. A fluoroscope may be used for guidance and a pacing electrode is inserted in the ventricular chamber of the heart, usually in the coronary sinus tributary. The electrode is connected to the generator and the generator pocket is closed.

Coding Clarification
Code 00.50 includes the following:

- Implantation of cardiac resynchronization (biventricular) pulse generator pacing device
- Formation of pocket
- Transvenous leads including placement of lead into left ventricular coronary venous system
- Intraoperative procedures for evaluation of lead signals

Report implantation of cardiac resynchronization defibrillator (CRT-D) with 00.51.

Insertion or replacement of any other type of pacemaker device is correctly reported with a code from range 37.80-37.87.

For replacement of cardiac resynchronization, report 00.54 for CRT-D and 00.53 for CRT-P. Note that these codes report the pulse generator only.

Do not assign a code for device testing performed during the procedure.

Documentation Tip
Also known as biventricular or BiV pacemaker, biventricular pacing without internal cardiac defibrillator, or that with CRT-P generator and one or more leads.

The wires leading from the pacemaker to the electrode are referred to as the lead. The end of a lead includes an electrode. Since the two cannot be separated, they are referred to as a lead [electrode] in the procedural section of ICD-9-CM.

Coding Guidance
AHA: 4Q, '02, 100; 3Q, '05, 3-5, 7; 3Q, '08, 18

00.51   Implantation of cardiac resynchronization defibrillator, total system (CRT-D)

Description
In order to monitor and provide electrical stimulation to the right atrium, right ventricle, and left coronary sinus/cardiac vein, CRT-D requires the use of a resynchronization pulse generator with defibrillation capabilities and three transvenous leads. The additional third lead is implanted within the coronary venous system of the left ventricle in order to synchronize ventricular contractions. Indications for CRT-D including the treatment of congestive heart failure, cardiomyopathy, and ventricular dysfunction.

● New Code   ▲ Revised Code   ▶◀ Revised Text   © 2010 Ingenix

An implantable cardioverter-defibrillator (ICD) is a device designed to administer an electric shock to control cardiac arrhythmias and restore a normal heartbeat. Transvenous placement through the subclavian or jugular vein is currently the most common technique for placing ICD electrodes. Local anesthesia is administered. An incision is made in the infraclavicular area. The subcutaneous tissue is opened and a pocket is created for the pulse generator. Transvenous electrode placement is performed under fluoroscopic guidance. The electrode catheter is advanced through the superior vena cava into the heart and placed in the appropriate site in the right ventricle and atrium. Since biventricular pacing is required, an additional electrode is placed in the left ventricular chamber of the heart, usually in the coronary sinus tributary. Once all leads are placed, they are tested and connected to the pulse generator, which is then placed in the previously prepared pocket. All incisions are closed.

Coding Clarification
Code 00.51 includes the following:

- Implantation of cardiac resynchronization (biventricular) pulse generator with defibrillator (AICD)
- Formation of pocket
- Transvenous leads including placement of lead into left ventricular coronary venous system
- Intraoperative procedures for evaluation of lead signals
- Obtaining defibrillator threshold measurements

Report implantation of cardiac resynchronization pacemaker (CRT-P) with 00.50.

Implantation or replacement of automatic cardioverter/defibrillator, total system (AICD) is correctly reported with 37.94.

For replacement of a cardiac resynchronization defibrillator, report 00.54. Note that this code reports the pulse generator only.

When the device and one or more leads are implanted/replaced, report 00.51.

Do not assign a code for device testing performed during the procedure.

Documentation Tip
Also known as BiV ICD, BiV pacing with defibrillation, biventricular pacing with internal cardiac defibrillator, or that with CRT-D generator and one or more leads.

The wires leading from the pacemaker to the electrode are referred to as the lead. The end of a lead includes an electrode. Since the two cannot be separated, they are referred to as a lead [electrode] in the procedural section of ICD-9-CM.

Coding Scenario
This 70-year-old female with worsening congestive heart failure and a history of coronary artery disease presents for an upgrade from her conventional, dual-chamber AICD system that was implanted six years ago to a cardiac resynchronization therapy defibrillator (CRT-D) system. The conventional AICD pulse generator was removed and replaced with a cardiac resynchronization therapy defibrillator (CRT-D) pulse generator, and an additional electrode was placed into the coronary vein of the left ventricle.

Code Assignment:

428.0   Congestive heart failure, unspecified
414.01 Coronary atherosclerosis of native coronary artery
00.51   Implantation of cardiac resynchronization defibrillator, total system [CRT-D]

Coding Guidance
AHA: 4Q, '02, 100; 3Q, '05, 3-9; 1Q, '07, 16; 3Q, '08, 18

00.52   Implantation or replacement of transvenous lead (electrode) into left ventricular coronary venous system

Description
With the pacemaker or pacing cardioverter-defibrillator already in place, the physician gains access transvenously through the subclavian or jugular vein. A fluoroscope may be used for guidance and a pacing electrode is inserted in the ventricular chamber of the heart, usually in the coronary sinus tributary. The electrode is connected to the generator and the pocket is closed.

Coding Clarification
Code 00.52 excludes the implantation of a total system CRT-D (00.51) or CRT-P (00.50).

Initial insertion of transvenous leads other than those into the left ventricular coronary system are reported with a code from range 37.70-37.72.

Replacement of transvenous atrial and/or ventricular leads is reported with 37.76.

Documentation Tip
The wires leading from the pacemaker to the electrode are referred to as the lead. The end of a lead includes an electrode. Since the two cannot be separated, they are referred to as a lead [electrode] in the procedural section of ICD-9-CM.

Coding Guidance
AHA: 3Q, '05, 3-6; 3Q, '08, 14

00.53 Implantation or replacement of cardiac resynchronization pacemaker pulse generator only (CRT-P)

Description
This operation proceeds under the assumption that permanent pacing wires are already in place. In a replacement procedure, the previous pocket is opened and any existing CRT-P or other pacemaker device is removed. In an initial insertion, a new pocket is created for the generator device. The pacing wires are tested and then connected to the new generator. The generator is placed into the pocket and the pocket is closed.

Coding Clarification
This code is used only when the CRT-P generator is inserted or replaced, and no leads are placed.

Do not assign a code for device testing performed during the procedure.

Implantation of a total system cardiac resynchronization pacemaker (CRT-P) is reported with 00.50.

Implantation or replacement of the pulse generator of a CRT-D (cardiac resynchronization defibrillator) is reported with 00.54.

Insertion or replacement of pacemaker devices, other than those described in this chapter, are reported with a code from range 37.80-37.87.

Coding Guidance
AHA: 3Q, '05, 3-9

00.54 Implantation or replacement of cardiac resynchronization defibrillator pulse generator device only (CRT-D)

Description
This operation is performed only when defibrillator electrodes are already in place. In a replacement procedure, the previous pocket is opened and any existing CRT-D, CRT-P, pacemaker, or defibrillator device is removed. In an initial insertion, a new pocket is created for the defibrillator generator. AICD pulse generators are implanted subcutaneously usually in an infraclavicular or abdominal pocket. The electrodes are tested. The electrodes are then connected to the defibrillator and it is placed in the pocket. The pocket is closed.

Coding Clarification
This code is used when only the CRT-D generator is inserted or replaced, and no leads are placed.

Do not assign a code for device testing performed during the procedure.

Implantation of a total system cardiac resynchronization defibrillator (CRT-D) is reported with 00.51.

Implantation or replacement of the pulse generator of a CRT-P (cardiac resynchronization pacemaker) is reported with 00.53.

Implantation of an automatic cardioverter-defibrillator pulse generator is reported with 37.96.

Coding Guidance
AHA: 4Q, '02, 100; 3Q, '05, 3-9

▲ 00.55 Insertion of drug-eluting stent(s) of other peripheral vessels

Description
Thrombotic occlusion and vessel restenosis are postoperative complications that may occur following stent insertion. Drug-eluting stents are those in which an active drug designed to reduce restenosis has been applied. Following stent insertion, the drug is gradually released into the vessel wall tissue over a period of 30 to 45 days to prevent the accumulation of scar tissue that can occlude the reopened artery.

In the percutaneous insertion technique, the physician places a drug-eluting intravascular stent(s) through a catheter into a peripheral blood vessel. A guidewire is threaded through the needle into the blood vessel and the needle is removed. A catheter with a stent-transporting tip is threaded over the guidewire into the vessel and the wire is extracted. The catheter travels to the point where the vessel needs additional support. The compressed stent(s) is then passed from the catheter out into the vessel, where it deploys, expanding to support the vessel walls. The catheter is removed and pressure is applied over the puncture site.

In the open technique, the physician makes an incision in the skin overlying the peripheral vessel to be catheterized. The vessel is dissected, and nicked with a small blade. A catheter with a stent-transporting tip is then threaded into the vessel. The catheter travels to the point where the vessel needs additional support, and the compressed drug-eluting stent(s) is passed from the catheter into the vessel, where it expands to support the vessel walls. The catheter is then removed and the vessel may be repaired. The skin incision is repaired with layered closure.

Coding Clarification
Drug-coated peripheral stents are reported with 39.90.

The following should also be coded when performed concurrently:

- Angioplasty/atherectomy of other non-coronary vessels (39.50)
- Number of stents inserted (00.45-00.48)

● New Code   ▲ Revised Code   ▶◀ Revised Text   © 2010 Ingenix

- Number of vessels treated (00.40-00.43)
- Procedure on a bifurcated vessel (00.44)

Insertion of cerebrovascular stents are reported with a code from range 00.63-00.65.

Insertion of drug-eluting coronary artery stents are reported with 36.07.

▶Code 00.55 excludes stents inserted as part of other endovascular procedures classifiable to codes 39.71–39.79.◀

▶Also note that code 00.55 excludes insertion of a drug-eluting stent in the superficial femoral artery, which is assigned code 00.60.◀

Insertion of non-drug-eluting stents are reported with the following codes:

- Coronary artery—36.06
- Peripheral vessel—39.90

Documentation Tip
Examples of the drugs in drug-eluting stents include paclitaxel, sirolimus, and taxol.

Drug-eluting stents and drug-coated or drug-covered stents are not synonymous. A drug-coated stent is layered with biocompatible substances such as phosphorylcholine or bonded with drugs such as heparin to prevent the formation of platelets on the stent. A covered stent is one that has been layered with silicone or a silicone derivative such as polyurethane or PTFE. The stents that are drug-coated do not release the drug; drug-eluting stents do.

Coding Guidance
AHA: 4Q, '02, 101

00.56   Insertion or replacement of implantable pressure sensor (lead) for intracardiac or great vessel hemodynamic monitoring

Description
Volume overload, also known as fluid retention, is one of the major precipitating factors for emergency and inpatient hospital treatment for patients with the more severe degrees of heart failure (NYHA Class III and IV). A key component in the control of volume overload episodes is close monitoring of the cardiac filling pressures. Prior to the intracardiac hemodynamic monitor (IHM), there was no reliable method for detection of variations in intracardiac pressure that might indicate clinical deterioration other than frequent physical examinations, reporting of symptoms by the patient, and periodic invasive right heart cardiac catheterizations. The monitor can provide daily clinically relevant information that may alert physicians of worsening heart failure symptoms to allow for medication adjustment or other treatment that could possibly

halt exacerbation of symptoms and subsequent hospitalization.

The intracardiac hemodynamic monitor is an implantable device consisting of a data storage system, a single lead with a pressure sensor tip, and a wireless antenna system. It allows continuous collection of data on heart rate, right ventricular diastolic and systolic pressure, physical activity, and body temperature, and is indicated for patients with moderate to severe heart failure.

The implanted hemodynamic monitoring system, which allows clinicians to distinguish early signs of volume overload prior to becoming apparent on physical exam, has two components. The monitoring device, which is similar in size to a pacemaker, is implanted in a subcutaneous pocket, usually in the upper chest. A lead-tipped pressure sensor is inserted transvenously into the heart's right ventricle. The monitor continuously measures cardiac pressures, body temperature, patient activity, and heart rate. Periodically this data is downloaded via telemetry for analysis and decision-making by the clinician.

Prior to the introduction of the lead into the venous circulation, it is attached to the implantable monitor in the sterile field. A calibration process is carried out to adjust the implantable components. The lead is placed transvenously via the subclavian vein in the right ventricle, with the tip of the lead in the RV outflow tract. The lead tip is subtly manipulated and secured to obtain fixation of the tines in the trabeculated portion of the right ventricle. Care is taken to make certain there is no unnecessary motion of the lead tip and that the sensor is situated in the right ventricle, free of the tricuspid valve.

Assessment is made of electrode stability by measuring the ventricular electrogram and the pacing threshold. The lead is then attached to the IHM device. Utilizing a standard suture sleeve for fixation to the pectoral muscle, both the IHM and the lead are positioned in the subclavian pocket. A programming head sheltered by a sterile plastic sleeve is positioned over the IHM and a pressure waveform is obtained to confirm that the sensor records the right ventricular pressure without any artifacts from mechanical interference.

Coding Clarification
Report 00.57 for any associated implantation or replacement of monitor.

Code 00.56 excludes circulatory monitoring (blood gas, arterial or venous pressure, cardiac output, and coronary blood flow). To report, see 89.60-89.69.

Coding Scenario
A 65-year-old male with documented Class III congestive heart failure presents for insertion of an implantable hemodynamic monitor (IHM). He

continues to be symptomatic despite treatment with ACE inhibitors and diuretics over the past nine months. He required one hospitalization six months ago for exacerbation of his congestive heart failure. Insertion of pressure sensor and implantation of IHM subcutaneous device were accomplished without complication.

Code Assignment:

428.0	Congestive heart failure, unspecified
00.56	Insertion or replacement of implantable pressure sensor (lead) for intracardiac hemodynamic monitoring
00.57	Implantation or replacement of subcutaneous device for intracardiac hemodynamic monitoring

Coding Guidance
AHA: 4Q, '06, 119

00.57 Implantation or replacement of subcutaneous device for intracardiac or great vessek hemodynamic monitoring

Description
The implanted hemodynamic monitoring system, which allows clinicians to distinguish early signs of volume overload prior to becoming apparent on physical exam, has two components. The monitoring device, which is similar in size to a pacemaker, is implanted in a subcutaneous pocket, usually in the upper chest. A lead-tipped pressure sensor is inserted transvenously into the heart's right ventricle. The monitor continuously measures cardiac pressures, body temperature, patient activity, and heart rate. Periodically this data is downloaded via telemetry for analysis and decision-making by the clinician.

Prior to the introduction of the lead into the venous circulation, it is attached to the implantable monitor in the sterile field. A calibration process is carried out to adjust the implantable components. The lead is placed transvenously via the subclavian vein in the right ventricle, with the tip of the lead in the RV outflow tract. The lead tip is subtly manipulated and secured to obtain fixation of the tines in the trabeculated portion of the right ventricle. Care is taken to make certain there is no unnecessary motion of the lead tip and that the sensor is situated in the right ventricle, free of the tricuspid valve.

Assessment is made of electrode stability by measuring the ventricular electrogram and the pacing threshold. The lead is then attached to the IHM device. Utilizing a standard suture sleeve for fixation to the pectoral muscle, both the IHM and the lead are positioned in the subclavian pocket. A programming head sheltered by a sterile plastic sleeve is positioned over the IHM and a pressure waveform is obtained to confirm that the sensor

records the right ventricular pressure without any artifacts from mechanical interference.

Coding Clarification
Code 00.57 reports implantation of the monitoring device and includes formation of the subcutaneous pocket and connection to the intracardiac pressure sensor (lead).

Report 00.56 for any associated insertion or replacement of the implanted pressure sensor (lead).

Coding Guidance
AHA: 4Q, '06, 119

00.58 Insertion of intra-aneurysm sac pressure monitoring device (intraoperative)

Description
This code is used to report the intraoperative insertion of intra-aneurysm sac pressure monitoring device during endovascular aneurysm repair of abdominal aortic aneurysms (AAA) and thoracic aortic aneurysms (TAA). An aneurysm forms in the wall of a blood vessel as a result of weakening of the vessel wall and the force of blood pressure can lead the aneurysm to rupture. Endovascular aneurysm repair of AAA and TAA includes the placement of a stent graft inside the blood vessel. To evaluate sac pressure within the aneurysm, pressure measurements are recorded before and after the stent graft is placed. These pressure measurements can also help detect an endoleak. Blood leaking around the graft and into the aneurysm sac is a potential complication of endovascular aneurysm repair procedures. Imaging may also be used alone or in conjunction to determine if an endoleak occurs during graft placement procedures.

Coding Clarification
The EndoSure® Wireless Pressure Measurement System is FDA approved for measuring intra-aneurysm sac pressure during endovascular repair of AAA and for measuring aneurysm sac pressure during endovascular repair of TAA. The system includes a wireless implantable sensor and an external module that wirelessly communicates with the sensor to deliver real-time sac pressure data.

Do not assign code 89.61 Systemic arterial pressure monitoring to report the intra-aneurysm sac pressure measurement. The intra-aneurysm sac pressure monitor device is implanted intraoperatively while systemic aterial pressure monitoring is a catheter technique that may be inserted at any time and is intended to be temporary.

Code intra-aneurysm sac pressure monitoring (00.58) in addition to the endovascular repair procedure (e.g., 39.71 Endovascular implantation of

● New Code   ▲ Revised Code   ▶◀ Revised Text   © 2010 Ingenix

graft in abdominal aorta or 39.73 Endovascular implantation of graft in thoracic aorta).

Coding Scenario

A patient with an abdominal aortic aneurysm is brought into the operating suite, draped and prepped for an endovascular aneurysm repair. The physician inserts a pressure measurement sensor to measure intra-aneurysm sac pressure during the procedure and subsequently performs the endovascular aneurysm graft repair. Pressure measurements are recorded again after the graft has been placed to help determine if an endoleak is present.

Code Assignment:

441.4	Abdominal aneurysm without mention of rupture
39.71	Endovascular implantation of graft in abdominal aorta
00.58	Insertion of intra-aneurysm sac pressure monitoring device (intraoperative)

Coding Guidance

AHA: 4Q, '08, 163-165

00.59 Intravascular pressure measurement of coronary arteries

Description

Fractional flow reserve (FFR) is another type of intracoronary pressure measurement used to evaluate blood flow using comparative pressure measurements. Fractional flow reserve is used to evaluate the severity of coronary artery stenosis and complex disease such as multivessel disease. Intravascular pressure measurement may be used as in addition to angiography to provide a more complete assessment of the severity of coronary disease.

Coding Clarification

Intravascular pressure measurement may be used in addition to angiography to provide a comprehensive assessment of the severity of coronary disease.

Report a separate code for any diagnostic or therapeutic procedures performed synchronously.

Coronary blood flow monitoring by coincidence counting technique, involving measurement of radioactive tracers to estimate blood flow, is reported with code 89.69 Monitoring of coronary blood flow.

Coding Scenario

A patient with coronary atherosclerosis presents for assessment of the coronary artery fractional flow reserve during diagnostic left heart angiography with selective coronary angiography (Judkins technique) to determine the most appropriate therapeutic intervention. The physician uses a pressure sensitive catheter to measure the intravascular pressure distal to the native coronary lesion to compare with the aortic pressure proximal to the lesion to assess the severity of the lesion in terms of limitation of blood flow.

Code Assignment:

414.01	Coronary atherosclerosis of native coronary artery
37.22	Left heart catheterization
88.53	Angiography of left heart structures
88.56	Coronary arteriography using two catheters
00.59	Intravascular pressure measurement of coronary arteries

Coding Guidance

AHA: 4Q, '08, 163-165

00.6 Procedures on blood vessels

Description

Subcategory 00.6 addresses other procedures on blood vessels, including percutaneous angioplasty or atherectomy of precerebral and intracranial vessels; percutaneous insertion of intracranial, carotid, and other precerebral artery stents; and PTCA. All codes within this subcategory require fourth-digit subclassification for further specificity with regard to the site and type of procedure performed. Documentation in the medical record and operative note must support code assignment.

● 00.60 Insertion of drug-eluting stent(s) of superficial femoral artery

Description

▶The Zilver® PTX stent is the first drug-eluting stent pending Food and Drug Administration approval in the United States for treating peripheral arterial disease (PAD) in the superficial femoral artery, the largest blood vessel in the leg. SFA lesions are particularly difficult to treat, often involving complex calcified plaque as well as total occlusions. The Zilver drug-eluting stent is a self-expanding device made of nitinol, a thin, specialized durable metal that targets delivery of a drug (paclitaxel) directly to the arterial lesion to restore blood flow. In contrast to other types of DES devices, the drug is attached to the nitinol frame of the Zilver stent, which achieves targeted drug delivery without using a polymer to adhere the drug to the stent. This eliminates potential complications associated with polymer-coated devices, including inflammation and clot formation.◄

Coding Clarification

▶Code also any additional procedures as appropriate, including number of stents inserted (00.45–00.48), and the number of vessels treated (00.40–00.43).

This code excludes DES insertions of other peripheral vessel sites (00.55). DES insertions inherent to endovascular procedures (e.g., stent grafts, endovascular repair, coil embolization) are reported separately in addition to the primary procedure (39.71–39.79).◄

Coding Scenario
►A 59-year-old patient with atherosclerotic PVD of the SFA presents for balloon angioplasty of the SFA with insertion of drug-eluting stent. Upon adequate dilation of the vessel, the DES was threaded over the guidewire and deployed into the SFA.

Code Assignment:

440.20	Atherosclerosis of the extremities, unspecified
39.50	Angioplasty or atherectomy of other non-coronary vessels
00.60	Insertion of drug-eluting stent(s) of superficial femoral artery
00.40	Procedure on single vessel
00.45	Insertion of one vascular stent◄

00.61 Percutaneous angioplasty or atherectomy of precerebral (extracranial) vessel(s)

Description
Stenting extracranial cerebrovascular arteries percutaneously through a catheter is an emerging alternative to open endarterectomies. The procedure is carried out by making a small incision in the leg to puncture an access artery and then threading a catheter to the target artery, such as the carotid. A stent delivery system that may also include an embolic capturing device is loaded into a delivery pod and advanced to the blocked or narrowed artery through the catheter. The embolic protection device is deployed first distal to the lesion so that any emboli are collected as the blood passes through the device. The stent is advanced out of the pod and expanded to open the narrowing. The position is confirmed by angiocardiography and/or transthoracic echocardiography.

Percutaneous angioplasty or atherectomy may also be performed before a stent is placed. Percutaneous angioplasty uses a balloon to expand a narrowed artery. A catheter with a special balloon tip is threaded through an access vein up to the target vessel. The physician inflates the balloon at the tip of the catheter to flatten obstructing plaque against the walls of the vessel and expand the lumen diameter.

Percutaneous atherectomy involves removing the obstructing plaque from inside the vessel using a device inserted through a catheter. The physician punctures the femoral artery with a large needle and passes a guidewire via the needle into the femoral artery. The physician removes the needle while leaving the guidewire in place, enlarges the arterial opening slightly with a blade, and slides an introducer sheath over the guidewire into the arterial

lumen. The physician then slides an appropriately sized guidewire through the atherectomy catheter or device, and inserts the guidewire/atherectomy catheter combination through the introducer sheath up the aorta and out into the involved precerebral vessel. The physician fluoroscopically positions the atherectomy device at the arterial stenosis and activates the device to remove the stenotic tissue. The physician then rechecks the diameter of the lesion by angiography. The physician may perform several passes with the atherectomy device. The physician removes the atherectomy catheter, guidewire, and introducer sheath, compressing the femoral artery manually until hemostasis is achieved.

Coding Clarification
Angioplasty or atherectomy of other non-coronary vessels, including upper and lower extremity vessels and the mesenteric and renal arteries, is reported with 39.50.

For removal of cerebrovascular obstruction of vessels by open approach, refer to codes found within category 38.

Codes should also be assigned for the following procedures when performed concurrently:

• Injection or infusion of thrombolytic agent (99.10)

• Number of vascular stents inserted (00.45-00.48)

• Number of vessels treated (00.40-00.43)

• Procedure on vessel bifurcation (00.44)

• Percutaneous insertion of carotid artery stents (00.63) or other precerebral artery stents (00.64)

Coding Scenario
A 70-year-old white male with arteriosclerosis of the carotid artery is diagnosed with stenosis or occlusion of the carotid artery. The patient is admitted for carotid artery atherectomy and insertion of a non-drug-eluting stent. This is done in an attempt to reduce his risk of cerebrovascular accident. The patient undergoes percutaneous angioplasty with TPA infusion of the area in question within the carotid artery before a non-drug-eluting stent deployment is carried out with cerebral protection from a thrombus or emboli also being used.

Code Assignment:

433.10	Occlusion and stenosis of carotid artery without mention of cerebral infarction
00.61	Percutaneous angioplasty or atherectomy of precerebral (extracranial) vessel(s)
00.63	Percutaneous insertion of carotid artery stent(s)
00.45	Insertion of one vascular stent
00.40	Procedure on single vessel
99.10	Injection or infusion of thrombolytic agent

● New Code   ▲ Revised Code   ►◄ Revised Text   © 2010 Ingenix

Coding Guidance
AHA: 4Q, '04, 114-116

00.62 Percutaneous angioplasty or atherectomy of intracranial vessel(s)

Description

The physician performs a percutaneous balloon angioplasty of an intracranial vessel, most often as an alternative to surgical carotid endarterectomy for carotid stenosis in high-risk patients. The patient undergoes an appropriate neurological and vascular work up preoperatively. A standard percutaneous transfemoral approach is most frequently used. Light intravenous sedation is administered. Standard diagnostic carotid and cerebral angiography is performed to confirm the suspected lesion and evaluate the cerebral circulation. The patient is anticoagulated and an antiplatelet agent is given. Using the femoral approach, the balloon is introduced on the tip of an angiographic catheter passed through the circulatory tree until it reaches the stenotic lesion. Once in place, the balloon is inflated, dilating the vessel and improving blood flow to the brain.

Coding Clarification

Angioplasty or atherectomy of other non-coronary vessels, including upper and lower extremity vessels and the mesenteric and renal arteries, is reported with 39.50.

For removal of cerebrovascular obstruction of vessels by open approach, refer to codes found within category 38.

Codes should also be assigned for the following procedures when performed concurrently:

- Injection or infusion of a thrombolytic agent (99.10)
- Number of vascular stents inserted (00.45-00.48)
- Number of vessels treated (00.40-00.43)
- Procedure on vessel bifurcation (00.44)
- Percutaneous insertion of intracranial stents (00.65)

Coding Guidance
AHA: 4Q, '04, 114-116

00.63 Percutaneous insertion of carotid artery stent(s)

Description

The physician places an intravascular stent percutaneously through a catheter into the cervical carotid artery. A needle is inserted through the skin into the access blood vessel, usually the brachial or femoral artery. A guidewire is threaded through the needle into the cervical carotid artery and the needle is removed. Long sheaths or guiding catheters are advanced into the stenosed cervical carotid artery. A filter protection device may be inserted distal to the stenosis to capture emboli. After filter opening, predilation of the stenosis with angioplasty balloons may be performed. A catheter with a stent-transporting tip is threaded over the guidewire into the vessel and the wire is extracted. The catheter travels to the point where the vessel needs additional support. The compressed stent is then passed from the catheter out into the vessel, where it deploys, expanding to support the vessel walls. The catheter is removed and pressure is applied over the puncture site.

Coding Clarification

Code 00.63 includes the use of any of the following:

- Embolic protection device
- Distal protection device
- Filter device
- Stent delivery system

This code is appropriate only for non-drug-eluting stents.

Codes should also be assigned for the following procedures when performed concurrently:

- Number of vascular stents inserted (00.45-00.48)
- Number of vessels treated (00.40-00.43)
- Procedure on vessel bifurcation (00.44)
- Percutaneous angioplasty/atherectomy of precerebral vessels (00.61)

Angioplasty or atherectomy of other non-coronary vessels is reported with 39.50.

Coding Guidance
AHA: 4Q, '04, 114-116

00.64 Percutaneous insertion of other precerebral (extracranial) artery stent(s)

Description

The physician places an intravascular stent(s) percutaneously through a catheter into a precerebral blood vessel other than the carotid. A guidewire is threaded through the needle into the blood vessel and the needle is removed. A catheter with a stent-transporting tip is threaded over the guidewire into the vessel and the wire is extracted. The catheter travels to the point where the vessel needs additional support. The compressed stent(s) is then passed from the catheter out into the vessel, where it deploys, expanding to support the vessel walls. The catheter is removed and pressure is applied over the puncture site.

Coding Clarification

Code 00.64 includes the use of any of the following:

00

● New Code   ▲ Revised Code   ►◄ Revised Text

- Embolic protection device
- Distal protection device
- Filter device
- Stent delivery system

Codes should also be assigned for the following procedures when performed concurrently:

- Number of vascular stents inserted (00.45-00.48)
- Number of vessels treated (00.40-00.43)
- Procedure on vessel bifurcation (00.44)
- Percutaneous angioplasty/atherectomy of precerebral vessels (00.61)

Angioplasty or atherectomy of other non-coronary vessels is reported with 39.50.

Coding Guidance
AHA: 4Q, '04, 114-116

00.65 Percutaneous insertion of intracranial vascular stent(s)

Description
The physician places an intravascular intracranial stent most often as an alternative to surgical carotid endarterectomy for carotid stenosis in high-risk patients. A percutaneous balloon angioplasty may also be performed. The patient undergoes an appropriate neurological and vascular work up preoperatively. A standard percutaneous transfemoral approach is most frequently used. Light intravenous sedation is administered. Standard diagnostic carotid and cerebral angiography is performed to confirm the suspected lesion and evaluate the cerebral circulation. The patient is anticoagulated and an antiplatelet agent is given. Using the femoral approach, a guiding catheter is placed from the groin into the common carotid artery. A microwire is passed through the guiding catheter and crosses the stenotic lesion in the artery. In the event that the stenosis is too tight to pass a stent primarily, an angioplasty balloon is used to predilate the stenosis prior to the stent placement. The microwire is left across the dilated segment, the balloon is removed, and the stent delivery device is placed. Once positioned, the stent is deployed across the region of the stenosis. If necessary, an additional balloon can be placed inside the deployed stent for postdilation to make sure the struts of the stent are pressed firmly against the inner surface of the wall of the vessel.

Coding Clarification
Code 00.65 includes the use of any of the following:

- Embolic protection device
- Distal protection device
- Filter device
- Stent delivery system

Codes should also be assigned for the following procedures when performed concurrently:

- Number of vascular stents inserted (00.45-00.48)
- Number of vessels treated (00.40-00.43)
- Procedure on vessel bifurcation (00.44)
- Percutaneous angioplasty/atherectomy of intracranial vessels (00.62)

Angioplasty or atherectomy of other non-coronary vessels is reported with 39.50.

Insertion of drug-eluting peripheral vessel stents is reported with 00.55.

Coding Guidance
AHA: 4Q, '04, 114-116

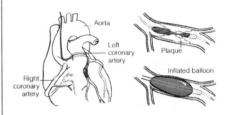

00.66 Percutaneous transluminal coronary angioplasty [PTCA] or coronary atherectomy

Description
In the PTCA procedure, the physician makes a small incision in the arm or leg. Two catheters are placed. A central venous catheter is inserted through the femoral or brachial artery and a second catheter with a balloon tip is threaded up to the heart. The physician inflates the balloon at the tip of the second catheter to flatten plaque obstructing the artery against the walls of the artery. If sufficient results are not obtained after the first inflation, the physician may reinflate the balloon for a longer period of time or at greater pressure. The catheter is removed and pressure is placed over the incision for 20 to 30 minutes to stem bleeding. The patient is observed for a period afterward.

In the percutaneous coronary atherectomy procedure, the physician removes the atherosclerotic plaque blocking the coronary artery. The physician makes a small incision in the arm or leg. Two catheters are placed. A central venous catheter is inserted through the femoral or brachial artery and a second catheter threaded up to the heart blockage. The blockage is removed using a rotary cutter introduced through a special catheter under radiographic guidance. The blockage may also require subsequent inflation of the balloon on the tip of the second catheter to flatten any remaining plaque. The catheters are removed. Pressure is placed over the incision for 20 to 30 minutes to stem

● New Code   ▲ Revised Code   ►◄ Revised Text   © 2010 Ingenix

bleeding. The patient is observed for a period afterward.

Coding Clarification
Codes should also be assigned for the following procedures when performed concurrently:

- Injection/infusion of thrombolytic agent (99.10)
- Insertion of coronary artery stents (36.06-36.07)
- Intracoronary artery thrombolytic infusion (36.04)
- Number of vascular stents inserted (00.45-00.48)
- Number of vessels treated (00.40-00.43)
- Procedure on vessel bifurcation (00.44)
- SuperSaturated oxygen therapy (00.49)

The use of the SpideRX® distal embolic protection device is integral to the total coronary angioplasty with stent insertion and is not coded separately.

Documentation Tip
Also known as balloon angioplasty, coronary atherectomy, percutaneous coronary angioplasty, and PTCA.

Coding Scenario
A 60-year-old female with coronary artery disease and ongoing unstable angina was admitted for PTCA with insertion of a drug-eluting stent. There is no prior surgical history. One stent was placed into the left anterior descending and one into the first diagonal artery. There were no complications.

Code Assignment:

414.01	Coronary atherosclerosis of native coronary artery
411.1	Intermediate coronary syndrome
00.66	Percutaneous transluminal coronary angioplasty [PTCA] or coronary atherectomy
36.07	Insertion of drug-eluting coronary artery stent(s)
00.41	Procedure on two vessels
00.46	Insertion of two vascular stents

Coding Guidance
AHA: 4Q, '05, 71, 101; 3Q, '06, 8; 2Q, '09, 12; ▶2Q, '10, 9◀

00.67   Intravascular pressure measurement of intrathoracic arteries

00.68   Intravascular pressure measurement of peripheral arteries

00.69   Intravascular pressure measurement, other specified and unspecified vessels

Description
Intravascular pressure measurements can be used in different arteries throughout the body other than the coronary arteries. These three codes under subcategory 00.6 Procedures on Blood Vessels, report the various uses of intravascular pressure measurements. Intravascular pressure provides of diagnostic information about underlying conditions and for assessing the need for vascular interventions. The procedure involves the use of guidewires and/or catheters to obtain a functional assessment.

Intravascular pressure measurement of intrathoracic arteries (00.67) is used to report assessment of the carotid, aorta and aortic arch. Code 00.68 is used to report assessment of other peripheral vessels and vessels of the arms and legs. Intravascular pressure measurement, other specified or unspecified vessels is reported with code 00.69. Other vessels reported with this code include iliac, intra-abdominal, mesenteric and renal vessels.

Coding Clarification
Also assign codes for any diagnostic or therapeutic procedures performed synchronously.

Do not use these codes to report intravascular pressure measurement of coronary arteries, rather assign code 00.59.

To report insertion of an EndoSure® wireless abdominal aortic aneurysm (AAA) pressure measurement system, assign code 00.58.

Documentation Tip
Intravascular pressure measurement may be documented as intravascular pressure measurement or FFR.

Intravascular pressure measurement is usually performed in conjunction with other coronary artery procedures; carefully review the documentation for specific information regarding the procedures performed to ensure complete and accurate code selection.

Coding Scenario
A patient with arteriosclerosis of the left anterior descending artery presents for assessment of the coronary artery by fractional flow reserve to determine the most appropriate therapeutic intervention. The physician uses a pressure sensitive catheter to measure the intravascular pressure to evaluate the severity of coronary artery stenosis.

Code Assignment:

414.0	Arteriosclerosis of native coronary artery
00.59	Intravascular pressure measurement of coronary arteries

Coding Guidance
AHA: 4Q, '08, 163-164

00.7 Other hip procedures

Description

Multiple factors contribute to the complexity of revision of hip replacement procedures, including the type of implant utilized in the original surgery, the cause of the replacement's failure, the quantity and condition of the patient's remaining bone, and the overall health status and anatomy of the patient. In procedures involving revision hip replacement, any or all of the implant components may be replaced. As well, major reconstruction of the bones and soft tissues around the hip may be necessary. Efforts are also being made to produce new bearing material in order to extend the life of these prosthetic implants and provide the patient with a higher level of functioning. Certain bearing surfaces, such as ceramic-on-ceramic, may extend the life of the implant by reducing the amount of friction and using a less biologically reactive material than surfaces utilizing polyethylene or metal.

Subcategory 00.7 addresses revisions of hip replacements and identification of the various types of bearing surfaces utilized. All codes within this subcategory require fourth-digit subclassification for further specificity with regard to the component replaced and the surface material involved in the replacement. Documentation in the medical record and operative note must support code assignment.

Coding Guidance
    AHA: 4Q, '05, 106

00.70   Revision of hip replacement, both acetabular and femoral components

Description

If both implants fail, revision of both the acetabular and femoral components may be necessary. Total hip revision has the highest complication rate and, of all revision hip replacement procedures, is the most labor and resource intensive. Frequently requiring specialized revision implants, extensive operative exposures, and specialized reconstructive techniques, this procedure has the least predictable outcomes of all revision hip replacement procedures.

The physician performs a revision of a total hip arthroplasty. With the patient in a lateral decubitus (lying on the side) position, the physician may access the hip through the previous hip surgery incision. Muscles are reflected. A trochanteric osteotomy may be performed with an oscillating saw. The physician incises the hip joint capsule. Any scar tissue is freed and removed. The physician then manually dislocates the hip. Cement is removed from the upper portion of the femoral stem with a motorized or hand instrument. The stem may be removed. If the stem has fractured, the physician may drill a

hole in the femoral shaft so that an instrument may remove the broken portion. Any remaining cement in the femoral shaft is then removed. The physician removes scar tissue and cement from around the acetabular component with chisels and gouges. The acetabular component is removed from its bed. The physician reconstructs the acetabulum with cement or screws and bone graft. The new femoral stem is inserted into the femoral shaft with or without cement. The physician may augment the area with an autograft or allograft. The physician harvests bone from the patient's iliac crest, repairing the surgically created graft donor site. An allograft (donor bone) may be used when additional bone is needed. The physician reduces (repositions) the hip and closes the capsule. The greater trochanter is wired into place. Suction drains may be placed in the wound. The incision is repaired in multiple layers with sutures, staples, and/or Steri-strips.

Coding Clarification

If the specific components replaced are not documented, assign 81.53 Revision of hip replacement, not otherwise specified.

Report any removal of cement or joint spacer performed at the same time with 84.57.

A code for the specific type of bearing surface (00.74-00.77) should also be assigned, if known.

Assign V43.64 Organ or tissue replaced by other means, joint, hip, to identify the prosthetic joint associated with the mechanical complication.

Conversion of a hemiarthoplasty that includes both acetabular and femoral components of the hip replacement is considered a total revision of hip replacement. Assign code 00.70.

Documentation Tip

This procedure is also called total hip revision.

Coding Guidance
    AHA: 4Q, '05, 113; 1Q, '08, 6; 2Q, '08, 3, 4

00.71   Revision of hip replacement, acetabular component

Description

Revision of the acetabular component entails the removal and replacement of the entire acetabular component, including both the metal shell and the bearing surface. Wearing of the modular bearing surface, loosening due to osteolysis, infection, or recurrent dislocations due to faulty positioning of the component are some of the most common indications for revision of the acetabular component. If the patient has sufficient remaining bone stock, the replacement may be performed with an implant that is similar but slightly larger than the original implant. If component malposition or osteolysis have resulted in a significant amount of bone destruction, specialized implants and a large amount of allograft bone or other bone substitutes may be required. Reconstruction in these cases is more complex, resulting in considerably prolonged surgery and recovery times and less predictable patient outcomes.

The physician performs a revision of the acetabular component of a total hip arthroplasty. With the patient in a lateral decubitus (lying on the side) position, the physician accesses the acetabular component through a previous hip surgery incision. Muscles are reflected. The physician may perform an osteotomy of the greater trochanter with an oscillating saw. The capsule is incised and the hip manually dislocated. Any scar tissue is removed from around the acetabulum. The physician removes cement from around the acetabular component with chisels and gouges. The acetabulum is then levered out from its bed. The acetabulum may need to be reamed out in preparation for the new component. The physician then reconstructs the acetabulum with or without cement. If the acetabulum is reconstructed without cement, the component is usually inserted and fixed with screws. Prior to the acetabulum placement, the physician may harvest a bone graft from the patient's iliac crest and close the surgically created graft donor site. Donor bone (allograft) may be used instead. If cement is used, it secures the new component in the acetabular bed. Once the cement has dried, the hip is reduced (repositioned) and the capsule closed. The physician may place suction drains in the wound. The incision is repaired in multiple layers with sutures, staples, and/or Steri-strips.

Coding Clarification
Code 00.71 includes exchange of the acetabular cup and liner and exchange of the femoral head.

If only the acetabular liner and/or femoral head are replaced, report 00.73.

If the specific components replaced are not documented, assign 81.53 Revision of hip replacement, not otherwise specified.

Report any removal of cement or joint spacer performed at the same time with 84.57.

A code for the specific type of bearing surface (00.74-00.77) should also be assigned, if known.

Assign V43.64 Organ or tissue replaced by other means, joint, hip, to identify the prosthetic joint associated with the mechanical complication.

Documentation Tip
This procedure is also known as partial replacement, acetabular component only.

Coding Scenario
A 68-year-old male, who had previously undergone a total hip arthroplasty (THA) 17 years ago, presents for replacement revision due to loosening of the acetabular component with resultant pain. The surgeon removed and replaced the acetabular component only using a ceramic-on-ceramic bearing surface. The procedure was accomplished without complications.

Code Assignment:

996.41 Mechanical loosening of prosthetic joint
V43.64 Organ or tissue replaced by other means, joint, hip
00.71 Revision of hip replacement, acetabular component
00.76 Hip replacement bearing surface, ceramic-on-ceramic

Coding Guidance
AHA: 4Q, '05, 112

00.72 Revision of hip replacement, femoral component

Description
Code 00.72 reports removal and exchange of the femoral component. Indications for this procedure commonly include infection, aseptic loosening due to osteolysis, recurrent dislocations due to faulty positioning of the components, or peri-prosthetic fracture. Specialized revision implants, surgical techniques, and/or instruments are often required. Allograft (cadaver) bone graft may or may not be utilized. Because many cases require protected weight bearing to allow the bone to heal to the prosthesis, recovery time tends to be longer than with revision of the acetabular component alone.

With the patient in a lateral decubitus position (lying on the side), the physician may access the femoral component through the previous hip surgery incision. Muscles are reflected. The physician may perform an osteotomy of the greater trochanter. The hip joint capsule is exposed and incised. The physician then dislocates the hip joint. If cement was used on the previous arthroplasty, the physician uses a motorized or hand instrument to remove it from around the upper portion of the femoral stem. If loose enough, the stem is removed with forceful blows. If the stem cannot be removed, additional cement may need to be removed from the femoral shaft, so the stem can be extracted. The physician may then place cement in the femoral shaft and insert the new femoral component. If the revision is cementless, donor bone (allograft) may be inserted as needed into the femoral shaft between the cortex and femoral component. The hip is reduced (repositioned). The physician reattaches the greater trochanter with wires. The incision is repaired in multiple layers with sutures, staples, and/or Steri-strips.

Coding Clarification
Code 00.72 reports exchange of the acetabular liner and exchange of the femoral stem and head.

If only the femoral head and/or acetabular liner are replaced, report 00.73.

If the specific components replaced are not documented, assign 81.53 Revision of hip replacement, not otherwise specified.

Report any removal of cement or joint spacer performed at the same time with 84.57.

A code for the specific type of bearing surface (00.74-00.77) should also be assigned, if known.

Assign V43.64 Organ or tissue replaced by other means, joint, hip, to identify the prosthetic joint associated with the mechanical complication.

Documentation Tip
This procedure is also known as partial replacement, femoral component only.

Coding Guidance
  AHA: 4Q, '05, 106-110

00.73   Revision of hip replacement, acetabular liner and/or femoral head only

Description
Code 00.73 reports removal and exchange of the modular femoral head and/or acetabular liner only, and is one of the most common revision hip replacement procedures performed. Recurrent dislocations or bearing surface wearing are the most frequent indications for replacement revision. If the bearing surface wear is due to osteolysis (peri-prosthetic bone loss) and prosthetic loosening, the entire acetabular and/or femoral component may require revision. However, the modular femoral head and acetabular liner may be replaced alone if bone defects can be accessed without difficulty and the components are positioned appropriately and are well fixed, resulting in decreased patient recovery times compared to procedures necessitating revision of the femoral or acetabular components.

Coding Clarification
If the specific components replaced are not documented, assign 81.53 Revision of hip replacement, not otherwise specified.

Report any removal of cement or joint spacer performed at the same time with 84.57.

A code for the specific type of bearing surface (00.74-00.77) should also be assigned, if known.

Assign V43.64 Organ or tissue replaced by other means, joint, hip, to identify the prosthetic joint associated with the mechanical complication.

Coding Guidance
  AHA: 4Q, '05, 106-110

00.74   Hip bearing surface, metal-on-polyethylene

Description
In order to address complications due to wear of the articular bearing surface and osteolysis caused by debris, metal on polyethylene bearings have been developed. Cross-linking of the polyethylene material has resulted in improved wear and enhanced resistance; up to a 90 percent reduction in the wear rate has been demonstrated over standard polyethylene.

Coding Clarification
Code 00.74 is an informational code. It should only be assigned when the information is available in the medical record, either on the manufacturer's sticker or in the provider's documentation. If the information is unavailable, omit the code.

Assign as an additional code only; this code cannot be used alone.

This code may be used for hip replacement procedures (81.51 and 81.52) or revision of hip replacement procedures (00.70-00.73, 81.53).

Coding Guidance
  AHA: 4Q, '05, 112

00.75   Hip bearing surface, metal-on-metal

Description
Compared with metal-on-polyethylene bearings, metal-on-metal bearings exhibit significantly lower wear rates. The long-term effects of accumulated metal ions is not known, although early clinical outcomes were excellent.

Coding Clarification
Code 00.75 is an informational code. It should only be assigned when the information is available in the medical record, either on the manufacturer's sticker or in the provider's documentation. If the information is unavailable, omit the code.

Assign as an additional code only; this code cannot be used alone.

This code may be used for hip replacement procedures (81.51 and 81.52) or revision of hip replacement procedures (00.70-00.73, 81.53).

Coding Guidance
  AHA: 4Q, '05, 112; 4Q, '06, 121

00.76   Hip bearing surface, ceramic-on-ceramic

Description
Ceramic-on-ceramic may offer numerous advantages over traditional bearing surfaces, including scratch resistance, superior wear resistance, and improved

lubrication. The alumina ceramic is hard and has a stronger affinity for water than polyethylene or metal. There is no metal ion release, and the alumina particulate debris is less bio-reactive.

Coding Clarification
Code 00.76 is an informational code. It should only be assigned when the information is available in the medical record, either on the manufacturer's sticker or in the provider's documentation. If the information is unavailable, omit the code.

Assign as an additional code only; this code cannot be used alone.

This code may be used for hip replacement procedures (81.51 and 81.52) or revision of hip replacement procedures (00.70-00.73, 81.53).

Coding Guidance
AHA: 4Q, '05, 112

00.77   Hip bearing surface, ceramic-on-polyethylene
Description
Both mechanical and clinical testing has shown that use of ceramic-on-polyethylene bearing surfaces significantly reduce polyethylene wear. In the majority of cases, a ceramic femoral head is assembled onto a metallic femoral stem, which articulates with a polyethylene cup or acetabular bearing. Complications may include fracture of the femoral head.

Coding Clarification
Code 00.77 is an informational code. It should only be assigned when the information is available in the medical record, either on the manufacturer's sticker or in the provider's documentation. If the information is unavailable, omit the code.

Assign as an additional code only; this code cannot be used alone.

This code may be used for hip replacement procedures (81.51 and 81.52) or revision of hip replacement procedures (00.70- 00.73, 81.53).

Coding Scenario
A 70-year-old active male who is 15 years status post total hip replacement (THR) complains of increasingly severe pain and inflammation. Radiographic studies reveal wear of the articular bearing surface of the prosthetic joint, necessitating revision of the acetabular component. This was carried out, utilizing a ceramic-on-polyethylene bearing surface. There were no complications.

Code Assignment:

996.46 Articular bearing surface wear of prosthetic joint

V43.64 Organ or tissue replaced by other means; hip

00.71   Revision of hip replacement, acetabular component only

00.77   Hip replacement bearing surface, ceramic-on-polyethylene

Coding Guidance
AHA: 4Q, '05, 110-113; 4Q, '06, 120

00.8   Other knee and hip procedures
Description
After an extended period of use, hip and knee replacements can fail, necessitating revision surgery. Common reasons for revision joint replacement surgery include:

- Mechanical loosening of the prosthesis
- Wear of the weight-bearing surface
- Infection
- Dislocation and instability
- Fracture of the bone around the implant (peri-prosthetic fracture)
- Implant fracture
- Technical error
- Painful results with decrease in mobility
- Mechanical failure

Treatment of failed hip and knee replacements varies in accordance with the clinical indications, general health of the patient, type and extent of diseased bone tissue, the nature of the injury, and status of the prosthetic implant that was used. Cases in which reconstruction of major bone loss is necessary make up the most resource-intensive hip and knee revision procedures. Bone reconstruction is estimated to be the most significant factor of higher costs among revision hip replacement procedures.

Subcategory 00.8 addresses revisions of knee replacements and resurfacing hip arthroplasties. Fourth-digit subclassifications are required in order to identify the components or sites involved.

Coding Clarification
Up to two components from range 00.81-00.83 may be reported to describe revision of knee replacements.

Report 00.80 if all three components of a knee replacement are revised.

Report an additional adjunct code from 00.85-00.87 with the appropriate fourth-digit subclassification that specifies the site of hip resurfacing.

Coding Guidance
AHA: 4Q, '05, 113

00

00.80 Revision of knee replacement, total (all components)

Description

The most common type of revision knee replacement procedure, complete total knee revision, often requires extensive operative approaches and specialized reconstructive implants, including those with long stems, metal augments, or hinged components. Bone grafts may also be necessary in order to fill bony defects. Cutting the tibia bone (osteotomizing) in order to gain access to the implants and adequately expose the joint is often necessary. Because of incompatibility of implants across vendors or types of prostheses, a complete revision of all the components is often necessary even when only one of the implants is broken or loose.

The physician performs a revision of a total knee arthroplasty. Typically, previous skin incisions are incorporated to expose the knee. In order to remove the components, an osteotome or saw may be used to loosen the cement or bone so that the prosthesis can be tapped out with a mallet. If any cement is present, it is removed in order to protect and preserve as much bone as possible. Bone cuts are made to accommodate the new prosthesis. If significant bone defects are present on the femur, tibia, or both, a bone graft may be needed. An allograft (donor bone) may be packed into the defect. The components of the new prosthesis are placed into position and may be cemented for fixation. The incision is repaired with sutures, staples, and/or Steri-strips.

Coding Clarification

Code 00.80 reports replacement of all components, including femoral, tibial, and patellar.

If the specific component is not documented, assign 81.55 Revision of knee replacement, not otherwise specified.

Report any removal of cement or joint spacer performed at the same time with 84.57 Removal of (cement) spacer.

If only one or two components are revised (tibial, femoral, or patellar), report with a code from range 00.81-00.84.

Coding Guidance

AHA: 4Q, '05, 117; 1Q, '08, 6

00.81 Revision of knee replacement, tibial component

Description

The most common indications for revision of the tibial component include modular bearing surface wearing, osteolysis-induced aseptic loosening, or infection. Depending on the condition of the ligaments around the knee and the amount of

associated bone loss, specialized implants, bone grafts, or metal augments may be necessary.

The physician performs a revision of the tibial component of a total knee arthroplasty. Typically, previous skin incisions are incorporated to expose the knee. The tibial component (including both the baseplate and liner) is removed, sometimes utilizing an osteotome or saw to loosen the cement or bone so that the prosthesis can be tapped out with a mallet. If any cement is present, it is removed in order to protect and preserve as much bone as possible. Bone cuts are made to accommodate the new prosthesis. If significant bone defects are present, a bone graft may be needed. An allograft (donor bone) may be packed into the defect. The components of the new prosthesis are placed into position and may be cemented for fixation. The incision is repaired with sutures, staples, and/or Steri-strips.

Coding Clarification

Code 00.81 reports the removal and exchange of the entire tibial component, including both the tibial baseplate and the tibial insert (liner).

If the specific component is not documented, assign 81.55 Revision of knee replacement, not otherwise specified.

Report any removal of cement or joint spacer performed at the same time with 84.57 Removal of (cement) spacer.

If all components are revised (tibial, femoral, and patellar), report 00.80.

Coding Guidance

AHA: 4Q, '05, 117

00.82 Revision of knee replacement, femoral component

Description

Indications for revision of the femoral component include infection or aseptic loosening of the implant that may occur with or without bone loss or associated osteolysis. If extensive bone loss is present, specialized implants, bone graft, or metal augments may be required.

The physician performs a revision of the femoral component of a total knee arthroplasty. Typically, previous skin incisions are incorporated to expose the knee. The femoral component is removed, sometimes utilizing an osteotome or saw to loosen the cement or bone so that the prosthesis can be tapped out with a mallet. If any cement is present, it is removed in order to protect and preserve as much bone as possible. Bone cuts are made to accommodate the new prosthesis. If significant bone defects are present, a bone graft may be needed. An allograft (donor bone) may be packed into the defect. The components of the new prosthesis are placed into position and may be cemented for fixation. The incision is repaired with sutures, staples, and/or Steri-strips.

Coding Clarification
Code 00.82 includes replacement of the tibial insert (liner).

If the specific component is not documented, assign 81.55 Revision of knee replacement, not otherwise specified.

Report any removal of cement or joint spacer performed at the same time with 84.57 Removal of (cement) spacer.

If all components are revised (tibial, femoral, and patellar), report 00.80.

Coding Scenario
A 65-year-old patient with localized osteoarthritis of the knees secondary to a past history of infectious arthritis presents for revision of his previously implanted knee replacement prosthesis. During the procedure, only the femoral and patellar components were replaced. This was accomplished without complication.

Code Assignment:

715.26 Secondary localized osteoarthrosis, lower leg
00.82   Revision of knee replacement, femoral component
00.83   Revision of knee replacement, patellar component

Coding Guidance
AHA: 4Q, '05, 117; 3Q, '06, 9

00.83   Revision of knee replacement, patellar component

Description
One of the most frequently occurring indications for revision knee replacement surgery is patello-femoral joint complication. Other indications include wear and fracture of the implant due to misalignment of the patella in the femoral groove, patellar fracture with or without implant loosening, tendon rupture involving the quadriceps or patellar tendons, and infectious processes.

The physician performs a revision of the patellar component of a total knee arthroplasty. Typically, previous skin incisions are incorporated to expose the knee. The patellar component is removed, sometimes utilizing an osteotome or saw to loosen the cement or bone so that the prosthesis can be tapped out with a mallet. If any cement is present, it is removed in order to protect and preserve as much bone as possible. Bone cuts are made to accommodate the new prosthesis. If significant bone

defects are present, a bone graft may be needed. An allograft (donor bone) may be packed into the defect. The components of the new prosthesis are placed into position and may be cemented for fixation. The incision is repaired with sutures, staples, and/or Steri-strips.

Coding Clarification
If the specific component is not documented, assign 81.55 Revision of knee replacement, not otherwise specified.

Report any removal of cement or joint spacer performed at the same time with 84.57 Removal of (cement) spacer.

If all components are revised (tibial, femoral, and patellar), report 00.80.

Coding Guidance
AHA: 4Q, '05, 117

00.84   Revision of total knee replacement, tibial insert (liner)

Description
Indications for revision of the modular tibial insert include loosening of the prosthetic knee joint or wear of the polyethylene bearing surface. The femoral, tibial, and patellar implants are not removed during this procedure; only the modular tibial bearing surface is removed and exchanged.

The physician performs a revision of the tibial insert (liner) of a total knee arthroplasty. Typically, previous skin incisions are incorporated to expose the knee. The tibial insert is removed, sometimes utilizing an osteotome or saw to loosen the cement or bone so that the prosthesis can be tapped out with a mallet. If any cement is present, it is removed in order to protect and preserve as much bone as possible. Bone cuts are made to accommodate the new tibial insert. The new insert is placed into position and may be cemented for fixation. The incision is repaired with sutures, staples, and/or Steri-strips.

Coding Clarification
If the specific component is not documented, assign 81.55 Revision of knee replacement, not otherwise specified.

Report any removal of cement or joint spacer performed at the same time with 84.57 Removal of (cement) spacer.

If all tibial components are revised, including tibial baseplate and liner, report 00.81.

Coding Guidance
AHA: 4Q, '05, 117

00.85 Resurfacing hip, total, acetabulum and femoral head

Description
This procedure differs from traditional hip replacement in that it involves grinding away only the worn surfaces of the femoral head and acetabulum and placing new bearing surfaces rather than resecting the head and the majority of the femoral neck. Intended as an initial joint replacement for patients who are likely to require more than one hip joint replacement in their lifetime, hip resurfacing is expected to delay total hip replacement and possibly eliminate the necessity of a revision hip replacement in patients who desire to continue a fairly active lifestyle.

Indications for a total hip resurfacing, which has consistently good pain relief, include inflammatory arthritis, such as rheumatoid arthritis, and end stage degenerative joint disease (DJD) in patients who have satisfactory anatomy and proximal femoral bone stock. Most patients who undergo a total hip resurfacing have osteoarthritis; approximately 10 percent have advanced osteonecrosis.

With the patient in a lateral position and using a posterior approach, the surgeon releases the external rotators from the piriformis to the gluteus maximus tendon. The surgeon performs a posterior capsulectomy and dislocates the femoral head. Anterior capsular release is accomplished and the neck diameter measured to determine the appropriate size of components to be utilized. The head is retracted anterosuperiorly and the acetabulum is exposed with the aide of a retractor. Utilizing hemispherical reamers, the surgeon shapes the acetabulum in 2 mm increments until the desired size is reached. The acetabular cup is fitted. The surgeon then prepares the femoral head in sequential steps in order to adapt to the resurfacing component. The surgeon reduces the components and fixes them into place using bone cement, and then performs layered closure of the soft tissues. Drainage tubes may be left in place for a couple of days following the surgery.

Documentation Tip
This procedure is also known as total hip resurfacing arthroplasty.

Coding Scenario
A 60-year-old male, an active hiker and skier, presents for total hip resurfacing arthroplasty due to worsening osteoarthritis. He does not desire a total hip replacement due to his relatively young age and active lifestyle. Resurfacing procedure was performed on the femoral head and acetabulum successfully and without incident.

Code Assignment:

715.95 Osteoarthrosis, unspecified whether generalized or localized, pelvic region and thigh

00.85 Resurfacing, hip, total, acetabulum and femoral head

Coding Guidance
AHA: 4Q, '06, 121

00.86 Resurfacing hip, partial, femoral head

Description
In comparison to traditional hip replacement arthroplasty or revision arthroplasty, hip resurfacing arthroplasty of the femoral head involves the grinding away of only the worn surfaces of the femoral head, retaining the greater part of the femoral head and the femoral neck. A cobalt chrome cap is positioned over the smoothed surfaces of the femoral head, articulating with a metal cup that has been pressed into the reamed acetabulum, thus the articulation is metal on metal. Since the head of the femur is preserved, hip resurfacing conserves more of the bone. Intended as an initial joint replacement for patients who are likely to require more than one hip joint replacement in their lifetime, partial hip resurfacing is expected to delay total hip replacement and possibly eliminate the necessity of a revision hip replacement in patients who desire to continue a fairly active lifestyle.

Indications for partial resurfacing include osteoarthritis, traumatic arthritis, avascular necrosis, and dysplasia/developmental dislocation of the hip (DDH). Partial resurfacing is not recommended for treating inflammatory disease since the implants that are presently available have comparatively unpredictable pain relief. Mechanical failure of partial resurfacing is rare; however, inadequate pain relief can result in conversion of the partial resurfacing to a total hip replacement within a five-year period.

Coding Clarification
If resurfacing of the acetabulum is also performed, report only 00.85.

Documentation Tip
This procedure is also known as hip resurfacing arthroplasty or partial hip resurfacing arthroplasty of the femoral head.

Coding Guidance
AHA: 4Q, '06, 121

00.87 Resurfacing hip, partial, acetabulum

Description
This procedure differs from traditional hip replacement in that it involves grinding away the worn surfaces of the acetabulum and placing new

● New Code ▲ Revised Code ▶◀ Revised Text © 2010 Ingenix

bearing surfaces. Intended as an initial joint replacement for patients who are likely to require more than one hip joint replacement in their lifetime, partial hip resurfacing is expected to delay total hip replacement and possibly eliminate the necessity of a revision hip replacement in patients who desire to continue a fairly active lifestyle.

Indications for partial resurfacing include osteoarthritis, traumatic arthritis, avascular necrosis, and dysplasia/developmental dislocation of the hip (DDH). Partial resurfacing is not recommended for treating inflammatory disease since the implants that are presently available have comparatively unpredictable pain relief. Mechanical failure of partial resurfacing is rare; however, inadequate pain relief can result in conversion of the partial resurfacing to a total hip replacement within a five-year period.

Coding Clarification
If resurfacing of the femoral head is also performed, report only 00.85.

Documentation Tip
This procedure is also known as hip resurfacing arthroplasty or partial hip resurfacing arthroplasty of the acetabulum.

Coding Guidance
AHA: 4Q, '06, 121

00.9   Other procedures and interventions

Description
Subcategory 00.9 addresses the status of allogenic donor transplants. Allogeneic refers to tissue transplanted from one individual to another of the same species but different genotypes—also referred to as homologous or allograft transplants. Allografts may be of three different types: cadaver donors, living related, and living unrelated donors. The source of the donor tissue affects outcomes and the amount of care that can be expected, as well as initial acquisition costs. Allogeneic bone marrow or hematopoietic stem cell transplants from unrelated donors are relatively new procedures that come with extensive procurement or donor cell acquisition costs, as well as an increased length of stay compared with other related procedures.

Transplants of organs from an unrelated donor source also require an increased use of expensive immunosuppressive drugs and costly prolonging of supportive care drugs, such as antibiotics. The incidence of graft vs. host disease and serious infections also increases as does the number of hospital admissions and need for ICU care.

Coding Clarification
Codes from this subcategory are assigned for statistical and informational purposes only and do not report the actual procedure.

Assign codes from subcategory 00.9 in addition to the appropriate code for the organ transplant procedure performed.

Codes from this subcategory cannot be reported alone.

Subcategory 00.9 codes must be reported in addition to the organ transplant procedure for the transplant encounter. These codes may not be reported for subsequent admissions.

00.91 Transplant from live related donor

Description
Code 00.91 is assigned in addition to the appropriate organ transplant code to identify the donor as a parent, sibling, or adult child. Patients whose organs are obtained from a live related donor have a decreased chance of rejection and may require fewer immunosuppressive drugs.

Coding Clarification
This code is assigned for statistical and informational purposes only and does not report the actual procedure.

Assign 00.91 in addition to the appropriate code for the organ transplant procedure performed.

Coding Scenario
A 48-year-old female with a history of hypertensive chronic kidney disease that has now progressed to stage V presented for kidney transplant; the donor was her 35-year-old sister. The transplant procedure was accomplished without complications.

> Code Assignment:
>
> 403.91   Hypertensive chronic kidney disease, unspecified benign or malignant, with chronic kidney disease stage V or end stage renal disease
>
> 585.5   Chronic kidney disease, stage V
>
> 55.69   Other kidney transplantation
>
> 00.91   Transplant from live related donor

Coding Guidance
AHA: 4Q, '04, 116

00.92   Transplant from live non-related donor

Description
Code 00.92 is reported in addition to the appropriate organ transplant code to identify a live donor who is not a relative of the patient, such as a spouse or friend. Fewer patients require temporary dialysis following a live, non-related donor kidney transplant than after a cadaver transplant.

Coding Clarification
This code is assigned for statistical and informational purposes only and does not report the actual procedure.

Assign 00.92 in addition to the appropriate code for the organ transplant procedure performed.

Coding Guidance
AHA: 4Q, '04, 117; 2Q, '08, 8

00.93   Transplant from cadaver

Description
Code 00.93 is reported in addition to the appropriate organ transplant code to identify a cadaveric organ. These organs are harvested from recently deceased donors, whose organs are kept viable by artificial means until they can be excised for transplantation.

Coding Clarification
This code is assigned for statistical and informational purposes only and does not report the actual procedure.

Assign 00.93 in addition to the appropriate code for the organ transplant procedure performed.

Coding Guidance
AHA: 4Q, '04, 116

00.94   Intra-operative neurophysiologic monitoring

Description
This code is used to report intra-operative neurophysiologic monitoring (IOM). Neurophysiologic testing techniques are used in real time during surgical procedures to assess the brain, spinal cord, and nerves and monitor intracranial

pressure and brain tissue oxygenation levels. IOM is used in the treatment of cerebrovascular or traumatic brain injuries. It is also used in the treatment of epilepsy, motion disorders, and severe pain.

Coding Clarification
Code 00.94 includes cranial nerve, peripheral nerve, and spinal cord testing performed intra-operatively.

The use of NIMS monitoring system during a procedure is reported with 00.94.

When reporting intraoperative anesthetic effect monitoring and titration (IAEMT), the official index indicates that two codes must be reported: code 00.94 and 89.14 Electroencephalogram. The most common IAEMT system is the BIS Monitoring System.

The following procedures are excluded from 00.94 and are more appropriately reported elsewhere:

- Brain temperature monitoring (01.17)
- Intracranial oxygen monitoring (01.16)
- Intracranial pressure monitoring (01.10)
- Plethysmogram (89.58)

Documentation Tip
This procedure may also be documented as the following:

- IOM
- Nerve monitoring
- Neuromonitoring

Coding Guidance
AHA: 4Q, '07, 104; 2Q, '09, 4

01-05

Operations on the Nervous System

2011 Changes

Two new codes were added to subcategory 01.2 Craniotomy and craniectomy to report the implantation, replacement, or removal of a responsive neurostimulator system (RNS) generator: 01.20 Cranial implantation or replacement of neurostimulator pulse generator, and 01.29 Removal of cranial neurostimulator pulse generator. The RNS are specifically designed to treat adults with medically refractory localization-related (focal) (partial) epilepsy.

Other changes include the addition of the inclusion term amygdalohippocampectomy to code 01.59 Other excision or destruction of lesion or tissue of brain. Code also notes were added and revised at code 02.93 Implantation or replacement of intracranial neurostimulator lead(s), to indicate that a code for insertion of the neurostimulator pulse generator for either the cranial or subcutaneous procedure should be assigned in addition to code 2.93 for the insertion of the lead(s). An exclusion term was added to code 04.92 Implantation or replacement of peripheral neurostimulator lead(s), which excludes carotid sinus stimulation lead(s) (39.82) procedures.

The ICD-9-CM classification system for operations performed on the nervous system is divided into categories of procedures according to sites as follows:

* Skull, Brain, and Cerebral Meninges (01-02)
* Spinal Cord and Spinal Canal Structures (03)
* Cranial and Peripheral Nerves (04)
* Sympathetic Nerves or Ganglia (05)

Coding Clarification
Many of the subcategories in this portion of the classification system require a fourth digit for further specificity with regard to type and/or site of the operation performed.

Documentation Tip
Documentation in the operative report must support code selection.

01   Incision and excision of skull, brain, and cerebral meninges

Description
Category 01 provides codes for cranial puncture, diagnostic procedures, craniotomy and craniectomy, and other incisional and excisional procedures. Other operations on the skull, brain, and cerebral meninges such as cranioplasty, repairs, and shunt procedures are located in category 02.

Specific procedural categories found within this category include:

* Cranial puncture
* Diagnostic procedures on skull, brain, and cerebral meninges
* Craniotomy/craniectomy
* Incision of brain and cerebral meninges
* Operations on thalamus and globus pallidus
* Other excision/destruction of brain/meninges
* Excision of skull lesions

01.0   Cranial puncture

Coding Clarification
All codes within this subcategory require assignment of a fourth digit in order to provide specificity with regard to site and/or type of procedure.

01.01   Cisternal puncture

Description
The physician performs a cisternal puncture at the base of the skull in the cisterna magna (cerebellomedullary cistern) for diagnostic or therapeutic procedures. The needle is placed at the base of the skull and through the tissues to obtain fluid from the cisterna magna. A diagnostic or therapeutic injection of a medication or other substance may be performed.

Coding Clarification
Code 01.01 does not represent pneumocisternogram, which is correctly reported with 87.02.

Documentation Tip
Cisternal puncture may also be referred to as a cisternal tap or cisternal aspiration.

01.02   Ventriculopuncture through previously implanted catheter

Description
Code 01.02 reports the piercing of an artificial, fluid-diverting tube in the brain for withdrawal of cerebrospinal fluid.

The physician injects or aspirates the shunt tubing or reservoir with a needle to determine function. Shunt tubing is a drain to eliminate excess cerebral spinal fluid in cases of hydrocephalus. The tubing is tunneled under the skin, behind the ear, through the neck and chest area, and into the abdominal cavity. The physician places a needle into the tube or reservoir and injects radiologic dye or aspirates to check for effective drainage.

Documentation Tip
May also be referred to as puncture of ventricular shunt tubing.

01.09   Other cranial puncture

Description
▶The placement of a subdural evacuating port system (SEPS) drain assists in evacuating hematomas from the brain. This procedure may be performed for chronic subdural hematoma for which a surgeon performs a twist drill and SEPS evacuation procedure.◀

Code 01.09 is used to report cranial puncture procedures that are not described by the other, more precise codes within subcategory 01.0.

Documentation Tip
Operative report terminology may include the following:

- Aspiration of subarachnoid or subdural space
- Cranial aspiration
- Puncture of anterior fontanel
- Subdural tap
- Subdural tap through fontanel
- ▶Placement of a subdural evacuating port system (SEPS)◀

Coding Guidance
   AHA: 4Q, '07, 107; ▶3Q, '09, 15, 16◀

01.1   Diagnostic procedures on skull, brain, and cerebral meninges

Description
Subcategory 01.1 includes subdivisions for closed and open biopsies, as well as codes to report intracranial pressure monitoring, intracranial oxygen monitoring, and brain temperature monitoring. In the case of an open biopsy, an incision is made and a tissue sample is taken by opening the skull. Closed biopsies include percutaneous, needle, and burr hole approach.

Coding Clarification
All codes within this subcategory require assignment of a fourth digit in order to provide specificity with regard to site and/or procedure performed.

01.10   Intracranial pressure monitoring

Description
Intracranial pressure monitoring devices are used in the management of cerebrovascular injury, traumatic brain injury, and other disorders of the brain that result in increased intracranial pressure. This increased pressure can result in a decrease in the tissue oxygenation levels in the brain. Intracranial pressure monitoring is achieved by a device placed inside the head that measures the pressure inside the brain cavity and then sends those measurements to a recording device. Monitoring may be performed in various ways, as detailed here.

An intraventricular catheter (a thin, flexible tube) may be threaded into one of the two lateral ventricles. A burr hole is drilled through the skull, through which the catheter is inserted. The catheter passes through the brain matter and into the lateral ventricle, which normally contains the cerebrospinal fluid (CSF) that protects the brain and spinal cord. The intracranial pressure can be monitored and also lowered if necessary by draining the CSF out via the catheter. This is felt to be the most accurate method of measurement.

Alternately, a bolt or screw may be placed just through the skull into the subarachnoid space (the space between the arachnoid membrane and the cerebral cortex). The subarachnoid bolt is typically used if immediate access is necessary. This device consists of a hollow screw that is inserted through an opening made in the skull and through the dura mater (the outermost membrane protecting the brain and spinal cord).

An epidural sensor, which is less invasive than the previous two methods, may also be utilized. Placed through a burr hole drilled into the skull just over the epidural covering, the epidural sensor cannot remove excess CSF since no hole is created in the epidural lining. Rather, it is inserted between the skull and the epidural tissue.

Coding Clarification
Code 01.10 includes the insertion of the catheter or probe for monitoring.

Documentation Tip
►Code 01.10 includes the Camino® ventricular bolt intracranial pressure monitoring catheter. Placement of the catheter can be performed at bedside.◄

Coding Guidance
AHA: 4Q, '07, 105, 107; ►3Q, '09, 15, 16◄

01.11   Closed (percutaneous) (needle) biopsy of cerebral meninges

Description
The physician uses a burr drill or trephine to create a hole in the cranium through which a biopsy needle is inserted to biopsy the tissue. Stereotactic guidance may be utilized.

Documentation Tip
Stereotactic instrumentation allows the physician to precisely position a biopsy probe to allow access to areas that are not easily reached so a physician may obtain a "closed" biopsy.

May also be referred to as a burr hole approach.

01.12   Open biopsy of cerebral meninges

Description
This code reports an open surgical excision of a tissue sample from the cerebral meninges. The meninges are three membranes that cover the brain and the spinal cord: the dura mater, the arachnoid, and the pia mater. Spinal fluid flows in the space between the arachnoid and the pia mater membranes, which is also called the subarachnoid space. In this procedure, the physician uses a special instrumentation to create a hole in the cranium through which a meningeal lesion is located. The physician incises the scalp and peels it away from the area to be drilled. A lesion biopsy is obtained using a forceps or curette.

01.13   Closed (percutaneous) (needle) biopsy of brain

Description
The physician may biopsy an intracranial lesion stereotactically. The lesion is mapped using a CT or MRI scanning technique. The physician uses the coordinates obtained from the scans to locate the area of interest. The physician incises and retracts the scalp. A burr hole is drilled. The physician inserts a biopsy needle into the area of interest to biopsy the tissue. The physician closes the dura and reapproximates the scalp and closes it in sutured layers.

Coding Clarification
Code 01.13 reports brain biopsy obtained by using a needle, not a surgical excision or other tissue removal.

Documentation Tip
When a stereotactic method is used there is a three-dimensional coordinate guidance for directing the needle. Stereotactic brain biopsy may be performed as open or percutaneous. Refer to the operative report or query the physician for clarification.

Coding Scenario
A patient was admitted to undergo stereotactic brain biopsy. Under CT guidance, the calvaria (roof of the skull) were entered using a burr drill. A biopsy needle was inserted through the burr hole and was used to obtain the specimen.

> Code Assignment:
>
>   01.13   Closed [percutaneous][needle]biopsy of brain

Coding Guidance
AHA: M-A, '87, 9

01.14   Open biopsy of brain

Description
Using a burr drill or trephine, the physician creates a hole in the cranium through which a brain lesion is located. The physician excises the scalp away from the area to be drilled and a biopsy is obtained using a forceps or curette.

Coding Clarification
Code 01.14 reports an open surgical excision of a sample of brain tissue.

01.15   Biopsy of skull

Description
Utilizing a trocar or needle, the physician performs a biopsy on bone to confirm a suspected growth, disease, or infection. The physician normally uses local anesthesia, however, general anesthesia may be used. The physician places a large needle into the bone to obtain the sample. If an open biopsy is performed, the patient is placed under general anesthesia and placed in the appropriate position. The physician makes an incision overlying the biopsy site and carries it down through the tissue to the level of the bone being biopsied. A piece of bone tissue is removed and sent for examination. The wound is sutured closed and the patient is moved to the recovery area.

01.16   Intracranial oxygen monitoring

Description
Intracranial oxygen monitoring devices are used in the management of cerebrovascular injury, traumatic brain injury, and other disorders of the

01–05

brain that result in a decrease in the tissue oxygenation levels in the brain. Cerebral hypoxia may result from an increased demand for cerebral oxygen or a decrease in the delivery of cellular oxygen. Underlying causes may include elevated intracranial pressure, pain, seizures, fever, hypotension, hypovolemia, and anemia. Cerebral hypoxia can result in irreversible neuronal cell damage and may occur even when the patient is in the normal ranges for intracranial and cerebral perfusion pressure. The monitoring of brain oxygen levels has been shown by recent studies to have the potential to improve the outcome of patients with severe brain injury, and is an essential tool in the management and treatment of these patients.

This procedure typically involves the insertion of a monitoring catheter or probe via a burr hole approach.

Coding Clarification
Code 01.16 includes the insertion of the catheter or probe for monitoring.

Documentation Tip
May also be documented in the medical record as partial pressure of brain oxygen (PbtO2).

Coding Scenario
After placing an intracranial pressure catheter and a brain tissue oxygen catheter in a patient with a traumatic subdural hematoma, the physician performs a craniotomy and aspirates a subdural hematoma to reduce the intracranial pressure and improve the partial pressure of oxygen in the brain tissue.

Code Assignment:

852.20	Subdural hemorrhage following injury, without mention of open intracranial wound, unspecified state of consciousness
01.09	Other cranial puncture
01.10	Intracranial pressure monitoring
01.16	Intracranial oxygen monitoring

Coding Guidance
AHA: 4Q, '07, 105, 107

01.17   Brain temperature monitoring

Description
Brain temperature monitoring devices are used in the management of patients with cerebrovascular injury, traumatic brain injury, and other disorders of the brain, and entails the insertion of a device such as a catheter or probe that is designed for this purpose.

Coding Clarification
Code 01.17 includes the insertion of the catheter or probe for monitoring.

Coding Guidance
AHA: 4Q, '07, 105

01.18   Other diagnostic procedures on brain and cerebral meninges

Description
Diagnostic procedures such as x-rays, arteriograms, thermography, ultrasound, and tomography on the brain and cerebral meninges are excluded from 01.18. They are found in the miscellaneous diagnostic and therapeutic procedures section. Report 01.18 for other diagnostic procedures on the brain and cerebral meninges that are not more specifically described by other codes in subcategory 01.1.

Coding Clarification
Code 01.18 excludes the following procedures:

- Brain temperature monitoring (01.17)
- Intracranial oxygen monitoring (01.16)
- Intracranial pressure monitoring (01.10)
- Cerebral arteriography (88.41) and thermography (88.81)
- Contrast radiogram of brain (87.01-87.02)
- CT of head (87.03)
- Echoencephalogram (88.71)
- Electroencephalogram (89.14)
- Microscopic examination of specimen from nervous system/spinal fluid (90.01-90.09)
- Neurological examination (89.13)
- Other tomography of head (87.04)
- Phlebography of head/neck (88.61)
- Pneumoencephalogram (87.01)
- Radioisotope scan—cerebral (92.11)
- Radioisotope scan—head NEC (92.12)

Coding Guidance
AHA: 3Q, '98, 12

01.19   Other diagnostic procedures on skull

Description
Diagnostic procedures such as skull x-ray and transillumination are excluded from 01.19 and are found in the miscellaneous diagnostic and therapeutic procedures section. Use this code to report diagnostic procedures on the skull that are not more specifically described by other codes within subcategory 01.1.

Coding Clarification
Report transillumination of skull with 89.16.

Report x-ray of skull with 87.17.

01.2   Craniotomy and craniectomy

Description
Craniotomy involves incision into the skull, while craniectomy refers to excision of a portion of the skull.

● New Code   ▲ Revised Code   ▶◀ Revised Text   © 2010 Ingenix

Coding Clarification
When craniotomy or craniectomy is performed as an operative approach, omit the code.

Report exploration of the orbit with a code from range 16.01-16.09.

Subcategory 01.2 does not include decompression or debridement of skull fractures or a strip craniectomy. The codes for these procedures are found under subcategory 02.0, cranioplasty.

All codes within this subcategory require fourth-digit classification in order to provide specificity regarding site and procedure.

Coding Guidance
AHA: 1Q, '91, 1

● **01.20   Cranial implantation or replacement of neurostimulator pulse generator**

Description
The responsive neurostimulator system (RNS) is specifically designed to treat adults with medically refractory localization-related (focal) (partial) epilepsy. Epilepsy is a chronic neurological condition characterized by abnormal electrical activity in the brain, which causes seizures. The RNS neurostimulator is a small, curved device designed to be implanted within the skull near the patient's specific foci (point of origin) of seizure. The entire procedure is performed in the hospital inpatient setting with patients under general anesthesia and takes approximately three hours to complete. The device is programmable, battery-powered, and microprocessor-controlled and delivers short bursts of mild electrical pulses to the brain through implanted leads.

The device continuously monitors brain electrical activity, detecting the abnormal electrical activity preceding seizure, and responds by delivering brief and mild electrical stimulation to normalize brain activity. Stimulation parameters are programmed specifically to meet the patient's individual needs. Additionally, the RNS software allows the physician programmer to view the electrocorticogram or ECoG in real-time. Patients may transmit ECoG and system data remotely to their physician. Battery life of a cranially implanted neurostimulator is approximately three years, at which time the battery may be surgically replaced. When necessary, removal of a cranially implanted neurostimulator requires surgical repair of the craniectomy defect using cranioplasty techniques.

Coding Clarification
These codes report cranial neurostimulator device procedures, which differ significantly from subcutaneous neurostimulator pulse generator (86.94–86.98) procedures in respect to anatomic site

(cranium) and surgical technique (via cranioplasty). Code also any associated lead implantation (02.93).

Coding Scenario
A patient with medically refractory localization-related epilepsy with complex partial seizures presents for implantation of an RNS. Via premeasured craniectomy, the ferrule was inserted into the cranium, upon which the neurostimulator and intracranial leads were fitted into place into the skull. Implanted intracranial leads were connected to the neurostimulator, and the neurostimulator was placed in the ferrule and anchored to the skull with bone screws. The scalp was replaced over the skull, covering the implanted neurostimulator, and the surgical site was sutured closed.

Code Assignment:

345.41   Localization-related (focal) (partial) epilepsy and epileptic syndromes with complex partial seizures

01.20   Cranial implantation or replacement of neurostimulator pulse generator

02.93   Implantation or replacement of intracranial neurostimulator lead(s)

01.21   Incision and drainage of cranial sinus

Description
The physician uses a burr drill or trephine to create a hole in the cranium, through which a cranial sinus is drained.

Coding Clarification
Report exploration of the orbit with a code from range 16.01-16.09.

01.22   Removal of intracranial neurostimulator lead(s)

Description
Intracranial neurostimulator devices are implanted into the brain for deep brain stimulation (DBS) to control tremors in patients diagnosed with essential tremor, epilepsy, or Parkinson's disease. The device consists of a pulse generator unit that transmits mild electrical pulses through a wire to a lead that is implanted in the thalamus. The pulses interrupt the thalamic signals that play a role in causing the tremor. The lead is surgically placed using stereotactic equipment and connected to the pulse generator that is surgically implanted in a subcutaneous pocket, usually near the collarbone.

The insertion of the pulse generator is similar regardless of the end target organ. However, the insertion of the leads varies in scope depending upon the target organ. Intracranial lead insertion is more difficult than peripheral lead insertion. Pulse generators are battery operated, and the batteries must be replaced periodically. The leads are considered permanent with the exception of a complication.

01–05

To remove intracranial neurostimulator leads, the physician incises and retracts the scalp and drills a burr hole in the cranium to locate the electrode. The electrode is removed, the dura is closed, and the scalp is reapproximated and closed in sutured layers.

Coding Clarification
If removal of a neurostimulator pulse generator is performed in the same operative episode, also assign 86.05.

Code 01.22 excludes removal with synchronous replacement, which is correctly reported with 02.93.

01.23   Reopening of craniotomy site

Description
Report this code for the reopening of a previous skull incision. This procedure may be performed utilizing stereotactic equipment, computer assistance, or microdissection techniques. A craniotomy may be reopened to treat postoperative complications such as edema or hemorrhage, to excise recurrent tumors, or for certain staged procedures.

01.24   Other craniotomy

Description
Report 01.24 for craniotomy procedures that are not more specifically described by another code in subcategory 01.2.

Coding Clarification
Code 01.24 may be used to report the following cranial procedures:

- Decompression
- Exploration
- Trephination
- Craniotomy not otherwise specified
- Craniotomy with removal of epidural abscess
- Craniotomy with removal of extradural hematoma
- Craniotomy with removal of foreign body of skull

This code excludes removal of foreign body with incision into brain, which is correctly reported with 01.39.

Coding Guidance
    AHA: J-A, '84, 20; 2Q, '91, 14

01.25   Other craniectomy

Description
Code 01.25 is reported for sequestrectomy of the skull, in which the physician removes a portion of dead bone. The physician incises and retracts the scalp and removes bone from the affected area. A bone graft or plastic replacement may be used to

reconstruct the skull. The scalp is anastomosed and closed in sutured layers.

This code also reports debridement of the skull, not otherwise specified. However, debridement of a compound skull fracture is excluded from 01.25 and is reported with a code from subcategory 02.0.

Coding Clarification
Debridement of a compound fracture of the skull is reported with 02.02.

Report strip craniectomy with 02.01.

Coding Guidance
    AHA: 1Q, '06, 6

01.26   Insertion of catheter(s) into cranial cavity or tissue

Description
Delivery of intracavitary radioisotope brachytherapy for brain tumors requires infusion of a liquid solution of iodine-125 via a catheter into the intracranial cavity. This treatment is performed post-resection of the malignancy. At the time of resection, a specialized cavity-conforming, barium-impregnated balloon catheter with reservoir is sized and placed temporarily inside the cavity. The patient is readmitted for infusion at a later time. Once the treatment regimen is completed, the intracavity catheter is removed.

Coding Clarification
Code 01.26 provides a means of coding and reporting the insertion of the catheter required for delivery of radioisotope solutions to treat malignancies in the brain. This code will most often be assigned at the time of surgical resection, when the catheter is usually placed. The patient is then readmitted for infusion with the catheter in situ.

Also assign a code for any concomitant procedures performed.

Code 01.26 excludes the placement of intracerebral catheters via burr holes, which is correctly reported with 01.28.

Coding Scenario
A patient was admitted for resection of a primary malignancy of the parietal lobe of the brain and placement of brachytherapy catheter into the tumor cavity.

    Code Assignment:
    191.3   Malignant neoplasm of the brain, parietal lobe
    01.59   Other excision or destruction of lesion or tissue of brain
    01.26   Insertion of catheter into cranial cavity

Coding Guidance
    AHA: 4Q, '05, 117-118; ▶3Q, 09, 16◀

● New Code   ▲ Revised Code   ▶◀ Revised Text   © 2010 Ingenix

01.27 Removal of catheter(s) from cranial cavity or tissue

Description
Delivery of intracavitary radioisotope brachytherapy for brain tumors requires infusion of a liquid solution of iodine-125 via a catheter into the intracranial cavity. This treatment is performed post-resection of the malignancy. At the time of resection, a specialized cavity-conforming, barium-impregnated balloon catheter with reservoir is sized and placed temporarily inside the cavity. The patient is readmitted for infusion at a later time. Once the treatment regimen is completed, the intracavity catheter is removed. The physician incises and retracts the scalp over the placement origin. The dura is incised, and the catheter is located and removed. The dura is sutured closed and the scalp is reapproximated and sutured in layers.

Coding Guidance
AHA: 4Q, '05, 117-118; ▶3Q, '09, 16◀

01.28 Placement of intracerebral catheter(s) via burr hole(s)

Description
The physician creates a burr hole in the patient's skull and, using stereotactic guidance, implants a catheter into the targeted area of the brain. This area will be treated with a drug infusion.

The blood-brain barrier is a closely woven group of cells that helps to protect the brain from infection or from exposure to molecules that are potentially harmful. However, this barrier also prevents the majority of antineoplastic drugs from entering the brain, making it difficult to treat brain tumors.

Primary brain tumors are now the leading cause of cancer-related deaths in children. Glioblastoma multiforme (GBM) is a type of glioma, the most commonly diagnosed primary malignant tumors of the central nervous system in adults. GBM, which is resistant to radiation and chemotherapy, has shown some response to a receptor-targeting tumor cytotoxin known as cintredekin besudotox. Infusion of this macromolecular agent into the affected parts of the brain has been a significant obstacle to therapy because of the blood-brain barrier.

Convection-enhanced delivery (CED) is a technique that penetrates the blood-brain barrier without damage. It entails the strategic placement of catheters directly into the targeted brain tissue, through which therapeutic agents such as antineoplastics are microinfused. This method of administering small and large molecules involves the placement by neurosurgeons of two to four catheters

under stereotactic guidance through cranial burr holes into the brain parenchyma that is infiltrated by tumor cells. Since the antineoplastic agent must be distributed uniformly throughout the tumor-infiltrated tissue, the catheters cannot be placed into any previous resection cavity.

Approximately two weeks following the hospitalization for craniotomy with tumor resection, the patient returns for a second admission during which the catheters are placed via burr holes in a delicate neurosurgical procedure. The antineoplastic is then administered via a microinfusion pump through these catheters. Cintredekin besudotox, a biological response modifier and large molecule compound that cannot normally cross the blood-brain barrier, is often the agent of choice for this drug delivery technique. Upon completion of the infusion, which takes approximately 96 hours, the catheters are removed and the patient discharged.

Other indications for CED include the treatment of Alzheimer's disease and epilepsy. Therapeutic agents are not limited to antineoplastics but may include any large molecule compound required for the treatment of brain tissue.

Coding Clarification
Code 01.28 excludes the insertion of catheters into the cranial cavity or tissues; this is correctly reported with 01.26.

A code should also be assigned for any infusion of medication.

Documentation Tip
May also be documented in the medical record as convection-enhanced delivery or stereotactic placement of intracerebral catheter(s).

Coding Scenario
A patient with recurrent glioblastoma multiforme presents for convection-enhanced delivery of cintredekin besudotox. Under stereotactic guidance, four infusion catheters were placed via cranial burr holes into the targeted brain parenchyma. Cintredekin besudotox was administered by a microinfusion pump for 96 hours. Upon completion of the infusion, the catheters were removed and the patient discharged in satisfactory condition.

Code Assignment:

191.9 Glioblastoma multiforme
01.28 Placement of intracerebral catheter(s) via burr hole(s)
99.28 Injection or infusion of biological response modifier (BRM) as an antineoplastic agent

Coding Guidance
AHA: 4Q, '06, 122; ▶3Q, '09, 16◀

01–05

● **01.29   Removal of cranial neurostimulator pulse generator**

Description
The responsive neurostimulator system (RNS) is specifically designed to treat adults with medically refractory localization-related (focal) (partial) epilepsy. The device continuously monitors brain electrical activity, detecting the abnormal electrical activity preceding seizure, and responds by delivering brief and mild electrical stimulation to normalize brain activity. Battery life of a cranially implanted neurostimulator is approximately three years, at which time the battery may be surgically replaced. When necessary, removal of a cranially implanted neurostimulator requires surgical repair of the craniectomy defect using cranioplasty techniques.

Coding Clarification
Code 01.29 should not be reported when an RNS device is removed, and a new device inserted during the same operative episode. In those circumstances, assign code 01.20 Cranial implantation or replacement of neurostimulator pulse generator for device replacement procedures.

01.3   Incision of brain and cerebral meninges

Description
Subcategory 01.3 reports procedures in which the brain and/or cerebral meninges are incised. All codes within this subcategory require fourth-digit classification in order to provide specificity regarding site and procedure.

01.31   Incision of cerebral meninges

Description
The procedure consists of opening and draining the abscess; however, the specific surgical procedure depends on the depth or size of the abscess. A needle aspiration guided by CT scan or MRI may be performed, surgical incision may be made to remove a portion, or medications may be directly injected into the abscess.

Coding Clarification
Code 01.31 reports incision with drainage of intracranial hygroma, subarachnoid abscess, and subdural empyema.

01.32   Lobotomy and tractotomy

Description
Lobotomy refers to incision of the nerve fibers of a brain lobe, usually the frontal. Tractotomy is the severing of a nerve fiber in order to relieve pain.

When performing a lobotomy and cingulotomy, the physician incises and retracts the scalp, then removes bone in the frontal or parietal region. For a midline lobotomy, the physician dissects between the two cerebral hemispheres and creates a lesion through the gyrus cinguli. The bone is replaced and stabilized. The scalp is anastomosed and closed in sutured layers.

When performing a tractotomy, the physician performs a suboccipital craniectomy to resect a nerve tract as it passes through the medulla, the mesencephalon, or the cerebellar or cerebral peduncle. The physician incises and retracts the scalp, then removes bone from the occiput. The brain is retracted to reveal the brain stem. The affected nerve tract is resected and the bone is replaced and stabilized. The scalp is anastomosed and closed in sutured layers.

Documentation Tip
The operative report may contain the following verbiage to describe procedures reported by this code:

- Division of brain tissue
- Division of cerebral tracts
- Percutaneous cingulotomy
- Percutaneous radiofrequency cingulotomy

01.39   Other incision of brain

Description
Report 01.39 for procedures involving incision of the brain that are not reported by the more specific codes in subcategory 01.3. Descriptions below depict some of the procedures that may be reported with 01.39.

Amygdalohippocampectomy (AH) is done to treat intractable mesial temporal lobe epilepsy. This surgical procedure describes AH in which excision is limited to the anterior hippocampus, amygdala, and parahippocampal gyrus and preserves the fusiform gyrus and the lateral temporal lobe. MRI is done before surgery to map the margins of the involved brain structures. The patient is prepped with a general anesthetic and placement of a lumbar drain. With the patient's head in position, the scalp is incised and the underlying temporalis muscle is dissected to expose the skull. Burr holes are drilled around the periphery of the bone flap area to be raised. Using a craniotome, the bone flap is freed and lifted to expose the dura, which is dissected and retracted out of the operative field. An operating microscope is used. A brain retractor is inserted, and cerebrospinal fluid is carefully suctioned from the ambient cistern. The uncus is elevated with the retractor and the anatomical positioning of the related structures (fusiform and parahippocampal gyri, uncus, ambient cistern, and tentorium) is examined. Landmarks for cortical incisions are identified, such as the oculomotor nerve. Cortical incisions are made and the temporal horn of the

01–05

lateral ventricle is exposed, using careful suction dissection of the cortex and white matter. The horn is opened and the amygdala and hippocampus are identified. The parahippocampal gyrus is then incised, exposing the posterior aspect of the temporal horn and anterior hippocampus. The thin layer of neural tissue connecting the hippocampus and the amygdala is divided with subpial aspiration. The parahippocampal gyrus is removed subpially, the hippocampus is divided transversely, and anterior choroidal and posterior cerebral arteries are coagulated and divided. The hippocampus is completely separated from the arachnoid membrane and removed. The amygdala facing the temporal horn is excised with an ultrasonic aspirator. Closure is done by suturing the dura meticulously and replacing the bone flap into position. Screws or plates are placed to secure the bone flap to surrounding skull bone. The divided muscles are sutured and the galea and the scalp are closed.

The physician drains an intracerebral hematoma by craniectomy, craniotomy, or drilling a burr hole in the cranium. The hematoma is identified using a CT scan. The physician incises the scalp and peels it away from the area to be drilled. The physician drills or cuts through the cranium to the dura mater, which is incised. The brain is dissected and gently retracted until the hematoma is located. The hematoma is then aspirated using a syringe if the fluid is to be sent to pathology. Otherwise, the fluid is irrigated and suctioned. The dura mater is sutured closed and the scalp is repositioned and sutured into place.

Coding Clarification
This code may be used to report the following procedures:

- Drainage of intracerebral hematoma
- Incision of brain

Do not report division of cortical adhesions with 01.39; rather, report with 02.91.

▶Note: Amygdalohippocampotomy is now assigned code 1.59.◀

Coding Guidance
   AHA: ▶4Q, '09, 83◀

01.4   Operations on thalamus and globus pallidus
Description
This subcategory reports the following procedures on the thalamus and globus pallidus, and requires fourth-digit subclassification for specificity with regard to site:

- Chemothalamectomy
- Thalamotomy

- Pallidoansectomy
- Pallidotomy

Coding Clarification
Stereotactic guidance may be used with procedures reported by this subcategory.

This subcategory excludes stereotactic radiosurgical procedures, which involve noninvasive, precise delivery of radiation to a brain tumor and are correctly reported with a code from range 92.30-92.39.

01.41   Operations on thalamus
Description
The physician creates a lesion of the thalamus through stereotactic methods. The tissue to be lesioned is mapped by using a CT or MRI scanning technique. The physician uses the coordinates obtained from the scans to locate the area of interest. The physician incises and retracts the scalp. A burr hole is drilled. An electrocautery unit or surgical knife is then directed to the area of interest. When the precise location is reached and confirmed by the coordinates, the lesion is made in the thalamus. After the lesion is made, the dura is sutured and the scalp is reapproximated and closed in sutured layers.

Coding Clarification
Operations reported by this code include chemothalamectomy and thalamotomy, and may be performed under stereotactic guidance.

Report stereotactic radiosurgical procedures with the appropriate code from range 92.30-92.39.

01.42   Operations on globus pallidus
Description
The physician creates a lesion of the globus pallidus through stereotactic methods. The tissue to be lesioned is mapped by using a CT or MRI scanning technique. The physician uses the coordinates obtained from the scans to locate the area of interest. The physician incises and retracts the scalp. A burr hole is drilled. An electrocautery unit or surgical knife is then directed to the area of interest. When the precise location is reached and confirmed by the coordinates, the lesion is made in the globus pallidus. After the lesion is made, the dura is sutured and the scalp is reapproximated and closed in sutured layers.

Coding Clarification
Operations reported by this code include pallidoansectomy and pallidotomy, and may be performed using stereotactic guidance.

Report stereotactic radiosurgical procedures with the appropriate code from range 92.30-92.39.

01–05

01.5   Other excision or destruction of brain and meninges

Description
Subcategory 01.5 provides subdivisions for excision or destruction of lesion or tissue. However, the codes for biopsy of the cerebral meninges or brain are classified under subcategory 01.1.

This subcategory reports the following procedures on the brain and cerebral meninges, and requires fourth-digit subclassification for specificity with regard to procedure and site:

- Excision of meningeal lesion or tissue
- Hemispherectomy
- Lobectomy
- Other brain lesion/tissue excision or destruction

Coding Guidance
AHA: 4Q, '93, 33

01.51   Excision of lesion or tissue of cerebral meninges

Description
The physician removes a lesion or tissue from the posterior fossa or from infratentorial or supratentorial structures. Infratentorial structures are those located below the tentorium cerebelli, the membrane that separates the cerebellum from the basal surface of the occipital and temporal lobes of the cerebrum, while supratentorial structures are located above. The physician incises and retracts the scalp, then removes bone from the affected area. The lesion or tissue is identified and excised. The bone is then replaced and stabilized. The scalp is anastomosed and closed in sutured layers.

Coding Clarification
Procedures reported with 01.51 include the following:

- Decortication
- Resection
- Stripping of subdural membrane

Biopsy of cerebral meninges is not reported with this code; rather, assign 01.11 or 01.12.

01.52   Hemispherectomy

Description
Hemispherectomy, or removal of one half of the brain, is most often performed for malignant neoplasms or intractable epilepsy.

The physician cuts the fibers within the corpus callosum or removes all or part of a brain hemisphere. An electrode array is used to monitor brain function during surgery. The dura is sutured around the remaining brain tissue, and the bone flap

is replaced and stabilized. The scalp is anastomosed and closed in sutured layers.

01.53   Lobectomy of brain

Description
A temporal lobectomy with or without electrocorticography is done for intractable epileptic seizures when the focal point of the seizures has been identified by previous exams to originate in that lobe. Partial or total lobectomy with or without electrocorticography may be performed on lobes other than the temporal lobe (often the frontal lobe) if the focal point of the seizures has been identified to originate there. An access incision is made through the scalp and overlying muscle to reach the skull. Burr holes are drilled around the periphery of the bone flap area to be raised. Using a craniotome, the bone flap is freed and lifted to expose the dura, which is dissected and retracted out of the operative field. If electrocorticography is utilized, electrodes are prepared and placed on the brain. The electrical activity of the brain is recorded and mapped while the cortex is kept irrigated. The recording grids may be moved a few times to gain enough information about various sites. After the electrocorticography, the electrodes are removed and markers are placed. Incisions are made into the cortex and dissection is carried down deep into the cortex. The extent of the lobe to be removed and placement of the cortical incisions are carefully determined. In temporal lobectomy, the temporal horn of the lateral ventricle and the hippocampus are identified. The pia is next encountered and is incised and opened and then the temporal lobe is removed, including any part of the hippocampus, amygdala, and uncus that are to be removed with the temporal lobe. In frontal lobectomy, the pia is incised and opened to gain access to the frontal lobe. The predetermined amount of frontal lobe is removed. Arteries are appropriately transected and coagulated, while preserving the main cerebral/choroidal arteries and the pia-arachnoid. With the lobe removed, closure is done by suturing the dura meticulously and replacing the bone flap into position. Screws or plates are placed to secure the bone flap to surrounding skull bone. The divided muscles are sutured and the galea and the scalp are closed.

Coding Clarification
Code 01.53 is not site-specific and may be reported for excision of any lobe of the brain.

01.59   Other excision or destruction of lesion or tissue of brain

Description
Code 01.59 should be used to report procedures not more specifically described by other codes within

● New Code   ▲ Revised Code   ▶◀ Revised Text   © 2010 Ingenix

subcategory 01.5 in which brain lesions/tissues are destroyed or excised.

Coding Clarification
Code 01.59 reports the following procedures on lesions or tissues of the brain:

- Curettage
- Debridement
- Marsupialization
- Transtemporal excision
- ▶Amygdalohippocampectomy◀

Code 01.59 excludes the following procedures, which are appropriately classified elsewhere:

- Biopsy of brain (01.13, 01.14)
- Laser interstitial thermal therapy [LITT] of lesions or tissue of the brain under guidance (17.61)
- Laser interstitial thermal therapy [LITT] of lesions or tissue of the neck under guidance (17.62)
- Stereotactic radiosurgery (92.30-92.39)

Documentation Tip
Stereotactic guidance refers to a three-dimensional coordinate guidance used for directing localizing probes, while stereotactic radiosurgery refers to noninvasive delivery of radiation to a brain tumor.

The exclusion of stereotactic radiosurgery does not preclude the use of stereotactic guidance utilized during a procedure.

Coding Guidance
AHA: 1Q, '98, 6; 3Q, 98, 12; 1Q, 99, 9; 3Q, '99, 7; 4Q, '05, 118

01.6 Excision of lesion of skull

Description
The physician removes a portion of the skull invaded by tumor or infection. The physician incises and retracts the scalp and removes bone from the affected area. A bone graft or plastic replacement may be used to reconstruct the skull. The scalp is anastomosed and closed in sutured layers.

Coding Clarification
Excluded from this code is biopsy of the skull, which is reported with 01.15, and sequestrectomy, which is reported with 01.25.

Documentation Tip
The medical record may document the removal of granulation tissue of the cranium, which is also appropriately reported with 01.6.

02 Other operations on skull, brain, and cerebral meninges

Description
Category 02 addresses nervous system operative procedures that include cranioplasty, cerebral meningeal repair, ventricular shunt procedures, and various other operations on the skull, brain, and cerebral meninges.

02.0 Cranioplasty

Description
Subcategory 02.0 excludes cranioplasty with synchronous repair of encephalocele, which is correctly reported with 02.12.

All codes within this subcategory require fourth-digit classification in order to provide specificity regarding site and procedure.

02.01 Opening of cranial suture

Description
The physician incises and retracts the scalp over a fused suture line. The bones are cut to reshape the skull into an anatomically correct position. The recreated suture line is left open and the scalp is reanastomosed and closed in sutured layers. Single or multiple sutures may be reformed.

Coding Clarification
Report cranioplasty with synchronous repair of encephalocele with 02.12.

Documentation Tip
This procedure may also be referred to in the operative report as strip craniectomy or linear craniectomy.

02.02 Elevation of skull fracture fragments

Description
The physician elevates a depressed skull fracture to restore anatomical position. The scalp is incised and retracted to expose the skull depression. The physician may drill a burr hole and pull up on the skull to elevate the bone. If there are multiple fracture lines, the bony pieces are stabilized in anatomic position. If the fracture has damaged the dura and brain, the physician removes the bony fragments and debrides the brain and dura in a separately reportable procedure. The dura is sutured closed and the bony fragments are approximated and stabilized in anatomic position. The scalp is reapproximated and closed in sutured layers.

Coding Clarification
Also report any synchronous debridement of brain with 01.59.

01-05

Code 02.02 excludes debridement of the skull, not otherwise specified, which is correctly reported with 01.25.

Report removal of granulation tissue of the cranium with 01.6.

Report cranioplasty with synchronous repair of encephalocele with 02.12.

Documentation Tip
Operative report terminology may include the following:

- Debridement of compound skull fracture
- Decompression of skull fracture
- Reduction of skull fracture

02.03   Formation of cranial bone flap

Description
Code 02.03 reports repair of the skull utilizing a bone flap. The physician corrects a defect in the cranium by incising and retracting the scalp. The bone flaps are lifted and remodeled. A prosthesis may be used to reapproximate the bony edges. The skull is stabilized and the scalp is reapproximated and closed in sutured layers.

Coding Clarification
Report cranioplasty with synchronous repair of encephalocele with 02.12.

02.04   Bone graft to skull

Description
A cranial bone graft is placed onto a part of the skull for repair following craniectomy, craniotomy, or other intracranial surgery. The donor site is already exposed for the primary procedure. The cranial bone graft harvested may be split- or full-thickness, a shaving graft, or bone dust. When a full-thickness graft is required, the dura around the edge of the graft is exposed with a burr or neurosurgical craniotomy technique. A split graft requires removing lateral bone from a contoured area, which leaves it exposed like an island, and an osteotome is then correctly placed and tapped through to produce the bone graft. Shaving grafts are acquired similar to wood shaving and bone dust is produced by using a craniotome. The graft is placed to repair the defect and rigidly fixed, if necessary. Bone dust is placed and packed to fill the skull defect.

Coding Clarification
Report cranioplasty with synchronous repair of encephalocele with 02.12.

Documentation Tip
May also be referred to in the operative report as autogenous or heterogenous pericranial graft.

02.05   Insertion of skull plate

Description
The physician inserts or replaces a prosthetic plate of the skull. The physician incises the scalp and retracts it to expose the dura. The prosthetic plate is placed over dura to correct the defect. The plate is stabilized and the scalp is reapproximated and closed in sutured layers.

Coding Clarification
If skull plate is removed without synchronous replacement, report only 02.07.

02.06   Other cranial osteoplasty

Description
Code 02.06 is used to report other cranial osteoplasty procedures for which there is no more specific code in subcategory 02.0.

Coding Clarification
Procedures that may be reported by this code include:

- Repair of skull, NOS
- Revision or replacement of bone flap of skull
- Correction of synostosis
- Revision of cranial wounds

Report cranioplasty with synchronous repair of encephalocele with 02.12.

Coding Scenario
A 55-year-old female presents for replacement of a bone flap that was removed during a previous admission in which she had undergone a decompressive hemicraniectomy. The bone flap was retrieved from the hospital's bone bank, where it had been saved. Right hemicranioplasty utilizing the saved bone flap was accomplished without complication.

Code Assignment:

738.19   Other acquired deformity of head, other specified deformity
02.06   Other cranial osteoplasty

Coding Guidance
AHA: 3Q, '98, 9; 1Q, '05, 11; 1Q, '06, 6

02.07   Removal of skull plate

Description
The physician removes a prosthetic plate of the skull. The physician incises the scalp above the area to be resected and retracts it. The stabilizers are removed and the bone flap lifted. The scalp is reapproximated over the dura and closed in sutured layers.

Coding Clarification
Report removal of skull plate with synchronous replacement with 02.05.

02.1 Repair of cerebral meninges

Description

Subcategory 02.1 excludes marsupialization of a cerebral lesion, which is correctly reported with 01.59.

All codes within this subcategory require fourth-digit classification in order to provide specificity regarding site and procedure.

02.11 Simple suture of dura mater of brain

Description

The physician repairs a dural/cerebrospinal fluid leak. The physician determines the location of the skull fracture using an MRI scan. The skin over the damaged area is incised. A bone flap is removed to access the dura, which is sutured closed. The bone flap is replaced and stabilized. The scalp is reapproximated and closed in sutured layers.

Coding Clarification

Report marsupialization of a cerebral lesion with 01.59.

02.12 Other repair of cerebral meninges

Description

The following describes certain procedures that may be reported by 02.12.

In repairing an encephalocele, the physician corrects a herniation in the brain into or through a defect in the cranium. The physician incises and retracts the scalp and raises a bone flap. The bone is reshaped to increase skull size. The skull is stabilized and the scalp is reapproximated and closed in sutured layers.

When the physician repairs a dural/cerebrospinal fluid leak, the location of the skull fracture is determined using an MRI scan. The skin over the damaged area is incised. A bone flap is removed to access the dura, which is sutured closed. The bone flap is replaced and stabilized. The scalp is reapproximated and closed in sutured layers.

Coding Clarification

Report marsupialization of a cerebral lesion with 01.59.

Code 02.12 may be used to report the following procedures:

- Closure of fistula of cerebrospinal fluid
- Dural graft
- Repair of encephalocele (including synchronous cranioplasty)
- Repair of meninges NOS
- Subdural patch

02.13 Ligation of meningeal vessel

Description

The physician makes an opening in the vault of the skull, and the dura is opened over the site (e.g., over the superior longitudinal sinus). Using a vascular clip or ligature, the vessel is ligated.

Coding Clarification

Report marsupialization of a cerebral lesion with 01.59.

Documentation Tip

Operative report terminology may include ligation of longitudinal sinus or ligation of middle meningeal artery.

02.14 Choroid plexectomy

Description

Code 02.14 reports the excision or destruction of the ependymal cells that form the membrane lining in the third, fourth, and lateral ventricles of the brain and secrete cerebrospinal fluid.

The physician excises or destroys the choroid plexus, which produces spinal fluid. The physician cuts and retracts the scalp in the affected region. A bone flap is raised and tissues are dissected to the ventricle where the affected choroid plexus is located. The choroid plexus is resected or destroyed using electrocautery. The bone is replaced and stabilized. The scalp is anastomosed and closed in sutured layers.

Coding Clarification

Report marsupialization of a cerebral lesion with 01.59.

Documentation Tip

May also be referred to as cauterization of the choroid plexus.

02.2 Ventriculostomy

Description

Ventriculostomy is the surgical creation of an opening to a ventricle, and is often performed to drain cerebrospinal fluid in treating hydrocephalus.

In a Torkildsen type procedure, the physician performs a ventriculocisternostomy to form a communicating duct from the lateral ventricles to the cisterna magna to drain excess CSF into the spinal cord where it can be absorbed. The scalp is incised and retracted posterior to the ear. The physician drills a burr hole and inserts the proximal portion of the shunt toward the lateral ventricles, with or without the aid of an endoscope, until CSF flows through the shunt. The distal end of the shunt is directed toward the cisterna magna until CSF flows through the shunt. The two ends are connected and tested. The dura is sutured closed

01–05

and the scalp is reapproximated and closed in sutured layers.

In a second ventriculostomy, the physician forms a communicating duct from the third ventricle to the cisterna magna to drain excess CSF into the spinal cord where it can be absorbed. The scalp is incised and retracted posterior to the ear. The physician drills a burr hole and inserts the proximal portion of the shunt toward the third ventricle until CSF flows through the shunt. The distal end of the shunt is directed toward the cisterna magna until CSF flows through the shunt. The two ends are connected and tested. The dura is sutured closed and the scalp is reapproximated and closed in sutured layers.

In a third ventriculostomy performed utilizing stereotactic, neuroendoscopic techniques, the physician performs a ventriculocisternostomy of the third ventricle. Performed in hydrocephalus cases to create a pathway for obstructed cerebrospinal fluid (CSF) by opening a communication between the third ventricle and the subarachnoid space to allow the fluid to drain internally, this method prevents the need for shunt placement in many cases. A small incision is made in the scalp and a small burr hole is made in the skull just large enough to allow passage of the endoscopic instrument. Computerized tomography (CT) guidance for stereotactic positioning is used. The neuroendoscope is inserted through the burr hole into the third ventricle. A contact laser fiber is inserted through the endoscope onto the floor of the third ventricle and the contact tip perforates the intracranial tissue at different points, avoiding arteries. The newly opened communication is verified when the circulation of CSF is unobstructed. Hemostasis is achieved, the instruments are removed, and the incision is closed.

Documentation Tip
The following terminology may be seen in the operative report:

- Anastomosis of ventricle to the cervical subarachnoid space

- Anastomosis of ventricle to the cisterna magna

- Insertion of Holter monitor

- Ventriculocisternal intubation

- Torkildsen, Dandy, or Stookey-Scarff type procedure

02.3   Extracranial ventricular shunt

Description
Codes in this subcategory report the placement of a shunt or the creation of an artificial passage leading from skull cavities to a site outside the skull to relieve excess cerebrospinal fluid created in the

choroid plexuses of the third and fourth ventricles of the brain.

Coding Clarification
Valve insertion is included in codes from subcategory 02.3.

All codes within this subcategory require fourth-digit classification in order to provide specificity regarding site and procedure.

02.31   Ventricular shunt to structure in head and neck

Description
The physician creates a shunt to form a communicating duct from the lateral ventricles to a structure in the head or neck to drain excess CSF. The scalp is incised and retracted posterior to the ear. The physician drills a burr hole and inserts the proximal portion of the shunt toward the lateral ventricles, with or without the aid of an endoscope, until CSF flows through the shunt. The distal end of the shunt is directed and tunneled subcutaneously toward the selected drain site. The two ends are connected and tested. The dura is sutured closed and the scalp is reapproximated and closed in sutured layers. If an incision is required at the distal end, the operative incision is closed in sutured layers.

Coding Clarification
Code 02.31 includes valve insertion.

Documentation Tip
Also known as ventriculomastoid anastomosis or ventricle to nasopharynx shunt

02.32   Ventricular shunt to circulatory system

Description
The physician creates a shunt to form a communicating duct from the lateral ventricles to the circulatory system to drain excess CSF. The scalp is incised and retracted posterior to the ear. The physician drills a burr hole and inserts the proximal portion of the shunt toward the lateral ventricles, with or without the aid of an endoscope, until CSF flows through the shunt. The distal end of the shunt is directed and tunneled subcutaneously toward the selected drain site. The two ends are connected and tested. The dura is sutured closed and the scalp is reapproximated and closed in sutured layers. If an incision is required at the distal end, the operative incision is closed in sutured layers.

Coding Clarification
Code 02.32 includes valve insertion.

Documentation Tip
Also known as ventriculoatrial anastomosis or ventriculocaval shunt.

● New Code   ▲ Revised Code   ►◄ Revised Text   © 2010 Ingenix

02.33   Ventricular shunt to thoracic cavity

Description
The physician creates a shunt to form a communicating duct from the lateral ventricles to the thoracic cavity to drain excess CSF. The scalp is incised and retracted posterior to the ear. The physician drills a burr hole and inserts the proximal portion of the shunt toward the lateral ventricles, with or without the aid of an endoscope, until CSF flows through the shunt. The distal end of the shunt is directed and tunneled subcutaneously toward the selected drain site. The two ends are connected and tested. The dura is sutured closed and the scalp is reapproximated and closed in sutured layers. If an incision is required at the distal end, the operative incision is closed in sutured layers.

Coding Clarification
Code 02.33 includes valve insertion.

Documentation Tip
Also known as ventriculopleural anastomosis.

02.34   Ventricular shunt to abdominal cavity and organs

Description
The physician creates a shunt to form a communicating duct from the lateral ventricles to the abdominal cavity and/or organs to drain excess CSF. The scalp is incised and retracted posterior to the ear. The physician drills a burr hole and inserts the proximal portion of the shunt toward the lateral ventricles, with or without the aid of an endoscope, until CSF flows through the shunt. The distal end of the shunt is directed and tunneled subcutaneously toward the selected drain site. The two ends are connected and tested. The dura is sutured closed and the scalp is reapproximated and closed in sutured layers. If an incision is required at the distal end, the operative incision is closed in sutured layers.

Coding Clarification
Code 02.34 includes valve insertion.

Documentation Tip
Also known as ventriculocholecystostomy or ventriculoperitoneostomy.

02.35   Ventricular shunt to urinary system

Description
The physician creates a shunt to form a communicating duct from the lateral ventricles to the ureter to drain excess CSF. The scalp is incised and retracted posterior to the ear. The physician drills a burr hole and inserts the proximal portion of the shunt toward the lateral ventricles, with or without the aid of an endoscope, until CSF flows through the shunt. The distal end of the shunt is directed and tunneled subcutaneously toward the

selected drain site. The two ends are connected and tested. The dura is sutured closed and the scalp is reapproximated and closed in sutured layers. If an incision is required at the distal end, the operative incision is closed in sutured layers.

Coding Clarification
Code 02.35 includes valve insertion.

Documentation Tip
This procedure is also known as ventricle to ureter shunt.

02.39   Other operations to establish drainage of ventricle

Description
Use 02.39 to report an extracranial ventricular shunt procedure that is not more precisely described by another code in subcategory 02.3.

The physician creates a shunt to form a communicating duct from the lateral ventricles to an extracranial site to drain excess CSF. The scalp is incised and retracted posterior to the ear. The physician drills a burr hole and inserts the proximal portion of the shunt toward the lateral ventricles, with or without the aid of an endoscope, until CSF flows through the shunt. The distal end of the shunt is directed and tunneled subcutaneously toward the selected drain site. The two ends are connected and tested. The dura is sutured closed and the scalp is reapproximated and closed in sutured layers. If an incision is required at the distal end, the operative incision is closed in sutured layers.

Coding Clarification
Code 02.39 includes valve insertion.

Code 02.39 is used to report ventricle to bone marrow shunt and ventricular shunt to an extracranial site not elsewhere classified.

02.4   Revision, removal, and irrigation of ventricular shunt

Description
Subcategory 02.4 provides three subdivisions for coding these procedures. If irrigation is necessary, use 02.41. For reinsertion of Holter valve, replacement of ventricular catheter, or revision of ventriculoperitoneal shunt at ventricular site, use 02.42. The complete removal is coded 02.43.

02.41   Irrigation and exploration of ventricular shunt

Description
A ventriculoperitoneal shunt drains excess cerebrospinal fluid from the brain into the abdomen. It is commonly used as a therapy in hydrocephalus, spina bifida, meningitis, brain tumor, or head injuries. Exploration may be attempted when there is a malfunction or blockage or when an infection is

01–05

suspected. Symptoms of a problem with a ventriculoperitoneal shunt include headache, fever, drowsiness, or seizures.

The physician performs irrigation, exploration, or reprogramming of a previously placed ventricular shunt system or component. The physician incises and retracts the scalp over the placement origin and drills a burr hole to gain access. The dura is incised and the inoperative portion of the shunt system is located and irrigated, explored, or reprogrammed. The shunt system is reconnected and tested. The dura is sutured closed and the scalp is reapproximated and sutured in layers.

Coding Clarification
If the exploration is at the ventricular site, report 02.41; if at the peritoneal site, report 54.95 Incision of peritoneum.

Documentation Tip
Operative report terminology may include the following:

- Exploration of ventriculoperitoneal shunt at ventricular site

- Reprogramming of ventriculoperitoneal shunt

02.42   Replacement of ventricular shunt

Description
The physician replaces or revises a previously placed ventricular shunt at the ventricular site. The physician incises and retracts the scalp over the placement origin and drills a burr hole to gain access. The dura is incised, and the inoperative portion of the shunt system is located and replaced or revised. The shunt system is reconnected and tested. The dura is sutured closed and the scalp is reapproximated and sutured in layers.

Coding Clarification
If the revision is at the ventricular site, report 02.42; if at the peritoneal site, report 54.95 Incision of peritoneum.

Documentation Tip
Operative note terminology may include the following:

- Reinsertion of Holter valve

- Replacement of ventricular catheter

- Revision of ventriculoperitoneal shunt at ventricular site

Coding Guidance
AHA: N-D, '86, 8; 5th issue, '94, 4; 4Q, '95, 65

02.43   Removal of ventricular shunt

Description
The physician removes a ventricular shunt without replacement. The physician incises and retracts the

scalp over the placement origin. The dura is incised and the shunt is located and removed. The dura is sutured closed and the scalp is reapproximated and sutured in layers.

Coding Clarification
Do not assign a code for the removal or shortening by puncture wound approach or trial clamping of the peritoneal portion of the ventriculoperitoneal shunt.

Documentation Tip
Review the medical record documentation closely to determine when the procedure involves removal. There usually is a specific code for removal alone. However, if removal and then replacement occurs during the same operative session, the classification may refer you to the code for insertion or replacement.

Coding Guidance
AHA: N-D, '86, 8

02.9   Other operations on skull, brain, and cerebral meninges

Description
All codes within this subcategory require fourth-digit classification in order to provide specificity regarding site and procedure.

This subcategory excludes the following operative sites, which are more appropriately classified elsewhere:

- Pineal gland (07.17, 07.51-07.59)

- Pituitary gland (07.13-07.15, 07.61-07.79)

02.91   Lysis of cortical adhesions

Description
This code describes the breaking up of fibrous structures in the brain's outer layer.

02.92   Repair of brain

Description
This code describes a repair of brain tissue that is not more appropriately classified elsewhere, such as a non-incisional removal of a foreign body or other repair or surgical treatment of trauma to the brain. If the procedure describes a removal of a foreign body from the brain, the physician incises the scalp and cuts the bone or creates a bone flap as necessary to reach the foreign body. The object is identified and removed. If the brain tissue has been damaged by the foreign object, it is debrided and irrigated. The dura is sutured closed and the bone is fastened into place.

02.93 Implantation or replacement of intracranial neurostimulator lead(s)

Description
Neurostimulator systems consist of a battery-operated pulse generator inserted into a subcutaneous pocket connected to an electrode (lead) situated at the target organ via a subcutaneous tunnel. The insertion of the pulse generator is similar regardless of the end target organ. However, the insertion of the leads varies in scope depending upon the target organ. Intracranial lead insertion is more difficult than peripheral lead insertion. The leads are considered permanent with the exception of a complication. Pulse generators, on the other hand, are battery operated, and the batteries must be replaced periodically.

Thalamic stimulator implantation for the control of tremor consists of implanting a lead in the thalamus connected to an indwelling battery pack inserted subcutaneously in the abdomen or below the clavicle. Code 02.93 includes all components of this procedure: the implantation of the lead in the thalamus, the tunneling, the pocket creation, and the insertion of the subcutaneous battery pack. If the procedure is staged, that is the insertion of the battery pack into the pocket is performed during a separate operative episode, assign 86.09 Other incision of the skin and subcutaneous tissue, and 86.99 Other operations on skin and subcutaneous tissue.

The physician uses a twist or burr drill or performs a craniectomy or craniotomy to reach the cortex or subcortex and implant neurostimulator electrodes. The physician incises the scalp and retracts it. The physician drills or cuts the cranium to expose the cortex for neurostimulator electrode placement. Bone may be removed. The physician places an electrode through an introducer needle into the tissue to be stimulated. The electrodes are tested to verify placement and the incision is closed in sutured layers.

Coding Clarification
Code 02.93 reports the implantation, insertion, placement, or replacement of the following intracranial devices:

- Brain pacemaker
- Neuropacemaker
- Depth electrodes
- Epidural pegs
- Electroencephalographic receiver
- Foramen ovale electrodes
- Intracranial electrostimulator
- Subdural grids

- Subdural strips

▶Assign an additional code for insertion of cranial implantation or replacement of neurostimulator pulse generator (01.20).◀

Assign an additional code from range 86.94-86.98 to report the insertion of a ▶subcutaneous◀ neurostimulator pulse generator.

Coding Guidance
AHA: 4Q, '92, 28; 4Q, '97, 57; 4Q, '04, 133-135

02.94 Insertion or replacement of skull tongs or halo traction device

Description
A halo traction device consists of a metal or plastic band encircling the head or neck and secured to the skull with four pins. Attached to a metal chest plate by rods, it provides support and stability for the head and neck. Skull tongs, a device inserted into each side of the skull, are used to apply parallel traction to the long axis of the cervical spine.

The physician applies a cranial halo to stabilize an injured cervical spine for radiography, traction, or to facilitate surgery. The physician places the patient supine (lying on the back) with the head supported just over the end of the stretcher. Skin and scalp are sterilized with a povidone-iodine solution. The halo is positioned about the patient's head below the area of greatest skull diameter. A local anesthetic is injected into the areas selected for frame pin insertion. The anterior pins are inserted first, followed by the posterior pins. Two diagonally opposed pins are tightened simultaneously until all four engage the skin and bone. Using a torque screwdriver, all are tightened and secured with nuts or set screws before attachment to a traction setup or to a halo vest or cast.

Coding Clarification
Report 02.94 in addition to the primary procedure, as appropriate.

If closed reduction of a vertebral fracture is accomplished by the application of a halo device and spinal traction, report 02.94 and 93.41 for the procedure. In this case, it is not necessary to report 03.53 Repair of vertebral fracture, if the fracture is reduced through traction alone.

When traction is used with the halo device, also assign 93.41 Spinal traction using skull device. The halo provides stabilization; spinal traction is an additional measure used with the halo device.

Coding Scenario
A 35-year-old patient was admitted with a C1-2 vertebral fracture dislocation. There was no spinal cord injury. Reduction was accomplished by the placement of a halo apparatus and spinal traction.

01–05

Code Assignment:

805.01   Fracture of vertebral column without mention of spinal cord injury, cervical, closed, first cervical vertebra

805.02   Fracture of vertebral column without mention of spinal cord injury, cervical, closed, second cervical vertebra

02.94   Insertion or replacement of skull tongs or halo traction device

93.41   Spinal traction using skull device

Coding Guidance
   AHA: 3Q, '96, 14; 3Q, '01, 8

02.95   Removal of skull tongs or halo traction device

Description
The physician removes tongs or a halo traction device. Maintaining alignment of the cervical spine, the physician unscrews the frame pins from the skull and removes the tongs or halo. Bone wax may be applied to the wounds to promote healing of the skull. Dressing may be applied to the skin wounds and the skin may be sutured.

02.96   Insertion of sphenoidal electrodes

Description
The physician places sensors in or near the sphenoid process. Often performed in a treatment room, this is a nonoperative, invasive procedure used to determine the localization of seizure activity and involving the insertion of electrodes deep inside the face. The physician inserts spinal needles threaded with the sphenoidal electrodes and attached receivers bilaterally into the temporomandibular joint space. The electrodes are placed near the underside of the skull for the purpose of continuous electroencephalographic monitoring.

Coding Clarification
Review the record carefully in order to differentiate the placement of intracranial neurostimulator leads from sphenoidal electrodes. The implantation of depth electrodes, foramen ovale electrodes, subdural grid placement, and epidural pegs should be reported with 02.93.

Coding Guidance
   AHA: 4Q, '92, 28

02.99   Other operations on skull, brain, and cerebral meninges

Description
Code 02.99 is used to report other operations on the skull, brain, and cerebral meninges for which there is no more specific code in subcategory 02.9. However, chemical shock therapy and subconvulsive and other electroshock therapy are excluded from 02.99 and are found in the miscellaneous diagnostic and therapeutic procedures section.

Coding Clarification
Report shock therapy as:

*   Chemical shock therapy (94.24)
*   Subconvulsive electroshock therapy (94.26)
*   Other electroshock therapy (94.27)

03   Operations on spinal cord and spinal canal structures

Description
There are nine subdivisions within category 03, with more than half requiring a fourth digit to complete the code. The various types of procedures that can be found here are decompression laminectomy or laminotomy, spinal tap, vertebral fracture repair, injections into the spinal canal, and others.

Coding Clarification
When reporting codes from category 03, also assign 99.77 for any application or administration of an adhesion barrier substance.

03.0   Exploration and decompression of spinal canal structures

Coding Guidance
   AHA: 4Q, '99, 14

03.01 Removal of foreign body from spinal canal

Description
A small incision (usually about 3 to 4 inches) is made in the back and the physician uses a retractor to spread apart the muscles and fatty tissue of the spine to expose the lamina.

An alternative to this is a micro-disc surgery in which the physician makes an incision and removes the lamina to access the dura through which the catheter is inserted for visualization of the surgical field with an operating microscope. Upon adequate visualization, the foreign body is located and removed.

03.02   Reopening of laminectomy site

Description
Laminectomy patients often require reoperation, typically at the site and level of previous surgery; so the physician must navigate scar tissue from the previous surgery. Retained fragments are frequently removed during reoperations or a new laminotomy may be performed because of nerve root compression due to herniation of the adjacent disc.

Coding Clarification
Do not assign this code when the reopening is performed as a surgical approach for a more definitive procedure.

● New Code   ▲ Revised Code   ▶◀ Revised Text   © 2010 Ingenix

01–05

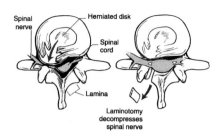

Spinal nerve

Herniated disk

Spinal cord

Spinal cord

Lamina

Laminotomy decompresses spinal nerve

03.09   Other exploration and decompression of spinal canal

Description
Decompression of the spinal canal consists of excision of bone pieces, hematoma, or other lesions in order to relieve spinal cord pressure. Expansile laminoplasty involves incision of the lamina at the level of the pedicle to relieve pressure; no tissue is excised. Foraminotomy consists of removal of the root opening between the vertebrae to relieve nerve root pressure.

Coding Clarification
Excision of an intervertebral disc includes decompression of the spinal canal. If any of these decompression procedures and excision are performed at the same vertebral level, do not assign 03.09 in addition.

Code also any synchronous insertion, replacement, or revision of posterior spinal motion preservation device(s), if performed, with a code from range 84.80-84.85.

Insertion of Mersilene sutures for stabilization is inherent in the exploration and decompression of the spinal canal and is not coded separately.

The following procedures are more accurately described elsewhere and are excluded from 03.09:

- Drainage of spinal fluid by anastomosis (03.71-03.79)

- Laminectomy with excision of intervertebral disc (80.51)

- Spinal tap (03.31)

Decompressive laminotomy or foraminotomy as an operative approach is not separately coded, but is included in the code for the primary procedure.

Documentation Tip
Medical record documentation may include the following descriptors of procedures reported by 03.09:

- Decompression laminectomy

- Decompression laminotomy

- Expansile laminoplasty

- Exploration of the spinal nerve root

- Foraminotomy

Coding Guidance
AHA: S-0, '86, 12; 2Q, '90, 22; 2Q, '95, 9; 2Q, '97, 6; 4Q, '99, 14; 2Q, '00, 22; 2Q, '02, 15; 4Q, '02, 109; 3Q, '04, 6; 1Q, '07, 10; 4Q, '07, 117, 120; 2Q, '08, 12; 4Q, '08, 109

03.1   Division of intraspinal nerve root

Description
Code 03.1 reports rhizotomy, which is the surgical severing of spinal nerve roots within the spinal canal.

A rhizotomy is performed on the anterior nerve roots to stop involuntary spasmodic movements associated with paraplegia or torticollis. It is also performed on the posterior nerve roots to eliminate pain in a restricted area. The patient is placed prone. The physician makes a midline incision overlying the affected vertebrae. The fascia is incised. The paravertebral muscles are retracted. Laminectomy is performed. The physician identifies the anterior or posterior nerve roots to be divided. Each is lifted with a nerve hook and severed. Fascia, muscles, and ligaments are allowed to fall back into place. The incision is closed with layered sutures.

03.2   Chordotomy

Description
Subcategory 03.2 reports chordotomy, which is the surgical cutting of the lateral spinothalamic tract of the spinal cord in order to relieve pain. Codes within this subcategory require fourth-digit subclassification in order to identify the type of chordotomy performed.

03.21 Percutaneous chordotomy

Description
The physician performs a neurosurgical procedure to relieve pain by cutting the nerves of the spinal cord that transmit pain impulses through the nerve pathways. Cordotomy is usually done percutaneously with fluoroscopic guidance under local anesthesia. Open cordotomy requires a laminectomy.

Documentation Tip
This procedure may also be referred to as stereotactic chordotomy.

Also spelled as cordotomy.

03.29   Other chordotomy

Description
Code 03.29 reports chordotomy other than that performed percutaneously or stereotactically. Tractotomy of the spinal cord involves the surgical incision or severing of a nerve tract of the spinal

01-05

Coders' Desk Reference for ICD-9-CM Procedures

cord. Transection of spinal cord tracts involves the use of a transverse incision to divide the spinal nerve root.

The following describes a chordotomy (tractotomy) with section of one spinothalamic tract.

The patient is placed prone. The physician makes a midline incision overlying the affected vertebrae. The fascia are incised. The paravertebral muscles are retracted. A laminectomy is performed. The physician identifies the anterolateral tracts in the appropriate level on the side opposite the pain. The dentate ligament is divided at the level of the chordotomy. The ligament is drawn posteriorly toward the midline to expose the anterolateral part of the cord. A chordotomy knife is introduced into the spinal cord anterior to the dentate ligament and directed toward the anterior spinal artery. The tissue in front of this artery is divided with the knife. The incision is closed with layered sutures.

Coding Clarification
Procedures reported with 03.29 include the following:

- Chordotomy not otherwise specified
- Tractotomy of spinal cord
- Transection of spinal cord tracts

03.3   Diagnostic procedures on spinal cord and spinal canal structures

03.31   Spinal tap

Description
This procedure is performed to lessen cerebrospinal fluid pressure. The patient is placed in a spinal tap position. The L3 and L4 vertebrae are located and local anesthesia is administered. The lumbar puncture needle is inserted. In some cases, spinal fluid is drawn through the needle as in a lumbar puncture test. In other cases, a catheter is inserted and the fluid empties into a reservoir. Pressure reading is performed with a manometer. When the procedure is completed, the needle is removed and the wound is dressed. In many cases, the patient lies prone to prevent fluid leakage.

Coding Clarification
Report lumbar puncture for injection of dye (myelogram) with 87.21.

Documentation Tip
This code reports a puncture into the lumbar subarachnoid space to remove cerebrospinal fluid or for the removal of dye; if the documentation indicates that the puncture was performed for injection of dye, this code will not be used.

Coding Guidance
   AHA: 2Q, '90, 22; 3Q, '05, 13

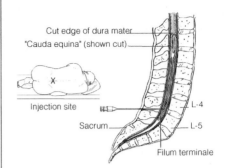

03.32   Biopsy of spinal cord or spinal meninges

Description
A biopsy of the spinal cord is performed to determine the nature and extent of a suspected lesion. The patient is placed in a spinal tap position. The affected vertebrae are located and local anesthesia is administered. The biopsy needle is inserted. In some cases, blood is drawn through the needle for testing. Imaging equipment is used to confirm placement, and samples are drawn from the lesion for inspection. When the procedure is completed, the needle is removed and the wound is dressed.

The patient is placed in the prone position during an intraspinal neoplasm biopsy. The physician makes a midline incision. Fascia is incised. Paravertebral muscles are retracted. The physician removes the laminae and the spinous processes of the vertebrae to the dura. A biopsy is taken of the neoplasm. Muscles, fascia, and ligaments are repaired and the incision is closed with layered sutures.

03.39   Other diagnostic procedures on spinal cord and spinal canal structures

Description
Code 03.39 reports other diagnostic procedures performed on the spinal cord and spinal canal structures that are not more precisely described by other codes within subcategory 03.3.

Coding Clarification
Report a microscopic examination of a specimen from the nervous system or of spinal fluid with a code from range 90.01-90.09.

Code 03.39 excludes x-ray of the spine, which is correctly reported with a code from range 87.21-87.29.

03.4   Excision or destruction of lesion of spinal cord or spinal meninges

Description
The physician removes a growth in the spine. The patient is placed prone. The physician makes a midline incision and the fascia is incised. Paravertebral muscles are retracted. The physician

Image caption labels: Cut edge of dura mater, "Cauda equina" (shown cut), Injection site, Sacrum, L-4, L-5, Filum terminale

01–05

77
77

removes the laminae and the spinous processes of the vertebrae to expose the outside of the dura. The extradural intraspinal lesion is excised or evacuated. If the lesion is intradural, the dura is exposed and incised. The pia-arachnoid is incised as necessary and the lesion is removed. The incision is closed with layered sutures.

Coding Clarification
Also report the application or administration of an adhesion barrier substance with 99.77.

Code 03.4 excludes biopsy of the spinal cord or meninges, which is correctly reported with 03.32.

Laminectomy is inherent to the excision of the lesion and is not coded separately.

Documentation Tip
Medical record documentation may contain the following terminology to describe procedures on the spinal cord or spinal meninges that are appropriately reported with this code:

- Curettage
- Debridement
- Marsupialization of cyst
- Resection

Coding Guidance
AHA: 3Q, '95, 5; 2Q, '08, 10

03.5 Plastic operations on spinal cord structures
Description
Subcategory 03.5 addresses the repair of various spinal cord defects and abnormalities, including meningocele, myelomeningocele, vertebral fractures and arch defects, and spina bifida.

Coding Clarification
When reporting codes from subcategory 03.5, also report any application or administration of an adhesion barrier substance with 99.77.

03.51 Repair of spinal meningocele
Description
Code 03.51 reports the restoration of a hernial protrusion of spinal meninges through a defect in the vertebral column.

The physician corrects a defect in which the outer coverings of the spinal cord, meninges, and (sometimes) nervous tissue bulge through a bony defect. The patient is placed prone, and the physician makes a midline incision and retraction through the skin, muscles, and paravertebral ligaments. The dura is incised to avoid herniated neural tissue. The physician places the neural tissue in the spinal canal. In the lumbar region, filum terminale are often identified tethering the cord and

divided. The dural defect, subcutaneous tissues, and skin are closed with layered sutures.

03.52 Repair of spinal myelomeningocele
Description
Code 03.52 reports the restoration of a hernial protrusion of the spinal cord and meninges through a defect in the vertebral column.

The physician corrects a defect in which the spinal cord, malformed nerve roots, and meninges all protrude through the defect, often directly exposed to the outside of the body. Surgery can be performed in one of many ways, though most require fusion from the thoracic region to the sacrum. The physician places the patient prone and incises the defect to the subarachnoid space. Using a microscope, the edges of the neural placode are trimmed of skin, dural remnants, and fat. The lateral edges of the placode are sutured together to form a tube. The dura is then incised and closed. Skin is closed with sutures.

03.53 Repair of vertebral fracture
Description
The following describes various closed and open methods of repairing vertebral fractures.

Closed treatment of a vertebral process fracture is only indicated if the spine is stable and the type of fracture does not require intervention. In the case of the cervical spine, the physician initially immobilizes the patient's neck and spine with sandbags or a cervical collar, as necessary.

Following dislocation or traumatic or pathological fracture of the vertebrae, the physician may decompress the spine into proper alignment and immobilize the vertebrae. The fracture or dislocation may be realigned by manual manipulation of the spine. If traction is employed, the patient is placed supine with a halo or tongs affixed to the skull. General anesthesia may be administered. Traction is applied to the feet and the halo or tongs, decompressing the vertebrae. As the traction is increased in stages, the physician assures that there is no additional neurological deficit. Traction is removed when the desired correction of the spine is accomplished. The patient is immobilized with bracing or casting, such as a halo cast.

The physician performs open treatment and/or reduction of a vertebral fracture or dislocation from a posterior approach. The patient is placed prone and the skin, fascia, and paravertebral muscles are incised and retracted to expose the fractured vertebra or dislocated segment. The proper rod (e.g., Harrington, Edwards) is selected and anatomic or C-shaped hooks are placed on vertebrae above and below the injury. The rod is inserted in the hooks and the spine is aligned. If fusion is desired, the physician may place separately reportable grafts between the vertebrae or place sleeves on the rod and position them to stabilize the injured vertebrae. The incision is closed by layered sutures.

The physician performs open treatment and/or reduction of an odontoid fracture and/or dislocation, including the os odontoideum. The os odontoideum (dens) is the tooth-like process located on the second cervical vertebra in the neck. The patient is placed in a supine position and the fracture or dislocation is reduced with skeletal traction. The physician then makes an anterior 6 to 7 cm transverse skin incision at the level of the C5-C6 disc space. Dissection is carried down to the odontoid process by longitudinally splitting the muscle and by careful blunt dissection of the space between the carotid, trachea, and esophagus. A retractor is placed and the anterior longitudinal ligament is incised. The superior thyroid artery may be ligated. Using imaging intensification, internal fixation is applied to hold the fracture in proper reduction. Guidewires are inserted into an area of the dens and screws are placed over the wires. Bone grafts may be placed to stabilize the fracture or dislocation. When the procedure is completed, a drain may be placed and the wound is closed with layered sutures.

Coding Clarification
Kyphoplasty and vertebroplasty are not reported with 03.53. Report kyphoplasty (percutaneous vertebral augmentation) with 81.66 and percutaneous vertebroplasty with 81.65.

Documentation Tip
The operative note may contain the following terminology for procedures reported by this code:

- Elevation of spinal bone fragments
- Reduction of fracture of vertebrae
- Removal of bony spicules from the spinal canal

Coding Guidance
AHA: 3Q, 96, 14; 4Q, '99, 11-13; 2Q, '02, 14; 4Q, '04, 126

03.59 Other repair and plastic operations on spinal cord structures

Description
Code 03.59 should be reported for repairs and/or plastic operations on the spinal cord that are not more specifically described by other codes within subcategory 03.5.

Documentation Tip
The medical record may contain documentation of repair of the following sites, which would be appropriately reported by this code:

- Diastematomyelia

- Spina bifida NOS
- Spinal cord NOS
- Spinal meninges NOS
- Vertebral arch defect

Coding Guidance
AHA: 4Q, '08, 109

03.6 Lysis of adhesions of spinal cord and nerve roots

Description
Spinal adhesiolysis may be performed utilizing various techniques, depending on the nature and site of the adhesions. Interventions may include a decompressive laminectomy or foraminotomy approach with direct, incisional division of adhesive tissues, or other endoscopic techniques and injection methods.

Epidural adhesions may be lysed endoscopically with direct vision using mechanical means or solution injection. The patient is mildly sedated and placed prone with a pillow under the abdomen. The site to be entered is sterilized and a local anesthetic is administered. Contrast medium is injected under fluoroscopy through a needle inserted into the floor of the canal for identification of nerve roots, fat, and adhesions. A guidewire is placed through the needle and threaded cephalad. The needle is removed and the canal passage is widened with a scalpel. A dilator and sheath are passed over the wire and then the dilator and guidewire are removed. The sheath is flushed with saline. A hand-controlled fiberoptic catheter system is passed through the sheath and the epidural space is distended with normal saline. The tip of the catheter is directed to adhesive bands that are tethered to adjacent tissues with intermittent distension and irrigation. Once the adhesiolysis is complete, an epidurogram is repeated. Depo-Medrol and lidocaine with normal saline may be injected for additional adhesiolysis. The catheter system is removed and the wound is dressed.

Epidural adhesions may also be lysed percutaneously by an injection, such as hypertonic saline or an enzyme solution, or by mechanical means. The patient is placed in the sitting or lateral decubitus position for insertion of a needle into a vertebral interspace. The site to be entered is sterilized, local anesthesia is administered, and the needle is inserted. Contrast media with fluoroscopy may be injected to confirm proper needle placement and to identify epidural adhesions. The physician injects the adhesiolytic solution or performs mechanical adhesion destruction, such as with a catheter, to lyse epidural adhesions. With the procedure completed, the needle and/or catheter is removed and the wound is dressed.

When performed for the treatment of epidural fibrosis, a guidewire is introduced into the epidural space under fluoroscopic guidance. The physician passes a dilator introducer over the guidewire. The tip of a myeloscope is placed inside the myeloscope steering catheter and is introduced into the caudal canal. Upon visualization of the fibrous tissue, saline is injected via the myeloscope to loosen the adhesions and fibrous tissue. Following the lysis of the fibrous tissue, an anesthetic or analgesic such as cortisone or Marcaine may be injected.

Coding Clarification
If anesthetic or analgesic injection is performed following the lysis, report with 03.91 or 03.92.

Also report the application or administration of an adhesion barrier substance with 99.77.

Coding Guidance
  AHA: 2Q, '98, 18

03.7   Shunt of spinal theca

Description
Codes within this subcategory report a surgical passage created from the spinal cord dura mater to another channel.

Coding Clarification
Codes included in subcategory 03.7 include those procedures with valves.

When reporting codes from subcategory 03.7, also report any application or administration of an adhesion barrier substance with 99.77.

All codes within this subcategory require fourth-digit subclassification to specify site.

03.71   Spinal subarachnoid-peritoneal shunt

Description
This procedure drains excess cerebral spinal fluid that may cause hydrocephalus. The patient is placed in a spinal tap position and the fascia, paravertebral muscles, and ligaments are incised and separated. The physician may remove the lamina, inserting the shunt through the dura into the subarachnoid space. The shunt is passed around the flank to the peritoneal space for drainage. The incisions are closed with layered sutures.

Coding Clarification
Code 03.71 includes shunt of spinal theca with valve.

03.72   Spinal subarachnoid-ureteral shunt

Description
This procedure drains excess cerebral spinal fluid that may cause hydrocephalus. The patient is placed in a spinal tap position and the fascia, paravertebral

muscles, and ligaments are incised and separated. The physician may remove the lamina, inserting the shunt through the dura into the subarachnoid space. The shunt is passed around the flank to the ureteral space for drainage. The incisions are closed with layered sutures.

Coding Clarification
Code 03.72 includes shunt of spinal theca with valve.

03.79   Other shunt of spinal theca

Description
This procedure drains excess cerebral spinal fluid that may cause hydrocephalus. The patient is placed in a spinal tap position and the fascia, paravertebral muscles, and ligaments are incised and separated. The physician may remove the lamina, inserting the shunt through the dura into the subarachnoid space. The shunt is passed around the flank to the specified drainage space. The incisions are closed with layered sutures.

Coding Clarification
Code 03.79 includes that with valve.

Documentation Tip
Operative note terminology associated with this code may include:

• Lumbar-subarachnoid shunt NOS

• Pleurothecal anastomosis

• Salpingothecal anastomosis

Coding Guidance
  AHA: 1Q, '97, 7

03.8   Injection of destructive agent into spinal canal

Description
This procedure is performed to destroy nerve tissue or adhesions. The patient is placed in a spinal tap position. The site is sterilized, and the needle is inserted under fluoroscopic guidance. The needle is placed at the proper level and the neurolytic substance is administered. Once the injection/infusion is completed, the needle is removed and the wound dressed.

Coding Clarification
Since chemotherapy is not classified as a destructive agent, this code is inappropriate for reporting the intrathecal injection of a chemotherapeutic agent, which would be correctly reported with 99.25 Injection or infusion of cancer chemotherapeutic substance, and 03.92 Injection of other agent into spinal canal.

Coding Guidance
  AHA: 2Q, '03, 6

03.9 Other operations on spinal cord and spinal canal structures

Coding Clarification
When reporting codes from subcategory 03.9, also report any application or administration of an adhesion barrier substance with 99.77.

All codes within this subcategory require fourth-digit subclassification in order to specify the procedure performed.

03.90 Insertion of catheter into spinal canal for infusion of therapeutic or palliative substances

Description
When the procedure is performed to allow long-term administration of medication via an external pump or implantable reservoir/infusion pump, the patient is placed in a spinal tap position and the fascia, paravertebral muscles, and ligaments are incised and separated. The physician inserts the catheter tip into the epidural space (the space outside the dura) or through the dura placing the catheter tip into the subarachnoid space. Tissue around the catheter may be sutured to hold the catheter in place. The catheter end is tunneled to the site where an implantable reservoir or implantable infusion pump has been previously placed or where an infusion pump is to be placed in a separately reportable procedure.

When performed to provide a continuous infusion or intermittent bolus of a therapeutic substance, the patient is placed in the sitting or lateral decubitus position for the physician to insert a catheter into the vertebral interspace of the cervical or thoracic region. The site to be entered is sterilized, local anesthesia is administered, and the infusion catheter is inserted. Contrast media with fluoroscopy may be injected to confirm proper catheter placement. The physician provides continuous infusion or intermittent bolus injection of solution to provide a therapeutic or a palliative outcome. The solution is injected into the epidural or subarachnoid space. With the procedure complete, the needle is removed and the wound is dressed.

Coding Clarification
Patients who have infusion pumps in order to release medication through a catheter for purposes of pain relief, such as those with cancer, require multiple codes to report the complete procedure.

For example when morphine sulfate is used to control pain, procedure code assignments are:

- 03.90 for the insertion of the catheter into the subarachnoid space
- 03.91 for the infusion of morphine
- 86.06 for the subcutaneous implantation of the pump

Documentation Tip
May be documented as insertion of catheter into epidural, subarachnoid, or subdural space of spine with intermittent or continuous infusion of drug.

03.91 Injection of anesthetic into spinal canal for analgesia

Description
The patient is placed in a sitting or lateral decubitus position for the physician to insert a needle into the appropriate vertebral interspace for injection or for continuous or intermittent infusion of anesthetic. The site to be entered is sterilized, local anesthesia is administered, and the needle is inserted. Contrast media with fluoroscopy may be injected to confirm proper needle placement. The physician injects or infuses the anesthetic into the epidural or subarachnoid space. With the procedure complete, the needle is removed and the wound is dressed.

The physician may also inject anesthetic into the epidural space using a transforaminal approach. This approach is used primarily in the treatment of herniated discs and requires fluoroscopic direction. The injection may be performed on single or multiple levels.

Coding Clarification
Omit this code if the anesthetic is injected for operative anesthesia.

Coding Guidance
AHA: 2Q, '90, 11; 2Q, '98, 18; 1Q, '99, 8; 3Q, '00, 15

03.92 Injection of other agent into spinal canal

Description
The patient is placed in a sitting or lateral decubitus position for the physician to insert a needle into the appropriate vertebral interspace for injection of an agent such as a steroid or refrigerated saline. The site to be entered is sterilized, local anesthesia is administered, and the needle is inserted. Contrast media with fluoroscopy may be injected to confirm proper needle placement. The physician injects or infuses the agent into the epidural or subarachnoid space. With the procedure complete, the needle is removed and the wound is dressed.

The physician may also inject the substance into the epidural space using a transforaminal approach. This approach is used primarily in the treatment of herniated discs and requires fluoroscopic direction. The injection may be performed on single or multiple levels.

Coding Clarification
Code 03.92 excludes the following procedures, which are more appropriately classified elsewhere:

- Injection of contrast material for myelogram (87.21)

01–05

- Injection of destructive agent into spinal canal (03.8)

Documentation Tip
Documentation may consist of the following:

- Intrathecal injection of steroid
- Subarachnoid perfusion of refrigerated saline

Coding Guidance
AHA: 2Q, '98, 18; 3Q, '00, 15; 2Q, '03, 6

03.93   Implantation or replacement of spinal neurostimulator lead(s)

Description
Spinal cord neurostimulator devices block pain conduction pathways to the brain, possibly also stimulating endorphins, and are used as a last resort to treat chronic, intractable pain from conditions such as nerve root injuries, phantom limb syndrome, end-stage peripheral vascular disease, cauda equina injury, and incomplete spinal cord injury. The electrodes are implanted percutaneously in the epidural space through a special needle and sometimes by an open procedure requiring laminectomy. The pulse generator, activated through a radiofrequency device, is inserted subcutaneously and connected to the implanted electrodes.

For percutaneous epidural electrode placement, the patient is placed prone. A standard epidural puncture is made. A thin-walled needle is placed at the appropriate segment. A flexible wire electrode is threaded through the needle under fluoroscopic control. Intraoperative testing is carried out to assure correct electrode positioning, creating maximum paresthesia in the pain region. The needle is removed and a dressing applied. A transmitter (pulse generator or receiver) is inserted in a separately reportable procedure. Stimulation may be applied as soon as four days following the procedure.

In an open procedure, the patient is placed prone. The physician makes a midline incision overlying the affected vertebrae. The fascia is incised. The paravertebral muscles are retracted. The lamina is removed to expose the epidural space. The physician places passive electrodes or plates or paddles in the epidural space proximate to the desired spine segment. Paravertebral muscles are reapproximated and the incision is closed with layered sutures. A transmitter (pulse generator or receiver) is inserted in a separately reportable procedure. Stimulation may be applied as soon as four days following the procedures.

Coding Clarification
Also assign a code from range 86.94-86.98 for the insertion of the neurostimulator pulse generator.

Coding Scenario
A 67-year-old man with post-herpetic neuralgia had a dual array spinal cord neurostimulator implanted a year ago. He was admitted for replacement of the leads due to a malfunction. The surgeon tests the leads and the pulse generator and finds only the leads to be nonfunctioning. The leads only are replaced and are reconnected after being tested and found to be in working order.

    Code Assignment:

    996.2   Mechanical complication of nervous system device, implant, and graft
    03.93   Implantation or replacement of spinal neurostimulator lead(s)

Coding Guidance
AHA: 2Q, '00, 22; 1Q, '00, 19

03.94   Removal of spinal neurostimulator lead(s)

Description
This procedure is performed to remove neurostimulator electrodes, plates, or paddles. The patient is placed prone. The physician makes a midline incision overlying the affected vertebrae. The fascia is incised. The paravertebral muscles are retracted. If the original electrodes were placed percutaneously, a laminectomy of the vertebra would not be performed. The physician removes the electrodes.

Coding Clarification
If there is concurrent removal of the neurostimulator pulse generator, also report 86.05.

03.95   Spinal blood patch

Description
Code 03.95 reports the injection of blood into the epidural space to patch a hole in the outer spinal membrane.

This procedure is performed following a spinal puncture to prevent spinal fluid leakage. The patient remains in a spinal tap position. The patient's blood is injected outside the dura to clot and plug the wound, preventing spinal fluid leakage. The wound is dressed and monitored.

03.96   Percutaneous denervation of facet

Description
Percutaneous facet denervation is also referred to as radiofrequency facet ablation, facet rhizotomy, radiofrequency facet denervation, and facet thermocoagulation. This procedure is used to treat back pain transmitted through the sensory nerves within the facet joint of spinal vertebrae. Radiofrequency delivers heat and destroys selected nerve fibers, blocking pain transmission.

01-05

03.97   Revision of spinal thecal shunt

Description
The physician makes an incision at the site of the original incision. Scar tissue, colloidal tissues, and adhesions are removed. The physician may irrigate the shunt with saline or other substances. If it is malfunctioning, the shunt is freed and replaced. A new shunt is placed in the site. Incisions are closed using layered sutures.

Coding Guidance
    AHA: 2Q, '99, 4

03.98   Removal of spinal thecal shunt

Description
The physician makes an incision at the site of the original incision. Scar tissue, colloidal tissues, and adhesions are removed. The shunt is freed and removed. Incisions are closed using layered sutures.

03.99   Other operations on spinal cord and spinal canal structures

Description
Code 03.99 is reported for any operations on the spinal cord and spinal canal structures that are not more precisely described by other codes from subcategory 03.9.

---

04   Operations on cranial and peripheral nerves

Description
Operations on the cranial and peripheral nerves include incision, division, and excision; diagnostic procedures; cryoanalgesia; lysis of adhesions; grafts; nerve transplantations; neuroplasty; injections; and other procedures.

04.0   Incision, division, and excision of cranial and peripheral nerves

Coding Clarification
Excluded from subcategory 04.0 are opticociliary neurectomy, which is correctly reported with 12.79, and sympathetic ganglionectomy, which is reported with a code from range 05.21-05.29.

04.01   Excision of acoustic neuroma

Description
The procedures detailed below describe the various approaches utilized in the excision of an acoustic neuroma.

The physician removes a brain tumor at the cerebellopontine angle. The physician makes a lateral posterior incision and removes an occipital bone flap. The cerebellum is retracted and the brain stem is examined. The tumor at the cerebellopontine

angle is resected. The bone is replaced and stabilized. The scalp is anastomosed and closed in sutured layers.

The physician excises a tumor at the cerebellopontine angle. Using a transmastoid approach, the physician incises the scalp and removes a bone flap. The tumor is identified and excised. The bone is replaced and stabilized. The scalp is anastomosed and closed in sutured layers. A multiple approach technique may be utilized, with the tumor being accessed from both a transtemporal and a middle or posterior fossa approach.

Coding Clarification
Code 04.01 includes that by craniotomy but excludes that by stereotactic radiosurgery, which is reported with 92.3.

Documentation Tip
Cerebellopontine angle tumors are benign neoplasms of the 8th cranial nerve and are more often referred to as acoustic neuromas. Other terms include acoustic tumor, vestibular schwannoma, or angle tumor.

Coding Guidance
    AHA: 4Q, '92, 26; 2Q, '95, 8; 2Q, '98, 20

04.02   Division of trigeminal nerve

Description
Code 04.02 reports the transection of sensory root fibers of the trigeminal nerve for relief of trigeminal neuralgia.

The physician incises and retracts the scalp and removes bone from the occiput. The brain is retracted to reveal the brain stem. The affected nerve tract is explored, decompressed, or resected. The bone is replaced and stabilized. The scalp is anastomosed and closed in sutured layers.

Documentation Tip
May also be referred to as retrogasserian neurotomy.

04.03   Division or crushing of other cranial and peripheral nerves

Description
Code 04.03 reports the division or crushing of cranial and peripheral nerves other than those more specifically described by other codes within the 04.0 subcategory.

Coding Clarification
Excluded from 04.03 is the division or crushing of the following sites:

• Glossopharyngeal nerve (29.92)

• Laryngeal nerve (31.91)

• Nerves to adrenal glands (07.42)

• Phrenic nerve for collapse of lung (33.31)

● New Code   ▲ Revised Code   ►◄ Revised Text   © 2010 Ingenix

- Vagus nerve (44.00-44.03)

Coding Guidance
AHA: 2Q, '98, 20

04.04   Other incision of cranial and peripheral nerves

Description
The following describes some of the procedures that may be reported with 04.04.

The physician makes an incision overlying a nerve of the hip joint. The physician uses a posterior approach to the sciatic nerve or an anterior approach to its branches (the femoral or obturator nerves). The physician dissects the tissue to locate and isolate the nerve. The nerve is then cut and the incision repaired in multiple layers.

This procedure is performed to alleviate chronic pain. The patient is placed prone. The physician makes a midline incision overlying the affected vertebrae. The fascia is incised. The paravertebral muscles are retracted. The physician removes the lamina. The physician identifies and incises the spinal accessory nerve. The lesion is removed and sutures are placed in the perineurium of the nerves. The sutures are approximated and tied. Fascia, muscles, and ligaments are allowed to fall back into place. The incision is closed with layered sutures.

04.05   Gasserian ganglionectomy

Description
The gasserian ganglion supplies sensory innervation to the face via the trigeminal nerve. The physician makes a periauricular incision and retracts the scalp and raises a bone flap. The gasserian ganglion is located and decompressed or stimulated. If indicated, the nerve or a nerve branch is sectioned. The bone flap is replaced and fastened. The scalp is reanastomosed and closed in sutured layers.

04.06   Other cranial or peripheral ganglionectomy

Description
The physician excises a neuroma of a major peripheral nerve. A neuroma is a benign tumor that may be formed by a disease process or secondary to trauma to the nerve. The physician incises the area over the affected major peripheral nerve. After locating the nerve with the symptomatic neuroma, the physician excises the tumor. The incision is closed in sutured layers.

Coding Clarification
Report sympathetic ganglionectomy with a code from range 05.21-05.29 rather than with 04.06.

04.07   Other excision or avulsion of cranial and peripheral nerves

Description
Code 04.07 reports excision or avulsion of cranial or peripheral nerves other than those procedures that are more precisely reported by other codes within subcategory 04.0. An example is excision of a Morton's neuroma.

Surgery for Morton's neuroma involves removal of the fibrous nerve growth from between the toes. The physician places a tourniquet at the ankle and a small incision is made on the top of the foot between the third and fourth metatarsal bones. The soft tissue is reflected in the web space and the bones are separated. Pressure is applied to the bottom of the foot under the web space causing the neuroma to protrude upward. The neuroma is removed and the nerve trunk is cut to prevent regrowth. The tourniquet is removed and the incision is closed with sutures.

Coding Clarification
Report biopsy of cranial or peripheral nerve with 04.11 or 04.12 rather than 04.07.

Documentation Tip
The operative note may contain the following verbiage regarding procedures on the peripheral nerve:

- Curettage
- Debridement
- Resection

Coding Guidance
AHA: 4Q, '92, 26; 2Q, '95, 8

04.1   Diagnostic procedures on peripheral nervous system

Description
Codes within this subcategory report open and closed biopsies, as well as other diagnostic procedures on a cranial or peripheral nerve or ganglion.

Documentation Tip
Some examples of peripheral nerves include the following:

- Abducens (cranial)
- Accessory (cranial)
- Axillary
- Brachial or cervical plexus
- Facial (cranial)
- Glossopharyngeal (cranial)
- Greater occipital
- Hypoglossal (cranial)
- Ilioinguinal, iliohypogastric

- Intercostal
- Lumbar plexus
- Oculomotor (cranial)
- Olfactory (cranial)
- Optic (cranial)
- Paracervical/uterine
- Paravertebral facet joint
- Phrenic
- Pudendal
- Sacral plexus
- Sciatic
- Spinal accessory
- Trigeminal (cranial)
- Trochlear (cranial)
- Vagus (cranial)
- Vestibulocochlear (cranial)

04.11 Closed (percutaneous) (needle) biopsy of cranial or peripheral nerve or ganglion

Description
Code 04.11 reports a biopsy of a cranial or peripheral nerve or ganglion performed by closed technique (percutaneous or needle biopsy).

04.12 Open biopsy of cranial or peripheral nerve or ganglion

Description
The physician biopsies a nerve. The physician makes an incision overlying the suspect nerve. The tissues are dissected to locate the nerve and a biopsy specimen is obtained. The incision is closed in sutured layers.

04.19 Other diagnostic procedures on cranial and peripheral nerves and ganglia

Description
This code reports diagnostic procedures on cranial and peripheral nerves and ganglia other than those that are described more precisely by other codes within subcategory 04.1.

Coding Clarification
Code 04.19 excludes the following procedures, which are more appropriately classified elsewhere:

- Microscopic examination of specimen from nervous system (90.01-90.09)
- Neurologic examination (89.13)

04.2 Destruction of cranial and peripheral nerves

Description
These procedures are performed to treat chronic pain. The affected nerve is destroyed using chemical, thermal, electrical, or radiofrequency techniques.

These techniques may be used singly or in combination. These procedures are designed to destroy the specific site(s) in the nerve root that produce(s) the pain while leaving sensation intact. Generally, intravenous conscious sedation is utilized during the initial phase of the procedure so that the patient can assist the physician in identifying the site of pain and the correct placement of the neurolytic agent, and local anesthesia is administered during the destruction phase of the procedure. Using fluoroscopic guidance, a needle is inserted into the affected nerve root. An electrode is then inserted through the needle and a mild electrical current is passed through the electrode. The current produces a tingling sensation at a site on the nerve. The electrode is manipulated until the tingling sensation is felt at the same site as the pain. Once the physician has determined that the electrode is positioned at the site responsible for the pain, a local anesthetic is administered and a neurolytic agent applied. Chemical destruction involves injection of a neurolytic substance (e.g., alcohol, phenol, glycerol) into the affected nerve root. Thermal techniques utilize heat. Electrical techniques utilize an electrical current. Radiofrequency, also referred to as radiofrequency rhizotomy, utilizes a solar or microwave current.

Documentation Tip
The operative note may contain the following terminology to describe cranial or peripheral nerve destruction:

- Cryoanalgesia
- Injection of neurolytic agent
- Radiofrequency neurolysis
- Radiofrequency ablation

Coding Scenario
A 62-year-old female who sustained an L2 osteoporotic compression fracture was admitted for radiofrequency neuroablation for pain reduction.

Code Assignment:

733.13 Pathological fracture of vertebra
733.00 Osteoporosis, unspecified
04.2 Destruction of cranial and peripheral nerves

Coding Guidance
AHA: 5th issue, '94, 12; 4Q, '95, 74; 3Q, '02, 10, 11

04.3 Suture of cranial and peripheral nerves

Description
The peripheral nerves consist of those outside the central nervous system. Comprised of the nerves that exit the brain and spinal cord, the peripheral nervous system serves the limbs and organs of the body.

01-05

The physician repairs a cranial or peripheral nerve. The physician locates the damaged nerve in a previously opened incision or wound. The nerve is sutured to restore sensory or motor function.

Coding Clarification
Report the delayed repair of an old injury to the cranial or peripheral nerves with 04.76.

04.4 Lysis of adhesions and decompression of cranial and peripheral nerves

Description
The operative approach (craniotomy) and closure (cranioplasty) are integral to the procedure described by codes within this category and therefore would not be coded separately.

04.41 Decompression of trigeminal nerve root

Description
The physician makes an incision overlying the nerve and dissects it free of the surrounding tissue. If the nerve is in bone and must be decompressed, freed, or moved, the overlying bone is first removed using drills and/or osteotomes. The physician makes an incision in the area of nerve tension and locates the nerve. Surrounding soft tissues are dissected from the nerve to release pressure on the nerve. Microvascular decompression (MVD) surgery is performed under general anesthesia, through an incision, and microsurgical instruments are used to mobilize the offending vessels away from the trigeminal nerve root.

04.42 Other cranial nerve decompression

Description
Code 04.42 is reported for the decompression of cranial nerves other than the trigeminal nerve root.

Documentation Tip
The 12 pairs of cranial nerves consist of the following:

- Abducens (VI)
- Accessory (XI)
- Facial (VII)
- Glossopharyngeal (IX)
- Hypoglossal (XII)
- Oculomotor (III)
- Olfactory (I)
- Optic (II)
- Trigeminal (V)
- Trochlear (IV)
- Vagus (X)
- Vestibulocochlear (VIII)

Coding Guidance
AHA: M-A, '87, 8; 3Q, '02, 13

04.43 Release of carpal tunnel

Description
In the open approach, the physician decompresses or transposes a portion of the ulnar or median nerve to restore feeling to the hand. The physician makes a horizontal incision in the wrist at the metacarpal joints and locates the affected nerve. Soft tissues are resected and the nerve is freed from the underlying bed. Care is taken to ensure tension is released and the incision is closed in sutured layers.

If performed endoscopically, the patient is placed supine with the arm positioned on a hand table. Endoscopic release may be accomplished by a one or two portal technique. In a single portal technique, a small, 1 1/2 cm, horizontal incision is made at the wrist. Using a two portal technique, two small incisions are made: one in the palm and one at the wrist. The palmar skin, underlying cushioning fat, protective fascia, and muscle are not cut. The endoscope is introduced underneath the transverse carpal ligament. The endoscope allows the physician to view the procedure on a monitor. A special blade attached to the arthroscope is then used to incise the transverse carpal ligament from the inside of the carpal tunnel. The instruments are removed and the portal(s) closed with sutures or Steri-strips. A splint may be applied.

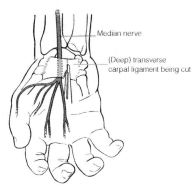

Median nerve

(Deep) transverse carpal ligament being cut

04.44 Release of tarsal tunnel

Description
The physician releases the tarsal tunnel, decompressing the posterior tibial nerve. The tarsal tunnel is located on the inside of the ankle. A curved incision is made along the inner ankle, behind the medial malleolus. Dissection is carried down to expose the flexor retinaculum. The retinaculum is carefully released along the tunnel. The posterior tibial nerve is identified by blunt dissection and traced as it courses down through the tarsal tunnel.

01–05

Three branches of the posterior tibial nerve are also traced at the point. Once the posterior tibial nerve and its terminal branches are released, the nerve is inspected to see if any other constrictions are present. The incision is closed in layers without closing the retinaculum.

04.49 Other peripheral nerve or ganglion decompression or lysis of adhesions

Description
Code 04.49 reports the decompression or lysis of adhesions of other peripheral nerves or ganglia that is not more precisely reported by other codes within subcategory 04.4.

Documentation Tip
May also be documented as peripheral nerve neurolysis.

Coding Guidance
AHA: 2Q, '93, 8

04.5 Cranial or peripheral nerve graft

Description
The physician obtains and places a nerve graft to restore innervation to the head, neck, arm, leg, hand, or foot. A typical graft harvest is obtained from the sural nerve. To harvest the graft, the physician makes a lateral incision of the lateral malleolus of the ankle. The nerve is identified and freed. The physician cuts the nerve to obtain the length needed for the graft, elongating the incision as necessary. The proximal and distal sural nerve endings are anastomosed. The physician makes an incision over the damaged nerve and dissects the tissues to locate the nerve. The damaged area of the nerve is resected and removed. Innervation is restored by suturing the graft to the proximal and distal ends of the damaged nerve. A single nerve strand or multiple nerve strands (cable) may be grafted.

04.6 Transposition of cranial and peripheral nerves

Description
Code 04.6 reports the relocation of a cranial or peripheral nerve without detaching or severing the nerve.

The physician moves an intact nerve to a new position (transposition). The physician makes an incision overlying the nerve, dissects it free of the surrounding tissue, and, if necessary, moves the nerve to a new position. If the nerve is in bone and must be decompressed, freed, or moved, the overlying bone is first removed using drills and/or osteotomes.

Documentation Tip
Also known as nerve transplantation.

04.7 Other cranial or peripheral neuroplasty

Description
Codes within subcategory 04.7 report anastomotic procedures on cranial and peripheral nerves, as well as revision, repair, and other neuroplastic procedures. All codes within this subcategory require fourth-digit subclassification in order to specify the site or procedure performed.

04.71 Hypoglossal-facial anastomosis

Description
Code 04.71 reports the surgical connection of a hypoglossal nerve to a facial nerve.

The physician creates an anastomosis (connection of two nerves that are not normally connected) to restore motor innervation to the face. The physician makes a horizontal lateral neck incision and isolates the hypoglossal nerve. The nerve is brought forward and sutured to the facial nerve.

Documentation Tip
Also known as Korte-Ballance anastomosis.

04.72 Accessory-facial anastomosis

Description
This code reports the surgical connection of an accessory nerve to a facial nerve.

The physician creates a connection of two nerves that are not normally connected (anastomosis) to restore motor innervation to the face. The physician makes a horizontal incision in the posterior lateral neck and isolates the spinal accessory nerve. The nerve is isolated and brought forward and sutured to the facial nerve.

04.73 Accessory-hypoglossal anastomosis

Description
This code reports the surgical connection of an accessory nerve to a hypoglossal nerve.

04.74 Other anastomosis of cranial or peripheral nerve

Description
This code reports the surgical connection of cranial or peripheral nerves other than those that are more specifically described by other codes within the 04.7 subcategory.

04.75 Revision of previous repair of cranial and peripheral nerves

Description
This code reports the surgical revision of a repair that was previously performed on cranial or peripheral nerves.

04.76 Repair of old traumatic injury of cranial and peripheral nerves

Description
The physician repairs a nerve where repair was delayed due to contamination or other factors. The wound is explored to locate the distal portion of the nerve. The proximal and distal nerves are sutured together to restore innervation. If the nerve was shortened during damage, in order to reanastomose the nerve, the distal and proximal portions of the nerve are freed from surrounding tissues. They are then approximated and sutured to restore innervation. If excessive trauma caused loss of a significant section of a major nerve, a portion of the parallel bone is resected in order to approximate the distal and proximal ends of the nerve.

04.79 Other neuroplasty

Description
Code 04.79 reports cranial or peripheral neuroplastic procedures that are not more specifically described by other codes within the 04.7 subcategory.

Coding Clarification
Code 04.79 is appropriate for reporting the application of the NeuraWrap Nerve Protector.

Documentation Tip
NeuraWrap is an absorbable collagen implant used in the treatment of peripheral nerve injuries where the nerve tissue damage is not significant. Designed to be an interface between the nerve and surrounding tissue, it encases the injured peripheral nerves in a non-constrictive manner.

Coding Guidance
AHA: 1Q, '06, 11

04.8 Injection into peripheral nerve

Coding Clarification
Subcategory 04.8 excludes nerve destruction by injection of a neurolytic agent, which is correctly reported with 04.2.

All codes within this subcategory require fourth-digit subclassification in order to specify the procedure performed.

04.80 Peripheral nerve injection, not otherwise specified

Description
The physician draws a substance into the syringe and injects it into the peripheral nerve for other than anesthetic (04.81) or neurolytic (04.2) purposes.

Coding Clarification
Report destruction of nerve by injection of neurolytic agent with 04.2.

04.81 Injection of anesthetic into peripheral nerve for analgesia

Description
The physician anesthetizes a peripheral nerve to provide pain control or blockage. The physician draws a local anesthetic into the syringe and injects it into the branch of the nerve to be anesthetized. Alternately, the physician may administer the anesthetic by continuous infusion via an indwelling catheter.

Coding Clarification
Omit code if performed for operative anesthesia.

Report destruction of a nerve by injection of a neurolytic agent with 04.2.

Coding Guidance
AHA: 5th issue, '94, 12; 1Q, '00, 7

04.89 Injection of other agent, except neurolytic

Description
Code 04.89 reports the injection of agents other than neurolytics into a peripheral nerve.

Coding Clarification
Report injection of a neurolytic agent with 04.2.

04.9 Other operations on cranial and peripheral nerves

04.91 Neurectasis

Description
Code 04.91 reports the surgical stretching of a peripheral or cranial nerve or nerve trunk.

04.92 Implantation or replacement of peripheral neurostimulator lead(s)

Description
Code 04.92 reports the placement of or removal and replacement of neurostimulator leads during the same operative episode.

Peripheral neurostimulator devices may be implanted to stimulate motor nerves in cases of muscle paralysis to prevent atrophy or sensory nerves to decrease pain sensation along the nerve distribution. Sacral nerve neurostimulation is done to help control bladder behavior, voiding, and pelvic floor muscles. Autonomic nerves may be stimulated to relieve sympathetically mediated pain. The electrodes are placed into the target tissue through an introducer needle percutaneously or through an open incision. The pulse generator may be placed anywhere appropriate within a subcutaneous pocket created to hold it.

In a percutaneous approach, the physician places an electrode through the skin through an introducer needle into the tissue to be stimulated. In the open

01–05

● New Code   ▲ Revised Code   ▶◀ Revised Text

approach, the physician makes an incision to place the electrode. The physician uses a scalpel to incise the skin and dissects to the anatomical location. The incision aides the physician in accurately placing and testing the electrode while visualizing results. After stimulating the area, the incision is closed with layered sutures. Electrodes placed over sensory nerves decrease pain sensation in the distribution of the nerve. Electrodes placed over motor nerves stimulate paralyzed muscles to prevent atrophy.

Coding Clarification
▶Code 04.92 excludes implantation or replacement of carotid sinus stimulation lead(s) (39.82).◀

A code should also be assigned from range 86.94-86.98 for any insertion of a neurostimulator pulse generator.

Coding Guidance
   AHA: 3Q, '96, 12; 2Q, '00, 22; 3Q, '01, 16; 2Q, '04, 7; 2Q, '06, 5; 2Q, '07, 8

04.93   Removal of peripheral neurostimulator lead(s)

Description
The physician removes previously placed neurostimulator electrodes. The physician makes an incision overlying the electrodes. The electrodes are removed and the incision is closed with layered sutures.

Coding Clarification
Also report 86.05 for the removal of any neurostimulator pulse generator.

Coding Guidance
   AHA: 3Q, '01, 16

04.99   Other operations on cranial and peripheral nerves

Description
Report 04.99 for other operations on cranial or peripheral nerves that are not more precisely described by other codes within the 04.9 subcategory.

05   Operations on sympathetic nerves or ganglia

Description
This group of codes for operations on sympathetic nerves or ganglia is limited to a few codes to identify division, diagnostic procedures, sympathectomy, injections, and other operations.

Coding Clarification
Category 05 excludes paracervical uterine denervation, which is correctly reported with 69.3.

05.0   Division of sympathetic nerve or ganglion

Description
The following is an example of a procedure involving division of a sympathetic nerve.

The physician severs the laryngeal nerve. The recurrent laryngeal nerve controls the action of the vocal cords. The physician makes a vertical incision and retracts the strap muscles and dissects the tissue until the nerve is exposed and identified. The physician severs the recurrent laryngeal nerve prior to its point of branching. The incision is repaired in sutured layers.

Coding Clarification
Code 05.0 excludes division of nerves to the adrenal glands, which is reported with 07.42.

05.1   Diagnostic procedures on sympathetic nerves or ganglia

05.11   Biopsy of sympathetic nerve or ganglion

Description
When performing an open biopsy of a nerve, the physician makes an incision overlying the suspect nerve. The tissues are dissected to locate the nerve and a biopsy specimen is obtained. The incision is closed in sutured layers.

05.19   Other diagnostic procedures on sympathetic nerves or ganglia

Description
Report 05.19 for diagnostic procedures other than biopsy on sympathetic nerves or ganglia.

05.2   Sympathectomy

Description
The codes in subcategory 05.2 report the division of a nerve pathway at a specific site of a sympathetic nerve.

Coding Clarification
All codes within this subcategory require fourth-digit subclassification to specify site and/or procedure.

05.21   Sphenopalatine ganglionectomy

Description
Code 05.21 reports the excision of a sphenopalatine ganglion, which is a small parasympathetic ganglion whose postsynaptic fibers supply the nasal and lacrimal glands.

Documentation Tip
This ganglion may also be documented as Meckel's ganglion or a pterygopalatine ganglion.

● New Code   ▲ Revised Code   ▶◀ Revised Text   © 2010 Ingenix

05.22   Cervical sympathectomy

Description

The cervical sympathetic chain supplies sympathetic innervation to the head, neck, and upper extremities, while the thoracic chain supplies sympathetic innervation to the chest and its contents.

The physician performs a cervical or cervicothoracic sympathectomy. In a cervical sympathectomy, the physician makes a midlateral incision of the neck and dissects the tissues to locate the sympathetic chain. In a cervicothoracic sympathectomy, the physician makes a thoracotomy and dissects the tissues to locate the sympathetic chain along the vertebral bodies. The ganglia (nerve cell bodies located outside the spinal cord) are identified and resected. The incision is closed in sutured layers.

05.23   Lumbar sympathectomy

Description

Code 05.23 reports the excision or resection of a lumbar chain nerve group to relieve causalgia, Raynaud's disease, or lower extremity thromboangiitis.

The physician makes a lateral incision through the lumbar area or the thoracic area to reach the sympathetic ganglia, which lie on the lateral border of the vertebral column. The physician determines at which level to remove the ganglia and dissects to the vertebral bodies. The sympathetic plexus is located and resected. The wound is closed in sutured layers.

Documentation Tip

May also be documented as thoracolumbar sympathectomy.

05.24   Presacral sympathectomy

Description

A portion of the presacral sympathetic nerve is removed or destroyed to alleviate pelvic pain. Often performed in conjunction with uterine suspension, the procedure may be done through a small abdominal incision or through the vagina.

05.25   Periarterial sympathectomy

Description

Code 05.25 reports the removal of an arterial sheath containing sympathetic nerve fibers.

The physician performs a digital sympathectomy using a microscope for visualization. The physician makes an incision along the digital artery in the medial and lateral aspects of the digit. The artery is identified and the adventitia is stripped from the blood vessel. Peripherally, the sympathetic nerves follow the arteries and lie in the adventitia layer. The incision is closed in layers. This procedure may also

be performed on the radial artery, the ulnar artery, or the superficial palmar arch.

05.29   Other sympathectomy and ganglionectomy

Description

Code 05.29 reports the excision or avulsion of sympathetic nerves that are not otherwise specified and not reported by a more specific code within subcategory 05.2. This code also reports sympathetic ganglionectomy not otherwise specified.

Coding Clarification

Code 05.29 excludes the following procedures, which are more appropriately classified elsewhere:

- Biopsy of sympathetic nerve or ganglion (05.11)
- Opticociliary neurectomy (12.79)
- Periarterial sympathectomy (05.25)
- Tympanosympathectomy (20.91)

05.3   Injection into sympathetic nerve or ganglion

Description

Subcategory 05.3 reports the injection of anesthetics, neurolytic agents, or other substances into sympathetic nerves or ganglia. All codes within this subcategory require fourth-digit subclassification in order to specify the substance injected.

Coding Clarification

Subcategory 05.3 excludes injection of a ciliary sympathetic ganglion, which is correctly reported with 12.79.

05.31   Injection of anesthetic into sympathetic nerve for analgesia

Description

Code 05.31 reports the injection of an anesthetic agent to block sympathetically-mediated pain. Fluoroscopic imaging may be utilized. The physician guides the needle into correct placement into the sympathetic nerve fibers and injects the anesthetic agent.

Coding Clarification

Report injection of a ciliary sympathetic ganglion with 12.79.

Coding Scenario

A 35-year-old female presents with severe, intractable menstrual pain for presacral nerve block. She is placed in the prone position and prepped. Under fluoroscopic guidance, a 6-inch needle is guided into the ventral lateral spine and through the L5/S1 interspace. Needle position is checked by injecting contrast material and aspirating for the return of any blood, urine, or cerebral spinal fluid. With negative aspiration results and imaging verifying that the needle position is in the

01–05

prevertebral space and not within a blood vessel, a ureter, or spinal nerves, local anesthetic is injected on both sides.

Code Assignment:

625.3   Dysmenorrhea

05.31   Injection of anesthetic into sympathetic nerve for analgesia

05.32   Injection of neurolytic agent into sympathetic nerve

Description
The celiac plexus is a network of nervous tissue that mediates sympathetic pain from the abdomen. This neurolytic block is often performed for pain relief of unresectable cancer in the upper abdomen.

The physician destroys the celiac plexus by applying a neurolytic agent. The celiac plexus is destroyed usually by chemodenervation, injecting phenol or alcohol to paralyze the network of nervous tissue. This procedure may be performed with or without radiologic monitoring, but is normally performed under CT guidance.

The superior hypogastric plexus, also called the presacral nerve, is located in front of the upper part of the sacrum and is formed by lower lumbar nerves responsible for pain sensation in the pelvic area. Nerve destruction is done in such cases as severe, intractable menstrual pain and pain due to pelvic area metastases from cancer such as prostatic malignancy when an anesthetic nerve block does not offer sufficient relief.

The physician performs a neurolysis on the superior hypogastric plexus by injecting a chemical, thermal, or electrical agent through a needle inserted in the L5/S1 interspace. The patient is placed in the prone position and prepped. A 6-inch needle is guided under radiological imaging, such as fluoroscopy (reported separately), into the ventral lateral spine and through the L5/S1 interspace. Needle position is checked by injecting contrast material and aspirating for the return of any blood, urine, or cerebral spinal fluid. With negative aspiration results and imaging verifying that the needle position is in the prevertebral space and not within a blood vessel, a ureter, or spinal nerves, the neurolytic agent is injected, or delivered, to both sides.

Coding Clarification
Report injection of a ciliary sympathetic ganglion with 12.79.

05.39   Other injection into sympathetic nerve or ganglion

Description
Code 05.39 reports other injections into sympathetic nerves or ganglia for which there is no more specific code in subcategory 05.3. An example is an injection of a medicinal substance into a ganglion cyst, which is a benign mass consisting of a thin capsule containing clear, mucinous fluid arising from an aponeurosis or tendon sheath, such as on the back of the wrist or foot.

The physician injects a ganglion cyst. After administering a local anesthetic, the physician inserts a needle through the skin and into the ganglion cyst. A medicinal substance is injected for therapy. The needle is withdrawn and pressure is applied to stop any bleeding.

Coding Clarification
Report injection of a ciliary sympathetic ganglion with 12.79.

05.8   Other operations on sympathetic nerves or ganglia

05.81   Repair of sympathetic nerve or ganglion

Description
The physician repairs a sympathetic nerve where repair was delayed because the initial wound was contaminated. The wound is explored to locate the distal portion of the nerve, and the proximal and distal nerves are sutured together to restore innervation. In order to reanastomose the nerve if the nerve was shortened during damage, the distal and proximal portions of the nerve are freed from surrounding tissues, approximated, and sutured to restore innervation. If excessive trauma caused loss of a significant section of a major nerve, a portion of the parallel bone is resected in order to approximate the distal and proximal ends of the nerve.

05.89   Other operations on sympathetic nerves or ganglia

Description
Code 05.89 reports other operations performed on sympathetic nerves or ganglia for which there is no more specific code elsewhere in the chapter.

05.9   Other operations on nervous system

Description
Code 05.9 reports other operations performed on the nervous system for which there are no more specific codes elsewhere in the chapter.

06-07

Operations on the Endocrine System

2011 Changes

An exclusion term was revised at category 07 Operations on other endocrine glands, to reflect that the codes in this category exclude operations on aortic and carotid bodies (39.81–39.89).

The ICD-9-CM classification system for operations performed on the endocrine system is divided into categories of procedures according to sites as follows:

- Thyroid and Parathyroid Glands (06)
- Other Endocrine Glands (07)

Coding Clarification
Many of the subcategories in this portion of the classification system require a fourth digit for further specificity with regard to type and/or site of the operation performed.

Documentation Tip
Documentation in the operative report must support code selection.

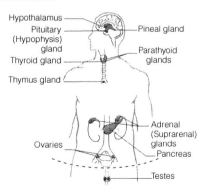

Hypothalamus
Pituitary (Hypophysis) gland
Thyroid gland
Thymus gland
Pineal gland
Parathyroid glands
Ovaries
Adrenal (Suprarenal) glands
Pancreas
Testes

06 Operations on thyroid and parathyroid glands

Description
The thyroid gland is a butterfly-shaped gland located in the lower neck. Its two lobes are positioned on either side of the upper trachea (windpipe) just beneath the larynx (voice box). The isthmus is a slender central portion situated just above the trachea and connects the two lobes. The thyroid gland secretes hormones that control metabolism. Tumors, both benign and malignant, may develop in the thyroid and manifest as a swelling in the lower neck. The majority of tumors are benign. Malignant tumors may cause hoarseness, enlargement of lymph nodes, pain, or breathing difficulties.

Category 06 provides codes for incisions, diagnostic procedures, excisions, and other operations on the thyroid and parathyroid. Explorations, diagnostic procedures, excisions, and other operations on the adrenal, pituitary, and pineal glands, and thymus are found in category 07.

Coding Clarification
Codes in category 06 include the incidental resection of the hyoid bone.

06.0 Incision of thyroid field

Coding Clarification
Subcategory 06.0 excludes division of the isthmus, which is reported with 06.91.

06.01 Aspiration of thyroid field

Description
This code is reported for the aspiration of a thyroid cyst. The physician localizes the thyroid cyst by palpation or ultrasound. A needle is passed through the skin into the cyst. The cyst is aspirated and the tissue captured is sent for analysis.

Coding Clarification
The following procedures are excluded from 06.01 and are more appropriately reported elsewhere:

- Aspiration biopsy of thyroid (06.11)

© 2010 Ingenix

06-07

- Drainage by incision (06.09)
- Postoperative aspiration of field (06.02)

Documentation Tip
This procedure may also be documented as percutaneous or needle drainage of the thyroid field.

06.02 Reopening of wound of thyroid field

Description
Through an incision in the neck over the previous incision, the physician explores the area for postoperative complications such as hemorrhage, thrombosis, or infection. If a vessel has ruptured, the physician isolates the vessel and dissects any adjacent critical structures as necessary to facilitate access. The complication is identified and corrected. A hemorrhage may be controlled by ligation or suture repair of the artery. Thrombosis often requires opening of the artery and the removal of the clot. An abscess or pocket of infection is drained, and a temporary tube may be placed so the infection can continue to drain. The physician sutures the skin incision with layered closure once the postsurgical complication has been treated.

Documentation Tip
Documented indications for reopening of the operative wound may include:

- Control of postoperative hemorrhage
- Removal of hematoma
- Examination/exploration

06.09 Other incision of thyroid field

Description
This code is reported, among other indications, for the incision and drainage of an infected thyroglossal tract. The physician incises and drains an infected thyroglossal (also called thyrolingual) cyst in the neck caused by incomplete closure or persistence of the embryonic thyroglossal duct between the developing thyroid and the back of the tongue. After the physician incises the cyst and drains the infected fluid, the wound may be irrigated with normal saline and a drainage system inserted. The drainage tubes may be stitched in place. A collection unit applies gentle suction to collect fluid from the incision site.

Coding Clarification
Code 06.09 also reports the following incisional procedures performed on the thyroid field:

- Drainage of hematoma (excluding that by aspiration)
- Exploration of the neck or thyroid field (excluding postoperative exploration)
- Removal of foreign body
- Thyroidotomy not otherwise specified

Report postoperative exploration with 06.02.

Report aspiration of a hematoma with 06.01.

Coding Guidance
AHA: J-A, '84, 3

06.1 Diagnostic procedures on thyroid and parathyroid glands

Description
This subcategory reports open and closed biopsies on the thyroid and parathyroid glands, as well as other diagnostic procedures. Fourth-digit subclassification is required for specificity of procedures.

06.11 Closed (percutaneous) (needle) biopsy of thyroid gland

Description
The physician removes tissue from the thyroid for examination. The physician localizes the area to be biopsied by palpation or ultrasound. A large, hollow bore needle is passed through the skin into the thyroid. The tissue is removed and sent for analysis.

Fine needle aspiration (FNA) is a percutaneous procedure that uses a fine gauge needle (22 or 25 gauge) and a syringe to sample fluid from a cyst or remove clusters of cells from a solid mass. First, the skin is cleansed. If a lump can be felt, the radiologist or surgeon guides a needle into the area by palpating the lump. If the lump is non-palpable, the FNA procedure is performed under image guidance using fluoroscopy, ultrasound, or computed tomography (CT), with the patient positioned according to the area of concern. In fluoroscopic guidance, intermittent fluoroscopy guides the advancement of the needle. CT image guidance allows computer-assisted targeting of the area to be sampled.

Ultrasonography-guided aspiration biopsy involves inserting an aspiration catheter needle device through the accessory channel port of the echoendoscope. The needle is placed into the area to be sampled under endoscopic ultrasonographic guidance. After the needle is placed into the region of the lesion, a vacuum is created and multiple in and out needle motions are performed. Several needle insertions are usually required to ensure that an adequate tissue sample is taken.

Documentation Tip
This procedure may also be documented as aspiration biopsy.

Coding Scenario
A 62-year-old female was admitted with a painless, palpable, solitary thyroid nodule discovered on routine physical examination last week. Because of this suspicious finding, compounded by a family history of thyroid cancer, needle core biopsy was

● New Code ▲ Revised Code ▶◀ Revised Text © 2010 Ingenix

performed. Biopsy results yielded a diagnosis of papillary carcinoma.

Code Assignment:

193   Malignant neoplasm of thyroid gland
06.11   Closed [percutaneous][needle]biopsy of thyroid gland

06.12 Open biopsy of thyroid gland

Description
Code 06.12 reports an incisional (open) biopsy of the thyroid gland.

06.13 Biopsy of parathyroid gland

Description
Code 06.13 reports a biopsy of the parathyroid gland. This code does not differentiate between an open and closed procedure.

Coding Guidance
AHA: J-A, '84, 3

06.19 Other diagnostic procedures on thyroid and parathyroid glands

Description
Code 06.19 reports other diagnostic procedures on the thyroid and parathyroid glands that are not more precisely described by other codes within subcategory 06.1.

Coding Clarification
The following procedures are excluded from 06.19 and are found in the miscellaneous diagnostic and therapeutic procedures chapter:

- Radioisotope scan of parathyroid (92.13)
- Radioisotope scan of thyroid (92.01)

- Soft tissue x-ray of thyroid field (87.09)

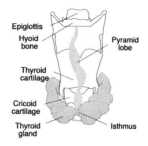

Both lobes of the thyroid gland are removed along with any tissues associated with the isthmus

Typical incision for total thyroidectomy

06.2 Unilateral thyroid lobectomy

Description
The physician removes all of a lobe of a thyroid with or without isthmusectomy. The physician exposes the thyroid via a transverse cervical incision in the skin line. The platysmas is divided and the strap muscles separated in the midline. The thyroid lobe to be excised is isolated and superior and inferior thyroid vessels serving that lobe are ligated. Parathyroid glands are preserved. The thyroid gland is divided in the midline of the isthmus over the anterior trachea. The entire thyroid lobe is resected. The platysmas and skin are closed. Alternately, the physician may remove all of a lobe of a thyroid with contralateral subtotal lobectomy, including isthmusectomy.

Coding Clarification
Code 06.2 excludes partial substernal thyroidectomy, which is reported with 06.51.

Documentation Tip
This procedure is also known as hemithyroidectomy.

06.3 Other partial thyroidectomy

06.31 Excision of lesion of thyroid

Description
The physician removes a cyst, adenoma, or other lesion from the thyroid. The physician exposes the thyroid via a transverse cervical incision in the skin line. The platysmas is divided and the strap muscles separated in the midline. The thyroid lesion is identified. Blood supply to and from the lesion is

06–07

controlled and the lesion is locally excised. The skin and platysmas are closed.

Coding Clarification
Report thyroid biopsy with 06.11 or 06.12. Report interstitial thermal therapy [LITT] of a thyroid lesion under guidance with 17.62.

06.39   Other partial thyroidectomy

Description
Report isthmectomy or partial thyroidectomy not otherwise specified with 06.39.

Coding Clarification
Report partial substernal thyroidectomy with 06.51.

06.4   Complete thyroidectomy

Description
The physician removes the entire thyroid. The physician exposes the thyroid via a transverse cervical incision in the skin line. The platysmas is divided and the strap muscles separated in the midline. The thyroid gland is mobilized and the superior and inferior thyroid vessels are ligated. The parathyroid glands are preserved and the thyroid is resected free of the trachea and removed. The platysmas and skin are closed. This procedure may be performed in conjunction with a limited or radical neck dissection with removal of lymph nodes in cases of malignancy.

Coding Clarification
Code 06.4 excludes the following procedures, which are more appropriately classified elsewhere:

- Complete substernal thyroidectomy (06.52)
- Complete thyroidectomy with laryngectomy (30.3, 30.4)

06.5   Substernal thyroidectomy

Description
Codes in subcategory 06.5 report the removal of thyroid tissue below the breastbone. This subcategory has subdivisions for partial, complete, and not otherwise specified. If the physician has not documented substernal, other codes are available. For example, use 06.4 for complete thyroidectomy. Code 06.6 is used for excision of the thyroid by submental or transoral route. When removing the parathyroid, only two code choices exist, one for complete and one for other, which includes partial parathyroidectomy.

06.50   Substernal thyroidectomy, not otherwise specified

Description
The physician removes the thyroid, including the substernal thyroid gland. The physician exposes the thyroid via a sternal split/transthoracic approach or

via a transverse cervical incision in the skin line. The platysmas is divided and the strap muscles separated in the midline. The thyroid gland is mobilized and the superior and inferior thyroid vessels are ligated. The parathyroid glands are preserved and the thyroid is resected free of the trachea and removed. Any substernal thyroid is bluntly dissected. Upper sternal incision may be necessary for complete excision of substernal thyroid. The platysmas and skin are closed.

Coding Clarification
Review the documentation in the medical record to determine if the thyroidectomy was partial or complete.

Avoid using 06.50 Substernal thyroidectomy, not otherwise specified, as this is considered a nonspecific operating room procedure.

06.51   Partial substernal thyroidectomy

Description
The physician partially removes the thyroid, including the substernal thyroid gland. The physician exposes the thyroid via a sternal split/transthoracic approach or via a transverse cervical incision in the skin line. The platysmas is divided and the strap muscles separated in the midline. The thyroid gland is mobilized and the superior and inferior thyroid vessels are ligated. The parathyroid glands are preserved and the thyroid is resected free of the trachea and removed. Any substernal thyroid is bluntly dissected. Upper sternal incision may be necessary for complete excision of substernal thyroid. The platysmas and skin are closed.

Documentation Tip
Carefully review the documentation in the medical record to ascertain whether the thyroidectomy was partial or complete. If unclear, the physician may be queried.

06.52   Complete substernal thyroidectomy

Description
The physician removes the total thyroid, including the substernal thyroid gland. The physician exposes the thyroid via a sternal split/transthoracic approach or via a transverse cervical incision in the skin line. The platysmas is divided and the strap muscles separated in the midline. The thyroid gland is mobilized and the superior and inferior thyroid vessels are ligated. The parathyroid glands are preserved and the thyroid is resected free of the trachea and removed. Any substernal thyroid is bluntly dissected. Upper sternal incision may be necessary for complete excision of substernal thyroid. The platysmas and skin are closed.

Documentation Tip
Carefully review the documentation in the medical record to ascertain whether the thyroidectomy was partial or complete. If unclear, the physician may be queried.

06.6   Excision of lingual thyroid
Description
Code 06.6 reports excision of thyroid tissue at the base of the tongue.

Coding Clarification
Report 06.6 when the thyroid excision is performed via the submental or transoral route.

06.7   Excision of thyroglossal duct or tract
Description
The physician excises a thyroglossal duct cyst or sinus. The physician circumferentially incises the skin around the cyst or sinus and extends the incision along the tract to its origin. The midpart of the hyoid bone is excised. The wound is packed and allowed to heal by secondary intention.

06.8   Parathyroidectomy
Description
Subcategory 06.8 provides two subclassification codes to differentiate complete and other parathyroidectomy.

06.81   Complete parathyroidectomy
Description
The physician removes the glands adjacent to the thyroids (parathyroids). The physician exposes the thyroid via a transverse cervical incision in the skin line. Alternately, the physician may perform the excision with mediastinal exploration, sternal split, or transthoracic approach. The platysmas is divided and the strap muscles separated in the midline. The parathyroid glands are identified and removed. A port often remains following excision. The platysmas and skin are closed.

06.89   Other parathyroidectomy
Description
The physician removes the glands adjacent to the thyroids (parathyroids). The physician exposes the thyroid via a transverse cervical incision in the skin line. Alternately, the physician may perform the excision with mediastinal exploration, sternal split, or transthoracic approach. The platysmas is divided and the strap muscles separated in the midline. The parathyroid glands are identified and removed. A port often remains following excision. The platysmas and skin are closed.

Coding Clarification
Code 06.89 reports the following procedures:

- Partial parathyroidectomy
- Parathyroidectomy not otherwise specified

Report biopsy of parathyroid with 06.13.

Documentation Tip
Carefully review the documentation in the medical record to ascertain whether the parathyroidectomy was partial or complete. If unclear, the physician may be queried.

06.9   Other operations on thyroid (region) and parathyroid
Description
This subcategory provides seven subclassification codes to report such operations on the thyroid region and parathyroid as division, ligation, suture, reimplantation, and other procedures.

06.91   Division of thyroid isthmus
Description
Code 06.91 reports the cutting or division of tissue at the narrowest point of the thyroid.

The physician transects the isthmus. The physician exposes the thyroid via a transverse cervical incision in the skin line. The platysmas is divided and the strap muscles separated in the midline. The skin and platysmas are closed.

Documentation Tip
May also be documented as transection of the thyroid isthmus.

06.92   Ligation of thyroid vessels
Description
Through an incision in the skin in the side of neck, usually in front of the sternocleidomastoid muscle, the physician isolates and dissects the ruptured or otherwise traumatized vessel, separating it from critical structures. Using a vascular clip or ligature, the vessel is ligated with sutures. Once the vessel has been tied off, the skin incision is repaired with layered closure.

06.93   Suture of thyroid gland
Description
Code 06.93 reports the repair of the thyroid gland by suturing.

06.94   Thyroid tissue reimplantation
Description
Code 06.94 reports placement of a thyroid tissue graft into a functional site.

Coding Clarification
This code is also reported for autotransplantation of thyroid tissue (tissue graft from patient's thyroid tissue to another site on the thyroid).

06-07

06.95   Parathyroid tissue reimplantation

Description
Following radical surgery on the thyroid gland, the development of hypocalcemia, osteomalacia with severe bone pain, and multiple fractures were noted in many patients. Parathyroid autotransplantation is often indicated to treat these conditions in patients who have undergone thyroid gland surgery or other operations on head and neck organs in which the parathyroids have been damaged or have questionable viability. Code 06.95 reports the placement of a parathyroid tissue graft into a functional site.

The physician excises and reimplants a portion of the parathyroid. The physician exposes the thyroid via a transverse cervical incision in the skin line. The platysmas is divided and the strap muscles separated in the midline. Tissue is excised for pathological examination. All four parathyroid glands are completely removed. One half of one gland is secured to the muscle of the sternocleidomastoid or upper arm. The platysmas and skin of the neck and transplant site are closed.

Documentation Tip
May also be documented as autotransplantation of parathyroid tissue.

Coding Guidance
AHA: 1Q, '95, 9

06.98   Other operations on thyroid glands

Description
Report 06.98 for operations on the thyroid glands for which there is no more precise code in subcategory 06.9.

06.99   Other operations on parathyroid glands

Description
Report 06.99 for operations on the parathyroid glands for which no more precise code exists in subcategory 06.9.

07   Operations on other endocrine glands

Description
The subdivisions in category 07 for procedures performed on the other endocrine glands—adrenal, pituitary, pineal, and thymus—are broken out similar to the thyroid category. There are codes for exploration, biopsy, excision, and other operations.

In some cases, ICD-9-CM provides a code for bilateral procedures on the endocrine glands. For example, use 07.3 for bilateral adrenalectomy.

There are also a number of codes in category 07 that subdivide based on the amount of the gland excised (partial or complete) and the approach taken to remove the gland. The operative report should be examined in order to choose the correct code.

Coding Clarification
If there is no code to distinguish bilateral from unilateral procedures, assign the same code twice for bilateral.

Operations on the aortic and carotid bodies, ovaries, pancreas, and testes are excluded from category 07 and are classified elsewhere.

07.0   Exploration of adrenal field

Description
Subcategory 07.0 provides three subclassification codes to report exploration of the adrenal field by laterality.

Coding Clarification
Report incision of the adrenal gland with 07.41 rather than with a code from subcategory 07.0.

07.00   Exploration of adrenal field, not otherwise specified

Description
The physician exposes the adrenal gland(s) via an upper anterior midline abdominal or posterior incision. The adrenal field is explored for diagnostic reasons. The physician closes the incision with sutures.

Alternately, the physician may perform a laparoscopic exploration of the adrenal gland through the abdomen or back. In the abdominal approach, a trocar is placed at the level of the umbilicus and the abdomen is insufflated. The laparoscope is placed through the umbilical port and additional trocars are placed into the abdominal cavity as needed. In the back approach, the trocar is placed at the back proximal to the retroperitoneal space superior to the kidney, adjacent to the adrenal gland. The physician uses the laparoscope fitted with a fiberoptic camera to explore all or part of the adrenal gland(s). The abdomen is then deflated, the trocars are removed, and the incisions are closed with sutures.

Coding Clarification
Avoid the use of this code on an inpatient record. Review the operative report thoroughly to ascertain whether the procedure was unilateral or bilateral. If documentation is unclear, the physician may be queried.

● New Code   ▲ Revised Code   ▶◀ Revised Text   © 2010 Ingenix

07.01 Unilateral exploration of adrenal field

Description

The physician exposes the adrenal gland via an upper anterior midline abdominal or posterior incision. The adrenal field is explored unilaterally for diagnostic reasons. The physician closes the incision with sutures.

Alternately, the physician may perform a laparoscopic unilateral exploration of the adrenal gland through the abdomen or back. In the abdominal approach, a trocar is placed at the level of the umbilicus and the abdomen is insufflated. The laparoscope is placed through the umbilical port and additional trocars are placed into the abdominal cavity as needed. In the back approach, the trocar is placed at the back proximal to the retroperitoneal space superior to the kidney, adjacent to the adrenal gland. The physician uses the laparoscope fitted with a fiberoptic camera to explore all or part of the adrenal gland. The abdomen is then deflated, the trocars are removed, and the incisions are closed with sutures.

07.02 Bilateral exploration of adrenal field

Description

The physician exposes the adrenal glands via an upper anterior midline abdominal or posterior incision. The adrenal field is explored bilaterally for diagnostic reasons. The physician closes the incision with sutures.

Alternately, the physician may perform a laparoscopic bilateral exploration of the adrenal glands through the abdomen or back. In the abdominal approach, a trocar is placed at the level of the umbilicus and the abdomen is insufflated. The laparoscope is placed through the umbilical port and additional trocars are placed into the abdominal cavity as needed. In the back approach, the trocar is placed at the back proximal to the retroperitoneal space superior to the kidney, adjacent to the adrenal gland. The physician uses the laparoscope fitted with a fiberoptic camera to explore all or part of the adrenal glands. The abdomen is then deflated, the trocars are removed, and the incisions are closed with sutures.

07.1 Diagnostic procedures on adrenal glands, pituitary gland, pineal gland, and thymus

Description

Subcategory 07.1 provides eight subclassification codes to report diagnostic procedures, including open and closed biopsies and other diagnostic procedures. Microscopic examination of specimens from the endocrine glands and radioisotope scans of the pituitary gland are found in the miscellaneous diagnostic and therapeutic procedures chapter.

07.11 Closed (percutaneous) (needle) biopsy of adrenal gland

Description

Code 07.11 reports a percutaneous or needle biopsy of the adrenal gland.

The physician may also perform a laparoscopic biopsy of the adrenal gland. In the abdominal approach, a trocar is placed at the level of the umbilicus and the abdomen is insufflated. The laparoscope is placed through the umbilical port and additional trocars are placed into the abdominal cavity as needed. In the back approach, the trocar is placed at the back proximal to the retroperitoneal space superior to the kidney, adjacent to the adrenal gland. The physician uses the laparoscope fitted with a fiberoptic camera and an operating tool to explore and biopsy all or part of the adrenal gland. The abdomen is then deflated, the trocars are removed, and the incisions are closed with sutures.

07.12 Open biopsy of adrenal gland

Description

The physician performs an open biopsy of the adrenal gland. The physician exposes the adrenal gland via an upper anterior midline abdominal or posterior incision. The retroperitoneal space is explored and the physician biopsies tissue for pathological study. The physician closes the incision with sutures.

07.13 Biopsy of pituitary gland, transfrontal approach

Description

The physician excises the pituitary gland tissue for examination via the frontal bone. The physician uses a craniotomy of the frontal bone to remove a portion of the pituitary gland. The physician cuts and retracts the frontal scalp and raises a bone flap. The tissues are dissected to the sella turcica and the pituitary is identified. The tumor or hypertrophic gland is biopsied. The frontal bone is replaced and fastened. The scalp is anastomosed and closed in sutured layers.

07.14 Biopsy of pituitary gland, transsphenoidal approach

Description

The physician excises the pituitary gland tissue for examination via the sphenoid bone. The physician uses an incision of the nasal mucosa to access the sphenoid sinus (sphenoidotomy). The sphenoid sinus separates the nose from the pituitary fossa, through which a portion of the pituitary gland is removed. The physician may use a combination of minimally invasive equipment (key-hole surgery) such as an operative microscope or neuro-endoscopes. A portion of sphenoid bone may

06-07

be elevated. The tumor or hypertrophic gland is biopsied. If a bone flap was created, it is replaced. The incision is closed in sutured layers.

07.15   Biopsy of pituitary gland, unspecified approach

Description
The physician excises the pituitary gland tissue for examination. No approach is specified. The physician may use a combination of equipment such as an operative microscope or neuro-endoscopes. If a bone flap was created, it is replaced. If a burr hole was made, it is packed with Gelfoam, with or without bone chips. The incision is closed in sutured layers.

07.16   Biopsy of thymus

Description
The physician excises tissue of the thymus for examination. Use of anesthesia depends on the surgical approach, which can range from a local anesthetic for needle biopsy to a general anesthetic for those including incision or endoscope. The approach may include a mediastinotomy (incision), CT-guided percutaneous needle aspiration, or endoscopy (mediastinoscopy or thorascopy). Upon removal of the tissue for examination, instrumentation is removed and the incision is closed in sutured layers, if necessary.

07.17   Biopsy of pineal gland

Description
The physician excises the tissue of the pineal gland for examination. The physician may biopsy, aspirate, or excise a portion of an intracranial lesion for tissue examination stereotactically. The lesion is mapped using a CT or MRI scanning technique. The physician uses coordinates to locate the pineal gland lesion and to accurately position the instrumentation. The scalp is incised and retracted. A burr hole or bone flap is created. A biopsy needle is inserted to aspirate or biopsy the pineal gland. The physician closes the dura, reapproximates the scalp, and closes the incision in sutured layers.

07.19   Other diagnostic procedures on adrenal glands, pituitary gland, pineal gland, and thymus

Description
Report 07.19 for diagnostic procedures on the adrenal, pituitary, and pineal glands and the thymus that are not more specifically addressed in other codes in subcategory 07.1.

Coding Clarification
Report microscopic examination of a specimen from an endocrine gland with a code from subcategory 90.1.

Report radioisotope scan of the pituitary gland with 92.11.

07.2   Partial adrenalectomy

Description
Subcategory 07.2 provides three codes for reporting partial adrenalectomy.

07.21   Excision of lesion of adrenal gland

Description
The physician excises a lesion of the adrenal gland. The physician exposes the adrenal gland via an upper anterior midline abdominal or posterior incision. The retroperitoneal space is explored. The capsule of the kidney is incised and the adrenal capsule is opened. Blood supply to the adrenal gland is ligated and a lesion of the gland is removed. The physician may remove tissue from the site for separately reportable pathological study. The physician closes the incision with sutures.

Coding Clarification
Report biopsy of the adrenal gland with 07.11 or 07.12.

07.22   Unilateral adrenalectomy

Description
Using an open approach, the physician removes one adrenal gland. The physician exposes the adrenal gland via an upper anterior midline abdominal or posterior incision. The retroperitoneal space is explored. The capsule of the kidney is incised and the adrenal capsule is opened. Blood supply to the adrenal gland is ligated and the gland is removed. The physician closes the incision with sutures.

Alternately, the physician may perform a laparoscopic unilateral adrenalectomy. In the abdominal approach, a trocar is placed at the level of the umbilicus and the abdomen is insufflated. The laparoscope is placed through the umbilical port and additional trocars are placed into the abdominal cavity as needed. In the back approach, the trocar is placed at the back proximal to the retroperitoneal space, superior to the kidney, and adjacent to the adrenal gland. The physician uses the laparoscope fitted with a fiberoptic camera and an operating tool to remove one of the adrenal glands. The abdomen is then deflated, the trocars are removed, and the incisions are closed with sutures.

Coding Clarification
This code is also used to report adrenalectomy not otherwise specified.

Report excision of the remaining adrenal gland with 07.3.

Coding Scenario
A 50-year-old female with benign pheochromocytoma of the left adrenal gland was admitted for unilateral adrenalectomy performed by laparoscopic technique. Following induction of

● New Code   ▲ Revised Code   ▶◀ Revised Text   © 2010 Ingenix

anesthesia and patient preparation, a port was inserted via a small transverse incision lateral to the edge of the right rectus muscle beneath the costal margin. Following peritoneal insufflation, the videolaparoscope was inserted through the port. Two additional ports were placed and diagnostic laparoscopic evaluation of the peritoneal cavity was performed. Following this, peritoneal ligaments were divided as necessary and the left colon and left lobe of the liver were mobilized. Instruments were placed for liver retraction. The retroperitoneal space was opened over the superior aspect of the kidney and adrenal gland, and an additional port was inserted in the posterior axillary line. Following identification, the adrenal gland was mobilized using a combination of blunt and sharp dissection. Hemostatic clips were placed and adrenal attachments were divided. The adrenal vein was divided with a laparoscopic stapler, a specimen bag was inserted through a port, and the adrenal gland was placed inside the bag. The bag was withdrawn through the port and the operative field irrigated. Once adequate homeostasis was achieved, the port sheaths were removed and the fascia was closed at the port sites. All skin sites were closed with subcuticular sutures.

Code Assignment:

227.0 Benign neoplasm of adrenal gland
07.22 Unilateral adrenalectomy

07.29 Other partial adrenalectomy

Description
The physician removes a portion of an adrenal gland, unilaterally or bilaterally. The physician exposes the adrenal gland via an upper anterior midline abdominal or posterior incision. The retroperitoneal space is explored. The capsule of the kidney is incised and the adrenal capsule is opened. Blood supply to the adrenal gland is ligated and a portion of the gland is removed. The physician closes the incision with sutures.

Alternately, the physician may perform a laparoscopic bilateral or unilateral partial adrenalectomy. In the abdominal approach, a trocar is placed at the level of the umbilicus and the abdomen is insufflated. The laparoscope is placed through the umbilical port and additional trocars are placed into the abdominal cavity as needed. In the back approach, the trocar is placed at the back proximal to the retroperitoneal space, superior to the kidney, and adjacent to the adrenal gland. The physician uses the laparoscope fitted with a fiberoptic camera and an operating tool to remove one of the adrenal glands. The abdomen is then deflated, the trocars are removed, and the incisions are closed with sutures.

Coding Guidance
AHA: 2Q, '05, 4-5

07.3 Bilateral adrenalectomy

Description
The physician removes both adrenal glands or excises a remaining adrenal gland. The physician exposes the adrenal gland via an upper anterior midline abdominal or posterior incision. The retroperitoneal space is explored. The capsule of the kidney is incised and the adrenal capsule is opened. Blood supply to the adrenal gland is ligated and the gland is removed. The physician closes the incision with sutures.

Alternately, the physician may perform a laparoscopic bilateral adrenalectomy or excision of a remaining adrenal gland. In the abdominal approach, a trocar is placed at the level of the umbilicus and the abdomen is insufflated. The laparoscope is placed through the umbilical port and additional trocars are placed into the abdominal cavity as needed. In the back approach, the trocar is placed at the back proximal to the retroperitoneal space, superior to the kidney, and adjacent to the adrenal gland. The physician uses the laparoscope fitted with a fiberoptic camera and an operating tool to remove the adrenal gland(s). The abdomen is then deflated, the trocars are removed, and the incisions are closed with sutures.

Coding Clarification
Report this code if excision of a remaining adrenal gland is performed.

Report bilateral partial adrenalectomy with 07.29.

07.4 Other operations on adrenal glands, nerves, and vessels

Description
This subcategory provides six subclassification codes to report other operations on adrenal glands, nerves, and vessels to include incision, division, ligation, repair, reimplantation, and other procedures.

07.41 Incision of adrenal gland

Description
Use this code to report adrenalotomy with drainage. The physician exposes the adrenal gland via an upper anterior midline abdominal or posterior incision. The retroperitoneal space is explored. The capsule of the kidney is incised and the adrenal capsule is opened. Abscesses or lesions are located and drained. The physician may insert a catheter for continued drainage and close the remaining incision with sutures.

06-07

07.42   Division of nerves to adrenal glands

Description
The physician cuts or avulses nerves to the adrenal glands. The physician incises the skin overlying the nerve, the tissues are dissected, and the nerve is exposed. The nerve is divided and the incision is closed in sutured layers.

07.43   Ligation of adrenal vessels

Description
The physician performs an abdominal incision to best expose the involved vessel. The physician identifies the vessel and quickly clamps it to reduce blood loss. The physician then ties off the vessel completely (ligation) and closes the abdomen. Drains may be left in place.

07.44   Repair of adrenal gland

Description
Report 07.44 when the operative procedure is described as repair of an adrenal gland.

07.45   Reimplantation of adrenal tissue

Description
Report 07.45 when autotransplantation (the use of a tissue graft from the patient's body) is performed. Adrenal tumors may be treated with partial adrenalectomy or bench surgery with autotransplantation into the thigh or arm. This method serves to preserve adrenal function after bilateral adrenalectomy or if blood supply to the adrenal glands is insufficient to sustain viability.

07.49   Other operations on adrenal glands, nerves, and vessels

Description
Report 07.49 for all other operations on adrenal glands, nerves, and tissues for which there is no more specific code in subcategory 07.4.

07.5   Operations on pineal gland

Description
This subcategory provides five subclassifications to report operations on the pineal gland to include exploration, incision, partial and total excision, and other procedures.

07.51   Exploration of pineal field

Description
The physician drills a burr hole or trephine. The physician makes an incision in the scalp over the area to be drilled, and uses a burr hole drill or a trephine (a specialized round saw for cutting circular holes in bone, especially the skull) to create an opening to the brain. The physician explores the pineal field and then closes the wound.

Alternately, the exploration may be performed by craniectomy or craniotomy. A craniectomy involves removal of skull bone. A craniotomy involves incision without bone removal. The physician incises the scalp and retracts it. The physician drills or cuts the cranium to access the area to be explored. Bone is removed and the pineal field is explored. If performing a craniotomy, the bone is replaced. The skull pieces are screwed together, and the scalp is closed in sutured layers.

Coding Clarification
Report exploration with incision of the pineal gland with 07.52.

07.52   Incision of pineal gland

Description
Code 07.52 reports incision into the pineal gland. This code includes exploration with incision.

The physician drills a burr hole or trephine. The physician makes an incision in the scalp over the area to be drilled, and uses a burr hole drill or a trephine to create an opening to the brain. The physician explores the pineal field and makes an incision into the pineal gland. The wound is closed.

Alternately, the exploration and incision may be performed by craniectomy or craniotomy. A craniectomy involves removal of skull bone. A craniotomy involves incision without bone removal. The physician incises the scalp and retracts it. The physician drills or cuts the cranium to access the area to be explored. Bone is removed, the pineal field is explored, and incision is made into the pineal gland. If performing a craniotomy, the bone is replaced. The skull pieces are screwed together and the scalp is closed in sutured layers.

07.53   Partial excision of pineal gland

Description
The physician performs partial excision of the pineal gland. The physician drills a burr hole or trephine. The physician makes an incision in the scalp over the area to be drilled, and uses a burr hole drill or a trephine to create an opening to the brain. The physician explores the pineal field and excises a portion of the pineal gland. The wound is closed.

Alternately, the exploration and incision may be performed by craniectomy or craniotomy. A craniectomy involves removal of skull bone. A craniotomy involves incision without bone removal. The physician incises the scalp and retracts it. The physician drills or cuts the cranium to access the area to be explored. Bone is removed, the pineal field is explored, and a portion of the pineal gland is excised. If performing a craniotomy, the bone is replaced. The skull pieces are screwed together and the scalp is closed in sutured layers.

● New Code   ▲ Revised Code   ▶◀ Revised Text   © 2010 Ingenix

Coding Clarification
This code excludes biopsy of the pineal gland, which is correctly reported with 07.17.

07.54   Total excision of pineal gland

Description
Code 07.54 reports a total or complete pinealectomy. The physician drills a burr hole or trephine. The physician makes an incision in the scalp over the area to be drilled, and uses a burr hole drill or a trephine to create an opening to the brain. The physician explores the pineal field and removes the pineal gland. The wound is closed.

Alternately, the exploration and incision may be performed by craniectomy or craniotomy. A craniectomy involves removal of skull bone. A craniotomy involves incision without bone removal. The physician incises the scalp and retracts it. The physician drills or cuts the cranium to access the area to be explored. Bone is removed, the pineal field is explored, and the pineal gland is excised. If performing a craniotomy, the bone is replaced. The skull pieces are screwed together and the scalp is closed in sutured layers.

07.59   Other operations on pineal gland

Description
Report other operations on the pineal gland that are not more precisely described by other codes within subcategory 07.5.

07.6   Hypophysectomy

Description
This subcategory provides seven subclassification codes to report various methods of excision and destruction of the pituitary gland.

07.61   Partial excision of pituitary gland, transfrontal approach

Description
The physician performs partial excision of the pituitary gland via the frontal bone. The physician uses a craniotomy to remove a pituitary tumor or resect a portion of the gland. The physician cuts and retracts the frontal scalp and raises a bone flap. The tissues are dissected to the sella turcica and the pituitary is identified. The tumor or a portion of the hypertrophic gland is resected. The bone is replaced and fastened. The scalp is anastomosed and closed in sutured layers.

Coding Clarification
Report biopsy of the pituitary gland via a transfrontal approach with 07.13.

Documentation Tip
The operative report may include the following terminology for procedures reported with this code:

- Partial cryohypophysectomy
- Division of hypophyseal stalk
- Excision of pituitary lesion
- Subtotal hypophysectomy
- Hypophyseal infundibulectomy

07.62   Partial excision of pituitary gland, transsphenoidal approach

Description
The physician performs partial excision of the pituitary gland via the sphenoid bone. The physician uses a transnasal or transseptal approach to remove a pituitary tumor or resect a portion of the gland. The physician accesses the base of the sella turcica through the nose. The incision may be made in the mouth underneath the upper lip to avoid facial scarring (transseptal approach). A small hole is drilled in the skull base through the inferior aspect of the sella turcica. The pituitary is identified and the tumor or a portion of the hypertrophic gland is resected. The hole is packed with Gelfoam, with or without bone chips. The nasal and oral mucosa are sutured closed.

When employing transsphenoidal neuroendoscopic techniques, the physician preps the face and nostrils. The abdomen is also prepped in case a fat graft must be harvested. Vasoconstriction is achieved in the nasal mucosa and blunt dissection is used on the middle turbinate to view the uncinate process, which is then removed with rongeurs. A complete ethmoidectomy is done with removal of the posterior half of the middle turbinate. A Freer elevator is used to identify the sphenoid sinus ostia behind the posterior ethmoid wall and the ostium is enlarged with pituitary rongeurs. The sphenoid anterior wall is removed for insertion of the endoscope. The sinus mucosa is removed with rongeurs and blunt dissection to expose the posterior sphenoid sinus wall and the sella floor. The pituitary fossa is entered and the sella floor is opened with an osteotome, if possible, or small, high-speed drills. The dura is coagulated with bipolar cautery and an incision is made. The tumor can now be removed with suction and angled curettes. The scope is advanced into the empty pituitary fossa as the tumor is removed to check for complete resection with the assistance of angled telescopes. Hemostasis is ensured after tumor removal. If cerebrospinal fluid is seen, the sella is packed with a fat graft harvested from the abdomen. The instruments are removed and no nasal packing is required.

Coding Clarification
Report a biopsy of the pituitary gland via a transsphenoidal approach with 07.14.

07–06

07.63 Partial excision of pituitary gland, unspecified approach

Description
Code 07.63 reports the partial excision of the pituitary gland. The approach is not specified.

Coding Clarification
The coder should avoid the use of this code when reporting an inpatient procedure. Review the operative note carefully to ascertain the approach. If documentation is insufficient, the physician should be queried.

Biopsy of the pituitary gland, not otherwise specified, is reported with 07.15.

07.64 Total excision of pituitary gland, transfrontal approach

Description
The physician uses a craniotomy to excise the entire pituitary gland via the frontal bone. The physician cuts and retracts the frontal scalp and raises a bone flap. The tissues are dissected to the sella turcica and the pituitary is identified. The gland is resected and the bone is replaced and fastened. The scalp is anastomosed and closed in sutured layers.

Documentation Tip
The operative report may include the following terminology for procedures reported with this code:

- Complete cryohypophysectomy
- Pituitary ablation by implantation
- Pituitary ablation by strontium yttrium implantation

07.65 Total excision of pituitary gland, transsphenoidal approach

Description
The physician excises the pituitary gland via the sphenoid bone. When employing transsphenoidal neuroendoscopic techniques, the physician preps the face and nostrils. The abdomen is also prepped in case a fat graft must be harvested. Vasoconstriction is achieved in the nasal mucosa and blunt dissection is used on the middle turbinate to view the uncinate process, which is then removed with rongeurs. A complete ethmoidectomy is done with removal of the posterior half of the middle turbinate. A Freer elevator is used to identify the sphenoid sinus ostia behind the posterior ethmoid wall and the ostium is enlarged with pituitary rongeurs. The sphenoid anterior wall is removed for insertion of the endoscope. The sinus mucosa is removed with rongeurs and blunt dissection to expose the posterior sphenoid sinus wall and the sella floor. The pituitary fossa is entered and the sella floor is opened with an osteotome, if possible, or small, high-speed drills. The dura is coagulated

with bipolar cautery and an incision is made. The tumor can now be removed with suction and angled curettes. The scope is advanced into the empty pituitary fossa as the tumor is removed to check for complete resection with the assistance of angled telescopes. Hemostasis is ensured after tumor removal. If cerebrospinal fluid is seen, the sella is packed with a fat graft harvested from the abdomen. The instruments are removed and no nasal packing is required.

Alternately, the physician uses a transnasal or transseptal approach to remove a pituitary tumor or resect the gland. The physician accesses the base of the sella turcica through the nose. The incision may be made in the mouth underneath the upper lip to avoid facial scarring (transseptal approach). A small hole is drilled in the skull base through the inferior aspect of the sella turcica. The pituitary is identified and the tumor or a portion of the hypertrophic gland is resected. The hole is packed with Gelfoam, with or without bone chips. The nasal and oral mucosa are sutured closed.

07.68 Total excision of pituitary gland, other specified approach

Description
Code 07.68 reports the complete removal of the pituitary gland by a specified approach other than those listed elsewhere in subcategory 07.6.

07.69 Total excision of pituitary gland, unspecified approach

Description
Code 07.69 reports the complete removal of the pituitary gland. The approach is not specified.

Coding Clarification
The coder should avoid the use of this code when reporting an inpatient procedure. Review the operative note carefully to ascertain the approach. If documentation is insufficient, the physician should be queried.

07.7 Other operations on hypophysis

Description
Subcategory 07.7 offers three subclassification codes to report other operations on the hypophysis, including exploration, incision, and other procedures.

07.71 Exploration of pituitary fossa

Description
The physician explores the depression in the sphenoid bone that houses the pituitary gland (pituitary fossa).

In one approach, the physician drills a burr hole or trephine. The physician makes an incision in the scalp over the area to be drilled, and uses a burr hole drill or a trephine to create an opening to the brain. The physician explores the area and closes the wound.

Alternately, the physician performs an exploratory craniectomy or craniotomy. A craniectomy involves removal of skull bone. A craniotomy involves incision without bone removal. The physician incises the scalp and retracts it. The physician drills or cuts the cranium to access the area to be explored. Bone is removed and the area of the brain is explored. If performing a craniotomy, the bone is replaced. The skull pieces are screwed together and the scalp is closed in sutured layers.

Coding Clarification
Report exploration with incision of the pituitary gland with 07.72.

07.72   Incision of pituitary gland

Description
The physician performs incision and aspiration of the pituitary gland through a burr hole or craniotomy approach. Once the gland is located stereotactically and isolated, it is aspirated or a therapeutic incision is made. Fine needle aspiration of the pituitary is used for cytologic diagnosis or to direct treatment of medical disorders based on pituitary function. The wound is closed in accordance with the approach.

A Rathke's cyst is a developmental cyst that arises from cells located in what is called Rathke's cleft, which is found in the region of the pituitary gland. Rathke's cysts may cause symptoms by creating pressure on adjacent structures such as the optic nerves (causing vision problems) and the pituitary gland with resultant loss of pituitary function. The pressure may be relieved with aspiration of the cyst or incision and drainage.

Documentation Tip
The medical record may contain the following terminology to describe sites of aspiration or incision reported by this code:

*   Craniobuccal pouch
*   Craniopharyngioma
*   Hypophysis
*   Rathke's pouch

07.79   Other operations on hypophysis

Description
Report 07.79 for other operations on the hypophysis that are not more accurately described by other codes in subcategory 07.7.

Coding Clarification
This code is appropriate for reporting the insertion of a pack into the sella turcica.

07.8   Thymectomy

Description
Subcategory 07.8 consists of five codes that report excision of the thymus. Fourth-digit subclassification provides specificity regarding extent of excision and approach.

Coding Clarification
Various codes are available based upon the operative technique employed and whether the removal is partial or total. The operative note should be reviewed carefully for specific information regarding the procedure prior to final code selection in order to ensure the most appropriate code is assigned.

07.80   Thymectomy, not otherwise specified

Description
The physician removes all or part of the thymus gland. The physician exposes the thymus via a sternal split or a transthoracic approach. The sternum is retracted and strap muscles separated. The superior lobe of the thymus is separated from the inferior aspect of the thyroid. The blood supply to the thymus is divided and the thymus is dissected free from the pericardium and removed. A radical mediastinal dissection may also be performed. The incision is closed.

Coding Clarification
Review the operative note carefully to determine whether the excision was partial or total. If documentation is unclear, the physician should be queried.

07.81   Other partial excision of thymus

Description
The physician removes part of the thymus gland. The physician exposes the thymus via a cervical incision in the skin line, a sternal split, or a transthoracic approach. The sternum is retracted and strap muscles separated. The superior lobe of the thymus is separated from the inferior aspect of the thyroid. The blood supply to the thymus is divided and a portion of the thymus is dissected free from the pericardium and removed. A radical mediastinal dissection may also be performed. The incision is closed.

Coding Clarification
Report biopsy of the thymus with 07.16.

Code 07.81 reports partial excision of the thymus that is specified as that by open approach.

06-07

Code 07.81 excludes thoracoscopic partial excision of the thymus, which is correctly reported with 07.83.

07.82   Other total excision of thymus

Description
The physician removes the entire thymus gland. The physician exposes the thymus via a cervical incision in the skin line, a sternal split, or a transthoracic approach. The sternum is retracted and strap muscles separated. The superior lobe of the thymus is separated from the inferior aspect of the thyroid. The blood supply to the thymus is divided and the thymus is dissected free from the pericardium and removed. A radical mediastinal dissection may also be performed. The incision is closed.

Coding Clarification
Code 07.82 reports total excision of the thymus that is specified as that by open approach.

Report thoracoscopic total excision of the thymus with 07.84.

07.83   Thoracoscopic partial excision of thymus

07.84   Thoracoscopic total excision of thymus

Description
These codes report the partial (07.83) and total (07.84) excision of the thymus performed thoracoscopically. A thoracoscope is a flexible, fiberoptic tube that is inserted into the thorax through a small incision for direct visualization, enabling removal of the thymus without opening the chest.

Coding Clarification
These codes exclude other partial and total excision of the thymus, which are correctly reported with 07.81 and 07.82, respectively.

Coding Scenario
A patient with acute exacerbation of myasthenia gravis is admitted for a total thymectomy. Using a video-assisted thoracoscopic technique, the physician performs total thymectomy. The surgeon makes three small incisions on the side of the chest and inserts a thoracoscope and dissecting instruments. The thymus gland is visualized and removed through the trocar incision.

Code Assignment:

358.01	Myasthenia gravis with (acute) exacerbation
07.84	Thoracoscopic total excision of thymus
17.45	Thoracoscopic robotic assisted procedure

Coding Guidance
AHA: 4Q, '07, 108-109

07.9   Other operations on thymus

Description
Subcategory 07.9 consists of seven subclassification codes to report other operations on the thymus, including exploration, incision, repair, transplantation, and other procedures. Fourth digits provide specificity regarding procedure and approach.

Coding Clarification
Various codes are available based on the operative technique documented and the approach utilized. Carefully review the operative report for specific information regarding the procedure prior to final code selection in order to ensure the most appropriate code is assigned.

07.91   Exploration of thymus field

Description
The physician explores the thymus field. The physician exposes the thymus via a cervical incision in the skin line, a sternal split, or a transthoracic approach. The sternum is retracted and strap muscles separated and the thymus field is explored. The incision is closed.

Coding Clarification
Report exploration with incision of the thymus with 07.92.

07.92   Other incision of thymus

Description
The physician performs an open incision of the thymus. The physician exposes the thymus via a cervical incision in the skin line, a sternal split, or a transthoracic approach. The sternum is retracted and strap muscles separated. An incision is made into the thymus. The thymus field may also be explored. The incision is closed.

Coding Clarification
This code reports an open incision of the thymus. Report thoracoscopic incision of the thymus with 07.95.

07.93   Repair of thymus

Description
The physician repairs the thymus. The physician exposes the thymus via a cervical incision in the skin line, a sternal split, or a transthoracic approach. The sternum is retracted and strap muscles separated. The thymus defect is located and repaired with suture, ligation, or coagulation. The incision is closed.

● New Code   ▲ Revised Code   ▶◀ Revised Text   © 2010 Ingenix

07.94   Transplantation of thymus

Description
The physician places thymus tissue grafts into a functional area of the gland. The physician exposes the thymus via a cervical incision in the skin line, a sternal split, or a transthoracic approach. The sternum is retracted and strap muscles separated. If a defect exists, it is located and tissue grafts are placed into a functional area of the thymus gland. The incision is closed.

07.95   Thoracoscopic incision of thymus

Description
The physician incises the thymus through thoracoscopic approach. A thoracoscope is a flexible, fiberoptic tube that is inserted into the thorax through a small incision for direct visualization, enabling the thymus to be incised without opening the chest.

Coding Clarification
Code 07.95 also appropriately reports the following thoracoscopic procedures on the thymus:

- Aspiration
- Exploration

Report incision of the thymus by other than thoracoscopic approach with 07.92.

Coding Guidance
AHA: 4Q, '07, 108

Review the operative report carefully for specific information regarding the procedure and approach prior to final code selection in order to ensure the most appropriate code is assigned.

07.98   Other and unspecified thoracoscopic operations on thymus

Description
Code 07.98 reports thoracoscopic procedures on the thymus not more specifically reported by other codes within subcategory 07.9.

Coding Clarification
Various codes are available based upon the operative technique documented. Review the operative report carefully for specific information regarding the procedure and approach prior to final code selection in order to ensure the most appropriate code is assigned.

Coding Guidance
AHA: 4Q, '07, 108

07.99   Other and unspecified operations on thymus

Description
Code 07.99 reports other operations on the thymus that are not more specifically described by other codes within subcategory 07.9, including transcervical thymectomy.

The physician removes part or the entire thymus gland. The physician exposes the thymus via a cervical incision in the skin line. The sternum is retracted and strap muscles separated. The superior lobe of the thymus is separated from the inferior aspect of the thyroid. The blood supply to the thymus is divided and the thymus is dissected free from the pericardium and removed. The incision is closed.

Coding Clarification
Report other operations on the thymus that are performed thoracoscopically with 07.98.

Various codes are available based upon the operative technique documented. Review the operative report carefully for specific information regarding the procedure and approach prior to final code selection in order to ensure the most appropriate code is assigned.

07-06

08-16

Operations on the Eye

The ICD-9-CM classification system for operations performed on the eye is divided into categories of procedures according to site as follows:

- Eyelids (08)
- Lacrimal System (09)
- Conjunctiva (10)
- Cornea (11)
- Iris, Ciliary Body, Sclera, and Anterior Chamber (12)
- Lens (13)
- Retina, Choroid, Vitreous, and Posterior Chamber (14)
- Extraocular Muscles (15)
- Orbit and Eyeball (16)

Coding Clarification
The majority of the subcategories in this portion of the classification system require a fourth digit for further specificity with regard to type and/or site of the operation performed.

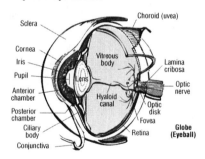

08   Operations on eyelids

Description
Category 08 provides codes for incisions, diagnostic procedures, excision or destruction of lesions or tissues, repairs, reconstructions, and other operations on the eyelids. This category also includes operations on the eyebrow.

08.0   Incision of eyelid

Description
Subcategory 08.0 consists of three codes that report various incisional procedures of the eyelid.

08.01   Incision of lid margin

Description
Trichiasis is a condition wherein eyelashes are ingrown or misdirected in their growth so that they irritate the tissues of the eye. The physician treats the area of trichiasis with a local anesthetic and preps and drapes the face and eye. The physician uses a scalpel to split the eyelid margin at the gray line (the junction of the palpebral mucosa and skin). The area of abnormal eyelash growth is excised and sutures may be required.

To treat an abscess in this area, the eyelid is prepped and draped and a local anesthetic is applied. A transverse incision is made to drain the abscess. The wound is irrigated and may be closed with sutures.

08.02   Severing of blepharorrhaphy

Description
The physician frees eyelids that were previously sutured shut. The eyelid is prepped and draped and a local anesthetic is applied. The previously formed seam or union between the upper and lower lid is then carefully delineated and divided using sharp scissors.

Coding Clarification
This procedure generally follows a previously performed tarsorrhaphy (closure of the eyelid), usually attempted to protect the cornea.

Documentation Tip
May be referred to in the operative report as division, severing, or reopening of blepharrhaphy, canthorrhaphy, or tarsorrhaphy.

08.09   Other incision of eyelid

Description
Code 08.09 is used to report an incision of the eyelid that is not more precisely reported by other codes within subcategory 08.0. Some of the procedures that are appropriately represented by this code are detailed below.

To treat an abscess, the eyelid is prepped and draped and a local anesthetic is applied. A transverse incision is made to drain the abscess. The wound is irrigated and may be closed with sutures.

To remove a foreign body embedded in the eyelid, the physician administers local anesthetic, and the patient's face and eyelid are draped and prepped for surgery. The physician locates the foreign body through palpation. An incision is made through the anterior surface if the foreign body is principally on the anterior of the lid; the lid is everted if the foreign body is near the posterior surface. An attempt is made to conceal the incision line in the crease of the upper lid, or through a subciliary incision, when possible. The foreign body is removed and the wound is irrigated and repaired with layered sutures.

Coding Clarification
The following are procedures that may also be appropriately reported with 08.09:

- Incision of eyebrow, chalazion without removal of capsule, hordeolum, stye, or meibomian gland
- Blepharotomy
- Exploration of eyelid
- Lysis of eyelid

08.1   Diagnostic procedures on eyelid

Description
Subcategory 08.1 includes two subclassification codes to report biopsy and other diagnostic procedures on the eyelid.

08.11   Biopsy of eyelid

Description
A local anesthetic is applied and the face and eyelid are prepped and draped. A small amount of tissue is excised from the suspect portion of the eyelid. Sutures may be required to repair the incision.

08.19   Other diagnostic procedures on eyelid

Description
Code 08.19 is used to report diagnostic procedures on the eyelid other than biopsy.

Coding Clarification
Diagnostic procedures on the canthus are appropriately reported with this code.

08.2   Excision or destruction of lesion or tissue of eyelid

Description
The six codes within subcategory 08.2 report the removal, excision, or destruction of lesions or tissues of the eyelid. Fourth-digit subclassification is

required in order to provide specificity to site and procedure.

Coding Clarification
If any synchronous reconstruction is performed with the excision, use an additional code from range 08.61-08.74.

If the lesion is biopsied and not excised or destroyed, use 08.11.

Both 08.23 and 08.24 are for excision of a major lesion of the eyelid. The difference is whether the removal was partial thickness (08.23) or full thickness (08.24).

08.20   Removal of lesion of eyelid, not otherwise specified

Description
To perform a blepharectomy, the physician administers a local anesthetic and the face and eyelid are draped and prepped for surgery. The eyelid lesion is outlined with a marking pen. The lesion is excised and the surgical wound is repaired with sutures if necessary.

To remove a benign or malignant lesion from the eyebrow, the physician administers a local anesthetic. The physician then makes a full-thickness incision through the dermis with a scalpel, usually in an elliptical shape around and under the lesion, and removes it. The physician may suture the wound.

Coding Clarification
Other procedures that may be appropriately reported with 08.20 include:

- Ciliectomy or cyclectomy of eyelid margin
- Resection of the orbicularis oculi muscle
- Tarsectomy
- Excision of the cilia base, meibomian gland, eyelid, or tarsal plate of eyelid

Report any synchronous reconstruction with a code from range 08.61-08.74.

Documentation Tip
Code 08.20 reports the removal of a lesion of the eyelid or eyebrow that is not more specifically described by other codes within subcategory 08.2.

08.21   Excision of chalazion

Description
A chalazion is a small mass in the eyelid that results in chronic inflammation. The face and eye are prepped and draped and local or general anesthesia is administered. Usually, general anesthesia is reserved for very young or otherwise uncooperative patients. The physician applies a chalazion clamp to expose the posterior surface of the eyelid. The chalazion is incised with a blade and a curette is

● New Code   ▲ Revised Code   ►◄ Revised Text   © 2010 Ingenix

used to explore the lid after the incision has been drained. Any pockets of infection are drained. The lips of the wound are generally cauterized to prevent excessive bleeding. The clamp is released.

Coding Clarification

Code 08.21 reports the excision of a single chalazion or of multiple chalazia.

Report any synchronous reconstruction with a code from range 08.61-08.74.

08.22   Excision of other minor lesion of eyelid

Description

The physician removes a minor lesion of the eyelid, such as a verruca or wart. After administering a local anesthetic, the physician makes a full-thickness incision through the dermis with a scalpel, usually in an elliptical shape around and under the lesion, and removes it. The physician may suture the wound simply.

Coding Clarification

Report any synchronous reconstruction with a code from range 08.61-08.74.

08.23   Excision of major lesion of eyelid, partial-thickness

Description

The physician performs a partial-thickness excision involving one-fourth or more of the lid margin. After administering a local anesthetic, the physician makes a partial-thickness incision through the dermis with a scalpel, usually in an elliptical shape around and under the lesion, and removes it. A rim of normal tissue is also removed in cases of malignancy. The physician may suture the wound.

Coding Clarification

Report any synchronous reconstruction with a code from range 08.61-08.74.

08.24   Excision of major lesion of eyelid, full-thickness

Description

The physician removes a benign or malignant lesion from the eyelid. After administering a local anesthetic, the physician makes a full-thickness incision through the skin, usually in an elliptical shape around and under the lesion, and removes it. A rim of normal tissue is also removed in cases of malignancy. The skin incision is sutured.

Coding Clarification

Report any synchronous reconstruction with a code from range 08.61-08.74.

Documentation Tip

May also be referred to as a wedge resection of the eyelid.

08.25   Destruction of lesion of eyelid

Description

For cauterization of a chalazion, meibomian gland, or other eyelid lesion, the physician administers a local anesthetic and the face and eyelid are draped and prepped for surgery. An electrocautery tool or photocoagulation is used to destroy the lesion.

Alternately, the physician may use a laser, electrosurgery, cryosurgery, chemical treatment, or surgical curettement to obliterate abnormal tissue. The physician destroys premalignant lesions after administration of local anesthesia.

Coding Clarification

Report any synchronous reconstruction with a code from range 08.61-08.74.

Documentation Tip

The medical record may refer to cauterization, cryotherapy, curettage, or destruction when describing procedures reported by 08.25.

08.3   Repair of blepharoptosis and lid retraction

Description

Subcategory 08.3 provides eight subclassification codes to report various forms of repair, reduction, and correction of specific conditions of the eyelid. When coding repairs of blepharoptosis, it is necessary to review the operative report for the technique used by the surgeon. ICD-9-CM provides different codes depending on the method described in the record.

08.31   Repair of blepharoptosis by frontalis muscle technique with suture

Description

The physician performs a repair of blepharoptosis by frontalis muscle technique using suture or other material. Blepharoptosis refers to a droop or displacement of the upper eyelid resulting from paralysis. The physician makes an incision directly above the brow (supraciliary). The frontalis fixation technique is a mechanical suspension that transfers the movement of the upper lid to the frontalis muscle above the eyelid. Banked fascia from a cadaver donor or other material such as Mersilene mesh may be used to create a sling to the frontalis muscle. It is sutured in place. The operative incision is repaired with sutures.

Documentation Tip

May also be documented in the medical record as a lid suture operation.

08–16

08.32 Repair of blepharoptosis by frontalis muscle technique with fascial sling

Description
The physician performs a repair of blepharoptosis by frontalis muscle technique using an autologous fascial sling. Blepharoptosis refers to a droop or displacement of the upper eyelid resulting from paralysis. The physician makes an incision directly above the brow (supraciliary). The frontalis fixation technique is a mechanical suspension that transfers the movement of the upper lid to the frontalis muscle above the eyelid. It is sutured in place. The physician obtains fascia from the patient's thigh and uses this fascia to create a sling to the frontalis muscle. This sling helps suspend the lid. The operative incisions are repaired with sutures.

Documentation Tip
May also be documented in the medical record as a Crawford operation, fascial graft of the eyelid, or frontalis fascial sling operation.

08.33 Repair of blepharoptosis by resection or advancement of levator muscle or aponeurosis

Description
The physician performs a repair of blepharoptosis by resection or advancement of the levator muscle or aponeurosis using an internal approach. Blepharoptosis refers to a droop or displacement of the upper eyelid resulting from paralysis. The physician administers a local anesthetic and the patient's face and eyelid are draped and prepped for surgery. The eyelid is everted and the physician makes an incision along the upper posterior edge of the tarsus. The levator complex, including Mueller's muscle, is then isolated for a distance superiorly to correspond with the amount of ptosis to be corrected. The levator aponeurosis is advanced onto the tarsal plate internally until the eyelid margin falls at the appropriate location below the limbus. The incision is repaired.

Alternately, the physician may perform a repair of blepharoptosis by resection or advancement of the levator muscle or aponeurosis using an external approach. Blepharoptosis refers to a droop or displacement of the upper eyelid resulting from paralysis. The physician administers a local anesthetic and the patient's face and eyelid are draped and prepped for surgery. An incision line is outlined along the crease of the upper eyelid. A dissection is carried down the normal insertion point of the distal point of the levator tendon. The levator tendon is then isolated. The physician uses sutures to advance the levator tendon onto the tarsal plate in an adjustable fashion. If the patient is old enough to undergo the procedure under local anesthetic, the patient is placed in a sitting position and eyelid height and contour are evaluated under the effect of gravity. The amount that the levator tendon is advanced corresponds to the degree of preoperative ptosis. If the patient is not able to undergo the procedure under local anesthetic, general anesthesia is used and a predetermined amount of advancement is performed. In either case, the incision is repaired with sutures once the tendon has been secured in its new location.

Documentation Tip
May also be documented as a Berke operation, Blascovic operation, myectomy of the levator palpebrae, levator muscle sling for eyelid ptosis repair, resection or shortening of the levator palpebrae muscle, tarsolevator resection, or tenectomy of the levator palpebrae.

08.34 Repair of blepharoptosis by other levator muscle techniques

Description
Code 08.34 reports blepharoptosis repair by levator muscle techniques other than resection or advancement.

Documentation Tip
Procedures that may be appropriately reported with 08.34 may be documented in the medical record as:

- Levator plication for blepharoptosis
- Repair of blepharoptosis by levator muscle technique
- Tucking of levator palpebrae

08.35 Repair of blepharoptosis by tarsal technique

Description
Code 08.35 reports the correction of blepharoptosis (a droop or displacement of the upper eyelid resulting from paralysis) with the tarsal muscle. Fasanella-Servatt (blepharoptosis repair) procedure is indexed in ICD-9-CM under 08.35.

In a Fasanella-Servatt type procedure, the physician administers local anesthetic and the patient's face and eyelid are draped and prepped for surgery. The physician everts the upper eyelid and a series of curved clamps are placed across the everted undersurface of the upper lid. All of the tissue distal to the clamps is removed or resected. This includes conjunctiva, tarsus, Müller's muscle, and the distal insertion of the levator aponeurosis. A running suture or purse string suture is used to consolidate the remaining tissues.

Documentation Tip
Medical record documentation may contain the following verbiage when describing this procedure:

- De Grandmont operation
- De Grandmont tarsectomy
- Tarsus muscle sling

- Resection of Müller's muscle
- Resection of tarsal muscle

08.36   Repair of blepharoptosis by other techniques

Description
Code 08.36 reports the correction of blepharoptosis by techniques other than those reported by other codes within subcategory 08.3, including orbicularis oculi muscle sling.

For correction of blepharoptosis using an orbicularis oculi muscle sling, the physician administers local anesthetic and the patient's face and eyelid are draped and prepped for surgery. The physician performs a repair that provides a mechanical suspension of the upper lid, transferring the movement of the upper lid to the frontalis muscle action of the eyebrow. The most common technique involves the creation of three horizontal incisions extending to the level of the tarsal plate approximately 3 mm above the upper eyelid margin in the midline, nasal, and lateral quarters. Three corresponding incisions are made just above the brow down to the periosteum of the bone. The lid is suspended in a double rhomboid configuration. The physician passes the suspending material deep in the lid tissue at the depth of the anterior surface of the levator aponeurosis through the orbital septum in front of the bone and out through the medial and lateral brow incisions. The knots are pulled up and tied to elevate the eyelid margin to the level of the superior limbus. The ends of the sutures are burned in the wound. The incisions are repaired with sutures.

Coding Clarification
This code is used to report correction or repair of blepharoptosis, not otherwise specified, and correction of eyelid ptosis, not otherwise specified.

Documentation Tip
This procedure may also be referred to in the operative report as:

- Attachment of the orbicularis oculi to the eyebrow
- Division of the canthal ligament
- Fixation of the palpebral ligament
- Orbicularis muscle sling
- Palpebral ligament sling

08.37   Reduction of overcorrection of ptosis

Description
The physician corrects or releases a previous plastic repair of a drooping eyelid. The physician administers local anesthetic and the patient's face and eyelid are draped and prepped for surgery. With an incision usually at the previous incision line, the

physician attempts to reduce a previous overcorrection of ptosis. The levator aponeurosis is cut free or disinserted from its attachment to the levator aponeurosis, and the operative incision is repaired with sutures.

08.38   Correction of lid retraction

Description
The physician administers local anesthetic and the patient's face and eyelid are draped and prepped for surgery. The physician outlines the incision line, usually in the crease of the upper lid. The distal portion of the tendon responsible for elevating the lid (levator aponeurosis) is isolated from its attachment to the tarsal plate. The levator aponeurosis is then allowed to retract itself posteriorly or autogenous graft materials are inserted between the levator aponeurosis and the tarsal plate. The patient is generally placed in a sitting position and the amount of the retraction of the levator aponeurosis is judged by the position of the eyelid while the patient is sitting on the table. Alternatively, the eyelid margin may be placed approximately 2 mm below the limbus. When the lid is positioned satisfactorily, it is affixed. The operative incision is closed with sutures.

Documentation Tip
May also be referred to in the operative report as eyelid retraction or as lengthening, myotomy, tenotomy, or recession of the levator palpebrae muscle.

08.4   Repair of entropion or ectropion

Description
Subcategory 08.4 contains five subclassification codes to report the various forms of entropion or ectropion repair. When coding repairs of entropion or ectropion, it is necessary to review the operative report for the technique used by the surgeon. ICD-9-CM provides different codes depending on the method described in the record.

Documentation Tip
An ectropion is a turning outward of the margin of the eyelid, while an entropion is an inversion of the margin of the eyelid.

08.41   Repair of entropion or ectropion by thermocauterization

Description
The physician restores the eyelid margin to a normal position by use of heat cautery. To repair an entropion, the physician administers local anesthetic and the patient's face and eyelid are draped and prepped for surgery. The physician uses bipolar or monopolar cautery to create central tissue shrinkage to rotate the eyelid margin anteriorly. This

08-16

corrects the malposition of the eyelid. No incisions are made in this procedure.

In an alternate method to repair an ectropion, the physician may use bipolar or unipolar cautery to shrink the posterior tissues of the eyelid margin in an effort to rotate the lid margin posteriorly toward the globe. Again, no incision is made.

08.42   Repair of entropion or ectropion by suture technique

Description
The physician restores the eyelid margin to a normal position by the use of sutures. To repair an entropion, the physician administers local anesthetic and the patient's face and eyelid are draped and prepped for surgery. The physician threads sutures through the inferior fornix or inferior cul-de-sac externally to the lash line. The sutures are placed in the medial, middle, and lateral third of the eyelid in a mattress fashion. These absorbable sutures are tied on the skin side. The sutures act to evert the eyelid margin anteriorly, correcting the malposition of the eyelid. No incision is made in this procedure.

To repair an ectropion, the physician administers local anesthetic and the patient's face and eyelid are draped and prepped for surgery. The physician uses absorbable sutures to foreshorten the posterior tissues of the eyelid in an effort to redirect the rotation of the eyelid posteriorly. No incisions are required for this treatment of ectropion.

Documentation Tip
The operative note may also refer to this procedure as tautening of the eyelid.

08.43   Repair of entropion or ectropion with wedge resection

Description
The physician restores the eyelid margin to a normal position by removing tissue. The following are examples of procedures that would be reported with this code.

To repair an entropion, the physician administers a local anesthetic and the patient's face and eyelid are draped and prepped for surgery. A triangular section of tarsus is excised from the eyelid. A large chalazion clamp may be used to evert the lid and excise the triangle of tarsus, which usually measures 8 to 10 mm at the base. A piece of exposed orbicularis muscle is removed with the wedge. The edges of the excision site are approximated and repaired with sutures.

Alternately, a section of tarsus and conjunctiva in the configuration of a diamond or rhomboid is taken

from the posterior or back surface of the lower lid. Incisions are then closed with interrupted absorbable sutures to rotate the eyelid margin posteriorly toward the globe.

Documentation Tip
This procedure is also known as a Fox operation.

08.44   Repair of entropion or ectropion with lid reconstruction

Description
The physician performs extensive blepharoplasty in which the eyelid margin is reconstructed. To repair an entropion, the physician administers local anesthetic and the patient's face and eyelid are draped and prepped for surgery. The physician makes the incision along approximately 80 percent of the width of the eyelid for extensive repair. The physician uses deep sutures to sever the eyelid margin outwardly. Strips of tarsus may also be excised from the eyelid. All incisions are repaired with sutures. This procedure is sometimes performed under general anesthesia.

Alternately, to repair an ectropion, the physician can make an incision in the lower lid and isolates a tongue or strip of tarsus in the lateral one third of the lower lid. Nonabsorbable sutures are passed through the tarsal strip. The periosteum of tough fibrous tissue that lines the bone of the lateral orbital rim is then isolated. The sutures from the tarsal strip are passed through the periosteum overlying the bone of the lateral orbital rim. The physician tightens the sutures. Eyelid margin tension and contour are evaluated and adjusted. The incision(s) is repaired with sutures.

Documentation Tip
Extensive entropion repair may also be referred to as a Wheeler operation or Wier operation.

This procedure may also be referred to as a Kuhnt-Szymanowski operation or a V-Y operation.

Coding Scenario
A patient underwent a blepharoplasty with an extensive ectropion repair of the right eyelid.

> Code Assignment:
>
> 374.10   Unspecified ectropion
> 08.44   Repair of entropion or ectropion with lid reconstruction

08.49   Other repair of entropion or ectropion

Description
Code 08.49 reports the restoration of the eyelid margin to a normal position by means other than those described with other codes within subcategory 08.4.

● New Code   ▲ Revised Code   ▶◀ Revised Text   © 2010 Ingenix

08.5   Other adjustment of lid position

Description
Subcategory 08.5 includes three codes to report other adjustment of lid position, including canthotomy, blephorrhaphy, and other procedures.

08.51   Canthotomy

Description
The physician incises the outer canthus of the eye. Under local anesthesia, the face and eyelids are draped and prepped. Scissors cut the lateral canthus to further divide the upper and lower lid to extend the division.

Coding Clarification
Use this code to report narrowing of the palpebral fissure.

Documentation Tip
This procedure may also be documented as enlargement of the palpebral fissure.

08.52   Blepharorrhaphy

Description
The constant action of the eyelid opening and closing against the cornea can cause problems in patients with chronic corneal conditions. Temporary closure of the eyelid may provide relief for an eroded or painful cornea. The physician administers a local anesthetic and preps and drapes the face and eyelids for surgery. Tissue along the mucocutaneous junction at the margins of the eyelids is excised. A suture is passed through the skin and eyelid margin at the gray line of the upper lid and corresponding portion of the lower lid. This process is repeated several times in each eye, creating a permanent marginal adhesion. The sutures are usually tied over a bolster to prevent erosion of the suture through the lid. The sutures are removed a week to 10 days later, after the lid margins have adhered.

Alternately, the physician may perform this procedure with transposition of the tarsal plate. The physician administers a local anesthetic and preps and drapes the face and eyelids for surgery. Tissue along the mucocutaneous junction at the margins of the eyelids is excised. A tongue of tarsal plate is isolated from above the upper or lower lid. The tarsal plate is sutured into a corresponding area of the opposite lid. The physician then passes a suture through the skin and eyelid margin at the gray line of the upper lid and corresponding portion of the lower lid. This process is repeated several times in each eye, creating a permanent marginal adhesion. The sutures are usually tied over a bolster to prevent erosion of the suture through the lid. The sutures are removed a week to 10 days later, after the lid margins have adhered.

Documentation Tip
This procedure may also be documented as canthorrhaphy or tarsorrhaphy.

08.59   Other adjustment of lid position

Description
Code 08.59 reports other adjustments of lid position that are not more specifically described by other codes within subcategory 08.5. Descriptions of some of the operative techniques reported by this code are included below.

Canthoplasty: The physician administers local anesthetic and the patient's face and eyelid are draped and prepped for surgery. The physician increases the lid margin by cutting the medial or lateral canthus (juncture of upper and lower eyelid). The physician rearranges the anterior tissues of the lids to prevent adherence.

Lateral canthopexy: The physician reattaches the lateral canthal ligament to correct soft tissue structures of the lateral aspect of the eye and eyelids. The lateral canthal ligament is attached laterally to the orbital aspect of the zygoma and medially to the orbital fascia, the upper eyelid, and the lower eyelid. The ligament is isolated through a horizontal skin incision placed beside the ligament. After locating the ligament, the physician places stainless steel suture or wire through the ligament. A hole is made in the zygoma with a drill. The physician then passes the suture or wire through the bony hole. The suture or wire is ligated to the bone. Skin incisions are repaired with a layered closure.

Medial canthopexy: The physician reattaches the medial canthal ligament. The medial canthal ligament is attached medially to nasal-orbital bones and laterally to the orbital fascia, the upper eyelid, and the lower eyelid. The ligament is isolated through a bicoronal incision or through skin incisions placed beside the ligament. After locating the ligament, stainless steel suture or wire is placed through the ligament. A hole is made in the nasal bones on the opposite side with a drill or awl. The suture or wire is passed under the nasal complex to the opposite side through the bony hole. The suture or wire is ligated to the bone. Any incisions are repaired with layered closure.

Coding Clarification
Other procedures that may be correctly reported with 08.59 include:

- Advancement of eyelid muscle
- Repair of canthus, epicanthus, telecanthus, or epicanthal fold
- Repair of blepharophimosis
- Revision of canthus

08-16

- Suture of palpebral fissure
- Tensing of orbicularis oculi
- Z-plasty of epicanthus

08.6   Reconstruction of eyelid with flaps or grafts

Description
Reconstruction of the eyelid or eyebrow may involve the use of a flap or graft. The fourth digits for subcategory 08.6 identify the type of flap or graft utilized in reconstructing the eyelid. Check the medical record for documentation of graft type: skin, mucous membrane, hair follicle, tarsoconjunctival, or other.

Coding Clarification
Repair of entropion or ectropion associated with eyelid reconstruction is appropriately reported with 08.44.

08.61   Reconstruction of eyelid with skin flap or graft

Description
The physician administers a local anesthetic and the patient's face and eyelid are draped and prepped for surgery. A section of full-thickness eyelid is excised from the upper or lower eyelid. The section includes the defect and a margin of normal tissue. The edges of the excision site are approximated to reconstitute the eyelid contour. In order to achieve proper cosmetic results, a skin graft or flap is performed.

When direct wound closure or adjacent tissue transfer is not possible, the physician may take a split-thickness skin autograft from one area of the body and graft it to the area needing repair. The physician harvests a split-thickness skin graft with a dermatome. The epidermis or top layer of skin is taken along with a small portion of the dermis or bottom layer of the skin. This graft is then sutured or stapled onto the recipient area on the eyelid.

08.62   Reconstruction of eyelid with mucous membrane flap or graft

Description
The physician transfers or rearranges adjacent tissue to repair traumatic or surgical wounds of the eyelids. This includes, but is not limited to, such rearrangement procedures as Z-plasty, W-plasty, ZY-plasty, or tissue transfers such as rotational flaps or advancement flaps.

Coding Clarification
Report 08.62 when the method of reconstruction is specified as a mucous membrane flap or graft.

08.63   Reconstruction of eyelid with hair follicle graft

Description
The primary goal of reconstructing eyelid defects is to restore the normal anatomy and function of the

eyelid. Code 08.63 is reported when the method of reconstruction is specified as a hair follicle graft.

Coding Clarification
Restoration of the eyebrow with graft and transposition of eyelash flaps is also reported with this code.

08.64   Reconstruction of eyelid with tarsoconjunctival flap

Description
In a one-stage or first-stage procedure, the patient's face and eyelid are draped and prepped for surgery. Local or general anesthesia may be administered. The patient has already undergone a separately reportable excision that has created a significant eyelid defect requiring reconstruction of up to two-thirds of the eyelid. Because the defect is too large for direct closure, portions of the opposing eyelid are excised and grafted to reconstruct the eyelid. The opposite lid is everted and a horizontal incision through the tarsus and conjunctiva, approximately 4 mm from the eyelid margin, is performed. Vertical incisions are then made through the conjunctiva to match the width of the flap. The dissection is carried down through Müller's muscle toward the fornix or cul-de-sac. The advancing tarsal conjunctival flap is then grafted to the opposing lid and secured with sutures. A full-thickness skin graft may be applied to complete the reconstruction.

In a second-stage procedure, the patient's face and eyelid are draped and prepped for surgery. Local or general anesthesia may be administered. Approximately six weeks after a reconstruction of the eyelid, the tissue is divided to create an upper and lower lid. Any redundant tissue is trimmed.

08.69   Other reconstruction of eyelid with flaps or grafts

Description
Code 08.69 reports other flap or graft reconstruction of the eyelids or eyebrow that are not more specifically reported with other codes within subcategory 08.6.

A free tarsal graft can be harvested from the contralateral upper lid and used as a posterior lamellar replacement for lower eyelid defects. This graft does not have a blood supply so it must be covered with a myocutaneous advancement flap.

Coding Clarification
A graft of the tarsal cartilage is appropriately reported with this code.

08.7   Other reconstruction of eyelid

Description
Just as in excision of lesions of the eyelid, subcategory 08.7 is subdivided based on the removal

08-16

● New Code   ▲ Revised Code   ▶◀ Revised Text   © 2010 Ingenix

thickness, partial or full. Additional differentiation is made based on whether the lid margin was involved in the procedure.

Coding Clarification
Report the repair of an entropion or ectropion associated with eyelid reconstruction with 08.44.

08.70 Reconstruction of eyelid, not otherwise specified

Description
Report 08.70 when the method of eyelid or eyebrow reconstruction is not more precisely reported by other codes within subcategory 08.7. Descriptions of some of the procedures appropriately reported by this code are included below.

Blepharoplasty, upper eyelid: Through an incision usually in the crease of the upper eyelid, the physician dissects the skin of the upper eyelid to the subcutaneous/muscle fascial layers. The skin is pulled tight and redundant skin is excised. Muscle fascia may be sutured to support sagging muscles. Orbital fat may be removed from the tissues, as well as excessive redundant skin that mechanically weighs down the eyelid, obstructing the visual field. The incision is closed with multiple layers.

Blepharoplasty, lower eyelid: Through an incision beneath the eyelash line, the physician dissects the skin of the lower eyelid to the subcutaneous/muscle fascial layers. The skin is pulled tight and excess skin is excised. Muscle fascia may be sutured to support sagging muscles. Orbital fat or an extensive herniated fat pad may be removed from the tissues. The incision is closed with multiple layers.

Z-plasty of the eyelid: The physician transfers or rearranges adjacent tissue to repair a traumatic or surgical wound of the eyelid.

Documentation Tip
This procedure may also be referred to in the operative report as tarsoplasty.

Coding Guidance
  AHA: 2Q, '96, 11

08.71 Reconstruction of eyelid involving lid margin, partial-thickness

Description
To perform an excision and repair of the eyelid involving the lid margin, the physician administers a local anesthetic and the patient's face and eyelid are draped and prepped for surgery. A section of partial-thickness eyelid is excised from the upper or lower eyelid. The section includes the defect and a margin of normal tissue. The edges of the excision site are approximated to reconstitute the eyelid contour and the wound is closed with layered sutures.

Coding Clarification
Code 08.71 also reports the following procedures:

- Repositioning or reopening of the cilia base
- Shortening of the eyelid margin
- Stretching of the eyelid

08.72 Other reconstruction of eyelid, partial-thickness

Description
The physician performs other partial-thickness reconstruction of the eyelid that does not involve the lid margin.

08.73 Reconstruction of eyelid involving lid margin, full-thickness

Description
For a full-thickness excision and repair of the eyelid (involving the lid margin), the physician administers a local anesthetic and the patient's face and eyelid are draped and prepped for surgery. A section of full-thickness eyelid is excised from the upper or lower eyelid. The section includes the defect and a margin of normal tissue. The edges of the excision site are approximated to reconstitute the eyelid contour and the wound is closed with layered sutures.

08.74 Other reconstruction of eyelid, full-thickness

Description
The physician performs other full-thickness reconstruction of the eyelid that does not involve the lid margin.

08.8 Other repair of eyelid

Description
Just as in excision of lesions of the eyelid, subcategory 08.8 is subdivided based on the removal thickness, partial or full. Additional differentiation is made based on whether the lid margin was involved in the procedure.

Coding Clarification
If the same procedure is performed bilaterally during a single operative session, the code may be assigned twice.

Documentation Tip
Carefully review the operative report for the site when a rhytidectomy is performed. ICD-9-CM differentiates between the lower eyelid (08.86) and the upper eyelid (08.87).

08.81 Linear repair of laceration of eyelid or eyebrow

Description
The physician performs a linear repair of a laceration of the eyelid or eyebrow. A local anesthetic is injected around the laceration and the wound is

08-16

thoroughly cleansed, explored, and often irrigated with a saline solution. The physician performs a simple, one-layer repair with sutures or may perform a layered closure. Due to deeper or more complex lacerations, deep subcutaneous or layered suturing techniques are required. The physician sutures tissue layers under the skin with dissolvable sutures before suturing the skin.

08.82 Repair of laceration involving lid margin, partial-thickness

Description
To suture a recent wound through a partial thickness of the eyelid that involves the lid margin, the physician administers a local anesthetic and the patient's face and eyelid are draped and prepped for surgery. The physician irrigates the wound and approximates its edges. The wound is repaired in layered sutures.

08.83 Other repair of laceration of eyelid, partial-thickness

Description
Report 08.83 for other partial-thickness repair of an eyelid laceration that does not involve the lid margin.

08.84 Repair of laceration of eyelid involving lid margin, full-thickness

Description
To suture a recent wound through the full thickness of the eyelid that involves the lid margin, the physician administers local anesthetic and the patient's face and eyelid are draped and prepped for surgery. The physician irrigates the wound and approximates its edges. The wound is repaired in layered sutures.

08.85 Other repair of laceration of eyelid, full-thickness

Description
Report 08.85 for other full-thickness laceration repair of the eyelid that does not involve the lid margin.

08.86 Lower eyelid rhytidectomy

Description
Through an incision beneath the eyelash line, the physician dissects the skin of the lower eyelid to the subcutaneous/muscle fascial layers. The skin is pulled tight and excess skin is excised. Muscle fascia may be sutured to support sagging muscles. Orbital fat or an extensive herniated fat pad may be removed from the tissues. The incision is closed with multiple layers.

08.87 Upper eyelid rhytidectomy

Description
Through an incision usually in the crease of the upper eyelid, the physician dissects the skin of the upper eyelid to the subcutaneous/muscle fascial layers. The skin is pulled tight and redundant skin is excised. Muscle fascia may be sutured to support sagging muscles. Orbital fat may be removed from the tissues, as well as excessive redundant skin that mechanically weight down the eyelid, obstructing the visual field. The incision is closed with multiple layers.

Coding Guidance
   AHA: 2Q, '96, 11

08.89 Other eyelid repair

Description
Code 08.89 should be reported when repair of the eyelid or eyebrow is not more precisely reported by another code in category 08.8.

Coding Guidance
   AHA: 1Q, '00, 22

08.9 Other operations on eyelids

Description
Subcategory 08.9 provides codes to report the various forms of epilation of the eyelid, as well as a code for other eyelid operations.

08.91 Electrosurgical epilation of eyelid

Description
Electrosurgical epilation may be used to treat trichiasis, a condition wherein eyelashes are ingrown or misdirected in their growth so that they irritate the tissues of the eye. The physician applies local anesthetic. Electrolysis directed at the follicles destroys them.

08.92 Cryosurgical epilation of eyelid

Description
Cryosurgical epilation may be used to treat trichiasis, a condition wherein eyelashes are ingrown or misdirected in their growth so that they irritate the tissues of the eye. The physician applies a local anesthetic. In cryotherapy, the freezing probe is applied to the affected area. After a period of repeated freezing and thawing, the lash follicles are usually destroyed.

08.93 Other epilation of eyelid

Description
Epilation by forceps may be used to treat trichiasis, a condition wherein eyelashes are ingrown or misdirected in their growth so that they irritate the tissues of the eye. Using a biomicroscope, the

● New Code   ▲ Revised Code   ►◄ Revised Text   © 2010 Ingenix

physician plucks the offending eyelashes with forceps. The lash follicles are not treated.

08.99 Other operations on eyelids

Description
Report 08.99 for operations on the canthus, eyelids, and tarsus when they are not elsewhere classified.

09 Operations on lacrimal system

Description
The lacrimal system serves to keep the conjunctiva and cornea moist through the production, distribution, and elimination of tears. Tears are produced in the lacrimal gland. Tears produced by the lacrimal gland are drained from the eye through the lacrimal punctum, a small opening near the margin of each eyelid. Ducts distribute the tears to the eye and nose. The lacrimal sac is an enlarged portion of the lacrimal duct that eliminates tears. Category 09 lists codes for a variety of diagnostic and therapeutic procedures on the lacrimal system and is organized by site and type of procedure. Given that different types of procedures may be performed on the same site, examine the operative report for this information for correct code assignment.

09.0 Incision of lacrimal gland

Description
The physician administers a local anesthetic along the edge of the supratemporal portion of the orbital rim over the lacrimal gland. An incision is made beneath the superior orbital rim or in the lid crease of the upper lid. The incision is extended to the lacrimal fossa where the abscess is drained. The wound is irrigated and then repaired with layered sutures.

Documentation Tip
This procedure may be also reported using the following terminology:

- Dacryoadenotomy
- Division of lacrimal ductules
- Exploration of the lacrimal gland
- Removal of the lacrimal gland by incision
- Incision and drainage of lacrimal cyst

09.1 Diagnostic procedures on lacrimal system

Description
Subcategory 09.1 provides three codes for reporting biopsy and other diagnostic procedures on the lacrimal system.

09.11 Biopsy of lacrimal gland

Description
The physician makes an incision beneath the superior orbital rim or in the lid crease of the upper lid. The incision is extended to lacrimal fossa. A previously determined portion of the lacrimal gland is excised for analysis. The wound is repaired with layered sutures.

09.12 Biopsy of lacrimal sac

Description
The physician administers a local anesthetic along the medial canthal tendon. An incision is made midway between the bridge of the nose and the medial canthal tendon. The dissection is carried down to the periosteum overlying the bone of the superior lacrimal crest. A portion of the lacrimal sac is removed. The wound is repaired with layered sutures.

09.19 Other diagnostic procedures on lacrimal system

Description
Code 09.19 reports diagnostic procedures (other than biopsy) on the lacrimal system.

Coding Clarification
Diagnostic procedures on the tarsus are also included in 09.19.

Report contrast dacryocystogram with 87.05.

Report soft tissue x-ray of the nasolacrimal duct with 87.09.

09.2 Excision of lesion or tissue of lacrimal gland

Description
Subcategory 09.2 is used to report excisional procedures involving the lacrimal gland. The lacrimal gland secretes tears and is located in the upper lateral part of the orbit, and is partially divided into a smaller palpebral portion (pars palpebralis) and a larger orbital part (pars orbitalis).

09.20 Excision of lacrimal gland, not otherwise specified

Description
The physician makes an incision beneath the superior orbital rim or in the lid crease of the upper lid. The incision is extended to the periosteum overlying the bone of the supraorbital rim. A periosteal elevator is used to isolate and dissect the lacrimal gland from its position in the lacrimal fossa. The gland is partially or totally removed and the wound is repaired with layered sutures.

Documentation Tip
This procedure is also known as dacryoadenectomy.

08–16

09.21   Excision of lesion of lacrimal gland

Description
To perform an excision of a lacrimal gland tumor via a frontal approach, the physician makes an incision beneath the superior orbital rim or in the lid crease of the upper lid. The incision is extended to the periosteum overlying the bone of the supraorbital rim or to the lacrimal fossa. The lesion or tumor is isolated and removed with a rim of normal lacrimal gland tissue. The wound is repaired with layered sutures.

When the excision of a lacrimal gland tumor involves an osteotomy, the physician makes an incision beneath the superior orbital rim or in the lid crease of the upper lid. The incision is extended to the periosteum overlying the bone of the supraorbital rim or to the lacrimal fossa. The tumor has invaded the lacrimal fossa, so an osteotome is used to remove the portion of affected bone. The wound is repaired with layered sutures.

Coding Clarification
Other lacrimal gland procedures reported with 09.21 include cauterization and fistulectomy.

Report lacrimal gland biopsy with 09.11.

09.22   Other partial dacryoadenectomy

Description
The physician makes an incision beneath the superior orbital rim or in the lid crease of the upper lid. The incision is extended to the periosteum overlying the bone of the supraorbital rim. A periosteal elevator is used to isolate and dissect the lacrimal gland from its position in the lacrimal fossa. A portion of the gland is removed and the wound is repaired with layered sutures.

Coding Clarification
Report lacrimal gland biopsy with 09.11.

Documentation Tip
This procedure is also known as partial lacrimal gland excision.

09.23   Total dacryoadenectomy

Description
The physician makes an incision beneath the superior orbital rim or in the lid crease of the upper lid. The incision is extended to the periosteum overlying the bone of the supraorbital rim. A periosteal elevator is used to isolate and dissect the lacrimal gland from its position in the lacrimal fossa. The gland is removed in total and the wound is repaired with layered sutures.

Documentation Tip
This procedure is also known as total lacrimal gland excision.

09.3   Other operations on lacrimal gland

Description
Code 09.3 is reported for operations on the lacrimal gland that are not more specifically reported by other codes within category 09.

09.4   Manipulation of lacrimal passage

Description
Subcategory 09.4 provides four codes to report probing and intubation of various portions of the lacrimal passage. Dilation and removal of calculus are included in these codes.

Coding Clarification
Report contrast dacryocystogram with 87.05.

09.41   Probing of lacrimal punctum

Description
The physician treats a suspected injury or blockage of the lacrimal punctum, the opening on the medial eyelids, to assist in drainage of secretions. The physician inserts a plastic probe, catheter, or large suture. The physician may irrigate the punctum to evaluate the patency of the lacrimal drainage system.

09.42   Probing of lacrimal canaliculi

Description
The physician threads a probe along the canaliculi. No incisions are made and no repairs are necessary. The canaliculi may be irrigated during the procedure.

Coding Clarification
Procedures that are correctly reported by this code include the following:

- Cannulation of the lacrimal apparatus
- Evacuation of streptothrix from lacrimal duct
- Lacrimal intubation for dilation
- Canaliculus irrigation
- Removal of calculus from the lacrimal canaliculi
- Removal of foreign body from the lacrimal canaliculi
- Slitting of the canaliculus for tube passage

Documentation Tip
This procedure is also known as an Anel operation.

09.43   Probing of nasolacrimal duct

Description
The physician dilates the proximal portion of the lacrimal system and threads a probe along the canaliculus to the lacrimal sac. No incisions are made and no repairs are necessary. This may be performed under local anesthesia or, in the case of

08–16

less patent ducts or a less cooperative patient, the use of general anesthesia may be required.

Coding Clarification
Report probing of the nasolacrimal duct with concurrent stent or tube insertion with 09.44.

09.44 Intubation of nasolacrimal duct
Description
The physician dilates the proximal portion of the lacrimal system and threads a probe along the canaliculus to the lacrimal sac. Canalicular stents are passed through the duct and placed in the distal portion of the lacrimal system. The tubes remain in place for three to six months before they are removed. No incisions are made and no repairs are necessary.

Coding Guidance
   AHA: 2Q, '94, 11

09.49 Other manipulation of lacrimal passage
Description
Report 09.49 for procedures involving manipulation of the lacrimal passage that are not more specifically reported by other codes within subcategory 09.4.

09.5 Incision of lacrimal sac and passages

09.51 Incision of lacrimal punctum
Description
The physician administers a local anesthetic at the lacrimal punctum and uses sharp scissors to snip the lacrimal punctum, usually posteriorly. A dilating probe is introduced to ensure that enlargement of the punctum has been achieved.

09.52 Incision of lacrimal canaliculi
Description
Report 09.52 when an incisional procedure is performed on the lacrimal canaliculi.

09.53 Incision of lacrimal sac
Description
The physician administers a local anesthetic along the medical canthal tendon. A stab incision is made directly into the lacrimal sac and the pressure created by the sequestered abscess is relieved. The wound may be irrigated and then repaired with layered sutures.

09.59 Other incision of lacrimal passages
Description
Report 09.59 for other incisional procedures on the lacrimal passages that are not more specifically reported by other codes within category 09.5.

Coding Clarification
Procedures that may be appropriately reported with 09.59 include the following:

* Division or incision of a nasolacrimal duct stricture
* incision and drainage of the lacrimal passage
* Incisional removal of calculus from the lacrimal passages
* Incisional foreign body removal from the lacrimal passages

09.6 Excision of lacrimal sac and passage
Description
The physician administers a local anesthetic along the medial canthal tendon. An incision is made midway between the bridge of the nose and the medial canthal tendon. The dissection is carried down to the periosteum overlying the bone of the superior lacrimal crest. A periosteal elevator is used to separate the lacrimal sac from its normal location. The sac is removed and the wound is repaired with layered sutures.

Coding Clarification
Report a biopsy of the lacrimal sac with 09.12.

09.7 Repair of canaliculus and punctum
Description
The three codes within subcategory 09.7 report the various forms of repair of the canaliculus and punctum. Repair of the eyelid is not addressed here, but in subcategory 08.8.

09.71 Correction of everted punctum
Description
The physician administers a local anesthetic at the lacrimal punctum and applies bipolar or monopolar cautery to the palpebral conjunctiva just below the level of the inferior punctum. The result is a repositioning of the punctum itself. No incisions are made and no repairs required in this procedure.

Coding Clarification
Report eyelid repair with a code from range 08.81-08.89.

09.72 Other repair of punctum
Description
Code 09.72 reports other repairs of the punctum, including cauterization. In a cauterization procedure, the physician administers a local anesthetic at the lacrimal punctum and uses cautery to close the proximal portion of the canalicular and lacrimal system, including the lacrimal punctum.

08-16

Coding Clarification
Report eyelid repair with a code from range
08.81-08.89.

09.73 Repair of canaliculus

Description
Lacrimal canaliculi are the ducts that carry the tears
from the lacrimal gland where they are produced to
the nose. The physician uses a probe to locate the
distal and proximal ends of the canaliculi in the
injured eye. The ends are freshened and reattached
with sutures. The wound is closed with layered
sutures.

Coding Clarification
Report eyelid repair with a code from range
08.81-08.89.

09.8 Fistulization of lacrimal tract to nasal cavity

09.81 Dacryocystorhinostomy (DCR)

Description
The physician uses an endoscope to visually and
surgically assist during a dacryocystorhinostomy.
When the lacrimal system is obstructed and
excessive tearing is a problem for the patient, a
dacryocystorhinostomy is performed. In this
procedure, the new lacrimal drainage system is
surgically created from the lower eyelid into the
nose. An endoscope allows the physician both
increased visualization and magnification of the
internal anatomy. Topical vasoconstrictive agents
are applied to the nasal mucosa and nerve blocks
with local anesthesia are performed. The endoscope
is placed into the nose. The nasolacrimal duct and
other lacrimal structures are visualized. Endoscopy
may aid in location of structures or enhance
intranasal procedures like osteotomies and internal
splinting with Teflon tubes.

Alternately, the physician administers a local
anesthetic along the medial canthal tendon. A 1 cm
incision is made in the skin midway between the
bridge of the nose and the medial canthal tendon.
The dissection is carried down to the periosteum
overlying the bone of the superior lacrimal crest. The
lacrimal sac is opened and a communication is
established between the lacrimal sac and underlying
bone and nasal mucosa. The lacrimal mucosa is
exposed and a connection between the medial
portion of the lacrimal sac and the nasal mucosa is
created and secured with sutures. The incision is
repaired with layered sutures.

Documentation Tip
The medical record may refer to this procedure as a
canaliculorhinostomy or
canaliculodacryocystorhinostomy.

This procedure is also known as a Jones,
Summerskill, Toti, or West operation.

09.82 Conjunctivocystorhinostomy

Description
The physician administers a local anesthetic along
the medial canthal tendon. A 1 cm incision is made
in the skin midway between the bridge of the nose
and the medial canthal tendon. The dissection is
carried down to the periosteum overlying the bone of
the superior lacrimal crest. The lateral portion of
lacrimal sac is connected by a series of interrupted
sutures to the nasal mucosa. The incision is repaired
with layered sutures.

Coding Clarification
When conjunctivocystorhinostomy is performed with
concurrent insertion of a tube or stent, report 09.83.

Documentation Tip
This procedure is also known as a Stallard
operation.

The medical record may refer to this procedure as a
canthocystostomy,
conjunctivodacryocystorhinostomy, CDCR, or
conjunctivodacryocystostomy.

09.83 Conjunctivorhinostomy with insertion of tube or stent

Description
The physician administers a local anesthetic along
the medial canthal tendon. A 1 cm incision is made
in the skin midway between the bridge of the nose
and the medial canthal tendon. The dissection is
carried down to the periosteum overlying the bone of
the superior lacrimal crest. The lateral portion of
lacrimal sac is connected by a series of interrupted
sutures to the nasal mucosa. A glass tube is inserted
to create a connection from the lacrimal system to
the nasal mucosa. The incision is repaired with
layered sutures.

Coding Clarification
This procedure is also known as a Stallard operation
with tube/stent insertion.

The medical record may refer to this procedure as a
conjunctivodacryocystorhinostomy with tube/stent
insertion, CDCR with tube/stent insertion, or
conjunctivodacryocystostomy with tube/stent
insertion.

09.9 Other operations on lacrimal system

09.91 Obliteration of lacrimal punctum

Description
The physician administers a local anesthetic at the
lacrimal punctum and uses a heat source, such as
cautery or argon laser, to close the proximal portion

of the canalicular and lacrimal system including the lacrimal punctum. Alternately, the physician may close the punctum by inserting a plug. The plug may be a permanent silicone plug or a temporary collagen plug.

09.99   Other operations on lacrimal system

Description
Report 09.99 for repairs or other operations on the lacrimal system that are not more specifically reported elsewhere in subcategory 09.9.

To perform closure of a lacrimal fistula, the physician administers a local anesthetic at the lacrimal punctum and uses a probe to locate the lacrimal fistula. The fistula is dissected and its core is removed. The incision is repaired with layered sutures.

Coding Clarification
ICD-9-CM does not provide a specific code for removal of a nasal lacrimal stent. Use 09.99 for this procedure.

Coding Guidance
   AHA: 2Q, '94, 11

---

10   Operations on conjunctiva

Description
Operations on the conjunctiva have subcategories, 0–6 and 9, to describe the different kinds of procedures (e.g., incision, excision, or repair) that may be performed on this site. In some cases, a subcategory is further subdivided with fourth digits providing greater specificity as to type.

10.0   Removal of embedded foreign body from conjunctiva by incision

Description
A small incision may be required to remove an embedded conjunctival foreign body. In this case, the physician may cut a V-shaped incision to access the defect through a flap, or a straight incision may be made. The incision may penetrate the conjunctiva, but it does not penetrate the sclera. Generally, a slit lamp is used when removing any embedded foreign body. After the removal, the physician may apply a broad spectrum antibiotic and a moderate pressure patch over the closed lid for 24 to 48 hours.

Coding Clarification
Report the removal of an embedded conjunctival foreign body without incision with 98.22.

Report the removal of a superficial foreign body with 98.21.

Coding Scenario
A patient presented to the emergency department with a metal shaving in the left eye. Using a slit lamp, the physician made an incision to remove the metal shaving, which was embedded in the conjunctiva.

   Code Assignment:

   930.1   Foreign body in conjunctival sac
   E914   Foreign body accidentally entering eye and adnexa
   10.0   Removal of embedded foreign body from conjunctiva by incision

10.1   Other incision of conjunctiva

Description
For incision and drainage of a conjunctival cyst, the patient's face and eyelid are draped and prepped for surgery. Local anesthesia is administered. A vertical or horizontal incision is made in the posterior surface of the eyelid margin. The incision does not extend to the eyelid margin itself. The contents of the cyst are drained with a cotton-tipped probe or a curette.

Coding Clarification
Report 10.1 for incisional procedures on the conjunctiva other than for foreign body removal. Code 10.1 appropriately reports the following procedures:

* Division of corneal blood vessels
* Conjunctival incision without foreign body removal
* Peritomy

10.2   Diagnostic procedures on conjunctiva

10.21   Biopsy of conjunctiva

Description
The patient's face and eyelid are draped and prepped for surgery. Local anesthesia may be administered. A portion of the bulbar or palpebral conjunctiva is excised with a curette. Sutures may be required to repair the wound.

10.29   Other diagnostic procedures on conjunctiva

Description
Report 10.29 for diagnostic procedures on the conjunctiva other than biopsy.

10.3   Excision or destruction of lesion or tissue of conjunctiva

10.31   Excision of lesion or tissue of conjunctiva

Description
The patient's face and eyelid are draped and prepped for surgery. Local anesthesia is administered. A

lesion on the bulbar or palpebral conjunctiva is excised with a curette. Sutures may be required to repair the wound.

If the excision includes the adjacent sclera, the patient's face and eyelid are draped and prepped for surgery. Local anesthesia is administered and a lid speculum is inserted. A lesion on the conjunctiva and adjacent superficial sclera is excised with a curette. No sutures are usually required.

Coding Clarification
Report conjunctival biopsy with 10.21.

Documentation Tip
This procedure may also be referred to in the operative note as conjunctival grattage, peridectomy, or peritectomy.

Coding Guidance
AHA: 3Q, '96, 7; 4Q, '00, 41

10.32   Destruction of lesion of conjunctiva

Description
The patient's face and eyelid are draped and prepped for surgery. Local anesthesia is administered and a lid speculum is inserted. A freezing probe (cryotherapy) is applied to a lesion on the conjunctiva. No repair is required.

Coding Clarification
This code is not used for lesion destruction by excision. Instead, report 10.31. If thermocauterization is performed for entropion repair, report 08.41.

10.33   Other destructive procedures on conjunctiva

Description
Trachoma is a chronic inflammation of the eye causing granulations to form on conjunctival tissue. The patient's face and eyelid are draped and prepped for surgery. Local anesthesia may be administered. Under biomicroscopic guidance, the physician everts the eyelid margin and removes the conjunctival follicles with a cotton-tipped swab or a curette. No incision is required.

Coding Clarification
Report 10.33 for other destructive procedures on the conjunctiva, such as the removal of trachoma follicles.

Documentation Tip
The operative report may contain the following terminology for procedures reported with 10.33:

- Rolling of conjunctiva
- Scarification of conjunctiva
- Scraping of trachoma follicles
- Cauterization of conjunctiva
- Conjunctival curettage

- Expression of trachoma follicles

10.4   Conjunctivoplasty

Description
Subcategory 10.4 reports conjunctival correction by plastic surgery and is further subdivided with fourth digits providing greater specificity as to type.

10.41   Repair of symblepharon with free graft

Description
A symblepharon is an adhesion between the conjunctiva on the eyeball (bulbar conjunctiva) and the conjunctiva on the inner eyelid (tarsal conjunctiva). The patient's face and eyelid are draped and prepped for surgery. Local anesthesia is administered. The physician separates the conjunctival adhesions and grafts replacement tissue over the site of the symblepharon. The tissue for graft can be a free graft of conjunctival tissue from the same or other eye, or buccal mucosa obtained from inside the patient's mouth. The site to which the donor tissue is to be grafted is then prepared to accept the tissue. Its margins are freshened and the conjunctival graft is sutured in place. A silicon stent or contact lens may be placed in the eye to prevent the development of further adhesions during the healing process.

Coding Clarification
Repair of symblepharon with conjunctival graft to the area of granuloma overlying the lateral rectus muscle is reported with code 10.41

Assign code 10.31, Excision of lesion or tissue of conjunctiva, for an excision of the granuloma.

Coding Guidance
AHA: 3Q, '96, 7

10.42   Reconstruction of conjunctival cul-de-sac with free graft

Description
The patient's face and eyelid are draped and prepped for surgery. Local anesthesia is administered. With the aid of an operating microscope, the physician separates the conjunctival epithelial tissue from the underlying Tenon's capsule. The tissue for graft can be a free graft of conjunctival tissue from the same or other eye, or buccal mucosa obtained from inside the patient's mouth. If employing a buccal mucous membrane graft, the physician separates the buccal mucous membrane that will be used for the graft from its location within the patient's mouth. The donor graft site does not usually require a repair. The site to which the donor tissue is to be grafted is then prepared to accept the tissue. Its margins are freshened and the conjunctival graft is sutured into a foreshortened or scarred inferior cul-de-sac or fornix. The fornix can be reformed with the use of a

08-16

cul-de-sac suture fixation or with the use of a silicon stent attached to the orbital rim. The stent is used to mold the fornix and is sutured into place securely and left for up to two weeks.

Coding Clarification
This code is not appropriate for reporting the revision of an enucleation socket with a graft; rather, report 16.63.

10.43   Other reconstruction of conjunctival cul-de-sac
Description
The physician performs plastic surgery for correction of a defect of the conjunctiva cul-de-sac. The patient's face and eyelid are draped and prepped for surgery. Local anesthesia is administered. With the aid of an operating microscope, the physician separates the conjunctival epithelial tissue from the underlying Tenon's capsule. The tissue for graft can be a free graft or extensive rearrangement of existing tissue. The fornix can be reformed with the use of a cul-de-sac suture fixation or with the use of a silicon stent attached to the orbital rim. The stent is used to mold the fornix and is sutured into place securely and left for up to two weeks.

Coding Clarification
This code is not appropriate for reporting the revision of an enucleation; rather, report 16.64.

Documentation Tip
The conjunctival cul-de-sac is also referred to as the conjunctival fornix.

10.44   Other free graft to conjunctiva
Description
The patient's face and eyelid are draped and prepped for surgery. Local anesthesia is administered. With the aid of an operating microscope, the physician separates the conjunctival epithelial tissue from the underlying Tenon's capsule. If utilizing a buccal mucous membrane graft, the physician separates the buccal mucous membrane that will be used for the graft from its location within the patient's mouth. The site to which the harvested tissue is to be grafted is then prepared to accept the tissue. Its margins are freshened and the conjunctival graft is arranged and sutured into place.

Coding Clarification
Report 10.44 for free grafts to the conjunctiva other than when performed for symblepharon repair.

10.49   Other conjunctivoplasty
Description
Report 10.49 for other forms of conjunctivoplasty that are not more precisely reported with other codes from subcategory 10.4.

To perform a bridge or partial conjunctival flap, the patient's face and eyelid are draped and prepped for surgery. Local anesthesia is administered. The physician elevates the conjunctiva from the Tenon's capsule and a small tongue of free conjunctiva is advanced via a flap to another site where it is secured with sutures.

If performing a total conjunctival flap, such as a Gunderson thin flap or purse string flap, the physician elevates the conjunctiva from the Tenon's capsule and the conjunctiva is advanced to cover the de-epithelialized cornea. The leading edge of the conjunctival flap is sutured along the medial extent of the corneal defect.

Coding Clarification
Code 10.49 is also appropriate for reporting the following procedures:

- Conjunctival repair of a late effect of trachoma
- Symblepharon repair by means other than division or free graft

This code is inappropriate for reporting corneal repair with a conjunctival flap; report 11.53.

10.5   Lysis of adhesions of conjunctiva and eyelid
Description
A symblepharon is an adhesion between the conjunctiva on the eyeball (bulbar conjunctiva) and the conjunctiva on the inner eyelid (tarsal conjunctiva). The patient's face and eyelid are draped and prepped for surgery. Local anesthesia is administered. The physician divides the adhesions between the globe and palpebral conjunctiva. No other repair is usually needed, although a conformer or contact lens may be placed in the eye to prevent the development of further adhesions during the healing process.

10.6   Repair of laceration of conjunctiva
Description
An ocular speculum may be placed in the patient's eye. The physician irrigates the laceration and sutures the conjunctival wound.

Coding Clarification
This code is inappropriate for reporting conjunctival laceration repair when performed concurrently with repair of the sclera; report 12.81.

10.9   Other operations on conjunctiva
Description
The two codes in subcategory 10.9 report other operations on the conjunctiva, including subconjunctival injections.

08–16

10.91   Subconjunctival injection

Description
The physician applies a drop of topical anesthetic to the eye. A small gauge needle is inserted to deliver a medication such as a cortical steroid or antibiotic into the subconjunctival space.

Coding Clarification
Report the injection of steroid (99.23) or antibiotic (99.21) in addition to 10.91 when appropriate.

Coding Guidance
   AHA: 3Q, '96, 7

10.99   Other operations on conjunctiva

Description
Code 10.99 reports operations on the conjunctiva that are not more specifically addressed by other codes within category 10. One example is the harvesting of a conjunctival allograft from a living donor.

A conjunctival allograft is harvested from a living donor for transplantation to another recipient to help the process of re-epithelialization in cases of corneal epithelial damage and disease when the normal population of conjunctival/limbal stem cells has been depleted. The donor eye is prepped and draped. The lid speculum is inserted to maintain the lids and lashes from the operative field. The conjunctival borders of the graft to be removed are marked with a surgical marking pen to approximate the recipient bed dimensions. Saline solution is injected subconjunctivally to raise the conjunctiva from the Tenon's layer. Incisions are made on the lateral borders of the graft first, with undermining done between those borders. The posterior ridge is incised and the graft is reflected. Dissection is carried to the conjunctival/limbal junction and anterior dissection is finished, moving into the peripheral cornea. The epitheliectomy from a living donor is kept at a superficial level like that of a keratectomy with limbal and peripheral corneal tissue; no sclera or corneal stroma. The free graft is removed and prepared in an appropriate storage medium. The wound is closed. Topical antibiotics and steroids are instilled and the lids are closed and patches applied.

11   Operations on cornea

Description
The breakdown for the codes for operations on the cornea follows a format similar to other procedures on the eye. The flow of procedure codes is by type of procedure such as removal of foreign body, incision, diagnostic procedures, excision, repair, reconstruction, and other operations. Also, as in

many areas of the procedure classification, the patient's diagnosis is a factor in code selection.

11.0   Magnetic removal of embedded foreign body from cornea

Description
Code 11.0 reports the magnetic extraction of an embedded corneal foreign body.

Coding Clarification
Report the incisional removal of an embedded corneal foreign body with 11.1.

11.1   Incision of cornea

Description
To remove an embedded foreign body from the cornea by incision, the physician may cut a V-shaped incision to access the defect through a flap, or a straight incision may be made. The incision does not penetrate the cornea. Generally, a slit lamp is used with any embedded foreign body. After the removal, the physician may apply a broad spectrum antibiotic and a moderate pressure patch over the closed lid for 24 to 48 hours.

11.2   Diagnostic procedures on cornea

Description
Subcategory 11.2 provides three codes for reporting diagnostic procedures on the cornea, including scraping, biopsy, and other nonspecified procedures.

11.21   Scraping of cornea for smear or culture

Description
The physician scrapes the surface of the corneal defect with a spatula. The scrapings will be cultured to determine a diagnosis.

Documentation Tip
This procedure may also be referred to as abrasion, curettage, excision, removal, or shaving of the corneal epithelium for smear or culture.

11.22   Biopsy of cornea

Description
The physician removes a portion of a corneal lesion for diagnostic purposes using a blade and forceps or scleral scissors. The edges of the lesion are undermined following a superficial incision in the cornea. Sutures are not required. Antibiotic ointment and possibly a 24-hour pressure patch is applied. The cornea is not perforated by the excision.

11.29   Other diagnostic procedures on cornea

Description
Report 11.29 for diagnostic procedures on the cornea other than those more specifically reported by other codes within subcategory 11.2.

● New Code   ▲ Revised Code   ▶◀ Revised Text   © 2010 Ingenix

11.3   Excision of pterygium

Description
A pterygium is a fleshy wedge of the bulbar conjunctiva covering a portion of the medial cornea. Codes within subcategory 11.3 report various methods of pterygium excision. Review the operative note carefully to determine correct code assignment.

11.31   Transposition of pterygium

Description
The physician dissects the pterygium with a blade and forceps or scleral scissors. The edges of the pterygium are undermined following a superficial incision in the clear cornea. Forceps retract the freed pterygium and it is dissected as gentle pressure pulls it away from the corneal tissue and across the limbus and sclera. The physician applies sutures to the sclera and conjunctiva as needed. The physician transposes the pterygium with normal conjunctival tissue to move it out of the field of vision. A topical antibiotic and a pressure patch may be applied.

Documentation Tip
The following terminology may also be used when referring to this procedure:

- Dissection of pterygium with reposition
- McReynold's operation

11.32   Excision of pterygium with corneal graft

Description
The physician excises the pterygium with a blade and forceps or scleral scissors. The edges of the pterygium are undermined following a superficial incision in the clear cornea. Forceps retract the freed pterygium and it is excised as gentle pressure pulls it away from the corneal tissue and across the limbus and sclera. The physician applies sutures to the sclera and conjunctiva as needed or may make a circumcorneal incision and use a conjunctival flap to repair the pterygium site. A topical antibiotic and a pressure patch may be applied.

Documentation Tip
This procedure is also known as a D'Ombrain operation.

11.39   Other excision of pterygium

Description
The physician excises the pterygium with a blade and forceps or scleral scissors. The edges of the pterygium are undermined following a superficial incision in the clear cornea. Forceps retract the freed pterygium and it is excised as gentle pressure pulls it away from the corneal tissue and across the limbus and sclera. The physician applies sutures to the sclera and conjunctiva as needed. No graft or transposition is performed. A topical antibiotic and a pressure patch may be applied.

Coding Clarification
The same procedure may be performed for different reasons. In some cases, ICD-9-CM may list a diagnosis in the procedure description. For example, 11.39 Other excision of pterygium, is used when the patient's diagnosis is pterygium. If the patient does not have this condition, this code should not be assigned.

Documentation Tip
Ensure the medical record documentation supports the condition; if not, a different code should be selected.

11.4   Excision or destruction of tissue or other lesion of cornea

Description
Subcategory 11.4 provides four codes to report the various methods of excision or destruction of corneal lesions or tissue. Subclassification is determined by the method employed; therefore, the operative note should be carefully reviewed to ensure correct code assignment.

11.41   Mechanical removal of corneal epithelium

Description
In cases of corneal erosion or degeneration, the physician may attempt to stimulate new growth of the cornea's outermost layer by essentially "wounding" it. The physician removes the outermost layer of the cornea (epithelium) by scraping or cutting it with a spatula or curette. Chemical cauterization may then be applied. An alternative to cutting or scraping is the application by swab of ethylenediaminetetraacetic acid (EDTA), an acid that destroys the corneal epithelium. In either case, an antibiotic ointment or pressure patch may be applied once the procedure is complete.

Coding Clarification
In cases of keratolimbal stem cell allograft transplants, report 11.41 on the donor's chart for the removal of the stem cells.

If performed for smear or culture, report 11.21 instead.

Documentation Tip
The medical record may contain the following terminology to describe the mechanical removal of the corneal epithelium:

- Abrasion
- Chemocauterization
- Curettage
- Excision

08-16

- Scraping
- Shaving

Coding Guidance
AHA: 3Q, '02, 20

11.42 Thermocauterization of corneal lesion

Description
The physician applies a heat probe directly to a corneal lesion or ulcer. Antibiotic ointment and sometimes a pressure patch are applied.

Documentation Tip
This procedure is also known as electrocauterization.

11.43 Cryotherapy of corneal lesion

Description
The physician applies a freezing probe directly to a corneal defect to destroy it. Freezing is the most common method used for this procedure. The physician then applies antibiotic ointment and sometimes a pressure patch.

11.49 Other removal or destruction of corneal lesion

Description
The physician may remove a corneal lesion using a blade and forceps or scleral scissors. The edges of the lesion are undermined following a superficial incision in the cornea. Sutures are not required. Antibiotic ointment and possibly a 24-hour pressure patch are applied. The lesion is superficial; the cornea is not perforated by the excision.

Alternately, the physician may apply a laser beam to a corneal defect to destroy it. The physician then applies antibiotic ointment and sometimes a pressure patch.

Coding Clarification
Report biopsy of the cornea with 11.22.

Documentation Tip
Code 11.49 is also appropriate for reporting the following corneal procedures:

- Abscission (the removal of tissue by cutting away)
- Closure of corneal fistula
- Electrokeratotomy
- Keratectomy

11.5 Repair of cornea

Description
Codes within subcategory 11.5 report suture and other forms of corneal repair.

11.51 Suture of corneal laceration

Description
The physician removes any foreign body from the cornea with a hollow needle or forceps and the wound is irrigated. A perforating or nonperforating tear in the cornea is repaired with sutures. The cornea may be splinted using a soft contact lens bandage. An air or saline injection may be required to reestablish proper ocular pressure in the anterior chamber. If the laceration involves the uveal tissue (the vascular layer beneath the sclera), injured tissue may be cut out or repositioned before the uvea is sutured and the sclera and conjunctiva may each require separate closure. In any of these procedures, a topical antibiotic or a pressure patch may be applied.

Coding Clarification
Repair of a filtering bleb by suture is also correctly reported with 11.51.

Coding Guidance
AHA: 3Q, '96, 7

11.52 Repair of postoperative wound dehiscence of cornea

Description
The physician reexplores an eye wound that is the site of previous surgery to revise postoperative defects. The physician uses a number of techniques, based on the wound and previous surgery. Surgery may be major or minor.

Coding Clarification
If a conjunctival flap is utilized in the repair of postcataract wound dehiscence, report 11.53.

11.53 Repair of corneal laceration or wound with conjunctival flap

Description
The physician removes any foreign body from the cornea with a hollow needle or forceps and the wound is irrigated. A perforating or nonperforating tear in the cornea is repaired with sutures. The cornea may be splinted using a soft contact lens bandage. An air or saline injection may be required to reestablish proper ocular pressure in the anterior chamber. If the laceration involves the uveal tissue (the vascular layer beneath the sclera), injured tissue may be cut out or repositioned before the uvea is sutured and the sclera and conjunctiva may each require separate closure. A conjunctival flap is also utilized. In any of these procedures, a topical antibiotic or a pressure patch may be applied.

In a bridge or partial conjunctival flap, the patient's face and eyelid are draped and prepped for surgery. Local anesthesia is administered. The physician elevates the conjunctiva from the Tenon's capsule and a small tongue of free conjunctiva is advanced via a flap to another site where it is secured with sutures.

When performing a total conjunctival flap, the patient's face and eyelid are draped and prepped for surgery. Local anesthesia is administered. The physician elevates the conjunctiva from the Tenon's capsule and the conjunctiva is advanced over the de-epithelialized cornea. The leading edge of the conjunctival flap is sutured along the medial extent of the corneal defect.

11.59   Other repair of cornea

Description
Report 11.59 for corneal repairs other than those more specifically described by other codes in category 11.

Tissue glue, also called medical adhesive or Cyanoacrylate tissue adhesive, acts as a suture in laceration repairs of the cornea and/or sclera. If the cornea is perforated, the physician may seal the perforation with tissue adhesive after debriding the outermost layer of cornea (the epithelium) to enhance adhesion. The patient may be fitted with a soft contact lens to be worn during the healing process. Antibiotic ointment is applied. A pressure patch may be used.

11.6   Corneal transplant

Description
Corneal transplants is subdivided with fourth digits that identify keratoplasty not otherwise specified, lamellar keratoplasty with autograft, other lamellar keratoplasty, penetrating keratoplasty with autograft, other penetrating keratoplasty, and other corneal transplant. When coding corneal transplants, it will be necessary to review the operative report for this information.

Coding Clarification
Do not assign a code from subcategory 11.6 when reporting corneal grafts with the excision of a pterygium; report 11.32.

Documentation Tip
A penetrating keratoplasty involves the replacement of the full thickness of the cornea, while a lamellar keratoplasty involves the replacement of superficial layers of the cornea.

In autografts, the donor and recipient are the same individual. In allografts, the donor is a different individual than the recipient.

11.60   Corneal transplant, not otherwise specified

Description
Code 11.60 reports a corneal transplant in which the technique (partial thickness or full thickness) is not specified. The donor tissue may be an autograft or homograft.

Coding Clarification
Code 11.60 is also used to report the repair of a filtering bleb by corneal graft.

If known, assign an additional code from range 00.91-00.93 to report the donor source.

11.61   Lamellar keratoplasty with autograft

Description
Lamellar keratoplasty is a partial thickness technique and is technically more difficult than a full-thickness corneal excision. Removal is limited to the cornea's diseased outer layers, preserving the deeper layers, and corneal transplant tissue is positioned over the resulting defect. This technique results in a reduced risk of tissue rejection or infection.

Code 11.61 reports a partial-thickness keratoplasty using the patient's own corneal tissue as the donor cornea. The physician measures the patient's cornea to select the size of trephine that will be used to excise corneal tissue. The physician punches a circular hole in the outermost layers of the cornea of the donor eye, using the trephine. The physician removes the round layer of corneal tissue, threads it with sutures, and sets it aside. The trephine is used to repeat this process in the cornea of the patient, removing the defective corneal tissue. The donor cornea is of similar diameter and thickness as the removed tissue. The donor cornea is positioned with the preplaced sutures, and then additional sutures secure it to the cornea. The physician may use a saline or air injection into the anterior chamber during the procedure. When the procedure is complete, the speculum is removed. Antibiotic ointment and a pressure patch may be applied.

Documentation Tip
Lamellar keratoplasty is indicated for corneal changes that are limited to the outer layers of the cornea, and for treating a thinning or unevenly shaped cornea. Review the documentation carefully to determine if a penetrating (i.e., full-thickness) keratoplasty was performed.

11.62   Other lamellar keratoplasty

Description
The physician measures the patient's cornea to select the size of trephine that will be used to excise corneal tissue. The physician punches a circular hole in the outermost layers of the cornea of a donor eye, using the trephine. The physician removes the round layer of corneal tissue, threads it with sutures, and sets it aside. The trephine is used to repeat this process in the cornea of the patient, removing the defective corneal tissue. The donor cornea is of similar diameter and thickness as the removed tissue. The donor cornea is positioned with

08-16

the preplaced sutures, and then additional sutures secure it to the cornea. The physician may use a saline or air injection into the anterior chamber during the procedure. When the procedure is complete, the speculum is removed. Antibiotic ointment and a pressure patch may be applied.

Coding Clarification
Report epikeratophakia with 11.76.

Coding Guidance
> **AHA:** S-O, '85, 6

11.63   Penetrating keratoplasty with autograft

Description
Penetrating keratoplasty entails the removal of corneal tissue and its replacement with autograft or homograft tissue. Unlike lamellar (partial thickness) keratoplasty, penetrating keratoplasty involves the full thickness removal of the diseased cornea while leaving healthy peripheral corneal tissue intact. The autograft or homograft donor corneal tissue is fashioned to fit the resulting defect and is sutured to the patient's remaining healthy cornea, often resulting in the restoration of good visual acuity.

The physician measures the patient's cornea to select the size of trephine that will be used to excise corneal tissue. The physician punches a circular hole in the cornea of the donor eye using the trephine. The physician removes the disk of corneal tissue, threads it with preplaced sutures, and sets it aside. In aphakic patients, vitreous and/or aqueous may be withdrawn from the eye before the cornea is removed. A metal ring may be sutured to the sclera of an aphakic patient to stabilize the operative field. The defective cornea of the patient is removed with the trephine. The donor cornea is positioned with sutures, and then additional sutures secure it to the cornea. The physician may use a saline or air injection to restore proper intraocular pressure.

Coding Clarification
Code 11.63 reports a full-thickness keratoplasty performed using the patient's own corneal tissue as the donor cornea.

Indications for this procedure include corneal degeneration or scarring, keratoconus, keratitis, bullous keratopathy, and corneal transplant tissue rejection.

Documentation Tip
Penetrating refers to the thickness of the donor cornea, indicating its full thickness.

11.64   Other penetrating keratoplasty

Description
The physician measures the patient's cornea to select the size of trephine that will be used to excise corneal tissue. The physician punches a circular

hole in the cornea of the donor eye using the trephine. The physician removes the disk of corneal tissue, threads it with preplaced sutures, and sets it aside. In aphakic patients, vitreous and/or aqueous may be withdrawn from the eye before the cornea is removed. A metal ring may be sutured to the sclera of an aphakic patient to stabilize the operative field. The defective cornea of the patient is removed with the trephine. The donor cornea is positioned with sutures, and then additional sutures secure it to the cornea. The physician may use a saline or air injection to restore proper intraocular pressure.

Coding Clarification
Perforating keratoplasty with homograft is reported with 11.64.

Documentation Tip
Penetrating refers to the thickness of the donor cornea, indicating its full thickness.

11.69   Other corneal transplant

Description
Code 11.69 reports a specified type of keratoplasty that is not more accurately reported by other codes within subcategory 11.6.

11.7   Other reconstructive and refractive surgery on cornea

Description
The cornea is one of several structures in the eye that contributes to refraction. Altering the shape of the cornea therefore alters visual acuity. Subcategory 11.7 provides seven codes to report other corneal reconstructive and refractive surgeries. Subclassification is based on the type of procedure performed.

11.71   Keratomileusis

Description
The physician retracts the patient's eyelids with an ocular speculum. Using a planing device, the physician removes a partial-thickness central portion of the patient's cornea, freezes it, and then reshapes it on an electronic lathe. The revised cornea is positioned and secured with sutures. This is done to correct optical error. The physician may use a saline or air injection into the anterior chamber during the procedure. The speculum is removed. Antibiotic ointment and a pressure patch may be applied.

11.72   Keratophakia

Description
The physician retracts the patient's eyelids with an ocular speculum and measures the patient's cornea to select the size of trephine that will be used to excise corneal tissue. The physician punches a

08-16

circular hole in the cornea of the donor eye using the trephine. The physician removes the disk of corneal tissue and sets it aside. An incision is made at the juncture of the cornea and the sclera (the limbus) and the patient's cornea is separated into two layers. The physician inserts the donor cornea between layers of the recipient's cornea. The resulting change in the corneal curvature alters the refractive properties of the cornea to correct the preexisting refractive error. The speculum is removed. Antibiotic ointment and a pressure patch may be applied.

Coding Scenario

A 30-year-old male with hyperopia desires surgical correction of vision. The physician removes a partial-thickness, disc-shaped portion of corneal tissue from the anterior corneal surface. Donor corneal tissue that has been previously lathed is positioned on the eye. The resected corneal tissue is then placed over the donor tissue and affixed. Antibiotic ointment and a pressure patch were applied. There were no complications.

Code Assignment:

367.0 Hypermetropia
11.72 Keratophakia

11.73 Keratoprosthesis

Description

Keratoprosthesis is indicated for certain patients with corneal blindness unable to undergo a transplant procedure or have a decreased likelihood of a successful transplant.

The physician creates a new anterior chamber with a plastic optical implant that replaces a severely damaged cornea that cannot be repaired. Sometimes the corneal prosthesis is sutured to the sclera. At other times, extensive damage to the eye requires that the implant be sutured to the closed and incised eyelid.

11.74 Thermokeratoplasty

Description

Code 11.74 reports the correction of hyperopia and astigmatism using an infrared laser. Laser thermokeratoplasty (LTK) treats farsightedness and astigmatism. This procedure is performed under local anesthesia and does not involve cutting or removal of tissue; rather, heat from a laser beam shrinks and reshapes the cornea. Vision is corrected in a matter of seconds, although the results are not permanent.

Documentation Tip

This procedure may also be referred to as TKP.

11.75 Radial keratotomy

Description

The physician retracts the patient's eyelids with an ocular speculum and measures the patient's cornea. The physician places multiple nonpenetrating cuts in the cornea in a bicycle spoke pattern to reduce myopia, or a variety of peripheral corneal tangential cuts for astigmatic correction. There are two basic surgical approaches: Russian, in which the incisions are made from the edges to the center of the cornea, and American, in which the incisions are made from the center to the periphery. The number and length of the incisions depend upon the patient's age and degree of myopia. The resulting change in the corneal curvature alters the refractive properties of the cornea to correct the preexisting refractive error. The speculum is removed. Antibiotic ointment and a pressure patch may be applied.

Documentation Tip

This procedure is also known as a Gifford operation.

11.76 Epikeratophakia

Description

A "living lens procedure" or epikeratophakia involves the removal of the corneal epithelium and the suturing of a donor corneal graft onto the patient's corneal surface. The physician retracts the patient's eyelids with an ocular speculum and measures the patient's cornea to select the size of trephine that will be used to excise corneal tissue. The physician punches a circular hole in the cornea of the donor eye using the trephine. The physician removes the disk of corneal tissue and sets it aside. On a lathe, the physician shapes a lens made of two layers from a donor cornea, the stroma and Bowman's membrane. The physician sutures this donor cornea to the surface of the patient's cornea. The resulting change in the corneal curvature alters the refractive properties of the cornea to correct the preexisting refractive error. The speculum is removed. Antibiotic ointment and a pressure patch may be applied.

11.79 Other reconstructive surgery on cornea

Description

Code 11.79 reports corneal reconstructive and refractive surgeries that are not more specifically addressed by other codes within subcategory 11.7.

When a previous surgery (e.g., for insertion of an intraocular lens or a corneal procedure) results in astigmatism, the physician at a later date returns the patient to the operating room to correct the problem. The physician retracts the patient's eyelids with an ocular speculum. In corneal relaxing, an "X" cut is made on the cornea to repair the error. Slices along the "X" are removed and its edges are sutured. The resulting change in the corneal curvature alters

08-16

the refractive properties of the cornea to correct the preexisting refractive error. The speculum is removed. Antibiotic ointment and a pressure patch may be applied.

Coding Clarification
Cryotherapy performed in order to reshape the cornea is correctly reported with 11.79.

11.9   Other operations on cornea

Description
Most surgical procedures involving the cornea involve various refractive eye surgery techniques to change the shape of the cornea in order to improve the refractive state of the eye.

11.91   Tattooing of cornea

Description
The physician places a speculum in the eye and uses a fine needle to create hundreds of tiny pricks in the surface of the outermost layer of the cornea (the epithelium). A topical antibiotic and patch may be applied.

Documentation Tip
This procedure is sometimes called a corneal tattoo.

11.92   Removal of artificial implant from cornea

Description
Corneal implants, which are small acrylic disks or rings similar to a contact lens, are removed from just under the surface of the cornea in the stroma, originally inserted to reshape the curvature of the irregular cornea shape and correct refraction.

Coding Scenario
An ophthalmologist makes a small incision in the cornea of the eye and removes two crescent shaped ring segments between the layers of the corneal stroma, one on each side of the pupil.

  Code Assignment:

  11.92   Removal of artificial implant from cornea

11.99   Other operations on cornea

Description
Corneal transplantation is a surgical procedure where a damaged or diseased cornea is replaced by donated corneal tissue.

With anesthesia induced, the surgical team prepares the eye to be operated on and drapes the face around the eye. An eyelid speculum is placed to keep the lids open, and the eye is lubricated to prevent drying. A metal ring is then stitched to the sclera providing a base for a trephine, which is placed over the cornea and used by the surgeon to cut the host cornea. The trephine is then removed and the surgeon cuts a circular graft (a "button") from the donor cornea.

Once this is done, the surgeon returns to the patient's eye and removes the host cornea. The donor cornea is brought into the surgical field and maneuvered into place with forceps. Once in place, the surgeon fastens the cornea to the eye with a running stitch or in multiple interrupted stitches. The surgeon reforms the anterior chamber with a sterile solution injected by a cannula and tests to assure that it is watertight by placing a dye on the wound exterior. With the metal ring removed and antibiotic eyedrops placed, the eye is patched and the patient is taken to a recovery area.

Coding Clarification
Corneal transplantation is also known as corneal grafting or penetrating keratoplasty.

Coding Guidance
  AHA: 3Q, '02, 20

---

12   Operations on iris, ciliary body, sclera, and anterior chamber

Description
Category 12 encompasses procedures on four different areas of the eye: iris, ciliary body, sclera, and anterior chamber. Every subcategory for this group of operations requires a fourth digit.

12.0   Removal of intraocular foreign body from anterior segment of eye

Documentation Tip
Subcategory 12.0 has fourth digits based on whether a magnet was used in the extraction. Review the physician documentation for information regarding use of a magnet prior to final code selection in order to ensure accurate code assignment.

12.00   Removal of intraocular foreign body from anterior segment of eye, not otherwise specified

Description
The physician removes an intraocular foreign body from the anterior chamber of the eye or lens. The physician makes a small incision in the connective tissue between the cornea and the sclera (the limbus) and retrieves the foreign body through the opening with intraocular forceps or another small instrument. Generally, foreign bodies that pierce the lens are self-sealing and removal is not attempted. The incision is sutured. The physician applies an antibiotic ointment. Sometimes a pressure patch is placed on the eye for 24 to 48 hours.

Coding Clarification
The removal of an intraocular foreign body from the anterior chamber, subcategory 12.0, has fourth

digits based on whether a magnet was used in the extraction.

Do not assign a separate code for iridectomy when it is associated with a cataract extraction, removal of a lesion, or scleral fistulization.

Documentation Tip
Review the physician documentation for information regarding use of a magnet prior to final code selection in order to avoid the "not otherwise specified" code.

12.01 Removal of intraocular foreign body from anterior segment of eye with use of magnet

Description
The physician will use an electromagnetic or magnetic probe to retrieve a metallic foreign body from the anterior chamber of the eye. In the anterior route, the physician first dilates the patient's pupil. In a series of moves aligning the magnet to the metallic foreign body, the physician draws the foreign body to the front of the eye and around the lens into the anterior chamber. The physician makes an incision in the connective tissue between the cornea and the sclera (the limbus) and retrieves the foreign body. In the posterior route, the physician makes a small incision in the conjunctiva over the site of the foreign body. A magnet is applied and the foreign body removed. The incision is repaired, and an injection may be required to reestablish proper fluid levels in the chambers of the eye. A broad spectrum antibiotic or a pressure patch may be applied. Among the tools common to this procedure are Gruning's, Haab's, or Hirschberg's magnets.

Coding Clarification
Do not assign a separate code for iridectomy when it is associated with a cataract extraction, removal of a lesion, or scleral fistulization.

12.02 Removal of intraocular foreign body from anterior segment of eye without use of magnet

Description
The physician uses intraocular forceps to retrieve the nonmetallic foreign body from the anterior segment of the eye. Nonmetallic foreign bodies in the vitreous or retina may be removed through a pars plana approach. The physician makes an incision through the conjunctiva overlying the site of the foreign body and the foreign body is retrieved with intraocular forceps. The incision is repaired with layered closure, and an injection may be required to reestablish proper fluid levels in the anterior or posterior chambers of the eye. A broad spectrum antibiotic or a pressure patch may be applied.

Coding Clarification
Do not assign a separate code for iridectomy when it is associated with a cataract extraction, removal of a lesion, or scleral fistulization.

12.1 Iridotomy and simple iridectomy

Description
This subcategory consists of four subclassification codes to report iridotomy with transfixion, other forms of iridotomy, excision of prolapsed iris, and other forms of iridectomy.

Coding Clarification
This subcategory excludes iridectomies associated with cataract extraction (13.11-13.69), lesion removal (12.41-12.42), and scleral fistulization (12.61-12.69).

An *iridotomy* is typically used to decrease intraocular pressure in patients with angle-closure glaucoma. It is often performed with a laser and involves making puncture-like openings through the iris without the removal of iris tissue.

An *iridectomy* is also known as a *corectomy* and involves the removal of a portion of iris tissue.

A *basal iridectomy* is the removal of iris tissue from the far periphery, near the iris root; a *peripheral iridectomy* is the removal of iris tissue at the periphery; and a *sector iridectomy* is the removal of a wedge-shaped section of iris that extends from the pupil margin to the iris root, leaving a keyhole-shaped pupil.

12.11 Iridotomy with transfixion

Description
Though constantly flushed and renewed, the overall pressure of aqueous is constant in a healthy eye's anterior chamber. Too little or too much fluid can cause permanent damage. In the iris bombe, where the iris balloons forward blocking aqueous outflow channels, the surgeon pierces the iris in two places. The physician closes the incision with sutures and may restore intraocular pressure with an injection of water or saline. A topical antibiotic or pressure patch may be applied.

12.12 Other iridotomy

Description
Though constantly flushed and renewed, the overall pressure of aqueous is constant in a healthy eye's anterior chamber. Too little or too much fluid can cause permanent damage. To enhance the flow of fluids in the anterior chamber, the physician makes an incision in the corneal-scleral juncture (the limbus). The physician slices through the iris in a side-to-side motion in an effort to increase the flow of aqueous hampered by a pupilary block. No tissue

is removed. The physician closes the incision with sutures and may restore intraocular pressure with an injection of water or saline. A topical antibiotic or pressure patch may be applied.

When performing iridotomy by laser surgery, a topical anesthetic is applied. The physician places a special contact lens on the eye of the patient. The argon or YAG laser is focused on the iris and multiple short bursts of laser light create holes in the iris. This procedure allows fluids in the eye to pass from behind the iris through the openings into the space between the iris and the cornea (the anterior chamber). This lowers intraocular pressure.

Documentation Tip
A laser peripheral iridotomy (LPI) may be performed with an argon laser or YAG laser.

12.13   Excision of prolapsed iris

Description
In the excision of a prolapsed iris, the iris is cut flush with the corneal surface. The iris defect may then be sutured.

12.14   Other iridectomy

Description
Code 12.14 reports other forms of iridectomy that are not more appropriately described by other codes within subcategory 12.1. The following scenarios describe certain surgical techniques that would be appropriately reported by this code.

When performing an iridectomy by laser surgery, a topical anesthetic is applied. The physician places a special contact lens on the eye of the patient. The argon or YAG laser is focused on the iris and multiple short bursts of laser light create holes in the iris. This procedure allows fluids in the eye to pass from behind the iris through the openings into the space between the iris and the cornea (the anterior chamber). This lowers intraocular pressure.

In order to widen an abnormally small pupil and improve vision, an ocular speculum is placed in the patient's eye. The physician makes an incision at the juncture of the cornea and sclera (the limbus). The physician trims an inner ring of iris as a means of widening an abnormally small pupil and improving vision. The physician may close the incision with sutures and may restore the intraocular pressure with an injection of water or saline. A topical antibiotic or pressure patch may be applied.

In a basal, buttonhole, or stenopeic iridectomy, an ocular speculum is placed in the patient's eye. The physician makes an incision at the juncture of the cornea and sclera (the limbus). The physician removes a piece of iris, providing a direct passageway for aqueous. This causes the intraocular

pressure to fall as aqueous from behind the iris can flow forward and drain from the eye. The physician may close the incision with sutures and may restore the intraocular pressure with an injection of water or saline. A topical antibiotic or pressure patch may be applied.

Though constantly flushed and renewed, the overall pressure of aqueous is constant in a healthy eye's anterior chamber. Too little or too much fluid can cause permanent damage. To enhance the flow of fluids in the eye, the physician makes an incision at the juncture of the cornea and sclera (the limbus). The physician removes a wedge piece from the iris leaving what is often referred to as a keyhole pupil. This causes the intraocular pressure to fall as aqueous from behind the iris can flow forward and drain from the eye. The physician may close the incision with sutures and may restore the intraocular pressure with an injection of water or saline. A topical antibiotic or pressure patch may be applied.

12.2   Diagnostic procedures on iris, ciliary body, sclera, and anterior chamber

12.21   Diagnostic aspiration of anterior chamber of eye

Description
Though constantly flushed and renewed, the overall pressure of aqueous is constant in a healthy eye's anterior chamber. Too little or too much fluid can cause permanent damage. In some cases, the removal of the fluid is diagnostic; in cases where the ocular pressure is high, a therapeutic removal of aqueous may be performed. Code 12.21 describes a procedure that uses suction to withdraw fluid for diagnostic purposes from the anterior chamber of the eye.

The physician aspirates aqueous from between the iris and the cornea (the anterior chamber) with a needle in what is typically called an "anterior chamber tap." The needle usually enters the anterior chamber through the corneal-scleral juncture (the limbus).

Coding Clarification
The physician may inject air to normalize eye pressure after fluid has been removed.

12.22   Biopsy of iris

Description
The physician uses a sharp-needle inserted through the cornea to obtain tissue or cells to diagnose anterior segment conditions. Another technique involves using a small, rounded, needle-shaped device called an "aspiration-cutter" to slice off bits of anterior segment tissue for biopsy.

12.29 Other diagnostic procedures on iris, ciliary body, sclera, and anterior chamber

Description
The angle of the anterior chamber of the eye is examined in a gonioscopy to assess for injury or disease process in the anterior chamber. The patient is given anesthesia (general anesthesia may be utilized if the patient has significant injury or otherwise cannot tolerate the examination while conscious), the goniolens is prepared, and the physician places it on the patient's cornea. The gonioscopy is accomplished and the angle of the anterior chamber of the eye is examined. The lens is removed, the eye is irrigated, and the cornea is checked again.

Coding Clarification
A gonioscopy is performed to assess for angle closure glaucoma, iris neovascularization, or other injury or disease process in the anterior chamber. Since the cornea's curvature creates internal reflection when the anterior angle structures are viewed directly, a gonioscopic lens is used to observe the angle. The lens puts a concave surface against the cornea, eliminating its refracting surface and allowing the angle to be observed with oblique mirrors.

Documentation Tip
Review the documentation carefully to determine if the physician performs a diagnostic fluid removal. If ocular pressure is high, a therapeutic removal of aqueous may be performed.

Coding Scenario
The physician first determines corneal integrity using fluorescein, and then the patient is given anesthesia. The goniolens is prepared and the physician places it on the patient's cornea. With the illumination lamp and microscope set, the gonioscopy is accomplished and the angle of the anterior chamber of the eye is examined. The lens is removed, the eye is irrigated, and the cornea is checked again.

Code Assignment:

12.29 Other diagnostic procedures on iris, ciliary body, sclera, and anterior chamber

12.3 Iridoplasty and coreoplasty

Description
Iridoplasty is a form of laser treatment often used in the treatment of angle closure glaucoma. A laser lightbeam is directed at the iris in order to bypass the blockage of the drainage angle caused by the iris allowing the aqueous humour to reach the trabecular meshwork. In goniosynechia, the outer portion of the iris adheres to the cornea. Lysis means to set free and removal may be accomplished in any number of ways.

12.31 Lysis of goniosynechiae

Description
Sometimes scar tissue or adhesions bind structures within the eye, interfering with vision or with intraocular pressure. Through an incision in the corneal-scleral juncture (the limbus), the physician enters the anterior segment to sever vitreal, corneal, or ciliary strands or adhesions binding the iris to adjunct structures interfering with vision. The strands or adhesions are not removed; they simply fall out of the visual field.

Coding Clarification
Adhesion of the iris to the posterior surface of the cornea in the angle of the anterior chamber associated with angle-closure glaucoma is also known as peripheral anterior synechia.

Lysis of goniosynechiae by injection of air or liquid is reported using 12.31.

12.32 Lysis of other anterior synechiae

Description
The physician enters the anterior segment through the limbus to sever strands or adhesions binding the iris to adjunct structures interfering with vision. Once the adhesions have been severed, the intraocular pressure may be restored with an injection of fluid or air. The incision is closed and an antibiotic and pressure patch may be applied.

Coding Clarification
For anterior synechiae, the physician severs adhesions of the base of the iris to the cornea. For posterior synechiae, the adhesions between the iris to the capsule of the lens or to the surface of the vitreous body are severed.

Lysis of other anterior synechiae includes lysis of anterior synechiae by injection of air or liquid.

Code 12.32 is also reported when the specific site of the anterior synechiae is not specified in the documentation.

12.33 Lysis of posterior synechiae

Description
The physician enters the anterior segment through the limbus to sever the adhesions between the iris to the capsule of the lens or to the surface of the vitreous body. Once the adhesions have been severed, the intraocular pressure may be restored with an injection of fluid or air. The incision is closed and an antibiotic and pressure patch may be applied.

Coding Clarification
Report 12.33 for lysis of iris adhesions not otherwise specified in the documentation

08–16

12.34   Lysis of corneovitreal adhesions

Description
The physician enters the anterior segment through the limbus to sever strands or adhesions binding the cornea to the gel-like vitreous that has prolapsed into the anterior chamber. Once the adhesions have been severed, the intraocular pressure may be restored with an injection of fluid or air. The incision is closed and an antibiotic and pressure patch may be applied.

Coding Clarification
Plastic surgery for correction of abnormality of the iris or pupil is reported using 12.34.

12.35   Coreoplasty

Description
Coreoplasty, or needling of pupillary membrane, is plastic surgery of the iris typically performed to correct a misshapen, miotic, or occluded pupil. The physician places a special contact lens on the eye of the patient and uses multiple bursts of light from an argon laser to create an additional hole in the iris.

Coding Clarification
Pupillary membranes are dense and therefore resistant to knife incision so that trauma to attached intraocular structures may occur during discission techniques. Needling techniques permit membrane stabilization on a fixation needle, which allows controlled incision of the pupillary membrane at an angle without tension on surrounding structures.

12.39   Other iridoplasty

Description
Code 12.39 reports a specified type of iridoplasty that is not more accurately reported by other codes within subcategory 12.3.

For example, when suturing the iris or ciliary body, an ocular speculum is placed in the patient's eye. The physician makes an incision at the juncture of the cornea and sclera (the limbus) to approach and repair a trauma-caused tear of the iris from the ciliary body. The wedge shaped tear is affixed to the ciliary body with dissolving sutures, or with stitches that can be removed through an incision prepared for that retrieval. The physician may close the incision with sutures and may restore the intraocular pressure with an injection of water or saline. A topical antibiotic or pressure patch may be applied.

In another example, the physician uses a YAG laser to selectively sever vitreal, corneal, or ciliary strands or adhesions binding the iris to adjunct structures and interfering with vision. This lens allows the physician to view the angle structures of the eye and the trabecular network while using the laser. The

strands or adhesions are not removed; they simply fall out of the visual field.

Coding Clarification
The YAG laser can be used to treat refractive errors and to perform corneal collagen shrinkage for the treatment of hyperopia by shrinking collagen in the peripheral cornea.

The codes for lysis of adhesions (i.e., synechiae) are found in subcategory 12.3. Fourth digits are selected based on the site of the adhesions.

12.4   Excision or destruction of lesion of iris and ciliary body

12.40   Removal of lesion of anterior segment of eye, not otherwise specified

Description
Code 12.40 reports a lesion removal from the anterior segment that is not more accurately described in the documentation.

Documentation Tip
Report 12.40 if the documentation does not provide further specification of the lesion removal from the anterior segment of the eye.

12.41   Destruction of lesion of iris, nonexcisional

Description
The physician places a special contact lens on the eye of the patient. The YAG or Argon laser is focused on the cyst or lesion and multiple short bursts of light destroy the abnormal tissue.

Coding Clarification
Destruction of a lesion of iris by cauterization, cryotherapy, or photocoagulation is reported with 12.41.

Documentation Tip
Review the documentation carefully to determine the operative method used (e.g., excisional, nonexcisional) because code selection is based on the site and surgical technique.

12.42   Excision of lesion of iris

Description
The physician places a contact lens on the patient's eye to help direct the laser's beam. The excision of a full-thickness piece of the iris is usually accomplished with an argon laser. The physician uses the "chipping away technique" until the iris is penetrated for the excision.

Coding Clarification
Do not use 12.42 to report biopsy of iris; rather use 12.22.

Documentation Tip
Review the documentation carefully to determine the operative method used (e.g., excisional,

08-16

nonexcisional) because code selection is based on the site and surgical technique.

12.43 Destruction of lesion of ciliary body, nonexcisional

Description
The physician places a special contact lens on the eye of the patient. The YAG or Argon laser is focused on the cyst or lesion and multiple short bursts of light destroy the abnormal tissue.

Coding Clarification
Do not report 12.43 when a lesion of ciliary body is excised. Lesions of the iris and ciliary body may be removed by excision or using a nonexcisional process such as by cryotherapy. Subdivisions for subcategory 12.4 are based on the site and surgical technique.

Documentation Tip
Review the documentation carefully to determine the operative method used (e.g., excisional, nonexcisional) because code selection is based on the site and surgical technique.

12.44 Excision of lesion of ciliary body

Description
The physician places a contact lens on the patient's eye to help direct the laser's beam. The excision of a full-thickness piece of the iris is usually accomplished with an argon laser. The physician uses the "chipping away technique" until the iris is penetrated for the excision.

Coding Clarification
Lesions of the iris and ciliary body may be removed by excision or using a nonexcisional process such as by cryotherapy. Subdivisions for subcategory 12.4 are based on the site and surgical technique.

Documentation Tip
Review the documentation carefully to determine the operative method used (e.g., excisional, nonexcisional) because code selection is based on the site and surgical technique.

With cyclectomy the burn is deeper, going through the iris into the ciliary body.

12.5 Facilitation of intraocular circulation

Description
To facilitate intraocular circulation, there are a number of different procedures physicians can perform. Subcategory 12.5 provides five subclassification codes specific to a type of operation and one "other" subclassification for any procedure not having its own code for facilitation of intraocular pressure.

Coding Clarification
If only a goniopuncture is performed, report 12.51 Goniopuncture without goniotomy. For a goniotomy alone, report 12.52 Goniotomy without goniopuncture.

If the surgeon performs a goniotomy with a goniopuncture, report 12.53 Goniotomy with goniopuncture.

Trabeculoplasty by laser used to treat open-angle glaucoma is coded with 12.59 Other facilitation of intraocular circulation.

12.51 Goniopuncture without goniotomy

Description
Goniopuncture is a procedure in which the physician makes a puncture in the filtration angle of the anterior chamber, usually to treat congenital glaucoma. The physician inserts a knife blade through the clear cornea within the limbus, across the anterior chamber of the eye and through the opposite corneoscleral wall.

Coding Clarification
If only a goniopuncture is performed, report 12.51 Goniopuncture without goniotomy. If the surgeon performs a goniotomy with a goniopuncture, report 12.53 Goniotomy with goniopuncture.

12.52 Goniotomy without goniopuncture

Description
Goniotomy is a surgical opening of the trabecular meshwork by way of the angle of the anterior chamber of the eye typically to treat congenital glaucoma. Essentially, the operation attempts to restore the natural pathway of aqueous drainage by incising the angle tissue. The physician uses a lens called a goniolens to view the structures of the front part of the eye (i.e., anterior chamber). The physician enters the anterior chamber through an incision in the scleral-corneal juncture (the limbus) and cuts with a gonioknife to open the angle of the ring of meshlike tissue at the iris-scleral junction (the trabecular meshwork). An opening is made in the trabecular meshwork. The new opening improves drainage of fluids in the eye.

Coding Clarification
De Vincentiis operation and Barkan's operation are both goniotomy procedures.

If the surgeon performs a goniotomy with a goniopuncture, report 12.53 Goniotomy with goniopuncture.

12.53 Goniotomy with goniopuncture

Description
To improve drainage of fluids in the eye, the physician enters the anterior chamber through an

08–16

incision in the scleral-corneal juncture (the limbus) and cuts with a gonioknife. The blade passes across the anterior to the opposite limbus and a sweep is made to open the angle of the ring of meshlike tissue at the iris-scleral junction (the trabecular meshwork) of the opposite portion of the eye.

Coding Clarification
De Vincentiis operation and Barkan's operation are both goniotomy procedures.

Goniotomy is a surgical opening of the trabecular meshwork by way of the angle of the anterior chamber of the eye to treat congenital glaucoma.

Goniopuncture is a procedure in which a puncture is made in the filtration angle, usually to treat congenital glaucoma.

12.54   Trabeculotomy ab externo

Description
To improve drainage of fluids in the eye, the physician inserts a special tool called a trabeculotome into Schlemm's canal and rotates it into the anterior chamber to open the ring of meshlike tissue (the trabecular meshwork). The name (ab) externo, meaning outside the eye, refers to the surgical approach from outside the eye cutting toward the anterior chamber.

12.55   Cyclodialysis

Description
The ciliary body supplies the anterior chamber with aqueous humor. In cases where high intraocular pressure cannot otherwise be controlled, portions of the ciliary body are destroyed to reduce the production of aqueous humor. The physician makes an incision in the conjunctiva and sclera in the pars plana adjacent to the portion of ciliary body to be treated. The physician passes a spatula through the incision and into the suprachoroidal space of the anterior chamber. The spatula separates the ciliary body from the scleral spur. This may result in a lowering of intraocular pressure by a decrease in aqueous humor formation from the now detached ciliary body or by increasing uveovascular scleral outflow of aqueous. The physician closes the incision with layered sutures and may restore the intraocular pressure with an anterior and/or posterior injection. A topical antibiotic or pressure patch may be applied.

12.59   Other facilitation of intraocular circulation

Description
The physician uses an argon laser to selectively burn the ring of meshlike tissue at the iris-scleral junction (the trabecular meshwork) to improve the drainage of fluids in the anterior segment. After applying a topical anesthetic, the physician places a special

contact lens on the eye of the patient. This lens allows the physician to view the angle structures of the eye and the trabecular network while using the laser. The argon or YAG laser is focused on the iris and multiple short bursts of laser light create holes in the iris. This procedure allows fluids in the eye to pass from behind the iris through the openings into the space between the iris and the cornea (the anterior chamber). This lowers intraocular pressure.

Coding Clarification
Though the trabecular network runs along the entire circumference of the iris, the physician burns holes in only a portion of that circumference during a single treatment session. In this way, the physician can measure the effects of each treatment upon the eye's fluid and suspend treatment once the proper intraocular fluid pressure is reached. No incision is made during this procedure.

12.6   Scleral fistulization

Description
Do not use a code from subcategory 12.6 to report exploratory sclerotomy (12.89).

12.61   Trephination of sclera with iridectomy

Description
To create a new pathway for fluids in the eye, the physician makes an incision in the conjunctiva near the limbus (the corneal-scleral juncture). Using a trephine to remove a circular portion of sclera and iris, the physician creates a collection area to improve the flow of aqueous. The physician closes the incision with sutures and may restore the intraocular pressure with an injection of water or saline. A topical antibiotic or pressure patch may be applied.

Coding Clarification
Report exploratory sclerotomy with 12.89.

Documentation Tip
This procedure may also be referred to as an Elliot operation.

12.62   Thermocauterization of sclera with iridectomy

Description
To create a new pathway for fluids in the eye, the physician makes an incision in the conjunctiva near the limbus (the corneal-scleral juncture) and destroys a portion of the sclera and iris by burning it with a hot probe to create a collection area to improve the flow of aqueous. The physician closes the incision with sutures and may restore the intraocular pressure with an injection of water or saline. A topical antibiotic or pressure patch may be applied.

Coding Clarification
Report exploratory sclerotomy with 12.89.

● New Code   ▲ Revised Code   ▶◀ Revised Text   © 2010 Ingenix

Documentation Tip

This procedure may also be documented in the medical record using the following terminology:

- Iridectomy with scleral thermocauterization
- Scheie operation
- Scheie cautery of sclera
- Scheie sclerostomy
- Thermosclerectomy

12.63   Iridencleisis and iridotasis

Description

To improve the flow of fluids in the eye, the physician places an ocular speculum in the patient's eye, and accesses the anterior chamber through an incision through the limbus (the corneal-scleral juncture). The physician creates a permanent drainage route through the anterior chamber by taking a piece of iris tissue clipped with scleral scissors from the edge of the iris and wedging it into an incision in the iris so that it will act as a wick to draw aqueous from one side of the iris to the other. The physician closes the incision with sutures and may restore the intraocular pressure with an injection of water or saline. A topical antibiotic or pressure patch may be applied.

Coding Clarification

Report exploratory sclerotomy with 12.89.

12.64   Trabeculectomy ab externo

Description

The physician places an ocular speculum in the patient's eye, and accesses the anterior chamber through an incision through the limbus (the corneal-scleral juncture).To promote better drainage of fluid, the physician removes a partial thickness portion of the ring of meshlike tissue at the iris-scleral junction (the trabecular meshwork). A scleral trap door is left open so that aqueous may flow through the new channel into the space between the conjunctiva and the sclera or cornea (bleb). The physician closes the incision with sutures and may restore the intraocular pressure with an injection of water or saline. A topical antibiotic or pressure patch may be applied.

Coding Clarification

This procedure is performed in absence of previous surgery or as a repeated surgery where adhesions are reduced. The adhesions may also have been caused by trauma.

Report exploratory sclerotomy with 12.89.

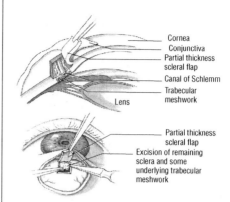

Cornea
Conjunctiva
Partial thickness scleral flap
Canal of Schlemm
Trabecular meshwork
Lens
Partial thickness scleral flap
Excision of remaining sclera and some underlying trabecular meshwork

12.65   Other scleral fistulization with iridectomy

Description

To improve the flow of aqueous, the physician makes an incision in the conjunctiva near the limbus (the corneal-scleral juncture). By using a punch or scleral scissors, the physician removes a portion of sclera and iris, creating a collection area for fluids in the anterior chamber. Various methods of sclerectomy include Lindner's, LaGrange, Knapp's, Holth's, and Herbert's operations. The physician closes the incision with sutures and may restore the intraocular pressure with an injection of water or saline. A topical antibiotic or pressure patch may be applied

Coding Clarification

In a scleral fistulization procedure with iridectomy a valve may be inserted (12.65). Code 12.65 also is the appropriate code if the operative report states the patient had a laser iridectomy for the purpose of re-establishing communication between posterior and anterior chambers in the treatment of angle-closure glaucoma.

Report exploratory sclerotomy with 12.89.

12.66   Postoperative revision of scleral fistulization procedure

Description

To improve the flow of fluids in the eye, the physician places an ocular speculum in the patient's eye, and accesses the anterior chamber through an incision through the limbus (the corneal-scleral juncture). The physician creates a permanent drainage route through the anterior chamber by taking a piece of iris tissue clipped with scleral scissors from the edge of the iris and wedging it into an incision in the iris so that it will act as a wick to draw aqueous from one side of the iris to the other. The physician closes the incision with sutures and may restore the intraocular pressure with an

08-16

injection of water or saline. A topical antibiotic or pressure patch may be applied.

Alternately, the physician may reexplore an eye wound that is the site of previous surgery to revise post-operative defects. The physician uses a number of techniques, based on the wound and previous surgery. Surgery may be major or minor.

Coding Clarification
Revision of filtering bleb is reported with 12.66 but this code is not used to report repair of fistula (12.82).

Report exploratory sclerotomy with 12.89.

Coding Guidance
   AHA: 2Q, '01, 16

12.69   Other scleral fistulizing procedure

Description
The physician performs fistulization of the sclera through the ciliary body for glaucoma. To create a new pathway for fluids in the eye, the physician makes an incision in the sclera through the ciliary body of the eye. Using an operating microscope, a small conjunctival flap is first created. One technique uses an electromagnetic plasma ablation device to create a tiny pit through the sclera. The metal tip creates a pore or a tract through the ciliary body into the posterior chamber of the eye beginning at the base of the scleral pit created above. The conjunctival flap is reattached.

Coding Clarification
In advanced cases of glaucoma, the physician can use a laser, cryotherapy probe, or other method to burn a hole in the ciliary body, reducing the production of aqueous humour and providing an opening to reduce the intraocular pressure.

A revision is done if the first procedure is unsuccessful and must be altered.

Report exploratory sclerotomy with 12.89.

12.7   Other procedures for relief of elevated intraocular pressure

Description
Subcategory 12.7 includes a variety of procedures to treat glaucoma including cyclodiathermy, cyclocryotherapy, and cyclophotocoagulation.

12.71   Cyclodiathermy

Description
The ciliary body supplies the anterior chamber with aqueous humor. In cases where high intraocular pressure cannot otherwise be controlled, portions of the ciliary body are destroyed to reduce the production of aqueous humor. The physician makes an incision in the conjunctiva and through the sclera

in the pars plana opposite the site of the ciliary body to be treated. The physician uses a heat probe (diathermy) to burn holes in the ciliary body. The physician closes the incision with layered sutures and may restore the intraocular pressure with an anterior and/or posterior injection. A topical antibiotic or pressure patch may be applied.

Coding Clarification
Cyclodiathermy is diathermy applied to the sclera adjacent to the ciliary body in the treatment of glaucoma. Diathermy heats the body tissues using electromagnetic radiation, electric currents, or ultrasonic waves.

Documentation Tip
Review the documentation carefully to determine the method of treatment used in order to ensure accurate code assignment from subcategory 12.7.

12.72   Cyclocryotherapy

Description
The ciliary body supplies the anterior chamber with aqueous humor. In cases where high intraocular pressure cannot otherwise be controlled, portions of the ciliary body are destroyed to reduce the production of aqueous humor. The physician applies a freezing probe to the sclera over the ciliary body with the purpose of destroying the ciliary process. This is especially useful in aphakic patients.

Coding Clarification
Subcategory 12.7 includes a variety of procedures to treat glaucoma including cyclodiathermy, cyclocryotherapy, and cyclophotocoagulation.

Documentation Tip
Review the documentation carefully to determine the method of treatment used and to ensure accurate code assignment.

12.73   Cyclophotocoagulation

Description
In this procedure, the ciliary body of the eye, which creates aqueous fluid, is treated with laser to decrease production of aqueous. This in turn reduces pressure inside the eye. In cases where high intraocular pressure cannot otherwise be controlled, portions of the ciliary body are destroyed to reduce the production of aqueous humor. Endoscopic cyclophotocoagulation is done on the ciliary body and may be accomplished by different methods.

With the pupil dilated, a limbal incision is made and any posterior synechiae are lysed. Viscoelastic material is injected under the iris to partially fill and expand the ciliary sulcus. The endoscopic cyclophotocoagulation probe is inserted under the iris. The probe allows simultaneous visualization with the photocoagulation. Approximately half the circumference of the ciliary body is treated through

● New Code   ▲ Revised Code   ▶◀ Revised Text   © 2010 Ingenix

the first limbal incision. Another incision is made 180 degrees from the first and the other half of the ciliary body circumference is treated. The viscoelastic material is removed by irrigation and aspiration and the wounds are closed.

Coding Clarification

For aphakic or pseudoaphakic eyes, the procedure is done from a posterior pars plana approach to reach the ciliary body and a limited vitrectomy is also performed.

Documentation Tip

Subcategory 12.7 includes a variety of procedures to treat glaucoma including cyclodiathermy, cyclocryotherapy, and cyclophotocoagulation. Review the documentation carefully to determine the method of treatment used and to ensure accurate code assignment.

12.74   Diminution of ciliary body, not otherwise specified

Description

In this procedure, the ciliary body of the eye, which creates aqueous fluid, is treated to modify the aqueous drainage or secretion, which in turn reduces pressure inside the eye.

Coding Clarification

Endoscopic treatment of the ciliary body may be accomplished by different methods, so careful review of the documentation is necessary to determine the method of treatment used and to ensure accurate code assignment.

Use this code to report destruction or diminution of the ciliary body that is not more specifically described by other codes within subcategory 12.7.

Documentation Tip

The medical record may contain the following terminology to describe procedures that are correctly reported with 12.74:

* Cycloanemization
* Destruction of ciliary body

12.79   Other glaucoma procedures

Description

Several glaucoma treatment methods are available including drugs, laser surgery, and incisional surgery. The type of glaucoma determines the appropriate method. Drugs and most laser surgeries modify the aqueous drainage and secretion systems, while incisional surgeries or glaucoma drainage implant devices (e.g., tube shunts) create a new drainage system. Careful review of the documentation is necessary to determine the method used and to ensure accurate code assignment.

Coding Clarification

The following procedures are appropriately reported with 12.79:

* Injection of sympathetic ciliary ganglion
* Catheter insertion into the anterior chamber of the eye for permanent drainage
* Opticociliary neurectomy
* Filtering operation for glaucoma
* Release of intraocular pressure
* Suture lysis required following trabeculectomy

Coding Guidance

AHA: 2Q, '98, 16

12.8   Operations on sclera

Description

The sclera, coming from the Greek word for "hard," is the tough, white, outer coat of the eye. Current surgical techniques for scleral defects include fascia lata, corneal, and scleral grafts.

Subcategory 12.8 consists of nine subclassification codes for operations on the sclera to include suture, repair, revision, excision, destruction, reinforcement, and other operations. All codes within this subcategory require fourth-digit subclassification to provide specificity to site and/or procedure.

Coding Clarification

Subcategory 12.8 is not used to report operations on the sclera associated with retinal reattachment (14.41-14.59), scleral fistulization (12.61-12.69), or postoperative revision of scleral fistulization procedure (12.66).

12.81   Suture of laceration of sclera

Description

An ocular speculum may be placed in the patient's eye. The physician irrigates the laceration and sutures the conjunctival wound. Alternately, the perforating tear in the cornea and any tear in the sclera may be sutured and the cornea may be splinted using a soft contact lens bandage. An air or saline injection may be required to reestablish proper ocular pressure in the anterior chamber. Topical antibiotic or a pressure patch may be applied.

Coding Clarification

Suture of sclera with synchronous repair of conjunctiva is reported with 12.81.

Documentation Tip

Review the operative documentation carefully. If the laceration involves the uveal tissue (the vascular layer beneath the sclera), injured tissue may be cut out or repositioned before the uvea is sutured and the sclera and conjunctiva may each require separate closure.

08-16

12.82   Repair of scleral fistula

Description
The physician reexplores an eye wound that is the site of previous surgery to revise postoperative defects. The physician uses a number of techniques, based on the wound and previous surgery. Surgery may be major or minor.

Coding Clarification
Do not use 12.82 to report postoperative revision of scleral fistulization procedure; rather, use 12.66.

Other procedures that are correctly reported with 12.82 include the following:

*   Repair of corneal or scleral filtering bleb by excision

*   Repair of filtering bleb by scleroplasty

12.83   Revision of operative wound of anterior segment, not elsewhere classified

Description
The physician reexplores an eye wound that is the site of previous surgery to revise postoperative defects. The physician uses a number of techniques, based on the wound and previous surgery. Surgery may be major or minor.

Coding Clarification
Do not use 12.83 to report postoperative revision of scleral fistulization procedure (12.66).

12.84   Excision or destruction of lesion of sclera

Description
To remove a scleral lesion, the physician cuts through the thin, transparent conjunctiva and then snips the lesion with scleral scissors. The scleral and conjunctival wounds may not require sutures. The physician then applies antibiotic ointment and possibly a 24-hour pressure patch.

In an alternate technique, a lesion on the conjunctiva and adjacent superficial sclera is excised with a curette. Typically, no sutures are required.

12.85   Repair of scleral staphyloma with graft

Description
A staphyloma is a bulging protrusion of the vascular coating of the eyeball (uvea) into a thin, stretched portion of the sclera. To repair the staphyloma, the physician places an ocular speculum in the patient's eye, and makes an incision in the conjunctiva and sclera over the site of a staphyloma. The physician excises the full-thickness staphyloma. A graft usually indicates that size of the staphyloma required that donor sclera tissue be grafted across the wound. The physician uses sutures or tissue glue in the layered repair. Antibiotic ointment and a patch may be applied.

12.85   Repair of scleral staphyloma with graft

To repair the stretched, bulging sclera and uveal tissue, the physician places an ocular speculum in the patient's eye, makes an incision in the conjunctiva and sclera over the site, and excises the full-thickness staphyloma. A piece of stretched sclera may also be removed. The physician uses sutures or tissue glue in the layered repair. Antibiotic ointment and a patch may be applied.

12.87   Scleral reinforcement with graft

Description
Graft materials used in surgical management of scleral defects include fascia lata, cornea, and sclera. To reinforce thin or weakened sclera, the physician places a patch of donor sclera over the weakened area. The physician uses sutures or tissue glue in the layered repair. Antibiotic ointment and a patch may be applied.

12.88   Other scleral reinforcement

Description
To repair a thin, weakened sclera, the physician places an ocular speculum in the patient's eye, and makes an incision in the conjunctiva and sclera over the site of the defect. The sclera is cinched and overlapped for reinforcement. Antibiotic ointment and a patch may be applied.

Coding Clarification
For scleral reinforcement involving a graft, report 12.87.

12.89   Other operations on sclera

Description
The physician performs an exploration of sclera by incision to confirm the presence or absence of suprachoroidal hemorrhage. In cases of corneal perforation, the physician may seal the perforation with tissue adhesive after debriding the outermost layer of cornea (the epithelium) to enhance adhesion. The patient may be fitted with a soft contact lens to be worn during the healing process. Antibiotic ointment is applied. A pressure patch may be used.

Coding Clarification
Code 12.89 is also used to appropriately report the following procedures:

*   Anterior or posterior exploratory sclerotomy

*   Incision and drainage of scleral abscess

*   Corneoscleral trephination

*   Scleroplasty

Documentation Tip
Tissue glue, which acts as a suture in laceration repairs of the cornea and/or sclera, is also called medical adhesive or Cyanoacrylate tissue adhesive.

● New Code   ▲ Revised Code   ▶◀ Revised Text   © 2010 Ingenix

12.9 Other operations on iris, ciliary body, and anterior chamber

Coding Clarification
Use this subcategory to report paracentesis of anterior chamber and injection of air, liquid, or medication into anterior chamber.

Subcategory 12.9 is not used to report diagnostic aspiration (12.21) or removal or destruction of growth from the anterior chamber with iridectomy (12.41-12.42).

12.91 Therapeutic evacuation of anterior chamber

Description
The overall pressure of aqueous is constant in a healthy eye's anterior chamber, but too little or too much fluid can cause permanent damage. Surgical management includes various methods. In one method, the physician aspirates aqueous from between the iris and the cornea (the anterior chamber) with a needle in what is typically called an "anterior chamber tap." The needle usually enters the anterior chamber through the corneal-scleral juncture (the limbus). In some cases, the removal of the fluid is diagnostic; however, if ocular pressure is high, a therapeutic removal of aqueous may be performed.

In other techniques, the physician aspirates the gel-like vitreous that has pushed forward into the anterior chamber. Using a needle that enters the eye through the limbus, the prolapsed vitreous is removed. In the same manner, the physician also uses a needle to aspirate a blood clot or blood from the anterior chamber. In some cases, the physician may inject saline to flush the blood and make its removal easier. Topical antibiotic or a patch may be applied when the procedure is complete.

Coding Clarification
Use this code to report paracentesis of the anterior chamber; however, 12.91 is not used to report diagnostic aspiration (12.21).

12.92 Injection into anterior chamber

Description
To manage the aqueous pressure, the physician administers a needle injection of air, liquid, or medication to the anterior of the eye. The needle may enter the anterior segment through the cornea or through the limbus (the juncture of the cornea and sclera).

Coding Guidance
AHA: J-A, '84, 1

12.93 Removal or destruction of epithelial downgrowth from anterior chamber

Description
Epithelial downgrowth describes the improper healing of surgical or traumatic wound to the cornea. The outer lining of the cornea (the epithelium) fails to close properly over the wound, instead growing around to the inner side of the cornea, sometimes continuing its growth to other structures of the eye. Disturbances in intraocular pressure and vision can result.

The physician retracts the patient's eyelids with an ocular speculum. The physician locates and excises the extraneous epithelial tissue from where it has spread into the anterior chamber. The original wound may be trimmed and revised. Injections may be required to restore pressure in the anterior or posterior chambers. The procedure may require sutures or tissue glue, antibiotic ointment, or a pressure patch.

Coding Clarification
To report removal of epithelial downgrowth with iridectomy, use 12.41 or 12.42.

12.97 Other operations on iris

Description
This code is used to report other procedures on the iris that are not more precisely documented or described by other codes in the 12.9 subcategory, including anterior iris sweep and reopening of the iris in the anterior chambers.

12.98 Other operations on ciliary body

Description
This code is used to report other procedures on the ciliary body that are not more precisely documented or described by other codes in the 12.9 subcategory.

12.99 Other operations on anterior chamber

Description
The physician reexplores an eye wound that is the site of previous surgery to revise postoperative defects. The physician uses a number of techniques, based on the wound and previous surgery. Surgery may be major or minor.

Coding Clarification
Removal of a Krupin-Denver valve is an anterior chamber procedure reported with 12.99.

Coding Guidance
AHA: M-J, '85, 15

08-16

13   Operations on lens

Description
The majority of codes under category 13 (subcategories 1-6 and 8) are for removal of a lens. The codes for lens removal are based on the type of extraction. Subcategories also exist under category 13 for foreign body removal from lens and insertion of a lens. Foreign body from the lens, subcategory 13.0, has fourth digits based on whether a magnet was used in the extraction.

Coding Clarification
Use 13.9 for the fixation procedure (i.e., placement of sutures to hold the lens in place) for a displaced or loose intraocular lens.

If the physician has also performed any synchronous insertion of a lens, an additional code is necessary.

Any mechanical vitrectomy is coded separately but installation of Helon in the anterior chamber is not.

Documentation Tip
Review the physician documentation to determine whether a magnet was used in the extraction prior to final code selection in order to avoid the use of a "not otherwise specified" code.

13.0   Removal of foreign body from lens

Description
Subcategories exist under category 13 for foreign body removal from lens and insertion of a lens. Foreign body from the lens, subcategory 13.0, has fourth digits based on whether a magnet was used in the extraction.

Coding Clarification
Codes from subcategory 13.0 are not used to report removal of pseudophakos; report a code from subcategory 13.8.

13.00   Removal of foreign body from lens, not otherwise specified

Description
The physician removes a foreign body, intraocular, from the anterior chamber of the eye or lens. The physician makes a small incision in the connective tissue between the cornea and the sclera (the limbus) and retrieves the foreign body through the opening with intraocular forceps or another small instrument. The incision is sutured. The physician applies an antibiotic ointment. Sometimes a pressure patch is placed on the eye for 24 to 48 hours.

Coding Clarification
Generally, foreign bodies that pierce the lens are self-sealing and removal is not attempted.

13.01   Removal of foreign body from lens with use of magnet

Description
The physician will use an electromagnetic or magnetic probe to retrieve a metallic foreign body from the lens. In the anterior route, the physician first dilates the patient's pupil. In a series of moves aligning the magnet to the metallic foreign body, the physician draws the foreign body to the front of the eye and around the lens into the anterior chamber. The physician makes an incision in the connective tissue between the cornea and the sclera (the limbus) and retrieves the foreign body.

In the posterior route, the physician makes a small incision in the conjunctiva over the site of the foreign body. A magnet is applied and the foreign body removed. The incision is repaired, and an injection may be required to reestablish proper fluid levels in the anterior and/or posterior chamber of the eye. A broad spectrum antibiotic or a pressure patch may be applied.

Coding Clarification
Among the tools common to this procedure are Gruning's, Haab's, or Hirschberg's magnets.

Generally, foreign bodies that pierce the lens are self-sealing and removal is not attempted.

Documentation Tip
Review the physician documentation to determine whether a magnet was used in the extraction prior to final code selection.

13.02   Removal of foreign body from lens without use of magnet

Description
The physician will use intraocular forceps to retrieve the nonmetallic foreign body from the lens. The physician makes an incision through the conjunctiva overlying the site of the foreign body. The foreign body is retrieved with intraocular forceps. The incision is repaired with layered closure, and an injection may be required to reestablish proper fluid levels in the anterior or posterior chambers of eye. A broad spectrum antibiotic or a pressure patch may be applied.

Coding Clarification
Nonmetallic foreign bodies in the vitreous or retina may be removed through a pars plana approach.

Documentation Tip
Review the physician documentation to determine whether a magnet was used in the extraction prior to final code selection.

08-16

13.1 Intracapsular extraction of lens

Description
Subcategory 13.1 is used to report cataract or lens extraction that is not further specified, cryoextraction of lens, and erysiphake extraction of a cataract.

Coding Clarification
Also code any synchronous insertion of pseudophakos (13.71).

Coding Guidance
AHA: S-O, '85, 6

13.11 Intracapsular extraction of lens by temporal inferior route

Description
Intracapsular cataract extraction (ICCE) is when the lens and capsule are removed intact. The physician extracts the lens and capsule using an anterior approach through the outer side of the eyeball. In general, the physician inserts an ocular speculum and an incision is made. The physician may close the incision with sutures and may restore the intraocular pressure with an injection of water or saline. A topical antibiotic or pressure patch may be applied.

13.19 Other intracapsular extraction of lens

Description
In an intracapsular cataract extraction (ICCE), the lens and capsule are removed intact. For other intracapsular lens extraction procedures that are not more specifically described by other codes in subcategory 13.1, report 13.19.

Coding Clarification
Code 13.19 is also used to report extraction of lens or cataract extraction, cryoextraction of lens, and erysiphake extraction of cataract that are not further specified in the documentation.

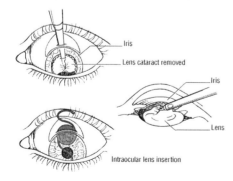

Iris
Lens cataract removed
Iris
Lens
Intraocular lens insertion

13.2 Extracapsular extraction of lens by linear extraction technique

Description
In an extracapsular cataract extraction (ECCE), the anterior shell and the nucleus of the lens capsule are both removed, leaving the posterior shell of the lens capsule in place. The physician inserts a lid speculum between the patient's eyelids and makes an incision in the corneal-scleral juncture (the limbus). To enhance the flow of fluids in the eye, the physician may punch a hole in the iris. Using a method other than aspiration or phacofragmentation, the physician removes the lens in parts: first the anterior lens, then the inner, hard nucleus. The clear, posterior capsule remains. The physician may close the incision with sutures and may restore the intraocular pressure with an injection of water or saline. A topical antibiotic or pressure patch may be applied.

Coding Clarification
There are two main types of extracapsular surgery:

• Phacoemulsification involves the use of a machine with an ultrasonic handpiece with a titanium or steel tip.

• Conventional extracapsular cataract extraction (ECCE) involves manual extraction of the lens through an incision made in the cornea or sclera.

Insertion of pseudophakos (13.71) is reported in addition to extracapsular lens extraction when performed synchronously.

Documentation Tip
Code 13.2 is used to report excision of the lens by means of a linear incision; review the documentation carefully to determine the surgical approach used.

Coding Guidance
AHA: S-O, '85, 6

13.3 Extracapsular extraction of lens by simple aspiration (and irrigation) technique

Description
In an extracapsular cataract extraction (ECCE), the anterior shell and the nucleus of the lens capsule are both removed, leaving the posterior shell of the lens capsule in place. A local anesthetic is injected into the periorbital area. The physician makes a small horizontal incision where the cornea and sclera meet. The anterior wall of the lens is incised. A probe attached to an irrigating/aspirating machine is inserted into the lens and the lens is destroyed and sucked away. The physician may close the incision with sutures and may restore the intraocular pressure with an injection of water or saline. A topical antibiotic or pressure patch may be applied.

08–16

Coding Clarification
Used 13.3 to report irrigation of a traumatic cataract.

Insertion of pseudophakos (13.71) is reported in addition to extracapsular lens extraction when performed synchronously.

Coding Guidance
AHA: S-O, '85, 6

13.4 Extracapsular extraction of lens by fragmentation and aspiration technique

Coding Guidance
AHA: S-O, '85, 6

13.41 Phacoemulsification and aspiration of cataract

Description
Phacoemulsification is a procedure in which ultrasonic vibrations are used to break the cataract into smaller fragments. These fragments are then aspirated from the eye using the same instrumentation.

The physician creates an opening in the thin membrane surrounding the cataract and places the phacoemulsification tip into the substance of the cataract. The "phaco" aspect of the procedure is used to remove the denser central nucleus of the cataract. Alternately, the physician may elect to create grooves in the cataract and subsequently break the cataract into smaller pieces using the phacoemulsification tip and a second instrument passed through a smaller incision. The physician uses irrigation and suction to remove the once hard nucleus, now liquefied. Once the denser central nucleus of the cataract has been removed, the peripheral cortex of the cataract, which is softer, is removed using an irrigation/aspiration handpiece. The posterior of the lens capsule is left intact to support the intraocular lens (IOL) implant. The area is irrigated and aspirated and an intraocular lens (IOL) is inserted. The physician may close the incision with sutures or may design a sutureless "self-sealing" incision. The physician may restore the intraocular pressure with an injection of water or saline. A topical antibiotic or pressure patch may be applied.

Coding Clarification
The same type of irrigating/aspirating machine used for extracapsular surgery is used for phacofragmentation, but in this case the probe is a needle that vibrates 40,000 times per second (phacofragmentation), or sound waves (phacoemulsification, ultrasound) that break up the lens.

Standard phacoemulsification may be performed if the lens capsule is intact and sufficient zonular support remains.

Coding Guidance
AHA: 3Q, '96, 4; 1Q, '94, 16

13.42 Mechanical phacofragmentation and aspiration of cataract by posterior route

Description
To remove a cataract obstructing the view of the retina during retinal surgery, or to remove a piece of natural lens retained following cataract surgery, the physician makes an incision in the conjunctiva, sclera, and choroid of the pars plana. The physician approaches the lens capsule from behind. If the entire lens is being removed, the wall of the posterior lens capsule is removed and a small suction device is inserted into the lens. The lens material is aspirated and the physician irrigates the area during aspiration. If a retained portion of the lens is removed, a portion of the clear gel in the back of the eye may be removed as well (vitrectomy). The incision is closed with layered sutures. The physician may restore anterior or posterior intraocular pressure with an injection of water or saline. A topical antibiotic or pressure patch may be applied.

Coding Clarification
Code also any synchronous vitrectomy (14.74).

Insertion of pseudophakos (13.71) is reported in addition to extracapsular lens extraction when performed synchronously.

13.43 Mechanical phacofragmentation and other aspiration of cataract

Description
A relatively simple cataract surgery technique uses mechanical phacofragmentation (MPF). Mechanical phacofragmentation ensures cataract removal through small tunnel incisions. The physician makes an incision in the cornea or the pars plana. The anterior wall of the lens is cut out.

The same type of irrigating/aspirating machine used for extracapsular surgery is used for phacofragmentation, but in this case the probe is a needle that vibrates 40,000 times per second that breaks up the lens. The physician uses irrigation and suction to remove the once hard nucleus, now liquefied by mechanical or sound vibrations. The physician may close the incision with sutures or may design a sutureless "self-sealing" incision. The physician may restore the intraocular pressure with an injection of water or saline. A topical antibiotic or pressure patch may be applied.

● New Code ▲ Revised Code ▶◀ Revised Text © 2010 Ingenix

08-16

Coding Clarification
The NASA-McGannon cataract fragmentor is a mechanical phacofragmentor powered by compressed air.

The phacosection, or the mechanical phacofragmentation (MPFC), is done through scleral tunnels or pockets.

Insertion of pseudophakos (13.71) is reported in addition to extracapsular lens extraction when performed synchronously.

13.5   Other extracapsular extraction of lens
Coding Clarification
Code also any synchronous insertion of pseudophakos (13.71).

Coding Guidance
   AHA: S-O, '85, 6

13.51   Extracapsular extraction of lens by temporal inferior route

Description
In extracapsular cataract extraction (ECCE), the anterior shell and the nucleus of the lens capsule are both removed, leaving the posterior shell of the lens capsule in place. The physician inserts a lid speculum between the patient's eyelids and makes an incision in the corneal-scleral juncture (the limbus). To enhance the flow of fluids in the eye, the physician may punch a hole in the iris. Using a method other than aspiration or phacofragmentation, the physician removes the lens in parts: first the anterior lens, then the inner, hard nucleus. The clear, posterior capsule remains. The physician may close the incision with sutures and may restore the intraocular pressure with an injection of water or saline. A topical antibiotic or pressure patch may be applied.

Documentation Tip
Review the documentation carefully to determine the surgical approach used in order to ensure accurate coding.

13.59   Other extracapsular extraction of lens

Description
In extracapsular cataract extraction (ECCE), the anterior shell and the nucleus of the lens capsule are removed, leaving the posterior shell of the lens capsule intact. Code 13.59 is used to report extracapsular lens extractions that are not more precisely described by other codes in this subcategory.

Documentation Tip
Review documentation carefully to determine the surgical technique used in order to ensure accurate coding.

Coding Scenario
The physician performed an extracapsular cataract extraction and inserted an intraocular lens to treat a patient with a senile cataract of the left eye.

   Code Assignment:

   366.10   Unspecified senile cataract
   13.59   Other extracapsular extraction of lens
   13.71   Insertion of intraocular lens prosthesis at time of cataract extraction, one-stage

13.6   Other cataract extraction
Description
Subcategory 13.6 is used to report other methods of cataract extractions that are not described by other codes in this subcategory. It includes subclassification codes for discission, excision, and mechanical fragmentation of the secondary membrane, as well as a code for other cataract extraction.

Coding Clarification
Code in addition any synchronous insertion of pseudophakos (13.71) performed.

Coding Guidance
   AHA: S-O, '85, 6

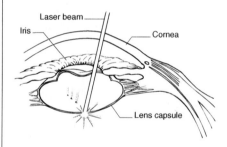

13.64   Discission of secondary membrane (after cataract)

Description
The patient initially had extracapsular cataract surgery in which the posterior shell of the lens was not removed from the eye. But the capsule and/or the membrane adjacent to it (the anterior hyaloid) has since become opaque and must be opened in this new surgery.

After placing an ocular speculum in the patient's eye, the pupil is dilated. The physician inserts a small needle, a Ziegler or Wheeler knife, or special scissors into the corneal-scleral juncture (the limbus) and advances it to the edge of the capsule and through to the membrane, cutting a flap in the opaque membrane in the field of vision. The physician maneuvers the instrument around any artificial lens. No tissue is removed from the eye; the

08–16

flap simply opens a window of vision. The physician may close the incision with sutures and may restore the intraocular pressure with an injection of water or saline. A topical antibiotic or pressure patch may be applied.

In an alternate technique, after a topical anesthetic is applied to the eye, the pupil is dilated and a number of YAG laser shots are focused to a point on the capsule, cutting it. Bursts from the YAG open a flap in the capsule, resulting in immediate improvement in vision. Multiple sessions may be needed to create an adequate opening in the lens capsule.

13.65   Excision of secondary membrane (after cataract)

Description
The patient initially had extracapsular cataract surgery, in which the posterior shell of the lens was not removed from the eye. The capsule and/or the membrane adjacent to it (the anterior hyaloid) has since become opaque and must be removed in this new surgery. The physician inserts an ocular speculum into the patient's orbit, and makes an incision at the juncture of the cornea and sclera (the limbus). A small cutting needle and suction device (an irrigating cystotome) is inserted to chip away the posterior lens capsule. In some cases, the iris must be cut or a piece of iris removed to access the lens capsule. The adjacent membrane (the anterior hyaloid) may also removed. The physician irrigates the area during aspiration. The physician may close the incision with sutures and may restore the intraocular pressure with an injection of water or saline. A topical antibiotic or pressure patch may be applied.

Coding Clarification
Capsulectomy is reported with 13.65.

13.66   Mechanical fragmentation of secondary membrane (after cataract)

Description
The patient initially had extracapsular cataract surgery in which the posterior shell of the lens was not removed from the eye. The capsule and/or the membrane adjacent to it (the anterior hyaloid) has since become opaque and must be opened in this new surgery. After placing an ocular speculum in the patient's eye, the pupil is dilated. The physician inserts a small needle, a Ziegler or Wheeler knife, or special scissors into the corneal-scleral juncture (the limbus) and advances it to the edge of the capsule and through to the membrane, cutting a flap in the opaque membrane in the field of vision. The physician maneuvers the instrument around any artificial lens. No tissue is removed from the eye; the

flap simply opens a window of vision. The physician may close the incision with sutures and may restore the intraocular pressure with an injection of water or saline. A topical antibiotic or pressure patch may be applied.

13.69   Other cataract extraction

Description
Code 13.69 is used to report other cataract extractions that are not more precisely described by other codes in this subcategory, including congenital cataract discission.

13.7   Insertion of prosthetic lens (pseudophakos)

Description
Pseudophakia is the presence of an intraocular lens after cataract extraction. Codes from subcategory 13.7 report various methods of insertion of an ocular implant following lens extractions.

Coding Clarification
Implantation of intraocular telescope prosthesis is not reported with a code from subcategory 13.7; report 13.91.

Coding Guidance
   AHA: J-A, '84, 1

13.70   Insertion of pseudophakos, not otherwise specified

Description
Physicians use many variations of surgical approaches and techniques for intraocular lens insertion. Code 13.70 is used to report insertions that are not more precisely described by other codes in this subcategory.

For an anterior lens, the physician places an intraocular lens in the fluid-filled space between the iris and cornea (the anterior chamber). The haptics (securing attachments) of the implant are wedged between the iris and cornea, fixating the implant so it cannot move. For a posterior lens, the physician injects a bubble of air into the anterior chamber to protect the cornea. The physician then guides the intraocular implant into the eye. The haptics lodge into the ciliary sulcus or the lens capsule. The physician may close the incision with sutures and may restore the intraocular pressure with an injection of water or saline. A topical antibiotic or pressure patch may be applied.

Documentation Tip
Review the operative documentation for specific information regarding the procedure prior to final code selection in order to avoid improper use of the "not otherwise specified" code.

08–16

● New Code   ▲ Revised Code   ▶◀ Revised Text   © 2010 Ingenix

13.71 Insertion of intraocular lens prosthesis at time of cataract extraction, one-stage

Description

Cataract surgery involves using a microincision procedure, phacoemulsification, and a foldable lens implant. Surgeons use many variations case-by-case based on the type of cataract being removed.

In one variation, the physician performs a complex extracapsular cataract removal with insertion of an intraocular lens prosthesis in a one-stage procedure. A local anesthetic is injected into the periorbital area. The physician makes a small horizontal incision where the cornea and sclera meet and, upon entering the eye through the incision, gently opens the front of the capsule and removes the hard center, or nucleus, of the lens. Standard phacoemulsification may be performed if the lens capsule is intact and sufficient support remains. Using a microscope, the physician suctions out the soft lens cortex, leaving the capsule in place. The area is irrigated and aspirated and an intraocular lens (IOL) (plastic disc that replaces the natural lens) is inserted. The physician sutures the incision and instills antibiotic ointment and applies an eye patch. A metal shield is secured over the eye with tape.

In an extracapsular cataract extraction (ECCE), the anterior shell and the nucleus of the lens capsule are both removed, leaving the posterior shell of the lens capsule in place. Using a cutting and suction or ultrasonic device, the physician removes the lens; the clear, posterior capsule remains. The physician then guides the intraocular implant into the eye. The haptics (securing attachments) lodge into the ciliary sulcus or the lens capsule, occupying the exact position of the original cataract.

In capsulorrhexis, after fragmentation of the cataract nucleus with an ultrasonic oscillating probe, the phaco probe is inserted into the eye and the cataract is suctioned out through an irrigation-aspiration probe. An IOL is inserted once all of the material is removed. Suture fixation is done if capsular and zonular supports are insufficient and the angle is minimally damaged.

Another variation is intracapsular cataract extraction (ICCE) in which the lens and capsule are removed intact. The physician inserts a surgical instrument filled with coolant (cryoprobe) into the anterior chamber; the lens adheres to the cryoprobe as it freezes, and when the cryoprobe is removed, the lens comes with it. The physician places an intraocular lens in the anterior chamber and the haptics (securing attachments) of the implant are wedged in the anterior chamber, fixating the implant so it cannot move.

In all variations, the physician may close the incision with sutures and may restore the

intraocular pressure with an injection of water or saline. A topical antibiotic or pressure patch may be applied.

Coding Clarification

Code also synchronous extraction of cataract (13.11-13.69).

Coding Guidance

AHA: 3Q, '96, 4

13.72 Secondary insertion of intraocular lens prosthesis

Description

The physician inserts an ocular speculum. An incision is made in the corneal-scleral juncture (the limbus). For an anterior lens, the physician places an intraocular lens in the fluid-filled space between the iris and cornea (the anterior chamber). The optic, or center, of the implant lies just in front of the pupil and the haptics (securing attachments) of the implant are wedged between the iris and cornea, fixating the implant so it cannot move. For a posterior lens, the physician injects a bubble of air into the anterior chamber to protect the cornea. The physician then guides the intraocular implant into the eye. The haptics lodge into the ciliary sulcus or the lens capsule. The physician may close the incision with sutures and may restore the intraocular pressure with an injection of water or saline. A topical antibiotic or pressure patch may be applied.

Coding Clarification

Use 13.72 to report insertion of a secondary intraocular lens implant, not associated with concurrent cataract removal.

In cases that cannot be corrected with a single implant, the physician may elect to implant a secondary piggyback lens.

13.8 Removal of implanted lens

Description

Early models of intraocular lens (IOL) implants sometimes cause irritation in the patient's eye. They can also become dislocated. Here, the physician removes the problematic lens. For anterior IOL, the physician removes an intraocular lens in the fluid-filled space between the iris and cornea (the anterior chamber). For posterior IOL, the physician injects a bubble of air into the anterior chamber through a syringe to protect the cornea. The physician then removes the intraocular implant in the eye. The physician may close the incision with sutures and may restore the intraocular pressure with an injection of water or saline. A topical antibiotic or pressure patch may be applied.

08-16

Coding Clarification
Report 13.8 for removal of pseudophakos.

13.9   Other operations on lens

Coding Clarification
Subcategory 13.9 is not used to report secondary insertion of ocular implants; report 16.61.

Coding Guidance
AHA: 1Q, '00, 9; 4Q, '06, 123

13.90   Operation on lens, not elsewhere classified

Description
Code 13.90 is used to report procedures on the lens that are not more precisely described by other codes in the subcategory, such as when an intraocular lens (IOL) implant becomes dislocated and the physician adjusts the problematic lens. The physician adjusts the artificial lens so that the attachments (haptics) of the implant are secured.

13.91   Implantation of ultracolor telescrope prosthesis

Description
The physician implants an intraocular, miniature telescope. An intraocular telescope is typically inserted to improve visual function in patients with severe visual impairment due to end-stage, age-related macular degeneration (AMD).

Coding Clarification
Code 13.91 includes removal of lens by any method.

If a secondary insertion of an ocular implant is performed, report 16.61.

---

14   Operations on retina, choroid, vitreous, and posterior chamber

Description
Category 14 includes procedures on four different areas of the eye: retina, choroid, vitreous, and posterior chamber. The retina may tear or detach. ICD-9-CM provides different subcategory codes depending on diagnosis. Method (e.g., diathermy, cryotherapy, photocoagulation) is also an issue in choosing the correct code in this category.

Coding Clarification
Except for subcategories 6 and 9, every subcategory for this group of operations requires a fourth digit.

Subcategory 14.2 Destruction of lesion of retina and choroid, has seven fourth digit subclassification codes from which to choose based on how the lesion was destroyed, as well as one code for other and unspecified technique.

The method (e.g., diathermy, cryotherapy, photocoagulation) is a factor in choosing the fourth

digit from category 14.3 Repair of retinal tear and 14.5 Other repair of retinal detachment.

When the surgeon removes vitreous, different approaches and techniques may be used. Subcategory 14.7 Operations on vitreous, has subdivisions for these options.

If the surgeon also performs a membrane peeling in conjunction with a vitrectomy, assign 14.74 for the vitrectomy and 14.9 for the peeling. Any drainage of subretinal fluid and gas/fluid exchange is considered integral to these procedures and therefore not coded separately.

If the operative report indicates the insertion of a Ganciclovir implant, report 14.79 and 99.29.

Documentation Tip
As previously indicated for foreign body removals of other sites, check the documentation for use of a magnet in the extraction of a posterior chamber foreign body, as fourth digits in subcategory 14.0 are dependent on this information.

Anterior approach: The surgeon approaches the vitreous from the front of the iris.

Open sky technique: A 180-degree incision is made at the limbus.

Posterior approach: The surgeon approaches the vitreous from behind the iris.

Mechanical vitrectomy: The vitreous is extracted by cutting and suction, using tools such as a rotoextractor or a vitreous infusion suction cutter (VISC).

14.0   Removal of foreign body from posterior segment of eye

Description
Codes from subcategory 14.0 are used to report other foreign body removal procedures of the posterior segment that are not more precisely described by other codes in this subcategory.

Coding Clarification
Report removal of surgically implanted material with 14.6.

Documentation Tip
Review the documentation for specific information regarding the procedure prior to final code selection in order to ensure accurate code assignment.

14.00   Removal of foreign body from posterior segment of eye, not otherwise specified

Description
This code is reported when the documentation does not further specify the foreign body removal from the posterior segment of the eye.

● New Code   ▲ Revised Code   ▶◀ Revised Text   © 2010 Ingenix

Documentation Tip
Review the operative documentation for specific
information regarding the procedure prior to final
code selection in order to avoid improper use of the
"not otherwise specified" code.

14.01   Removal of foreign body from posterior segment of eye with use of magnet

Description
Diagnostic tests locate the foreign body before
surgery is attempted. The physician will use an
electromagnetic or magnetic probe to retrieve a
metallic foreign body from the area behind the lens
(the posterior segment). In the anterior route, the
physician first dilates the patient's pupil. In a series
of moves aligning the magnet to the metallic foreign
body, the physician draws the foreign body to the
front of the eye and around the lens into the anterior
chamber. The physician then makes an incision in
the connective tissue between the cornea and the
sclera (the limbus) and retrieves the foreign body. In
the posterior route, the physician makes a small
incision in the conjunctiva over the site of the foreign
body. A magnet is applied and the foreign body
removed. The incision from either is repaired, and an
injection may be required to reestablish proper fluid
levels in the anterior and/or posterior chamber of
the eye. A broad spectrum antibiotic or a pressure
patch may be applied. Among the tools common to
this procedure are Gruning's, Haab's, or
Hirschberg's magnets.

14.02   Removal of foreign body from posterior segment of eye without use of magnet

Description
Diagnostic tests locate the foreign body before
surgery is attempted. The physician will use
intraocular forceps to retrieve the nonmetallic
foreign body from the area behind the lens (the
posterior segment). The physician makes an incision
through the conjunctiva overlying the site of the
foreign body. The foreign body is retrieved with
intraocular forceps. Nonmetallic foreign bodies in
the vitreous or retina may be removed through a
pars plana approach. Either incision is repaired with
layered closure and an injection may be required to
reestablish proper fluid levels in the anterior
segment.

14.1   Diagnostic procedures on retina, choroid, vitreous, and posterior chamber

Description
Codes in this subcategory report other diagnostic
procedures of the retina, choroids, vitreous, and
posterior chamber that are not more precisely
described by other codes in this subcategory.

Documentation Tip
Review the documentation for specific information
regarding the procedure prior to final code selection
in order to ensure accurate code assignment.

14.11   Diagnostic aspiration of vitreous

Description
The physician inserts a needle into the posterior
chamber through the pars plana to aspirate
vitreous. Sometimes a posterior sclerotomy is made
to release the fluid. When this is done, the physician
extracts the vitreous, using a mechanical cutting
and suctioning process that may involve a special
instrument like a rotoextractor or vitreous infusion
suction cutter (VICS). Once completed, the incision
is repaired with sutures. Intraocular pressure may
be adjusted with an injection. A pressure patch may
be applied.

Documentation Tip
This extraction of the vitreous is often called a
vitreous chamber tap in operative reports.

14.19   Other diagnostic procedures on retina, choroid, vitreous, and posterior chamber

Description
Code 14.19 is used to report diagnostic procedures
on the retina, choriod, vitreous, or posterior
chamber of the eye that are not more precisely
described by other codes in this subcategory. This
code is also reported when the documentation does
not further specify the procedure.

Documentation Tip
Review the documentation for specific information
regarding the procedure prior to final code selection
in order to avoid improper use of the "not otherwise
specified" code.

14.2   Destruction of lesion of retina and choroid

Description
Codes in the 14.2 subcategory are used to report
destruction of damaged retina and choroid tissue,
such as chorioretinopathy or an isolated
chorioretinal lesion.

Coding Clarification
Do not use 14.2x for repair of the retina; report
14.31-14.59.

Documentation Tip
This procedure may also be documented as
retinochoroid.

14.21   Destruction of chorioretinal lesion by diathermy

Description
The physician destroys a lesion of the retina by heat
(diathermy). The physician explores the sclera and

08–16

stay sutures are placed under the involved rectus muscles so the eye can be rotated to expose the area to be treated. Sometimes, a rectus muscle is temporarily detached to permit adequate exposure. Diathermy is performed without entering the posterior chamber; the probe is pressed against the sclera overlying the site of the retinal lesion until it is destroyed or until the session is completed. Any muscle incision is repaired and any stay sutures removed. A topical antibiotic or pressure patch may be applied.

Coding Clarification
Diathermy may be performed with a laser light or xenon arc aimed through a dilated pupil without an incision. This procedure is often referred to as "scattered destruction." Multiple sessions may be required.

Documentation Tip
A chorioretinal lesion is a lesion relating to the choroid coat of the eye and the retina.

14.22 Destruction of chorioretinal lesion by cryotherapy

Description
The physician destroys a lesion of the retina by freezing (cryotherapy). The physician explores the sclera and stay sutures are placed under the involved rectus muscles so the eye can be rotated to expose the area to be treated. Sometimes, a rectus muscle is temporarily detached to permit adequate exposure. Cryotherapy is performed without entering the posterior chamber. The probe is pressed against the sclera overlying the site of the retinal lesion until it is destroyed or until the session is complete. Any muscle incision is repaired and any stay sutures removed. A topical antibiotic or pressure patch may be applied.

14.23 Destruction of chorioretinal lesion by xenon arc photocoagulation

Description
The physician destroys a lesion of the retina using a xenon arc. After the patient's eye has been dilated, the physician places a special contact on the eye of the patient. At least 500 Xenon arc burns are applied. This procedure is often referred to as "scattered destruction." Multiple sessions may be required. Photocoagulation by xenon arc is performed without entering the posterior chamber; the destructive light beam is guided through the contact and to the retinal lesion, which is destroyed in one session or in a series of sessions. A topical antibiotic or pressure patch may be applied.

14.24 Destruction of chorioretinal lesion by laser photocoagulation

Description
The physician destroys a lesion of the retina using laser photocoagulation. After the patient's eye has been dilated, the physician places a special contact on the eye of the patient. Photocoagulation by laser is performed without entering the posterior chamber; the destructive light beam is guided through the contact and to the retinal lesion, which is destroyed in one session or in a series of sessions. A topical antibiotic or pressure patch may be applied.

14.25 Destruction of chorioretinal lesion by photocoagulation of unspecified type

Description
The physician destroys a lesion of the retina using photocoagulation that is not further specified. The physician destroys lesions on the retina by photocoagulation using various methods including freezing (cryotherapy), heat (diathermy), or laser light or xenon arc.

14.26 Destruction of chorioretinal lesion by radiation therapy

Description
The physician treats a malignancy, tumor, growth, or edema by various methods of radiation therapy.

14.27 Destruction of chorioretinal lesion by implantation of radiation source

Description
The physician treats a malignancy, tumor, growth, or edema by exposing it to a radioactive implant. The plaque-like implant is secured with sutures to the sclera overlying the site of a malignancy. At a future time, the physician recovers the implant. The incision is repaired. An antibiotic ointment and pressure patch may be applied.

14.29 Other destruction of chorioretinal lesion

Description
Code 14.29 is used to report destruction of a chorioretinal lesion that is not more precisely described by other codes in this subcategory. This code is also reported when the documentation does not further specify the destruction procedure.

Coding Clarification
Report 14.29 for destruction of a lesion of the retina and choroid that is not otherwise specified.

Documentation Tip
Review the documentation for specific information regarding the procedure prior to final code selection in order to avoid improper use of the "not otherwise specified" code.

08-16

14.3 Repair of retinal tear

Description
Subcategory 14.3 is used to report repairs of a retinal defect.

Coding Clarification
Do not use 14.3x to report repair of a retinal detachment; report 14.41-14.59.

14.31 Repair of retinal tear by diathermy

Description
When the retina detaches, it separates from its nourishing blood supply and falls into the posterior cavity of the eye. Loss of vision results. The physician secures a degenerating retina by diathermy, where heat is used to seal the retinal tissue to the back of the eye. The physician explores the sclera and stay sutures are placed under the involved rectus muscles so the eye can be rotated to expose the area to be treated. Sometimes a rectus muscle is temporarily detached to permit adequate exposure. Diathermy is performed without entering the posterior chamber; a probe is pressed against the sclera overlying the site of the retinal defect, sealing it against the choroid.

14.32 Repair of retinal tear by cryotherapy

Description
When the retina detaches, it separates from its nourishing blood supply and falls into the posterior cavity of the eye. Loss of vision results. The physician reattaches the retina by freezing (cryotherapy) and thus sealing the retinal tissue to the back of the eye. The physician explores the sclera and stay sutures are placed under the involved rectus muscles so the eye can be rotated to expose the area to be treated. Sometimes, a rectus muscle is temporarily detached to permit adequate exposure. Cryotherapy is performed without entering the posterior chamber; a probe is pressed against the sclera overlying the site of the retinal defect, sealing it against the choroid. If subretinal fluid must be drained, the physician makes an incision in the sclera (sclerotomy) to permit access to the middle layer of the eye's shell (the choroid), which is perforated so that fluid drains out. Any incisions are repaired with layered closures. Injections may be required to reestablish proper intraocular pressure. A topical antibiotic or pressure patch may be applied.

14.33 Repair of retinal tear by xenon arc photocoagulation

Description
Using a xenon arc that goes through a dilated pupil without an incision, the physician burns spots at the site of the retinal weakness to seal the retina into place against the choroid (vascular, middle layer of the eye's shell). No incision is made. Multiple sessions may be required.

In alternate techniques, the physician makes three small incisions in the eyeball and uses xenon arc photocoagulation to treat retinal problems, like retinal detachments, diabetic retinopathy, or retinal holes. Injections may be required to reestablish the intraocular pressure. A topical antibiotic or pressure patch may be applied.

14.34 Repair of retinal tear by laser photocoagulation

Description
When the retina detaches, it separates from its nourishing blood supply and falls into the posterior cavity of the eye. Loss of vision results. Using a laser light that goes through a dilated pupil without an incision, the physician burns spots at the site of the retinal detachment or retinal tear to seal the retina back into place. With focal endolaser photocoagulation, the physician uses a laser to treat minor retinal disorders. If the physician performs endolaser panretinal photocoagulation, a stronger laser treats larger retinal problems, like retinal detachments, diabetic retinopathy, or retinal holes. If subretinal fluid must be drained, the physician cuts through the conjunctiva and into the sclera (sclerotomy) to access the choroid, which is perforated so that fluid drains out. Any incisions are repaired with layered closures. Injections may be required to reestablish the intraocular pressure. A topical antibiotic or pressure patch may be applied.

Coding Guidance
AHA: 1Q, '94, 17

14.35 Repair of retinal tear by photocoagulation of unspecified type

Description
Code 14.35 is used to report repairs of a retinal tear when the documentation does not further specify the photocoagulation procedure.

Documentation Tip
Review the documentation for specific information regarding the procedure prior to final code selection in order to avoid improper use of the "not otherwise specified" code.

14.39 Other repair of retinal tear

Description
Code 14.39 reports repair of a retinal tear or defect that is not more precisely described by other codes in this subcategory. This code is also reported when the documentation does not further specify the destruction procedure.

08-16

Documentation Tip
Review the documentation for specific information regarding the procedure prior to final code selection in order to ensure appropriate code assignment.

14.4 Repair of retinal detachment with scleral buckling and implant

Description
Codes within this subcategory report the placement of material around the eye to indent the sclera and close a hole or tear, or to reduce vitreous traction. Fourth-digit specificity is required.

14.41 Scleral buckling with implant

Description
The physician explores the sclera to locate the site overlying a retinal detachment. Stay sutures are placed under involved rectus muscles so the eye may be exposed to the area that will be treated. The physician treats the retinal tear externally, by placing a cold or hot probe over the scleral and depressing it. The burn seals the choroid to the retina at the site of the tear. The physician cuts a groove in the sclera and mattress sutures are placed across this incision. Any subretinal fluid is drained. A Silastic band is laid in the scleral bed and sutured in place. Sometimes, a silicone sponge is placed under the band. Additional cryotherapy or photocoagulation may be accomplished at this time. When the tear has been adequately repaired and supported, the rectus muscle sutures are removed.

Coding Clarification
Because the band is implanted at the same time as the retinal detachment, it is considered an implant and is therefore an inherent part of the scleral buckle procedure.

Coding Guidance
　　AHA: 3Q, '96, 6

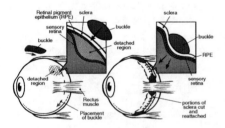

14.49 Other scleral buckling

Description
Code 14.49 is used to report scleral buckling with air tamponade, resection of sclera, or vitrectomy.

Documentation Tip
Review the documentation for specific information regarding the procedure prior to final code selection in order to ensure appropriate code assignment.

Coding Guidance
　　AHA: 1Q, '94, 16, 17

14.5 Other repair of retinal detachment

Description
When the retina detaches, it separates from its nourishing blood supply and falls into the posterior cavity of the eye. Loss of vision results. All codes within subcategory 14.5 include repair of retinal detachment with drainage.

14.51 Repair of retinal detachment with diathermy

Description
The physician reattaches the retina by diathermy, where heat is used to seal the retinal tissue to the back of the eye. Diathermy is performed without entering the posterior chamber. The probe is pressed against the sclera overlying the site of the retinal defect, sealing it against the choroid. Any incisions are repaired with layered closures. Injections may be required to reestablish proper intraocular pressure. A topical antibiotic or pressure patch may be applied.

14.52 Repair of retinal detachment with cryotherapy

Description
The physician reattaches the retina by freezing (cryotherapy) and thus sealing the retinal tissue to the back of the eye. The physician explores the sclera and stay sutures are placed under the involved rectus muscles so the eye can be rotated to expose the area to be treated. Sometimes, a rectus muscle is temporarily detached to permit adequate exposure. Cryotherapy is performed without entering the posterior chamber. A probe is pressed against the sclera overlying the site of the retinal defect, sealing it against the choroid. If subretinal fluid must be drained, the physician makes an incision in the sclera (sclerotomy) to permit access to the middle layer of the eye's shell (the choroid), which is perforated so that fluid drains out. Any incisions are repaired with layered closures. Injections may be required to reestablish proper intraocular pressure. A topical antibiotic or pressure patch may be applied.

14.53 Repair of retinal detachment with xenon arc photocoagulation

Description
The physician uses a xenon arc, which goes through a dilated pupil without an incision, to seal the retina back into place against the choroid (vascular, middle

08–16

layer of the eye's shell). If subretinal fluid must be drained, the physician cuts through the conjunctiva and into the sclera (sclerotomy) to access the choroid, which is perforated so that fluid drains out. Any incisions are repaired with layered closures. Injections may be required to reestablish the intraocular pressure. A topical antibiotic or pressure patch may be applied.

14.54 Repair of retinal detachment with laser photocoagulation

Description
The vitreous is the clear gel filling the posterior cavity of the eyeball. The physician applies a special contact lens to the cornea to better visualize the back of the eye. With focal endolaser photocoagulation, the physician uses a laser to treat minor retinal disorders. In endolaser panretinal photocoagulation, a stronger laser treats larger retinal problems, such as retinal detachments, diabetic retinopathy, or retinal holes. The cannulas are extracted and the incisions repaired with layered closures. Injections may be required to reestablish the intraocular pressure. A topical antibiotic or pressure patch may be applied. The physician may also use an alternate technique in which a laser is used. The light goes through a dilated pupil without an incision to burn spots at the site of the retinal detachment or retinal tear and seals the retina back into place against the choroid (vascular, middle layer of the eye's shell).

Coding Guidance
   AHA: N-D, '87, 10

14.55 Repair of retinal detachment with photocoagulation of unspecified type

Description
Use 14.55 to report photocoagulation repair of a retinal tear that is not more precisely described in the documentation and when the physician does not further specify the photocoagulation procedure.

Documentation Tip
Review the documentation for specific information regarding the procedure prior to final code selection in order to ensure accurate code assignment.

14.59 Other repair of retinal detachment

Description
Code 14.59 is used to report other retinal detachment repairs, such as when the physician uses a needle to inject expandable gas into the eye to flatten the retinal tear, and applies laser or cryotherapy to seal the retinal tear. Also report 14.59 for cases in which the physician performs a reoperative procedure to correct retinal detachment following failed surgery.

Coding Clarification
This procedure is used to report pneumatic retinopexy.

14.6 Removal of surgically implanted material from posterior segment of eye

Description
Several different techniques may be used to remove implanted material from the posterior segment of the eye. Typically, the physician inserts an ocular speculum and removes a previously implanted extraocular tube, reservoir, buckle, or other prosthetic device from the eye. To release the tension in a previously placed scleral buckle, the physician makes an incision in the conjunctiva and sclera, adjusts the buckle, and repairs the surgical wound with sutures.

In cases in which the physician removes an extracapsular IOL from the eye, an incision is made in the pars plana near the site of an intraocular lens that has fallen into the posterior segment of the eye. The physician may close the incision with sutures and may restore the intraocular pressure with an injection of water or saline. A topical antibiotic or pressure patch may be applied.

14.7 Operations on vitreous

Description
The vitreous of the eye is the semifluid substance that comprises the contents of the eyeball core. Subcategory 14.7 reports procedures on the vitreous of the eye including the removal of all or part of the eyeball fluid via the anterior segment and removal of abnormal tissue in the eyeball fluid to control fiberoptic overgrowth in severe intraocular injury.

14.71 Removal of vitreous, anterior approach

Description
The physician inserts a needle at the limbus or through the cornea and passes the needle to the back of the anterior segment where a portion of displaced vitreous humor is aspirated. If most or all of the vitreous is extracted, the physician extracts the vitreous using a mechanical cutting and suctioning process that may involve a special instrument like a rotoextractor or vitreous infusion suction cutter (VICS). In either case, the aspirated vitreous is usually replaced by an injection of a vitreous substitute or aqueous. Expandable gas may also be injected into the eye to flatten out the retinal detachment against the choroids and the physician also removes any vitreous opacity or vitreous traction. The lens may also be removed if it interferes with the physician's view of the retina or if the lens is in the way of the removal of scar tissue. Any incisions may be repaired with sutures.

08–16

Antibiotic ointment and a pressure patch may be applied.

Coding Clarification
Code 14.71 is used to report the removal of vitreous via an anterior approach with replacement.

Do not use this code to report mechanical vitrectomy by posterior approach; report 14.74.

Documentation Tip
This procedure may also be documented as open sky technique.

14.72   Other removal of vitreous

Description
The physician performs aspiration of vitreous by posterior sclerotomy. Once completed, the incision is repaired with sutures. Intraocular pressure may be adjusted with an injection. A pressure patch may be applied.

Documentation Tip
This is often called a vitreous chamber tap in operative reports.

14.73   Mechanical vitrectomy by anterior approach

Description
The physician extracts the vitreous, using a mechanical cutting and suctioning process that may involve a special instrument like a rotoextractor or vitreous infusion suction cutter (VICS). In either case, the aspirated vitreous is usually replaced by an injection of a vitreous substitute or aqueous. Any incision is closed with sutures.

Coding Clarification
Code 14.73 is not used to report membrane peeling, which is done at the junction between the cornea and the sclera, in front of the iris. This is reported with 14.9.

Coding Guidance
    AHA: 3Q, '96, 4, 5

14.74   Other mechanical vitrectomy

Description
This code is reported when the physician performs a mechanical vitrectomy using a posterior approach. Code 14.74 is also used to report other procedures that are not more precisely described by other codes in subcategory 14.7.

▶Report code 14.74 for the pars plana vitrectomy for the removal of retroprosthetic membrane.◀

Coding Guidance
    AHA: ▶2Q, '10, 5◀

Coding Clarification
▶Assign code 14.74 for pars plana vitrectomy to remove retroprosthetic membrane. Code also 99.29

Injection or infusion of other therapeutic or prophylactic substance, for the intravitreal injection of Avastin, as appropriate.◀

Do not use this code to report the removal of vitreous via an anterior approach; report 14.71.

Documentation Tip
Review the documentation for specific information regarding the procedure prior to final code selection in order to ensure accurate code assignment.

Coding Guidance
    AHA: 3Q, '96, 5; ▶2Q, '10, 5◀

14.75   Injection of vitreous substitute

Description
The physician inserts a syringe in the pars plana to inject a material like healon or silicone. The injection may be required to replace vitreous and to restore intraocular pressure.

Coding Clarification
Do not use 14.75 to report injection of a vitreous substitute that is associated with removal; report 14.71-14.72.

Use 14.75 to report a fluid/gas exchange.

Code 14.75 is not used to report insertion of an intravitreal Ganciclovir implant because Ganciclovir is not a vitreous substitute.

Coding Guidance
    AHA: 1Q, '94, 17; 3Q, '96, 4-5; 1Q, '98, 6

14.79   Other operations on vitreous

Description
Report 14.79 for other procedures on the vitreous that are not more precisely described by other codes in subcategory 14.7 and when the physician does not further specify the vitreous procedure. One example is when the physician implants an intravitreal drug delivery system to provide consistent delivery of a drug to an area of the eye affected by disease. In another case, the physician uses a YAG laser to cut vitreous strands, adhesions, or opacities that obstruct the patient's vision.

Documentation Tip
Review the documentation for specific information regarding the procedure prior to final code selection in order to ensure accurate code assignment.

Coding Guidance
    AHA: 1Q, '98, 6; 1Q, '99, 11; 3Q, '99, 12

14.9   Other operations on retina, choroid, and posterior chamber

Description
Report 14.9 for other procedures on the retina, choriod, and posterior chamber that are not more

● New Code   ▲ Revised Code   ▶◀ Revised Text   © 2010 Ingenix

precisely described by other codes in this subcategory. This code is also used when the physician does not further specify the procedure performed.

Documentation Tip
Review the documentation for specific information regarding the procedure prior to final code selection in order to ensure accurate code assignment.

Coding Guidance
AHA: 5th issue, '93, 13; 3Q, '96, 4, 5

---

15   Operations on extraocular muscles

Description
Category 15 has subcategories differentiating operations on one extraocular muscle and two or more extraocular muscles. Other criteria for code selection include the specific procedure performed and whether the surgery involved the temporary detachment of the extraocular muscle from the globe.

Coding Clarification
If the procedure was performed on one muscle in one or both eyes, use 15.11. If the procedure is performed on two or more muscles in one or both eyes, use 15.3. For bilateral procedures, report the code twice.

Documentation Tip
A resection shortens the muscle; in a recession, the muscle is lengthened.

15.0   Diagnostic procedures on extraocular muscles or tendons

Description
The extraocular muscles of the eye control the positioning of the eyes and coordinate movement between the eyes. There are two horizontal muscles and four vertical muscles in each eye.

Although many diagnostic techniques are useful, only direct intraoperative inspection can accurately diagnose a slipped extraocular muscle. The physician may diagnose a lost muscle using a traditional conjunctival approach, by an external orbitotomy, or by an endoscopic transnasal approach.

15.01   Biopsy of extraocular muscle or tendon

Description
A speculum is placed in the patient's eye and the physician makes incisions in the conjunctiva and sclera to expose the muscle. The extraocular muscle to be biopsied is isolated and the physician uses a scalpel to remove a small portion of the muscle. The excision will not affect overall action of the eye muscle. The surgical wound is closed with sutures.

15.09   Other diagnostic procedures on extraocular muscles and tendons

Description
Code 15.09 is used to report other diagnostic procedures on the extraocular muscles and tendons that are not more precisely described by other codes in subcategory 15.0.

Documentation Tip
Review the documentation for specific information regarding the procedure prior to final code selection in order to ensure accurate code assignment.

15.1   Operations on one extraocular muscle involving temporary detachment from globe

Description
Codes in subcategory 15.1 describe procedures such as detachment of exterior eye muscle with posterior reattachment or forward reattachment to correct strabismus and advancement of one extraocular muscle. Strabismus, or crooked eyes, is ocular misalignment due to extraocular muscle imbalance. Strabismus is an imbalance in the muscles of the eyeball that control eyeball movement. Surgery can sometimes correct this imbalance. Pseudoesotropia is a common condition that presents with the false appearance of strabismus.

15.11   Recession of one extraocular muscle

Description
The physician performs a posterior reattachment to correct strabismus. A speculum is placed in the patient's eye (no previous surgery). The physician makes incisions in the conjunctiva about 7 mm posterior to the juncture of the sclera and cornea (the limbus) in the superior nasal quadrant of the globe. An incision is made to expose the sclera and a muscle hook is used to engage the superior rectus muscle initially. The tendon of the superior oblique may be located about 12 mm behind the medial or nasal edge of the insertion of the superior rectus. The physician repairs or recesses the superior oblique muscle. The operative wound is closed with layered sutures.

During strabismus surgery, the extraocular muscle is isolated far posterior to its insertion. The borders or edges of the muscle are sutured to the eye far back of the insertion in what is commonly called the Faden procedure. The surgical wound is closed with sutures. This posterior fixation suturing technique on an extraocular muscle is done in conjunction with the strabismus surgery.

Coding Clarification
Assign 15.11 when the procedure is performed on one muscle in one or both eyes. Code 15.11 is assigned since the operation is on only one muscle in each eye.

08-16

Assign 15.3 when the procedure is performed on two or more muscles in one or both eyes.

Coding Scenario

A patient was admitted for surgery to correct mechanical strabismus. A speculum was placed in the patient's eye and the physician made incisions in the conjunctiva. The extraocular muscle was isolated and weakened by recession. The muscle was secured with sutures and the operative wound closed.

Code Assignment:

378.60 Unspecified mechanical strabismus
15.11 Recession of one extraocular muscle

Coding Guidance

AHA: 3Q, '96, 3, 4

15.12 Advancement of one extraocular muscle

Description

In this procedure, one detached muscle is treated with forward reattachment to correct strabismus. The physician makes incisions in the conjunctiva at the juncture of the sclera and cornea (the limbus) or in the cul-de-sac (Parks incision). Radial relaxing incisions in the conjunctiva are made and the muscle (medial or lateral rectus) is isolated with a muscle hook. The muscle is then strengthened by resection (removal of a measured segment) or weakened by recession (retroplacement of the muscle attachment). The muscles are secured with sutures. The operative wound is closed with sutures.

15.13 Resection of one extraocular muscle

Description

A speculum is placed in the patient's eye (no previous surgery). The physician makes incisions in the conjunctiva about 7 mm posterior to the juncture of the sclera and cornea (the limbus) in the superior nasal quadrant of the globe. An incision is made to expose the sclera and a muscle hook is used to engage the muscle initially. The physician resects the muscle. The operative wound is closed with layered sutures.

15.19 Other operations on one extraocular muscle involving temporary detachment from globe

Description

A speculum is placed in the patient's eye, and the physician makes incisions in the conjunctiva at the

juncture of the sclera and cornea (the limbus) to expose the muscle. The extraocular muscle or muscles involved are isolated, and the primary strabismus surgery is performed such as recession or resection on horizontal or vertical muscles, or any procedure on oblique extraocular muscles.

Coding Clarification

Do not use 15.19 to report transposition of muscle; report 15.5.

15.2 Other operations on one extraocular muscle

Description

Codes from subcategory 15.2 are used to report other procedures on one extraocular muscle that are not more precisely described by other codes from category 15.

Coding Clarification

There is an increased level of difficulty involved in both the planning and performance of strabismus surgery on an eye with previous surgery or injury. The extraocular muscles involved are isolated, and the appropriate definitive primary strabismus surgery is performed (e.g., recession or resection on horizontal or vertical muscles).

Documentation Tip

Review the documentation for specific information regarding the procedure prior to final code selection in order to ensure accurate code assignment.

15.21 Lengthening procedure on one extraocular muscle

Description

Strabismus surgery typically involves lengthening or shortening eye muscles, which includes detachment of one of the muscles attached to the eye and reattachment of the muscle further back on the eye, or excising a portion of the distal end of the muscle and subsequent reattachment to the eye. Adjustable suture eye muscle surgery allows postoperative adjustment to improve the final outcome in some cases. The procedure is completed and the eye is patched. Approximately 24 hours later, the patch is removed and ocular alignment is evaluated. The treated muscle can then be tightened or loosened based on the alignment of the eyes. The adjustable suture is permanently tied once the desired alignment is achieved and the procedure is complete.

 ● New Code　▲ Revised Code　▶◀ Revised Text　© 2010 Ingenix

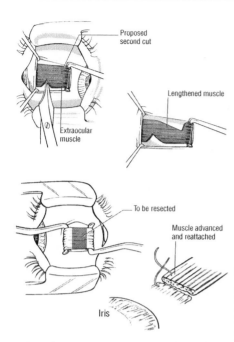

Proposed second cut

Lengthened muscle

Extraocular muscle

To be resected

Muscle advanced and reattached

Iris

15.22 Shortening procedure on one extraocular muscle

Description
Strabismus surgery typically involves lengthening or shortening eye muscles. It may involve detachment of one of the muscles attached to the eye and reattachment of the muscle further back on the eye, or excising a portion of the distal end of the muscle and subsequent reattachment to the eye. Adjustable suture eye muscle surgery allows postoperative adjustment to improve the final outcome in some cases. The procedure is completed and the eye is patched. Approximately 24 hours later, the patch is removed and ocular alignment is evaluated. The treated muscle can then be tightened or loosened based on the alignment of the eyes. The adjustable suture is permanently tied once the desired alignment is achieved, and the procedure is complete.

15.29 Other operations on one extraocular muscle

Description
Code 15.29 is used to report other procedures on one extraocular muscle that are not more precisely described by other codes in subcategory 15.2.

Coding Clarification
There is an increased level of difficulty involved in both the planning and performance of strabismus surgery on an eye that has had previous surgery or injury. The extraocular muscles involved are isolated, and the appropriate definitive primary

strabismus surgery is performed (e.g., recession or resection on horizontal or vertical muscles).

Documentation Tip
Review the documentation for specific information regarding the procedure prior to final code selection in order to ensure accurate code assignment.

15.3 Operations on two or more extraocular muscles involving temporary detachment from globe, one or both eyes

Description
A speculum is placed in the patient's eye (no previous surgery). The physician makes incisions in the conjunctiva at the juncture of the sclera and cornea (the limbus) or in the cul-de-sac (Parks incision). Radial relaxing incisions in the conjunctiva are made and the muscles (medial or lateral rectus, superior or inferior rectus) are isolated with a muscle hook. The muscles are then strengthened by resection (removal of a measured segment) or weakened by recession (retroplacement of the muscle attachment). The muscles are secured with sutures. The operative wound is closed with sutures.

Coding Clarification
Code 15.3 is reported when the procedure is performed on two or more muscles in one or both eyes.

Coding Guidance
AHA: 3Q, '96, 3-4

15.4 Other operations on two or more extraocular muscles, one or both eyes

Description
Strabismus is an imbalance in the muscles of the eyeball that control eyeball movement. Surgery can sometimes correct this imbalance. The muscles to be placed on an adjustable suture are isolated in the usual fashion during strabismus surgery. Instead of permanently suturing the muscle to the eyeball by tying and cutting the suture distal to the knot, the sutures are tied and brought out through the overlying conjunctiva. Tension on the muscle is adjusted later when the anesthetic is no longer affecting the position of the globe.

15.5 Transposition of extraocular muscles

Description
In this procedure, the physician relocates an exterior eye muscle to a more functional site. A speculum is placed in the patient's eye, and the physician makes incisions in the conjunctiva at the juncture of the sclera and cornea (the limbus) to expose the muscle. The extraocular muscle or muscles to be transposed are isolated, and the physician exposes the area of sclera to which the transposed muscles are to be attached. The insertions of the transposed muscles

08-16

are then relocated generally adjacent to the paretic or weak muscle. They are attached to the sclera with sutures, and the surgical wound is closed with sutures. Occasionally, the transposed muscle may be split and one-half of the muscle relocated.

Coding Clarification

Do not report 15.5 when the transposition is performed for correction of ptosis; report 08.31-08.36.

15.6   Revision of extraocular muscle surgery

Description

There is an increased level of difficulty involved in both the planning and performance of surgery on an eye that has had previous surgery due to scarring, previous strabismus or retinal detachment surgery, injury, or myopathy. The extraocular muscle is isolated and the physician performs the appropriate strabismus surgery after freeing the muscle from surrounding fibrotic or scarred tissues. The muscle or muscles are then dissected posteriorly to ensure lack of incarceration and repositioned if necessary. The surgical wound is closed with sutures.

15.7   Repair of injury of extraocular muscle

Description

The physician makes an extensive incision of the conjunctiva at the juncture of the cornea and the sclera (the limbus). This is known as a peritomy. In the plane of the detached muscle, retractors afford increased visibility. Extensive posterior dissection may be necessary in an effort to locate the severed, lost, or detached muscle and reapproximate it to the eyeball with sutures. Once the repair is complete, the incision is repaired.

Coding Clarification

Use 15.7 to report lysis of adhesions of extraocular muscle and repair of laceration of extraocular muscle, tendon, or Tenon's capsule.

This code is also appropriately used to report the freeing of an entrapped extraocular muscle.

15.9   Other operations on extraocular muscles and tendons

Description

Code 15.9 is used to report other procedures on extraocular muscles and tendons that are not more precisely described by other codes in category 15.

Documentation Tip

Review the documentation for specific information regarding the procedure prior to final code selection in order to ensure accurate code assignment.

16   Operations on orbit and eyeball

Description

Many of the codes found under category 16 are combination codes. When combination codes are available, assign the single code to indicate both procedures were performed. For example, 16.52 describes the exenteration of the orbit with therapeutic removal of the orbital bone.

Coding Clarification

Do not assign codes from category 16 to report reduction of orbital fractures; report 76.78 or 76.79.

16.0   Orbitotomy

Description

The physician makes an incision into the orbital bone and inserts a small piece of bone. Techniques include anterior orbitotomy, lateral orbitotomy, transconjunctival medial orbitotomy, and mediolateral orbitotomy. Lateral orbitotomy is frequently used for the removal of orbital tumors and for orbital decompression. In lateral orbitotomy, the physician cuts through the lateral orbital rim and removes the bone.

Coding Clarification

The surgical approach is based on the anatomical location of the tumor or lesion. Lateral orbital tumors are approached by lateral orbitotomy route, while medial orbitotomy is performed for tumors of nasal hemiorbit. A paraorbital tumor is typically approached by lateral rhinotomy.

16.01   Orbitotomy with bone flap

Description

Techniques include anterior orbitotomy, lateral orbitotomy, transconjunctival medial orbitotomy, and mediolateral orbitotomy. The physician makes an incision in the lateral aspect of the orbit. A C-shaped incision is made down to the periosteum overlying the lateral orbital rim. The periosteum is incised posterior to the rim itself. The temporalis muscle is moved aside and the globe is protected with pliable retractors. A vibrating saw removes the bone of the lateral orbital rim. A piece of orbital bone is removed for decompression. The bone flap is then replaced and wired into position. The operative wound is closed in layers.

Coding Clarification

Report 16.01 for orbitotomy with lateral approach.

16.02   Orbitotomy with insertion of orbital implant

Description

The physician inserts a prosthesis in the eye. An orbital implant lies outside the muscle cone and is usually secured with sutures.

● New Code   ▲ Revised Code   ▶◀ Revised Text   © 2010 Ingenix

08-16

Coding Clarification

Do not report 16.02 for obitotomy with bone flap; report 16.01.

16.09   Other orbitotomy

Description

In orbitotomy, the physician makes an incision into the orbital bone and inserts a small piece of bone. Techniques include anterior orbitotomy, lateral orbitotomy, transconjunctival medial orbitotomy, and mediolateral orbitotomy. The surgical approach is based on the anatomical location of the tumor or lesion. Lateral orbital tumors are approached by lateral orbitotomy route, while medial orbitotomy is performed for tumors of nasal hemiorbit. A paraorbital tumor is typically approached by lateral rhinotomy.

Documentation Tip

Review the documentation for specific information regarding the procedure prior to final code selection in order to ensure accurate code assignment.

16.1   Removal of penetrating foreign body from eye, not otherwise specified

Description

Code 16.1 is used to report removal of a foreign body from an unspecified part of the eye. Typically, the physician explores the orbit and removes lesions or foreign bodies.

Coding Clarification

Do not use 16.1 to report removal of nonpenetrating foreign body of the eye; report 98.21.

Documentation Tip

Review the documentation for specific information regarding the procedure prior to final code selection in order to ensure accurate code assignment.

16.2   Diagnostic procedures on orbit and eyeball

Description

Codes within subcategory 16.2 are used to report diagnostic procedures on the orbit and eyeball, such as ophthalmoscopy, diagnostic aspiration of orbit, and biopsy of eyeball and orbit.

16.21   Ophthalmoscopy

Description

Ophthalmoscopy allows a complete view of the back of the eye. After the pupils have been dilated, views of the retina are seen with the indirect ophthalmoscope. The direct ophthalmoscope allows the highly magnified view of the posterior portion of the retina; an indirect ophthalmoscope gives a broader view that includes the posterior and anterior retina and vitreous. An extended ophthalmoscopy can also be performed with a contact lens,

three-mirror lens, or 90-diopter lens. One or both eyes are viewed and the physician sketches views of the patient's retinas and their defects.

Coding Scenario

After dilating the patient's pupils, the physician used an indirect ophthalmoscope to obtain a magnified view of the posterior and anterior portions of the retina and vitreous.

Code Assignment:

16.21   Ophthalmoscopy

16.22   Diagnostic aspiration of orbit

Description

With the aid of fluoroscope or x-ray visualization, the physician directs the needle toward the targeted area and aspirates a small amount. No incision is made and no repair is required.

16.23   Biopsy of eyeball and orbit

Description

In this procedure soft tissue or bone may be excised for examination. The physician accesses the orbit through a subciliary, extraperiosteal, or transconjunctival incision. In the subciliary incision, an incision is made in the upper eyelid. In the extraperiosteal incision, the approach is through an incision anterior, superior, interior, or medial to the eye, allowing access to the bone beneath the periosteum. In the transconjunctival approach, the lower lid is everted and an incision is made over the infraorbital rim through the inferior cul-de-sac. In either case, the operative incision is closed with layered sutures.

16.29   Other diagnostic procedures on orbit and eyeball

Description

Code 16.29 is used to report other diagnostic procedures on the orbit and eyeball that are not more precisely described by other codes in subcategory 16.2.

Coding Clarification

Do not use 16.29 to report examination of the form and structure of the eye (95.11-95.16), general and subjective eye examinations (95.01-95.09), microscopic examination of a specimen from eye (90.21-90.29), objective functional tests (95.21-95.26), ocular thermography (88.82), tonometry (89.11), or x-rays of the orbit (87.14, 87.16).

Documentation Tip

Review the documentation for specific information regarding the procedure prior to final code selection in order to ensure accurate code assignment.

08-16

16.3   Evisceration of eyeball

Description
Subcategory 16.3 describes procedures for removal of the eyeball, leaving the sclera and occasionally the cornea.

16.31   Removal of ocular contents with synchronous implant into scleral shell

Description
The physician removes the contents of the eyeball: the vitreous, retina, choroid, lens, iris, and ciliary muscles. Retained is the tough, white outer shell (the sclera). After an ocular speculum has been inserted, the physician dissects the conjunctiva free from the sclera. An elliptical incision is made in the sclera surrounding the cornea, and the contents of the anterior chamber are removed. The physician uses a spoon to remove the contents of the posterior chamber, and then scrapes the inside of the sclera with gauze on a curette. Only the scleral shell remains. The conjunctiva may be removed. A permanent implant is inserted into the scleral shell at this time. The sclera is attached to the implant, usually with sutures.

Coding Clarification
Code 16.31 reports the removal of the eyeball, leaving the outer eyeball layer for synchronous ocular implant.

16.39   Other evisceration of eyeball

Description
Code 16.39 is used to report other evisceration of the eyeball that is not more precisely described by 16.31.

Documentation Tip
Review the documentation for specific information regarding the procedure prior to final code selection in order to ensure accurate code assignment.

16.4   Enucleation of eyeball

Description
Enucleation is the surgical removal of the entire eyeball from its orbit. The procedure is usually performed under general anesthesia. Immediately after the eyeball is removed, an orbital implant is typically inserted into the socket; this implant is covered surgically with conjunctiva.

16.41   Enucleation of eyeball with synchronous implant into Tenon's capsule with attachment of muscles

Description
The physician severs the eyeball from the extraorbital muscles and optic nerve and removes it.

After an ocular speculum has been inserted, the physician dissects the conjunctiva free at the corneal-scleral juncture (the limbus). The physician cuts each extraocular muscle at its juncture to the eyeball and severs the optic nerve. The eyeball is removed but the extraocular muscles remain attached at the back of the eye socket. A spherical implant is placed in the eye socket. The extraocular muscles are attached to the permanent implant to allow normal movement of the prosthesis.

Coding Clarification
Report 16.41 for an integrated implant of the eyeball.

The most common type of ocular prosthesis is the Hydroxyappetite Integrated Implant.

16.42   Enucleation of eyeball with other synchronous implant

Description
An ocular prosthesis is an artificial eye that is placed in the eye socket after the enucleation procedure. The implant is inserted deep into the socket after removal of the eye and may be surgically attached to the eye muscles. The procedure is usually performed under general anesthesia. Immediately after the eyeball is removed, an orbital implant is inserted in the socket and covered surgically with conjunctiva.

16.49   Other enucleation of eyeball

Description
Report 16.49 for other enucleation procedures that are not more precisely described by other codes in subcategory 16.4.

Coding Clarification
Code 16.49 is reported for removal of an eyeball that is not further specified in the documentation.

Documentation Tip
Review the documentation for specific information regarding the procedure prior to final code selection in order to ensure accurate code assignment.

16.5   Exenteration of orbital contents

Description
Exenteration is the radical removal of the contents of the orbit, sometimes including surrounding structures. Orbital exenteration is typically performed on orbital malignancies and to treat life-threatening orbital infections. Orbital exenteration can be divided into two categories: total and subtotal orbital exenteration.

Documentation Tip
A subtotal orbital exenteration is a partial removal of orbital tissues sacrificing the eye and is sometimes referred to as an extended enucleation.

● New Code   ▲ Revised Code   ▶◀ Revised Text   © 2010 Ingenix

16.51 Exenteration of orbit with removal of adjacent structures

Description
The physician removes the maxilla, eye, and orbital soft tissue. Incisions may be intraoral or may include skin incisions such as a modified Weber-Ferguson incision that includes incision into the upper eyelid. Dissection is continued to expose and isolate the planned bony excision. The physician uses drills, saws, and chisels to fracture the maxilla from the midface. The fractured maxilla and adjacent tissue are loosened and removed to "free margins" as determined with intraoperative tissue specimens sent to the pathologist for immediate microscopic examination. The upper eyelid incision is dissected to the periosteum of the superior orbit. The maxilla is retracted downward, so the physician can visualize the optic nerve and blood vessels. The optic nerve is severed and the vessels are ligated. The maxilla, adjacent soft tissue, and orbital contents are removed in one specimen. All sinus mucosa is removed. Exposed bone is covered with a separately reportable split thickness skin graft. A splint may be placed to obturate (block) the mouth from the surgical area. All skin incisions are repaired with layered closure.

Documentation Tip
This procedure is also referred to as a radical orbitomaxillectomy.

16.52 Exenteration of orbit with therapeutic removal of orbital bone

Description
The physician performs a radical removal of the contents of the orbit. The orbital contents are removed and pieces of orbital bone are excised. The orbit is packed with dry gauze and pressure is applied to control bleeding.

16.59 Other exenteration of orbit

Description
Code 16.59 is used to report other enucleation procedures that are not more precisely described by other codes in subcategory 16.5.

Coding Clarification
Report 16.59 for exenteration of orbit with temporalis muscle transplant.

Code 16.59 is also used to report evisceration of orbit that is not further specified in the documentation.

Documentation Tip
Review the documentation for specific information regarding the procedure prior to final code selection in order to ensure accurate code assignment.

16.6 Secondary procedures after removal of eyeball

Description
Subcategory 16.6 provides seven subclassification codes to report various secondary procedures following removal of the eyeball. Included in this subcategory are insertion, revision, and reinsertion of ocular implants; grafts; other forms of revision to enucleation sockets and exenteration cavities; and other secondary procedures that are performed post eyeball removal.

Coding Clarification
Do not use subcategory 16.6 to report those procedures with synchronous enucleation of eyeball (16.41-16.42) or evisceration of eyeball (16.31).

16.61 Secondary insertion of ocular implant

Description
After removal of the eyeball (e.g., enucleation or evisceration), an implant can be introduced as a secondary procedure at a later date. The physician inserts a permanent ocular prosthesis into a patient's orbit. In each case, an ocular speculum is placed in the eye, any conjunctiva is retracted, and any temporary prosthesis is removed. In a patient whose eye has been eviscerated, the implant is attached to the remaining sclera. In a patient following enucleation, the implant is otherwise secured. In some cases, eye muscles are attached to corresponding niches in the prosthesis to provide for more natural movement of the artificial eye following enucleation.

16.62 Revision and reinsertion of ocular implant

Description
The physician revises or removes an orbital implant and returns an ocular prosthesis to the patient's eye socket. After an ocular speculum is inserted, the physician places the ocular prosthesis back into an eye from which it had been previously removed. The prosthesis is attached to the sclera in an eviscerated eye, or otherwise secured in an enucleated eye. Foreign material may be required to better secure the prosthesis and/or the prosthesis may be reattached to extraocular muscles. In either procedure, conjunctival tissue may be grafted over the prosthesis once it is secured.

16.63 Revision of enucleation socket with graft

Description
The patient's face and eyelid are draped and prepped for surgery. Local anesthesia is administered. With the aid of an operating microscope, the physician separates the conjunctival epithelial tissue from the underlying Tenon's capsule. The tissue for graft can be a free graft or extensive rearrangement of existing tissue. For example, the physician may separate

© 2010 Ingenix

08-16

buccal mucous membrane from its location within the patient's mouth to be used for the graft. In this case, the donor graft site does not usually require a repair.

The site to which the donor tissue is to be grafted is then prepared to accept the tissue. Its margins are freshened and the conjunctival graft is sutured into a foreshortened or scarred inferior cul-de-sac or fornix. The fornix can be reformed with the use of a cul-de-sac suture fixation or with the use of a silicon stent attached to the orbital rim. The stent is used to mold the fornix and is sutured into place securely and left for up to two weeks.

16.64   Other revision of enucleation socket

Description
Report 16.64 for other revisions of the enucleation socket that are not more precisely described by other codes in subcategory 16.6.

Documentation Tip
Review the documentation for specific information regarding the procedure prior to final code selection in order to ensure accurate code assignment.

16.65   Secondary graft to exenteration cavity

Description
After orbital exenteration is performed, the resulting defect is reconstructed with implants and a pericranial flap onto which a split thickness skin graft is placed. In another reconstructive technique, the physician performs a rectus abdominis free-tissue transfer to the orbital cavity. Other variations use the temporalis or the pectoralis major muscle as a pedicle flap.

16.66   Other revision of exenteration cavity

Description
Code 16.66 is used to report other revisions of the exenteration cavity that are not more precisely described by other codes in subcategory 16.6.

Documentation Tip
Review the documentation for specific information regarding the procedure prior to final code selection in order to ensure accurate code assignment.

16.69   Other secondary procedures after removal of eyeball

Description
Report 16.69 for other procedures performed secondary to eyeball removal that are not more precisely described by other codes in subcategory 16.6.

Documentation Tip
Review the documentation for specific information regarding the procedure prior to final code selection in order to ensure accurate code assignment.

16.7   Removal of ocular or orbital implant

Description
This subcategory provides two subclassification codes to report removal of ocular and orbital implants.

16.71   Removal of ocular implant

Description
The physician removes the ocular implant from the eye socket. After placing an ocular speculum, the physician cuts and retracts any conjunctival tissue or Tenon's capsule overlying the prosthesis. Any connection between the implant and extraocular muscle or sclera is severed and the ocular implant is removed.

16.72   Removal of orbital implant

Description
The physician removes an orbital implant from the eye. An orbital implant lies outside the muscle cone and is usually secured with sutures.

16.8   Repair of injury of eyeball and orbit

Description
Codes in this subcategory are used to report repairs of injuries to the eyeball and orbit. Fourth-digit specificity is required.

16.81   Repair of wound of orbit

Description
The physician repairs a deep laceration to the orbital complex. This laceration extends through the extraocular muscles that aid the eye in directional movement. The laceration extends through tendinous attachment of the muscles to the bony orbit and may include the deep connective tissue envelope encasing the eyeball. Each anatomic structure is identified and reapproximated with sutures. The wound is closed in multiple layers.

Coding Clarification
The physician may also use a bone graft to repair an orbital injury. Bone grafts offer physicians excellent building blocks when repairing skeletal injuries.

Code 16.81 is not used to report reduction of orbital fractures (76.78-76.79) or repair of extraocular muscles (15.7).

● New Code   ▲ Revised Code   ▶◀ Revised Text   © 2010 Ingenix

08–16

16.82   Repair of rupture of eyeball

Description
Tissue glue, also called medical adhesive or Cyanoacrylate tissue adhesive, acts as a suture in laceration repairs of the cornea and/or sclera. If the cornea is perforated, the physician may seal the perforation with tissue adhesive after debriding the outermost layer of cornea (the epithelium) to enhance adhesion. The patient may be fitted with a soft contact lens to be worn during the healing process. Antibiotic ointment is applied. A pressure patch may be used.

Coding Clarification
Use 16.82 to report repair of multiple structures of the eye.

Do not use 16.82 to report repair of corneal lacerations (11.51-11.59) or scleral lacerations (12.81).

16.89   Other repair of injury of eyeball or orbit

Description
Report 16.89 for other forms of repair to the eyeball or orbit that are not more precisely described by other codes within subcategory 16.8.

For example, the physician repairs a deep laceration to the orbital complex. This laceration extends through the extraocular muscles that aid the eye in directional movement. The laceration extends through tendinous attachment of the muscles to the bony orbit and may include the deep connective tissue envelope encasing the eyeball. Each anatomic structure is identified and reapproximated with sutures. The wound is closed in multiple layers.

16.9   Other operations on orbit and eyeball

Description
Codes in subcategory 16.9 describe injections, excisions, and other procedures performed on the orbit and eyeball that are not more precisely described by other codes in category 16.

Coding Clarification
Do not use codes from subcategory 16.9 to report irrigation of eye (96.51) or prescription and fitting of low vision aids (95.31-95.33).

Codes from subcategory 16.9 are also inappropriate for reporting the removal of an eye prosthesis NEC (97.31) or non-incisional removal of a nonpenetrating foreign body from the eye (98.21).

Documentation Tip
Review the documentation for specific information regarding the procedure prior to final code selection in order to ensure accurate code assignment.

16.91   Retrobulbar injection of therapeutic agent

Description
The physician injects a therapeutic or anesthetic medication or alcohol into the orbit through the lower eyelid or in a transconjunctival method.

Coding Clarification
Do not use this code to report injection of radiographic contrast material (87.14) or an opticociliary injection (12.79).

16.92   Excision of lesion of orbit

Description
The physician explores the orbit and removes lesions or foreign bodies. The physician incises the frontal scalp area and retracts the scalp posteriorly and the forehead anteriorly. The frontal bone is cut and removed. The forebrain is retracted until the superior margins of the orbit are visualized; a lesion is then excised. The roof of the orbit is reconstructed and freedom of movement of extraocular eye muscles is ensured. The dura is closed and the skull is replaced. The forehead and scalp are reanastomosed and closed in sutured layers.

Coding Clarification
Do not use 16.92 to report biopsy of the orbit; report 16.23.

16.93   Excision of lesion of eye, unspecified structure

Description
Report 16.93 for other lesion excision procedures of the eye that are not more precisely described by the physician documentation.

Coding Clarification
Do not use 16.39 to report biopsy of the eye that is not further specified; report 16.23.

Documentation Tip
Review the documentation for specific information regarding the procedure prior to final code selection in order to ensure accurate code assignment.

16.98   Other operations on orbit

Description
Report 16.98 for other orbital procedures that are not more precisely described by other codes in subcategory 16.9.

Documentation Tip
Review the documentation for specific information regarding the procedure prior to final code selection in order to ensure accurate code assignment.

08-16

16.99   Other operations on eyeball

Description
Report 16.99 for other procedures on the eyeball that are not more precisely described by other codes in subcategory 16.9.

Documentation Tip
Review the documentation for specific information regarding the procedure prior to final code selection in order to ensure accurate code assignment.

● New Code   ▲ Revised Code   ►◄ Revised Text   © 2010 Ingenix

17

Other Miscellaneous Diagnostic and Therapeutic Procedures

2011 Changes

New code 17.71 Noncoronary intraoperative fluorescence vascular angiography [IFVA] was added to subcategory 17.7 Other diagnostic and therapeutic procedures to report noncoronary IFVA. This technology is used during bypass surgery to assess function of venous and arterial vessels and blood perfusion in tissues and organs.

17 Other Miscellaneous Procedures

Description

Category 17 includes codes that describe a laparoscopic approach to certain procedures. Laparoscopic surgery, described as minimally invasive surgery, provides benefits over the open procedure such as less pain and scarring and faster recovery time. During laparoscopic surgery the physician makes a series of small incisions then places a "scope" with a small camera in one of the incisions for a magnified view of the patient's internal organs. Surgical instruments can also be placed in other incisions (i.e., trocars) allowing the physician to work inside the body cavity.

17.1	Laparoscopic unilateral repair of inguinal hernia
17.11	Laparoscopic repair of direct inguinal hernia with graft or prosthesis
17.12	Laparoscopic repair of indirect inguinal hernia with graft or prosthesis
17.13	Laparoscopic repair of inguinal hernia with graft or prosthesis, not otherwise specified

Description

Subcategory 17.1 provides codes for laparoscopic repairs of hernias. ICD-9-CM procedure codes did not previously distinguish between laparoscopic and open repairs of hernias. Laparoscopic hernia repair is similar to other minimally invasive laparoscopic procedures. The physician makes a small incision in or just below the navel and inflates the abdomen with air to visualize the abdominal organs. The laparoscope is inserted through the incision and the instruments to repair the hernia are inserted through other small incisions in the lower abdomen. Mesh is typically placed over the defect to reinforce the abdominal wall.

Coding Clarification

ICD-9-CM procedure codes distinguish between laparoscopic and open repairs of hernias. To report open repair of hernias, refer to codes 53.00–53.05 and 53.10–53.17.

Although separate laparoscopic ICD-9-CM procedure codes exist for many procedures including cholecystectomy, appendectomy, and hysterectomy, ICD-9-CM procedure codes did not previously distinguish between laparoscopic and open repairs of hernias or between open and laparoscopic approaches to colo-rectal surgery. Careful review of the documentation for specific information regarding the procedure prior to final code selection will be necessary to ensure accurate code assignment.

Documentation Tip

Review the documentation carefully for specific information regarding the surgical approach and technique prior to final code selection will be necessary to ensure accurate code assignment.

Coding Scenario

A 31-year-old male with an inguinal hernia is brought into the operating room. Once the patient is anesthetized, the physician makes three incisions, three millimeters long and a fiber optic camera is threaded into the patient's abdomen. Using a headset, the physician directs a robot positioning system known as AESOP (automated endoscopic system for optimal positioning) to locate the hernia. The repair is accomplished with a polypropylene mesh patch placed it inside the abdominal wall through the operating port.

17

Code Assignment:

550.90	Inguinal hernia without mention of obstruction or gangrene, unilateral or unspecified, (not specified as recurrent)
17.13	Laparoscopic repair of inguinal hernia with graft or prosthesis, not otherwise specified
17.42	Laparoscopic robotic assisted procedure

Coding Guidance
AHA: 4Q, '08, 165-166

17.2 Laparoscopic bilateral repair of inguinal hernia

17.21 Laparoscopic bilateral repair of direct inguinal hernia with graft or prosthesis

17.22 Laparoscopic bilateral repair of indirect inguinal hernia with graft or prosthesis

17.23 Laparoscopic bilateral repair of inguinal hernia, one direct and one indirect, with graft or prosthesis

17.24 Laparoscopic bilateral repair of inguinal hernia with graft or prosthesis, not otherwise specified

Description
Subcategory 17.2 includes codes for bilateral laparoscopic repairs of hernias. In a laparoscopic repair of bilateral inguinal hernias, the physician places a trocar at the umbilicus and insufflates the abdominal cavity. The laparoscope is placed through the umbilical port and additional trocars are placed into the peritoneal or retroperitoneal space. The hernia sac is identified and reduced into the abdominal cavity. A sheet of mesh is placed into the abdominal or retroperitoneal cavity and secured in place covering the defect. After the procedure is repeated on the opposite side, the trocars are removed and the incisions are closed.

Coding Clarification
ICD-9-CM procedure codes distinguish between laparoscopic and open repairs of hernias or between open and laparoscopic approaches to colorectal surgery. To report open repairs of hernias, refer to codes 53.00–53.05 and 53.10–53.17.

Documentation Tip
Review the documentation carefully for specific information regarding the surgical approach and technique prior to final code selection will be necessary to ensure accurate code assignment.

Coding Scenario
The physician performs a repair of bilateral direct inguinal hernias. Using a three port technique, the laparoscope is placed through the umbilical port and additional trocars are placed through the other two ports. The two sides are repaired using a single long mesh. The mesh is placed on one side behind the

bladder and across the inguinal orifice on the opposite side and secured in place. The trocars are removed and the incisions are closed.

Code Assignment:

550.92	Inguinal hernia without mention of obstruction or gangrene, bilateral, (not specified as recurrent)
17.21	Laparoscopic bilateral repair of direct inguinal hernia with graft or prosthesis

Coding Guidance
AHA: 4Q, '08, 165-166

17.3 Laparoscopic partial excision of large intestine

17.31 Laparoscopic multiple segmental resection of large intestine

17.32 Laparoscopic cecectomy

17.33 Laparoscopic right hemicolectomy

17.34 Laparoscopic resection of transverse colon

17.35 Laparoscopic left hemicolectomy

17.36 Laparoscopic sigmoidectomy

17.39 Other laparoscopic partial excision of large intestine

Description
Subcategory 17.3 provides ICD-9-CM procedure codes to distinguish between open and laparoscopic colorectal surgery. There are specific ICD-9-CM procedure codes to describe other laparoscopic procedures such as cholecystectomy, appendectomy, and hysterectomy, but codes describing laparoscopic colectomy procedures did not exist prior to the creation of this subcategory. Colectomy is a surgical treatment for colon cancer or other diseases of the colon such as ulcerative colitis and Crohn's disease. Colectomy, which removes portions of the large intestine, can be performed as an open surgical procedure as well as laparoscopically. Laparoscopic colectomy procedures are done with the patient under general anesthesia. Pneumoperitoneum is established with a laparoscopic port placed through the umbilicus; the laparoscope is positioned in the abdominal cavity and the remaining laparoscopic ports are placed. The physician incises peritoneum to mobilize the colon. For example, in a laparoscopic sigmoidectomy, the physician mobilizes the sigmoid colon and incises the right pelvic peritoneum. The colon is divided with an endoscopic stapler, and the specimen is removed through an enlarged trocar site. The abdomen is deflated and the laparoscope and trocar incisions are closed.

● New Code   ▲ Revised Code   ▶◀ Revised Text   © 2010 Ingenix

Coding Clarification

In ICD-9-CM classification, partial excision and segmental excision of a single section are synonymous. Coding specificity is provided in ICD-9-CM for multiple segmental excision verses single segment or partial excision of the large intestines. Code 17.31 is assigned to report a laparoscopic multiple segmental excision and code 17.39 reports laparoscopic partial excision or segmental. The index contains two entries under main term *Excision/intestine/large/segmental* to direct the coder to the appropriate code: 17.39 Excision/intestine/large/segmental/laparoscopic and 17.31 Excision/intestine/large/segmental/multiple/laparoscopic.

Codes in the 17.3 and 45.7 subcategories report procedures on the large intestines (cecum, colon, rectum, anal canal) and include specificity such as multiple or partial, laparoscopic versus open, and other specificity. Small intestines (duodenum, jejuneum, ileum) procedure codes, however, do not. There are also no laparoscopic procedure codes. Only when the ileum of the small intestine is involved within the multiple or partial laparoscopic procedure of the large intestines, is there specificity for small intestines. For example, ileocolectomy is coded 17.33 or 45.73; hemicolectomy includes ileum and cecum.

Documentation Tip

Review the documentation carefully for specific information regarding the operative site, surgical approach and technique prior to final code selection will be necessary to ensure accurate code assignment.

Coding Scenario

A patient with adenocarcinoma of the terminal ileum is admitted for hemicolectomy. With the patient under general anesthesia, the physician places a trocar at the umbilicus and insufflates the abdominal cavity and additional trocars are placed. The physician mobilizes the right colon up to proximal transverse colon. The terminal ileum is divided and the specimen is retrieved. The abdomen is deflated and the laparoscope and trocar incisions are closed.

Code Assignment:

152.2   Malignant neoplasm of ileum
17.33   Laparoscopic right hemicolectomy

Coding Guidance

AHA: 4Q, '08, 169-170

17.4   Robotic assisted procedures

17.41   Open robotic assisted procedure

17.42   Laparoscopic robotic assisted procedure

17.43   Percutaneous robotic assisted procedure

17.44   Endoscopic robotic assisted procedure

17.45   Thoracoscopic robotic assisted procedure

17.49   Other and unspecified robotic assisted procedure

Description

Robotic-assisted surgery refers to the technology used to assist the surgeon. Robotic-assisted surgery involves the use of 3-D computer imaging (e.g., CT, MRI) visualization and instrumentation combined with the use of robotic arms, devices, or systems to diagnose and perform the operation. Subcategory 17.4 provides six codes to identify the use of robotics during open, thoracoscopic, percutaneous, endoscopic, and laparoscopic procedures. Report the code for the primary procedure first, followed by the appropriate robotic assisted surgery code.

Robotic-assisted surgery was first used with general laparoscopic surgeries such as gall bladder removal and for treatment of severe heartburn. Since then, use of the robotic-assisted surgical systems has expanded into assisting in several other surgical areas including gynecological laparoscopic procedures such as hysterectomy and myomectomy; radical prostatectomy; certain procedures of the heart, such as coronary artery bypass surgery and mitral valve repair; and procedures involving the lungs, esophagus, and internal thoracic artery. Prior to the creation of this subcategory, ICD-9-CM, volume 3, did not recognize the use of robotics in surgical procedures and according to the index, only the specific procedure performed was coded.

Coding Clarification

These codes exclude computer-assisted surgery (00.31–00.35, 00.39). Computer-assisted and robotic surgeries have similarities such as preoperative planning and registration; however, the main distinction is computer-assisted surgeries do not use robots. Computer-assisted surgery (CAS), uses 3-D imaging to provide better visualization and targeting of operative sites and improved diagnostic capabilities. Robotic surgery, on the other hand, requires the use of a surgical robot in performing surgical interventions.

Documentation Tip

Robotic-assisted and computer-assisted surgeries have similarities, so to ensure accurate code assignment, it will be necessary to review the

17

medical record documentation carefully for the approach and surgical technique. Examples of robotic surgical devices include the da Vinci® Surgical System and the ZEUS™ Robotic Surgical System. Computer-assisted surgery may be documented as 3-D computer surgery, image-guided surgery, or surgical navigation.

Coding Scenario
A patient with chronic cholecystitis is admitted for gallbladder surgery. Three incisions are made in the patient's abdomen and three stainless-steel rods are inserted. One of the rods is equipped with a camera and the other two are fitted with surgical instruments to dissect and suture the tissue of the gallbladder. These rods are held in place by three robotic arms. Sitting at the control console, a few feet from the operating table, the physician views a magnified, three-dimensional image of the surgical site and manipulates the surgical instruments using two fingertip controls. The physician guides the arms of the robot that hold the surgical tools and the gallbladder is dissected from the liver bed and removed through a trocar site. The trocars are removed and the incisions are closed.

Code Assignment:

575.11   Chronic cholecystitis
51.23   Laparoscopic cholecystectomy
17.42   Laparoscopic robotic assisted procedure

Coding Scenario
A patient with acute exacerbation of myasthenia gravis is admitted for a total thymectomy. The physician makes a small 2 cm incision at the fifth intercostal space and introduces the 3-dimensional stereoendoscope of the da Vinci system. Two additional thoracic ports were inserted and two of the robotic arms were attached to these while a third arm was attached to the inserted endoscope. The left arm was used to grasp the thymus and an endo-dissector device with electric cautery attached to the right arm was used to perform the dissection. The thymic gland was radically dissected and the specimen was removed through the trocar incision. A drainage tube was inserted and the other wounds were closed.

Code Assignment:

358.01   Myasthenia gravis with (acute) exacerbation
07.84   Thoracoscopic total excision of thymus
17.45   Thoracoscopic robotic assisted procedure

Coding Guidance
AHA: 4Q, '08, 172-174; ▶3Q, '09, 5◀

17.5   Additional cardiovascular procedures

17.51   Implantation of rechargeable cardiac contractility modulation [CCM], total system

17.52   Implantation or replacement of cardiac contractility modulation [CCM] rechargeable pulse generator only

Description
During the absolute refractory period (ARP), the heart muscle is incapable of responding to the next excitatory stimulus. Cardiac contractility modulation signals are non-excitatory signals that enhance cardiac strength and performance rather than initiating a new heartbeat. Automatic implantable cardioverter/defibrillators (AICD) and pacemakers control and restore normal rhythm of the heart. The cardiac contractility modulation (CCM) system delivers non-excitatory impulses to the right ventricular septum during the absolute refractory period to improve the strength and performance of the heart muscle. The implantable pulse generator (IPG) delivers the CCM signals to the heart through standard pacemaker leads. Implantation of a CCM system includes formation of a pocket, placement of a catheter and transvenous leads, and intraoperative evaluation of lead signals and sensing threshold and defibrillator threshold measurements. CCM systems are used for the treatment of moderate to severe heart failure. The CCM system is used alone or in combination with AICD.

Coding Clarification
Implantation of a cardiac contractility modulation system is more complex and involves more intraoperative time than insertion of pacemakers or defibrillators due to the extensive testing and programming required.

Testing of this device is included in the code and should not be reported separately. In addition to the implantation of the total CCM system (17.51), report any concomitant coronary bypass (36.01-36.19), extracorporeal circulation (39.61), or insertion or replacement of automatic cardioverter/defibrillator, total system (37.94). When reporting the replacement of the pulse generator of the CCM system only (17.52), also report any revision of device pocket (37.79) or revision of leads or electrodes (37.75). Caution: The ICD-9-CM index lists CCM procedures under the main term "Implantation" and does not include the term under the main term "Insertion."

Documentation Tip
Review documentation for specific information regarding the procedure prior to final code selection in order to ensure accurate code assignment. The physician may implant the device along with an automatic implantable cardioverter/defibrillator

● New Code   ▲ Revised Code   ▶◀ Revised Text   © 2010 Ingenix

(AICD) or the device may be implanted in patients with pre-existing AICDs. In other cases, replacement of a cardiac contractility modulation rechargeable pulse generator may be the only procedure performed.

Coding Scenario

A patient with chronic systolic and diastolic congestive heart failure with a preexisting AICD is admitted for implantation of a cardiac contractility modulation system implantation to improve heart function. The patient received a total Optimizer III® system. During the procedure, a catheter-based transducer was introduced for hemodynamic measurements during the positioning of three standard pacemaker leads: two placed in the right ventricular septum and one in the right atrium. The leads were connected to the implantable pulse generator (IPG), which was placed in a subcutaneous pectoral pocket. Intraoperative testing of the device was performed to ensure appropriate function.

Code Assignment:

428.42   Chronic combined systolic and diastolic heart failure
428.0   Congestive heart failure, unspecified
17.51   Implantation of rechargeable cardiac contractility modulation [CCM], total system

Coding Guidance

AHA: ▶4Q, '09, 139-141◀

17.6   MRI-guided laser interstitial thermal therapy (LITT)

17.61   Laser interstitial thermal therapy [LITT] of lesion or tissue of brain under guidance

17.62   Laser interstitial thermal therapy [LITT] of lesion or tissue of head and neck under guidance

17.63   Laser interstitial thermal therapy [LITT] of lesion or tissue of liver under guidance

17.69   Laser interstitial thermal therapy [LITT] of lesion or tissue of other and unspecified site under guidance

Description

Treatment options for patients with brain cancer typically include a combination of surgical resection, stereotactic radiosurgery, external beam or intracranial radiation, and chemotherapy. Laser interstitial thermal therapy (LITT) under real time MRI guidance has been developed for ablation of brain tumors. LITT for tumor ablation uses a laser probe that focuses the laser's energy on the targeted tumor tissue reducing or avoiding damage to surrounding tissue. LITT under guidance, such as

MRI or ultrasound, has been effective at destroying or reducing the size of tumors in the brain, head and neck, thyroid, lung, breast, liver, bone, prostate, uterus, and rectum. The treating physician visualizes the procedure in realtime using a standard 1.5T MRI scanner with software and controls to remotely monitor and position devices allowing precise control of the thermal ablation in real time. A thin, side-firing laser combined with gas cooling within the probe tip is inserted through a small burr hole in the skull. The laser energy discharged heats the targeted tissue while cooling all surrounding tissue allowing the physician to selectively treat the tumor tissue without damaging other tissue.

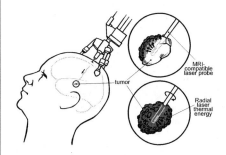

Coding Clarification

A subcategory was created in 2010 to include site-specific codes for laser interstitial thermal therapy (LITT) of the brain (17.61), the head and neck (17.62), and the liver (17.63). Prior to the creation of subcategory 17.6, MRI-guided LITT of a brain lesion or tissue was coded with 01.59 Other excision or destruction of lesion or tissue of brain.

Documentation Tip

Laser interstitial thermal therapy may also be documented in the medical record as focused laser interstitial thermal therapy (f-LITT).

Coding Scenario

A patient is admitted for treatment of medulloblastoma in the fourth ventricle, between the brain stem and the cerebellum. After a 1 cm burr hole is drilled through the skull at the location of the tumor, the physician uses the AutoLITT™ workstation in the MRI control room to monitor and control the thermal ablation in real time. A standard MRI scanner guides the placement of the MRI compatible laser probe through the transcranial burr hole. The laser is used to thermally ablate the tumor tissue while simultaneously cooling the surrounding tissue to prevent that tissue from being damaged. The physician repositions the probe to treat different areas of the tumor. After the treatment is completed, the physician withdraws the probe and the burr hole is closed.

Code Assignment:

191.5   Malignant neoplasm of ventricles of brain

17.61   Laser interstitial thermal therapy [LITT] of lesion or tissue of brain under guidance

Coding Guidance

AHA: ▶4Q, '09, 141-143◀

17.7   Other diagnostic and therapeutic procedures

17.70   Intravenous infusion of clofarabine

Description

Clofarabine is an anti-neoplastic treatment option for acute lymphoblastic leukemia (ALL) and acute myeloid leukemia (AML). Clofarabine is a purine nucleoside antimetabolite that interferes with cell division and the development of new cancer cells. Clofarabine was originally approved by the Food and Drug Administration (FDA) to treat relapsed or refractory acute lymphoblastic leukemia (ALL) in pediatric patients who have previously received at least two other types of treatment. Clofarabine has also proven effective in the treatment of adults 70 years of age or older with acute myeloid leukemia (AML) and an unfavorable prognosis factor such as poor performance status, advanced age, or an antecedent hematologic disorder. Myeloid leukemia is a rapid proliferation of malignant myeloblasts. Patients with acute myelogenous leukemia (AML) typically present with symptoms resulting from bone marrow failure such as anemia, neutropenia, and thrombocytopenia or from organ infiltration with leukemic cells.

Coding Clarification

Do not assign code 99.25 Injection or infusion of cancer chemotherapeutic substance, for intravenous infusion of clofarabine. Subcategory 17.7 Other pharmaceuticals, and code, 17.70 Intravenous infusion of clofarabine, were created specifically to report an intravenous infusion of clofarabine.

Documentation Tip

Carefully review the medical record documentation for the chemotherapy agent used in order to ensure correct code assignment.

Coding Scenario

A 75-year-old patient with myelodysplastic syndrome secondary to aggressive cancer treatment is admitted for the first cycle of CLOLAR® therapy for treatment of acute myeloid leukemia (AML). The clofarabine is administered intravenously at a dose of 52 mg/m2, over a two hour period. The initial dosing cycle is once daily for five consecutive days. This dosing cycle is repeated in two to six weeks depending on the patient's response to treatment.

Code Assignment:

V58.11   Encounter for antineoplastic chemotherapy

205.00   Myeloid leukemia, Acute, without mention of remission

238.75   Myelodysplastic syndrome, unspecified

17.70   Intravenous infusion of clofarabine

Coding Guidance

AHA: ▶4Q, '09, 144◀

● 17.71   Noncoronary intraoperative fluorescence vascular angiography

Description

▶Intraoperative fluorescence vascular angiography (IFVA) is used during bypass graft surgery to assess function of venous and arterial vessels and blood perfusion in tissues and organs. IFVA is distinguished from other forms of angiography by the ability to perform the procedure intraoperatively; without exposing patients to risks associated with toxic dye used in x-ray angiography. IFVA may be performed for patients contraindicated for x-ray angiography due to renal insufficiency. Intraoperative angiography is a valuable tool for timely identification and correction of bypass graft defects, improving operative outcomes, and reducing complications. In some instances, intraoperative angiography replaces and eliminates the need for postoperative angiography. Fluorescence angiography is contraindicated in patients with poor vascularization due to prior radiation exposures, history of smoking, diabetes, congestive heart failure, peripheral vascular disease, low body weight, obesity, or advanced age.◀

Coding Clarification

▶Previously, code 88.59 was assigned for both coronary and noncoronary surgical procedures.

Code 17.71 specifically identifies noncoronary intraoperative angiography, distinguishing between procedures performed on coronary vs. noncoronary sites.

Code 17.71 excludes intraoperative coronary fluorescence vascular (coronary) angiography (88.59).◀

Documentation Tip

▶IFVA may also be documented as intraoperative laser arteriogram, or SPY arteriogram.◀

Coding Scenario

▶A patient with islet cell cancer presents for a pancreatic transplant. Intraoperative imaging was performed with fluorescence angiography (IFVA) of the allografts. Vessel filling and perfusion were assessed with IFVA as grade 3, with complete perfusion and patency.

17

Code Assignment:

157.4	Malignant neoplasm of pancreas, islets of Langerhans
52.80	Pancreatic transplant, not otherwise specified
17.71	Noncoronary intraoperative fluorescence vascular angiography◄

18-20

Operations on the Ear

The ICD-9-CM classification system for operations performed on the ear is divided into categories of procedures according to site and type as follows:

- External Ear (18)
- Middle Ear Reconstruction (19)
- Other Operations on Middle and Inner Ear (20)

The ear is comprised of three main parts: the outer, middle, and inner ear. The outer ear (the visible part) opens into the ear canal. The eardrum separates the ear canal from the middle ear. Small bones in the middle ear help transfer sound to the inner ear. The middle ear also includes the tympanic membrane, auditory ossicles, muscles, and conduction pathways. The inner ear contains the cochlea, saccule, semicircular canals, and the auditory acoustic nerve, which leads to the brain.

Ear surgery is performed for the treatment of diseases, injuries, or deformations of the external ear or the ear's auditory tube, middle ear, inner ear, and auditory and vestibular systems. Ear surgery is most commonly performed to treat conductive hearing loss, chronic ear infections, perforated eardrums, congenital ear defects, and tumors. Types of ear surgery include stapedectomy, tympanoplasty, myringotomy and ear tube surgery, ear surgery to repair a perforated eardrum, cochlear implants, and tumor removal.

The structures of the ear are very small; therefore, surgery is usually performed with an operating microscope. Microsurgery of the ear is often referred to as otomicrosurgery or otologic surgery. A stapedectomy is an example of an ear operation performed entirely with an operating microscope.

Lasers provide a bloodless method of operating on the delicate structures of the ear without sacrificing precision. The CO2 (carbon dioxide), Argon, and KTP lasers are the primary types of lasers used in ear surgery. Lasers can stop bleeding (coagulation) and can also vaporize tissue. Lasers are typically used in stapedectomies (see otosclerosis) and in removing inflamed tissue (see cholesteatoma).

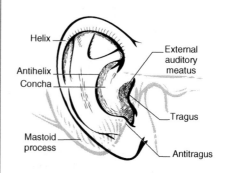

18   Operations on external ear

Description

Category 18 provides codes for incisions, diagnostic procedures, excision or destruction of lesions, repairs, reconstructions, and other operations on the external ear. The external ear includes the external auditory meatus (ear canal) and the skin and cartilage of the auricle (pinna).

Coding Clarification

Subcategory 18.2 Excision or destruction of lesion of external ear, and 18.3 Other excision of external ear, provide fourth digits for excision of lesion or tissue depending on the diagnosis and procedure method.

The code for biopsy of the external ear is 18.12. A biopsy may be performed and afterwards further surgery may be necessary. In this circumstance, code the more extensive surgery followed by the code for the biopsy.

18.0   Incision of external ear

Coding Clarification

Do not use these codes to report removal of intraluminal foreign body; report 98.11.

18.01   Piercing of ear lobe

Description

The physician or technician uses a sharp instrument such as a sterile needle or a piercing gun to form an opening in the ear lobe. After the puncture is complete, the area is cleaned with a disinfectant and an earring is inserted to keep the opening patent. No further treatment is usually necessary.

Coding Clarification
This code is also reported for piercing of the pinna.

18.02   Incision of external auditory canal

Description
The physician makes an incision in the skin and drains an abscess in the external auditory canal. Occasionally, packing is inserted to absorb the drainage and facilitate healing. Usually no further treatment is needed and no closure is required.

18.09   Other incision of external ear

Description
Through a small incision in the skin or at times into the perichondrium external ear at the site of the abscess or hematoma (collection of blood), the physician drains the contents of the abscess in a simple procedure. Occasionally, a small drain tube is inserted and packing is placed to facilitate healing. A bolster with through-and-through sutures is placed to help prevent accumulation of fluid. In a complicated procedure, the physician also devotes time to cleaning the abscess cavity, and a soft sponge is placed in the canal after antibiotic ear drops have been applied.

Coding Clarification
Incision and drainage of the external ear is reported with 18.09.

Documentation Tip
Review the documentation for specific information regarding the procedure prior to final code selection in order to ensure accurate code assignment.

Coding Guidance
AHA: 1Q, '05, 18

18.1   Diagnostic procedures on external ear

Description
Diagnostic procedures performed on the ear often include the use of specialized equipment such as an otoscope to visualize the outer and middle ear. Physicians use otoscopes to screen for illness or to investigate a symptom involving the ears.

18.11   Otoscopy

Description
The physician examines the ear with instrument designed for visualization called an otoscope (auriscope). The head of the otoscope contains a light source and a magnifying lens. The physician straightens the ear canal by pulling on the pinna and inserts the ear speculum side of the otoscope into the external ear.

Coding Clarification
Many otoscope models have a detachable sliding window that allows instruments to be inserted through the otoscope into the ear canal, such as for removing cerumen. Most models are also capable of pushing air through the speculum to allow the physician to test the mobility of the tympanic membrane.

18.12   Biopsy of external ear

Description
The physician uses a scalpel or punch forceps to excise a portion of a lesion on the external ear for diagnostic purposes. Unless the incision is large, a sutured closure is usually unnecessary. In an alternate technique, the physician uses a scalpel, curette, or small biopsy forceps to excise a portion of a lesion on the external ear for diagnostic purposes. Ear canal packing may be required.

18.19   Other diagnostic procedures on external ear

Description
Code 18.19 is used to report other diagnostic procedures of the ear that are not more precisely described by other codes in this subcategory. For example, the physician uses an operating binocular microscope to examine the ear for direct, detailed visualization.

Coding Clarification
Do not use 18.19 to report a microscopic examination of a specimen from the ear; report 90.31-90.39.

18.2   Excision or destruction of lesion of external ear

Description
Excisional biopsy is commonly performed for diagnosis of external ear lesions. Several techniques are employed in lesion excision and destruction, including wedge resection, partial and total auriculectomy, wide excision and skin grafting, and Mohs micrographic surgery.

18.21   Excision of preauricular sinus

Description
Preauricular sinuses are common congenital malformations that usually present as a small dell or depression near the front of the ear. Magnification with an operating microscope is used, and an elliptical incision is made around the sinus and extended to the postauricular area. The soft tissue between the plane of temporalis fascia and the skin anterior to the sinus is excised along with a piece of adjoining helical cartilage. With bipolar dissecting forceps hemostasis is attained, no drain is used, and primary closure is performed.

Coding Clarification
Preauricular sinus is a benign congenital malformation of the preauricular soft tissues.

● New Code   ▲ Revised Code   ▶◀ Revised Text   © 2010 Ingenix

Documentation Tip
A preauricular sinus is also referred to as a preauricular pit or preauricular fistula.

18.29 Excision or destruction of other lesion of external ear

Description
Code 18.29 is used to report other excision or destruction of external ear lesions. Methods may include curettage, cauterization, electrocoagulation, cryosurgery, or enucleation.

Coding Clarification
This code is also used to report excision of the exostosis of the external auditory canal or a preauricular appendage and partial excision of the ear.

Do not use 18.29 to report biopsy of the external ear (18.12), a radical excision of a lesion (18.31), or removal of cerumen (96.52).

Documentation Tip
Review the documentation for specific information regarding the procedure prior to final code selection in order to ensure accurate code assignment.

18.3 Other excision of external ear

Description
This category includes fourth-digit subclassification codes for radical and other excisions of the external ear.

Coding Clarification
Do not use codes from subcategory 18.3 to report biopsy of the external ear; report 18.12.

18.31 Radical excision of lesion of external ear

Description
Through a postauricular incision, the physician uses a scalpel to remove an extensive lesion in the ear canal. Depending upon whether the lesion involves bone, a section of supporting hard tissue may be excised. The tympanic membrane, parotid gland, facial nerve, and portions of the mandible and mastoid may also be removed. A graft or flap may be performed at this time, or the surgical wound may be repaired with layered closure.

A section of supporting hard tissue may be excised, as well as the tympanic membrane, parotid gland, facial nerve, and portions of the mandible and mastoid. The physician may perform a neck dissection, removing the lymph nodes from that side of the neck. The jugular vein, spinal accessory nerve, or sternocleidomastoid muscle may also be removed. The carotid artery, vagus, sympathetic, phrenic, brachial plexus, hypoglossal, and lingual nerves are spared. A graft or flap may be performed at this

time, or the surgical wound may be repaired with layered closure.

Coding Clarification
Do not use 18.31 to report radical excision of preauricular sinus; report 18.21.

18.39 Other excision of external ear

Description
Using a scalpel or electric knife, the physician amputates the external ear. The wound is closed during a second procedure involving a skin graft or flap.

Alternately, the physician removes a full-thickness section of the external ear, often as a triangular wedge. The portion of the ear removed will vary from case to case, but most frequently it is in the curved upper portion of the ear. A small portion of normal tissue surrounding the defect is also removed. The wound is closed with layered sutures.

Coding Clarification
Code 18.39 is used to report amputation of the external ear

Do not use this code to report excision of a lesion; see 18.21-18.29 and 18.31.

18.4 Suture of laceration of external ear

Description
The physician repairs lacerations of the external ear. Three types of repairs are performed: simple, intermediate, and complex. Simple repair is performed when the wound is superficial (partial- or full-thickness damage to the skin or subcutaneous tissues) without involvement of deeper structures. Only simple, one layer, primary suturing is required, which typically includes local anesthetic. Intermediate repair is performed for lacerations involving the deeper layers of subcutaneous tissue and non-muscle fascia in addition to the skin and subcutaneous tissue. Complex repair includes repair of lacerations requiring more than layered closure, such as those requiring revision, debridement, extensive undermining, stents, or retention sutures and those requiring creation of a defect and special preparation of the site.

18.5 Surgical correction of prominent ear

Description
The physician corrects a protruding ear. The physician makes an incision on the posterior auricle and raises the posterior skin off the cartilage. A new antihelical fold is created with multiple sutures through the cartilage. Some techniques employ limited cartilage cutting. A small ellipse of posterior skin is removed and the skin is closed with sutures.

18-20

Packing corresponding to the anterior ear contours is placed. The size of the auricle may be reduced.

Coding Scenario
A teenager was admitted for otoplasty to correct a protruding ear that she has had since birth.

Code Assignment:

744.29 Other congenital anomaly of ear
18.5   Surgical correction of prominent ear

18.6 Reconstruction of external auditory canal

Description
Code 18.6 is used to report repair of the outer ear canal such as reconstruction of the external auditory canal, canaloplasty of the external auditory meatus, or construction of the external meatus of the ear (osseous portion or skin-lined portion with skin graft).

In a single stage reconstructive procedure for congenital atresia, the physician makes a postauricular incision and drills just behind and above the temporomandibular joint region. Drilling is continued until the ossicles are identified. The new bony canal is enlarged. The eardrum is reconstructed and split thickness skin grafts are used to line the new canal. A large canal opening is made by removing skin and soft tissue. The canal is packed and the incision is repaired with sutures.

In a reconstruction performed for stenosis due to injury or infection, the physician makes a postauricular incision and removes the thick, stenotic plug of soft tissue from the external auditory canal. Some drilling of the bony canal may be needed to enlarge the bony canal. Thin skin grafts are used to reline the canal and are held in place by packing. The posterior incision is repaired with sutures.

18.7 Other plastic repair of external ear

Description
Other plastic repairs include prosthetic appliance for absent ear, reconstruction of the ear or auricle, and reformation or repair of the external ear flap.

18.71 Construction of auricle of ear

Description
The auricle is a complex, cartilaginous structure with multiple folds, draped closely with thin skin. The amount of cartilage decreases and subcutaneous tissue increases to end in a lobule that is primarily skin and subcutaneous tissue. In cases where the entire auricular structure is lost, the standard reconstruction is a staged procedure in which contralateral costal cartilage is harvested, carved, and placed in a subcutaneous pocket. Later

procedures are performed to reconstruct the lobule and tragus, and elevate the reconstructed auricle away from the scalp.

An alternative procedure involves implanting a silastic mold into the forearm to form a prefabricated flap; microvascular techniques are subsequently used to transfer the mold and forearm skin to the head. A prosthetic auricle is also a viable option in some cases.

18.72 Reattachment of amputated ear

Description
Replantation of an amputated ear is performed using different techniques ranging from microsurgical techniques to simple reattachment of the amputated part as a composite graft. Both the graft and the amputated stump of the ear are meticulously cleaned. The epidermis and outer layer of the dermis of the posterior aspect of the graft are sharply excised with a scalpel. The anterior skin of the graft is sutured in layers to the amputated stump of the ear and the skin of the helical rim is sutured to the elevated postauricular flap. Sutures are placed for fixation of the graft to the tissues of the mastoid bed.

18.79 Other plastic repair of external ear

Description
Otoplasty ear surgery involves a combination of moving, reshaping, adding, or removing structural ear elements including reconstructive procedures such as postauricular skin graft and reconstruction of an ear that is at a right angle to the head (lop ear).

To correct a protruding ear, the physician makes an incision on the posterior auricle and raises the posterior skin off the cartilage. A new antihelical fold is created with multiple sutures through the cartilage. Some techniques employ limited cartilage cutting. A small ellipse of posterior skin is removed and the skin is closed with sutures. Packing corresponding to the anterior ear contours is placed. The size of the auricle may be reduced.

In a postauricular skin graft, the physician may reconstruct an area of the ear with a cartilage graft harvested from the ribs. The physician makes a small incision near the sternum through the pectoralis muscle exposing the rib where the bone and cartilage meet. Cartilage is removed from the area and the donor site is closed directly. The physician prepares the recipient sites of the ear for the rib cartilage graft. The graft is placed and held in place with wires, plates, or screws. The incisions are sutured with a layered closure. In an alternate procedure, cartilage from the other ear may be harvested to use as the graft.

Coding Clarification
Code 18.79 is also used to report otoplasty procedures that are not further specified in the documentation.

Coding Guidance
    AHA: 3Q, '03, 12

18.9   Other operations on external ear

Description
Code 18.9 is used to report other procedures of the external ear that are not more precisely described by other codes in this subcategory.

Coding Clarification
Code 18.9 is not used to report irrigation of the ear (96.52) or packing of the external auditory canal (96.11)

Do not use this code to report removal of cerumen (96.52) or removal of a foreign body without incision (98.11)

Documentation Tip
Review the documentation for specific information regarding the procedure prior to final code selection in order to ensure accurate code assignment.

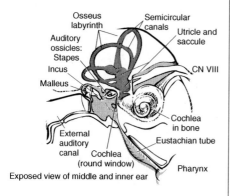

Exposed view of middle and inner ear

---

19   Reconstructive operations on middle ear

Description
Category 19 reports reconstructive procedures on the middle ear such as stapes mobilization, initial stapedectomy as well as revision, other ossicular chain procedures, myringoplasty, tympanoplasty and revisions, and other methods of middle ear repair. Many of the codes within this section require fourth-digit subclassification in order to provide greater specificity as to type.

Coding Clarification
A TORP procedure is a tympanoplasty with a total ossicular reconstruction and prosthesis (19.53).

Documentation Tip
Tympanoplasty, myringoplasty, ossiculoplasty, and mastoidectomy are sometimes used interchangeably by physicians. A tympanoplasty can often mean one or more of these procedures.

A myringoplasty is a repair of the eardrum.

An ossiculoplasty involves removal, replacement, or revision of the three bones of the ear.

A mastoidectomy involves drilling the bones over the mastoid air cells to improve aeration or remove cholesteatoma.

19.0   Stapes mobilization

Description
The stapes is the third of the three bones in the middle ear that transmits sound vibrations from the eardrum to the inner ear fluid so we can hear. Otosclerosis refers to a growth of bone in the ear that develops around the stapes, fixing it in place so that it will not vibrate properly.

The physician makes an incision in the posterior canal skin through the external ear canal opening. Under microscopic visualization, the physician reflects the skin flap and posterior eardrum forward. A small amount of the posterior bony canal may need to be removed with a curette or drill. The incus and stapes are visualized and palpated. If the stapes is fixated it can be mobilized by applying pressure to it with delicate instruments. The canal skin and eardrum are repositioned and the ear canal is packed.

19.1   Stapedectomy

Description
Stapedectomy is the removal of all or part of the stapes, one of the bones in the middle ear, and replacement with a tiny prosthesis. Stapedectomy is a microsurgical procedure that can be done through the ear canal. Anesthesia can be general or local.

Coding Clarification
Stapedectomy is performed to restore hearing loss. The conductive type of hearing loss caused by otosclerosis is usually correctable by a surgery called stapedectomy, although this type of hearing loss is possible to overcome with a hearing aid.

19.11   Stapedectomy with incus replacement

Description
The incus, or anvil, is one of three ossicles in the ear located between the malleus and stapes. A common ossicular problem is the eroded incus. When the incus is eroded the ossicular chain is reconstructed with an incus replacement prosthesis.

The surgeon makes an incision in the posterior canal skin through the external canal opening.

Occasionally, a postauricular incision may be substituted. Under microscopic guidance, the physician reflects the canal skin flap and posterior eardrum forward. Some posterior canal bone may be removed with a curette or drill. The ossicular chain is palpated. If the stapes is fixed, it is separated from the incus. The stapes can be removed (stapedectomy) or an opening can be made in the stapes footplate with a laser or drill (stapedotomy). A prosthesis is placed on the incus to replace the stapes. A piece of fascia, vein, perichondrium, or fat might be applied around or under the prosthesis. The skin and eardrum are repositioned and the ear canal is packed.

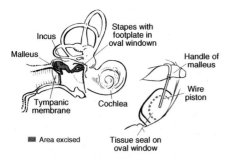

Incus

Malleus

Stapes with footplate in oval windown

Handle of malleus

Wire piston

Tympanic membrane

Cochlea

▨ Area excised

Tissue seal on oval window

19.19   Other stapedectomy

Description
Stapedectomy involves removal of the fixed stapes and replacing it with a prosthesis that allows sound vibrations to be transmitted properly to the inner ear fluids for hearing. Code 19.19 is used to report other stapedectomy procedures that are not more precisely described by other codes in this subcategory.

Documentation Tip
Procedures that are correctly reported by 19.19 include:

- Bisection or fenestration of stapes foot plate
- Ossiculectomy with stapedectomy
- Incudectomy with stapedectomy
- Incudopexy
- Incudostapediopexy
- Malleostapediopexy

This code is also reported when the documentation does not further specify the procedure. Review the documentation for specific information regarding the procedure prior to final code selection in order to ensure accurate code assignment.

19.21   Revision of stapedectomy with incus replacement

Description
The physician revises a stapedectomy. The physician makes an incision over the previous incision site in

the posterior canal or through the external canal opening. Alternately, a previous postauricular incision may be reincised. Under microscopic guidance, the physician reflects the canal skin flap and posterior eardrum forward. Some posterior canal bone may be removed with a curette or drill. The ossicular chain is palpated. If the stapes has become fixed since the previous surgery it is separated from the incus. The footplate may be opened with a laser or drilled out. The prosthesis may be repositioned, revised, or removed and replaced. A piece of fascia, vein, perichondrium, or fat previously placed may be removed and replaced around or under the prosthesis. The skin and eardrum are repositioned and the ear canal is packed.

Coding Clarification
One of the most common problems requiring revision stapedectomy is an eroded incus. Incus erosion is frequently associated with multiple revisions. Conductive hearing loss is another common reason for revision surgery. Other causes of stapedectomy revision include prosthesis malfunction, fibrous adhesions, and otosclerotic regrowth.

19.29   Other revision of stapedectomy

Description
Code 19.29 is used to report other stapedectomy revision procedures that are not more precisely described by other codes in this subcategory. This code is also reported when the documentation does not further specify the procedure.

Documentation Tip
Review the documentation for specific information regarding the procedure prior to final code selection in order to ensure accurate code assignment.

19.3   Other operations on ossicular chain

Description
Code 19.3 is used to report other operations on the ossicular chain that are not more precisely described elsewhere.

Coding Clarification
Excisions of middle ear bones (incudectomy, ossiculectomy) that are not otherwise specified are reported with 19.3.

Other procedures that are also appropriately reported with 19.3 include repair of middle ear bones following previous surgery and second-stage reconstruction of the ossicles.

19.4   Myringoplasty

Description
Myringoplasty is surgical repair of a perforated eardrum with a tissue graft. This procedure is

typically used to close a hole in the eardrum primarily to prevent recurrent infection. Myringoplasty may be performed with cauterization to accomplish a plastic repair of the tympanic membrane of eardrum by heat.

Through the external ear canal, the physician visualizes the tympanic membrane and the eardrum defect. The edges of the eardrum perforation are roughened ("rimming the perforation"). Some dissolvable packing may be placed through the perforation into the middle ear space. A fat graft plug may be placed in the perforation or a piece of fascia may be placed medial to the eardrum over the dissolvable packing. A tympanomeatal flap may be raised. Any incisions are sutured and a dressing is applied.

Coding Clarification
Other procedures reportable with 19.4 include epitympanic, type I, which is a repair over or upon an eardrum, or tympanoplasty, which is a reconstruction of the eardrum to restore hearing.

Documentation Tip
A graft repair is a plastic repair using implanted tissue.

Coding Scenario
A patient presented for surgical repair of a perforated eardrum.

Code Assignment:

384.20   Unspecified perforation of tympanic membrane
19.4   Myringoplasty

19.5   Other tympanoplasty

Description
Tympanoplasty is performed to reconstruct the eardrum in patients with partial or total conductive hearing loss, which is usually caused by chronic middle ear infections or perforations.

After making an incision in the ear to view the perforation, the eardrum is elevated away from the ear canal and lifted forward. If the bones of hearing (ossicular chain) are functioning, tissue is taken from the ear and grafted to the eardrum to close the perforation. The ear is stitched together, and a sterile patch is placed on the outside of the ear canal.

Coding Clarification
There are five basic types of tympanoplasty. Type I is myringoplasty, reported with 19.4. Types II, III, IV, and V are reported within subcategory 19.5 The technique used to repair the tympanic membrane (medial or lateral placement of the graft or the ossiculoplasty to be performed) is determined based on where the conductive mechanism will be constructed.

19.52   Type II tympanoplasty

Description
Type II tympanoplasty is performed for tympanic membrane perforations with erosion of the malleus. It involves grafting onto the incus or the remains of the malleus.

19.53   Type III tympanoplasty

Description
Type III tympanoplasty is performed when an intact, mobile stapes is present and involves placing a graft onto the stapes.

In a total ossicular replacement prosthesis (TORP) procedure, the physician makes an incision in the ear canal skin through a postauricular or transcanal approach. The edges of the tympanic membrane are roughened ("rimming the perforation"). The physician reflects the eardrum forward. The middle ear is explored, and lysis of any adhesions is performed. Any squamous debris or middle ear cholesteatoma is removed and the physician inspects and palpates the ossicles. The ossicular chain is reconstructed using a synthetic reconstructive prosthesis. A partial ossicular prosthesis (PORP) is used when the stapes suprastructure is present. If the stapes suprastructure is absent, a TORP is used. A piece of cartilage may be placed between the eardrum and prosthesis. Some packing may be placed in the middle ear to support the reconstructed ossicle prior to final positioning of the eardrum graft. Some drilling or curetting of the canal wall may be necessary. Some fascia from the temporalis muscle or other tissues is harvested as a graft to repair the tympanic membrane perforation. The graft may be placed under (underlay or medial graft technique) or on top of the remaining eardrum (overlay or lateral graft technique). The canal skin is repositioned and the canal is packed.

Coding Guidance
AHA: M-A, '85, 15

19.54   Type IV tympanoplasty

Description
Type IV tympanoplasty describes destruction of all or part of the stapes arch and involves placing a graft onto or around a mobile stapes footplate.

19.55   Type V tympanoplasty

Description
Type V tympanoplasty is used when the footplate of the stapes is fixed and involves fenestration created in the horizontal semicircular canal.

18-20

19.6   Revision of tympanoplasty

Description
In this subcategory, the physician repairs or corrects a previous plastic surgery on eardrum. Patients for revision tympanoplasty have typically experienced a failed attempt at repair of the tympanic membrane and are at higher risk for subsequent repair failure. Revision tympanoplasty is frequently performed using cartilage grafting. The use of mastoidectomy with tympanoplasty is often used to decrease the risk for subsequent failure.

19.9   Other repair of middle ear

Description
Code 19.9 is used to report closure of a mastoid fistula (abnormal channel in the mastoid), restoration or repair of the mastoid muscle (mastoid myoplasty), and total removal of the functional elements of the middle ear.

Documentation Tip
Review the documentation for specific information regarding the procedure prior to final code selection in order to ensure accurate code assignment.

---

20   Other operations on middle and inner ear

Description
There are nine subcategories within category 20. The majority require fourth-digit subclassification to complete the code. Subcategories 0-8 report myringotomy, incisional procedures on the mastoid and middle ear, tympanostomy tube removal, middle/inner ear diagnostic procedures, various forms of mastoidectomy and other middle ear excisions, inner ear fenestration, Eustachian tube operations, and incision, excision, and destruction of inner ear.

Subcategory 9 is used for all other operations on the inner and middle ear not classified to subcategories 0-8. Subcategory 20.9 includes codes for the implantation or replacement of cochlear implants (20.96-20.98). This procedure involves the implantation of the complete device (i.e., a receiver within the skull and insertion of one or more electrodes in the cochlea). The choice between these three codes is dependent upon a single channel, 20.97; multiple channel, 20.98; or unspecified, 20.96, transmission process.

Coding Clarification
Use 20.1 for the removal of a myringotomy tube.

Assign 20.99 Other operations on middle and inner ear, when only the internal coils and/or electrode(s) of a cochlear prosthetic device are replaced. This code is also used for repair or removal without replacement of the complete device.

Any adjustments to the external components of the cochlear prosthetic device are coded to 95.49.

20.0   Myringotomy

Description
Myringotomy and ear tube surgery are performed to drain ear fluid and to prevent ear infections when ear infections are chronic. The surgeon makes a small hole in the eardrum and uses suction to remove fluid. A small ear tube is inserted into the eardrum to allow continual drainage. The tube prevents infections as long as it stays in place, which can vary from six months to three years.

20.01   Myringotomy with insertion of tube

Description
In a patient who has received a local or a general anesthetic, the physician inserts a ventilating tube. Under direct visualization with a microscope, the physician makes a small incision in the tympanum (eardrum). Any middle ear fluid is suctioned and may be reserved for analysis. The physician inserts a ventilating tube into the opening in the tympanum. No other treatment is required.

Documentation Tip
This procedure may also be documented in the medical record as myringostomy.

20.09   Other myringotomy

Description
After the application of a local anesthetic or a general anesthetic and using a microscope for guidance, the physician makes an incision in the patient's tympanic membrane. Fluid is suctioned from the middle ear space and may be reserved for analysis. The eustachian tube may be inflated. No closure is required.

Coding Clarification
Report 20.09 for aspiration of the middle ear that is not otherwise specified.

20.1   Removal of tympanostomy tube

Description
Assisted by microscopic visualization and using delicate forceps or hook, the physician removes from the tympanic membrane a previously placed ventilating tube with the patient under general anesthesia. No other treatment is required.

Coding Guidance
AHA: N-D, '87, 9; 3Q, '94, 7

18-20

20.2   Incision of mastoid and middle ear

Description
Code 20.2 describes incisional procedures on the mastoid and middle ear including atticotomy, division of tympanum, and lysis of adhesions of middle ear. The mastoid bone is located behind the ear. The inside of the mastoid bone is similar to a honeycomb with the spaces filled with air. These air cells are connected to the middle ear through an air-filled cavity called the mastoid antrum.

Coding Clarification
Do not use codes from subcategory 20.2 to report the division of otosclerotic process or stapediolysis (19.0), or for incision of the middle ear with stapedectomy (19.11-19.19).

20.21   Incision of mastoid

Description
This code reports incision or exploration of the mastoid bone.

Documentation Tip
This procedure may also be documented in the medical record as mastoidotomy. The mastoid bone is located behind the ear. The inside of the mastoid bone is similar to a honeycomb with the spaces filled with air. These air cells are connected to the middle ear through an air-filled cavity called the mastoid antrum.

20.22   Incision of petrous pyramid air cells

Description
Entering through the external ear canal opening or through a postauricular incision (behind the ear) and into the ear canal, the physician performs exploratory surgery of the middle ear. The eardrum is lifted posteriorly and the middle ear is explored including testing the mobility of the ossicular chain. No major treatment is rendered at this time. The eardrum and canal skin are repositioned and the canal is packed. Any postauricular incision is sutured.

Documentation Tip
This procedure may also be referred to in the medical record as:

- Almoor operation
- Eagleton operation
- Exploration of petrous pyramid air cells
- Extrapetrosal drainage
- Frenckner operation
- Intrapetrosal drainage

20.23   Incision of middle ear

Description
Through the external ear canal opening, the physician treats a lesion or other irritation to the tympanic membrane. The physician makes an incision in the posterior canal skin and reflects the eardrum forward. Under microscopic guidance, the physician removes adhesions from the tympanic membrane (tympanolysis). When tympanolysis is complete, the eardrum and canal skin are repositioned and packing is placed in the ear canal.

Coding Clarification
Code 20.23 is used to report an atticotomy, which is an operative opening into the tympanic attic.

20.3   Diagnostic procedures on middle and inner ear

Description
This subcategory provides three subclassification codes to report such diagnostic procedures on the middle and inner ear as electrocochleography and biopsy, as well as other diagnostic procedures that are not further specified.

20.31   Electrocochleography

Description
An electrode is placed through the tympanic membrane into the promontory of the inner ear. The ear is stimulated and recordings are made of the electrical response of the cochlear nerve. This can be done under local, topical, or general anesthesia.

20.32   Biopsy of middle and inner ear

Description
The physician performs a biopsy to diagnose polyps, inflammation, or tumors of the middle or inner ear. Tumors in different areas of the ear behave differently. Polyps in the middle ear may be indistinguishable from more serious problems of the middle ear. If unresponsive to medical therapy, polyps should be biopsied.

Coding Clarification
Cholesteatoma are the most common of all middle ear tumors and are usually benign.

One of the less common benign tumors of the middle ear is the facial neuroma, a tumor of the facial nerve.

Malignant tumors in the middle ear and mastoid are uncommon; among these, the squamous cell cancers are the most prevalent.

20.39   Other diagnostic procedures on middle and inner ear

Description
Code 20.39 is used to report other diagnostic procedures of the middle or inner ear that are not

18-20

more precisely described by other codes in this subcategory.

Coding Clarification
Do not use 20.39 to report auditory and vestibular function tests (89.13, 95.41-95.49) or microscopic examination of specimen from ear (90.31-90.39).

Documentation Tip
Review the documentation for specific information regarding the procedure prior to final code selection in order to ensure accurate code assignment.

20.4   Mastoidectomy

Description
A **mastoidectomy** is a surgical procedure designed to remove infection or lesions in the mastoid bone. Mastoidectomy is often indicated for other diseases that spread to the mastoid bone, such as cholesteatoma. Depending on the amount of infection or cholesteatoma present, various degrees of mastoidectomies can be performed.

In a **simple mastoidectomy**, the surgeon opens the bone and removes any infection. A tube may be placed in the eardrum to drain any pus or secretions present in the middle ear. Antibiotics are then given.

A **radical mastoidectomy** removes the most bone and is indicated for extensive spread of a cholesteatoma. The eardrum and middle ear structures may be completely removed. Usually the stapes is spared if possible.

In a **modified radical mastoidectomy**, some middle ear bones are left in place and the eardrum is rebuilt (tympanoplasty). Both a modified radical and a radical mastoidectomy usually result in less than normal hearing.

Coding Clarification
Also report in addition any skin graft (18.79) or tympanoplasty (19.4-19.55) performed.

20.41   Simple mastoidectomy

Description
Through a postaural or endaural incision, the physician removes the mastoid cortex (outer bone) and drills out some of the mastoid air cells to enter the mastoid antrum. This is usually done as a drainage procedure for mastoid disease limited to the antrum region. A myringotomy with or without tube placement may be performed. A temporary drain may be placed and the incision is sutured.

Coding Clarification
In a simple mastoidectomy, the surgeon opens the bone and removes any infection. A tube may be placed in the eardrum to drain any pus or secretions present in the middle ear.

20.42   Radical mastoidectomy

Description
The physician makes incisions in the ear canal to develop a posterior tympanomeatal flap that is reflected forward. Through a postaural or endaural incision, the physician drills out the mastoid cells. The posterior and superior bony canal walls are taken down to the level of the facial nerve. The ossicles, except for the stapes if possible, are removed, as well as the eustachian tube orifice mucosa, middle ear mucosa, granulations, and cholesteatoma. The middle ear and mastoid are exposed to the exterior through the ear canal. A large meatoplasty is performed. Packing is placed, the incision is sutured, and a dressing is applied.

Coding Clarification
A radical mastoidectomy removes the most bone and is usually performed for extensive spread of a cholesteatoma. The eardrum and middle ear structures may be completely removed. Usually the stapes is spared if possible.

20.49   Other mastoidectomy

Description
Code 20.49 is used to report mastoidectomy that is not more precisely described by other codes in this subcategory such as an atticoantrostomy (also called antroatticotomy), which is a surgical opening of the mastoid antrum and the attic of the middle ear, or a modified radical mastoidectomy in which some middle ear bones are left in place and the eardrum is rebuilt (tympanoplasty).

Coding Clarification
Code 20.49 is used to report atticoantrostomy; also use this code to report modified radical mastoidectomy and mastoidectomy that is not further specified in the documentation.

Documentation Tip
Review the documentation for specific information regarding the procedure prior to final code selection in order to ensure accurate code assignment.

20.5   Other excision of middle ear

Description
This subcategory provides two codes to report excisional procedures of the middle ear, including lesion excision, epicectomy of the petrous pyramid, and tympanectomy. Both require fourth-digit subclassification for procedure specificity.

20.51   Excision of lesion of middle ear

Description
When excising an aural polyp, the physician removes the polyp with a cup forceps or an ear snare through the external ear canal opening. Bleeding is

controlled with packing or epinephrine on a cotton ball. Antibiotic drops may be instilled.

When performing a transcanal excision of an aural glomus tumor, the physician approaches through the external auditory canal. The physician makes an incision in the posterior canal skin and reflects the skin flap and eardrum forward. Under microscopic visualization, the small vascular tumor is grasped with a cup forceps and gently removed. Hemostasis is obtained with packing soaked in epinephrine. Once bleeding is controlled, the middle ear is packed with absorbable material. The eardrum and skin flap are repositioned and the ear canal is packed.

In a transmastoid excision of an aural glomus tumor, the physician drills out the mastoid cavity through a postaural incision. The mastoid sinus is exposed posteriorly. The tegmen (bony plate separating the mastoid and middle cranial fossa) is exposed superiorly. The posterior ear canal wall remains intact. An extended facial recess is sometimes needed to completely visualize the tumor. The vascular tumor is grasped and removed with cup forceps. Hemostasis is obtained using absorbable packing. Usually the ossicles can be left undisturbed. For larger tumors, the posterior canal wall and ossicles may be removed. The incision is repaired with sutures and a dressing is applied.

When performing an extended excision of an aural glomus tumor, the surgeon makes an incision in front of the ear. The facial nerve, hypoglossal nerve, spinal accessory nerve, internal jugular vein, and carotid artery are identified in the neck. A complete mastoidectomy with extended facial recess is performed. The tip of the mastoid is removed and the jugular bulb is exposed and ligated inferiorly. The mastoid sinus is skeletonized, opened, and packed. Hemostasis is obtained with packing. If the tumor extends intracranially, a craniotomy may be necessary. A parotidectomy may also be needed if further mobilization of the facial nerve is required. The ear canal and ossicles may be removed. The incision is repair with layered closure. Dressings are applied.

Coding Clarification
Glomus tumors are common vascular lesions of the middle ear. There are several lesions of the middle ear that mimic a glomus tumor, including vascular, neoplastic, and inflammatory lesions.

Code 20.51 excludes biopsy of the middle ear, which is correctly reported with 20.32.

Coding Scenario
A previous computed tomography scan showed a possible glomus tumor at the right hypotympanium near the eustachian tube area. The lesion was totally excised from the middle ear using an endural approach. Some bleeding occurred during excision, controlled with cotton swabs soaked with adrenaline solution.

Code Assignment:

388.8   Disorders of ear NEC

20.51   Excision of lesion of middle ear

20.59   Other excision of middle ear

Description
The physician performs an apicectomy of petrous pyramid. The petrous apex is a pyramid-shaped bone. Petrous apex lesions may be approached surgically in different ways (e.g., pterional, subtemporal, presigmoid, and retrosigmoid) based on the extent and nature of the pathology. In a common approach to a petrous apicectomy, a radical mastoidectomy is performed. The anterior canal wall is removed and so is the mandibular condyle. The bony covering is taken off the internal carotid artery and the petrous apex is entered through a triangular opening between the cochlea, middle fossa dura, and internal carotid artery.

Coding Clarification
Lesions of the petrous apex are rare but most often are inflammatory and infective lesions of the petrous apex such as petrous apex cholesteatomas.

Code 20.59 is also used to report a tympanectomy.

20.6   Fenestration of inner ear

Description
Two subclassification codes are provided within this subcategory to report initial and revision fenestrations of the inner ear.

20.61   Fenestration of inner ear (initial)

Description
A fenestration is an opening or window. An inner ear fenestration is a surgical treatment for hearing problems in which the physician makes an artificial opening (fenestration) in the labyrinth of the ear.

Through an endaural incision, the physical performs a partial mastoidectomy. The mastoid antrum and horizontal semicircular canal are identified. The posterior ear canal wall is removed down to the level of the facial nerve after elevating and protecting the posterior canal wall and eardrum. The incus and head of the malleus are removed. A small opening is created in the horizontal canal. The eardrum and canal skin are repositioned to cover the opening (fenestration). The mastoid is packed, the incision repaired, and a dressing placed.

Coding Clarification
Report fenestration associated with type V tympanoplasty with 19.55.

18-20

20.62   Revision of fenestration of inner ear

Description
Through an endaural incision, the physician revises a previous fenestration of the lateral semicircular canal. The physician drills through the mastoid bone to reach the lateral semicircular canal. Additional canal bone is removed, leaving the inner membrane intact. The eardrum and canal skin are repositioned to cover the opening (fenestration). The mastoid is packed, the incision repaired, and a dressing placed.

20.7   Incision, excision, and destruction of inner ear

Description
This subcategory provides three subclassification codes to report endolymphatic shunt, inner ear injection, and other incisional, excisional, and destructive procedures on the inner ear.

20.71   Endolymphatic shunt

Description
Through a postauricular incision, the physician drills out the mastoid cavity. The posterior ear canal wall remains intact. The horizontal and posterior semicircular canals are visualized. Drilling is continued until the endolymphatic sac is identified. The physician may use a diamond burr to remove the bone around the sac (i.e., decompression). A shunt is inserted into the sac. The mastoid cavity is packed with absorbable packing and the outer incision is sutured and a pressure dressing applied.

20.72   Injection into inner ear

Description
In a transcanal approach, the physician makes an incision in the posterior ear canal skin through the external ear opening and reflects the skin flap and posterior tympanic membrane forward. For a mastoid approach, the physician drills out the mastoid cavity. In either case, the posterior ear canal wall remains intact. The horizontal semicircular canal is visualized. Under microscopic guidance, a variety of procedures may be performed, including placement of a small temporary or permanent tack through the stapes footplate, placement of a hook through the round window, or ultrasonography or cryotherapy of the round window.

20.79   Other incision, excision, and destruction of inner ear

Description
Code 20.79 reports other incisional, excisional, or destruction procedures of the inner ear that are not more precisely described by other codes in this subcategory.

Coding Clarification
Report biopsy of the inner ear with 20.32

Procedures reported with 20.79 include:

- Decompression of labyrinth: Controlled relief of pressure in cavities of inner ear
- Drainage of inner ear: Removal of fluid from inner ear
- Fistulization of endolymphatic sac: Creation of passage to fluid sac in inner ear cavities
- Fistulization of labyrinth: Creation of passage to inner ear cavities
- Incision of endolymphatic sac: Cutting into fluid sac in inner ear cavities
- Labyrinthectomy (transtympanic): Excision of cavities across eardrum
- Opening of bony labyrinth: Cutting into inner ear bony cavities
- Perilymphatic tap: Puncture or incision into fluid sac of inner ear cavities

Documentation Tip
Code 20.79 is also used to report incisional, excisional, or destruction procedures on the inner ear that are not further specified in the documentation.

Review the documentation for specific information regarding the procedure prior to final code selection in order to ensure accurate code assignment.

20.8   Operations on Eustachian tube

Description
In a transtympanic eustachian tube catheterization, the physician makes an incision in the posterior ear canal skin and raises the eardrum. The eustachian tube opening in the middle ear is visualized and a small catheter is inserted into the eustachian tube to stent it open. This can be left in place indefinitely. No repair is made.

In transnasal eustachian tube inflation, the physician topically decongests and anesthetizes the nose and nasopharynx. The eustachian tube is cannulated with a small catheter through the nose, often with the aid of a nasopharyngoscope. Air is forced into the catheter to inflate the eustachian tube. The catheter is removed.

Alternately, the physician inflates a blocked or collapsed eustachian tube by increasing the air pressure in the nasopharynx. One method is to blow air against the resistance of the closed mouth and nose. Another method is to close one side of the nose and force air into the other nostril with a Politzer bag as the patient swallows.

Coding Clarification
Procedures reported with 20.8 include:

- Catheterization: Passing a catheter into the passage between the pharynx and middle ear

● New Code   ▲ Revised Code   ▶◀ Revised Text   © 2010 Ingenix

- Inflation: Blowing air, gas, or liquid into the passage between the pharynx and middle ear to inflate
- Injection (Teflon paste): Forcing fluid (Teflon paste) into the passage between the pharynx and middle ear
- Insufflation (boric acid-salicylic acid): Blowing gas or liquid into the passage between the pharynx and middle ear
- Intubation: Placing a tube in the passage between the pharynx and middle ear
- Politzerization: Inflating the passage between the pharynx and middle ear with a Politzer bag

20.9 Other operations on inner and middle ear

Description
Subcategory 20.9 consists of nine subclassification codes to report such operations on the inner and middle ear as tympanosympathectomy, mastoidectomy revision, oval and round window repair, and injection of tympanum. There are also codes for reporting various cochlear prosthetic device implantation and replacement procedures, as well as a general code for other operations on the middle and inner ear.

20.91 Tympanosympathectomy

Description
Tympanosympathectomy is an excision or chemical suppression of impulses of middle ear nerves.

The physician makes an incision in the posterior canal wall skin and raises a skin flap and the eardrum forward. Jacobson's nerve is identified in the middle ear and is divided. The eardrum and canal skin are repositioned and packing is placed in the ear canal.

20.92 Revision of mastoidectomy

Description
The physician performs a correction of a previous removal of mastoid cells from temporal or mastoid bone. Using a postaural incision, the physician revises a previously performed simple mastoidectomy with a complete mastoidectomy. The physician drills out the mastoid cavity. The mastoid sinus is exposed posteriorly. The tegmen (bony plate separating the mastoid and middle cranial fossa) is exposed superiorly. The posterior ear canal wall remains intact. The horizontal semicircular canal and part of the incus are visualized. Cholesteatoma or diseased mastoid mucosa are removed. The incision is sutured. A temporary drain may be placed and a dressing is applied.

Alternately, the physician revises a previously performed simple or complete mastoidectomy with a modified radical mastoidectomy by removing all the mastoid cells, granulations, pus, and the bony partitions of the mastoid cavity, using a postaural incision. A tympanomeatal flap is developed and reflected anteriorly. The posterior and superior bony canal walls are taken down to the level of the facial nerve. If cholesteatoma is present around the ossicles, the ossicles are removed. The tympanomeatal flap is repositioned over the facial ridge and into the mastoid cavity. Some middle ear space is thus maintained. A large meatoplasty is made. The ear canal and mastoid cavity are packed and the incision is closed with sutures.

When revising a previously performed complete or modified radical mastoidectomy with a radical mastoidectomy, the physician uses an endaural or postauricular incision. The posterior and superior bony canal walls are taken down to the level of the facial nerve. The ossicles, except for the stapes if possible, are removed, as well as the eustachian tube orifice mucosa, middle ear mucosa, granulations, and cholesteatoma. The middle ear and mastoid are exposed to the exterior through the ear canal. A large meatoplasty is performed. Packing is placed, the incision is sutured, and a dressing is applied.

Coding Guidance
AHA: 2Q, '98, 20

20.93 Repair of oval and round windows

Description
The physician makes a posterior canal incision through the external ear canal opening. Sometimes a postauricular incision is performed instead. Under microscopic guidance, the physician reflects the skin flap and posterior eardrum forward. The oval window area is inspected for fluid leak from the inner ear. The lining around the oval window is gently roughened. The area is packed with fat, fascia, or muscle tissue. The eardrum and skin flap are replaced and the canal is packed. If a postauricular incision is made, it is sutured.

Coding Clarification
Code 20.93 reports procedures performed to restore middle ear openings, such as closure of fistula described as perilymph, oval window, or round window.

20.94 Injection of tympanum

Description
Gentamycin injection is used as a treatment in some patients with severe dizziness. The ear is examined with a microscope, and the eardrum numbed with anesthetic. The physician inserts a tiny needle for the injection. This is repeated periodically until

18-20

dizziness stops. Hearing is assessed before each injection.

20.95   Implantation of electromagnetic hearing device

Description
The physician implants a bone conduction hearing device. Through a postauricular incision, the physician drills a circular depression in the outer skull cortex behind the mastoid cavity. The internal coil is seated in the circular depression and secured to the skull with titanium screws. The subcutaneous tissue over the internal coil may be thinned. The wound is irrigated and repaired with sutures. A dressing is applied.

Coding Clarification
Do not use 20.95 to report a cochlear prosthetic device; report 20.96-20.98.

Coding Guidance
AHA: 4Q, '89, 5, 6; 3Q, '07, 4

20.96   Implantation or replacement of cochlear prosthetic device, not otherwise specified

Description
The physician implants a receiver within the skull and inserts an electrode in the cochlea. Cochlear implants stimulate nerve ends within the inner ear, enabling deaf people to hear. The device has a microphone that remains outside the ear, a processor that selects and codes speech sounds, and a receiver/stimulator to convert the coded sounds to electric signals that stimulate the hearing nerve and are recognized by the brain as sound.

The physician makes a U-shaped incision, creating a skin flap well behind the mastoid, and drills a circular depression in the squamous portion of the temporal bone in which the internal coil will be housed. The mastoid air cells are removed with a drill, and a facial recess approach is used. The bony ear canal is preserved. The internal coil is secured in the depressed area of the temporal bone, and the electrode is introduced through the facial recess and the round window into the cochlea. The ground wire attached to the internal coil is introduced into the temporalis muscle. The incision is sutured.

Coding Clarification
Use this code to report the implantation of a receiver (within skull) and insertion of an electrode(s) in the cochlea.

Do not use 20.96 to report insertion of an electromagnetic hearing device; report 20.95.

Coding Guidance
AHA: 4Q, '89, 5, 6

20.97   Implantation or replacement of cochlear prosthetic device, single channel

Description
The physician makes a U-shaped incision, creating a skin flap well behind the mastoid, and drills a circular depression in the squamous portion of the temporal bone in which the internal coil will be housed. The mastoid air cells are removed with a drill, and a facial recess approach is used. The bony ear canal is preserved. The internal coil is secured in the depressed area of the temporal bone, and the electrode is introduced through the facial recess and the round window into the cochlea. The ground wire attached to the internal coil is introduced into the temporalis muscle. The incision is sutured.

Coding Clarification
Use this code to report the implantation of a receiver (within skull) and insertion of an electrode(s) in the cochlea.

Do not use 20.97 to report insertion of an electromagnetic hearing device; report 20.95.

Coding Guidance
AHA: 4Q, '89, 5, 6

20.98   Implantation or replacement of cochlear prosthetic device, multiple channel

Description
Through a postauricular incision, the physician drills a circular depression in the outer skull cortex behind the mastoid cavity. The internal coil is seated in the circular depression and secured to the skull with titanium screws. The subcutaneous tissue over the internal coil may be thinned. The wound is irrigated and repaired with sutures. A dressing is applied.

Coding Clarification
Use this code to report the implantation of a receiver (within skull) and insertion of an electrode(s) in the cochlea.

Do not use 20.98 to report insertion of an electromagnetic hearing device; report 20.95.

Coding Guidance
AHA: 4Q, '89, 5, 6

20.99   Other operations on middle and inner ear

Description
Through a postauricular incision, the physician accesses a previously implanted electromagnetic bone conduction hearing device. The device is repaired or removed. The wound is irrigated and repaired with sutures. A dressing is applied.

Coding Clarification
Code 20.99 is used to report the repair or removal of a cochlear prosthetic device (receiver or electrode).

● New Code   ▲ Revised Code   ▶◀ Revised Text   © 2010 Ingenix

Do not use 20.99 to report adjustment of the external components of a cochlear prosthetic device (95.49) or fitting of a hearing aid (95.48).

An inclusion term indicates that 20.99 includes attachment of a percutaneous abutment (screw) for prosthetic device.

Coding Guidance
   AHA: 4Q, '89, 7; 3Q, '07, 4

21-29

Operations on the Nose, Mouth and Pharynx

The ICD-9-CM classification system for operations performed on the nose, mouth, and pharynx is divided into categories of procedures according to sites as follows:

- Operations on the Nose (21)
- Operations on the Nasal Sinuses (22)
- Removal and Restoration of Teeth (23)
- Other Operations on Teeth, Gums, and Alveoli (24)
- Operations on Tongue (25)
- Operations on Salivary Glands and Ducts (26)
- Other Operations on Mouth and Face (27)
- Operations on Tonsils and Adenoids (28)
- Operations on Pharynx (29)

Coding Clarification
Many of the subcategories in this portion of the classification system require a fourth digit for further specificity with regard to type and/or site of the operation performed.

Documentation Tip
Documentation in the operative report must support code selection.

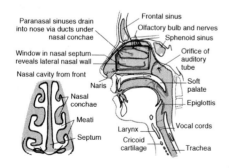

Paranasal sinuses drain into nose via ducts under nasal conchae
Window in nasal septum reveals lateral nasal wall
Nasal cavity from front
Naris
Nasal conchae
Meati
Septum
Frontal sinus
Olfactory bulb and nerves
Sphenoid sinus
Orifice of auditory tube
Soft palate
Epiglottis
Vocal cords
Larynx
Cricoid cartilage
Trachea

21   Operations on nose

Description
The nose consists of external and internal sections that serve as passageways for air. These nasal passageways warm and moisten inhaled air through the nostril openings. Inside the nostrils, or nares, the cilia (hairs inside the nose) work as a filter to trap foreign matter, such as dust and pollen. The cilia contain olfactory receptors, or nerves that facilitate the sense of smell. A partition known as the septum separates the nasal passageways into right and left-sided cavities. These cavities divide into superior, middle, and inferior air passages that connect to pharynx, eustachian tubes of the ears, and nasolacrimal ducts of the eyes. There are many conditions, inflammatory and non-inflammatory in nature, that may adversely affect the structure or function of nasal passages of the upper airway and cause breathing difficulties.

Category 21 provides codes for control of hemorrhage, incisions, diagnostic and therapeutic procedures including excisions, resections and repairs, and other operations. Procedures performed on the nasal sinuses are classified to category 22.

Coding Clarification
Codes in category 21 include operations on the bone and skin of the nose.

Coding Guidance
   AHA: 1Q, '94, 5

21.0   Control of epistaxis

Description
This code subcategory classifies control of nose bleed (epistaxis). Clinically, epistaxis can be divided into two categories, anterior bleeds and posterior bleeds, based on the site of the hemorrhage. Epistaxis often occurs when the nasal mucosa becomes eroded, causing the vessel walls to become weakened and break. Approximately 90 percent of nose bleeds occur in the anterior nasal at a network of vessels called the Kiesselbach plexus, near the nasal septum. This vascular plexus contains convergence of the internal and external carotid and maxillary venous and arterial branches. Posterior epistaxis occurs in the posterior nasal cavity and is often of arterial origin. Posterior nasal hemorrhages are often more complex or difficult to control than anterior epistaxis, and present a greater risk of

airway difficulty and aspiration of blood into the respiratory tract.

Coding Clarification
This subcategory reports control of epistaxis (nose bleed). Fourth-digit subclassification is required for specificity. The fourth digit describes the site of treatment that corresponds to the site of hemorrhage, as well as the technique utilized to control the hemorrhage.

21.00   Control of epistaxis, not otherwise specified
Description
This code describes control of epistaxis that is not otherwise specified. The physician commonly uses an endoscope for a diagnostic evaluation of the bleeding nose. Electrical or chemical coagulation or packing materials may be applied to the anterior (front) section of the nose or limited electrical or chemical coagulation may be utilized to control a simple nose bleed (epistaxis). The physician may use extensive electrical coagulation or extensive packing in the anterior (front) section of the nose if the epistaxis is complicated, or otherwise resistant to control. To control bleeding that is coming from the posterior (back) of the nose (nasopharynx), the physician places packing into the nasal cavity through the back of the throat. Extensive electrical coagulation may be required. The patient may return if the bleeding recurs. When nasal packing and coagulation fail to control nasal hemorrhage, the physician may administer a local anesthetic and control the epistaxis by ligation of the nasal arteries that supply the nose or other surgical means such as skin grafting. Depending on the location of the artery ligated for hemorrhage control, the site of the incision and access may vary. Bone flaps may be elevated. An operating microscope may be utilized for assistance in locating the vessel. Once the vessel is isolated, a clip or suture is utilized to control the hemorrhage. The incision is repaired with layered closure.

Coding Clarification
Review the documentation in the medical record to determine the site of epistaxis and method of hemorrhage control (e.g., packing, cauterization, or ligation).

Avoid using 21.00 Control of epistaxis, not otherwise specified.

Documentation Tip
Carefully review the documentation in the medical record to ascertain whether the epistaxis is specified as an anterior or posterior nasal site. If unclear, the physician should be queried.

21.01   Control of epistaxis by anterior nasal packing
Description
This code describes control of epistaxis by packing of the anterior nasal cavity. Several types of nasal packing products exist and may be utilized, depending on the nature of the hemorrhage. Common packing products include nasal tampon sponges, gauze impregnated with petroleum jelly, or small, inflatable balloon-type devices with a hemostatic sleeve. Some devices are impregnated with a vasoconstrictor such as phenylephrine 0.25% and a topical anesthetic (e.g., lidocaine 2%). Topical decongestants and anesthetic agents may also be applied.

Examination of the nasal cavity may be performed with a headlight or head mirror, nasal speculum, otoscope and speculum, and nasal suction. Once the site of hemorrhage has been visualized, blood and clots are debrided with a straight, rigid nasal suction, flexible suction catheter, or bayonet forceps. Anterior packing is commonly left in for up to 72 hours. The patient may need to return for removal of packing, depending on the type of packing utilized.

Coding Clarification
Review the documentation in the medical record for documentation of electrical or chemical coagulation in addition to the packing.

Report 21.03 for control of anterior nasal hemorrhage with packing and cauterization.

21.02   Control of epistaxis by posterior (and anterior) packing
Description
The physician may apply electrical or chemical coagulation or packing materials to the anterior (front) section of the nose. To control bleeding that is coming from the posterior (back) of the nose (nasopharynx), the physician places packing into the posterior nasal cavity through the back of the throat. Several types of nasal packing products exist and may be utilized, depending on the nature of the hemorrhage. Common posterior packing products include coated gauze, impregnated sponge tampons, Foley catheters with gauze pack, and other double-balloon (anteroposterior) inflatable nasal devices. IV sedation, analgesia, and supplementary O2 may be necessary. The posterior packing material may be tied to a catheter and threaded through the nasal cavity on the side of the bleeding and through the mouth. As the catheter is withdrawn from the nose, the postnasal pack may be pulled into place above the soft palate in the nasopharynx. The packing may remain in place for up to five days. An antibiotic may be given to prevent infection.

Coding Clarification
Assign this code for epistaxis control by posterior (and anterior) packing with catheter assistance or balloon device. The catheter and balloon devices are included in the packing procedure, and are not reported separately.

Review the documentation in the medical record for documentation of electrical or chemical coagulation in addition to the packing.

Report 21.03 for control of anterior nasal hemorrhage with packing and cauterization.

Coding Scenario
A 45-year-old female presented to the emergency department with severe epistaxis of two hours duration. Upon physical examination, she was hemodynamically stable and neurologically intact, although she had bleeding from the left nostril. Hemostasis was ultimately achieved by placing anteroposterior packing soaked in bacitracin, oxymetazoline, and 4% cocaine solution.

Code Assignment:

784.7 Epistaxis
21.02 Control of epistaxis by posterior (and anterior) packing

Coding Guidance
AHA: 1Q, '95, 5

21.03 Control of epistaxis by cauterization (and packing)

Description
The physician applies heat energy (electrocautery) or chemical coagulation (silver nitrate) to seal the bleeding vessel(s) and inserts packing materials to the anterior (front) section of the nose or posterior (back) section of the nasal cavity to control epistaxis. The physician may apply electrocautery or chemical coagulation with packing materials to the anterior (front) section of the nose and use limited electrical or chemical coagulation to control a simple nose bleed (epistaxis). To control bleeding that is coming from the posterior (back) of the nose (nasopharynx), the physician may cauterize the bleeding vessel and/or place packing into the posterior nasal cavity through the back of the throat. The physician may use extensive electrical coagulation or extensive packing with inflatable devices and catheters if the epistaxis is complicated or otherwise resistant to control. Posterior packing may remains in place for up to five days. An antibiotic may be given to prevent infection.

Coding Clarification
Assign this code for epistaxis treated with both packing and cauterization.

Epistaxis controlled by packing only is classified to 21.01 (anterior) or 21.02, as appropriate.

Epistaxis controlled by arterial ligation is reported with codes that describe the anatomic site of vessels treated (21.04-21.06).

Documentation Tip
Carefully review the documentation in the medical record to confirm that epistaxis is specified treated with both cauterization and packing. If treatment methods are unclear, the physician should be queried.

21.04 Control of epistaxis by ligation of ethmoidal arteries

Description
When site of bleeding is determined to be the ethmoid arteries, the physician may administer a local anesthetic and control the epistaxis by ligation of the ethmoid vessels. The physician administers a local anesthetic and makes an incision along the side of the nose near the inner canthus of the eye to expose the ethmoid arteries. The periosteum (periorbitum) is elevated. The anterior ethmoid artery is identified in the suture line between the frontal and ethmoid bones. The posterior ethmoid artery is located entering the posterior medial wall near the orbital apex. A clip or suture completes the ligation. The incision is repaired with layered closure.

Coding Clarification
Assign this code for ligation of vessels by a surgical tying or binding procedure.

Report control of epistaxis by cauterization of vessels with 21.03.

This procedure includes nasal packing.

21.05 Control of epistaxis by (transantral) ligation of the maxillary artery

Description
When site of bleeding is determined to be the maxillary artery, the physician may administer a local anesthetic and control the epistaxis by ligation of the maxillary artery. The physician makes an incision in the mucous membrane under the upper lip. The incision above the canine tooth on the side of the hemorrhage is commonly referred to as a Caldwell-Luc approach. An opening is created through the bone into the normal maxillary sinus. Through an operating microscope, the physician locates and incises the posterior wall of the maxillary sinus. Through this incision, the maxillary artery is isolated and ligated with sutures or a clip. The posterior maxillary sinus wall is repaired. The incision is repaired with a layered closure.

Coding Clarification
Assign this code for ligation of vessels by a surgical tying or binding procedure.

Report control of epistaxis by cauterization of vessels with 21.03.

21.06 Control of epistaxis by ligation of the external carotid artery

Description
Posterior epistaxis may result from hemorrhage of the sphenopalatine artery, a branch of the external carotid artery. This type of epistaxis usually occurs in patients with chronic hypertension and may be controlled with ligation of the external carotid in the neck. The patient is sedated and kept in a head-elevated position. Nasal endoscopy, a catheter, or an operating microscope may be used to assist in visualization and access of the vessels. The physician applies a vasoconstrictor and topical anesthetic to both nasal passages. Once the vessel is isolated, it is ligated with sutures or a clip. If an operative incision was made, it is repaired with layered closure.

Coding Clarification
Assign this code for ligation of vessels by a surgical tying or binding procedure.

Report control of epistaxis by cauterization of vessels with 21.03.

This procedure includes nasal packing.

21.07 Control of epistaxis by excision of nasal mucosa and skin grafting of septum and lateral nasal wall

Description
The physician removes diseased intranasal mucosa and replaces it with a separately reportable split thickness graft. The surgery is performed on one nasal side. A lateral rhinotomy is made to expose the intranasal mucosa. The diseased mucosal tissue is excised from the septum, nasal floor, and anterior aspect of the inferior turbinate. A split thickness graft is sutured to the recipient bed, covering the exposed cartilage and submucosal surfaces. Gauze packing and splints are placed in the grafted nasal cavity.

Coding Clarification
Assign this code for epistaxis control by tissue excision and graft.

Documentation Tip
This procedure may also be documented as a septal or intranasal dermatoplasty.

21.09 Control of epistaxis by other means

Description
Report 21.09 for control of epistaxis by other means for which there is no more precise code in subcategory 21.0.

Control of epistaxis may be achieved by embolization of an artery. Embolization is most commonly utilized for control of posterior epistaxis and other severe or recurrent intranasal hemorrhages. Embolization is accomplished by interventional radiology measures that involve the insertion of a catheter, or tube, through an artery in the groin. The tube is guided up through the blood vessels to the site of the epistaxis, where it delivers small particles of a spongy material that embolize, or clog up, the artery that feeds the epistaxis to allow the hemorrhage to heal. This material eventually will break down. Alternatively, small pieces of soft flexible platinum wire that induce clotting may be used to embolize the artery. The access instrumentation is removed and the groin incision is closed in layers.

Coding Clarification
This code includes control of epistaxis by ligation of an unspecified artery or vessel.

This procedure includes nasal packing.

Coding Guidance
AHA: 1Q, '95, 5

21.1 Incision of nose

Description
This code classifies incisions of the nose, nasal septum, cartilage, and other nasal tissues. Nasal incisions can be performed for a variety of reasons including:

- **Foreign body removal:** The physician removes a foreign body from deep within the nasal cavity, accessing the area with a lateral rhinotomy. This foreign body is located in an area of difficult access and requires complex surgery to remove it. Foreign bodies are defined as objects not normally found in the body. The object may be embedded in normal tissue as a result of some type of trauma. Topical vasoconstrictive agents and local anesthesia are applied to the nasal mucosa. A full-thickness skin incision is made from the nostril extending along the nasal alar rim and continuing superiorly. The incision can extend to the medial aspect of the eyebrow if necessary. The lateral aspect of the nose is retracted, exposing the bony structures beneath the soft tissue. Blunt dissection and retrieval of the object is performed with hemostats or forceps. The surgical wound is closed in layers.

- **Abscess or hematoma drainage:** The physician makes an incision to decompress and drain a collection of pus or blood in the nasal mucosa or septal mucosa. A hemostat bluntly penetrates the pockets and allows the fluid to evacuate. Once decompressed, a small latex drain may be placed into the incision site. This allows an escape for any fluids that may continue to enter the pocket. If a drain is used, it is removed within 48 hours. The nasal cavity may be packed with gauze or Telfa to provide pressure against the mucosa and assist decompression after drainage. The incision may be closed primarily or may be left to granulate without closure.

Coding Clarification
This code classifies incisions of the nose, nasal septum, cartilage, and other nasal tissues. It is not to be reported separately if performed as an operative approach to another procedure.

Documentation Tip
The operative report may include the following terminology for procedures reported with this code:

- Nasal chondrotomy
- Nasal septotomy

21.2   Diagnostic procedures on nose

Description
This subcategory classifies diagnostic nasal procedures including rhinoscopy, biopsy, and other diagnostic procedures.

Coding Clarification
Fourth-digit subclassification is required for specificity. The fourth digit describes the type of procedure as an endoscopy, biopsy, or other diagnostic procedure.

21.21   Rhinoscopy

Description
The physician performs an endoscopic intranasal examination. An endoscope has a rigid fiberoptic telescope that allows the physician both increased visualization and magnification of internal anatomy. Topical vasoconstrictive agents are applied to the nasal mucosa and nerve blocks with local anesthesia are performed. The endoscope is placed into the nose and a thorough inspection of internal nasal structures is accomplished.

The physician may also examine the nasopharynx via a diagnostic rhinoscopy procedure, whereby the examination is performed with the patient lying on his back. Under a local anesthetic with topical Lidocaine sprayed onto the back of the throat and into the nasal passages, the physician introduces the flexible fiberoptic endoscope through the nose and advances it into the pharynx. Endoscopic

examination may be made to determine whether there are any fixed blockages such as a deviated septum, nasal polyps, or enlarged adenoids and tonsils. The physician may position the tip of the endoscope at the level of the hard palate and instruct the patient to perform simple maneuvers that demonstrate airway activity under conditions that promote or prevent collapse. The test may also be performed to identify anatomic factors contributing to sleep disorder, stability of the upper airway, and determining treatments.

Coding Clarification
This procedure includes intranasal or nasopharyngeal endoscopy.

Endoscopy of the nasal sinuses is classified to 22.19 Other diagnostic procedures on nasal sinuses.

21.22   Biopsy of nose

Description
This procedure code describes a nasal biopsy, whether by direct (intranasal) approach or via an endoscopy In a direct biopsy, the physician removes mucosa from inside the nose for biopsy. This biopsy is performed when the mucosa is suspicious for disease. Some normal tissue adjacent to the diseased mucosa is also removed during the biopsy. This allows the pathologist to compare diseased vs. non-diseased tissues. The excision site may be closed primarily with sutures or may be allowed to granulate without closure.

In an endoscopic biopsy, the physician uses an endoscope for a diagnostic evaluation of the nose. An endoscope has a rigid fiberoptic telescope that allows the physician both increased visualization and magnification of internal anatomy. Topical vasoconstrictive agents are applied to the nasal mucosa and nerve blocks when local anesthesia are performed. The endoscope is placed into the nose and a thorough inspection of the internal nasal structures is accomplished. Any identified lesions can be removed by intranasal instruments placed parallel to the endoscope. Scalpels, forceps, snares, and other instruments are used to remove diseased mucosa or lesions from the internal nose. The nose may be packed if excessive bleeding occurs.

Documentation Tip
The operative report may include the following terminology for procedures reported with this code:

- Biopsies of the skin of the nose
- Endoscopic intranasal biopsy
- Other direct intranasal biopsy (non-endoscopic)
- Biopsy of nasal mucosa
- Biopsy of nasal septum

21.29   Other diagnostic procedures on nose

Description
Code 21.29 reports other diagnostic nasal
procedures that are not more specifically described
by other codes within subcategory 21.2.

Coding Clarification
The following procedures are excluded from 21.29
and are more appropriately reported elsewhere:

- Microscopic examination of specimen from nose
  (90.31-90.39)
- Nasal function study (89.12)
- Nasal x-ray (87.16)
- Rhinomanometry (89.12)

21.3   Local excision or destruction of lesion of nose

Description
This code subcategory includes excision or
destruction of nasal lesions described as "local" or
not otherwise specified, including lesions of the skin
of the nose and intranasal lesions. Tissue excision or
destruction may be performed under direct
visualization (transnasal) or with the assistance of
an endoscope.

Endoscopic excision/destruction: The physician
uses an endoscope for a diagnostic evaluation of the
nose. An endoscope has a rigid fiberoptic telescope
that allows the physician both increased
visualization and magnification of internal anatomy.
Topical vasoconstrictive agents are applied to the
nasal mucosa and nerve blocks with local anesthesia
are performed. The endoscope is placed into the
nose and a thorough inspection of the internal nasal
structures is accomplished. Any identified lesions
can be removed by intranasal instruments placed
parallel to the endoscope. Scalpels, forceps, snares,
and other instruments are used to remove diseased
mucosa or lesions from the internal nose. The nose
may be packed if excessive bleeding occurs.

Coding Clarification
Fourth-digit subclassification is required for
specificity.

The following procedures are excluded from 21.29
and are more appropriately reported elsewhere:

- Biopsy of nose (21.22)
- Nasal fistulectomy (21.82)

21.30   Excision or destruction of lesion of nose, not otherwise specified

Description
This code describes excision or destruction of nasal
lesions that cannot be appropriately classified to
21.31 or 21.32.

The physician removes or destroys soft tissue lesions
using techniques such as cryosurgery, chemical
application, or laser surgery. The lesion may be
approached intranasally or through external skin
incisions. The physician performs a lateral
rhinotomy by retracting the lateral ala to expose the
internal nose. Cryosurgery will freeze and kill soft
tissue lesions. Laser surgery will vaporize and
emulsify the lesions. Chemical application of topical
vasoconstrictive agents and local anesthesia
cauterizes vessels and limits post-surgical
hemorrhage. No postoperative wound closure or
intranasal packing is usually necessary.

21.31   Local excision or destruction of intranasal lesion

Description
This code describes excision or destruction of
intranasal lesions, specifically. The physician
removes or destroys intranasal soft tissue lesions
using techniques such as cryosurgery, chemical
application, or laser surgery. The lesion is
approached intranasally or through external skin
incisions. The physician performs a lateral
rhinotomy by retracting the lateral ala to expose the
internal nose. Cryosurgery will freeze and kill soft
tissue lesions. Laser surgery will vaporize and
emulsify the lesions. Chemical application of topical
vasoconstrictive agents and local anesthesia
cauterizes vessels and limits post-surgical
hemorrhage. No postoperative wound closure or
intranasal packing is usually necessary.

The physician may remove a lesion specified as a
polyp from inside the nose. Nasal polyps can grow to
a large size, which may obstruct both the airway
passages and sinus drainage ducts. The polyp is
usually approached intranasally. Topical
vasoconstrictive agents are applied to the nasal
mucosa. Local anesthesia is injected underneath
and around the polyp. A scalpel or biting forceps can
be used to excise the polyp. Small polyps may leave
mucosal defects that do not require closure. With
larger defects, the mucosa is closed with sutures in a
single layer. The physician may place Telfa to pack
the nasal cavity during the first 24 hours.

21.32   Local excision or destruction of other lesion of nose

Description
This code describes excision or destruction of nasal
lesions that cannot be appropriately classified to
codes 21.30 or 21.31.

The physician may destroy or excise skin lesions
using a laser, electrosurgery, cryosurgery, chemical
treatment, or surgical curettement. Local anesthesia
is included.

● New Code   ▲ Revised Code   ►◄ Revised Text   © 2010 Ingenix

The physician surgically removes diseased tissue caused by rhinophyma from the external nasal tip. A rhinophyma is a descriptive term for a large, bulbous, ruddy appearance of the nose caused by granulomatous tissue, or untreated rosacea. It is characterized by hypertrophy of the sebaceous glands and connective tissue, as well as multiple telangectasias. Local anesthesia is injected into the nasal tip. The excess tissue is removed by carving and recontouring hyperplastic tissue from the area. Scalpels, dermabrasion (planing with fine sandpaper or wire brushes), and lasers are common methods for removing this excess tissue. A thin layer of epithelium is maintained over the nasal cartilages to ensure adequate healing.

Coding Clarification
This code includes wide (radical) excision of lesions of the skin of the nose.

Coding Guidance
   AHA: 2Q, '89, 16

21.4   Resection of nose

Description
This code describes a resection or amputation of all or part of the nose. The physician resects the nose, leaving a surgical defect. The extent of the resection is determined by the extent of the tumor or trauma. A full-thickness incision is made through the external nose. All diseased or damaged soft tissue is excised to clear margins. Underlying bone or cartilage may be removed. Exposed bone or cartilage is covered with mucosal flaps or separately reportable skin grafts.

Documentation Tip
The operative report may include the following terminology:

- Resection of nose
- Amputation of nose (total) (partial)

21.5   Submucous resection of nasal septum

Description
This code describes a resection of the nasal septum whereby the physician reshapes the nasal septum, correcting airway obstruction caused by trauma, neoplasm, or other structural abnormality or inflammation. Topical vasoconstrictive agents are applied to shrink the blood vessels and local anesthesia is injected in the nasal mucosa. The physician makes a vertical incision in the septal mucosa and elevates the mucoperichondrium from the septal cartilage. The deviated portion of the bony and cartilaginous septum is excised or augmented by grafting. If the cartilaginous septum remains bowed, partial or full-thickness incisions are made in the cartilage to straighten the septum. Excess

cartilage is excised from the bone-cartilage junction. Incisions are closed in single layers. Transseptal sutures are placed. Septal splints may support the septum during healing.

Documentation Tip
The operative report may include the following terminology:

- Septoplasty with submucous resection

21.6   Turbinectomy

Description
This subcategory classifies the removal, partial or total, of turbinate bones. The inferior turbinate is most often excised. Turbinectomy is often performed for the treatment of chronic sinusitis, but may also be indicated in the presence of neoplasm or to correct certain nasal fractures or other structural abnormalities that obstruct the airway (e.g., sleep apnea).

Coding Clarification
Fourth-digit subclassification is required for specificity. The fourth digit describes the surgical technique or associated procedures.

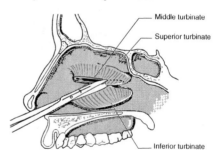

Middle turbinate
Superior turbinate
Inferior turbinate

21.61   Turbinectomy by diathermy or cryosurgery

Description
This code describes turbinectomy by diathermy or cryosurgery, which uses heat or freezing temperatures to destroy the nasal turbinate bones. The physician removes a part or all of the inferior turbinate bone through a submucous incision. The physician places vasoconstrictive drugs on the turbinate to shrink the blood vessels. A full-thickness incision is made over the anterior-inferior surface of the turbinate and continued deep to bone. The physician lifts the mucoperiosteum with an elevator to expose the bony turbinate. The bony turbinate is destroyed using high frequency electrical current (diathermy) or freezing (cryosurgery). The turbinate mucosa may be closed in a single layer or electrocautery may be used to control the bleeding. The nasal mucosa may be sutured in single layers. The nasal cavity may be packed with gauze.

21.62   Fracture of the turbinates

Description
The physician fractures a portion of the inferior turbinate bone to reposition the nasal turbinate. This procedure is performed on a hypertrophied (enlarged) inferior turbinate obstructing the nasal airway. With repositioning, the hypertrophied turbinate should shrink in size, allowing normal airflow. Topical vasoconstrictive drugs are placed on the turbinate to shrink the blood vessels. Commonly, the physician uses a blunt instrument to out-fracture the turbinate. This can be performed with or without incisions. If visualization is necessary, the physician makes a full-thickness incision over the anterior-inferior surface of the turbinate and continues it deep to bone. An elevator lifts the mucoperiosteum, exposing the bony turbinate. The physician fractures the bony turbinate with a chisel. Electrocautery may control bleeding. The turbinate mucosa is closed in a single layer.

21.69   Other turbinectomy

Description
Code 21.69 reports other turbinectomies that are not more specifically described by other codes within subcategory 21.6. Procedures classified to this code include:

- **Turbinectomy with submucous resection of turbinate bones:** The physician removes a part or all of the inferior turbinate bone through a submucous incision. The physician places vasoconstrictive drugs on the turbinate to shrink the blood vessels. A full-thickness incision is made over the anterior-inferior surface of the turbinate and continued deep to bone. The physician lifts the mucoperiosteum with an elevator to expose the bony turbinate. A chisel or forceps is used to remove portions of the bony turbinate. Electrocautery may control bleeding. The turbinate mucosa is closed in a single layer.

- **Turbinectomy with cauterization of mucosa:** The physician uses electrocautery and/or ablation to reduce inflammation or remove excessive mucosa from the inferior nasal turbinates unilaterally or bilaterally. Cauterization may be superficial or may be placed deep into the mucosa. Topical vasoconstrictive agents are applied to the nasal mucosa. Excessive or hypertrophied mucosa is cauterized or ablated and may be excised. Postoperative bleeding is minimal and there is no need for intranasal packing.

- **Other turbinectomy:** The physician removes a part of or the entire inferior nasal turbinate located on the lateral wall of the nose. The

turbinate is primarily removed in cases of hypertrophy that obstruct the nasal airway. The physician places topical vasoconstrictive drugs on the turbinate to shrink the blood vessels. A mucosal incision is made around the base of the turbinate. The physician fractures the bony turbinate from the lateral nasal wall with a chisel or drill. The turbinate is excised. Electrocautery may control bleeding. The nasal mucosa is sutured in single layers. The nasal cavity may be packed with gauze.

Coding Clarification
Turbinectomy associated with sinusectomy is excluded from 21.69. Turbinectomy is included with sinusectomy procedure codes 22.31-22.39, 22.42, and 22.60-22.64.

21.7   Reduction of nasal fracture

Description
This subcategory classifies reduction of nasal fracture by open or closed technique.

Coding Clarification
Fourth-digit subclassification is required for specificity. The fourth digit describes the surgical technique as an open or closed approach.

A fracture reduction not specified as open or closed is assumed to be closed.

Closed reduction of a fracture may be defined as a manipulative correction of fracture to anatomic position without an incision or exposure of the bone through the skin.

Open reduction of a fracture may be defined as a manipulative correction of a fracture to anatomic position through exposure of the fracture site by an incision carried down through the skin to the fractured bone.

Coding Guidance
AHA: 2Q, '94, 3

21.71   Closed reduction of nasal fracture

Description
The physician treats a displaced nasal fracture by manipulating the nasal bones. The physician places nasal elevators or forceps into the nose and realigns the nasal bones. After the bones are realigned, they remain slightly mobile and require additional stabilization with splints. External splinting may consist of a cast taped to the reduced nose. Internal splinting consists of supporting the nasal septum by splints or packing with gauze strips.

In closed treatment of a nasoethmoid fracture, the physician may repair a fracture of the nasoethmoid region with a percutaneous (through the skin) approach. Percutaneous pins or screws are placed into stable bone and attached to external support such as splints, headcaps, or wire fixation to aid in reduction of the fractures. If the medial canthal ligaments are detached, they are repaired through a percutaneous approach with awls or K-wires and transnasal stainless steel sutures or wire. Injuries of the nasolacrimal complex are repaired using non-resorbable sutures and polyethylene tubing.

In closed treatment of a fracture of the nasal septum, no intranasal incisions are made. The physician may use nasal elevators and forceps to realign the septal fracture. Transseptal sutures may be placed to prevent formation of a septal hematoma. Internal splints or packing with gauze strips may be used for stabilization to support the septum during healing.

21.72   Open reduction of nasal fracture

Description
This procedure code describes open treatment of nasal fractures, and includes various anatomic sites and restorative techniques. In open treatment of uncomplicated fracture, the physician treats a displaced nasal fracture. After unsatisfactory results with closed manipulation of the fractured bones, the physician performs open treatment. Open reduction allows the physician to visualize the fracture. Lacerations may be present, allowing direct visualization. Incisions are made inside the nose to expose the nasal septum and portions of the nasal bones. The physician realigns the fractured bones using nasal elevators and forceps. It may be necessary to remove small segments of bone for adequate realignment. Intranasal incisions are closed in a single layer. Any lacerated skin areas are closed in layers. After the bones are realigned, they remain slightly mobile and require additional stabilization with splints. External splinting may consist of a cast taped to the reduced nose. Internal splinting consists of supporting the nasal septum by splints or packing with gauze strips.

In open treatment of a complicated fracture with fixation, the physician treats a displaced nasal fracture. After unsatisfactory results with closed manipulation of the fractured bones, the physician performs open treatment. Open reduction allows the physician to visualize the fracture. Lacerations may be present, allowing direct visualization. Incisions are made inside the nose to expose the nasal septum and portions of the nasal bones. Additionally, bicoronal or other local skin incisions may be used to expose the fractured nasal bones. The physician realigns the fractured bones using nasal elevators and forceps. The bones are fixed in reduction with wires, plates, and/or screws. Intranasal incisions are closed in a single layer. Lacerations and other skin incisions are repaired with layered closure.

In open treatment of a septal fracture, the physician makes an incision to treat a displaced nasal fracture and also repairs the fractured nasal septum. Open treatment is necessary after unsatisfactory results with closed manipulation of the fractured bones and allows the physician to visualize the fractures. Lacerations overlying the fractures may allow direct visualization. Incisions may be made inside the nose to expose the nasal septum and portions of the nasal bones. Additionally, bicoronal and other local skin incisions may be used to expose the fractured nasal bones. The nasal septum is exposed and portions of the fractured cartilaginous and bony septum are removed. The physician realigns the nasal bones using nasal elevators and forceps. Transseptal sutures are placed to prevent formation of a septal hematoma. Intranasal incisions are closed in a single layer. Lacerations and other skin incisions are repaired with layered closure. After the bones are realigned, they remain slightly mobile and require additional stabilization with splints. External splinting may consist of a cast taped to the reduced nose. Internal splinting consists of supporting the nasal septum by splints or packing with gauze strips.

In open septal fracture treatment without stabilization, the physician makes an incision to repair a nasal septal fracture. Open treatment is necessary after unsatisfactory results with closed manipulation of the fractured septum and allows the physician to visualize the septal fracture. Incisions are made inside the nose. The nasal septum is exposed and portions of the fractured cartilaginous and bony septum are removed. Transseptal sutures are placed to prevent formation of a septal hematoma. Intranasal incisions are closed in single layers. Stabilization such as internal splinting may be used to support the septum during healing. Internal splinting consists of supporting the nasal septum by splints or packing with gauze strips.

In open treatment of a nasoethmoid fracture, the physician repairs fractures of the nasoethmoid region, which includes nasal and ethmoid bones and the medial wall of the orbit. Lacerations may be present allowing direct visualization. The physician may use bicoronal, local skin, and lower eyelid incisions to expose the fractured bones. The medial canthal ligaments are examined and, if detached, are repaired in a separately reportable procedure with transnasal stainless steel sutures or wire. The physician realigns the fractured bones and holds them in rigid reduction with internal wires, plates, and/or screws. Any lacerated skin areas are repaired and other skin incisions are closed in layers. Although external fixation is not always required, it may be needed to support grossly depressed fractures.

21.8 Repair and plastic operations on the nose

Description
This subcategory classifies repairs of the nose, which includes sutures and fistula repairs, variations of rhinoplasty, and nasal reconstructions.

Coding Clarification
Fourth-digit subclassification is required for specificity. The fourth digit describes the specific procedure according to surgical technique and extent of procedure performed, as well as providing classification options for procedures not classifiable elsewhere.

21.81 Suture of laceration of nose

Description
The physician sutures lacerations of the nose, ranging from simple to complex in severity. A local anesthetic is injected around the laceration and the wound is cleansed, explored, and irrigated with a saline solution. For suture of simple lacerations, the physician may perform a simple, one-layer repair of the epidermis, dermis, or subcutaneous tissue with sutures.

Lacerations of intermediate complexity may require a layered closure. A local anesthetic is injected around the laceration and the wound is cleansed, explored, and often irrigated with a saline solution. Due to deeper or more complex lacerations, deep subcutaneous or layered suturing techniques are required. The physician sutures tissue layers under the skin with dissolvable sutures before suturing the skin. Extensive cleaning or removal of foreign matter from a heavily contaminated wound that is closed with a single layer may also be reported as an intermediate repair.

The physician may repair complex lacerations of the nose with complex, layered suturing of torn, crushed, or deeply lacerated tissue. The physician debrides the wound by removing foreign material or damaged tissue. Irrigation of the wound is performed and antimicrobial solutions are used to decontaminate and cleanse the wound. The physician may trim skin margins with a scalpel or scissors to allow for proper closure. The wound is closed in layers. Stents or retention sutures may also be used in complex repair of a wound.

Coding Clarification
This code reports suture of a laceration of the nose. To report suture of nose for control of epistaxis, see subcategory 21.0 Control of epistaxis.

This code includes suture or closure of wound dehiscence.

21.82 Closure of nasal fistula

Description
A nasal fistula is an abnormal passageway between the nose and another structure. Fistulas may be a complication from previous injury or surgery or can result from chronic infection or inflammatory conditions. The following types of nasal fistulas are classified to this code:

- **Oronasal:** The physician closes an opening between the mouth and nasal cavity. The communication is through the maxillary hard palate and the tract is lined with epithelium. Local anesthesia is injected into the mucosa. The physician uses a scalpel to excise the epithelized tract. An incision is made into the palatal mucosa and a local mucosal flap is developed. The flap is sutured in layers, covering the oronasal tract.

- **Nasolabial:** The physician repairs a fistula communication from the nasal or sinus regions to the nasolabial region of the midface. The repair is dependent on the size of the fistular tract. For small defects, an excision of the epithelized tract is made from source to skin surface. This wound is sutured in layers. In larger defects, a nasolabial flap may be necessary after excision of the fistula. A nasolabial flap is designed, incised, and rotated to the defect region. The flap is sutured over the defect in layers.

- **Oromaxillary/Oroantral:** The physician closes an opening between the mouth and the maxillary sinus. The communication is through the maxillary bone and this tract is lined with epithelium. Local anesthesia is injected into the mucosa. The physician uses a scalpel to excise the epithelized tract. An incision is made into the palatal mucosa and a local mucosal flap is developed. The flap is sutured in layers, covering the oromaxillary tract. Careful postoperative instructions are given to limit sinus pressure by not allowing nose blowing, which would reopen the tract and impair healing.

Coding Clarification
This code classifies fistulas of the nose and lip, the nose and pharynx, or the nose and mouth.

Fistula repair of the nasal sinuses is classified to 22.71 Closure of nasal sinus fistula.

21.83 Total nasal reconstruction

Description
The physician performs surgery to reshape the external nose. No surgery to the nasal septum is necessary. This surgery can be performed open (external skin incisions) or closed (intranasal

incisions). Topical vasoconstrictive agents are applied to shrink the blood vessels and local anesthesia is injected in the nasal mucosa. After incisions are made, dissections expose the external nasal cartilaginous and bony skeleton. The cartilages may be reshaped by trimming or may be augmented by grafting. Local grafts from adjacent nasal bones and cartilage are not reported separately. The physician may reshape the dorsum with files. The physician fractures the lateral nasal bones with chisels. Fat may be removed from the subcutaneous regions. Incisions are closed in single layers. Steri-strip tape is used to support cartilaginous surgery of the nasal tip. An external splint or cast supports changes in bone position.

Coding Clarification
This code includes nasal reconstruction with arm flap graft or forehead flap graft.

This code reports the recreation, restoration, or rebuilding of the nose.

21.84 Revision rhinoplasty

Description
The physician performs a second surgery to reshape the external nose and correct unfavorable results from the initial rhinoplasty. Secondary rhinoplasties can be performed open (external skin incisions) or closed (intranasal incisions). Topical vasoconstrictive agents are applied to shrink the blood vessels and local anesthesia is injected in the nasal mucosa. After incisions are made, dissections expose the external nasal cartilaginous and bony skeleton. The cartilages and nasal tip may be reduced by trimming or may be augmented by grafting. The bony dorsum may receive grafts. Local grafts from adjacent nasal bones and cartilage are not reported separately. Incisions are closed in single layers. Steri-strip tape is used to support cartilaginous surgery of the nasal tip. An external splint or cast supports changes in bone position.

Coding Clarification
This code also includes rhinoplasty for repair of nasal deformity secondary to cleft lip and/or palate.

Augmentation rhinoplasty is classified to 21.85. Tip rhinoplasty is classified to 21.86.

Documentation Tip
The operative report may include the following terminology:

- Rhinoseptoplasty
- Twisted nose rhinoplasty

21.85 Augmentation rhinoplasty

Description
The physician performs surgery to reshape or enlarge the external nose. No surgery to the nasal

septum is necessary. This surgery can be performed open (external skin incisions) or closed (intranasal incisions). Topical vasoconstrictive agents are applied to shrink the blood vessels and local anesthesia is injected in the nasal mucosa. After incisions are made, dissections expose the external nasal cartilaginous and bony skeleton. The cartilages may be reshaped by trimming or may be augmented by grafting. Local grafts from adjacent nasal bones and cartilage are not reported separately. The physician may reshape the dorsum with files. The physician fractures the lateral nasal bones with chisels. Fat may be removed from the subcutaneous regions. Incisions are closed in single layers. Steri-strip tape is used to support cartilaginous surgery of the nasal tip. An external splint or cast supports changes in bone position.

Coding Clarification
This code includes augmentation rhinoplasty with graft or synthetic implant.

21.86 Limited rhinoplasty

Description
In tip rhinoplasty, the physician performs surgery to reshape the external nose. No surgery to the nasal septum is necessary. The physician may perform surgery open (external skin incisions) or closed (intranasal incisions). Topical vasoconstrictive agents are applied to shrink the blood vessels and local anesthesia is injected into the nasal mucosa. After incisions are made, dissections expose the external nasal cartilaginous and bony skeleton. The cartilages may be reshaped with files. Fat may be removed from the subcutaneous regions. Incisions are closed in single layers. Steri-strip tape is used to support cartilaginous surgery of the nasal tip.

Alternately, the physician reshapes the external nose and corrects secondary developmental cleft lip and/or palate deformities. Rhinoplasties can be performed open (external skin incisions) or closed (intranasal incisions). Topical vasoconstrictive agents are applied to shrink the blood vessels and local anesthesia is injected in the nasal mucosa. After incisions are made, dissections expose the external nasal cartilaginous and bony skeleton. The cartilages and nasal tip may be reduced by trimming or may be augmented by grafting. Local grafts from adjacent nasal bones and cartilage are not reported separately. Incisions are closed in single layers. Steri-strip tape supports cartilaginous surgery of the nasal tip.

Documentation Tip
The operative report may include the following terminology:

- Plastic repair of nasolabial flaps
- Tip rhinoplasty

21.87   Other rhinoplasty

Description
Code 21.87 reports other rhinoplasty procedures that are not more specifically described by codes 21.84-21.86.

21.88   Other septoplasty

Description
The physician removes abnormal, diseased, or injured intranasal mucosa and replaces it with a separately reportable split-thickness graft. The surgery is performed on one nasal side. A lateral rhinotomy is made to expose the intranasal mucosa. Mucosal tissue is excised from the septum, nasal floor, and anterior aspect of the inferior turbinate. A split-thickness graft is sutured to the recipient bed, covering the exposed cartilage and submucosal surfaces. Gauze packing and splints are placed in the grafted nasal cavity.

Coding Clarification
Septoplasty associated with submucous resection of the nasal septum is classified to 21.5 Submucous resection of nasal septum.

Documentation Tip
The operative report may include the following terminology:

- Crushing of nasal septum
- Septoplasty with insertion of septal button prosthesis
- Septoplasty for repair of nasal septum perforation or defect

21.89   Other repair and plastic operations on nose

Description
Code 21.89 reports other rhinoplasties, repairs, and plastic operations on the nose that are not more specifically described by other codes within subcategory 21.8.

Coding Clarification
This code includes reattachment of an amputated nose.

21.9   Other operations on nose

Description
This subcategory classifies other operations on the nose not classifiable elsewhere in category 21 Operations on nose.

Coding Clarification
Fourth-digit subclassification is required for specificity.

21.91   Lysis of adhesions of nose

Description
The physician removes mucosal scarring, which blocks the passage of air in the nose. Nasal synechiae are formed when two bleeding mucosal surfaces contact, forming scar tissue and eventual fibrosis. These patients are unable to breath through the nose. The physician makes an intranasal approach to the synechia. Topical vasoconstrictive agents are applied and local anesthesia is injected in the nasal mucosa. An attempt to minimize intra- and postoperative mucosal bleeding is made. A scalpel is used to excise the mucosal tissue. Mucosal edges are sutured with resorbable sutures. Postoperative gauze packing or splints may be used to absorb hemorrhage until mucosal healing occurs. Long-term splinting may be necessary to prevent reformation of the synechiae.

Documentation Tip
The operative report may include the following:

- Posterior nasal scrub

21.99   Other operations on nose

Description
Code 21.99 reports other nasal operations that are not more specifically described by other codes within category 21.

Coding Clarification
The following procedures are excluded from 21.29 and are more appropriately reported elsewhere:

- Dilation of frontonasal duct (96.21)
- Irrigation of nasal passages (96.53)
- Removal of intraluminal foreign body without incision (98.12)
- Removal of nasal packing (97.32)
- Replacement of nasal packing (97.21)

Documentation Tip
Carefully review the documentation in the medical record to determine if a more specific code can be reported. If unclear, the physician should be queried.

22   Operations on nasal sinuses

Description
The nasal sinuses consist of cavities in the cranial bones. These cavities divide into superior, middle, and inferior air passages that connect to pharynx, eustachian tubes of the ears, and nasolacrimal ducts of the eyes. The main functions of the nasal sinuses include warming, moistening, and filtering air inhaled into the respiratory system. There are many conditions, inflammatory and non-inflammatory in nature, may adversely affect

● New Code   ▲ Revised Code   ▶◀ Revised Text   © 2010 Ingenix

the structure or function of nasal passages of the upper airway and cause breathing difficulties.

Coding Clarification
Category 22 provides codes for a variety of diagnostic and therapeutic sinus procedures.

Procedures performed on the nose and nasal septum are classified to category 21 Operations on nose.

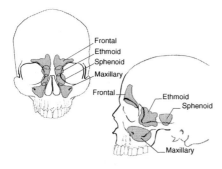

22.0   Aspiration and lavage of nasal sinus

Description
This subcategory classifies aspiration and lavage of nasal sinus. Aspiration may be defined as the withdrawal of fluid from the nasal sinus, and is commonly performed by puncture of the cavity. Lavage may be defined as the washing of the nasal cavity through a natural opening; through the nostril.

Coding Clarification
Fourth-digit subclassification is required for specificity. The fourth digit describes the technique utilized as aspiration or lavage by puncture, transnasal approach, or not otherwise specified.

22.00   Aspiration and lavage of nasal sinus

Description
This code is used to report aspiration and lavage of the nasal sinus that is not more precisely described by other codes in subcategory 22.0.

Documentation Tip
Carefully review the documentation in the medical record to determine if a more specific code can be reported. If unclear, the physician should be queried.

22.01   Puncture of nasal sinus for aspiration or lavage

Description
Aspiration may be defined as the withdrawal of fluid from the nasal sinus, and is commonly performed by puncture of the cavity. The physician irrigates infected sinuses through cannulas. Topical vasoconstrictive agents are applied. The maxillary sinus is entered through an antral puncture beneath the inferior nasal turbinate. The sphenoid sinus may

be entered through the sphenoethmoidal recess in the superior nasal cavity. A flexible cannula is inserted into this opening and the sinuses are irrigated with saline solutions. These lavages will reduce inflammation and remove purulent (pus) discharge in the sinuses.

22.02   Aspiration or lavage of nasal sinus through natural ostium

Description
Aspiration may be defined as the withdrawal of fluid from the nasal sinus, and is commonly performed by puncture of the cavity. Lavage may be defined as the washing of the nasal cavity through a natural opening—through the nostril. The physician irrigates infected sinuses through cannulas. Topical vasoconstrictive agents are applied. The maxillary sinus is entered through the natural ostium or opening in the middle meatus of the nasal cavity. The sphenoid sinus may be entered through the sphenoethmoidal recess in the superior nasal cavity. A flexible cannula is inserted into these openings and the sinuses are irrigated with saline solutions. These lavages will reduce inflammation and remove purulent (pus) discharge in the sinuses.

22.1   Diagnostic procedures on nasal sinus

Description
This subcategory classifies diagnostic procedures on nasal sinuses, removal of tissue for examination (biopsy), and diagnostic endoscopy.

Coding Clarification
Fourth-digit subclassification is required for specificity.

A biopsy not specified as performed by an open approach is assumed to be a closed biopsy, and is reported accordingly.

Carefully review the documentation in the medical record to determine if a more specific code can be reported. If unclear, the physician should be queried.

22.11

Description
The physician uses an endoscope for a diagnostic evaluation of the nose. An endoscope has a rigid fiberoptic telescope that allows the physician both increased visualization and magnification of internal anatomy. Topical vasoconstrictive agents are applied to the nasal mucosa and nerve blocks with local anesthesia are performed. The endoscope is placed into the nose and a thorough inspection of the internal nasal structures is accomplished. Any identified lesions can be removed by intranasal instruments placed parallel to the endoscope. Scalpels, forceps, snares, and other instruments are

used to remove diseased mucosa or lesions from the internal nose. The nose may be packed if excessive bleeding occurs.

Coding Clarification
This code describes a closed nasal sinus biopsy. Nasal sinus biopsy performed by an incision (open approach) into the nasal sinus is reported with 22.12.

Documentation Tip
The operative report may include the following terminology:

- Endoscopic
- Percutaneous
- Needle

Coding Scenario
A 34-year-old female presented for biopsy of a suspicious lesion of the maxillary sinus previously located on CT scan in evaluation of her chronic maxillary sinusitis. Because of these suspicious images, a needle core biopsy of the maxillary sinus was performed. Biopsy results yielded a diagnosis of maxillary sinus squamous cell carcinoma.

Code Assignment:

160.2	Malignant neoplasm of maxillary sinus
473.0	Chronic sinusitis, maxillary
22.11	Closed [endoscopic] [needle] biopsy of nasal sinus

22.12   Open biopsy of nasal sinus

Description
The physician may make an external skin incision or an internal incision with the assistance of an endoscope to access the specific sinus cavity. The dissection may continue to the bone, depending on the anatomic location of the lesion. The physician may use a drill or forceps to create an opening through the bone into sinus and an additional sinusotomy for access, if necessary. A specimen may be removed with forceps, sharp excision, or curette. A portion of the sinus wall can be removed, increasing the drainage from the sinus into the nose. The wound is closed in layers.

Coding Clarification
This code describes an open, incisional nasal sinus biopsy. Nasal sinus biopsy performed by a closed (percutaneous, needle, endoscopic without incision) approach into the nasal sinus is reported with 22.11.

22.19   Other diagnostic procedures on nasal sinuses

Description
Code 22.19 reports other nasal operations that are not more specifically described by other codes within

subcategory 22.1. This procedure includes diagnostic endoscopy of the nasal sinuses.

The physician uses an endoscope for a diagnostic evaluation of the nose and the sinus. An endoscope has a rigid fiberoptic telescope that allows the physician both increased visualization and magnification of internal anatomy. Topical vasoconstrictive agents are applied to the nasal mucosa and nerve blocks with local anesthesia are performed. The endoscope is placed into the nose and a thorough inspection of the internal nasal structures is accomplished. To access the maxillary sinus, a trocar puncture is made directly into the inferior meatus area of the nose or after a mucosal incision into the canine fossa of the maxilla. The endoscope is placed into the maxillary sinus for evaluation. The intraoral mucosa may be closed in a single layer. The nasal puncture wound does not normally require closure. To access the sphenoid sinus, a trocar puncture is made directly into the sphenoid sinus after negotiation through the ethmoids or by cannulation of the sphenoid drainage system that enters the sphenoethmoidal recess. The endoscope is placed into the sphenoid sinus for evaluation. The sphenoidal puncture wound does not normally require closure. No other procedure is performed on the sinus at this time of diagnostic endoscopy classifiable to this code.

Coding Clarification
The following procedures are excluded from 22.19 and are more appropriately reported elsewhere:

- Transillumination of sinus (89.15)
- X-ray of sinus (87.15-87.16)

Other diagnostic and therapeutic nasal sinus procedures performed during the same encounter are classifiable elsewhere.

Diagnostic rhinoscopy (endoscopy of nasal passages without sinus endoscopy) and nasopharyngoscopy are more appropriately classified to 21.21.

Documentation Tip
Carefully review the documentation in the medical record to determine if a more specific code can be reported. If unclear, the physician should be queried.

22.2   Intranasal antrotomy

Description
The physician surgically creates an opening from the nasal cavity into the sinus to allow adequate sinus drainage. An antral "window" is made in the inferior meatus or by enlargement of the natural ostium in the middle meatus. Topical vasoconstrictive agents are applied to the nasal mucosa. Local anesthesia is injected into the nasal mucosa. Then a trocar is used to create an opening into the desired antral window location. The opening is enlarged with biting forceps.

● New Code   ▲ Revised Code   ▶◀ Revised Text   © 2010 Ingenix

The sinus can then be inspected and irrigated with direct visualization. A temporary irrigation catheter may be placed into the sinus and secured with sutures to the nose. The nasal cavity may be packed for 24 to 48 hours if excessive bleeding occurs during the procedure.

Coding Clarification
This procedure excludes antrotomy with external approach classifiable to 22.31-22.39.

22.3   External maxillary antrotomy

Description
This code subcategory describes an incision of the maxillary sinus by external approach.

Coding Clarification
Fourth-digit subclassification is required for specificity. The fourth digit describes the extent of the procedure as radical (22.31) or other (22.39).

22.31   Radical maxillary antrotomy

Description
The physician creates an opening or several maxillary sinus openings to allow adequate sinus drainage for treatment of irreversible maxillary sinus disease. An intraoral incision is made in the labial mucosa, exposing the canine fossa. The canine fossa is perforated with a trocar and biting forceps increase the opening into the maxillary sinus. Sinus mucosa is removed with curettes. A second opening may be made from the nasal cavity into the inferior meatus. Topical vasoconstrictive agents are applied to the nasal mucosa and local anesthesia is injected. The mucosa adjacent to the natural ostium is removed with the polyps. The intraoral incision is repaired in a single layer.

22.39   Other external maxillary antrotomy

Description
The physician may use an endoscope for surgical resection of the maxillary sinus. Topical vasoconstrictive agents are applied to the nasal mucosa and nerve blocks with local anesthesia are performed. The endoscope is placed into the nose and a thorough inspection of internal nasal structures is accomplished. A scalpel or biting forceps is introduced parallel to the endoscope and is used to remove diseased tissues. Polyps may be excised. An external maxillary antrostomy is performed creating an opening for drainage from the maxillary sinus. The maxillary sinus may be opened and the mucosa removed. Electrocautery may be used for hemostasis. The nasal cavity may be packed with Telfa or gauze for 24 to 48 hours.

22.4   Frontal sinusotomy and sinusectomy

Description
This code subcategory describes an incision of the frontal sinus with or without excision of frontal sinus lesion.

22.41   Frontal sinusotomy

Description
This code describes an incision of the frontal sinus. Surgical approach and techniques may vary, including:

- **Brow or coronal incision approach:** The physician enters the frontal sinus to remove pathologic lesions and diseased sinus mucosa. In the frontal sinus access, an osteoplastic flap is used in which the periosteum of the excised frontal bone is preserved. When the frontal sinus is accessed by brow incision, an incision is made from the superior aspect of one eyebrow, extending through the nasofrontal junction to the opposite eyebrow. A bicoronal flap also may be used to access the frontal sinus. Dissection is carried to the periosteal layer. A template is made from a radiograph outlining the frontal sinus. The template is placed over the frontal sinus and the periosteum is excised around the template. The physician removes the frontal bone with attached periosteum overlying the frontal sinus using drills, saws, and chisels. The contents of the exposed sinus are removed with curettes and burrs. No obliteration of the sinus is necessary. The frontal bone flap is returned and secured with sutures, wires, plates, and/or screws. The incisions are repaired in layers.

- **External approach (Trephine):** The physician uses a trephine (a cylindrical or crown saw used to remove a disc of bone) to access the frontal sinus. A small skin incision is made beneath the unshaven medial eyebrow. The dissection is carried to the frontal bone overlying the frontal sinus. The physician uses a round burr to make an opening into the sinus cavity. Tissue for culture may be taken at this time. The sinus is irrigated with saline solutions. Two irrigation catheters are placed into the sinus through the bony opening. The wound is closed in layers. The catheters are sutured to the skin. The exposed catheters are used to irrigate the sinus and are removed once the sinus inflammation subsides and the irrigation fluid starts to exit through the nose.

- **With Endoscopic assistance:** The physician uses an endoscope for diagnostic evaluation or therapeutic drainage of the frontal sinus. Topical vasoconstrictive agents are applied to the nasal mucosa and nerve blocks with local anesthesia are performed. The endoscope is placed into the nose and a thorough inspection of the internal nasal structures is accomplished. An antrostomy is performed, creating an opening for drainage. Electrocautery may be used for hemostasis. The nasal cavity may be packed with Telfa or gauze for 24 to 48 hours.

22.42   Frontal sinusectomy

Description
This code describes an excision of the frontal sinus or sinus lesion. Surgical approach and techniques may vary, including:

- **Lynch approach/transorbital:** The physician makes an external skin incision in the medial orbit to access the frontal sinus. The curvilinear incision is made beneath the eyebrow along the medial orbit extending to the superior aspect of the orbit. The dissection continues to the bone. The physician uses a drill and forceps to create an opening into the frontal sinus and, if needed, the ethmoid sinus. Pathologic tissue and diseased tissue membrane is removed with curettes. The inferior wall of the sinus can be removed, increasing the drainage from the sinus into the nose. The wound is closed in layers.

- **With endoscopic assistance:** The physician uses an endoscope for a diagnostic evaluation or surgical resection of the frontal sinus. An endoscope has a rigid fiberoptic telescope that allows the physician both increased visualization and magnification of internal anatomy. Topical vasoconstrictive agents are applied to the nasal mucosa and nerve blocks with local anesthesia are performed. The endoscope is placed into the nose and a thorough inspection of the internal nasal structures is accomplished. Any identified lesions can be removed by intranasal instruments placed parallel to the endoscope. Scalpels, forceps, snares, and other instruments are used to remove diseased mucosa or lesions from the internal nose. An antrostomy is sometimes performed, creating an opening for drainage from the maxillary sinus. Electrocautery may be used for hemostasis. The nasal cavity may be packed with Telfa or gauze for 24 to 48 hours. The nose may be packed if excessive bleeding occurs.

- **Coronal or brow incision without osteoplastic flap:** The physician removes the frontal sinus mucosa and places material into the sinus cavity to prevent regrowth of the sinus mucosa. To access the frontal sinus through a brow incision, a full-thickness incision is made from the superior aspect of one eyebrow, extending through the nasofrontal junction to the opposite eyebrow. A bicoronal flap may also be used to access the frontal sinus. After the physician exposes the sinus, the frontal bone overlying the frontal sinus is removed with drills, saws, and chisels. The contents of the exposed sinus are removed with curettes and burrs. The nasofrontal duct is obstructed with an alloplastic or autogenous material (bone). The removed frontal bone is returned and secured with wires, plates, and/or screws. Incisions are repaired in layers.

- **Obliterative sinusotomy with osteoplastic flap:** The physician removes the frontal sinus mucosa and places material into the sinus cavity to prevent regrowth of the sinus mucosa. In the frontal sinus access, an osteoplastic flap may be used. The periosteum of the excised frontal bone is preserved. When the frontal sinus is accessed by brow incision, an incision is made from the superior aspect of one eyebrow, extending through the nasofrontal junction to the opposite eyebrow. A bicoronal flap may also be used to access the frontal sinus. Dissection is carried to the periosteal layer. A template is made from a radiograph outlining the frontal sinus. The template is placed over the frontal sinus and the periosteum is excised around the template. The physician removes the frontal bone, with attached periosteum overlying the frontal sinus, using drills, saws, and chisels. The contents of the exposed sinus are removed with curettes and burrs. The nasofrontal duct is obstructed with an alloplastic (synthetic) or autogenous material (i.e., bone). The sinus cavity is obliterated with autologous fat harvested from the abdomen or buttocks. The frontal bone flap is returned and secured with sutures, wires, plates, and/or screws. The incisions are repaired in layers.

Coding Clarification
This code excludes biopsy of the nasal sinus, classifiable to 22.11-22.12.

22.5   Other nasal sinusotomy

Description
This subcategory describes an incision of the nasal sinus, without excision of sinus lesion.

22.50   Sinusotomy, not otherwise specified

Description
This code describes the incision of a sinus, without further description of anatomic site involved.

● New Code   ▲ Revised Code   ▶◀ Revised Text   © 2010 Ingenix

Coding Clarification
Avoid assigning 22.50 Sinusotomy, not otherwise specified

Documentation Tip
Carefully review the documentation in the medical record to determine if a more specific code can be reported. If unclear, the physician should be queried.

22.51   Ethmoidotomy

Description
The physician makes an incision into ethmoid sinuses. A curvilinear incision is made between the nasal dorsum and the medial canthus of the eye. Dissection is carried to the medial orbital bone. A bony window is made through the lamina papyracea bone, exposing the lateral ethmoid sinus. The physician removes all diseased tissue. The nasal cavity is penetrated through the medial ethmoid region. Nasal gauze packing is placed through the extranasal incision. The external skin incision is repaired with layered closure.

The physician uses an endoscope for a diagnostic evaluation or surgical resection of the ethmoid sinus. Disease of the anterior ethmoid sinus may block maxillary sinus drainage. An endoscope allows both increased visualization and magnification of internal anatomy. Topical vasoconstrictive agents are applied to the nasal mucosa and nerve blocks with local anesthesia are performed. The endoscope is placed into the nose and a thorough inspection of internal nasal structures is accomplished. Electrocautery may be used for hemostasis. The nasal cavity may be packed with Telfa or gauze for 24 to 48 hours.

22.52   Sphenoidotomy

Description
The physician enters the diseased sphenoid sinus. While open, biopsies may be taken of the sphenoidal masses. The sinus mucosa or mucosal polyps are removed. Due to its location deep within the skull, the sphenoid sinus surgery is accessed through structures overlying the sinus. Most commonly, an intraoral incision is made in the maxillary labial vestibule. The nasal septal cartilage is dissected from the nasal floor and is detached from the anterior nasal spine. The anterior cartilaginous septum is displaced and dissection continues to the bony nasal septum. The physician uses rongeurs to remove the bony septum, exposing the sphenoid region. The anterior wall of the sphenoid sinus is also removed with rongeurs. The physician uses an operating microscope to remove sinus contents. The nasal midline is reestablished and the cartilage is reattached to the nasal spine. Transseptal sutures are placed. The intraoral incision is closed in a single

layer. The nose is packed and external nasal dressings may be placed.

22.53   Incision of multiple nasal sinuses

Description
The physician enters three or more sinuses to remove diseased sinus contents using multiple approaches. Sinus disease may involve any of the maxillary, ethmoid, sphenoid, and/or frontal sinuses. The physician uses multiple approaches to the sinus, including intraoral, intranasal, skin, and/or bicoronal incisions. Once the sinus is accessed, the physician removes its contents with curettes. Incisions are repaired in both single and multiple layers, depending on the access.

22.6   Other nasal sinusectomy

Description
This code subcategory describes an excision of nasal sinus lesions, without excision of sinus lesion.

Coding Clarification
This subcategory includes sinusectomy with incidental turbinectomy.

Biopsy of the nasal sinus is excluded and reported with 22.11-22.12.

22.60   Sinusectomy, not otherwise specified

Description
This code describes the excision of sinus lesions, without further description of the anatomic site involved.

Coding Clarification
Avoid assigning 22.60 Sinusectomy, not otherwise specified

Documentation Tip
Carefully review the documentation in the medical record to determine if a more specific code can be reported. If unclear, the physician should be queried.

22.61   Excision of lesion of maxillary sinus with Caldwell-Luc approach

Description
The physician creates several maxillary sinus openings to allow adequate sinus drainage for treatment of irreversible maxillary sinus disease. An intraoral incision is made in the labial mucosa, exposing the canine fossa. The canine fossa is perforated with a trocar and biting forceps increase the opening into the maxillary sinus. Sinus mucosa is removed with curettes. A second opening is made from the nasal cavity into the inferior meatus. Topical vasoconstrictive agents are applied to the nasal mucosa and local anesthesia is injected. A trocar perforates an opening into the inferior

meatus. The opening is enlarged with biting forceps, and the diseased tissue is excised, curetted, and removed. The intraoral incision is repaired in a single layer.

Coding Clarification
This code includes maxillary sinusectomy by external (Caldwell-Luc) approach.

Maxillary sinusectomy by approach other than external (Caldwell-Luc) is classified to 22.62.

22.62 Excision of lesion of maxillary sinus with other approach

Description
This code describes a sinusectomy or excision of sinus lesion not classifiable elsewhere. If sinusectomy includes maxillary resection, the physician may remove a portion of or all of the diseased maxillary bone. Incisions may be intraoral or may include skin incisions such as the Weber-Ferguson approach. Dissection is continued to expose and isolate the planned bony and tissue excision. The physician may use drills, saws, and chisels to fracture the maxilla from the midface. Fractured maxilla and adjacent tissue are loosened and removed to "free margins" as determined with intraoperative tissue specimens sent to the pathologist for immediate microscopic examination. All sinus mucosa is removed. Exposed bone may be covered with a separately reportable split-thickness skin graft. A splint may be placed to obturate (block) the mouth from the surgical area. All skin incisions are repaired with layered closure.

The physician may use an endoscope for surgical resection of the maxillary sinus. Topical vasoconstrictive agents are applied to the nasal mucosa and nerve blocks with local anesthesia are performed. The endoscope is placed into the nose and a thorough inspection of internal nasal structures is accomplished. A scalpel or biting forceps is introduced parallel to the endoscope and is used to remove diseased tissues. Polyps may be excised. An antrostomy may be performed in creating an opening for drainage from the maxillary sinus. The maxillary sinus is opened and the mucosa removed. Electrocautery may be used for hemostasis. The nasal cavity may be packed with Telfa or gauze for 24 to 48 hours.

Coding Clarification
Maxillary sinusectomy by external (Caldwell-Luc) approach is classified to 22.61.

22.63 Ethmoidectomy

Description
This procedure code describes excision or removal of ethmoid sinus tissue. Surgical technique and operative approach may vary, including:

- **Intranasal:** The physician removes diseased tissue from the ethmoid sinuses. The physician accesses the ethmoid sinuses through the nose. Topical vasoconstrictive agents are placed on the nasal mucosa to shrink the blood vessels. Local anesthesia is injected into the nasal mucosa. The physician retracts the middle turbinate anteriorly, exposing the sinus opening. A small curette may be advanced into the anterior ethmoid cells. The physician uses the curette to remove any diseased tissue of the anterior sinus, and allows the sinus to drain.

- **Extranasal (via skin incision):** The physician removes diseased tissue of the ethmoid sinuses. A curvilinear incision is made between the nasal dorsum and the medial canthus of the eye. Dissection is carried to the medial orbital bone. A bony window is made through the lamina papyracea bone, exposing the lateral ethmoid sinus. The physician removes all diseased tissue. The nasal cavity is penetrated through the medial ethmoid region. Nasal gauze packing is placed through the extranasal incision. The external skin incision is repaired with layered closure.

- **Endoscopic:** The physician uses an endoscope for surgical resection of the anterior or posterior ethmoidectomy. Disease of the anterior ethmoid sinus may block maxillary sinus drainage. An endoscope allows both increased visualization and magnification of internal anatomy. Topical vasoconstrictive agents are applied to the nasal mucosa and nerve blocks with local anesthesia are performed. The endoscope is placed into the nose and a thorough inspection of internal nasal structures is accomplished. A scalpel or biting forceps is introduced parallel to the endoscope and is used to remove diseased tissues. Polyps may be excised. Electrocautery may be used for hemostasis. The nasal cavity may be packed with Telfa or gauze for 24 to 48 hours.

22.64 Sphenoidectomy

Description
This procedure code describes excision or removal of sphenoid sinus tissue. The physician enters the diseased sphenoid sinus. While open, biopsies may be taken of the sphenoidal masses. The sinus mucosa or mucosal polyps may be removed. Due to its location deep within the skull, the sphenoid sinus is accessed through structures overlying the sinus. Most commonly, an intraoral incision is made in the maxillary labial vestibule. The nasal septal cartilage is dissected from the nasal floor and is detached from the anterior nasal spine. The anterior cartilaginous septum is displaced and dissection

continues to the bony nasal septum. The physician uses rongeurs to remove the bony septum, exposing the sphenoid region. The anterior wall of the sphenoid sinus is also removed with rongeurs. The physician uses an operating microscope to remove sinus contents. The nasal midline is reestablished and the cartilage is reattached to the nasal spine. Transseptal sutures are placed. The intraoral incision is closed in a single layer. The nose is packed and external nasal dressings may be placed.

The physician may use an endoscope for surgical access of the sphenoid sinus. The sphenoid can be explored with direct access or through the posterior ethmoid sinus. The isolated access to the sphenoid sinus is through dilation of the sphenoid ostium. The middle turbinate may be fractured or partially removed for access. The ostium is cannulated and dilated. The physician uses forceps or a sphenoid punch to open the sinus cavity. Diseased mucosa or tissue is removed. The nose may be packed if excessive bleeding occurs.

22.7   Repair of nasal sinus

Description
This subcategory describes repair procedures of the nasal sinuses, classified as fistula closure or other sinus repair.

22.71   Closure of nasal sinus fistula

Description
The physician closes an opening between the mouth and the maxillary sinus. The communication is through the maxillary bone and the tract is lined with epithelium. Local anesthesia is injected into the mucosa. The physician uses a scalpel to excise the epithelized tract. An incision is made into the palatal mucosa and a local mucosal flap is developed. The flap is sutured in layers, covering the oromaxillary tract. Careful postoperative instructions are given to limit sinus pressure by not allowing nose blowing, which would reopen the tract and impair healing.

Coding Clarification
Closure of nasal fistula is classified to 21.82.

Documentation Tip
This procedure may also be described with the following terminology:

- Oroantral fistula
- Oronasal fistula

22.79   Other repair of nasal sinus

Description
Code 22.79 reports other nasal repair procedures.

The physician performs reconstruction of the frontonasal duct for reduction of a fracture. Depending upon the complexity of fracture, surgical technique may vary. For an uncomplicated fracture, the physician realigns a depressed frontal bone fracture overlying the frontal sinus. This fracture does not involve injury to the nasofrontal duct drainage of the frontal sinus. The physician may access the frontal bone with a bicoronal incision or local skin incisions overlying the fracture. Sinus mucosa may be removed. The bone is realigned and stabilized with wires, plates, and/or screws. The incisions are repaired with layered closure.

When the procedure is performed for treatment of a complicated frontal sinus fracture, the physician realigns a complicated frontal bone fracture and obliterates the frontal sinus. This fracture injures the duct drainage of the frontal sinus and requires obliteration of the nasofrontal duct to prevent postoperative sinus complications. The physician may access the frontal bone with a bicoronal incision or local skin incisions overlying the fracture. Sinus mucosa is removed from the frontal sinus. If the posterior wall of the sinus is fractured, the bony wall may be removed, thus cranializing the sinus. The nasofrontal duct is plugged (i.e., bone) and obliterating material (i.e., fat, muscle) is placed into the sinus cavity. The frontal bone is realigned and stabilized with wires, plates, and/or screws. The incisions are repaired with layered closure

Coding Clarification
This code may be used to report repair of bone of the accessory sinus.

22.9   Other operations on nasal sinuses

Description
This code classifies other operations on the nasal sinuses that are not more appropriately classified elsewhere in category 22.

Coding Clarification
This code may be used to classify:

- Exteriorization of maxillary sinus
- Fistulization of sinus

This code excludes dilation of the frontonasal duct (96.21).

Documentation Tip
Carefully review the documentation in the medical record to determine if a more specific code can be reported. If unclear, the physician should be queried.

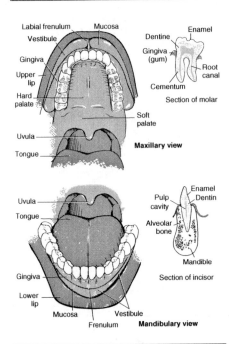

Labial frenulum — Mucosa
Vestibule
Gingiva
Upper lip
Hard palate
Uvula
Tongue

Enamel
Dentine
Gingiva (gum)
Root canal
Cementum
Section of molar
Soft palate

Maxillary view

Uvula
Tongue
Gingiva
Lower lip
Mucosa
Frenulum

Enamel
Dentin
Pulp cavity
Alveolar bone
Mandible
Section of incisor
Vestibule

Mandibulary view

23   Removal and restoration of teeth

Description
A tooth may be removed for therapeutic reasons due to tooth or gum disease, or to assist in restorative procedures and orthodonture. Restorations are defined as materials or devices used to replace lost tooth structure, such as fillings or crowns, or to replace a lost tooth or teeth, such as bridges or complete or partial dentures. A variety of dental restorative materials are currently in use, including amalgam, composite resin, silicate, acrylic, synthetic, and plastic. Crowns, jackets, inlays, onlays, and cast restorations are also used as restorative materials. These materials are not permanent and therefore may suffer from failure.

Two sets of teeth are produced during a lifetime: deciduous and permanent.

During childhood, permanent teeth begin to erupt and replace the first set of deciduous teeth (baby teeth) at approximately 6 years of age, continuing until the adult set is completed at approximately 21 years of age.

Adult teeth are identified as upper or lower, within four categories that extend from the front of the mouth around the sides of the oral cavity to the jaw bones, including:

- Incisors: Eight sharp teeth adapted for cutting and biting food.

- Canines (cuspids): Four large, strong teeth with roots deep in the facial bones, also referred to as the "eye teeth."

- Premolars (bicuspid): Eight teeth situated behind the canines that function similarly to the molars in grinding food.

- Molars: Twelve permanent grinding teeth that are the largest of the permanent set.

Each tooth is comprised of three main anatomic parts:

- Crown: Portion that is visible above the gingiva (gums).

- Neck: Portion embedded in the gingiva between the crown and the root.

- Root: Portion embedded in the alveolus (tooth sockets) of the jaws.

Teeth are anchored into the jaw at the root of the tooth in the alveoli (socket) by periodontal ligaments and the cementum (the surface lining the tooth neck and root). Alveolar blood vessels and nerves supply a support system for the teeth, and extend from the root of the tooth, up the root canal into the pulp cavity. A tooth is a multi-layered structure that includes the following parts:

- Enamel: External hard coating.

- Dentin: Solid, bulk portion of the tooth.

- Pulp cavity: Contains the loose connective tissue, vessels, and nerves of the tooth.

The following dental and periodontal conditions are common indications for removal or restoration of teeth:

- Dental caries: Tooth decay caused by erosive bacteria.

- Gingivitis: Inflammation of the connective tissue or gingiva (gums) that support the teeth.

- Periodontitis: Complication of gingivitis in which the inflammation, infection, and weakening of the gums results in the loss of bone that supports teeth.

- Malocclusions: Teeth that do not close properly, overlap, or protrude that may create pressure on the temporomandibular joint or tooth structures.

Coding Clarification
Category 23 describes procedures of tooth restoration or removal.

Other dental and periodontal procedures are classified to category 24 Other operations on teeth, gums and alveoli.

● New Code   ▲ Revised Code   ▶◀ Revised Text   © 2010 Ingenix

23.0   Forceps extraction of tooth

Description
This subcategory classifies extraction (pulling out) or removal of the teeth, with the assistance of forceps or other non-surgical, non-incisional instrumentation.

Coding Clarification
Surgical extraction of teeth and extraction by incision are classified to subcategory 23.1

23.01   Extraction of deciduous tooth

Description
The dentist extracts a deciduous tooth; a "baby tooth" or naturally occurring temporary tooth that is expected to shed or fall out at a particular stage of growth and development. A deciduous tooth may fail to shed, and obstruct or otherwise impair the eruption of permanent, adult teeth. The dentist or physician performs a simple extraction on teeth that are visible in the mouth. Under a local anesthetic, the tooth is elevated and grasped with dental forceps and rocked back and forth to loosen the periodontal ligament and supportive alveolar structures, until the tooth is removed. The wound is irrigated. Packing and sutures may be used, but are usually not necessary.

23.09   Extraction of other tooth

Description
The dentist or physician extracts a permanent tooth, an "adult" tooth, or a tooth that is not otherwise specified. The dentist or physician performs a simple extraction on teeth that are visible in the mouth. Under a local anesthetic, the tooth is elevated and grasped with dental forceps and rocked back and forth to loosen the periodontal ligament and supportive alveolar structures, until the tooth is removed. The wound is irrigated. Packing and sutures may be used, but are usually not necessary.

Documentation Tip
Carefully review the documentation in the medical record to determine if a more specific code can be reported. If unclear, the physician should be queried.

23.1   Surgical removal of tooth

Description
The dentist or physician performs a surgical extraction to remove teeth that cannot be easily accessed. Surgical extractions are often indicated for teeth that are impacted (obstructed), non-erupted (lying below the gum line), or partially-erupted. Under local anesthesia, conscious sedation, or general anesthesia, an incision is made into the gum to access the tooth. General anesthesia may be necessary to extract teeth from young children.

Instrumentation is used to elevate the soft tissues that overly or surround the tooth. With the assistance of a drill or osteotome, the tooth is split or fragmented to facilitate removal.

23.11   Removal of residual root

Description
The dentist removes remnants of root or residual tooth root that had been retained in the oral soft tissue after deciduous shedding or other extraction. Local anesthesia is administered and the gum is incised. The root remnants are grasped with hand instruments and removed. If the remnants have become embedded, small incisions may be necessary to locate and remove them in entirety. The wound may be sutured closed.

23.19   Other surgical extraction of tooth

Description
This code classifies surgical tooth extractions other than extraction of residual root. The dentist removes the tooth from the oral soft tissue. Local anesthesia is administered and the gum is incised. The tooth is grasped with hand instruments and removed. If the tooth is embedded or impacted, the physician may make several incisions and instrumentation may be applied to elevate the tooth. The tooth may be split or fragmented to facilitate removal. The wound may be packed or sutured closed.

Coding Clarification
This code may be used to classify:

*   Odontectomy NOS
*   Removal of impacted teeth
*   Tooth extraction with elevation of mucoperiosteal flap

Coding Scenario
A 19-year-old female presented for surgical extraction of two painfully impacted, partially-erupted third mandibular molars (wisdom teeth). The patient was anesthetized and the soft tissue impaction overlying the teeth was trimmed. The right mandibular molar was extracted with forceps, and the left molar was fractured into pieces to facilitate removal. The sockets were irrigated and packed.

Code Assignment:

520.6   Disturbances in tooth eruption
23.19   Other surgical extraction of tooth

23.2   Restoration of tooth by filling

Description
The dentist uses a filing to close off spaces where bacteria can enter, preventing further tooth decay. Materials used for fillings include gold, porcelain, a

composite resin (tooth-colored fillings), and an amalgam (an alloy of mercury, silver, copper, tin, and sometimes zinc). If an old filling is present, it is removed along with any decay. The cleaned-out cavity is then filled with any of the variety of materials described above. Under local anesthesia, the dentist uses a drill, air abrasion, or laser to remove decay from the tooth. The cleaned cavity space is then prepared for the filling. A base or a liner made of composite resin, glass ionomer, zinc oxide, and eugenol or another material may be used to protect the tooth nerve. Depending on the type of filling used, the dentist may stop several times to shine a light on the tooth to cure (harden) the material and make it strong. After the filling is placed, it is finished and polished.

23.3   Restoration of tooth by inlay

Description
A metallic, porcelain, ceramic, or resin inlay covering a tooth surface (top of the tooth or a single side of the tooth) is applied. An inlay, like a filling or a crown, is a type of dental restoration procedure. Inlays are constructed of metallic or nonmetallic materials and are considered indirect restorations. An inlay fits like a puzzle piece into the tooth and is used to restore teeth that require more than a filling, but do not require a crown. The tooth is anesthetized and prepared for the inlay. If an old filling is present, it is removed, along with any decay. A mold is made of the tooth, the opposing tooth that the inlay bites against, and adjacent teeth. When a ceramic or porcelain inlay is used, the dentist also uses a color chart to match the color of the inlay to the color of the tooth. The mold and the tooth color information are sent to a laboratory where the inlay is constructed. While the inlay is being constructed, temporary inlay material is placed into the tooth. When the permanent inlay is returned from the laboratory, the patient returns to the dentist office and the inlay is cemented (luted) into the tooth.

23.4   Other dental restoration

Description
This subcategory describes other dental restoration procedures, including crowns and bridges, that restore the functional integrity, aesthetics, or health of the tooth. Dental restorations may be fashioned from a variety of materials including amalgam, ceramic, porcelain, acrylic, metals, and resins.

23.41   Application of crown

Description
Crowns, or pre-fabricated crowns, are available in a variety of materials that are used for both short- and long-term coverage. The tooth is anesthetized. The dentist prepares the tooth for crown by removing the

old filling, if present, along with any decay. The crown is selected in a size and configuration that will best match the tooth being replaced. It is placed over the tooth and checked for fit, then reconfigured and adjusted as needed. When a good fit is achieved, it is cemented into place.

23.42   Insertion of fixed bridge

Description
This procedure code describes the insertion of a fixed partial denture. A fixed dental prosthesis is indicated in partially edentulous patients for restoration of dental function and aesthetics. Fixed partial dentures are anchored or cemented to the remaining teeth and are intended to remain in place and should be removed only by a dentist.

23.43   Insertion of removable bridge

Description
This procedure code describes the insertion of a removable partial denture, or a denture that can be removed and reinserted by the patient without professional help. Indications include restoration of dental function and aesthetics for partially edentulous patients. Removable partial dentures feature clasps of metal or plastic that "clip" onto the remaining teeth that stabilize the device. Partial dentures are composed of a metal framework with plastic teeth and gum areas. The framework contains metal clasps or other attachments that hold the denture in place. Two types of attachments are available: metal clasps and precision attachments. Metal clasps consist of C-shaped pieces of denture framework that fit around adjacent natural teeth. The adjacent teeth sometimes require shaping to hold the clasps and keep the denture securely in place. A precision attachment uses a receptacle created within a remaining tooth. The receptacle typically is covered with a crown. The precision attachment extends into the receptacle securing the partial denture. Precision attachments have no visible clasps and the forces of chewing usually are better distributed along the teeth. However, precision attachments are more expensive than metal clasps, so most partial dentures still use metal clasps for retention. Both types of dentures are easily removed for cleaning.

23.49   Other dental restoration

Description
This code describes dental restoration procedures not otherwise classifiable to subcategory 23.4.

Documentation Tip
Carefully review the documentation in the medical record to determine if a more specific code can be reported. If unclear, the physician should be queried.

23.5   Implantation of tooth

Description
The dentist performs dental implantation, whereby one of the patient's own teeth or other non-prosthetic implant is placed into a site of extraction or edentulism due to trauma or disease.

Reimplantation is often indicated when a tooth is put back into its alveolus after being partially or completely avulsed (knocked out), which occurs most commonly in the front teeth. The success of a tooth reimplantation is dependent upon timely reinsertion after injury. The sooner the tooth can be reimplanted, the better the outcome. Upon evulsion, the tooth should be handled by the crown (not the roots) and placed in a glass of milk until it is able to be reimplanted. After the tooth is inserted into the socket or alveolus, it may be splinted for stabilization and to facilitate healing.

Coding Clarification
This code includes reimplantation of a patient's own tooth.

Implantation of prosthetic dental implants is reported with 23.6.

23.6   Prosthetic dental implant

Description
A prosthetic dental implant is an artificial tooth replacement. There are several types of dental implants available, including the endosseous implant, which is successfully incorporated into the patient's jaw bone when osteoblasts (bone forming cells) grow onto the surface of the implant. The formation of osteoblasts provides structural and functional support between the jaw bone and dental implant.

Depending on the type of implant, the entire scope of a surgical placement of endosseous implants may require two to three surgical sessions. However, in some cases a prosthetic tooth can be attached to the implants at the same time as a tooth extraction. The physician administers a local anesthetic. An incision is made to expose the bone at the site where the implant will be placed. The bone is prepared using a drill and a screw-like implant is twisted into position. The incision is closed or splinted and the implant site is allowed to heal. During staged procedures, the patient returns after osteointegration of the implant is confirmed, and a second surgery is performed. A local anesthetic is administered and a small incision is made over the implant site. At this time a healing abutment or a permanent abutment is placed. If a healing abutment is placed, the gum grows over the abutment and a third procedure is required about two to three weeks later to remove the healing abutment and to place the permanent abutment.

Once the permanent abutment is in place, teeth are fabricated and attached to the implant. Dental implants can be made of a variety of materials, such as titanium, aluminum oxide, and surgical stainless steel.

Coding Clarification
This code includes insertion of prosthetic dental implants.

Reimplantation of a patient's own tooth is reported with 23.5.

23.7   Apicoectomy and root canal therapy

Description
The dentist or physician removes the root tip of the tooth and irrigates or removes surrounding infected tissue of an abscessed tooth (apicoectomy). The dentist may also perform root canal procedures whereby diseased or infected apical pulp is removed, filled, and sealed. These procedures may be performed at separate operative episodes or in combination therapy as indicated.

Root canal therapy is performed on the primary or permanent anterior teeth, which include the upper and lower incisors and cuspids. Underneath each tooth is a soft tissue area, called the pulp, which contains nerves, veins, arteries, and lymph vessels. The pulp, with its network of nerves, veins, arteries, and lymph vessels, extends from the top of the tooth down to its root by way of a root canal. Each tooth has at least one root and one root canal, but some teeth have as many as four or five root and root canals. Root canal therapy is performed when the pulp becomes inflamed or infected due to deep decay, repeated dental procedures on the tooth, a crack or chip in the tooth, or an injury to the tooth with or without visible damage to the exterior tooth.

23.70   Root canal, not otherwise specified

Description
After discussing treatment options with the patient, a plan for the root canal therapy is developed. The tooth is anesthetized. An opening may be made in the tooth and the diseased pulp removed. The root canal is thoroughly cleaned and enlarged. Temporary antibacterial filler may be placed into the canal to prevent bacteria from reentering the canal. Once the infection has healed, the canal is permanently sealed and separately reportable restoration work such as a filling, crown, or bridgework may be performed. Root canal therapy may be performed during a single visit or multiple visits. This code should be reported only once regardless of the number of visits required.

Coding Clarification
Code 23.70 describes root canal therapy not otherwise specified.

Documentation Tip

Carefully review the documentation in the medical record to determine if a more specific code can be reported. If unclear, the physician should be queried.

This procedure may also be documented in the medical record as extirpation of a tooth nerve, pulpectomy, or pulpotomy.

23.71   Root canal therapy with irrigation

Description

After discussing treatment options with the patient, a plan for root canal therapy is developed. The tooth is anesthetized. An opening is made in the tooth and the diseased pulp is removed. Debris is flushed with large amounts of water (irrigated), and the root canal is thoroughly cleaned and enlarged. Temporary antibacterial filler is placed into the canal to prevent bacteria from reentering the canal. Once the infection has healed, the canal is permanently sealed and separately reportable restoration work such as a filling, crown, or bridgework is performed. Root canal therapy may be performed during a single visit or multiple visits. This code should be reported only once regardless of the number of visits required.

23.72   Root canal therapy with apicoectomy

Description

After discussing treatment options with the patient, a plan for root canal therapy with apicoectomy is developed. The tooth is anesthetized. An opening is made in the tooth and the diseased pulp is removed. The root canal is thoroughly cleaned and enlarged. Temporary antibacterial filler is placed into the canal to prevent bacteria from reentering the canal. Once the infection has healed, the canal is permanently sealed and separately reportable restoration work such as a filling, crown, or bridgework is performed. Root canal therapy may be performed during a single visit or multiple visits.

Root canal therapy may be performed in conjunction with apicoectomy (a surgical procedure that attempts to remove infection). Apicoectomy is often performed only after a tooth has had at least one failed root canal procedure. Since root canal systems are complicated, with multiple minute branches, infected debris can remain following a root canal procedure and can result in non-healing or later reinfection.

The gum is incised and lifted away from the tooth so that the root can be more easily accessible. The infected tissue is excised, in addition to the last few millimeters of the root tip. Following this excision, three to four millimeters of the tooth's canal are cleaned and filled. An x-ray of the area is taken, and the tissue is sutured back into place.

23.73   Apicoectomy

Description

An apicoectomy (a surgical procedure that attempts to remove infection) is often performed only after a tooth has had at least one failed root canal procedure. Since root canal systems are complicated, with multiple minute branches, infected debris can remain following a root canal procedure and can result in non-healing or later reinfection.

Following appropriate anesthesia, the surgeon or endodontist incises and lifts the gum away from the tooth so that the root can be more easily accessible. The infected tissue is excised, in addition to the last few millimeters of the root tip. Following this excision, three to four millimeters of the tooth's canal are cleaned and filled. An x-ray of the area is taken and the tissue is sutured back into place.

24   Other operations on teeth, gums and alveoli

Description

This category provides codes for a variety of diagnostic and therapeutic procedures not classifiable to category 23 Removal and restoration of teeth. These procedures include biopsies, therapeutic incisions, plastic repairs, and other dental and periodontal operations.

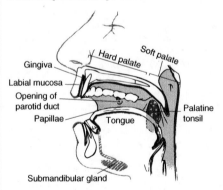

24.0   Incision of gum or alveolar bone

Description

This code classifies an incision of the gum or alveolus, including apical alveolotomy. An incision of the gum or alveolar bone may be indicated for the following:

- **Incision and drainage:** The physician drains an abscess, cyst, or hematoma from dentoalveolar structures. The physician may make gingival incisions to provide drainage. An artificial drain may be placed and removed at a later time. On

● New Code   ▲ Revised Code   ▶◀ Revised Text   © 2010 Ingenix

occasion, drainage may be obtained by probing the gingival sulcus.

- **Removal of foreign body from alveolar bone:** The physician removes a foreign body embedded in the bone of dentoalveolar structures. The physician may simply grasp the object with an instrument and remove it. If the object is further embedded, mucosal incisions may be made to reach the foreign body in the bone, which is removed, possibly with drills or osteotomes as necessary. The incision is sutured simply.

- **Removal of foreign body from soft tissue:** The physician removes a foreign body embedded in the soft tissue of the dental alveolus (gingival or alveolar mucosa). The physician may simply grasp the object with an instrument and remove it. If the object is further embedded, incisions may be made in the mucosa near the object to remove it. Sutures may be necessary.

24.1   Diagnostic procedures on teeth, gums, and alveoli

Description
This subcategory describes diagnostic procedures on teeth, gums, and alveoli.

Coding Clarification
Other specified therapeutic procedures such as repairs, excisions, and application of orthodontic devices are classified elsewhere in category 24.

24.11   Biopsy of gum

Description
The physician performs a biopsy on a lesion of the soft tissue of the gums. Under local anesthesia, the physician makes an incision in the area of the gum to be biopsied and removes a portion of the lesion and some surrounding tissue. The incision may be closed with electrocautery or simple suture.

24.12   Biopsy of alveolus

Description
The physician performs a biopsy on a lesion of the alveolus; the socket-like structures of the jaw in which the teeth are embedded. Under local anesthesia, the physician makes an incision in the dentoalveolar tissue to be biopsied and removes a portion of the lesion and some surrounding tissue. The incision may be closed with electrocautery or simple suture.

24.19   Other diagnostic procedures on teeth, gums, and alveoli

Description
The physician performs other diagnostic procedures on teeth, gum, and alveoli not classified elsewhere in subcategory 24.1.

Coding Clarification
The following procedures are excluded from 24.19 and are found in the miscellaneous diagnostic and therapeutic procedures chapter:

- Dental examination (89.31)
- Dental x-rays, full mouth (87.11) and other (87.12)
- Microscopic examination of dental specimen (90.81-90.89)

24.2   Gingivoplasty

Description
Gingivoplasty may be defined as a surgical repair of gum tissue. It may be performed with or without bone or soft tissue graft. The physician alters the contours of the gums by performing gingivoplasty. Areas of gingiva may be excised or incisions may be made through the gingiva to create a gingival flap. The flap may be sutured in a different position, trimmed, or both. Any incisions made are closed with sutures. When the repair requires a graft, the physician takes mucosa from one area of the mouth and grafts it around the teeth to repair areas of gingival recession. The physician uses a scalpel to remove a small piece of mucosa, usually from the hard palate. After preparing the recipient site, the physician sutures the graft in the area of gingival recession.

24.3   Other operations on gum

Description
This subcategory describes other therapeutic operations on gums not classifiable elsewhere. These procedures include lesion excisions and repair by suture.

Coding Clarification
Biopsy of gum is a diagnostic procedure reported with 24.11.

Gingivoplasty is reported with 24.2.

24.31   Excision of lesion or tissue of gum

Description
The physician removes a lesion of the dentoalveolar structures. If the lesion is within the mucosa, the physician makes incisions around the lesion and dissects it away from adjacent structures. If the lesion is within the bone, the mucosa is incised and the underlying bone exposed. The lesion is removed

from the bone and the incision closed with layered sutures.

Coding Clarification
This code excludes biopsy of gum (24.11) and excision of odontogenic lesion (24.4).

24.32   Suture of laceration of gum

Description
A local anesthetic is injected around the laceration and the wound is cleansed, explored, and often irrigated with a saline solution. The physician performs a suture repair of the gum laceration.

Coding Clarification
A repair of the gum by gingivoplasty is reported with 24.2.

24.39   Other operations on gum

Description
This code describes other gum procedures not classified elsewhere in subcategory 24.3.

24.4   Excision of dental lesion of jaw

Description
The physician removes a dental or odontogenic lesion of the dentoalveolar structures of the jaw. If the lesion is within the mucosa, the physician makes incisions around the lesion and dissects it away from adjacent structures. If the lesion is within the bone, the mucosa is incised and the underlying bone exposed. The lesion is removed from the bone and the incision may be closed with electrocautery or with sutures.

24.5   Alveoloplasty

Description
The physician repairs alveolar tissue. Surgical techniques vary depending on the nature of the alveolar lesion, including:

- **Alveoloplasty/alveolar repair:** The physician alters the contours of the alveolus by selectively performing alveoloplasty to remove sharp areas or undercuts of alveolar bone. The physician makes incisions in the mucosa overlying the alveolus, exposing the alveolar bone. Drills, osteotomes, or files are used to contour the bone. The mucosa is sutured in place over the contoured bone.

- **Alveolectomy including sequestrectomy:** The physician removes a portion of the alveolus. Incisions are made through the mucosa to expose the alveolar bone. Curettes, drills, or osteotomes are used to remove the diseased alveolar bone or sequestrum. The mucosa may be sutured directly over the surgical wound, or

it may be packed and allowed to heal secondarily.

- **Excision of hyperplastic alveolar mucosa:** The physician excises hyperplastic or excessive mucosa from the alveolus. Incisions are made in the hyperplastic tissue, separating it from the normal mucosa. The excessive tissue is removed. The resultant defect may be directly sutured or left to heal without suturing. With large amounts of excess tissue, more than one surgical session may be required to eliminate all of the tissue. Use this code for each specified quadrant excised.

24.6   Exposure of tooth

Description
The physician exposes an impacted tooth that fails to naturally erupt into place. Surgical exposure facilitates eruption—often to assist in the completion of orthodontic treatment. The physician administers a local anesthetic and makes an incision into the gum tissue. The gum tissue retracted may be moved, along with bony tissue that may be surrounding the crown of the tooth. If exposure is to assist in orthodonture, an orthodontic bracket may be placed and fixated with dissolvable sutures to the patient's gum tissue.

24.7   Application of orthodontic appliance

Description
The physician applies interdental fixation to wire the jaws together for conditions other than a fracture or dislocation. Arch bars, ivy loops, or other wires are attached to the teeth and wired together. For edentulous patients (without teeth), or partially edentulous patients, dentures or splints may be wired to the jaws first and wired together to provide intermaxillary fixation. Orthodontic appliances may also be used.

24.8   Other orthodontic operation

Description
This code reports other orthodontic procedures not classified to 24.7 Application of orthodontic appliance.

Coding Clarification
Code 24.8 includes the following procedures:

- Closure of diastema
- Occlusal adjustment
- Removal of arch bars
- Repair of dental arch

Removal of nonorthodontic wiring is excluded from this code; report 97.33.

● New Code   ▲ Revised Code   ►◄ Revised Text   © 2010 Ingenix

24.9   Other dental operations

Description
This subcategory describes other dental operations not classified elsewhere in categories 23 or 24.

24.91   Extension or deepening of buccolabial or lingual sulcus

Description
The physician performs extension or deepening of the buccolabial or lingual sulcus. Surgical technique may vary, including:

- **Complex procedure with grafts:** The surgeon performs a vestibuloplasty and deepens the vestibule of the mouth by any series of surgical procedures for the purpose of increasing the height of the alveolar ridge, allowing a complete denture to be worn. The vestibule refers to the mucosal and submucosal tissue of the inner lips and cheeks, the part of the oral cavity outside of the dentoalveolar structures. This procedure is performed for complex cases, such as those in which the physician must lower muscle attachments to provide enough space for deepening the vestibule. Soft tissue grafting from other areas of the body into the mouth is often required. Hypertrophied and hyperplastic tissue may need to be trimmed and soft tissue revised by dissecting it from the alveolar ridge and rearranging its attachment.

- **Other vestibuloplasty:** The surgeon performs a vestibuloplasty and deepens the vestibule of the mouth by any series of surgical procedures for the purpose of increasing the height of the alveolar ridge, allowing a complete denture to be worn. The vestibule refers to the mucosal and submucosal tissue of the inner lips and cheeks, the part of the oral cavity outside of the dentoalveolar structures. This procedure may be performed in several ways. The surgeon may rearrange the patient's own tissue or the submucosal tissue may be dissected and freed from the bone. The mucosa is moved deeper into the vestibule. Soft tissues may also be grafted into the mouth.

Documentation Tip
This procedure code may also be documented as a vestibuloplasty.

24.99   Other dental operations

Description
This procedure code describes other dental operations not classifiable elsewhere.

Coding Clarification
Multiple dental procedure exclusions are listed for 24.99, including fittings, examinations, wiring, microscopic examinations, and removal of dental

appliances classified to the miscellaneous diagnostic and therapeutic procedures chapter.

Documentation Tip
Carefully review the documentation in the medical record to ascertain whether further information exists to classify the procedure to a more specific code. If the documentation is ambiguous or unclear, the physician should be queried.

25   Operations on tongue

Description
The tongue is a muscular organ, surrounded by a mucous membrane. The oral tongue can be divided into three major portions: the root, central body, and tip. The root of the tongue may also be referred to as the pharyngeal portion, which lies at the back of the oral cavity and arises from the upper pharynx. The surface of the tongue is covered with papillae (taste buds) that receive the sensations of taste (in combination with olfaction, or smell), which are processed by the central nervous system. The tongue facilitates the manipulation of food for mastication (chewing) and swallowing, as well as manipulating phonation into specific sounds to assist with speech.

Category 25 provides codes for diagnostic and therapeutic procedures that include incisions, excisions, repairs, and other operations.

Coding Clarification
Codes in category 25 exclude associated labial procedures classified to category 27.

25.0   Diagnostic procedures on tongue

Description
Subcategory 25.0 describes diagnostic procedures on the tongue.

Coding Clarification
Subcategory 25.0 excludes therapeutic and other operations on the tongue classifiable elsewhere within category 25.

25.01   Closed (needle) biopsy of tongue

Description
The physician performs a biopsy on a lesion of the tongue. Under local anesthesia, the physician obtains a needle specimen of the lesion. Any bleeding that occurs may be controlled with electrocautery.

25.02   Open biopsy of tongue

Description
The physician makes an incision around the lesion as appropriate. Depending on the nature and size of the lesion, multiple types of incisions may be made to collect a specimen for biopsy. An elliptical-shaped

incision or wedge biopsy is typically used to include the diseased tissue and part normal tissue. Incisions are carried beneath the tissue sample and the specimen is removed. The surgical wound is usually sutured simply.

25.09   Other diagnostic procedures on tongue

Description
This procedure code describes other diagnostic procedures on the tongue not classifiable as a closed (25.01) or open (25.02).

25.1   Excision or destruction of lesion or tissue of tongue

Description
The physician removes a lesion in any area of the tongue by electric current, laser destruction, or sharp excision. Incisions may be made in an elliptical shape completely around and under the lesion to facilitate excision. If the lesion is of small size, no suturing or closure of the surgical wound is necessary. Otherwise, the wound may be sutured closed. Bleeding may be controlled with electrocautery.

For patients with sleep apnea, the physician may perform an automated radiofrequency thermal energy somnoplasty to shrink the soft tissue of the upper airway including the base of the tongue. This technique is performed under local anesthesia, during which the area of tissue causing the obstruction is heated with the thermal energy unit for approximately five to 10 minutes per application. The body gradually absorbs the heat and the obstruction is minimized. Multiple treatments may be required to achieve desired results.

Coding Clarification
Code 25.1 excludes biopsy of tongue classifiable to 25.01-25.02 and frenulectomy, labial (27.41) and lingual (25.92).

Documentation Tip
This procedure may also be documented as a somnoplasty.

Coding Scenario
A 52-year-old male with obstructive sleep apnea presented for a somnoplasty of the tongue. The patient was positioned and prepped. Under local anesthesia, the target area of soft tissue obstruction at the base of the tongue was heated to approximately 85° C (185° F) with automated radiofrequency thermal energy for 10 minutes, creating finely controlled coagulative lesions.

Code Assignment:

327.23   Obstructive sleep apnea
25.1   Excision or destruction of lesion or tissue of tongue

Coding Guidance
    AHA: 2Q, '02, 5

25.2   Partial glossectomy

Description
The physician makes incisions around the portion of the tongue to be removed and extends the incisions through the thickness of the tongue. Scalpels, scissors, electrocautery, or lasers may be used. The diseased portion is removed. After obtaining good hemostasis (controlled bleeding), the tongue is sutured closed to repair the surgical wound.

25.3   Complete glossectomy

Description
The physician removes the entire tongue, with or without a tracheostomy. The physician makes incisions through the thickness of the tongue. Scalpels, scissors, electrocautery, or lasers may be used. The tongue is removed. A tracheostomy may be performed. An incision is made in the front of the neck below the larynx. The physician dissects the tissues down to the trachea. An incision is made through the tracheal wall and an artificial airway is inserted, which extends out of the neck. The patient breathes through this airway.

Coding Clarification
Code 25.3 reports glossectomy, not otherwise specified (NOS).

Code also any neck dissection (40.40-40.42).

Code also any tracheostomy (31.1-31.29).

25.4   Radical glossectomy

Description
The physician removes part or all of the diseased or cancerous tongue and resects the mandible and the tissue of the floor of the mouth. The physician uses incisions both extraorally in the skin and intraorally through the mucosa. The physician removes the tongue by making incisions through the thickness of the tongue. Scalpels, scissors, electrocautery, or lasers may be used. The affected tissue of the mouth floor is removed with a scalpel and the diseased portion of the mandible is also accessed and resected. After removal of the diseased section, continuity of the mandible is reestablished. This is done with metal plates initially and bone grafting at a later time, or with immediate bone grafting. Skin or mucosal grafting may also be needed. A radical neck dissection is performed and lymph nodes, muscles, blood vessels, and other tissue are removed from one side of the neck. A tracheostomy may be performed. An incision is made in the front of the neck below the larynx. The physician dissects the tissues down to the trachea. An incision is made through the tracheal wall and an artificial airway is inserted,

● New Code   ▲ Revised Code   ▶◀ Revised Text   © 2010 Ingenix

which extends out of the neck. The patient breathes through this airway. The skin and mucosal incisions are repaired with layered sutures.

Coding Clarification
Code also any neck dissection (40.40-40.42).

Code also any tracheostomy (31.1-31.29).

25.5   Repair of tongue and glossoplasty

Description
This subcategory describes repair of the tongue (glossoplasty), classified as a suture (25.51) or other repair and plastic operation (25.59).

25.51   Suture of laceration of tongue

Description
The physician sutures a laceration of the tongue, either simply without tissue rearrangement or requiring more complex closure techniques. These may include tissue rearrangement, extensive submucosal suturing, debridement of grossly contaminated lacerations, or repair of through-and-through lacerations.

25.59   Other repair and plastic operations on tongue

Description
The physician performs a repair or plastic operation of the tongue. A variety of techniques may be used depending on the defect or nature of the repair, including:

- **Douglas tongue-lip fusion:** The physician makes an incision in the commissure (corner) of the mouth. The tongue is sutured to the lip in the area previously incised to enlarge the mouth. The tongue is later sectioned from the mouth in a second surgical session.

- **Frenoplasty:** The physician performs a frenoplasty and surgically alters the frenum by rearranging the tissue, usually with a Z-plasty technique. The lingual frenum is the connecting fold or membrane under the tongue that attaches it to the floor of the mouth. An incision in the shape of a "Z" is made through the frenum and the tissues are reapproximated in a different position and sutured.

- **Fixation of tongue:** The physician applies K-wire (Kirschner wire) for temporary fixation of the tongue. The K-wire is threaded through one side of the mandible, through the tongue, and through the opposite side of the mandible.

Coding Clarification
Code 25.59 reports the following procedures:

- Fascial sling of tongue
- Fusion of tongue (to lip)
- Graft of mucosa or skin to tongue

- Genioglossus advancement

Code 25.59 excludes lysis of adhesions of tongue (25.93).

Coding Guidance
  AHA: 1Q, '97, 5

25.9   Other operations on tongue

Description
This subcategory provides five subclassification codes to report other operations on the tongue including frenotomy, frenectomy, lysis of tongue adhesions, other glossotomy, and other procedures.

25.91   Lingual frenotomy

Description
The physician makes an incision in the lingual frenum, freeing the tongue and allowing greater range of motion. The lingual frenum is the connecting fold or membrane under the tongue that attaches it to the floor of the mouth. Sutures may be placed. The frenum is simply incised and not removed.

25.92   Lingual frenectomy

Description
The physician removes a tight or short lingual frenum to free the tongue and allow greater range of motion. The lingual frenum is the connecting fold or membrane under the tongue that attaches it to the floor of the mouth. The physician makes incisions in the frenum both near the tongue and near the mandible, which ultimately connect as they move posteriorly. The frenum is excised. The surgical wound may be sutured.

25.93   Lysis of adhesions of tongue

Description
The physician removes or releases tight adhesions to free the tongue and allow greater range of motion. The physician makes incisions in the adhesion. The adhesion may be excised. The surgical wound may be sutured.

25.94   Other glossotomy

Description
Glossotomy may be defined as an incision of the tongue. The physician may make a small intraoral incision into the tongue, or through the mucosa of the tongue overlying an abscess, cyst, hematoma, or other lesion. Fluid may be drained.

25.99   Other operations on tongue

Description
Report 25.99 for operations on the tongue for which no more precise code exists in subcategory 25.

---

26 Operations on salivary glands and ducts

Description
The salivary glands secrete fluid, mucus, and digestive enzymes in the form of saliva, to lubricate the oral cavity and digestive system. Saliva assists in mastication by moistening food as it moves from the oral cavity to the stomach.

There are three main pairs of salivary glands, which are connected by a ductal system (tubed passageways) that empties into the mouth. These glands include:

- Parotid: Largest gland that extends from the area at the bottom of the ear to the top of the pharynx.
- Submandibular: Located "under the mandible" in the soft tissue of the lower jaw area.
- Sublingual: Located "under the tongue" in the soft tissues.

A calculus (stone) may develop as a complication of chronic infection or due to other and idiopathic causes. Surgical removal is often required to relieve the obstruction and thoroughly eradicate any secondary infection.

Category 26 provides codes for diagnostic and therapeutic salivary gland and duct procedures that include incisions, excisions, repairs, and other operations.

Coding Clarification
Code also any neck dissection procedures (40.40-40.42) performed with procedures classifiable to category 26.

Codes in category 26 include operations on the following glands and ducts:

- Lesser salivary
- Parotid
- Sublingual
- Submaxillary

26.0 Incision of salivary gland or duct

Description
The physician performs an incision into a salivary gland or duct. Surgical technique and anatomic site (parotid, salivary, sublingual, or submaxillary) varies depending on the reason for the procedure, including:

- **Drainage of abscess:** The physician drains an abscess of the salivary gland. An incision is made intraorally or extraorally, through the tissue overlying the gland. The physician dissects through the tissue overlying the abscess. The abscess is opened with a surgical instrument and the fluid is drained. A drain may be placed.
- **Removal of calculus:** The physician makes an incision in the gland to remove a sialolith (a stone). An incision is made intraorally or extraorally in the skin overlying the gland and dissected to reach the stone, or the intraoral mucosa overlying the duct is incised. Tissue is dissected to the gland. The physician removes the stone. The incision may be sutured closed.

Coding Scenario
A 47-year-old female presented for sialolithotomy to remove a sialolith from her right submandibular gland, causing significant local pain and swelling. The patient was prepped and anesthetized and an intraoral incision was made overlying the gland with ultrasound assistance. The overlying tissue was dissected and the stone was located and removed. The wound was closed in layered sutures.

Code Assignment:

527.5   Sialolithiasis
26.0   Incision of salivary gland or duct

26.1 Diagnostic procedures on salivary glands and ducts

Description
Subcategory 26.1 describes operations on salivary glands and ducts that are classified as biopsies or other diagnostic procedures.

26.11 Closed (needle) biopsy of salivary gland or duct

Description
The physician performs a needle biopsy of a salivary gland. A needle is inserted through the skin overlying the salivary gland. The physician takes a tissue sample from the gland and withdraws the needle.

26.12 Open biopsy of salivary gland or duct

Description
The physician performs an incisional biopsy of a salivary gland. An incision is made in the skin overlying the salivary gland. Tissues are dissected to the gland. An incision is made in the tissue of the gland and a small piece of the gland is removed. The surgical wound is sutured.

26.19 Other diagnostic procedures on salivary glands and ducts

Description
Report 26.19 for other diagnostic operations on the salivary glands or ducts not classifiable as a closed (25.11) or open (25.12) biopsy.

● New Code   ▲ Revised Code   ▶◀ Revised Text   © 2010 Ingenix

Coding Clarification
Code 26.19 excludes x-ray of the salivary gland (87.09).

26.2   Excision of lesion of salivary gland

Description
Subcategory 26.2 describes excisions of lesions of the salivary glands described as marsupialization of a cyst or other lesion excision.

26.21   Marsupialization of salivary gland cyst

Description
The physician incises and removes the mucosa overlying a salivary gland cyst. The roof of the cyst is removed and the remaining sides of the cyst wall are sutured to the mucosa, creating a pouch. The saliva drains through the pouch. The pouch shrinks in size to a small opening in the floor of the mouth. Saliva from the sublingual gland flows through this opening.

26.29   Other excision of salivary gland lesion

Description
Report 26.29 for other excision of a salivary gland lesion that is not described as marsupialization of a salivary cyst.

Coding Clarification
Code 26.29 excludes biopsy of salivary gland (26.11-26.12) and salivary fistulectomy (26.42).

26.3   Sialoadenectomy

Description
Subcategory 26.3 describes removal of all or part of the salivary gland.

26.30   Sialoadenectomy, not otherwise specified

26.31   Partial sialoadenectomy

26.32   Complete sialoadenectomy

Description
The physician removes a portion or all of a salivary gland. Depending on the specific gland (parotid, submandibular, sublingual) excised and the extent of the excision (partial or complete), surgical technique may vary:

- **Parotid gland:** The physician excises a portion or all of the parotid gland with or without facial nerve preservation and unilateral neck dissection. The physician makes a preauricular incision with a curved cervical extension to the midpoint of the mandible. The anterior and posterior skin flaps are retracted and the tissues are retracted to expose the parotid gland, leaving the fascia over the gland intact. If

a facial nerve dissection is performed, the main trunk of the facial nerve is visualized and the lateral (superficial) lobe of the parotid gland may be freed and excised, depending on the extent of excision, or the facial nerve may identified and the lateral lobe lifted off the branches of the nerve using dissection. A nerve stimulator may be used to test nerve integrity. The nerve may be retracted so the deep parotid gland can be removed without damaging the facial nerve. The physician removes the gland, and may or may not sacrifice the facial nerve, depending on the extent of dissection necessary. The incision may extend inferiorly to dissect the unilateral neck for lymph node excision.

- **Submandibular gland:** The physician removes a diseased, infected, blocked, or injured submandibular gland. The physician makes an incision in the skin of the neck below the inferior border of the mandible and near the angle of the mandible. The underlying tissues are dissected to the submandibular gland. The gland is exposed, freed from the surrounding tissue, and removed. The incision is closed with sutures.

- **Sublingual gland:** The physician removes a diseased, infected, blocked, or injured sublingual gland. The physician makes an intraoral incision in the mucosa overlying the gland. Tissues are dissected down to the gland. The gland is exposed, freed from surrounding tissue, and removed. The incision is closed with sutures.

Coding Clarification
Review the documentation in the medical record to determine if the sialoadenectomy was partial or complete.

Avoid using 26.30 Sialoadenectomy, not otherwise specified.

26.4   Repair of salivary gland or duct

Description
Subcategory 26.4 describes repair procedures of the salivary gland or duct, including suture of laceration, closure of fistula, or other repairs.

26.41   Suture of laceration of salivary gland

Description
The physician repairs a laceration of a salivary gland. Depending on the specific gland (parotid, submandibular, sublingual) surgical approach may vary:

- **Parotid laceration:** The physician makes or extends a pre-auricular incision with a curved cervical extension to the midpoint of the mandible. The anterior and posterior skin flaps are retracted and the tissues are retracted to expose the parotid gland. The laceration is identified, irrigated, and sutured. The wound is closed in layers.

- **Submandibular laceration:** The physician makes or extends an incision in the skin of the neck below the inferior border of the mandible and near the angle of the mandible. The underlying tissues are dissected to the submandibular gland. The laceration is identified, irrigated, and sutured. The incision is closed in layers.

- **Sublingual laceration:** The physician makes or extends an intraoral incision in the mucosa overlying the gland. Tissues are dissected down to the gland. The laceration is identified, irrigated, and sutured. The incision is closed with sutures.

26.42   Closure of salivary fistula

Description
The physician closes an abnormal opening in a salivary gland. The physician makes an incision around the fistula and excises the fistula down to the level of the duct. The incision is closed directly.

26.49   Other repair and plastic operations on salivary gland or duct

Description
The physician performs other repair and plastic operation of a salivary gland or duct. Depending on the nature of the defect or repair, surgical technique may vary, including:

- **Fistulization of salivary gland:** The physician repairs a salivary duct by inserting a hollow plastic or silicone tube into the duct. The tube is threaded through the duct. The duct is allowed to heal and may be sutured around the tube. The tube is later removed and patency is restored.

- **Parotid duct diversion (Wilke procedure):** The physician repairs a salivary duct by inserting a hollow plastic or silicone tube into the duct. The tube is threaded through the duct. The duct is allowed to heal and may be sutured around the tube. The repair may be complex or delayed. The tube is later removed and patency is restored.

- **Other repair of salivary duct:** The physician may repair a salivary duct by inserting a hollow plastic or silicone tube into the duct. The tube is threaded through the duct. The duct is allowed to heal and may be sutured around the tube. The repair may be simple, complex, or delayed. The tube is later removed and patency is restored.

26.9   Other operations on salivary gland or duct

Description
This subcategory describes other operations on salivary glands or ducts not elsewhere classifiable to category 26.

26.91   Probing of salivary duct

Description
The physician inserts a probe into the salivary duct to dilate a narrowed section. The physician repeats the procedure with progressively larger probes until the desired amount of dilation is achieved.

The physician may introduce a catheter and dilate or expand the salivary duct. A radiopaque dye may be injected into the duct to outline the structure of the duct and any disease process. The catheter is removed.

Coding Clarification
Salivary duct or gland probing with incision is classified to an incision procedure (26.0).

26.99   Other operations on salivary gland or duct

Description
This code describes other operations on the salivary glands or ducts not elsewhere classified in category 26.

Documentation Tip
Carefully review the documentation in the medical record to determine if a more specific procedure code can be assigned.

If the documentation is ambiguous or unclear, query the physician.

27   Other operations on mouth and face

Description
This category includes operations on the lips, palate, and soft tissues of the face and mouth that include incisions, excisions, repairs, and other operations.

Coding Clarification
This category excludes operations on the gingiva (24.0-24.99) and tongue (25.01-25.99).

27.0   Drainage of face and floor of mouth

Description
The physician performs incision and drainage of the face and floor of the mouth. Surgical technique varies depending on the type of lesion and approach necessary, including:

- **Extraoral approach:** The physician drains an abscess, a cyst, or a hematoma from the floor of the mouth by making an extraoral incision in the skin below the inferior border of the mandible and dissecting through the tissue to reach the affected space. The physician may dissect through the supramylohyoid muscle and submental space into the sublingual space below the tongue to drain the abscess. The dissection may be taken to the supramylohyoid muscle to drain an abscess in the submental space. The physician makes an incision under the angle of the mandible, or between the angle and the chin, and below the inferior border of the mandible. Dissection may be limited to the submandibular space. An incision is made just below the angle of the ramus of the mandible, the posterior part of the mandible, and into the masticator space containing the masticator muscles to drain the abscess, cyst, or hematoma. A drain may be placed to facilitate healing, which is later removed.

- **Intraoral approach:** The physician makes a small intraoral incision through the mucosa of the tongue or floor of the mouth overlying an abscess, cyst, or hematoma and drains the fluid. The physician may dissect through the anterior floor of the mouth into the supramylohyoid muscle to drain an abscess in the submental space. The physician may incise through the mucosa of the floor of the mouth to the supramylohyoid muscle or carry the dissection deeper into the tissue to reach the submandibular space. The physician may dissect down through the mucosa in the posterior floor of the mouth and into the masticator space, containing the ramus, the posterior part of the mandible, and the masticator muscles to drain a deep abscess or other lesion.

- **Pterygomaxillary fossa drainage:** The physician opens the pterygopalatine space to access the nerves or blood vessels located within the fossa. An intraoral incision is made in the maxillary buccal vestibule. An opening is made in the anterior maxillary wall with drills and chisels. Electrocautery of the sinus membrane of the posterior maxillary wall is performed to control bleeding. Chisels create an opening in the posterior maxillary wall. This bone is removed, providing an entrance into the pterygopalatine space. Fat is abundant and protects the fossas vidian nerve, the sphenopalatine ganglion, and the branches of the internal maxillary artery. These structures are dissected free from fat and may be ligated and sectioned. The intraoral incision is closed in a single layer.

Coding Clarification
This code excludes drainage of the thyroglossal tract (06.09). Incision of palate is reported with 27.1.

27.1   Incision of palate
Description
The physician drains an abscess of the hard (bony) palate. The abscess is opened with a surgical instrument and the fluid is drained. The wound is allowed to heal without closure.

27.2   Diagnostic procedures on oral cavity
Description
Subcategory 27.2 describes diagnostic procedures on the oral cavity including biopsies of the mouth, lips, palate, and intraoral structures.

27.21   Biopsy of bony palate
Description
The physician performs a biopsy on a lesion of the hard (bony) palate. An incision is made in the tissue, usually in an elliptical shape and typically including part diseased and part normal tissue. Incisions are made beneath the tissue and the specimen is removed. The surgical wound is closed with sutures.

27.22   Biopsy of uvula and soft palate
Description
The physician performs a biopsy on a lesion of the uvula or soft palate. An incision is made in the tissue, usually in an elliptical shape and typically including part diseased and part normal tissue. Incisions are made beneath the tissue and the specimen is removed. The surgical wound is closed with sutures.

27.23   Biopsy of lip
Description
The physician removes a biopsy sample of skin, subcutaneous tissue, and/or mucous membrane of a lesion on the lip. An incision is made in the lip and a portion of the lesion together with some normal tissue is removed. The surgical wound is closed directly. Some normal tissue adjacent to the diseased tissue may also be removed for comparison purposes. The excision site may be closed simply or may be allowed to granulate without closure.

27.24   Biopsy of mouth, unspecified structure
Description
When the physician performs an excisional biopsy on a lesion of the floor of the mouth, an incision is made around the lesion, usually in an elliptical shape, which typically includes the diseased tissue and part normal tissue. Incisions are carried beneath the tissue sample and the specimen is removed. The surgical wound is usually sutured simply.

When the physician performs a biopsy on a lesion in the vestibule of the mouth, the physician makes an incision in the area of the vestibule to be biopsied and removes a portion of the lesion and some surrounding tissue. The incision is closed simply. The vestibule consists of the mucosal and submucosal tissue of the lips and cheeks within the oral cavity, not including the dentoalveolar structures.

27.29   Other diagnostic procedures on oral cavity

Description
This code describes other diagnostic procedures on the oral cavity, not specified as biopsy.

Coding Clarification
This code excludes soft tissue x-ray of the mouth (87.09).

Documentation Tip
Carefully review the documentation in the medical record to determine if a more specific procedure code can be assigned. If the documentation is ambiguous or unclear, query the physician.

27.3   Excision of lesion or tissue of bony palate

Description
This subcategory includes excision of a lesion or tissue of the hard (bony) palate, specified as local or wide (en bloc).

27.31   Local excision or destruction of lesion or tissue of bony palate

Description
The physician performs destruction or surgical excision and removal of a lesion of the hard (bony) palate. Destruction may be accomplished by using a laser or electrocautery to burn the lesion, cryotherapy to freeze the lesion, or chemicals to destroy the lesion. The physician may surgically remove a lesion of the hard palate by incisions that are made completely around and under a lesion, typically in an elliptical shape, removing the lesion. If the lesion excised is small in diameter, no suturing or closure of the surgical wound may be necessary. Removal of larger lesions may require simple closure or local flap closure.

Coding Clarification
This procedure excludes biopsy of the bony palate (27.21).

27.32   Wide excision or destruction of lesion or tissue of bony palate

Description
The physician resects the palate or area of a lesion. The physician excises the lesion and any adjacent tissue where the lesion may have spread. The

surgical wound is repaired by intermediate or complex closure, adjacent tissue transfer, or graft.

27.4   Excision of other parts of mouth

Description
This subcategory describes excision of other parts of the mouth, including excision of lip lesions and lesions of the mouth not classified elsewhere.

27.41   Labial frenectomy

Description
The physician removes the labial or buccal frenum. The buccal frenum is a band of mucosal membrane that connects the alveolar (dental) ridge to the cheek and separates the lip vestibule from the cheek vestibule. The labial frenum is a connecting fold of mucous membrane that joins the lip to the gums at the inside mid-center. Incisions are made around the frenum and through the mucosa and submucosa. The underlying muscle is removed as well. The excision may extend to the interincisal papilla. The mucosa is closed simply, or the physician may rearrange the tissue as in a Z-plasty technique.

Coding Clarification
Code 27.41 excludes division of labial frenulum (27.91).

27.42   Wide excision of lesion of lip

Description
The physician performs a wide lip excision or resection by incision made through the midline of the lip and extended over the portion of the lip to be removed. The tumor and surrounding tissues are removed. The oral cavity is closed primarily, and the lip and surrounding structures are closed with layered sutures.

27.43   Other excision of lesion or tissue of lip

Description
The physician removes a lesion of the lip. After administering a local anesthetic, the physician makes a full-thickness incision through the dermis with a scalpel, usually in an elliptical shape around and under the lesion, and removes it. The physician may suture the wound simply, or complex or layered closure may be required.

27.49   Other excision of mouth

Description
This procedure code describes other excision of mouth lesion or tissue not elsewhere classified to category 27.4.

Coding Clarification
Composite resection floor of mouth is classified to 27.49 as other excision of mouth.

● New Code   ▲ Revised Code   ►◄ Revised Text   © 2010 Ingenix

Code 27.49 excludes multiple procedures that can be more specifically classified to category 25 or 27. Biopsy of the mouth (27.24), excision of lesions of the palate (27.31-27.32), tongue (25.1), and uvula (27.72), fistulectomy (27.53), and frenectomy (27.41, 27.91) can be more specifically classified elsewhere.

Coding Scenario
A 43-year-old female with a long history of tobacco abuse presented for an excision of irritative hyperplastic lesion of the oral soft tissues. Previous needle biopsies revealed dysplastic changes associated with an undefined possible precancerous pathology. The patient was positioned, prepped, and anesthetized. The lesions were identified under direct visualization and sharply excised. Minor bleeding was controlled with electrocautery.

Code Assignment:

528.9   Other and unspecified diseases of the oral soft tissues
27.49   Other excision of mouth

Coding Guidance
AHA: 2Q, '05, 8

27.5   Plastic repair of lip and mouth

Description
This subcategory describes plastic repair of mouth, including suture repairs, fistula closures, and other repairs.

Coding Clarification
Subcategory 27.5 excludes palatoplasty (27.61-27.69).

27.51   Suture of laceration of lip

Description
The physician sutures lacerations of the lips and/or mucous membranes. A local anesthetic is injected around the laceration and the wound is cleansed, explored, and often irrigated with a saline solution. The physician may perform a simple, one-layer repair or layered closure of the epidermis, dermis, or subcutaneous tissue with sutures.

27.52   Suture of laceration of other part of mouth

Description
The physician sutures lacerations of the buccal cavity and/or mucous membranes. A local anesthetic is injected around the laceration and the wound is cleansed, explored, and often irrigated with a saline solution. The physician may perform a simple, one-layer repair or layered closure of the epidermis, dermis, or subcutaneous tissue with sutures.

27.53   Closure of fistula of mouth

Description
The physician closes an abnormal fistula of the buccal cavity and/or mucous membranes and an adjacent tissue, organ, or structure. A local anesthetic is injected around the fistula and the fistula tract is cleansed, explored, and often irrigated with a saline solution. The fistula tract is excised and the wound is sutured in layers. A temporary drain may be placed.

Coding Clarification
Code 27.53 excludes nasolabial (21.82), oroantral (22.71), and oronasal (21.82) fistulectomy.

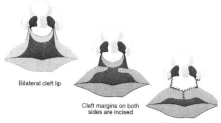

Bilateral cleft lip

Cleft margins on both sides are incised

Margins are closed, correcting cleft

27.54   Repair of cleft lip

Description
The physician surgically corrects a partial or complete unilateral developmental cleft lip/nasal deformity. A cleft lip may range in appearance as a "notch" in the upper lip to a complete separation running into the nose. The cleft margins are incised on either side from the mouth toward the nostril and through the full-thickness layers of mucosa, muscle, and skin. The vermilion border of the cleft lip is turned downward to restore the normal shape of the lip and the muscle and skin are brought together to close the cleft separation and preserve muscle function. The nasal deformity often caused by the cleft lip may be repaired. The physician closes the prepared margins in layers from the intraoral mucosa through the muscle with final closure of the skin.

27.55   Full-thickness skin graft to lip and mouth

Description
The physician harvests a full-thickness skin graft with a scalpel from one area of the body and grafts it to an area needing repair. A full-thickness skin graft consists of both the superficial and deeper layers of skin (epidermis and dermis). The resulting surgical wound at the donor site is closed by lifting the remaining skin edges and placing sutures for direct closure. Fat is removed from the graft, which is sutured onto the recipient bed to cover a defect of lips and mouth.

27.56   Other skin graft to lip and mouth

Description
This code describes a skin graft to the lip or mouth, specified as other than full-thickness. Surgical techniques may vary depending on the defect and type of graft, including:

- The physician transfers or rearranges adjacent tissue to repair traumatic or surgical wounds of the mouth and/or lips. This includes, but is not limited to, such rearrangement procedures as Z-plasty, W-plasty, ZY-plasty, or certain tissue transfers.

- The physician takes an epidermal autograft from one area of the body and grafts it to an area needing repair. This procedure is performed when direct wound closure or adjacent tissue transfer is not possible. The physician harvests an epidermal skin graft with a dermatome. The epidermal autograft should be as thin as possible: 0.05 mm (0.002 inches) to 0.13 mm (0.005 inches). Only the epidermis or top layer of skin is taken. The dermis or bottom layer of the skin is left behind and will regenerate new skin. The epidermal autograft is sutured or stapled onto the recipient area.

- The physician takes a split-thickness skin autograft from one area of the body and grafts it to an area needing repair. This procedure is performed when direct wound closure or adjacent tissue transfer is not possible. The physician harvests a split-thickness skin graft with a dermatome. The epidermis or top layer of skin is taken, along with a small portion of the dermis or bottom layer of the skin. This graft is sutured or stapled onto the recipient area.

27.57   Attachment of pedicle or flap graft to lip and mouth

Description
This procedure may be defined as a repair of the lip or mouth with tissue pedicle or flap still connected to original vascular base. Surgical technique may vary depending on size of defect and type of graft, including:

- The physician transfers or rearranges adjacent tissue to repair traumatic or surgical wounds of the mouth or lips. This includes, but is not limited to, tissue transfers such as rotational or advancement flaps.

- The physician forms a direct or tubed pedicle flap to reconstruct traumatic defects. A pedicle flap of full-thickness skin and subcutaneous tissue that retains its supporting blood vessels is developed in the donor area. A tubed pedicle flap maintains two vascular ends and the cut edges of the raised flap are sutured together to

form a tube. The flap may be rotated or transferred to the defect area and sutured to the recipient bed in layers. The physician closes the harvest region in layers or covers it with a split thickness skin graft. Repairs to the donor area using skin grafts or flaps are reported separately. Other exposed regions, including portions of the pedicle, may also be covered with a split thickness skin graft. Once the recipient site has healed, a second surgery will detach the pedicle and return the unused flap to its anatomic location.

Coding Guidance
    AHA: 1Q, '06, 14

27.59   Other plastic repair of mouth

Description
This code describes other plastic repair of mouth not classified elsewhere in subcategory 27.5.

Documentation Tip
Carefully review the documentation in the medical record to determine if a more specific code can be assigned. If the documentation is ambiguous or unclear, query the physician.

27.6   Palatoplasty

Description
This subcategory describes palatoplasty procedures, which may be defined as a surgical repair of the palate to restore form and function.

27.61   Suture of laceration of palate

Description
The physician repairs a laceration of the palate. The physician may suture the wound in a simple closure without submucosal sutures, or sutures a laceration that requires complex closure, such as tissue rearrangement, submucosal sutures, or extensive cleaning due to tissue damage or crushing.

Documentation Tip
This procedure may be documented as palatorrhaphy.

27.62   Correction of cleft palate

Description
This procedure code describes an initial cleft palate repair, with or without bone graft or soft tissue closure of the alveolar ridge. Surgical techniques may vary depending on the characteristics of the cleft and necessary repair, including:

- The physician repairs the developmental cleft opening of the palate. The cleft size and location will dictate the type of repair to be performed. The physician closes the opening between the oral and nasal cavities with a partition of soft tissue. Typically, incisions are made in the palatal mucosa adjacent to the alveolar (tooth-bearing) bone. The mucosa is elevated and loosened from the bony palate. The margins of the cleft are incised and dissected to develop mucosal and muscular layers. These incised midline margins are closed in layers, thus closing the communication between the oral and nasal cavities.

- The physician repairs the developmental cleft opening of the palate and reconstructs the alveolar ridge (tooth-bearing region) of the maxilla. The cleft size and location will dictate the type of repair performed. The physician closes the opening between the oral and nasal cavities with a partition of soft tissue. Bony reconstruction of the alveolar ridge can stabilize maxillary segments, benefit development of the teeth, and aid dental rehabilitation of chewing functions. Typically, incisions are made in the palatal mucosa adjacent to the alveolar bone. The mucosa is elevated and loosened from the bony palate. The midline margins of the cleft mucosa and gingiva are incised and dissected to develop mucosal and muscular layers. Through a separate incision, the physician harvests bone from the hip or skull and closes the surgically created wound. The bone is placed in the alveolar cleft, reestablishing normal contours of the maxilla. The physician closes all midline incisions in layers and gingival incisions in a single layer.

- The physician repairs the developmental cleft opening of the palate, which extends through the alveolar ridge (tooth-bearing region) of the maxilla. The cleft size and location will dictate the type of repair performed. The physician closes the opening between the oral and nasal cavities with a partition of soft tissue. Closure of the alveolar ridge will benefit development of both the maxilla and the teeth. Typically, incisions are made in the palatal mucosa adjacent to the alveolar bone. The mucosa is elevated and loosened from the bony palate. The midline margins of the cleft are incised and dissected to develop mucosal and muscular layers. The physician closes the midline margins in layers.

Coding Clarification
Subsequent repair or cleft palate revision procedures are reported with 27.63 Revision of cleft palate repair.

Documentation Tip
This code includes correction of cleft palate documented as a "push back" operation or uranostaphylorrhaphy for cleft palate repair.

27.63   Revision of cleft palate repair

Description
This procedure code describes a secondary repair or revision of a previous cleft palate procedure. Surgical techniques may vary depending on the characteristics of the cleft and necessary repair, and may include:

- **Secondary lengthening procedure:** The physician revises the previous cleft palate incisions to lengthen the soft palate. Wound dehiscence (splitting), infection, or scarring after initial surgeries could cause developmental growth restrictions or velopharyngeal incompetence. The defect will dictate the repair performed. Typically, the soft palate lengthening is accomplished with the use of mucosal advancement flaps. Incisions are made in the palatal mucosa adjacent to the alveolar (tooth-bearing) bone. The mucosa is elevated and loosened from the bony palate. The pedicle flaps utilizing posterior palatine blood supply are developed and sutured to increase the anterior-posterior length of the soft palate. The physician sutures all remaining midline incisions in layers.

- **Attachment of pharyngeal flap:** The physician revises previous cleft palate incisions with pharyngeal flap techniques. Through the soft palate, a midline incision is made to expose the posterior pharyngeal wall. The physician incises a flap from the posterior pharyngeal wall through the mucosa, submucosa, and muscle. This flap is sutured to the soft palate. Revision of previous surgical incisions may be necessary. All remaining midline incisions are sutured in layers.

- **Other cleft palate revision:** The physician revises previous repairs of the cleft palate. Wound dehiscence (splitting), infection, or scarring after initial surgeries could cause oral/nasal recommunication, developmental growth restrictions, or velopharyngeal incompetence. The defect will dictate the repair to be performed. Typically, incisions are made in the palatal mucosa adjacent to the alveolar (tooth-bearing) bone. The mucosa is elevated and loosened from the bony palate. The previous midline incisions are excised and dissected to develop mucosal and muscular layers. The physician resutures all midline incisions in layers and gingival incisions are closed in a single layer.

Coding Clarification
Code 27.63 is reported for an advancement flap graft repair/revision of a cleft palate procedure.

Coding Guidance
AHA: 1Q, '96, 14

27.64   Insertion of palatal implant

Description
This code describes the insertion of implants into the palate to correct form and function. Although palatial implants may be used in orthodonture, they have recently been utilized in the treatment of obstructive sleep apnea. Palatal implants are sometimes intended to stiffen and change the airflow characteristics of the soft palate tissue. The change is intended to reduce the severity of snoring and the incidence of airway obstructions for individuals with mild to moderate obstructive sleep apnea (OSA). The devices are cylindrical shaped segments of braided polyester filaments. A delivery tool comprised of a handle and needle assembly allows for positioning and placement of three implants submucosally in the soft palate. The procedure is often performed under local anesthetic in an outpatient setting or it may be performed in conjunction with other nasopharyngeal procedures, such as tonsillectomies, uvulopalatopharyngoplasties, laser-assisted uvulopalatoplasties, and various tongue-based procedures.

Coding Guidance
AHA: 4Q, '04, 17

27.69   Other plastic repair of palate

Description
This procedure code describes other plastic repairs of the palate and palatoplasty operations not classified elsewhere in subcategory 27.6. Surgical techniques vary according to the characteristics of the palatial defect and necessary repair, including:

- **Anterior palate repair:** The physician repairs the hard palate by closing the communication between the oral and nasal cavities. A combination of mucosal and mucoperiosteal flaps are used to repair the defect. The margins of the defect are incised and dissected to develop mucosal, muscular, and mucoperiosteal layers. The mucoperiosteum of the vomer (nasal septum) is elevated and sutured to the mucoperiosteum of the hard palate. This closes the communication between the oral and nasal cavities. Incisions are made in the palatal mucosa adjacent to the alveolar (tooth-bearing) bone. The mucosa is elevated and loosened from the bony palate. The palatal mucosa is closed in layers.
- **Palate lengthening with island flap:** The physician uses mucosal island flaps to lengthen

the soft palate. Incisions are made in the palatal mucosa adjacent to the alveolar (tooth-bearing) bone. The mucosa is elevated and loosened from the bony palate. Advancement flaps utilizing posterior palatine blood vessels are used to lengthen the soft palate by suturing techniques that increase the anterior-posterior length of the soft palate. All remaining incisions are sutured in layers.

Coding Clarification
Code also any insertion of palatal implant (27.64).

Code 27.69 excludes fistulectomy of mouth (27.53).

Documentation Tip
Carefully review the documentation in the medical record to determine if a more specific procedure code can be assigned. If the documentation is ambiguous or unclear, query the physician.

If this procedure is documented as uvulopalatopharyngoplasty (UPPP), two codes are required to report the procedure: 29.4 Plastic operation on pharynx, and 27.69 Other plastic repair of palate.

This procedure may also be documented as uranostaphylorrhaphy, NOS.

Coding Guidance
AHA: 3Q, 92, 18; 1Q, '97, 14; 3Q, '99, 22

27.7   Operations on uvula

Description
This subcategory describes operations on the uvula, including incisions, excision, repairs, and other procedures.

27.71   Incision of uvula

Description
The physician drains an abscess of the uvula. The abscess is opened with a surgical instrument and the fluid is drained. The wound is allowed to heal without closure.

27.72   Excision of uvula

Description
The physician removes all or part of the uvula. If a lesion is excised, incisions are made completely around and under a lesion, typically in an elliptical shape, removing the lesion. The physician removes the uvula with a full-thickness incision. Electrocautery may be used to control hemorrhage. Sutures may be used to close the mucosa in a single layer or local flap closure.

Coding Clarification
Code 27.72 excludes biopsy of uvula (27.22).

● New Code   ▲ Revised Code   ▶◀ Revised Text   © 2010 Ingenix

27.73   Repair of uvula

Description
This code describes uvula repair procedures and uvuloplasty procedures. Some uvuloplasty procedures are performed to treat certain sleep disorder symptoms such as obstructive sleep apnea (OSA) and snoring. A coblation uvuloplasty is performed with a cold ablation plasma beam, under local anesthesia. A laser-assisted uvuloplasty (LAUP) is performed with a laser beam under local anesthesia.

Coding Clarification
This procedure excludes uvuloplasty with synchronous cleft palate repair (27.62) and uranostaphylorrhaphy (27.62).

27.79   Other operations on uvula

Description
This code describes other operations on the uvula not specifically classifiable to other codes in subcategory 27.

Coding Guidance
    AHA: 3Q, '92, 18

27.9   Other operations on mouth and face

Description
This subcategory describes other operations on mouth and face not elsewhere classified in category 27.

27.91   Labial frenotomy

Description
The physician performs a frenotomy by incising the labial frenum. The labial frenum is a connecting fold of mucous membrane that joins the lip to the gums at the inside mid-center. This procedure is often performed to release tension on the frenum and surrounding tissues. The frenum is simply incised and not removed.

Coding Clarification
This code excludes lingual frenotomy (25.91).

Documentation Tip
Code 27.91 may also be documented as a division of the labial frenum.

27.92   Incision of mouth, unspecified structure

Description
This code describes an incision of an unspecified structure of the mouth, including:

*   **Incision of skin and subcutaneous tissue of mouth:** The physician removes a foreign body embedded in subcutaneous tissue. The physician makes a simple incision in the skin overlying the foreign body. The foreign body is

retrieved using hemostats or forceps. The skin may be sutured or allowed to heal secondarily. If the wound is more complicated, dissection of underlying tissues may be required.

*   **Incision of mouth:** The physician drains an abscess, a cyst, or a hematoma from the floor of the mouth by making an extraoral or intraoral incision, dissecting through the tissue to reach the affected space. A drain may be placed to facilitate healing, which is later removed.

Coding Clarification
Code 27.92 excludes incision of specific structures of the mouth classifiable as:

*   Gum (24.0)
*   Palate (27.1)
*   Salivary gland or duct (26.0)
*   Tongue (25.94)
*   Uvula (27.71)

27.99   Other operations on oral cavity

Description
This code describes other operations on the oral cavity not elsewhere classified in category 27.

Coding Clarification
This code includes graft of the buccal sulcus, which can be defined as an implant of tissue into the groove of the inferior cheek lining.

This code excludes removal of intraluminal foreign body (98.01) and penetrating foreign body from mouth without incision (98.22).

Documentation Tip
Carefully review the documentation in the medical record to determine if a more specific code can be assigned. If the documentation is ambiguous or unclear, query the physician.

28   *Operations on tonsils and adenoids*

Description
The tonsils and adenoids are areas of lymphoid tissue located in the pharynx and nasopharynx. They function as part of the immune system, producing antibodies and protecting the body against infection—especially of the upper respiratory system. The tonsils and adenoids atrophy as part of the natural aging process, which is why hypertrophy and infection of these tissues are most common among the pediatric population. Airway obstruction caused by hypertrophied or infected nasopharyngeal lymphoid tissues poses the greatest risk to the patient, whereby the entire airway can become seriously compromised. Airway obstruction is the most common indication for tonsil and adenoid excision and removal procedures.

Category 28 provides codes for diagnostic and therapeutic tonsil and adenoid operations including incisions, biopsy, excision, hemorrhage control, and other procedures.

28.0 Incision and drainage of tonsil and peritonsillar structures

Description
Code 28.0 describes incision and drainage of the tonsil and peritonsillar structures, which can be performed by intraoral or extraoral approach:

- **Tonsil incision and drainage:** The physician drains an abscess near or on a tonsil. The patient is given a topical anesthetic or placed under general anesthesia. Using an intraoral approach with a mouth gag, the physician incises the mucus membrane of the abscess. The abscess cavity is opened with angulated closed forceps or hemostat. The wound is irrigated and left open.

- **Peritonsillar incision and drainage:** The physician drains an abscess located on or near the pharynx. Retropharyngeal indicates the abscess is located on the back of the pharynx; parapharyngeal indicates the abscess is near the pharynx. The patient is given a topical anesthetic or placed under general anesthesia. Though an intraoral approach, the physician locates the abscess using a diagnostic needle puncture and aspiration at the point of maximal fluctuation on the pharynx. The physician incises the mucus membrane to open the abscess. The pus is evacuated using suction and sponging.

- **Extraoral approach:** The physician drains an abscess located on or near the pharynx. The patient may be placed under general anesthesia. The physician makes an incision beneath the angle of the jaw and carries out a blunt dissection to locate and isolate the abscess. The physician incises the mucus membrane of the abscess. The pus is evacuated; a gauze or rubber drain may be inserted into the abscess cavity. The incision is repaired in sutured layers.

Coding Clarification
Code 28.0 includes oral (intraoral) or transcervical (extraoral) drainage of abscesses specified as:

- Parapharyngeal
- Peritonsillar
- Retropharyngeal
- Tonsillar

28.1 Diagnostic procedures on tonsils and adenoids

Description
Subcategory 28.1 describes diagnostic procedures on tonsils and adenoids including biopsy and other procedures.

28.11 Biopsy of tonsils and adenoids Description

Description
The physician obtains a biopsy of the tonsil or adenoid. After the airway is secured with an endotracheal tube, a mouth gag is placed. The physician obtains a tissue sample through an incisional or snare technique. Bleeding is controlled through electrocautery; the wound is not closed.

28.19 Other diagnostic procedures on tonsils and adenoids

Description
Code 28.19 reports other diagnostic procedures on tonsils and adenoids not described as biopsy.

Coding Clarification
Code 28.19 excludes soft tissue x-ray (87.09).

28.2 Tonsillectomy without adenoidectomy

Description
The physician removes the tonsils. The tonsillectomy can be the first the patient has undergone, or a secondary procedure to remove tonsil regrowth since the primary procedure. The physician accesses the tonsils in an intraoral approach. First, the physician removes the tonsils by grasping the tonsil with a tonsil clamp and dissecting the capsule of the tonsil. The tonsil is removed. Bleeding vessels are clamped and tied. Bleeding may also be controlled using silver nitrate and gauze packing. Alternate surgical techniques for a tonsillectomy include electrocautery, laser surgery, and cryogenic surgery.

Coding Clarification
Code 28.2 includes laser tonsillectomy.

Coding Guidance
  AHA: 2Q, '90, 23; 1Q, '97, 5

28.3 Tonsillectomy with adenoidectomy

Description
The physician removes the tonsils and adenoids. The physician accesses the tonsils and adenoids in an intraoral approach. First, the physician removes the tonsils by grasping the tonsil with a tonsil clamp and dissecting the capsule of the tonsil. The tonsil is removed. Bleeding vessels are clamped and tied. Bleeding may also be controlled using silver nitrate and gauze packing. Using a mirror or nasopharyngoscope for visualization, the physician uses an adenotome or a curette and basket punch to excise the adenoids. Alternate surgical techniques

● New Code   ▲ Revised Code   ▶◀ Revised Text   © 2010 Ingenix

for a tonsillectomy and adenoidectomy include electrocautery, laser surgery, and cryogenic surgery.

Coding Clarification
Code 28.3 includes tonsillectomy and adenoidectomy by fulguration.

Coding Scenario
A 7-year-old female with chronic obstructive adenotonsillar hypertrophy presented for tonsillectomy and adenoidectomy (T&A). The patient was positioned, prepped, and anesthetized. Bilateral tonsils were identified in the oropharynx, dissected from the capsule and removed. Bleeding vessels were controlled with electrocautery. A mirror was used to visualize the adenoid tissue, which upon identification, were fulgurated.

> Code Assignment:
>
> 474.10   Hypertrophy of tonsils and adenoids
> 28.3   Tonsillectomy with adenoidectomy

Coding Guidance
> **AHA:** 2Q,'05, 16

28.4   Excision of tonsil tag

Description
The physician removes portions of the tonsils not excised during primary resection or that have developed polyps. The physician cauterizes and/or snares the affected tissue. No closure is required.

28.5   Excision of lingual tonsil

Description
The physician removes or destroys the lingual tonsils. Because the abscessed tonsils may restrict the airway passage, the physician is present during intubation in case an emergency airway is needed. The physician uses an endotracheal tube or an operating laryngoscope with jet ventilation to ventilate the patient. Using an intraoral approach, the physician uses a laser to destroy the lingual tonsils.

28.6   Adenoidectomy without tonsillectomy

Description
The physician removes the adenoids. Using an intraoral approach and a mirror or nasopharyngoscope for visualization, the physician uses an adenotome or a curette and basket punch to excise the adenoids. Alternate surgical techniques for an adenoidectomy include electrocautery, laser surgery, and cryogenic surgery.

28.7   Control of hemorrhage after tonsillectomy and adenoidectomy

Description
The physician controls bleeding of the oropharynx. Primary hemorrhaging occurs within 24 hours after surgery; secondary hemorrhaging occurs 24 hours to two weeks after tonsillectomy. Hemorrhaging is controlled using methods such as clot evacuation and applying pressure with sponges, electrocautery, or application of vasoconstrictor solutions such as tannic acid, silver nitrate, and epinephrine. Cellulose sponges that expand when placed in the tonsillar cavity may be used. When extensive bleeding requires hospitalization, surgery is required to control hemorrhaging. Surgical intervention methods include suture ligation of bleeding vessels. In cases of profuse bleeding, emergency ligation of the external carotid artery may be performed. The tonsillar pillars may be approximated with sutures to control post-tonsillectomy bleeding.

Coding Guidance
> **AHA:** 2Q,'05, 16

28.9   Other operations on tonsils and adenoids

Description
Subcategory 28.9 describes other operations on tonsils and adenoids not classified elsewhere in category 28.

28.91   Removal of foreign body from tonsil and adenoid by incision

Description
The physician removes a foreign body from tonsillar or adenoid tissue by incision. Topical or local anesthesia may be used to anesthetize the patient. An incision is made and the object is grasped and removed with bayonet forceps, a hemostat, or other instrumentation. An endoscope may assist in visualization.

Coding Clarification
This code excludes removal of foreign body without incision (98.13).

28.92   Excision of lesion of tonsil and adenoid

Description
The physician removes a lesion of the tonsil or adenoid. The physician cauterizes snares or sharply excises the affected tissue. The wound may be sutured or cauterized closed.

Coding Clarification
This code excludes biopsy of the tonsil and adenoid (28.11).

28.99   Other operations on tonsils and adenoids

Description
Code 28.99 describes other operations on the tonsils or adenoids not classifiable elsewhere in subcategory 28.

Coding Guidance
> **AHA:** 2Q, '90, 23

29   Operations on pharynx

Description
The pharynx (throat) is a tubed passageway that extends from the mouth to the esophagus. There are three main regions of the pharynx, named for their anatomic locations:

- Oropharynx—behind the mouth
- Nasopharynx—behind the nose
- Laryngopharynx—behind the larynx

The pharynx contains openings and passageways from the eustachian tubes, nasopharynx, oropharynx, and laryngopharynx to other structures. Adjacent to the pharynx, accessory lymphatic organs known as the tonsils serve to filter bacteria and foreign substances. The lower portion of the pharynx opens into the esophagus and larynx.

Category 29 provides codes for diagnostic and therapeutic pharynx operations including incisions, biopsy, excision, fistula closure, and other procedures.

Coding Clarification
This category includes procedures specific to the following anatomic sites:

- Hypopharynx
- Nasopharynx
- Oropharynx
- Pharyngeal pouch
- Pyriform sinus

29.0   Pharyngotomy

Description
Code 29.0 describes an incision of the pharynx. This incision may be used for drainage of an abscess or bursa or as access for long-term feeding. If the purpose of the incision is to insert a feeding tube, the physician makes a horizontal incision below the jaw line to create a communication between the pharyngeal lumen and the exterior of the patient's neck. The incision is sutured to create an opening for placement of a feeding tube.

Coding Clarification
Code 29.0 excludes incision and drainage of retropharyngeal abscess (28.0) and removal of foreign body without incision (98.13).

29.1   Diagnostic procedures on pharynx

Description
Subcategory 29.1 describes diagnostic procedures on the pharynx, including endoscopy, biopsy, and other procedures.

29.11   Pharyngoscopy

Description
The examination is performed with the patient lying on his back and under a local anesthetic, topical Lidocaine is sprayed onto the back of the throat and into the nasal passages. The physician introduces the flexible fiberoptic endoscope through the nose and advances it into the pharynx to determine whether there are any fixed blockages such as a deviated septum, nasal polyps, or enlarged adenoids and tonsils. The physician may position the tip of the endoscope at the level of the hard palate and instruct the patient to perform simple maneuvers that demonstrate airway activity under conditions that promote or prevent collapse. The test may be performed to identify anatomic factors contributing to sleep disorder, stability of the upper airway, and determining treatments.

29.12   Pharyngeal biopsy

Description
The physician obtains a biopsy of the pharynx. After the airway is secured with an endotracheal tube, a mouth gag is placed. The physician obtains a tissue sample through an incisional or snare technique. Bleeding may be controlled with electrocautery. The wound is usually not closed. A portion of tissue visible in the nasopharynx is biopsied. If the lesion is deep in the nasopharynx, an operating laryngoscope is used to visualize the area.

Coding Scenario
The physician performed a biopsy to diagnose a patient with obstructive supraglottis.

Code Assignment:

464.51 Unspecified supraglottis, with obstruction
29.12   Pharyngeal biopsy

29.19   Other diagnostic procedures on pharynx

Description
This procedure code describes other diagnostic procedures on the pharynx, not specified as endoscopy or biopsy.

Coding Clarification
This procedure excludes x-ray of the nasopharynx (87.06, 87.09).

29.2   Excision of branchial cleft cyst or vestige

Description
The physician removes a branchial cleft cyst or vestige that is confined to the skin and subcutaneous tissues of the neck. A branchial cleft is an abnormal embryological remnant that resembles gills. The physician makes a horizontal neck incision just below the jaw line to access and

● New Code   ▲ Revised Code   ▶◀ Revised Text   © 2010 Ingenix

remove the cyst or vestige. The incision is repaired in sutured layers.

Alternately, the physician may remove a branchial cleft cyst or vestige that has extended beyond the skin and subcutaneous tissue. A branchial cleft is an abnormal embryological remnant that resembles gills. The physician makes one or two horizontal neck incisions just below the jaw line. The cyst or vestige is dissected from the surrounding muscle and fascia. If a fistula is present, a surrounding elliptical skin excision is performed. Any ducts of the cyst are dissected and traced to a pharyngeal communication. The cyst, vestige, and ducts are removed. A tissue drain is placed and the wound is sutured in layers.

Coding Clarification
This procedure excludes branchial cleft fistulectomy (29.52).

29.3   Excision or destruction of lesion or tissue of pharynx

Description
Subcategory 29.3 describes excision or destruction of a lesion of tissue of the pharynx, including myotomy, diverticulectomy, and other procedures.

29.31   Cricopharyngeal myotomy

Description
The physician incises the cricopharyngeal muscle, also known as the upper esophageal sphincter (UES). The physician makes a lateral neck incision to expose the UES, and a second lateral incision through the UES. The incision is repaired with sutured layers.

Coding Clarification
Code 29.31 excludes cricopharyngeal myotomy with pharyngeal diverticulectomy (29.32).

29.32   Pharyngeal diverticulectomy

Description
The physician removes a diverticulum from the hypopharynx or esophagus. A diverticulum is a pouch that occurs normally or because of a defect in the muscular membrane. In the cervical approach, the physician makes a lateral incision in the neck. In the thoracic approach, the physician incises and dissects the left posterior chest wall. The physician may dissect or incise the cricopharyngeus muscle to expose the diverticulum. The physician clamps the diverticulum and closes using sutures or staples. The incision is closed with sutured layers.

Coding Guidance
    AHA: 2Q, '89, 18

29.33   Pharyngectomy (partial)

Description
The physician removes the affected portion of the pharyngeal wall. The physician makes a vertical incision in the neck and retracts the strap muscles. The affected area of the pharynx is excised and the pharyngeal walls are reapproximated and closed with sutures. The incision is sutured in layers. Occasionally, the area removed includes part of the thyroid ala, hyoid bone, and wall of the pyriform fossa. Reconstructive surgery is often required for closure.

Coding Clarification
Code 29.33 excludes laryngopharyngectomy (30.3).

29.39   Other excision or destruction of lesion or tissue of pharynx

Description
The physician removes or destroys a lesion of the pharynx. The physician uses an intraoral approach to excise or destroy the lesion. Destruction may be accomplished using a laser, cryosurgery, or electrocoagulation to cause the tissue to coagulate. Methods of excision may include avulsion or curettage.

29.4   Plastic operation on pharynx

Description
A variety of techniques may be used for pharyngoplasty including skin grafts, tongue flaps, regional cutaneous flaps, and microvascular free-tissue transfer. Skin grafts are commonly harvested from the forehead, deltopectoral, nape of the neck, and pectoralis major. Reconstruction procedures are often performed when direct wound closure or reapproximation is not possible. The following pharyngoplasty procedures are classified to 29.4:

*   **Repair of choanal (nasopharyngeal) atresia:** The physician reconstructs the congenitally absent openings between the nasal cavity and the pharynx (throat). Topical vasoconstrictive agents are applied to the nasal mucosa. Local anesthesia is injected in the nasal mucosa and maxilla. A midpalatal incision is made extending posterior to the nasopalatine foramen to the soft palate. The mucoperiosteum is elevated, exposing the hard palate. Using drills and chisels, the physician creates bony windows at the posterior hard palate, removing bony obstructions between the nasal floor and the pharynx. The physician places rubber tubes along the nasal floor through the new openings into the nasopharynx. The rubber tubes are sutured to the nasal columella. The palatal incision is closed in a single layer. The rubber

tubes remain for a three- to eight-week healing period to ensure patency of the new posterior nares after removal.

- **Palatopharyngoplasty:** The physician removes elongated and excessive tissues of the uvula, soft palate, and pharynx. Incisions are made in the soft palate mucosa and a wedge of mucosa is excised. Excessive submucosal tissue is removed and the uvula is partially excised. The midline at the uvula is sutured first. The physician closes the remaining mucosa in a single layer, reapproximating the soft palate and thus increasing the diameter of the oropharynx.

- **Pharyngoesophageal repair:** The physician repairs a tear at the pharyngeal esophageal junction. After the airway is secured, the physician makes a horizontal neck incision and retracts superficial tissues to expose the pharyngeal esophageal junction. The defect is identified, irrigated to reduce infection, and sutured in layers.

Documentation Tip
If this procedure is documented as uvulopalatopharyngoplasty (UPPP), two codes are required to report the procedure: 29.4 Plastic operation on pharynx, and 27.69 Other plastic repair of palate.

Coding Guidance
AHA: 3Q, '92, 18; 1Q, '97, 5; 3Q, '99, 22

29.5   Other repair of pharynx
Description
Subcategory 29.5 reports repair of the pharynx, including suture, closures, adhesiolysis, and other procedures.

29.51   Suture of laceration of pharynx
Description
The physician locates and sutures a wound or injury to the pharynx. The physician uses an intraoral or transhyoid approach, depending on the location and extent of the wound. For an intraoral approach, the physician uses a mirror for visualization. For a transhyoid approach, the physician makes a horizontal incision directly below the jaw line. The physician sutures the wound. If a transhyoid approach is used, the incision is sutured in layers.

29.52   Closure of branchial cleft fistula
Description
The physician removes a branchial cleft fistula. A branchial cleft is an abnormal embryological remnant that resembles gills. The physician makes one or two horizontal neck incisions just below the jaw line. An elliptical skin excision is performed surrounding the fistula. Any ducts are dissected and

traced to a pharyngeal communication and removed. A tissue drain is placed and the wound is sutured in layers.

29.53   Closure of other fistula of pharynx
Description
This procedure code describes a closure of other pharynx fistula, including pharyngoesophageal fistula. After the airway is secured, the physician makes a horizontal neck incision and retracts superficial tissues to expose the pharyngeal esophageal junction. The fistula is identified and irrigated. The fistula tract or ducts may be excised and sutured. The wound is closed in layers.

29.54   Lysis of pharyngeal adhesions
Description
The physician divides and releases adhesions of the pharynx. The physician uses an intraoral or transhyoid approach, depending on the anatomic location of the adhesions. For an intraoral approach, the physician uses a mirror for visualization. For a transhyoid approach, the physician makes a horizontal incision directly below the jaw line. The physician identifies the adhesions and sharply divides and releases the adhesive tissue. If a transhyoid approach is used, the incision is sutured in layers.

29.59   Other repair of pharynx
Description
This procedure code describes other repair operations of the pharynx, not elsewhere classifiable in subcategory 29.5.

Coding Clarification
Code 29.59 includes cricopharyngeal myotomy with suspension of the pharyngoesophageal diverticulum to allow drainage.

Coding Guidance
AHA: 2Q, '89, 18

29.9   Other operations on pharynx
Description
This subcategory includes other operations on the pharynx not elsewhere classifiable in category 29, including dilations, divisions, and other procedures.

29.91   Dilation of pharynx
Description
This procedure code describes a mechanical dilation of the pharynx and nasopharynx to expand a constricted or otherwise obstructed anatomic space. The patient is anesthetized and may be sedated as dilating devices are threaded through the space, often with the assistance of an endoscope or

● New Code   ▲ Revised Code   ▶◀ Revised Text   © 2010 Ingenix

guidewire, and the area is dilated. The devices are removed and the pharynx or nasopharynx tested for patency.

29.92   Division of glossopharyngeal nerve

Description
The physician cuts or avulses the glossopharyngeal nerve. The physician makes an incision on the face or neck overlying the extradural portion of the nerve. The tissues are dissected and the nerve is exposed and destroyed. The incision is sutured in layers.

29.99   Other operations on pharynx

Description
This procedure code describes other operations on the pharynx not classifiable elsewhere in category 29.

Coding Clarification
Code 29.99 excludes insertion of radium into the pharynx and nasopharynx (92.27) and removal of an intraluminal foreign body (98.13).

30-34

Operations on the Respiratory System

2011 Changes

New code 32.27 Bronchoscopic bronchial thermoplasty, ablation of airway smooth muscle reports a bronchoscopic procedure in which radiofrequency (RF)-based technology is applied to the smooth muscle of the tracheobronchial tree and lungs for the treatment of severe asthma.

Exclusion terms were added to codes 33.24 Closed [endoscopic] biopsy of bronchus and 33.29 Other diagnostic procedures on lung and bronchus to differentiate between BAL (33.24) and mini-BAL (33.29) classifications.

Inclusion and exclusion terms were added to or revised in codes 33.27 Closed endoscopic biopsy of lung and 33.24 Closed [endoscopic] biopsy of bronchus to differentiate between TBNA of the bronchus (33.27) and TBNA of the lung (33.27).

Inclusion terms were added to code 33.73 Endoscopic insertion or replacement of bronchial valve(s), multiple lobes.

The ICD-9-CM classification system for operations performed on the respiratory system is divided into categories of procedures according to site and type as follows:

- Excision of Larynx (30)
- Other Operations on Larynx and Trachea (31)
- Excision of Lung and Bronchus (32)
- Other Operations on Lung and Bronchus (33)
- Operations on Chest Wall, Pleura, Mediastinum, and Diaphragm (34)

Coding Clarification

Two categories, 30 and 32, are used strictly for excisions of larynx and lung and bronchus, respectively. If an excision has not occurred, see categories 31 and 33.

Since these procedures require the use of high magnification and specially designed micro-instruments, an operating microscope or telescope should not be reported separately.

30   Excision of larynx

Description

Category 30 Excision of larynx, provides codes for excision or destruction, including laser, of lesions or tissue of the larynx, and laryngectomies.

Documentation Tip

Six codes are available when the surgeon documents a laryngectomy. Check both the operative and pathology reports to determine the precise excision in order to assign the most appropriate code.

A complete laryngectomy is a block dissection of the larynx and may include a thyroidectomy with synchronous tracheostomy.

A radical laryngectomy is complete (total) laryngectomy with radical neck dissection and may include a thyroidectomy and synchronous tracheostomy.

30.0   Excision or destruction of lesion or tissue of larynx

Coding Clarification

Since many of these procedures require the use of high magnification and specially designed micro-instruments, an operating microscope or telescope is included and should not be reported separately.

Do not use 30.0 subclassification codes to report biopsy of larynx (31.43), laryngeal fistulectomy (31.62), or laryngotracheal fistulectomy (31.62).

30.01   Marsupialization of laryngeal cyst

Description

Marsupialization is the incision of a cyst of larynx with the edges sutured open to create a pouch. Using a horizontal neck incision, the physician exposes the larynx, opening the larynx at the midline of the thyroid cartilage. The physician sutures the cut edges of the remaining wall to adjacent edges of the skin, creating a pouch. The incision is repaired in sutured layers.

30.09 Other excision or destruction of lesion or tissue of larynx

Description

This code can be used to report a variety of procedures, some of which are detailed below.

When performing a diagnostic laryngotomy, the physician first performs a tracheostomy on the patient. Using a horizontal neck incision, the physician exposes the larynx and performs a thyrotomy and laryngofissure, opening the larynx at the midline of the thyroid cartilage. The larynx is explored, but no other procedure is performed. The incision is repaired in sutured layers.

A laryngocele is an air-filled dilation of the laryngeal ventricle that connects with the laryngeal cavity. When performing a laryngotomy with removal of a tumor or laryngocele, the physician first performs a tracheostomy on the patient. Using a horizontal neck incision, the physician exposes the larynx and performs a thyrotomy and laryngofissure, opening the larynx at the midline of the thyroid cartilage. The laryngocele or tumor is isolated, dissected, and excised. A cordectomy, the excision of all or part of the vocal cord, may also be performed. The incision is repaired in sutured layers.

The physician performs a direct operative laryngoscopy with excision of tumor and/or stripping of the vocal cords or epiglottis. A topical anesthetic is administered to the oral cavity, pharynx, and larynx and the laryngoscope is inserted into the patient's mouth. The interior of the larynx is examined and a laryngeal tumor may be isolated, dissected, and excised. The vocal cords or epiglottis may also be removed using stripping forceps. An operating microscope or a telescope may be used. This is usually done for smaller lesions.

Coding Clarification

Do not use 30.09 to report biopsy of the larynx (31.43), laryngeal fistulectomy (31.62), or laryngotracheal fistulectomy (31.62).

30.1 Hemilaryngectomy

Description

The physician excises half of the larynx. First the physician performs a tracheostomy on the patient. Using a horizontal neck incision, the physician excises one side of the larynx. Frequently, a rib graft is obtained and sewn to provide posterior stability to the larynx and adjacent trachea. The incision is sutured in layers.

Coding Clarification

The hemilaryngectomy can be horizontal, laterovertical, anterovertical, or antero-laterovertical.

30.2 Other partial laryngectomy

Description

Other partial laryngectomy includes procedures on the epiglottis (epiglottidectomy) and excisional procedures on vocal cords and laryngeal cartilage.

30.21 Epiglottidectomy

Description

The physician excises all or part of the epiglottis, the cartilage that protects the entrance to the larynx. The physician uses an intra-oral approach to access and remove the epiglottis or lesions involving the tip of the epiglottis. If the affected area is minor, no sutures are needed. If the area involves most or the entire epiglottis, the remaining tissues are sutured together.

30.22 Vocal cordectomy

Description

A vocal cordectomy is an excision of the vocal cords. The physician first performs a tracheostomy on the patient. Using a horizontal neck incision, the physician exposes the larynx and performs a thyrotomy and laryngofissure, opening the larynx at the midline of the thyroid cartilage. The vocal code excision is performed and the incision is repaired in sutured layers.

30.29 Other partial laryngectomy

Description

Code 30.29 is used to report excision of laryngeal cartilage and other partial laryngectomy procedures that are not more precisely described by other codes in subcategory 30.2.

Documentation Tip

Review the documentation for specific information regarding the procedure prior to final code selection in order to ensure accurate code assignment.

30.3 Complete laryngectomy

Description

The physician performs a block dissection of the larynx and thyroidectomy with synchronous tracheostomy. First, a tracheostomy is performed. The physician makes a low collar or midline cervical incision or a horizontal neck incision. The strap muscles of the neck and thyroid isthmus are cut. Part or all of the hyoid bone is removed. The trachea and inferior pharyngeal constrictor muscles are transected. By cutting the hypopharyngeal walls, the larynx is freed and removed. The incision is sutured in layers.

Coding Clarification

Use 30.3 to report laryngopharyngectomy.

● New Code   ▲ Revised Code   ▶◀ Revised Text   © 2010 Ingenix

Do no use this code to report radical neck dissection; report 30.4.

Documentation Tip

A complete laryngectomy is a block dissection of the larynx. It may include thyroidectomy with synchronous tracheostomy.

A radical laryngectomy is a complete (total) laryngectomy with radical neck dissection. It may also include thyroidectomy and synchronous tracheostomy.

30.4   Radical laryngectomy

Description

The physician performs a complete or total laryngectomy with radical neck dissection with thyroidectomy and synchronous tracheostomy. An extensive dissection may include removal of the sternocleidomastoid muscle, the submandibular salivary gland, the internal jugular vein and the lymph nodes of the lateral neck, under the chin and mandible, and the supraclavicular nodes.

Coding Clarification

Report 30.4 for a complete or total laryngectomy (i.e., with radical neck dissection, with thyroidectomy, and with synchronous tracheostomy).

Documentation Tip

A complete laryngectomy is a block dissection of the larynx. A thyroidectomy with synchronous tracheostomy may be performed.

A radical laryngectomy is a complete (total) laryngectomy with radical neck dissection. A thyroidectomy and synchronous tracheostomy may also be performed.

Coding Scenario

A patient was admitted for surgical treatment of malignant neoplasms throughout the larynx. The physician performed a tracheostomy then removed the larynx and surrounding tissues in an extensive neck dissection that included removal of the thyroid, the lymph nodes of the neck, and the supraclavicular nodes.

Code Assignment:

161.8   Malignant neoplasm of other specified sites of larynx

30.4   Radical laryngectomy

31   Other operations on larynx and trachea

Description

Category 31 provides codes for operations on the larynx (except excisions) and trachea. There are nine subcategories (0–7 and 9) because with both sites

represented under one category, site specificity occurs on the subcategory level.

Coding Clarification

Assign 31.1 for a temporary tracheostomy.

31.0   Injection of larynx

Description

The physician performs a direct laryngoscopy and injects material into the larynx or vocal cords. The physician administers a topical anesthetic to the oral cavity, pharynx, and larynx and inserts the laryngoscope into the patient's mouth. The interior of the larynx is examined and the physician injects the vocal cord at one to three sites with the selected therapeutic substance. No other procedure is performed. An operating microscope or a telescope is used.

Coding Clarification

An injection with a therapeutic substance into an affected vocal cord can augment its size and help bring it into apposition with the other vocal cord, creating a more complete glottic closure. For a therapeutic injection of the vocal cords, the physician injects the vocal cords with a therapeutic substance such as glycerin, sesame oil, Gelfoam, or Teflon paste (Polytef). The injected material hardens and retains its shape for improvement in voice quality. A Teflon paste injection is used when a permanent augmentation is desired. A glycerin, sesame oil, or Gelfoam injection is used to create a temporary augmentation until a permanent solution to an incomplete glottic closure is found.

31.1   Temporary tracheostomy

Description

The physician performs a tracheotomy for assistance in breathing. The physician creates a tracheostomy by first making a horizontal neck incision and dissects the muscles to expose the trachea. The thyroid isthmus is cut if necessary. The trachea is incised and an airway is inserted. After bleeding is controlled, a stoma is created by suturing the skin to the tissue layers.

Temporary percutaneous dilatational tracheostomy (PDT) (31.29) is typically performed at the bedside as opposed to a tracheostomy done in the operating room using the traditional surgical approach. Percutaneous dilatational tracheostomy involves making an incision in the skin over the tracheal cartilage and inserting a needle and guide wire into the trachea. The physician uses a dilator to enlarge the opening then inserts a standard tracheostomy tube. Bronchoscopy may be performed synchronously in order to visualize and confirm the placement of the needle, guide wire, and dilator.

30-34

Documentation Tip
Report code 31.1 for procedures documented as temporary percutaneous dilational tracheostomy. PDT described as permanent is reported with code 31.29.

Coding Clarification
In a permanent tracheostomy, skin flaps are used to create a more permanent stoma.

When reporting code 31.1, code also any synchronous bronchoscopy, if performed (33.21–33.24, 33.27).

Coding Scenario
A 60-year-old female was admitted for lung volume reduction surgery. A temporary tracheostomy was also performed.

Code Assignment:

32.22	Lung volume reduction surgery
31.1	Temporary tracheostomy

Coding Guidance
AHA: 4Q, '90, 5; 1Q, '97, 6

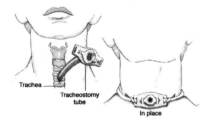

Trachea
Tracheostomy tube
In place

31.2   Permanent tracheostomy

Description
The physician creates a tracheostomy. The physician makes a horizontal neck incision and dissects the muscles to expose the trachea. The thyroid isthmus is cut if necessary. The trachea is incised and an airway is inserted. After bleeding is controlled, skin flaps are used to create a more permanent stoma, which is created by suturing the skin to the tissue layers.

31.21   Mediastinal tracheostomy

Description
Upper airway obstruction is often associated with carcinomas extending into the mediastinum and requires surgical intervention so the physician creates a tracheostomy for placement of an artificial breathing tube in the windpipe through mediastinum, for long-term use. Several types of myocutaneous flaps have been used for mediastinal tracheostomy. In one technique, the physician resects the anterior chest wall and places the distal end of the trachea low between the superior vena

cava and aortic arch. The physician then brings omentum up to the neck through the posterior mediastinum and the omentum is put around the trachea, main arteries, and the anastomosis.

Coding Clarification
Anterior mediastinal tracheostomy surgical approach is not commonly performed; however, it is typically performed to facilitate resection of cervicothoracic, tracheal, and esophageal malignancy.

31.29   Other permanent tracheostomy

Description
Code 31.29 is used to report other permanent tracheostomy procedures that are not more precisely described by other codes in subcategory 31.2. For example, permanent percutaneous dilatational tracheostomy (PDT) (31.29) is typically performed at the bedside as opposed to a tracheostomy done in the operating room using the traditional surgical approach. Percutaneous dilatational tracheostomy involves making an incision in the skin over the tracheal cartilage and inserting a needle and guide wire into the trachea. The physician uses a dilator to enlarge the opening then inserts a standard tracheostomy tube. Bronchoscopy may be performed synchronously in order to visualize and confirm the placement of the needle, guide wire, and dilator.

Coding Clarification
To report other permanent tracheostomy with laryngectomy, see 30.3-30.4.

Bronchoscopy (33.21–33.24, 33.47) performed synchronously should be reported in addition to the tracheostomy.

Report code 31.29 for procedures documented as permanent percutaneous dilatational tracheostomy. Temporary PDT is reported with code 31.1.

Documentation Tip
Review the documentation for specific information regarding the procedure prior to final code selection in order to ensure accurate code assignment.

Coding Guidance
AHA: 2Q, '02, 6; 2Q, '05, 8

31.3   Other incision of larynx or trachea

Description
This code is used to report such procedures as vocal cordotomy, incisional laryngeal or tracheal exploration, laryngocentesis, laryngotomy, thyrochondrotomy, and thyrotomy.

Coding Clarification
When larynx or tracheal incisions are performed for assistance in breathing, do not use 31.3; instead use 31.1-31.29.

● New Code   ▲ Revised Code   ▶◀ Revised Text   © 2010 Ingenix

31.4   Diagnostic procedures on larynx and trachea

Description

Tracheoscopy and laryngoscopy are endoscopic procedures that involve the use of a viewing tube to examine a hollow structure. For these procedures, the endoscope is inserted through the mouth or nose.

Biopsy may be performed using a closed or an open method. Closed methods are performed through the trachea (windpipe). An open biopsy is performed in the operating room under general anesthesia.

Coding Clarification

There are various biopsy procedures and techniques, including:

- **Needle biopsy:** After a local anesthetic is given, the physician uses a needle that is guided through the chest wall into a suspicious area with computed tomography (CT or CAT scan) or fluoroscopy (a type of x-ray "movie") to obtain a tissue sample. This type of biopsy may also be referred to as a closed, transthoracic, or percutaneous (through the skin) biopsy.

- **Transbronchial biopsy:** This type of biopsy is performed through a fiberoptic bronchoscope (a long, thin tube that has a close-focusing telescope on the end for viewing) through the main airways of the lungs (bronchoscopy).

- **Thoracoscopic biopsy:** After a general anesthetic is given, an endoscope is inserted through the chest wall into the chest cavity. Various types of biopsy tools can be inserted through the endoscope to obtain lung tissue for examination. This procedure may be referred to as video-assisted thoracic surgery (VATS) biopsy. In addition to obtaining tissue for biopsy, therapeutic procedures such as the removal of a nodule or other tissue lesion may be performed.

- **Open biopsy:** An open biopsy is performed in the operating room under general anesthesia. After a general anesthetic is given, the physician makes an incision in the skin of the chest and surgically removes a piece of tissue from the larynx or trachea.

31.41   Tracheoscopy through artificial stoma

Description

The physician examines the trachea by inserting the scope through an artificial opening.

Coding Clarification

When a tracheoscopy or laryngoscopy is performed with biopsy, see 31.43-31.44.

31.42   Laryngoscopy and other tracheoscopy

Description

Tracheoscopy and laryngoscopy are endoscopic procedures that involve the use of a viewing tube to examine a hollow structure. For these procedures, the endoscope is inserted through the mouth or nose.

When performing an indirect diagnostic laryngoscopy or tracheoscopy, the physician typically administers a topical anesthetic to the oral cavity, pharynx, and larynx and positions the patient's head and laryngoscopic mirror so as to view the larynx or pharynx through the reflection. The interior of the larynx or pharynx is examined for diagnostic purposes.

When performing a direct diagnostic laryngoscopy or tracheoscopy, the physician places a rigid laryngoscope to examine the patient's larynx. The physician administers a topical anesthetic to the oral cavity, pharynx, and larynx and inserts the laryngoscope through the patient's mouth. The interior of the larynx is examined. If a tracheoscopy is performed, a bronchoscope is inserted through the laryngoscope for visualization of the trachea and bronchi. No other procedure is performed at this time.

Coding Clarification

Do not use 31.42 to report laryngoscopy and tracheoscopy with biopsy; see 31.43-31.44.

31.43   Closed (endoscopic) biopsy of larynx

Description

Tracheoscopy and laryngoscopy are endoscopic procedures that involve the use of a viewing tube to examine a hollow structure. The endoscope is inserted through the mouth or nose. Endoscopic biopsy is a commonly performed type of biopsy that is done through a fiberoptic endoscope which the physician inserts into the trachea and bronchial system (laryngoscopy and bronchoscopy), through a natural body orifice or a small surgical incision. The physician directly visualizes the in question and removes tissue with biopsy forceps.

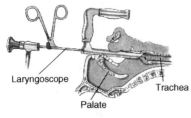

Laryngoscope

Trachea

Palate

Growth on vocal cord

31.44   Closed (endoscopic) biopsy of trachea

Description
When performing an indirect laryngoscopy with tracheal biopsy, the physician administers a topical anesthetic to the oral cavity, pharynx, and larynx and positions the patient's head and laryngoscopic mirror so as to view the larynx through the reflection. The interior of the larynx is examined, and suspect tissue or a lesion may be stained for identification and a biopsy of the tissue is taken.

Alternately, the physician may perform a direct, operative laryngoscopy with biopsy. A topical anesthetic is administered to the oral cavity, pharynx, and larynx and the laryngoscope is inserted into the patient's mouth. The interior of the larynx is examined and a lesion is biopsied with a sharp basket or cup forceps. Sometimes staining with toluidine blue is used to delineate the biopsy site. The physician may use an operating microscope or a telescope to isolate and biopsy the lesions. This is usually done for smaller lesions.

When utilizing a flexible fiberoptic laryngoscope, the physician administers a topical anesthetic to the oral cavity, pharynx, and larynx and uses a nasal or oral approach to insert the laryngoscope. The interior of the larynx is examined and a lesion is biopsied with a sharp basket or cup forceps. Sometimes staining with toluidine blue is used to delineate the biopsy site.

31.45   Open biopsy of larynx or trachea

Description
After a general anesthetic is given, the physician makes an incision in the skin on the chest and surgically removes a piece of tissue from the larynx or trachea.

31.48   Other diagnostic procedures on larynx

Description
Code 31.48 is used to report other diagnostic procedures of the larynx that are not more precisely described by other codes in subcategory 31.4.

Coding Clarification
Do not report 31.48 for contrast laryngogram (87.07), microscopic examination of specimen from the larynx (90.31-90.39), or soft tissue x-ray of the larynx NEC (87.09).

Documentation Tip
Review the documentation for specific information regarding the procedure prior to final code selection in order to ensure accurate code assignment.

31.49   Other diagnostic procedures on trachea

Description
Code 31.49 is used to report other diagnostic procedures of the trachea that are not more precisely described by other codes in subcategory 31.4.

Coding Clarification
Do not report 31.48 for microscopic examination of specimen from the trachea (90.41-90.49) or x-ray of the trachea (87.49)

Documentation Tip
Review the documentation for specific information regarding the procedure prior to final code selection in order to ensure accurate code assignment.

31.5   Local excision or destruction of lesion or tissue of trachea

Description
The physician excises a tracheal lesion. The physician makes a horizontal neck incision to access the stenosis. The trachea is incised and the lesion is resected. The proximal and distal portions of the trachea are brought together and closed with sutures. The wound is sutured in layers. Alternately, lesion removal may be accomplished with laryngoscopy.

Coding Clarification
Do not report 31.5 for biopsy of the trachea (31.44-31.45), laryngotracheal fistulectomy (31.62), or tracheoesophageal fistulectomy (31.73).

31.6   Repair of larynx

Description
Fourth-digit subclassifications identify specific types of repair procedures on the larynx, including suturing and fracture repairs, cordopexy, graft procedure on the larynx, and transposition of vocal cords.

31.61   Suture of laceration of larynx

Description
The physician first performs a low tracheostomy on the patient. Using a horizontal neck incision, the physician performs the laryngoplasty. A stent may be placed to maintain cricotracheal continuity. The incision is repaired in sutured layers.

31.62   Closure of fistula of larynx

Description
Fistula is a common complication following total laryngectomy that requires surgical closure by direct suture of the laryngeal mucosa. In some cases, a pectoral myocutaneous flap is used in the closure procedure.

Coding Clarification
Laryngotracheal fistulectomy is an excision and closing of passage between voice box and trachea.

Take-down of laryngostomy describes the removal of a laryngostomy tube and restoration of the voice box.

31.63   Revision of laryngostomy

Description
A laryngostomy is the creation of an artificial opening into the larynx from the neck. In this procedure, the physician revises a previous laryngostomy.

31.63   Revision of laryngostomy

Description
The physician aligns and positions harder structures of the larynx, such as the hyoid bone, following fracture. The physician reduces a fractured larynx to its anatomical position. The physician first performs a low tracheostomy on the patient to secure the airway and prevent extravasation of air into the surrounding tissues. Using a horizontal neck incision, the physician exposes the thyroid cartilage and repairs the mucosal defects. The thyroid cartilage is stabilized with wire stents. The incision is repaired in sutured layers.

31.69   Other repair of larynx

Description
Code 31.69 is used to report other repairs of the larynx that are not more precisely described by other codes in subcategory 31.6.

Coding Clarification
Use 31.69 to report arytenoidopexy (fixation of pitcher-shaped cartilage in voice box), a graft of larynx (implant of graft tissue into voice box), and transposition of the vocal cords (placement of vocal cords into a more functional position).

Report the construction of artificial larynx with 31.75, rather than 31.69.

Documentation Tip
Review the documentation for specific information regarding the procedure prior to final code selection in order to ensure accurate code assignment.

31.7   Repair and plastic operations on trachea

Description
Subcategory 31.7 provides codes for operations on the trachea with further procedure and site specificity.

31.71   Suture of laceration of trachea

Description
The physician closes a wound or injury of the trachea. The physician debrides the wound and closes the trachea with sutures. The tissues are sutured in layers.

31.72   Closure of external fistula of trachea

Description
The physician closes a tracheostomy or fistula. The physician excises the scarred tissue forming the tracheostomy or fistula. If the trachea has healed, it is closed with sutures. The remaining tissues of the tracheostomy or fistula are pulled together and the wound is sutured in layers. The tracheostomy or fistula is closed with or without plastic repair of the skin made to hide the repair.

Documentation Tip
This procedure may also be documented in the medical record as closure of tracheotomy.

31.73   Closure of other fistula of trachea

Description
Tracheoesophageal fistulectomy is an excision and closure of an abnormal opening between the windpipe and esophagus. The physician performs an anterior cervical incision and dissects surrounding tissues and muscles to expose the trachea. An airway is inserted and the trachea is incised. Surgical repair of the trachea is undertaken. End-to-end anastomosis of the trachea may be performed. For satisfactory reconstruction, it may be necessary for the physician to surgically repair the trachea using splints constructed from rib or costal cartilage to patch the length of the trachea. Once repair is achieved, the airway is removed and the incisions are closed.

Coding Clarification
To report a laryngotracheal fistulectomy, report 31.72.

31.74   Revision of tracheostomy

Description
The physician revises a tracheal stoma. The physician incises the stoma area and resects redundant scar tissue or a poorly healing wound. The skin is re-anastomosed and sewn to the stoma in sutured layers. A simple revision may be performed or a complex procedure with flap rotation.

31.75   Reconstruction of trachea and construction of artificial larynx

Description
Initially, a bronchoscopy is performed to reassess the patient's airway. The physician then harvests the appropriate size section of grafting material (e.g., rib cartilage for an anterior cartilage graft), which is used to rebuild the patient's airway. In some cases, a graft flap is taken at the forearm, which consists of subcutaneous tissue and fascia for tracheal wrapping to give the trachea a new blood supply, skin for temporary closure of the hemilaryngectomy defect, and a vascular pedicle. The physician transfers the forearm flap to the neck, the fascia flap is wrapped around the trachea, and the skin is sutured into the laryngeal defect. The blood vessels of the forearm flap are sutured to the neck vessels. A tracheostome is left between the reconstructed larynx and fascia-wrapped trachea.

Coding Clarification
Tracheoplasty with artificial larynx is reported with 31.75.

31.79   Other repair and plastic operations on trachea

Description
Code 31.79 is used to report other repair and plastic procedures of the trachea that are not more precisely described by other codes in subcategory 31.7.

Documentation Tip
Review the documentation for specific information regarding the procedure prior to final code selection in order to ensure accurate code assignment.

The following procedures may be appropriately reported with 31.79:

- Tracheoplasty
- Grafting of trachea
- Tracheal repair not elsewhere classified

31.9   Other operations on larynx and trachea

Description
Fourth-digit subclassifications describe other procedures on the larynx and trachea such as lysis of adhesions, tracheoesophageal fistulization, replacement of laryngeal or tracheal stent, and therapeutic injection procedures.

31.91   Division of laryngeal nerve

Description
The physician severs the laryngeal nerve. The recurrent laryngeal nerve controls the action of the vocal cords. The physician makes a vertical incision, retracts the strap muscles, and dissects the tissue until the nerve is exposed and identified. The physician severs the recurrent laryngeal nerve prior to its point of branching. The incision is repaired in sutured layers.

31.92   Lysis of adhesions of trachea or larynx

Description
Lysis of adhesions is the process of cutting scar tissue within the body. In this procedure, the adhesions are between the esophagus and the anterior cervical spine. The incision is repaired in sutured layers.

31.93   Replacement of laryngeal or tracheal stent

Description
The physician removes and replaces a tracheal stent or stents using a flexible fiberoptic or rigid bronchoscope introduced through the nasal or oral cavity, using local anesthesia of the patient's airway. The physician introduces a wire through the narrowed part of the trachea and removes the bronchoscope. If dilation is required, a series of dilators are passed over the wire to open the airway until sufficient tracheal/bronchial dilation is accomplished. A stent is then passed over the wire to the target area in the trachea and positioned in place to maintain an open airway. This may be done with or without fluoroscopic guidance.

31.94   Injection of locally-acting therapeutic substance into trachea

Description
The physician punctures the trachea with a needle to inject a therapeutic agent. The physician palpates the site, inserts a hollow point needle, and a therapeutic agent is injected. The needle is removed.

31.95   Tracheoesophageal fistulization

Description
The physician constructs a tracheal esophageal fistula for vocalization. The physician makes a horizontal neck incision and dissects the tissues between the tracheostoma and the esophagus. The esophagus is incised and a laryngeal speech prosthesis is inserted between the esophagus and the trachea, creating a fistula. The prosthesis, called a voice button or Blom-Singer prosthesis, is a one-way valve enabling the patient to phonate. The physician closes the incision around the prosthesis.

31.98 Other operations on larynx

Description
Code 31.98 reports other procedures of the larynx that are not more precisely described by other codes in subcategory 31.9, such as dilation (increasing larynx size by stretching), division of congenital web (cutting and separating congenital membranes around larynx), and removal of keel or stent (removal of prosthetic device from larynx).

Coding Clarification
Report removal of an intraluminal foreign body from the larynx without incision with 98.14.

Documentation Tip
Review the documentation for specific information regarding the procedure prior to final code selection in order to ensure accurate code assignment.

31.99 Other operations on trachea

Description
Code 31.99 is used to report other procedures of the trachea that are not more precisely described by other codes in subcategory 31.9.

Coding Clarification
Removal of an intraluminal foreign body from the trachea without incision (98.15), tracheostomy tube (97.37), replacement of tracheostomy tube (97.23), and tracheostomy toilette (96.55) are not reported with 31.99.

Documentation Tip
Review the documentation for specific information regarding the procedure prior to final code selection in order to ensure accurate code assignment.

Coding Guidance
AHA: 1Q, '97, 14

---

32 Excision of lung and bronchus

Description
Excision of the lung and bronchus includes rib resection, sternotomy, sternum-splitting incision, and thoracotomy as operative approaches. An operative approach is not assigned a code because these processes are an integral part of the procedure. Many of the codes within this category require fourth-digit subclassification to provide specificity regarding approach.

Coding Clarification
Codes in this section include the cutting or removal of the ribs (rib resection), sternotomy, sternum-splitting incision, or thoracotomy to access the operative field.

Code also any synchronous bronchoplasty (33.48).

The destruction of a lesion or tissue of bronchus by laser is included in 32.01.

A segmental resection of the lung is the same as a partial lobectomy (32.3); however, if the surgeon performs a lobectomy with segmental resection of adjacent lobes of the lung, this is coded as 32.4, Lobectomy of lung.

A complete pneumonectomy, code 32.5, is a pneumonectomy with mediastinal dissection.

Documentation Tip
Various codes are available when the surgeon documents a lung excision. Check both the operative and pathology reports to determine the specific excision, as this will determine the most appropriate code.

A radical procedure involves the dissection of bronchus, lobe of lung, brachial plexus, intercostal structure, ribs, and sympathetic nerves.

Thoracoscopic and endoscopic biopsies are not one and the same. An endoscopic biopsy is performed using an endoscope passed through a lumen. For example, an endoscopic biopsy of the bronchus is performed using an endoscope passed through the lumen of the trachea and bronchus. A thoracoscopic wedge biopsy of the lung involves insertion of a thoracoscope through a small incision in the chest wall to visualize the excision of tissue for a biopsy.

32.0 Local excision or destruction of lesion or tissue of bronchus

Description
Endoscopic excision or destruction of a lesion or tissue of bronchus is reported with codes from subcategory 32.0.

Coding Clarification
Do not report 32.0 for biopsy of the bronchus (33.24-33.25) or bronchial fistulectomy (33.42).

Coding Guidance
AHA: 4Q, '88, 11

32.01 Endoscopic excision or destruction of lesion or tissue of bronchus

Description
The physician views the airway using a flexible fiberoptic or rigid bronchoscope introduced through the nasal or oral cavity, using local anesthesia of the patient's airway. The physician uses the views obtained through the bronchoscope to identify the tumor from within the airway. The physician may use fluoroscopy (x-ray) to assist with navigation of the bronchoscope tip to the abnormal tissue. The physician passes special forceps through channels in the bronchoscope to grasp and excise the tumor. The bronchoscope is removed. The physician may use separately reportable fluoroscopy (x-ray) to assist with navigation of the bronchoscope tip to the abnormal tissue. The physician passes a laser or

freezing (cryo) probe through a channel in the bronchoscope to destroy the tumor or any areas of stenosis. The bronchoscope is removed.

Coding Clarification
The destruction of a lesion or tissue of bronchus by laser is included in 32.01.

32.09 Other local excision or destruction of lesion or tissue of bronchus

Description
Code 32.09 is used to report other local excision or destruction procedures of the bronchus that are not more precisely described by other codes in subcategory 32.0.

Coding Clarification
Do not use 32.09 to report that by endoscopic approach (32.01).

Documentation Tip
Review the documentation for specific information regarding the procedure prior to final code selection in order to ensure accurate code assignment.

32.1 Other excision of bronchus

Description
The physician performs a local excision or destruction of a lesion of the lung. A wide sleeve resection of bronchus involves an excision and partial, lengthwise removal of a lung branch.

Coding Clarification
Do not use 32.1 to report a radical dissection of the bronchus; see 32.6.

32.2 Local excision or destruction of lesion or tissue of lung

Description
Procedures in subcategory 32.2 are used to report ablations of lung lesions or tissue including open, percutaneous, thoracoscopic, and other endoscopic ablation, excision, or destruction of lung lesions.

Coding Clarification
Closed endoscopic biopsy involves a much smaller incision than open biopsy. The small incision is made to allow insertion of a visualization device. In an open biopsy, an incision is made in the skin, the organ is exposed, and a tissue sample is taken.

32.20 Thoracoscopic excision of lesion or tissue of lung

Description
The physician excises a lesion or tissue of the lung, typically a wedge shaped portion, with the use of a thoracoscope.

Coding Clarification
Assign 32.20 for a thoracoscopic wedge resection.

Documentation Tip
A variety of codes are available when the surgeon documents a lung excision. Check both the operative and pathology reports to determine the specific excision, as this will determine the most appropriate code.

Coding Guidance
AHA: 4Q, '07, 109, 110

32.21 Plication of emphysematous bleb

Description
An emphysematous bleb is a thin, air-filled blister, usually located in the upper lung regions. Plication is defined as a folding or pleating procedure for reducing the size of a swollen vesicle by making folds or tucks in its walls.

In the plication technique, the lung tissue is rolled and a non-cutting stapler is placed over the layers of lung held by a clamp. A stapler is positioned over the plicated tissue and the grasping mechanism is withdrawn. The stapler is then fired and the tissue remains in place but the bleb has been sealed or the volume of the lung has been reduced without removing any tissue.

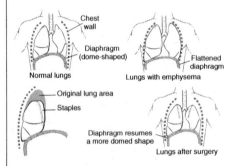

Normal lungs / Lungs with emphysema / Lungs after surgery

32.22 Lung volume reduction surgery

Description
Lung volume reduction surgery (LVRS) is a surgical treatment for patients with specific types of emphysema. LVRS is an extensive, invasive surgical procedure that involves excision of a portion of the lung(s) to reduce respiratory effort. Various surgical approaches to access the lung cavity are used. Open methods involve splitting the breastbone (sternotomy) or making an incision between the ribs on each side of the chest. An alternative method uses video-assisted thoracoscopic technique.

The physician removes part of an emphysematous lung. The physician opens the chest cavity widely to gain access to the lung to be removed. The physician makes a long incision around the side of the chest between two of the ribs, or the physician may use an incision through the center of the sternum. The incision is carried through all the tissue layers into the chest cavity, and rib spreaders are used to expose the lung. The lung tissue to be removed is identified and isolated in the operative field by pushing aside the deflated lung with a gloved hand and large moist gauze sponges. The lung tissue may be further isolated using a row of staples. The tissue is excised and instruments and gauze sponges are removed. The chest incision is sutured closed in layers (sternal wires are used if the chest was entered through a midline sternal incision). A chest tube(s) may be used to provide drainage for the chest cavity.

Coding Guidance
AHA: 4Q, '95, 64; 3Q, '96, 20; 1Q, '97, 6

32.23   Open ablation of lung lesion or tissue

Description
Code 32.23 is used to report other open ablation procedures on the lungs that are not more precisely described by other codes in subcategory 32.2.

Documentation Tip
Review the documentation for specific information regarding the procedure prior to final code selection in order to ensure accurate code assignment.

Coding Guidance
AHA: 4Q, '06, 124

32.24   Percutaneous ablation of lung lesion or tissue

Description
The physician performs a percutaneous ablation therapy for reduction or eradication of a lung lesion. Percutaneous thermal tissue ablation is performed with a needle electrode inserted into the lesion under imaging guidance.

Coding Guidance
AHA: 4Q, '06, 124

32.25   Thoracoscopic ablation of lung lesion or tissue

Description
The physician performs a thoracoscopic ablation therapy for reduction or eradication of a lung lesion. Thoracoscopic tissue ablation is performed as an alternative to lung resection for treatment of blebs using an electrocautery. A video-assisted thoracoscopic technique and thoracoscopic ligation using an Endoloop are alternate methods used.

Coding Clarification
Thoracoscopic excision of a lesion or tissue of the lung is not reported with this code; report 32.20.

Coding Scenario
A 56-year-old male with non-small cell cancer of the right upper lobe presented for thoracoscopic thermal ablation of his primary lesion. Following

administration of general anesthesia, the ablation device was inserted via thoracoscopic approach. Following completion of the ablation cycle, the ablation device and thoracoscope were removed and the incision was sutured.

Code Assignment:

162.3   Malignant neoplasm of upper lobe, bronchus or lung

32.25   Thoracoscopic ablation of lung lesion or tissue

Coding Guidance
AHA: 4Q, '06, 124

32.26   Other and unspecified ablation of lung lesion or tissue

Description
Code 32.26 is used to report ablation procedures on the lungs that are not more precisely described by other codes in subcategory 32.2. This code is also reported when the documentation does not further specify the ablation procedure performed.

▶Report ablation of smooth airway muscle by bronchoscopic bronchial thermoplasty with code 32.27.◀

Documentation Tip
Review the documentation for specific information regarding the procedure prior to final code selection in order to avoid improper use of the "not otherwise specified" code and to ensure accurate code assignment.

Coding Guidance
AHA: 4Q, '06, 124

● 32.27   Bronchoscopic bronchial thermoplasty, ablation of smooth airway muscle

Description
Bronchial thermoplasty is a new bronchoscopic procedure in which radiofrequency (RF)-based technology is applied to the smooth muscle of the tracheobronchial tree and lungs for the treatment of severe asthma. Patients who suffer severe asthma attacks exhibit increased smooth airway muscle mass, which causes increased bronchoconstriction in response to external stimuli (e.g., allergens, irritants). Bronchoconstriction is an integral part of an asthma attack; therefore, reducing the attacks provides significant therapeutic benefit for patients with severe asthma. The Alair® Bronchoscopic Bronchial Thermoplasty System is pending Food and Drug Administration approval for patients 18 years or older with severe persistent asthma, recalcitrant to medical therapy. This system contains a specialized sensory catheter to deliver therapeutic heat, an RF controller, foot switch, and return electrode. The ablation is performed via standard flexible bronchoscopy, whereby controlled thermal

energy is delivered via the catheter to the targeted regions of the bronchus and lung, repositioning as necessary to deliver consistent treatment. The procedure is approximately one hour in duration for each region treated.

Coding Clarification
This procedure was previously identified by code 32.26 Other and unspecified ablation of lung lesion or tissue, which did not clearly describe the procedure. Code 32.27 reports ablation of smooth airway muscle of the bronchus and lung specifically by thermoplasty.

Coding Scenario
A patient with severe asthma presents for bronchoscopic thermoplasty. Via bronchoscopy, a catheter was inserted into the bronchus through which a sensory electrode was passed to deliver thermal energy to three targeted sites along the bronchial airway.

Code Assignment:

493.90 Asthma, unspecified

32.27 Bronchoscopic bronchial thermoplasty, ablation of smooth airway muscle

32.28 Endoscopic excision or destruction of lesion or tissue of lung

Description
The physician views the airway using a flexible fiberoptic or rigid bronchoscope introduced through the nasal or oral cavity, using local anesthesia of the patient's airway. The physician uses the views obtained through the bronchoscope to identify the tumor from within the airway. The physician may use fluoroscopy (x-ray) to assist with navigation of the bronchoscope tip to the abnormal tissue. The physician passes forceps through channels in the bronchoscope to grasp and excise the tumor. The bronchoscope is removed. This may be done with or without fluoroscopic guidance.

Coding Clarification
Do not use this code to report ablation of a lung lesion or tissue: open (32.23), other (32.26), percutaneous (32.24), thoracoscopic (32.25), or biopsy of lung (33.26-33.27).

Coding Guidance
AHA: 4Q, '06, 124

32.29 Other local excision or destruction of lesion or tissue of lung

Description
The physician removes a wedge-shaped portion(s) of a lobe(s) of one or both lungs. The physician opens the chest cavity widely to gain access to the lung to be removed. Using a scalpel, the surgeon makes a long incision around the side of the chest between two of the ribs. The incision is carried through all the

tissue layers into the chest cavity. Rib spreaders are inserted into the wound and the ribs are spread apart exposing the lung. The area to be removed is identified and isolated in the operative field by pushing aside the deflated lung with a gloved hand and large moist gauze sponges. The healthy portions of the lung surrounding the area(s) to be removed are clamped and the portion is removed by cutting the lung tissue isolated by the clamps. Sutures or surgical clips are used to repair the cut portion of the remaining lung tissue. After the removal of the instruments and gauze sponges, the chest incision is sutured closed in layers. A chest tube(s) may be used to provide drainage for the chest cavity.

In another technique, the chest cavity can by opened and the operation performed through a vertical incision in the center of the chest through the sternum. The skin incision is carried down to the sternum bone and a saw is used to split the sternum. With the sternum split in half, the chest is entered by using a set of rib spreaders to separate the sternum. When the procedure is complete, wires are used to bring the halves of the sternum together. The skin is closed over the sternum by suturing.

Coding Clarification
Do not assign this code to report a thoracoscopic excision of lesion or tissue of lung; report 32.20.

Do not assign 32.29 to report ablation of lung lesion or tissue: open (32.23), other (32.26), percutaneous (32.24), thoracoscopic (32.25), biopsy of lung (33.26-33.27), endoscopic approach (32.28), or wide excision of lesion of lung (32.3).

Documentation Tip
Code 32.29 is used to report wedge resections and other lung resections that are not further specified. Review the documentation for specific information regarding the procedure prior to final code selection in order to avoid improper use of the "not otherwise specified" code.

Coding Guidance
AHA: 3Q, '99, 3

32.3 Segmental resection of lung

Description
Subcategory 32.3 contains codes to describe thoracoscopic segmental lung resection, as well as other and unspecified segmental resection of the lung. A partial lobectomy is appropriately reported by codes in this subcategory.

Coding Guidance
AHA: 4Q, '07, 109

32.30 Thoracoscopic segmental resection of lung

Description
The physician removes all or a segmental portion of a lobe of one lung through a rigid or flexible

● New Code   ▲ Revised Code   ►◄ Revised Text   © 2010 Ingenix

fiberoptic endoscope. The physician makes a small incision between two ribs and by blunt dissection and the use of a trocar enters the thoracic cavity. The endoscope is passed through the trocar and into the chest cavity. The lung is usually partially collapsed by instilling air into the chest through the trocar or the lung may be collapsed through a double lumen endotracheal tube inserted through the mouth into the trachea. The contents of the chest cavity are examined by direct visualization and/or by the use of a video camera. Still photographs may be taken as part of the procedure. Additional instruments may be inserted into the chest cavity through a second and/or third wound in the chest. Under direct visualization through the endoscope, the physician manipulates the instruments inserted through the secondary sites and clamps the blood vessels and bronchial tubes going to the area of lung to be removed. With the clamps in place, the portion of lung is removed by dividing the vessel and bronchial tubes isolated by the clamps. Any cut portions of the remaining lung tissue are repaired by suturing or clipping with surgical clips. At the conclusion of the procedure, the endoscope and the trocar(s) are removed. A chest tube for drainage and re-expansion of the lung is usually inserted through the wound used for the thoracoscopy.

Coding Guidance
AHA: 4Q, '07, 110

32.39   Other and unspecified segmental resection of lung

Description
The physician removes a segment of a lobe of one lung. The physician opens the chest cavity widely to gain access to the lung to be removed. Using a scalpel, the surgeon makes a long incision around the side of the chest between two of the ribs. The incision is carried through all the tissue layers into the chest cavity. Rib spreaders are inserted into the wound and the ribs are spread apart exposing the lung. The segment to be removed is identified and isolated in the operative field by pushing aside the deflated lung with a gloved hand and large moist gauze sponges. Within the segment of the lung, the main blood vessels and bronchial tubes are clamped, tied off, and cut. The segment is then removed through the wide chest incision. After the removal of the instruments and gauze sponges, the chest incision is sutured closed in layers. A chest tube(s) may be used to provide drainage for the chest cavity. Alternately, the chest cavity can be opened and the operation performed through a vertical incision in the center of the chest through the sternum. The skin incision is carried down to the sternum bone and then a saw is used to split the sternum. With the sternum split in half, the chest is

entered by spreading the sternum apart with a set of rib spreaders. When the procedure is complete, the wound is closed by using wires to bring the two halves of the sternum together and the skin is closed over the sternum by suturing.

Coding Clarification
This code is also used to report partial lobectomy.

Do not assign this code to report a thoracoscopic segmental resection of lung; report 32.3.

32.4   Lobectomy of lung

Description
This subcategory provides two subclassification codes to report lobectomy of the lung. Fourth-digit specificity identifies approach.

Coding Clarification
Lobectomy of the lung with radical dissection or excision of thoracic structures is excluded from this subcategory; report 32.6.

Coding Guidance
AHA: 4Q, '07, 109

32.41   Thoracoscopic lobectomy of lung

Description
This procedure is performed with the aid of a camera (thoracoscope). The physician removes a large section of a lobe of one lung through a rigid or flexible fiberoptic endoscope. The physician makes a small incision between two ribs and by blunt dissection and the use of a trocar enters the thoracic cavity. The endoscope is passed through the trocar and into the chest cavity. The lung is usually partially collapsed by instilling air into the chest through the trocar or the lung may be collapsed through a double lumen endotracheal tube inserted through the mouth into the trachea. The contents of the chest cavity are examined by direct visualization and/or by the use of a video camera. Still photographs may be taken as part of the procedure. Additional instruments may be inserted into the chest cavity through a second and/or third wound in the chest. Under direct visualization through the endoscope, the physician manipulates the instruments inserted through the secondary sites and clamps the blood vessels and bronchial tubes going to the area of lung to be removed. With the clamps in place, the portion of lung is removed by dividing the vessel and bronchial tubes isolated by the clamps. Any cut portions of the remaining lung tissue are repaired by suturing or clipping with surgical clips. At the conclusion of the procedure, the endoscope and the trocar(s) are removed. A chest tube for drainage and re-expansion of the lung is usually inserted through the wound used for the thoracoscopy.

Coding Clarification
Do not use this code to report that with radical dissection or excision of the thoracic structures; report 32.6.

Coding Guidance
> **AHA:** 4Q, '07, 110

32.49   Other lobectomy of lung

Description
Using a scalpel, the surgeon makes a long incision around the side of the chest between two of the ribs. The incision is carried through all the tissue layers into the chest cavity. Rib spreaders are inserted into the wound and the ribs are spread apart exposing the lung. The lobe(s) to be removed is identified and isolated in the operative field by pushing aside the deflated lung with a gloved hand and large moist gauze sponges. Within the lobe(s) of the lung, the main blood vessels and bronchial tubes are clamped, tied off, and cut. The lobe(s) is removed through the wide chest incision. After the removal of the instruments and gauze sponges, the chest incision is sutured closed in layers. A chest tube(s) may be used to provide drainage for the chest cavity. Alternately, the chest cavity can be opened and the operation performed through a vertical incision in the center of the chest through the sternum. The skin incision is carried down to the sternum bone and a saw is used to split the sternum. With the sternum split in half, the chest is entered by spreading the sternum apart with a set of rib spreaders. When the procedure is complete, the wound is closed by using wires to bring the two halves of the sternum together and the skin is closed over the sternum by suturing.

Coding Clarification
Do not use this code to report that with radical dissection or excision of the thoracic structures; report 32.6.

32.5   Pneumonectomy

Description
Pneumonectomy is frequently performed as treatment for patients with cancer who require complete pneumonectomy for cure. Common techniques include conventional, intrapericardial, and extrapleural pneumonectomies. This subcategory provides two subclassification codes to report thoracoscopic and other pneumonectomy.

Coding Clarification
Subcategory 32.5 correctly reports pneumonectomy with mediastinal dissection, as well as excision of the lung that is not otherwise specified.

Coding Guidance
> **AHA:** 1Q, '99, 6

32.50   Thoracoscopic pneumonectomy

Description
Code 32.50 reports pneumonectomy that is performed via a thoracoscopic technique.

Coding Guidance
> **AHA:** 4Q, '07, 110

32.59   Other and unspecified pneumonectomy

Description
Code 32.59 is assigned to report pneumonectomy that is not more precisely described by other codes in this category or when the documentation does not further specify the procedure. In one technique, the physician removes one lung in its entirety. The physician opens the chest cavity widely to gain access to the lung to be removed. Using a scalpel, the surgeon makes a long incision around the side of the chest between two of the ribs. The incision is carried through all the tissue layers into the chest cavity. Rib spreaders are inserted into the wound and the ribs are spread apart exposing the lung, heart, and other structures. The root of the lung is found by pushing aside the deflated lung with a gloved hand and large moist gauze sponges. Within the root of the lung, the blood vessels and bronchial tubes are clamped, tied off, and cut. The lung is then removed through the wide chest incision. After the removal of the instruments and gauze sponges, the chest incision is sutured closed in layers. A chest tube(s) may be used to provide drainage for the chest cavity.

Alternately, the chest cavity can be opened and the operation performed through a vertical incision in the center of the chest through the sternum. The skin incision is carried down to the sternum bone and a saw is used to split the sternum. With the sternum split in half, the chest is entered by spreading the sternum apart with a set of rib spreaders. When the procedure is complete, the wound is closed by using wires to bring the two halves of the sternum together and the skin is closed over the sternum by suturing.

Coding Clarification
Thoracoscopic pneumonectomy is not reported with this code; report 32.50.

32.6   Radical dissection of thoracic structures

Description
In a radical dissection procedure of thoracic structures, the physician performs resection of an apical lung tumor including chest wall resection, rib(s) resection(s), neurovascular dissection, and chest wall reconstruction.

The physician removes a tumor from the apex of the lung, such as a Pancoast tumor, as well as a portion of the chest wall. The patient may be intubated with

● New Code   ▲ Revised Code   ►◄ Revised Text   © 2010 Ingenix

a double lumen endotracheal tube to verify correct positioning and to evaluate endobronchial disease. The chest cavity is entered using an anterior or posterior incision. The posterior incision is made along the outline of the scapula, entering the pleural space at the third or fourth intercostal space. In some cases, an anterior transcervical approach is used. The necessary extended en bloc resection of the chest wall includes posterior portions of the first three ribs, part of the upper thoracic vertebrae (including the transverse process), the intercostal nerves, the lower trunk of the brachial plexus, the stellate ganglion, a section of the dorsal sympathetic ganglion, and the portion of the involved lung. For tumors that are situated peripherally, the apical segment of the upper lobe of the lung is separated from the remaining superior lobe by using a GIA-75 stapler. The apex of the lung is left attached to the chest wall. The first through third, fourth, or fifth ribs are then sectioned anteriorly. The subclavian artery is sharply dissected from the surrounding structures. A subperiosteal dissection is performed around the first rib, which is transected, and the subclavian vessels are mobilized superiorly. If preoperative magnetic resonance imaging demonstrated vessel involvement, an initial anterior approach is performed to dissect or graft the vessels. The ribs are disarticulated and the tumor, along with the involved chest wall, is gradually mobilized. Next, the segmental vessels are identified, doubly ligated, and transected. The parietal pleura are bluntly dissected along the anterior border of the spinal column. The tumor and the involved chest wall that has remained attached to the inferior trunk of the brachial plexus is excised, using caution to spare the T1 nerve root as it crosses beneath the angle of the first rib to join the C8 nerve root. If a tumor has invaded the vertebral bodies, the subclavian artery, or the C8 to T1 nerve routes, a multidisciplinary approach may be necessary. At the completion of the procedure, two large chest tubes are placed: one at the apex of the chest to drain any residual air and the other to drain fluids.

Coding Clarification
This code appropriately reports block dissection of bronchus, lobe of lung, brachial plexus, intercostal structure, ribs (transverse process), and sympathetic nerves.

32.9   Other excision of lung

Description
Code 32.9 is used to report excisional procedures on the lung that are not more precisely described by other codes in category 32.

Coding Clarification
Do not use this code to report biopsy of lung and bronchus (33.24-33.27) or pulmonary decortication (34.51).

Documentation Tip
Review the documentation for specific information regarding the procedure prior to final code selection in order to ensure accurate code assignment.

33   Other operations on lung and bronchus Description

Codes with category 33 include rib resection, sternotomy, sternum-splitting incision, and thoracotomy. Do not assign a code for these operative approaches, as they are an integral part of the procedure.

There are a number of different codes available from which to choose for an endoscopy in conjunction with excision. Review the operative report for the site (bronchus or lung) and type of procedure performed (excision of tissue or lesion or open or closed biopsy) to determine the proper code.

33.0   Incision of bronchus

Description
Code 33.0 is used to report incisional procedures on the bronchus that are not more precisely described by other codes.

Documentation Tip
The medical record may contain the following descriptive terms for procedures correctly reported with 33.0:

- Incisional removal of bronchial foreign body
- Bronchostomy
- Bronchotomy
- Incisional bronchial exploration

Review the documentation for specific information regarding the procedure prior to final code selection in order to ensure accurate code assignment.

33.1   Incision of lung

Description
Code 33.1 is used to report incisional procedures on the lung that are not more precisely described by other codes.

Coding Clarification
Do not use this code to report puncture of lung; report 33.93.

The medical record may contain the following descriptive terms for procedures correctly reported with 33.1:

- Cavernostomy

- Incisional drainage of the lung
- Incisional exploration of the lung
- Pneumonotomy (with or without exploration)
- Incisional removal of foreign body from the lung

33.2   Diagnostic procedures on lung and bronchus

Description
Subcategory 33.2 describes diagnostic procedures on the lung or bronchus that are not more precisely reported with other codes from this category. Diagnostic procedures on the lungs may be performed using a variety of surgical techniques.

Coding Clarification
An endoscopic biopsy of the bronchus is reported as a closed biopsy, 33.24.

33.20   Thoracoscopic lung biopsy

Description
Code 33.20 describes a biopsy procedure on the lung that is performed through a thoracoscope. A thoracoscope, or flexible fiberoptic tube, is inserted into the thorax through a small incision. The physician examines the inside of the chest cavity and takes a sample(s) of tissue. The procedure can be done under local or general anesthesia. The surgeon makes a small incision between two ribs and by blunt dissection and the use of a trocar enters the thoracic cavity. The thoracoscope is passed through the trocar and into the chest cavity. The lung is partially collapsed by instilling air into the chest through the trocar or, if general anesthesia is used, the lung may be collapsed through a double lumen endotracheal tube inserted through the mouth into the trachea. The contents of the chest cavity are examined by direct visualization and/or the use of a video camera. Still photographs may be taken as part of the procedure. The tissue selected for biopsy is identified and a biopsy taken using a device through the thoracoscope or the insertion of an instrument through a second incision in the chest. At the conclusion of the procedure, the thoracoscope and the trocar are removed. A chest tube for drainage and re-expansion of the lung is usually inserted through the wound used for the thoracoscopy.

Coding Clarification
Code 33.20 excludes closed endoscopic biopsy of lung (33.27), closed biopsy of lung specified as percutaneous or needle (33.26), and open biopsy of lung (33.28).

Coding Guidance
   AHA: 4Q, '07, 110

33.21   Bronchoscopy through artificial stoma

Description
The physician performs a visual exam of the lung and its branches via a tube inserted through an artificial opening. The physician views the airway using a bronchoscope placed through an existing tracheostomy. The physician examines the conducting airways. The bronchoscope is removed.

Coding Clarification
Do not use 33.21 to report a bronchoscopy with biopsy; see 33.24 and 33.27.

33.22   Fiber-optic bronchoscopy

Description
The physician examines the lung and bronchus via a flexible optical instrument for visualization. A flexible fiberoptic bronchoscope is introduced through the nasal or oral cavity. The airway is anesthetized. The bronchoscope is inserted and advanced through the nasal or oral cavity, past the larynx to inspect the bronchus. This may be done with or without fluoroscopic guidance. The bronchoscope is removed.

Coding Clarification
Do not use 33.21 to report a bronchoscopy with biopsy; see 33.24 and 33.27.

Coding Guidance
   AHA: 1Q, '04, 4

33.23   Other bronchoscopy

Description
Code 33.23 is used to report bronchoscopy procedures that are not more precisely described by other codes in subcategory 33.2.

The physician views the airway using a rigid bronchoscope that is introduced through the nasal or oral cavity. The airway is anesthetized. The bronchoscope is inserted and advanced through the nasal or oral cavity, past the larynx to inspect the bronchus. This may be done with or without fluoroscopic guidance. The bronchoscope is removed.

Coding Clarification
Do not use 33.23 to report a bronchoscopy with biopsy; see 33.24 and 33.27.

Bronchoscopy for aspiration is reported with 96.05.

Documentation Tip
Review the documentation for specific information regarding the procedure prior to final code selection in order to ensure accurate code assignment.

Coding Guidance
   AHA: 1Q, '99, 6; 3Q, '02, 18

30-34

33.24   Closed [endoscopic] biopsy of bronchus

Description
The physician performs a bronchoscopy (fiberoptic, rigid) with a lung brushing or washing for specimen collection. In an alternate technique, saline is introduced into the subsegment of a lobe and retrieved using gentle suction, which is called liquid biopsy or diagnostic bronchoalveolar lavage (BAL).

Coding Clarification
Code 33.24 appropriately reports the following fiberoptic or rigid bronchoscopic procedures:

- Brush biopsy of lung
- Brushing or washing for specimen collection
- Excision (bite) biopsy
- BAL
- Transbronchoscopic needle aspiration [TBNA] ▶of bronchus◀

▶Code 33.24 includes transbronchoscopic needle aspiration [TBNA] of bronchus. Transbronchoscopic needle aspiration [TBNA] of the lung is reported with code 33.27.◀

▶Code 33.24 includes BAL. Procedures documented as mini-BAL are classified to code 33.29 Other diagnostic procedures on lung and bronchus.◀

An endoscopic biopsy of the bronchus is coded as a closed biopsy (33.24).

If biopsies are taken from the bronchus and lung endoscopically, use two codes (33.27 and 33.24).

Do not use 33.24 to report whole lung lavage (33.99).

Coding Guidance
AHA: 3Q, '91, 15; 4Q, '92, 27; 3Q, '02, 16; 3Q, '04, 9; 2Q, '06, 20; 2Q, '09, 16

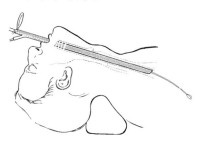

33.25   Open biopsy of bronchus

Description
The physician performs an open biopsy on the bronchus. In one method, the physician makes a lateral thoracotomy incision to access the bronchus. An excision and anastomosis may also be performed with this procedure. A chest tube(s) may be used to provide drainage for the chest cavity. The chest incision is sutured closed in layers (sternal wires are used if the chest was entered through a midline sternal incision).

Coding Clarification
Do not use 33.25 to report open biopsy of lung; see 33.28.

33.26   Closed [percutaneous] (needle) biopsy of lung

Description
The physician obtains a sample of the lung by puncturing through the space between two of the ribs with a needle. The procedure is often done under radiological guidance to assure more precise placement of the needle. Using a biopsy needle, the physician carefully passes the needle over the top of a rib, punctures through the chest tissues, enters the pleural cavity, and punctures into the area of concern in the lung. With the end of the needle in the chest cavity, the physician withdraws a piece of tissue. The needle is then withdrawn and the puncture site covered with a bandage.

Coding Clarification
Fine needle aspiration (FNA) and transthoracic needle biopsy (TTNB) are appropriately reported with 33.26.

This code excludes thoracoscopic lung biopsy, which is correctly reported with 33.20.

When the biopsy is of the lung, separate codes exist for a closed biopsy (33.26) and a closed endoscopic biopsy (33.27).

To report endoscopic biopsy of the lung, see 33.27.

Coding Guidance
AHA: 3Q, '92, 12

33.27   Closed endoscopic biopsy of lung

Description
The physician views the airway using a flexible fiberoptic or rigid bronchoscope that is introduced through the nasal or oral cavity. The airway is anesthetized. The bronchoscope is inserted and advanced through the nasal or oral cavity, past the larynx to inspect the bronchus, including fluoroscopic guidance, if used. The physician uses the views obtained through the bronchoscope to identify abnormal structures in the lung to be biopsied. After diagnostic visualization of the bronchus, a sample of bronchial or endobronchial tissue is removed for study; more than one site may be biopsied. Fluoroscopy may be used to assist with navigation of the bronchoscope tip to the abnormal tissue. The physician passes special closed biopsy forceps through a channel in the bronchoscope and through the bronchial wall to obtain one or more lung tissue samples from a single lobe. Bleeding is assessed and controlled, and the bronchoscope is removed.

Coding Clarification
Code 33.27 is used to report flexible bronchoscopy with biopsy using fluoroscopic guidance and transbronchial lung biopsy.

Do not use 33.27 to report brush biopsy of the lung (33.24) or percutaneous biopsy of the lung (33.26).

Code 33.27 also excludes thoracoscopic lung biopsy, which is correctly reported with 33.20.

▶Code 33.27 may also be used to report procedures documented as transbronchoscopic needle aspiration [TBNA] of the lung.◀

Coding Guidance
AHA: S-O, '86, 11; 3Q, '91, 15; 4Q, '92, 27; 3Q, '02, 16; 3Q, '04, 9; 2Q, '09, 16

33.28   Open biopsy of lung

Description
The physician removes a sample of tissue from the lung or the pleura (the tissue covering the inside surface of the chest cavity or the surface of the lung). Using a scalpel, the skin between two ribs is incised and the tissues separated to expose the inside of the chest cavity. A representative sample of tissue is removed using a biopsy needle or by cutting with a scalpel or scissors. The surgical wound created is closed by suturing.

In a more extensive procedure, the physician opens the chest cavity widely to directly visualize and assess the organs and structures in the chest and/or to obtain tissue for study and analysis. Using a scalpel, the surgeon makes a long incision around the side of the chest between two of the ribs. The incision is carried through all the tissue layers into the chest cavity. Rib spreaders are inserted into the wound and the ribs are spread apart, exposing the lung, heart, and other structures. The area of the chest cavity is explored by pushing aside the deflated lung with a gloved hand and large gauze sponges. Tissue can be sampled by using a biopsy needle or by grasping tissue and cutting it with a scalpel or scissors. After the removal of the instruments and gauze sponges, the incision is closed in sutured layers. A chest tube(s) may be used to provide drainage for the chest cavity.

Alternately, the chest cavity can be opened and the operation performed through a vertical incision in the center of the chest through the sternum. The skin incision is carried down to the sternum bone and a saw is used to split the sternum. With the sternum split in half, the chest is entered by spreading the sternum apart with a set of rib spreaders. When the procedure is complete, the wound is closed by using wires to bring the two

halves of the sternum together and the skin is closed over the sternum by suturing.

Coding Guidance
AHA: 3Q, '92, 12; 3Q, '99, 3

33.29   Other diagnostic procedures on lung or bronchus

Description
Use 33.29 to report diagnostic procedures of the lung and bronchus that are not more precisely described by other codes in subcategory 33.2.

Coding Clarification
▶Code 33.29 includes mini-BAL. Procedures documented as BAL are classified to code 33.24 Closed [endoscopic] biopsy of bronchus.◀

Various diagnostic procedures on the lung and bronchus are coded elsewhere including:

- Endoscopic pulmonary airway flow measurement (33.72)
- Endotracheal contrast bronchogram (87.31)
- Other contrast bronchogram (87.32)
- Lung scan (92.15)
- Magnetic resonance imaging (88.92)
- Microscopic examination of specimen from bronchus or lung (90.41-90.49)
- Routine chest x-ray (87.44)
- Ultrasonography of lung (88.73)
- Vital capacity determination (89.37)
- X-ray of bronchus or lung NOS (87.49)

Documentation Tip
Review the documentation for specific information regarding the procedure prior to final code selection in order to ensure accurate code assignment.

33.3   Surgical collapse of lung

Description
This subcategory provides five subclassification codes to report the various methods of surgical lung collapse. Fourth-digit specificity is required in order to identify the precise procedure.

33.31   Destruction of phrenic nerve for collapse of lung

Description
The physician transects or removes a portion of the phrenic nerve. The phrenic nerve supplies innervation to the diaphragm. The physician makes a horizontal neck incision and dissects the surrounding tissue and locates the nerve. The nerve is transected and the proximal portion of the nerve is buried in the surrounding tissue to prevent neuroma formation.

● New Code   ▲ Revised Code   ▶◀ Revised Text   © 2010 Ingenix

33.32 Artificial pneumothorax for collapse of lung

Description

In one technique, the physician forces air or gas into the diaphragmatic space to achieve therapeutic collapse of the lung. The physician partially collapses a lung by injecting air into the chest cavity by puncturing through the space between the ribs. Using a needle attached to a syringe, the physician passes the needle over the top of a rib and punctures through the chest tissues entering the pleural cavity. With the end of the needle in the chest cavity, the physician injects air into the chest cavity to create a partial collapse of one lung, most commonly used to treat tuberculosis. A small plastic tube may be passed through the chest and left in place for repeated injections of air.

In an alternate technique for therapeutic collapse of the lung, the physician makes an incision into the chest (thoracotomy). The physician removes fluid from the chest cavity by puncturing through the space between the ribs. To enter the chest cavity, the physician passes a trocar over the top of a rib, punctures through the chest tissues between the ribs, and enters the pleural cavity. With the end of the trocar in the chest cavity, the physician advances the plastic tube into the chest cavity. The sharp trocar is removed leaving one end of the plastic catheter in place within the chest cavity. A large syringe is attached to the outside end of the catheter and the fluid (blood or pus) is removed from the chest cavity by pulling back on the plunger of the syringe. The outside end of the tube may be connected to a water seal system to prevent air from being sucked into the chest cavity and to allow continuous or intermittent removal of fluid.

33.33 Pneumoperitoneum for collapse of lung

Description

The physician injects air into the peritoneal cavity. Forcing air or gas into the abdominal serous membrane is done to achieve therapeutic collapse of lung. The physician inserts a needle or catheter into the peritoneal cavity and injects air as a diagnostic procedure. An x-ray is usually obtained to define the pattern of air in the abdomen. The needle or catheter is removed at the completion of the procedure.

33.34 Thoracoplasty

Description

The physician performs a thoracoplasty, which is the removal of the skeletal support of a portion of the chest. The procedure is carried out primarily on the upper chest. An incision is made through the skin down to the ribs. The Schede operation consists of the extensive unroofing of an empyema space by resecting the overlying ribs and portions of membrane lining the chest cavity (parietal pleural

peel). The muscles in the area are partially closed over gauze packing and the skin partially closed by suturing in layers. As the packing is withdrawn in stages a few days later, it is hoped that fresh granulation tissue fills in the space formerly occupied by the empyema. The original Schede type operation is rarely performed but several modifications are currently done.

33.39 Other surgical collapse of lung

Description

Code 33.39 reports surgical collapse of the lung procedures that are not more precisely described by other codes in subcategory 33.3. This code is also reported when the documentation does not further specify the destruction procedure.

Documentation Tip

Review the documentation for specific information regarding the procedure prior to final code selection in order to avoid improper use of the "not otherwise specified" code and to ensure accurate code assignment.

Coding Guidance

AHA: 2Q, '99, 12

33.4 Repair and plastic operation on lung and bronchus

Description

Fourth-digit specificity is required in this subclassification to describe repair procedures on the lung and bronchus, such as closure of a bronchostomy and fistulectomy.

Coding Clarification

Do not use codes in this subcategory to report closure of a fistula that is specified as bronchomediastinal, bronchopleural, or bronchopleuromediastinal. These are correctly reported with 34.73.

33.41 Suture of laceration of bronchus

Description

The physician repairs a bronchial laceration by suture technique.

33.42 Closure of bronchial fistula

Description

Code 33.42 is used to report various procedures such as closure of a bronchostomy and bronchocutaneous, bronchoesophageal, or bronchovisceral fistulectomy.

The physician repairs a major bronchial fistula (an abnormal passageway between the remaining end of a bronchial tube and the chest that occurs sometimes after the removal of a lung or portion of a lung). The physician enters the chest cavity through

30-34

a vertical incision made in the middle of the front of the chest. The incision is carried down to the sternum, which is split in order to enter the chest cavity at the root of the lung near the center of the chest. The fistula exposure often requires the resection of one or two of the upper ribs. The end of the bronchial tube is located and the stump of the bronchial tube is reamputated. The inside lining of the bronchial tube is treated with silver nitrate to destroy the mucus-forming cells lining the bronchus. The stump is sutured or stapled. The chest defect created is repaired, the sternum closed using wire sutures, and the skin closed in sutured layers. A chest tube may be inserted into the chest cavity for drainage.

Coding Clarification
Do not use codes in this subcategory to report closure of a fistula that is specified as bronchomediastinal, bronchopleural, or bronchopleuromediastinal. These are correctly reported with 34.73.

Documentation Tip
An understanding of the following terms may be helpful in code selection:

- **Bronchocutaneous:** Between the skin and lung branch.
- **Bronchoesophagus:** Between the esophagus and lung branch.
- **Bronchovisceral:** Between an internal organ and lung branch.
- **Closure of bronchostomy:** Removal of a bronchostomy tube and repair of a surgical wound.
- **Fistulectomy:** Closure of an abnormal passage.

33.43   Closure of laceration of lung

Description
The physician opens the chest cavity widely to directly visualize and assess the organs and structures in the chest and to control bleeding and/or repair injury to the lung. Using a scalpel, the surgeon makes a long incision around the side of the chest between two of the ribs. The incision is carried through all the tissue layers into the chest cavity. Rib spreaders are inserted into the wound and the ribs are spread apart exposing the lung, heart, and other structures. The area of the chest cavity is explored by pushing aside the deflated lung with a gloved hand and large gauze sponges. The site of the injury is identified and repaired. After the removal of the instruments and gauze sponges, the incision is closed in sutured layers. A chest tube(s) may be used to provide drainage for the chest cavity. Alternately, the chest cavity can be opened and the operation performed through a vertical incision in the center of the chest through the sternum. The skin incision is

carried down to the sternum bone and a saw is used to split the sternum. With the sternum split in half, the chest is entered by spreading the sternum apart with a set of rib spreaders. When the procedure is complete, the wound is closed by using wires to bring the two halves of the sternum together and the skin closed over the sternum by suturing.

33.48   Other repair and plastic operations on bronchus

Description
The physician repairs a bronchus. The physician makes a lateral thoracotomy incision to access the bronchus. An autograft or Silastic stent may be used to repair the bronchus. A chest tube is inserted and the wound is sutured in layers. An excision stenosis and anastomosis may also be performed with this procedure.

33.49   Other repair and plastic operations on lung

Description
This code is used to report repairs and plastic procedures of the lung that are not more precisely described by other codes in subcategory 33.4.

In one procedure, the physician opens the chest cavity widely to directly visualize and assess the organs and structures in the chest and to control bleeding and/or repair injury to the lung. Using a scalpel, the surgeon makes a long incision around the side of the chest between two of the ribs. The incision is carried through all the tissue layers into the chest cavity. Rib spreaders are inserted into the wound and the ribs are spread apart exposing the lung, heart, and other structures. The area of the chest cavity is explored by pushing aside the deflated lung with a gloved hand and large gauze sponges. The site of the injury is identified and repaired. After the removal of the instruments and gauze sponges, the incision is closed in layers of sutures. A chest tube(s) may be used to provide drainage for the chest cavity.

Alternately, the chest cavity can be opened and the operation performed through a vertical incision in the center of the chest through the sternum. The skin incision is carried down to the sternum bone and a saw is used to split the sternum. With the sternum split in half, the chest is entered by spreading the sternum apart with a set of rib spreaders. When the procedure is complete, the wound is closed by using wires to bring the two halves of the sternum together and the skin closed over the sternum by suturing.

Documentation Tip
Review the documentation for specific information regarding the procedure prior to final code selection in order to ensure accurate code assignment.

● New Code   ▲ Revised Code   ▶◀ Revised Text   © 2010 Ingenix

Coding Clarification
Do not use 33.29 to report closure of a pleural fistula; see 34.73.

33.5   Lung transplant

Description
Fourth-digit subclassifications describe unilateral and bilateral lung transplantation (33.51, 33.52) and lung transplantation that is not otherwise specified (33.50).

Coding Clarification
To report donor source, see 00.91-00.93.

Code also cardiopulmonary bypass, extracorporeal circulation, heart-lung machine; see 39.61.

Do not use these codes for combined heart-lung transplantation; see 33.6.

Documentation Tip
Bilateral lung transplantation is also referred to as double-lung transplantation or an en bloc transplantation that describes a sequential excision and implant of both lungs.

Coding Guidance
  AHA: 4Q, '95, 75

33.50   Lung transplantation, NOS

Description
Code 33.50 is reported when the procedure performed is not more precisely described by other codes in subcategory 33.5. This code is also reported when the documentation does not further specify the transplantation procedure.

Documentation Tip
Review the documentation for specific information regarding the procedure prior to final code selection in order to avoid improper use of the not otherwise specified code.

33.51   Unilateral lung transplantation

Description
The physician performs a single lung transplantation of the recipient patient. During the transplantation of the lung, the patient is placed on a cardiopulmonary bypass machine to maintain circulation to the organs. The physician makes a long, midline vertical incision through all of the layers of the skin down to the sternum bone. The sternum is split and the chest cavity entered. The patient's original lung is deflated, the root of the lung is isolated, and the major arteries and veins that carry blood to and from the heart are identified and divided. The main bronchial tube to that lung is severed and the lung removed. The donor lung is placed in the chest cavity and the bronchial tube and arteries and veins are sutured to the patient

where the former lung was attached. Circulation and functioning of the donor lung is assured and the chest is closed. The sternum is closed using wire sutures and the skin closed in sutured layers. A chest tube(s) is inserted into the chest cavity for drainage.

33.52   Bilateral lung transplantation

Description
When the physician performs a double-lung transplantation of the recipient patient, the patient's original lungs are deflated sequentially, the root of the lung is isolated, and the major arteries and veins that carry blood to and from the heart are identified and divided. The tracheal tube to the lungs is severed and the lungs removed. The donor lungs are placed in the chest cavity as a single unit or one at a time. The tracheal tube and arteries and veins are sutured to the site where the former lungs were attached. Circulation and functioning of the donor lungs are assured and the chest is closed. The sternum is closed using wire sutures and the skin is closed in sutured layers. Chest tubes are inserted into the chest cavities for drainage.

33.6   Combined heart-lung transplantation

Description
The physician performs a standard backbench preparation of the heart and lungs following procurement from a cadaver donor. Backbench or back table preparation refers to procedures performed on the donor organs following procurement to prepare the donor organs for transplant. The heart and lungs are removed en bloc. The heart and lungs are inspected following procurement to identify any injury or abnormality not noted prior to procurement. The physician prepares the heart and lungs by dissecting free any residual soft tissue. Attention is focused on the aorta, superior vena cava, inferior vena cava, and the trachea. The aorta, which was divided at the aortic arch, is inspected and residual tissue removed. The superior vena cava is inspected and residual tissue removed. The inferior vena cava is inspected to assure adequate length has been preserved. Any residual tissue is removed from the inferior vena cava. The trachea, which was divided as far above the carina as possible, is inspected and residual tissue removed. When all residual soft tissue has been removed and the vessels prepared, the heart and lungs are ready for transplant.

The patient is placed on cardiopulmonary bypass and the heart and lungs are removed. The donor's organs are placed by sewing the left atrium of the donor to the left atrium of the recipient's first, and sewing together the atrial septum and the right atrium. The donor aorta is trimmed to an

30-34

appropriate length and sewn to the ascending aorta of the recipient. Immunosuppressive drugs may be given to the patient before, during, and after the operation. Cardiopulmonary bypass is discontinued when the donor's heart function returns.

Coding Clarification
To report donor source, see 00.91-00.93.

Code also cardiopulmonary bypass, extracorporeal circulation, heart-lung machine; see 39.61.

Coding Guidance
AHA: 4Q, '03, 96

33.7   Other endoscopic procedures in bronchus or lung

Description
Subcategory 33.7 includes codes to report insertion, removal, or replacement of bronchial valves, biological reagents, and other therapeutic devices when performed through an endoscope.

Specific codes in subcategory 33.7 Other endoscopic procedures in bronchus or lung, differentiate endoscopic bronchial valve interventions on a single lobe vs. multiple lobes. Endobronchial valve insertion is currently being used for the treatment of severe emphysema (multiple lobes are typically treated) and for the control of prolonged air leaks (typically only one lobe is treated). Bronchial valve insertion in multiple lobes of the lungs requires more clinical resources and time to perform than single lobe treatment.

33.71   Endoscopic insertion or replacement of bronchial valve(s), single lobe

Description
This code reports the endoscopic insertion or replacement of endobronchial and intrabronchial airflow redirection valve interventions on a single lobe of the lung. Endobronchial valve insertion is commonly performed on a single lobe for the control of prolonged air leaks. Air leaks most commonly develop following surgery and are caused by lung tissue that has not completely sealed, which results in an accumulation of air in the pleural cavity. Most air leaks are small and resolve naturally in a few days. Air leaks lasting longer than five to seven days are classified as prolonged and may result in significant morbidity or mortality. Prolonged air leaks are typically limited to a single lobe. For this indication, the valve limits airflow to the affected areas while still allowing air movement in the direction of uninjured tissue. Valve interventional procedures for treatment of prolonged air leaks is temporary with removal of the valve within six weeks.

Coding Clarification
Code 33.71 Endoscopic insertion or replacement of bronchial valve(s), was created in 2006; however, this code did not capture the difference in the extent of treatment of multiple lobes vs. a single lobe during bronchial valve procedures. As a result, the title of code 33.71 was revised to specify treatment involving a single lobe.

Documentation Tip
To ensure accurate code assignment, review procedural documentation for endoscopic approach and to determine whether a single lobe or multiple lobes of the lung were treated.

Coding Scenario
A patient is admitted for temporary endobronchial valve insertion for treatment of postsurgical air leak in the left lower lobe. The physician determines the targeted placement of the valve based on the extent of the diseased tissue in the lobe. To determine the appropriate valve size for the airway, a balloon is inflated with saline at the targeted implant site. The physician deploys the endobronchial valve into the bronchial tree through the bronchoscope.

Code Assignment:

33.71   Endoscopic insertion or replacement of bronchial valve(s), single lobe

997.39 Other respiratory complications

E879.8 Other procedures, without mention of misadventure at the time of procedure, as the cause of abnormal reaction of patient, or of later complication

Coding Guidance
AHA: 4Q, '06, 126; 4Q, '08, 175; ▶4Q, '09, 144◀

33.72   Endoscopic pulmonary airway flow measurement

Description
Endoscopic pulmonary airway flow measurement is a new method of assessing intrapulmonary air flow in patients with various types of lung disease to measure the effectiveness of current treatments and the disease progression. This procedure measures intrapulmonary airflow using intrapulmonary balloon catheters inserted into diseased portions of the lung via bronchoscopy.

Evaluating the airflow in isolated lung regions can also enable therapies to be directed to the optimal site for treatment.

Coding Clarification
Also code any diagnostic or therapeutic procedures that are performed.

Documentation Tip
The Chartis System Functional Assessment System (FAS) is pending FDA approval in 2008.

● New Code   ▲ Revised Code   ▶◀ Revised Text   © 2010 Ingenix

Coding Scenario
A patient is admitted with severe emphysema and undergoes bronchoscopy to determine the most appropriate treatment (e.g., endobronchial valve therapy or lung volume reduction surgery). The physician views the airway using a bronchoscope that is inserted through the oral cavity and advanced past the larynx to inspect the bronchus. The physician also assesses the patient's intrapulmonary air flow using intrapulmonary balloon catheters inserted into diseased portions of the lung during the bronchoscopy.

> Code Assignment:
>
> 492.8   Other emphysema
> 33.72   Endoscopic pulmonary airway flow measurement

33.73   Endoscopic insertion or replacement of bronchial valve(s), multiple lobes

Description
Bronchial valve insertion is typically performed to treat severe emphysema or to manage prolonged air leaks. Emphysema is a chronic, progressive disease characterized by the destruction of lung tissue in multiple lobes. Air leaks can be a result of traumatic, iatrogenic, or spontaneous causes, but air leaks most commonly occur following surgery (e.g., lobectomy, segmentectomy, or lung volume reduction surgery) as a result of lung tissue that has not completely closed and sealed. Endoscopic bronchial valve insertion is a minimally invasive procedure because the valves are placed via a bronchoscopic procedure that does not require a surgical incision. Other treatments for air leaks include surgical intervention such as pleurodesis or insertion of drain tubes into the chest.

The right lung, which is slightly larger than the left, is divided into three lobes: upper, middle, and lower. The left lung has two lobes, an upper and a lower (basal). Bronchial valve insertion in multiple lobes of the lungs during a single procedural episode requires more clinical time and resources to perform than single lobe treatment. Consequently, a code was created in subcategory 33.7 Other endoscopic procedures in bronchus or lung, for endoscopic insertion or replacement of bronchial valves in multiple lobes. Code 33.73 Endoscopic insertion or replacement of bronchial valve(s), multiple lobes, is used to report endoscopic bronchial valve treatment of multiple lobes. Prior to creation of this code, endoscopic insertion or replacement of bronchial valves was reported with 33.71 Endoscopic insertion or replacement of bronchial valve(s). Because this code did not capture the extent of treatment for multiple lobes vs. a single lobe during bronchial valve procedures, the title of existing code 33.71 was revised to specify single lobe treatment.

Coding Clarification
Review the operative report for the time and clinical resources (e.g., length of anesthesia, number of valves) required to perform the procedure because valve insertion in multiple lobes (33.73) during the same procedural episode involves more time and resources than a single lobe (33.71).

Documentation Tip
To ensure accurate code assignment, review procedural documentation for endoscopic approach and to determine whether a single lobe or multiple lobes of the lung were treated.

▶Bronchial valves classified to code 33.73 may be documented as endobronchial airflow redirection valves or intrabronchial airflow redirection valves.◀

Coding Scenario
A patient is admitted for endobronchial valve insertion for treatment of severe emphysema. Due to the severity of the patient's emphysema, multiple lobes require treatment during the operative session. The physician uses a CT scan to determine the location and number of valves to be placed based on the extent of the disease in each lobe. Using an airway sizing kit, a balloon is inflated with saline at the target implantation site to determine the appropriate valve size for each airway. A catheter is passed through the bronchoscope and the small umbrella-shaped valves are deployed into the segmental and subsegmental bronchi.

> Code Assignment:
>
> 33.73   Endoscopic insertion or replacement of bronchial valve(s), multiple lobes
> 492.8   Other emphysema

Coding Guidance
     AHA: ▶4Q, '09, 144-145◀

33.78   Endoscopic removal of bronchial device(s) or substances

Description
This code reports the endoscopic removal of other bronchial devices or substances.

Coding Guidance
     AHA: 4Q, '06, 126

33.79   Endoscopic insertion of other bronchial device or substances

Description
This code reports the endoscopic insertion of other bronchial devices or substances, including biologic lung volume reduction that is not otherwise specified. With BLVR, biological reagents are instilled in the lungs, during bronchoscopy, to remodel and shrink damaged regions of the lung.

Coding Clarification
Insertion of a tracheobronchial stent is reported with 96.05 rather than 33.7 codes.

Coding Scenario
This 65-year-old female presents with severe emphysema. She has a 30-year history of cigarette abuse, although she quit smoking five years ago and has remained abstinent. Under general anesthesia, the patient underwent BLVR treatment, which was administered via bronchoscope. There were no complications.

Code Assignment:

492.8   Emphysema
V15.82   Personal history of tobacco use
33.79   Endoscopic insertion of other bronchial device or substances.

Coding Guidance
   AHA: 4Q, '06, 126

33.9   Other operations on lung and bronchus

Description
Subcategory 33.9 includes five subclassification codes to report bronchial dilation, tying off (ligation) a lung branch (bronchus), whole lung lavage, punctures of the lung other than needle biopsy (96.05), and other operations on the bronchus and lung.

33.91   Bronchial dilation

Description
The physician performs tracheal/bronchial dilation using a flexible fiberoptic or rigid bronchoscope introduced through the nasal or oral cavity. The physician uses the views obtained through the bronchoscope to identify any narrowing or fracture of the trachea or bronchus. The physician introduces a wire through the narrowed or fractured part of the airway and removes the bronchoscope. A series of dilators or stents are passed over the wire to open the airway until sufficient dilation is accomplished. This may be done with or without fluoroscopic guidance.

Coding Guidance
   AHA: 1Q, '97, 14

33.92   Ligation of bronchus

Description
The physician ties off a lung branch. The physician uses a direct access thoracotomy and performs vascular ligation with port-access endostapling instrumentation.

33.93   Puncture of lung

Description
The physician pierces a lung with surgical instrument. The physician removes a collection of fluid in a lung by puncturing through the space between the ribs and entering the lung. Using an aspirating needle attached to a syringe, the physician passes the needle over the top of a rib, punctures through the chest tissues, enters the pleural cavity, and directs the needle into the fluid area of the lung. With the end of the needle in the fluid cavity within the lung, the physician withdraws the fluid by pulling back on the plunger of the syringe.

Coding Clarification
Code 33.93 is not used to report needle biopsy of the lung; see 33.26.

33.98   Other operations on bronchus

Description
Code 33.98 is used to report procedures of the bronchus that are not more precisely described by other codes in subcategory 33.9.

Coding Clarification
Do not use 33.98 to report bronchial lavage (96.56) or removal of intraluminal foreign body from bronchus without incision (98.15).

Documentation Tip
Review the documentation for specific information regarding the procedure prior to final code selection in order to ensure accurate code assignment.

33.99   Other operations on lung

Description
Whole lung lavage is performed under general anesthesia using mechanical ventilation. The physician inserts an endotracheal tube and the lungs are lavaged one at a time. The physician performs repeated cycles of filling and emptying using saline solution.

Coding Clarification
Code 33.99 excludes other continuous mechanical ventilation (96.70-96.72) and respiratory therapy (93.90-93.99).

Coding Guidance
   AHA: 3Q, '02, 17

---

34   Operations on chest wall, pleura, mediastinum, and diaphragm

Description
Included under category 34 are operations on the chest wall, pleura, mediastinum, and diaphragm. Procedures on the breast are located in the chapter on operations on the integumentary system. As one

would expect when multiple sites are classified under one category, the various types of procedures found at the subcategory level are further broken out by site.

Coding Clarification
To report operations on the breast, see 85.0-85.99.

34.0   Incision of chest wall and pleura

Coding Clarification
Codes in this subcategory are not reported when the incision is used as an operative approach.

34.01   Incision of chest wall

Description
The physician incises the bone cortex of infected bone in the thorax to treat an abscess or osteomyelitis. The physician makes an incision over the affected area. Dissection is carried down through the soft tissues to expose the bone. The periosteum is split and reflected back from the bone overlying the infected area. A curette may be used to scrape away the abscess or infected portion down to healthy bony tissue, or drill holes may be made through the cortex into the medullary canal in a window outline around the infected or abscessed bone. The area is drained and debrided of infected bony and soft tissue. The physician then irrigates the area with antibiotic solution, the periosteum is closed over the bone, and the soft tissues are sutured closed. Alternately, the wound may be packed and left open, allowing the area to drain. Secondary closure is performed approximately three weeks later. Dressings are changed daily.

Coding Clarification
To report incision of the pleura, use 34.09.

Extrapleural drainage is an incisional procedure to drain fluid from the external pleura.

Coding Guidance
    AHA: 1Q, '92, 13; 3Q, '00, 12

34.02   Exploratory thoracotomy

Description
The physician opens the chest cavity widely to directly visualize and assess the organs and structures in the chest and/or to obtain tissue for study and analysis. Using a scalpel, the surgeon makes a long incision around the side of the chest between two of the ribs. The incision is carried through all the tissue layers into the chest cavity. Rib spreaders are inserted into the wound and the ribs are spread apart exposing the lung, heart, and other structures. The area of the chest cavity is explored by pushing aside the deflated lung with a gloved hand and large gauze sponges. Tissue can be sampled by using a biopsy needle or by grasping

tissue and cutting it with a scalpel or scissors. After the removal of the instruments and gauze sponges, the incision is closed in sutured layers. A chest tube(s) may be used to provide drainage for the chest cavity. Alternately, the chest cavity can be opened and the operation performed through a vertical incision in the center of the chest through the sternum. The skin incision is carried down to the sternum bone and a saw is used to split the sternum. With the sternum split in half, the chest is entered by spreading the sternum apart with a set of rib spreaders. When the procedure is complete, the wound is closed by using wires to bring the two halves of the sternum together and the skin is closed over the sternum by suturing.

34.03   Reopening of recent thoracotomy site

Description
The physician uses the site of a previous thoracotomy. The physician reopens the chest cavity widely to directly visualize and assess the organs and structures in the chest after recent surgery in the chest. Repairs can be made as indicated and discovered while exploring the chest cavity. A second and/or third trocar and instruments may be inserted into the chest cavity through a second and/or third wound in the chest. The hemorrhage is controlled by clipping or cauterizing the damaged blood vessel. At the conclusion of the procedure, the endoscope and trocar(s) are removed. After the removal of the instruments and gauze sponges, the incision is closed in sutured layers. A chest tube(s) may be used to provide drainage for the chest cavity.

34.04   Insertion of intercostal catheter for drainage

Description
The physician removes fluid from the chest cavity by puncturing through the space between the ribs. To enter the chest cavity, the physician carefully passes a trocar (a long, thin, sharp pointed instrument within a plastic tube) over the top of a rib, punctures through the chest tissues between the ribs, and enters the pleural cavity. With the end of the trocar in the chest cavity, the physician advances the plastic tube (catheter). The sharp instrument is removed, leaving one end of the plastic catheter in place within the chest cavity. A syringe is attached to the outside end of the catheter and fluid is removed from the chest cavity by pulling back on the plunger of the syringe. The outside end of the tube may be connected to a water seal system to prevent air from being sucked into the chest cavity and to allow continuous or intermittent removal of fluid.

Insertion of a tunneled, indwelling pleural catheter is done to aid quality of life and long-term management of malignant effusion. The catheter allows drainage on an outpatient or home basis and consists of flexible rubber tubing with a safety drainage valve to provide access to the pleural cavity and prevent air and fluid entering. A polyester cuff secures the catheter in place and helps prevent infection. Under conscious sedation with local anesthesia, and using ultrasonic and/or fluoroscopic guidance, the physician inserts the catheter percutaneously through a small incision in the anterior axillary area. The pleural catheter is threaded over a guidewire to access the pleural cavity, tunneled under the skin along the chest wall, and brought out that side in the lower chest. After placement, the patient may drain pleural fluid at home periodically into special vacuum bottles by connecting the matching drainage line access tip to the valve.

Coding Clarification
Code 34.04 excludes thoracoscopic drainage of the pleural cavity, which is correctly reported with 34.06.

Coding Guidance
AHA: 1Q, '92, 12; 1Q, '95, 5; 1Q, '99, 10; 2Q, '99, 12; 2Q, '03, 7; 1Q, '07, 14

34.05   Creation of pleuroperitoneal shunt

Description
Pleuroperitoneal shunting is frequently performed for treatment of intractable pleural effusions. The shunt is a silicone rubber conduit consisting of a one-way valve and pumping chamber located between pleural and peritoneal catheters. This procedure can be performed under local or general anesthesia.

Documentation Tip
Pleuroperitoneal shunts are often referred to by the trade name of the shunt manufactured by Denver Biomaterials (e.g., "Denver shunt'). Although other shunts differ from the Denver shunt in design and function, the terminology often remains the same.

Coding Guidance
AHA: 4Q, '94, 50

34.06   Thoracoscopic drainage of pleural cavity

Description
The physician removes fluid from the chest cavity by puncturing through the space between the ribs using thoracoscopy. The procedure can be done under local or general anesthesia. The physician makes a small incision between two ribs and by blunt dissection and a trocar (a long, thin, sharp pointed instrument within a plastic tube) enters the thoracic cavity. The endoscope is passed through the trocar and into the chest cavity. Under direct vision through this opening, a syringe is attached to the outside end of the catheter and fluid is removed from the chest cavity by pulling back on the plunger of the syringe. The outside end of the tube may be

connected to a water seal system to prevent air from being sucked into the chest cavity during fluid removal.

Coding Clarification
Evacuation of empyema is correctly reported with 34.06.

Coding Scenario
A patient is admitted for drainage of a loculated pocket of pleural fluid, which is encysted between layers of visceral pleural. The physician inserts a thoracoscopic port, visualizes the effusion and several ounces of purulent fluid is drained.

Code Assignment:

511.89 Pleurisy with other specified forms of effusion, except tuberculous

34.06   Thoracoscopic drainage of pleural cavity

Coding Guidance
AHA: 4Q, '07, 110, 112

34.09   Other incision of pleura

Description
Insertion of a tunneled, indwelling pleural catheter is done to aid quality of life and long-term management of malignant effusion. The catheter allows drainage on an outpatient or home basis and consists of flexible rubber tubing with a safety drainage valve to provide access to the pleural cavity and prevent air and fluid entering. A polyester cuff secures the catheter in place and helps prevent infection. Under conscious sedation with local anesthesia, and using ultrasonic and/or fluoroscopic guidance, the physician inserts the catheter percutaneously through a small incision in the anterior axillary area. The pleural catheter is threaded over a guidewire to access the pleural cavity, tunneled under the skin along the chest wall, and brought out that side in the lower chest. After placement, the patient may drain pleural fluid at home periodically into special vacuum bottles by connecting the matching drainage line access tip to the valve.

Coding Clarification
This procedure excludes thoracoscopy (34.21) and thoracotomy for lung collapse (33.32).

Documentation Tip
An understanding of the following terms may aid in correct code assignment:

- **Creation of pleural window:** Creation of a circumscribed drainage hole in the serous membrane of the chest.

- **Intercostal stab:** Creation of a penetrating stab wound between the ribs.

- **Open chest drainage:** Insertion of a tube through the ribs and serous membrane of the chest for drainage.

● New Code   ▲ Revised Code   ►◄ Revised Text   © 2010 Ingenix

Coding Guidance

AHA: 1Q, '94, 7; 4Q, '94, 50; 3Q, '02, 22; 1Q, '07, 14

34.1   Incision of mediastinum

Description

The physician performs a mediastinotomy with exploration and/or drainage. The surgical approach can be cervical, transthoracic, or median sternotomy.

The physician makes an incision low in the front of the neck, pulling back the sternomastoid muscles and the cranial vessels to the side and drawing the trachea and thyroid to the center. The space behind the esophagus is exposed. The area is explored and Penrose drains may be placed. The incision is closed with sutures or staples.

Coding Clarification

Do not report 34.1 for mediastinoscopy (34.22) or for mediastinotomy associated with pneumonectomy (32.5). Any biopsy performed in conjunction with an incision of the mediastinum (34.1) should be reported separately.

34.2   Diagnostic procedures on chest wall, pleura, mediastinum, and diaphragm

Description

Fourth-digit subclassifications describe diagnostic procedures on the chest wall, pleura, and diaphragm including transpleural thoracoscopy, mediastinoscopy, and biopsies (open, closed, percutaneous needle) of the diaphragm, mediastinum, chest wall, and pleura.

34.20   Thoracoscopic pleural biopsy

Description

The physician removes a sample of tissue from the pleura (the tissue covering the inside surface of the chest cavity or the surface of the lung) through a small opening created in the chest for a rigid or flexible fiberoptic endoscope. The procedure can be done under local or general anesthesia. The physician makes a small incision between two ribs and by blunt dissection and the use of a trocar enters the thoracic cavity. The endoscope is passed through the trocar and into the chest cavity. Under direct vision through this opening, a sample of tissue is removed using a biopsy needle or by cutting the tissue with a scalpel or scissors. The tissue selected for biopsy is identified and a biopsy taken using a device through the endoscope or the insertion of an instrument through a second incision in the chest. The surgical wound created is then closed by suturing. At the conclusion of the procedure, the endoscope and trocar are removed. A chest tube for drainage and re-expansion of the lung

is usually inserted through the wound used for the thoracoscopy.

Coding Clarification

Biopsies of the pleura can be open, closed, or percutaneous needle biopsies.

Coding Guidance

AHA: 4Q, '07, 110

34.21   Transpleural thoracoscopy

Description

The physician performs an exam of the chest through the serous membrane using either a rigid or flexible fiberoptic endoscope. The procedure can be done under local or general anesthesia. The surgeon makes a small incision between two ribs and by blunt dissection and the use of a trocar enters the thoracic cavity. The endoscope is passed through the trocar and into the chest cavity. The lung is usually partially collapsed by instilling air into the chest through the trocar, or if general anesthesia is used, the lung may be collapsed through a special double lumen endotracheal tube inserted through the mouth into the trachea. The contents of the chest cavity are examined by direct visualization and/or the use of a video camera. Still photographs may be taken as part of the procedure. At the conclusion of the procedure, the endoscope and the trocar are removed. A chest tube for drainage and re-expansion of the lung is usually inserted through the wound used for the thoracoscopy.

Coding Guidance

AHA: 3Q, '02, 27

34.22   Mediastinoscopy

Description

In an exam of the lung cavity and heart using a scope, the physician makes a small incision in the notch above the sternum. The mediastinoscope is inserted and the explorations are carried out between the trachea and the major vessels. The mediastinal lymph nodes, thymus, and thyroid are visualized, and biopsy is performed through the mediastinoscope. The scope is removed and the incision is closed with sutures or Steri-strips.

Coding Clarification

Code also any biopsy performed.

34.23   Biopsy of chest wall

Description

The physician performs a biopsy of the soft tissues of the thorax. With proper anesthesia administered, the physician identifies the mass through palpation and x-ray (reported separately), if needed. An incision is made over the site and dissection is taken down to the subcutaneous fat or further into the

30-34

30-34

fascia or muscle to reach the lesion. A portion of the tissue mass is excised and submitted for pathology. The area is irrigated and the incision is closed with layered sutures.

34.24   Other pleural biopsy

Description
Code 34.24 reports pleural biopsies that are not more appropriately reported by other codes within subcategory 34.2.

Biopsies of the pleura can be open, closed, or percutaneous needle biopsies. The physician obtains a sample of the lining of the lung and/or the lining of the inside of the chest cavity by needle biopsy. Using a special pleural biopsy needle, the physician carefully passes the needle over the top of a rib, punctures through the chest tissues between two ribs, enters the pleural cavity, and slightly punctures the surface of the lung. With the end of the needle in the chest cavity, the physician withdraws a piece of tissue. The needle is then withdrawn and the puncture site covered with a bandage. The procedure is often done under radiological guidance to assure more precise placement of the needle.

In an alternate method, the physician removes a sample of tissue from the pleura (the tissue covering the inside surface of the chest cavity or the surface of the lung). A small opening is created in the chest. The skin between two ribs is incised and the tissues separated to create a small opening in the chest. Under direct vision through this opening, a representative sample of tissue is removed using a biopsy needle or by cutting the tissue with a scalpel or scissors. The surgical wound created is then closed by suturing.

Coding Guidance
AHA: 1Q, '92, 14; 3Q, '02, 22, 27

34.25   Closed (percutaneous) (needle) biopsy of mediastinum

Description
The physician obtains a sample of the mediastinum (the tissues in the center of the chest between the two lung cavities) by puncturing through the space between two of the ribs with a needle. The procedure is often done under radiological guidance to assure more precise placement of the needle. Using a biopsy needle, the physician carefully passes the needle over the top of a rib, punctures through the chest tissues, enters the pleural cavity, and punctures into the area of concern in the mediastinum. With the end of the needle in the chest cavity, the physician withdraws a piece of tissue. The needle is then withdrawn and the puncture site covered with a bandage.

In an alternate procedure, the physician examines the inside of the mediastinal space, through a rigid or flexible fiberoptic endoscope. The endoscope is passed through a trocar and into the chest cavity. The lung is usually partially collapsed by instilling air into the chest through the trocar or, if general anesthesia is used, the lung may be collapsed through a special double lumen endotracheal tube inserted through the mouth into the trachea. As the physician views the structures and the anatomy of the area through the endoscope, the endoscope is advanced into the mediastinum (area inside the center of the chest cavity between the lungs). The contents of the mediastinal space are examined by direct visualization and/or by the use of a video camera. Still photographs may be taken as part of the procedure. The tissue selected for biopsy is identified and a biopsy is taken using a device inserted through the endoscope. At the conclusion of the procedure, the endoscope and the trocar are withdrawn. A chest tube for drainage and re-expansion of the lung is usually inserted through the wound.

34.26   Open biopsy of mediastinum

Description
The physician makes an incision low in the front of the neck, pulling back the sternomastoid muscles, moving the cranial vessels to the side, and drawing the trachea and thyroid to the center. The space behind the esophagus is exposed. The biopsy of any abnormal mass is performed and Penrose drains are placed. The incision is closed with sutures or staples. The procedure may also be accomplished using a transthoracic approach.

34.27   Biopsy of diaphragm

Description
To biopsy the diaphragm, the physician makes a large incision extending from just above the pubic hairline to the rib cage. The physician takes tissue samples of the organ for diagnosis. The incision is then closed with sutures.

34.28   Other diagnostic procedures on chest wall, pleura, and diaphragm

Description
Code 34.28 is used to report diagnostic procedures that are not more precisely described by other codes in subcategory 34.2.

Coding Clarification
Do not use 34.28 to report diagnostic procedures on the chest wall, pleura, and diaphragm that are listed elsewhere, such as:

*   Angiocardiography (88.50-88.58)
*   Aortography (88.42)

● New Code   ▲ Revised Code   ▶◀ Revised Text   © 2010 Ingenix

- Arteriography of intrathoracic vessels NEC (88.44) or pulmonary arteries (88.43)
- Microscopic examination of specimen from chest wall, pleura, and diaphragm (90.41-90.49)
- Phlebography of intrathoracic vessels NEC (88.63) or pulmonary veins (88.62)

Radiological examinations of the thorax are also listed elsewhere and are not reported by 34.28, including:

- C.A.T. scan (87.41)
- Diaphragmatic x-ray (87.49)
- Intrathoracic lymphangiogram (87.34)
- Routine chest x-ray (87.44)
- Sinogram of chest wall (87.38)
- Soft tissue x-ray of chest wall NEC (87.39)
- Tomogram of thorax NEC (87.42)
- Ultrasonography of thorax (88.73)

Documentation Tip
Review the documentation for specific information regarding the procedure prior to final code selection in order to avoid improper use of the "not otherwise specified" code.

34.29   Other diagnostic procedures on mediastinum

Description
Code 34.29 is used to report diagnostic procedures of the mediastinum that are not more precisely described by other codes in subcategory 34.2.

Coding Clarification
This code excludes mediastinal pneumogram (87.33) and mediastinal x-ray not classified elsewhere (87.49).

Documentation Tip
Review the documentation for specific information regarding the procedure prior to final code selection in order to ensure accurate code assignment.

34.3   Excision or destruction of lesion or tissue of mediastinum

Description
The physician makes an incision in front of the axilla just below the nipple line. The incision extends below the tip of the shoulder blade and ascends to halfway between the spinal column and the shoulder blade. The physician exposes the rib cage, retracting muscles. A rib spreader is used to ease access to the thoracic cavity. The cyst is located and removed. The rib spreader is removed, and the wound is closed with sutures or staples.

In an alternate approach, the physician removes a cyst, tumor, or mass from the mediastinum through a rigid or flexible fiberoptic endoscope. The procedure can be done under local or general

anesthesia. The physician makes a small incision between two ribs and by blunt dissection and the use of a trocar enters the thoracic cavity. The endoscope is passed through the trocar and into the chest cavity. The lung is usually partially collapsed by instilling air into the chest through the trocar or, if general anesthesia is used, the lung may be collapsed through a special double lumen endotracheal tube inserted through the mouth into the trachea. As the physician views the structures and the anatomy of the area through the endoscope, the endoscope is advanced into the mediastinum (area inside the center of the chest cavity between the lungs). The contents of the mediastinal space are examined by direct visualization and/or by the use of a video camera. Still photographs may be taken as part of the procedure. The cyst, tumor, or mass is identified and removed using instruments guided through the endoscope or by using instruments introduced into the area through a second and/or third insertion site in the chest. At the conclusion of the procedure, the endoscope and the trocar are withdrawn. A chest tube for drainage and re-expansion of the lung is usually inserted through the wound used for the thoracoscopy.

34.4   Excision or destruction of lesion of chest wall

Description
The physician excises a chest wall tumor, possibly including ribs. An incision in the skin of the chest overlying the site of the tumor is made. The tumor and surrounding tissue are excised. The tissue removed includes at least one adjacent rib above and below the tumor site and all intervening intercostal muscles. It may also include an en bloc resection of muscles, including the pectoralis minor or major, the serratus anterior, or the latissimus dorsi. The physician ligates or cauterizes bleeding vessels. A chest tube may be placed to re-expand the lung. The incision is repaired with layered closure and a pressure dressing is applied to the wound.

Coding Clarification
This code is reported when the documentation does not further specify the lesion excision procedure.

Code 34.4 is not used to report the following procedures, which are more appropriately reported elsewhere:

- Biopsy of mediastinum (34.25-34.26)
- Mediastinal fistulectomy (34.73)
- Biopsy of chest wall (34.23)
- Costectomy not incidental to thoracic procedure (77.91)
- Fistulectomy (34.73)
- Excision of a lesion of the breast (85.20-85.25), cartilage (80.89), or skin (86.2-86.3)

34.5   Pleurectomy

Description

Pleurectomy is an excision of the pleura and usually involves the parietal pleura. The physician removes the membranous tissue lining the inside surface of the chest cavity (the parietal pleura). The physician opens the chest cavity widely. Using a scalpel, the surgeon makes a long incision around the side of the chest between two of the ribs. The incision is carried through all the tissue layers into the chest cavity. Rib spreaders are inserted into the wound and the ribs are spread apart exposing the lung. The constricting membrane is then stripped off the surface of the lung. The parietal pleura is stripped from the inside surface of the chest. The chest wall incision is then sutured closed in layers. A chest tube(s) may be used to provide drainage for the chest cavity.

Alternately, the chest cavity can be opened and the operation performed through a vertical incision in the center of the chest through the sternum. The skin incision is carried down to the sternum bone and then a saw is used to split the sternum. With the sternum split in half, the chest is entered by spreading the sternum apart with a set of rib spreaders. When the procedure is complete, the wound is closed by using wires to bring the two halves of the sternum together and the skin is closed over the sternum by suturing.

34.51   Decortication of lung

Description

The physician removes a constricting membrane or layer of tissue from the surface of the lung (decortication) in order to permit the lung to fully expand. The physician opens the chest cavity widely. Using a scalpel, the surgeon makes a long incision around the side of the chest between two of the ribs. The incision is carried through all the tissue layers into the chest cavity. Rib spreaders are inserted into the wound and the ribs are spread apart exposing the lung. The constricting membrane is then stripped off the entire surface of the lung; other times, only a portion of the lung surface is removed. The chest wall incision is then sutured closed in layers. A chest tube(s) may be used to provide drainage for the chest cavity. Alternately, the chest cavity can be opened by a vertical incision in the front of the chest through the sternum. The skin incision is carried down to the sternum bone and then a saw is used to split the sternum. With the sternum split in half, the chest is entered by spreading the sternum apart with a set of rib spreaders. When the procedure is complete, the wound is closed by using wires to bring the two halves of the sternum together and the skin is closed by suturing.

Coding Clarification

Decortication of the lung is the removal of thickened serous membrane for lung expansion.

This procedure is typically performed for the removal of a clot or scar tissue following a hemothorax or from an untreated empyema.

Thoracoscopic decortication of the lung is appropriately reported with 34.52.

34.52   Thoracoscopic decortication of lung

Description

The physician removes a constricting membrane or layer of tissue from the surface of the lung (decortication) in order to permit the lung to fully expand using thoracoscopy. The surgeon makes a small incision between two ribs and by blunt dissection and the use of a trocar enters the thoracic cavity. The endoscope is passed through the trocar and into the chest cavity. The constricting membrane is then stripped off the entire surface of the lung; at other times, only a portion of the lung surface is removed using a device through the endoscope or the insertion of an instrument through a second incision in the chest. At the conclusion of the procedure, the endoscope and the trocar are removed. A chest tube for drainage and re-expansion of the lung is usually inserted through the wound used for the thoracoscopy.

Coding Scenario

A patient with pleurisy was admitted for surgical decortication of the visceral pleura of one lung. Under direct visualization through an endoscope, the physician stripped away the membranous tissues covering a portion of the lung. A chest tube for drainage and re-expansion of the lung was inserted through the wound used for the thoracoscopy.

> Code Assignment:
>
> 511.0   Pleurisy, without mention of effusion or current tuberculosis
>
> 34.52   Thoracoscopic decortication of lung

Coding Guidance
  AHA: 4Q, '07, 111, 113

34.59   Other excision of pleura

Description

Code 34.59 is used to report pleural lesion excision procedures that are not more precisely described by other codes in subcategory 34.5.

The physician removes the membranous tissue lining the inside surface of the chest cavity (the parietal pleura). The physician opens the chest cavity widely to gain access to the inside surface of the chest. Using a scalpel, the surgeon makes a long incision around the side of the chest between two of

● New Code   ▲ Revised Code   ▶◀ Revised Text   © 2010 Ingenix

the ribs. The incision is carried through all the tissue layers into the chest cavity. Rib spreaders are inserted into the wound and the ribs are spread apart exposing the lung. The parietal pleura is stripped from the inside surface of the chest. The chest wall incision is then sutured closed in layers. A chest tube(s) may be used to provide drainage for the chest cavity. Alternately, the chest cavity can be opened and the operation performed through a vertical incision in the center of the chest through the sternum. The skin incision is carried down to the sternum bone and then a saw is used to split the sternum. With the sternum split in half, the chest is entered by spreading the sternum apart with a set of rib spreaders. When the procedure is complete, the wound is closed by using wires to bring the two halves of the sternum together and the skin is closed over the sternum by suturing.

Coding Clarification
Code 34.59 is not used to report biopsy of pleura (34.24) or pleural fistulectomy (34.73).

Documentation Tip
Review the documentation for specific information regarding the procedure prior to final code selection in order to ensure accurate code assignment.

34.6   Scarification of pleura

Description
Scarification of the pleura destroys fluid-secreting serous membrane cells of chest. The physician treats repeat pneumothorax by producing adhesions between the surface of the lung and the inside surface of the chest cavity. To create the adhesions, a chemical solution is injected into the chest cavity and allowed to circulate over the surface of the lung and the inside surface of the chest cavity. The physician injects the solution by passing a tube into the chest cavity. The physician carefully passes a trocar (a long, thin, sharp pointed instrument within a plastic tube) over the top of a rib and punctures through the chest tissues between the ribs and enters the pleural cavity. With the end of the trocar in the chest cavity, the physician advances the plastic tube (catheter) into the chest cavity. The sharp instrument is removed, leaving one end of the plastic catheter in place within the chest cavity. A syringe is attached to the outside end of the catheter and fluid is injected into the chest cavity. The fluid selected is designed to cause the formation of adhesive scar tissue between the surface of the lung and the inside surface of the chest cavity. Once the lung is stuck to the chest wall it can no longer collapse and allow the formation of a pneumothorax.

Alternately, the physician makes a small incision between two ribs and by blunt dissection and the use of a trocar enters the thoracic cavity. The endoscope is passed through the trocar and into the

chest cavity. The lung is usually partially collapsed by instilling air into the chest through the trocar or, if general anesthesia is used, the lung may be collapsed through a special double lumen endotracheal tube inserted through the mouth into the trachea. The contents of the chest cavity are examined by direct visualization and/or by the use of a video camera. Still photographs may be taken as part of the procedure. A second trocar and instruments may be inserted into the chest cavity through a second wound in the chest. Adhesion may be induced in one of two ways: by abrading the surfaces of the lung and the inside of the chest cavity or by the instillation of chemicals into the chest cavity that bathe the surfaces of the lung and the inside of the chest cavity. Most commonly, a chemical solution is instilled into the chest through the endoscope or second puncture site. At the conclusion of the procedure, the endoscope and the trocar are removed. A chest tube for drainage and re-expansion of the lung is usually inserted through the wound used for the thoracoscopy.

Coding Clarification
To report injection of a sclerosing agent, see 34.92.

Coding Guidance
AHA: 1Q, '92, 12

34.7   Repair of chest wall

Description
The various types of repair procedures are described at the subcategory level.

34.71   Suture of laceration of chest wall

Description
The physician explores a penetrating wound in the operating room, such as a gunshot or stab wound, to help identify damaged structures. Nerve, organ, and blood vessel integrity is assessed. The wound may be enlarged to help assess the damage. Debridement, removal of foreign bodies, and ligation or coagulation of minor blood vessels in the subcutaneous tissues, fascia, and muscle are also included in this range of codes. Damaged tissues are debrided and repaired when possible. The wound is closed (if clean) or packed open if contaminated by the penetrating body.

Coding Clarification
This procedure excludes suture of skin and subcutaneous tissue alone (86.59).

34.72   Closure of thoracostomy

Description
The physician treats a draining empyema (accumulation of pus in the chest cavity) by resecting a rib, irrigating the empyema space with an antibiotic solution intermittently over an

30-34

extended period of time, and then closing the empyema space in six to eight weeks. This code reports the closure portion only.

Coding Clarification
Closure of the chest wall following open flap drainage for empyema is also known as a Clagett type procedure.

34.73   Closure of other fistula of thorax

Description
The physician closes a bronchopleural fistula and performs a thoracoplasty, which is the removal of the skeletal support of a portion of the chest to treat chronic thoracic empyema (accumulation of pus in the chest cavity) when there is insufficient lung tissue to fill the chest space. The procedure is carried out primarily on the upper chest. An incision is made through the skin down to the ribs. The Schede operation consists of the extensive unroofing of an empyema space by resecting the overlying ribs and portions of membrane lining the chest cavity (parietal pleural peel). The bronchopleural fistula (an abnormal passageway between the remaining end of a bronchial tube that occurs sometimes after the removal of a lung or portion of a lung) is identified and resected, then closed by suturing. Closure of the fistula sometimes requires the use of muscle flap grafts taken from outside the chest cavity. After repair of the fistula, the muscles in the area are partially closed over gauze packing and the skin partially closed by suturing in layers. As the packing is withdrawn in stages a few days later, it is hoped that fresh granulation tissue fills in the space formerly occupied by the empyema. The original Schede type operation is rarely performed but several modifications are currently done.

Coding Clarification
Code 34.73 is used to report closure of bronchopleural, bronchopleurocutaneous, and bronchopleuromediastinal fistulas.

34.74   Repair of pectus deformity

Description
The physician performs reconstructive surgery on the anterior chest to correct pectus excavatum (a depression in the chest wall) or pectus carinatum (a forward projection of the chest wall). With the patient under anesthesia, the physician makes an incision overlying the anterior sternum. This is carried deep to the bone. The costal cartilages are exposed and deformed rib ends are freed from their sternal attachments. The sternum is mobilized and restored to its normal position. Internal fixation devices are employed to hold the sternum in corrected alignment. The physician irrigates the wound and closes it in sutured layers.

In an alternate technique, the physician performs a Nuss procedure, which is also known as minimally invasive repair of pectus excavatum, or MIRPE. The chest is first marked at strategic points and the length of a curved steel bar, called the Lorenz pectus bar, to be inserted into the sternum is measured and shaped to fit the individual's chest. Midaxillary line incisions are made on the right and left side aligned with the deepest depression point. A skin tunnel is raised from the incisions and another small lateral incision is made for insertion of a thoracoscope. The skin incisions are elevated and a long introducer instrument is inserted through the right intercostal space at the top of the pectus ridge and slowly advanced across the anterior mediastinal space with videoscopic guidance. The sternum is forcefully lifted as the introducer is passed to the other side. Once behind the sternum, the tip is pushed through the intercostal space at the top of the pectus ridge on the left side and brought out through that skin incision. Umbilical tape is pulled through the tunnel and used to guide the prepared bar. The bar is inserted with the convex curve facing posteriorly and rotated with a flipping instrument until the convex curve faces anteriorly. The bar can be pulled back out and bent in a more ideal curvature for correction as many times as needed. Usually only one bar is placed. With the bar in position, a stabilizing bar is sutured around the pectus bar and to the muscle. Sutures are placed in the lateral chest wall musculature, as well as one other fixation point to the side of the sternum around one rib and the pectus bar.

Coding Clarification
The Nuss procedure is a minimally invasive technique that involves using a convex steel bar placed beneath the pectus deformity to correct pectus excavatum.

The Lorenz Pectus Bar allows the physician to correct a concave chest deformity by applying an outward force to the sternum.

An understanding of the following terms may aid in code selection:

- **Pectus carinatum repair:** Restoration of prominent chest bone defect with implant.
- **Pectus excavatum:** Restoration of a depressed chest bone defect with implant.

Coding Guidance
   AHA: 2Q, '04, 6

34.79   Other repair of chest wall

Description
Code 34.79 is used to report chest wall repair procedures that are not more precisely described by other codes in subcategory 34.7, including exploration of penetrating wounds of the chest,

● New Code   ▲ Revised Code   ▶◀ Revised Text   © 2010 Ingenix

repair of a lung hernia through the chest wall, and posttraumatic reconstruction of the chest wall. This code is also reported when the documentation does not further specify the repair procedure.

Documentation Tip
Review the documentation for specific information regarding the procedure prior to final code selection in order to ensure accurate code assignment.

Coding Guidance
> **AHA:** J-F,'87, 13; 5th issue, '94, 15; 2Q, '04, 6

34.8   Operations on diaphragm

Description
Codes in category 34.8 contain fourth-digit specificity to report other repair procedures on the diaphragm.

Documentation Tip
Review the documentation for specific information regarding the procedure prior to final code selection in order to ensure accurate code assignment.

34.81   Excision of lesion or tissue of diaphragm

Description
The surgeon removes all or part of the diaphragm, the large muscle separating the chest and abdominal cavities. The patient is taken to the operating room, the abdomen and/or chest are surgically opened, and the operation is performed. This code involves a simple repair using sutures or a complex repair using muscle or synthetic material for patching some of the area.

Coding Clarification
Biopsy of the diaphragm is reported with 34.27.

34.82   Suture of laceration of diaphragm

Description
The physician makes an abdominal or chest incision and exposes a tear in the diaphragm. The tear is repaired with nonabsorbable sutures. Occasionally the tear may be so extensive that an artificial patch is used to repair defects or reinforce sutures. The incision is closed with sutures or staples, and a dressing is applied.

34.83   Closure of fistula of diaphragm

Description
The physician excises or incises a diaphragmatic fistula. The physician identifies the location of the fistula. An incision is made; the skin, subcutaneous tissue, and muscle overlying the fistula is excised or incised to open the fistula tract and the fistula is completely unroofed or may be excised.

Coding Clarification
Code 34.83 is reported for a thoracicoabdominal, thoracicogastric, or thoracicointestinal fistulectomy.

34.84   Other repair of diaphragm

Description
The physician makes an abdominal or chest incision and exposes a tear in the diaphragm. If the tear is so extensive that it cannot be repaired with sutures, an artificial patch is used to repair defects or reinforce sutures. The incision is closed with sutures or staples, and a dressing is applied.

Alternately, the physician makes an incision across the chest or abdomen, the abdominal contents are drawn back into the abdomen, and the diaphragm is exposed. The connective tissue is used to stitch folds or tucks into the diaphragm to restore it to its original position. The incision is closed with sutures or staples.

Coding Clarification
To report the repair of a diaphragmatic hernia, see 53.71-53.82.

Suture repair of diaphragmatic lacerations is reported with 34.82.

Documentation Tip
This procedure may also be referred to in the medical record as phrenoplasty or reconstruction of the diaphragm.

34.85   Implantation of diaphragmatic pacemaker

Description
Diaphragmatic pacing is an alternative to mechanical ventilation. A diaphragmatic pacemaker is a device that is surgically implanted to help patients breathe through pacing of the diaphragm. With a diaphragmatic pacemaker, pacing is accomplished via electrodes surgically implanted into the diaphragm, which is controlled by the phrenic nerve. Breathing is helped by setting the respiratory rate by electrical stimulation (pacing) of the phrenic nerve.

Diaphragm pacing originally required a surgical opening of the chest cavity (thoracotomy) to implant the electrodes; but is now performed as a laparoscopic implantation of electrodes in the muscle of the diaphragm and initial electrical stimulation.

The pacing system electrodes are sutured to the phrenic nerves. The external transmitter controls the intensity, duration, and rate of impulse of the respiratory rate. Fluoroscopy may be used to determine the current needed for optimal contraction of the diaphragm and maximal tidal volume using the lowest applied current.

34.89   Other operations on diaphragm

Description
Code 34.89 is used to report other procedures of the diaphragm that are not more precisely described by other codes in this subcategory.

Documentation Tip
Review documentation for specific information regarding the procedure prior to final code selection in order to ensure accurate code assignment.

34.9   Other operations on thorax

Description
Fourth-digit specificity in this subcategory is included to report chemical pleurodesis, thoracentesis, and injections or instillation of therapeutic substances into thoracic cavity.

34.91   Thoracentesis

Description
The physician removes fluid from the chest cavity by puncturing through the space between the ribs. Using an aspirating needle attached to a syringe, the physician carefully passes the needle over the top of a rib, punctures through the chest tissues, and enters the pleural cavity. With the end of the needle in the chest cavity, the physician withdraws the fluid from the chest cavity by pulling back on the plunger of the syringe.

Documentation Tip
This procedure is also known as pleurocentesis (puncture of pleural cavity for fluid aspiration).

Coding Guidance
    AHA: S-O, '85, 6

34.92   Injection into thoracic cavity

Description
The physician instills fluid into the chest cavity by puncturing through the space between the ribs. To enter the chest cavity, the physician carefully passes a trocar (a long, thin, sharp, pointed instrument within a plastic tube) over the top of a rib, punctures through the chest tissues, and enters the pleural cavity. With the end of the trocar in the chest cavity, the physician advances the plastic tube (catheter) into the chest cavity. The sharp instrument is removed leaving one end of the plastic catheter in place within the chest cavity. A syringe is attached to the outside end of the catheter and fluid is injected into the chest cavity. The fluid selected is designed to cause the adhesion of the surface of the lung to the inside surface of the chest cavity.

Coding Clarification
Code 34.92 correctly reports the following procedures:

- Chemical pleurodesis

- Injection of a cytotoxic agent or tetracycline
- Instillation into the thoracic cavity

Do not report 34.92 for thoracic cavity injections performed for collapse of lung; see 33.32.

Instillation into the thoracic cavity requires an additional code for any cancer chemotherapeutic substance (99.25).

Documentation Tip
Chemical pleurodesis involves the injection of a cytotoxic agent or tetracycline hydrochloride injections, to create adhesions between parietal and visceral pleura for treatment of pleural effusion.

Coding Guidance
    AHA: 2Q, '89, 17; 1Q, '92, 12; 1Q, '07, 14; 4Q, '07, 112

Coding Scenario
A patient with malignant pleural effusion undergoes chemical pleurodesis with drainage of the pleural fluid. Using video assistance, the physician inserts the thoracoscope through a small incision in the chest and removes the pleural fluid. A talc solution is then blown over the lung and pleural surfaces. A chest tube is inserted and a dressing placed over it.

    Code Assignment:

    511.81   Malignant pleural effusion
    34.06   Thoracoscopic drainage of pleural cavity
    34.92   Injection into thoracic cavity

34.93   Repair of pleura

Description
Code 34.93 is used to report repair procedures on the pleura that are not more precisely described by other codes in subcategory 34.9, including pleural closure not elsewhere classified or that by suture.

Documentation Tip
Review the documentation for specific information regarding the procedure prior to final code selection in order to ensure accurate code assignment.

34.99   Other operations on thorax

Description
Code 34.99 is used to report procedures of the thorax that are not more precisely described by other codes in subcategory 34.9, such as creation of a pleural tent.

The physician performs an extrapleural mobilization of the parietal pleura in the apex of the chest cavity, allowing it to drape down over the visceral pleura of the remaining lung and allows the parietal pleura to seal air leaks.

Coding Clarification
This code also correctly reports the following procedures:

- Lysis of mediastinal or thoracic adhesions

● New Code   ▲ Revised Code   ►◄ Revised Text   © 2010 Ingenix

- Operations on the chest cavity, pleural cavity, or thorax that are not elsewhere classified
- Pleuropexy

This code excludes removal of a mediastinal drain (97.42), sutures (97.43), or thoracotomy tube (97.41).

Documentation Tip
A pleural tent is extrapleural mobilization of the parietal pleura that allows draping of membrane

over visceral pleura to eliminate intrapleural dead space and seal visceral pleura.

Review the documentation for specific information regarding the procedure prior to final code selection in order to ensure accurate code assignment.

Coding Guidance
AHA: 1Q, '88, 9; 1Q, '00, 17

35-39

Operations on the Cardiovascular System

2011 Changes

Multiple additions, deletions, and revisions were made to codes classified within this section including:

New code 35.97 Percutaneous mitral valve repair with implant, specifically reports a minimally invasive transcatheter approach for intracardiac mitral valve repair. It is performed by interventional cardiologists in the cardiac catheterization laboratory or operating room as an alternative to the open heart surgical approach.

Multiple inclusion and exclusion term changes were made to codes in subcategory 37.3 Pericardiectomy and excision of lesion of heart. New code 37.37 Excision or destruction or other lesion or tissue of heart, thoracoscopic approach reports an ablation procedure performed via thoracoscope to treat atrial fibrillation. This procedure creates lesions in the tissue of the left and right atria of the heart that interrupt the abnormal electrical currents of atrial fibrillation to restore normal sinus rhythm.

New code 38.97 Central venous catheter placement with guidance reports CVC placement assisted by guidance technologies, including electrocardiogram, fluoroscopy, and ultrasound.

Code 39.8 has been expanded to the fourth-digit level to include new codes 39.81–39.88, which report baroreflex activation device procedures. These procedures report implantable medical devices designed to electrically activate the baroreflex. The baroreflex activation system helps regulate cardiovascular function to treat primary hypertension and hypertensive heart failure recalcitrant to medical therapy. Other procedures previously classified to code 39.8 are now classified to new code 39.89 Other operations on carotid body, carotid sinus, and other vascular bodies.

The ICD-9-CM classification system for operations performed on the cardiovascular system is divided into categories of procedures according to sites as follows:

- Operations on the Valves and Septa of Heart (35)
- Operations on the Vessels of Heart (36)
- Other Operations on Heart and Pericardium (37)
- Incision, Excision and Occlusion of Vessels (38)
- Other Operations on Vessels (39)

Coding Clarification

Many of the subcategories in this portion of the classification system require a fourth digit for further specificity with regard to type and/or site of the operation performed.

Documentation Tip

Documentation in the operative report must support code selection.

35 Operations on the valves and septa of the heart

Description

The heart is a dual-pumping mechanism, which is divided by a partition called the septum, into left and right sections. Both the right and left heart sections are further divided into upper and lower sections called chambers. The upper chambers are referred to as the atria and the lower chambers are referred to as the ventricles. The atria receive blood from the veins of the body via the vena cava, while the ventricles pump blood through the aorta to the arteries of the body.

Valves allow for the controlled flow of blood, and when functioning normally, prevent the back-flow of blood, ensuring that circulation occurs to and from the heart in the proper, uninterrupted direction. Valves are defined as follows:

- **Mitral (bicuspid) valve:** Separates the left atrium and left ventricle, allowing blood to flow from the left atrium into the left ventricle.

- **Aortic (semilunar) valve:** Separates the left ventricle and aorta, allowing the blood to flow from the heart to the arteries of the body via the aorta.

- **Pulmonary (semilunar) valve:** Separates the right ventricle and the pulmonary artery, allowing blood to flow to the lungs for oxygenation.

- **Tricuspid (atrioventricular) valve:** Separates the right atrium and ventricle, allowing the blood to flow into the right ventricle from the right atrium.

Category 35 provides codes for incisions, repairs, replacements, and other operations on the valves, septa, and certain adjacent cardiac structures.

Coding Clarification
Codes in category 35 include those performed by the following surgical approaches:

- Median sternotomy

- Transverse sternotomy

- Thoracotomy

Code also any associated cardiopulmonary bypass (extracorporeal circulation) (heart-lung machine) (39.61).

35.0   Closed heart valvotomy

Description
This subcategory classifies closed valvotomy, which may be defined as incisions into the heart valve to restore function. A closed valvotomy is performed utilizing endocardiac approach—without incision through the heart wall.

Coding Clarification
Subcategory 35.0 excludes percutaneous balloon valvuloplasty (35.96).

Documentation Tip
May also be documented in the medical record as valvulotomy.

35.00   Closed heart valvotomy, unspecified valve

Description
This code describes a closed valvulotomy of an unspecified heart valve. The left chest is opened. The pericardium is opened. A gloved finger is used to open the heart valve. Blunt tearing is used to open the areas between the leaflets, which may have been obliterated by scar tissue and inflammation. The finger is removed and the chest is closed.

Documentation Tip
Carefully review documentation in the medical record to determine the specific valve treated. If the documentation is ambiguous or unclear, the physician should be queried.

35.01   Closed heart valvotomy, aortic valve

Description
The left chest is opened. The aorta is opened near the valve. The spaces where the heart valve leaflets

meet have been fused by inflammation and scarring in diseases requiring this operation. The scars between the leaflets are cut with a knife or torn bluntly with a gloved finger. The aorta is closed and the clamp is removed.

35.02   Closed heart valvotomy, mitral valve

Description
The left chest is opened. The pericardium is opened. A gloved finger is used to invert the left atrial appendage into the left atrium. The finger is placed across the mitral valve. Blunt tearing is used to open the areas between the leaflets, which have been obliterated by scar tissue and inflammation. The finger is removed and the chest is closed.

35.03   Closed heart valvotomy, pulmonary valve

Description
Cardiopulmonary bypass is usually not required. The heart is exposed through the sternum. A U-stitch reinforced with small patches of Teflon felt is placed in the right ventricular outflow tract muscle. A hole is made in the center of this U-stitch. Dilators are passed through the hole and across the valve. Gradually larger dilators are passed until the valve opening is large enough. The last dilator is removed and the U-stitch is tied to stop any bleeding. The chest is closed. In this operation, the valve is dilated from below.

35.04   Closed heart valvotomy, tricuspid valve

Description
The left chest is opened. The pericardium is opened. The heart is exposed through the sternum. Via the right atrium, the tricuspid valve is accessed. The spaces where the heart valve leaflets meet have been fused by inflammation and scarring in diseases requiring this operation. The scars between the leaflets are cut with a knife or torn bluntly with a gloved finger the diameter of the tricuspid valve. The chest is closed.

35.1   Open heart valvuloplasty without replacement

Description
This code subcategory classifies open heart repair of the heart valve in lieu of heart valve replacement.

Coding Clarification
Subcategory 35.1 includes open heart valvulotomy.

Subcategory 35.1 excludes valvuloplasty associated with:

- Endocardial cushion defect (35.54, 35.63, 35.73)

- Percutaneous (balloon) valvuloplasty (35.96)

- Valvular defect associated with atrial and ventricular septal defects (35.54, 35.63, 35.73)

● New Code   ▲ Revised Code   ▶◀ Revised Text   © 2010 Ingenix

Code also cardiopulmonary bypass (extracorporeal circulation)(heart-lung machine) (39.61)

Valvuloplasty (repair of the entire heart valve, ring, and leaflets) includes the annuloplasty (repair of the heart ring). If only an annuloplasty is performed, it is reported with 35.33. Repair of the ring and leaflets are reported with the appropriate valvuloplasty code from subcategory 35.1.

Coding Guidance
> AHA: 1Q, '97, 13

35.10 Open heart valvuloplasty without replacement, unspecified valve

Description
This code describes open heart valvulotomy or valvuloplasty without specification of anatomic site.

Coding Clarification
This is a non-specific procedure code that should not be assigned for inpatient hospital admissions. The medical record should contain sufficient information to facilitate coding at a higher level of specificity.

Documentation Tip
Carefully review documentation in the medical record to determine the specific valve treated. If the documentation is ambiguous or unclear, the physician should be queried.

35.11 Open heart valvuloplasty of aortic valve without replacement

Description
Cardiopulmonary bypass is initiated. The aorta is clamped from above the heart and a cold preserving solution is pumped through the heart. The aorta is opened near the valve. The spaces where the heart valve leaflets meet have been fused by inflammation and scarring in diseases requiring this operation. The scars between the leaflets are cut with a knife. The aorta is closed and the clamp is removed. Cardiopulmonary bypass is discontinued when heart function returns.

Coding Clarification
Resuspension of the aortic valve is assigned code 35.11.

Coding Guidance
> AHA: 2Q, '08, 13

35.12 Open heart valvuloplasty of mitral valve without replacement

Description
This operation is done to improve the ability of the mitral valve to close completely when the ventricle contracts. It is done in patients whose mitral valve has lost the ability to close normally. In almost all cases, this is the result of a mitral valve prolapse in

which the mitral leaflets and the cords that tether them on the ventricle have become elongated. Cardiopulmonary bypass is initiated. The left atrium is opened and the mitral valve is exposed. Redundant leaflet tissue is excised and defects in the valve leaflets are closed with sutures. The cords are also shortened with sutures. Valve closure is assessed after the repair. The left atrium is closed and cardiopulmonary bypass is discontinued when heart function returns. The mitral valve diameter may be enlarged requiring placement of a prosthetic ring, or more extensive repair, including transfer of cords from the posterior leaflet to the anterior leaflet, may be performed. A prosthetic ring may be required with extensive reconstruction.

Coding Scenario
A 60-year-old female with mitral valve incompetence was admitted for a mitral valve reconstruction. Posterior leaflet repair and Carpenter-Edwards ring annuloplasty were performed with the assistance of extracorporeal circulation. Redundant leaflet tissue was excised. Defects in the valve leaflets were closed with sutures. The chordae tendineae were shortened with sutures. Valve closure was assessed after the repair and determined to be adequate.

> Code Assignment:
>
> 424.0 Mitral valve disorders
> 35.12 Open heart valvuloplasty of mitral valve without replacement

Coding Clarification
►Use code 35.12 to report open heart mitral valve repair via a heart port device. Port access valve surgery is a minimally invasive technique that can lessen operating time and aortic cross-clamping by allowing surgeons to operate via small incisions (ports) underneath the breast instead of cutting through the sternum.

If cardiopulmonary bypass is performed, report separately in addition to the primary procedure.

Thoracoscopic mitral valve repair via a heart port device or a port access approach is excluded from 35.12. Instead, report this procedure with code 37.37.◄

Coding Guidance
> AHA: 1Q, '88, 10; 1Q,'97,13; ►1Q, '10, 14◄

35.13 Open heart valvuloplasty of pulmonary valve without replacement

Description
Cardiopulmonary bypass is initiated. The right ventricular infundibular muscle is opened and the obstructing muscle bands are cut out. The valve may also need to be opened. If so, the valve is cut open. The hole in the right ventricle is closed with a patch of pericardium. Cardiopulmonary bypass is

discontinued when heart function returns. The operation may be performed with a gusset, with or without commissurotomy or infundibular resection.

35.14 Open heart valvuloplasty of tricuspid valve without replacement

Description
Cardiopulmonary bypass is initiated with venous uptake tubes in both of the caval veins. The right atrium is opened. Valvuloplasty of the tricuspid valve almost always requires nothing more than reducing the diameter of the tricuspid valve. A double purse string of sutures is place around the circumference of the valve and tightened to reduce the valve diameter. The right atrium is closed. A stiff ring may be used to reduce the valve's diameter rather than purse strings.

35.2 Replacement of heart valve

Description
This subcategory describes heart valve replacement procedures. The excision or removal of the diseased valve is included in the code for the heart valve replacement. The valve replacement may be synthetic or organic in nature; made of prosthetic (synthetic) materials or biological tissue grafts from other humans or animals.

Coding Clarification
Subcategory 35.2 excludes heart valve replacement associated with:

- Endocardial cushion defect (35.54, 35.63, 35.73)
- Valvular defect associated with atrial and ventricular septal defects (35.54, 35.63, 35.73)

Code also cardiopulmonary bypass (extracorporeal circulation)(heart-lung machine) (39.61)

35.20 Replacement of unspecified heart valve

Description
This code describes open heart replacement of a heart valve with tissue graft or prosthetic implant, without specification of anatomic site.

Coding Clarification
This is a non-specific procedure code that should not be assigned for inpatient hospital admissions. The medical record should contain sufficient information to facilitate coding at a higher level of specificity.

Documentation Tip
Carefully review the documentation in the medical record to determine the specific valve replaced. If the documentation is ambiguous or unclear, the physician should be queried.

35.21 Replacement of aortic valve with tissue graft

Description
This code describes a replacement of the aortic valve with a tissue graft. Cardiopulmonary bypass is initiated. A clamp is placed on the aorta well above the heart. A cold preserving solution is pumped into the coronary arteries to stop the heart. The aorta is opened just above the aortic valve. The valve leaflets are cut out and the annulus of the valve (ring of tissue where the valve leaflets normally attach to the aorta) is cleaned of calcium. At this point an allograft is selected. The tissue valve is trimmed so that it can be sewn to the valve annulus. The aorta above the graft valve is trimmed so that the valve cusps can be suspended when the graft is in place. By doing so, the coronary arteries are not obstructed by the graft. The new valve is sewn in place. The valve annulus size is measured and an appropriate artificial valve is selected. The artificial valve is sewn to the valve annulus. The aorta is closed and the clamp is taken off. Cardiopulmonary bypass is discontinued when heart function returns.

Coding Clarification
When an aortic valve replacement is performed by transplanting a patient's pulmonary valve and replacing the pulmonary valve with a homograft, code both the aortic valve replacement with tissue graft (35.21) and replacement of the pulmonary valve with tissue graft.

This procedure may also be documented as:

- Ross procedure
- Aortic switch procedure

Coding Guidance
AHA: 2Q, '97, 8

35.22 Other replacement of aortic valve

Description
The physician performs prosthetic or synthetic replacement of the aortic valve. Cardiopulmonary bypass is initiated. A clamp is placed on the aorta well above the heart. A cold preserving solution is pumped into the coronary arteries to stop the heart. The aorta is opened just above the aortic valve. The valve leaflets are cut out and the annulus of the valve (ring of tissue where the valve leaflets normally attach to the aorta) is cleaned of calcium. The valve annulus size is measured and an appropriate artificial valve is selected. The artificial valve is sewn to the valve annulus. The aorta is closed and the clamp is taken off. Cardiopulmonary bypass is discontinued when heart function returns.

Coding Guidance
AHA: 1Q, '96, 11; 4Q, '08, 179

35.23   Replacement of mitral valve with tissue graft

Description
The physician performs replacement of the mitral valve tissue graft. Cardiopulmonary bypass is initiated. The left atrium is opened and the mitral valve is exposed. All leaflet tissue and its attached cords are cut out. Sutures are placed in the mitral annulus. The valvular tissue graft valve is seated against the valve annulus by sutures and the stitches are tied. The sutures are passed through the sewing ring of the annulus and tied down so the sewing ring is adherent to the annulus. The left atrium is closed. Cardiopulmonary bypass is discontinued when heart function returns.

35.24   Other replacement of mitral valve

Description
The physician performs prosthetic or synthetic replacement of the mitral valve. Cardiopulmonary bypass is initiated. The left atrium is opened and the mitral valve is exposed. All leaflet tissue and its attached cords are cut out. Sutures are placed in the mitral annulus. The annulus is sized and an appropriate artificial valve is selected (a totally mechanical valve or a valve with plastic supports and tissue leaflets). The sutures are passed through the sewing ring of the annulus and tied down so the sewing ring is adherent to the annulus. The left atrium is closed. Cardiopulmonary bypass is discontinued when heart function returns.

Coding Clarification
▶Code 35.24 excludes percutaneous repair with implant or leaflet clip (35.97).◀

Coding Guidance
AHA: 4Q, '97, 55

35.25   Replacement of pulmonary valve with tissue graft

Description
The physician replaces the pulmonary valve with tissue graft. Cardiopulmonary bypass is initiated with venous uptake tubes in both caval veins. The pulmonary artery is opened and the pulmonary valve leaflets are cut out. Stitches are placed around the circumference of the pulmonary annulus and the valve is sized. The valvular tissue graft valve is seated against the valve annulus by sutures and the stitches are tied. The hole in the pulmonary artery is closed. Cardiopulmonary bypass is discontinued when heart function returns.

Coding Clarification
Pulmonary valve replacement procedures are often performed in association with other heart operations. Code also any other associated procedures. For example, when an aortic valve replacement is performed by transplanting a patient's pulmonary valve and replacing the pulmonary valve with a homograft, code both the aortic valve replacement with tissue graft (35.21) and replacement of the pulmonary valve with tissue graft (35.25).

This procedure may also be documented as:

*   Ross procedure
*   Aortic switch procedure

Coding Guidance
AHA: 2Q, '97, 8; 1Q, '04, 16; 1Q, '07, 14

35.26   Other replacement of pulmonary valve

Description
The physician replaces the pulmonary valve with a synthetic graft or prosthesis. Cardiopulmonary bypass is initiated with venous uptake tubes in both caval veins. The pulmonary artery is opened and the pulmonary valve leaflets are cut out. Stitches are placed around the circumference of the pulmonary annulus and the valve is sized. An appropriate artificial valve is selected. The stitches are passed through the sewing ring of the valve. The sewing ring is seated against the valve annulus and the stitches are tied. The hole in the pulmonary artery is closed. Cardiopulmonary bypass is discontinued when heart function returns.

35.27   Replacement of tricuspid valve with tissue graft

Description
The physician replaces the tricuspid valve with a tissue graft. Cardiopulmonary bypass is initiated with venous uptake tubes in both caval veins. The right atrium is opened and the tricuspid valve leaflets are excised. The tissue graft is trimmed and placed into position. Sutures are placed around the tricuspid valve annulus circumference. They are brought through the sewing ring of the valve. The valve is seated so the sewing ring is resting on the annulus. The sutures are tied tightly. The right atrium is closed. Cardiopulmonary bypass is discontinued when heart function returns.

35.28   Other replacement of tricuspid valve

Description
Cardiopulmonary bypass is initiated with venous uptake tubes in both caval veins. The right atrium is opened and the tricuspid valve leaflets are excised. A valve of an appropriate diameter is selected (usually it is a plastic or other synthetic material). Sutures are placed around the tricuspid valve annulus circumference. They are brought through the sewing ring of the valve. The valve is seated so that the sewing ring is resting on the annulus. The sutures are tied tightly. The right atrium is closed.

35-39

Cardiopulmonary bypass is discontinued when heart function returns.

35.3   Operations on structures adjacent to heart valves

Description
This subcategory includes operations on cardiac anatomic structures adjacent to the heart valves, which includes certain repair, excision, division, and reattachment procedures.

Coding Clarification
Code also cardiopulmonary bypass (extracorporeal circulation)(heart-lung machine) (39.61)

35.31   Operations on papillary muscle

Description
The physician repairs or restores anatomic function to the papillary heart muscle. The papillary muscles contract the chordae tendineae, limiting the motion of the mitral and tricuspid valves and thereby preventing inversion of the valve leaflets. This inversion is demonstrated by regurgitation of blood flow, resulting in congestive heart failure. The papillary muscle may rupture as a complication of myocardial infarction, congestive heart failure, or certain types of cardiomyopathy. Papillary muscle rupture is commonly treated with mitral valve replacement. Reimplantation of a ruptured muscle head into a viable area of the myocardium may be performed; however, due to the possibility of recurrent rupture or reimplantation failure, it is not usually the preferred treatment. Papillary muscle repairs are frequently performed in conjunction with heart valve operations; the treatment of choice is often a prosthetic mitral valve replacement. Papillary muscle elongation or shortening techniques may often be employed; however, these techniques may be accompanied by resection of the valve leaflets or chordal transfer procedures.

35.32   Operations on chordae tendineae

Description
This procedure code describes an operation to repair the chordae tendineae. Rupture of the chordae tendineae may be associated with mitral valve regurgitation, whereby mitral valve replacement, annuloplasty, or other valve repair is indicated. Surgical techniques such as wedge leaflet resection with primary closure may be used to repair the rupture and associated valve dysfunction. Elongated or broken chordae tendineae may be repaired with Gore-Tex sutures to create new chords.

35.33   Annuloplasty

Description
The physician repairs or placates (folding; taking tucks in a structure to reduce its size) the annulus. The annulus is the ring-shaped structure encircling the heart valve leaflets. Cardiopulmonary bypass is initiated. A clamp is placed on the aorta well above the heart. A cold preserving solution is pumped into the coronary arteries to stop the heart. The aorta is opened just above the aortic valve. The valve leaflets are cut out and the annulus of the valve (ring of tissue where the valve leaflets normally attach to the aorta) is cleaned of calcium. At this point a homograft or a xenograft is selected. The tissue valve is trimmed so that it can be sewn to the valve annulus. The aorta above the graft valve is trimmed so the valve cusps can be suspended when the graft is in place and so the coronary arteries are not obstructed by the graft. When the valve is sized, it must be greater than or equal to 19 mm on a normal sized adult. If a smaller valve is inserted, the heart will slowly fail. To enlarge the valve, the aorta is cut longitudinally toward the heart and through the commissure (connecting point where two valve leaflets meet on the aortic wall) between the non-coronary leaflet (no coronary is near this leaflet) and the left coronary leaflet (leaflet near the left coronary artery) and across the valve annulus for a variable distance. The cut may need to extend onto the roof of the left atrium and onto the anterior leaflet of the mitral valve. The end of the cut is determined by the point at which the aortic root will accommodate at least a 19 mm valve. The anterior mitral leaflet, left atrial roof, and the aorta are repaired with patches. The new valve is sewn in place. The aorta is closed and the clamp is taken off. Cardiopulmonary bypass is discontinued when heart function returns.

Coding Clarification
Annuloplasty (35.33) includes eccentric annuloplasty, Carpentier annuloplasty, and leaflet plication procedures.

An annuloplasty (35.33) is an operation on the ring only. If the procedure includes operations on the heart valve leaflets, 35.12 should be reported. Code 35.12 includes an annuloplasty; no additional code is necessary.

Coding Guidance
AHA: 1Q, '88, 10; 1Q, '97, 13

35.34   Infundibulectomy

Description
The physician excises the funnel-shaped passage of the right upper chamber of the heart. Cardiopulmonary bypass is initiated. The right ventricular infundibular muscle is opened and the

obstructing muscle bands are cut out. The valve may also need to be opened. If so, the valve is cut open. The hole in the right ventricle is closed with a patch of pericardium. Cardiopulmonary bypass is discontinued when heart function returns.

35.35   Operations on trabeculae carneae cordis

Description
This code describes procedures performed on the trabeculae carneae cordis, the muscular projections from the inner surface of the ventricles that serve as points of origin for chordae tendineae. Cardiopulmonary bypass is initiated. The aorta is opened and the left ventricular outflow tract is assessed below the valve. There is usually a clearly definable ring or shelf below the valve. This is taken off with a tool designed for the purpose. Usually, the left ventricular septal muscle is thickened. A trough of muscle tissue is cut out of the left ventricular septal muscle. The aorta is closed. Cardiopulmonary bypass is discontinued when heart function returns.

35.39   Operations on other structures adjacent to valves of heart

Description
This code describes operations on other heart structures not classifiable elsewhere in subcategory 35.3. These procedures may include repair of abnormal sinus tract, fistula closure, or repair of aneurysm of the sinus of Valsalva. Surgical technique depends on the nature of the procedure and specific anatomic heart structure involved.

In fistula of sinus of Valsalva repair, cardiopulmonary bypass is required. After the heart is stopped, the aorta is opened and the fistula is identified. Repair of fistula may be performed through the aorta or through the right atrium. The fistula is closed with a patch of pericardium or other graft. Any aortic valve incompetence is repaired by shortening the redundant valve leaflet diameter with stitches that reef in its free edge. If the repair was made by incision into the aorta, the hole in the aorta is closed.

35.4   Production of septal defect in heart

Description
This subcategory includes operations on the heart whereby an existing natural defect is enlarged or a defect is created in order to facilitate normal heart function.

35.41   Enlargement of existing atrial septal defect

Description
This procedure code describes an enlargement of an existing defect in the partition that divides the lower heart chambers in order to improve heart function.

Surgical technique may vary depending on the nature of the defect, including:

- **Open septostomy:** In most pediatric cardiac surgery centers, this procedure has been supplanted by balloon dilation of a naturally occurring hole in the wall between the atrial chambers. No incision is needed for balloon dilation. Operative septostomy/septectomy requires cardiopulmonary bypass with venous uptake tubes in both caval veins. The right atrium is opened and the thin part of the wall between the right and left atria is cut out or opened widely. The goal is to allow free mixing of the blood from the right and left atria. Cardiopulmonary bypass is discontinued when heart function returns. Tourniquets may be placed around the caval veins and the patient is placed head down so no air entering the right atrium crosses the wall between the right and left atria.

- **Rashkind procedure:** Certain congenital heart defects, particularly those involving transposition of the great vessels, require surgical creation or enlargement of an opening in the interatrial septum (wall) that separates the upper right and left chambers of the heart. The physician makes a small incision in the arm or leg. Two catheters are placed: a central venous catheter and a second catheter threaded up to the heart. When the foramen ovale has not closed, a deflated balloon (Rashkind-type) is passed through the foramen ovale, inflated, and pulled through the atrial septum, enlarging the opening and improving oxygenation of the blood. When the septum is intact, the deflated balloon (Rashkind-type) is passed from the right atrium through the septum to the left atrium, inflated, and withdrawn, creating an interatrial septal defect and improving oxygenation of the blood. The catheters are removed. Pressure is placed over the incision for 20 to 30 minutes to stem bleeding. A cardiac catheterization may be included. The patient is observed for a period afterward.

- **Blade septostomy:** The purpose of this procedure is to increase blood flow across the atrial septum in children with certain forms of cyanotic congenital heart disease. This procedure is used as an alternative to the Rashkind procedure (balloon method of atrial septostomy), typically in infants older than one month of age. The physician makes a small incision in the femoral vein. The physician places a transseptal sheath in the right femoral vein using standard methods, advancing the sheath to the superior vena cava under fluoroscopic or echocardiographic guidance.

The physician uses a transseptal needle to cross the atrial septum, entering the left atrium. The physician introduces a guidewire into the left atrium and removes the transseptal catheter while leaving the wire in place. The physician advances a septostomy catheter over the wire into the left atrium. This catheter has a retracted blade, which the physician extends. The physician pulls the blade slowly across the atrial septum from the left into the right atrium, under fluoroscopic or echocardiographic guidance. The physician may make several passes with the blade catheter in this fashion. The physician removes the septostomy catheter and venous sheath. Pressure is placed over the incision for 20 to 30 minutes to stem bleeding. The patient is observed for a period afterward.

Documentation Tip
This procedure may also be documented as a closed (e.g., balloon, blade, park) or open septostomy.

35.42   Creation of septal defect in heart

Description
This procedure code describes the creation of a septal defect by removal of a partition wall defect in the lower heart chamber to facilitate normal function. Surgical technique may vary.

The procedure requires a median sternal opening or a right chest opening. A purse string is placed in the right atrial appendage and the appendage is opened in the middle of the purse string. A finger or a dilating tool is passed through the hole in the atrium and the wall between the right and left atria is torn open. The dilating instrument is removed and the purse string is tied to stop the bleeding.

In most pediatric cardiac surgery centers, this procedure is supplanted by balloon dilation of a naturally occurring hole in the wall between the atrial chambers. No incision is needed for balloon dilation. Operative septostomy/septectomy requires cardiopulmonary bypass with venous uptake tubes in both caval veins. The right atrium is opened and the thin part of the wall between the right and left atria is cut out or opened widely. The goal is to allow free mixing of the blood from the right and left atria. Cardiopulmonary bypass is discontinued when heart function returns. Tourniquets may be placed around the caval veins and the patient is placed head down so no air entering the right atrium crosses the wall between the right and left atria.

35.5   Repair of atrial and ventricular septa with prosthesis

Description
Subcategory 35.5 describes repair of septa with a prosthesis: a synthetic implant or patch.

Coding Clarification
Code also cardiopulmonary bypass (extracorporeal circulation)(heart-lung machine) (39.61)

35.50   Repair of unspecified septal defect of heart with prosthesis

Description
The physician repairs an unspecified septal defect with a prosthesis.

Coding Clarification
This is a non-specific procedure code that should not be assigned for inpatient hospital admissions. The medical record should contain sufficient information to facilitate coding at a higher level of specificity.

This code excludes septal defect repair associated with repair of:

- Endocardial cushion defect (35.54)
- Atrial septal defect associated with valvular and ventricular septal defects (35.54)

Documentation Tip
Carefully review documentation in the medical record to determine the specific anatomic site treated. If the documentation is ambiguous or unclear, the physician should be queried.

35.51   Repair of atrial septal defect with prosthesis, open technique

Description
This procedure code describes an open repair of atrial septal defect with synthetic prosthesis. Cardiopulmonary bypass is necessary. Two venous tubes are placed for the bypass machine: one draining the superior caval vein and one draining the inferior caval vein. The right atrium is isolated by placing tourniquets around the superior vena cava and inferior vena cava and their corresponding tubes. The right atrium is opened and the size and location of the arterial septal defect are assessed. A patch of Dacron or other synthetic material is sewn to the edge of the defect to close it.

Coding Clarification
This code excludes septal defect repair associated with repair of:

- Endocardial cushion defect (35.54)
- Atrial septal defect associated with valvular and ventricular septal defects (35.54)

Documentation Tip
This procedure may be documented using the following terms, with prosthesis:

- Atrioseptoplasty
- Correction of atrial septal defect
- Repair of foramen ovale (patent) or ostium secundum defect

● New Code   ▲ Revised Code   ►◄ Revised Text   © 2010 Ingenix

35.52   Repair of atrial septal defect with prosthesis, closed technique

Description

This procedure code describes closure of an atrial septal defect by closed technique. An atrial septal defect may be closed percutaneously by catheter. This procedure may be performed on infants or adults, usually under conscious sedation. After heparinization is induced, a combined right and left heart catheterization is first undertaken through the existing septal opening. Contrast material is injected for atrial and ventricular angiograms to map the anatomy. Using a specialized catheter, the atrial defect is crossed from the right atrium into the left. The catheter is threaded into the upper left pulmonary vein. A guidewire is inserted, the catheter is removed, and a balloon is threaded over the guidewire into position across the defect and inflated with low pressure. The stretched diameter of the defect is measured. Testing is carried out to ensure that the repair will remain hemodynamically stable by occluding the defect temporarily with the balloon while taking right-side pressures and saturation measurements. A dilator and sheath holding the device are advanced over the guidewire and positioned in the left atrium. Positioning is checked using echocardiography or fluoroscopy before releasing the device. The implant is deployed across the atrial opening and positioning is checked again. Any leaks, abnormal placement, or an improperly sized device may require removal of the implant and placement of a second device. The catheters and guidewires are removed.

Coding Clarification

Closure of an atrial septal defect may require reporting of associated procedures, such as:

- Cardiac catheterization
- Diagnostic ultrasound of the heart
- Esophagoscopy

Documentation Tip

Balloon occlusion of the atrial septal defect/patent foramen ovale may be documented as an Amplatzer occlusion procedure, which is reported with 35.52. Code also any associated procedures.

Coding Guidance

AHA: 3Q, '98, 11; 2Q, '05, 17

35.53   Repair of ventricular septal defect with prosthesis, open technique

Description

The physician repairs a solitary defect in the tissue separating the right and left ventricles of the heart in an open heart procedure. Cardiopulmonary bypass is established with tubes in both the caval veins. The ventricular septal defect can almost always be accessed and repaired through an incision in the right atrium, except in the case of a supracristal ventricular septal defect, in which the ventricle is higher in the outflow part of the right ventricle. This type of ventricular septal defect is most often accessed and repaired through an incision in the pulmonary artery. All types of ventricular septal defects can be accessed and repaired through an incision in the muscle of the right ventricle, but this causes more damage and is avoided if possible. The ventricular septal defect is usually repaired with a patch of Dacron or pericardium, but may be closed using only sutures. After the ventricular septal defect is closed, the hole that has been created in the right atrium, right ventricle, or pulmonary artery is closed. The chest incision is repaired. Cardiopulmonary bypass is discontinued when heart function returns.

Coding Clarification

Code 35.53 includes correction of a ventricular septal defect or supracristal defect with prosthesis.

This code excludes septal defect repair associated with repair of:

- Endocardial cushion defect (35.54)
- Atrial septal defect associated with valvular and ventricular septal defects (35.54)

Coding Guidance

AHA: 1Q, '07, 14

35.54   Repair of endocardial cushion defect with prosthesis

Description

Cardiopulmonary bypass is established with the venous uptake tubes in both the superior and inferior caval veins. A hole in the right atrium or, if needed, a hole in one of the ventricles is made. The hole in the ventricle is made in the area of scar (if the ventricular septal defect is due to ischemia) or in the anterior part of the right ventricle (if the ventricular septal defect is congenital). All dead heart muscle is cut out (in ischemic ventricular septal defect) and the ventricular septal defect is closed with a patch of Dacron or pericardium. The hole in the atrium or ventricle is closed. Cardiopulmonary bypass is discontinued when heart function is restored.

Coding Clarification

Code 35.54 excludes repair of isolated:

- Atrial septal defect (35.51-35.52)
- Valvular defect (35.20, 35.22, 35.24, 35.26, 35.28)
- Ventricular septal defect (35.53)

Documentation Tip

Code 35.54 may also be documented as a prosthetic septal grafted repair of:

- Atrioventricular canal
- Ostium primum defect
- Valvular defect associated with atrial and ventricular septal defects

35.55   Repair of ventricular septal defect with prosthesis, closed technique

Description
The physician performs prosthetic repair of a ventricular septal defect by closed technique. In a transmyocardial transcatheter approach, the physician performs endoscopic operative repair of a ventricular septal defect using an implant. Through multiple endoscopic incisions in the chest, the physician accesses and visualizes the outer (epicardial) surface of the heart. The myocardium is incised, and the endoscopic tool carrying the septal plug implant is advanced to the site of the ventricular defect. The defect is closed with the implant, and the endoscope is removed and access incisions are sutured in layers.

35.6   Repair of atrial and ventricular septa with tissue graft

Description
This subcategory describes repair of atrial and ventricular septal with tissue graft.

Coding Clarification
Code also cardiopulmonary bypass (extracorporeal circulation)(heart-lung machine) (39.61).

35.60   Repair of unspecified septal defect of heart with tissue graft

Description
This procedure code describes repair of an unspecified septal defect with tissue graft.

Coding Clarification
This is a non-specific procedure code that should not be assigned for inpatient hospital admissions. The medical record should contain sufficient information to facilitate coding at a higher level of specificity.

Documentation Tip
Carefully review the documentation in the medical record to determine the specific anatomic site treated. If the documentation is ambiguous or unclear, the physician should be queried.

35.61   Repair of atrial septal defect with tissue graft

Description
The physician repairs an atrial septal defect with tissue graft. Cardiopulmonary bypass is necessary. Two venous tubes are placed for the bypass machine, one draining the superior caval vein and one draining the inferior caval vein. The right atrium

is isolated by placing tourniquets around the superior vena cava and inferior vena cava and their corresponding tubes. The right atrium is opened and the size and location of the arterial septal defect are assessed. If it is small enough or if the atrial septal tissue is sufficiently redundant, the defect is closed with a patch of pericardium or other tissue graft is sewn to the edge of the defect to close it.

Coding Clarification
Code 35.61 excludes atrial septal defect with repair of:

- Atrial septal defect associated with valvular and ventricular septal defects (35.63)
- Endocardial cushion defect (35.63)

Documentation Tip
Code 35.61 may be documented as a tissue graft repair with the following terminology:

- Atrioseptoplasty
- Correction of atrial septal defect
- Repair of foramen ovale (patent) or ostium secundum defect

35.62   Repair of ventricular septal defect with tissue graft

Description
The physician repairs a solitary defect in the tissue separating the right and left ventricles of the heart in an open heart procedure. Cardiopulmonary bypass is established with tubes in both the caval veins. The ventricular septal defect can almost always be accessed and repaired through an incision in the right atrium, except in the case of a supracristal ventricular septal defect, in which the ventricle is higher in the outflow part of the right ventricle. This type of ventricular septal defect is most often accessed and repaired through an incision in the pulmonary artery. All types of ventricular septal defects can be accessed and repaired through an incision in the muscle of the right ventricle, but this causes more damage and is avoided if possible. The ventricular septal defect is usually repaired with a patch of Dacron or pericardium or other tissue graft. After the ventricular septal defect is closed, the hole that has been created in the right atrium, right ventricle, or pulmonary artery is closed. The chest incision is repaired. Cardiopulmonary bypass is discontinued when heart function returns.

Coding Clarification
Code 35.62 excludes ventricular septal defect repair with tissue graft of:

- Endocardial cushion defect (35.63)
- Ventricular defect associated with valvular and atrial septal defects (35.63)

Documentation Tip
Code 35.62 may be documented as a tissue graft repair with the following terminology:

- Correction of ventricular septal defect
- Repair of supracristal defect

35.63 Repair of endocardial cushion defect with tissue graft

Description
The physician performs closure of an endocardial cushion defect with tissue graft. Surgical technique may vary:

- **Repair of complete atrioventricular canal:** Cardiopulmonary pulmonary bypass is established using venous uptake tubes in both the superior and inferior caval veins. The right atrium is opened. A radially oriented cleft or division in the anterior leaflet of the mitral valve is closed with the interrupted sutures. Care is taken to assure that the valve closes properly after it is repaired. There is a raphe or line of denser valve tissue marking the anatomic line between the two AR valves. The ventricular septal defect is obliterated by sewing this line to the top of the septal muscle. The atrial septal defect is closed with a patch of pericardium or other tissue graft. The right atrium is closed and cardiopulmonary pulmonary bypass discontinued after heart function is restored. An opening in the right atrium is made. The competency of the single AV valve is assessed as is the imaginary line where the plane extending upward from the ventricular septal defect intersects the AV valve. The AV valve leaflets are divided along this line. The ventricular septal defect patch is placed. The valve leaflets are resuspended by sewing them to the ventricular septal defect patch. The competency of the valves is assessed. The atrial septal defect is closed with a patch sewn to the top of the ventricular septal defect patch or an extension of the ventricular septal defect patch is used to close the atrial septal defect (single patch technique). The hole in the right atrium is closed. Cardiopulmonary bypass is discontinued when cardiac function has returned.
- **Repair of intermediate or transitional atrioventricular canal:** Cardiopulmonary bypass is established with the venous uptake tubes in both the superior and inferior caval veins. A hole in the right atrium or, if needed, a hole in one of the ventricles is made. The hole in the ventricle is made in the area of scar (if the ventricular septal defect is due to ischemia) or in the anterior part of the right ventricle (if the

ventricular septal defect is congenital). The AV valve anatomy can be highly variable, ranging from normal mitral and tricuspid anatomy with a sub valvular ventricular septal defect to grossly abnormal AV valve leaflet number position, but with two separate "valve" present separated by a line of tissue. The AV valves are repaired. Repair is all that is done if valvular competence can be restored to the left AV valve. If not, this valve is replaced with a mechanical valve or a tissue valve.

- **Repair of ostium primum defect:** Cardiopulmonary bypass is established using venous uptake tubes in both the superior and inferior caval veins. The right atrium is opened. A radially oriented cleft or division in the anterior leaflet of the mitral valve is closed with the interrupted sutures. Care is taken to assure that the valve closes properly after it is repaired. There is a raphe or line of denser valve tissue marking the anatomic line between the two AR valves. The ventricular septal defect is obliterated by sewing this line to the top of the septal muscle. The arterial septal defect is closed with a patch of pericardium or other tissue graft. The right atrium is closed and cardiopulmonary pulmonary bypass discontinued after heart function is restored.

Coding Clarification
Code 35.63 excludes repair of isolated:

- Atrial septal defect (35.61)
- Valvular defect (35.20-35.21, 35.23, 35.25, 35.27)
- Ventricular septal defect (35.62)

Documentation Tip
Code 35.63 may be documented with the following terminology as a repair of:

- Atrioventricular canal
- Ostium primum defect
- Valvular defect associated with atrial and ventricular septal defects

35.7 Other and unspecified repair of atrial and ventricular septa

Description
This subcategory describes other repair of atrial and ventricular septa.

Coding Clarification
Code also cardiopulmonary bypass (extracorporeal circulation)(heart-lung machine) (39.61).

This subcategory includes codes for septal repair procedures not otherwise specified in subcategories 35.4-35.6.

35.70 Other and unspecified repair of unspecified septal defect of heart

Description
This procedure code describes other and unspecified repair of a septal defect.

Coding Clarification
This is a non-specific procedure code that should not be assigned for inpatient hospital admissions. The medical record should contain sufficient information to facilitate coding at a higher level of specificity.

Documentation Tip
Carefully review the documentation in the medical record to determine the anatomic site treated. If the documentation is ambiguous or unclear, the physician should be queried.

35.71 Other and unspecified repair of atrial septal defect

35.72 Other and unspecified repair of ventricular septal defect

35.73 Other and unspecified repair of endocardial cushion defect

Description
Codes 35.71-35.73 include other and unspecified repairs of atrial, ventricular, and endocardial cushion defects not otherwise specified. Those procedures that are further specified according to the presence of prosthesis or tissue graft are more appropriately classified in subcategories 35.4-35.6.

35.8 Total repair of certain congenital cardiac anomalies

Description
Subcategory 35.8 describes total repair procedures of specified congenital cardiac anomalies. These procedures employ multiple surgical techniques to correct complex conditions, depending on the nature of the anomaly.

Coding Clarification
Partial defect repairs are excluded from this subcategory, and more appropriately classified to the specific procedure.

35.81 Total repair of tetralogy of Fallot

Description
The physician completely repairs tetralogy of Fallot with or without pulmonary atresia, including construction of a conduit from the right ventricle to the pulmonary artery and closure of the ventricular septal defect. Cardiopulmonary bypass is required. A hole is made in the right ventricle and any muscular obstruction in the outflow tract of the right ventricle is removed. The pulmonary artery or its branches are opened longitudinally until normal-sized vessels

are encountered. The ventricular septal defect is closed. An aortic graft from an organ donor is trimmed to form a patch over the opened pulmonary artery. Any excess artery from the donor graft or a patch of pericardium or Dacron is sewn to the graft below the valve to use as a secondary patch for closing the hole in the right ventricle. The graft valve becomes the new pulmonary valve. After the patches and graft are sewn in place and heart function returns, cardiopulmonary bypass is stopped.

35.82 Total repair of total anomalous pulmonary venous connection

Description
The goal of total anomalous pulmonary venous repair procedures (TAPVR) is to return pulmonary vein blood to the left atrium where it can be pumped to the body. Pulmonary vein blood is replete with oxygen. The means by which this is done varies with whether the common vein and sinus (abnormal structures present only in these patients) returns above the heart, below the diaphragm, or at the level of the heart. Cardiopulmonary bypass is required. Sometimes, one pulmonary vein does not drain into the common vein or sinus. Usually, this is the left upper lobe vein. Its blood is directed into the left atrium by creating a connection between it and the left atrial appendage.

35.83 Total repair of truncus arteriosus

Description
The physician gains access to the mediastinum through an incision through the sternum (median sternotomy). The physician places cardiopulmonary bypass catheters usually through incisions in the right atrial appendage and aorta or femoral artery. The physician stops the heart by infusing cardioplegia solution into the coronary circulation. The physician applies a large Dacron patch to direct oxygenated blood from the left ventricle through the large ventricular septal defect into the aortic valve and ascending aorta. The physician ligates the proximal main pulmonary artery or oversews the pulmonic valve. The physician places a fabric conduit or a human cadaveric homograft to direct unoxygenated blood from the right ventricle to the branch pulmonary arteries after removing them from their origin(s) at the truncal vessel. The physician sews a pericardial patch in place to close the defect(s) in the truncal vessel. The physician may place a bioprosthetic valve in the pulmonary outflow conduit if the pulmonary vascular resistance is elevated. The physician closes the cardiac incisions, takes the patient off cardiopulmonary bypass, closes the remaining surgical incisions, and dresses the sternal or chest wall wound. The physician may leave chest tubes and/or a mediastinal drainage tube in place following the procedure.

● New Code ▲ Revised Code ▶◀ Revised Text © 2010 Ingenix

35.84 Total correction of transposition of great vessels, not elsewhere classified

Description
The physician gains access to the mediastinum through an incision through the sternum (median sternotomy). The physician places cardiopulmonary bypass catheters through incisions in the low inferior vena cava, the superior vena cava, and aorta or femoral artery. The physician stops the heart by infusing cardioplegia solution into the coronary circulation. The physician removes the pulmonary artery band placed during a previous surgery and dilates the pulmonary artery to normal size. If this is not possible, the physician removes the pulmonary band and constricted area of pulmonary artery, and applies a woven Dacron patch over the hole. The physician removes the coronary ostia from the aortic root and sews them into the root of the pulmonary trunk. The pulmonary trunk and aortic root are each transected and interchanged to direct blood from the pulmonary veins through the left ventricle to the aorta, and the systemic venous drainage to the pulmonary trunk via the right ventricle. The physician closes the cardiac incisions, takes the patient off cardiopulmonary bypass, closes the remaining surgical incisions, and dresses the sternal or chest wall wound. The physician may leave chest tubes and/or a mediastinal drainage tube in place following the procedure.

Coding Clarification
Code 35.84 excludes procedures documented as the following:

- Baffle operation [Mustard] [Senning] (35.91)
- Creation of shunt between right ventricle and pulmonary artery [Rastelli] (35.92)

35.9 Other operations on valves and septa of heart

Description
Subcategory 35.9 describes other operations on valves and septa of heart that are not more specifically classifiable elsewhere in category 35.

Coding Clarification
Code also cardiopulmonary bypass [extracorporeal circulation][heart-lung machine] (39.61).

35.91 Interatrial transposition of venous return

Description
The physician corrects blood flow by creating an intra-arterial baffle to correct great vessel transposition. The physician gains access to the mediastinum through an incision through the sternum (median sternotomy). The physician places cardiopulmonary bypass catheters through incisions in the low inferior vena cava, the superior vena cava, and the aorta or femoral artery. The physician stops the heart by infusing cardioplegia solution into the

coronary circulation. The physician excises the interatrial septum. The physician sews baffle material (pericardium or Dacron) to direct blood from the pulmonary veins to the right ventricle and the systemic venous drainage to the left ventricle. The physician may enlarge the pulmonary venous chamber with a woven Dacron or pericardial patch. The physician closes the cardiac incisions, takes the patient off cardiopulmonary bypass, closes the remaining surgical incisions, and dresses the sternal or chest wall wound. The physician may leave chest tubes and/or a mediastinal drainage tube in place following the procedure.

35.92 Creation of conduit between right ventricle and pulmonary artery

Description
Mechanical, extracorporeal circulation is established and the heart is stopped (cardiopulmonary bypass). A hole is made in the pulmonary artery. This last hole is enlarged to cross any areas of narrowing. A cadaver ascending aorta is trimmed to the right length. A tube of artery or Dacron is sewn to the valve end of the cadaver aorta. The cadaver artery is connected to the hole in the pulmonary artery. The tube of aorta or Dacron is sewn to the hole in the ventricle to close the hole and allow blood to flow through the new valved tube that now connects the ventricle to the pulmonary artery.

Coding Clarification
Code 35.92 excludes conduit creation associated with total repair truncus arteriosus (35.83).

Coding Guidance
AHA: 1Q, '07, 14

35.93 Creation of conduit between left ventricle and aorta

Description
Cardiopulmonary bypass is required. A hole is made in the tip of the left ventricle and another is made in the aorta above the coronary arteries. The conduit is oriented so that the valve in it will only let blood flow out of the heart, but not back in. One end of the conduit is sewn to the hole in the tip of the heart. The other end is sewn to the hole in the aorta. Air is removed from the heart and from the conduit. Cardiopulmonary bypass is discontinued when heart function returns.

Coding Guidance
AHA: 2Q, '09, 8

35.94 Creation of conduit between atrium and pulmonary artery

Description
The right pulmonary artery (or left in situs inverses) is exposed from the main pulmonary trunk to the

35-39

hilum of the lung. The superior vena cava is detached from the right atrium. The atrial hole is closed. A hole is made in the top part of the pulmonary artery and the cut end of the superior vena cava is connected to the hole in the pulmonary artery. Pulmonary blood flow comes directly from the venous system and bypasses the heart. Cardiopulmonary bypass with or without circulatory arrest is required. Blood flow is directed from the inferior caval vein, through a tunnel created inside the right atrium to the pulmonary artery. All systemic venous return is diverted away from the heart and directly into the pulmonary circulation. The right atrium is widely opened. A large patch of pericardium or Dacron is used for one wall of the tunnel. The lateral wall of the right atrium forms the other half of the tunnel. The tunnel leads from the inferior caval vein, where it joins the right atrium, to the undersurface of the pulmonary artery. The mouth of the tunnel is connected to a hole on the undersurface of the pulmonary artery.

Coding Clarification
This procedure may be performed at separate operative episodes as a staged procedure.

Documentation Tip
This procedure may be documented as a Fontan procedure.

35.95   Revision of corrective procedure on heart

Description
This procedure code describes a revision of a previous corrective heart procedure. Surgical technique varies depending on the procedure or device revised.

Coding Clarification
Code 35.95 includes:

- Replacement of prosthetic heart valve poppet
- Resutures of septal or valve prosthesis

Code 35.95 excludes complete revision or replacement of prosthesis or graft, which is coded to the specific revision procedure.

▲ 35.96   Percutaneous balloon valvuloplasty

Description
Procedures referred to as minimally invasive valvulotomy or balloon valvulotomy involve the use of an endoscope and inflatable balloon that are guided into the heart from a small incision in the chest through a long catheter. The balloon is used to widen the opening of the heart valve.

Valvuloplasty is a procedure for opening a blocked valve. The physician makes a small incision in the arm or leg. Two catheters are placed: a central venous catheter and a second catheter threaded up to the heart. The physician inflates a balloon at the

tip of the second catheter to open the blocked valve. The catheter is removed. Pressure is placed over the incision for 20 to 30 minutes to stem bleeding. The patient is placed on observation post-procedure.

Coding Clarification
►Code 35.96 excludes mitral valve repair with implant (35.97).◄

Documentation Tip
►Code 35.96 may be documented as mitral valve reconstruction by the Evalve® Cardiovascular Repair System or MitraClip® implant.◄

Coding Guidance
   AHA: N-D, '85, 10; M-J, '86, 6; ►3Q, '09, 19◄

● 35.97   Percutaneous mitral valve repair with implant

Description
►The American College of Cardiology and the American Heart Association recommend that mitral regurgitation (MR) be corrected surgically before disease progression leads to left ventricular dysfunction. However, due to the substantial risks associated with open heart mitral valve surgery, many patients are not surgical candidates and are treated medically. The MitraClip® percutaneous mitral valve implant is a minimally invasive transcatheter approach for intracardiac MR repair. Since the procedure is performed while the heart is beating, it is an alternative to the open heart surgical approach. The procedure is performed by interventional cardiologists in the cardiac catheterization laboratory or operating room. Surgical prep is similar to that for an open heart surgical mitral valve procedure. The left atrium is accessed by puncturing the interatrial septum with the use of a transseptal needle and sheath under fluoroscopic and continuous transesophageal echocardiographic (TEE) guidance. The patient is anticoagulated, and a 24 French steerable guide catheter-dilator assembly of the MitraClip system is advanced into the left atrium. The clip delivery system with the attached MitraClip implant is inserted through the steerable guide catheter. Using the steering controls on the guide catheter and the clip delivery system under careful manipulation, the MitraClip implant is precisely steered until it is axially aligned and centered over the origin of the regurgitant MR jet. The implant is advanced into the left ventricle and is retracted until the leaflets are grasped and then closed to bring the leaflets together. After adequate reduction of MR has been achieved and proper leaflet insertion is confirmed, the MitraClip implant is deployed and the clip delivery system and guide catheter are withdrawn. Approximately half of patients achieve adequate reduction of their MR with a single implant, while others may require a second.◄

● New Code   ▲ Revised Code   ►◄ Revised Text   © 2010 Ingenix

35-39

Coding Clarification
▶Code 35.97 includes endovascular mitral valve repair, implantation of mitral valve leaflet clip and transcatheter mitral valve repair.

Code also any transesophageal echocardiography (TEE) performed during the operative episode (88.72).

Code 35.97 excludes percutaneous balloon valvuloplasty performed (35.96).◀

Coding Scenario
▶A patient with nonrheumatic mitral valve regurgitation presents for percutaneous mitral valve repair with deployment of the MitraClip implant with TEE guidance.

Code Assignment:

424.0   Mitral valve disorders
35.97   Percutaneous mitral valve repair with implant
88.72   Diagnostic ultrasound of heart◀

35.98   Other operations on septa of heart

Description
This code describes other heart septa operations that cannot be more specifically classified to other codes within category 35.

Coding Clarification
This procedure code should not be assigned if the medical record contains sufficient information to facilitate coding at a higher level of specificity.

Documentation Tip
If the documentation is ambiguous or unclear, the physician should be queried.

Coding Guidance
  AHA: 1Q, '07, 11

35.99   Other operations on valves of heart

Description
This code reports other heart valve operations that cannot be more specifically classified to other codes within category 35.

Coding Clarification
This procedure code should not be assigned if the medical record contains sufficient information to facilitate coding at a higher level of specificity.

Documentation Tip
If the documentation is ambiguous or unclear, the physician should be queried.

36   Operations on the vessels of heart

Description
The blood vessels of the heart (coronary vessels) provide the oxygen-rich blood that the heart requires

to peform its primary function as a central pumping mechanism. Coronary veins collect deoxygenated blood from the heart muscle. Coronary arteries deliver blood to the heart muscle, and serve as the heart's only source of blood supply. Therefore, coronary artery blockages are critical and require emergent care.

Allowing for normal variations in anatomy, and those patients with congenital anomalies, the two main coronary vessels, the right coronary artery (RCA) and left coronary artery (LCA), branch into the vascular structures summarized below:

- **RCA:** The right coronary artery normally originates just below the sinotubular junction of the right (right anterior) sinus of Valsalva. It supplies the right ventricular wall, extending either posteriorly as far as the obtuse margin of the heart or, in most patients, the RCA supplies the posterior descending coronary artery, which then supplies the atrioventricular (AV) node and the posterior aspect of the interventricular septum. The RCA branches into:
  - conal or infundibular branch, which courses anteriorly to supply the muscular right ventricular outflow tract or infundibulum
  - small branches that supply blood to the atria
  - sinus node artery, which arises from the proximal RCA in approximately 50 percent of patients
- **LCA:** The left coronary artery normally originates at the left anterior portion of the sinus of Valsalva, behind the cusps of the aortic valve. The left coronary main branch is usually single, giving rise to a short, common trunk that branches into:
  - the left anterior descending (LAD)
  - the circumflex coronary arteries
  - anterior septal branches that extend to the cardiac apex
  - small branches that may arise from the LAD and supply the anterior wall of the right ventricle
  - diagonal branches: that arise from the LAD to supply the wall of the left ventricle
- **Cx:** The circumflex coronary artery extends long from the atrioventricular margin, the obtuse margin, and posteriorly toward the crux of the heart in circumference (hence, circumflex).The circumflex artery branches into:
  - atrial branches that supply the sinus
  - obtuse marginal branches that supply the left ventricle

– a coronary branch to supply an area between the LAD diagonal branches and obtuse branches

Ischemic heart disease refers to a group of conditions characterized by a decreased supply of blood to the heart. This restriction of blood is often referred to as an insufficiency. An insufficiency results from an obstruction or constriction of the coronary arteries or myocardium. Although the most common cause for coronary insufficiency has been attributed to arteriosclerosis, or coronary artery disease, other contributing factors to the development of ischemic heart disease include the secondary effects of infectious or inflammatory diseases and congenital anomalies of the heart or coronary vasculature.

Category 36 provides codes for obstruction removal, stent insertion, infusions, revascularizations, and other restorative and exploratory operations on heart vessels.

Coding Clarification
Codes in category 36 include those performed by the following surgical approaches:

• Median sternotomy

• Transverse sternotomy

• Thoracotomy

Code also any associated cardiopulmonary bypass [extracorporeal circulation] [heart-lung machine] (39.61).

Code also any associated procedures such as:

• Injection or infusion of platelet inhibitor (99.20)

• Injection or infusion of thrombolytic agent (99.10)

36.0 Removal of coronary artery obstruction and insertion of stent(s)

Description
This subcategory classifies removal of coronary obstructions by various surgical techniques and the insertion of stents (prosthetic devices that restore the vessel's patency).

Coding Guidance
AHA: N-D, '86, 8; 2Q, '90, 23; 1Q, '94, 3

36.03 Open chest coronary artery angioplasty

Description
The physician performs open-chest coronary artery vessel repair for removal of coronary artery obstruction. This operation is performed when a coronary artery is so full of disease along its length that a good site for sewing on the bypass graft cannot be found. Coronary artery bypass grafts are performed in association with the arterectomy. The coronary artery is opened along its length for a

distance greater than that usually opened for a bypass alone, along its entire length. The plaque within the artery is separated from the outer layer of the arterial wall with a tool designed for the purpose. The plaque is removed from as much of the artery as is possible. The rest of the hole is closed directly with suture or a patch of opened vein graft is laid over the open artery and sewn to the coronary artery wall to close the hole.

Coding Clarification
An open chest approach includes that by sternotomy (median) (transverse) or thoracotomy.

Code also:

• Insertion of drug-eluting coronary stent(s) (36.07)

• Insertion of non-drug eluting coronary stent(s) (36.06)

• Number of vascular stents inserted (00.45-00.48)

• Number of vessels treated (00.40-00.43)

• Procedure on vessel bifurcation (00.44)

Code 36.03 excludes coronary artery angioplasty with a bypass graft (36.10-36.19). If a coronary artery bypass graft (CABG) and endarterectomy are performed on the same vessel, report only the CABG (36.1x). If an endarterectomy is performed on a separate vessel from a bypassed vessel, then both the endarterectomy (36.03) and CABG (36.1x) should be reported.

Documentation Tip
This procedure may be documented as:

• Coronary endarterectomy (with patch graft)

• Thromboendarterectomy (with patch graft)

Coding Guidance
AHA: 3Q, '93, 7; 2Q, '01, 24

36.04 Intracoronary artery thrombolytic infusion

Description
The physician performs infusion of a thrombolytic (clot-dissolving) agent into a coronary artery. A small incision is made. The physician places a hollow catheter in the aorta from the arm or leg. Using fluoroscopic guidance, the physician advances the catheter tip to the coronary artery and confirms the presence of thrombus (blood clot) in the artery by injecting contrast material through the catheter into the artery. The physician infuses a thrombolytic agent (urokinase, for example) into the affected artery in order to dissolve the thrombus. The physician may perform contrast injections to assess the size and extent of the thrombus after infusion of the thrombolytic agent. The catheter is removed from the patient's body. Pressure is placed over the

incision for 20 to 30 minutes to stem bleeding. The patient is observed for a period afterward.

Coding Clarification
Code 36.04 includes direct coronary artery injection, infusion, or catheterization of a thrombolytic enzyme, platelet inhibitor, or other clot-dissolving agent.

Code 36.04 excludes peripheral vessel intravenous infusion of a thrombolytic agent.

When a thrombolytic intracoronary artery infusion is performed on the same vessel as an open chest coronary angioplasty (36.03), report only the angioplasty. The infusion is included in the angioplasty code.

Coding Guidance
AHA: 4Q, '95, 67; 1Q, '97, 3; 4Q, '98, 85; 2Q, '01, 24

36.06   Insertion of non-drug-eluting coronary artery stent(s)

Description
This code describes the percutaneous catheter-deployed implant of a non-drug eluting stent to restore patency to a blocked or collapsed blood vessel in the heart. The physician makes a small incision in the arm or leg. Two catheters are placed. A central venous catheter is inserted through the femoral or brachial artery and a second catheter is threaded up to the heart. Any obstruction is first treated by inflating a balloon at the tip of the second catheter (PTCA) and/or by using a rotary cutter (atherectomy) to flatten or remove the obstruction. A stent is introduced through a catheter and placed under radiographic guidance. Pressure is placed over the incision for 20 to 30 minutes to stem bleeding. The patient is placed on observation.

Coding Clarification
Code also:

- Percutaneous transluminal coronary angioplasty (00.66)
- Open chest coronary artery angioplasty (36.03)
- Coronary atherectomy (00.66)
- Number of vascular stents inserted (00.45-00.48)
- Number of vessels treated (00.40-00.43)
- Procedure on vessel bifurcation (00.44)

Code 36.06 excludes insertion of a drug-eluting coronary artery stent(s) (36.07)

Intravascular stents are tubular implants made of various synthetic materials, such as metal, mesh or plastic, designed to restore vessel patency and facilitate normal circulation. Stent procedures may be performed in the inpatient or outpatient setting by trained physicians or surgeons as an

interventional radiology or catheterization laboratory procedure. The stent is deployed via catheterization into the narrowed vessel.

Documentation Tip
Non-drug eluting stents may also be documented as:

- Bare stents
- Bonded stents
- Drug-coated stents
- Endografts or endovascular grafts
- Stent grafts

Coding Guidance
AHA: 1Q, '99, 17; 1Q, '00, 11; 2Q, '01, 24; 1Q, '01, 9; 4Q, '02, 101; 2Q, '09, 12

36.07   Insertion of drug-eluting coronary artery stent(s)

Description
This code describes the percutaneous, catheter-deployed implant of a drug-eluting stent to restore patency to a blocked or collapsed blood vessel in the heart. The physician makes a small incision in the arm or leg. Two catheters are placed. A central venous catheter is inserted through the femoral or brachial artery and a second catheter is threaded up to the heart. Any obstruction is first treated by inflating a balloon at the tip of the second catheter (PTCA) and/or by using a rotary cutter (atherectomy) to flatten or remove the obstruction. A stent is introduced through a catheter and placed under radiographic guidance. Pressure is placed over the incision for 20 to 30 minutes to stem bleeding. The patient is placed on observation.

Coding Clarification
Code also:

- Percutaneous transluminal coronary angioplasty or atherectomy (00.66)
- Open chest coronary artery angioplasty (36.03)
- Number of vascular stents inserted (00.45-00.48)
- Number of vessels treated (00.40-00.43)
- Procedure on vessel bifurcation (00.44)

Code 36.07 excludes drug-coated stents reportable with 36.06.

Drug-eluting stents slowly release certain anti-thrombus medication (Taxol, paclitaxel) in a controlled manner over a period of 30 to 45 days to assist in the prevention of scar tissue formation or restenosis of the vessel. Although the characteristics of the stent may vary according to the manufacturer, most drug-eluting stents (36.07) are coated with a layer of medication mixed with polymer. A diffusion barrier is placed over the coated stent to facilitate the sustained release of the drug over a period of time. By contrast, non-drug eluting coated stents (36.06) do not release a drug or medication, but are simply coated or bonded with a medication to prevent platelets from forming on the stent.

Documentation Tip
Drug-eluting stents may be documented as drug-eluting:

- Endografts or endovascular grafts
- Stent grafts

Coding Guidance
AHA: 4Q, '02, 101; 4Q, '05, 105-106

36.09   Other removal of coronary artery obstruction

Description
This code describes removal of coronary artery obstruction not otherwise specified in subcategory 36.0.

Coding Clarification
This code should not be assigned if the medical record contains sufficient information to facilitate coding at a higher level of specificity.

Documentation Tip
If the documentation is ambiguous or unclear, the physician should be queried.

36.1   Bypass anastomosis for heart revascularization

Description
This code subcategory classifies bypass anastomosis for coronary vessel revascularization. In the context of this subcategory, anastomosis may be defined as the surgical formation of a communication between vessels by connecting the one vessel to another. This anastomosis facilitates revascularization by the restoration of blood flow or blood supply to the heart.

Coding Clarification
▶A vein patch angioplasty may be performed when the surgeon determines that the current vessel bypass graft is of inadequate size. In these cases, do not assign a separate code for the vein patch angioplasty, as it is considered an inherent component of the CABG procedure.◀

Coding Guidance
AHA: 4Q, '89, 3; 2Q, '90, 24; 1Q, '91, 7; 3Q, '93, 8; 3Q, '95, 7; 2Q, '96, 7; 4Q, '07, 121; ▶1Q, '10, 9◀

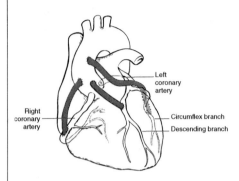

36.10   Aortocoronary bypass for heart revascularization, not otherwise specified

Description
This code describes a bypass for heart revascularization that is not further specified according to the specific anatomic vessels involved or the number of vessels bypassed.

The chest is opened via a midline sternotomy and the heart is examined by the surgeon. Vessels are harvested for formation of conduits. Common conduit grafts include the saphenous veins, internal thoracic arteries, and brachial and radial arteries. The surgeon stops the heart, initiates cardiopulmonary bypass, and places devices to stabilize the heart. One end of each graft is sewn onto the coronary arteries, bypassing the occluded segments. The other end is attached to the aorta. The heart is restarted and any stabilizing devices are removed. The sternotomy is wired together and the incisions are sutured closed.

Coding Clarification
This is a non-specific procedure code that should not be assigned if the medical record contains sufficient information to facilitate coding at a higher level of specificity.

Documentation Tip
If the documentation is ambiguous or unclear, the physician should be queried.

Coding Guidance
AHA: 2Q, '96, 7

● New Code   ▲ Revised Code   ▶◀ Revised Text   © 2010 Ingenix

36.11   (Aorto)coronary bypass of one coronary artery

36.12   (Aorto)coronary bypass of two coronary arteries

36.13   (Aorto)coronary bypass of three coronary arteries

36.14   (Aorto)coronary bypass of four or more coronary arteries

Description
Cardiopulmonary bypass is initiated with a single, two-stage venous uptake tube. Saphenous vein is harvested from either leg. Other arterial or vein graft may also be taken from the arm, the back of the leg, or from a cadaver. A clamp is placed on the aorta above the heart. Cold preserving solution is pumped through the coronary arteries to stop the heart. A point is chosen on the diseased coronary (arteries) beyond the area of disease and a longitudinal incision is cut in it. The proximal part of the graft is trimmed to the same length as the cut in the coronary artery and is cleaned off. One end of each graft is sewn onto the coronary arteries, bypassing the occluded segments and the other end is attached to the aorta. A 3 to 6 mm hole is punched in the ascending aorta and the other end of the vein graft is sewn to this hole. The clamp on the aorta is released. Cardiopulmonary bypass is discontinued when heart function returns.

Coding Guidance
AHA: 4Q, '89, 3; 2Q, '96, 7; 3Q, '97, 14; 4Q, '99, 15; 3Q, '02, 4, 6, 7, 8, 9; 4Q, '07, 122

36.15   Single internal mammary-coronary artery bypass

36.16   Double internal mammary-coronary artery bypass

Description
These procedures describe internal mammary-coronary artery bypass grafts. The internal mammary arteries (IMA), also known as the internal thoracic arteries (ITA), are paired vessels which extend parallel to the inside edge of the sternum to the left and right. These arteries supply the skeletal and soft tissues of the chest wall, and are significantly resistant to atherosclerosis. Due to the left internal mammary artery's (LIMA) proximity to the left anterior descending (LAD) artery, it can be readily transferred to the heart surface to use as a bypass graft. Therefore, the LIMA is commonly grafted to the left anterior descending (LAD) coronary artery.

Cardiopulmonary bypass is initiated with a single, two-stage venous uptake tube. A clamp is placed on the aorta above the heart. Cold preserving solution is

pumped through the coronary arteries to stop the heart. The IMA is detached with its origin left intact. A small opening is made in the coronary artery to be bypassed and the tip of the IMA is attached to this opening to create a bypass conduit. The clamp on the aorta is released. Cardiopulmonary bypass is discontinued when heart function returns.

Coding Guidance
AHA: 2Q, '96, 7; 3Q, '02, 5

36.17   Abdominal-coronary artery bypass

Description
The physician performs anastomosis of an abdominal artery to a coronary artery to create a bypass conduit. Cardiopulmonary bypass is initiated with a single, two-stage venous uptake tube. A clamp is placed on the aorta above the heart. Cold preserving solution is pumped through the coronary arteries to stop the heart. Arterial grafts are commonly obtained from the gastroepiploic, inferior epigastric, or other abdominal artery or vessel. A small opening is made in the coronary artery to be bypassed and the tip of the abdominal vessel is attached to this opening to create a bypass conduit. The clamp on the aorta is released. Cardiopulmonary bypass is discontinued when heart function returns.

Coding Guidance
AHA: 4Q, '96, 64; 3Q, '97, 14

36.19   Other bypass anastomosis for heart revascularization

Description
This code describes other specified bypass of coronary artery obstruction by vessel conduit-formation; creating an anastomosis between vessels to restore circulation.

Coding Clarification
This code should not be assigned if the medical record contains sufficient information to facilitate coding at a higher level of specificity.

Documentation Tip
If the documentation is ambiguous or unclear, the physician should be queried.

Coding Guidance
AHA: 2Q, '96, 7

36.2   Heart revascularization by arterial implant

Description
The physician performs an indirect anastomosis for revascularization of the heart whereby the aorta, internal mammary arteries, or other arteries are used to form a direct conduit to the heart wall, myocardium, or ventricle instead of a coronary artery. Cardiopulmonary bypass is initiated with a

single, two-stage venous uptake tube. A clamp is placed on the aorta above the heart. Cold preserving solution is pumped through the coronary arteries to stop the heart. The chosen vessel is grafted or otherwise implanted to the heart wall or other cardiac structure. A small opening is made in the heart and the tip of the vessel is implanted into this opening. The clamp on the aorta is released. Cardiopulmonary bypass is discontinued when heart function returns.

36.3   Other heart revascularization

Description

This subcategory includes heart revascularization by other methods than those classified elsewhere (bypass anastomosis or arterial implant) in category 36.

36.31   Open chest transmyocardial revascularization

Description

The physician performs transmyocardial laser revascularization to restore the flow of blood and oxygen to the heart. The procedure is frequently performed on the beating heart, although cardiopulmonary bypass may be initiated. In the beating heart, the physician uses a scalpel and makes a 10 to 15 cm incision on the left side of the chest between the ribs and exposes the surface of the heart. The area of ischemia (in still vital tissue) is identified. A laser is inserted through the chest opening and is fired (between heartbeats) through the filled left ventricle. Ten to 40 channels (small holes) are created to encourage new capillary growth in the area. As the channels are created, pressure is applied to each to help close the openings. When the procedure is complete, the laser is removed and the wound is closed with layered sutures. If cardiopulmonary bypass was initiated it is discontinued, the patient is rewarmed, and the heartbeat is restored.

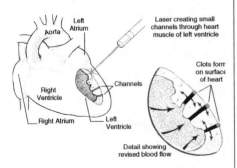

36.32   Other transmyocardial revascularization

Description

This procedure code describes other transmyocardial revascularization (TMR) by methods

or techniques other than those classified as open chest (36.31), endoscopic (36.33), or percutaneous (36.34).

Coding Clarification

This code should not be assigned if the medical record contains sufficient information to facilitate coding at a higher level of specificity.

Documentation Tip

If the documentation is ambiguous or unclear, the physician should be queried.

Coding Guidance

   AHA: 4Q, '98, 74

36.33   Endoscopic transmyocardial revascularization

36.34   Percutaneous transmyocardial revascularization

Description

These procedure codes describe a transmyocardial revascularization (TMR) procedure performed using the percutaneous or endocardial approach, in which the transmural channels are initiated at the endocardial surface and extended toward the pericardium using the laser.

The percutaneous, catheter-based transmyocardial revascularization procedure has been developed as an alternative approach to thoracotomy. Rather than utilizing an incision to access the heart, in this less invasive approach a laser-tipped catheter is inserted through the femoral artery and is advanced to the heart, where the laser forms small channels in the myocardium of the left ventricle. The trauma associated with open thoracic surgery is minimized, general anesthesia is not required, length of hospitalization is reduced, and there is decreased risk of serious complications.

The endoscopic technique employs the assistance of an endoscope for visualization of the heart, providing a minimally invasive alternative to the open-chest approach. Under general anesthesia, thoracoscopic ports are inserted through small incisions. An endoscope is utilized for visualization, using a single channel for 2-D (thoracoscopic) vision or a dual channel for 3-D (robotic) vision. Pleural adhesions are lysed if present, the pericardium is opened and scar tissue is divided, and the laser energy is used to create transmyocardial channels in the left ventricular wall. This method permits a broader selection of patients, including those considered unsuitable for sternotomy or thoracotomy approaches. Advantages to this approach include a shorter recovery period.

Coding Scenario

A 70-year-old male with diagnosed coronary artery disease has had increasing instances of unstable

● New Code   ▲ Revised Code   ▶◀ Revised Text   © 2010 Ingenix

angina over the past year. Because of multiple comorbidities, he was considered high risk for coronary artery bypass grafting. Decision was made to treat with endoscopic transmyocardial revascularization. Under general anesthesia, he was placed in the right lateral decubitus position with independent lung ventilation. Via small (<3 cm) incisions, four thoracoscopic ports were placed. Visualization took place through the endoscope utilizing a single channel for 2-D (thoracoscopic) vision. No pleural adhesions were observed. The pericardium was opened and the scar tissue divided to expose the surface of the heart. Subsequently, transmyocardial channels were formed in the left ventricular free wall with laser energy. Once hemostasis was achieved, drains were placed, the endoscopic equipment removed, and the port sites closed. There were no complications.

> Code Assignment:
>
> 414.01   Coronary atherosclerosis of native coronary artery
> 411.1   Intermediate coronary syndrome
> 36.33   Endoscopic transmyocardial revascularization

Coding Guidance
   AHA: 4Q, '06, 127

36.39   Other heart revascularization

Description
This code describes other heart revascularization procedures not classifiable elsewhere in category 36. Surgical techniques vary, including:

- **Cardio-omentopexy:** The omental graft is excised after drawing a segment through an incision in the diaphragm. The physician sutures a segment of the omentum to the heart to improve blood supply.

- **Intrapericardial poudrage:** The physician applies powder to the heart lining to promote fusion.

36.9   Other operations on vessels of heart

Description
This subcategory includes other operations on the heart that are not classifiable elsewhere in category 36, including repair of a coronary artery aneurysm or arteriovenous fistula.

Coding Clarification
Code also any associated cardiopulmonary bypass [extracorporeal circulation] [heart-lung machine] (39.61).

36.91   Repair of aneurysm of coronary vessel

Description
This procedure code describes repair of a coronary vessel aneurysm by surgical technique other than

bypass revascularization or stent insertion. Cardiopulmonary bypass may be initiated. The site of the aneurysm has been previously determined by cardiac catheterization. Surgical approach may vary. The physician may expose the heart by midline sternotomy if an open chest approach is utilized. The physician repairs an aneurysm of the coronary artery by excision of the diseased segment of artery and reapproximation of the viable ends of the vessel with sutures. Cardiopulmonary bypass is discontinued. The heart is restarted and any stabilizing devices are removed. The sternotomy is wired together and the incisions are sutured closed.

36.99   Other operations on vessels of heart

Description
This code describes other operations on the heart vessels not classifiable elsewhere in category 36, including fistula repair. Cardiopulmonary bypass is initiated. The site of the fistula has been previously determined by cardiac catheterization. The venous end of the fistula is ligated with sutures. Cardiopulmonary bypass is often discontinued. If the fistula is to a cardiac chamber, that chamber is opened and the chamber end of the fistula is closed with a stitch.

Coding Clarification
Code 36.99 includes coronary artery:

- Repair by direct suture
- Exploration
- Incision
- Ligation
- Repair of arteriovenous fistula

Coding Guidance
   AHA: 1Q,'94, 3; 3Q, '03, 18

37   Other operations on heart and pericardium

Description
Category 37 includes other operations on the heart and pericardium not classifiable to categories 35-36, including punctures, incisions, catheter-based interventional procedures, biopsies, excisions, implantations, and other repairs.

Coding Clarification
Code also any injection or infusion of platelet inhibitor (99.20).

37.0   Pericardiocentesis

Description
The physician drains fluid from the pericardial space. The physician may perform this procedure using anatomic landmarks or under fluoroscopic or

35-39

echocardiographic (ultrasound) guidance. The physician places a long needle below the sternum and directs it into the pericardial space. When pericardial fluid is aspirated, the physician may advance a guidewire through the needle into the pericardial space and exchange the needle over the guidewire for a drainage catheter. The physician removes as much pericardial fluid as is required, removes the needle or catheter, and dresses the wound.

Coding Guidance
   AHA: 1Q, '07, 11

37.1   Cardiotomy and pericardiotomy
Description
This subcategory classifies incision procedures into the heart or pericardium.

Coding Clarification
Code also any associated cardiopulmonary bypass [extracorporeal circulation] [heart-lung machine] (39.61).

37.10   Incision of heart, not otherwise specified
Description
This procedure code describes an incision into the heart.

Coding Clarification
This is a nonspecific code that should not be assigned if the medical record contains sufficient information to facilitate coding at a higher level of specificity.

Documentation Tip
If the documentation is ambiguous or unclear, the physician should be queried.

37.11   Cardiotomy
Description
This code reports an incision into the heart. Cardiotomy may be performed for foreign body removal or other diagnostic or therapeutic intervention. Cardiopulmonary bypass may be necessary. The physician exposes the heart via the sternum and makes an incision into the heart. If the cardiotomy is to facilitate removal of a foreign body, the foreign body is located by feeling the heart. If possible, the object is removed from the surface of the heart. A hole may be made in one of the ventricles or atria to remove an object or thrombus lodged there. The holes are closed with sutures and small reinforcing patches of Teflon felt.

37.12   Pericardiotomy
Description
The physician may remove a clot, foreign body, or fluid collection from the pericardial space by

incision. The physician performs a midline sternotomy, incising skin, fascia, and the sternum. The pericardium is incised. The pericardium is repaired loosely, leaving gaps for blood and fluid to drain into the pleural space. A tube may be placed to facilitate drainage. The sternum is re-anastomosed with sternal wires and the skin is sutured in layers.

37.2   Diagnostic procedures on heart and pericardium
Description
This subcategory includes diagnostic procedures on the heart and pericardium, including biopsy, echocardiography, cardiac catheterization, and other procedures.

37.20   Noninvasive programmed electrical stimulation [NIPS]
Description
Full scale EPS is an invasive diagnostic procedure that involves threading specialized catheters into the chambers of the heart in order to assess the heart's electrical activity. The identification of inducible arrhythmias is important in determining appropriate treatment, such as the need for a defibrillator. It is also a useful tool in deciding what type of device is chosen, and how it is programmed.

In comparison, NIPS is noninvasive and is performed in order to test a cardioverter-defibrillator that was previously implanted. During this procedure, the patient is sedated, arrhythmia is induced, and the defibrillation thresholds are monitored. The purpose of this study is to ensure that the cardioverter-defibrillator (ICD) and ICD leads are positioned well and working properly, to guarantee proper function of this device in the future. The physician records cardiac electrical signals from the leads and paces the heart through the leads to determine pacing threshold. The physician uses the ICD pulse generator to pace the heart into an arrhythmia, such as ventricular tachycardia or fibrillation. The ICD detects and terminates the arrhythmia using pacing or shocking the heart through the ICD lead. The physician may reprogram the ICD treatment parameters to optimize the device function to best treat the patient's arrhythmia.

Coding Clarification
Code 37.20 excludes the following procedures:

- Catheter based invasive electrophysiologic testing (37.26)
- Device interrogation only without arrhythmia induction (bedside check) (89.45-89.49)
- That as part of intraoperative testing—omit code

● New Code   ▲ Revised Code   ▶◀ Revised Text   © 2010 Ingenix

Coding Scenario
A 68-year-old male underwent ICD implantation last year for primary prevention of sudden cardiac death. However, with defibrillation threshold testing at increasing outputs he had high defibrillation thresholds and required external shocks. He is referred at this time for noninvasive assessment of defibrillation threshold testing before consideration of alternative options for device configuration. After informed consent was obtained, the patient was transported to the EP lab in a fasting, non-sedated state where baseline rhythm, heart rate, oxygen saturation, and blood pressure were monitored. General induction anesthesia was administered by the anesthesia staff with IV propofol. Induction of ventricular fibrillation was performed noninvasively with T-wave shocks through the device. VF was induced and converted cleanly with a single biphasic 30-joule shock. No further defibrillation threshold testing was performed. The patient was awakened, exhibited no complications, and was returned to the Heart Institute for observation prior to discharge.

Code Assignment:

V53.32 Fitting and adjustment of implantable cardiac defibrillator
37.20 Noninvasive programmed electrical stimulation

Coding Guidance
AHA: 4Q, '06, 128

37.21   Right heart cardiac catheterization

Description
The physician threads a catheter to the heart most frequently through an introducing sheath placed percutaneously or by cutdown into the femoral vein. However, the physician may elect to use the subclavian, internal jugular, or antecubital vein instead. The catheter is threaded into the right atrium, through the tricuspid valve into the right ventricle, and across the pulmonary valve into the pulmonary arteries. ECG monitoring for the entirety of the procedure is included. Blood samples, pressure and electrical recordings, and/or other tests are performed through the catheter. This code applies to catheterizing the heart's right side only.

Coding Clarification
Right heart cardiac catheterization includes the study of the right atrium and ventricle, the tricuspid and pulmonic valves, the main pulmonary artery and its branches, and the superior and inferior vena cava.

Code 37.21 includes cardiac catheterization NOS.

Code 37.21 excludes that with catheterization of the left heart (37.23).

Code also any associated angiocardiography (88.40-88.49).

Diagnostic cardiac catheterizations (37.21-37.23) include:

• Recording of intracardiac and intravascular pressures
• Tracings
• Obtaining blood samples for measurement of blood gases
• Measuring cardiac output (dye dilution, Fick, or other method)

Coding Guidance
AHA: M-J, '87, 11; 2Q, '90, 23; 3Q, '03, 9; 3Q, '04, 10

37.22   Left heart cardiac catheterization

Description
The physician threads a catheter to the heart most frequently through an introducing sheath placed percutaneously or by cutdown into the femoral, brachial, or axillary artery using retrograde technique. Using this technique, the catheter passes through the aortic valve into the left ventricle. Blood samples, pressure and electrical recordings, and/or other tests are performed. ECG monitoring for the entirety of the procedure is included.

Coding Clarification
Left heart cardiac catheterization includes the study of the left atrium and ventricle, the mitral and aortic valves, the ascending left aorta, and possibly the pulmonary veins.

Code 37.22 excludes that with catheterization of the right heart (37.23).

Code also any associated angiocardiography (88.40-88.49).

Diagnostic cardiac catheterizations (37.21-37.23) include:

• Recording of intracardiac and intravascular pressures
• Tracings
• Obtaining blood samples for measurement of blood gases
• Measuring cardiac output (dye dilution, Fick, or other method)

Coding Guidance
AHA: M-J, '87, 11; 4Q, '88, 4; 2Q, '90, 23; 1Q, '00, 21; 2Q, '04, 3; 3Q, '04, 10; 3Q, '05, 14; 4Q, '05, 71; ▶2Q, '10, 9◀

37.23   Combined right and left heart cardiac catheterization

Description
This procedure is performed to evaluate both right and left heart function. To accomplish right heart catheterization, the physician threads a catheter through an introducing sheath placed percutaneously into the femoral, subclavian, internal jugular, or antecubital vein. The catheter is threaded into the right atrium, through the tricuspid valve into the right ventricle, and across the pulmonary valve into the pulmonary arteries. Left heart catheterization is also performed in this case using retrograde technique. The catheter is inserted through an introducing sheath placed percutaneously into the femoral, brachial, or axillary artery. The catheter is passed through the aortic valve into the left ventricle. ECG monitoring for the entirety of the procedure is included. Blood samples, pressure and electrical recordings, and/or other tests are performed through the catheter.

Coding Clarification
Combined right and left heart cardiac catheterization is a single procedure with study and evaluation of both right and left heart.

Code also any associated angiocardiography (88.50-88.58).

Diagnostic cardiac catheterizations (37.21-37.23) include:

* Recording of intracardiac and intravascular pressures
* Tracings
* Obtaining blood samples for measurement of blood gases
* Measuring cardiac output (dye dilution, Fick, or other method)

Coding Guidance
AHA: M-J, '87, 11; 2Q, '90, 23; 3Q, '98, 11; 1Q, '00, 20; 2Q, '01, 8; 3Q, '04, 10; 2Q, '05, 17; 1Q, '07, 11

37.24   Biopsy of pericardium

Description
This procedure code describes a biopsy of the pericardium; the protective outer membrane surrounding the heart. A portion of tissue is excised for diagnostic purposes. The tissue may be obtained by incision (open approach) or by thoracoscopy (endoscopic approach).

A biopsy by thoracoscopic approach is obtained by the physician examining the inside of the chest cavity through a rigid or flexible fiberoptic endoscope. The procedure can be done under local or general anesthesia. The surgeon makes a small incision between two ribs and by blunt dissection

and the use of a trocar enters the thoracic cavity. The endoscope is passed through the trocar and into the chest cavity. The pericardium is visualized and a portion of tissue is obtained with transendoscopic forceps or other sharp instrumentation. At the conclusion of the procedure, the endoscope and the trocar are removed. A chest tube for drainage and re-expansion of the lung is usually inserted through the wound used for the thoracoscopy.

37.25   Biopsy of heart

Description
The physician threads a catheter to the heart through a central intravenous line often inserted up the femoral vein to take tissue samples of the heart's septum.

Coding Clarification
Code 37.25 includes the heart catheterization used as the operative approach for this procedure. The heart catheterization is not reported separately.

Report any other associated procedures (e.g., Swan-Ganz).

Coding Guidance
AHA: 3Q, '94, 8; 3Q, '03, 16

37.26   Catheter based invasive electrophysiologic testing

Description
Electrophysiologic studies use electric stimulation and monitoring in the diagnosis of conduction abnormalities that predispose patients to bradyarrhythmias and to determine a patient's chance of developing ventricular and supraventricular tachyarrhythmias. The physician inserts an electrode catheter percutaneously into the right subclavian vein and, under fluoroscopic guidance, positions the electrode catheter at the right ventricular apex, both for recording and stimulating the right atrium and the right ventricle. A second electrode catheter is inserted percutaneously into the right femoral vein and positioned across the tricuspid valve for recording the His bundle electrogram.

For intra-atrial pacing, the physician attaches the catheter to an electrical pacing device to allow transmission of pacing impulses through the catheter to the right atrium. The physician may pace the left atrium by placing the catheter in the coronary sinus or by crossing the interatrial septum. Alternatively, the physician may pace the left atrium by placing an arterial catheter into the aorta and crossing both the aortic and mitral valves in a retrograde fashion.

For intraventricular pacing, the physician attaches the catheter to an electrical pacing device to allow

● New Code   ▲ Revised Code   ▶◀ Revised Text   © 2010 Ingenix

transmission of pacing impulses through the catheter to the right ventricle. Alternatively, the physician may pace the left ventricle by placing the catheter in the right atrium, crossing the intraatrial septum and mitral valve. Finally, the physician may pace the left ventricle by advancing a catheter through an arterial sheath, via the aorta, across the aortic valve into the left ventricle.

For comprehensive EPS evaluation with atrial and ventricular pacing, the physician places three venous sheaths, usually in one or both femoral veins, using standard techniques. The physician advances three electrical catheters through the venous sheaths and into the right heart under fluoroscopic guidance. The physician attaches the three catheters to an electrical recording device to allow depiction of the intracardiac electrograms obtained from electrodes on the catheter tips.

Coding Clarification
Code 37.26 excludes:

- Device interrogation only without arrhythmia induction (bedside check) (89.45-89.49)

- HIS bundle recording (37.29)

- Non-invasive programmed electrical stimulation (NIPS) (37.20)

- That as part of intraoperative testing—omit code

Documentation Tip
The bedside check of an implantable automatic cardioverter/defibrillator (AICD) differs from an EPS study because the bedside check is a test performed on the AICD device; however, the EPS study is a test performed on the patient's heart.

Coding Guidance
   AHA: 3Q, 03, 23

37.27   Cardiac mapping
Description
The physician may place pacing or mapping catheters inside the heart prior to or during surgery using a standard transvenous approach. Additionally, the surgeon will place electrical probes on the outside (epicardium) of the heart in order to allow additional mapping. The physician attaches the catheters and probes to an electrical recording device to allow depiction of the electrograms obtained from electrodes on the catheter and probe tips. The surgeon's electrical probe can be moved around the outside of the heart to allow comparison of electrical activation times from different regions. The physician may attach the catheters to an electrical pacing device to allow transmission of pacing impulses through the catheters to the different heart chambers. The physician may stimulate the heart with rapid pacing or

programmed electrical stimulation in an attempt to induce an arrhythmia.

An electrode catheter may be inserted percutaneously from the right femoral artery and advanced into the left ventricle. Ventricular tachycardia is induced by programmed ventricular stimulation from both the right and left ventricular apexes. The earliest activation site is determined and the diastolic pressure is recorded on the endocardial activation map during the ventricular tachycardia. Intracardiac electrograms with surface electrocardiograms are simultaneously displayed and recorded on a multichannel oscilloscopic photographic recorder.

Coding Clarification
Code also any associated or complementary procedure.

Code 37.27 excludes electrocardiogram (89.52) and HIS bundle recording (37.29).

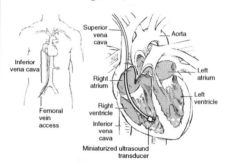

37.28   Intracardiac echocardiography
Description
During separately reportable electrophysiologic evaluation or intracardiac catheter ablation of arrhythmogenic focus, intracardiac echocardiography (ICE) is performed. ICE uses intravascular ultrasound imaging systems in the cardiac chambers providing direct endocardial visualization. A single rotating transducer that provides a 360-degree field of view in a plane transverse to the long axis of the catheter is introduced through a long vascular sheath. Access is typically via the femoral vein. The transducer is directed to various sites within the heart. During electrophysiologic evaluation, ICE is used to guide placement of mapping and stimulating catheters. During intracardiac ablation procedures, ICE allows for precise anatomic localization of the ablation catheter tip in relation to endocardial structures. Since the focus of some arrhythmias can be anatomically determined, it also allows the ablative procedure to be performed using anatomic landmarks.

35-39

Coding Clarification
Code 37.28 excludes intravascular imaging of coronary vessels (intravascular ultrasound) (IVUS) (00.24)

Intracardiac echocardiography (ICE) differs from IVUS (00.24) by the tools utilized, and the imaging that ICE allows that provide real-time visualization of the entire heart. IVUS is used only in target peripheral vessels and coronary arteries.

Documentation Tip
This procedure may also be documented as:

- Echocardiography of heart chambers
- ICE

Code also any synchronous Doppler flow mapping (88.72).

Coding Guidance
AHA: 4Q, '01, 62

37.29   Other diagnostic procedures on heart and pericardium

Description
This code describes other diagnostic heart and pericardium procedures not classified elsewhere in subcategory 37.2.

Bundle of His recordings may be obtained as part of a comprehensive EPS evaluation with atrial and ventricular pacing whereby the physician places three venous sheaths, usually in one or both femoral veins, using standard techniques. The physician advances three electrical catheters through the venous sheaths and into the right heart under fluoroscopic guidance. The physician attaches the three catheters to an electrical recording device to allow depiction of the intracardiac electrograms obtained from electrodes on the catheter tips. The physician moves the tips of the three catheters to the right atrium, the bundle of His, and the right ventricle and obtains recording.

Coding Clarification
Code 37.29 lists multiple exclusions. Before reporting 37.29, confirm that there is no other more specific code available.

37.3   Pericardiectomy and excision of lesion of heart

Description
This subcategory describes excisions of lesions of the heart or excisions of the pericardium (the outer protective membrane encasing the heart).

Coding Clarification
Code also any cardiopulmonary bypass [extracorporeal circulation] [heart-lung machine] (39.61) ▶if performed.◀

37.31   Pericardiectomy

Description
This code describes excision of pericardial tissue, by a thoracoscopic (endoscopic) or open (incisional) approach.

In an endoscopic approach, the physician removes the pericardial sac through a rigid or flexible fiberoptic endoscope. The physician makes a small incision between two ribs and by blunt dissection and the use of a trocar enters the thoracic cavity. The endoscope is passed through the trocar and into the chest cavity. The lung is usually partially collapsed by instilling air into the chest through the trocar, or the lung may be collapsed through a double lumen endotracheal tube inserted through the mouth into the trachea. The endoscope is advanced to and into the pericardial sac as the physician views the structures and the anatomy of the area through the scope. The contents of the pericardial sac are examined by direct visualization and/or by the use of a video camera. Still photographs may be taken as part of the procedure. Using instruments introduced through a second and/or third wound in the chest, and manipulated by direct vision through the endoscope, the physician removes the pericardial sac. At the conclusion of the procedure, the endoscope and the trocar are withdrawn. A chest tube for drainage and re-expansion of the lung is usually inserted through the wound used for the thoracoscopy.

In an open approach, the physician gains access to the pericardium through an incision through the sternum (median sternotomy). The physician cuts away most or all of the pericardial tissue while the heart is still beating (without cardiopulmonary bypass), taking care to leave the phrenic nerves intact. The physician closes the sternal or chest wall incision and dresses the wound. The physician may leave chest tubes and/or a mediastinal drainage tube in place following the procedure.

Coding Clarification
Code 37.21 includes excision of pericardial or epicardial adhesions or constrictive scar tissue.

37.32   Excision of aneurysm of heart

Description
The physician performs excision or repair of an aneurysm of the heart, which may be performed in conjunction with coronary artery bypass grafting. Prior to placing the bypass grafts, or as the primary procedure, the aneurysm is opened and any clot is removed from the ventricle. The aneurysm is opened widely, but not excised. The hole created by opening the aneurysm is closed with sutures directly or with a patch of Gortex, for example, or Dacron sewn into the hole. All stitches are placed in healthy (not

aneurysm) heart tissue and care is taken to avoid the coronary arteries.

37.33   Excision or destruction of other lesion or tissue of heart, open approach

Description
An open excision or destruction of a lesion or tissue of the heart may be performed utilizing various surgical techniques, depending on the nature and location of the lesion or tissue.

For excision of an intracardiac tumor, the physician gains access to the pericardium through an incision through the sternum (median sternotomy) or the chest wall (lateral thoracotomy). The physician places cardiopulmonary bypass catheters usually through incisions in the right atrial appendage and aorta or femoral artery. The physician stops the heart by infusing cardioplegia solution into the coronary circulation. The physician cuts away the pericardial cyst or tumor while the heart is still. The physician takes the patient off cardiopulmonary bypass, closes the surgical incisions, and dresses the sternal or chest wall wound. The physician may leave chest tubes and/or a mediastinal drainage tube in place following the procedure.

For resection of an external cardiac tumor, cardiopulmonary bypass is employed. Venous tubes are placed in both caval veins. The part of the heart that is opened depends on where the tumor is located. Every effort is made to avoid making an incision in any ventricular wall. After the heart is opened, the tumor is resected with a margin of normal heart tissue. Any problems created by this resection (damage to heart valves, holes in the walls between heart chambers or the outside of the heart, or injury to coronary arteries) are repaired. All holes in the heart are closed. Cardiopulmonary bypass is stopped when heart function returns.

In operative ablation procedures of arrhythmogenic focus, cardiopulmonary bypass may be required. The heart is exposed through the sternum. A mapping grid of electrodes is placed over the surface of the beating heart. The location of the arrhythmia source is determined. The source is destroyed using electrical current, freezing, or cutting. Any bleeding is controlled with sutures. The right atrium may be opened and a long cut made around the tricuspid valve until the cut on the outside of the heart is seen. Any other focuses of the arrhythmia are destroyed with electrical current or freezing. The right atrium is closed. The chest is closed. Cardiopulmonary bypass is discontinued when heart function returns.

The physician may perform operative ablation and reconstruction of the atria to treat arrhythmias. In a maze procedure, the physician seeks to permanently interrupt aberrant electrical conduction within the atria to restore normal sinus rhythm. The physician performs a midline sternotomy, incising the skin, fascia, muscles, and sternum. The pericardium is incised and an incision is made into the left or right atrium. A combination of surgical incision and/or energy sources such as heat, microwave, laser, ultrasound, or cryoprobe is used to create lesions that will heal into scars that disrupt conduction. In an extensive procedure, the right and/or left atrial tissue and/or atrial septum is treated and additional operative ablation involving the atrioventricular annulus is performed. In any of these procedures, the left atrial appendage may be excised or isolated. Lines may be placed for cardiopulmonary bypass. When cardiopulmonary bypass is achieved, an extensive ablation and reconstruction procedure is performed. The atrial incision lines are reanastomosed. The pericardium is repaired loosely, leaving gaps for blood and fluid to drain into the pleural space. The sternum is reanastomosed with sternal wires and the skin is sutured in layers.

Coding Clarification
Code 37.33 excludes such procedures performed by endovascular approach (37.34) ▶and thoracoscopic approach (37.37).◀

Code 37.33 is not used to report excision or destruction of left atrial appendage (LAA); rather, report code 37.36.

The Maze procedure is so named because the treatment creates lines of conduction block in the heart, similar to a maze. The classic maze procedure involves creating the maze lines with sharp scalpel incision, resulting in scar tissue formation and subsequent therapeutic conduction block. The incision method proved to be a lengthy, demanding, highly-invasive procedure. Surgical techniques have evolved from surgical incisions to tissue ablation by energy sources such as radiofrequency, laser, and cryoablation to create the conduction blocks.

Documentation Tip
Procedures classified to 37.33 may be documented as:

*   Cox-maze procedure

*   Modified open maze procedure

*   Transaortic septal myomectomy

Coding Guidance
   AHA: 2Q,'94, 12; 4Q, '03, 93-94; 3Q, '06, 13

▲ 37.34   Excision or destruction of other lesion or tissue of heart, endovascular approach

Description
The physician performs endoscopic, endovascular, or catheter-based operative ablation or other

Coders' Desk Reference for ICD-9-CM Procedures

destruction of heart tissues or lesions to correct arrhythmia.

By endoscopic approach, the physician seeks to permanently interrupt aberrant electrical conduction within the atria to restore normal sinus rhythm. Through multiple endoscopic incisions in the chest, the physician accesses and visualizes the outer (epicardial) surface of the heart. For a limited or modified maze procedure performed endoscopically, the pulmonary veins or other anatomically defined triggers are isolated in the left or right atrium and a heat, microwave, laser, ultrasound, or cryoprobe is used to create lesions from the outside of the left atrium that will heal into scars that disrupt conduction. The right and/or left atrial tissue and/or atrial septum may be so treated, and additional operative ablation involving the atrioventricular annulus may be performed. In either of these procedures, the left atrial appendage may be excised or isolated. Once sufficient interruption of electrical conduction has been accomplished, the endoscope is removed and access incisions are sutured in layers.

By catheter-based approach, the physician places a venous sheath, usually in a femoral vein, using standard techniques. The physician advances an electrical catheter through the venous sheath and into the right heart under fluoroscopic guidance. The physician attaches the catheter to an electrical recording device to allow depiction of the intracardiac electrograms obtained from electrodes on the catheter tip. The physician moves the catheter tip to the bundle of His, on the anteroseptal tricuspid annulus, and obtains recordings. Alternatively, the physician may obtain similar recordings by placing a catheter into the left ventricular outflow tract via the aorta. The physician maps the His bundle area and ablates the His bundle by sending cautery (radiofrequency) current through the catheter. The physician may also place a temporary pacing catheter in the right ventricle for this procedure.

Coding Clarification
▶Code 37.34 excludes ablation, excision, or destruction of lesion of heart tissue by open approach (37.33) or thoracoscopic approach (37.37).◀

Tissue ablation by endovascular (also "percutaneous") approach enables the physician to accomplish similar goals as in the maze procedure (37.33), but by isolating a smaller area. This approach allows precision location of the area of the heart that is producing the arrhythmia.

Code 37.34 includes such procedures performed by endovascular approach or peripherally-inserted catheter.

Documentation Tip
Procedures classified to 37.34 may be documented as:

- Pulmonary vein ablation
- Modified maze procedure, ▶percutaneous◀ approach

Coding Guidance
AHA: 1Q, '00, 20; 4Q, '03, 93-95

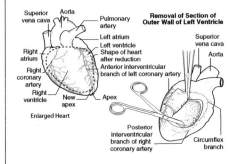

37.35   Partial ventriculectomy

Description
The physician may perform a surgical ventricular restoration (SVR) procedure to treat congestive heart failure subsequent to a myocardial infarction that has caused scarring or aneurysm of the left ventricle resulting in an enlarged rounded heart. SVR restores the heart to a more normal size and shape thereby improving function. Cardiopulmonary bypass is initiated. The ventricle is collapsed. A small incision is made in the bottom of the left ventricle through the scar tissue. The heart is opened and the area between the scar and the good heart muscle is identified. Using a plastic model of the heart selected based on the body surface area of the patient, the physician reshapes the heart. Rather than closing the defect, the physician sutures a patch over the defect to restore the normal spherical shape of the heart.

Coding Clarification
This procedure is often performed for patients with end-stage congestive heart failure that may be caused by idiopathic dilated cardiomyopathy, myocardial infarction or other ventricular aneurysm, hypertrophy, or scarring. SVR may be performed as an alternative for some patients in lieu of heart transplant.

Code also any synchronous mitral valve repair (35.02, 35.12) or replacement (35.23-35.24).

Documentation Tip
Procedures classified to 37.35 may be documented as:

- Batista procedure

35-39

320   ● New Code   ▲ Revised Code   ▶◀ Revised Text   © 2010 Ingenix

- Ventricular reduction surgery
- Ventricular remodeling

Coding Guidance
AHA: 4Q, '97, 54-55

37.36 Excision or destruction of left atrial appendage (LAA)

Description
To surgically close the left atrial appendage (LAA), the surgeon uses a surgical stapler, clip, or suture to pull together the walls of the LAA to permanently close the opening from the left atrium.
Cardiovascular surgeons routinely perform closure of the left atrial appendage during major cardiovascular procedures such as coronary artery bypass graft, mitral valve repair, and maze procedures. In patients with atrial fibrillation, prophylactic left atrial appendage removal or exclusion is recommended whenever the chest has been opened for another cardiovascular procedure to prevent future strokes.

Coding Clarification
Also code any concomitant procedure performed; however, do use this code to report ablation, excision or destruction of lesion or tissue of heart via an endovascular approach (37.34).

Documentation Tip
To ensure accurate code assignment, review the medical record documentation carefully to determine the operative approach (thoracoscopic approach, minithoracotomy approach) and surgical technique (clipping, exclusion, oversewing, or stapling of left atrial appendage).

Coding Scenario
A patient with atrial fibrillation that is unresponsive to anticoagulation therapy is admitted for thoracotomy to occlude the LAA. Under direct visualization using a small left anterior thoracotomy, the physician exposes the heart through the fourth intercostal interspace. The physician uses a clip to occlude the LAA to interrupt the abnormal atrial conduction causing the patient's atrial fibrillation.

Code Assignment:

427.31 Atrial fibrillation
37.36 Excision or destruction of left atrial appendage (LAA)

Coding Guidance
AHA: 4Q, '08, 182

● 37.37 Excision or destruction of other lesion or tissue of heart, thoracoscopic approach

Description
Cardiac ablation procedures treat atrial fibrillation by surgically creating lesions in the tissue of the left

and right atria of the heart. These lesions are designed to interrupt the abnormal electrical currents that characterize atrial fibrillation and redirect them so as to restore normal sinus rhythm. Over the years, three different surgical approaches have been developed by which the maze procedure can be performed: open, endovascular, and thoracoscopic. The thoracoscopic, or thoracoscopic-assisted, approach is the most recently developed technique. The thoracoscope is used for illumination and visualization only, while the surgical and ablation instruments are inserted via a (mini) thoracotomy or subxiphoid incision rather than through the thoracoscope. A total thoracoscopic approach has recently been developed. Both the thoracoscopic-assisted and total thoracoscopic techniques require opening the pericardium. Significant dissection of the pericardial sinuses and other vital structures is necessary to gain access to the target sites of the heart. Similar to the open technique, sharp incisions can be made into the atria thoracoscopically to create the therapeutic lesions; however, linear ablation is the preferred technique. Lesion creation is visualized via the thoracoscope. Similar to the open procedure, the thoracoscopic approach must be performed in an operating room by a cardiac or cardiothoracic surgeon.

In a thoracoscopic approach, the physician examines the inside of the pericardial sac through a rigid or flexible fiberoptic endoscope and removes a cyst, tumor, or mass lesion inside the pericardial sac. The procedure can be performed under local or general anesthesia. The physician makes a small incision between two ribs and by blunt dissection and the use of a trocar enters the thoracic cavity. The endoscope is passed through the trocar and into the chest cavity. The lung is usually partially collapsed by instilling air into the chest through the trocar or, if general anesthesia is used, the lung may be collapsed through a double lumen endotracheal tube inserted through the mouth into the trachea. The endoscope is advanced into the pericardial sac as the physician views the structures and the anatomy of the area through the scope. The contents of the pericardial sac are examined by direct visualization and/or by the use of a video camera. Still photographs may be taken as part of the procedure. The cyst, tumor, or mass is identified and removed using instruments guided through the endoscope or by using instruments introduced into the area through a second and/or third insertion site in the chest. At the conclusion of the procedure, the endoscope and the trocar are withdrawn. A chest tube for drainage and re-expansion of the lung is usually inserted through the wound initially created for the thoracoscope insertion.

35-39

35-39

Coding Clarification
Also known as the modified maze procedure, this code includes ablation by multiple delivery methods (e.g., cryoablation, electrocautery, ultrasound, radiofrequency) by thoracoscopic approach.

Thoracoscopic approach includes thoracotomy (subxiphoid incision) to establish port access.

Ablation procedures performed via open approach (37.33) or endovascular approach (37.34) are excluded from this code.

Coding Scenario
A patient presents for treatment of atrial fibrillation by modified maze procedure via thoracoscopic approach. Via small subxiphoid incision, a thoracoscope is inserted, and lesions are created in the left atrium with laser ablation.

> Code Assignment:
>
> 427.31 Atrial fibrillation
> 37.37 Excision or destruction of other lesion or tissue of heart, thoracoscopic approach

37.4   Repair of heart and pericardium

Coding Guidance
AHA: 2Q, '90, 24

37.41   Implantation of prosthetic cardiac support device around the heart

Description
A Cardiac Support Device (CSD) is a treatment option available for some heart failure patients and is designed to reduce heart wall stress dilation. This device is a permanent, textile mesh implant that is placed around the heart. It is adjusted to conform to the heart and support the heart's structures without changing its hemodynamics. It can be considered a preventive as well as therapeutic measure. The benefits of CSDs include reducing the need for acute care intervention to manage the disease (thus decreasing the long term associated costs) and to improve and prolong the patient's life.

The CSD implant may be accomplished by the following basic procedural steps. A sternotomy is performed and the pericardium is opened to expose the heart. Baseline measurements of heart size are obtained by transesophageal echocardiography (TEE).

Additional measurements of the heart's outside circumference and base-to-apex are taken using specially designed tools provided by the manufacturer. One of the available six sizes of the device is selected for implant. The CSD is positioned around the ventricles and aligned near the atrioventricular (AV) groove. Tacking sutures are placed every 2 to 4 cm along the base of the heart to secure the device along the AV groove. The device is custom fitted and clamped. The tension of the CSD is evaluated for even distribution. Left ventricular and end diastolic dimensions (LVEDD) are re-measured via TEE. Intra-cardiac pressures are monitored by Swan-Ganz catheters to ensure stability of hemodynamics. Any excess fabric is trimmed and adjusted, then stitched to make a new seam. The seam is reinforced and the hemline of the CSD is completed using tacking sutures. The device is inspected for adequate fit and function. The structures are irrigated and the chest is closed.

The CSD implant procedure can be performed alone in an approximate two-hour procedure, or as an approximate 30-minute addition to valve replacements/repairs and CABGs. Whether or not the procedure is performed off pump or with cardiopulmonary bypass is based upon the risk assessment of the surgeon.

Coding Clarification
A code also note prompts the coder to assign the proper codes for other associated procedures performed during the operative episode.

Code 37.41 excludes circulatory assist systems (37.61-37.68).

Documentation Tip
Procedures classified to code 37.41 may be documented as:

- Epicardial support device
- Fabric (textile) (mesh) device
- Ventricular support device.

Coding Guidance
AHA: 4Q, '05, 119-120

Coding Scenario
A hospital patient was taken to the operative suite for scheduled prosthetic mitral valve replacement and CSD implant for management of mitral valve insufficiency and chronic diastolic heart failure. Measurements for CSD were taken via TEE. The patient was placed on cardiopulmonary bypass and both procedures were performed successfully and without incident.

> Code Assignment:
>
> 424.0 Mitral valve insufficiency
> 428.32 Diastolic heart failure, chronic
> 35.24 Other replacement of mitral valve
> 37.41 Implantation of prosthetic cardiac support device around the heart
> 39.61 Cardiopulmonary bypass
> 88.72 Transesophageal echocardiography

● New Code   ▲ Revised Code   ▶◀ Revised Text   © 2010 Ingenix

37.49   Other repair of heart and pericardium

Description
This procedure code describes other repairs of the heart and pericardium not more specifically classified elsewhere.

Repair of a cardiac wound may be performed with cardiopulmonary bypass. The physician gains access to the heart using an incision through the sternum (median sternotomy) or the left anterior chest wall (thoracotomy). A pericardial window may be created if the diagnosis of penetrating cardiac trauma is not confirmed. Once penetrating trauma has been confirmed, the pericardial sac is incised and clotted blood and fluid removed. The entire heart is inspected and wound site(s) identified. Small lacerations are repaired with sutures and reinforced with Teflon felt pledges to anchor the sutures. Lacerations to small coronary vessels are ligated. Lacerations to larger coronary vessels are repaired. Large myocardial wounds may require synthetic grafting to cover the wound. The surgical incision is closed. Chest tubes and/or a mediastinal drainage tube may be left in place following the procedure.

37.5   Heart transplantation

Description
This subcategory includes heart replacement procedures, including implantation and repair or replacements of implantable heart replacement systems or components.

Coding Clarification
Heart replacement procedures are reserved for patients suffering from end-stage heart disease, recalcitrant to other treatment options.

Coding Guidance
    AHA: 4Q, '03, '96; 3Q, '08, 9

37.51   Heart transplantation

Description
The patient is placed on cardiopulmonary bypass. Cardiac transplantation may be performed by one of two techniques: total orthotopic heart replacement or heterotropic implantation. A total orthotopic heart replacement involves excising the ventricles, atrial appendages, and most of the coronary sinus from the donor heart. The recipient heart is opened. The atria, aorta, and pulmonary artery of the recipient heart are anastomosed to the donor heart. The sinoatrial nodes of both the donor and recipient heart are left intact. In a heterotropic implantation, the donor's organs are placed by sewing the left atrium of the donor heart to the left atrium of the recipient and sewing together the atrial septum and the right atrium. The donor aorta is trimmed to an appropriate length and sewn to the ascending aorta of the recipient. Immunosuppressive drugs may be given to the patient before, during, and after the operation. Cardiopulmonary bypass is discontinued when the donor heart begins functioning in the recipient.

Coding Clarification
Code 37.51 excludes combined heart-lung transplantation (33.6)

Coding Guidance
    AHA: 2Q, '05, 14; 4Q, '08, 182

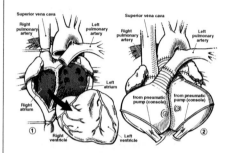

37.52   Implantation of internal biventricular heart replacement system

Description
The physician exposes the heart by median sternotomy. Pockets are created for the components of the system. The sites of pocket implantation may vary depending on the patient's anatomy. The implanted battery and controller may be implanted below the ribs, anterior to the rectus abdominus muscle sheath. The transcutaneous energy transfer (TET) coil may be implanted anterior to the pectoral muscle. The patient is placed on cardiopulmonary bypass, and a ventriculectomy is performed, whereby the thoracic unit is attached to the left atrium, right atrium, pulmonary artery, and aorta. The device is tested and the sternotomy wired closed.

Coding Clarification
Code 37.52 includes ventriculectomy and a substantial removal of part or all of the biological heart. Both ventricles are resected, and the native heart is no longer intact. Do not report a separate code for the ventriculectomy portion of the procedure.

Code 37.52 excludes implantation of a heart assist system (VAD), which is more appropriately classified elsewhere.

Documentation Tip
Procedures classified to 37.52 may be documented as implantation of artificial heart.

Coding Guidance
    AHA: 4Q, '08, 181

35-39

37.53 Replacement or repair of thoracic unit of (total) replacement heart system

Description

This code reports repair or removal and replacement of the thoracic unit of a total replacement heart system or artificial heart. The thoracic unit is the pump that consists of the artificial ventricles, which are attached to the natural atria, containing their corresponding valves, and the motor-driven hydraulic pumping system, or the pneumatic air pressure valves, depending on the system. Repair or removal and replacement of this component requires open chest access in a procedure following the same kind of steps for implantation, except that the other internal components are already in position and must be reconnected after repair or replacement is complete. The physician exposes the heart by median sternotomy and the patient is placed on cardiopulmonary bypass. The physician trims any scar tissue or overgrowth. The thoracic unit is disconnected, repaired, or replaced. The unit is reattached and reconnected, replacing cuffs and grafts as necessary.

Coding Clarification

Code 37.53 excludes replacement and repair of a heart assist system (VAD), which is more appropriately classified elsewhere.

Coding Guidance
> **AHA:** 4Q, '08, 181

37.54 Replacement or repair of other implantable component of (total) replacement heart system

Description

This code reports repair or removal and replacement of an internal component of a total replacement heart system or artificial heart, excluding the thoracic unit. Internal components include the implanted rechargeable battery, which is continually charged by external battery packs, the internal transcutaneous coil for receiving the battery charge across the skin, or the control unit, which monitors and controls the pumping speed of the artificial heart. These components are repaired or removed and replaced back in their prepared subcutaneous/submuscular pockets, and tunneled back to their connection with the thoracic unit, which is not replaced or repaired in this code.

Under general anesthesia, the physician performs a blunt dissection of the skin pockets containing the component and hardware to be replaced, disconnects the cables and components, removing and replacing as necessary. External controllers are used during the component replacement to maintain system function during maintenance.

Coding Clarification

Code 37.54 includes replacement or repair of an implantable battery or controller or TET device.

Code 37.54 excludes replacement and repair of a heart assist system (VAD) (37.63) and thoracic unit of total replacement heart system (37.53).

Coding Guidance
> **AHA:** 4Q, '08, 181

37.55 Removal of internal biventricular heart replacement system

Description

The physician removes a biventricular heart replacement system, which is sutured to the patient's atria. The device is composed of implantable artificial ventricles and valves, which are connected to an external pneumatically driven pump that replaces the patient's diseased ventricle and valves.

Coding Clarification

Biventricular mechanical heart assist devices are also known as an artificial hearts. An artificial heart differs from a ventricular assist device. The artificial heart requires resection of the ventricles so the native heart is no longer intact; however, a VAD is attached to the heart at the ventricle leaving the heart intact after being assisted by a VAD.

Documentation Tip

To ensure accurate code assignment, it will be necessary to review the medical record documentation carefully for the type and model of the device used. Examples of biventricular mechanical heart assist devices, also known as an artificial hearts, include:

- CardioWest™ temporary total artificial heart (TAH-t), which is used as a bridge in cardiac transplant eligible candidates at risk of death from biventricular failure.

- Abiomed™ AbioCor® Implantable Replacement Heart, which is used for patients who are not eligible candidates for heart transplantation.

Coding Scenario

A patient with end-stage congestive heart failure who is awaiting cardiac transplantation is admitted for implantation of a mechanical circulatory-support device as a bridge to transplantation. Cardiopulmonary bypass is instituted and the excision of the heart proceeds. A bilateral ventriculectomy is performed and the total artificial heart device is implanted.

Code Assignment:

428.0	Congestive heart failure, unspecified
37.52	Implantation of internal biventricular heart replacement system

● New Code   ▲ Revised Code   ►◄ Revised Text   © 2010 Ingenix

39.61 Extracorporeal circulation auxilary to open heart surgery

Coding Guidance
AHA: 4Q, '08, 180-182

37.6 Implantation of heart and circulatory assist systems

Description
This subcategory classifies the implantation of heart and circulatory assist systems, which may be used after acute myocardial infarction (AMI), after open heart surgery, or as a temporary life support (bridge procedure) for end-stage disease patients awaiting heart transplantation. These systems may be implantable, internal or non-implantable, external devices. This subcategory provides codes for insertion, implantation, repair, and removal of heart and circulatory assist systems and devices.

Coding Clarification
Codes classified to subcategory 37.6 list multiple exclusions for procedures performed on devices and systems more appropriately classified elsewhere, such as:

- Implantation of a prosthetic cardiac support system (37.41)
- Total heart replacement system procedures (37.5X)

Coding Guidance
AHA: 4Q, '95, 68; 4Q, '08, 177-179

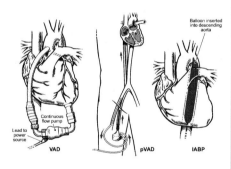

Balloon inserted into descending aorta

Continuous flow pump

Lead to power source

VAD   pVAD   IABP

37.60 Implantation or insertion of biventricular external heart assist system

Description
A biventricular external heart assist system is a device with external circulation pump outside the body but connected to heart that provides temporary cardiac support for both left and right ventricles.

Coding Clarification
Biventricular mechanical heart assist devices are also known as an artificial hearts. An artificial heart differs from a ventricular assist device. The artificial heart requires resection of the ventricles so the native heart is no longer intact; however, a VAD is attached to the heart at the ventricle leaving the heart intact after being assisted by a VAD. Code 37.60 includes sternotomy procedure for cannula attachments. Ventriculotomy is also included; so do not code it separately.

Coding Scenario
A patient is admitted with acute and chronic systolic/diastolic congestive heart failure. The physician inserts temporary cardiac support for both left and right ventricles using a sternotomy procedure to insert cannula attachments. The blood pump is positioned outside the body and connected to the cannulas inserted into the heart.

Code Assignment:

428.43 Combined systolic and diastolic heart failure, acute or chronic
37.60 Implantation or insertion of biventricular external heart assist system

Coding Guidance
AHA: 4Q, '08, 179

37.61 Implant of pulsation balloon

Description
Implantation of an intra-aortic pulsation balloon pump (IABP) consists of placing a balloon catheter into the descending thoracic aorta that inflates and deflates with the patient's heartbeat. This pump circulates the blood to the heart and the body, allowing the heart to rest or recover from injury, trauma, or shock.

This operation is done to help support the function of the left ventricle of the heart. The left or right femoral artery is exposed in the groin. After the vessel is occluded above and below the proposed insertion site, the artery is opened transversely. Occasionally, the end of a small tube of Gortex may be sewn to the side of the artery. The tip of the balloon catheter is inserted into the artery (or Gortex tube). The clamp occluding the artery upstream is released and the balloon catheter is advanced to the femoral artery and into the aorta above the level of the kidney arteries, but not beyond the left arm artery. It is connected to a pump and the pump is turned on. The pump inflates and deflates the balloon during each heartbeat cycle.

Documentation Tip
Procedures classified to 37.61 may be documented as an intra-aortic balloon pump (IABP).

Coding Guidance
AHA: 3Q, '05, 14; 3Q, '08, 9

© 2010 Ingenix   ● New Code   ▲ Revised Code   ▶◀ Revised Text

37.62   Insertion of temporary non-implantable extracorporeal circulatory assist device

Description
In internal circulatory assist, the femoral artery is cannulated and a catheter with balloon or other device is inserted into the aorta. Various devices may be used to assist circulation. This code should be reported for the internal insertion of such a device, but should not be used to report intra-aortic balloon pump (IABP) or implantation of ventricular assist devices that are reported elsewhere.

Coding Clarification
Code 37.62 may be used to classify the insertion of a heart assist system or pump, not otherwise specified (NOS).

Code 37.62 includes explantation of this device; do not report explantation separately.

Report separately any removal of heart assist system (37.64), if appropriate.

Code 37.62 lists multiple exclusions for implantation of devices more appropriately classified elsewhere, such as:

- Implantation of total internal biventricular heart replacement heart system [artificial heart] (37.52)
- Implant of external heart assist system (37.65)

Documentation Tip
This procedure may also be documented as a Symbion biventricular assist device.

Coding Guidance
AHA: 2Q, '90, 25; 4Q, '03, 116

37.63   Repair of heart assist system

Description
This code describes the repair or replacement of parts of an existing ventricular assist device (VAD). Surgical approach and technique vary depending on the component part repaired or replaced.

Coding Clarification
Code 37.63 reports repair of heart assist system, procedures such as replacement or repair of other implantable component of (total) replacement heart system (artificial heart) (37.54) and replacement or repair of thoracic unit of (total) replacement heart system (artificial heart) (37.53) are excluded from this code, and more appropriately classified elsewhere.

37.64   Removal of external heart assist system(s) or devices

Description
The physician removes a heart assist system. Surgical approach and technique may vary depending on the type of device(s) removed.

A previously placed balloon pump is withdrawn and the artery is occluded above and below the hole. If a Gortex sleeve has been used, it is simply tied off and no other repair is needed. If the balloon was directly introduced into the artery, the hole is sewn shut. If sewing the hole shut narrows the artery significantly, the hole can be patched with a piece of saphenous vein or Dacron. If the arterial diameter has been damaged, the segment of artery containing the hole can be removed and the artery replaced with an interposition graft of saphenous vein or Dacron tube.

The physician removes an ascending aortic intra-aortic balloon assist device during performance of a primary procedure. If the sternum is open, the physician removes the aortic balloon while tightening purse-string sutures around the hole. When hemostasis is assured, the pericardium is repaired loosely with or without graft, leaving gaps for blood and fluid to drain into the pleural space. The sternum is reanastomosed with sternal wires and the skin is sutured in layers. If the sternum is closed, a Dacron-tube graft is used as a vehicle for balloon removal. As the balloon is removed, the Dacron-tube graft tightens around the aortic incision to create aortic hemostasis.

Coding Clarification
Code 37.64 includes explantation of external device(s) providing left and right ventricular support and explantation of single external device and cannulae. Do not report these procedures separately.

Removal of temporary nonimplantable extracorporeal circulatory assist device is excluded from this code, and more appropriately reported with code 37.62.

Coding Guidance
AHA: 4Q, '08, 177-178, 180

37.65   Implant of single ventricular extracorporeal external heart assist system

Description
Cardiopulmonary bypass is required. For right ventricular failure, a pump uptake tube is placed in the right ventricular apex. A pump delivery tube is placed in the pulmonary artery. The pump is turned on and the patient is weaned off cardiopulmonary bypass. For left ventricular failure, the pump uptake tube is placed in one of the pulmonary veins or in the left ventricle apex. The arterial delivery tube is placed in the aorta. The pump is turned on and the patient is removed from cardiopulmonary bypass. The implanted pump is placed in a pocket formed in the upper abdominal wall, but outside the abdominal cavity. Tubes for the pump drive are brought out through separate incisions in the skin.

● New Code   ▲ Revised Code   ▶◀ Revised Text   © 2010 Ingenix

The pump is started and the patient is weaned off cardiopulmonary bypass. The device is removed when the patient's ventricle recovers, a total artificial heart is placed, or the patient undergoes heart transplantation.

Coding Clarification
Code 37.65 lists multiple exclusions for procedures more appropriately classified elsewhere, such as:

- Implantation of total internal biventricular heart replacement heart system (37.52)
- Insertion of implantable heart assist system (37.66)

Implantation or insertion of a temporary external heart assist system or device without sternotomy is reported with code 37.62.

Documentation Tip
Code 37.65 may be documented as:

- Insertion of one extracorporal heart ventricular assist device into one ventricle
- Insertion or implantation of one external VAD for left or right heart support

37.66   Insertion of implantable heart assist system

Description
This procedure code describes an implantable system connected to the heart and implanted in the left upper quadrant of the peritoneal cavity. It provides circulatory support to the vital organs by pumping blood through the body by providing a type of "back up" pump for the heart, when it is unable to maintain adequate circulation. These systems may be used as destination therapy (DT) or as bridge-to-transplant (BTT), meaning that a heart assist system may be permanent and life-sustaining or as a temporary means to facilitate heart function pending organ transplant.

Coding Clarification
Temporary, percutaneous heart assist devices that are intended for short-term use (37.61, 37.68) are excluded from 37.66.

Implantation of an artificial heart (37.52) is excluded from 37.66.

Documentation Tip
Advances in technology have been made whereby there are several types of heart assist systems available, depending on the patient's individual needs. They may be documented as:

- Axial flow heart
- Diagonal pump
- Rotary pump
- DeBakey Ventricular assist device (VAD)
- Left or right VAD

Coding Guidance
AHA: 1Q, '98, 7; 4Q, '03, 116

37.67   Implantation of cardiomyostimulation system

Description
This procedure code describes a two-step open procedure consisting of transfer of one end of the latissimus dorsi muscle, wrapping it around the heart, rib resection, implantation of epicardial cardiac pacing leads into the right ventricle, and tunneling and pocket creation for the cardiomyostimulator device. This approximate six-hour procedure essentially uses electrical stimulation to convert skeletal muscle into a fatigue-resistant muscle.

The first step of the procedure entails latissimus dorsi muscle dissection, with preservation of nerve and blood supply. Intramuscular electrodes are placed for pacing. The chest cavity is opened by resection of a portion of the posterior second rib through an incision in the back. The latissimus dorsi muscle and pacing leads are placed in the chest and the incision is closed.

For the second step of the procedure, the physician performs a median sternotomy. The pericardium is opened and a flap is preserved. Two pacing leads are inserted into the right ventricle. The latissimus muscle is threaded up over the apex of the lung and wrapped around the heart. The pericardium flap is used as a patch graft over the right heart. The pacing leads are tunneled into a pocket into the left upper abdominal quadrant and attached to a cardiomyostimulator device. During the healing phase, the stimulator conditions the skeletal muscle to become fatigue-resistant. Approximately two weeks post-op, the muscle is ready to be electrically stimulated to synchronize with the heart.

Coding Clarification
This procedure is most commonly performed for advanced end-stage heart failure patients with underlying idiopathic dilated cardiomyopathy who are unresponsive to other medical therapy. This procedure is not considered curative; the patient may still require future heart transplant.

Coding Guidance
AHA: 1Q, '98, 8; 4Q, '98, 75

37.68   Insertion of percutaneous external heart assist device

Description
This procedure code describes an external heart assist device that is tunneled percutaneously through venous access and threaded through a catheter into the atrium of the heart. In the atrium, it is threaded through the atrial septum into the left

35–39

atrium. An inflow cannula is advanced over the guidewire. Positioning is confirmed and the cannula is secured. A second cannula is placed in the femoral artery for return of blood flow. Both cannulae are connected to the external heart assist device or pump and adjusted to provide short-term mechanical circulatory support.

Coding Clarification
These devices are intended to provide temporary circulatory support for terminal patients who are not surgical candidates.

Code 37.68 includes the percutaneous insertion of femoral cannulae.

Documentation Tip
Procedures classifiable to 37.68 may be documented as percutaneous or external:

- Circulatory or heart assist devices
- Extrinsic (external) heart assist devices
- Percutaneous ventricular assist devices (pVAD)

Assign code 37.68 for the percutaneous insertion of an Orqis device which is an extracorporeal, minimally invasive cardiac system that increases blood velocity through the thoracic aorta.

▶Assign code 37.68 for the insertion of Impella. Impella is a minimally invasive, catheter-based cardiac assist device that supports the patient's cardiac function during various procedures. It functions by direct unloading of the left ventricle, reducing myocardial workload and oxygen consumption, and increasing cardiac output and coronary and end-organ perfusion.◀

Coding Guidance
    AHA: 2Q, '08, 12; ▶3Q, '09, 12◀

37.7   Insertion, revision, replacement, and removal of leads; insertion of temporary pacemaker system; or revision of cardiac device pocket

Description
This subcategory includes a wide range of procedures associated with specific pacemaker leads including:

- Insertion of lead by site (atrium, ventricle, epicardium)
- Revision or relocation
- Repair
- Removal

Cardiac pacemaker devices may be used as temporary or permanent treatment to control the rate of the heart by electrical stimulation and response mechanism. Common indicators for the procedure include:

- Arrhythmias
- Conduction disorders

- Low cardiac output
- Ventricular irritation

Coding Clarification
Code also any insertion and replacement of a pacemaker device or pulse generator (37.80-37.87). The pulse generator or device contains the battery and electronic component.

This subcategory excludes implantation or replacement of transvenous lead into the left ventricular cardiac venous system (00.52).

Coding Guidance
    AHA: M-J, '87, 1; 3Q, '92, 3; 1Q, '94, 16

37.70   Initial insertion of lead (electrode), not otherwise specified

Description
Access to the central caval veins is obtained through the subclavian or jugular vein. The vein is penetrated with a large needle and a wire is passed through. A fluoroscope may be used to guide the wire into the right atrium. A pocket for the pacemaker generator is created and the wire is tested. The wire is connected to the generator and the generator is closed in its pocket. The guide and pacemaker wires are placed appropriately.

Coding Clarification
This is a non-specific procedure code that should not be assigned if the medical record contains sufficient information to facilitate coding at a higher level of specificity. Check the medical record to confirm anatomic site of lead insertion.

Documentation Tip
If the documentation is ambiguous or unclear, the physician should be queried.

37.71   Initial insertion of transvenous lead (electrode) into ventricle

Description
Access to the central caval veins is obtained through the subclavian or jugular vein. The vein is penetrated with a large needle and a wire is passed through. A fluoroscope (separately reported) is used to guide the wire into the right atrium. A pocket for the pacemaker generator is created and the wire is tested. The guide and pacemaker wires are placed in the right ventricle.

37.72   Initial insertion of transvenous leads (electrodes) into atrium and ventricle

Description
Access to the central caval veins is obtained through the subclavian or jugular vein. The vein is penetrated with a large needle and a wire is passed through. A fluoroscope may be used to guide the wire into the right atrium. A pocket for the pacemaker generator is created and the wire is

tested. The wire is connected to the generator and the generator is closed in its pocket. The guide and pacemaker wires are placed in the atrium and ventricle.

Coding Guidance
> AHA: 2Q, '97, 4; 4Q, '08, 102

37.73   Initial insertion of transvenous lead (electrode) into atrium

Description
Access to the central caval veins is obtained through the subclavian or jugular vein. The vein is penetrated with a large needle and a wire is passed through. A fluoroscope may be used to guide the wire into the right atrium. A pocket for the pacemaker generator is created and the wire is tested. The wire is connected to the generator and the generator is closed in its pocket. The guide and pacemaker wires are placed in the atrium.

37.74   Insertion or replacement of epicardial lead (electrode) into epicardium

Description
The physician places electrical leads on the outside of the heart (epicardial electrodes) using an endoscopic approach. Three trocars are placed in the left anterior chest wall and the left lung is collapsed. A small incision is made in the chest (thoracostomy) and a 12 mm trocar is placed. The thoracoscope (endoscope) is inserted. Two additional trocars are placed under thoracoscopic visualization in the inframammary anterolateral region. Under thoracoscopic guidance, the pericardium is grasped and incised. The lateral trocar is removed and the incision enlarged to allow passage of the epicardial electrode placement device and the electrodes through the intercostal space. The electrodes are placed intrapericardially. The pericardium is approximated with a single stitch to hold the electrodes in place. The electrodes are tested and then tunneled under the costal margin to the upper abdomen to a pulse generator or over the ribs to the infraclavicular area if the generator is in that area. The thoracoscope is removed and a thoracostomy tube is placed at this site. The lung is expanded and the incisions closed in layered sutures.

Coding Guidance
> AHA: 3Q, '05, 3-9; 1Q, '07, 20

37.75   Revision of lead (electrode)

Description
This procedure code describes the revision of a lead (electrode) including repair or repositioning procedures.

A previously placed transvenous right atrial or right ventricular electrode is repositioned. This is done when the system does not function due to improper placement of the electrode wire itself. The generator is removed and the wire is tested to ensure that the wire is not defective, but simply in the wrong place. It is reattached to the generator in its new position and tested again.

Alternately, the pacemaker or cardioverter/defibrillator pocket is opened and the generator is removed. The electrode wire is tested. Repairs are performed. The wire is retested and reconnected to the generator. The generator is placed back in its pocket and the pocket is closed.

Coding Guidance
> AHA: 2Q, '99, 11; 3Q, '05, 8

37.76   Replacement of transvenous atrial and/or ventricular lead(s) (electrode(s))

Description
The pacemaker or cardioverter/defibrillator pocket is opened and the electrode wires are tested. Repairs are performed. The wire is retested and reconnected to the generator. The generator is placed back in its pocket and the pocket is closed.

Coding Guidance
> AHA: 3Q, '05, 3-5

37.77   Removal of lead(s) (electrodes) without replacement

Description
The generator pocket is opened and the wire is disconnected from the generator. The wire is dissected from the scar tissue that has formed around it. Once the wire is completely freed, it is twisted in a direction opposite to that used for insertion (counter clockwise). The wire is withdrawn. Bleeding from the tracts leading to the vein is controlled with sutures.

37.78   Insertion of temporary transvenous pacemaker system

Description
Access to the central caval veins is obtained through the subclavian vein or jugular vein. The vein is penetrated with a large needle and a wire is passed through it. A fluoroscope may be used to guide the wire into the right atrium. The pacemaker generator is not implanted but temporarily placed outside the body and a transvenous single chamber cardiac electrode, pacemaker catheter, or transvenous dual chamber electrode(s) is inserted.

Coding Guidance
> AHA: 1Q, '89, 2; 3Q, '93, 12; 3Q, '05, 7

35-39

37.79   Revision or relocation of cardiac device pocket

Description
This operation is done for patient comfort, impending exposure of the generator through the skin, or complications from the original generator placement (e.g., infection, bleeding). The pocket is opened. The generator is removed and the pocket is assessed. If it can be reused, it is revised. If not, a new pocket is formed somewhere within the reach of the pacemaker wires. The wires are brought through a new subcutaneous tunnel into the new pocket and connected to a new or the old generator. The old pocket is closed and the generator is placed in the new pocket, which is closed. If the old pocket is to be used, the generator is simply reinserted and the pocket closed.

Coding Guidance
AHA: 3Q, '05, 3-9

37.8   Insertion, replacement, removal and revision of pacemaker device

Description
This subcategory describes a wide range of procedures associated with specific pacemaker generator procedures including:

- Insertion of generator by type (single chamber, dual chamber)

- Replacement

- Repair

- Removal

Cardiac pacemaker devices may be used as temporary or permanent treatment to control the rate of the heart by electrical stimulation and response mechanism. Common indicators for the procedure include:

- Arrhythmias

- Conduction disorders

- Low cardiac output

- Ventricular irritation

Coding Clarification
Code also any insertion and replacement of pacemaker leads (electrodes) (37.70-37.77). The pulse generator or device contains the battery and electronic component.

This subcategory excludes implantation of a cardiac resynchronization pacemaker (00.50, 00.53).

Report pacemaker procedures according to the nature of the procedure (e.g., initial insertion, replacement, revision) and type of device inserted.

Coding Guidance
AHA: M-J, '97, 1

37.80   Insertion of permanent pacemaker, initial or replacement, type of device not specified

Coding Clarification
This procedure code should not be assigned if the medical record contains sufficient information to facilitate coding at a higher level of specificity.

Documentation Tip
The medical record should specify the type of device implanted. If the documentation is ambiguous or unclear, the physician should be queried.

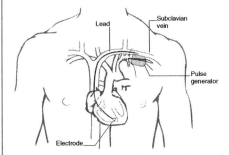

37.81   Initial insertion of single-chamber device, not specified as rate responsive

37.82   Initial insertion of single-chamber device, rate responsive

37.83   Initial insertion of dual-chamber device

37.85   Replacement of any type of pacemaker device with single-chamber device, not specified as rate responsive

37.86   Replacement of any type of pacemaker device with single-chamber device, rate responsive

37.87   Replacement of any type of pacemaker device with dual-chamber device

37.89   Revision or removal of pacemaker device

Description
A single or dual chamber pacemaker pulse generator is inserted or replaced. If this is an initial insertion, a pocket for the pacemaker generator is created subcutaneously in the subclavicular region or underneath the abdominal muscles just below the ribcage. The generator is inserted into the pocket. If the generator is being replaced, the old pacemaker generator pocket is opened and the old generator removed. The new generator is then placed into the existing pocket. The pacer wire(s) is tested and connected to the generator. The pocket is closed.

A single chamber system may be converted to a dual chamber system. The existing pacemaker generator pocket is opened and the single chamber generator removed. The dual chamber generator is then placed into the existing pocket. The existing pacer wire is tested and connected to the generator. A second lead is placed and tested. The pocket is closed.

A pacemaker device may be revised or repaired. The existing pacemaker generator pocket is opened and the generator is removed, revised, or repaired. The existing pacer wire is tested and connected to the generator. A second lead is placed and tested. The pocket is closed.

Coding Guidance
AHA: 4Q, '08, 102

37.9   Other operations on heart and pericardium

Description
This subcategory describes other therapeutic operations on the heart and pericardium not classifiable elsewhere in category 37, including other device insertions, injections, AICD procedures, and other operations.

Coding Guidance
AHA: 3Q, '90, 11

37.90   Insertion of left atrial appendage device

Description
This procedure code describes the implantation of a filtering device within the left atrial appendage to block emboli from exiting and causing stroke or thromboembolism. Under conscious sedation, the physician inserts the device percutaneously via a catheter delivery system. Associated procedures such as transesophageal echocardiography, fluoroscopy, or intracardiac echocardiography may be used to locate the left atrial appendage. The filtering or occluding device is implanted distal to the ostium of the left atrial appendage.

Coding Clarification
Filtering devices are commonly used to prevent clot formation in patients with atrial fibrillation.

Documentation Tip
Procedures classifiable to this code may be documented as:

* Left atrial filter
* Left atrial occluder

Coding Guidance
AHA: 4Q, '04, 121

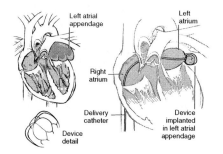

Left atrial appendage
Left atrium
Right atrium
Delivery catheter
Device implanted in left atrial appendage
Device detail

37.91   Open chest cardiac massage

Description
The physician opens the chest cavity widely to perform direct manual cardiac massage in the treatment of a cardiac arrest. Using a scalpel, the surgeon makes a long incision around the side of the chest between two of the ribs. The incision is carried through all the tissue layers into the chest cavity. Rib spreaders are inserted into the wound and the ribs are spread apart, exposing the lung. Space is made in the chest by packing the uninvolved lung away from the operative field by using large moist gauze sponges. The heart is exposed and squeezed rhythmically to mimic cardiac contractions thus pumping blood through the body. The heart may be directly contra-shocked to produce spontaneous heartbeats. After the procedure is complete, the instruments and gauze sponges are removed and the incision is closed in sutured layers. A chest tube(s) may be used to provide drainage for the chest cavity.

Alternately, the chest cavity can be opened and the operation performed through a vertical incision in the center of the chest through the sternum. The skin incision is carried down to the sternum bone and a saw is used to split the sternum. With the sternum split in half, the chest is entered by spreading the sternum apart with a set of rib spreaders. When the procedure is complete, the wound is closed by using wires to bring the two halves of the sternum together and the skin is closed over the sternum by suturing.

Coding Guidance
AHA: 4Q, '88, 12

37.92   Injection of therapeutic substance into heart

37.93   Injection of therapeutic substance into pericardium

Description
These procedures codes describe injection of therapeutic substances into the heart or pericardium.

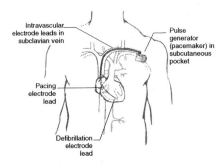

37.94   Implantation or replacement of automatic cardioverter/ defibrillator, total system (AICD)

37.95   Implantation of automatic cardioverter/defibrillator leads(s) only

37.96   Implantation of automatic cardioverter/defibrillator pulse generator only

37.97   Replacement of automatic cardioverter/defibrillator leads(s) only

37.98   Replacement of automatic cardioverter/defibrillator pulse generator only

Description
These codes report the implantation or replacement of defibrillator with leads, including formation of a subcutaneous pocket, placement of transvenous leads, and intraoperative testing procedures for evaluation of signals and threshold measurements. Operative approach for AICD placement includes lateral thoracotomy, median sternotomy, and subxiphoid techniques.

The physician inserts a pulse generator with transvenous electrode placement. Transvenous placement is currently the most common technique for placing implantable cardioverter-defibrillator (ICD) electrodes. An ICD is a device designed to administer an electric shock to control cardiac arrhythmias and restore a normal heartbeat. Local anesthesia is administered. An incision is made in the infraclavicular area. The subcutaneous tissue is opened and a pocket is created for the pulse generator. Transvenous electrode placement is

performed under separately reportable fluoroscopic guidance. The electrode catheter is advanced through the superior vena cava into the heart and placed in the appropriate site in the right ventricle (single chamber system) or in the right ventricle and atrium (dual chamber system). Multiple leads may be required for both single and dual chamber systems. Once all leads are placed, they are tested and connected to the pulse generator that is placed in the previously prepared pocket. All incisions are closed.

Coding Clarification
AICD devices may be upgraded to CRT-D devices (00.51) for patients who require biventricular pacing. These procedures are reported as insertion of a cardiac resynchronization defibrillator (00.51) system, and include the removal of the existing AICD for upgrade.

Device testing during implantation or replacement of an AICD is included in 37.94. Do not report testing separately.

Implantation of cardiac resynchronization defibrillator (00.51) is a biventricular pacing device that is excluded from 37.94.

Code also extracorporeal circulation, if performed (39.61).

Code also any concomitant procedure [e.g., coronary bypass (36.10-36.19) or CCM total system (17.51)].

Coding Guidance
    AHA: 3Q, '90, 11; ▶4Q, '09, 141◀

37.99   Other operations on heart and pericardium
Description
This procedure includes other operations on the heart and pericardium not classified elsewhere in category 37.

Coding Clarification
This is a nonspecific code that should not be assigned if the medical record contains sufficient information to facilitate coding at a higher level of specificity.

Code 37.99 lists multiple exclusions for procedures classifiable to specific codes in category 37 or to Chapter 16 Miscellaneous diagnostic and therapeutic procedures (87-99).

Documentation Tip
If the documentation is ambiguous or unclear regarding the nature of the operation, the physician should be queried.

Coding Guidance
    AHA: 3Q, '90, 11

● New Code   ▲ Revised Code   ▶◀ Revised Text   © 2010 Ingenix

38   Incision, excision and occlusion of vessels

Description
The vessels of the cardiovascular system consist of a complex roadmap of arteries and veins that transport blood to and from the organs and tissues of the body. An understanding of the following terms may help in code selection:

- **Arteries:** Branching system of elastic tubes that transport blood from the heart to all parts of the body via rhythmic, wave-like contractions called pulses. This arterial pulse echoes the beating of the heart. The heart's rate and rhythm can be taken at arterial "pulse points" throughout the body. The heart has its own vascular supply, the coronary arteries. The thickness of the heart muscle necessitates that specialized arteries and veins are necessary to filter the blood through the heart.

- **Veins:** Branching system of vessels that transport blood from body tissues to the heart. Veins contain valves that serve to prevent the back-flow of blood, since vein walls are relatively delicate and thin and do not contract as the arteries.

- **Capillaries:** Consist of microscopic blood vessels with single-celled walls that connect venules (tiny veins) to arterioles (tiny arteries), and facilitate both the flow of oxygen and nutrients to the tissues of the body via the arterioles, and elimination of waste products and carbon dioxide from the tissues of the body via the venules. The delicate membranes of the capillaries facilitate this vital intake and output exchange.

Category 38 provides codes for incisions, excision, surgical occlusion, and puncture of vessels.

Throughout category 38, many codes (except 38.7 Interruption of the vena cava) are acceptable only with certain fourth digits. In the ICD-9-CM text, the applicable digits are listed under the code number, enclosed in brackets.

The following fourth-digit subclassification is for use with appropriate categories in section 38.0, 38.1, 38.3, 38.5, 38.6, and 38.8 according to site.

- 0 unspecified
- 1 intracranial vessels
  - Cerebral (anterior) (middle)
  - Circle of Willis
  - Posterior communicating artery
- 2 other vessels of head and neck
  - Carotid artery (common) (external) (internal)
  - Jugular vein (external) (internal)
- 3 upper limb vessels
  - Axillary
  - Brachial
  - Radial
  - Ulnar
- 4 aorta
- 5 other thoracic vessels
  - Innominate
  - Pulmonary (artery) (vein)
  - Subclavian
  - Vena cava, superior
- 6 abdominal arteries
  - Celiac
  - Gastric
  - Hepatic
  - Iliac
  - Mesenteric
  - Renal
  - Splenic
  - Umbilical
  - Excludes abdominal aorta (4)
- 7 abdominal veins
  - Iliac
  - Portal
  - Renal
  - Splenic
  - Vena cava (inferior)
- 8 lower limb arteries
  - Femoral (common) (superficial)
  - Popliteal
  - Tibial
- 9 lower limb veins
  - Femoral
  - Popliteal
  - Saphenous
  - Tibial

Valid fourth digits are in [brackets] under each code.

For example:

38.1   Endarterectomy
[0-6, 8]

Valid: 38.10-38.16, 38.18

Invalid: 38.17

Rationale: The fourth digit 7, abdominal arteries, is invalid with subcategory 38.1 Endarterectomy.

Coding Clarification
Category 38 procedures exclude those performed on coronary vessels classifiable to subcategory 36 or Chapter 1 Procedures and interventions, NEC.

Code also any associated cardiopulmonary bypass [extracorporeal circulation] [heart-lung machine] (39.61).

35-39

Code also any application or administration of an adhesion barrier substance (99.77).

38.0   Incision of vessel

Description
This subcategory classifies incision of vessel procedures, whereby therapeutic procedures such as embolectomy or thrombectomy are performed to remove a blood clot.

To remove a blood clot in a vessel, the physician makes an incision in the skin over the site of the clot or immediately above or below it. The vessel is isolated and dissected from adjacent critical structures. The vessel may be clamped above and below the clot and incised. The physician removes the blood clot. The clamps are removed. The blood vessel is repaired with sutures and the skin incision is repaired with layered closure.

Coding Clarification
Subcategory 38.0 excludes endovascular removal of obstruction from head and neck vessels (39.74) and puncture or catheterization of an artery or a vein classified elsewhere.

Codes classified to subcategory 38.0 require fourth-digit subclassifications 0-9, which specify the anatomic region or site of the vascular procedure as:

    0   unspecified vessel
    1   intracranial vessels
    2   other vessels of head and neck
    3   upper limb vessels
    4   aorta
    5   other thoracic vessels
    6   abdominal arteries
    7   abdominal veins
    8   lower limb arteries
    9   lower limb veins

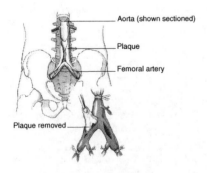

Aorta (shown sectioned)
Plaque
Femoral artery
Plaque removed

38.1   Endarterectomy

Description
This subcategory classifies endarterectomy procedures whereby the tunical intima (the innermost membrane of the vessel) is clogged by disease or other obstruction. Surgical technique may vary depending on the nature of the obstruction or disease, including endarterectomy by:

- **Embolectomy:** Surgical removal of an embolus, which is a mass or clot that has detached from its point of origin and traveled in the bloodstream, eventually becoming lodged in a blood vessel causing obstruction.

- **Patch graft:** Surgical repair of a defect by implantation or transplantation of a piece of tissue from one anatomic location to another.

- Temporary bypass during a procedure.

- **Thrombectomy:** Excision of a thrombus, which is a stationary clot causing vessel obstruction.

The physician makes an incision in the skin over the site of a blood clot, plaque, or abnormal lining of the affected vessel. The vessels are isolated and dissected from adjacent critical structures and vessel clamps are applied. The vessels are incised. Using a blunt, spatula-like tool, the plaque and the vessel lining are separated from the arteries and removed. The edge of the normal artery linings may be sutured to the artery walls to prevent separation when blood flow resumes. After the plaque and lining are removed, patch grafts taken from another portion of the patient's body, a cadaver, or a synthetic source may be applied and sutured to the vessels. This enlarges the diameter of the arteries. The vessel clamps are removed and the skin incision is repaired with layered closure.

Coding Clarification
Code also the number of vessels treated (00.40-00.43), and if applicable:

- Number of vascular stents inserted (00.45-00.48)

- Procedure on vessel bifurcation (00.44)

Codes classified to subcategory 38.1 require fourth-digit subclassifications 0-6 or 8-9. Fourth-digit 7, abdominal arteries, is invalid with subcategory 38.1. The following valid fourth digits specify the anatomic region or site of the vascular procedure as:

    0   unspecified vessel
    1   intracranial vessels
    2   other vessels of head and neck
    3   upper limb vessels
    4   aorta
    5   other thoracic vessels
    6   abdominal arteries
    8   lower limb arteries
    9   lower limb veins

● New Code   ▲ Revised Code   ▶◀ Revised Text   © 2010 Ingenix

38.2 Diagnostic procedures on blood vessels

Description
This subcategory classifies diagnostic procedures on blood vessels including biopsy, percutaneous angioscopy, and other procedures.

Coding Clarification
Subcategory 38.2 excludes adjunct vascular system procedures classified to 00.40-00.43. This exclusion indicates that it is not necessary to assign adjunct vascular procedures to describe the number of vessels treated for this range of codes. Imaging of vessels is assumed to be an inherent part of these procedures. Reporting the adjunct codes would be redundant.

38.21 Biopsy of blood vessel

Description
Through an incision in the skin overlying the targeted vessel, the physician isolates and dissects the vessel, separating it from critical structures. Using a clip or ligature, the vessel is ligated or tissue samples are taken for biopsy. The vessel may be tied off or repaired. The skin incision is repaired with layered closure.

38.22 Percutaneous angioscopy

Description
This procedure code describes exam by a fiberoptic catheter inserted through a peripheral artery to visualize the inner lining of blood vessels. The purpose of this procedure is to use an endoscope to look inside a blood vessel. The physician places an introducer sheath in the vessel to be examined, using percutaneous puncture or a cutdown technique. The physician places an angioscopy catheter through the introducer sheath into the vessel to be examined. The physician advances the angioscope through the vessel, clearing the view with injections of saline. Once the inside of the vessel has been examined, the angioscope and sheath are withdrawn. Vessel hemostasis is achieved using sutures or manual pressure.

Coding Clarification
Code 38.22 excludes angioscopy of eye (95.12).

38.23 Intravascular spectroscopy

Description
During a cardiac catheterization stenting procedure, the interventional cardiologist uses an intravascular spectroscopy system to assess coronary plaques. The ability to identify the chemical composition of coronary artery plaques in a patient undergoing a percutaneous coronary intervention can assist in determining whether a drug eluting stent is the most appropriate type of stent. For example, lipid rich plaques may cause secondary events such as

thrombosis after stenting, so determining whether plaques are lipid rich can guide the choice of stent used. Near-infrared (NIR) spectroscopy involves near-infrared imaging of the coronary artery with an intravascular spectroscopy catheter. The spectroscopy system consists of a laser light source, a small fiber optic catheter, and a console.

Coding Clarification
Infrared spectroscopy technique is different from other types of imaging that utilize ultrasound or visualization for peripheral and coronary vessel imaging. Code 38.23 includes spectroscopy of both coronary and peripheral vessels, intravascular chemography, and near infrared (NIR) spectroscopy; however, intravascular imaging of coronary vessels (00.24, 38.24) or peripheral vessels (00.23, 38.25) are not included. Coronary intravascular ultrasound (IVUS) is used to assess arterial wall architecture and identify intravascular stenosis or deposits, but it does not provide information regarding the chemical composition of atherosclerotic plaque. The IVUS codes do have separate codes for coronary, peripheral, renal extracranial cerebral and intrathoracic (00.2 series). Use code 38.23 to report either coronary or peripheral IVCG.

Documentation Tip
Review the medical record documentation carefully to confirm intravascular spectroscopy to ensure accurate code assignment. A number of alternative intravascular imaging methods are currently in use, such as ultrasound, near-infrared spectroscopy (NIR), angioscopy, optical coherence tomography (OCT), computed tomography (CT) and magnetic resonance imaging (MRI). Spectroscopy may employ nuclear magnetic resonance, Raman, fluorescence and near-infrared (NIR) technologies. For example, InfraReDx™ is a fiber-optic, catheter-based NIR spectroscopy system designed for detection of lipid rich coronary plaques. Raman spectroscopy can be used to quantify the weight of cholesterol, calcium salts, triglycerides, and phospholipids in arterial tissue.

Coding Scenario
Prior to a cardiac stenting procedure, the interventional cardiologist uses a fiber-optic, catheter-based near-infrared intravascular spectroscopy system to assess coronary plaques in the coronary vessels in order to determine whether a drug eluting or metal stent is the most appropriate type of stent. The final diagnosis is arteriosclerotic heart disease due to lipid rich plaque.

Code Assignment:

414.00 Coronary atherosclerosis of unspecified type of vessel, native or graft

414.3 Coronary atherosclerosis due to lipid rich plaque

38.23   Intravascular spectroscopy

Coding Guidance
   AHA: 4Q, '08, 182-183

38.24   Intravascular imaging of coronary vessel(s) by optical coherence tomography [OCT]

38.25   Intravascular imaging of non-coronary vessel(s) by optical coherence tomography [OCT]

Description
Coronary angiography is a commonly performed, two-dimensional imaging technique used to visualize atherosclerotic disease. Due to its limited imaging aspect, coronary angiography cannot identify details of a particular lesion such as the presence and composition of coronary atherosclerotic plaques. Intravascular ultrasound (IVUS) is also frequently used to assess coronary vascular lesions; however, IVUS uses sound waves to view the lumen and is limited by its low resolution. Optical coherence tomography (OCT) is a technology developed for coronary plaque characterization. OCT provides enhanced resolution imaging that enables better assessment of the vessel and the coronary atherosclerotic plaque. OCT produces cross-sectional images of coronary and peripheral vessels using fiberoptic catheter probes and near-infrared electromagnetic radiation light. Intravascular OCT high-resolution images can identify intraluminal thrombus, thin cap fibroatheromas, and can also quantify macrophages within the plaque. OCT provides images of the coronary and peripheral vessel lumen and wall structures to assist in stenting procedures and to assess endothelial growth over stented vessels in the treatment of late stent thrombosis and re-stenosis.

Two codes were created for 2010 to report the use of intravascular optical coherence tomography (OCT) of coronary and non-coronary vessels: 38.24 Intravascular imaging of coronary vessel(s) by optical coherence tomography [OCT], and 38.25 Intravascular imaging of non-coronary vessel(s) by optical coherence tomography [OCT].

Coding Clarification
Coronary angiography is performed using a variety of techniques and careful review of the documentation for specific information regarding the procedure is necessary to ensure accurate code assignment. Intravascular ultrasound (IVUS) of the coronary vessels is a catheter-based ultrasound imaging technique reported with 00.24. Similar to a rotational IVUS catheter, the inner portion of the OCT catheter is a rotating optical fiber with an imaging lens attached to it except using near infrared light instead of ultrasound. Code 88.57

Other and unspecified coronary arteriography, describes an unspecified coronary angiography procedure that is not classified elsewhere. SPY angiography (88.59 SPY intraoperative fluorescence vascular angiography) is an imaging technology used to test cardiac graft patency and technical adequacy at the time of coronary artery bypass grafting (CABG).

Documentation Tip
To ensure accurate code assignment, review medical record documentation to determine the specific imaging technique used.

Coding Scenario
A patient with coronary artery disease (CAD) undergoes optical coherence tomography imaging of the coronary atherosclerotic plaque. The physician uses a catheter-based system to assess vascular morphology, the vessel lumen, and plaque components. After the imaging catheter has been placed in the coronary artery, the physician uses a power injector connected to a catheter to flush saline and contrast to clear vessel and begins acquiring the images. The inner member of the catheter is a rotating optical fiber with an imaging lens attached. The lens is moved across the targeted area while the recording takes place. After the image acquisition, the physician reviews the images and analyzes various measurements to guide clinical decision making.

   Code Assignment:

   414.01   Coronary atherosclerosis of unspecified type of vessel, native or graft
   38.24   Intravascular imaging of coronary vessel(s) by optical coherence tomography [OCT]

Coding Guidance
   AHA: ▶1Q, '10, 16-17◀

38.29   Other diagnostic procedures on blood vessels
Description
This code describes other diagnostic procedures on blood vessels not classified elsewhere in subcategory 38.2.

Coding Clarification
This code should not be assigned if the medical record contains sufficient information to facilitate coding at a higher level of specificity.

Code 38.29 lists multiple exclusions for procedures classifiable to specific codes in Chapter 16 Miscellaneous diagnostic and therapeutic procedures (87-99).

Documentation Tip
If the documentation is ambiguous or unclear regarding the nature of the operation, the physician should be queried.

● New Code   ▲ Revised Code   ▶◀ Revised Text   © 2010 Ingenix

Coding Guidance
AHA: 1Q, '99, 7; 3Q, '00, 16

38.3   Resection of vessel with anastomosis

Description
This subcategory classifies vessel resection with anastomosis procedures whereby a vessel is reconstructed or reconnected after a partial excision. Surgical technique may vary depending on the type of lesion resected and the anatomic site of the procedure, including:

- Angiectomy
- Excision of:
  - aneurysm (arteriovenous)
  - blood vessel (lesion)

The physician makes an incision in the skin overlying the vessel. The enlarged or blocked section of the vessel is isolated and dissected from adjacent critical structures. Vessel clamps are affixed above and below the defect, which may be repaired or removed. The repair may be accomplished by removing the segment of artery and suturing the exposed ends of the vessel in an end-to-end fashion. Once the vessel is repaired, the clamps are removed. The skin incision is repaired with layered closure.

Coding Clarification
Codes classified to subcategory 38.3 require fourth-digit subclassifications 0-9, which specify the anatomic region or site of the vascular procedure as:

0   unspecified vessel
1   intracranial vessels
2   other vessels of head and neck
3   upper limb vessels
4   aorta
5   other thoracic vessels
6   abdominal arteries
7   abdominal veins
8   lower limb arteries
9   lower limb veins

38.4   Resection of vessel with replacement

Description
This subcategory classifies vessel resection with replacement whereby a portion of a vessel is excised, and that portion is replaced with a bypass graft or other means. Surgical technique may vary depending on the type of lesion resected, the anatomic site of the procedure, and type of replacement performed, including:

- Angiectomy with replacement
- Excision of aneurysm or vessel lesion with replacement

- Partial vessel resection with replacement
- Repair of a vessel with graft replacement

An incision is made overlying the vessel. The vessel is exposed, the affected portion identified, and vessels are inspected for other injury or disease. Repair may be accomplished by temporarily clamping the vessel both above and below the affected portion. Blood flow to the legs is interrupted while the vessel is clamped. The vessel is opened lengthwise and any thrombi (blood clots) removed. If an aneurysm is present, the aneurysm wall may or may not be removed. A harvested or synthetic graft is inserted into the defect. The vessel is cut above and below the lesion, and a replacement graft may be sutured in place between the two ends or the vessel wall may be wrapped around a synthetic graft. The clamps are removed allowing blood to flow through the graft and into the vessels of the lower extremities. The surgical wound is closed.

Coding Clarification
Subcategory 38.4 excludes endovascular aneurysm repair (39.71-39.79).

Codes classified to subcategory 38.4 require fourth-digit subclassifications 0-9, which specify the anatomic region or site of the vascular procedure as:

0   unspecified vessel
1   intracranial vessels
2   other vessels of head and neck
3   upper limb vessels
4   aorta
5   other thoracic vessels
6   abdominal arteries
7   abdominal veins
8   lower limb arteries
9   lower limb veins

Coding Guidance
AHA: 2Q, '99, 5-6; 2Q, '08, 13

38.5   Ligation and stripping of varicose veins

Description
This subcategory classifies ligation and stripping of varicose veins. Varicose veins are enlarged, twisted veins that can occur anywhere in the body and cause significant and progressive swelling, pain, and itching. They occur due to insufficiency of the valves that prevent backflow of blood. When these valves are not working properly, blood pools in the veins and the veins enlarge. Varicose veins may occur due to congenital defects, positional pressures associated with prolonged standing or sitting, and are often a complication associated with pregnancy in women. Surgical technique may vary depending on the anatomic site of the varicosity and the patient's state of cardiovascular health.

35-39

35-39

The physician ligates (i.e., ties-off), divides, and/or excises (i.e., stripping) a varicose vein. The physician makes an incision or several incisions, as necessary in the skin and tissue over the varicosity. These veins are isolated and dissected free of neighboring tissue, tied with sutures and divided, or stripped out bluntly. Pressure is applied over the site to stop bleeding. All incisions are repaired with layered closure. If the varicosities are in the legs, the legs are wrapped in an elastic pressure dressing postoperatively.

Coding Clarification

Codes classified to subcategory 38.5 require fourth-digit subclassifications 0-3, 5, 7, or 9, which specify the anatomic region or site of the vascular procedure as:

0   unspecified vessel
1   intracranial vessels
2   other vessels of head and neck
3   upper limb vessels
5   other thoracic vessels
7   abdominal veins
9   lower limb veins

Fourth digits 4, 6, and 8 are invalid with subcategory 38.5, since those subclassifications pertain to arterial vessels and these procedures apply only to veins (varicose).

Subcategory 38.5 excludes ligation of varices of the esophagus (42.91) and stomach (44.91).

38.6   Other excision of vessels

Description

This subcategory classifies excision of blood vessels not otherwise specified in category 38, including excision of a lesion of blood vessel, not otherwise specified.

The physician makes an incision or several incisions in the skin and tissue overlying the affected vessel. The vessel is isolated and dissected free of neighboring tissue and the physician dissects around any other structures. The physician dissects around the vessel, and applies vessel clamps above and below the portion to be excised. The physician sharply divides the vessel, removing the affected segment. The blood vessel is repaired with sutures. The incision is closed in layers.

Coding Clarification

Subcategory 38.6 excludes vessel excision procedures that are specifically classifiable elsewhere, such as:

- Excision of vessel with anastomosis (38.30-38.39)

- Excision of vessel with graft replacement (38.40-38.49)

- Excision of vessel with implant (38.40-38.49)

Codes classified to subcategory 38.6 require fourth-digit subclassifications 0-9, which specify the anatomic region or site of the vascular procedure as:

0   unspecified vessel
1   intracranial vessels
2   other vessels of head and neck
3   upper limb vessels
4   aorta
5   other thoracic vessels
6   abdominal arteries
7   abdominal veins
8   lower limb arteries
9   lower limb veins

Coding Guidance

AHA: 3Q, '90, 17

38.7   Interruption of the vena cava

Description

This is a valid, three-digit procedure code that describes a surgical interruption of the vena cava. This procedure may be defined as an interruption of the blood flow through the venous heart vessels to prevent clots from reaching the chambers of the heart by means of implanting a sieve or implant, separating off a portion, or by narrowing the venous blood vessels.

The physician performs an upper midline abdominal incision and dissects to expose the inferior vena cava. The physician interrupts vena caval flow by tying the cava off with suture, folding it (plication), or clipping it. The physician closes the abdomen, leaving drains in place. The physician may place an intravascular umbrella device using a percutaneous (venous) approach. The physician places a needle in the femoral (or internal jugular) vein, advances a guidewire through the needle, removes the needle over the wire, and advances an introducer sheath over the wire into the femoral vein. The physician advances the umbrella device through the introducer sheath into the inferior vena cava under fluoroscopic guidance. The physician removes the introducer sheath and compresses the femoral vein manually until hemostasis is achieved.

Documentation Tip

Procedures classifiable to 38.7 may be documented as vena caval:

- Plication

- Ligation

- Insertion of implant or sieve

- Insertion of femoral tulip filter

Coding Guidance

AHA: S-O, '85, 5; 2Q, '94, 9; 2Q, '07, 5

● New Code   ▲ Revised Code   ▶◀ Revised Text   © 2010 Ingenix

38.8   Other surgical occlusion of vessels

Description

This subcategory includes other surgical occlusion of vessels, including surgical techniques that may be described as:

- **Clamping:** Surgical occlusion by application of compression device.

- **Division:** Surgical occlusion by separation of the vessel.

- **Ligation:** Surgical occlusion by binding or tying the vessel.

- **Occlusion:** Surgical occlusion by sealing the vessel with an implanted device (coil or plug) or other technique.

Surgical occlusion may be defined as the process of reducing or eliminating blood flow to an area of the body by blocking a blood vessel. Surgical occlusion may be used to treat circulatory or other diseases by:

- Reducing the pressure on weakened or malformed vessels that result in vessel leakage.

- Reducing blood supply to growths or tumors.

- Reducing blood supply to an organ or area of the body prior to other therapies or procedures.

- Rerouting blood supply to a different blood vessel or part of the body.

This procedure code describes the surgical occlusion of a vessel. Surgical technique depends on the nature and anatomic site of the vascular disease.

The physician performs occlusion of a vessel by ligation or clamping. Through an incision in the skin of an extremity, usually over the damaged or traumatized vessel, the physician isolates and dissects the vessel, separating it from critical structures. Using a vascular clip or ligature, the vessel is ligated with sutures or vascular clips. Once the vessel has been tied off, the skin incision is repaired with layered closure.

Alternately, the physician can perform occlusion by ligation and division of a vessel. The physician makes an incision in the skin overlying the affected vessel. Tissues are dissected free and the vessel is isolated. Ties are placed around the vessel, which is divided between the ties. Once the ties are in place and the vein has been divided, the skin incision is repaired with layered closure.

Coding Clarification

Subcategory 38.8 lists multiple exclusions including occlusions of certain anatomic sites, occlusion for control of postoperative hemorrhage, and percutaneous transcatheter embolization, which are appropriately classified elsewhere.

Codes classified to subcategory 38.8 require fourth-digit subclassifications 0-9, which specify the anatomic region or site of the vascular procedure as:

- 0 unspecified vessel
- 1 intracranial vessels
- 2 other vessels of head and neck
- 3 upper limb vessels
- 4 aorta
- 5 other thoracic vessels
- 6 abdominal arteries
- 7 abdominal veins
- 8 lower limb arteries
- 9 lower limb veins

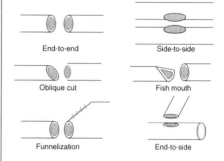

End-to-end   Side-to-side

Oblique cut   Fish mouth

Funnelization   End-to-side

38.9   Puncture of vessel

Description

This subcategory includes procedures in which a vessel is punctured, for catheterization, vascular access, or other reason.

Coding Clarification

Subcategory 38.9 excludes puncture of a vessel for circulatory monitoring (89.60-89.69).

38.91   Arterial catheterization

Description

This procedure code describes the puncture of an artery for the purpose of introducing an intra-arterial catheter. Technique may vary, depending on the purpose for the catheterization and anatomic site.

The physician inserts a needle through the skin and into an underlying artery, and threads a guidewire through the needle and into the artery. The needle is removed. The wire is threaded into the specific vessel. A catheter follows the wire into the artery branch. The wire is removed and the catheter is secured.

38.92   Umbilical vein catheterization

Description

The physician catheterizes the umbilical vein for diagnostic or therapeutic purposes. The physician cleanses the umbilical cord stump and locates the umbilical vein. A catheter is inserted in the vein for reasons including blood sampling or administering medication.

38.93 Venous catheterization, not elsewhere classified

Description

This code describes venous catheterization. Technique may vary depending on the purpose for the catheterization and anatomic site. The physician places a needle or a catheter through a puncture in the skin and into a peripheral vein.

For insertion of a non-tunneled catheter, the site over the access vein (e.g., subclavian, jugular) is injected with local anesthesia and punctured with a needle. A guidewire is inserted. The central venous catheter is placed over the guidewire. Ultrasound guidance may be used to gain venous access and/or fluoroscopy to check the positioning of the catheter tip. The catheter is secured into position and dressed.

A tunneled catheter has an entrance site at a distance from its entrance into the vascular system; they are "tunneled" through the skin and subcutaneous tissue to a great vein. The site over the access vein (e.g., subclavian, jugular) is injected with local anesthesia and punctured with a needle or accessed by cutdown approach. A guidewire is inserted. A subcutaneous tunnel is created using a blunt pair of forceps or sharp tunneling tools, often over the clavicle from the anterior chest wall to the venotomy site, which is dilated to the right size. The catheter is passed through this tunnel over the guidewire and into the target vein. Ultrasound guidance may be used to gain venous access and/or fluoroscopy to check the positioning of the catheter tip. The catheter is secured into position and any incisions are sutured.

Coding Clarification

Code 38.93 excludes venous catheterization for cardiac catheterization (37.21-37.23) and catheterization performed to facilitate renal dialysis (38.95).

▶Central venous catheterizations placed with guidance (e.g., electrocardiogram, fluoroscopy, ultrasound) are reported with code 38.97.◀

Documentation Tip

Procedures classifiable to code 38.93 may be documented as:

- Peripherally inserted central catheter (PICC line)
- Central venous catheter (CVC)
- Vascular access device (without implantable port or reservoir)
- Hickman catheter

- Broviac catheter
- Double or triple lumen catheter

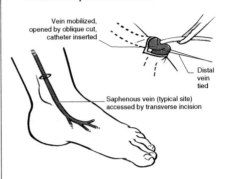

Vein mobilized, opened by oblique cut, catheter inserted

Distal vein tied

Saphenous vein (typical site) accessed by transverse incision

38.94 Venous cutdown

Description

This procedure code describes venous cutdown, which may be defined as an incision of a vein for needle or catheter placement. The physician makes an incision in the skin directly over the vessel and dissects the area surrounding the vein. A needle is passed into the vein for the withdrawal of blood or for the infusion of intravenous medication or other reason. Once the procedure is complete, the incision is repaired with layered closure.

38.95 Venous catheterization for renal dialysis

Description

This procedure code reports a venous catheterization to facilitate renal dialysis. Technique may vary.

For insertion of a non-tunneled catheter, the site over the access vein (e.g., subclavian, jugular) is injected with local anesthesia and punctured with a needle. A guidewire is inserted. The central venous catheter is placed over the guidewire. Ultrasound guidance may be used to gain venous access and/or fluoroscopy to check the positioning of the catheter tip. The catheter is secured into position and dressed.

A tunneled catheter has an entrance site at a distance from its entrance into the vascular system; they are tunneled through the skin and subcutaneous tissue to a great vein. The site over the access vein (e.g., subclavian, jugular) is injected with local anesthesia and punctured with a needle or accessed by cutdown approach. A guidewire is inserted. A subcutaneous tunnel is created using a blunt pair of forceps or sharp tunneling tools, often over the clavicle from the anterior chest wall to the venotomy site, which is dilated to the right size. The catheter is passed through this tunnel over the guidewire and into the target vein. Ultrasound guidance may be used to gain venous access and/or fluoroscopy to check the positioning of the catheter tip. The catheter is secured into position and any incisions are sutured.

Coding Clarification
Code 38.95 excludes insertion of a totally implantable vascular access device [VAD] (86.07).

Coding Guidance
   AHA: 4Q, '08, 193

● **38.97   Central venous catheter placement with guidance**

Description
▶The majority of patients admitted to hospitals require vascular access for delivery of IV medications (e.g., pain medication, antibiotic therapy), TPN, chemotherapy, and fluid replacement. Central venous catheters are typically inserted into a vein in the arm and then threaded into the superior vena cava. The proper placement of the tip of the catheter is important in order to avoid complications, repeated insertion procedures, and delays in catheter-related therapy. To ensure proper placement, catheters are often placed using imaging guidance assistance. Guidance technologies may include fluoroscopy, ultrasound, and more recently, electrocardiography. When a CVC is inserted blindly (without imaging guidance), positioning may be confirmed by chest x-ray.◀

Coding Clarification
▶This code includes guidance by electrocardiogram, fluoroscopy, and ultrasound. CVC placement without guidance is excluded from this code and reported with code 38.93.◀

Scenario
▶The patient presents for insertion of vascular access catheter via ECG guidance utilizing the Sherlock 3CG TPS System. Using two standard exterior ECG electrodes placed on the left shoulder and the lower left abdomen, and an intravascular electrode located on the tip of the catheter, a signal is generated using magnet technology to guide the tip of the catheter to ensure optimal placement.

   Code Assignment:
   38.97   Central venous catheter placement with guidance◀

38.98   Other puncture of artery

38.99   Other puncture of vein

Description
These codes describe other punctures of vessels not classifiable elsewhere in category 38.

Coding Clarification
These procedures should not be assigned if the medical record contains sufficient information to facilitate coding at a higher level of specificity.

Both codes list multiple exclusions for procedures classifiable to specific codes in category 39 or to Chapter 16 Miscellaneous diagnostic and therapeutic procedures (87-99).

Documentation Tip
If the documentation is ambiguous or unclear regarding the nature of the operation, the physician should be queried.

39   Other operations on vessels

Description
Category 39 provides a wide variety of codes which include vascular shunts, bypass procedures, fistulizations, sutures, repairs, revisions, procedures performed by endovascular approach, and other operations on vessels not classifiable to category 38.

Coding Clarification
Category 39 excludes procedures performed on coronary vessels (36.03-36.99).

39.0   Systemic to pulmonary artery shunt

Description
This procedure describes a surgically created shunt by vascular anastomosis or grafting between systemic arteries to the pulmonary artery. Surgical techniques may vary, including:

• **Potts-Smith shunt:** The operation is performed through the left side of the chest. Cardiopulmonary bypass is not required. One end of a 3 to 5 mm diameter tube made of PTFE (e.g., Gortex) is sewn to the side of the descending aorta and the other end is sewn to some part of the pulmonary artery. The ductus arteriosus (a connection between the aorta and pulmonary artery that has been supplying blood to the lungs, but usually closes at birth) is tied off.

• **Blalock-Taussig shunt:** In its unmodified form, this operation involves dividing the left subclavian artery, tying off the end of the artery going to the arm, and creating a connection between the end of this artery coming from the heart and the side of the pulmonary artery. The difficulty with this operation is making the connection to the pulmonary artery exactly the right size to supply adequate, but not excessive, blood flow to the lungs. Instead, a modified version of the operation is usually performed. The artery to the arm is not divided. Instead, one end of a 3 to 5 mm diameter tube of Gortex is sewn to the side of the artery to the arm and the other end is sewn to the side of the pulmonary artery. The size of the tube determines the amount of blood flow to the lungs. Cardiopulmonary bypass is not required.

The ductus arteriosus (a connection between the aorta and pulmonary artery that has been supplying blood to the lungs, but usually closes at birth) is tied off.

Coding Clarification
Code also any associated cardiopulmonary bypass [extracorporeal circulation] [heart-lung machine] (39.61).

39.1   Intra-abdominal venous shunt

Description
This procedure code reports on intra-abdominal venous shunt. Surgical technique may vary, including:

- **Mesocaval anastomosis:** The physician performs an upper midline vertical abdominal incision and retracts the transverse colon in a cephalad direction. The physician exposes the anterior surface of the inferior vena cava and frees the posterior surface of the superior mesenteric vein after careful dissection through the root of the transverse mesocolon. The physician isolates a long segment of the superior mesenteric vein with ties and partially occludes the inferior vena cava. The physician removes an ellipse of tissue from the inferior vena cava and performs an end-to-side anastomosis of Dacron graft to the inferior vena cava. The physician occludes the superior mesenteric vein, cuts an ellipse from its anterior surface, and sews the end of the Dacron graft to the side of the superior mesenteric vein. The physician assesses patency of the anastomosis and may measure venous pressures before closing the abdomen.

- **Portacaval venous anastomosis:** The physician places a long right thoracoabdominal incision and exposes the liver. The physician exposes the inferior vena cava and portal vein through careful dissection. The physician places a plastic sling around the portal vein and ties it closed, just proximal to its bifurcation. The physician clamps and divides the portal vein. The physician applies a partial exclusion vascular clamp to the front of the vena cava and removes a small oval of tissue from the vena cava to allow end-to-side anastomosis of portal vein to the inferior vena cava. The physician removes the clamps and checks for appropriate flow without anastomotic leakage. The physician closes the incision, leaving a chest tube in place (but no abdominal drains, as this may lead to protein loss from postoperative drainage of ascites).

- **Transvenous intrahepatic portosystemic shunt (TIPS):** Shunts are placed percutaneously to manage the complications of portal hypertension and control variceal bleeding and ascites. Once the patient is under general anesthesia or conscious sedation, the right internal jugular vein is accessed and a catheter is placed into the right hepatic vein. Catheter placement is verified with separately reportable venography. A Colapinto needle is advanced through the catheter into the wall of the right hepatic vein to access the right portal vein. A guidewire and catheter are advanced along this route into the portal vein and venography again is performed to verify placement. A self-expanding metallic stent is deployed through the catheter and dilated to the desired diameter where it bridges the portal and hepatic veins, using an angioplasty balloon. Post-placement venography and pressure measurements confirm adequate position and flow through the TIPS. The balloon, catheter, and other endoscopic tools are removed and pressure is applied to the insertion site, which may require suture.

Coding Clarification
Code 39.1 includes intraabdominal venous shunts by anastomosis described as:

- Mesocaval

- Portacaval

- Portal vein to inferior vena cava

- Splenic and renal veins

- Transjugular hepatic portosystemic shunt (TIPS)

Code 39.1 excludes peritoneovenous shunt (54.94)

39.2   Other shunt or vascular bypass

Description
Subcategory 39.2 classifies a variety of other vascular shunt and bypass procedures involving specific vessels or for a specified purpose (dialysis).

Coding Clarification
Code also a pressurized treatment of venous bypass graft with pharmaceutical substance, if performed (00.16).

39.21   Caval-pulmonary artery anastomosis

Description
Circulatory arrest and deep cooling of the body are usually employed. The right (or the persistent left) superior caval vein is occluded and its connection with the heart is divided. The heart end of the superior caval vein is closed. The free end of the superior caval vein is sewn to the side of the corresponding pulmonary artery. It is assumed that the corresponding pulmonary artery is isolated from the opposite lung congenitally or surgically. The goal is to permit blood to flow directly from the superior

● New Code   ▲ Revised Code   ▶◀ Revised Text   © 2010 Ingenix

caval vein to the lungs, thereby bypassing the right side of the heart.

Or, the main pulmonary artery may be tied-off. The superior caval vein is detached from its connection to the right atrium. The hole left in the right atrium is closed with sutures. The free end of the superior caval vein is sewn to a hole in the side of the pulmonary artery. In this way, blood can flow to the lungs without passing through the right side of the heart

Coding Clarification
Code also any associated cardiopulmonary bypass [extracorporeal circulation] [heart-lung machine] (39.61).

39.22   Aorta-subclavian-carotid bypass

Description
Surgical technique may vary depending on the vessels involved in the bypass procedure.

The physician exposes the aorta by median sternotomy and exposes the carotid or subclavian artery extending this incision in the appropriate direction. The physician clamps the middle part of the right anterolateral aspect of the anterior ascending aorta with a J clamp. The physician makes a 2 to 3 cm longitudinal incision in the clamped portion of the aorta and sews the venous graft to the aortic incision. The physician clamps the vein and releases the aortic clamp to assess the anastomosis for leaks. The physician clamps the distal end of the diseased artery (carotid or subclavian). The physician makes a longitudinal incision in the diseased artery, distal to the blockage, and sews the venous graft to the arterial incision. The physician may also use harvested vein to enlarge the arterial lumen (patch graft). The physician removes the clamp from the vein graft. The physician may perform arteriography or use a Doppler probe to establish patency of the graft. The physician closes the sternotomy or thoracotomy, leaving a chest tube in place.

Coding Clarification
Code 39.22 includes arterial bypass specified as:

- Aorta to carotid and brachial
- Aorta to subclavian and carotid
- Carotid to subclavian

39.23   Other intrathoracic vascular shunt or bypass

Description
The physician gains access to the mediastinum through an incision through the sternum (median sternotomy) or the chest wall (lateral thoracotomy). The physician uses purse string incisions to place a shunt (bypass) catheter around the abnormal area of the vessel to be repaired. The physician sews in the

aortic or great vessel graft while the heart is still beating. The physician removes the bypass catheter, closes the surgical incisions, and dresses the sternal or chest wall wound. The physician may leave chest tubes and/or a mediastinal drainage tube in place following the procedure.

Coding Clarification
Code 39.23 excludes coronary artery bypass (36.10-36.19).

39.24   Aorta-renal bypass

Description
The physician exposes the involved abdominal aorta and renal artery using an abdominal incision, retracting and dissecting past large and small bowel. The physician partially clamps the aorta below the renal takeoff and places a small longitudinal incision down the clamped portion of the aorta. The physician sutures in a venous graft, clamps the graft, and removes the aortic clamp to assess the anastomosis for leaks. The physician clamps the renal artery distal to the stenosis, incises the renal artery, and attaches the distal venous graft to the distal renal artery. The physician may also use harvested vein to enlarge the renal arterial lumen (patch graft). The physician may perform arteriography or use a Doppler probe to establish patency of the graft. The physician closes the abdominal wound, leaving drains in place.

39.25   Aorta-iliac-femoral bypass

Description
This code describes a bypass procedure involving combinations of the aorta, iliac, or femoral arteries. Surgical technique may vary, depending on the specific vessels utilized for bypass, such as:

- **Aorto-iliac-femoral:** The physician makes an incision in the skin of the abdomen over a section of damaged or blocked lower aorta. The artery is isolated and dissected from adjacent critical structures. Through a separate skin incision in the upper thigh, the femoral artery is isolated and dissected from adjacent critical structures. The physician creates a bypass around the damaged or blocked artery using a harvested vein. Once vessel clamps have been affixed above the defect, the lower aorta may be cut through or tied off with sutures above the damaged area and sutured to one end of the harvested vein. The vein graft is sutured to the iliac artery. A second vein is sutured to the iliac artery and the other end is passed through a tunnel on the inside of the upper thigh and sutured to a point on the femoral artery. When clamps are removed, the grafted vein forms a new path through which blood can easily bypass the blocked area. After the graft is

© 2010 Ingenix

● New Code   ▲ Revised Code   ▶◀ Revised Text

35-39

complete, the skin incisions are repaired with layered closures.

- **Iliofemoral:** Through incisions in the skin of the lower abdomen overlying the iliac artery and in the skin of the upper thigh overlying the femoral artery, the physician isolates and dissects a section of common iliac artery. The physician creates a bypass around the iliac artery, using a harvested vein and one of two methods of repair. Once vessel clamps have been affixed above and below the defect, the iliac artery may be cut or tied off with sutures above the damaged area and sutured to one end of a harvested vein. The graft is passed through a tunnel on the inside of the upper thigh and is sutured to the side of the femoral artery. In the second method, the end of the harvested vein is sutured to the side of the iliac artery. Either method results in a bypass of the damaged area. When the clamps are removed, the section of vein forms a new path through which blood can easily bypass the blocked area. After the graft is complete, the skin incisions are repaired with layered closures.

Coding Clarification
Code 39.25 includes bypass procedures documented as:

- Aortofemoral
- Aortoiliac
- Aortoiliac to popliteal
- Aortopopliteal
- Iliofemoral

39.26   Other intra-abdominal vascular shunt or bypass

Description
This code describes a vascular shunt or bypass utilizing other intraabdominal vessels. Surgical technique may vary, depending on the specific vessels utilized, including:

- **Aortoceliac:** The physician exposes the involved mesenteric or celiac artery using an upper midline abdominal incision, retracting and dissecting past large and small bowel. The physician exposes the distal thoracic aorta, administers heparin for anti coagulation, and clamps the aorta both proximal and distal to the celiac axis origin. The physician cuts out an elliptical disk of aortic wall from the anterior surface of the aorta. The physician exposes the involved vessel (mesenteric or celiac artery) and divides it proximal to the occlusion, closing off the proximal stump with suture. The physician sews a venous graft from the clamped aorta to the undiseased distal artery. The physician may use harvested vein to enlarge the arterial lumen (patch graft). The physician may perform

arteriography or use a Doppler probe to establish patency of the graft. The physician closes the abdominal wound, leaving drains in place.

Coding Clarification
Code 39.26 excludes peritoneovenous shunt (54.94).

39.27   Arteriovenostomy for renal dialysis

Description
This procedure code describes arteriovenostomy or formation of an internal arteriovenous fistula (shunt) for dialysis. Surgical technique may vary depending on the site selected for dialysis access and associated factors.

Through an incision, usually in the skin over an artery in the nondominant wrist or antecubital fossa, the physician isolates a desired section of artery and neighboring vein. Vessel clamps are placed on the vein and adjacent artery. The vein is dissected free, divided, and the downstream portion of the vein is sutured to an opening created in the adjacent artery, usually in an end-to-side fashion, allowing blood to flow both down the artery and into the vein. Large branches of the vein may be tied off to cause flow down a single vein. The skin incision is repaired with layered closure. This arteriovenous anastomosis will allow an increased blood flow through the vein, usually for hemodialysis.

Coding Clarification
Code also any renal dialysis (39.95).

Transposition of the vein is an inherent part of the formation of the arteriovenous fistula creation.

Coding Guidance
AHA: 1Q, '06, 10; 1Q, '07, 18

39.28   Extracranial-intracranial (EC-IC) vascular bypass

Description
Through an incision in the skin of the neck, the physician isolates and dissects the vertebral and carotid arteries, separating them from adjacent critical structures. The physician creates a bypass around a section of vertebral artery that is damaged or blocked, using a harvested vein and one of two methods of repair. After vessel clamps have been affixed above and below the damaged area, the graft is sewn to the side of the carotid artery and sewn to the side of the vertebral artery beyond the affected area (end-to-side) or sewn over the cut end of the vertebral artery after dividing it beyond the affected area (end-to-end). The damaged or blocked section of the vertebral artery is not removed. When the clamps are removed, the section of vein graft forms a new path through which blood can easily bypass the blocked area. After the graft is complete, the skin incision is repaired with layered closure.

● New Code   ▲ Revised Code   ▶◀ Revised Text   © 2010 Ingenix

Coding Guidance
> **AHA:** 4Q, '91, 22; 2Q, '92, 7

39.29   Other (peripheral) vascular shunt or bypass

Description
This code reports other peripheral vascular shunt or bypass. Surgical technique may vary depending on the specific vessels utilized for bypass, including:

- **Femoropopliteal:** Through incisions in the skin of the leg overlying the femoral and popliteal arteries, the physician isolates and dissects a section of artery that is damaged or blocked. The physician creates a bypass around the superficial femoral artery, using a harvested vein and one of two methods of repair. Once vessel clamps have been affixed above and below the defect, the superficial femoral artery may be cut through above the damaged or blocked area and sutured to one end of a harvested vein. The vein is passed through a tunnel down the thigh muscles and behind the knee and sutured to the popliteal artery. In the second method, the ends of the harvested vein are sutured into the side of the femoral and popliteal arterial walls, resulting in a bypass of the damaged area. When the clamps are removed, the section of vein forms a new path through which blood can easily bypass the blocked area. The blocked or damaged portion of artery is not removed. After the graft is complete, the skin incisions are repaired with layered closures.

- **Femoral-femoral:** Through incisions in the skin of the upper thighs, the physician isolates and dissects a section of the femoral arteries. The physician creates a bypass using a harvested vein. Once vessel clamps have been affixed above and below the area of anastomosis, the femoral artery may be cut through below the damaged area and sutured to one end of a harvested vein, which is sutured to the femoral artery in the opposite leg, resulting in a bypass of the damaged or blocked area. When the clamps are removed, the section of vein forms a new path through which blood can easily bypass the blocked area. The blocked or damaged portion of the artery is not removed. After the graft is complete, the skin incisions are repaired with layered closures.

- **Axillary-femoral:** The physician makes incisions in the skin of the axilla and upper thigh. The axillary and femoral arteries are isolated and dissected from adjacent critical structures. The physician creates a bypass around a section of lower aorta or iliac artery that is damaged or blocked using a harvested vein and one of two methods of repair. Once vessel clamps have been affixed above and below the areas of anastomosis, the harvested vein is sutured to an incision in the side of the axillary artery and passed through a subcutaneous tunnel on the side of the body and to the upper thigh. The harvested vein is sutured to the femoral artery (common, deep, or superficial) in an end-to-side or end-to-end fashion. The blocked or damaged portion of lower aorta or iliac artery is not removed. When the clamps are removed, the section of vein graft forms a new path through which blood can easily bypass the blocked area. After the graft is complete, the skin incisions are repaired with layered closures.

39.3   Suture of vessel

Description
Subcategory 39.3 classifies suture of an artery, vein, or unspecified vessel, including suture procedure for repair of vessel laceration.

Coding Clarification
Subcategory 39.3 lists many exclusions. Suture of vessel for control of postoperative hemorrhage or suture of aneurysm are specifically classified elsewhere.

Suture of vessel is not reported when performed in association with any other vascular puncture closure device.

39.30   Suture of unspecified blood vessel

39.31   Suture of artery

39.32   Suture of vein

Description
The physician makes an incision in the skin overlying the affected blood vessel. The vessel is isolated and dissected from adjacent critical structures, and vessel clamps are applied. The edges of the vessel may be trimmed to ease repair. The vessel is repaired with sutures. The clamps are removed and the skin incision is repaired with layered closure.

Coding Clarification
Suturing of the carotid artery may be required following decannulation of extracorporeal membrane oxygenation (ECMO). Report 39.31 if the artery requires suture repair upon decannulation.

Coding Guidance
> **AHA:** 3Q,'06, 9

39.4 Revision of vascular procedure

Description
Subcategory 39.4 provides four subclassification codes to report various revision procedures on the vascular system, including hemorrhage control post vascular surgery, revision and removal of arteriovenous shunts for renal dialysis, and other revision procedures.

39.41 Control of hemorrhage following vascular surgery

Description
Through an incision in the extremity over the affected area, the physician isolates the vessel and explores it for site of hemorrhage. The physician dissects any adjacent critical structures as necessary to access the vessel. The complication is identified and corrected. A hemorrhage is controlled by ligation or suture repair of the vessel. The physician sutures the skin incision with layered closure once the postsurgical complication has been treated.

Coding Clarification
Code 39.41 reports the control of a (vascular) hemorrhage following a vascular surgery. This code excludes control of a postoperative hemorrhage of other specified organ sites classifiable elsewhere.

39.42 Revision of arteriovenous shunt for renal dialysis

Description
This procedure code describes a revision of a previously placed internal arteriovenous shunt for renal dialysis. Surgical technique may vary, depending on the type of anastomosis or re-fistulization required to restore shunt function.

The physician makes an incision at the site of an already existing artificial fistula between an artery and a vein. The fistula is dissected free. Vessel clamps are affixed above and below the fistula, which is incised. Revisions are made to the fistula at its juncture to the vein and/or artery and may require creating a new anastomosis with a graft obtained from a separate site or created with synthetic material. After the repair has been made, the fistula is sutured, the clamps removed, and the skin incision repaired with layered closure. The physician may also remove a blood clot at the fistula site in addition to, or instead of, revising the existing arteriovenous fistula.

Coding Clarification
Code 39.42 excludes replacement of a vessel to vessel cannula (39.94).

39.43 Removal of arteriovenous shunt for renal dialysis

Description
This code describes removal of a surgically created arteriovenous shunt for renal dialysis. The physician removes an external cannula, followed by closure of the insertion site using sutures on the vessels or skin as necessary.

Coding Clarification
Code 39.43 excludes removal of a shunt with shunt replacement (revision)(39.42).

39.49 Other revision of vascular procedure

Description
This procedure code reports a wide range of vascular procedure revisions including:

- **Thrombectomy of AV fistula:** Under radiologic guidance, a percutaneously placed catheter is advanced to the site of a thrombus or clot that has formed in a previously created connection between an artery and a vein (arteriovenous fistula). The catheter is inserted into the clot and the clot is fragmented. Injection of urokinase may be required to dissolve the clot or percutaneous pharmacomechanical thrombolysis may be performed. Pharmacomechanical thrombolysis involves both injection of urokinase and mechanical fragmentation of the clot. Suction is applied and the clot fragments are removed through the catheter. The catheter is removed and pressure is applied at the insertion site.

- **Declotting of cannula:** To remove a blood clot lodged in a previously placed cannula, the physician may inject a solution containing enzymes into the cannula to dissolve the clot or the physician may, after injecting a solution containing enzymes, insert a balloon catheter into the cannula to retrieve a clot there. The balloon is inserted and inflated beyond the clot. The catheter is slowly pulled out, capturing and retrieving the clot. Once the clot is dissolved or retrieved, the catheter is removed and the cannula is left in place.

- **Revision of infected graft (extremity):** Through an incision in the skin of the extremity overlying the graft, the physician dissects around any muscle, vessels, or other structures to access the graft site. The physician dissects around the vessel and applies vessel clamps above and below the graft. The physician excises above and below the existing infected graft. The blood vessel is repaired with sutures. A catheter may be left in place to help drain infection. The skin is loosely closed. If the excised graft is replaced with a new graft, report the appropriate revascularization code.

Coding Clarification
Code 39.49 describes revision of a previous vascular procedure, such as re-anastomosis of a vessel or declotting of a vascular graft.

39.5   Other repair of vessels

Description
Subcategory 39.5 includes other repair of vessels including angioplasty, aneurysm repair, arteriovenous fistula repair, and other restorative vascular operations.

39.50   Angioplasty or atherectomy of other non-coronary vessel(s)

Description
In an open transluminal angioplasty, the physician makes an incision in the skin overlying the artery. The artery is dissected from adjacent critical structures and vessel clamps are applied. The physician may nick the vessel to create an opening into which a catheter with a balloon attached is inserted and threaded through. The catheter may be fed into the narrowed portion of the vessel, where its balloon is inflated in the narrowed area. The blood vessel is stretched to a larger diameter, allowing a more normal outflow of blood through the area. Several inflations may be performed along the narrowed area. The catheter is slowly withdrawn after deflation. Occasionally, the opening in the artery is repaired with sutures. The skin incision is repaired with layered closure.

In percutaneous transluminal balloon angioplasty (PTA), the physician isolates the targeted artery or vein and inserts a large needle through the skin and into the vessel. A guidance wire is threaded through the needle into the vessel. The needle is removed. A catheter with a balloon attached follows the wire into the vessel. The wire is removed. The catheter is fed through the arterial system and into the narrowed portion of the tibioperoneal trunk and, if necessary, one of its branches. There, the balloon is inflated. The blood vessel is stretched to a larger diameter, allowing a more normal outflow of blood through the area. Several inflations may be performed along the narrowed area. The catheter is slowly withdrawn after deflation. Pressure is applied to the puncture site to stop the bleeding after the catheter is removed.

In transluminal open peripheral atherectomy, the physician creates a femoral cutdown incision to expose one of the femoral arteries. The physician punctures the femoral artery with a large needle and passes a guidewire via the needle into the femoral artery. The physician removes the needle while leaving the guidewire in place, enlarges the arterial opening slightly with a blade, then slides an introducer sheath over the guidewire into the arterial lumen. The physician slides a guidewire through the atherectomy catheter or device, and inserts the guidewire/atherectomy catheter combination through the introducer sheath into the aorta. The physician fluoroscopically positions the atherectomy device at the aortic stenosis and activates the device to remove the stenotic tissue. The physician rechecks the diameter of the lesion by angiography. The physician may perform several passes with the atherectomy device. The physician removes the atherectomy catheter, guidewire, and introducer sheath, closing the femoral arteriotomy with suture. The physician closes the femoral cutdown incision with suture.

In transluminal percutaneous peripheral atherectomy, the physician punctures the femoral artery with a large needle and passes a guidewire via the needle into the femoral artery. The physician removes the needle while leaving the guidewire in place, enlarges the arterial opening slightly with a blade, and slides an introducer sheath over the guidewire into the arterial lumen. The physician slides a guidewire through the atherectomy catheter or device, and inserts the guidewire/atherectomy catheter combination through the introducer sheath up the aorta and out into the involved renal or other visceral artery. The physician fluoroscopically positions the atherectomy device at the arterial stenosis and activates the device to remove the stenotic tissue. The physician rechecks the diameter of the lesion by angiography. The physician may perform several passes with the atherectomy device. The physician removes the atherectomy catheter, guidewire, and introducer sheath, compressing the femoral artery manually until hemostasis is achieved.

Coding Clarification
Code also any:

- Drug-eluting peripheral vessel stent insertion (00.55)
- Injection or infusion of thrombolytic agent (99.10)
- Insertion of non-drug-eluting peripheral vessel stent(s) or stent graft(s) (39.90)
- Number of vascular stents inserted (00.45-00.48)
- Number of vessels treated (00.40-00.43)
- Procedure on vessel bifurcation (00.44)

Code 39.50 excludes percutaneous angioplasty or atherectomy on precerebral or cerebral vessels (00.61-00.62).

Coding Clarification

▶Code 39.50 includes insertion of pulmonary vein stent via a cardiac catheterization procedure. This procedure is considered noncoronary, regardless of the location for the procedure performed. Assign additional adjunct vascular codes as appropriate (00.40–00.48).◀

Coding Guidance
> **AHA:** 4Q, '06, 119; ▶3Q, '09, 13◀

39.51   Clipping of aneurysm

Description

This code describes clipping of an aneurysm. Surgical technique may vary depending on the anatomic site of the aneurysm.

The physician makes an incision over the affected vessel and isolates the aneurysm. The affected vessel is dissected from adjacent critical structures. The aneurysm is then obliterated with a tiny metal clip. The clip prevents blood from entering the aneurysm and future bleeding is prevented, protecting the surrounding tissues and organs. The skin incision is repaired with layered closure.

Coding Clarification

Code 39.51 excludes clipping of an arteriovenous fistula (39.53).

39.52   Other repair of aneurysm

Description

This code reports aneurysmal repairs accomplished by the following techniques:

- Coagulation (clotting or solidifying)
- Electrocoagulation (electrically produced clotting)
- Filipuncture (insertion of wire or thread)
- Methyl methacrylate (insertion or injection of plastic material)
- Suture (stitching)
- Wiring (insertion of wire)
- Wrapping (compression)

Coding Clarification

Code 39.52 excludes repair of aneurysm by endovascular approach (39.71-39.79) or by resection (38.30-38.49, 38.60-38.69) or graft replacement (38.40-38.49).

39.53   Repair of arteriovenous fistula

Description

This code describes the correction of an arteriovenous fistula by application of clamps, coagulating the vessel, or by tying off and dividing the vessel connection. The physician exposes the arteriovenous fistula by careful dissection. The physician isolates the fistula with ties or clamps. The physician may tie the arteriovenous fistula off completely (ligation) with suture, or the physician may partially obstruct (banding) or clip the lumen of the fistula with a broader band in order to reduce flow. The physician closes the skin incision.

Coding Clarification

Code 39.53 includes repair of an arteriovenous fistula by:

- Clipping
- Coagulation
- Ligation and division
- Embolization of carotid cavernous fistula

Code 39.53 lists multiple exclusions, such as repair of an arteriovenous shunt for renal dialysis (39.42) and repair with graft replacement or resection classifiable to category 38.

Coding Guidance
> **AHA:** 1Q, '00, 8

39.54   Re-entry operation (aorta)

Description

This code reports a fenestration (creation of small openings) used to treat dissecting aneurysm of the aorta whereby a passage is created between the stretched arterial heart vessel and the functional part of the vessel.

Coding Clarification

Code also any associated cardiopulmonary bypass [extracorporeal circulation] [heart-lung machine] (39.61).

39.55   Reimplantation of aberrant renal vessel

Description

The physician corrects an obstruction by cutting across or repositioning renal vessels that deviate from proper anatomical placement. To access the kidney, the physician makes an incision in the skin of the flank, cuts the muscles, fat, and fibrous membranes (fascia) overlying the kidney, and sometimes removes a portion of the twelfth rib. After repositioning the aberrant vessels to a more functional anatomic placement, the physician performs layered closure.

39.56   Repair of blood vessel with tissue patch graft

Description

The physician makes an incision in the skin over the site of the affected blood vessel. The vessel is isolated and dissected from adjacent critical structures, and vessel clamps are applied. A patch graft is sutured over any defect. The clamps are removed and the skin incision is repaired with layered closure.

● New Code   ▲ Revised Code   ▶◀ Revised Text   © 2010 Ingenix

Coding Clarification
Code 39.56 excludes vessel repair with resection (38.40-38.49).

Coding Guidance
AHA: 1Q, '04, 16

39.57 Repair of blood vessel with synthetic patch graft

Description
The physician makes an incision over the site of the affected blood vessel. The vessel is isolated and dissected from adjacent critical structures and vessel clamps are applied. The physician repairs the injured vessel with a length of synthetic graft material. The synthetic vein is sutured over the defect. The clamps are removed and the skin incision is repaired with layered closure.

Coding Clarification
Code 39.57 excludes vessel repair with resection (38.40-38.49).

39.58 Repair of blood vessel with unspecified type of patch graft

Description
The physician makes an incision over the site of the affected blood vessel. The vessel is isolated and dissected from adjacent critical structures and vessel clamps are applied. The physician repairs the injured vessel with a length graft material. The graft material is sutured over the defect. The clamps are removed and the skin incision is repaired with layered closure.

Coding Clarification
Code 39.58 excludes vessel repair with resection (38.40-38.49).

39.59 Other repair of vessel

Description
This code describes a wide range of vessel repair procedures. Surgical technique may vary, depending on the nature of the defect, anatomic site of vessel, and type of repair required

- **Valvuloplasty (femoral vein):** The physician makes an incision in the skin overlying the site of the incompetent valve. The femoral vein is isolated and dissected from adjacent critical structures. The physician affixes vessel clamps above and below the malfunctioning valve. The physician opens the vein and repairs the valve leaflets by suture plication (tacking the excess valve material). The vein is repaired with sutures. The clamps are removed and the skin incision is repaired with layered closure.
- **Direct repair of blood vessel (upper extremity):** The physician makes an incision in the skin of an upper extremity over the site of an injured blood vessel. The vessel is isolated and dissected from adjacent critical structures and vessel clamps are applied. The edges of the injured vessel may be trimmed to ease repair. The defect or hole in the vessel is repaired with sutures. The clamps are removed and the skin incision is repaired with layered closure.

- **Transposition and/or reimplantation (subclavian to carotid artery):** The physician performs a supraclavicular incision and exposes the carotid and subclavian arteries by careful dissection. The physician clears the adventitia of the chosen translocation site in the posterolateral wall of the common carotid artery. The physician anticoagulates the patient's blood with heparin and divides the subclavian artery distal to the stenotic area. The physician ligates the proximal subclavian stump with suture and makes a small arteriotomy in the common carotid artery wall with an aortic punch. The physician attaches the subclavian artery using an end-to-side anastomosis to the carotid artery. The physician may perform arteriography or use a Doppler probe to establish patency of the graft. The physician closes the supraclavicular wound, leaving a drain in place.

Coding Clarification
This code should not be assigned if the medical record contains sufficient information to facilitate coding at a higher level of specificity.

Code also any associated cardiopulmonary bypass [extracorporeal circulation] [heart-lung machine] (39.61).

Code 39.59 lists multiple exclusions for procedures classifiable to specific codes in category 38 or 39.

Documentation Tip
If the documentation is ambiguous or unclear regarding the nature of the operation, the physician should be queried.

Procedures classifiable to 39.59 may be documented as :

- Aorticopulmonary window operation
- Arterioplasty NOS
- Construction of (peripheral) venous valves
- Plication of vein
- Reimplantation of artery

39.6 Extracorporeal circulation and procedures auxiliary to open heart surgery

Description
Subcategory 39.6 classifies procedures associated with open heart surgery.

35-39

Coding Clarification

It is appropriate to report 39.61 in addition to the open heart surgery such as coronary artery bypass graft (CABG); however, do not separately report procedures that are integral to the surgery, such as hypothermia (39.62), cardioplegia (39.63), intraoperative cardiac pacing (39.64), and chest tube insertion (34.04).

Coding Guidance

AHA: 1Q, '95, 5-6

39.61 Extracorporeal circulation auxiliary to open heart surgery

Description

This procedure code describes a form of extracorporeal (situated or occurring outside the body) circulation utilized to temporarily assume the function of heart and lungs during surgery and maintain the circulation of blood and the oxygen content of the body. Cardiopulmonary bypass pumps (i.e., heart-lung machines) may be operated by Perfusionists; allied health professionals in association with surgeons who connect the CPB to the patient's body and monitor the machine and the patient. The machine consists of two main functional units—the CPB pump and the oxygenator—that remove oxygen-deprived blood from the patient and replace it with oxygen-rich blood through a series of hoses.

Coding Clarification

Code 39.61 excludes other specific types of extracorporeal circulation classified elsewhere.

Documentation Tip

Procedures classifiable to code 39.61 may be documented as :

- Artificial heart and lung
- Cardiopulmonary bypass
- Pump oxygenator

Coding Guidance

AHA: 2Q, '08, 13; 3Q, '08, 9; 2Q, '09, 8; ▶1Q, '10, 14◀

39.62 Hypothermia (systemic) incidental to open heart surgery

Description

Medically induced hypothermia (auxiliary to open heart surgery) may be described as a state of low body temperature in which the body can be maintained for an hour or more in the absence of blood flow. If blood flow is stopped at normal body temperature, it is fatal to the patient, with permanent brain damage occurring in approximately three to four minutes and resulting in death.

39.63 Cardioplegia

Description

This auxiliary component of cardiopulmonary bypass stops the heart and provides protection of the myocardium during surgery. A cannula is sewn into the heart to deliver a cardioplegia solution to cause the heart to stop beating.

39.64 Intraoperative cardiac pacemaker

Description

This component procedure provides a temporary pacemaker to regulate the heart rate and rhythm during and immediately following cardiac surgery.

Coding Guidance

AHA: 1Q, '95, 5

39.65 Extracorporeal membrane oxygenation (ECMO)

Description

ECMO is a simplified form of cardiopulmonary bypass (extracorporeal circulation) that may be used as life support for patients awaiting organ transplantation or for newborns with serious birth complications or defects. ECMO provides both cardiac and respiratory support to oxygenate severely ill patients whose heart and lungs cannot function without assistance.

Coding Clarification

Code 39.65 includes associated cannula placement.

ECMO auxiliary to open heart surgery is classified to 39.61.

39.66 Percutaneous cardiopulmonary bypass

Description

This procedure code describes the use of a mechanical pump to oxygenate and pump blood through the body via a percutaneously placed catheter in the femoral artery and vein.

When the IntraVascular Oxygenator (IVOX) device is utilized, it is designed to pump oxygen through the access line and filter the blood and carbon dioxide through specialized microfibers, which provides additional support to the lungs, while minimizing surgical trauma, and facilitating faster healing.

Coding Clarification

Code 39.66 excludes other specific types of extracorporeal circulation classified elsewhere.

Documentation Tip

This procedure may also be documented as an IntraVascular Oxygenator (IVOX).

Coding Guidance

AHA: 3Q, '96, 11

● New Code ▲ Revised Code ▶◀ Revised Text © 2010 Ingenix

39.7   Endovascular procedures on vessels

Description

This subcategory classifies a type of vascular surgery that is less invasive than the traditional open approach under general anesthesia. Endovascular procedures may be performed using local or regional anesthesia, decreasing the risks associated with general anesthesia. The term endovascular describes a procedure that is contained within the blood vessel, usually by access through a catheter placed in an access vessel such as the femoral artery.

Endovascular procedures include embolization, implantations, occlusion, removal, and repair. Radiological imaging assists in guiding the catheter to the diseased vessel to perform the repair inside the vessel. Endovascular procedures have been successful in treating aneurysm and vessel narrowing (due to occlusion or stenosis) with less surgical trauma to the patient, while expediting healing time.

Coding Clarification

Codes from subcategory 39.7 Endovascular procedures on vessel(s), should not be assigned unless the embolization involves a transcatheter coil. Codes to report endovascular treatment of the vessels of the head or neck using microcoils were created in 2010 in order to distinguish between the use of bare platinum coils and bioactive coils. Bioactive coils, which include an active biological agent to enhance occlusion and thrombus formation, have proven effective in aneurysm occlusion as compared to treatment using bare platinum coils and a specific code is necessary to track procedures that involve bioactive coils.

Subcategory 39.7 lists multiple exclusions, such as procedures on coronary vessels, percutaneous procedures, and vessel resections, which are more appropriately classified elsewhere.

Documentation Tip

Procedures classified to this subcategory may be documented as endoluminal repair. The term endoluminal describes a procedure performed inside the lumen (the inner, open space within the vascular structure).

Other terms that may be used in the medical record include endovascular embolization, implantation, occlusion, removal, or repair.

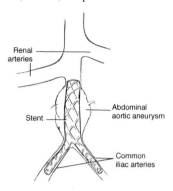

39.71   Endovascular implantation of graft in abdominal aorta

Description

The physician performs catheter-guided deployment of graft material into an aortic aneurysm to prevent continued blood flow into the diseased portion of the vessel and strengthen the weakened vessel walls. Two small incisions are made into the femoral arteries by cut-down. With radiological guidance and imaging, a balloon-tipped catheter containing the graft material is guided through the femoral into the femoral artery to the aorta. Once properly positioned at the site of aneurysm, the balloon is inflated, deploying the graft. The graft is secured into position by the balloon inflation to the proper diameter, and small hooks that attach to the inner walls of the aorta. The balloon is deflated and removed along with the catheter.

Coding Clarification

Code also any associated intra-aneurysm sac pressure monitoring (intraoperative) (00.58).

Documentation Tip

This procedure may be documented as endovascular repair of an abdominal aortic aneurysm with stent graft.

Coding Guidance

AHA: 4Q, '00, 63-64

39.72   Endovascular embolization or occlusion of head and neck vessels

Description

The physician performs an endovascular repair or occlusion by multiple possible surgical occlusive tools and techniques. Under general anesthesia and with x-ray guidance, a neuro-microcatheter is guided from entry vessel to the site of the aneurysm of the head and neck vessels for access to stop blood flow to an aneurysm or arteriovenous malformation. Occluding materials such as liquid tissue adhesives, particles, and other materials may be used to facilitate vessel repair. The catheter is removed and the access incision is closed.

Coding Clarification
Code 39.72 excludes mechanical thrombectomy (39.74) and embolization of the head or neck vessels using bare coils (39.75) or bioactive coils (39.76).

This procedure is commonly performed for repair of an aneurysm, arteriovenous malformation (AVM), or fistula.

Documentation Tip
Procedures classifiable to 39.72 may be documented as:

* Endograft
* Liquid tissue adhesive embolization or occlusion

Coding Guidance
    AHA: 4Q, '02, 103

39.73   Endovascular implantation of graft in thoracic aorta

Description
This code describes aortic dissection, aneurysm, or other repair to be performed intravascularly, without opening the chest. Through a small incision in the leg or groin, an image-guided catheter is used to advance the endoprosthesis from the peripheral access arteries through the abdominal aorta and into the thoracic aorta. The prosthesis consists of a self-expanding stent-graft deployed through a conduit (or sleeve). The graft is made of ePTFE (expanded polytetrafluoroethylene). Each endovascular graft is compressed into the end of a long, thin, tube-like device called a delivery catheter. The device is positioned and fitted into the damaged section of the vessel, restoring hemodynamic status. The catheter is removed and the access incision is closed.

Coding Clarification
Code 39.73 excludes fenestration of dissecting thoracic aneurysm (39.54).

This procedure is commonly performed for repair of aneurysm, dissection, or injury.

Code also any associated intra-aneurysm sac pressure monitoring (intraoperative) (00.58).

Documentation Tip
Procedures classifiable to 39.73 may be documented as:

* Endograft
* Endovascular repair with graft
* Stent graft

Coding Scenario
A patient was admitted for repair of a thoracic aorta aneurysm. The procedure was performed endovascularly through a small surgical cut in the skin (incision) for femoral arterial access. The catheter was guided through the abdomen and into the chest at the site of the aortic defect. The graft was deployed. Imaging confirmed adequate seal of the arterial wall.

    Code Assignment:

    441.2   Thoracic aneurysm without mention of rupture
    39.73   Endovascular implantation of graft in thoracic aorta

Coding Guidance
    AHA: 4Q, '05, 120

39.74   Endovascular removal of obstruction from head and neck vessel(s)

Description
Through a small access incision, an image-guided catheter is used to advance a thrombectomy device into position. The physician removes the clot or thrombus from the blocked vessel utilizing a balloon catheter, guidewire, microcatheter, and retrieval device. The catheter is removed and the access incision is closed.

Coding Clarification
Code 39.74 excludes endarterectomy procedures (38.11-38.12), occlusive endovascular embolization of the head or neck vessels using bare coils (39.75) or bioactive coils (39.76), and open embolectomy or thrombectomy (38.01-38.02) classifiable elsewhere.

Code also:

* Number of vessels treated (00.40-00.43) (if unknown, code and report 00.40 by default)
* Any injection or infusion of thrombolytic agent (99.10)
* Procedure on vessel bifurcation, if performed (00.44)

Coding Scenario
A 75-year-old male was admitted through the emergency room with slurred speech and unilateral weakness, which has worsened in severity over the past five hours. MRI and CT revealed acute ischemic cerebral thrombosis. Once the location of the stroke-inducing thrombus was identified using angiography, the balloon guide catheter was inserted employing standard catheterization techniques via a femoral artery approach. Under x-ray guidance, the catheter was maneuvered to the carotid artery. A guidewire and the microcatheter were deployed through the balloon guide catheter and then placed just beyond the clot in the appropriate intracranial artery. The retriever device was deployed in order to

● New Code   ▲ Revised Code   ▶◀ Revised Text   © 2010 Ingenix

engage and ensnare the thrombus. Upon capture of the thrombus, the balloon guide catheter was inflated to momentarily halt forward flow. The thrombus was pulled into the balloon guide catheter and completely out of the body. The balloon was then deflated and blood flow was restored. The patient was taken to the floor in stable condition.

Code Assignment:

434.01	Cerebral thrombosis
39.74	Endovascular removal of obstruction from head and neck vessel(s)
00.40	Procedure on single vessel

Coding Guidance
AHA: 4Q, '06, 129; ▶4Q, '09, 141◀

39.75   Endovascular embolization or occlusion of vessel(s) of head or neck using bare coils

39.76   Endovascular embolization or occlusion of vessel(s) of head or neck using bioactive coils

Description
Endovascular coil embolization is a minimally invasive procedure used to treat brain aneurysms or artery wall weaknesses that result in dilation and ballooning of a blood vessel. Left untreated, an aneurysm may lead to stroke or death. Filling an aneurysm with coils initiates a healing response and prevents rupture of the aneurysm. ICD-9-CM code 39.72 Endovascular repair or occlusion of head and neck vessels, does not differentiate between the use of bare platinum coils (BPC) and biodegradable polymer coils and so codes for endovascular treatment of the vessels of the head or neck using BPCs and bioactive coils were created in subcategory 39.7 Endovascular repair of vessel. Bioactive coils include an active biological agent to enhance occlusion and thrombus formation and have shown improved clinical outcomes for treating cerebral aneurysms. Filling the aneurysm with coils initiates a healing response and prevents rupture of the aneurysm.

Coding Clarification
Endovascular procedures on vessels include embolization, implantation, occlusion, removal, or repair. Endovascular embolization or occlusion of head and neck vessels without the use of bare or bioactive coils is reported with 39.72.

Documentation Tip
Review procedure documentation for specific information regarding the type of microcoil used prior to final code selection in order to ensure accurate code assignment.

Coding Scenario
A patient with a brain aneurysm is admitted for endovascular coiling. The physician inserts a catheter into the femoral artery and guides it to the site of the aneurysm in the brain. Next, the physician places a Cerecyte® bioactive microcoil through the catheter into the aneurysm, which disrupts the flow of blood into the aneurysm and prevents rupture of the aneurysm.

Code Assignment:

39.76	Endovascular embolization or occlusion of vessel(s) of head or neck using bioactive coils
437.3	Cerebral aneurysm, nonruptured

Coding Guidance
AHA: ▶4Q, '09, 145◀

39.79   Other endovascular procedures on other vessels

Description
The physician performs endovascular repair or occlusion by multiple possible surgical occlusive tools and techniques. With x-ray guidance, a catheter is guided from the entry vessel to the site of the diseased vessels for delivery of micro-coils, liquid adhesive, particulates or other implant deployment to stop blood flow to an aneurysm, or arteriovenous malformation to facilitate vessel repair. The catheter is removed and the access incision is closed.

Use code 39.79 to report endovascular procedures, including coil embolization on vessels other than the head and neck.

Coding Clarification
Code 39.79 lists multiple exclusions for aneurysm repair procedures more appropriately classified elsewhere.

▶When percutaneous uterine artery embolization is performed using embospheres or spherical embolics, procedure code 99.29 Injection or infusion of other therapeutic or prophylactic substance should be assigned.◀

Documentation Tip
Procedures classifiable to 39.79 may be documented as:

- Aneurysm repair
- Coil embolization or occlusion
- Endograft
- Liquid tissue adhesive embolization or occlusion
- Transcatheter embolism with polyvinyl alcohol (PVA) microspheres

Coding Guidance
AHA: 4Q, '02, 103; 2Q, '09, 7-8; ▶4Q, 09, 145-146;1Q, '10, 21; 2Q, '10, 9◀

35-39

39.8   Operations on carotid body, carotid sinus, and other vascular bodies

● **39.81   Implantation or replacement of carotid sinus baroreflex activation device, total system**

● **39.82   Implantation or replacement of carotid sinus lead(s) only**

● **39.83   Implantation or replacement of carotid sinus pulse generator only**

● **39.84   Removal of carotid sinus baroreflex activation device, total system**

● **39.85   Removal of carotid sinus lead(s) only**

● **39.86   Removal of carotid sinus pulse generator, only**

Description
These codes report the implantation, replacement, or removal of carotid sinus baroreflex activation systems devices, including the insertion of total system or components, repositioning, relocation, revision, and removal. The Rheos™ carotid sinus baroreflex activation system is a type of baroreflex activation device currently under clinical trial. It is a surgically implantable medical device designed to electrically activate the baroreflex; the system helps regulate cardiovascular function to treat primary hypertension and hypertensive heart failure recalcitrant to medical therapy. This system contains one implantable pulse generator, bilateral carotid sinus leads, and the programming system software. When activated by the device, signals are sent to the brain, which are interpreted as a rise in blood pressure. The brain works to counteract this perceived rise by modulating the nervous system and body hormones to dilate blood vessels to allow blood to flow more freely, thereby reducing the heart rate and affecting fluid handling by the kidneys. The intended result is a reduction in excessive blood pressure and workload by the heart, improved circulation, and a more optimal neurohormonal balance. Potential complications of chronic carotid sinus baroreflex activation therapy include hypotension, stimulation of extravascular tissues and cranial nerves, and vascular injury (e.g., vessel wall rupture) or stenosis.

Coding Clarification
▶Code 38.95 includes repositioning of the pulse generator, debridement and revision of skin and subcutaneous pocket, relocation of pocket, and creation of a new pocket.

Do not report code 38.92 or 38.93 separately when both the leads and pulse generator are implanted or replaced during the same operative episode; instead,

report code 38.91 Implantation or replacement of carotid sinus stimulation device, total system.◀

Coding Scenario
▶A patient presents for treatment of hypertensive cardiovascular disease with diastolic heart failure by implantation of the Rheos carotid sinus baroreflex activation system. The total system was placed by inserting the generator under the skin near the collarbone. The electrodes were placed on the carotid arteries, with the leads tunneled under the skin and connected to the device. The programmer system was retested and activated.

Code Assignment:

402.91   Hypertensive heart disease with heart failure
428.30   Diastolic heart failure, unspecified
39.81   Implantation or replacement of carotid sinus baroreflex activation device, total system◀

39.89   Operations on carotid body, carotid sinus and other vascular bodies

Description
This code reports various procedures on the carotid and other vascular bodies. Surgical technique is dependent upon the nature of the disease and anatomic sites involved. Some of the procedures classifiable to this code include the following techniques:

● **Chemodectomy:** Removal of a chemoreceptor vascular body.

● **Denervation of aortic body:** Destruction of nerves attending the major heart blood vessels.

● **Destruction of carotid body:** Destruction of nerves of the carotid body.

● **Glomectomy, carotid:** Removal of the carotid artery framework.

Surgical techniques include:

● **Glomectomy or chemodectomy with excision of tumor:** The physician removes a tumor from a small epithelioid structure (carotid body) just above the bifurcation of the carotid. The physician exposes the carotid body via an incision anterior to the sternocleidomastoid. After dissection down to the carotid sheath, the vein is retracted and the carotid bifurcation exposed. The blood supply to the tumor is ligated and the tumor resected. The incision is closed. The carotid body tumor excision may be performed with excision of the carotid artery.

● **Carotid sinus nerve injection:** The physician injects the carotid sinus nerve with an anesthetic agent to block sympathetically mediated pain or cardiovascular responses

● **Denervation of carotid body:** The physician exposes the carotid body via an incision anterior to the sternocleidomastoid. After dissection down to the carotid sheath, the vein is retracted and the carotid bifurcation exposed. The blood supply to the tumor is ligated. The incision is closed.

Coding Clarification
Code 39.89 excludes excision of the glomus jugulare (20.51).

Coding Guidance
AHA: 2Q, '07, 10

39.9   Other operations on vessels

Description
This subcategory classifies other operations on vessels not classifiable elsewhere in category 38 or 39.

39.90   Insertion of non-drug-eluting peripheral (non-coronary) vessel stents(s)

Description
The physician places a non-drug-eluting intravascular stent(s) percutaneously through a catheter into a peripheral vessel. A guidewire is threaded through the needle into the blood vessel and the needle is removed. A catheter with a stent-transporting tip is threaded over the guidewire into the vessel and the wire is extracted. The catheter travels to the point where the vessel needs additional support. The compressed stent(s) is passed from the catheter out into the vessel, where it deploys, expanding to support the vessel walls. The catheter is removed and pressure is applied over the puncture site.

Alternately, the physician makes an incision in the skin overlying the vessel to be catheterized. The vessel is dissected and nicked with a small blade. A catheter with a stent-transporting tip is threaded into the vessel. The catheter travels to the point where the vessel needs additional support, and the compressed stent(s) is passed from the catheter into the vessel, where it expands to support the vessel walls. The catheter is removed and the vessel may be repaired. The skin incision is repaired with layered closure.

Coding Clarification
Code 39.90 lists multiple exclusions for stent insertion procedures more appropriately classified elsewhere, such as those by percutaneous placement classified to chapter 00 Procedures and interventions, not elsewhere classified, and insertion of stent for aneurysm repair (39.71-39.79).

Code also any:

- Non-coronary angioplasty or atherectomy (39.50)
- Number of vessels treated (00.40-00.43)
- Number of vascular stents inserted (00.45-00.48)
- Procedure on vessel bifurcation (00.44)

Documentation Tip
Stent insertion procedures classifiable to 39.90 may be documented as:

- Bare or bonded
- Drug-coated
- Endografts or endovascular grafts
- Endovascular recanalizations
- Stent grafts

Coding Guidance
AHA: 4Q, '06, 119; ▶3Q, 09,13◀

39.91   Freeing of vessel

Description
Through an incision in the skin overlying the vessel to be examined, the physician dissects around any muscle, vessels, and/or other structures as necessary to access the vessel. The physician dissects out around the vessel, freeing it so it can be examined. The artery is freed from any surrounding scar tissue that may be compressing it. Finding no perforations or other signs of injury, the physician repairs the skin incision with layered closure.

Coding Clarification
Code 39.91 includes dissection and freeing of adherent tissue such as:

- Artery-vein-nerve bundle
- Vascular bundle

39.92   Injection of sclerosing agent into vein

Description
The physician injects a sclerosing solution into a vein or selected veins. This procedure is commonly performed on the vessels of the leg. The physician inserts a tiny needle through the skin and directly into any single vein or multiple veins of the same anatomic site. A solution (hypertonic saline and other solutions) is injected into these veins. The patient stands while the injection is given. The leg is elevated thereafter and wrapped in an elastic dressing. The solution causes the walls of the veins to become inflamed, collapse, and stick together so the veins close.

© 2010 Ingenix

Coding Clarification
Code 39.92 excludes injection of certain types of veins of specific sites, such as of esophageal varices (42.33) and hemorrhoids (49.42).

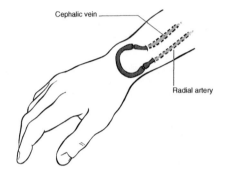

Cephalic vein

Radial artery

39.93   Insertion of vessel-to-vessel cannula

39.94   Replacement of vessel-to-vessel cannula

Description
These procedures describe the formation or replacement of an arteriovenous fistula or shunt by external cannula, which is most commonly performed to facilitate renal dialysis access.

The physician isolates two veins, usually in the nondominant forearm, and inserts a needle through the skin and into each vessel. A guidance wire may be threaded through the needle into each vessel. The needle is removed. An end of a single cannula is inserted into each puncture, and any guidance wire removed. The cannula remains external, and may be left in place for several days. This hemodialysis cannula is used to remove blood from the vein, route it through the dialysis machine, and reinfuse it.

Coding Clarification
Code also any renal dialysis (39.95).

39.95   Hemodialysis

Description
This code describes a replacement method for non-functioning kidneys that artificially removes waste products such as free water, urea, and potassium from the blood. Dialysis may be performed in a hospital, clinic, or home environment. The dialysis machine operates on the principle of diffusion of solutes across a semipermeable membrane using counter-current flow; whereby the dialysate flows in the opposite direction to the blood flow. This counter-current flow keeps the concentration gradient across the membrane at a consistent maximum by hydrostatic pressure, which assists in filtering of the waste products. Hemodialysis requires intravenous access

by venous catheter, arteriovenous fistula, or synthetic graft.

Documentation Tip
This procedure may also be documented as:

• Artificial kidney

• Hemofiltration

• Hemodiafiltration

• Renal dialysis

Coding Clarification
Code 39.95 excludes peritoneal dialysis (54.98)

Coding Guidance
    AHA: 4Q, '08, 193

39.96   Total body perfusion

Description
Perfusion may be defined as an injection of fluid and or nutrients through blood vessels in order to nourish, oxygenate, or otherwise support tissues and organs in the body. Perfusion consists of artificial pumping of fluid through the body, usually to deliver medication or nutrients.

Coding Clarification
Code also the substance perfused (99.21-99.29).

39.97   Other perfusion

Description
This procedure code describes perfusion other than total body perfusion (39.96). Perfusion classifiable to this code includes local or regional treatment. In regional or local perfusion procedures, a specific area of the body is saturated with high doses of medications, fluid, or nutrients. This type of therapy may be used to treat cancer patients.

Coding Clarification
Code also the substance perfused (99.21-99.29).

Code 39.97 excludes perfusion of certain organ sites, such as the kidney (55.95), intestine (46.95, 46.96), and liver (50.93).

Code 39.97 excludes SuperSaturated oxygen therapy (00.49).

39.98   Control of hemorrhage, not otherwise specified

Description
Through an incision over the affected area, the physician isolates the vessel and explores it for site of hemorrhage. The physician dissects any adjacent critical structures as necessary to access the vessel. The complication is identified and corrected. A hemorrhage may be controlled by ligation, electrocoagulation, or suture repair of the artery. The physician sutures the skin incision with layered closure.

● New Code   ▲ Revised Code   ►◄ Revised Text   © 2010 Ingenix

Coding Clarification

Code 39.98 excludes control of (postoperative) hemorrhage classifiable elsewhere and similar vascular procedures performed by ligation (38.80-38.89) or suture (39.30-39.32).

39.99   Other operations on vessels

Description

This code describes other vascular procedures not otherwise specified in category 39.

Coding Clarification

This code should not be assigned if the medical record contains sufficient information to facilitate coding at a higher level of specificity.

Code 39.99 excludes infusions, injections, or transfusions classifiable to Chapter 16 Miscellaneous diagnostic and therapeutic procedures.

Documentation Tip

If the documentation is ambiguous or unclear, the physician should be queried.

35-39

40-41

Operations on the Hemic and Lymphatic Systems

2011 Changes

In this section, an inclusion term was added to clarify the classification of transbronchoscopic needle aspiration (TBNA) of lymph node to code 40.11 Biopsy of lymphatic structure.

The ICD-9-CM classification system for operations performed on the hemic and lymphatic systems is divided into categories of procedures according to site as follows:

- Lymphatic System (40)
- Bone Marrow and Spleen (41)

40   Operations on lymphatic system

Description

Category 40 provides codes for incisions, diagnostic procedures, excisions, and other operations on the lymphatic system. When assigning a procedure code for the excision of lymph nodes, code the procedure based upon physician documentation.

Coding Clarification

To choose the correct code for an excision, check the operative report for the lymph node site.

For axillary lymph node excision, identify whether the excision was simple, regional, or radical.

If the report indicates radical excision of cervical lymph nodes, subcategory 40.4, review the documentation for location and whether the procedure was unilateral or bilateral in order to assign a fourth digit.

Code 40.9 Other operations on lymphatic structures, classifies a number of different procedures including anastomosis, dilation, ligation, obliteration, reconstruction, repair, or transplantation of peripheral lymphatics.

Documentation Tip

Lymph node biopsy and lymphadenectomy usually describe removal of a portion of the node or one node from a group of nodes.

Lymph node dissection usually describes complete removal of a particular area of lymph nodes.

A regional lymph node excision usually describes an excision of the regional lymph node with the lymphatic drainage area including skin, subcutaneous tissue, and fat.

A radical excision of lymph nodes usually involves the muscle and deep fascia.

40.0   Incision of lymphatic structures

Description

The physician performs this procedure to drain inflamed lymph nodes. The physician makes an incision over the affected lymph node and the abscess or infection is drained. The wound is irrigated and closed with sutures or Steri-strips.

A more extensive procedure is performed to correct lymphangiomas, which are primarily found in the neck. The physician makes an incision over the site of the tumor. The tissue, muscles, nerves, and blood vessels are dissected away from the tumor. The tumor is removed. The incision is closed with sutures, wound drains are placed, and a sterile dressing is applied.

Coding Scenario

The physician creates an opening in a lymphatic swelling or cavity (lymphocele) located outside the abdominopelvic walls to drain the material contained within to a cavity of the peritoneum. Irrigation of the lymphocele is performed. The incision is sutured closed.

Code Assignment:

40.0   Incision of lymphatic structures

40.1   Diagnostic procedures on lymphatic structures

Description

Fourth-digit subclassifications are provided to report diagnostic procedures on lymphatic structures.

Coding Clarification

Do not use subcategory 40.1 to report lymphangiograms of the following sites: abdominal

(88.04), cervical (87.08), intrathoracic (87.34), or upper or lower limb (88.34, 88.36).

Codes from subcategory 40.1 are also inappropriate for reporting microscopic examination of a specimen (90.71-90.79), radioisotope scan (92.16), or thermography (88.89).

40.11 Biopsy of lymphatic structure

Description
The physician performs a biopsy on or removes tissue from a lymph node for histologic examination. The physician makes a small incision through the skin overlying the lymph node. The tissue is dissected to the node. A small piece of the node and surrounding tissue is removed, or the entire node may be removed. The incision is then repaired with layered closure. Alternately, a biopsy needle may be utilized.

Coding Clarification
▶Transbronchoscopic needle aspiration (TBNA) of the lymph node is classified to 40.11.◀

Coding Scenario
The physician performs an open biopsy of an internal mammary node.

  Code Assignment:

  40.11 Biopsy of lymphatic structure

Coding Guidance
  AHA: 4Q, '08, 91; ▶4Q, '09, 74◀

40.19 Other diagnostic procedures on lymphatic structures

Description
Vital blue dye is injected into the subcutaneous tissues for outlining of skin lymphatics. As soon as the lymphatic vessels are visualized by their blue color, the radiologist makes a small longitudinal incision over the area. Exposure of the lymph vessel is accomplished, the vessel is made taut, and it is cannulated with a 27 or 30 gauge needle with a fine catheter attached. A small amount of dye is injected to ensure correct placement, and the needle is advanced 2 to 3 mm into the vessel. The needle and catheter are secured. Dye is injected with a 10 cc syringe. X-rays are made and repeated 24 hours later. The physician removes the needle and closes the incision with sutures.

Coding Clarification
Do not use subcategory 40.1 to report lymphangiograms of the following sites: abdominal (88.04), cervical (87.08), intrathoracic (87.34), or upper or lower limb (88.34, 88.36). Codes from subcategory 40.1 are also inappropriate for reporting microscopic examination of a specimen (90.71-90.79), radioisotope scan (92.16), or thermography (88.89).

40.2 Simple excision of lymphatic structure

Coding Clarification
To report a biopsy of a lymphatic structure, see 40.11.

When assigning a procedure code for the excision of lymph nodes, code the procedure based upon physician documentation.

Documentation Tip
Lymph node biopsy and lymphadenectomy usually describe removal of a portion of the node or one node from a group of nodes.

Lymph node dissection usually describes complete removal of a particular area of lymph nodes.

A regional lymph node excision is an excision of the regional lymph node with excision of lymphatic drainage area including skin, subcutaneous tissue, and fat.

A radical excision of lymph nodes involves the muscle and deep fascia.

40.21 Excision of deep cervical lymph node

Description
The physician performs a biopsy on or removes one or more deep cervical nodes, frequently with excision of scalene fat pads. The physician makes a small incision through the skin overlying the lymph node. The tissue is dissected to the node and part of the node and surrounding tissue are removed, or the entire node may be removed. The incision is then repaired with layered closure.

Coding Clarification
A regional lymph node excision is an excision of the regional lymph node with excision of lymphatic drainage area including skin, subcutaneous tissue, and fat.

A radical excision of lymph nodes involves the muscle and deep fascia.

Coding Guidance
  AHA: 4Q, '99, 16

40.22 Excision of internal mammary lymph node

Description
The physician removes one or more internal mammary nodes. The physician makes a small incision through the skin overlying the lymph node. The tissue is dissected to the node and the node is removed. The incision is then repaired with layered closure.

Documentation Tip
A regional lymph node excision is an excision of the regional lymph node with excision of the lymphatic drainage area including skin, subcutaneous tissue, and fat.

A radical excision of lymph nodes involves the muscle and deep fascia.

40.23   Excision of axillary lymph node

Description
Axillary lymph node excision involves removal of the lymph nodes under the armpit. The physician makes a diagonal incision across the lower axilla, exposing the axillary vein. The fatty tissue, lymph nodes, and vessels beneath the vein are dissected free. A drain is placed and connected to suction. The tissue and skin are closed with sutures.

Coding Clarification
To choose the correct code for an excision, check the operative report for the lymph node site.

For axillary lymph node excision, identify whether the excision was simple, regional, or radical.

Coding Guidance
AHA: 2Q, '02, 7

40.24   Excision of inguinal lymph node

Description
The physician makes an incision across the groin area. The surrounding tissue, nerves, and blood vessels are dissected away, and the inguinal and femoral lymph nodes are visualized. The nodes are removed by group. The wound is closed with sutures or staples. A pelvic lymphadenectomy may also be performed concurrently.

In an alternate procedure, the physician removes one or more superficial lymph nodes. The physician makes a small incision through the skin overlying the lymph node. The tissue is dissected to the node and the node is removed. The incision is repaired with layered closure.

Coding Clarification
To choose the correct code for an excision, check the operative report for the lymph node site.

Coding Scenario
The physician makes an incision through the skin overlying an inguinal lymph node and dissects to the node. The node and a portion of the surrounding tissue are removed and the incision is repaired with layered closure.

Code Assignment:

40.24   Excision of inguinal lymph node

40.29   Simple excision of other lymphatic structure

Description
The physician removes one or more superficial lymph nodes. The physician makes a small incision through the skin overlying the lymph node. The tissue is dissected to the node and the node is

removed. The incision is repaired with layered closure.

Coding Clarification
Report 40.29 for excision of a cystic hygroma, lymphangioma, and simple lymphadenectomy.

Documentation Tip
An understanding of the following terms may aid in code selection:

*   **Lymphangioma:** Abnormal mass of lymphatic vessels.

*   **Simple lymphadenectomy:** Removal of lymph node.

Coding Guidance
AHA: 1Q, '99, 6

40.3   Regional lymph node excision

Description
Code 40.3 is used to report an extended regional lymph node excision or a regional lymph node excision with excision of the lymphatic drainage area including skin, subcutaneous tissue, and fat. The physician makes a midline abdominal incision just below the navel. The surrounding tissue, nerves, and blood vessels are dissected away, and the pelvic and/or para-aortic lymph nodes are visualized. The nodes are removed. The wound is closed with sutures or staples. A retroperitoneal lymphadenectomy may also be performed.

Coding Clarification
An extended regional lymph node excision is the removal of a lymph node group, including the area around nodes.

Coding Guidance
AHA: 2Q, '92, 7

Coding Scenario
The physician performed a regional abdominal lymphadenectomy via a midline abdominal incision. The abdominal contents were exposed, allowing location of the lymph nodes. Each lymph node grouping was dissected away from the surrounding tissue, nerves, and blood vessels, and removed. The incision was closed with sutures or staples.

Code Assignment:

40.3   Regional lymph node excision

40.4   Radical excision of cervical lymph nodes

Description
The physician performs a resection of cervical lymph nodes down to the muscle and deep fascia. If the report indicates radical excision of cervical lymph nodes, subcategory 40.4, review the documentation for location and whether the procedure was

40-41

unilateral or bilateral in order to assign a fourth digit.

Coding Clarification

To choose the correct code for an excision, check the operative report for the lymph node site. For cervical or axillary lymph node excision, identify whether the excision was simple, regional, or radical.

These codes are not used to report cervical lymph node excisions that are associated with radical laryngectomy (30.4)

40.40   Radical neck dissection, not otherwise specified

Description

Code 40.40 is used to report radical neck dissection that is not more precisely described by other codes in subcategory 40.4. This code is also reported when the documentation does not further specify the procedure.

The physician makes a large curved incision starting at the ear, going down the neck, and continuing to the chin. Incision may also be made starting at the original incision and continuing down the neck. The skin flaps are folded back and held in place with retractors. The tissue, lymph tissue, blood vessels, nerves, and muscles targeted for removal are dissected away and removed. The incision is closed with sutures.

An alternate lymph-removal procedure is performed to preserve the spinal accessory nerve, jugular vein, and the sternocleidomastoid muscles. The physician makes a large curved incision starting at the ear, going down the neck, and continuing to the chin. Other incisions may be made down the neck from the original incision. Skin and tissue are retracted and the physician removes the lymph nodes. The incision is closed with sutures, including wound drains connected to suction. A tracheotomy may be performed

Documentation Tip

Review the documentation for specific information regarding the procedure prior to final code selection in order to avoid improper use of the "not otherwise specified" code and to ensure accurate code assignment.

40.41   Radical neck dissection, unilateral

Description

The physician performs a total dissection of the cervical lymph nodes on one side of neck. Radical neck dissection is performed to remove lymph nodes, muscles, blood vessels, and other tissue from one side of the neck.

Coding Scenario

The physician makes a preauricular incision with a curved cervical extension and the incision is extended inferiorly to the cervical lymph node. Skin and tissue are retracted and the physician removes the lymph nodes on the right side of the neck. The incision is closed with sutures, including wound drains connected to suction.

    Code Assignment:

        40.41 Radical neck dissection, unilateral

Coding Guidance
    AHA: 2Q, '05, 8; 2Q, '99, 6

40.42   Radical neck dissection, bilateral

Description

The physician performs a total dissection of the cervical lymph nodes on both sides of neck. The physician makes a large curved incision starting at the ear, going down the neck, and continuing to the chin. Incision may also be made starting at the original incision and continuing down the neck. The skin flaps are folded back and held in place with retractors. The tissue, lymph tissue, blood vessels, nerves, and muscles targeted for removal are dissected away and removed. The incision is closed with sutures.

In an alternate procedure, the physician makes a large curved incision starting at the ear, going down the neck, and continuing to the chin. Other incisions may be made down the neck from the original incision. Skin and tissue are retracted and the physician removes the lymph nodes. The incision is closed with sutures, including wound drains connected to suction. A tracheotomy may be performed.

Coding Clarification

To choose the correct code for an excision, check the operative report for the lymph node site, whether the procedure was unilateral or bilateral, and to identify the excision as simple, regional, or radical.

40.5   Radical excision of other lymph nodes

Description

Subcategory 40.5 describes radical excision of lymph nodes other than cervical lymph nodes. A radical excision of lymph nodes involves the muscle and deep fascia.

Coding Clarification

To choose the correct code for an excision, check the operative report for the lymph node site, whether the procedure was unilateral or bilateral, and to identify the excision as simple, regional, or radical.

To report radical excision of lymph nodes associated with radical mastectomy, see 85.45-85.48.

● New Code   ▲ Revised Code   ▶◀ Revised Text   © 2010 Ingenix

40-41

Documentation Tip
Review the documentation for specific information regarding the procedure prior to final code selection in order to avoid improper use of the "not otherwise specified" code.

40.50   Radical excision of lymph nodes, not otherwise specified

Description
Code 40.50 is used to report radical lymph node dissection that is not more precisely described by other codes in subcategory 40.5. This code is also reported when the documentation does not further specify the lymph node involved in the procedure.

Coding Clarification
To choose the correct code for an excision, check the operative report for the lymph node site.

For lymph node excision, identify the excision as simple, regional, or radical.

If the report indicates radical excision of cervical lymph nodes, see subcategory 40.4.

40.51   Radical excision of axillary lymph nodes

Description
The physician makes a diagonal incision across the lower axilla, exposing the axillary vein. The fatty tissue, lymph nodes, and vessels beneath the vein are dissected free. A drain is placed and connected to suction. The tissue and skin are closed with sutures.

Coding Clarification
To choose the correct code for an excision, check the operative report for the lymph node site and review the documentation for location, whether the procedure was unilateral or bilateral, and to identify the excision as simple, regional, or radical.

If the report indicates radical excision of cervical lymph nodes, refer to subcategory 40.4.

Documentation Tip
Excision of the regional lymph node involves excision of the lymphatic drainage area including skin, subcutaneous tissue, and fat.

A radical excision of lymph nodes involves the muscle and deep fascia.

40.52   Radical excision of periaortic lymph nodes

Description
The physician makes a large midline abdominal incision. The surrounding tissue, nerves, and blood vessels are dissected away, and the lymph nodes are visualized. The nodes are then removed by group. Some surrounding tissues may also be removed. The wound is closed with sutures or staples.

Coding Clarification
To choose the correct code for an excision, check the operative report for the lymph node site and review the documentation for location, whether the procedure was unilateral or bilateral, and to identify the excision as simple, regional, or radical.

Documentation Tip
Excision of the regional lymph node involves excision of the lymphatic drainage area including skin, subcutaneous tissue, and fat.

A radical excision of lymph nodes involves the muscle and deep fascia.

40.53   Radical excision of iliac lymph nodes

Description
The physician makes a low abdominal vertical incision. The surrounding tissue, nerves, and blood vessels are dissected away, and the pelvic lymph nodes are visualized. The nodes are removed by group. The wound is closed with sutures or staples.

Coding Clarification
To choose the correct code for an excision, check the operative report for the lymph node site and review the documentation for location, whether the procedure was unilateral or bilateral, and to identify the excision as simple, regional, or radical.

Documentation Tip
Excision of the regional lymph node involves excision of the lymphatic drainage area including skin, subcutaneous tissue, and fat.

A radical excision of lymph nodes involves the muscle and deep fascia.

Coding Scenario
The physician makes a low abdominal vertical incision and the surrounding tissue, nerves, and blood vessels are dissected away. The pelvic lymph nodes are visualized and removed. The wound is closed with sutures or staples.

> Code Assignment:
>
> 40.53   Radical excision of iliac lymph nodes

40.54   Radical groin dissection

Description
The physician makes a large midline abdominal incision. The surrounding tissue, nerves, and blood vessels are dissected away, and the lymph nodes are visualized. The nodes are then removed by group. Some surrounding tissues may also be removed. The wound is closed with sutures or staples.

Coding Clarification
To choose the correct code for an excision, check the operative report for the lymph node site and review the documentation for location, whether the

40-41

procedure was unilateral or bilateral, and to identify the excision as simple, regional, or radical.

Documentation Tip
Excision of the regional lymph node involves excision of the lymphatic drainage area including skin, subcutaneous tissue, and fat.

A radical excision of lymph nodes usually involves the muscle and deep fascia.

40.59   Radical excision of other lymph nodes

Description
The physician performs a surgical procedure to remove most or all of the lymph nodes that drain lymph from the area around a tumor for pathologic examination.

Coding Clarification
To choose the correct code for an excision, check the operative report for the lymph node site and review the documentation for location, whether the procedure was unilateral or bilateral, and to identify the excision as simple, regional, or radical.

To report a radical neck dissection, see 40.40-40.42.

Documentation Tip
Excision of the regional lymph node involves excision of the lymphatic drainage area including skin, subcutaneous tissue, and fat.

A radical excision of lymph nodes involves the muscle and deep fascia.

40.6   Operations on thoracic duct

Description
Fourth-digit subclassifications describe procedures of the thoracic duct such as fistulization, closure of a fistula, and ligation.

40.61   Cannulation of thoracic duct

Description
The physician places a cannula in the main lymphatic duct of the chest. Exposure of the lymph vessel is accomplished, the vessel is made taut, and it is cannulated with a 27 or 30 gauge needle with a fine catheter attached. The needle and catheter are secured. Medication is injected. The physician removes the needle and closes the incision with sutures.

40.62   Fistulization of thoracic duct

Description
The physician creates a passage in the main lymphatic duct of the chest using a thoracic or an abdominal approach. This procedure is performed to suture or tie the thoracic duct to correct chylothorax, the presence of lymphatic fluid within the pleural or lung space. The physician makes an

incision at the base of the neck, dissects the tissue, and visualizes the origin of the duct near C2 vertebra. The duct is tied or tied and cut. The incision is sutured.

40.63   Closure of fistula of thoracic duct

Description
This procedure is performed to suture or tie the thoracic duct to correct chylothorax, the presence of lymphatic fluid within the pleural or lung space. Using a thoracic approach, the physician makes an incision at the base of the neck, dissects the tissue, and visualizes the origin of the duct near C2 vertebra. The duct is tied or tied and cut. The incision is sutured. An abdominal approach may also be used.

Coding Scenario
The physician makes an incision in the abdomen. The involved thoracic duct compartment is drained of all effluent and the duct is ligated.

> Code Assignment:
>
> 40.63   Closure of fistula of thoracic duct

40.64   Ligation of thoracic duct

Description
In this procedure, the physician ties off the main lymphatic duct of the chest. This procedure is usually performed to suture or tie the thoracic duct to correct chylothorax, the presence of lymphatic fluid within the pleural or lung space. The physician makes an incision at the base of the neck, dissects the tissue, and visualizes the origin of the duct near C2 vertebra. The duct is tied or tied and cut. The incision is sutured.

40.69   Other operations on thoracic duct

Description
Code 40.69 is used to report other procedures of the thoracic duct that are not more precisely described by other codes in subcategory 40.6.

Documentation Tip
In order to ensure accurate code assignment, review the documentation for specific information regarding the procedure prior to final code selection.

40.9   Other operations on lymphatic structures

Description
Subcategory 40.9 classifies a number of different procedures including anastomosis, dilation, ligation, obliteration, reconstruction, repair, or transplantation of peripheral lymphatics.

Coding Clarification
To report reduction of elephantiasis of scrotum, see 61.3.

Documentation Tip

The following procedures are correctly reported with 40.9:

- Anastomosis of lymphatic channel
- Charles operation
- Correction of lymphedema by excision with graft, obliteration of lymphatics, or transplantation of autogenous lymphatics
- Dilation of lymphatic structures
- Grafting of lymphatic structures
- Homan operation
- Kondoleon operation
- Ligation of lymphatic structure
- Lymphangioplasty
- Lymphangiorrhaphy
- Lymphaticostomy
- Obliteration of lymphatic structures
- Thompson operation
- Reconstruction, repair, or transplant of lymphatic structures

41   Operations on bone marrow and spleen

Description

Bone marrow is the soft, sponge-like material inside bones that contains hematopoietic (blood-forming stem cells); these cells divide to form more blood-forming stem cells, or white blood cells, red blood cells, and platelets.

Bone marrow transplantation is performed as treatment for patients with aplastic anemia and certain types of cancer; however, there must be a genetic match between the donor and recipient for the bone marrow transplant. There are three procedures involved in all bone marrow transplant: harvesting, infusion, and regeneration.

Spleen procedures are also classified under category 41. The spleen is a dark purple, bean-shaped organ behind the bottom of the rib cage in the upper left side of the abdomen. The spleen filters the blood, regulates blood flow to the liver, and stores blood cells (sequestration). The spleen also functions as part of the immune system. Splenectomies are performed for a variety of different reasons including hypersplenism (a syndrome or group of symptoms), idiopathic thrombocytopenia purpura, and hemolytic anemia, which typically requires a spleen removal. Also, hereditary conditions such as spherocytosis, sickle cell disease, or thalassemia can result in the need for splenectomy. Often patients with cancers of the cells that fight infection, known as lymphoma or certain types of leukemia, require

spleen removal. When the spleen becomes enlarged, it sometimes removes too many platelets from the blood and has to be removed. Sometimes the spleen is removed to diagnose or treat a tumor. Removal may also be necessary if the blood supply to the spleen becomes blocked (infarct) or the artery abnormally expands (aneurysm).

Coding Clarification

Bone marrow or hematopoietic stem cell transplant, biopsy, splenectomy, and repair are some of the operations found under category 41.

Subcategory 41.0 requires a fourth digit to identify whether it was a bone marrow, hematopoietic stem cell, or cord blood transplant and origin of bone marrow or hematopoietic stem cell.

If the patient has both bone marrow and peripheral stem cells transplanted during the same episode of care, assign two codes: one for the bone marrow transplant and another for the stem cell transplant.

Documentation Tip

Many of the codes for operations on the spleen are for removal. Check the operative and a pathology report to determine precisely what was excised in order to assign the most appropriate code.

Autologous bone marrow transplants are assigned to 41.01 Autologous bone marrow transplant without purging or 41.09 Autologous bone marrow transplant with purging.

Autograft of bone marrow not otherwise specified is not the same as autograft of bone (78.0x).

Marsupialization is the conversion of a closed cavity into an open pouch.

41.0   Bone marrow transplant

Description

Subcategory 41.0 requires a fourth digit to identify whether it was a bone marrow, hematopoietic stem cell, or cord blood transplant and origin of bone marrow or hematopoietic stem cell. Hematopoietic stem cells are found in the bone marrow and in the bloodstream (peripheral blood stem cells); umbilical cord blood also contains hematopoietic stem cells. Cells from each of these sources may be used in transplants.

An **autologous transplant** uses the patient's own bone marrow or stem cells for the transplant, while an **allogeneic transplant** uses a donor's bone marrow or stem cells. Hematopoietic progenitor cells or stem cells harvested for transplantation are used to regenerate bone marrow and immune systems destroyed by chemotherapy and/or radiation therapy. For stem cell harvesting from peripheral blood, the progenitor cells are collected by apheresis, often after the donor is given a hematopoietic growth

40-41

40-41

factor to mobilize progenitor cells into the bloodstream.

The harvested bone marrow is usually obtained from a large bone of the donor. The donor is given general or regional anesthesia. Needles are inserted through the skin over the pelvic (hip) bone and into the bone marrow to draw the marrow out of the bone. The harvested bone marrow is then processed to remove blood and bone fragments. Harvested bone marrow may be cryopreserved. After the bone marrow is processed, the processed marrow is infused into the bloodstream of the recipient through an intravenous catheter. Purging is a process to remove certain types of cells, such as cancer cells and T-lymphocytes, from stem cells prior to infusion.

Coding Clarification
Code 41.00 for bone marrow transplant not otherwise specified should rarely, if ever, be assigned. Check the medical record documentation for the source of the transplant. If unclear, the physician should be queried.

Use code 41.02 with purging of T-cells or 41.03 without purging of T-cells for syngeneic transplants.

To report the donor source, see 00.91-00.93.

Documentation Tip
In order to ensure accurate code assignment, review the documentation for specific information regarding the type of bone marrow transplant used. Three types of bone marrow are used:

- Syngeneic transplant uses genetically identical marrow from an identical twin

- Allogeneic transplant uses marrow from individuals other than an identical twin

- Autologous transplant uses the patient's own marrow that has been stored

Coding Guidance
AHA: 1Q, '91, 3; 4Q, '91, 26; 4Q, '00, 64

41.00   Bone marrow transplant, not otherwise specified

Description
Code 41.00 is used to report other bone marrow transplant procedures that are not more precisely described by other codes in subcategory 41.0.

Coding Clarification
Code 41.00 should rarely, if ever, be assigned. If documentation is unclear, the physician should be queried.

Documentation Tip
Review the documentation for specific information regarding the procedure and source of the transplant prior to final code selection in order to

avoid improper use of the "not otherwise specified" code and to ensure accurate code assignment.

41.01   Autologous bone marrow transplant without purging

Description
This procedure is for the implantation of stem cells from the patient's own marrow that are removed, stored, and then returned to the body. The recipient's immune system is first suppressed using radiation or chemotherapy. The harvested bone marrow cells are injected into the recipient by intravenous drip therapy in a sterile environment.

Coding Clarification
For autologous bone marrow transplant with purging, see 41.09.

41.02   Allogeneic bone marrow transplant with purging

Description
Allogenic bone marrow transplant uses bone marrow from a donor, in this case after donor marrow is purged of undesirable cells. Purging techniques are used to clean the cells of residual tumor cells prior to transplanting, leaving only hematopoietic stem cells and progenitor cells that are infused into the recipient. Marrow and stem cell purging techniques involve using drugs or immunologic agents such as monoclonal antibodies. An allogeneic approach combines the concepts of high-dose therapy with immunotherapy. High-dose therapy is administered, followed by an infusion of hematopoietic cells.

Coding Clarification
Use 41.02 to report allograft of bone marrow with in vitro removal or purging of T-cells.

41.03   Allogeneic bone marrow transplant without purging

Description
In this procedure, bone marrow is obtained from a sibling or other HLA-compatible donor, purged of T-cells, and infused in the patient. Human leukocyte antigens (HLA) are genetic markers of our immune system; donor cells are obtained from a closely or completely HLA matched individual. This procedure is for the implantation of donor bone marrow cells. The recipient's immune system is first suppressed using radiation or chemotherapy. The harvested bone marrow or peripheral blood stem cells are injected into the recipient by intravenous drip therapy in a sterile environment.

Coding Clarification
Use this code to report allograft of bone marrow that is not otherwise specified.

 ● New Code   ▲ Revised Code   ▶◀ Revised Text   © 2010 Ingenix

41.04 Autologous hematopoietic stem cell transplant without purging

Description

Hematopoietic progenitor cells, or stem cells, harvested for transplantation are used to regenerate bone marrow and immune systems destroyed by chemotherapy and/or radiation therapy. These progenitor cells are not only acquired from bone marrow, but are also found in peripheral blood, collected by apheresis. For stem cell harvesting from peripheral blood by apheresis, the donor is often given a hematopoietic growth factor to mobilize progenitor cells into the bloodstream. The patient is prepared much the same as when giving a regular blood donation. Whole blood is drawn out of one arm and into an instrument called a cell separator. A special column in the separator sorts out the desired cells from the other cells with the help of computerized calibration. The stem cells are collected while the remainder of the blood is returned to the donor through a tube and needle in the other arm. More than one collection session may be required to acquire the amount needed for transplanting. Blood-derived progenitor cells may also be harvested from placental and umbilical cord blood after delivery for transplantation to the neonate later in life or to others.

An alternate procedure is for the implantation of donor bone marrow or blood-derived peripheral stem cells. The recipient's immune system is first suppressed using radiation or chemotherapy. The harvested bone marrow or peripheral blood stem cells are injected into the recipient by intravenous drip therapy in a sterile environment. Leukemia patients who show molecular or clinical evidence of relapse after transplantation are infused with additional lymphocytes collected from their donor to help boost the graft vs. leukemia effect.

Coding Clarification

To report autologous hematopoietic stem cell transplant with purging, see 41.07.

Coding Guidance

AHA: 4Q, '94, 52

41.05 Allogeneic hematopoietic stem cell transplant without purging

Description

Hematopoietic progenitor cells, or stem cells, harvested for transplantation are used to regenerate bone marrow and immune systems destroyed by chemotherapy and/or radiation therapy. These progenitor cells are not only acquired from bone marrow, but are also found in peripheral blood, collected by apheresis. For stem cell harvesting from peripheral blood by apheresis, the donor is often given a hematopoietic growth factor to mobilize

progenitor cells into the bloodstream. The patient is prepared much the same as when giving a regular blood donation. Whole blood is drawn out of one arm and into an instrument called a cell separator. A special column in the separator sorts out the desired cells from the other cells with the help of computerized calibration. The stem cells are collected while the remainder of the blood is returned to the donor through a tube and needle in the other arm. More than one collection session may be required to acquire the amount needed for transplanting. Blood-derived progenitor cells may also be harvested from placental and umbilical cord blood after delivery for transplantation to the neonate later in life or to others.

An alternate procedure is for the implantation of donor bone marrow or blood-derived peripheral stem cells. The recipient's immune system is first suppressed using radiation or chemotherapy. The harvested bone marrow or peripheral blood stem cells are injected into the recipient by intravenous drip therapy in a sterile environment. Leukemia patients who show molecular or clinical evidence of relapse after transplantation are infused with additional lymphocytes collected from their donor to help boost the graft vs. leukemia effect.

Coding Clarification

To report allogeneic hematopoietic stem cell transplant with purging, see 41.08.

Coding Guidance

AHA: 4Q, '97, 55; 1Q, '09, 9

41.06 Cord blood stem cell transplant

Description

Hematopoietic progenitor cells, or stem cells, harvested for transplantation are used to regenerate bone marrow and immune systems destroyed by chemotherapy and/or radiation therapy. Blood-derived progenitor cells may also be harvested from placental and umbilical cord blood after delivery for transplantation to the neonate later in life or to others. Cord blood is also used to treat disease because it contains stem-progenitor cells. Harvesting is usually performed immediately after delivery of the baby. After the umbilical cord is clamped and separated from the baby, the physician inserts a syringe into the umbilical cord and blood is drawn. The recipient's immune system is first suppressed using radiation or chemotherapy. The harvested cord blood stem cells are injected into the recipient by intravenous drip therapy in a sterile environment.

Coding Guidance

AHA: 4Q, '97, 56

41.07 Autologous hematopoietic stem cell transplant with purging

Description

Hematopoietic progenitor cells, or stem cells, harvested for transplantation are used to regenerate bone marrow and immune systems destroyed by chemotherapy and/or radiation therapy. These progenitor cells are not only acquired from bone marrow, but are also found in peripheral blood, collected by apheresis. For stem cell harvesting from peripheral blood by apheresis, the donor is often given a hematopoietic growth factor to mobilize progenitor cells into the bloodstream. Purging techniques are used to clean the cells of residual tumor cells prior to transplanting, leaving only hematopoietic stem cells and progenitor cells. These hematopoietic and progenitor cells are put back into the body. Marrow and stem cell purging techniques involve using drugs or immunologic agents such as monoclonal antibodies.

The patient is prepared much the same as when giving a regular blood donation. Whole blood is drawn out of one arm and into an instrument called a cell separator. A special column in the separator sorts out the desired cells from the other cells with the help of computerized calibration. The stem cells are collected while the remainder of the blood is returned to the donor through a tube and needle in the other arm. More than one collection session may be required to acquire the amount needed for transplanting. Blood-derived progenitor cells may also be harvested from placental and umbilical cord blood after delivery for transplantation to the neonate later in life or to others.

An alternate procedure is for the implantation of donor bone marrow or blood-derived peripheral stem cells. The recipient's immune system is first suppressed using radiation or chemotherapy. The harvested bone marrow or peripheral blood stem cells are injected into the recipient by intravenous drip therapy in a sterile environment. Leukemia patients who show molecular or clinical evidence of relapse after transplantation are infused with additional lymphocytes collected from their donor to help boost the graft vs. leukemia effect.

Coding Guidance

AHA: 2Q, '06, 20-22

41.08 Allogeneic hematopoietic stem cell transplant with purging

Description

Hematopoietic progenitor cells, or stem cells, harvested for transplantation are used to regenerate bone marrow and immune systems destroyed by chemotherapy and/or radiation therapy. These progenitor cells are not only acquired from bone marrow, but are also found in peripheral blood, collected by apheresis. For stem cell harvesting from peripheral blood by apheresis, the donor is often given a hematopoietic growth factor to mobilize progenitor cells into the bloodstream. Purging techniques are used to clean the cells of residual tumor cells prior to transplanting, leaving only hematopoietic stem cells and progenitor cells which are infused into the recipient. Marrow and stem cell purging techniques involve using drugs or immunologic agents such as monoclonal antibodies. An allogeneic approach combines the concepts of high dose therapy with immunotherapy. High dose therapy is administered, followed by an infusion of hematopoietic cells.

The patient is prepared much the same as when giving a regular blood donation. Whole blood is drawn out of one arm and into an instrument called a cell separator. A special column in the separator sorts out the desired cells from the other cells with the help of computerized calibration. The stem cells are collected while the remainder of the blood is returned to the donor through a tube and needle in the other arm. More than one collection session may be required to acquire the amount needed for transplanting. Blood-derived progenitor cells may also be harvested from placental and umbilical cord blood after delivery for transplantation to the neonate later in life or to others.

An alternate procedure is for the implantation of donor bone marrow or blood-derived peripheral stem cells. The recipient's immune system is first suppressed using radiation or chemotherapy. The harvested bone marrow or peripheral blood stem cells are injected into the recipient by intravenous drip therapy in a sterile environment. Leukemia patients who show molecular or clinical evidence of relapse after transplantation are infused with additional lymphocytes collected from their donor to help boost the graft vs. leukemia effect.

41.09 Autologous bone marrow transplant with purging

Description

Hematopoietic progenitor cells, or stem cells, harvested for transplantation are used to regenerate bone marrow and immune systems destroyed by chemotherapy and/or radiation therapy. These progenitor cells are not only acquired from bone marrow, but are also found in peripheral blood, collected by apheresis. For stem cell harvesting from peripheral blood by apheresis, the donor is often given a hematopoietic growth factor to mobilize progenitor cells into the bloodstream. Purging techniques are used to clean the cells of residual tumor cells prior to transplanting, leaving only hematopoietic stem cells and progenitor cells, which

40-41

are infused into the recipient. Marrow and stem cell purging techniques involve using drugs or immunologic agents such as monoclonal antibodies. An allogeneic approach combines the concepts of high dose therapy with immunotherapy. High dose therapy is administered, followed by an infusion of hematopoietic cells.

The patient is prepared much the same as when giving a regular blood donation. Whole blood is drawn out of one arm and into an instrument called a cell separator. A special column in the separator sorts out the desired cells from the other cells with the help of computerized calibration. The stem cells are collected while the remainder of the blood is returned to the donor through a tube and needle in the other arm. More than one collection session may be required to acquire the amount needed for transplanting. Blood-derived progenitor cells may also be harvested from placental and umbilical cord blood after delivery for transplantation to the neonate later in life or to others.

An alternate procedure is for the implantation of donor bone marrow or blood-derived peripheral stem cells. The recipient's immune system is first suppressed using radiation or chemotherapy. The harvested bone marrow or peripheral blood stem cells are injected into the recipient by intravenous drip therapy in a sterile environment. Leukemia patients who show molecular or clinical evidence of relapse after transplantation are infused with additional lymphocytes collected from their donor to help boost the graft vs. leukemia effect.

Coding Clarification
Use 41.09 to report autologous bone marrow transplant with extracorporeal purging of malignant cells from marrow.

Code 41.09 is also used to report cell depletion.

41.1   Puncture of spleen

Description
The physician grasps the spleen with the forceps and inserts a cannula percutaneously into the abdominal cavity to puncture the spleen.

Coding Clarification
To report aspiration biopsy of the spleen, see 41.32.

41.2   Splenotomy

Description
Code 41.2 is used to report an incisional procedure on the spleen that is not more precisely described by other codes in category 41. This code is also reported when the documentation does not further specify the incisional procedure.

Coding Clarification
An understanding of the following terms may aid in code selection:

- **Splenotomy:** Surgical incision into the spleen or the dissection of the spleen. It can also mean the removal of the spleen by incision.

- **Splenectomy:** Total or partial surgical removal of the spleen.

Documentation Tip
Review the documentation for specific information regarding the procedure prior to final code selection in order to ensure accurate code assignment.

41.3   Diagnostic procedures on bone marrow and spleen

Description
Fourth-digit subclassifications describe various diagnostic procedures on the spleen and bone marrow. Bone marrow biopsy, open and closed splenic biopsies, and other diagnostic procedures on the bone marrow and spleen are reported with codes from this subcategory.

41.31   Biopsy of bone marrow

Description
Bone marrow samples are usually taken from the pelvic bone or sternum. The skin over the bone is first cleaned with an antiseptic solution. A local anesthetic is injected and the needle is inserted, rotated to the right, then to the left, withdrawn, and reinserted at a different angle. This procedure is repeated until a small chip is separated from the bone marrow. The needle is again removed, and a piece of fine wire threaded through its tip transfers the specimen onto sterile gauze. Samples contain bone marrow of which the structure has not been disturbed or destroyed. The bone must be decalcified overnight before it can be properly stained and examined.

41.32   Closed (aspiration) (percutaneous) biopsy of spleen

Description
In a needle or percutaneous biopsy, the tissue sample is obtained using a syringe. The physician inserts a needle into the tissue to be biopsied and cells are removed through the needle. Needle biopsies are often performed under radiologic guidance, usually a CT scan. Local or general anesthesia is used.

Coding Clarification
Code 41.32 is used to report needle biopsy of the spleen.

When the tissue to be sampled cannot be safely accessed with a needle or a closed procedure, an open biopsy is performed in the operating room. In an open biopsy, an incision is made in the skin, the organ is exposed, and a tissue sample is taken.

41.33   Open biopsy of spleen

Description
An open biopsy is performed in the operating room. The physician makes an incision in the skin, the spleen is exposed, and a tissue sample is taken.

Coding Clarification
When the tissue to be sampled cannot be safely accessed with a needle or a closed procedure, an open biopsy is performed in the operating room. In an open biopsy, an incision is made in the skin, the organ is exposed, and a tissue sample is taken.

41.38   Other diagnostic procedures on bone marrow

Description
Code 41.38 is used to report other diagnostic procedures of the bone marrow that are not more precisely described by other codes in subcategory 41.3.

Coding Clarification
Do not use 41.38 to report microscopic examination of specimen from bone marrow (90.61-90.69) or radioisotope scan (92.05).

Documentation Tip
Review the documentation for specific information regarding the procedure prior to final code selection in order to ensure accurate code assignment.

41.39   Other diagnostic procedures on spleen

Description
Code 41.39 is used to report other diagnostic procedures of the spleen that are not more precisely described by other codes in subcategory 41.3. One example is an injection procedure for splenoportography in which the physician makes an incision in the left lower axilla. An 18 or 20 gauge sheath catheter is inserted into the middle of the soft, sponge-like tissue of the spleen. The splenic vein is visualized and the catheter is placed. Around 2 to 3 cc of dye are injected per second totaling 15 to 20 cc of radiopaque dye. X-rays are taken every second for 12 seconds. The catheter is removed and the incision is covered with a dressing.

Coding Clarification
Report separately any microscopic examination of specimen from spleen (90.61-90.69) or radioisotope scan (92.05).

Documentation Tip
Review the documentation for specific information regarding the procedure prior to final code selection in order to ensure accurate code assignment.

41.4   Excision or destruction of lesion or tissue of spleen

Description
Fourth-digit subclassification describes various procedures to excise or destroy splenic lesions or other tissue.

Coding Clarification
Code also any application or administration of an adhesion barrier substance (99.77).

To report an excision of an accessory spleen, see 41.93.

Documentation Tip
Review the documentation for specific information regarding the procedure prior to final code selection in order to ensure accurate code assignment.

41.41   Marsupialization of splenic cyst

Description
In a marsupialization procedure, the physician makes an incision of a cyst of the spleen and sutures the edges open to create a pouch.

41.42   Excision of lesion or tissue of spleen

Description
The physician makes a midline incision and dissects tissue around the spleen. The short stomach vessels are doubly ligated and cut. The splenic recess is dissected and the splenic artery and vein are divided and cut individually. The physician removes the splenic tissue. A drain may be placed and the wound is irrigated. The incision is closed with sutures or staples and a dry sterile dressing is applied.

Coding Clarification
Do not use 41.42 to report biopsy of a spleen; see 41.32-41.33.

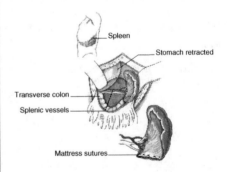

Spleen

Stomach retracted

Transverse colon

Splenic vessels

Mattress sutures

41.43   Partial splenectomy

Description
In a partial splenectomy, the physician removes only a portion of the spleen, usually to treat pain caused by an enlarged spleen. The physician makes a midline incision and dissects tissue around the

spleen. The short stomach vessels are doubly ligated and cut. The splenic recess is dissected and the splenic artery and vein are divided and cut individually as needed and the physician removes a portion of the spleen. A drain may be placed and the wound is irrigated. The incision is closed with sutures or staples and a dry sterile dressing is applied.

In an alternate technique, the physician performs a laparoscopic splenectomy. With the patient under anesthesia, the physician makes a small incision in the abdominal wall and inserts a trocar just below or above the umbilicus. The physician insufflates the abdominal cavity and places the laparoscope through the umbilical incision. Additional small incisions are performed and trocars are placed into the peritoneal space to be used as ports for instruments, video camera (the camera allows the physician to operate both by viewing through the laparoscope and on a video monitor), and/or an additional light source. Dissection is carried down to the level of the spleen with care taken to identify tail of the pancreas. A portion of the spleen is excised using special instruments to ensure hemostasis. The freed splenic tissue is isolated and pouched. Pieces of the spleen are then suctioned from the pouch through a trocar. The laparoscope and trocars are removed. The incisions are closed with sutures.

Coding Clarification
There are two operative approaches to access the spleen for a splenectomy:

- In an open procedure, which is performed under general anesthesia, the physician makes an incision in the abdomen, the artery to the spleen is tied, and the ligaments holding the spleen in place are detached and the spleen is removed.

- Laparoscopic splenectomy is the removal of the spleen in piecemeal through several small incisions using smaller surgical instruments, with the assistance of a camera.

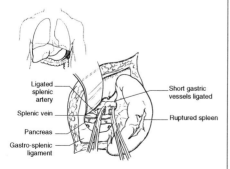

Ligated splenic artery

Short gastric vessels ligated

Splenic vein

Ruptured spleen

Pancreas

Gastro-splenic ligament

41.5 Total splenectomy

Description
There are two operative approaches to access the spleen for a splenectomy. In an open procedure, which is performed under general anesthesia, the physician makes an incision in the abdomen, the artery to the spleen is tied, and the ligaments holding the spleen in place are detached and the spleen is removed. Laparoscopic splenectomy is the removal of the spleen in piecemeal through several small incisions using smaller surgical instruments, with the assistance of a camera.

The physician makes a midline incision and dissects tissue around the spleen. The short stomach vessels are doubly ligated and cut. The splenic recess is dissected and the splenic artery and vein are divided and cut individually. The physician removes the spleen. A drain may be placed and the wound is irrigated. The incision is closed with sutures or staples and a dry sterile dressing is applied.

Alternately, the physician performs a laparoscopic splenectomy. The patient is placed in a right lateral decubitus position, left arm over the head. With the patient under anesthesia, the physician makes a small incision in the abdominal wall and inserts a trocar just below or above the umbilicus. The physician insufflates the abdominal cavity and places the laparoscope through the umbilical incision. Additional small incisions are performed and trocars are placed into the peritoneal space to be used as ports for instruments, video camera (the camera allows the physician to operate both by viewing through the laparoscope and on a video monitor), and/or an additional light source. Dissection is carried down to the level of the spleen with care taken to identify tail of the pancreas. Electrocautery is used to divide ligaments and the spleen is mobilized. Short gastric vessels may be transected to gain additional exposure. The splenic vessels are transected and the spleen is excised using special instruments to ensure hemostasis. The freed spleen is isolated and pouched. Pieces of the spleen are then suctioned from the pouch through a trocar. The laparoscope and trocars are removed. The incisions are closed with sutures.

Coding Clarification
Use 41.5 to report splenectomy that is not further specified in the documentation.

Code in addition any application or administration of an adhesion barrier substance (99.77).

41.9 Other operations on spleen and bone marrow

Description
Codes in subcategory 41.9 describe other procedures of the spleen and bone marrow that are

40-41

not more precisely described by other codes in category 41.

Coding Clarification
When reporting 41.9x, also report any application or administration of an adhesion barrier substance with 99.77.

Documentation Tip
Review the documentation for specific information regarding the procedure prior to final code selection in order to ensure accurate code assignment.

41.91   Aspiration of bone marrow from donor for transplant

Description
Bone marrow samples are usually taken from the pelvic bone or sternum. The skin over the bone is first cleaned with an antiseptic solution. A local anesthetic is injected and the physician inserts a needle beneath the skin and rotates it until the needle penetrates the cortex and into the marrow cavity of the sternum, iliac crest, or ribs. At least half a teaspoon of marrow is aspirated from the bone by a syringe attached to the needle. If more marrow is needed, the needle is repositioned slightly, a new syringe is attached, and a second sample is taken. The samples are transferred from the syringes to slides and sent to a laboratory for analysis. The puncture wound is covered with a sterile dressing.

Coding Clarification
To report biopsy of bone marrow, see 41.31.

Coding Guidance
    AHA: 1Q, '91, 3

41.92   Injection into bone marrow

Description
The physician inserts a special needle through the skin and through the muscle tissue to puncture the bone marrow cavity, usually in the tibia or femur, of a patient whose vessels otherwise seem inaccessible. This needle is then used as a method of infusing fluids into the blood vessels in the bone marrow.

Coding Clarification
To report a bone marrow transplant, see 41.00-41.03.

Coding Guidance
    AHA: 3Q, '96, 17

41.93   Excision of accessory spleen

Description
A common congenital anomaly, an accessory spleen is healthy splenic tissue that is separate from the spleen; it can be an outlying portion of the spleen, connected or detached.

The physician typically performs a laparoscopic excision of an accessory spleen. With the patient under anesthesia, the physician makes a small incision in the abdominal wall and inserts a trocar just below or above the umbilicus. The physician insufflates the abdominal cavity and places the laparoscope through the umbilical incision. Additional small incisions are performed and trocars are placed into the peritoneal space to be used as ports for instruments, video camera (the camera allows the physician to operate both by viewing through the laparoscope and on a video monitor), and/or an additional light source. Dissection is carried down to the level of the spleen with care taken to identify tail of the pancreas. Electrocautery is used to divide ligaments and the spleen is mobilized. Short gastric vessels may be transected to gain additional exposure. The splenic vessels are transected and the spleen is excised using special instruments to ensure hemostasis. The laparoscope and trocars are removed. The incisions are closed with sutures.

41.94   Transplantation of spleen

Description
Spleen transplantation is the transfer of the spleen, or portions of the spleen, from one patient to another. Spleen transplantation is frequently performed to prevent harmful antibodies from returning after incompatible transplantation. Patients who have had their spleen removed need to be protected from most bacteria through immunizations.

The physician can remove the spleen through an open incision or via laparoscopic surgery. In an open procedure, an incision is made in the abdomen over the spleen, the spleen is located, and the splenic artery and vein are tied off. The spleen is removed and any bleeding is controlled with a cautery.

In a laparoscopic removal, the physician makes a small incision in the abdomen through which a laparoscope is inserted. Two or three additional incisions are made in the abdomen through which the surgeon inserts specialized instruments. The spleen is located, isolated, and blood vessels are tied off. The spleen is then rotated and removed. At this time, the transplant is introduced into the abdominal cavity and a splenic-to-common iliac artery and vein bypass is performed laparoscopically using a 7-0 polytetrafluoroethylene running suture. The incisions are closed with stitches and covered with surgical tape. After the transplant, the patient begins taking medications to prevent rejection of the new spleen.

● New Code   ▲ Revised Code   ▶◀ Revised Text   © 2010 Ingenix

41.95   Repair and plastic operations on spleen

Description
The physician repairs a ruptured spleen with or without partial splenectomy. The physician makes an upper midline incision and dissects around the spleen until it is exposed. Lacerations are sutured. The damaged segment of the spleen is resected and removed and the edges are sutured. The wound is irrigated and the incision is closed using sutures or staples and a dry dressing.

41.98   Other operations on bone marrow

Description
Code 41.98 is used to report other procedures of the bone marrow that are not more precisely described by other codes in subcategory 41.9.

Documentation Tip
Review the documentation for specific information regarding the procedure prior to final code selection in order to avoid improper use of the "not otherwise specified" code and to ensure accurate code assignment.

Coding Guidance
   AHA: 3Q, '08, 19

41.99   Other operations on spleen

Description
Code 41.99 is used to report other procedures of the spleen that are not more precisely described by other codes in subcategory 41.9.

Documentation Tip
Review the documentation for specific information regarding the procedure prior to final code selection in order to avoid improper use of the "not otherwise specified" code and to ensure accurate code assignment.

42-54

Operations on the Digestive System

2011 Changes

In this section, an inclusion term was added to clarify the classification of hernia of the abdominal wall by laparoscopic approach to code 53.59 Repair of other hernia of anterior abdominal wall.

The ICD-9-CM classification system for operations performed on the digestive system is divided into categories of procedures according to sites as follows:

- Operations on Esophagus (42)
- Incision and Excision of Stomach (43)
- Other Operations on Stomach (44)
- Incision, Excision and Anastomosis of Intestine (45)
- Other Operations on Intestine (46)
- Operations on Appendix (47)
- Operations on Rectum, Rectosigmoid and Perirectal Tissue (48)
- Operations on Anus (49)
- Operations on Liver (50)
- Operations on Gallbladder and Biliary tract (51)
- Operations on Pancreas (52)
- Repair of Hernia (53)
- Other Operations on Abdominal Region (54)

Coding Clarification

Many of the subcategories in this portion of the classification system require a fourth digit for further specificity with regard to type and/or site of the operation performed.

Documentation Tip

Documentation in the operative report must support code selection.

42   Operations on esophagus

Description

The esophagus is a tube that extends approximately 10 inches from the pharynx to the stomach for the passage of food. Peristalsis is a series of wave-like involuntary muscle contractions that move the food along the digestive tract, starting at the esophagus. The esophagus may be divided into three parts: the upper, middle and distal portions. The upper portion extends from the pharynx, the middle portion extends into the thoracic cavity, and the distal portion empties into the stomach.

Category 42 provides codes for esophageal diagnostic and therapeutic procedures, including incisions, excisions, resections, repairs, anastomoses, and other procedures.

42.0 Esophagotomy

Description

This subcategory classifies esophagotomy (incisions into the esophagus).

42.01   Incision of esophageal web

Description

This code describes the cutting into of an anomalous congenital esophageal membrane.

42.09   Other incision of esophagus

Description

The physician makes a horizontal or an oblique incision in the lateral neck and into the esophagus. If the procedure is performed for foreign body removal, forceps may be used to grasp and extract the foreign body. The incision is closed with sutured layers.

Coding Clarification

Code 42.09 excludes incision procedures specified as esophagomyotomy (42.7) and esophagostomy (42.10-42.19.)

42.1   Esophagostomy

Description

This subcategory classifies esophagostomy procedures (surgically-created artificial openings in the esophagus).

42-54

42.10   Esophagostomy, not otherwise specified

Description
The physician performs esophagostomy without specification of surgical approach or type.

Coding Clarification
This is a non-specific procedure code that should not be assigned for inpatient hospital admissions. The medical record should contain sufficient information to facilitate coding at a higher level of specificity.

Documentation Tip
If the documentation is ambiguous or unclear, the physician should be queried.

42.11   Cervical esophagostomy

Description
The physician creates an opening into the upper region of the esophagus. The physician makes a cervical incision to access the esophagus. The proximal limb of the esophagus is exteriorized and sutured into place, creating a connection from the exterior of the body to the esophageal lumen for mucus drainage. The incision is sutured in layers.

Coding Clarification
Different approaches are used to access the esophagus. For example, in 42.11, access is gained through a cervical incision; however in 42.19, the physician uses a lateral thoracotomy to access the esophagus. An abdominal approach using an upper midline abdominal incision may also be used.

42.12   Exteriorization of esophageal pouch

Description
The physician transfers a section of esophageal pouch to the exterior of the body.

42.19   Other external fistulization of esophagus

Description
The physician connects the esophagus to the exterior of the body, creating a fistula for drainage. To access the esophagus, the physician makes an incision in the anterior chest (lateral thoracotomy). The physician makes an incision in the esophagus, or uses the esophageal stump as an opening. The proximal limb of the esophagus is exteriorized and sutured into place to create a connection for mucus drainage from the exterior of the body to the esophageal lumen. The incision is sutured in layers.

Coding Clarification
Code also any resection (42.40-42.42).

Different approaches are used to access the esophagus. For example, in 42.11, access is gained through a cervical incision; however in 42.19, the physician uses a lateral thoracotomy to access the esophagus. An abdominal approach using an upper midline abdominal incision may also be used.

42.2   Diagnostic procedures on esophagus

Description
This subcategory classifies diagnostic procedures on the esophagus including endoscopy, biopsy, and other procedures.

42.21   Operative esophagoscopy by incision

42.22   Esophagoscopy through artificial stoma

42.23   Other esophagoscopy

Description
The physician views the esophagus. The physician introduces a rigid esophagoscope through an operative incision or the patient's mouth and into the esophagus under general anesthesia, or a flexible esophagoscope under topical anesthesia with sedation.

Coding Clarification
Codes 42.22-42.23 exclude esophagoscopy with biopsy (42.24).

Coding Guidance
   AHA: 3Q, '98, 11; 1Q, '00, 20

42.24   Closed (endoscopic) biopsy of esophagus

Description
The physician introduces a rigid esophagoscope through the patient's mouth and into the esophagus under general anesthesia or a flexible esophagoscope under topical anesthesia with sedation. The physician views the esophagus and may take a specimen collection of cells by brushing or washing and aspirating the esophageal lining.

Coding Clarification
Code 42.24 excludes esophagogastroduodenoscopy (EGD) with closed biopsy (45.16).

Coding Scenario
A patient with chronic esophagitis was admitted to the endoscopy unit. After using topical anesthesia with sedation, the physician introduced a flexible esophagoscope into the esophagus where bite biopsy forceps were used to obtain samples of the esophageal mucosa that appeared abnormal.

   Code Assignment:

   530.10   Unspecified esophagitis
   42.24   Closed [endoscopic] biopsy of esophagus

42.25   Open biopsy of esophagus

Description
The physician makes an incision into the esophagus. A biopsy specimen is removed. The incision is closed in layers.

● New Code   ▲ Revised Code   ▶◀ Revised Text   © 2010 Ingenix

42.29 Other diagnostic procedures on esophagus

Description
This code reports other diagnostic procedures on the esophagus not classifiable elsewhere in subcategory 42.2

Coding Clarification
This code should not be assigned if the medical record contains sufficient information to facilitate coding at a higher level of specificity.

Code 42.29 excludes certain radiological and microscopic diagnostic procedures classifiable to Chapter 16 Miscellaneous diagnostic and therapeutic procedures.

Documentation Tip
If the documentation is ambiguous or unclear, the physician should be queried.

Coding Guidance
AHA: 3Q, '96, 12

42.3 Local excision or destruction of lesion or tissue of esophagus

Description
This subcategory classifies excision or destruction of esophageal lesions either by open (incisional) or endoscopic approach.

42.31 Local excision of esophageal diverticulum

Description
The physician removes a diverticulum from the hypopharynx or esophagus. A diverticulum is a pouch that occurs normally or because of a defect in the muscular membrane. The physician incises and dissects the left posterior chest wall. The physician may dissect or incise the cricopharyngeus muscle to expose the diverticulum. The physician clamps the diverticulum and closes using sutures or staples. The incision is closed with sutured layers.

42.32 Local excision of other lesion or tissue of esophagus

Description
The physician removes a lesion in the esophagus. The physician makes a horizontal or oblique incision of the lateral neck. Next, the physician makes an incision in the esophagus and excises the lesion. The remaining esophageal borders are sutured together. The incision is sutured in layers.

Coding Clarification
Code 42.32 excludes biopsy of esophagus (42.24-42.25) and esophageal fistulectomy (42.84).

42.33 Endoscopic excision or destruction of lesion or tissue of esophagus

Description
This code reports the endoscopic excision or destruction of a lesion or tissue of the esophagus. Surgical technique may vary depending on the size and nature of the lesion or tissue.

The physician uses an esophagoscope to remove tumors, polyps, or lesions from the esophagus. The physician passes a rigid or flexible esophagoscope through the patient's mouth and into the esophagus and locates the lesion. The base of the lesion may be electrocoagulated and severed using biopsy forceps or bipolar cautery. A snare loop may be placed around the base of the lesion and closed (the tissue is electrocoagulated and severed as the loop is closed). The severed tissue is withdrawn through the scope. The lesion may also be removed using laser therapy, electrocoagulation, or injection of toxic agents.

Coding Clarification
Code 42.33 includes the following endoscopic procedures:

- Ablation
- Control of hemorrhage
- Polypectomy
- Injection or control of bleeding esophageal varices

Code 42.33 excludes endoscopic biopsy of esophagus (42.24-42.25), fistulectomy (42.84), and open ligation of esophageal varices (42.91).

42.39 Other destruction of lesion or tissue of esophagus

Description
The physician removes or destroys a lesion in the esophagus by electrocautery or other method. The physician makes a horizontal or an oblique incision of the lateral neck. Next, the physician makes an incision in the esophagus and excises the lesion. The lesion is destroyed and any bleeding is controlled. The remaining esophageal borders are sutured together. The incision is sutured in layers.

Coding Clarification
Code 42.39 excludes lesion or tissue destruction by endoscopic approach (42.33).

42.4 Excision of esophagus

Description
This subcategory describes partial, total, or unspecified excision of the esophagus.

Coding Clarification
This subcategory excludes esophagogastrectomy (excision of both esophageal and stomach tissue) that is not otherwise specified (43.99).

42.40   Esophagectomy, not otherwise specified
Description
This code reports excision of esophageal, unspecified as partial or total.

Coding Clarification
This non-specific code should not be assigned if the medical record contains sufficient information to facilitate coding at a higher level of specificity.

Documentation Tip
If the documentation is ambiguous or unclear, the physician should be queried.

42.41   Partial esophagectomy Description
Description
The physician surgically removes part of the esophagus. Surgical approach and technique may vary, depending on the nature and anatomic site of esophageal resection. The physician removes the affected portion of the esophagus, which may be replaced as a graft from the large or small intestine. The physician gains access to the esophagus through a cervical, thoracic, thoracoabdominal, or abdominal incision. The physician resects the affected portion of the esophagus. The physician may obtain a graft from the large or small intestine. This is most commonly necessary when removing the proximal esophagus. To do this, the physician makes a midline abdominal incision and frees a portion of the large or small intestine of muscular and vascular attachments. The intestine is resected and interposed to reestablish gastrointestinal continuity in the cervical esophagus. Microsurgical techniques are used to create a new blood supply for the graft. The distal and proximal portions of the remaining intestine are reconnected (anastomosis).

If the physician resects the distal esophagus, the physician makes a midline abdominal incision. The stomach is dissected free of surrounding structures and the esophagus is mobilized as it passes through the diaphragm to the stomach. The esophagus is divided at its connection to the stomach. Part of the esophagus is excised and removed, without synchronous resection of gastric tissue. Next, a right chest incision is made between the ribs to expose the esophagus. The distal esophagus is mobilized under direct vision and divided above its diseased segment. The distal esophagus, attached proximal stomach, and the esophageal segment are removed. The remaining stomach is pulled into the chest and connected to the stump of the proximal esophagus.

Drains are placed into the chest near the new anastomosis and the incisions are closed.

Coding Clarification
Code also any synchronous:

- Anastomosis other than end-to-end (42.51-42.69)
- Esophagostomy (42.10-42.19)
- Gastrostomy (43.11-43.19)

42.42   Total esophagectomy
Description
The physician surgically removes the entire esophagus. Surgical technique may vary depending on whether a thoracotomy approach is utilized and the type of anastomosis required.

- **Resection with anastomosis:** The physician removes the esophagus and attaches the stump to the stomach and the pharynx. The physician gains access to the esophagus through two incisions: an oblique cervical incision and a horizontal upper midline abdominal incision. The physician divides the esophagus at the cervical level (for an esophagogastrostomy) or at its origin at the pharynx (for a pharyngogastrostomy). The esophagus is removed through the abdominal incision and divided from the stomach. The stomach is pulled through the posterior mediastinum and anastomosed to the pharynx or the remaining cervical esophagus. The incisions are repaired in sutured layers.

- **Resection with bowel graft:** The physician removes the esophagus and uses a bowel or colon graft for reconstruction. The physician gains access to the esophagus through two incisions: an oblique cervical incision and a horizontal upper midline abdominal incision. The physician divides the esophagus at the cervical level (for an esophagogastrostomy) or at its origin at the pharynx (for a pharyngogastrostomy). The esophagus is removed through the abdominal incision and divided from the stomach. A portion of the colon or small bowel is excised and freed of attachments, taking care to preserve its major vascular supply. Gastrointestinal continuity is reestablished by securing the distal and proximal bowel margins. Finally, the excised portion of the colon or bowel is attached to the pharynx or cervical esophagus and the stomach. This anastomosis creates a usable esophagus. If the stomach is used as the esophageal conduit, a pyloroplasty may be performed to open the pyloric sphincter. The incisions are repaired in sutured layers.

- **Resection with thoracotomy and anastomosis:** The physician removes the esophagus through abdominal, chest, and neck incisions and replaces the esophagus with stomach. The physician makes a midline abdominal incision. Next, the stomach is dissected free of surrounding structures and the esophagus is mobilized as it passes through the diaphragm to the stomach. The physician makes an incision in the right chest between the ribs and exposes the esophagus. The esophagus is mobilized under direct vision in the chest from the diaphragm to the neck. Next, a longitudinal incision is made in the left or right neck and the esophagus is identified and mobilized in the neck. The esophagus is divided at its junction with the stomach and in the neck and the esophagus is removed. The stomach is pulled through the middle of the chest into the neck and the stomach is connected to the stump of the esophagus. The incisions are closed.

- **Resection with thoracotomy and bowel graft:** The physician removes the esophagus through abdominal, chest, and neck incisions and replaces the esophagus with colon or small bowel. The physician makes a midline abdominal incision. The stomach is dissected free of surrounding structures and the esophagus is mobilized as it passes through the diagram to the stomach. The physician makes an incision in the right chest between the ribs and exposes the esophagus. The esophagus is mobilized under direct vision in the chest from the diaphragm to the neck. The esophagus is divided at its junction with the stomach and in the neck and the esophagus is removed. The physician selects an appropriate segment of colon or small bowel. The bowel is divided proximal and distal to this segment and the bowel ends are reapproximated. The selected segment of colon or small bowel is pulled through the middle section of the chest and connected to the stump of the esophagus in the neck and to the stomach in the abdomen. The incisions are closed.

Coding Clarification
Code also any synchronous:

- Gastrostomy (43.11-43.19)
- Interposition or anastomosis other than end-to-end (42.51-42.69)

Code 42.42 excludes esophagogastrectomy (excision of both esophageal and stomach tissue) that is not otherwise specified (43.99).

Coding Guidance
AHA: 4Q, '88, 11

42.5   Intrathoracic anastomosis of esophagus
Description
This subcategory classifies surgical connection of the esophagus to a conduit within the chest.

Coding Clarification
Code also any synchronous:

- Esophagectomy (42.40-42.42)
- Gastrostomy (43.1)

42.51   Intrathoracic esophagoesophagostomy
Description
The physician connects both ends of the esophagus within the chest cavity after resection.

42.52   Intrathoracic esophagogastrostomy
Description
The physician connects the esophagus to stomach in the chest following resection.

A right chest incision is made between the ribs to expose the esophagus. The distal esophagus is mobilized under direct vision and divided above its diseased segment. The distal esophagus, attached proximal stomach, and the esophageal segment resected are removed. The remaining stomach is pulled into the chest and connected to the stump of the proximal esophagus.

42.53   Intrathoracic esophageal anastomosis with interposition of small bowel
Description
The physician removes all or part of the esophagus through abdominal, chest, and neck incisions and replaces the esophagus with colon or small bowel. The physician makes a midline abdominal incision. The stomach is dissected free of surrounding structures and the esophagus is mobilized as it passes through the diaphragm to the stomach. The physician makes an incision in the right chest between the ribs and exposes the esophagus. The esophagus is mobilized under direct vision in the chest from the diaphragm to the neck. The esophagus is divided at its junction with the stomach and in the neck and the esophagus is removed. The physician selects an appropriate segment of small bowel. The bowel is divided proximal and distal to this segment and the bowel ends are reapproximated. The selected segment of small bowel is pulled through the middle section of the chest and connected to the stump of the esophagus in the neck and to the stomach in the abdomen. The incisions are closed.

42-54

42.54   Other intrathoracic esophagoenterostomy

Description
This code reports the anastomosis of the esophagus to a segment of intestine, not otherwise specified.

Coding Clarification
This code should not be assigned if the medical record contains sufficient information to facilitate coding at a higher level of specificity.

Documentation Tip
If the documentation is ambiguous or unclear, the physician should be queried.

42.55   Intrathoracic esophageal anastomosis with interposition of colon

Description
The physician removes all or part of the esophagus through abdominal, chest, and neck incisions and replaces the esophagus with colon or small bowel. The physician makes a midline abdominal incision. The stomach is dissected free of surrounding structures and the esophagus is mobilized as it passes through the diaphragm to the stomach. The physician makes an incision in the right chest between the ribs and exposes the esophagus. The esophagus is mobilized under direct vision in the chest from the diaphragm to the neck. The esophagus is divided at its junction with the stomach and in the neck and the esophagus is removed. The physician selects an appropriate segment of colon. The bowel is divided proximal and distal to this segment and the bowel ends are reapproximated. The selected segment of colon is pulled through the middle section of the chest and connected to the stump of the esophagus in the neck and to the stomach in the abdomen. The incisions are closed.

42.56   Other intrathoracic esophagocolostomy

Description
This code reports the anastomosis of the esophagus to a segment of colon, not otherwise specified.

Coding Clarification
This code should not be assigned if the medical record contains sufficient information to facilitate coding at a higher level of specificity.

Documentation Tip
If the documentation is ambiguous or unclear, the physician should be queried.

42.58   Intrathoracic esophageal anastomosis with other interposition

Description
This code reports a thoracoabdominal esophageal anastomosis contiguous to or post-esophageal resection. The physician uses a thoracoabdominal

approach as a continuous incision or separate thoracic and abdominal incisions. The stomach is mobilized and repositioned in the chest in the original esophageal bed and sutured to the esophageal stump. The incision and esophageal stoma are closed. A jejunostomy tube may be left in place. This procedure may be performed with colon interposition or small bowel reconstruction, including bowel mobilization, preparation, and/or anastomosis.

42.59   Other intrathoracic anastomosis of esophagus

Description
This code reports other intrathoracic anastomosis of the esophagus not classifiable elsewhere in subcategory 42.5.

Coding Clarification
This code should not be assigned if the medical record contains sufficient information to facilitate coding at a higher level of specificity.

Documentation Tip
If the documentation is ambiguous or unclear, the physician should be queried.

Coding Guidance
   AHA: 4Q, '88, 11

42.6   Antesternal anastomosis of esophagus

Description
The physician connects the ends of the esophagus to the stomach, small bowel, or colon through a cervical incision.

42.61   Antesternal esophagoesophagostomy

42.62   Antesternal esophagogastrostomy

42.63   Antesternal esophageal anastomosis with interposition of small bowel

42.64   Other antesternal esophagoenterostomy

42.65   Antesternal esophageal anastomosis with interposition of colon

42.66   Other antesternal esophagocolostomy

42.68   Other antesternal esophageal anastomosis with interposition

42.69   Other antesternal anastomosis of esophagus

Description
The physician removes the affected portion of the esophagus, which may be replaced as a graft from the large or small intestine. The physician gains access to the esophagus through an antesternal or cervical incision. The physician resects the affected

● New Code   ▲ Revised Code   ▶◀ Revised Text   © 2010 Ingenix

42-54

portion of the esophagus. The physician may obtain a graft from the large or small intestine. This is most commonly necessary when the physician is removing the proximal esophagus. To do this, the physician makes a midline abdominal incision and frees a portion of the large or small intestine of muscular and vascular attachments. The intestine is resected and interposed to reestablish gastrointestinal continuity in the cervical esophagus. Microsurgical techniques are used to create new blood supply for the graft. The distal and proximal portions of the remaining intestine are reconnected (anastomosis).

42.7 Esophagomyotomy

Description
The physician accesses the esophagus through an upper abdominal or a thoracic incision. The physician may use a thoracic, abdominal, or other thoracoabdominal approach. The physician makes an incision into the muscular layers of the distal esophagus and cardia of the stomach (myotomy), leaving a gastric fundic flap. The flap is pulled along the esophagus and sutured onto the margins of the myotomy. Repair of a hiatal hernia is performed by restoring the herniated portion of the stomach back to the abdomen, then narrowing the hiatal opening of the diaphragm by suturing the left and right crura together. All incisions are sutured in layers.

42.8 Other repair of esophagus

Description
This subcategory lists esophageal repair procedures classified as "other," including esophagostomy, other suture of laceration, repair of esophageal fistula or stricture, and other procedures.

42.81 Insertion of permanent tube into esophagus

Description
The physician examines the esophagus to place a plastic tube or stent. This procedure usually follows dilation for an obstruction. The physician passes a rigid or flexible esophagoscope through the patient's mouth and into the esophagus. A guidewire is placed through the scope. The stent or plastic tube is advanced over the guidewire. The position of the stent is confirmed with the scope.

Coding Clarification
Insertion of stents classifiable to 42.81 may be used for treatment of esophageal stricture and fistula produced by the adverse effects of malignant neoplasm or other disease.

Coding Guidance
AHA: 1Q, '97, 15

42.82 Suture of laceration of esophagus

Description
The physician sutures a wound or injury to the esophagus. The physician accesses the esophagus through a lateral neck, midline abdominal, or thoracic incision. The physician exposes the affected segment of the esophagus, which is repaired by suturing. The incision is sutured in layers.

42.83 Closure of esophagostomy

Description
The physician closes an opening in the esophagus and returns it to its natural position. The physician accesses the defect through an oblique cervical incision along the border of the sternocleidomastoid muscle, a midline abdominal incision, or a thoracic incision. The physician closes the opening with sutures and repositions the esophagus to its normal anatomical position. The incision is sutured in layers.

42.84 Repair of esophageal fistula, not elsewhere classified

Description
This code reports the repair of esophageal fistula, without specification of anatomic site or type. Operative approach depends on the anatomic site or type of the fistula. The physician excises and removes the fistula tract or closes the fistula tract with sutures, and repositions the esophagus to its normal anatomical position, if necessary. The incision is sutured in layers.

Coding Clarification
This code should not be assigned if the medical record contains sufficient information to facilitate coding at a higher level of specificity. The site of incision and anatomic structures described in the procedure should assist in specification of the type of fistula repaired.

Code 42.84 lists multiple exclusions for specified fistula repairs more appropriately classified elsewhere, including:

- Bronchoesophageal (33.42)
- Esophagopleurocutaneous (34.73)
- Pharyngoesophageal (29.53)
- Tracheoesophageal (31.73)

Documentation Tip
If the documentation is ambiguous or unclear, the physician should be queried.

42.85 Repair of esophageal stricture

Description
This code reports surgical repair of an esophageal stricture, not specified as dilation, such as

42–54

esophageal or paraesophageal transection. The physician repairs a defect in the esophagus using plastic repair or reconstruction. The physician may make a thoracic incision to access the esophagus. The stricture is identified and surgically repaired. Surgical repair technique may vary depending on the site and nature of stricture. The incision is sutured in layers.

Coding Clarification

Dilation of esophageal stricture is classified to 42.92.

Repair of esophageal stricture by insertion of a permanent tube or stent is classified to 42.81.

Coding Guidance

> **AHA:** 1Q, '97, 15

42.86   Production of subcutaneous tunnel without esophageal anastomosis

Description

This procedure may be defined as the surgical formation of a subcutaneous esophageal passage without cutting and reconnection.

42.87   Other graft of esophagus

Description

This code reports graft procedure of the esophagus, which cannot be more specifically classified elsewhere in category 42.

Coding Clarification

This code should not be assigned if the medical record contains sufficient information to facilitate coding at a higher level of specificity.

Code 42.87 lists multiple exclusions for specified esophageal graft repairs more appropriately classified elsewhere in category 42.

42.89   Other repair of esophagus

Description

This code reports other esophageal repairs that cannot be specifically classified elsewhere in category 42.

Coding Clarification

This code should not be assigned if the medical record contains sufficient information to facilitate coding at a higher level of specificity.

Code 42.89 lists multiple exclusions for specified repairs classified elsewhere in category 42.

42.9   Other operations on esophagus

Description

This subcategory classifies other esophageal operations not classifiable elsewhere in category 42, including ligation, dilation, and other procedures.

42.91   Ligation of esophageal varices

Description

The physician accesses the esophagus through a midline abdominal or thoracic incision, and makes a longitudinal incision in the esophagus. The physician locates the varices (tortuous, dilated veins) and ligates them with sutures. The esophagotomy is closed with sutures. The incision is sutured in layers.

Coding Clarification

Code 42.91 excludes ligation by endoscopic approach (42.33).

42.92   Dilation of esophagus

Description

This code reports the passage of balloon or hydrostatic dilators through the esophagus to enlarge the esophagus and relieve obstruction. Technique and approach may vary, including:

* **Dilation by guidewire:** The physician dilates the esophagus by passing dilators over a guidewire. The physician uses a fluoroscope to place a guidewire into the patient's throat, down the esophagus, and into the stomach. A series of olive-shaped metal dilators (Eder-Puestow) are passed over the guidewire and withdrawn. The process is repeated until the esophagus is dilated to an acceptable size.

* **Retrograde dilation:** The physician dilates the esophagus using a dilator that passes from the stomach through the esophagus. The physician uses a fluoroscope to place a guidewire into the patient's throat, down the esophagus, and into the stomach. A dilator is inserted through a gastrostomy tube and attached to the guidewire. Tension on the oral end of the wire pulls the dilator into the distal esophagus. The process is repeated until the esophagus is dilated to an acceptable size.

* **Dilation by balloon or dilator device:** The physician dilates the esophagus using an unguided dilator. The physician passes a dilator into the patient's throat down into the esophagus until the end of the dilator passes the stricture. A stricture is a decrease in the esophagus opening as a result of cicatricial (scar) contraction or a deposit of abnormal tissue. The dilator is withdrawn after it passes the stricture. This may be repeated several times to dilate the esophagus to an acceptable size.

Coding Clarification

Code 42.92 excludes intubation of the esophagus classified to Chapter 16 Miscellaneous Diagnostic and Therapeutic Procedures (96.03, 96.06-96.08).

42-54

42.99 Other operations on esophagus

Description
This code reports other esophageal procedures not elsewhere classified in category 42.

Coding Clarification
This code should not be assigned if the medical record contains sufficient information to facilitate coding at a higher level of specificity.

Code 42.99 lists multiple exclusions for specified repairs classified elsewhere in category 42 and to Chapter 16 Miscellaneous Diagnostic and Therapeutic Procedures.

43 Operations on stomach

Description
The stomach is a sac-like organ into which food passes from the esophagus. The size of the stomach should be slightly larger than the size of a person's closed fist. The walls of the stomach are comprised of serosal, muscular, and mucosal layers. Two sphincters open and close as food is passed into and out of the stomach. The esophageal sphincter (cardiac sphincter) divides the stomach from the esophagus. The pyloric sphincter divides the stomach from the small intestine, allowing for the passage of digested food products into the intestine in small amounts. The stomach may be divided into four major sections:

- **Cardia:** Upper portion of the stomach.
- **Fundus:** Upper part of the stomach that curves upward.
- **Body:** Main, central portion of the stomach.
- **Pylorus (antrum):** Lower part of the stomach that empties into the small intestine.

With the assistance of hydrochloric acid and gastric enzymes, the stomach breaks down food into a digestible state in order to facilitate absorption of nutrients.

Category 43 provides codes for diagnostic and therapeutic stomach procedures including incisions, excision, resections with anastomosis, vagotomy, pyloroplasty, repairs, and other procedures.

43.0 Gastrotomy

Description
The physician performs a diagnostic or therapeutic gastrotomy and explores the gastric area or removes a foreign body. The physician makes a midline epigastric incision and retracts the skin and underlying tissues laterally. The stomach is incised and explored. The stomach is then sutured in layers, the soft tissues are returned to anatomical position, and the incision is sutured in layers.

Coding Clarification
Code also any application or administration of an adhesion barrier substance (99.77).

Code 43.0 excludes gastrostomy (43.11-43.19) and gastrotomy for control of hemorrhage (44.49).

Coding Guidance
AHA: 3Q, '89, 14

43.1 Gastrostomy

Description
This subcategory describes gastrostomy procedures (positioning of a tube through the abdominal wall into the stomach).

Coding Guidance
AHA: S-O, '85, 5

43.11 Percutaneous (endoscopic) gastrostomy (PEG)

Description
The physician uses an endoscope to examine the upper gastrointestinal tract to guide placement of a gastrostomy tube. The physician passes an endoscope through the patient's mouth into the esophagus. The esophagus, stomach, duodenum, and sometimes the jejunum are viewed. The endoscope is used to guide the placement of a percutaneous gastrostomy tube. The tube is inserted through an incision of the abdomen. When in place, the tube connects the gastric lumen with the exterior abdominal wall.

Coding Scenario
A patient presented for percutaneous placement of a gastrostomy tube into the stomach. Using gastric endoscopy for guidance in placing the tube, the physician made a small incision in the stomach and a large bore needle with a suture attached was passed through the incision into the lumen of the stomach. The gastrostomy tube was connected to the suture and passed through the mouth into the stomach and out the abdominal wall where it was sutured to the skin.

Code Assignment:

43.11   Percutaneous [endoscopic] gastrostomy [PEG]

Coding Guidance
AHA: 2Q, '94, 10

43.19 Other gastrostomy

Description
This code reports the construction or insertion of a gastrostomy tube into the stomach without the assistance of an endoscope as described in code 43.11. Percutaneous (non-endoscopic) and open techniques may be utilized. Surgical technique may vary.

The physician constructs a permanent gastrostomy for instillation of nutrients. After a small midline, upper abdominal incision, the physician creates a flap with its base at the greater curvature of the stomach. The flap is converted into a tube by closure of the stomach incision. The tube is brought through the skin surface via a stab wound or tunnel. The end of the tube is everted slightly and sutured to the skin. The abdominal incision is closed with sutures.

In an alternate procedure, the physician constructs a temporary or permanent gastrostomy for instillation of nutrients. After making a midline incision in the upper abdomen, the physician chooses a gastrostomy site on the middle anterior surface of the stomach. Stay sutures are placed and a small stab wound is made between purse string sutures. A gastrostomy tube is inserted and the purse string sutures are tied. The gastrostomy tube is withdrawn through a stab wound in the abdominal wall and stay sutures are placed in the posterior fascia. The abdominal incision is closed.

Coding Clarification
Code 43.19 excludes endoscopic placement of gastrostomy (43.11).

Coding Guidance
AHA: 3Q, '89, 14; 1Q, '92, 14

43.3   Pyloromyotomy

Description
The physician incises the pyloric muscle. The physician makes a small subcostal incision over the pyloric olive. The peritoneum is incised, the tissues are retracted, and the pylorus is identified. The serosa is incised and the tension of the pyloric muscle is released with longitudinal incisions. The peritoneum is sutured closed and the operative site is sutured in layers.

43.4   Local excision or destruction of lesion or tissue of stomach

Description
Subcategory 43.4 provides three subclassification codes to report various methods of stomach lesion excisions or destruction.

43.41   Endoscopic excision or destruction of lesion or tissue of stomach

Description
The physician uses an endoscope to examine the upper gastrointestinal tract and locate and remove tumors, polyps, or other lesions. The physician passes an endoscope through the patient's mouth into the esophagus. The lesion may be destroyed using laser therapy or electrocoagulation. The base of the lesion may be electrocoagulated and severed using biopsy forceps or bipolar cautery. A snare loop

may be placed around the base of the lesion and closed (the tissue is electrocoagulated and severed as the loop is closed). The severed tissue is withdrawn through the endoscope. The endoscope is removed.

Coding Clarification
Code 43.41 excludes excision for biopsy of stomach (44.14-44.15), electrocoagulation or other destruction for control of hemorrhage (44.43), and open ligation of gastric varices (44.91).

Coding Guidance
AHA: 3Q, '96, 10

43.42   Local excision of other lesion or tissue of stomach

Description
The physician performs a local excision of a lesion of the stomach. The physician makes a midline abdominal incision. Next, the stomach is dissected free of surrounding structures and the area of the lesion identified. The lesion is excised. The defect created in the stomach is closed with sutures or a stapling device. The incision is closed.

Coding Clarification
Code 43.42 excludes other excisional procedures classifiable elsewhere, such as biopsy of stomach (44.14-44.15), fistulectomy (44.62-44.63), and partial gastrectomy (43.5-43.89).

43.49   Other destruction of lesion or tissue of stomach

Description
This code reports other non-endoscopic destruction of a lesion of the stomach.

Coding Clarification
This code should not be assigned if the medical record contains sufficient information to facilitate coding at a higher level of specificity.

Code 43.49 excludes destruction of a stomach lesion by endoscopic approach (43.41).

Coding Guidance
AHA: S-O, '85, 6; N-D, '87, 5

43.5   Partial gastrectomy with anastomosis to esophagus

Description
This code reports a partial gastrectomy with esophageal anastomosis. Various surgical techniques may be employed.

The physician removes the distal esophagus and possibly the proximal stomach through abdominal and chest incisions and replaces the esophagus with the remaining stomach. The physician makes a midline abdominal incision. The stomach is dissected free of surrounding structures and the esophagus is mobilized as it passes through the diaphragm to the stomach. The esophagus is divided at its connection to the stomach or the stomach may be divided near its middle portion. Next, a right chest incision is made between the ribs to expose the esophagus. The distal esophagus is mobilized under direct vision and divided above its diseased segment. The distal esophagus and attached proximal stomach are then removed. The remaining stomach is pulled into the chest and connected to the stump of the proximal esophagus. Drains are placed into the chest near the new anastomosis and the incisions are closed.

In an alternate procedure, the physician removes the affected part of the esophagus and proximal stomach and reattaches the remaining stomach to the esophageal stump. The physician accesses the esophagus through a right posterolateral thoracotomy; no abdominal incision is made. The physician resects the affected portion of the distal esophagus and sometimes a portion of the proximal stomach. The resected area is removed. The stomach or gastric remnant is pulled into the thorax and sutured to the esophageal stump. If the stomach is used as the esophageal conduit, a pyloroplasty may be performed to open the pyloric sphincter. The incision is sutured in layers.

Documentation Tip
This procedure may also be documented as proximal gastrectomy.

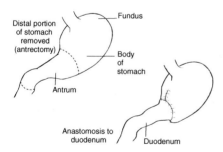

43.6 Partial gastrectomy with anastomosis to duodenum

Description
The physician removes the distal stomach and approximates the proximal stomach to the duodenum. The physician makes a midline abdominal incision. The distal stomach (antrum) is dissected free from surrounding structures and the blood supply to the antrum is divided. Next, the gastroduodenal junction is divided and the stomach is divided in its middle portion, removing the antrum. An anastomosis is made between the proximal stomach and the duodenum with staples or sutures. The incision is closed.

Documentation Tip
This procedure may also be documented as Billroth I operation, distal gastrectomy, or gastropylorectomy.

43.7 Partial gastrectomy with anastomosis to jejunum

Description
The physician removes the distal stomach and approximates the proximal stomach to the jejunum. The physician makes a midline abdominal incision. The distal stomach (antrum) is dissected free from surrounding structures and the blood supply to the antrum is divided. Next, the gastroduodenal junction is divided and the stomach is divided in its middle portion, removing the antrum. An anastomosis is made between the proximal stomach and the jejunum with staples or sutures. The incision is closed.

Documentation Tip
This procedure may also be documented as Billroth II operation, distal gastrectomy, or gastropylorectomy.

Coding Guidance
AHA: 3Q, '03, 3

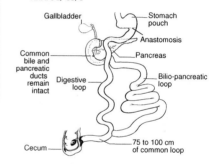

43.8 Other partial gastrectomy

Description
Subcategory 43.8 provides two codes to report partial gastrectomy procedures that are not more specifically described in other subcategories.

43.81 Partial gastrectomy with jejunal transposition

Description
The physician removes the distal stomach and approximates the proximal stomach to the jejunum. The physician makes a midline abdominal incision. The distal stomach (antrum) is dissected free from surrounding structures and the blood supply to the antrum is divided. Next, the gastroduodenal junction is divided and the stomach is divided in its middle portion removing the antrum. An anastomosis is made between the proximal stomach and the

jejunum with staples or sutures. The incision is closed.

Coding Clarification
Code also any synchronous intestinal resection (45.51).

43.89   Other partial gastrectomy

Description
A partial gastrectomy with pylorus-preserving duodenoileostomy and ileoileostomy is done to combine gastric restriction with limited intestinal absorption for weight loss. This procedure is called a biliopancreatic diversion with duodenal switch. The stomach is resected along the greater curvature, leaving the pyloric valve intact with the remaining stomach that maintains its functionality. A portion of the duodenum is also left within the food track to preserve the pylorus/duodenum pathway. The duodenum is divided near the pyloric valve. The small intestine is also divided. The distal end of the small intestine in continuity with the large intestine is brought up and anastomosed to the short duodenal segment on the stomach. The other end of the small intestine—the duodenal segment in connection with the gallbladder and pancreas, or the biliopancreatic loop—is attached to the newly anastomosed other limb further down near the large intestine. This forms a 75 to 100 cm common loop where the contents of both these segments channel together before dumping into the large intestine.

Coding Clarification
This procedure may be performed by laparoscopic or open approach.

Documentation Tip
This procedure may also be documented as partial gastrectomy with bypass gastrogastrostomy or sleeve resection of stomach.

Coding Guidance
AHA: 3Q,'03, 6-8

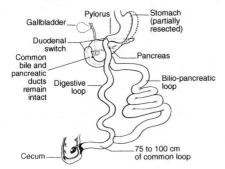

43.9   Total gastrectomy

Description
Subcategory 43.9 provides two subclassification codes to report total gastrectomy, including that with intestinal interposition and other forms.

43.91   Total gastrectomy with intestinal interposition

Description
The physician removes the stomach and approximates a limb of small bowel to the esophagus by performing an esophagoenterostomy or a Roux-en-Y esophagojejunostomy. The physician makes a midline abdominal incision. The stomach is dissected free of surrounding structures and its blood supply is divided. The stomach is divided at the gastroesophageal junction and at the gastroduodenal junction and removed. The remaining duodenal end of the intestine is simply mobilized to the end of the esophagus and connected. A measured limb of Roux, or limb of small intestine, is created by dividing the upper jejunum. The distal part of the now divided upper jejunum, the limb in continuity with the ileum, is brought up and anastomosed to the esophagus. The proximal end of the divided jejunum, the segment containing the duodenum, must be connected back into the limb of small bowel farther down from the esophageal anastomosis. This maintains continuity for the duodenal section, which was sealed upon removal of the stomach, but which is also receiving bile from the liver and gallbladder, as well as pancreatic juice.

43.99   Other total gastrectomy

Description
This code reports total gastrectomy (removal of stomach) not classifiable to 43.91. Surgical technique may vary, including:

- **With construction of intestinal pouch:** The physician removes the stomach and forms a pouch of small bowel and approximates this to the esophagus. The physician makes a midline abdominal incision. Next, the stomach is dissected free of surrounding structures and its blood supply divided. The stomach is divided at the gastroesophageal junction and the gastroduodenal junction removed. The proximal jejunum is divided and the distal end of bowel is folded upon itself and approximated in such a way to form a pouch. The pouch is connected to the esophagus. The divided proximal jejunum is connected to the limb of small bowel distal to the esophageal anastomosis to restore intestinal continuity. The incisions are closed.

42-54

Documentation Tip

Procedures classifiable to this code may be documented as:

- Complete (total) (radical) gastrectomy
- Complete gastroduodenectomy
- Esophagoduodenostomy NOS or with complete (total) gastrectomy
- Esophagojejunostomy with complete (total) gastrectomy

---

44 Other operations on stomach

Description

Category 44 provides eight subcategories for the reporting of various operations on the stomach, including vagotomy, diagnostic procedures, pyloroplasty, gastroenterostomy without gastrectomy, hemorrhage control, suture of stomach or duodenal ulcer, gastric anastomosis revision, and other repairs and operations on the stomach. The majority require fourth-digit subclassification to provide specificity to site and/or procedure.

Coding Clarification

For all codes within category 44, code also any application or administration of adhesion barrier substance (99.77).

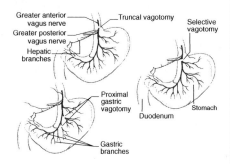

44.0 Vagotomy

Description

A vagotomy is performed under general anesthesia, using a closed (laparoscopic) or open (incisional) surgical approach. The physician makes an incision in the abdomen and locates the vagus nerve. The trunk or the specific branches leading to the stomach are transected or cut. The incision is closed with layered sutures.

Coding Clarification:

Vagotomy is often performed in association with other gastrointestinal surgery, such as gastrectomy and pyloroplasty. The vagotomy portion of the procedure interferes with the nerve stimulation that causes peristalsis (i.e., muscular contractions that move food and digestive secretions through the bowel) and delays gastric emptying.

Code also any application or administration of adhesion barrier substance (99.77).

44.00 Vagotomy, not otherwise specified

Description

This code reports vagotomy not specified to type.

Coding Clarification

This is a nonspecific code that should not be assigned if the medical record contains sufficient information to facilitate coding at a higher level of specificity.

Documentation Tip

If the documentation is ambiguous or unclear, the physician should be queried.

44.01 Truncal vagotomy

Description

The physician performs division of the trunks of the main vagal nerve(s).

44.02 Highly selective vagotomy

Description

The branches of the vagal nerves are divided from the esophagogastric junction to the point of division along the lesser curvature of the stomach.

Documentation Tip

Procedures classifiable to this code may be documented as:

- Parietal cell vagotomy
- Selective proximal vagotomy

44.03 Other selective vagotomy

Description

The main vagal trunks are dissected to the point of branch division and cut.

Documentation Tip

This procedure may be documented as selective (total gastric) vagotomy.

44.1 Diagnostic procedures on stomach

Description

This subcategory classifies diagnostic stomach procedures, including endoscopy, biopsy, and other procedures.

44.11 Transabdominal gastroscopy

Coding Clarification

Code 44.11 excludes gastroscopy with biopsy (44.14).

Documentation Tip
This procedure may be documented as intraoperative gastroscopy.

44.12 Gastroscopy through artificial stoma

Description
The physician examines the upper gastrointestinal tract. The physician passes an endoscope through the surgically created opening (stoma) into the esophagus. The esophagus and stomach are viewed. The endoscope is then removed.

Coding Clarification
Code 44.12 excludes gastroscopy with biopsy (44.14).

44.13 Other gastroscopy

Description
The physician examines the upper gastrointestinal tract. The physician passes an endoscope through the patient's mouth into the esophagus. The esophagus and stomach are viewed. The endoscope is then removed.

Coding Clarification
Code 44.13 excludes gastroscopy with biopsy (44.14).

Coding Guidance
 AHA: N-D, '87, 5; 1Q, '88, 15; 4Q, '90, 23

44.14 Closed [endoscopic] biopsy of stomach

Description
The physician examines the upper gastrointestinal tract for diagnostic purposes. The physician anesthetizes the oropharynx and sedates the patient. The physician passes an endoscope through the patient's mouth into the esophagus. The esophagus is viewed to determine if bleeding, tumors, erosions, ulcers, or other abnormalities are present. Specimens may be obtained by brushing or washing the esophageal lining with saline, followed by aspiration. Next, the stomach and the stomach mucosa are biopsied. The physician may take a biopsy of a random location or specific lesion. The base of the lesion may be electrocoagulated and severed using biopsy forceps or bipolar cautery. A snare loop may be placed around the base of the lesion and closed (the tissue is electrocoagulated and severed as the loop is closed). The severed tissue is withdrawn through the endoscope. The endoscope is removed.

Coding Clarification
Code 44.14 excludes EGD with closed biopsy (45.16).

Coding Guidance
 AHA: N-D, '87, 5; 1Q, '88, 15

44.15 Open biopsy of stomach

Description
The physician makes a midline abdominal incision. The peritoneum is incised and tissues are retracted to identify the anterior surface of the stomach. An incision is made in the stomach and the physician explores the mucosa to obtain biopsies. Once biopsies are acquired, the stomach incision is closed with sutures or staples. The peritoneum is sutured closed and the abdominal incision is closed using layered sutures.

44.19 Other diagnostic procedures on stomach

Description
This code reports other stomach diagnostic procedures not classifiable elsewhere in subcategory 44.1.

Coding Clarification
This code should not be assigned if the medical record contains sufficient information to facilitate coding at a higher level of specificity.

Code 44.19 excludes diagnostic procedures classifiable to Chapter 16 Miscellaneous Diagnostic and Therapeutic Procedures (87-99).

Documentation Tip
If the documentation is ambiguous or unclear, the physician should be queried.

44.2 Pyloroplasty

Description
The physician cuts and sutures the pylorus to relieve obstruction.

44.21 Dilation of pylorus by incision

Description
The physician repairs the pylorus. The physician makes an upper abdominal incision through skin, fascia, and muscles to expose the pylorus, a muscular band surrounding the distal opening of the stomach. A longitudinal incision is made in the pylorus. The incision is closed with a single full thickness suture layer.

44.22 Endoscopic dilation of pylorus

Description
The physician uses an endoscope to examine the upper gastrointestinal tract to locate an obstruction. The physician passes an endoscope through the patient's mouth into the esophagus. The esophagus, stomach, duodenum, and sometimes the jejunum are viewed. If the gastric outlet (pylorus) is obstructed, the physician dilates it using various methods, such as a balloon, guidewire, or bogie. If balloon dilation is performed, the balloon is inflated briefly several times to enlarge the gastric outlet.

● New Code ▲ Revised Code ▶◀ Revised Text © 2010 Ingenix

When the dilation is complete, the balloon and endoscope are removed.

Coding Guidance
   AHA: 2Q, '01, 17

44.29   Other pyloroplasty

Description
This code reports other pyloroplasty not classifiable to dilation (44.21) or endoscopy (44.22).

Coding Clarification
Pyloroplasty is often performed in conjunction with other gastrointestinal procedures such as hiatal hernia repair, vagotomy, or esophagectomy.

This code should not be assigned if the medical record contains sufficient information to facilitate coding at a higher level of specificity.

Documentation Tip
If the documentation is ambiguous or unclear, the physician should be queried.

Coding Guidance
   AHA: 3Q, '99, 3

44.3   Gastroenterostomy without gastrectomy

Description
Subcategory 44.3 provides four subclassification codes to report the various forms of gastroenterostomy without gastrectomy.

44.31   High gastric bypass

Description
The physician performs a gastric bypass for morbid obesity by partitioning the stomach and performing a small bowel division and anastomosis to the proximal stomach (Roux-en-Y gastrojejunostomy). This bypasses the majority of the stomach. The physician makes a midline abdominal incision. The stomach is mobilized and the proximal stomach is divided with a stapling device along the lesser curvature, leaving only a small proximal pouch in continuity with the esophagus. A short limb of the proximal small bowel (150 cm or less) is divided and the distal end of the short intestinal limb is brought up and anastomosed to the proximal gastric pouch. The other end of the divided bowel is connected back into the small bowel distal to the short limb's gastric anastomosis to restore intestinal continuity. The incision is closed.

Documentation Tip
This procedure may also be documented as Printen and Mason gastric bypass.

Coding Guidance
   AHA: M-J, '85, 17

44.32   Percutaneous [endoscopic] gastrojejunostomy

Description
▶The physician performs a percutaneous insertion of an endoscopically guided gastrostomy tube, which provides an artificial opening into the gastric lumen and portion of the jejunum via the exterior abdominal wall.◀

In an endoscopic insertion, the physician uses an endoscope to examine the upper gastrointestinal tract to guide placement of a gastrostomy tube. The physician passes an endoscope through the patient's mouth into the esophagus. The esophagus and stomach are viewed. The endoscope is used to guide the placement of a percutaneous gastrostomy tube. The tube is inserted through an incision of the abdomen. When in place, the tube connects the gastric lumen ▶and a portion of the jejunum◀ with the exterior abdominal wall.

Coding Clarification
Do not assign code 44.32 to report percutaneous endoscopic feeding jejunostomy, rather report code 46.32.

Documentation Tip
Percutaneous endoscopic gastrojejunostomy may also be documented as "PEGJJ."

44.38   Laparoscopic gastroenterostomy

Description
The physician performs a laparoscopic gastric bypass for morbid obesity by partitioning the stomach and performing a small bowel division with anastomosis to the proximal stomach (Roux-en-Y gastroenterostomy). This bypasses the majority of the stomach. The physician places a trocar though an incision above the umbilicus and insufflates the abdominal cavity. The laparoscope and additional trocars are placed through small portal incisions. The stomach is mobilized and the proximal stomach is divided with a stapling device along the lesser curvature, leaving only a small proximal pouch in continuity with the esophagus. A short limb of the proximal small bowel (150 cm or less) is divided and the distal end of the short intestinal limb is brought up and anastomosed to the proximal gastric pouch. The other end of the divided bowel is connected back into the small bowel distal to the short limb's gastric anastomosis to restore intestinal continuity. The instruments are removed.

Coding Guidance
   AHA: 4Q, '04, 122

42-54

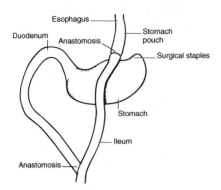

Esophagus

Duodenum

Anastomosis

Stomach pouch

Surgical staples

Stomach

Ileum

Anastomosis

44.39   Other gastroenterostomy without gastrectomy

Description
This code reports other gastroenterostomy not classifiable elsewhere in subcategory 44.3. Surgical technique may vary depending on bypass sites involved.

The physician performs a gastroduodenostomy. The physician uses an upper midline epigastric incision through fascia and muscle. The distal end of the greater curvature of the stomach is removed. The duodenum is mobilized and connected to the greater curvature. The anastomosis is closed with interrupted stitches and the abdominal incision is closed.

Coding Guidance
AHA: 1Q, '01, 16, 17; 3Q, '03, 6

44.4   Control of hemorrhage and suture of ulcer of stomach or duodenum

Description
This subcategory includes control of hemorrhage and suture of an ulcer of the stomach or duodenum by endoscopic, transcatheter embolization, and other surgical approach. Suture procedures are classified to anatomic site.

44.40   Suture of peptic ulcer, not otherwise specified

Description
The physician sutures a peptic ulcer for a site not otherwise specified.

Coding Clarification
This is a non-specific code that should not be assigned if the medical record contains sufficient information to facilitate coding at a higher level of specificity. Review the medical record for documentation of the specific anatomic site of the suture.

Documentation Tip
If the documentation is ambiguous or unclear, the physician should be queried.

44.41   Suture of gastric ulcer site

Description
The physician performs a gastrostomy and explores the gastric area. The physician makes a midline epigastric incision and retracts the skin and underlying tissues laterally. The stomach is incised and explored. The ulcer is identified and the mucosa is drawn over the ulcer and sutured. After exploration and repair, the stomach is sutured in layers, the soft tissues are returned to anatomical position, and the incision is sutured in layers.

Coding Clarification
Code 44.41 excludes ligation of gastric varices (44.91).

44.42   Suture of duodenal ulcer site

Description
The physician repairs an ulcer of the duodenum by suture. The ulcer is exposed by the physician via a midline upper abdominal incision or a transverse supraumbilical incision through skin, fascia, and muscle. The perforation is sutured closed and the peritoneal cavity is irrigated and suctioned to remove contamination. The abdominal fascia and peritoneum are closed in one layer. The skin and subcutaneous layers are not closed unless the perforation is less than two hours old.

Coding Guidance
AHA: J-F, '87, 11

44.43   Endoscopic control of gastric or duodenal bleeding

Description
The physician uses an endoscope to access and control bleeding of the upper gastrointestinal tract. The physician passes an endoscope through the patient's mouth and into the esophagus. Control of bleeding may be achieved using several endoscopic methods including laser therapy, electrocoagulation, rubber band ligation, and injection of the bleeding vessel with sclerosant, ethanol, or adrenaline. The endoscope is removed.

Coding Guidance
AHA: N-D, '87, 4; 2Q, '92, 17; 2Q, '04, 12

44.44   Transcatheter embolization for gastric or duodenal bleeding

Description
The physician performs a transcatheter embolization for gastric or duodenal bleeding. This is accomplished by introducing various substances using a catheter.

Coding Clarification
Code 44.44 excludes surgical occlusion of abdominal blood vessels (38.86-38.87).

● New Code   ▲ Revised Code   ►◄ Revised Text   © 2010 Ingenix

Coding Guidance
AHA: N-D, '87, 4; 1Q, '88, 15

44.49   Other control of hemorrhage of stomach or duodenum

Description
This code reports other control of hemorrhage of the stomach or duodenum, not specified as by endoscopic, transcatheter, or suture technique. Surgical technique may vary.

The physician performs a gastrostomy and explores the gastroduodenal area, removes a foreign body, or corrects a mucosal defect. The physician makes a midline epigastric incision and retracts the skin and underlying tissues laterally. The stomach and/or duodenum are incised and explored. A bleeding ulcer may be identified and bleeding is controlled with electrocautery or ligation of vessels. After exploration or repair, the stomach and/or duodenum is sutured in layers, the soft tissues are returned to anatomical position, and the incision is sutured in layers.

Coding Clarification
Code 44.49 excludes suture of ulcer (44.41).

44.5   Revision of gastric anastomosis

Description
The physician uses an open technique to revise a failed gastric restrictive procedure for morbid obesity. Indications for revision include stomal stenosis, stomal dilation, non-emptying gastric pouch, gastroesophageal reflux, staple dehiscence, intragastric foreign body, gastric fistula, gastroesophageal fistula, failure to maintain weight loss, breakdown of staple continuity, and restored gastric continuity. Revision techniques vary depending on the technique used in the initial gastric restrictive procedure and the nature of the gastric restrictive failure.

The physician makes a midline abdominal incision. Next, the stomach and previous anastomoses are dissected free of surrounding structures. This can involve painstaking lysis of adhesions between the liver, stomach, distal esophagus, colon, and/or spleen. The physician performs the required revision. A small strip of mesh or a Silastic ring may be wrapped around the stoma and stapled to itself. If a gastric bypass is performed, the stomach is partitioned, the small bowel divided, and the small bowel is reanastomosed to the proximal stomach.

44.6   Other repair of stomach

Description
Subcategory 44.6 provides nine subclassification codes to report other repairs of the stomach, including suture of laceration, gastrostomy and gastric fistula closure, gastropexy, esophagogastroplasty, laparoscopic and other procedures for creating esophagogastric sphincteric competence, laparoscopic gastroplasty, and other stomach repair.

44.61   Suture of laceration of stomach

Description
The physician repairs a laceration, wound, or injury to the stomach. The wound is exposed by the physician via a midline upper abdominal incision or a transverse supraumbilical incision through skin, fascia, and muscle. The perforation is sutured closed and the peritoneal cavity is irrigated and suctioned to remove contamination. The abdominal fascia and peritoneum are closed in one layer. The skin and subcutaneous layers are not closed unless the perforation is less than two hours old.

Coding Clarification
Code 44.61 excludes suture of ulcer (44.41).

44.62   Closure of gastrostomy

Description
The physician closes a gastrostomy no longer needed. The physician enters through a previous gastrostomy. The stomach is dissected free of the abdominal wall. The stomach gastrostomy site is closed with sutures. The abdominal incision is closed with layered sutures.

44.63   Closure of other gastric fistula

Description
The physician closes a gastric fistula. The physician exposes stomach and colon or jejunum via a midline abdominal incision through skin, fascia, and muscle. The fistula is excised and the bowel mobilized. The fistula is located and resected. The abdominal incision is closed.

44.64   Gastropexy

Description
The physician performs a gastropexy, which is suture repair of the stomach or the position of the stomach. The physician folds the intestine upon itself and attaches the edges with sutures for anchoring purposes. The physician makes an abdominal incision. Next, the bowel is folded upon itself and the edges are plicated with sutures without making an anastomosis to anchor the bowel in place. The incision is closed.

Coding Guidance
AHA: M-J, '85, 17

44.65   Esophagogastroplasty

Description
The physician mobilizes the lower end of the esophagus and folds the fundus of the stomach around it. The physician accesses the lower esophagus through an upper abdominal incision. The fundus of the stomach is moved up and wrapped around the terminal 3 to 4 cm of the esophagus and sutured into place. The lower esophageal sphincter passes through a short tunnel of stomach muscle, which prevents reflux through the sphincter. When performed for a hiatal hernia, this procedure may include a sutured tightening of the junction of the diaphragmatic crura behind the esophagus.

Documentation Tip:
Procedures classifiable to this code may be documented as:

- Belsey operation
- Esophagus and stomach cardioplasty
- Esophagogastropexy

Coding Guidance
AHA: M-J, '85, 17

44.66   Other procedures for creation of esophagogastric sphincteric competence

Description
The physician pulls up part of the gastric fundus to cover the affected distal esophagus. A bougie (dilating instrument) is placed in the distal esophagus to maintain the esophageal opening. The physician accesses the esophagus and stomach through a transverse abdominal incision. The physician picks up the stomach 1 cm below the gastroesophageal (GE) junction and attaches it 1 cm above the GE junction. This fundic patch is sutured to the esophagus. Next, a Nissen fundoplication is performed by wrapping the rest of the fundus around the esophagus and suturing it into place. The incision is sutured in layers.

The distal portion of the esophagus is lengthened by constructing a tube made of the stomach wall. The physician accesses the esophagus and stomach through a lateral thoracotomy. A bougie (dilating instrument) is passed through the esophagus into the stomach so the bougie spans the gastroesophageal junction. The stomach is divided along the bougie with a GIA stapler, forming a gastric tube that effectively lengthens the esophagus. The fundus of the stomach is dissected, wrapped around the distal esophagus and gastric tube, and sutured into place. The incision is sutured in layers.

Coding Clarification:
Code 44.66 excludes procedures performed by laparoscopic approach (44.67).

Documentation Tip:
Procedures classifiable to this code may be documented as:

- Fundoplication
- Gastric cardioplasty
- Nissen's fundoplication
- Restoration of cardioesophageal ring

Coding Guidance
AHA: M-J, '85, 17; 3Q, '98, 10; 2Q, '01, 3, 5-6; 2Q, '03, 12

44.67   Laparoscopic procedures for creation of esophagogastric sphincteric competence

Description
The physician performs an esophagogastric fundoplasty using a laparoscope. With the patient under anesthesia, the physician places a trocar at the umbilicus into the abdomen and insufflates the abdominal cavity. The physician places a laparoscope through the umbilical incision and additional trocars are placed into the peritoneal or space. Additional instruments are introduced through the trocars. The physician identifies the fundus and the esophagus and resects them. The fundus is wrapped around the lower end of the esophagus, which is rejoined to the stomach with sutures. The trocars are removed and the incisions are closed with sutures.

Coding Clarification:
Procedures classified to 44.66 are the same, except performed by laparoscopic approach.

44.68   Laparoscopic gastroplasty

Description
This code reports other specified laparoscopic gastroplasty operations not classifiable elsewhere in subcategory 44.6. Surgical techniques may vary.

Coding Clarification
Code 44.68 excludes laparoscopic insertion of an adjustable gastric band (44.95).

Code also synchronous laparoscopic gastroenterostomy (44.38).

Documentation Tip
Procedures classifiable to 44.68 may be documented as:

- Banding or silastic vertical banding
- Vertical banded gastroplasty (VBG)

Coding Guidance
AHA: 4Q, '04, 123

● New Code   ▲ Revised Code   ▶◀ Revised Text   © 2010 Ingenix

44.69   Other repair of stomach

Description
This code reports other stomach repair procedures not classifiable elsewhere in subcategory 44.6.

Coding Clarification
This code should not be assigned if the medical record contains sufficient information to facilitate coding at a higher level of specificity.

Documentation Tip
If the documentation is ambiguous or unclear, the physician should be queried.

Coding Guidance
   AHA: N-D, '84, 13; M-J, '85, 17; 3Q, '99, 3; 2Q, '01, 3; 3Q, '03, 8

44.9   Other operations on stomach

Description
Subcategory 44.9 provides nine subclassification codes to report various operations on the stomach, including gastric variceal ligation, manipulation, insertion and removal of a gastric balloon, various laparoscopic gastric restrictive procedures, and other procedures for which there is no more specific code.

44.91   Ligation of gastric varices

Description
The physician performs ligation of the gastric varices, which is destruction of dilated veins by suture or strangulation.

Coding Clarification
Code 44.91 excludes variceal ligation by endoscopic approach (43.41).

44.92   Intraoperative manipulation of stomach

Description
This code reports a physical manipulation (a skillful use of the hands) to correct a defect or other malposition of the stomach, such as reduction of the volvulus (twisting). Surgical technique may vary, depending on the nature of the defect or malposition.

The physician reduces a volvulus, intussusception, or other malposition of the stomach through an abdominal incision. The physician makes an abdominal incision. Next, the abdomen is explored and the defect is manually reduced. Adhesions may be sharply divided. The bowel is inspected to ensure viability. The incision is closed.

44.93   Insertion of gastric bubble (balloon)

44.94   Removal of gastric bubble (balloon)

Description
The physician inserts (44.93) or removes (44.94) a gastric balloon for the treatment of obesity. The balloon is a minimally invasive weight loss procedure that involves the insertion of a durable, elastic, high-quality, triple-layered silicone balloon into the stomach. The balloon is inserted endoscopically through the esophagus into the stomach, where it is filled with a sterile liquid solution. The stomach balloon may be left in place for up to six months, after which it is removed or replaced.

44.95   Laparoscopic gastric restrictive procedure

44.96   Laparoscopic revision of gastric restrictive procedure

44.97   Laparoscopic removal of gastric restrictive device(s)

Description
The physician performs a laparoscopic adjustable gastric banding and port insertion, revision, or removal of a gastric restrictive device for treatment of morbid obesity that does not permanently alter the gastrointestinal tract. The physician places a trocar though an incision, generally above the umbilicus, and insufflates the abdominal cavity. The laparoscope and additional trocars are placed through small portal incisions. The silicone gastric band is introduced into the peritoneal cavity via a trocar and is placed and secured around the upper stomach to form a smaller stomach pouch with a narrowed outlet. A small port, or reservoir, is placed under the skin at the time of surgery and connected to the silicone band by tubing to facilitate postoperative adjustments of the outlet size by the addition or removal of saline via the port. The device may be altered, adjusted, or removed as necessary. The instruments are removed and the incisions are closed.

Coding Clarification
These procedures exclude the incisional insertion, revision, or removal of gastric restrictive devices.

Coding Guidance
   AHA: 4Q, '04, 123

44.98   (Laparoscopic) adjustment of size of adjustable gastric restrictive device

Description
The physician performs a laparoscopic adjustment of an adjustable gastric band or device. The physician places a trocar though an incision,

42-54

generally above the umbilicus, and insufflates the abdominal cavity. The laparoscope and additional trocars are placed through small portal incisions. Saline is added to (for tightening) or removed from (for loosening) the gastric band.

Coding Clarification:
Laparoscopic adjustment techniques may vary depending on the nature or type of adjustable device. This code reports the laparoscopic adjustment of the size of the gastric restrictive device, as opposed to the revision or replacement procedures classifiable to 44.96. This procedure refers only to the adjustment of the size of the (adjustable) device, not a revision of the actual device.

Code also any associated imaging procedures classifiable to Chapter 16 Miscellaneous Diagnostic and Therapeutic Procedures (87-99).

Coding Guidance
AHA: 4Q, '04, 123

44.99   Other operations on stomach

Description
This code reports other operations on the stomach not elsewhere classifiable to category 44.

Coding Clarification
This code should not be assigned if the medical record contains sufficient information to facilitate coding at a higher level of specificity.

Code 44.99 lists multiple exclusions for procedures classifiable to Chapter 16 Miscellaneous Diagnostic and Therapeutic Procedures (87-99).

Documentation Tip
If the documentation is ambiguous or unclear, the physician should be queried.

Coding Guidance
AHA: 3Q, '04, 5

45   Incision, excision and anastomosis of intestine

Description
The digestive system may be considered a tube (with accessory organs) that runs from the mouth to the anus. This tube is approximately 30 feet long, stretched end-to-end. It may also be known as the gastrointestinal tract or alimentary canal. The primary function of this tube and its accessory organs is to facilitate the processes of digestion of food, absorption of nutrients, and elimination of wastes.

The small intestine is approximately a 1-inch diameter tube that would extend for just over 20 feet if stretched from end to end. However, it is tightly

coiled in the abdominal cavity from its origin at the pyloric orifice to the large intestine. The small intestine has three main parts:

- Duodenum, which is the approximate first 12 inches of the small intestine.

- Jejunum, which is the approximate next 8 feet of the small intestine.

- Ileum, which is the approximate remaining 12 feet of the small intestine

The stomach secretes gastric enzyme laden fluid (chyme) that mixes with bile from the liver and gallbladder and pancreatic enzymes, creating a digestive "cocktail" of fluid, which serves to break down food into smaller particles. The nutrients in these small particles are absorbed by the small intestine via tiny capillaries and lymph vessels, which are transmitted to the circulatory system to nourish the body.

The large intestine is approximately a 2.5 inch diameter tube that is nearly 5 feet in length. It extends from the cecum to the anus. The colon comprises the majority of the length of the large intestine and essentially wraps around the small intestine in ascending (sigmoid), transverse, and descending portions.

The large intestine absorbs liquid and nutrients not processed by the small intestine. The primary function of the colon is to absorb water and excrete the remaining digestive waste products (feces).

Category 45 provides codes for incision, excision, anastomoses (i.e., surgical creation of a connection of the ends or parts of the intestine to create a continuous channel), and creation of artificial openings of the intestines.

45.0   Enterotomy

Description
This subcategory classifies enterotomy (surgical incision into the intestine).

Coding Clarification
Subcategory 45.0 excludes intestinal incision procedures for the purpose of:

- Duodenocholedochotomy (51.41-51.42, 51.51)

- That for destruction of lesion (45.30-45.34)

- That for exteriorization of intestine (surgically-created intestinal stoma or fistula) (46.14, 46.24, 46.31)

45.00   Incision of intestine, not otherwise specified

Description
This code reports an incision of an unspecified site in the intestine.

● New Code   ▲ Revised Code   ►◄ Revised Text   © 2010 Ingenix

Coding Clarification
This is a non-specific code that should not be assigned if the medical record contains sufficient information to facilitate coding at a higher level of specificity.

Documentation Tip
If the documentation is ambiguous or unclear, the physician should be queried.

45.01   Incision of duodenum

Description
The physician opens the duodenum, explores the segment, and exposes the proximal duodenum via a midline upper abdominal incision through skin, fascia, and muscles. The duodenum is incised in a longitudinal fashion and the area of concern is exposed. The duodenum is closed with transverse interrupted sutures. The abdominal incision is closed.

45.02   Other incision of small intestine

Description
The physician makes an abdominal incision. Next, the selected segment of small intestine is mobilized and incised to expose the area of interest. The enterotomy is closed with staples or sutures. The abdominal incision is closed.

45.03   Incision of large intestine

Description
The physician makes an abdominal incision. Next, the selected segment of colon is mobilized and a colotomy is made in the area of interest. The colon is explored. The colotomy is closed with staples or sutures. The abdominal incision is closed.

Coding Clarification
Code 45.03 excludes proctotomy (incision of the rectum) (48.0).

45.1   Diagnostic procedures on small intestine

Description
This subcategory classifies diagnostic procedures on the small intestine, which is comprised of the duodenum, jejunum, and ileum. However, some of these procedures include examination of the esophagus and stomach as well, since these structures facilitate access to the small intestine sites by endoscopy.

Coding Clarification
When coding endoscopic procedures, the examination is classified to the furthest intestinal point examined. For example, an examination described as a gastroscopy in which the duodenum is also examined is classified to an esophagogastroduodenoscopy (45.13) since the

esophagus, stomach, and duodenum are all visualized by insertion of the endoscope.

Biopsies performed via endoscopy or percutaneous aspiration are referred to as closed biopsies. An incisional approach for removal of tissue is referred to as an open biopsy.

Code also any laparotomy (incision of the abdominal wall), if performed (54.11-54.19).

45.11   Transabdominal endoscopy of small intestine

Description
The physician uses an endoscope to examine the upper gastrointestinal tract. The physician passes an endoscope through an opening in the abdomen into the duodenum, and sometimes the jejunum. When the examination is complete, the endoscope is removed.

Coding Clarification
Code 45.11 includes intraoperative endoscopy of the small intestine.

Code 45.11 excludes transabdominal endoscopy of the small intestine with biopsy (45.14).

45.12   Endoscopy of small intestine through artificial stoma

Description
The physician performs endoscopy through a surgically created opening in the intestine. The physician places the endoscope into the opening and advances the endoscope into the small intestine. The small bowel lumen is visualized and brushings or washings may be obtained. The endoscope is withdrawn at the completion of the procedure.

Coding Clarification
Code 45.12 excludes endoscopy of the small intestine through artificial stoma with biopsy (45.14).

Coding Guidance
   AHA: M-J, '85, 17

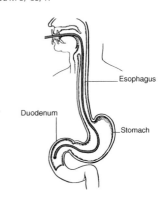

Esophagus

Duodenum

Stomach

45.13   Other endoscopy of small intestine

Description
The physician performs endoscopy of the proximal small bowel. The physician places an endoscope through the mouth and advances it into the small intestine. The lumen of the small bowel is examined. The endoscope is withdrawn at the completion of the procedure.

Coding Clarification
Code 45.13 excludes other endoscopy of the small intestine with biopsy (45.14, 45.16).

Coding Guidance
AHA: N-D, '87, 5; 4Q, '90, 20; 3Q, '04, 5

45.14   Closed [endoscopic] biopsy of small intestine

Description
The physician performs endoscopy of the proximal small bowel and obtains brushings or washings. The physician places an endoscope through the mouth and advances it into the small intestine. The lumen of the small bowel is examined and brushings or washings are obtained of suspicious areas. The endoscope is withdrawn at the completion of the procedure.

Coding Clarification
Code 45.14 excludes esophagogastroduodenoscopy [EGD] with closed biopsy (45.16).

45.15   Open biopsy of small intestine

Description
The physician makes an incision in the small intestine (enterotomy) for exploration and biopsy. The physician makes an abdominal incision. Next, the selected segment of small intestine is mobilized and incised to expose the area of interest. A biopsy is taken and removed. The enterotomy is closed with staples or sutures. The abdominal incision is closed.

Coding Guidance
AHA: 2Q, '05, 12

45.16   Esophagogastroduodenoscopy (EGD) with closed biopsy

Description
The physician examines the upper gastrointestinal tract for diagnostic purposes. The physician passes an endoscope through the patient's mouth into the esophagus. The esophagus, stomach, duodenum, and sometimes the jejunum are viewed to determine if bleeding, tumors, erosions, ulcers, or other abnormalities are present. Single or multiple tissue samples are obtained for biopsy specimens using bite forceps through the endoscope.

Coding Guidance
AHA: 2Q, '01, 9; 3Q, '05, 17

45.19   Other diagnostic procedures on small intestine

Description
This code reports other diagnostic procedures of the small intestine not classified elsewhere in subcategory 45.1.

Coding Clarification
This is a non-specific code that should not be assigned if the medical record contains sufficient information to facilitate coding at a higher level of specificity.

Documentation Tip
If the documentation is ambiguous or unclear, the physician should be queried.

45.2   Diagnostic procedures on other intestine

Description
Subcategory 45.2 provides nine subclassification codes to report numerous diagnostic procedures on the large intestine, including various endoscopic procedures, open and closed biopsy, and other diagnostic procedures that are not more specifically classified elsewhere.

Coding Clarification
Code also any laparotomy (incision into the abdominal wall) (54.11-54.19).

45.21   Transabdominal endoscopy of large intestine

Description
The physician performs transabdominal endoscopy of the large intestine, which is an endoscopic exam of the large intestine through the abdominal wall. The physician makes an abdominal incision. Next, the colon may be mobilized. An incision is made in the colon in the segment of interest and the colonoscope is inserted through the colotomy and advanced to visualize the lumen of the colon. At the completion of the procedure, the colonoscope is removed and the colotomy is closed with sutures or staples. The abdominal incision is closed.

Coding Clarification
Code 45.21 includes intraoperative colonoscopy performed during surgery.

45.22   Endoscopy of large intestine through artificial stoma

Description
The physician performs endoscopy of the large intestine through an artificial stoma, which is an endoscopic exam of the large intestine lining from rectum to cecum via a colostomy stoma. The physician places the endoscope into the colostomy and advances the endoscope into the colon. The lumen of the colon is visualized. The endoscope is withdrawn at the completion of the procedure.

● New Code   ▲ Revised Code   ►◄ Revised Text   © 2010 Ingenix

45.23 Colonoscopy

Description
The physician performs a colonoscopy, which is an endoscopic exam of the descending colon, splenic flexure, transverse colon, hepatic flexure, and cecum. The physician inserts the colonoscope into the anus and advances the scope through the colon past the splenic flexure. The lumen of the colon and rectum are visualized. The colonoscope is withdrawn at the completion of the procedure.

Coding Clarification
Code 45.23 excludes the following procedures classified elsewhere:

- Endoscopy of large intestine through artificial stoma (45.22)
- Flexible sigmoidoscopy (45.24)
- Rigid proctosigmoidoscopy (48.23)
- Transabdominal endoscopy of large intestine (45.21)

Documentation Tip
This procedure may also be documented as a flexible fiberoptic colonoscopy.

Coding Scenario
A patient was seen in the outpatient endoscopy suite for a screening colonoscopy.

Code Assignment:

V76.51 Special screening for malignant neoplasms, colon.
45.23 Colonoscopy

Coding Guidance
AHA: S-O, '85, 5; 4Q, '90, 20-24; 1Q, '95, 3-4; 3Q, '05, 17

45.24 Flexible sigmoidoscopy

Description
The physician performs flexible sigmoidoscopy, which is an endoscopic exam of the anus, rectum, and sigmoid colon. The physician inserts the sigmoidoscope into the anus and advances the scope into the sigmoid colon. The lumen of the sigmoid colon and rectum are visualized. The sigmoidoscope is withdrawn at the completion of the procedure.

45.25 Closed [endoscopic] biopsy of large intestine

Description
The physician performs colonoscopy through an abdominal wall colostomy and obtains brushings, washings, or biopsies. The physician places the endoscope into the colostomy and advances the endoscope into the colon. The lumen of the colon is visualized specimens are obtained. The endoscope is withdrawn at the completion of the procedure.

Coding Clarification
Code 45.25 excludes proctosigmoidoscopy with biopsy (48.24).

Coding Guidance
AHA: 1Q, '03, 10

45.26 Open biopsy of large intestine

Description
The physician makes an incision in the colon (colotomy) through which the colon is explored for biopsy. The physician makes an abdominal incision. Next, the selected segment of colon is mobilized and a colotomy is made in the area of interest. The colon is explored and biopsy performed. The colotomy is closed with staples or sutures. The abdominal incision is closed.

45.27 Intestinal biopsy, site unspecified

Description
The physician takes a biopsy of the intestine, not classified elsewhere according to site or type.

Coding Clarification
This code should not be assigned if the medical record contains sufficient information to facilitate coding at a higher level of specificity.

Documentation Tip
If the documentation is ambiguous or unclear, the physician should be queried.

45.28 Other diagnostic procedures on large intestine

Description
This code reports other diagnostic procedures of the large intestine (colon, rectum, and anus), not classifiable elsewhere in subcategory 45.2.

Coding Clarification
This code should not be assigned if the medical record contains sufficient information to facilitate coding at a higher level of specificity.

Documentation Tip
If the documentation is ambiguous or unclear, the physician should be queried.

45.29 Other diagnostic procedures on intestine, site unspecified

Description
This code reports other diagnostic procedures of the intestine of unspecified anatomic site not classifiable elsewhere in subcategory 45.2.

Coding Clarification
This code should not be assigned if the medical record contains sufficient information to facilitate coding at a higher level of specificity.

42-54

Code 45.29 lists multiple exclusions for procedures classifiable to Chapter 16 Miscellaneous Diagnostic and Therapeutic Procedures (87-99).

Documentation Tip
If the documentation is ambiguous or unclear, the physician should be queried.

45.3   Local excision or destruction of lesion or tissue of small intestine

Description
Subcategory 45.3 provides five subclassification codes to report various excisional or destructive procedures of lesions or tissues of the small intestine.

45.30   Endoscopic excision or destruction of lesion of duodenum

Description
The physician uses an endoscope to examine the upper gastrointestinal tract and locate and remove tumors, polyps, or other lesions. The physician passes an endoscope through the patient's mouth into the esophagus. The esophagus, stomach, duodenum, and sometimes the jejunum are viewed to locate the lesion in the small intestine. The base of the lesion may be electrocoagulated and severed using biopsy forceps or bipolar cautery, or snare loop may be placed around the base of the lesion and closed (the tissue is electrocoagulated and severed as the loop is closed). The esophagus, stomach, duodenum, and sometimes the jejunum are viewed to locate the lesion. If tissue is removed, the severed tissue is withdrawn through the endoscope. The endoscope is removed.

Coding Clarification
Code 45.30 excludes biopsy of duodenum (45.14-45.15), endoscopic control of hemorrhage (44.43), and fistulectomy (46.72).

45.31   Other local excision of lesion of duodenum

Description
The physician removes one or more lesions in the small intestine through an incision in the small intestine (enterotomy) without bowel resection. The physician makes an abdominal incision. Next, the segment of small intestine containing the lesions is mobilized. An incision is made in the small intestine and the lesions are removed. The enterotomy is closed with staples or sutures. The abdominal incision is closed.

Coding Clarification
Code 45.31 lists multiple exclusions for small intestine procedures more specifically classified elsewhere in category 45 or 46.

45.32   Other destruction of lesion of duodenum

Description
The physician destroys lesions in the small intestine through an incision in the small intestine (enterotomy) without bowel resection. The physician makes an abdominal incision. Next, the segment of small intestine containing the lesions is mobilized. An incision is made in the small intestine and the lesions are destroyed with electrocautery or other method. The enterotomy is closed with staples or sutures. The abdominal incision is closed.

Coding Clarification
Code 45.32 excludes endoscopic destruction of a small bowel lesion (45.30).

Coding Guidance
   AHA: S-O, '85, 6; N-D, '87, 5

45.33   Local excision of lesion or tissue of small intestine, except duodenum

Description
This code reports excision of a lesion(s) in the jejunum or ileum through an incision in the small intestine (enterotomy) without bowel resection. The physician makes an abdominal incision. Next, the segment of small intestine containing the lesion is mobilized. An incision is made in the small intestine and the lesion is removed. The enterotomy is closed with staples or sutures. The abdominal incision is closed.

Coding Clarification
Code 45.33 excludes certain small intestine procedures more specifically classified elsewhere in category 45 or 46.

45.34   Other destruction of lesion of small intestine, except duodenum

Description
This code reports other, nonexcisional destructive procedures of small intestine lesions, excluding those on the duodenum.

Coding Clarification
Procedures on the small intestine that may be correctly reported with 45.34 include:

*   Fulguration not elsewhere classified

*   Inversion of diverticulum

45.4   Local excision or destruction of lesion or tissue of large intestine

Description
This subcategory provides four subclassification codes to report various excisional and destructive procedures on large intestine lesions or tissues.

Coding Guidance
   AHA: N-D, '87, 11

45.41   Excision of lesion or tissue of large intestine

Description
The physician removes one or more lesions in the large intestine through an incision without bowel resection. The physician makes an abdominal incision. Next, the segment of large intestine containing the lesions is mobilized. An incision is made into the bowel and the lesions are removed. The incision is closed with staples or sutures. The abdominal incision is closed.

Coding Clarification
Code 45.41 excludes other excisional procedures classified elsewhere such as that for biopsy of large intestine (45.25-45.27), segmental resection (17.31, 45.71), and fistulectomy (46.76), as well as excisions performed by endoscopic approach (45.42-45.43).

45.42   Endoscopic polypectomy of large intestine

Description
The physician performs a colonoscopy and removes a polyp. The physician inserts the colonoscope into the anus and advances the scope past the splenic flexure. The lumen of the colon and rectum are visualized. The polyps are identified and removed by hot biopsy forceps or cautery. The colonoscope is withdrawn at the completion of the procedure.

Coding Guidance
AHA: 2Q, '90, 25; 2Q, '05, 16

45.43   Endoscopic destruction of other lesion or tissue of large intestine

Description
The physician performs a colonoscopy and controls an area of bleeding or destroys a lesion or area of tissue. The physician places the endoscope into the rectum and advances the endoscope into the colon. The lumen of the colon is visualized and the area of bleeding is identified and controlled. The physician may perform ablation of a tumor, polyp, or other lesion by ablation. The endoscope is withdrawn at the completion of the procedure.

Coding Clarification
Code 45.43 excludes endoscopic polypectomy of the large intestine (45.42).

Coding Guidance
AHA: 4Q, '02, 61

45.49   Other destruction of lesion of large intestine

Description
This code reports other open (incisional) destruction of a large intestine lesion not classifiable elsewhere in subcategory 45.4.

Coding Clarification
This code should not be assigned if the medical record contains sufficient information to facilitate coding at a higher level of specificity.

Code 45.49 excludes destruction by endoscopic approach (45.43).

Documentation Tip
If the documentation is ambiguous or unclear, the physician should be queried.

45.5   Isolation of intestinal segment

Description
Codes in this subcategory report the separation of a portion of intestine, usually performed as part of a greater procedure such as an interposition or bypass anastomosis.

45.50   Isolation of intestinal segment, not otherwise specified

45.51   Isolation of segment of small intestine

45.52   Isolation of segment of large intestine

Coding Clarification
Code also any anastomosis other than end-to-end (45.90-45.94) or enterostomy (46.10-46.39).

45.6   Other excision of small intestine

Description
This subcategory lists other excisional procedures of the small bowel not classifiable elsewhere in category 45.

Coding Clarification
In ICD-9-CM classification, partial excision and segmental excision of a single section are synonymous. Coding specificity is provided in ICD-9-CM for multiple segmental excision verses single segment or partial excision of the large intestines; however, specificity is not provided for small intestines (duodenum, jejuneum, ileum).

Code also any synchronous:

- Anastomosis other than end-to-end (45.90-45.93, 45.95)
- Enterostomy (46.10-46.39)
- Colostomy (46.10-46.13)

This subcategory excludes other specific bowel excision procedures classifiable elsewhere.

45.61   Multiple segmental resection of small intestine

Description
The physician resects segments of small intestine and performs an anastomosis between the remaining bowel ends. The physician makes an abdominal incision. Next, the selected segment of

42-54

small bowel is isolated and divided proximally and distally to the remaining bowel and removed. The remaining bowel ends are reapproximated using staples or sutures. The incision is closed.

45.62 Other partial resection of small intestine

Description
The physician resects and removes a section of small intestine and performs an anastomosis between the remaining bowel ends. The physician makes an abdominal incision. Next, the selected portion of small bowel is isolated and divided proximally and distally to the remaining bowel and removed. The remaining bowel ends are reapproximated using staples or sutures. The incision is closed.

Coding Clarification
Code 45.62 excludes duodenectomy with synchronous pancreatectomy (52.51-52.7) and resection of cecum and terminal ileum (17.32, 45.72).

Coding Guidance
  AHA: 1Q, '03, 18; 1Q, '04, 10; ►1Q, '10, 11◄

45.63 Total removal of small intestine

Description
The physician performs an enterectomy of the small bowel. The physician performs a midline abdominal incision. Tissue is incised and muscles are separated down to the level of the small intestine. The small intestine is mobilized and excised. The bowel ends are anastomosed to restore continuity. Any bleeding is controlled, the area is irrigated, and the incision is closed with layered sutures.

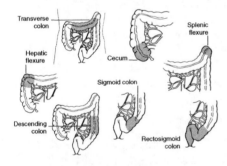

45.7 Partial excision of large intestine

Description
This subcategory classifies various partial large bowel excision procedures. The code descriptions state the portion of bowel surgically removed. The physician may perform end-to-end or other anastomoses, or may create a temporary or permanent enterostomy opening during the same operative episode.

Coding Clarification
Code also any synchronous anastomosis other than end-to-end (45.92-45.94) or enterostomy (46.10-46.39).

Subcategory 45.7 excludes laparoscopic partial excision of large intestine (17.31–17.39).

Coding Guidance
  AHA: 4Q, '92, 27

45.72 Open and other cecectomy

45.73 Open and other right hemicolectomy

45.74 Open and other resection of transverse colon

45.75 Open and other left hemicolectomy

45.76 Open and other sigmoidectomy

45.79 Other and unspecified partial excision of large intestine

Description
The physician resects segments of large intestine and sometimes a portion of the end of the small intestine and performs an anastomosis between the remaining bowel ends. The physician makes an abdominal incision. Next, the selected segments of bowel are isolated and divided proximally and distally to the remaining bowel and removed. The remaining bowel ends are reapproximated using staples or sutures. The incision is closed.

Coding Clarification
In ICD-9-CM classification partial excision and segmental excision of a single section are synonymous. Coding specificity is provided in ICD-9-CM for multiple segmental excision verses single segment or partial excision of the large intestines. Code 17.31 is assigned to report a laparoscopic multiple segmental excision and code 17.39 reports laparoscopic partial excision or segmental. The index contains two entries under main term *Excision/intestine/large/segmental*: laparoscopic (17.39) and multiple/laparoscopic (17.31) to direct the coder to the appropriate code.

Codes in the 45.7 and 17.3 subcategories report procedures on the large intestines (cecum, colon, rectum, anal canal) and include specificity such as multiple or partial, laparoscopic versus open, and laterality specificity. Small intestines (duodenum, jejuneum, ileum) procedure codes, however, do not, and there are also no laparoscopic procedure codes. Only when the ileum of the small intestine is involved within the multiple or partial laparoscopic procedure of the large intestines, is there specificity for small intestines. For example: ileocolectomy is coded 17.33 or 45.73; hemicolectomy includes ileum and cecum 17.32 and 45.72.

Coding Scenario
A patient is admitted for treatment of a malignant neoplasm. The physician performs a resection of the cecum and terminal ileum using an abdominal incision. An anastomosis is created between the distal ileum and the incision is closed with staples.

Code Assignment:

153.4 Malignant neoplasm of cecum
45.72 Open and other cecectomy

Coding Guidance
AHA: 3Q, '89, 15; 2Q, 91, 16; 1Q, '96, 9; 3Q, '97, 9; 1Q, '03, 18; 1Q, '09, 5

45.8 Total intra-abdominal colectomy

Description
Subcategory 45.8 includes codes to report intra-abdominal colectomy procedures, which vary depending on the surgical technique utilized.

Coding Guidance
AHA: 4Q, '08, 169-170

45.81 Laparoscopic total intra-abdominal colectomy

45.82 Open total intra-abdominal colectomy

45.83 Other and unspecified total intra-abdominal colectomy

Description
Laparoscopic colon surgery is a technique whereby the colon can be removed using several small incisions. Laparoscopic colectomy has advantages over open colectomy in regard to the length of hospital stay and postoperative morbidity and mortality. Laparoscopic colon removal involves a 1/2 inch incision near the umbilicus to place the camera with instruments placed through two 1/4 inch incisions. Using the inserted instruments the colon is mobilized. The colon is extracted using an incision about three inches long and the remaining ends of the colon are reattached.

In an open colectomy procedure, the physician removes the entire colon and performs an ileostomy or an anastomosis between the ileum and rectum. The physician makes an abdominal incision. Next, the colon is mobilized and the colorectal junction and terminal ileum is divided. The colon is removed. The terminal ileum is approximated to the rectum or brought out through a separate incision on the abdominal wall onto the skin as an ileostomy. The incisions are closed with staples.

Coding Scenario
A patient with cancer throughout the colon is admitted for treatment. The physician makes an abdominal incision, removes the entire colon and rectum, strips the mucosa from the distal rectum, and performs an anastomosis between the terminal ileum and anus.

Code Assignment:

153.8 Malignant neoplasm of other specified sites of large intestine
45.82 Open total intra-abdominal colectomy

Coding Clarification
Code 45.8 excludes coloproctectomy (48.41-48.69).

ICD-9-CM procedure codes did not previously distinguish between laparoscopic and open approaches to colectomy surgery. To ensure accurate code assignment, it will be necessary to review the medical record documentation for specific information regarding the surgical technique and procedure performed.

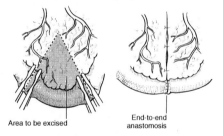

Area to be excised   End-to-end anastomosis

45.9 Intestinal anastomosis

Description
This subcategory describes a separately reportable anastomosis of the bowel. An end-to-end anastomosis is included in the code for the resection procedure, and not reported separately. The code descriptions state the portions of bowel sutured or stapled together post-resection.

Coding Clarification
Any synchronous resection should also be reported (45.31-45.8, 48.41-48.69).

45.90 Intestinal anastomosis, not otherwise specified

Coding Clarification
Code 45.90 is a non-specific code that should not be assigned if the medical record contains sufficient information to facilitate coding at a higher level of specificity.

45.91 Small-to-small intestinal anastomosis

Coding Guidance
AHA: ▶1Q, '10, 12◀

42–54

45.92   Anastomosis of small intestine to rectal stump

45.93   Other small-to-large intestinal anastomosis

45.94   Large-to-large intestinal anastomosis

Coding Guidance
> **AHA:** 1Q, '09, 5; ▶1Q, '10, 11◀

45.95   Anastomosis to anus

Coding Clarification
Anastomoses other than end-to-end require an additional code. All intestinal resections with synchronous anastomoses (other than end-to-end) require two codes: one code for the resection and a second code for the anastomosis.

Coding Guidance
> **AHA:** M-J, '85, 17; N-D, '86, 11; 3Q, '89, 15; 1Q, '03, 18; 3Q, '03, 6-8; 2Q, '05, 13

---

46   Other operations on intestine

Description
This category classifies other intestinal operations not classifiable elsewhere.

Coding Clarification
Code also any application or administration of an adhesion barrier substance (99.77).

46.0   Exteriorization of intestine

Description
This subcategory describes exteriorization of the intestine, or the creation of an artificial opening from the intestine to the exterior of the body. Indications include providing a temporary opening to facilitate healing post-surgery or as a permanent opening to allow for the elimination of waste products in a dysfunctional bowel.

46.01   Exteriorization of small intestine

46.02   Resection of exteriorized segment of small intestine

46.03   Exteriorization of large intestine

Description
A loop of bowel (e.g., colon, ileum) may be brought out through the abdominal wall onto the skin as a stoma proximal to an anastomosis. The bowel may be folded upon itself and approximated in order to form a pouch.

Documentation Tip
These procedures may also be documented as loop ileostomy or loop colostomy.

46.04   Resection of exteriorized segment of large intestine

Description
The physician resects a segment of colon and brings the proximal end of colon through the abdominal wall onto the skin as a colostomy. The physician makes an abdominal incision. Next, the selected segment of colon is isolated and divided proximally and distally to the remaining colon and removed. The proximal end of colon is brought through a separate incision on the abdominal wall and onto the skin as a colostomy. Alternately, the remaining bowel ends may be reapproximated and a loop of colon proximal to the anastomosis brought through a separate incision on the abdominal wall onto the skin as a loop colostomy. The initial incision is closed.

46.1   Colostomy

Description
This subcategory describes the creation of an opening from the large intestine through the abdominal wall and sutured to the skin. This leaves the patient with an artificial opening called a stoma, through which fecal matter can be excreted into a collection pouch. The code descriptions state whether the colostomy is temporary, permanent, delayed, or unspecified.

46.10   Colostomy, not otherwise specified

Coding Clarification
Code 46.10 is a non-specific code that should not be assigned if the medical record contains sufficient information to facilitate coding at a higher level of specificity.

46.11   Temporary colostomy

46.13   Permanent colostomy

46.14   Delayed opening of colostomy

Coding Clarification
Code also any synchronous bowel resection (45.49, 45.71-45.79, 45.8)

This subcategory excludes procedures documented as:

*   Loop colostomy (46.03)

*   With abdominoperineal resection of rectum (48.5)

*   With synchronous anterior rectal resection (48.62)

Coding Scenario
With the patient under general anesthesia, the physician constructed a permanent colostomy using a laparoscope. The physician brought a loop of colon

---

● New Code   ▲ Revised Code   ▶◀ Revised Text   © 2010 Ingenix

onto the skin as a stoma through a small incision in the abdominal wall.

> Code Assignment:
>
> 46.13   Permanent colostomy

46.2   Ileostomy

Description
This subcategory describes the creation of an opening from the ileum through the abdominal wall and sutured to the skin. This leaves the patient with an artificial opening called a stoma, through which intestinal waste can be excreted into a collection pouch. The code descriptions state whether the ileostomy is temporary, permanent, delayed, or unspecified.

46.20   Ileostomy, not otherwise specified

Coding Clarification
Code 46.20 is a non-specific code that should not be assigned if the medical record contains sufficient information to facilitate coding at a higher level of specificity.

46.21   Temporary ileostomy

46.22   Continent ileostomy

46.23   Other permanent ileostomy

46.24   Delayed opening of ileostomy

Coding Clarification
Code also any synchronous bowel resection (45.34, 45.61-45.63).

This subcategory excludes ileostomy specified as loop ileostomy (46.01).

Coding Guidance
AHA: M-J; '85, 17

46.3   Other enterostomy

Description
This subcategory describes the creation of an opening from the intestine through the abdominal wall and sutured to the skin. This leaves the patient with an artificial opening called a stoma, through which intestinal waste can be excreted into a collection pouch. The code descriptions state whether the enterostomy is temporary, permanent, delayed, or unspecified.

46.31   Delayed opening of other enterostomy

46.32   Percutaneous (endoscopic) jejunostomy (PEJ)

Description
▶The physician places a percutaneous jejunostomy (PEJ) tube. A percutaneous feeding enterostomy is the surgical placement of a (feeding) tube through the midsection of the small intestine through abdominal wall.◀

The physician places an endoscope into the mouth and advances it into the small intestine. The bowel lumen is visualized and transilluminated through the abdominal skin. A needle is placed through the skin into the lumen of the jejunum under visualization of the endoscope. A wire is threaded through the needle into the bowel lumen. The needle is removed. A jejunostomy tube is placed over the wire, through the skin, into the jejunum, and secured into place. The endoscope is withdrawn.

▶A conversion of gastrostomy to jejunostomy is the endoscopic advancement of a jejunostomy tube through an existing gastrostomy tube into the proximal jejunum. For conversion of a gastrostomy to a jejunostomy, the physician performs endoscopy of the proximal small bowel and places a percutaneous jejunostomy tube. The physician places an endoscope into the mouth and advances it into the small intestine. The bowel lumen is visualized and transilluminated through the abdominal skin. A needle is placed through the skin into the lumen of the jejunum under visualization of the endoscope. A wire is threaded through the needle into the bowel lumen. The needle is removed. A jejunostomy tube is placed over the wire, through the skin, into the jejunum, and secured into place. The endoscope is withdrawn.◀

Coding Clarification
Code 46.32 excludes percutaneous [endoscopic] gastrojejunostomy (bypass) (44.32).

Documentation Tip
Report code 46.32 for procedures documented as:

* Endoscopic conversion of gastrostomy to jejunostomy

* Percutaneous (endoscopic) feeding enterostomy

Coding Scenario
▶The physician performed endoscopy of the proximal small bowel and converts a percutaneous gastrostomy tube to a percutaneous jejunostomy tube by advancing a jejunostomy tube through the previously placed gastrostomy tube. The jejunostomy tube was grasped with forceps placed through the endoscope and advanced with the endoscope into the proximal jejunum.

> Code Assignment:
>
> 46.32   Percutaneous [endoscopic] gastrojejunostomy [PEJ]◀

46.39   Other enterostomy

Description
When performing a feeding enterostomy, the physician places a tube in the small bowel for feeding. The physician makes an abdominal incision. Next, a segment of proximal small bowel is isolated. A tube is placed into the small bowel and brought out through the abdominal wall. The incision is closed.

Coding Clarification
Code also any synchronous bowel resection (45.61-45.8).

Coding Guidance
AHA: 3Q, '89, 15

46.4   Revision of intestinal stoma

Description
This category describes a surgical correction or amendment of a previously created surgical opening from the intestine through the abdominal wall to the skin surface, in order to improve its function.

46.40   Revision of intestinal stoma, not otherwise specified

Description
The physician revises an intestinal stoma through an incision around the stoma with release of scar tissue. The physician makes an incision around the stoma site. Next, the stoma is dissected free of the surrounding abdominal wall and constricting scar tissue is released. The stoma is reapproximated to the skin, or the distal end of the stoma may be transected. Additional bowel tissue may be pulled through the abdominal wall and approximated to the skin.

Coding Clarification
Code 46.40 is a non-specific code that should not be assigned if the medical record contains sufficient information to facilitate coding at a higher level of specificity.

Code 46.40 excludes excision of redundant mucosa (45.41).

Documentation Tip
If the documentation is ambiguous or unclear, the physician should be queried.

46.41   Revision of stoma of small intestine

Description
The physician revises an intestinal stoma of the small intestine through an incision around the stoma with release of scar tissue. The physician makes an incision around the stoma site. Next, the stoma is dissected free of the surrounding abdominal wall and constricting scar tissue is released. The stoma is reapproximated to the skin or

the distal end of the stoma may be transected. Additional bowel tissue may be pulled through the abdominal wall and approximated to the skin.

Coding Clarification
Code 46.41 excludes excision of redundant mucosa (45.33).

Coding Guidance
AHA: 2Q, '05, 11

46.42   Repair of pericolostomy hernia

Description
The physician performs a colostomy revision and repairs a pericolostomy hernia. The physician makes an abdominal incision. Next, the previous colostomy site is taken down. The hernia at the former colostomy site is repaired. The end of colon is brought through a separate incision on the abdominal wall at a new site and onto the skin as a revised colostomy. The initial incision and previous stoma site are closed.

46.43   Other revision of stoma of large intestine

Description
The physician revises a large intestinal stoma through an incision around the stoma with release of scar tissue. The physician makes an incision around the stoma site. Next, the stoma is dissected free of the surrounding abdominal wall and constricting scar tissue is released. The stoma is reapproximated to the skin, or the distal end of the stoma may be transected. Additional bowel tissue may be pulled through the abdominal wall and approximated to the skin.

Coding Clarification
Code 46.43 is a non-specific code that should not be assigned if the medical record contains sufficient information to facilitate coding at a higher level of specificity.

Code 46.43 excludes excision of redundant mucosa (45.41).

Coding Guidance
AHA: 2Q, '02, 9

46.5   Closure of intestinal stoma

Description
This subcategory classifies take-down or closure of a stoma of the small or large intestine. The code descriptions specify the anatomic site of the stoma.

46.50   Closure of intestinal stoma, not otherwise specified

Coding Clarification
Code 46.50 is a nonspecific code that should not be assigned if the medical record contains sufficient

information to facilitate coding at a higher level of specificity.

46.51 Closure of stoma of small intestine

46.52 Closure of stoma of large intestine

Description
The physician takes down and closes an enterostomy (stoma) of the small intestine or colon. The physician makes an incision around the stoma or a separate abdominal incision may be made. Next, the stoma is mobilized and taken down from the abdominal wall and the stoma is closed. The abdominal incisions are closed.

Coding Clarification
Code also any synchronous bowel resection (45.34, 45.49, 45.61-45.8). Report code 46.52 for a colostomy reversal.

Coding Guidance
AHA: N-D, '87, 8; 2Q, '91, 16; 3Q, '97, 9; 2Q, '05, 4; 1Q, '09, 5

46.6 Fixation of intestine

Description
This subcategory classifies a surgical fixation (i.e., fastening, securing into position) or plication (i.e., folding with a surgical "tuck") of a portion of intestine into place. The code descriptions state the anatomic site or portion of bowel surgically treated.

46.60 Fixation of intestine, not otherwise specified

Coding Clarification
Code 46.60 is a nonspecific code that should not be assigned if the medical record contains sufficient information to facilitate coding at a higher level of specificity.

46.61 Fixation of small intestine to abdominal wall

46.62 Other fixation of small intestine

46.63 Fixation of large intestine to abdominal wall

46.64 Other fixation of large intestine

Description
The physician folds the intestine upon itself and attaches the edges with sutures for anchoring purposes. The physician makes an abdominal incision. Next, the bowel is folded upon itself and the edges are plicated with sutures without making an anastomosis to anchor the bowel in place. The incision is closed.

46.7 Other repair of intestine

Description
This subcategory classifies other intestinal repair procedures not elsewhere classifiable in category 46. The code descriptions state the anatomic site or portion of intestine being repaired.

Coding Clarification
Subcategory 46.7 excludes procedures specified as closure of ulcer of duodenum (44.42) or vesicoenteric fistula (57.83).

46.71 Suture of laceration of duodenum

Description
The physician performs suture closure of a duodenal perforation(s) or laceration(s). The physician makes an abdominal incision. Next, the abdomen is explored and the duodenal wounds are identified and repaired with sutures. The incision is closed.

46.72 Closure of fistula of duodenum

Description
This code reports closure of a duodenal fistula. Surgical technique may vary depending on the type of fistula.

In an intestinal cutaneous fistula, the physician takes down and closes an intestinal cutaneous fistula. The physician makes an abdominal incision. Next, the bowel is mobilized and the fistula is identified and taken down from the abdominal wall and skin. The segment of bowel containing the fistula is resected and the bowel ends reapproximated with staples or sutures. The abdominal wall incisions are closed.

In an enteroenteric fistula, the physician closes a connection (fistula) between loops of small bowel or between the small bowel and colon. The physician makes an abdominal incision. Next, the enteroenteric or enterocolic fistula is identified and divided. The ends of the fistula may be closed with sutures or the segments of bowel involved with the fistula may be resected and the bowel ends reapproximated in order to completely remove the involved areas. The incision is closed.

46.73 Suture of laceration of small intestine, except duodenum

Description
This code reports the suture closure of small bowel wounds. The physician performs suture closure of a small bowel perforation(s) or laceration(s). The physician makes an abdominal incision. Next, the abdomen is explored and the small bowel wounds are identified and repaired with sutures. The incision is closed.

42-54

Coding Clarification
Closure of small bowel wounds, perforations, or lacerations documented as duodenal are classified to 46.71.

Coding Guidance
AHA: ▶1Q, '10, 11◀

46.74 Closure of fistula of small intestine, except duodenum

Description
This code reports closure of a small bowel fistula. Surgical technique may vary depending on the type of fistula.

In an intestinocutaneous fistula, the physician takes down and closes an intestinal cutaneous fistula. The physician makes an abdominal incision. Next, the bowel is mobilized and the fistula is identified and taken down from the abdominal wall and skin. The segment of bowel containing the fistula is resected and the bowel ends reapproximated with staples or sutures. The abdominal wall incisions are closed.

In an enteroenteric fistula, the physician closes a connection (fistula) between loops of small bowel or between the small bowel and colon. The physician makes an abdominal incision. Next, the enteroenteric or enterocolic fistula is identified and divided. The ends of the fistula may be closed with sutures or the segments of bowel involved with the fistula may be resected and the bowel ends reapproximated in order to completely remove the involved areas. The incision is closed.

46.75 Suture of laceration of large intestine

Description
This code reports the suture closure of large bowel wounds. The physician performs suture closure of a large bowel perforation(s) or laceration(s). The physician makes an abdominal incision. Next, the abdomen is explored and the bowel wounds are identified and repaired with sutures. The incision is closed.

46.76 Closure of fistula of large intestine

Description
This code reports closure of a large bowel fistula. Surgical technique may vary depending on the type of fistula:

In an intestinocutaneous fistula, the physician takes down and closes an intestinal cutaneous fistula. The physician makes an abdominal incision. Next, the bowel is mobilized and the fistula is identified and taken down from the abdominal wall and skin. The segment of bowel containing the fistula is resected and the bowel ends reapproximated with staples or sutures. The abdominal wall incisions are closed.

In an enteroenteric fistula, the physician closes a connection (fistula) between loops of small bowel or between the small bowel and colon. The physician makes an abdominal incision. Next, the enteroenteric or enterocolic fistula is identified and divided. The ends of the fistula may be closed with sutures or the segments of bowel involved with the fistula may be resected and the bowel ends reapproximated in order to completely remove the involved areas. The incision is closed.

Coding Clarification
Code 45.75 lists multiple exclusions for certain types of fistula from the large bowel to other anatomic sites which are classified elsewhere, including:

- Large bowel-stomach [gastrocolic] (44.63)
- Rectal fistula (48.73)
- Sigmoid-vesical [bladder], vesicocolic, or vesicosigmoidovaginal (57.83)
- Stoma (46.52)
- Vaginal fistula (70.72-70.73)

Coding Guidance
AHA: 3Q, '99, 8

46.79 Other repair of intestine

Description
This code reports other repair of the intestine not classifiable to category 46, including duodenoplasty.

Coding Clarification
Code 46.79 should not be assigned if the medical record contains sufficient information to facilitate coding at a higher level of specificity.

Documentation Tip
If the documentation is ambiguous or unclear, the physician should be queried.

Coding Guidance
AHA: 3Q, '02, 11

46.8 Dilation and manipulation of intestine

Description
This subcategory classifies dilation and manipulation of the intestine. The code descriptions specify the site of manipulation as the small bowel, large bowel, or unspecified site. Dilation is classified separately.

Coding Guidance
AHA: 1Q, '03, 14

46.80 Intra-abdominal manipulation of intestine, not otherwise specified

Coding Clarification
Code 46.80 is a non-specific code that should not be assigned if the medical record contains sufficient

42-54

information to facilitate coding at a higher level of specificity.

Code 46.80 lists multiple exclusions for reduction procedures classifiable to Chapter 16 Miscellaneous diagnostic and therapeutic procedures (87-99).

Documentation Tip
If the documentation is ambiguous or unclear, the physician should be queried.

Coding Guidance
  AHA: 4Q, '98, 82

46.81   Intra-abdominal manipulation of small intestine

46.82   Intra-abdominal manipulation of large intestine

Description
The physician reduces a volvulus, intussusception, internal hernia, or other malposition of the intestine. The physician makes an abdominal incision. Next, the abdomen is explored and the twisted segment of bowel (volvulus), telescoped segment of bowel (intussusception), internal hernia, or other malposition is manually reduced. The bowel is inspected to ensure viability. The incision is closed.

46.85   Dilation of intestine

Description
The physician performs an endoscopy and dilates strictures by balloon catheter. The physician inserts the endoscope and advances the scope into the area of stricture. Areas of stenosis are identified and a balloon catheter is passed to the point of constriction and a little beyond. The balloon is inflated to the appropriate diameter and gradually withdrawn through the stenosed area, stretching the walls of the bowel at the strictured area.

A colonic stenting procedure would be assigned code 46.85 Dilation of the intestine. No additional code is available for the insertion of a colonic stent. If ICD-9-CM does not have a code for the stent insertion and the index does not provide any further instruction, code only the procedure performed.

Coding Clarification
Code 46.85 excludes dilation with insertion of colonic stent; refer to codes 46.86 and 46.87.

Coding Guidance
  AHA: 3Q, '89, 15; 3Q, '07, 6

46.86   Endoscopic insertion of colonic stent(s)

46.87   Other insertion of colonic stent(s)

Description
Colonic stents can be placed endoscopically, under fluoroscopic guidance, or using a combination of techniques. In a nonendoscopic, fluoroscopic stent

insertion, an angiography catheter is inserted into the anus and advanced to the level of obstruction. Radiographic contrast is injected and a guidewire is placed. The stent delivery system is inserted over the guidewire and the stent is deployed. Contrast is injected to rule out any perforation.

Colonic stent insertion using self-expandable metal stents is an alternative to surgery in the treatment of patients with acute malignant colonic obstruction.

Coding Clarification
Prior to 2010, the Volume 3 procedure classification did not include a code to report an endoscopic insertion of a colonic stent. Coding guidance advised coders to report endoscopic colonic stenting with procedure code 46.85 Dilation of intestine. Codes for endoscopic and other insertion of colonic stent(s) were added to subcategory 46.8 Dilation and manipulation of intestine.

Unique codes were created to report endoscopic and nonendoscopic insertion of colonic stent(s): code 48.86 is assigned to report insertion of colonic stent via endoscopic technique, and code 46.87 Other insertion of colonic stent(s), is used to report nonendoscopic insertion and colonic stenting with fluoroscopic guidance only or by rectal guiding tube.

In the United States there are currently three self-expandable colonic stents approved by the FDA: the Colonic Z-Stent®, the Enteral Wallstent®, and the Ultraflex™ Precision Colonic stent.

Assign separate codes for any diagnostic procedures performed synchronously.

Documentation Tip
To ensure accurate code assignment, review medical record documentation to determine the approach and surgical technique. Procedures reported with these codes may be documented as through the scope [TTS] stent placement, or stent endoprosthesis of the colon. Transendoscopic stent placement may be combined with fluoroscopic-guided insertion.

Coding Scenario
A patient is admitted for surgical treatment of an acute bowel obstruction. The physician inserts a colonic stent using endoscopic visualization with fluoroscopy. After the patient is sedated, the physician inserts the endoscope, visualizes the obstruction, and measures the length of the obstruction. Contrast is injected and a guidewire is placed through the scope and beyond the level of the obstruction. A Colonic Z-Stent® designed to fit through the scope is inserted over the guidewire and deployed under endoscopic visualization with fluoroscopic confirmation.

  Code Assignment:

  560.89 Other specified intestinal obstruction
  46.86   Endoscopic insertion of colonic stent(s)

42-54

Coding Guidance
AHA: ▶4Q, '09, 147◀

46.9 Other operations on intestines

Description
This subcategory describes other operations on the intestines not classifiable elsewhere in category 46, including myotomy, anastomosis revision, local perfusion, and transplantation.

46.91 Myotomy of sigmoid colon

46.92 Myotomy of other parts of colon

Description
The physician performs a myotomy of other parts of the colon. A myotomy is a surgical division of the muscular layer of the intestinal wall. A myotomy may be performed to treat intestinal motility disorders.

46.93 Revision of anastomosis of small intestine

46.94 Revision of anastomosis of large intestine

Description
These codes report a revision or correction of anastomosis of the intestine.

46.95 Local perfusion of small intestine

46.96 Local perfusion of large intestine

Coding Clarification
For codes 46.95 and 46.96, code also any substance perfused (99.21-99.29).

46.97 Transplant of intestine

Description
The physician performs an intestinal transplantation. The patient is placed supine on the operating room table. After adequate preparation, the physician performs a midline abdominal incision, tissue is incised, and muscles are separated down to the level of the intestine. The area of intestine to be transplanted is located. An incision is made through the intestine, the area is examined, and the free intestinal edges are debrided or excised in order to accept the intestinal transplant. The intestinal graft from a cadaver or partially excised small intestinal allograft from a living donor are removed from the maintenance solution and irrigated. The allograft is sized and is anastomosed first to one free end of the patient's intestine and then the opposite end of the patient's intestine. Any bleeding is controlled, the area is irrigated, and the bowel is anatomically positioned in the abdominal cavity. The wound is closed with layered sutures over a drain. A dressing is applied.

Coding Clarification
To report donor source, see 00.91-00.93.

Coding Guidance
AHA: 4Q, '00, 66

46.99 Other operations on intestines

Description
This code reports other intestinal procedures not classifiable elsewhere in category 46.

Coding Clarification
Code 46.99 should not be assigned if the medical record contains sufficient information to facilitate coding at a higher level of specificity.

Documentation Tip
If the documentation is ambiguous or unclear, the physician should be queried.

Coding Guidance
AHA: 1Q, '89, 11; 3Q, '99, 11

---

47 Operations on appendix

Description
This category classifies operations on the appendix, a small appendage-like pouch attached to the neck of the ascending colon, just proximal to the cecum.

Coding Clarification
Code also any application or administration of an adhesion barrier substance (99.77).

Operations on the appendiceal stump are also included in this category.

47.0 Appendectomy

47.01 Laparoscopic appendectomy

Description
The physician performs a laparoscopic appendectomy. The physician places a trocar at the umbilicus and insufflates the abdomen. The laparoscope is placed through the umbilical port and additional trocars are placed into the abdominal cavity. The appendix is identified, dissected from surrounding structures, and its blood supply divided. The appendix is transected with staples or suture and removed. The trocars are removed and the incisions are closed.

Coding Scenario
A patient presented to the emergency department with acute appendicitis. She was transported to the surgical suite for an emergency appendectomy. The physician placed a laparoscope through an umbilical port. Additional trocars were placed into the abdominal cavity and the appendix was dissected and removed.

● New Code ▲ Revised Code ▶◀ Revised Text © 2010 Ingenix

Code Assignment:

540.9   Acute appendicitis without mention of peritonitis

47.01   Laparoscopic appendectomy

Coding Guidance
AHA: 4Q, '96, 64; 1Q, '01, 15

47.09   Other appendectomy

Description
The physician removes the appendix. The physician makes an abdominal incision. Next, the appendix is identified and mobilized, its blood supply is divided, and the appendix is transected and removed. The incision is closed.

Coding Clarification
This subcategory excludes incidental appendectomy (47.11, 47.19).

Coding Guidance
AHA: 4Q, '97, 52

47.1   Incidental appendectomy

Description
This subcategory classifies appendectomy incidental to other surgery performed during the same operative episode.

47.11   Laparoscopic incidental appendectomy

Description
The physician performs a laparoscopic appendectomy incidental to other surgery. With the laparoscope placed in the abdominal cavity, the appendix is identified, dissected from surrounding structures, and its blood supply divided. The appendix is transected with staples or suture and removed. The trocars are removed and the incisions are closed after the entire scope of laparoscopic surgery is complete.

47.19   Other incidental appendectomy

Description
The physician removes the appendix incidental to other surgery performed by abdominal incision. The appendix is identified and mobilized, its blood supply is divided, and the appendix is transected and removed. The incision is closed upon completion of the entire scope of the abdominal procedure.

Coding Guidance
AHA: 4Q, '96, 65

47.2   Drainage of appendiceal abscess

Description
The physician performs open drainage of an appendiceal abscess. The physician makes an abdominal incision. Next, the abscess near the appendix is identified, incised, and drained. A drain may be left in the abscess cavity. The abdominal wall incision is closed and the skin incision may be left open to heal secondarily.

In an alternate procedure, the physician performs percutaneous drainage of an appendiceal abscess. The physician may create a small incision in the skin proximal to the appendiceal abscess to ease placement of drainage instruments through the skin. The physician uses a CAT scan or ultrasound to guide placement of a drainage needle or trocar into the appendiceal abscess. The physician advances the drainage needle or trocar through the abdominal wall into the peritoneum to gain access to the abscess cavity. The fluid is allowed to drain. Once drained, a catheter may be placed. Sutures may be secured to hold the drainage catheter in place. The operative site is subsequently cleaned and bandaged.

47.9   Other operations on appendix

47.91   Appendicostomy

Description
The physician performs an appendicostomy, which is a surgically-created opening of the vermiform appendix for the purpose of irrigation or drainage of the large intestine.

47.92   Closure of appendiceal fistula

Description
The physician closes a connection (fistula) between the appendix and bowel. The physician makes an abdominal incision. Next, the appendiceal fistula tract is identified and divided. Depending on the nature of the fistula and anatomic sites involved, the ends of the fistula may be closed with sutures or if segments of bowel are involved, the fistula may be resected and the bowel ends reapproximated in order to completely remove the involved areas. The incision is closed.

47.99   Other operations on appendix

Description
This code reports other operations on the appendix not classifiable elsewhere in category 47, including anastomosis of the appendix.

Coding Clarification
Code 47.99 should not be assigned if the medical record contains sufficient information to facilitate coding at a higher level of specificity.

Code 47.99 excludes diagnostic procedures on the appendix (45.21-45.29).

Documentation Tip
If the documentation is ambiguous or unclear, the physician should be queried.

Coding Guidance
> **AHA:** 3Q, '01, 16

---

48   Operations on rectum rectosigmoid, and perirectal tissue

Description
The rectum is the approximate 12 cm distal length of large intestine whereby fecal matter is temporarily stored before being evacuated from the body from the anus. When fecal matter fills the rectal ampulla walls, the expansion stimulates nervous system receptors and signals the need for defecation. When the rectum becomes full, the pressure forces the walls of the anal canal apart and the peristaltic contractions that moves the waste through the digestive tract propels the feces from the anal canal through internal and external sphincters.

Category 48 classifies operations on the rectum, rectosigmoid, and perirectal tissue, including incisions, artificial openings, diagnostic procedures, excisions, resections, repairs, and other operations.

Coding Clarification
Code also any application or administration of an adhesion barrier substance (99.77).

48.0   Proctotomy

Description
This code reports an incision into the rectal portion of the large intestine. Surgical approach and technique may vary.

A transanal incision may be made through the rectal lining in order to facilitate rectal abscess drainage. The incision may be left open to drain.

Documentation Tip
Procedures classifiable to this code may be documented as Panas' operation (linear proctotomy) or decompression of imperforate anus.

Coding Guidance
> **AHA:** 3Q, '99, 8

48.1   Proctostomy

Description
The physician performs a proctostomy, which is the formation of an artificial opening of the rectum.

48.2   Diagnostic procedures on rectum, rectosigmoid, and perirectal tissue

48.21   Transabdominal proctosigmoidoscopy

Description
The physician performs a transabdominal or intraoperative proctosigmoidoscopy. The physician inserts the proctosigmoidoscope through an operative incision in the abdomen and visualizes the sigmoid colon and rectal lumen. The proctosigmoidoscope is removed at the completion of the procedure.

Coding Clarification
Code 48.21 excludes proctosigmoidoscopy with biopsy (48.24).

48.22   Proctosigmoidoscopy through artificial stoma

Description
The physician performs a trans-stomal proctosigmoidoscopy. The physician inserts the proctosigmoidoscope into the stoma and advances the scope. The sigmoid colon and rectal lumen are visualized. The proctosigmoidoscope is removed at the completion of the procedure.

Coding Clarification
Code 48.22 excludes proctosigmoidoscopy with biopsy (48.24).

48.23   Rigid proctosigmoidoscopy

Description
The physician performs rigid proctosigmoidoscopy. The physician inserts the rigid proctosigmoidoscope into the anus and advances the scope. The sigmoid colon and rectal lumen are visualized. The proctosigmoidoscope is removed at the completion of the procedure.

Coding Guidance
> **AHA:** 1Q, '01, 8

48.24   Closed (endoscopic) biopsy of rectum

Description
The physician performs proctosigmoidoscopy and obtains brushings or washings. The physician inserts the proctosigmoidoscope into the anus and advances the scope. The sigmoid colon and rectal lumen are visualized and brushings, washings, or biopsy obtained. The proctosigmoidoscope is removed at the completion of the procedure.

Coding Guidance
> **AHA:** 1Q, '03, 14

42-54

48.25   Open biopsy of rectum

48.26   Biopsy of perirectal tissue

Description
The physician usually performs a biopsy of the rectal wall or perirectal tissue using a transanal approach. The physician performs an incisional biopsy or a suction biopsy of the low rectal wall. The biopsy may be closed with sutures.

48.29   Other diagnostic procedures on rectum, rectosigmoid, and perirectal tissue

Description
This code reports other diagnostic procedures on the rectum, rectosigmoid, and perirectal tissue not elsewhere classifiable in subcategory 48.2.

Coding Clarification
Code 48.29 should not be assigned if the medical record contains sufficient information to facilitate coding at a higher level of specificity.

Code 48.29 lists multiple exclusions for reduction procedures classifiable to Chapter 16 Miscellaneous diagnostic and therapeutic procedures (87-99).

Documentation Tip
If the documentation is ambiguous or unclear, the physician should be queried.

48.3   Local excision or destruction of lesion or tissue of rectum

Description
Subcategory 48.3 classifies local rectal excision or destruction procedures including those by electrocoagulation, laser, cryosurgery, or other methods. The code descriptions state the extent of procedure and surgical technique utilized.

48.31   Radical electrocoagulation of rectal lesion or tissue

48.32   Other electrocoagulation of rectal lesion or tissue

48.33   Destruction of rectal lesion or tissue by laser

48.34   Destruction of rectal lesion or tissue by cryosurgery

Description
The physician performs destruction of a rectal tumor, lesion, or tissue from a transanal approach. The physician explores the anal canal and exposes the lesion. It is ablated by electrosurgery, laser, or some other method. Bleeding is controlled and instrumentation removed.

Coding Guidance
   AHA: 2Q, '98, 18

48.35   Local excision of rectal lesion or tissue

Description
The physician excises a rectal lesion through a transanal or other surgical approach. If the excision is transanal, the physician explores the anal canal and exposes the lesion. The lesion is excised to include a full thickness of the rectal wall if necessary. The defect in the rectum is closed with sutures.

Coding Clarification
Code 48.35 excludes excision of rectal lesions described as biopsy, polypectomy, perirectal tissue, hemorrhoidectomy, and fistula, which are more appropriately classified elsewhere in category 48 and 49.

48.36   [Endoscopic] polypectomy of rectum

Description
The physician performs an endoscopic polypectomy of the rectum. The physician inserts the endoscope into the anus and advances the scope. The sigmoid colon and rectal lumen are visualized and the polyp or other lesion is identified and removed by hot biopsy forceps or snare excision. Bleeding is controlled with electrocautery. The endoscope is removed at the completion of the procedure.

Coding Guidance
   AHA: 4Q, '95, 65

48.4   Pull-through resection of rectum

Description
Subcategory 48.4 procedure codes report rectal resection by pull-through technique, which vary depending on the type of resection and type of pull-through technique utilized.

48.40   Pull-through resection of rectum, not otherwise specified

48.41   Soave submucosal resection of rectum

48.42   Laparoscopic pull-through resection of rectum

48.43   Open pull-through resection of rectum

48.49   Other pull-through resection of rectum

Description
The physician removes the rectum and performs an anastomosis between the colon and the anus. The physician makes an abdominal incision. The distal colon and rectum are mobilized within the abdomen to the level of the sphincter muscles. The colon is divided above the pelvic brim and the rectum at the level of the sphincter muscles and removed. The mucosa may be stripped from the remaining distal rectum from a perineal approach. The distal colon is

42-54

pulled through the sphincter complex and approximated to the anus with sutures. The incision is closed.

In an alternate procedure, the physician removes or bypasses the diseased rectal segment and performs an anastomosis of the colon and anus. The physician makes an abdominal incision. The rectum and distal colon are mobilized and the colon is divided just proximal to the diseased rectal segment. The rectal segment may be removed and the distal colon pulled through the sphincter complex and approximated to the anus with sutures from a perineal approach. Alternatively, the distal colon may be pulled down and approximated to the anus with sutures, bypassing the diseased rectal segment with a combined lengthwise anastomosis between the colon and the diseased rectal segment. The incision is closed.

In a Soave submucosal resection of rectum (48.41), the physician performs a resection of the submucosal rectal part of the large intestine by pull-through technique. The physician removes or bypasses the diseased rectal segment and performs an anastomosis of the colon and anus. The physician makes an abdominal incision. The rectum and distal colon are mobilized and the colon is divided just proximal to the diseased rectal segment. The rectal segment may be removed and the distal colon pulled through the sphincter complex and approximated to the anus with sutures from a perineal approach. Alternatively, the distal colon may be pulled down and approximated to the anus with sutures, bypassing the diseased rectal segment with a combined lengthwise anastomosis between the colon and the diseased rectal segment. The incision is closed.

Coding Clarification
A pull-through rectal resection refers to pulling the colon through for anastomosis. In an abdominoperineal resection of rectum (48.5), the physician removes the entire rectum and anus through both an abdominal and perineal operative approach and forms a colostomy; there is no anastomosis because all of the anal structures are removed. If the documentation states *pull-through resection* without further specification, report code 48.40. *Abdominoperineal pull-through* that is not further specified is coded as 48.50.

When reporting code 48.40, also code any synchronous anastomosis other than end-to-end (45.90, 45.92-45.95).

Documentation Tip
Review the medical record carefully to determine the surgical technique and approach. If a colostomy is formed, report a code from subcategory 48.5; however, if the colon is anastomosed to the anus and

no colostomy is formed, then a pull-through resection (48.4) was performed. If the physician describes an elliptical incision around the anus, removal of the anus and rectum, closure of the perineum, and formation of colostomy, do not report a code from the 48.4 series, rather see subcategory 48.5.

Coding Scenario
A patient with rectal cancer is admitted for a pull-through resection with sphincter preservation. After removing the diseased rectal segment the physician then performs a primary anastomosis by the double stapling technique at the anus.

Code Assignment:

154.1 Malignant neoplasm of rectum
48.40 Pull-through resection of rectum, not otherwise specified

Coding Guidance
AHA: 3Q, '01, 8; 2Q, '99, 13; 4Q, '08, 169-171

48.5 Abdominoperineal resection of rectum
Description
Subcategory 48.5 codes describe abdominoperineal resection of rectum. In an abdominoperineal resection of rectum, the physician removes the entire rectum and anus through both an abdominal and perineal operative approach and forms a colostomy.

48.50 Abdominoperineal resection of the rectum, not otherwise specified

48.51 Laparoscopic abdominoperineal resection of the rectum

48.52 Open abdominoperineal resection of the rectum

48.59 Other abdominoperineal resection of the rectum

Coding Clarification
In an abdominoperineal resection of rectum, the physician removes the entire rectum and anus through both an abdominal and perineal operative approach and forms a colostomy. Abdominoperineal pull-through resection involves incising around the anus and excising the anus and rectum. There is no anastomosis involved in this type of abdominoperineal resection because all of the anal structures are excised. If a colostomy is formed, report a code from subcategory 48.5; however, if the colon is anastomosed to the anus and no colostomy is formed, then an abdominoperineal pull-through resection (48.4) was performed.

Codes in subcategory 48.5 include synchronous colostomy, combined abdominoendorectal resection and complete proctectomy.

● New Code   ▲ Revised Code   ►◄ Revised Text   © 2010 Ingenix

Do not use these codes to report abdominoperineal resection described as Duhamel (48.65) or when performed as part of pelvic exenteration (68.8).

Also report the appropriate code for any synchronous anastomosis other than end-to-end (45.90, 45.92–45.95)

Documentation Tip
Review the medical record carefully to determine the surgical technique and approach. If a colostomy is formed, report a code from subcategory 48.5; however, if the colon is anastomosed to the anus and no colostomy is formed, then a pull-through resection (48.4) was performed. If the physician describes an elliptical incision around the anus, removal of the anus and rectum, closure of the perineum, and formation of colostomy, report a code from the 48.5 series rather than subcategory 48.4. If the documentation states *pull-through resection* without further specification, report code 48.40. *Abdominoperineal pull-through* that is not further specified is coded as 48.50.

Coding Scenario
A patient with Crohn's disease is admitted for removal of the sigmoid colon and rectum. The physician makes an elliptical incision around the anus, removes the anus and rectum, and pulls the colon through for anastomosis. The physician forms a colostomy and closure of the perineum.

> Code Assignment:
>
> 555.9 Regional enteritis, unspecified site
> 48.50 Abdominoperineal resection of the rectum, not otherwise specified

Coding Guidance
AHA: 2Q, '97, 5; 4Q, '08, 169-171

48.6 Other resection of rectum

Description
This subcategory describes other rectal resections. Rectal resection may be defined as surgical removal of a damaged or dysfunctional portion of the rectum. Indications for rectal resection include:

- Disease (e.g., diverticulitis, neoplasm, inflammatory conditions)
- Injury
- Obstruction
- Ischemia

Rectal resections remove damaged portions of the rectum in order to restore function. Disease or injury can result in scar tissue formation, obstruction, and impairment of the mechanisms that facilitate normal elimination of feces. Some disease processes can cause perforations in the bowel, which can cause serious intraabdominal infections. Surgical removal of the damaged tissues can facilitate the return of normal bowel function.

Coding Clarification
Code also any synchronous anastomosis other than end-to-end (45.90, 45.92-45.95).

48.61 Transsacral rectosigmoidectomy

Description
The physician performs a transsacral rectosigmoidectomy, which is an excision through sacral bone of an area of sigmoid and last parts of the large intestine. The physician removes a portion of the rectum through a transsacral approach. The physician makes a posterior incision at the junction of the sacrum and coccyx. The coccyx is excised. Dissection is continued posteriorly and the rectum and distal colon are mobilized. The rectum is transected proximally and distally and a portion of the rectum is removed. The distal end of colon is approximated to the remaining rectal stump with sutures or staples. The incision is closed.

48.62 Anterior resection of rectum with synchronous colostomy

Description
The physician resects the front terminal end of the large intestine and creates a colostomy.

48.63 Other anterior resection of rectum

Description
This code reports other anterior resection of the rectum without synchronous colostomy.

Coding Guidance
AHA: 1Q, '96, 9

48.64 Posterior resection of rectum

Description
This code reports other resection of the rectum described as a posterior resection.

48.65 Duhamel resection of rectum

Description
The physician removes or bypasses the diseased rectal segment and performs an anastomosis of the colon and anus. The physician makes an abdominal incision. The rectum and distal colon are mobilized and the colon is divided just proximal to the diseased rectal segment. The rectal segment may be removed and the distal colon pulled through the sphincter complex and approximated to the anus with sutures from a perineal approach. Alternately, the distal colon may be pulled down and approximated to the anus with sutures, bypassing the diseased rectal segment with a combined

longitudinal anastomosis between the colon and the diseased rectal segment. The incision is closed.

48.69   Other resection of rectum

Description
This code reports other resection of the rectum not classifiable elsewhere in category 48, including partial proctectomy.

Coding Clarification
Code 48.69 should not be assigned if the medical record contains sufficient information to facilitate coding at a higher level of specificity.

Documentation Tip
If the documentation is ambiguous or unclear, the physician should be queried.

Coding Guidance
   AHA: N-D, '86, 11; J-F, '87, 11; 2Q, '05, 13

48.7   Repair of rectum

Description
This subcategory classifies rectal repair procedures, including sutures, closures, anastomoses, proctopexies, and other procedures.

Coding Clarification
This subcategory excludes repair of current obstetric laceration (75.62) and vaginal rectocele repair (70.50, 70.52, 70.53, 70.55).

48.71   Suture of laceration of rectum

Description
The physician explores and repairs a rectal injury. The physician makes an abdominal incision. The rectal injury is explored and repaired with sutures if possible. An incision may be made between the coccyx and anus and drains placed in the presacral space. The abdominal incision is closed.

48.72   Closure of proctostomy

Description
The physician closes a surgically created artificial opening into the rectum. The stoma device is dissected free and removed, the rectum is repaired, and the defect is closed with layered sutures.

48.73   Closure of other rectal fistula

Description
A rectal sinus tract or fistula may be repaired by dissecting the tract from its external origin, the skin of the perineum or the lining of the vagina, to its source at the rectum, and closing the tissues.

Coding Clarification
Code 48.73 excludes fistulectomy described as:

* Perirectal (48.93)

* Rectourethral (58.43) or rectovesical (57.83)

* Rectovaginal (70.73)

* Rectovesicovaginal (57.83)

48.74   Rectorectostomy

Description
The physician performs rectorectostomy, which is the connection of two cut portions of the large intestine, rectal end.

Coding Clarification
Code 48.74 includes rectal anastomosis, not otherwise specified.

Code 48.74 also includes the stapled transanal rectal resection (STARR) procedure.

48.75   Abdominal proctopexy

Description
The physician performs abdominal proctopexy, which is the fixation of rectum to adjacent abdominal structures. The physician approximates the rectum to the sacrum (proctopexy) for rectal prolapse. The physician makes an abdominal incision. The rectum is completely mobilized from the sacrum and placed in upward tension to remove any redundancy. The rectum is reapproximated to the sacrum with sutures or a mesh may be wrapped around the rectum and attached to the sacrum. The incision is closed.

48.76   Other proctopexy

Description
This code reports other proctopexy not classifiable as abdominal (48.75). Surgical technique and approach may vary.

Through a perineal approach, the physician approximates the rectum to the sacrum (proctopexy) for rectal prolapse. The physician makes a transverse incision between the anus and coccyx. Dissection is continued through the levator muscles to mobilize the rectum from the sacrum. The rectum is placed on upward tension to remove the redundancy and approximated to the sacrum with sutures or with a mesh wrapped around the rectum and secured to the sacrum. The incision is closed.

In an alternate procedure, the physician performs a laparoscopic proctopexy (or rectopexy) for correction of rectal prolapse. With the patient under general anesthesia, the physician places trocars into the abdomen and insufflates the abdominal cavity. Using a laparoscope, the physician completely mobilizes the rectum down to the pelvic floor and attaches the rectum to the sacrum using polypropylene mesh. The mesh is initially stapled to the sacral hollow and sutured on both sides of the rectum. The trocars are removed and the incisions are closed with sutures.

42-54

Coding Clarification
Procedures classifiable to 48.76 include:

- Delorme repair of prolapsed rectum—fixation of collapsed large intestine, rectal part

- Proctosigmoidopexy—suturing of twisted large intestine, rectal part

- Puborectalis sling operation—fixation of rectal part of large intestine by forming the puborectalis muscle into a sling

Code 48.76 excludes manual reduction of rectal prolapse (96.26).

48.79   Other repair of rectum

Description
This code reports other repair of rectum not classifiable elsewhere in subcategory 48.7.

Coding Clarification
Code 48.79 should not be assigned if the medical record contains sufficient information to facilitate coding at a higher level of specificity.

Code 48.79 includes repair of old obstetric laceration of the rectum.

Code 48.79 lists many exclusions. Specific bowel anastomoses and rectal repairs of a gynecological nature are more appropriately classified elsewhere.

Documentation Tip
If the documentation is ambiguous or unclear, the physician should be queried.

48.8   Incision or excision of perirectal tissue or lesion

Description
This subcategory classifies incisions or excisions of perirectal tissue or lesion, including tissue specified as pelvirectal and rectovaginal septum.

48.81   Incision of perirectal tissue

Description
The physician makes an incision into perirectal or rectovaginal tissue. This procedure may be performed to drain an abscess. The physician identifies the location of the abscess. The skin over the abscess is incised and the abscess cavity is opened and drained. Or, the physician may make a transanal incision through the rectum into a perirectal abscess cavity and drain the contents. The incision may be packed open for continued drainage.

48.82   Excision of perirectal tissue

Description
This code reports an excision of a lesion of perirectal tissue. Operative approach and surgical technique may vary.

The physician may remove a lesion of perirectal tissue through a transsacral or transcoccygeal approach. The physician makes an incision at the junction of the sacrum and coccyx. The coccyx is excised and dissection is continued posteriorly to mobilize the rectum. The lesion is identified, an incision is made in the rectum (proctotomy), and the perirectal tissue is excised. The rectum and perirectal tissues are closed with sutures or staples. The initial incision is closed.

In an alternate procedure, the physician removes a rectal tumor through a transanal approach. The physician explores the anal canal and exposes the tumor. The tumor is excised to include a full thickness of the rectal wall. The defect in the rectum is closed with sutures.

Coding Clarification
Code 48.82 excludes perirectal excisional procedures specified as:

- Biopsy (48.26)
- Perirectofistulectomy (48.93)
- Rectal fistulectomy (48.73)

48.9   Other operations on rectum and perirectal tissue

Description
This subcategory classifies other operations on the rectum and perirectal tissue not classifiable elsewhere in category 48, including incision of rectal stricture, myomectomy, repair of perirectal fistula, and other procedures.

48.91   Incision of rectal stricture

Description
The physician performs division of a rectal stricture. The physician makes longitudinal incisions in the scar tissue in one or more places circumferentially around the strictured area of the rectal mucosa. A dilatation of the strictured area may be performed. In addition, the internal anal sphincter may be incised as part of the procedure.

48.92   Anorectal myectomy

Description
The physician removes a muscle tumor or a section of muscle from the anorectum. The physician identifies the anorectal muscle tumor or area of interest. A transanal incision is made through the rectal wall and the tumor or identified area of muscle is excised. The incision is closed by approximating the muscle edges and closing the incision in the rectal lining.

48.93   Repair of perirectal fistula

Description
The physician performs repair of a perirectal fistula, which involves closure of an abdominal passage in tissue around large intestine, rectal part.

Coding Clarification
Code 48.93 excludes repair of a perirectal fistula that opens into the rectum (48.73).

48.99   Other operations on rectum and perirectal tissue

Description
This code reports other operations of the rectum and perirectal tissue not elsewhere classifiable in category 48.

Coding Clarification
Code 48.99 should not be assigned if the medical record contains sufficient information to facilitate coding at a higher level of specificity.

Code 48.99 lists multiple exclusions for rectum and perirectal procedures classifiable to Chapter 16 Miscellaneous diagnostic and therapeutic procedures (87-99).

Documentation Tip
If the documentation is ambiguous or unclear, the physician should be queried.

---

49   Operations on anus

Description
The anus is the external opening at the distal end of the rectum through which fecal matter is expelled from the body. The primary function of the anus is to serve as a passageway that opens and closes utilizing specialized sphincter muscles. This physiological process is called defecation, which is the last stage of the digestive process whereby waste is eliminated from the body out of the digestive system. When the rectum becomes full, the pressure forces the walls of the anal canal apart and the peristaltic contractions that move the waste through the digestive tract propels the feces from the anal canal through internal and external sphincters.

Category 49 classifies operations on the anus, including incisions, excisions, endoscopies, repairs, and other diagnostic and therapeutic procedures.

Coding Clarification
Code also any application or administration of an adhesion barrier substance (99.77).

49.0   Incision or excision of perianal tissue

Description
This subcategory classifies incision and excision procedures of perianal tissue, including the treatment of abscesses, skin tags, and other conditions.

49.01   Incision of perianal abscess

Description
The physician drains a superficial perianal abscess. The physician identifies the location of the abscess. The perianal skin over the abscess is incised and the abscess cavity is opened and drained. The incision is packed open for continued drainage.

Coding Guidance
   AHA: 2Q, '05, 10

49.02   Other incision of perianal tissue

Description
The physician identifies the location of the abscess or other perianal tissue requiring incision. An incision is made in the perianal skin and the skin and connective tissues are opened and drained. The mucosa, skin, and internal sphincter muscle may be unroofed, if necessary. The incision may be left open to drain or closed with layered sutures.

49.03   Excision of perianal skin tags

Description
The physician performs excision of a perianal skin tag. The physician identifies the perianal skin tag and sharply excises and removes it. If the tag is situated at the anal sphincter, an incision is made around the skin tag whereby the lesion is dissected from the underlying sphincter muscle and removed. The incision is closed with sutures or may be left partially open to drain.

49.04   Other excision of perianal tissue

Description
The physician performs excision of a perianal lesion. The physician identifies the lesion and sharply excises and removes it. If the lesion is situated at the anal sphincter, an incision is made around the lesion and it is dissected from the underlying sphincter muscle and removed. The incision is closed with sutures or may be left partially open to drain.

Coding Guidance
   AHA: 1Q, '01, 8

49.1   Incision or excision of anal fistula

Description
This category describes incision or excision of an anal fistula.

Coding Clarification
Subcategory 49.1 excludes closure of an anal fistula (49.73).

49.11   Anal fistulotomy

Description
The physician identifies the location of the internal and external openings of the anal fistula in relation to the sphincter muscles. An incision is made in the perianal skin and the fistula tract may be opened and drained. The mucosa, skin, and internal sphincter muscle overlying the fistula is incised and the fistula is unroofed. If the fistula goes beneath the external sphincter muscle a stitch (seton) may be placed through the fistula tract to allow drainage and preserve continence. The incision may be left open to drain and the abscess cavity is packed open for continued drainage.

49.12   Anal fistulectomy

Description
The physician excises an anal fistula. The physician explores the anal canal and identifies the location of the fistula in relation to the sphincter muscles. The skin, subcutaneous, and connective tissue overlying the fistula are incised and the fistula tract is dissected free and removed. The incision may be left open to allow continued drainage or closed in layered sutures.

49.2   Diagnostic procedures on anus and perianal tissue

Description
This category describes diagnostic procedures on the anus and perianal tissue including endoscopy, biopsy, and other procedures.

49.21   Anoscopy

Description
The physician performs anoscopy and may obtain brushings or washings. The physician inserts the anoscope into the anus and advances the scope. The anal canal and distal rectal mucosa are visualized and brushings or washings may be obtained. The anoscope is withdrawn at the completion of the procedure.

49.22   Biopsy of perianal tissue

49.23   Biopsy of anus

Description
These codes report a perianal or anal biopsy, which may be performed under direct visualization, by incision, or endoscopically.

The physician may perform an anal or perianal biopsy by endoscopy for tissue samples. The physician inserts the anoscope into the anus and advances the scope. The anal canal and distal rectal mucosa are visualized and tissue samples are obtained. The anoscope is withdrawn at the completion of the procedure.

If the physician performs the anal or perianal biopsy under direct visualization, a biopsy sample of skin, subcutaneous tissue, and/or mucous membrane may be sharply excised and removed. Some normal tissue adjacent to the diseased tissue may also be removed for comparison purposes. The excision site may be closed simply or may be allowed to granulate without closure.

49.29   Other diagnostic procedures on anus and perianal tissue

Description
This code reports other diagnostic procedures on anal and perianal tissue that are not classifiable as anoscopy or biopsy.

Coding Clarification
Code 49.29 should not be assigned if the medical record contains sufficient information to facilitate coding at a higher level of specificity.

Code 49.29 excludes microscopic examinations of specimens classifiable to Chapter 16 Miscellaneous diagnostic and therapeutic procedures (87-99).

Documentation Tip
If the documentation is ambiguous or unclear, the physician should be queried.

49.3   Local excision or destruction of other lesion or tissue of anus

Description
This subcategory describes endoscopic or other local excision or destruction of anal lesions.

Coding Clarification
This subcategory excludes the following excisional or destruction procedures classified elsewhere:

* Biopsy of anus (49.23)
* Control of (postoperative) hemorrhage of anus (49.95)
* Hemorrhoidectomy (49.46)

Documentation Tip
Procedures classifiable to this section may be documented as:

* Anal cryptotomy
* Cauterization of lesion of anus

49.31   Endoscopic excision or destruction of lesion or tissue of anus

Description
The physician performs anoscopy and removes a tumor, polyp, or other lesion. The physician inserts the anoscope into the anus and advances the scope. The anal canal and distal rectal mucosa are

visualized. The lesion is identified and removed or destroyed by hot biopsy forceps, electrocautery, or other method. The anoscope is withdrawn at the completion of the procedure.

49.39   Other local excision or destruction of lesion or tissue of anus

Description

A lesion of anal skin, subcutaneous tissue, and/or mucous membrane may be sharply excised and removed. Some normal tissue adjacent to the diseased tissue may also be removed to ensure the entire lesion is removed. The excision site may be closed simply or may be allowed to granulate without closure.

In an alternate procedure, the physician performs destruction of anal lesions. The physician exposes the perianal skin and identifies the lesions. The lesions may be painted with destructive chemicals, destroyed, or excised with electrodesiccation or cautery. The physician may also perform a destruction of anal lesions with cryosurgery, usually with liquid nitrogen.

Coding Guidance
> **AHA:** 1Q, '01, 8

49.4   Procedures on hemorrhoids

Description

This subcategory classifies procedures for the treatment of hemorrhoids. Hemorrhoids are swollen, painful veins in the rectum and anus that are caused by increased pressure that causes the veins to bulge. Patients who suffer from hemorrhoids often have difficulty sitting due to the swelling of the veins, itching, and swelling of the anus. The most common causes of hemorrhoids include prolonged sitting, constipation, or straining during bowel movements. Hemorrhoids are also a common complication of pregnancy and childbirth, or may manifest secondary to the effects of other chronic diseases.

Hemorrhoids are classified as internal or external, meaning that external hemorrhoids are those around the outside of the anus, and internal hemorrhoids are inside the anus or rectum. Treatment of hemorrhoids usually consists of topical methods intended to decrease discomfort, unless complications develop that require further intervention. Complications of hemorrhoids include bleeding from the varicosities, or thrombus (clot) formations. These complications are treated with a variety of relatively minor surgical procedures that remove the clot, coagulate the area of hemorrhage, or excise, ligate (i.e., tie-off), and inject the offending vein.

49.41   Reduction of hemorrhoids

Description

The physician performs manual manipulation to reduce hemorrhoids.

49.42   Injection of hemorrhoids

Description

The physician performs sclerotherapy of internal hemorrhoids. The physician explores the anal canal and identifies the hemorrhoid columns. Sclerosing solution is injected into the submucosa of the rectal wall under the hemorrhoid columns.

49.43   Cauterization of hemorrhoids

Description

The physician performs destruction of hemorrhoids. The physician explores the anal canal and identifies the hemorrhoid columns. The physician explores the anal canal and identifies any internal or external hemorrhoids. The hemorrhoids are destroyed by clamping the vessel and cauterization of the blood supply. The hemorrhoid remnants may be removed.

49.44   Destruction of hemorrhoids by cryotherapy

Description

The physician performs destruction of hemorrhoids. The physician explores the anal canal and identifies the hemorrhoid columns. The hemorrhoids are destroyed by cryotherapy, usually liquid nitrogen. The hemorrhoid remnants may be removed.

49.45   Ligation of hemorrhoids

Description

The physician performs hemorrhoidectomy by ligation of a hemorrhoid. The physician identifies the hemorrhoid columns. The hemorrhoid may be ligated at its base (usually with a rubber band) or suture ligation of the hemorrhoid may be performed. The hemorrhoid tissue is allowed to slough over time.

49.46   Excision of hemorrhoids

Description

The physician performs excision of internal and external hemorrhoids. The physician explores the anal canal and identifies the hemorrhoid column. An incision is made in the rectal mucosa around the hemorrhoids and the lesions are dissected from the underlying sphincter muscles and removed. The incisions are closed with sutures.

Coding Guidance
> **AHA:** 1Q, '01, 8

● New Code   ▲ Revised Code   ►◄ Revised Text   © 2010 Ingenix

49.47   Evacuation of thrombosed hemorrhoids

Description

The physician performs an incision and drainage or excision of a thrombosed external hemorrhoid. The physician exposes the thrombosed external hemorrhoid. The hemorrhoid may be incised and the thrombus removed or completely excised. The incision may be closed or left open to allow continued drainage.

49.49   Other procedures on hemorrhoids

Description

This code reports other hemorrhoid treatment not classifiable elsewhere in subcategory 49.4.

Coding Clarification

Code 49.49 should not be assigned if the medical record contains sufficient information to facilitate coding at a higher level of specificity.

Documentation Tip

If the documentation is ambiguous or unclear, the physician should be queried.

This procedure may be documented as a Lord hemorrhoidectomy.

49.5   Division of anal sphincter

Description

This subcategory classifies division (incision) of the anal sphincter, which may be documented as anal sphincterotomy procedures. The code descriptions state the site of the division (incision). Sphincterotomy may be indicated for the treatment of anal fissure or stricture, whereby the sphincter is stretched or cut to prevent muscle spasm and assists in healing of the traumatized anal tissue.

49.51   Left lateral anal sphincterotomy

49.52   Posterior anal sphincterotomy

49.59   Other anal sphincterotomy

Description

The physician divides the anal sphincter. The patient is placed in jackknife or lithotomy position. The physician performs digital and instrumental dilation of the anus with exposure of the patient's anal canal. A small incision is made between the muscle layers of the anus and internal muscle is divided without opening the lining of the anus.

49.6   Excision of anus

Description

This code reports the excisional procedures such as excision and removal of the anal vault and sphincter or other radical excision of anal tissue. This type of procedure is most commonly performed to remove a malignant neoplasm and the extension of neoplasm into surrounding contiguous tissues. Although rectal cancer was traditionally treated by removing the anus, sphincter, and tumor, more recent surgical techniques are likely to preserve as much of the anus and sphincter as possible in order for the patient to retain bowel function.

49.7   Repair of anus

Description

This subcategory classifies anal repair procedures, including suture repairs, cerclage application, fistula closures, incontinence treatment, artificial sphincters, and other procedures.

Coding Clarification

This subcategory excludes repair of current obstetric laceration of the anus (75.62).

49.71   Suture of laceration of anus

Description

The physician sutures a laceration of the anus. A local anesthetic is injected around the laceration and the wound is cleansed, explored, and often irrigated with a saline solution. The physician performs suture repair of the epidermis, dermis, or subcutaneous tissues.

49.72   Anal cerclage

Description

The physician performs anal cerclage, which is encircling the anus with a ring or sutures. This procedure may be performed to treat anal fissure or anal prolapse.

49.73   Closure of anal fistula

Description

This code reports closure of an anal fistula. The closure technique may vary depending on the nature, location, and severity of fistula tract, including:

- **Closure by suture:** The physician explores the anal canal and identifies the location of the fistula in relation to the sphincter muscles. The skin and subcutaneous tissue overlying the fistula is incised to open the fistula tract, which is excised or repaired with sutures. The incision may be left open to allow continued drainage.

- **Closure with fibrin glue:** The physician repairs an anal fistula using fibrin glue. Fibrin glue is made with human fibrinogen pooled from the plasma of long-term donors under control methods that avoid passing infection to the recipient. The glue is composed of two components, usually applied through double lumen catheters to guide the component injections separately to the tissue and must be

42-54

applied at a temperature of 37 C. The fistula is first localized and cannulated, then prepped for the glue. The margins and canal of the fistula are de-epithelialized with electrocoagulation and/or roughening the fistulous canal with a brush. Some bleeding will actually improve the adhesion of the fibrin clot. The gluing is done so as to completely fill the defect and around the borders of the fistula, sealing it with a clot. Fibrin glue only works on tissue capable of local regeneration for wound healing since the glue does not actually function as a seal or a plug, but provides the substrate for fibroblasts to move in. After about four weeks, the glued surface is replaced by scar tissue and the fibrin glue totally decomposes. Mechanical stress must be avoided while this stage is developing.

- **Advancement flap closure:** The physician excises an anal fistula and closes the defect with a rectal advancement flap. The physician explores the anal canal and identifies the location of the fistula in relation to the sphincter muscles. The fistula tract is excised. An incision is made onto the perianal skin and a wedge of skin and subcutaneous tissue are mobilized and advanced into the defect created by the excision of the fistula. The incisions are closed with sutures.

Coding Clarification
Code 49.73 excludes simple excision and closure of anal fistula (49.12).

49.74   Gracilis muscle transplant for anal incontinence

Description
The physician performs sphincteroplasty with levator muscle imbrication for incontinence in an adult (Park repair). The physician makes a transverse incision anterior to the anus. Dissection is carried through the subcutaneous tissue to expose the anal canal. The external sphincter muscle is dissected from the internal sphincter and dissection is continued between the sphincters to expose the puborectalis muscle (levator). The edges of the puborectalis muscle are imbricated around the anal canal with sutures. The external sphincter muscle is imbricated around the anal canal with sutures. The incision is closed.

49.75   Implantation or revision of artificial anal sphincter

49.76   Removal of artificial anal sphincter

Description
The physician makes a midline abdominal incision. The physician dissects the perineum overlying the

rectal orifice. The external anal sphincter muscle is mobilized along with its fibrotic ends. Surgical repair of the defective sphincter is performed with the implantation of an artificial sphincter, or the previously implanted artificial sphincter is repaired or revised. The external sphincter muscle may be wrapped around the anal canal and approximated without tension. The surgeon may find it necessary to approximate the levator ani muscle to restore the anorectal angle to normal; the puborectalis and external sphincter muscles are also tightened with sutures. This procedure lengthens the anal canal. Once implantation of the artificial sphincter is complete and the sphincter is reconstructed, the perineum is closed.

Coding Clarification
Code 49.76 excludes revision with implantation during the same operative episode (49.75).

Coding Guidance
AHA: 4Q, '02, 105

49.79   Other repair of anal sphincter

Description
This code reports other repair of anal sphincter not classifiable elsewhere in subcategory 49.7.

Coding Clarification
Code 49.79 should not be assigned if the medical record contains sufficient information to facilitate coding at a higher level of specificity.

Code 49.79 excludes anoplasty with synchronous hemorrhoidectomy (49.46) and repair of current obstetric laceration (75.62).

Documentation Tip
If the documentation is ambiguous or unclear, the physician should be queried.

Coding Guidance
AHA: 1Q, '97, 9; 2Q, '98, 16

49.9   Other operations on anus

Description
This subcategory classifies other operations on the anus not classifiable elsewhere in category 49, including certain incisions, insertions, reductions, and other procedures.

49.91   Incision of anal septum

Description
The physician may incise a congenital anal septum. The physician identifies the anal opening and septum, usually in an infant patient. The septum is sharply incised.

49.92 Insertion of subcutaneous electrical anal stimulator

Description
This code reports the insertion or implantation of a neurostimulator to assist in maintaining control over the anal sphincter function in patients who suffer from chronic fecal incontinence. In a preliminary procedure, temporary electrodes may be placed percutaneously through the sacral foramina. If the test period of two to three weeks shows satisfactory continence, the permanent electrode is placed and a neurostimulator may be implanted, whereby an electrode and generator device are implanted and tunneled subcutaneously to stimulate the sacral nerve and assist in maintaining sphincter control.

49.93 Other incision of anus

Description
This code reports other incisions of the anus classifiable elsewhere, such as an incision for removal of a foreign body.

The physician removes an anal seton or other marker. The physician identifies the seton stitch or other marker at the anal verge. The seton is divided and removed. The external anal sphincter at the level of the seton may be divided.

Coding Clarification
Code 49.93 excludes incision of an anal fistula (49.11) and removal of an intraluminal foreign body without incision (98.05).

49.94 Reduction of anal prolapse

Description
The physician reduces an anal prolapse, which is the manipulation of displaced anal tissue to normal position. The physician places a wire, suture, or muscular graft around the anus for prolapse or incontinence (Thiersch procedure). The physician makes incisions on opposite sides of the anus in the lateral perianal subcutaneous tissue. A wire, suture, or muscular graft mobilized from the thigh is wrapped around the anus in the subcutaneous space and secured in place. The incisions are closed.

Coding Clarification
Code 49.94 excludes manual reduction of rectal prolapse (96.26).

49.95 Control of (postoperative) hemorrhage of anus

Description
The physician may perform an anoscopy to control an area of postoperative or other bleeding. The physician inserts the anoscope into the anus and advances the scope. The anal canal and distal rectal mucosa are visualized. The area of bleeding is identified and controlled. The anoscope is withdrawn at the completion of the procedure.

49.99 Other operations on anus

Description
This code reports other operations on the anus not classifiable elsewhere in category 49.

Coding Clarification
Code 49.99 should not be assigned if the medical record contains sufficient information to facilitate coding at a higher level of specificity.

Documentation Tip
If the documentation is ambiguous or unclear, the physician should be queried.

50 Operations on liver

Description
The liver is a large, multi-lobed, glandular organ that is located in the upper right abdominal quadrant, and serves multiple essential biochemical functions in the body. The liver is a vital organ without which the human organism cannot sustain life. The liver is essential to the digestive, metabolic, and hematologic processes by the following functions:

* Secreting digestive enzymes and bile
* Providing metabolism of nutrients from proteins, fats, and carbohydrates
* Storing nutrients such as glycogen for future use
* Filtering and detoxifying substances in the body such as alcohol and medications
* Producing body heat by metabolism
* Producing clotting factors for the blood

The liver performs many vital functions in the body, one of which is to filter out toxic substances. If the liver is not functioning properly, a build-up of toxins can occur, which can have a devastating affect on other organs.

Category 50 provides codes for diagnostic and therapeutic stomach procedures including incision, biopsy, excision, destruction, transplant, repair, and other operations.

Coding Clarification
Code also any application or administration of an adhesion barrier substance (99.77).

50.0 Hepatotomy

Description
The physician incises the liver, usually to drain an abscess or a cyst. The physician exposes the liver via an upper midline incision. The cyst is incised and suctioned with care so as not to contaminate the abdomen with purulent matter. The incision is closed.

50.1   Diagnostic procedures on liver

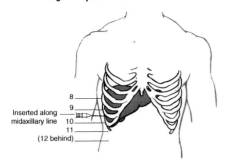

Inserted along midaxillary line

8
9
10
11
(12 behind)

50.11   Closed (percutaneous) (needle) biopsy of liver

Description
The physician takes tissue from the liver for examination. The physician may use ultrasound guidance to place a hollow bore needle between the ribs on the patient's right side. The liver biopsy is sent for pathology.

Coding Guidance
    AHA: 4Q, '88, 12; 3Q, '05, 24

50.12   Open biopsy of liver

Description
The physician takes a biopsy through an abdominal incision. A wedge-shaped section of liver tissue may be excised for biopsy. The physician exposes the abdomen via an upper abdominal incision through skin, fascia, and muscle. Interrupted mattress sutures are placed on the edge of the liver lobe. A specimen is excised or pie-shaped wedge of the liver is resected and sent for pathology in a separately reportable activity. Electrocautery is used to obtain hemostasis of the liver edge. The abdominal incision is closed with layered sutures.

Coding Guidance
    AHA: 2Q, '05, 13; 3Q, '05, 24

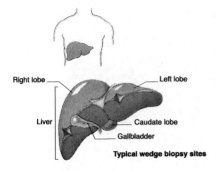

Right lobe

Left lobe

Liver

Caudate lobe

Gallbladder

Typical wedge biopsy sites

50.13   Transjugular liver biopsy

Description
The physician takes tissue from the liver for examination. A catheter is inserted into the jugular vein in the neck. Under fluoroscopic guidance, the catheter is threaded to the liver through the vena cava and heart to the hepatic vein. Through the hepatic vein access, tissue samples are removed from the liver and delivered out through the catheter for microscopic analysis.

Coding Clarification
Excluded from 50.13 are closed liver biopsy (50.11) and laparoscopic liver biopsy (50.14).

Documentation Tip
This procedure may also be documented as a transvenous liver biopsy.

Coding Scenario
A patient underwent a liver biopsy to diagnose the cause of chronic liver disease. Using imaging guidance, the radiologist inserted a catheter into the jugular vein in the neck and directed it into the primary vein in the liver. A small biopsy needle was then inserted through the tube and into the liver to obtain a sample of tissue.

    Code Assignment:

    571.9   Unspecified chronic liver disease without mention of alcohol
    50.13   Transjugular liver biopsy

Coding Guidance
    AHA: 4Q, '07, 113

50.14   Laparoscopic liver biopsy

Description
This procedure code describes a liver biopsy through laparoscope. The physician makes an incision in the umbilicus through which the abdomen is inflated and a fiberoptic laparoscope is inserted. Other incisions are made through which trocars can be passed into the abdominal cavity to deliver instruments, a fiberoptic camera, and light source. The physician manipulates the tools so that the liver can be viewed through the laparoscope and video monitor. Liver biopsy is obtained by utilizing special forceps to remove pieces of liver tissue or lesion. When the specimen is obtained, the abdomen is deflated, instrumentation is removed and incisions are closed with simple suture.

Coding Clarification
Excluded from 50.14 are closed liver biopsy (50.11), open liver biopsy (50.12), and transjugular liver biopsy (50.13).

Coding Guidance
    AHA: 4Q, '07, 113

● New Code   ▲ Revised Code   ▶◀ Revised Text   © 2010 Ingenix

50.19   Other diagnostic procedures on liver

Description

This code reports other diagnostic procedures on the liver, not described as open, closed, laparoscopic, or transjugular biopsy.

Coding Clarification

Code 50.19 excludes diagnostic liver procedures classifiable to Chapter 16 Miscellaneous diagnostic and therapeutic procedures (87-99).

50.2   Local excision or destruction of liver tissue or lesion

Description

This subcategory classifies other local excision or destruction of liver, including ablation, excision, and other procedures utilizing open, percutaneous, or laparoscopic operative approaches.

50.21   Marsupialization of lesion of liver

Description

The physician creates a pouch with the lining of a cyst on the liver. The physician exposes the liver via an upper midline abdominal incision through skin, fascia, and muscles. The cyst is incised and suctioned with care not to contaminate the abdomen. Electrocautery is used to resect the cyst wall to allow open drainage into the abdomen. The abdominal incision is closed with sutures.

50.22   Partial hepatectomy

Description

The physician removes a section of liver. The physician exposes the liver via an upper midline incision through skin, fascia, and muscle. The fibrous connections of the liver to the diaphragm are divided and the portal structures are controlled. The portal and hepatic vessels associated with the divided. The portal structures are clamped. The liver parenchyma is divided by pressure or coagulation hemostasis. The portal clamp is removed and hemostasis is assured before the abdomen is closed with sutures.

Coding Clarification

Code 50.22 includes wedge resection of the liver.

Code 50.22 excludes excision for biopsy of liver (50.11-50.12) and hepatic lobectomy (50.3).

50.23   Open ablation of liver lesion or tissue

50.24   Percutaneous ablation of liver lesion or tissue

50.25   Laparoscopic ablation of liver lesion or tissue

50.26   Other and unspecified ablation of liver lesion or tissue

Description

Surgery and liver transplant are considered to be the only curative treatments for hepatocellular carcinoma; however, due to contraindications such as multiple tumors, decreased liver function, or various medical complications, few patients are eligible. Ablative procedures offer an alternative to these major invasive procedures.

Radiofrequency ablation, or RFA, uses heat to destroy liver lesions by applying energy to a specific lesion. Performed by open, percutaneous, or laparoscopic technique, energy derived from the radiofrequency bandwidth comes from a base generator and is passed through the ablation device, causing lesion cell death by coagulation necrosis. Radiofrequency ablation may be most effective in primary liver cancer (hepatocellular carcinoma or hepatoma) since these tumors are most often soft and encapsulated. As well, these tumors usually occur in a cirrhotic liver, which allows the heat to be more effectively distributed and retained. Survival rates of patients undergoing radiofrequency ablation are felt to be similar to that of patients undergoing surgery or percutaneous ethanol injection (PEI) treatment.

HIFU, or high-intensity focused ultrasound, utilizes a probe that is inserted laparoscopically. A rapid temperature rise causes lesion ablation. Laser-induced interstitial thermotherapy (LITT) utilizes lasers to heat certain areas of the body. Directed to interstitial areas (areas between organs) that are near the tumor, the heat generated from the laser increases the temperature of the tumor and shrinks, damages, or destroys the cancer cells.

Cryoablation, a hypothermal technique, is the oldest thermal ablation and may be performed by open technique, laparoscopically, or percutaneously. Localization of the tumor is performed by laparoscopic and/or radiographic means; freezing of the tumor follows.

Ablation can be performed by one of three methods: open, percutaneous, or laparoscopic. Prior to the procedure, the patient receives general anesthesia or conscious sedation. The sedated patient is then positioned in order to provide the best angle necessary for accurate device placement.

The open approach to ablation (50.23) involves the creation of an incision in order to afford superior visual identification for placement of the ablation device. Following activation and completion of the ablation cycle, the device is removed and the incision closed by traditional methods.

42-54

In percutaneous ablation (50.24), the ablation device is inserted through the skin and into the lesion. Ultrasound or computed tomography guidance is employed in order to achieve accurate device placement. After activation and completion of the ablation cycle, the device is removed and a bandage is placed over the site of insertion.

Laparoscopic ablation (50.25) involves the insertion of the ablation device into the lesion with the assistance of a laparoscope and, if necessary, imaging guidance. Following cycle initiation and completion, the device is removed and the incision closed with a few sutures.

Coding Scenario
A 52-year-old male with primary hepatocellular carcinoma presented for laparoscopic radiofrequency ablation. Under general anesthesia, laparoscopic ultrasound was performed and the lesion within the liver was located and mapped. Utilizing laparoscopic technique, the radiofrequency thermal ablation catheter was placed into the liver using ultrasound guidance. The tip of the probe was inserted into the center of the tumor and the prongs were deployed. Upon initiation of the ablation cycle, a target temperature of 105x C was maintained for five minutes during each cycle. Following cycle completion, the ablation device and laparoscope were removed and the incision sutured. There were no complications.

Code Assignment:

155.0   Malignant neoplasm of liver, primary
50.25   Laparoscopic ablation of liver lesion or tissue

Coding Guidance
AHA: 4Q, '06, 124

50.29   Other destruction of lesion of liver
Description
This code reports other destruction, cauterization, enucleation, or evacuation of liver lesion or tissue not classifiable elsewhere in subcategory 50.2.

Coding Clarification
Code 50.29 excludes ablation of liver by specified method or approach classifiable elsewhere in subcategory 50.2, as well as percutaneous aspiration of liver (50.91).

Do not assign 50.29 to report laser interstitial thermal therapy [LITT] of lesions of the liver under guidance; assign code 17.63.

Code 50.29 should not be assigned if the medical record contains sufficient information to facilitate coding at a higher level of specificity.

Documentation Tip
If the documentation is ambiguous or unclear, the physician should be queried.

Coding Guidance
AHA: 2Q, '03, 9

50.3   Lobectomy of liver
Description
The physician removes a lobe of the liver (lobectomy). The physician exposes the liver via an upper midline incision through skin, fascia, and muscle. The fibrous connections of the liver to the diaphragm are divided and the portal structures are controlled. The portal and hepatic vessels associated with the affected lobe are divided. The portal structures are clamped. The liver parenchyma is divided by pressure or coagulation hemostasis. The portal clamp is removed and hemostasis is assured before the abdomen is closed with sutures.

50.4   Total hepatectomy
Description
The physician performs a donor hepatectomy by removing the liver from a cadaver donor for transplantation into another recipient. The physician accesses the liver, which is mobilized from its attachments. The blood supply and bile ducts to the liver are dissected free and isolated. The liver is removed with its attached blood vessels and bile ducts and perfused with a cold preservation solution and removed from the operative field. The liver is preserved for transplantation into the recipient. The organ remains under refrigeration, specially packed in a sealable container with some preserving solution and kept on ice in a suitable carrier.

Coding Guidance
AHA: 2Q, '08, 8

50.5   Liver transplant
Description
This subcategory lists liver transplant procedures, specified as auxiliary or other.

Coding Clarification
To report the donor source, see adjunct procedure codes 00.91-00.93.

50.51   Auxiliary liver transplant
Description
The physician performs a partial or whole liver transplantation to a position other than the normal anatomic position of the liver, as the patients own liver is left in situ. The physician makes an abdominal incision. The donor liver is placed in an acceptable position in the upper abdominal cavity that is not the normal liver bed location. Anastomoses are created between the donor hepatic vessels and the appropriate recipient vessels. The donor bile duct is approximated to the recipient bile

duct or to a limb of small bowel for drainage. Drains are placed and the abdominal incision is closed.

50.59   Other transplant of liver

Description
The physician performs a partial or whole liver transplantation. The physician makes an abdominal incision. The donor liver is placed in an acceptable position in the upper abdominal cavity that is not the normal liver bed location. Anastomoses are created between the donor hepatic vessels and the appropriate recipient vessels. The donor bile duct is approximated to the recipient bile duct or to a limb of small bowel for drainage. Drains are placed and the abdominal incision is closed.

Coding Guidance
   AHA: 2Q, '08, 8; 4Q, '08, 120

50.6   Repair of liver

50.61   Closure of laceration of liver

Description
The physician sutures a liver wound to control the bleeding or repair damage. The physician exposes the liver via an upper midline abdominal incision. The abdomen is packed to control bleeding. The patient is stabilized hemodynamically. The liver is systematically exposed with pressure on bleeding points. The liver tissue is divided to expose the points of bleeding and the bleeding is controlled by ligation of bleeding vessels. The abdominal incision is closed.

50.69   Other repair of liver

Description
The physician performs a hepatopexy (surgical repair of the liver). The physician exposes the liver via an upper midline abdominal incision. The abdomen is packed to control bleeding. The patient is stabilized hemodynamically. The liver is systematically exposed with pressure on bleeding points, if necessary. The liver is explored and tissue is divided to expose points of bleeding and the bleeding is controlled by ligation of bleeding vessels. Complex suture of liver wound or injury, extensive debridement, coagulation, sutures, and packing of the liver may be required. The abdominal incision is closed.

50.9   Other operations on liver

Description
This subcategory lists other operations on the liver not classifiable elsewhere in category 50.

Coding Clarification
Subcategory 50.9 excludes lysis of adhesions (54.5).

50.91   Percutaneous aspiration of liver

Description
The physician performs a hepatotomy for percutaneous drainage of an abscess or a cyst, one or two stages. The physician may create a small incision in the skin proximal to the liver abscess or cyst to ease placement of drainage instruments through the skin (percutaneous). The physician uses a CAT scan or ultrasound to guide placement of a drainage needle or trocar into the liver abscess or cyst. The physician advances the drainage needle or trocar through the abdominal wall into the peritoneum to gain access to the abscess or cystic cavity. The procedure sometimes requires multiple stages. The fluid is allowed to drain. Once drained, a catheter may be placed. Sutures may be secured to hold the drainage catheter in place. The operative site is subsequently cleaned and bandaged.

50.92   Extracorporeal hepatic assistance

Description
The physician performs extracorporeal hepatic assistance, which involves devices used outside the body to assist in liver function. Liver dialysis is used to treat patients in acute hepatic failure. It utilizes a mobile bedside device that is similar in function to a hemodialysis machine by alternately withdrawing and returning blood through an access catheter. Liver dialysis is designed to remove toxins from blood and assist in maintaining metabolic balance.

Coding Clarification
Code 50.92 includes liver dialysis.

Coding Guidance:
   AHA: 2Q,'01, 21

50.93   Localized perfusion of liver

Description
This code reports intravenous delivery of medication, fluid, or other substances through the vessels that directly supply the liver to nourish or treat the organ in a concentrated manner. In the treatment of liver cancer, liver perfusion is used to deliver high doses of chemotherapy to the liver through its blood supply, minimizing systemic circulation of the drugs.

50.94   Other injection of therapeutic substance into liver

Description
The physician performs an injection of the liver. The physician makes an abdominal incision. The liver is mobilized and the site of injection is identified. The remaining abdominal contents are packed off with sponges for protection. The abdominal incision is closed.

© 2010 Ingenix

● New Code   ▲ Revised Code   ►◄ Revised Text

42-54

50.99   Other operations on liver

Description
This code reports other operations on the liver not classifiable elsewhere in subcategory 50.9.

Coding Clarification
Code 50.99 should not be assigned if the medical record contains sufficient information to facilitate coding at a higher level of specificity.

Documentation Tip
If the documentation is ambiguous or unclear, the physician should be queried.

51   Operations on gallbladder and biliary tract

Description
The gallbladder is a pouch-like structure that is attached to the liver and duodenum by a network of biliary tracts (tubes). The cystic duct extends from the gallbladder and joins the common hepatic duct to form the common bile duct, which joins with the pancreatic duct and enters the duodenum. A small amount of bile is stored in the gallbladder in a concentrated form, which is released to assist with the digestion of fats.

Common diseases of the gallbladder include inflammation, infection, the presence of calculi (stones), and other causes of biliary obstruction. When the gallbladder or bile ducts become diseased or obstructed (blocked), the ability of the digestive system to break down fats is affected.

Diagnostic imaging assists in confirming the diagnosis and type of gallbladder and bile duct disease and determining the best course of treatment. Infections can be effectively treated with antibiotics. Removal of the stones from the bile duct can be effectively performed via an endoscopic procedure; however, many cases necessitate surgical removal of stones in the bile ducts or the gallbladder.

Category 51 provides codes for diagnostic and therapeutic biliary procedures including incision, biopsy, excision, destruction, anastomosis, repair, and other operations.

Coding Clarification
Code also any application or administration of an adhesion barrier substance (99.77).

Category 51 includes operations on the following anatomic sites:

- Ampulla of Vater
- Common bile duct
- Cystic duct
- Hepatic duct

- Intrahepatic duct
- Sphincter of Oddi

51.0   Cholecystotomy and cholecystostomy

Description
This category describes incisions for drainage or aspiration by open (incisional) approach, through trocar, or percutaneous approach through needle or catheter.

51.01   Percutaneous aspiration of gallbladder

Description
The physician inserts a tube into the gallbladder to allow drainage through the skin. The physician uses ultrasound guidance to place a subcostal drainage tube into the gallbladder. The physician places a needle between the ribs into the gallbladder. The needle position is checked by aspiration. A guidewire is passed through the needle. A catheter is passed over the wire into the biliary tree. The wire is removed and the tube is left in place.

Coding Clarification
Code 51.01 excludes needle biopsy of the gallbladder (51.12).

51.02   Trocar cholecystostomy

Description
The physician creates an opening in the gallbladder with a catheter to facilitate drainage or stone removal.

Coding Guidance
   AHA: 3Q, '89, 18

51.03   Other cholecystostomy

51.04   Other cholecystotomy

Description
The physician performs a cholecystotomy or cholecystostomy with exploration, drainage, or removal of calculus. The physician exposes the gallbladder through a subcostal or upper midline incision. The gallbladder is incised, explored, and may be drained. Calculi may be removed. The gallbladder is closed with interrupted sutures primarily or around a drainage tube. If placed, the drainage tube is brought out through the skin at a site separate from the incision. The abdominal incision is closed.

51.1   Diagnostic procedures on biliary tract

Description
This subcategory classifies diagnostic procedures on the biliary tract including those performed by percutaneous, open, and endoscopic techniques.

Coding Clarification
Subcategory 51.1 excludes endoscopic therapeutic biliary procedures classifiable elsewhere.

Coding Guidance
AHA: 2Q, '97, 7

51.10 Endoscopic retrograde cholangiopancreatography (ERCP)

Description
The physician performs a diagnostic endoscopic retrograde cholangiopancreatography (ERCP), which involves an endoscopic and radioscopic exam of the pancreatic and common bile ducts with contrast material injected in the opposite direction of normal flow through the catheter. The physician passes the endoscope through the patient's oropharynx, esophagus, stomach, and into the small intestine. The ampulla of Vater is cannulated and filled with contrast. The common bile duct and the whole biliary tract including the gallbladder are visualized.

Coding Clarification
This procedure differs from ERC and ERP in regard to the extent of the examination performed. ERCP is a comprehensive procedure in which the entire biliary tract is examined. ERC and ERP provide a limited examination of certain structures as specified in the code descriptions.

Code 51.10 excludes other endoscopic retrograde procedures that visualize only the gallbladder and bile ducts (51.11) or pancreas and pancreatic ducts (52.13).

Coding Guidance
AHA: 2Q, '99, 13; 1Q, '01, 8; 3Q, '03, 17; 4Q, '03, 118

51.11 Endoscopic retrograde cholangiography (ERC)

Description
The physician passes an endoscope to visualize portions of the biliary tract, which may be filled with contrast medium for identifying the common bile duct, biliary tree, and gallbladder (including areas of abnormality, stricture, or obstruction).

Coding Clarification
Code 51.11 excludes other endoscopic retrograde procedures such as ERCP (51.10) or pancreas and pancreatic ducts (52.13).

Coding Guidance
AHA: 4Q, '88, 7; 3Q, '89, 18; 1Q, '96, 12;

51.12 Percutaneous biopsy of gallbladder or bile ducts

Description
The physician uses ultrasound or other guidance to obtain a sample of tissue from the bile ducts. The physician places a needle between the ribs into the bile duct. A sample of tissue is extracted into the needle. If a small access incision was necessary, it is closed with layered sutures.

51.13 Open biopsy of gallbladder or bile ducts

Description
This code reports a sample of gallbladder or bile duct tissue excised and removed by open incision through the abdominal wall. When an adequate tissue sample is obtained, the physician closes the incision with layered sutures.

51.14 Other closed (endoscopic) biopsy of biliary duct or sphincter of Oddi

Description
The physician performs an endoscopic (closed) biopsy of the biliary duct or sphincter of Oddi. The physician passes the endoscope through the patient's oropharynx, esophagus, stomach, and into the small intestine. The ampulla of Vater is cannulated and filled with contrast. The common bile duct and the whole biliary tract including the gallbladder are visualized. Brushings or washings may be obtained. A tissue sample is excised or removed for biopsy through the endoscope.

Coding Clarification
Code 51.14 includes biopsy of the biliary duct or sphincter of Oddi by ERCP (51.10), ERC (51.11), or ERP (52.13).

51.15 Pressure measurement of sphincter of Oddi

Description
The physician performs pressure measurement tests of muscle tissue surrounding pancreatic and common bile ducts, usually performed in conjunction with other procedures. The physician passes the endoscope through the patient's oropharynx, esophagus, stomach, and into the small intestine. The ampulla of Vater is cannulated and filled with contrast. The common bile duct and the whole biliary tract including the gallbladder are visualized. A pressure measurement is recorded of the sphincter of Oddi. The instrumentation is removed.

Coding Clarification
Code 51.15 includes pressure measurement of sphincter by procedures classifiable to 51.10-51.11 and 52.13.

51.19 Other diagnostic procedures on biliary tract

Description
This code reports other diagnostic procedures on the biliary tract not classifiable elsewhere in subcategory 51.1.

42-54

Coding Clarification
Code 51.19 should not be assigned if the medical record contains sufficient information to facilitate coding at a higher level of specificity.

Code 51.19 excludes diagnostic procedures classifiable to Chapter 16 Miscellaneous diagnostic and therapeutic procedures (87-99).

Documentation Tip
If the documentation is ambiguous or unclear, the physician should be queried.

51.2   Cholecystectomy

Description
This subcategory classifies cholecystectomy procedures (surgical removal of the gallbladder).

Coding Guidance
AHA: 3Q, '89, 18; 4Q, '91, 26; 1Q, '93, 17

51.21   Other partial cholecystectomy

Description
The physician removes part of the gallbladder or revises a previous cholecystectomy. The physician exposes the liver and gallbladder via a right subcostal incision. The cystic duct and cystic artery are ligated and the gallbladder or portion of the gallbladder is removed using electrocautery. The incision is closed with layered sutures.

Coding Clarification
Code 51.21 excludes laparoscopic partial cholecystectomy (51.24).

Coding Guidance
AHA: 4Q, '96, 69

51.22   Cholecystectomy

Description
The physician removes the gallbladder. The physician exposes the liver and gallbladder via a right subcostal incision. The cystic duct and cystic artery are ligated and the gallbladder is removed using electrocautery. The incision is closed with layered sutures

Coding Clarification
Code 51.22 excludes laparoscopic total cholecystectomy (51.23).

Coding Guidance
AHA: 2Q, '91, 16; 4Q, '97, 52

51.23   Laparoscopic cholecystectomy

Description
The physician performs endoscopic removal of the gallbladder.

Coding Guidance
AHA: 4Q, '91, 26; 2Q, '95, 11; 1Q, '96, 12; 4Q, '97, 52; 3Q, '98, 10; 4Q, '08, 174

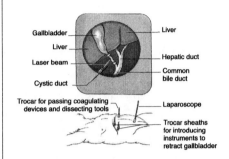

51.24   Laparoscopic partial cholecystectomy

Description
The physician performs endoscopic removal of part of the gallbladder or revision of a previous cholecystectomy. The physician removes the gallbladder through a laparoscope. The physician makes a 1 centimeter infraumbilical incision through which a trocar is inserted. Pneumoperitoneum is achieved by insufflating the abdominal cavity with carbon dioxide. A fiberoptic laparoscope fitted with a camera and light source is inserted through the trocar. Other incisions are made on right side of the abdomen and in the subxiphoid area to allow other instruments or an additional light source to be passed into the abdomen. The tip of the gallbladder is mobilized and placed in traction. The Hartmann's pouch (junction of the cystic duct and gallbladder neck) is identified. Tissue is dissected free from around the area for exposure of Calot's triangle (formed by the cystic artery, and cystic and common bile ducts). Clips are applied to the proximal area of the cystic duct and artery (close to the gallbladder) and the cystic duct and artery are cut. The gallbladder is dissected from the liver bed and removed through a trocar site. Any loose stones that have dropped into the abdominal cavity are retrieved with forceps. The intraabdominal cavity is irrigated. The trocars are removed and the incisions are closed.

Coding Guidance
AHA: 4Q, '96, 69

51.3   Anastomosis of gallbladder or bile duct

Description
This subcategory classifies anastomosis of the gallbladder or bile duct(s) to various intestinal sites. An anastomosis is an operation to create a therapeutic connection between body parts, usually performed to restore physiologic function after a diseased body part is surgically removed.

● New Code   ▲ Revised Code   ▶◀ Revised Text   © 2010 Ingenix

Coding Clarification
Subcategory 51.3 excludes resection with
end-to-end anastomosis (51.61-51.69), which is
included in the code for the resection.

These procedures may be performed by open
(incisional) or laparoscopic approach.

51.31   Anastomosis of gallbladder to hepatic ducts

51.32   Anastomosis of gallbladder to intestine

51.33   Anastomosis of gallbladder to pancreas

51.34   Anastomosis of gallbladder to stomach

51.35   Other gallbladder anastomosis

51.36   Choledochoenterostomy

Description
The physician performs a connection of common bile
duct to intestine.

**51.37   Anastomosis of hepatic duct to gastrointestinal
tract**

Coding Clarification
This procedure is also known as a Kasai
portoenterostomy, which is the creation of a duct to
drain bile from the liver formed by anastomosing
(connecting) the porta hepatis to a loop of bowel.

Coding Guidance
    AHA: 2Q, '02, 12

51.39   Other bile duct anastomosis

Description
The physician performs an anastomosis between the
gallbladder or bile duct and other intestinal site,
such as the hepatic ducts, intestine, pancreas, or
stomach. The gallbladder and anastomosis site are
identified and mobilized. An artificial communication
or passageway is created between the two sites with
staples or sutures. The incisions are closed.

51.4   Incision of bile duct for relief of obstruction

Description
This subcategory describes bile duct incision for
relief of obstruction by decompression or removal of
the calculus or other obstruction.

**51.41   Common duct exploration for removal of
calculus**

**51.42   Common duct exploration for relief of other
obstruction**

**51.43   Insertion of choledochohepatic tube for
decompression**

Description
The physician makes an incision into the common
bile duct, removing calculus, draining purulent
matter, and/or relieving other obstruction. The
physician exposes the common bile duct within the
portal triad through a subcostal or upper midline
incision. The common bile duct is incised, explored,
and drained. The common bile duct is closed with
interrupted sutures primarily or around a drainage
tube (choledochostomy). If placed, the drainage tube
is brought out through the skin at a site separate
from the incision. The abdominal incision is closed.

Coding Guidance
    AHA: 4Q, '88, 7; 3Q, '89, 18; 1Q, '96, 12

**51.49   Incision of other bile ducts for relief of
obstruction**

Description
The physician makes an incision into a bile duct,
removing calculus, draining purulent matter, and/or
relieving other obstruction. The physician exposes
the bile duct within the portal triad through a
subcostal or upper midline incision. The duct is
incised, explored, and drained. The duct may be
closed with interrupted sutures. If placed, the
drainage tube is brought out through the skin at a
site separate from the incision. The abdominal
incision is closed.

Coding Guidance
    AHA: 3Q, '89, 18

51.5   Other incision of bile duct

Description
The physician performs bile duct incision for
exploration.

Coding Clarification
Subcategory 51.5 excludes incision for relief of
obstruction (51.41-51.49).

51.51   Exploration of common bile duct

51.59   Incision of other bile duct

Description
The physician explores the common duct or other
bile duct. The physician exposes the liver and
gallbladder via a right subcostal incision. The
physician may perform a bile duct exploration

post-cholecystectomy during a subsequent operation. If the gallbladder is removed during this operation, the cystic duct and cystic artery are ligated and the gallbladder removed using electrocautery. The common bile duct is exposed in the portal triad, incised, and the stones removed. The common bile duct is closed and the abdominal incision is closed with sutures.

Coding Guidance

AHA: 3Q, '89, 12; 1Q, '96, 12; 2Q, '97, 16

51.6 Local excision or destruction of lesion or tissue of biliary ducts and sphincter of oddi

Coding Clarification
Subcategory 51.6 excludes excision of tissue for biopsy (51.12-51.13).

Code also anastomosis other than end-to-end (51.31, 51.36-51.39).

51.61 Excision of cystic duct remnant

Description
The physician performs an excision of a remaining portion of cystic duct post-cholecystectomy.

Coding Clarification
The cystic duct remnant (re-formed gallbladder) can cause or contribute a painful condition called post-cholecystectomy syndrome, whereby the patient continues to suffer upper abdominal pain after the gallbladder has been resected with no identifiable remaining stones.

Coding Guidance

AHA: 3Q, '89, 18

51.62 Excision of ampulla of Vater (with reimplantation of common duct)

Description
The physician excises the ampulla of Vater, a saccular dilation of liver and/or pancreas. The physician exposes the duodenum and pancreas via an upper midline abdominal incision. The duodenum is opened with a longitudinal incision. The ampulla of Vater is exposed and the abnormality is excised. The common bile duct and duodenal mucosa are re-approximated as needed. The duodenum is closed with transverse interrupted sutures. The abdominal incision is closed.

51.63 Other excision of common duct

Description
The physician performs an excision of the common bile duct. The physician exposes the liver and gallbladder via an upper midline or subcostal incision made through skin, fascia, and muscle. The common bile duct is exposed and a lesion or portion

excised. The defect of the biliary system is repaired. The abdominal incision is closed with layered sutures.

Coding Clarification
Code 51.63 excludes excision for fistulectomy (51.72).

51.64 Endoscopic excision or destruction of lesion of biliary ducts or sphincter of Oddi

Description
The physician performs an endoscopic examination by passing an endoscope through the patient's oropharynx, esophagus, stomach, and into the small intestine. The ampulla of Vater is cannulated and filled with contrast. The common bile duct and the whole biliary tract including the gallbladder are visualized. An ablation or other destruction of biliary duct or sphincter of Oddi lesion(s) is performed by bipolar cautery, sharp excision, electrocauterization, snare technique, or other method.

51.69 Excision of other bile duct

Description
The physician performs excision of a bile duct lesion. The physician makes an abdominal incision and explores the abdomen. The bile duct is dissected from surrounding structures and the lesion is identified and mobilized. The lesion is excised along with a margin of normal tissue, if necessary. An anastomosis may be performed to allow biliary drainage. The distal end of the bile duct is oversewn. The incision is closed.

Coding Clarification
Code 51.69 excludes excision for fistulectomy (51.79).

51.7 Repair of bile ducts

Description
This subcategory classifies suture or other plastic repair of the common or other bile duct.

51.71 Simple suture of common bile duct

51.72 Choledochoplasty

51.79 Repair of other bile ducts

Description
The physician performs suture repair of the common bile duct or other bile duct. The physician makes an abdominal incision. The affected bile duct is dissected from surrounding structures and the area necessitating suture of the duct is identified. The duct is closed or otherwise repaired with sutures. A drain may be placed and brought out through the abdominal wall. The incision is closed.

Coding Clarification
Code 51.79 excludes operative removal of a
prosthetic device from the biliary tract (51.95).

**51.8   Other operations on biliary ducts and sphincter
        of oddi**

Description
This subcategory classifies other operations on the
bile ducts and sphincter of Oddi not classifiable
elsewhere in category 51.

51.81   Dilation of sphincter of Oddi

Description
The physician performs dilation of muscle around
the common bile duct and pancreatic ducts to
mitigate constriction from obstructing bile flow.

Coding Clarification
Code 51.81 describes dilation by incisional (open)
approach through an incision in the abdominal wall.
Dilation by endoscopic approach is classified to
51.84.

Code 51.81 includes dilation of the ampulla of Vater.

Code 51.81 excludes endoscopic dilation (51.84).

51.82   Pancreatic sphincterotomy

51.83   Pancreatic sphincteroplasty

Description
The physician performs a transduodenal pancreatic
sphincterotomy or sphincteroplasty, which is the
division of muscle around common bile and
pancreatic ducts. The physician exposes the second
portion of the duodenum via a subcostal or upper
midline incision through skin, fascia, and muscle.
The duodenum is opened using a longitudinal
incision. The pancreatic sphincter is identified and
an incision is made at the two o'clock position. The
common bile duct mucosa may be reapproximated
to the duodenal mucosa and the duodenum
transversely closed with interrupted sutures. The
abdominal incision is closed.

Coding Clarification
Code 51.82 describes dilation by incisional (open)
approach through an incision in the abdominal wall.
Sphincterotomy by endoscopic approach is classified
to 51.85.

This procedure may be performed through a
transduodenal approach whereby the duct is
accessed through the fist section of small intestine,
requiring closure of intestine upon completion of the
sphincterotomy portion of the procedure. The access
incision and suture closure of the duodenum is
included in the code for the primary procedure
(51.82 or 51.83) and is not reported separately.

51.84   Endoscopic dilation of ampulla and biliary duct

51.85   Endoscopic sphincterotomy and papillotomy

**51.86   Endoscopic insertion of nasobiliary drainage
        tube**

**51.87   Endoscopic insertion of stent (tube) into bile
        duct**

**51.88   Endoscopic removal of stone(s) from biliary
        tract**

Description
The physician performs an endoscopic examination
(ERCP, ERC, ERP) by passing the endoscope through
the patient's oropharynx, esophagus, stomach, and
into the small intestine. The ampulla of Vater is
cannulated and filled with contrast. The common
bile duct and the whole biliary tract including the
gallbladder are visualized. The following procedures
may be performed:

*   Sphincterotomy/papillotomy
*   Removal of stones from biliary and/or
    pancreatic ducts
*   Insertion of a nasobiliary or nasopancreatic
    drainage tube
*   Insertion of a tube or stent into the bile or
    pancreatic duct
*   Balloon dilation of the ampulla, biliary, and/or
    pancreatic ducts

Upon completion of the procedure, the specimen(s)
and instrumentation are removed.

Coding Clarification
Code 51.87 excludes nasobiliary drainage tube
(51.86) or replacement of a stent or tube (97.05).

Code 51.88 excludes percutaneous extraction of
common bile duct stones (51.96).

Coding Guidance
  AHA: 2Q, '97, 7; 2Q, '00, 11; 3Q, '03, 17; 4Q, '03, 118

51.89   Other operations on sphincter of Oddi

Description
This code reports other operations on the sphincter
of Oddi not classifiable elsewhere in category 51.

Coding Clarification
Code 51.89 should not be assigned if the medical
record contains sufficient information to facilitate
coding at a higher level of specificity.

Documentation Tip
If the documentation is ambiguous or unclear, the
physician should be queried.

51.9   Other operations on biliary tract

Description
This subcategory classifies other operations on the biliary tract not classifiable elsewhere in category 51, including certain laceration repairs, closures, those performed by percutaneous approach, and other procedures.

51.91   Repair of laceration of gallbladder

Description
The physician exposes the gallbladder via a right subcostal incision. The cystic duct and cystic artery are ligated if necessary and the gallbladder laceration is identified and repaired with sutures, electrocautery, or other method. The incision is closed with layered sutures.

51.92   Closure of cholecystostomy

Description
This code reports closure of a surgical opening into the gallbladder or bile ducts for drainage. The previous incision may be reopened. The drainage tube is dissected free and the defect is repaired with sutures. The incision is closed in layers.

51.93   Closure of other biliary fistula

Description
The physician performs closure of a biliary tract fistula. The physician makes an abdominal incision. The affected bile duct is dissected from surrounding structures and the fistula tract is identified. The fistula tract is excised, closed, or otherwise repaired. A drain may be placed and brought out through the abdominal wall. The incision is closed.

51.94   Revision of anastomosis of biliary tract

Description
The physician performs a revision, correction, or repair of a previous anastomosis between the gallbladder or bile duct and other intestinal site, such as the hepatic ducts, intestine, pancreas, or stomach. The anastomosis site is identified and mobilized. The anastomosis between the two sites is repaired or revised with dissection, staples, or sutures. Bleeding is controlled with electrocautery. A drain may be placed and brought out through the abdominal wall. The incision is closed.

51.95   Removal of prosthetic device from bile duct

Description
This code reports the operative removal of a stent or other prosthetic device from the biliary tract.

Coding Clarification
Code 51.95 excludes other nonoperative removal of a stent (97.55).

51.96   Percutaneous extraction of common duct stones

Description
The physician removes a stone from the common bile duct by percutaneous approach. The physician places a choledochoscope, which is a radiologically-guided access catheter, into the common bile duct through a small incision in the abdominal wall. The biliary tree, liver, and ampulla are visualized. Using a basket or snare through the choledochoscope, the stones are extracted with fluoroscopy or other guidance. The instrumentation is removed, the defect in the common bile duct is closed, and the abdominal access incision is closed.

Coding Clarification
Code 51.96 includes percutaneous removal of common bile duct stones. Percutaneous stone extraction from the bile duct other than the common bile duct is reported with 51.98.

Coding Guidance
    AHA: 4Q, '88, 7

51.98   Other percutaneous procedures on biliary tract

Description
This code reports biliary tract procedures performed by percutaneous approach. Surgical technique may vary depending on the procedures performed.

The physician makes a small incision in the abdomen. The physician advances an endoscope through an opening in the abdominal wall or through a T-tube inserted through the abdominal wall into the bile duct. With the endoscope, the physician is able to directly visualize portions of the biliary tract, which may be filled with contrast medium for identifying the bile ducts, biliary tree, and gallbladder (if present). Calculi may be identified and removed. The endoscope is removed. The T-tube is withdrawn and the defect in the bile duct is sutured closed. The tract, peritoneum, and abdominal wall are closed using a layered technique.

Coding Clarification
Code 51.98 excludes percutaneous common bile duct stone extraction (51.96) and other percutaneous aspiration (51.01) or biopsy (51.12).

Coding Guidance
    AHA: N-D, '87, 1; 3Q, '89, 18; 1Q, '97, 14

51.99   Other operations on biliary tract

Description
This code describes other operations on the biliary tract not classifiable elsewhere in category 51.

Coding Clarification
Code 51.99 should not be assigned if the medical record contains sufficient information to facilitate coding at a higher level of specificity.

● New Code ▲ Revised Code ▶◀ Revised Text © 2010 Ingenix

42-54

Code 51.99 lists multiple exclusions for specific procedures classifiable elsewhere in category 51 or Chapter 16 Miscellaneous diagnostic and therapeutic procedures (87-99).

Documentation Tip
If the documentation is ambiguous or unclear, the physician should be queried.

---

52   Operations on pancreas

Description
The pancreas is a 6 to 9 inch long glandular organ that secretes enzymes and fluid to assist with digestion. It can be separated into three main portions: the body, head, and tail. It serves dual functions as both a digestive organ and an endocrine gland. The exocrine cells of the pancreas produce digestive enzymes and the endocrine cells secrete hormones. The hormones insulin and glucagon are secreted directly into the bloodstream by endocrine islets of Langerhans cells.

Due to the importance of the functions of the pancreas in maintaining metabolic balance and essential digestive enzymes, pancreatic infection, injury, or other disease is potentially very serious, and requires expedient medical intervention.

Category 52 provides codes for diagnostic and therapeutic pancreas procedures including incision, biopsy, excision, destruction, transplant, repair, and other operations.

Coding Clarification
Code also any application or administration of an adhesion barrier substance (99.77).

Category 52 includes operations on the pancreatic duct.

52.0   Pancreatotomy
Description
This subclassification lists pancreatotomy procedures, including diagnostic or therapeutic incisions into the pancreas.

52.01   Drainage of pancreatic cyst by catheter
Description
The physician performs percutaneous drainage of a pancreatic cyst. The physician may create a small incision in the flank or abdomen proximal to the cystic lesion in order to ease placement of drainage instruments through the skin and into the cyst for drainage to an external fluid collection system. The physician uses a CAT scan or ultrasound to guide placement of a drainage needle or trocar into the lesion. The physician advances the drainage needle or trocar through the skin into the cyst, which is allowed to drain. Once the cyst is drained, a drainage catheter may be placed. Sutures may be placed to secure the drainage catheter in place. The operative site is cleaned and bandaged.

52.09   Other pancreatotomy
Description
Code 52.09 describes incision of the pancreas. Surgical technique may vary depending on the nature of the diagnosis.

In a pancreatolithotomy, the physician removes a stone from the pancreas. The physician exposes the pancreas via an upper midline incision through skin, fascia, and muscle. The pancreatic duct is opened and the calculus removed. The pancreatic duct is connected directly to the small bowel for drainage. The abdominal incision is closed.

In an alternate procedure, the physician externally drains a pancreatic cyst. The physician approaches the pancreas through a midline abdominal incision. The physician locates the cyst through an incision and approaches the pancreas through the lesser sac of the omental bursa or through the transverse mesocolon. Once the drain is placed, the adjacent tissues are returned to anatomic position and the operative site is sutured in layers.

Coding Clarification
Code 52.09 excludes drainage of the pancreas by anastomosis (52.4, 52.96), incision of the pancreatic sphincter (51.82), and marsupialization of a cyst (52.3).

52.1   Diagnostic procedures on pancreas
Description
This subcategory lists diagnostic procedures on the pancreas, including biopsy, endoscopic examinations, and other procedures.

52.11   Closed (aspiration) (needle) (percutaneous) biopsy of pancreas
Description
The physician removes tissue from the pancreas. The physician passes the biopsy needle through the skin of the upper abdomen under computerized tomography guidance. The pancreatic lesion is removed and the specimen is sent for pathological examination.

52.12   Open biopsy of pancreas
Description
The physician obtains a biopsy of the pancreas. The physician makes a midline epigastric incision and retracts the skin and underlying tissues laterally. The physician approaches the pancreas through the lesser sac of the omental bursa. The pancreas is palpated, the lesion is identified, and a biopsy is

42-54

obtained by various methods, such as fine needle aspiration or needle core or wedge biopsy. Bleeding is controlled and the lesser sac is closed. Tissues are reapproximated to the anatomical position and the incision is sutured in layers.

52.13 Endoscopic retrograde pancreatography (ERP)

52.14 Closed (endoscopic) biopsy of pancreatic duct

Description
The physician performs an endoscopic retrograde pancreatography (ERP). Following sedation, the physician passes the endoscope through the patient's oropharynx, esophagus, stomach, and into the small intestine. From the major papilla, the pancreatic duct is visualized and injected with contrast. A tissue sample of the pancreatic duct is obtained for pathological examination. The specimen is removed through the endoscope. After examination is complete, the endoscope is removed.

Coding Clarification
A diagnostic endoscopy procedure code is not used as an additional code when the code assignment indicates a biopsy or other procedure performed through that endoscope.

When an endoscope is passed through more than one body cavity or anatomic structure, the code for the endoscopy identifies the most distant site examined.

Code 52.13 excludes procedures performed via ERC (51.11) or ERCP (51.10).

Code 52.14 includes closed biopsy of the pancreatic duct by procedures classifiable to 51.10-51.11 and 52.13.

52.19 Other diagnostic procedures on pancreas

Description
Code 52.19 describes other diagnostic pancreatic procedures not classifiable elsewhere in subcategory 52.1.

Coding Clarification
Code 52.19 should not be assigned if the medical record contains sufficient information to facilitate coding at a higher level of specificity.

Code 52.19 lists multiple exclusions for procedures specifically classifiable elsewhere including:

- ERP (52.13)
- Procedures classifiable to Chapter 16 Miscellaneous diagnostic and therapeutic procedures (87-99)

52.2 Local excision or destruction of pancreas and pancreatic duct

Coding Clarification
Subcategory 52.2 excludes excisional procedures classifiable elsewhere, such as biopsy of the pancreas (52.11-52.12, 52.14) and pancreatic fistulectomy (52.95).

52.21 Endoscopic excision or destruction of lesion or tissue of pancreatic duct

Description
The physician performs an endoscopic examination (ERCP, ERP) by passing the endoscope through the patient's oropharynx, esophagus, stomach, and into the small intestine. In ERCP, the ampulla of Vater is cannulated and filled with contrast. The common bile duct and the whole biliary tract including the gallbladder may be visualized, In ERP, the pancreatic duct is visualized and injected with contrast. Pancreatic duct lesions are identified and excised or destroyed. Upon completion of the procedure, the specimen(s) and instrumentation are removed.

52.22 Other excision or destruction of lesion or tissue of pancreas or pancreatic duct

Description
The physician excises a lesion of the pancreas. The physician makes a midline epigastric incision and retracts the skin and underlying tissues laterally. The physician approaches the pancreas through the lesser sac of the omental bursa or through the transverse mesocolon. The pancreas is palpated and the lesion is identified and excised. Bleeding is controlled and the lesser sac is closed. Tissues are reapproximated to anatomical position and the incision is sutured in layers.

52.3 Marsupialization of pancreatic cyst

Description
The physician marsupializes a pancreatic cyst. The physician approaches the pancreas through a midline abdominal incision and retracts the skin and underlying tissues laterally. The physician approaches the pancreas through the lesser sac of the omental bursa or through the transverse mesocolon. The cyst is located and the anterior cyst wall is incised. The cut edges of the cyst are sutured to the skin edges establishing a pouch of what was formally an enclosed cyst. The remainder of the operative site is sutured in layers.

Coding Clarification
Code 52.3 excludes drainage of a cyst by catheter insertion (52.01).

52.4   Internal drainage of pancreatic cyst

Description
The physician performs internal drainage of a pancreatic cyst. The physician creates an internal anastomosis of a pancreatic cyst to a portion of the gastrointestinal tract. The physician approaches the pancreas through a midline abdominal incision and retracts the skin and underlying tissues laterally. The physician approaches the pancreas through the lesser sac of the omental bursa or through the transverse mesocolon. The cyst is located. The physician approximates the stomach wall or a loop of duodenum or jejunum and incises it. The anterior cyst wall is incised and the cyst edges are approximated with the cut edges of the gastrointestinal tract and sutured. The cyst is decompressed through the drainage tract. The surrounding tissues are returned to anatomic position and the operative site is sutured in layers.

Documentation Tip
Procedures classifiable to code 52.4 may be documented as:

- Pancreaticocystoduodenostomy
- Pancreaticocystogastrostomy
- Pancreaticocystojejunostomy

52.5   Partial pancreatectomy

Description
This subcategory describes partial (subtotal) pancreatectomy procedures or excision of part of the pancreas. The code descriptions state the part of pancreas excised or the extent of the procedure (if described as radical, assign 52.53).

Coding Clarification
Subcategory 52.5 excludes pancreatic fistulectomy (52.95).

52.51   Proximal pancreatectomy

52.52   Distal pancreatectomy

52.53   Radical subtotal pancreatectomy

52.59   Other partial pancreatectomy

Description
The physician removes a portion of the pancreas. The physician makes a midline epigastric incision and retracts the skin and underlying tissues laterally. The physician may approach the pancreas through the lesser sac of the omental bursa or through the transverse mesocolon. The pancreas is identified and freed from attachments. If the blood supply to the pancreas also supplies the spleen, the spleen is sacrificed in the resection. The pancreas is transected and a portion is removed, with or without

the spleen. Bleeding is controlled and the lesser sac is closed. Tissues are reapproximated to anatomical position and the incision is sutured in layers.

52.6   Total pancreatectomy

Description
The physician removes the pancreas. The physician makes a midline epigastric incision and retracts the skin and underlying tissues laterally. The physician may approach the pancreas through the lesser sac of the omental bursa or through the transverse mesocolon. The pancreas is identified and freed from attachments. The pancreas is removed. Blood vessels are ligated and bleeding is controlled. The lesser sac is closed. Tissues are reapproximated to anatomical position and the incision is sutured in layers.

Coding Guidance
AHA: 4Q, '96, 71

52.7   Radical pancreaticoduodenectomy

Description
The physician performs excision of the proximal pancreas, duodenum, distal bile duct, and distal stomach with reconstruction (Whipple procedure) but with pancreatojejunostomy. The physician makes an abdominal incision and explores the abdomen. The duodenum, proximal pancreas, and bile duct are mobilized. The distal bile duct, distal stomach, and distal duodenum are divided. The pancreas is transected at the junction of the head and body and the pancreatic head, duodenum, distal stomach, and distal bile duct are removed en bloc. The anatomy is reconstructed by performing sequential anastomoses between the proximal jejunum and the distal bile duct and distal stomach. The edge of the remaining distal pancreas is closed with sutures or staples. The incision is closed.

Coding Clarification
Code 52.7 excludes radical subtotal (partial) pancreatectomy (52.53).

Documentation Tip
Procedures classifiable to 52.7 may be documented as:

- Whipple procedure
- Radical resection of the pancreas
- Two-stage pancreaticoduodenal resection

Coding Guidance
AHA: 1Q, '01, 13

52.8   Transplant of pancreas

Description
This subcategory describes pancreatic transplants.

42-54

Coding Clarification
To report the donor source, see 00.91-00.93.

52.80   Pancreatic transplant, not otherwise specified

Description
This code reports a pancreatic transplant procedure, not specified according to type.

Coding Clarification
Code 52.80 should not be assigned if the medical record contains sufficient information to facilitate coding at a higher level of specificity.

Documentation Tip
If the documentation is ambiguous or unclear, the physician should be queried.

52.81   Reimplantation of pancreatic tissue

Description
The physician performs surgical replacement of pancreatic tissue to the site from which it was previously removed.

52.82   Homotransplant of pancreas

Description
The physician transplants a pancreas obtained from another (cadaveric donor) person to the patient. (Also known as allotransplant, homograft, or homotransplant.)

52.83   Heterotransplant of pancreas

Description
The physician performs pancreas transplantation. The physician makes an abdominal incision. The iliac arteries and veins in the pelvis are exposed and isolated. An anastomosis is usually performed between the artery and vein supplying the pancreas to the iliac artery and vein on one side of the pelvis. An additional anastomosis is usually performed between the attached duodenal segment and the bladder. The incision is closed.

Coding Clarification
Heterotransplant of the pancreas involves transplanting a pancreas from another species (animal) and grafting it into a recipient of another species (human). (Also known as heterograft, heterotransplant, xenotransplant.)

52.84   Autotransplantation of cells of islets of Langerhans

Description
The physician transplants Islet cells from the pancreas to another (anatomic) location in the body of the same patient.

Coding Guidance
   AHA: 4Q, '96, 70, 71

52.85   Allotransplantation of cells of islets of Langerhans

Description
The physician transplants Islet cells from one individual to another.

Coding Guidance
   AHA: 4Q, '96, 70, 71

52.86   Transplantation of cells of islets of Langerhans, not otherwise specified

Description
Islet cells are insulin-producing cell clusters found only in the pancreas. In islet cell transplants, insulin-producing islet cells are infused into the liver by portal vein embolization. Islet cell transplant is considered a less invasive alternative to pancreatic transplant. The physician uses ultrasonic guidance to insert a catheter through a skin incision in the upper abdomen and into the portal vein of the liver. Islet cells are slowly infused through the catheter. The pressure within the portal vein is monitored during the procedure to ensure the vessel is not occluded. The catheter is removed and the incision closed. The islet cells will attach to the vessel walls in the portal vein and begin releasing insulin within a month. This procedure is limited to persons with Type 1 diabetes.

Coding Guidance
   AHA: 4Q, '96, 70

52.9   Other operations on pancreas

Description
This subcategory describes other operations on the pancreas not classifiable elsewhere in category 52, including certain endoscopic procedures, repairs, cannulations, and other procedures.

52.92   Cannulation of pancreatic duct

Description
The physician performs cannulation of the pancreatic duct, which is placement of a tube into the pancreatic duct.

Coding Clarification
Code 52.92 excludes cannulation by endoscopic approach (52.93).

52.93   Endoscopic insertion of stent (tube) into pancreatic duct

Description
The physician passes the endoscope (via ERCP, ERP) through the patient's oropharynx, esophagus, stomach, and into the small intestine. The ampulla of Vater and/or pancreatic duct is cannulated and filled with contrast to visualize biliary and/or pancreatic anatomy. A tube or stent is inserted into

the pancreatic duct. Upon adequate deployment, the endoscope is removed.

Coding Guidance
AHA: 2Q, '97, 7

52.94   Endoscopic removal of stone(s) from pancreatic duct

Description
The physician passes the endoscope (via ERCP, ERP) through the patient's oropharynx, esophagus, stomach, and into the small intestine. The ampulla of Vater and/or pancreatic duct is cannulated and filled with contrast to visualize biliary and/or pancreatic anatomy. Stones are identified and removed from the pancreatic duct. The endoscope is removed.

52.95   Other repair of pancreas

Description
The physician performs a pancreatic repair (pancreatorrhaphy). The physician makes an abdominal incision and the abdomen is explored. The pancreas is exposed and the pancreatic injury, defect, or lesion is identified and repaired with sutures. A peripancreatic drain is usually placed. The incision is closed.

52.96   Anastomosis of pancreas

Description
This code reports an anastomosis of the pancreas or pancreatic duct to another intestinal site, such as the jejunum or stomach. Surgical technique may vary.

The physician may create a pancreaticojejunostomy (passageway between the pancreas and jejunum) to drain pancreatic enzymes through a side-to-side anastomosis. The physician makes a midline epigastric incision and retracts the skin and underlying tissues laterally. The physician approaches the pancreas through the lesser sac of the omental bursa or through the transverse mesocolon. A jejunal loop is brought up to create a fistula for enzyme flow to the digestive tract. Bleeding is controlled and the lesser sac is closed. Tissues are reapproximated to the anatomical position and the incision is sutured in layers.

Coding Clarification
Code 52.96 excludes anastomosis to the bile duct (51.39) or gallbladder (51.33).

52.97   Endoscopic insertion of nasopancreatic drainage tube

Description
The physician passes the endoscope (via ERCP, ERP) through the patient's oropharynx, esophagus,

stomach, and into the small intestine. The ampulla of Vater and/or pancreatic duct is cannulated and filled with contrast to visualize biliary and/or pancreatic anatomy. A drainage tube is threaded for pancreatic drainage through the esophagus, stomach, and duodenum and into the pancreatic duct. The endoscope is removed.

Coding Clarification
Code 52.97 excludes catheter drainage of a pancreatic cyst (52.01) and replacement of s stent (97.05).

52.98   Endoscopic dilation of pancreatic duct

Description
The physician passes the endoscope (via ERCP, ERP) through the patient's oropharynx, esophagus, stomach, and into the small intestine. The ampulla of Vater and/or pancreatic duct is cannulated and filled with contrast to visualize biliary and/or pancreatic anatomy. The pancreatic duct is dilated, patency tested, and the endoscope is removed.

52.99   Other operations on pancreas

Description
Code 52.99 describes other pancreas procedures not classifiable elsewhere in category 52.

Coding Clarification
Code 52.99 should not be assigned if the medical record contains sufficient information to facilitate coding at a higher level of specificity.

Code 52.99 excludes non-operative irrigation of a pancreatic tube (96.42) and removal of a pancreatic tube (96.56).

Documentation Tip
If the documentation is ambiguous or unclear, the physician should be queried.

53   Repair of hernia

Description
A hernia of the abdominal cavity is a protrusion of a portion of bowel through a weak point in the abdominal wall that is characterized by pain, bulge, or swelling of the affected site. At this weakened place, the muscles and connective tissues that usually hold the bowel in place sustain injury or falter, and a portion of the bowel pokes through, resulting in a bulge of the abdominal wall. Congenital hernias are largely due to an incomplete closure or development in the lining of the abdominal wall. Hernias may occur spontaneously, may result from trauma or excess strain on the abdominal wall, or may be precipitated by bending, lifting heavy objects, or excessive coughing.

Most hernias are detectable upon physical exam or palpation of the abdominal wall. Some hernias may be reduced manually, although this is often a temporary measure, since the defect in the abdominal wall must be repaired or the hernia will recur. The defect may be repaired by suture or it may require a graft to reinforce the repair and prevent recurrence. Complications of a hernia include strangulation and obstruction, which can lead to necrosis (e.g., gangrene) of the intestine, and a potentially fatal infection.

Category 53 provides codes for hernia repair procedures according to site, type, and laterality.

Coding Clarification
Code also any application or administration of an adhesion barrier substance (99.77).

Category 53 includes:

- Hernioplasty—surgical repair of hernia
- Herniorrhaphy—suture of hernia
- Herniotomy—incision of hernia for division of strangulated or irreducible hernia

Category 53 excludes:

- Manual (non-operative) reduction of hernia (96.27)

Repair of inguinal hernia may be performed by open (incisional) or laparoscopic operative approach.

Coding Guidance
AHA: 3Q, '94, 8

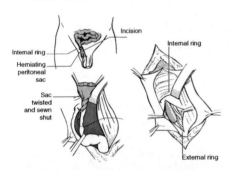

53.0   Other unilateral repair of inguinal hernia

Description
This subclassification lists unilateral (one sided) repair of inguinal (groin) hernia procedures.

An inguinal hernia is defined as a condition in which a loop of intestine enters the inguinal canal, a tubular passage through the lower layers of the abdominal wall. A hernia occurs when part of an organ protrudes through a weak point or tear in the thin muscular wall that holds the abdominal organs in place. A direct inguinal hernia creates a bulge in the groin area, and an indirect hernia descends into the scrotum. Inguinal hernias occur less often in women than men.

Hernias are caused by congenital (defects at birth) or age-related weaknesses in the abdominal walls. In males, they are often congenital and caused by an improper closure of the abdominal cavity. They can also be caused by an increase in pressure within the abdominal cavity due to heavy lifting, straining, violent coughing, obesity, or pregnancy.

Signs and symptoms include a protrusion in the groin area between the pubis and the top of the leg in the area known as the inguinal region of the abdomen or pain during urination or a bowel movement or when lifting a heavy object. The pain can be sharp and immediate. There may be a dull aching sensation, nausea, or constipation; these feelings typically get worse toward the end of the day or after standing for long periods of time and may disappear when lying down.

A hernia that can be pushed back into the abdominal cavity (called a reducible hernia) is not considered an immediate health threat, though it does require surgery to repair the hernia. A hernia that cannot be pushed back in (called a nonreducible hernia) may lead to dangerous complications such as the obstruction of the flow of the intestinal contents or intestinal blood supply (strangulation), leading to tissue death, and requires immediate surgery.

Coding Guidance
AHA: 4Q, '08, 165-167

53.00   Unilateral repair of inguinal hernia, not otherwise specified

Description
This code reports a unilateral repair of an inguinal hernia not specified as direct or indirect or as a repair with graft or prosthesis.

Coding Clarification
Code 53.00 should not be assigned if the medical record contains sufficient information to facilitate coding at a higher level of specificity.

Documentation Tip
If the documentation is ambiguous or unclear, the physician should be queried.

Coding Guidance
AHA: 3Q, '03, 10

53.01 Other and open repair of direct inguinal hernia

53.02 Other and open repair of indirect inguinal hernia

53.03 Other and open repair of direct inguinal hernia with graft or prosthesis

53.04 Other and open repair of indirect inguinal hernia with graft or prosthesis

53.05 Repair of inguinal hernia with graft or prosthesis, not otherwise specified

Description
The physician repairs an inguinal hernia. The physician makes a groin incision. Dissection is continued through scar tissue and the spermatic cord and hernia sac are identified and dissected from surrounding structures. The hernia contents may be reduced or the hernia sac opened and the contents examined. The hernia sac may be ligated and resected. The physician may implant a graft or prosthesis of mesh or other material to strengthen and reinforce the hernia repair. The incision is closed.

Coding Clarification
ICD-9-CM procedure codes distinguish between laparoscopic and open repairs of inguinal hernias. To report laparoscopic repair of inguinal hernias, refer to codes 17.11–17.13 and 17.21–17.23.

Coding Guidance
AHA: 4Q, '96, 66

53.1 Other bilateral repair of inguinal hernia

Description
This subclassification lists bilateral (two sided, right and left) repair of inguinal (groin) hernia procedures. The code descriptions state the type of hernia (direct or indirect) and whether the repair includes graft or prosthesis implantation.

Coding Guidance
AHA: 4Q, '08, 165-167

53.10 Bilateral repair of inguinal hernia, not otherwise specified

Description
This code reports bilateral (two-sided, right and left) repair of inguinal hernias not specified as direct or indirect or as a repair with graft or prosthesis.

Coding Clarification
Code 53.10 should not be assigned if the medical record contains sufficient information to facilitate coding at a higher level of specificity.

Documentation Tip
If the documentation is ambiguous or unclear, the physician should be queried.

53.11 Other and open bilateral repair of direct inguinal hernia

53.12 Other and open bilateral repair of indirect inguinal hernia

53.13 Other and open bilateral repair of inguinal hernia, one direct and one indirect

53.14 Other and open bilateral repair of direct inguinal hernia with graft or prosthesis

53.15 Other and open bilateral repair of indirect inguinal hernia with graft or prosthesis

53.16 Other and open bilateral repair of inguinal hernia, one direct and one indirect, with graft or prosthesis

53.17 Bilateral inguinal hernia repair with graft or prosthesis, not otherwise specified

Description
The physician repairs an inguinal hernia. The physician makes a groin incision. Dissection is continued through scar tissue and the spermatic cord and the hernia sac are identified and dissected from surrounding structures. The hernia contents may be reduced or the hernia sac opened and the contents examined. The hernia sac may be ligated and resected. The physician may implant a graft or prosthesis of mesh or other material to strengthen and reinforce the hernia repair. The incision is closed. The physician repeats the procedure, with variations as necessary, on the other side.

Coding Clarification
ICD-9-CM procedure codes distinguish between laparoscopic and open repairs of inguinal hernias. To report laparoscopic bilateral repair of inguinal hernia refer to codes 17.21–17.24.

53.2 Unilateral repair of femoral hernia

Description
This subcategory lists unilateral (one-sided) repair of femoral hernia (a groin herniation of an intraabdominal organ through a weakness in the abdominal wall). Femoral hernias occur below the inguinal ligament, at a vulnerable abdominal wall location known as the femoral canal.

42-54

53.21 Unilateral repair of femoral hernia with graft or prosthesis

53.29 Other unilateral femoral herniorrhaphy

Description
The physician repairs a femoral hernia. The physician makes a femoral or groin incision. The hernia sac is identified and dissected from surrounding structures. The hernia may be reduced and the hernia sac resected. The femoral defect may be closed with a prosthetic patch or sutures by plicating the fascia and muscles to cover the defect. The incision is closed.

53.3 Bilateral repair of femoral hernia

Description
This subcategory lists bilateral (two-sided) repair of femoral hernias (groin herniations of an intraabdominal organ through a weakness in the abdominal wall). Femoral hernias occur below the inguinal ligament, at a vulnerable abdominal wall location known as the femoral canal.

53.31 Bilateral repair of femoral hernia with graft or prosthesis

53.39 Other bilateral femoral herniorrhaphy

Description
The physician repairs a femoral hernia. The physician makes a femoral or groin incision. The hernia sac is identified and dissected from surrounding structures. The hernia may be reduced and the hernia sac resected. The femoral defect may be closed with a prosthetic patch or sutures by plicating the fascia and muscles to cover the defect. The incision is closed. The physician repeats the procedure, with variations as necessary on the other side.

53.4 Repair of umbilical hernia

Description
This subcategory lists repair of an umbilical hernia (a protrusion of bowel at the site of the umbilicus, commonly called a navel or belly button). This hernia usually occurs in a newborn patient. Paraumbilical hernia is more common in adults and involves a defect (or weak spot) in the midline of the abdominal wall near but not through the umbilicus.

53.41 Other and open repair of umbilical hernia with graft or prosthesis

53.42 Laparoscopic repair of umbilical hernia with graft or prosthesis

53.43 Other laparoscopic umbilical herniorrhaphy

53.49 Other open umbilical herniorrhaphy

Description
The physician repairs an umbilical hernia. The physician makes an umbilical incision. The hernia sac and fascial defect are identified and dissected from surrounding structures. The hernia sac is reduced and may be resected. The hernia defect is closed with sutures. The incision is closed. In some cases, a graft or prosthetic material is used to create a patch that is sutured over the defect to close the defect and hold the herniated contents.

In a laparoscopic repair, the physician makes a small abdominal incision and inflates the abdomen with air to visualize the abdominal organs. The laparoscope is inserted through the incision and the surgical instruments to repair the hernia are inserted through other small incisions in the lower abdomen. Mesh is typically placed over the defect to reinforce the abdominal wall.

Coding Clarification
ICD-9-CM procedure codes distinguish between laparoscopic and open repairs of hernias. Careful review of the documentation for specific information regarding the procedure, surgical technique and approach will be necessary to ensure accurate code assignment.

Coding Scenario
The physician repairs an umbilical hernia in a 5-year-old patient. The physician makes an umbilical incision and the laparoscope is placed through the umbilical port. Additional trocars are placed through small incisions in the lower abdomen. The hernia sac is identified and reduced and mesh is placed to reinforce the defect.

Code Assignment:

553.1   Umbilical hernia without mention of obstruction or gangrene
53.42   Laparoscopic repair of umbilical hernia with graft or prosthesis

Coding Guidance
AHA: 4Q, '08, 165-168

● New Code   ▲ Revised Code   ►◄ Revised Text   © 2010 Ingenix

53.5   Repair of other hernia of anterior abdominal wall (without graft or prosthesis)

Description
This subcategory lists repair of an anterior abdominal wall hernia without graft or prosthesis (e.g., mesh).

53.51   Incisional hernia repair

53.59   Repair of other hernia of anterior abdominal wall

Description
The physician repairs an incisional, ventral, or other anterior abdominal wall hernia. The physician makes an incision over the hernia. Dissection is continued through scar tissue and the hernia sac is identified and dissected from surrounding structures. The fascial defect is identified circumferentially. The hernia is reduced and the hernia sac may be resected. The hernia defect is closed with sutures. The incision is closed.

Documentation Tip
Code 53.59 includes repair of hernia of abdominal wall documented as by laparoscopic approach ▶without graft or prostheses.◀

Procedures classifiable to code 53.59 may be documented as repair of:

- Epigastric hernia
- Hypogastric hernia
- Spigelian hernia
- Ventral hernia

Coding Guidance
　AHA: 3Q, '96, 15; 3Q, '03, 6; 2Q, '06, 105

53.6   Repair of other hernia of anterior abdominal wall with graft or prosthesis

Description
This subcategory lists repair of an anterior abdominal wall hernia with graft or prosthesis (e.g., mesh).

Coding Guidance
　AHA: 4Q, '08, 165-168

53.61   Other open incisional hernia repair with graft or prosthesis

53.62   Laparoscopic incisional hernia repair with graft or prosthesis

53.63   Other laparoscopic repair of other hernia of anterior abdominal wall with graft or prosthesis

53.69   Other and open repair of other hernia of anterior abdominal wall with graft or prosthesis

Description
The physician repairs an incisional, ventral, or other anterior abdominal wall hernia. The physician makes an incision over the hernia. Dissection is continued through scar tissue and the hernia sac is identified and dissected from surrounding structures. The fascial defect is identified circumferentially. The hernia is reduced and the hernia sac may be resected. The hernia defect is closed with mesh or some other prosthetic material. The incision is closed.

In contrast, the laparoscopic repair of incisional, or ventral, hernias involves the placement of a synthetic patch into the abdomen through small trocar incisions.

Coding Clarification
Incisional, ventral, epigastric, and umbilical hernias involve defects of the anterior abdominal wall.

Documentation Tip
Incisional hernias may occur at any stage of wound healing (e.g., fresh, recent or old) and there are many types of procedures surgical techniques and approaches used to repair an incisional hernia. Careful review of the procedure documentation will be necessary to ensure accurate code assignment.

Coding Scenario
The patient presents for repair of an epigastric hernia. The physician makes small abdominal incisions. The hernia sac is identified and dissected from surrounding structures. The fascial defect is identified circumferentially. The hernia is reduced and the hernia sac resected. The hernia defect is reinforced with mesh.

　　Code Assignment:

　　553.29　Other ventral hernia without mention of obstruction or gangrene
　　53.63　Other laparoscopic repair of other hernia of anterior abdominal wall with graft or prosthesis

42-54

53.7   Repair of diaphragmatic hernia, abdominal approach

Description
Subcategory 53.7 contains codes that report repair of a diaphragmatic hernia using an abdominal approach which are further specified by technique, such as a laparoscopic repair (53.71) versus an open repair (53.72).

Coding Guidance
    AHA: 4Q, '08, 165-169

53.71   Laparoscopic repair of diaphragmatic hernia, abdominal approach

53.72   Other and open repair of diaphragmatic hernia, abdominal approach

53.75   Repair of diaphragmatic hernia, abdominal approach, not otherwise specified

Description
The physician makes an incision across the abdomen. The herniated stomach is returned to its appropriate position in the abdomen and the hernia sac is cut away and removed. The enlarged opening in the diaphragm through which the esophagus passes is narrowed by placing sutures in the two pillars connecting the spinal column and the diaphragm. Reforming the stomach, cutting the vagus nerve, or altering the size of the stomach-intestinal opening may be performed as well. Drains are placed and the wound is sutured closed.

Coding Scenario
The patient is brought to the operating room to repair a traumatic diaphragmatic hernia with organ protrusion into the chest cavity. The physician makes an incision across the abdomen and the abdominal contents are drawn back into the abdomen. The hole in the diaphragm is repaired with nonabsorbable sutures. The incision is closed with sutures or staples.

    Code Assignment:

    553.3   Diaphragmatic hernia without mention of obstruction or gangrene
    53.72   Other and open repair of diaphragmatic hernia, abdominal approach

53.8   Repair of diaphragmatic hernia, thoracic approach

Description
The physician repairs a diaphragmatic hernia through the abdomen and thorax.

53.80   Repair of diaphragmatic hernia with thoracic approach, not otherwise specified

53.81   Plication of the diaphragm

53.82   Repair of parasternal hernia

53.83   Laparoscopic repair of diaphragmatic hernia, with thoracic approach

53.84   Other and open repair of diaphragmatic hernia, with thoracic approach

Description
The physician makes an incision across the chest, which may be extended into the upper abdomen. Tissues are dissected and the esophagus, diaphragm, and upper part of the stomach are exposed. The connective tissue is used to stitch folds or tucks into the diaphragm to restore it to its original position. The incision is closed with sutures or staples.

Coding Scenario
A 6-month-old boy undergoes closure of a congenital diaphragmatic hernia using prosthetic mesh placed via the thoracic approach. The incision is closed with staples.

    Code Assignment:

    756.6   Congenital anomaly of diaphragm
    53.84   Other and open repair of diaphragmatic hernia, with thoracic approach

Coding Guidance
    AHA: 4Q, '08, 165-169

53.9   Other hernia repair

Description
This code reports other repair of a hernia not classifiable elsewhere in category 53.

Coding Clarification
Code 53.9 should not be assigned if the medical record contains sufficient information to facilitate coding at a higher level of specificity.

Code 53.9 excludes certain hernia repair procedures requiring intestinal operations classifiable to category 46 or requiring gynecological procedures classifiable to category 70.

Documentation Tip
If the documentation is ambiguous or unclear, the physician should be queried.

Procedures classifiable to 53.9 may be documented as repair of:

• Ischiatic or ischiorectal hernia

• Lumbar or sciatic hernia

• Obturator hernia

● New Code   ▲ Revised Code   ►◄ Revised Text   © 2010 Ingenix

- Omental hernia
- Retroperitoneal hernia

54 Other operations on abdominal region

Description
Category 54 classifies other abdominal region operations not classifiable elsewhere in Chapter 9 Operations on the digestive system.

Coding Clarification
Code also any application or administration of an adhesion barrier substance (99.77).

Category 54 excludes:

- Hernia repair (53.00-53.9)
- Obliteration of cul-de-sac (70.92)
- Retroperitoneal tissue dissection (59.00-59.09)
- Procedures on the skin and subcutaneous tissue of the abdominal wall (86.01-86.09)

Documentation Tip
Procedures classifiable to Category 54 include those as specified to the following anatomic sites:

- Epigastric region
- Flank or groin
- Hypochondrium
- Inguinal or loin region
- Pelvic cavity
- Mesentery
- Omentum
- Peritoneum
- Retroperitoneal space

54.0 Incision of abdominal wall

Description
The physician explores the abdominal wall for drainage of an abscess or other reason. The physician may approach the retroperitoneum or other extraperitoneal space through a flank or abdominal incision. The surface of the abdominal wall is inspected and any area of interest may be opened and the space or lesion explored or drained. The incision is closed.

Coding Guidance
AHA: N-D, '87, 12; 1Q, '97, 11; 4Q, '05, 77; 2Q, '06, 23

54.1 Laparotomy

Description
The physician performs a laparotomy, which is an incision into the abdominal cavity.

Coding Guidance
AHA: 1Q, '92, 13

54.11 Exploratory laparotomy

Description
The physician performs an exploratory laparotomy. To explore the intraabdominal organs and structures, the physician makes a large incision extending from just above the pubic hairline to the rib cage. The abdominal cavity is opened for a systematic examination of all organs. The physician may take tissue samples of any or all intraabdominal organs for diagnosis. The incision is closed with sutures.

Coding Clarification
Code 54.11 excludes exploration incidental to intraabdominal surgery. Omit code 54.11 as an operative approach and report only the definitive surgical procedure. By exception, code 54.11 should be reported during exploratory surgery when biopsies and/or incidental appendectomies are performed. In these cases, report both the exploratory laparotomy and any biopsy or incidental appendectomy, as appropriate.

Coding Guidance
AHA: J-F, '87; 4Q, '88, 12; 3Q, '89, 14

54.12 Reopening of recent laparotomy site

Description
The physician reopens the incision of a recent laparotomy before the incision has fully healed to control bleeding, remove packing, or drain a postoperative infection.

Coding Clarification
Code 54.12 includes reopening of a recent laparotomy site for:

- Control of hemorrhage
- Incision of hematoma
- Exploration

54.19 Other laparotomy

Description
This code describes other laparotomy not specified as exploratory or a reopening of a recent laparotomy site.

Coding Clarification
Code 54.19 should not be assigned if the medical record contains sufficient information to facilitate coding at a higher level of specificity.

Code 54.19 lists multiple exclusions for therapeutic procedures specifically classifiable elsewhere.

Code 54.19 should not be reported if the laparotomy is incidental to other intraabdominal surgery

42-54

performed during the same episode of care. Omit 54.19 as an operative approach and report only the definitive surgical procedure.

Documentation Tip
If the documentation is ambiguous or unclear, the physician should be queried.

Coding Guidance
    AHA: 3Q, '03, 17

54.2   Diagnostic procedures of abdominal region

54.21   Laparoscopy
Description
The physician makes a 1 cm incision in the umbilicus through which the abdomen is inflated and a fiberoptic laparoscope is inserted. Other incisions are also made through which trocars can be passed into the abdominal cavity to deliver instruments, a video camera, and when needed an additional light source. The physician manipulates the tools so that the pelvic organs, peritoneum, abdomen, and omentum can be viewed through the laparoscope and/or video monitor. When the procedure is complete, the laparoscope, instruments, and light source are removed and the incisions are closed with sutures.

Coding Clarification
Code 54.21 excludes therapeutic procedures such as laparoscopic cholecystectomy (51.23) and laparoscopy incidental to fallopian tube procedures (66.21-66.29).

Documentation Tip
This procedure may also be documented as peritoneoscopy.

54.22   Biopsy of abdominal wall or umbilicus

54.23   Biopsy of peritoneum
Description
These procedures describe an open (incisional) biopsy of suspicious lesions of the abdominal wall or umbilicus (54.22) or the peritoneum and associated intraabdominal sites (54.23). The physician makes an incision over the lesion or area to be biopsied. The abdominal cavity is opened and examined. The physician takes tissue samples of the peritoneum, abdominal wall, umbilicus, mesentery, or peritoneal implant or omentum as necessary for diagnosis. The incision is closed with sutures.

Coding Clarification
Code 54.23 excludes closed biopsy of omentum or peritoneum (54.24).

54.24   Closed (percutaneous) (needle) biopsy of intra-abdominal mass
Description
Using radiological supervision, the physician locates the mass within or immediately outside the peritoneal lining of the abdominal cavity. A biopsy needle is passed into the mass, a tissue sample is removed, and the needle is withdrawn. This may be repeated several times. No incision is necessary.

Coding Clarification
Code 54.24 excludes closed biopsy of specific female pelvic abdominal sites such as the fallopian tubes (66.11), ovary (65.11), and other structures.

Coding Guidance
    AHA: 4Q, '97, 57

54.25   Peritoneal lavage
Description
The physician performs infusion and drainage of fluid from the abdominal cavity (peritoneal lavage). The physician inserts a needle or catheter into the abdominal cavity and infuses and subsequently withdraws fluid for diagnostic or therapeutic purposes. The needle or catheter is removed at the completion of the procedure.

Documentation Tip
Peritoneal lavage is defined as irrigation of the peritoneal cavity with siphoning of liquid contents for analysis.

Coding Guidance
    AHA: 4Q, '93, 28; 2Q, '98, 19

54.29   Other diagnostic procedures on abdominal region
Description
This code reports other diagnostic abdominal region procedures not classifiable elsewhere in subcategory 54.2.

Coding Clarification
Code 54.29 should not be assigned if the medical record contains sufficient information to facilitate coding at a higher level of specificity.

Code 54.2 lists multiple exclusions for diagnostic procedures classifiable to Chapter 16 Miscellaneous diagnostic and therapeutic procedures (87-99).

Documentation Tip
If the documentation is ambiguous or unclear, the physician should be queried.

54.3   Excision or destruction of lesion or tissue of abdominal wall or umbilicus
Description
The physician makes an incision over the abdominal lesion. The lesions, growths, or other tissue is

removed using a laser, electrical cautery, or a scalpel. The incision is closed by suturing.

Coding Clarification
Code 54.3 excludes abdominal wall excision or destruction procedures for the purpose of biopsy (54.22), size reduction (86.83), or lesions specified as involving the skin only (86.22, 86.26, 86.3).

Documentation Tip
Procedures classifiable to code 54.3 may be documented as:

* Debridement of the abdominal wall
* Omphalectomy—excision of the navel or associated lesion

Coding Guidance
AHA: 1Q, '89, 11

54.4   Excision or destruction of peritoneal tissue
Description
The physician excises a lesion in the mesentery, omentum, peritoneum, or other intraabdominal connective tissue. The physician makes an incision in the abdomen over the lesion to be excised. Tissues are dissected free to the site of the lesion. The lesion may be removed by resecting a portion of the tissue with the lesion, or destroyed with electrocautery or other technique. The connective tissues are reapproximated together and the incision is closed in layers.

Coding Clarification
Code 54.4 excludes excision for biopsy (54.23) or excision of female pelvic organs or tissues classifiable to Chapter12 Operations on the female genital organs (65-71).

Code 54.4 reports sharp, surgical incision and division of intraabdominal adhesive tissues. Do not report 54.4 for adhesiolysis documented as:

* Blunt
* Digital
* Manual
* Mechanical
* Without instrumentation

Documentation Tip
Procedures classifiable to code 54.4 may be documented as excision or destruction of the following peritoneal and intraabdominal sites:

* Appendices epiploicae
* Falciform ligament
* Gastrocolic ligament
* Mesentery
* Omentum
* Presacral lesion NOS
* Retroperitoneal lesion NOS

54.5   Lysis of peritoneal adhesions
Coding Clarification
Code 54.5 excludes lysis of adhesions documented as associated with the following organs:

* Bladder (59.11)
* Fallopian tube and ovary (65.81, 65.89)
* Kidney (59.02)
* Ureter (59.02-59.03)

Documentation Tip
Adhesions may be defined as a fibrous band(s) of scar tissue that abnormally binds or connects body tissues and anatomical parts that are normally separate.

Procedures classifiable to 54.5 may be documented as lysis, division, or freeing of adhesions of the following intraabdominal structures:

* Biliary tract
* Liver
* Peritoneum
* Uterus
* Intestines
* Pelvic peritoneum

Coding Guidance
AHA: 4Q, '90, 18; 3Q, '94, 8

54.51   Laparoscopic lysis of peritoneal adhesions
Description
The physician performs laparoscopic enterolysis to free intestinal adhesions. With the patient under anesthesia, the physician places a trocar at the umbilicus into the abdominal or retroperitoneal space and insufflates the abdominal cavity. The physician places a laparoscope through the umbilical incision and additional trocars are placed into the abdomen. Intestinal adhesions are identified and instruments are passed through to dissect and remove the adhesions. The trocars are removed and the incisions are closed with sutures.

Coding Guidance
AHA: 4Q, '96, 65; 3Q, '03, 6-7; 4Q, '06, 134

54.59   Other lysis of peritoneal adhesions
Description
The physician frees intestinal adhesions. The physician enters the abdomen through a midline abdominal incision. The bowel is freed from its attachments to itself, the abdominal wall, and/or other abdominal organs. The abdominal incision is closed.

Coding Clarification
▶Extensive adhesiolysis may result in inadvertent serosal tear. Do not assign a separate code for the

42-54

repair of minor serosal tears. However, if
full-thickness injury occurs, report in addition to the
primary procedure the appropriate repair
procedures as documented (e.g., bowel resection,
anastomosis other than end-to-end, suture of
laceration of intestine).◄

Coding Guidance
   AHA: 4Q, '96, 66; 1Q, '03, 14; 3Q, '03, 11; 3Q,'06, 16;
   ►1Q, '10, 11◄

54.6   Suture of abdominal wall and peritoneum

54.61   Reclosure of postoperative disruption of abdominal wall

Description
The physician performs a secondary closure of the
abdominal wall for postoperative wound dehiscence.
The physician opens the former incision and
removes the remaining sutures. The abdominal wall
is closed with sutures.

54.62   Delayed closure of granulating abdominal wound

Description
The physician secondarily repairs a surgical skin
closure after granulations have formed on the
healing skin. This may be performed after resolution
of a wound infection, allowing the wound to heal and
infection to resolve prior to wound closure. The
physician uses a scalpel to excise granulation and
scar tissue. Skin margins are trimmed to bleeding
edges. The wound is sutured in several layers.

54.63   Other suture of abdominal wall

54.64   Suture of peritoneum

Description
These procedures describe other suture of the
abdominal wall (54.63) or peritoneum (54.64) not
classifiable elsewhere in subcategory 54.6 as a
reclosure or delayed closure of wound.

Coding Clarification
Codes 54.63 and 54.64 exclude routine suture for
closure of an operative wound, which is incidental
to, and included in, the code for the primary surgical
procedure.

Documentation Tip
Procedures classifiable to 54.63 or 54.64 may be
documented as suture of laceration or secondary
suture.

54.7   Other repair of abdominal wall and peritoneum

54.71   Repair of gastroschisis

Description
The physician repairs a gastroschisis. The peritoneal
sac is dissected from surrounding structures and
reduced. The herniated contents of the gastroschisis
are reduced into the abdominal cavity if possible.
The abdominal wall defect is identified. If possible,
the abdominal wall defect is closed with sutures. If
the defect is too large or if the herniated contents
cannot be reduced, a prosthetic material is used to
create a patch or silo that is sutured over the defect
to close the defect and accommodate the herniated
contents.

Documentation Tip
Repair of gastroschisis may be defined as surgical
repair of a fissure (usually congenital) in the
abdomen that is often associated with a protrusion
or herniation of the viscera (internal organs).

Coding Guidance
   AHA: 2Q, '02, 9

54.72   Other repair of abdominal wall

54.73   Other repair of peritoneum

54.74   Other repair of omentum

Description
These procedures describe other suture or repair of
the abdominal wall and peritoneum wounds or
defects not classifiable elsewhere in category 54.

Documentation Tip
Procedures classifiable to 54.74 may be documented
as:

*   **Epiplorrhaphy**—suture of abdominal serous membrane

*   **Omentopexy**—implantation of tissue into abdominal serous membrane

*   **Graft of omentum**—anchoring of abdominal serous membrane

*   **Reduction of torsion of omentum**—untwisting, straightening, or smoothing of abdominal serous membrane

Coding Clarification
Codes 54.63 and 54.64 exclude routine suture for
closure of an operative wound, which is incidental to
and included in the code for the primary surgical
procedure.

Coding Guidance
   AHA: J-F, '87, 11

● New Code   ▲ Revised Code   ►◄ Revised Text   © 2010 Ingenix

54.75   Other repair of mesentery

Description
The physician repairs a defect in the mesentery with sutures. The physician makes an abdominal incision. Next, the mesenteric defect is identified and closed with sutures. The incision is closed.

Documentation Tip
Procedures classifiable to code 54.74 may be documented as:

* Mesenteric plication—creation of folds in the mesentery for shortening
* Mesenteriopexy—fixation of torn mesentery

54.9   Other operations of abdominal region

Coding Clarification
Subcategory 54.9 excludes procedures on the female reproductive system classifiable to Chapter 12 Operations on female genital organs.

54.91   Percutaneous abdominal drainage

Description
The physician performs percutaneous abdominal drainage, which is puncture of the peritoneal space for removal of fluid. The physician makes a small skin incision in the abdomen or flank. Percutaneous needle aspiration and closed catheter drainage using computer tomographic (CT) or ultrasound guidance is performed. A needle, guidewire, or pigtail catheter is placed within the peritoneal cavity or space. Fluid is extracted via the needle.

Coding Guidance
AHA: 2Q, '90, 25; 1Q, '92, 14; 3Q, '98, 12; 2Q, '99, 14; 3Q,'99, 9; 4Q, '07, 96

54.92   Removal of foreign body from peritoneal cavity

Description
The physician removes a foreign body from the abdominal cavity. The physician makes an abdominal incision and explores the abdominal cavity. The foreign body is identified and removed. The incision is closed.

Coding Guidance
AHA: 1Q, '89, 11

54.93   Creation of cutaneoperitoneal fistula

Description
The physician creates a cutaneoperitoneal fistula, which is an opening between the skin and peritoneal cavity. The physician places a permanent intraperitoneal catheter for drainage or dialysis. The physician makes a small abdominal incision, opens the peritoneum, and inserts the catheter into the abdominal cavity. The proximal end of the catheter is tunneled subcutaneously away from the initial incision and brought out through the skin. The incision is closed.

Coding Guidance
AHA: N-D, '84, 6; 2Q, '95, 10

54.94   Creation of peritoneovascular shunt

Description
For a peritoneovenous shunt, the physician makes a small lateral upper abdominal incision. Dissection is carried through the abdominal wall layers, the peritoneum is entered and the peritoneal end of the catheter is inserted into the peritoneal cavity and sutured into place. A subcutaneous tunnel is created from the abdominal incision up to the neck and the catheter is pulled through the tunnel into the neck. A counter incision is made in the neck over the internal jugular vein and the venous end of the catheter is inserted into the jugular vein. The incisions are closed.

Documentation Tip
Creation of a peritoneal vascular shunt involves construction of a shunt to connect the peritoneal cavity with the vascular system.

Coding Guidance
AHA: S-O, '85, 6; 1Q, '88, 9; 1Q, '94, 7

54.95   Incision of peritoneum

Description
This code reports an incision of the peritoneum or peritoneal cavity. Surgical technique may vary, depending on the indication for the procedure. The peritoneal incision may be performed for diagnostic or therapeutic purposes or to remove implanted devices.

In a Ladd operation, the physician makes an abdominal incision. Next, the abdomen is explored and the physician performs a lysis of duodenal bands or reduction of midgut volvulus. The bowel is inspected to ensure viability. The incision is closed.

Coding Clarification
Code 54.95 excludes incision of the peritoneum incidental to laparotomy (54.11-54.19).

Coding Guidance
AHA: 4Q,'95, 65

54.96   Injection of air into peritoneal cavity

Description
The physician injects air contrast into the peritoneal cavity. The physician inserts a needle or catheter into the peritoneal cavity and injects air as a diagnostic procedure. An x-ray is usually obtained to define the pattern of air in the abdomen. The needle or catheter is removed at the completion of the procedure.

Coding Clarification

Code 54.96 excludes injection of air into the peritoneal cavity for:

- Collapse of lung (33.33)
- Radiography (88.12-88.13, 88.15)

Documentation Tip

Procedures classifiable to 54.96 may be documented as pneumoperitoneum

54.97   Injection of locally-acting therapeutic substance into peritoneal cavity

Description

This code describes the injection of a chemotherapeutic or other substance into the peritoneal cavity to treat diseases such as malignancy or infection. The physician inserts a needle into the abdominal cavity through a catheter placed in the peritoneum and injects the drug or substance.

54.98   Peritoneal dialysis

Description

Dialysis is a process to remove toxins from the blood and to maintain fluid and electrolyte balance when the kidneys no longer function. In peritoneal dialysis, a fluid is introduced into the peritoneal cavity that removes toxins and electrolytes, which passively leach into the fluid. Hemofiltration, similar to hemodialysis, employs passing large volumes of blood over extracorporeal, adsorbent filters that remove waste products from the blood.

Coding Guidance

AHA: N-D, '84, 6; 4Q, '93, 28

54.99   Other operations of abdominal region

Description

This code reports other abdominal operations not classifiable elsewhere in category 54.

Coding Clarification

Code 54.99 should not be assigned if the medical record contains sufficient information to facilitate coding at a higher level of specificity.

Code 54.99 lists multiple exclusions for procedures classifiable to Chapter 16 Miscellaneous diagnostic and therapeutic procedures (87-99).

Documentation Tip

If the documentation is ambiguous or unclear, the physician should be queried.

Coding Guidance

AHA: 1Q, '99, 4

● New Code   ▲ Revised Code   ►◄ Revised Text   © 2010 Ingenix

55-59

Operations on the Urinary System

The ICD-9-CM classification system for operations performed on the urinary system is divided into categories of procedures according to site and type as follows:

- Operations on Kidney (55)
- Operations on Ureter (56)
- Operations on Urinary Bladder (57)
- Operations on Urethra (58)
- Other Operations on Urinary Tract (59)

Coding Clarification
If a procedure was unsuccessful (i.e., could not be completed), assign the code to the extent that the procedure was carried out. For example, if the intended procedure was cystotomy with use of stone basket for extraction of the ureteral stone but the surgeon was unable to reach the stone or could not remove it, the code assignment would be 57.19 Cystotomy.

Documentation Tip
Review the operative report for clues regarding incomplete or failed procedures for correct code assignment.

55   Operations on kidney

Description
Category 55 provides codes for incisions, diagnostic procedures, excisions, transplant, repairs, and other operations on the kidney and renal pelvis. Category 55 includes operations on the renal pelvis; however, this category does not include procedures on the perirenal tissue. They are found under category 59.

Coding Clarification
Code separately any application or administration of an adhesion barrier substance (99.77) that is performed.

Assign 55.03 for percutaneous nephrostomy tube placement.

Assign 55.04 for percutaneous nephrostomy with ultrasonic disruption of kidney stone(s).

Use 55.92 for repeat nephroscopic removal or fragmentation if it occurs during the same episode as the initial procedure.

Assign 55.92 for percutaneous extraction of calculus from the renal pelvis and 59.95 for any use of ultrasound to break up the calculus.

Use 55.93 for replacement of a nephrostomy tube.

Category 55 is not used to report procedures on the perirenal tissue (59.00-59.09, 59.21-59.29, 59.91-59.92).

55.0   Nephrotomy and nephrostomy

Description
Nephrotomy is an incision into the kidney, typically performed for exploration of the kidney, to drain a renal cyst, or to remove a kidney stone. Nephrostomy is the creation of a passageway through the body wall into the renal pelvis using a tube, stent, or catheter. A nephrostomy, which creates an opening from the kidney to the exterior of the body, can be accomplished using a surgical incision or it can be placed percutaneously. A percutaneous nephrostomy catheter is a small, flexible, rubber tube that is placed through the incision into the kidney. Nephrostomy is performed to provide urinary drainage when the ureter is obstructed, but it also can be performed to gain access to the upper urinary tract for certain procedures, such as intracorporeal lithotripsy, stent placement, to remove or dissolve renal calculi, and diagnostic antegrade radiologic studies of the ureter.

Coding Clarification
Codes in subcategory 55.0 are not used to report drainage by anastomosis (55.86) or aspiration (55.92).

Code separately any application or administration of an adhesion barrier substance (99.77) that is performed.

Documentation Tip
Nephrotomy is an incision into kidney, typically performed for exploration of the kidney.

55-59

Evacuation of a renal cyst describes draining the contents of a renal cyst.

Nephrolithotomy is the removal of a kidney stone through an incision.

Nephroscopic nephrostolithotomy (percutaneous) is the insertion of a tube through the abdominal wall to remove stones.

Nephroscopic percutaneous pyelostolithotomy is the percutaneous removal of stones from the funnel-shaped portion of the kidney.

55.01   Nephrotomy

Description
Nephrotomy is an incision into kidney, typically performed for exploration of the kidney, to drain a renal cyst, or to remove a kidney stone. To access the kidney, the physician makes an incision in the skin of the flank, cuts the muscles, fat, and fibrous membranes (fascia) overlying the kidney, and sometimes removes a portion of the eleventh or twelfth rib. The physician makes an incision in the kidney (nephrotomy) and sometimes places fine traction sutures at the edges of the incision. After exploration, the physician sutures the incision, inserts a drain tube, bringing it out through a separate stab incision, and performs layered closure.

Coding Clarification
Evacuation of a renal cyst describes draining the contents of a renal cyst and is reported with 55.01.

Code separately any application or administration of an adhesion barrier substance (99.77) that is performed.

Documentation Tip
Nephrolithotomy, which is the removal of a kidney stone through incision, is also reported with this code.

55.02   Nephrostomy

Description
Nephrostomy is the creation of a passageway through the body wall into the renal pelvis using a tube, stent, or catheter. Nephrostomy is typically performed to provide urinary drainage when the ureter is obstructed, but it also can be performed to gain access to the upper urinary tract for certain procedures, such as intracorporeal lithotripsy, stent placement, to remove or dissolve renal calculi, and diagnostic antegrade radiologic studies of the ureter.

The physician creates an opening from the kidney to the exterior of the body by making an incision in the kidney. To access the kidney, the physician makes an incision in the skin of the flank, cuts the muscles, fat, and fibrous membranes (fascia) overlying the

kidney, and sometimes removes a portion of the eleventh or twelfth rib. Using an incision to open the renal pelvis (pyelotomy), the physician passes a curved clamp into the renal pelvis, middle or lower minor calyx, and the cortex of the kidney. The physician inserts a catheter tip through the same path as the clamp, and passes the tube through a stab incision in the skin of the flank. After suturing the incisions, the physician inserts a drain tube, bringing it out through a separate stab incision, and performs layered closure.

Coding Clarification
Code separately any application or administration of an adhesion barrier substance (99.77) that is performed.

Coding Guidance
    AHA: 2Q, '97, 4

55.03   Percutaneous nephrostomy without fragmentation

Description
The physician inserts a tube through the abdominal wall without breaking up stones. A nephrostomy, which creates an opening from the kidney to the exterior of the body, can be accomplished using a surgical incision or it can be placed percutaneously. It is often performed with placement of a catheter down the ureter.

Coding Clarification
Two codes, 55.03 and 55.04, are available to report percutaneous nephrostomy. If the removal of the kidney stone(s) was by basket or forceps extraction, code 55.03 is correct. Any disruption of kidney stones by ultrasonic energy and extraction through the endoscope is coded 55.04.

This code excludes repeat nephroscopic removal during current episode (55.92) and percutaneous removal by fragmentation (55.04).

Code separately any application or administration of an adhesion barrier substance (99.77) that is performed.

Documentation Tip
Nephroscopic or percutaneous nephrostolithotomy is the insertion of a tube through the abdominal wall to remove stones.

Nephroscopic or percutaneous pyelostolithotomy is the percutaneous removal of stones from the funnel-shaped portion of the kidney.

Nephroscopic forceps extraction, or basket extraction, is the percutaneous removal of a stone with grasping forceps.

Coding Guidance
    AHA: 2Q, '96, 5

● New Code   ▲ Revised Code   ▶◀ Revised Text   © 2010 Ingenix

55.04 Percutaneous nephrostomy with fragmentation

Description
The physician perform a percutaneous nephrostomy with disruption of kidney stone by ultrasonic energy and extraction (suction) through an endoscope, sometimes with placement of a catheter down the ureter. A nephrostomy, which creates an opening from the kidney to the exterior of the body, can be accomplished using a surgical incision or it can be placed percutaneously.

Coding Clarification
Two codes, 55.03 and 55.04, are available to report percutaneous nephrostomy. If the removal of the kidney stone(s) was by basket or forceps extraction, code 55.03 is correct. Any disruption of kidney stones by ultrasonic energy and extraction through the endoscope is coded 55.04.

Code 55.04 excludes repeat fragmentation during the current episode (59.95).

Code separately any application or administration of an adhesion barrier substance (99.77) that is performed.

Documentation Tip
Nephroscopic nephrostolithotomy (percutaneous) is the insertion of a tube through the abdominal wall to remove stones.

Nephroscopic pyelostolithotomy (percutaneous) is the percutaneous removal of stones from the funnel-shaped portion of the kidney.

Coding Guidance
AHA: S-O, '86, 11; 1Q, '89, 1

55.1 Pyelotomy and pyelostomy

Description
A pyelotomy in an incision into the pelvis of the kidney and a pyelostomy is the creation of an opening into the kidney pelvis to establish urinary drainage.

Coding Clarification
Do not use codes in the 55.1 subcategory to report drainage by anastomosis (55.86), percutaneous pyelostolithotomy (55.03), or removal of calculus without incision (56.0).

Code separately any application or administration of an adhesion barrier substance (99.77) that is performed.

55.11 Pyelotomy

Description
The physician makes an incision in the renal pelvis to explore the calyces and renal pelvis. To access the kidney, the physician makes an incision in the skin of the flank, cuts the muscles, fat, and fibrous membranes (fascia) overlying the kidney, and sometimes removes a portion of the eleventh or twelfth rib. The physician makes an incision in the renal pelvis (pyelotomy). The physician may place fine traction sutures at the edges of the pyelotomy while exploring the calyces and renal pelvis. After closing the pyelotomy, the physician inserts a drain tube, bringing it out through a separate stab incision, and performs layered closure.

Coding Clarification
Use 55.11 to report exploration of the renal pelvis or pyelolithotomy.

Code separately any application or administration of an adhesion barrier substance (99.77) that is performed.

Documentation Tip
Pyelolithotomy is the removal of a stone via the renal pelvis. In this procedure, the kidney is exposed with a posterolateral incision over the 12th rib.

Nephrolithotomy, or the removal of a stone through the renal substance, is typically used to remove the fragments following pyelolithotomy; residual fragments can also be disintegrated by ESWL.

55.12 Pyelostomy

Description
The physician makes an incision in the renal pelvis to insert a pyelostomy tube for drainage. To access the kidney, the physician makes an incision in the skin of the flank, cuts the muscles, fat, and fibrous membranes (fascia) overlying the kidney, and sometimes removes a portion of the eleventh or twelfth rib. After exposing the renal pelvis, the physician makes an incision in the renal pelvis (pyelotomy). The physician inserts the tip of a catheter into the renal pelvis and passes the tube out through a stab incision in the skin of the flank. The physician performs layered closure.

Coding Clarification
Code separately any application or administration of an adhesion barrier substance (99.77) that is performed.

55.2 Diagnostic procedures on kidney

Description
Subcategory 55.2 includes codes for open and closed biopsy. Flexible nephroscopy is a diagnostic and therapeutic tool used to diagnose and treat upper urinary tract conditions or as the primary endoscopic procedure to treat renal calculi. Flexible nephroscopy is frequently used as an adjunct procedure during percutaneous nephrolithotomy (percutaneous removal of urinary stones) to remove residual renal calculi.

55-59

55-59

Coding Clarification
The closed biopsy code, 55.23, includes not only a percutaneous or needle biopsy but also one via an existing nephrostomy, nephrotomy, pyelostomy, or pyelotomy.

Code separately any application or administration of an adhesion barrier substance (99.77) that is performed.

55.21   Nephroscopy
Description
The physician examines the kidney and ureter with an endoscope passed through an established opening between the skin and kidney (nephrostomy) or renal pelvis (pyelostomy). After inserting a guidewire, the physician removes the nephrostomy or pyelostomy tube and passes the endoscope through the opening into the kidney or renal pelvis. To better view renal and ureteric structures, the physician may flush (irrigate) or introduce by drops (instillate) a sterile saline solution. The physician may introduce contrast medium for radiologic study of the renal pelvis and ureter (ureteropyelogram). After examination, the physician removes the endoscope and guidewire and reinserts the nephrostomy tube or allows the surgical passageway to seal on its own.

Coding Clarification
Endoscopic exam of the renal pelvis can be performed retrograde through ureter, percutaneous, or open exposure.

Code separately any application or administration of an adhesion barrier substance (99.77) that is performed.

55.22   Pyeloscopy
Description
Pyeloscopy is a fluoroscopic exam of the kidney pelvis, calyces, and ureters following IV or retrograde injection of contrast. Percutaneous pyeloscopy is an endoscopic procedure of the renal pelvis in which an endoscope is introduced into the renal pelvis via a puncture using real-time ultrasonic guidance.

The physician examines the kidney and ureter with an endoscope passed through an incision in the kidney (nephrotomy) or renal pelvis (pyelotomy). After accessing the renal and ureteric structures with an incision in the skin of the flank, the physician incises the kidney or renal pelvis and guides the endoscope through the incision. To better view renal and ureteric structures, the physician may flush (irrigate) or introduce by drops (instillate) a saline solution. The physician may introduce contrast medium for radiologic study of the renal pelvis and ureter (ureteropyelogram). After

examination, the physician sutures the incision, inserts a drain tube, and performs a layered closure.

Coding Clarification
Code separately any application or administration of an adhesion barrier substance (99.77) that is performed.

55.23   Closed (percutaneous) (needle) biopsy of kidney
Description
For a percutaneous biopsy, the physician uses a local anesthetic, biopsy needle, and radiologic guidance to collect the sample tissue. The patient holds his or her breath as the physician inserts the biopsy needle and collects the tissue. The physician may need multiple passes to collect the samples.

The physician extracts a plug of biopsy tissue from the kidney by inserting a needle or trocar in the skin of the back. Using radiologic or ultrasonic guidance, the physician advances the instrument into the suspect tissue of the kidney. With the instrument's cutting sheath, the physician traps a specimen of renal tissue and removes the instrument. After usually repeating the process several times, the physician applies pressure to the puncture wound.

Coding Clarification
Code 55.23 is also used to report endoscopic biopsy via an existing nephrostomy, nephrotomy, pyelostomy, or pyelotomy.

Code separately any application or administration of an adhesion barrier substance (99.77) that is performed.

55.24   Open biopsy of kidney
Description
Some patients may undergo a kidney biopsy through an open procedure in which the surgeon makes an incision to visualize the kidney to obtain a biopsy sample. The physician excises a specimen of biopsy tissue from the kidney through an incision. To access the kidney, the physician makes an incision in the skin of the flank and cuts the muscles, fat, and fibrous membranes (fascia) overlying the kidney. After excising a specimen of the diseased or damaged renal tissue, the physician sutures the incision and performs layered closure.

Coding Clarification
Code separately any application or administration of an adhesion barrier substance (99.77) that is performed.

55.29   Other diagnostic procedures on kidney
Description
Code 55.29 is used to report other diagnostic kidney procedures that are not more precisely described by

● New Code   ▲ Revised Code   ▶◀ Revised Text   © 2010 Ingenix

other codes in subcategory 55.2. Another diagnostic method is the transjugular biopsy. To obtain the tissue sample, the physician inserts a needle through a catheter that enters the jugular vein at the neck. The needle is threaded through the blood vessel to the right kidney and the physician obtains the tissue from the inside without puncturing the outside skin of the kidney.

Coding Clarification
Code 55.29 is not used to report intravenous pyelogram (87.73), percutaneous pyelogram (87.75), or retrograde pyelogram (87.74).

Do not use 55.29 to report radioisotope scan (92.03), renal arteriography (88.45), or tomography (87.71, 87.72).

To report microscopic examination of a specimen from the kidney, see 91.21-91.29.

Code separately any application or administration of an adhesion barrier substance (99.77) that is performed.

Documentation Tip
Review the documentation for specific information regarding the procedure prior to final code selection in order to ensure accurate code assignment.

55.3 Local excision or destruction of lesion or tissue of kidney

Description
The destruction of kidney lesions ranges from open surgery to less invasive procedures, such as percutaneous techniques, retrograde ureteroscopy, and laparoscopy.

55.31 Marsupialization of kidney lesion

Description
Marsupialization is a surgical technique in which the lesion is exteriorized by incising the anterior wall and suturing the cut edges to the skin creating an open pouch.

Coding Clarification
Code separately any application or administration of an adhesion barrier substance (99.77) that is performed.

55.32 Open ablation of renal lesion or tissue

Description
Ablation is a form of treatment that destroys kidney lesions by applying energy to a specific lesion. The open approach to renal ablation involves the creation of an incision in order to afford superior visual identification for placement of the ablation device. Following activation and completion of the ablation cycle, the device is removed and the incision closed by traditional methods.

The physician performs open cryosurgical ablation of one or more renal mass lesions. The physician performs a laparotomy. Dissection is carried down to the kidney. Intraoperative ultrasound may be used to identify the lesion. Cryosurgical probes are inserted into the kidney lesion. The cryosurgical probe delivers cryogen, a coolant, at subfreezing temperatures to freeze the lesion. The renal tissue is slowly thawed. A minimum of two cycles of freezing and thawing are performed. This is repeated for each lesion. When all lesions have been treated, the incision is closed with layered sutures.

Coding Clarification
Code separately any application or administration of an adhesion barrier substance (99.77) that is performed.

Coding Guidance
AHA: 4Q, '06, 124

55.33 Percutaneous ablation of renal lesion or tissue

Description
Ablation is a form of treatment that destroys kidney lesions by applying energy to a specific lesion. Often utilizing minimally invasive nephron-sparing techniques, the kidney tumor is localized and treated with energy that kills the tumor cells but leaves the surrounding tissues intact and functioning. In percutaneous renal ablation, the ablation device is inserted through the skin and into the lesion. Ultrasound or computed tomography guidance is employed in order to achieve accurate device placement. After activation and completion of the ablation cycle, the device is removed and a bandage is placed over the site of insertion.

There are various hyperthermal ablation techniques. Radiofrequency ablation involves radiographic localization of the renal tumor, followed by delivery of heat through a needle that has been placed percutaneously. Cryoablation, a hypothermal technique, is the oldest thermal ablation and may be performed laparoscopically or percutaneously. Localization of the tumor is performed by radiographic means; freezing of the tumor follows.

The physician performs percutaneous radiofrequency ablation of one or more renal tumors. Using computerized tomography (CT), magnetic resonance imaging (MRI), or ultrasound guidance, the site for the electrode placement is identified. With the patient under conscious sedation, a small incision is made and an internally cooled radiofrequency needle electrode is introduced and placed into the renal tumor. Placement of the tip is confirmed with image guidance. Alternating current is applied as needed until correct core heat is reached in the electrode. The tumor tissue is heated to a specified temperature with monitoring done

55-59

before and after each treatment, depending on the ablation device used, until sufficient time results in permanent cell damage and tumor necrosis. Overlapping tumor tissue is ablated in the same manner until all margins are satisfactory. Hemostasis is maintained after the electrode needle is withdrawn, the site is cleaned, and dressings are applied. The ablated tissue remains in place and is absorbed over time and replaced with scar tissue.

Alternately, the physician may use percutaneously placed cryotherapy probes to destroy tumors of the kidney. The patient is positioned for best exposure of the affected kidney. Images are obtained to localize the tumor(s) and determine the site for cryoprobe placement. After planning the skin entry site, the cryoprobe(s) is placed in the lesion and the tip(s) confirmed in position. Cycles of freezing and thawing are monitored to ensure encapsulation of the tumor tissue and a sufficient margin within the ice ball created by the cryotherapy. After the second active thaw cycle, the cryoprobes are removed if the ice ball is judged to cover the tumor tissue. If freezing was insufficient, the probes may be removed and repositioned or additional probes may be added and freezing is continued until the tumor and margin receive two complete cycles. The instruments are removed, the incision site closed, and dressings are applied.

Coding Clarification
Code separately any application or administration of an adhesion barrier substance (99.77) that is performed.

Coding Guidance
AHA: 4Q, '06, 124

55.34 Laparoscopic ablation of renal lesion or tissue

Description
Ablation is a form of treatment that destroys kidney lesions by applying energy to a specific lesion. Often utilizing minimally invasive nephron-sparing techniques, the kidney tumor is localized and treated with energy that kills the tumor cells but leaves the surrounding tissues intact and functioning. Laparoscopic renal ablation involves the insertion of the ablation device into the lesion with the assistance of a laparoscope and, if necessary, imaging guidance. Following cycle initiation and completion, the device is removed and the incision closed with a few sutures.

There are various hyperthermal ablation techniques. HIFU, or high-intensity focused ultrasound, utilizes a probe that is inserted laparoscopically. A rapid temperature rise causes tissue ablation. Cryoablation, a hypothermal technique, is the oldest thermal ablation and may be performed laparoscopically or percutaneously. Localization of

the tumor is performed by laparoscopic and/or radiographic means; freezing of the tumor follows.

The physician can perform a laparoscopic surgical ablation of a renal mass or lesion through the abdomen or back. With the abdominal approach, an umbilical port is created by placing a trocar at the level of the umbilicus. The abdominal wall is insufflated. The laparoscope is placed through the umbilical port and additional trocars are placed into the abdominal cavity. In the back approach, the trocar is placed at the back proximate to the retroperitoneal space near to the kidney with additional ports placed nearby for appropriate access to the operative site. The physician uses the laparoscope fitted with a fiberoptic camera and/or an operating instrument. The renal cysts or lesions are visualized through the scope and are ablated by fulguration or another method that can be utilized endoscopically, such as cryotherapy or radiofrequency thermal coagulation. The instruments are removed and the abdominal or back incisions are closed by staples or sutures.

Coding Clarification
Code separately any application or administration of an adhesion barrier substance (99.77) that is performed.

Coding Scenario
A 55-year-old male presented with biopsy-proven renal cell carcinoma. He declined nephrectomy and desired treatment with laparoscopic ablation. Under general anesthesia, an umbilical port was created by placing a trocar at the level of the umbilicus. The abdominal wall was then insufflated, the laparoscope was placed through the umbilical port, and additional trocars placed into the abdominal cavity. The renal lesions were visualized through the scope and were ablated by radiofrequency thermal coagulation. The instruments were removed and the abdominal incisions closed with sutures. There were no complications.

Code Assignment:

189.0	Malignant neoplasm of kidney, except pelvis
55.34	Laparoscopic ablation of renal lesion or tissue

Coding Guidance
AHA: 4Q, '06, 124

55.35 Other and unspecified ablation of renal lesion or tissue

Description
Ablation is a form of treatment that destroys kidney lesions by applying energy to a specific lesion. Often utilizing minimally invasive nephron-sparing techniques, the kidney tumor is localized and treated with energy that kills the tumor cells but leaves the surrounding tissues intact and functioning.

● New Code ▲ Revised Code ▶◀ Revised Text © 2010 Ingenix

There are various ablation techniques. Laser-induced interstitial thermotherapy (LITT) utilizes lasers to heat certain areas of the body. Directed to interstitial areas (areas between organs) that are near the tumor, the heat generated from the laser increases the temperature of the tumor and shrinks, damages, or destroys the cancer cells.

Code 55.35 reports other renal ablation procedures that are not more precisely described by other codes in subcategory 55.3. This code is also reported when the documentation does not further specify the ablation procedure.

Coding Clarification
Code separately any application or administration of an adhesion barrier substance (99.77) that is performed.

Documentation Tip
Review the documentation for specific information regarding the procedure prior to final code selection in order to avoid improper use of the "not otherwise specified" code.

If documentation is unclear, the physician should be queried.

Coding Guidance
AHA: 4Q, '06, 124

55.39   Other local destruction or excision of renal lesion or tissue

Description
Until recently, treatment of calyceal diverticula has involved open surgery; however, treatment has evolved from open surgery to less invasive procedures, such as extracorporeal shock wave lithotripsy (ESWL), percutaneous techniques, retrograde ureteroscopy, CT-guided puncture of the diverticulum, and laparoscopy. Percutaneous nephrolithotomy (PCNL) is commonly used to treat calyceal diverticula, and includes stone removal, diverticular wall fulguration, and diverticular neck dilatation.

The physician excises a cyst on the kidney or in the surrounding renal tissue. To access the kidney, the physician makes an incision in the skin of the flank, cuts the muscles, fat, and fibrous membranes (fascia) overlying the kidney, and sometimes removes a portion of the twelfth rib. After clearing away the fatty tissue surrounding the kidney, the physician excises the cyst from the renal surface. The physician destroys tiny vessels bordering the cyst with high-frequency electric current (fulguration) to minimize the need for sutures. If the cyst requires a deep excision, the physician usually sutures renal tissue. The physician inserts a drain tube, bringing it out through a separate stab incision in the skin, and performs layered closure.

Coding Clarification
Use 55.39 to report obliteration of calyceal diverticulum.

Code 55.39 excludes ablation of renal lesion or tissue: laparoscopic (55.34), open (55.32), other (55.35), percutaneous (55.33), biopsy of kidney (55.23-55.24), partial nephrectomy (55.4), percutaneous aspiration of kidney (55.92), and wedge resection of kidney (55.4).

Code separately any application or administration of an adhesion barrier substance (99.77) that is performed.

Documentation Tip
The medical record may contain documentation of the following procedures on the kidney, which are also correctly reported with 55.39:

- Cavernotomy
- Diverticulectomy
- Unroofing of cyst

55.4   Partial nephrectomy

Description
The kidneys filter waste from the blood and produce urine. There are two kidneys located at the back of the abdomen, just below the diaphragm, behind the liver and the spleen. Depending on the reason for a nephrectomy, all or part of one kidney may be removed or both kidneys may be removed. Surgical techniques include open nephrectomy; however, these procedures can also be performed laparoscopically.

The physician removes a portion of the kidney. To access the kidney and ureter, the physician usually makes an incision in the skin of the flank, cuts the muscles, fat, and fibrous membranes (fascia) overlying the kidney, and sometimes removes a portion of the eleventh or twelfth rib. After mobilizing the kidney and the major renal blood vessels (renal pedicle), the physician clamps the renal vessels, and sometimes induces hypothermia of the kidney with iced saline slush. The physician excises a wedge containing the diseased or damaged kidney tissue. After clamping and ligating the exposed arteries and veins, the physician inserts a drain tube, bringing it out through a separate stab incision in the skin, removes the clamps, and performs layered closure.

In an alternate technique, the physician performs a laparoscopic partial nephrectomy. With an abdominal approach, an umbilical port is created by placing a trocar at the level of the umbilicus. The abdominal wall is insufflated. The laparoscope is placed through the umbilical port and additional trocars are placed into the abdominal cavity. In a back approach, the trocar is placed at the back proximate to the retroperitoneal space near to the

55-59

kidney with additional ports placed nearby for appropriate access to the operative site. The physician uses the laparoscope fitted with a fiberoptic camera for direct vision and/or an operating instrument. Direct vision and the use of laparoscopic ultrasonography allow the physician to identify the tumors and assess the appropriate surgical margin that should be allowed. The diseased kidney tissue is removed with emphasis on hemostasis. Methods such as electrocautery, argon beam coagulator, topical agents, and microwave thermotherapy may be employed to help reduce bleeding during resection. Retrieval pouches used in endoscopic surgery allow removal of the tumor specimen without spilling. The instruments are removed and the abdominal or back incisions are closed by staples or sutures.

Coding Clarification
Code 55.4 is also used to report calycectomy (the removal of indentations in kidney) wedge resection of the kidney.

Code also any synchronous resection of ureter (56.40-56.42).

Code separately any application or administration of an adhesion barrier substance (99.77) that is performed.

55.5   Complete nephrectomy

Description
A nephrectomy is the surgical removal of a kidney, the organ that filters waste from the blood and produces urine. There are two kidneys located at the back of the abdomen, just below the diaphragm, behind the liver and the spleen. Depending on the reason for a nephrectomy, all or part of one kidney may be removed or both kidneys may be removed. Open nephrectomy for kidney removal requires a large, abdominal incision and the removal of a rib. These procedures can also be performed laparoscopically. An abdominal or anterior nephrectomy is performed through an incision in the abdominal wall. A lumbar or posterior nephrectomy is done through an incision in the loin. A paraperitoneal nephrectomy is the removal of a kidney through an incision in the side along the twelfth rib.

Coding Clarification
There is no specific ICD-9-CM procedure code that fully describes a *radical nephrectomy* (removal of the kidney, the adrenal gland, and the adjacent lymph nodes); therefore, it is necessary to also assign codes for any excision of the adrenal gland (07.21-07.3), bladder segment (57.6), or lymph nodes (40.3, 40.52-40.59) performed synchronously with the complete nephrectomy.

Code separately any application or administration of an adhesion barrier substance (99.77) that is performed.

Documentation Tip
An understanding of the following terms may aid in code selection:

- **Bilateral nephrectomy:** Removal of both kidneys.

- **Partial nephrectomy:** Part of one kidney is removed.

- **Radical nephrectomy:** All of one kidney is removed, as well as the adjacent adrenal gland and lymph nodes.

- **Simple nephrectomy:** All of one kidney is removed.

- **Total nephrectomy:** Removal of only the kidney.

55.51   Nephroureterectomy

Description
Nephroureterectomy can be accomplished using various approaches and techniques, some of which are detailed below.

The physician removes the kidney and all of the ureter through a laparoscope. The physician makes a 1 cm periumbilical incision and inserts a trocar. The abdominal cavity is insufflated with carbon dioxide. A fiberoptic laparoscope fitted with a camera and light source is inserted through the trocar. Other incisions (ports) are made in the abdomen or flank to allow other instruments or an additional light source to be passed into the abdomen or retroperitoneum. The colon is mobilized and the laparoscope is advanced to the operative site. The physician mobilizes the kidney and clamps, ligates, and severs all of the ureter at the ureterovesical junction and major renal blood vessels (renal pedicle). The kidney and ureter are bagged and brought through one of the port sites (e.g., periumbilical) that have been slightly enlarged. The instruments are removed and the small abdominal or flank incisions are closed with staple or suture.

In an alternate approach, the physician removes the kidney, ureter, and small cuff of the bladder through one excision. To access the kidney and ureter, the physician usually makes an incision in the skin of the flank, cuts the muscles, fat, and fibrous membranes (fascia) overlying the kidney, and sometimes removes a portion of the eleventh or twelfth rib. After mobilizing the kidney, ureter, and bladder, the physician clamps, ligates, and severs the ureter, major renal blood vessels (renal pedicle), and a small cuff of the bladder. The physician pulls the kidney, ureter, and bladder cuff upward through the flank incision. In this procedure, the physician does not remove the adrenal gland, surrounding fatty tissue, or Gerota's fascia. After controlling bleeding, the physician irrigates the site with normal saline and places a drain tube, bringing it out through a separate stab incision in the skin. The physician sutures and catheterizes the bladder, removes the clamps, and performs layered closure.

Also by incisional approach, the physician may remove the kidney and upper portion of the ureter. To access the kidney and ureter, the physician usually makes an incision in the skin of the flank, cuts the muscles, fat, and fibrous membranes (fascia) overlying the kidney, and sometimes removes a portion of the eleventh or twelfth rib. After mobilizing the kidney and ureter, the physician clamps, ligates, and severs the upper ureter and major renal blood vessels (renal pedicle). The physician removes the kidney and upper ureter, but does not remove the adrenal gland, surrounding fatty tissue, or Gerota's fascia. After controlling bleeding, the physician irrigates the site with normal saline and places a drain tube, bringing it out through a separate stab incision in the skin. The physician removes the clamps and performs layered closure.

Coding Clarification
Code 55.51 is used to report nephroureterectomy with bladder cuff and total nephrectomy (unilateral); however, to report removal of transplanted kidney, use 55.53 instead.

Donation of a kidney by a live person is assigned diagnosis code V59.4 and the code for removal of the kidney, 55.51.

Code separately any application or administration of an adhesion barrier substance (99.77) that is performed.

Also assign codes for any synchronous excision of the following structures:

- Adrenal gland (07.21-07.3)
- Bladder segment (57.6)
- Lymph nodes (40.3, 40.52-40.59)

Documentation Tip
An understanding of the following terms may aid in code selection:

- **Nephroureterectomy:** Complete removal of the kidney and all or a portion of the ureter.

- **Nephroureterectomy with bladder cuff:** Removal of the kidney, ureter, and a portion of the bladder attached to ureter.

- **Total nephrectomy (unilateral):** Complete excision of one kidney.

Coding Guidance
AHA: 2Q, '05, 4

55.52 Nephrectomy of remaining kidney

Description
This code reports the removal of a solitary kidney. The physician makes an incision through the skin and muscle along the lower border of the eleventh or twelfth rib and extends the incision from the spine around to the front of the abdomen. If necessary to expose the kidney, a portion of one or two ribs will be removed. The kidney's blood vessels and ureter are tied off and the kidney is removed. The internal layers of the incision are closed with sutures, the upper layer of skin is closed with surgical staples, and a temporary drainage tube is inserted. Other techniques may also be utilized.

Coding Clarification
Do not use 55.52 to report the removal of a transplanted kidney; report 55.53.

Code separately any application or administration of an adhesion barrier substance (99.77) that is performed.

Also assign codes for any synchronous excision of the following structures:

- Adrenal gland (07.21-07.3)
- Bladder segment (57.6)
- Lymph nodes (40.3, 40.52-40.59)

55.53 Removal of transplanted or rejected kidney

Description
Kidney transplantation is a primary treatment for kidney failure; however, rejection is a common problem in transplantation. Immunosuppressive, or anti-rejection medications, help prevent rejections.

The physician removes a transplanted donor kidney from the recipient. To access the rejected kidney, the physician usually reopens the original kidney transplant incision and cuts the muscles, fat, and fibrous membranes (fascia) overlying the kidney. After mobilizing the kidney, the physician clamps, ligates, and severs the major renal blood vessels (renal pedicle). The physician removes the rejected kidney. After controlling bleeding, the physician irrigates the site with normal saline. The physician may place a drain tube, bringing it out through a separate stab incision in the skin. After removing the clamps, the physician performs layered closure.

Coding Clarification
Also assign codes for any synchronous excision of the following structures:

- Adrenal gland (07.21-07.3)
- Bladder segment (57.6)
- Lymph nodes (40.3, 40.52-40.59)

Code separately any application or administration of an adhesion barrier substance (99.77) that is performed.

Coding Guidance
AHA: 4Q, '08, 83

55.54   Bilateral nephrectomy

Description
The physician removes both kidneys during the same operative session. In one approach, with the patient under general anesthesia, a chevron incision is made and the physician removes the right kidney. Homeostasis is achieved with electrocautery, clamping, and ligatures. The left kidney is then removed in the same fashion.

Coding Clarification
To report complete nephrectomy that is not further specified in the documentation, see 55.51.

Code separately any application or administration of an adhesion barrier substance (99.77) that is performed.

Also assign codes for any synchronous excision of the following structures:

- Adrenal gland (07.21-07.3)
- Bladder segment (57.6)
- Lymph nodes (40.3, 40.52-40.59)

Documentation Tip
Review the documentation for specific information regarding the procedure prior to final code selection in order to avoid improper use of the "not otherwise specified" code.

55.6   Transplant of kidney

Description
In a kidney transplantation from a living donor, the donor's kidney is typically removed with laparoscopic surgery. Traditional open surgery requires a larger incision in the side between the ribs and the hip, and also involves the removal of a donor's rib. Once the donor kidney has been removed, the transplant procedure is the same as for a living or a cadaveric kidney donor.

During kidney transplant surgery, an incision is made in the transplant recipient's abdomen, usually on the lower right side, and the donor kidney is placed near the bladder on the right side of the recipient's pelvis. The recipient's own kidneys are often not removed. The physician attaches the donor ureter to the recipient's bladder, allowing urine to flow normally from the new kidney, and restores the blood supply to the donor kidney by connecting it to the recipient's blood vessels.

Coding Clarification
Kidney transplantation is replacement of a non-functioning kidney with a healthy kidney from another person (donor). It is often used to treat chronic renal failure or end-stage renal disease. Donor kidneys can be obtained from a living or a nonliving (cadaveric) kidney donor.

Use 00.91-00.93 to report the donor source.

Code separately any application or administration of an adhesion barrier substance (99.77) that is performed.

55.61   Renal autotransplantation

Description
The physician moves the kidney from its original anatomic site and revascularizes the kidney by connecting the renal and iliac vessels to a new site. To access the transplant site, the physician usually makes a midline transabdominal incision in the skin and cuts the muscles, fat, and fibrous membranes (fascia). After exposing the kidney, the physician clamps, ligates, and severs the renal vessels, keeping the ureter intact. The physician flushes the kidney with cold, anticoagulant electrolyte solution, and surgically connects the renal vessels to another appropriate arterial and venous site. The physician removes the clamps and checks for leakage, bleeding, and infarction. After placing a drain tube and bringing it out through a separate stab incision in the skin, the physician removes the clamps and performs layered closure.

Coding Clarification
Open surgical renal autotransplantation is an extensive operation that includes two procedures (a live-donor nephrectomy and autotransplantation), and requires two large incisions. Renal autotransplantation can also be performed laparoscopically.

Use 00.91-00.93 to report the donor source.

Code separately any application or administration of an adhesion barrier substance (99.77) that is performed.

55.69   Other kidney transplantation

Description
The physician implants a donor kidney and upper ureter after removing the recipient's kidney and upper ureter in a separately reportable procedure. To access the recipient's kidney and ureter, the physician usually makes an incision in the skin of the flank, cuts the muscles, fat, and fibrous membranes (fascia) overlying the kidney, and sometimes removes a portion of the eleventh or twelfth rib. The physician clamps, ligates, and severs the upper ureter and major renal blood vessels (renal

55-59

pedicle), and removes the kidney and upper ureter. To implant the donor kidney and upper ureter, the physician usually makes a curved lower quadrant incision in the skin. The physician surgically connects the renal vein and artery of the donor kidney to the recipient's clamped and dissected internal iliac vein and hypogastric artery. After incising the bladder, the physician passes the donor ureter through the bladder and sutures the ureter and opening in the bladder (cystotomy). The physician performs layered closure. The drain tube may be left in.

In an alternate technique, the physician surgically implants a human kidney and ureter from a living donor or cadaver into a transplant patient, without performing a concurrent nephrectomy on the recipient. To access the transplant site, the physician usually makes a curved, right or left lower quadrant incision in the skin. After cutting the muscles, fat, and fibrous membranes (fascia), the physician controls bleeding with clamps, ties, and electrocoagulation. The physician surgically connects the renal vein and artery of the donor kidney to the recipient's clamped and dissected internal iliac vein and hypogastric artery. After removing the clamps, the physician checks for leakage, bleeding, and insufficient blood supply. To implant the donor ureter, the physician makes an incision into the bladder and passes the ureter through the bladder. The physician sutures the ureter as well as the opening in the bladder (cystotomy). The physician performs layered closure. The drain tube may be left in.

Coding Clarification
Code separately any application or administration of an adhesion barrier substance (99.77) that is performed.

Coding Scenario
A female patient with chronic renal failure was admitted for a non-related, living donor kidney transplant.

Code Assignment:

585.9	Chronic kidney disease, unspecified
55.69	Other kidney transplantation
00.92	Transplant from live nonrelated donor

Coding Guidance
AHA: 4Q, '96, 71; 4Q, '04, 117

55.7   Nephropexy

Description
Nephropexy is performed to treat a floating, or movable, kidney. The traditional surgical treatment of a floating kidney is open surgery in which fixation of the mobile kidney is done in a high, retroperitoneal position. There are also various

techniques of laparoscopic nephropexy, most of which use a transperitoneal approach that entails a lengthy surgical procedure with intraabdominal dissection. A percutaneous nephropexy is a minimally invasive nephropexy in which the physician fixes the kidney to the posterior abdominal wall.

Coding Clarification
Code separately any application or administration of an adhesion barrier substance (99.77) that is performed.

55.8   Other repair of kidney

Description
Subcategory 55.8 provides eight codes to report various methods of kidney repair. Fourth-digit subclassification provides specificity to site and/or procedure performed.

Coding Clarification
The patient's diagnosis plays a role in code selection for repairs of the kidney. Be sure the medical record documentation states the condition referenced in the procedural descriptor, such as a laceration of the kidney (55.81), nephrostomy or pyelostomy (55.82), and other fistula of kidney (55.83).

Code separately any application or administration of an adhesion barrier substance (99.77) that is performed.

55.81   Suture of laceration of kidney

Description
The physician uses sutures to surgically fixate a wound or injury of the kidney. To access the kidney, the physician makes an incision in the skin of the flank, cuts the muscles, fat, and fibrous membranes (fascia) overlying the kidney, and sometimes removes a portion of the eleventh or twelfth rib. After using sutures to close or surgically fixate a kidney wound or injury, the physician places a drain tube, bringing it out through a separate stab incision in the skin, and performs layered closure.

Coding Clarification
The patient's diagnosis plays a role in code selection for repairs of the kidney. Be sure the medical record documentation states laceration of the kidney (i.e., the condition referenced in the procedural descriptor).

Code separately any application or administration of an adhesion barrier substance (99.77) that is performed.

55.82   Closure of nephrostomy and pyelostomy

Description
The physician performs removal of a tube from the kidney or renal pelvis and closure of the site of tube

55-59

insertion. After removing the ostomy tube, the physician sutures the clean percutaneous tissues together to create a smooth surface.

Coding Clarification
Be sure the medical record documentation states the condition referenced in the procedural descriptor (i.e., nephrostomy or pyelostomy).

Code separately any application or administration of an adhesion barrier substance (99.77) that is performed.

55.83   Closure of other fistula of kidney

Description
The physician closes a fistula that is an abnormal opening between the kidney and an organ of the digestive, respiratory, urogenital, or endocrine system. The physician usually makes an incision in the abdomen, cuts the muscles, fat, and fibrous membranes (fascia) overlying the kidney to access the fistula. In an alternate approach, the physician makes an incision in the skin of the chest, opens the chest cavity, collapses the lung, and separates the leaves of the diaphragm to expose the kidney. After excising the fistula, the physician sutures the clean tissues together to create a smooth surface. The physician places a drain tube, bringing it out through a separate stab incision in the skin, and performs layered closure. In some cases, the physician inserts a chest tube to re-expand the lung.

Coding Clarification
The patient's diagnosis plays a role in code selection for repairs of the kidney. Be sure the medical record documentation states the condition as fistula of the kidney as referenced in the procedural descriptor.

Code separately any application or administration of an adhesion barrier substance (99.77) that is performed.

55.84   Reduction of torsion of renal pedicle

Description
Torsion of the kidney vascular pedicle may compromise renal integrity. In this procedure, the physician restores a twisted renal pedicle into a normal position. The renal artery and vein and the lateral, posterior, and ureteral attachments to the kidney create a three-point fixation to the retroperitoneum to limit mobility of the kidney and prevent torsion of the kidney vascular pedicle.

Coding Clarification
Vascular complications and renal infarction resulting from torsion of the vascular pedicle are frequent surgical complications after kidney transplant.

Code separately any application or administration of an adhesion barrier substance (99.77) that is performed.

Coding Scenario
A patient who was 11 months post intraperitoneal kidney transplantation presented with abdominal pain and decreased urine output. The physician performed a diagnostic laparotomy and determined the symptoms were due to torsion of the vascular pedicle. The physician restored the twisted renal pedicle into a normal position.

   Code Assignment:

   593.89   Other specified disorders of kidney and ureter
   55.84   Reduction of torsion of renal pedicle

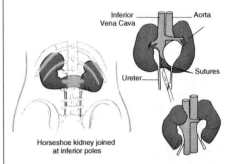

Horseshoe kidney joined at inferior poles

55.85   Symphysiotomy for horseshoe kidney

Description
Horseshoe kidney is a common congenital abnormality of the urinary system that occurs during fetal development. With horseshoe kidney, as the kidneys of the fetus rise from the pelvic area, they fuse together at the lower end or base forming a "U" or horseshoe shape. Horseshoe kidney usually causes no symptoms but in some cases it can impair the flow of urine, which can damage the kidney.

The physician divides an abnormal union of the kidneys to correct a horseshoe kidney. To access the horseshoe kidney, the physician usually makes an incision in the skin of the lower abdomen and cuts the muscles, fat, and fibrous membranes (fascia) overlying the kidney. After incising the union and placing two rows of sutures to control bleeding, the physician usually performs pyeloplasty or another plastic procedure on one or both sides of the divided kidney. After completion of repair, the physician may rotate the kidney to affect drainage. The physician irrigates the site with normal saline, places a drain tube, bringing it out through a separate stab incision in the skin, and performs layered closure.

Coding Clarification
Code separately any application or administration of an adhesion barrier substance (99.77) that is performed.

● New Code   ▲ Revised Code   ▶◀ Revised Text   © 2010 Ingenix

55.86 Anastomosis of kidney

Description
The physician surgically connects the upper ureter and renal pelvis to allow for urinary drainage. To access the renal pelvis and ureter, the physician makes an incision in the skin of the flank, cuts the muscles, fat, and fibrous membranes (fascia) overlying the kidney, and sometimes removes a portion of the eleventh or twelfth rib. The physician ligates the renal pelvis and ureter at the point of blockage. After excising the obstructing part of the ureter or pelvis, the physician surgically connects (anastomosis) the two structures, bypassing the obstructing point. To provide support during healing, the physician may insert a slender tube into the renal pelvis. After wrapping the anastomosis with perinephric fat, the physician inserts a drain tube and performs layered closure.

Coding Clarification
To report nephrocystanastomosis that is not further specified in the documentation, see 56.73.

Code separately any application or administration of an adhesion barrier substance (99.77) that is performed.

Documentation Tip
The following terms may aid in code selection:

- **Nephropyeloureterostomy:** Creation of a passage between the kidney and the ureter.

- **Pyeloureterovesical anastomosis:** Creation of a passage between the kidney and the bladder.

- **Ureterocalyceal anastomosis:** Creation of a passage between the ureter and kidney indentations.

55.87 Correction of ureteropelvic junction

Description
The physician uses plastic surgery to correct an obstruction or defect in the renal pelvis or ureteropelvic junction. To access the renal pelvis and ureter, the physician usually makes an incision in the skin of the flank. The physician incises, trims, and shapes the renal pelvis and ureter, using absorbable sutures or soft rubber drains for traction. The physician usually inserts a slender tube into the renal pelvis to provide support during healing. In Foley Y-pyeloplasty, the physician advances a Y-shaped flap of the renal pelvis into a vertical incision in the upper ureter. The physician may surgically fixate (nephropexy) a floating or mobile kidney, and/or establish an opening between the kidney (nephrostomy) or renal pelvis (pyelostomy) and the exterior of the body. The physician places a drain tube, bringing it out

through a separate stab incision in the skin, and performs layered closure.

Coding Clarification
Code separately any application or administration of an adhesion barrier substance (99.77) that is performed.

Documentation Tip
Ureteropelvic junction repair is sometimes referred to as an Anderson-Hynes pyeloplasty.

55.89 Other repair of kidney

Description
Code 55.89 is used to report other repair procedures of the kidney that are not more precisely described by other codes in subcategory 55.8.

Coding Clarification
Code separately any application or administration of an adhesion barrier substance (99.77) that is performed.

Documentation Tip
Review the documentation for specific information regarding the procedure prior to final code selection in order to ensure accurate code assignment.

55.9 Other operations on kidney

Description
Fourth-digit subclassifications describe various other kidney procedures such as capsulectomy and decortication of the kidney, aspiration and renipuncture of the kidney, replacement of nephrostomy and pyelostomy tubes, and injection procedures.

Coding Clarification
Do not use 55.9 subcategory codes to report a percutaneous biopsy of the kidney; report 55.23.

To report lysis of perirenal adhesions, see 59.02.

Code separately any application or administration of an adhesion barrier substance (99.77) that is performed.

55.91 Decapsulation of kidney

Description
The physician performs decapsulation of kidney by removing or stripping off the capsule of the kidney. Renal decapsulation may be performed as treatment for retroperitoneal tissue adhesions.

Coding Clarification
This procedure may also be documented as renal decapsulation, capsulectomy, or decortication and nephrocapsectomy.

Code separately any application or administration of an adhesion barrier substance (99.77) that is performed.

55-59

55.92   Percutaneous aspiration of kidney (pelvis)

Description
The physician inserts a needle through the skin to inject or drain fluid from the renal pelvis or a renal cyst. The physician usually inserts a long, thin needle in the skin of the back. Using radiologic guidance, the physician advances the needle toward the renal pelvis or renal cyst and injects or drains fluid.

Coding Clarification
Code 55.92 is used to report aspiration of renal cysts and renipuncture; however, do not use 55.92 to report a percutaneous biopsy of the kidney. Instead, see 55.23.

Code separately any application or administration of an adhesion barrier substance (99.77) that is performed.

Coding Guidance
    AHA: N-D, '84, 20

55.93   Replacement of nephrostomy tube

Description
The physician changes a nephrostomy tube. To remove the existing tube, the physician takes out the sutures securing the tube to the skin. The physician inserts a guidewire through the tube and passes the tube back over the guidewire. The physician passes a new tube over the guidewire, removes the guidewire, and sutures the tube to the skin.

Coding Clarification
Code separately any application or administration of an adhesion barrier substance (99.77) that is performed.

55.94   Replacement of pyelostomy tube

Description
The physician changes a pyelostomy tube. To remove the existing tube, the physician takes out the sutures securing the tube to the skin. The physician inserts a guidewire through the tube and passes the tube back over the guidewire. The physician passes a new tube over the guidewire, removes the guidewire, and sutures the tube to the skin.

Coding Clarification
Code separately any application or administration of an adhesion barrier substance (99.77) that is performed.

55.95   Local perfusion of kidney

Description
This procedure involves fluid passage through the kidney. For example, gravity perfusion and high-pressure perfusion are used in kidney transplantation. During a donor operation, the kidney is perfused by a gravity-hydrostatic pressure

(gravity perfusion) or an alternate technique in which perfusion solution is flushed under additional pressure (high-pressure perfusion) in order to perfuse the small parenchymal vessels. The perfusion solution is flushed under an additional pressure to create pressure similar to that in the normal arterial system.

Coding Clarification
Code separately any application or administration of an adhesion barrier substance (99.77) that is performed.

55.96   Other injection of therapeutic substance into kidney

Description
The physician instills a therapeutic agent, such as an anticarcinogenic or an antifungal, through the tube of an established opening between the skin and kidney (nephrostomy), renal pelvis (pyelostomy), or ureter (ureterostomy). This type of intracavitary topical therapy is reliably done through a tube left in place following a previous surgery. After inserting a guidewire, an endoscope or flexible delivery catheter is passed through the tube into the kidney, renal pelvis, or ureter. To better view renal and ureteric structures, the physician may flush (irrigate) or introduce by drops (instillate) a saline solution. The physician introduces the therapeutic agent to the target area. After examination, the physician removes the instruments and reinserts the nephrostomy, pyelostomy, or ureterostomy tube or allows the surgical passageway to seal on its own.

Alternately, the physician inserts a needle through the skin to inject fluid into the renal pelvis or a renal cyst. The physician usually inserts a long, thin needle in the skin of the back. Using radiologic guidance, the physician advances the needle toward the renal pelvis or renal cyst and injects fluid.

Coding Clarification
This code is also used to report injection into a renal cyst.

Code separately any application or administration of an adhesion barrier substance (99.77) that is performed.

55.97   Implantation or replacement of mechanical kidney

Description
The physician surgically implants an artificial mechanical device that performs the functions usually performed by the kidneys of patients in chronic kidney failure. An artificial kidney uses the principle of dialysis to purify the blood. Dialyzers use pure water to remove impurities and waste products from the patient's blood.

● New Code   ▲ Revised Code   ▶◀ Revised Text   © 2010 Ingenix

Coding Clarification
Artificial kidney or dialyzers are continually changing with advancements in bioengineering and nanotechnology toward developing a fully functioning artificial kidney for patients with end-stage renal disease.

Code separately any application or administration of an adhesion barrier substance (99.77) that is performed.

55.98   Removal of mechanical kidney

Description
The physician surgically removes an artificial mechanical device that performs the functions usually performed by the kidneys of patients in chronic kidney failure. An artificial kidney uses the principle of dialysis to purify the blood. Dialyzers use pure water to remove impurities and waste products from the patient's blood.

Coding Clarification
Artificial kidney or dialyzers are continually changing with advancements in bioengineering and nanotechnology toward developing a fully functioning artificial kidney for patients with end-stage renal disease.

Code separately any application or administration of an adhesion barrier substance (99.77) that is performed.

55.99   Other operations on kidney

Description
Code 55.99 is used to report other procedures of the kidneys that are not more precisely described by other codes in subcategory 55.9.

Coding Clarification
To report the removal of a pyelostomy or nephrostomy tube, see 97.61.

Code separately any application or administration of an adhesion barrier substance (99.77) that is performed.

Documentation Tip
Review the documentation for specific information regarding the procedure prior to final code selection in order to avoid improper use of the "not otherwise specified" code and to ensure accurate code assignment.

---

56   Operations on ureter

Description
Included under category 56 are codes for transurethral removal of obstruction, incisions, diagnostic procedures, excisions, ileostomy, anastomosis, repairs, and other operations on the ureter and renal pelvis. Subcategory 56.3 (diagnostic procedures on the ureter) includes codes for closed and open biopsy.

Coding Clarification
For all codes within category 56, code also any application or administration of an adhesion barrier substance (99.77).

Documentation Tip
Ureteral obstructions (e.g., blood clots, calculus, foreign body) may be removed transurethrally or by incision. Choose the most appropriate code for the method.

Different than endoscopic procedures classified elsewhere, a closed endoscopic biopsy of the ureter has two codes. It will be necessary to check the operative report to determine the type of closed biopsy prior to code selection.

56.0   Transurethral removal of obstruction from ureter and renal pelvis

Description
The physician removes an obstruction such as a blood clot, calculus, or foreign body from the ureter or renal pelvis without an incision using a tube inserted through the urethra to the ureter. The physician examines the urinary collecting system with endoscopes passed through the urethra into the bladder (cystourethroscope), ureter (ureteroscope), and renal pelvis (pyeloscope), and removes or manipulates a stone (calculus). To extract or manipulate a calculus, the physician passes a stone basket through an endoscope. The physician inserts a ureteral catheter and removes the endoscopes.

Coding Clarification
Use 56.0 for transurethral ureteroscopic lithotripsy using high-energy shock waves.

Assign 56.0 for transurethral ureteroscopic lithotripsy using a laser to break up the stone(s).

Assign 56.0 and 59.95 for transurethral ureteroscopic ultrasonic lithotripsy.

Code also any application or administration of an adhesion barrier substance (99.77).

Do not use 56.0 to report manipulation without removal of obstruction (59.8), that by incision (55.11, 56.2), or transurethral insertion of ureteral stent for passage of calculus (59.8).

Documentation Tip
Ureteral obstructions (e.g., blood clots, calculus, foreign body) may be removed transurethrally or by incision. Review the documentation carefully to ensure the appropriate code is assigned for the method used.

Coding Guidance
AHA: S-O, '86, 12; 1Q, '89, 1

56.1   Ureteral meatotomy

Description
The physician makes an incision into the ureteral meatus to enlarge the passage. The physician examines the urinary collecting system with a cystourethroscope passed through the urethra and bladder, and makes an incision in the opening of the ureter(s) into the bladder (ureteral meatotomy). The physician passes the cystourethroscope through the urethra into the bladder, and inserts a cutting instrument through the cystourethroscope to incise the opening of one or both ureters into the bladder. The physician removes the instrument and cystourethroscope.

Coding Clarification
Code also any application or administration of an adhesion barrier substance (99.77).

56.2   Ureterotomy

Description
Ureterotomy may be performed for drainage, exploration, or calculus removal. The physician makes an incision in the ureter (ureterotomy) to insert a catheter (stent) in the ureter. To access the ureter, the physician makes an incision in the skin of the flank, and cuts the muscles, fat, and fibrous membranes (fascia) overlying the ureter. The physician makes an incision in the ureter and sometimes places fine traction sutures at the edges of the incision. The physician inserts a slender rod or catheter into the ureter, sutures the incision, and performs layered closure.

Coding Clarification
A Davis ureterotomy is an open procedure involving a ureteral incision and intubation for multiple strictures below the ureteropelvic junction.

Code also any application or administration of an adhesion barrier substance (99.77).

Code 56.2 excludes cutting of ureterovesical orifice (56.1), removal of calculus without incision (56.0), transurethral insertion of ureteral stent for passage of calculus (59.8), and urinary diversion (56.51-56.79).

Coding Guidance
AHA: S-O, '86, 10

56.3   Diagnostic procedures on ureter

Description
Subcategory 56.3 includes codes for open, closed percutaneous, and endoscopic biopsy of the ureter, ureteroscopy, and cystourethroscopy with ureteral biopsy.

56.31   Ureteroscopy

Description
Ureteroscopy is an endoscopy of the upper urinary tract in which the physician passes a ureteroscope through the urethra into the bladder and then into the ureter to perform diagnostic endoscopy or a variety of minimally invasive procedures.

Coding Clarification
Code also any application or administration of an adhesion barrier substance (99.77).

Ureteroscopy is commonly used as a diagnostic tool to evaluate an obstruction or investigate abnormal imaging findings localizing the source of positive urine culture or cytology results.

Therapeutic uses of ureteroscopy include endoscopic lithotripsy (treating stones), treatment of upper urinary tract strictures, and ureteropelvic junction obstructions.

56.32   Closed percutaneous biopsy of ureter

Description
Percutaneous biopsy is performed under imaging guidance used to insert a small needle, usually 21 gauge, into the tissue. For a percutaneous biopsy, the physician may use a local anesthetic, biopsy needle, and radiologic guidance to collect the sample tissue. The physician may need multiple passes to collect the samples.

Coding Clarification
In a percutaneous biopsy, a needle is passed into the tissue and the sample is removed through the needle.

In an open biopsy, an incision is made in the skin, the area to be biopsied exposed, and a tissue sample is taken.

Closed biopsy involves a much smaller incision than open biopsy, made to allow insertion of an endoscopic visualization device. To report endoscopic biopsy of the ureter, see 56.33.

56.33   Closed endoscopic biopsy of ureter

Description
The physician examines the urinary collection system with a cystourethroscope passed through the urethra and bladder, and extracts biopsy tissue from the ureter. The physician passes a cutting instrument through the endoscope to the suspect tissue and traps a specimen of tissue. The physician removes the instrument and cystourethroscope. The physician may flush (irrigate) or introduce by drops (instillate) a sterile saline solution to better view structures. The physician removes the cystourethroscope after examination.

● New Code   ▲ Revised Code   ▶◀ Revised Text   © 2010 Ingenix

Coding Clarification
Code 56.33 is used to report the following procedures:

- Cystourethroscopy with ureteral biopsy
- Transurethral biopsy of ureter
- Ureteral endoscopy with biopsy through ureterotomy
- Ureteroscopy with biopsy

Do not use 56.33 to report percutaneous biopsy of the ureter; see 56.32.

A closed biopsy is performed by aspiration through a hypodermic needle, percutaneous needle, or using a brush or bristle to collect cells endoscopically (through a flexible tube inserted into an orifice or through a small skin incision).

Closed biopsy involves a much smaller incision than open biopsy, made to allow insertion of an endoscopic visualization device. To report endoscopic biopsy of the ureter, see 56.33.

Documentation Tip
The technique used to obtain the tissue sample determines the biopsy code; review the documentation for specific information regarding the procedure prior to final code selection in order to ensure accurate code assignment.

56.34   Open biopsy of ureter

Description
In an open biopsy, an incision is made in the skin, the area to be biopsied exposed, and a tissue sample is taken.

Coding Clarification
Biopsies are typically classified as open or closed. A closed biopsy is performed by aspiration through a hypodermic needle, percutaneous needle, or using a brush or bristle to collect cells endoscopically (through a flexible tube inserted into an orifice or through a small skin incision).

Closed biopsy involves a much smaller incision than open biopsy, made to allow insertion of an endoscopic visualization device. To report endoscopic biopsy of the ureter, see 56.33.

Documentation Tip
The technique used to obtain the tissue determines the biopsy code assigned. Review the documentation for specific information regarding the procedure prior to final code selection in order to ensure accurate code assignment.

56.35   Endoscopy (cystoscopy) (looposcopy) of ileal conduit

Description
This code reports an endoscopic exam of a created opening between the ureters and one end of small intestine with the other end used to form an artificial opening.

Coding Clarification
In an ileal conduit procedure, the surgeon creates a new urinary passage by connecting the ileum to the ureter, which is then brought through an incision in the abdominal wall, creating a stoma to empty urine.

56.39   Other diagnostic procedures on ureter

Description
Code 56.39 is used to report other diagnostic procedures of the ureter that are not more precisely described by other codes in subcategory 56.3.

Coding Clarification
This code does not include microscopic examination of specimen from ureter (91.21-91.29).

Documentation Tip
Review the documentation for specific information regarding the procedure prior to final code selection in order to ensure accurate code assignment.

56.4   Ureterectomy

Description
Ureterectomies can be performed using an open or laparoscopic surgical technique. Endoscopic ureterectomy is a minimally invasive surgical technique in comparison to conventional open ureterectomy. Surgical procedures to restore patency to the ureter include ureterotomy, partial ureterectomy, and ureteral resection and anastomosis.

Coding Clarification
Subcategory 56.4 codes are not used to report fistulectomy (56.84) or nephroureterectomy (55.51-55.54).

In addition to the ureterectomy procedure, code also anastomosis other than end-to-end (56.51-56.79).

56.40   Ureterectomy, not otherwise specified

Description
Code 56.40 is used to report ureterectomy that is not more precisely described by other codes in subcategory 56.4 or when the documentation does not further specify the procedure.

Documentation Tip
Review the documentation for specific information regarding the procedure prior to final code selection in order to ensure accurate code assignment and

avoid improper use of the "not otherwise specified" code.

If documentation is unclear, the physician should be queried.

56.41   Partial ureterectomy

Description
Ureterotomy is a surgical incision of a ureter, often performed for removal of a ureteral lesion. Ureteral reimplantation requires removing much of the abnormal distal ureter and preserving the blood supply to the proximal ureter. The laparoscopic technique of ureteral reimplantation, which involves minimal tissue dissection, reduces the risks of open reimplantation. Endoscopic intravesical mobilization of the ureter and a ureteral reimplantation using monofilament sutures is performed under videoscopic guidance. The ureter is dissected free from the intestinal wall and mobilized into the lumen. After excision of the distal ureteral segment, the physician performs a new direct mucosa-to-mucosa reimplantation.

The physician may divide and reconnect the ureter to bypass a defect or obstruction. To access the ureter, the physician makes an incision in the skin of the abdomen and cuts the muscles, fat, and fibrous membranes (fascia) overlying the ureter. For the upper or middle third of the ureter, the physician usually makes an incision in the skin of the flank; to access the lower third of the ureter, the physician usually makes a curved lower quadrant incision. The physician ligates and dissects the ureter at the point of blockage, and surgically rejoins (anastomosis) the two ends, bypassing the obstructing point. To provide support during healing, the physician may insert a slender tube into the ureter. The physician inserts a drain tube and performs layered closure.

Coding Clarification
This code is not used to report a biopsy of the ureter; see 56.32-56.34.

Other procedures correctly reported by code 56.41 include:

- Excision of ureterocele
- Excision of ureteral stricture
- Shortening of the ureter (with reimplantation)
- Ureterocelectomy
- Lumbar ureteroureterostomy
- Ureteroureterostomy resection with end-to-end anastomosis
- Spatulated ureteroureterostomy

56.42   Total ureterectomy

Description
To access the ureter, the physician makes an incision in the skin of the abdomen, perineum, and/or vagina. The physician cuts the muscles, fat, and fibrous membranes (fascia) overlying the ureter. After mobilizing the bladder and ureter, the physician ligates, dissects, and removes the ureter. The physician places a drain tube at the site of the incision and performs layered closure.

Coding Clarification
Ureterectomies can be performed using an open or laparoscopic (minimally-invasive) surgical technique.

56.5   Cutaneous uretero-ileostomy

Description
In cutaneous ureteroileostomy, the surgeon creates a new urinary passage by connecting the terminal section of the small intestine (ileum) to the ureter, which is then brought through an incision in the abdominal wall, creating a stoma for direct emptying of urine. In ureterointestinal anastomosis for internal urinary diversion, the ureter is connected to a segment of small intestine to divert urine flow. The urinary diversion is completely internal with no cutaneous fistula.

56.51   Formation of cutaneous uretero-ileostomy

Description
This procedure involves the creation of a urinary passage by connecting the terminal end of the small intestine to the ureter, which is connected to an opening through the abdominal wall. In an ileal conduit, the surgeon creates a new urinary passage by connecting the ileum to the ureter, which is then brought through an incision in the abdominal wall, creating a stoma to empty urine.

Coding Clarification
Code 56.51 is used to report the following procedures:

- Construction of ileal conduit
- External ureteral ileostomy
- Formation of open ileal bladder
- Ileal loop operation
- Ileoureterostomy (Bricker's) (ileal bladder)
- Transplantation of ureter into ileum with external diversion

This code is not used to report closed ileal bladder (57.87) or the replacement of ureteral defect by ileal segment (56.89).

● New Code   ▲ Revised Code   ▶◀ Revised Text   © 2010 Ingenix

55-59

56.52   Revision of cutaneous uretero-ileostomy

Description
The physician revises a surgical opening between the skin and ureter, bladder, or colon segment. The physician removes the sutures securing the anastomosis to the skin and revises the anastomosis. The physician may make a midline incision in the skin of the abdomen to access the urinary tract. In a separately reportable procedure, the physician may repair a defect in surrounding fibrous membranes (fascia) and/or a rupture (hernia) in ureteral tissues.

Coding Clarification
Patients with ileal conduits may develop upper urinary tract obstruction; treatment consists of removal of the conduit and replacement by a new ileal conduit or a continent reservoir.

Coding Guidance
AHA: 4Q, '88, 7; 3Q, '96, 15

56.6   Other external urinary diversion

Coding Clarification
In cutaneous ureteroileostomy, the surgeon creates a new urinary passage by connecting the terminal section of the small intestine (ileum) to the ureter, which is then brought through an incision in the abdominal wall, creating a stoma for direct emptying of urine.

In ureterointestinal anastomosis for internal urinary diversion, the ureter is connected to a segment of small intestine to divert urine flow. The urinary diversion is completely internal with no cutaneous fistula.

56.61   Formation of other cutaneous ureterostomy

Description
The physician connects the ureter to the skin for urinary drainage. To access the ureter, the physician makes a midline incision in the skin of the abdomen and cuts the corresponding muscles, fat, and fibrous membranes (fascia). The physician ligates the distal ureter and brings the proximal end to the skin. The physician splits the end of the ureter and sutures it to the skin with a double Z-plasty to prevent the ureter from narrowing. To provide support during healing, the physician may insert a slender tube into the ureter. The physician inserts a drain tube and performs layered closure.

Coding Clarification
Code 56.61 is used to report cutaneous ureterostomy that is not more precisely described by other codes in subcategory 56.6, such as anastomosis of the ureter to the skin, or when the documentation does not further specify the procedure.

Documentation Tip
Review the documentation for specific information regarding the procedure prior to final code selection in order to ensure accurate code assignment and avoid improper use of the "not otherwise specified" code.

56.62   Revision of other cutaneous ureterostomy

Description
The physician revises any surgical opening (anastomosis) between the skin and ureter, bladder, or colon segment. The physician removes the sutures securing the anastomosis to the skin and revises the anastomosis. The physician may make a midline incision in the skin of the abdomen to access the urinary tract.

Coding Clarification
To report nonoperative removal of a ureterostomy tube, see 97.62.

56.7   Other anastomosis or bypass of ureter

Coding Clarification
This subcategory excludes ureteropyelostomy (55.86).

56.71   Urinary diversion to intestine

Description
The physician connects the ureter to a segment of intestine to divert urine flow. To access the ureter and intestine, the physician makes an incision in the skin of the abdomen and cuts the corresponding muscles, fat, and fibrous membranes (fascia). The physician dissects the ureter, makes small incisions in the intestine segment, and surgically connects (anastomosis) the ureter to the intestine. To provide support during healing, the physician may insert a slender tube into the ureter. The physician inserts a drain tube and performs layered closure.

Coding Clarification
Code also any synchronous colostomy (46.10-46.13).

This code is also reported when the documentation does not further specify the internal urinary diversion procedure.

To report external ureteral ileostomy, see 56.51.

56.72   Revision of ureterointestinal anastomosis

Description
The physician revises a surgical opening (anastomosis) between the ureter and the bladder or colon segment. The physician removes the sutures securing the anastomosis to the skin and revises the anastomosis. The physician may make a midline incision in the skin of the abdomen to access the urinary tract.

55-59

Coding Clarification
Do not use 56.72 to report the revision of an external ureteral ileostomy; see 56.52.

56.73   Nephrocystanastomosis, not otherwise specified

Description
Code 56.73 is used to report kidney to bladder connection procedures that are not more precisely described by other codes in subcategory 56.7, or when the documentation does not further specify the procedure.

Documentation Tip
Review the documentation for specific information regarding the procedure prior to final code selection to avoid improper use of the "not otherwise specified" code.

56.74   Ureteroneocystostomy

Description
The physician removes diseased or damaged bladder tissue close to the ureteral orifice, and reimplants ureter(s) into the bladder (ureteroneocystostomy). To access the bladder and ureters, the physician makes a midline incision in the skin of the abdomen and cuts the corresponding muscles, fat, and fibrous membranes (fascia). The physician mobilizes the bladder, ureter(s), and the major vesical blood vessels, and may incise the bladder wall to access the diseased or damaged bladder tissue. The physician removes the diseased or damaged bladder tissue, requiring removal of the ureteral orifice and/or ureteral division. The physician brings the cut end of the ureter through a stab wound in the bladder and sutures the ureter to the bladder. To provide support during healing, the physician inserts a ureteral catheter, bringing the tube end out through the urethra or bladder incision. The physician inserts a drain tube and performs layered closure.

Coding Clarification
Use 56.74 to report replacement of the ureter with a bladder flap and implantation of the ureter into the bladder (ureterovesical anastomosis).

56.75   Transureteroureterostomy

Description
The physician divides and connects a diseased or obstructed ureter to the other ureter. To access the ureters, the physician usually makes a midline incision in the skin of the abdomen and cuts the muscles, fat, and fibrous membranes (fascia) overlying the ureters. The physician ligates and dissects the ureter at the point of disease or blockage and surgically attaches (anastomosis) the end of the usable ureteric portion to the other ureter. To

provide support during healing, the physician may insert a slender tube into the ureter. The physician inserts a drain tube and performs layered closure.

Coding Clarification
To report a ureteroureterostomy associated with partial resection, see 56.41.

56.79   Other anastomosis or bypass of ureter

Description
Code 56.79 is used to report other ureteral anastomosis or bypass procedures that are not more precisely described by other codes in subcategory 56.7, or when the documentation does not further specify the procedure.

Coding Clarification
Assign 56.79 for the Camay procedure used for creation of an ileal conduit without external urinary diversion.

The following procedures are also correctly reported with 56.79:

- Ureteral anastomosis not elsewhere classified
- Drainage of ureter by anastomosis not elsewhere classified

Documentation Tip
Review the documentation for specific information regarding the procedure prior to final code selection in order to ensure accurate code assignment and avoid improper use of the "not otherwise specified" code.

56.8   Repair of ureter

Description
Fourth-digit subclassifications describe various repair procedures of the ureter such as laceration suturing, closure of ureterostomy and fistulas, and graft procedures.

Coding Clarification
Repair of ureter, subcategory 56.8, includes a code for lysis of intraluminal adhesions of the ureter, 56.81. However, the codes for freeing of adhesions of the periureteral or perirenal area are located under subcategory 59.0.

Documentation Tip
Review the documentation for specific information regarding the procedure prior to final code selection in order to ensure accurate code assignment

56.81   Lysis of intraluminal adhesions of ureter

Description
The physician performs a destruction procedure on adhesions within the ureteral cavity. An incision is made and the dissection, including lysis, is performed and fibrous tissue removed. The incision is closed in layers.

Coding Clarification
Laparoscopic ureterolysis is often performed for idiopathic retroperitoneal fibrosis.

Do not use 56.81 to report lysis of periureteral adhesions or ureterolysis. (See codes 59.02-59.03.)

56.82   Suture of laceration of ureter
Description
The physician sutures a wound or defect in the ureter. To access the ureter, the physician makes an incision in the skin and cuts the muscles, fat, and fibrous membranes (fascia) overlying the ureter. For the upper or middle third of the ureter, the physician usually makes an incision in the skin of the flank; to access the lower third of the ureter, the physician usually makes a curved lower quadrant incision. The physician uses sutures to close or surgically fixate a ureteral wound or defect. To provide support during healing, the physician may insert a slender tube into the ureter. The physician inserts a drain tube and performs layered closure.

56.83   Closure of ureterostomy
Description
The physician restores continuity of a ureter through which urine flow was previously diverted. To access the ureter, the physician usually reopens the original ureteral diversion incision and cuts the corresponding muscles, fat, and fibrous membranes (fascia). The physician reverses the diversion by removing sutures connecting the ureter and colon, colon segment, and/or skin. The physician closes the opening in the skin used for the diversionary anastomosis. To restore ureteral continuity, the physician reconnects the upper and lower ureter segments, connects the ureter to the other ureter (ureteroureterostomy), or reimplants the ureter into the bladder (ureteroneocystostomy). To provide support during healing, the physician inserts a slender tube into the ureter. The physician inserts a drain tube and performs layered closure.

56.84   Closure of other fistula of ureter
Description
The physician closes an abnormal opening (fistula) between the skin and the ureter (ureterocutaneous). After excising the fistula, the physician sutures the clean percutaneous tissues together to create a smooth surface.

56.85   Ureteropexy
Description
A ureteropexy is the fixation of the urethra and bladder typically performed as treatment for stress incontinence. The physician performs a surgical suspension of the urethra from the posterior surface of the pubic symphysis.

Coding Clarification
Peritoneal flap ureteropexy is also performed for idiopathic retroperitoneal fibrosis.

56.86   Removal of ligature from ureter
Description
The physician removes a thread, wire, or constricting band (ligature) placed on the ureter during a previous operative session. To access the ureter, the physician usually reopens the incision used for the previous operative session. After removing the ligature(s) from the ureter, the physician places a drain tube, bringing it out through a separate stab incision in the skin, and performs layered closure.

56.89   Other repair of ureter
Description
Code 56.89 is used to report other repair procedures of the ureter that are not more precisely described by other codes in subcategory 56.8, including ureteroplication and grafting.

In one example, the physician performs replacement of the ureter with the ileal segment implanted into the bladder and ureter replacement with the terminal end of the small intestine. The physician replaces part or all of the ureter with a segment of intestine. To access the ureters and intestine, the physician makes a midline incision in the skin of the abdomen and cuts the corresponding muscles, fat, and fibrous membranes (fascia). After dissecting an isolated segment of intestine, the physician reconnects (anastomosis) the divided intestine to restore bowel continuity. The physician dissects and removes the diseased or defective ureteral segment, replacing it with the intestine segment. To provide support during healing, the physician may insert a slender tube into the ureter. The physician inserts a drain tube and performs layered closure.

When performing ureteroplasty, the physician uses plastic surgery to correct an obstruction or defect in the ureter. To access the ureter, the physician makes an incision in the skin and cuts the muscles, fat, and fibrous membranes (fascia) overlying the ureter. For the upper or middle third of the ureter, the physician usually makes an incision in the skin of the flank; to access the lower third of the ureter, the physician usually makes a curved lower quadrant incision. The physician inserts a catheter into the ureter to the point of obstruction. The balloon is inflated, sometimes using repeated inflation with increasing diameter of the catheter. The physician incises, trims, and shapes the ureter, using absorbable sutures or soft rubber drains for

55-59

traction. The physician may insert a slender tube into the ureter to provide support during healing. The physician places a drain tube, bringing it out through a separate stab incision in the skin, and performs layered closure.

Coding Clarification

When reporting replacement of the ureter with ileal segment implanted into the bladder, two codes are required: 56.89 and 45.51.

An understanding of the following terms may aid in code selection:

- **Graft of ureter:** Tissue from another site for graft replacement or repair of the ureter.

- **Ureteroplication:** Creation of tucks in the ureter.

56.9   Other operations on ureter

Description

Codes in subcategory 56.9 are used to report other procedures of the ureter that are not more precisely described by other codes in category 56.

Documentation Tip

Review the documentation for specific information regarding the procedure prior to final code selection in order to ensure accurate code assignment.

56.91   Dilation of ureteral meatus

Description

Urethral dilation is performed to treat urethral strictures and meatal stenosis. A fine probe is passed through followed by progressively larger diameter dilators that are attached to the distal end of the probe and passed to dilate the stricture until urine stream becomes adequate. The procedure is usually performed over several sessions.

Coding Clarification

An alternate technique for ureteral dilation is balloon dilatation.

56.92   Implantation of electronic ureteral stimulator

Description

An electronic stimulator implant consists of a tonicity signal generator, a self-contained power supply, an electrode with one end for connecting to implant, and a second end for connecting to a sacral nerve, for transmitting said tonicity and voiding signals to the nerve. The tonicity signal generator is manually activated by the patient. When activated, the voiding signal is generated, which activates detrusor muscle contraction, causing bladder voiding.

Coding Clarification

An electronic stimulator implant is used to treat different forms of lower urinary tract dysfunction such as bladder voiding and bladder hyperreflexia.

Patients with spinal cord injury often cannot empty their bladder voluntarily; this can be restored by intermittent electrical stimulation of the sacral nerve roots to cause bladder contraction.

56.93   Replacement of electronic ureteral stimulator

Description

The physician removes and replaces a thin lead wire with a small electrode tip that was surgically implanted near the sacral nerve to control voiding function. An electronic stimulator implant consists of a tonicity signal generator, a self-contained power supply, an electrode with one end for connecting to implant, and a second end for connecting to a sacral nerve, for transmitting said tonicity and voiding signals to the nerve. The tonicity signal generator is manually activated by the patient. When activated, the voiding signal is generated, which activates detrusor muscle contraction, causing bladder voiding.

56.94   Removal of electronic ureteral stimulator

Description

The physician removes a thin lead wire with a small electrode tip that was surgically implanted near the sacral nerve to control voiding function. An electronic stimulator implant consists of a tonicity signal generator, a self-contained power supply, an electrode with one end for connecting to implant, and a second end for connecting to a sacral nerve, for transmitting said tonicity and voiding signals to the nerve. The tonicity signal generator is manually activated by the patient. When activated, the voiding signal is generated, which activates detrusor muscle contraction, causing bladder voiding.

Coding Clarification

To report removal with synchronous replacement, see 56.93.

56.95   Ligation of ureter

Description

The physician places a thread, wire, or constricting band (ligature) placed on the ureter. To access the ureter, the physician usually makes an incision. After placing the ligature(s) on the ureter, the physician places a drain tube, bringing it out through a separate stab incision in the skin, and performs layered closure.

56.99   Other operations on ureter

Description

Code 56.99 is used to report procedures of the ureter that are not more precisely described by other codes.

● New Code   ▲ Revised Code   ▶◀ Revised Text   © 2010 Ingenix

Coding Clarification
This code is not used to report removal of a ureterostomy tube and ureteral catheter (97.62) or ureteral catheterization (59.8).

Documentation Tip
Review the documentation for specific information regarding the procedure prior to final code selection in order to ensure accurate code assignment.

57 Operations on urinary bladder

Description
Category 57 lists codes for transurethral procedures, incisions, diagnostic procedures, excisions, repairs, and other operations on the urinary bladder. Operations on the perivesical tissue and ureterovesical orifice are classified elsewhere.

Coding Clarification
For all codes within category 57, code also any application or administration of an adhesion barrier substance (99.77).

Category 57 excludes perivesical tissue (59.11-59.29, 59.91-59.92) and ureterovesical orifice (56.0-56.99).

Documentation Tip
Different codes are available if the surgeon documents a transurethral approach vs. that by incision. Check the operative report to determine the method used by the surgeon.

Sphincterotomy of the bladder is also referred to as the release of the bladder neck contracture by radial incision or incision of the bladder neck at 5 o'clock, 7 o'clock, and 12 o'clock.

57.0 Transurethral clearance of bladder

Description
The physician performs drainage of the bladder without making an incision via a device inserted through the urethra to cleanse the bladder.

When performing a Bigelow operation, the physician uses ultrasound to crush or fragment a calculus. The physician examines the urinary collecting system with a cystourethroscope passed through the urethra and bladder to remove a foreign body. The physician inserts an instrument that generates shock waves through the cystourethroscope. The physician crushes the calculus in the bladder (litholapaxy) and washes out the fragments through a catheter. Post-shockwave fragments too large to be easily suctioned may require manual crushing.

Alternately, the physician may examine the urinary collecting system with a cystourethroscope passed through the urethra and bladder, and removes a foreign body or calculus from the bladder. The physician passes the cystourethroscope through the

urethra into the bladder, and inserts an instrument through the cystourethroscope to extract a foreign body or calculus. The physician removes the instrument and cystourethroscope.

Coding Clarification
Use 57.0 to report the removal of a blood clot, calculus, or foreign body from the bladder without an incision.

To report clearance of the bladder by incision, see 57.19.

Use 57.0 and 59.95 for ultrasound destruction of bladder calculi (lithotripsy).

Documentation Tip
The medical record may contain the following verbiage to describe procedures that are correctly reported with 57.0:

- Aspiration of bladder via catheter
- Aspiration of bladder calculus
- Bigelow operation
- Litholapaxy
- Crushing of urinary bladder calculus
- Cystolitholapaxy
- Nonincisional bladder drainage
- Lithotripsy of bladder
- Nonincisional removal of bladder blood clot
- Nonincisional removal of bladder calculus
- Nonincisional removal of foreign body of bladder

Coding Guidance
AHA: S-O, '86, 11

57.1 Cystotomy and cystostomy

Description
A cystotomy is a surgical incision of the bladder, while a cystostomy is the surgical creation of an opening into the bladder.

The physician passes the cystourethroscope through the urethra into the bladder, and inserts an instrument through the cystourethroscope to extract a foreign body, calculus, or ureteral stent from the urethra or bladder. The physician removes the instrument and cystourethroscope.

Coding Clarification
Do not report cystotomy and cystostomy when used as operative approaches.

57.11 Percutaneous aspiration of bladder

Description
The physician inserts a needle through the skin into the bladder to withdraw urine. Alternately, the physician inserts a trocar or intracatheter through the skin into the bladder. In an alternate technique,

55-59

a suprapubic catheter is placed into the bladder. This procedure may also be performed after the abdomen has been surgically incised.

57.12 Lysis of intraluminal adhesions with incision into bladder

Description
This code reports the incisional division of adhesions that are located within the wall (lumen) of the bladder, including the bladder neck.

If an open abdominal surgery (laparotomy) is done, the patient receives aLysis of intraluminal adhesions with incision into bladder

general anesthetic, and a large incision is made in the abdomen to allow direct access to the bladder.

Coding Clarification
This procedure excludes transurethral lysis of intraluminal adhesions (57.41).

57.17 Percutaneous cystostomy

Description
A percutaneous cystostomy is generally performed when it is not possible to insert a catheter or tube into the bladder through the urethra. The catheter is inserted into the urinary bladder through the lower abdominal wall. The procedure involves numbing the skin of the lower abdomen with a local anesthetic agent and inserting first a needle and then a catheter from the skin into the bladder.

Coding Clarification
An understanding of the following terms may aid in code selection:

- **Closed cystostomy:** Incision through the body wall into the bladder to insert a tube.

- **Percutaneous (closed) suprapubic cystostomy:** Incision above the pubic arch, through the body wall, and into the bladder to insert a tube.

This code is not used to report removal of a cystostomy tube (97.63) and replacement of a cystostomy tube (59.94).

57.18 Other suprapubic cystostomy

Description
Code 57.18 is used to report suprapubic cystostomy procedures that are not more precisely described by other codes in subcategory 57.1.

For example, the physician inserts a needle, trocar, or intracatheter through the skin into the bladder to withdraw urine, or a suprapubic catheter is placed into the bladder. This procedure may also be performed after the abdomen has been surgically incised.

In a Franco operation, the physician creates an opening into the bladder (cystostomy) through an incision in the bladder (cystotomy). To access the bladder, the physician makes an incision in the skin of the lower abdomen and cuts the corresponding muscles, fat, and fibrous membranes (fascia). The physician makes a small incision and inserts a catheter (cystostomy tube) into the bladder, passing the tube through a stab incision in the skin of the abdomen. After closing the cystotomy, the physician may insert a drain tube, bringing it out through a separate stab incision, and performs layered closure with absorbable sutures.

Coding Clarification
This procedure excludes percutaneous cystostomy (57.17), removal of a cystostomy tube (97.63), and replacement of a cystostomy tube (59.94).

Documentation Tip
Review the documentation for specific information regarding the procedure prior to final code selection in order to ensure accurate code assignment.

The medical record may contain the following verbiage to describe procedures correctly reported with 57.18:

- Suprapubic catheterization (not elsewhere classified)

- Open suprapubic cystostomy

- Franco operation

- Suprapubic drainage of the bladder (not elsewhere classified)

- Fistula formation, bladder to skin

- Suprapubic incision of the bladder

57.19 Other cystotomy

Description
Code 57.19 reports cystotomy procedures other than those more specifically described by other codes within subcategory 57.1. For example, when performing a cystolithotomy, the physician makes an incision in the bladder to remove a calculus. To access the bladder, the physician makes an incision in the skin of the lower abdomen and cuts the corresponding muscles, fat, and fibrous membranes (fascia). The physician performs a cystotomy, isolates the calculus, and removes it. The bladder neck is not excised. After examining the bladder for other defects, the physician sutures the incision and performs layered closure using absorbable sutures, inserting a drain tube through a stab incision in the skin.

Coding Clarification
A cystotomy is a surgical incision of the bladder, while a cystostomy is the surgical creation of an opening into the bladder.

Code 57.19 is also used to report a cystolithotomy.

Assign 57.19 and 59.95 for disruption of bladder stone(s) by ultrasonic energy, cystotomy approach.

This code excludes percutaneous cystostomy (57.17) and suprapubic cystostomy (57.18).

Documentation Tip
Review the documentation for specific information regarding the procedure prior to final code selection in order to ensure accurate code assignment.

The medical record may contain the following verbiage to describe procedures that are correctly reported with 57.19:

- Cystolithotomy
- Open cystotomy
- Incisional bladder exploration
- Kock pouch procedure with removal of calculus
- Incisional bladder litholapaxy
- Lithotomy of bladder
- Incisional removal of bladder blood clot
- Incisional removal of bladder calculus
- Incisional removal of bladder foreign body
- Vesicolithotomy

Coding Guidance
   AHA: S-O, '86, 11; 4Q, '95, 73

57.2   Vesicostomy

Description
Vesicostomy is the creation of a permanent opening from bladder to skin using a bladder flap. Vesicostomy is usually considered synonymous with cystostomy. This classification specifically includes cutaneous vesicostomy, which is the surgical creation of an opening from the bladder to the skin.

Coding Clarification
This procedure excludes percutaneous cystostomy (57.17) and suprapubic cystostomy (57.18).

57.21   Vesicostomy

Description
The physician connects the bladder to the skin (cutaneous vesicostomy) for direct urinary drainage. The Blocksom technique is usually performed on newborns. To access the bladder, the physician makes a suprapubic incision in the abdomen and cuts the corresponding muscles, fat, and fibrous membranes (fascia). After securing the bladder dome to the rectus fascia, the physician incises the bladder to create an opening that is sutured to a small incision in the skin. To support the opening during healing, the physician inserts a catheter or stent into the bladder. The physician inserts a drain

tube and performs layered closure. In adults, the Lapides technique passes a flap of bladder beneath the skin to replace a retracted section of abdominal skin. The abdominal skin is passed below the abdominal surface and sutured to the opening in the bladder, making a long-term tubular passage for urine. A catheter is placed through the stoma for two or three days.

When performing a cutaneous appendicovesicostomy, the physician connects a segment of cecum colon (vermiform appendix) to the bladder to directly divert urine flow through an opening in the skin. To access the bladder and cecum colon, the physician makes a midline incision in the skin of the abdomen and cuts the corresponding muscles, fat, and fibrous membranes (fascia). After dissecting vermiform appendix, the physician sutures the colon to restore bowel continuity. The physician makes an incision in the bladder and surgically connects the proximal end of the vermiform appendix to the bladder. The physician brings the distal end of vermiform appendix through an incision in the skin of the abdomen to establish an opening (stoma) for direct emptying of urine. The physician inserts a drain tube and performs layered closure.

Documentation Tip
A cutaneous appendicovesicostomy may also be documented in the medical record as a Mitrofanoff procedure.

57.22   Revision or closure of vesicostomy

Description
The physician revises a previously performed procedure that connects the bladder to the skin (cutaneous vesicostomy) for direct urinary drainage. To access the bladder, the physician makes a suprapubic incision in the abdomen and cuts the corresponding muscles, fat, and fibrous membranes (fascia).

Coding Clarification
Do not use 57.22 to report closure of a cystostomy; see 57.82.

57.3   Diagnostic procedures on bladder

Description
Subcategory 57.3 includes codes for various diagnostic procedures on the bladder, such as transurethral cystoscopy, cystoscopy performed through an artificial stoma, bladder biopsy, and other diagnostic procedures.

Documentation Tip
Review the documentation for specific information regarding the procedure prior to final code selection in order to ensure accurate code assignment.

55-59

57.31   Cystoscopy through artificial stoma

Description
The physician performs a cystoscopy through an artificial opening created to empty urine (stoma). The physician inserts an instrument called a cystoscope through the stoma and into the bladder.

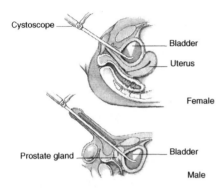

57.32   Other cystoscopy

Description
Through the urethra, the physician performs a transurethral cystoscopic urinary tract evaluation. The cystourethroscope is introduced into the meatus and the urethra is inspected. Instruments may be inserted through the cystourethroscope if needed.

Coding Clarification
This procedure excludes cystourethroscopy with ureteral biopsy (56.33), retrograde pyelogram (87.74), and that for control of hemorrhage (postoperative) of the bladder (57.93) and prostate (60.94).

Do not assign 57.32 when the cystoscopy is used as an operative approach in the diagnosis and treatment of a urinary condition.

Coding Guidance
    AHA: 1Q, '01, 14

57.33   Closed (transurethral) biopsy of bladder

Description
The physician examines the urinary collecting system with a cystourethroscope passed through the urethra and bladder, and extracts biopsy tissue from the bladder or urethra. To do so, the physician passes a cutting instrument through the endoscope to the suspect tissue and traps a specimen of tissue. Multiple samples may be collected. The physician removes the instrument and cystourethroscope.

57.34   Open biopsy of bladder

Description
In an open biopsy, an incision is made in the skin, the bladder is exposed, and a tissue sample is taken.

Coding Clarification
An open biopsy is the removal of tissue by way of an incision. The incision is inherent to an open biopsy, so an additional code for the incision is unnecessary.

Coding Guidance
    AHA: 2Q, '05, 12

57.39   Other diagnostic procedures on bladder

Description
Code 57.39 is used to report diagnostic procedures on the bladder that are not more precisely described by other codes in subcategory 57.3.

Coding Clarification
This procedure excludes cystogram NEC (87.77), microscopic examination of specimen from bladder (91.31-91.39), retrograde cystourethrogram (87.76), and therapeutic distention of bladder (96.25).

Documentation Tip
Review the documentation for specific information regarding the procedure prior to final code selection in order to ensure accurate code assignment.

This procedure may also be documented as a diagnostic procedure of the vesical.

57.4   Transurethral excision or destruction of bladder tissue

Description
Subcategory 57.4 includes destruction procedures of bladder tissue using an instrument inserted through the urethra.

57.41   Transurethral lysis of intraluminal adhesions

Description
The physician examines the urinary collecting system with a cystourethroscope passed through the urethra and bladder. The physician passes a cutting instrument through the endoscope to dissect the adhesion. The physician removes the instrument and cystourethroscope.

57.49   Other transurethral excision or destruction of lesion or tissue of bladder

Description
The physician examines the urinary collecting system with a cystourethroscope passed through the urethra and bladder, and destroys or removes a tumor, lesion, or other tissue of the bladder by electric current (fulguration) or excision. The physician may also use liquid nitrogen or carbon dioxide (cryosurgery) or lasers to destroy lesions. The physician removes the instruments and cystourethroscope.

Coding Clarification
The following transurethral procedures are correctly reported with 57.49:

- Coagulation or electrocoagulation of urethrovesical junction lesion
- Bladder curettage
- Diverticulectomy of bladder
- Cystoscopic electrocoagulation
- Endoscopic resection of bladder lesion

This code excludes transurethral biopsy of bladder (57.33) and transurethral fistulectomy (57.83-57.84).

57.5 Other excision or destruction of bladder tissue

Description
Fourth-digit subclassifications describe various other excision and destruction procedures of the bladder.

Coding Clarification
This procedure excludes that with transurethral approach (57.41-57.49).

Documentation Tip
Review the documentation for specific information regarding the procedure prior to final code selection in order to ensure accurate code assignment

57.51 Excision of urachus

Description
The urachus is a remnant from fetal development that persists throughout life as the median umbilical ligament. Anomalies may develop in the urachus, such as a sinus at the inferior end, or even a fully patent lumen that leaks urine from the umbilicus.

The physician excises a urachal bladder sinus. The physician removes a cyst or dilated urachus (the remnant of bladder development that attaches from bladder to umbilicus). To access the urachus, the physician makes an incision in the skin of the lower abdomen through the umbilicus and cuts the corresponding muscles, fat, and fibrous membranes (fascia). After isolating the urachus with a clamp, the physician excises the urachal cyst or sinus and a small cuff of the bladder. The physician sutures the bladder and removes the urachal tissue, leaving the navel intact. The physician may also repair a rupture (hernia) of tissue in the umbilicus. After inserting a drain tube and urethral catheter, the physician performs layered closure.

Coding Clarification
This code excludes excision of a urachal cyst of the abdominal wall; see 54.3.

57.59 Open excision or destruction of other lesion or tissue of bladder

Description
A suprapubic excision of bladder lesion involves an incision in the bladder to remove a tumor of the bladder. To access the bladder, the physician makes an incision in the skin of the lower abdomen and cuts the corresponding muscles, fat, and fibrous membranes (fascia). The bladder is incised (cystotomy). After removing the tumor and surrounding diseased vesical tissue, the physician inserts a drain tube and performs layered closure. Endometrectomy of bladder is performed using laparoscopic diagnostics and laser removal of the tissue to restore normal function to reproductive tissue.

Coding Clarification
This procedure excludes biopsy of bladder (57.33-57.34) and fistulectomy of bladder (57.83-57.84).

An understanding of the following terms may aid in code selection:

- **Endometrectomy of bladder:** Removal of inner lining.

- **Suprapubic excision of bladder lesion:** Removal of lesion by excision above the suprapubic bone arch.

57.6 Partial cystectomy

Description
The physician removes a portion of diseased or damaged bladder tissue. To access the bladder, the physician makes an incision in the skin above the pubic bone and cuts the corresponding muscles, fat, and fibrous membranes (fascia). The physician mobilizes the bladder and the major vesical blood vessels and incises the bladder wall to access the diseased or damaged bladder tissue. After removing the tissue, the physician inserts catheters into the bladder and urethra and sutures the bladder tissues. The physician performs layered closure and inserts a drain tube, bringing it out through a separate stab incision in the skin. The cystectomy procedure may be complicated because of prior administration of radiation, a previous surgery, or difficult access to the diseased or damaged bladder tissue.

Coding Clarification
Code 57.6 is used to report excision of the bladder dome, trigonectomy, and wedge resection of the bladder.

57.7 Total cystectomy

Description
The physician removes the bladder (cystectomy). To access the bladder, the physician makes an incision in the skin of the lower abdomen and cuts the corresponding muscles, fat, and fibrous membranes (fascia). The physician dissects and ties (ligates) the hypogastric and vesical vessels, and severs the

55-59

bladder from the urethra, rectum, surrounding peritoneum, vas deferens, and prostate (if applicable). After removing the bladder and controlling bleeding, the physician inserts drain tubes and performs layered closure.

Coding Clarification
Subcategory 57.7 includes total cystectomy with urethrectomy.

57.71   Radical cystectomy

Description
A radical cystectomy is a surgical procedure typically performed for the treatment of bladder cancer. The surgery involves an incision in the lower abdomen and removal of the bilateral pelvic lymph nodes, bladder, and, in some cases, the urethra. In men, the prostate gland and seminal vesicles are also removed and in women, the uterus and ovaries if present.

The physician removes the bladder (cystectomy). To access the bladder, the physician makes an incision in the skin of the lower abdomen and cuts the corresponding muscles, fat, and fibrous membranes (fascia). The physician dissects and ties (ligates) the hypogastric and vesical vessels, and severs the bladder from the urethra, rectum, surrounding peritoneum, vas deferens, and prostate (if applicable). Lymphadenectomy and urinary diversion may also be performed and are reported separately. After removing the bladder and controlling bleeding, the physician inserts drain tubes and performs layered closure.

When performing a pelvic exenteration on a male, the physician removes the bladder (cystectomy) and pelvic lymph nodes, and diverts urine by connecting the ureters to a ureteroileal conduit or sigmoid bladder with an opening into the skin. To access the bladder and ureters, the physician makes a midline incision in the skin of the abdomen and cuts the corresponding muscles, fat, and fibrous membranes (fascia). The physician dissects and ligates the hypogastric and vesical vessels, and severs the bladder from the ureters and urethra. Blunt dissection from adherent rectum, surrounding peritoneum, and vas deferens and prostate may be needed. The physician also removes external iliac, hypogastric, and obturator lymph nodes. After controlling bleeding, the physician diverts urine by connecting the ureters to a segment of ileal or sigmoid colon fashioned into a conduit or bladder, with an opening into the skin. The physician inserts a slender tube into each ureter. After completing the urinary diversion procedure, the physician inserts drain tubes and performs layered closure.

Coding Clarification
Code also any lymph node dissection (40.3, 40.5) or urinary diversion (56.51-56.79).

This procedure excludes that as part of pelvic exenteration in a female (68.8).

This procedure includes that as part of pelvic exenteration in a male.

Documentation Tip
An understanding of the following terms may aid in code selection:

*   **Pelvic exenteration in male:** Removal of bladder, prostate, seminal vesicles, and fat.

*   **Pelvic exenteration in female:** Removal of bladder, urethra, and fat.

57.79   Other total cystectomy

Description
The physician removes the bladder (cystectomy). To access the bladder, the physician makes an incision in the skin of the lower abdomen and cuts the corresponding muscles, fat, and fibrous membranes (fascia). In some case, the physician dissects and ties (ligates) the hypogastric and vesical vessels, and severs the bladder from the urethra, rectum, surrounding peritoneum, vas deferens, and prostate (if applicable). After removing the bladder and controlling bleeding, the physician inserts drain tubes and performs layered closure. In other cases, the physician bilaterally removes the pelvic lymph nodes.

57.8   Other repair of urinary bladder

Description
Fourth-digit subclassifications describe various repair procedures of the urinary bladder such as laceration suturing, closure of cystostomy and fistulas, and other reconstruction procedures.

Coding Clarification
Codes from this subcategory are not used to report repair of current obstetric laceration (75.61), cystocele (70.50-70.51), or when performed for stress incontinence (59.3-59.79).

Documentation Tip
Review the documentation for specific information regarding the procedure prior to final code selection in order to ensure accurate code assignment.

57.81   Suture of laceration of bladder

Description
The physician sutures a wound, injury, or rupture in the bladder. To access the bladder, urethra, and ureters, the physician makes an incision in the skin of the abdomen and cuts the corresponding muscles, fat, and fibrous membranes (fascia). To provide support during healing, the physician may insert a catheter through the urethra. The physician inserts a drain tube and performs layered closure. Constant irrigation is provided to help prevent infection. The

55-59

procedure may be complicated due to a previous surgery, congenital defect, or other reason.

Coding Clarification
Do not use 57.81 to report repair of a current obstetric laceration (75.61), cystocele (70.50-70.51), or when performed for stress incontinence (59.3-59.79).

57.82   Closure of cystostomy

Description
The physician closes an artificial opening into the bladder (cystostomy). To access the cystostomy, the physician uses the original incision creating the cystostomy or makes an incision in the skin of the lower abdomen. After removing the sutures securing the cystostomy tube to the skin and bladder, the physician removes the cystostomy tube and sutures the bladder musculature to repair the opening. The physician places a drain tube, bringing it out through a separate stab incision in the skin, and performs layered closure.

Documentation Tip
Review the documentation for specific information regarding the procedure prior to final code selection in order to ensure accurate code assignment.

57.83   Repair of fistula involving bladder and intestine

Description
The physician closes a connection between the small or large intestine and bladder (enterovesical fistula) by resecting a portion of the intestine or bladder. The physician makes an abdominal incision. Next, the enterovesical fistula is identified and divided. The connection of the fistula to the bladder is resected and the bladder is closed with sutures. The segment of intestine containing the fistula is resected and the ends are reapproximated. The incision is closed.

The physician closes a connection between the rectum and the bladder (rectovesical fistula). The physician makes an abdominal incision. The sigmoid colon and rectum are mobilized and the connection between the rectum and bladder is identified and divided. The fistulous openings in the rectum and bladder are debrided and closed with sutures.

Coding Clarification
Use 57.83 to report rectovesicovaginal fistulectomy and vesicosigmoidovaginal fistulectomy.

57.84   Repair of other fistula of bladder

Description
The physician excises a vesicouterine fistula, which is an abnormal opening between the uterus and the bladder, then sutures the clean tissues together, closing the resulting defect and creating a smooth surface. The procedure is done through the bladder

with a small abdominal incision or during a laparotomy. This procedure may also be performed concurrently with a hysterectomy, which is assigned a separate code.

Alternately, the physician excises a vesicovaginal fistula, which is an abnormal opening between the vagina and the bladder. The procedure is done through a vertical abdominal incision from just above the umbilicus to the pubic symphysis. The anterior bladder wall is opened and the bladder interior explored. The fistula is excised along with the surrounding tissue to assure preservation of only healthy tissue. The resulting defect is closed with layered sutures starting with the vaginal wall, then the bladder walls, and finally the abdominal incision. A catheter is left in the bladder to prevent distension of the bladder and tension to the sutured areas.

Coding Clarification
Use 57.84 to report these fistulectomy procedures:

- Urethroperineovesical
- Uterovesical
- Vaginovesical

Do not use this code to report vesicoureterovaginal fistulectomy (56.84).

57.85   Cystourethroplasty and plastic repair of bladder neck

Description
The physician uses plastic surgery to correct an obstruction or defect in the bladder or vesical neck and urethra. The bladder is distended using a Foley catheter. To access the bladder, the physician makes an incision in the skin of the lower abdomen and cuts the corresponding muscles, fat, and fibrous membranes (fascia). The physician incises, trims, and shapes the bladder or vesical neck and urethra, using absorbable sutures or soft rubber drains for traction. The physician may insert a catheter through the urethra to provide support during healing. In anterior Y-plasty, the physician makes a Y-shaped flap of the bladder extending the vertical incision into the vesical neck. The vertical part of this incision is then pulled up into the V-shaped incision, which becomes a straight line when sutured. The physician may remove a portion of the vesical neck. The physician places a drain tube, bringing it out through a separate stab incision in the skin, and performs layered closure.

The physician uses plastic surgery to correct a defect in the bladder and urethra, and reimplants one or both ureters into the bladder (ureteroneocystostomy). To access the bladder, urethra, and ureters, the physician makes a midline incision in the skin of the abdomen and cuts the

● New Code   ▲ Revised Code   ▶◀ Revised Text

corresponding muscles, fat, and fibrous membranes (fascia). The physician incises, trims, and shapes the bladder and urethra, using absorbable sutures or soft rubber drains for traction. The physician brings the cut end of one or both ureters through a stab wound in the bladder and sutures the ureter(s) to the bladder. To provide support during healing, the physician inserts a ureteral catheter, bringing the tube end out through the urethra or bladder incision. The physician inserts a drain tube and performs layered closure.

Coding Clarification
Code 57.85 is used to report:

- **Cystourethroplasty:** Reconstruction of a narrowed portion of the bladder.

- **Plication of sphincter or urinary bladder:** Creation of a tuck in the bladder sphincter.

- **V-Y plasty of bladder neck:** Surgical reconstruction of the narrowed portion of bladder by V-Y technique.

When reporting cystourethroplasty performed in conjunction with ureteroneocystostomy, two codes are necessary to capture the complete procedure: 57.85 and 56.74.

57.86   Repair of bladder exstrophy

Description
This code reports the surgical correction of bladder exstrophy, a congenital bladder wall defect. Bladder exstrophy is a rare and serious abnormality wherein the bladder is everted and exposed due to incomplete midline closure of the abdominal wall. The anterior wall of the bladder is also often defective.

The physician closes a congenital defect in the front of the bladder wall, which is associated with lack of closure of the pubic bone at the symphysis pubis. The physician makes an incision around the exposed bladder and around the urethra to develop thick skin flaps. The physician brings the skin flaps together in the midline to close the roof of the urethra and allow the bladder and prostatic urethra to drop back beneath the bony pelvis (male patients), or lengthen the urethra (female patients). To invert the bladder and establish a functional vesical neck, the physician dissects the edge of the bladder from the rectus muscle and divides the fibromuscular bar that unites the pubic bone to the bladder base. To support the urethra and bladder neck, the physician brings the muscles of the urogenital diaphragm toward the midline. The physician places drain tubes and performs layered closure.

Coding Clarification
Code also any application or administration of an adhesion barrier substance (99.77).

57.87   Reconstruction of urinary bladder

Description
The physician reconstructs or enlarges a bladder with a segment of intestine. To access the intestine and bladder, the physician makes a transverse or longitudinal incision on the lower abdomen and cuts the corresponding muscles, fat, and fibrous membranes (fascia). After dissecting an isolated segment of colonic intestine, the physician reconnects (anastomosis) the ileum end-to-end to the ascending colon, restoring continuity to the bowel. The dissected segment of colon is opened and the distal ends are sutured. An incision is made at the bladder dome, a portion of the top of the bladder is removed in preparation, and the colonic segment is sutured to the bladder. After controlling bleeding, the physician inserts a catheter and closes the abdomen in layers over the catheter for support.

Coding Clarification
Code 57.87 is used to report:

- Anastomosis of bladder with isolated segment of ileum: Creation of a connection between the bladder and the separated terminal end of the small intestine

- Anastomosis of bladder with isolated segment of ileum

- Augmentation of bladder

- Replacement of bladder with ileum or sigmoid (closed ileal bladder)

Code also any resection of intestine (45.50-45.52).

Coding Guidance
    AHA: 3Q, '00, 7; 2Q, '03, 11; 2Q, '05, 12

57.88   Other anastomosis of bladder

Description
Code 57.88 is used to report bladder anastomosis procedures that are not more precisely described by other codes in subcategory 57.8. This code is also reported when the documentation does not further specify the anastomosis procedure.

Coding Clarification
Code 57.88 is used to report anastomosis of bladder to intestine NOS and cystocolic anastomosis.

This code is not used to report formation of a closed ileal bladder; see 57.87.

Documentation Tip
Review the documentation for specific information regarding the procedure prior to final code selection in order to avoid improper use of the "not otherwise specified" code and to ensure accurate code assignment.

57.89   Other repair of bladder

Description
Code 57.89 is used to report bladder repair procedures that are not more precisely described by other codes in subcategory 57.8. This code is also reported when the documentation does not further specify the repair.

Coding Clarification
Use code 57.89 to report:

- Bladder suspension, not elsewhere classified
- Cystopexy NOS
- Repair of old obstetric laceration of bladder

Code 57.89 is not used to report repair of a current obstetric laceration; see 75.61.

Documentation Tip
Review the documentation for specific information regarding the procedure prior to final code selection in order to avoid improper use of the "not otherwise specified" code and to ensure accurate code assignment.

57.9   Other operations on bladder

Description
Subcategory 57.9 contains fourth-digit subclassifications that describe various bladder procedures that are not more precisely described by other codes in this chapter.

Documentation Tip
Review the documentation for specific information regarding the procedure prior to final code selection in order to ensure accurate code assignment.

57.91   Sphincterotomy of bladder

Description
The physician examines the urinary collecting system with a cystourethroscope passed through the urethra and bladder, and makes an incision (sphincterotomy) in the musculature of the urethral closure (urethral sphincter). The physician passes a cutting instrument through the cystourethroscope for resection of the external sphincter. After the sphincterectomy, the physician removes the instrument and cystourethroscope.

Coding Guidance
AHA: 2Q, '90, 26

57.92   Dilation of bladder neck

Description
The physician examines the urinary collecting system with a cystourethroscope passed through the urethra and bladder and dilates the bladder with a balloon to relieve chronic inflammation of the bladder (interstitial cystitis). The physician removes the instrument and cystourethroscope.

Coding Clarification
This procedure may be done under local, general, or spinal anesthesia.

57.93   Control of (postoperative) hemorrhage of bladder

Description
Postoperative bladder hemorrhage can occur after urologic procedures, gynecologic surgery, or cesarean section. Most bladder hemorrhages can be treated using suprapubic continuous bladder drainage and a Foley catheter. If this is insufficient, the hemorrhage must be controlled using a suprapubic cystotomy or it may be necessary to perform a laparotomy.

57.94   Insertion of indwelling urinary catheter

Description
The patient is catheterized with a non-indwelling bladder catheter (e.g., for residual urine) such as simple catheterization with a temporary indwelling bladder catheter (Foley). The area is properly cleaned and sterilized. A water-soluble lubricant may be injected into the urethra before catheterization begins. The distal part of the catheter is coated with lubricant. In males, the penis is held perpendicular to the body and pulled up gently and the catheter is steadily inserted about 8 inches until urine is noted. In females, the catheter is gently inserted until urine is noted. With an indwelling catheter, insertion continues into the bladder until the retention balloon can be inflated. The catheter is gently pulled until the retention balloon is snuggled against the neck of the bladder. The catheter is secured to the abdomen or thigh and the drainage bag is secured below bladder level.

Coding Clarification
A change in anatomy, such as enlarging of the prostate or a fractured catheter or balloon, can complicate the catheterization process.

57.95   Replacement of indwelling urinary catheter

Description
The physician replaces a non-indwelling bladder catheter in a catheterized patient. In a simple catheterization with a temporary indwelling bladder catheter (Foley), the area is properly cleaned and sterilized. A water-soluble lubricant may be injected into the urethra before catheterization begins. The distal part of the catheter is coated with lubricant. In males, the penis is held perpendicular to the body and pulled up gently and the catheter is steadily inserted about eight inches until urine is noted. In females, the catheter is gently inserted until urine is noted. With an indwelling catheter, insertion continues into the bladder until the retention balloon can be inflated. The catheter is gently pulled

until the retention balloon is snuggled against the neck of the bladder. The catheter is secured to the abdomen or thigh and the drainage bag is secured below bladder level.

Coding Clarification
A change in anatomy, such as enlarging of the prostate or a fractured catheter or balloon, can complicate the catheterization process.

57.96   Implantation of electronic bladder stimulator

Description
Patients with spinal cord injury often cannot empty their bladder voluntarily; this can be restored by intermittent electrical stimulation of the sacral nerve roots to cause bladder contraction. An electronic stimulator implant can also be used to treat different forms of lower urinary tract dysfunction such as bladder voiding and bladder hyperreflexia.

An electronic stimulator implant consists of a tonicity signal generator, a self-contained power supply, an electrode with one end for connecting to implant, and a second end for connecting to a sacral nerve, for transmitting said tonicity and voiding signals to the nerve. The tonicity signal generator is manually activated by the patient. When activated, the voiding signal is generated, which activates detrusor muscle contraction causing bladder voiding.

57.97   Replacement of electronic bladder stimulator

Description
The physician removes and replaces a thin lead wire with a small electrode tip that was surgically implanted near the sacral nerve to control voiding function. An electronic stimulator implant consists of a tonicity signal generator, a self-contained power supply, an electrode with one end for connecting to implant, and a second end for connecting to a sacral nerve, for transmitting said tonicity and voiding signals to the nerve. The tonicity signal generator is manually activated by the patient. When activated, the voiding signal is generated, which activates detrusor muscle contraction causing bladder voiding.

Coding Clarification
Report removal without replacement with 57.98.

57.98   Removal of electronic bladder stimulator

Description
The physician removes a thin lead wire with a small electrode tip that was surgically implanted near the sacral nerve to control voiding function. An electronic stimulator implant consists of a tonicity signal generator, a self-contained power supply, an electrode with one end for connecting to implant,

and a second end for connecting to a sacral nerve, for transmitting said tonicity and voiding signals to the nerve. The tonicity signal generator is manually activated by the patient. When activated, the voiding signal is generated, which activates detrusor muscle contraction causing bladder voiding.

Coding Clarification
This procedure excludes that with synchronous replacement (57.97).

57.99   Other operations on bladder

Description
Code 57.99 is used to report procedures of the bladder that are not more precisely described by other codes in this chapter.

Coding Clarification
Code 57.99 excludes the following procedures, which are more appropriately classified elsewhere:

• Irrigation of cystostomy (96.47)

• Irrigation of other indwelling urinary catheter (96.48)

• Lysis of external adhesions (59.11)

• Removal of cystostomy tube (97.63)

• Removal of other urinary drainage device (97.64)

• Therapeutic distention of bladder (96.25).

Documentation Tip
Review the documentation for specific information regarding the procedure prior to final code selection in order to ensure accurate code assignment.

58   Operations on urethra

Description
The different types of procedures performed on the urethra (e.g., incisions, diagnostic procedures, excisions, repair, release of stricture, dilation) are located under category 58. Operations on the bulbourethral gland and periurethral tissue are also found here.

Coding Clarification
For all procedures reported by codes from category 58, code also any application or administration of an adhesion barrier substance (99.77).

Documentation Tip
To choose the correct code for a biopsy, determine the site as documented in the operative record. For example, use 58.23 for the urethra and 58.24 for periurethral tissue.

Procedures on Cowper's gland [bulbourethral gland] are included in this category.

● New Code   ▲ Revised Code   ▶◀ Revised Text   © 2010 Ingenix

58.0   Urethrotomy

Description
The physician makes an external incision in the urethra or creates an opening between the urethra and the skin. The physician places the patient in the lithotomy position and passes a sound into the urethra until it meets the obstructing stricture. A longitudinal incision is made down to the urethra directly over the sound. After the stricture is identified, the urethra is incised the length of the stricture so defects may be removed. The sound is removed and a catheter is passed through the urethra into the area of the incision and guided past it into the bladder. The urethra is then repaired over the catheter, using sutures. Occasionally, the urethra is not repaired by suturing but is simply allowed to grow epithelial cells (epithelize) around the catheter.

Coding Clarification
Code 58.0 is used to report:

- Excision of urethral septum
- Formation of urethrovaginal fistula
- Perineal urethrostomy
- Removal of calculus from urethra by incision

Do not use 58.0 to report drainage of the bulbourethral gland or periurethral tissue (58.91), internal urethral meatotomy (58.5), or removal of urethral calculus without incision (58.6).

58.1   Urethral meatotomy

Description
The physician makes an incision in the opening of the urethra (urethral meatus) using a small pointed knife and a meatotomy clamp. The meatus is opened on the ventral surface and the meatus may be dilated. Sutures may be required on the mucosa of the meatus. The physician often uses a hemostat to separate the tissue in the urethra prior to making the incision.

Coding Clarification
This code describes an incision of the urethra to enlarge the passage; to report internal urethral meatotomy, see 58.5.

58.2   Diagnostic procedures on urethra

Description
Fourth-digit subclassifications describe various diagnostic procedures on the urethra, such as urethroscopy and biopsy.

Documentation Tip
Review the documentation for specific information regarding the procedure prior to final code selection in order to ensure accurate code assignment.

58.21   Perineal urethroscopy

Description
The physician examines the urethra, bladder, and ureteric openings with a cystourethroscope passed through the urethra and bladder. No other procedure is performed at this time. After examination, the physician removes the cystourethroscope.

58.22   Other urethroscopy

Description
The physician examines the urinary collecting system with a cystourethroscope passed through the urethra and bladder. The physician passes the cystourethroscope through the urethra into the bladder, moving the scope to visualize the urethra and bladder. After insertion of a catheter into the ureter, the physician may flush (irrigate) or introduce by drops (instillate) a sterile saline solution to better view structures and/or may introduce contrast medium for radiologic study of the renal pelvis and ureter (ureteropyelogram, retrograde pyelogram). The physician removes the cystourethroscope after examination.

Coding Clarification
If performing a biopsy of the urethra, report 58.23.

58.23   Biopsy of urethra

Description
Using an open approach, the physician excises a specimen of tissue from the urethra for biopsy. At the site to be analyzed, a portion of the suspect tissue is excised by blunt or sharp dissection. The incision is closed in layers.

In an alternate procedure, the physician examines the urinary collecting system with a cystourethroscope passed through the urethra and bladder, and extracts biopsy tissue from the urethra. To do so, the physician passes a cutting instrument through the endoscope to the suspect tissue and traps a specimen of tissue. Multiple samples may be collected. The physician removes the instrument and cystourethroscope.

Coding Clarification
When coding urethral biopsy, no differentiation is made with regard to approach; all are reported with 58.23.

In a percutaneous biopsy, a needle is passed into the tissue and the sample is removed through the needle.

In an open biopsy, an incision is made in the skin, the area to be biopsied exposed, and a tissue sample is taken.

© 2010 Ingenix   ● New Code   ▲ Revised Code   ►◄ Revised Text

Documentation Tip

To choose the correct code for a biopsy, determine the site as documented in the operative record. For example, use 58.23 for the urethra and 58.24 for periurethral tissue.

58.24   Biopsy of periurethral tissue

Description

The physician removes tissue around the urethra for biopsy. At the site to be analyzed, a portion of the suspect tissue is excised by blunt or sharp dissection. The incision is closed in layers.

Coding Clarification

In a percutaneous biopsy, a needle is passed into the tissue and the sample is removed through the needle.

In an open biopsy, an incision is made in the skin, the area to be biopsied is exposed, and a tissue sample is taken.

Closed biopsy involves a much smaller incision than open biopsy, made to allow insertion of a endoscopic visualization device.

Documentation Tip

To choose the correct code for a biopsy, determine the site as documented in the operative record. For example, use 58.23 for the urethra and 58.24 for periurethral tissue.

58.29   Other diagnostic procedures on urethra and periurethral tissue

Description

Code 58.29 is used to report diagnostic procedures of the urethra and periurethral tissue that are not more precisely described by other codes in this category 58.

Coding Clarification

Do not use 58.29 to report microscopic examination of specimen from urethra (91.31-91.39), retrograde cystourethrogram (87.76), urethral pressure profile (89.25), or urethral sphincter electromyogram (89.23).

Documentation Tip

Review the documentation for specific information regarding the procedure prior to final code selection in order to ensure accurate code assignment.

58.3   Excision or destruction of lesion or tissue of urethra

Description

Subcategory 58.3 provides two codes to report excision and destruction of urethral lesions or tissues via endoscopic or other approaches. Fourth-digit subclassification provides specificity of operative approach.

Coding Clarification

Do not use subcategory 58.3 to report biopsy of the urethra (58.23), excision of the bulbourethral gland (58.92), or fistulectomy (58.43).

This code is also not used to report urethrectomy as part of a complete cystectomy (57.79), pelvic evisceration (68.8), or radical cystectomy (57.71).

58.31   Endoscopic excision or destruction of lesion or tissue of urethra

Description

The physician examines the urinary collecting system with endoscopes passed through the urethra into the bladder (cystourethroscope), ureter (ureteroscope), and renal pelvis (pyeloscope), and takes a biopsy and/or uses electric current (fulguration) to destroy a ureteral lesion. The physician passes instruments through the endoscope to take a biopsy of suspect tissue and/or destroy a lesion with electric current. The physician removes required instruments and endoscopes.

Coding Clarification

Code 58.31 is used to report fulguration of a urethral lesion.

58.39   Other local excision or destruction of lesion or tissue of urethra

Description

A urethrectomy is performed for the excision of a congenital valve of the urethra, a lesion, or urethral stricture. The physician makes a slightly curved, suprapubic (Cherney) incision down to the ureter and bladder. The bladder is opened and the urethral orifice is circumcised and usually tied off with sutures. Tumors of the urethra are removed by partial or complete urethrectomy or by electric current (fulguration).

Coding Clarification

Although a urethrectomy is classified to 58.39, this code should not be reported if the urethrectomy is a part of a larger procedure.

To report this procedure using an endoscopic approach, see 58.31.

58.4   Repair of urethra

Description

Subcategory 58.4 provides eight codes to report various urethral repair procedures, including suture, closure of urethrostomy or other fistula, reanastomosis, meatoplasty, and other forms of repair. Fourth-digit subclassifications provide specificity to site and/or procedure.

Coding Clarification

This subcategory excludes repair of current obstetric laceration; see 75.61.

● New Code   ▲ Revised Code   ▶◀ Revised Text   © 2010 Ingenix

58.41   Suture of laceration of urethra

Description
The physician repairs a urethral wound or injury, including the skin, and even more traumatic wounds requiring more than layered closure. Examples include debridement of cuts (lacerations) or tears (avulsion). Suturing of the urethra is done in layers to prevent later complications and fistula formations. The tissue can be constructed around a catheter.

58.42   Closure of urethrostomy

Description
The physician closes a urethrostomy or urethrocutaneous fistula. An elliptical incision is made around the opening of the urocutaneous fistula and carried deeper into the supporting tissue toward the urethra. The entire tract is freed up and excised unless it involves other important structures, such as the external sphincters. When the tract cannot be completely removed, the remaining part is cut. The defect of the urethra is closed in layers over a catheter.

58.43   Closure of other fistula of urethra

Description
The following descriptions detail the closure of various forms of urethral fistula:

*   **Rectourethral:** The physician makes an abdominal incision. The rectum is dissected from the prostate and the fistula is identified and divided. The fistulous opening in the rectum is closed with sutures and the opening in the urethra may be closed or left open. A pedicle of omentum is usually mobilized and placed between the areas of repair. The incision is closed. As an alternate method, an incision may be made between the anus and urethra from a perineal approach and dissection continued between the rectum and urethra. The fistula is identified and divided and the openings in the rectum and urethra are closed. The incision is closed.

*   **Urethrovaginal:** The physician closes a urethrovaginal fistula, which is an abnormal passage between the urethra and vagina. With a catheter in the urethra, the fistula tract is excised and the defect in the urethra is sutured closed. A pad of fatty tissue is sutured between the repaired urethral defect and the vaginal defect. If a separately reportable bulbocavernosus transplant is also performed, a pad of fatty tissue and a strip of the bulbocavernosus muscle are brought through a tunnel created between the vagina and one labium. The fat and muscle flap are sutured

between the repaired urethral defect and the vaginal defect. In either case, the involved area in the vagina is excised and the defect is sutured closed. The catheter is left in place for several days to allow healing of the urethra.

Coding Clarification
If a bulbocavernosus transplant is performed in conjunction with the closure of a urethrovaginal fistula, two codes are needed to fully report the procedure: 71.79 and 58.43.

This procedure excludes repair of a urethroperineovesical fistula (57.84).

58.44   Reanastomosis of urethra

Description
This code reports both anastomosis and reanastomosis of the urethra. This procedure is often performed in order to repair a severed urethra.

Documentation Tip
An anastomosis is a surgically created connection between two tubular structures.

58.45   Repair of hypospadias or epispadias

Description
This code reports multiple forms of repair of hypospadias (an abnormal opening of the urethra on the underside of the penis or on the perineum) and epispadias (congenital absence of the urethral upper wall), some of which are detailed in the following descriptions.

The physician corrects epispadias, which is the congenital absence of the upper wall of the urethra. The urethra has its opening anywhere on the top surface of the penis. A closed urethra is created by reapproximating the tissues, and by using skin grafts, tube grafts, free tissue grafts, or a combination of techniques depending on the extent of the defect.

In an alternate procedure, the physician corrects epispadias and associated urinary incontinence in one or more stages. Epispadias with incontinence is the congenital absence of the upper wall of the urethra and the lack of function of the muscles that control the bladder neck. Through an incision in the lower abdomen, the surgeon reconstructs the bladder neck and reimplants the ureters from the kidneys away from the bladder neck outlet. A closed urethra is created by reapproximating the tissues and by using skin grafts, tube grafts, free tissue grafts, or a combination of techniques depending on the extent of the defect.

In yet another variation, the physician corrects epispadias and exstrophy of the bladder in stages. Epispadias is the congenital absence of the upper wall of the urethra. Bladder exstrophy is the turning

55-59

inside out of the bladder so that the bladder is open directly to the outside and, as such, urine does not collect in the bladder but simply drains without any control to the outside onto the lower abdomen. The separately reportable first stage is to close the bladder through incisions in the lower abdomen. The surgeon frees the bladder from the abdominal wall and proceeds to close the bladder and reimplant the ureters from the kidneys away from the bladder neck outlet. In the second stage, a closed urethra is created by reapproximating the tissues and by using skin grafts, tube grafts, free tissue grafts, or a combination of techniques depending on the extent of the defect. In the following stages, the physician reconstructs the bladder neck to provide urinary control and, if necessary, does additional surgery on the penis and urethra.

Coding Clarification
If the correction of epispadias is performed concurrently with bladder exstrophy repair, assign 57.86 in addition to 58.45.

Hypospadias is a congenital abnormality of the penis in which the urethral opening is positioned along the shaft of the penis on its underside or on the scrotum or perineum instead of being located at the tip of the penis. With increasing degrees of severity, the penis is curved downward (referred to as chordee).

Chordee is a condition in which the penis curves downward. In most cases, chordee is associated with hypospadias.

Coding Guidance
AHA: 4Q, '96, 35; 3Q, '97, 6

58.46   Other reconstruction of urethra

Description
This code reports multiple forms of urethral reconstruction, some of which are detailed in the following descriptions.

Urethroplasties are performed to open a stricture, repair trauma, or correct a prolapse. In the first stage, the physician identifies the injured area using a catheter or a urethrograph. The incision is made over the injury and carried through the skin, fat, and other tissues (fascia). If a urethral prolapse is involved, other incisions may be involved. The problem is repaired or excised and layered sutures are made to provide adequate support. A catheter is placed and left for at least six to 12 days. In the second stage, to close the urethra, the physician cuts around the urethral defect, using skin from the scrotal flap to make a urethra. The right size urethra must be constructed to allow a catheter and prevent obstructions. The physician pulls the loose skin around the urethra and closes the incisions.

In a Johanson-type operation, the physician reconstructs the urethra in two stages. In the first stage, the area of the stricture is identified by a catheter and urethrography and its location is marked with ink or dye. All strictures distal to the perineum are handled in the same manner. The incision is made over the stricture area. When no further strictures can be identified, the area involved is removed. Otherwise, the stricture is opened widely and the normal skin of the male or female is sutured to the edge of the mucosa on each side. In those areas in which mucosa had to be removed, the skin is sutured edge-to-edge. Six to eight weeks are required for complete healing of this stage. In the second stage, the physician makes parallel incisions around the defect and continues around the urethral opening both proximally and distally. The lateral skin edges are closed over an indwelling catheter to create a new urethra. The corpora and muscles are then closed, respectively, becoming the new urethra structure.

In the Tenago or Leadbetter procedures, the physician elongates the urethra by using bladder musculature. Continence is achieved due to contraction of the bladder musculature. The physician exposes the bladder through a suprapubic incision. The bladder is opened and the bladder neck incision is made 2 cm lateral to the urethra on each side. The musculature is drawn together in a tube and attached to the urethra. The urethral canal is closed in a two-layer technique. For the Tenago procedure, they are moved laterally.

Documentation Tip
The medical record may contain the following terminology when referring to procedures reported with 58.46:

- Cecil operation
- Johanson operation
- Leadbetter operation
- Swinney operation
- Tenago procedure

58.47   Urethral meatoplasty

Description
The physician performs surgery to open or reconstruct the urethra, improving voiding or allowing insertion of an instrument. The meatus, which may be congenitally small or narrowed as the result of infection, is opened and a mucosal flap is advanced and sutured to the glans. Alternately, the physician makes an incision on the ventral surface of the penis and skin is freed from the shaft. Fibrous tissue is removed. An erection is artificially induced to confirm all fibrous tissue has been removed.

● New Code   ▲ Revised Code   ▶◀ Revised Text   © 2010 Ingenix

Documentation Tip
The medical record may refer to this procedure as a Richardson type procedure.

58.49 Other repair of urethra

Description
Code 58.49 is used to report repair procedures of the urethra that are not more precisely described by other codes in category 58, including:

- Benenenti rotation of bulbous urethra
- Repair of old obstetric laceration of urethra
- Urethral plication
- Repair or revision of urethral stoma
- Urethropexy (other than anterior)
- Urethroplasty

When performing a urethral plication, the physician accesses the urethral sphincter from the vagina. With a catheter in the urethra, the physician dissects the midline vaginal wall, separating it from the bladder and the proximal urethra. Sutures are placed at the junction of the bladder and urethra on each side of the urethra. This supports the area. Excess vaginal tissue is excised and the vaginal wall is closed.

Coding Clarification
Do not use 58.49 to report repair of a current obstetric laceration (75.61) or urethrocele (70.50-70.51).

Coding Guidance
AHA: 1Q, '09, 15

58.5 Release of urethral stricture

Description
The physician widens the urethra. With the patient under anesthesia, the physician examines the urinary collection system with a cystourethroscope passed through the urethra and dilates a stricture. The physician inserts a balloon catheter to dilate a urethral stricture or stenosis. The physician may pass a cutting instrument through the cystourethroscope to make an incision (meatotomy) in the opening of the urethra or inject radiocontrast for radiologic study of the bladder. In other cases, the physician inserts a stent to dilate the urethral stricture or stenosis. After dilation, the physician removes the instrument and cystourethroscope.

Coding Clarification
Use 58.5 for an internal urethrotomy with an endourethral prosthesis and 58.6 for a sequential dilation of the urethral stricture with endourethral prosthesis.

Code 58.5 is used to report internal urethral meatotomy and urethrolysis.

Coding Guidance
AHA: 1Q, '97, 13

58.6 Dilation of urethra

Description
The physician uses fine tools to dilate the urethra. A filiform (a small, silk-like instrument with woven spiral tips, to which followers made of a similar material can be attached by a screw-like mechanism) is used when a stricture cannot be passed. With a filiform as a guide, the follower is passed through the urethra. Increasing sizes of followers are introduced, dilating the stricture. The filiform is manipulated up a lubricated urethra to the stricture. The physician attaches a follower to the filiform and the stricture is widened. The physician uses dilators of increasing size to widen the urethra. A suppository or instillation of a saline solution may be used.

Coding Clarification
General or spinal anesthesia is administered for dilation of a female urethral stricture.

Use 58.6 to report dilation of the urethrovesical junction.

To report urethral calibration, see 89.29.

Coding Guidance
AHA: 1Q, '97, 13; 1Q, '01, 14

58.9 Other operations on urethra and periurethral tissue

Description
The different types of procedures performed on the urethra and periurethral tissue (e.g., incisions, excisions, repairs) that are not more precisely described by other codes are located under subcategory 58.9.

Documentation Tip
Review the documentation for specific information regarding the procedure prior to final code selection in order to ensure accurate code assignment.

58.91 Incision of periurethral tissue

Description
The physician drains an abscess in the urethra resulting from a urethral infection or traumatic injury. The physician makes an incision through the skin, subcutaneous tissue, and overlying layers of muscle, fat, and tissue (fascia) over the site of the abscess. By blunt or sharp dissection, the incision is carried into the abscessed area to provide drainage. Several drains are inserted and the incision is closed in layers.

Coding Clarification
Report 58.91 for drainage of a deep periurethral abscess, an abscess or cyst in the Skene's or paraurethral glands in the female, and incision of tissue around the urethra and drainage of bulbourethral gland.

58.92   Excision of periurethral tissue

Description
The physician excises the bulbourethral (Cowper's) gland. The bulbourethral glands are located on each side of the prostate gland near the external sphincter and are connected to the urethra with 1-inch ducts. The glands secrete what becomes part of the seminal fluid. The physician completes this procedure through transurethral or segmental resection with end-to-end sutures (anastomosis).

Coding Clarification
Do not use 58.92 to report biopsy of periurethral tissue (58.24) or lysis of periurethral adhesions (59.11-59.12).

58.93   Implantation of artificial urinary sphincter (AUS)

Description
An artificial urinary sphincter is a device that mimics the function of a biological urinary sphincter. Due to recent advances in mechanical design and new technology, some minimally invasive treatment options have become available for stress urinary incontinence.

The physician implants an artificial sphincter to stem urinary incontinence. In male patients where the incontinence is caused by anything other than prostatic surgery, the entire prosthesis is inserted through a subpubic incision. In female patients, the sphincter is inserted through a suprapubic incision. The space of Retzius (between the bladder and the pubis) is opened and the bladder neck is cut free, making space for the device. The bladder neck circumference is measured and a cuff of slightly larger size is chosen and sutured around the bladder neck. A space is created below the skin low in the scrotum, and the control pump passed into this position from the subpubic incision. The pressure balloon is placed in a pocket behind the rectus muscle on the same side as the control pump. The physician injects fluid into the pressure balloon. In females, the plane between the bladder neck and vagina is dissected to serve the same purpose as the scrotum.

The physician removes and replaces an artificial sphincter (including pump, reservoir, and cuff) used to stem urinary incontinence. In male patients where the incontinence is caused by anything other than prostatic surgery, the entire prosthesis is accessed

through a subpubic incision. In female patients, the sphincter is accessed through a suprapubic incision. The sphincter and pump are examined, removed, and replaced. The bladder neck circumference is measured and a cuff of slightly larger size is chosen and positioned around the bladder neck. A space is created below the skin low in the scrotum and the control pump passed into this position from the subpubic incision. The pressure balloon is placed in a pocket behind the rectus muscle on the same side as the control pump. The physician injects fluid into the pressure balloon and the connections are then permanently established. In females, the plane between the bladder neck and vagina is dissected.

Coding Clarification
This code reports the placement of inflatable sphincters of the urethra and bladder.

Removal with replacement of sphincter device is also reported with 58.93.

Pump and/or reservoir are included in this code.

Coding Guidance
    AHA: 1Q, '09, 15

58.99   Other operations on urethra and periurethral tissue

Description
The physician repairs an artificial urinary sphincter pump and/or reservoir to stem incontinence. The rectus muscles are separated bluntly and a space is created behind the muscle of one side large enough to gain access to the reservoir of the prosthesis. The physician checks the reservoir for any malfunctions or abnormalities. The physician follows the tubing (this may require a second incision in the rectus sheath). A space is dilated within the spongy carpal tissue where the cylinder tubing is checked. After both cylinders are examined, they are test-inflated to ensure that they reach into the glans portion of the corpora and that there is no buckling when they are inflated. The physician closes the incisions. The reservoir is filled and all connections are made. Several test inflations and deflations are performed during closure. The physician places a catheter in the bladder for about one day.

The physician removes an artificial urinary sphincter. In female patients, the physician makes a midline lower abdominal incision to gain access to the space of Retzius. The artificial urinary sphincter is exposed and the plane between the bladder neck and vagina is dissected. The device is removed and the opening is closed using suture for the rectus fascia. The subcutaneous tissues are closed and staples are used for skin closure. In male patients, the urethral bulb is exposed and the bulbospongiosus muscles are left intact over the urethra. The strap of the prosthesis is grasped under

● New Code   ▲ Revised Code   ▶◀ Revised Text   © 2010 Ingenix

the crus and the muscle and the procedure is repeated distally to grasp the second lateral strap. The same maneuvers are repeated on the opposite site. The proximal straps are untied, as are the lateral straps. The incision is closed and a Foley catheter remains for several days.

Coding Clarification
Code 58.99 is used to report procedures on the urethra and periurethral tissue that are not more precisely described by other codes in subcategory 58.9, such as repair of an inflatable sphincter pump and/or reservoir, surgical correction of hydraulic pressure of an inflatable sphincter device, and removal of an inflatable urinary sphincter without replacement.

This code is not used to report the removal of an intraluminal foreign body from the urethra without incision (98.19) and urethral stent (97.65).

Documentation Tip
Review the documentation for specific information regarding the procedure prior to final code selection in order to ensure accurate code assignment.

59   Other operations on urinary tract

Description
Category 59 lists codes for procedures on the perirenal, periureteral, and perivesical tissue, and other operations on the urinary tract such as plication of urethrovesical junction, suprapubic sling operation, retropubic urethral suspension, repairs for stress incontinence, and replacement of ostomy tubes.

Coding Clarification
For all procedures reported by codes within category 59, code also any application or administration of an adhesion barrier substance (99.77).

59.0   Dissection of retroperitoneal tissue

Description
Codes in this subcategory report the different types of procedures performed on the retroperitoneal tissue (e.g., incision, excision, lysis, dissection) that are not more precisely described by other codes in category 59.

Documentation Tip
Review the documentation for specific information regarding the procedure prior to final code selection in order to ensure accurate code assignment.

59.00   Retroperitoneal dissection, not otherwise specified

Description
Code 59.00 is used to report retroperitoneal dissection that is not more precisely described by

other codes in subcategory 59.0. This code is also reported when the documentation does not further specify the dissection procedure.

Documentation Tip
Review the documentation for specific information regarding the procedure prior to final code selection in order to avoid improper use of the "not otherwise specified" code.

59.02   Other lysis of perirenal or periureteral adhesions

Description
The physician surgically frees the ureter from localized inflammatory disease of retroperitoneal fibrous tissue. To access the ureter, the physician makes a midline incision in the skin of the abdomen and cuts the muscles, fat, and fibrous membranes (fascia) overlying the ureter. The physician incises surrounding fibrotic tissue to free the ureter, and may use sutures to reposition the ureter away from obstructive fibrous tissue. The physician places a drain tube, bringing it out through a separate stab incision in the skin, and performs layered closure.

Coding Clarification
To report lysis of perirenal or periureteral adhesions by laparoscope, see 59.03.

59.03   Laparoscopic lysis of perirenal or periureteral adhesions

Description
The physician performs a laparoscopic procedure to surgically free the ureter from localized inflammatory disease of retroperitoneal fibrous tissue. To access the ureter, the physician makes a small incision in the skin of the abdomen. The physician uses the laparoscope fitted with a fiberoptic camera and an operating instrument. The perirenal or periureteral adhesions are visualized through the scope and the physician incises surrounding fibrotic tissue to free the ureter from obstructive fibrous tissue. The physician performs layered closure.

Coding Clarification
Surgical procedures on the perirenal or periureteral tissue are performed using a variety of surgical techniques and approaches ranging from open surgery to less invasive procedures, such as laparoscopy, percutaneous techniques, or transurethrally via cystoscopy.

Documentation Tip
Review the documentation for specific information regarding the procedure prior to final code selection in order to ensure accurate code assignment.

Coding Guidance
AHA: 4Q, '06, 134

59.09 Other incision of perirenal or periureteral tissue

Description
The physician drains an infection (abscess) on the kidney or on the surrounding renal tissue. To access the renal or perirenal abscess, the physician makes a small incision in the skin of the flank, cuts the muscles, fat, and fibrous membranes (fascia) overlying the kidney, and sometimes removes a portion of the eleventh or twelfth rib. After exploring the abscess cavity, the physician irrigates the site, inserts multiple drain tubes through separate stab wounds, and sutures the drain tube ends to the skin. The physician packs the wound with gauze and sutures the fascia and muscles. The skin and subcutaneous tissue are usually left open to prevent formation of a secondary body wall abscess.

In an alternate procedure, the physician performs percutaneous drainage of a perirenal or renal abscess. The physician may create a small incision in the skin between two ribs proximal to the abscess or in the flank in order to ease placement of drainage instruments through the skin into an abscess located within the kidney or immediately adjacent to it. The physician uses a CAT scan or ultrasound to guide placement of a drainage needle or trocar into the abscess. The physician advances the drainage needle or trocar through the skin to gain access to the abscess. The fluid is allowed to drain. Once the abscess is drained, a drainage catheter may be placed (and later removed) to maintain drainage. Sutures may be placed to secure the drainage catheter in place. The operative site is cleaned and bandaged.

Coding Clarification
Use 59.09 to report exploration of the perinephric area and incision of a perirenal abscess.

Exploration of the perinephric area entails exam of the tissue around the kidney by incision.

Incision of a perirenal abscess involves incising an abscess in the tissue around the kidney.

59.1 Incision of perivesical tissue

Description
The different types of procedures involving incising tissue around the bladder are reported with subcategory 58.1.

Documentation Tip
Review the documentation for specific information regarding the procedure prior to final code selection in order to ensure accurate code assignment.

59.11 Other lysis of perivesical adhesions

Description
Code 59.11 is used to report lysis procedures on the urinary bladder tissue that are not more precisely described by other codes in subcategory 59.1.

Documentation Tip
Review the documentation for specific information regarding the procedure prior to final code selection in order to ensure accurate code assignment.

59.12 Laparoscopic lysis of perivesical adhesions

Description
The physician performs a laparoscopic procedure to surgically free perivesical tissue adhesions. To access the ureter, the physician makes a small incision in the skin of the abdomen. The physician uses the laparoscope fitted with a fiberoptic camera and an operating instrument. The adhesions are visualized through the scope and the physician incises surrounding tissue to free the obstructive fibrous tissue. The physician performs layered closure.

Coding Clarification
Surgical procedures on the perirenal or periureteral tissue are performed using a variety of surgical techniques and approaches ranging from open surgery to less invasive procedures, such as laparoscopy, percutaneous techniques, or transurethrally via cystoscopy.

Review the documentation for specific information regarding the procedure prior to final code selection in order to ensure accurate code assignment.

59.19 Other incision of perivesical tissue

Description
The physician drains an infection (abscess) near the bladder. To access the bladder, the physician makes an incision in the skin of the lower abdomen and cuts the corresponding muscles, fat, and fibrous membranes (fascia). After exploring the abscess cavity, the physician irrigates the site, inserts multiple drain tubes through separate stab wounds, and sutures the drain tube ends to the skin. The physician inserts a urethral catheter and performs layered closure.

Coding Clarification
Code 59.19 is used to report exploration of perivesical tissue, incision of a hematoma of the space of Retzius, and retropubic exploration.

● New Code　▲ Revised Code　▶◀ Revised Text　© 2010 Ingenix

59.2 Diagnostic procedures on perirenal and perivesical tissue

Description
Subcategory 59.2 includes different types of diagnostic procedures involving the perirenal tissue and perivesical tissue.

59.21 Biopsy of perirenal or perivesical tissue

Description
Code 59.21 reports biopsy of the tissues surrounding the kidneys or bladder, regardless of approach.

59.29 Other diagnostic procedures on perirenal tissue, perivesical tissue, and retroperitoneum

Description
Code 59.29 is used to report diagnostic procedures of the perirenal tissue, perivesical tissue, and retroperitoneum that are not more precisely described by other codes in subcategory 59.2.

Coding Clarification
Do not use this code to report microscopic examination of specimens from perirenal tissue (91.21-91.29), perivesical tissue (91.31-91.39), retroperitoneum NEC (91.11-91.19), or to report retroperitoneal x-ray (88.14-88.16).

Documentation Tip
Review the documentation for specific information regarding the procedure prior to final code selection in order to ensure accurate code assignment.

59.3 Plication of urethrovesical junction

Description
The physician sutures a tuck in tissues around the urethra at its junction with the bladder, which changes the angle of the junction and provides support. The physician accesses the urethral sphincter from the vagina. With a catheter in the urethra, the physician dissects the midline vaginal wall separating it from the bladder and the proximal urethra. Sutures are placed at the junction of the bladder and urethra on each side of the urethra. This pushes up the urethrovesical junctions and supports the area. Excess vaginal tissue is excised and the vaginal wall is closed.

Coding Clarification
This procedure is also known as a Kelly-Kennedy operation on the urethra or a Kelly-Stoeckel urethral plication.

59.4 Suprapubic sling operation

Description
The physician performs a suspension of the urethra from the suprapubic periosteum to restore support to the bladder and urethra. Through vaginal and abdominal incisions, the physician places a sling under the junction of the urethra and bladder. The physician places a catheter in the bladder, makes an incision in the anterior wall of the vagina, and folds and tacks the tissues around the urethra. A sling is formed out of synthetic material or from fascia harvested from the sheath of the rectus abdominus muscle. The loop end of the sling is sutured around the junction of the urethra. An incision is made in the lower abdomen and the ends of the sling are grasped with a clamp and pulled up into the incision and sutured to the rectus abdominus sheath. The abdominal and vaginal incisions are closed in layers by suturing.

If performed laparoscopically, the physician inserts an instrument through the cervix into the uterus to manipulate the uterus. Next, the physician makes a 1 cm incision just below the umbilicus through which a fiberoptic laparoscope is inserted. A second incision is made and a second instrument is passed into the abdomen. The physician manipulates the tools so that the pelvic organs can be observed through the laparoscope. The physician places a sling under the junction of the urethra and bladder. The physician places a catheter in the bladder, makes an incision in the anterior wall of the vagina, and folds and tacks the tissues around the urethra. A sling is formed out of synthetic material or from fascia harvested from the sheath of the rectus abdominus muscle. The loop end of the sling is sutured around the junction of the urethra. An incision is made in the lower abdomen and the ends of the sling are grasped with a clamp and pulled into the incision and sutured to the rectus abdominus sheath. The instruments are removed and incisions are closed with sutures.

Coding Clarification
This procedure is also known as a Goebel-Frangenheim-Stoeckel urethrovesical suspension, a Millin-Read urethrovesical suspension, an Oxford operation for urinary incontinence, or a urethrocystopexy by suprapubic suspension.

59.5 Retropubic urethral suspension

Description
Suspension of the urethra from the pubic bone with a suture placed from the symphysis pubis to paraurethral tissues elevates the urethrovesical angle and restores urinary continence. The physician performs a "Burch procedure." An incision is made in the lower part of the abdomen and the top edges of the vagina are pulled up and stitched to ligaments connected to the pubic bone. As a result, the urethra is held upward in a hammock of vaginal tissue.

55-59

Coding Clarification
The Burch procedure is performed to treat urinary stress incontinence. The Burch procedure is performed through vertical or low transverse incision.

Code 59.5 is also used to report a Marshall-Marchetti-Krantz operation, suturing of periurethral tissue to the symphysis pubis, and urethral suspension that is not otherwise specified.

Coding Guidance
AHA: 1Q, '97, 11

59.6   Paraurethral suspension

Description
The physician performs suspension of the bladder neck from fibrous membranes of the anterior abdominal wall with upward traction applied, which changes the angle of the urethra and improves urinary control. The physician makes an inverted U-shaped incision in the area between the vagina and the urethra. By blunt and sharp dissection, the physician creates an opening in the space on each side of the urethra as it passes into the bladder. Using a continuous suture for each side, the physician stitches the fascial tissues along the urethra to the urethrovesical junction. The physician then makes an incision in the abdomen above the pubis and, doing each side in turn, drives a special Pereyra ligature carrier through the tissues just lateral to the midline and takes it down to the sutured tissue. The sutures are threaded into the instrument and brought back through the abdominal incision. The urethrovesical junction is elevated by pulling up on the sutures and fixing them around the rectus abdominus muscle. In addition, the physician performs an anterior colporrhaphy using a vaginal approach, which corrects a cystocele and repairs the tissues between the vagina, bladder, and urethra.

Coding Clarification
The procedure is also know as a Pereyra paraurethral suspension or periurethral suspension.

59.7   Other repair of urinary stress incontinence

Description
Subcategory 59.7 is used to report urinary stress incontinence repair procedures that are not more precisely described by other codes in category 59.

Documentation Tip
Review the documentation for specific information regarding the procedure prior to final code selection in order to ensure accurate code assignment.

59.71   Levator muscle operation for urethrovesical suspension

Description
Through vaginal and abdominal incisions, the physician places a sling under the junction of the urethra and bladder. The physician places a catheter in the bladder, makes an incision in the anterior wall of the vagina, and folds and tacks the tissues around the urethra. A sling is formed out of synthetic material or from fascia harvested from the sheath of the rectus abdominus muscle. The loop end of the sling is sutured around the junction of the urethra. An incision is made in the lower abdomen and the ends of the sling are grasped with a clamp and pulled up into the incision and sutured to the rectus abdominus sheath. The abdominal and vaginal incisions are closed in layers by suturing.

If performed laparoscopically, the physician inserts an instrument through the cervix into the uterus to manipulate the uterus. Next, the physician makes a 1 cm incision just below the umbilicus through which a fiberoptic laparoscope is inserted. A second incision is made and a second instrument is passed into the abdomen. The physician manipulates the tools so that the pelvic organs can be observed through the laparoscope. The physician places a sling under the junction of the urethra and bladder. The physician places a catheter in the bladder, makes an incision in the anterior wall of the vagina, and folds and tacks the tissues around the urethra. A sling is formed out of synthetic material or from fascia harvested from the sheath of the rectus abdominus muscle. The loop end of the sling is sutured around the junction of the urethra. An incision is made in the lower abdomen and the ends of the sling are grasped with a clamp and pulled into the incision and sutured to the rectus abdominus sheath. The instruments are removed and incisions are closed with sutures.

Coding Clarification
The code is also used to report cystourethropexy with levator muscle sling, gracilis muscle transplant for urethrovesical suspension, and pubococcygeal sling.

59.72   Injection of implant into urethra and/or bladder neck

Description
The physician injects natural proteins or synthetic material into the urethra and bladder neck, helping to prevent urinary incontinence. Before the injection, an endoscope is placed through the urethra into the bladder. Using local anesthesia, the physician makes one to three injections into the transurethral submucous. The injections are made through the endoscope into the affected area. The procedure can also be performed through the lower abdomen.

Coding Clarification
Collagen implant, reported with 59.72, is an injection of collagen into submucosal tissues to increase tissue bulk and improve urinary control in patients with intrinsic sphincter deficiency.

Code 59.72 is also used to report endoscopic injection of implant, fat implant, or Polytef implant.

Coding Guidance
AHA: 4Q, '95, 72-73

59.79   Other repair of urinary stress incontinence

Description
This code is reported when the procedure documented is not more precisely described by other codes in subcategory 59.7 and when the documentation does not further specify the stress incontinence repair procedure. Examples of procedures appropriately reported by this code include:

- **Pubovaginal sling for treatment of stress incontinence:** A strip of fascia is harvested and the vaginal epithelium is mobilized and sutured to the midline at the urethral level to the rectus muscle to create a sling supporting the bladder.

- **Vaginal wall sling with bone anchors for treatment of stress incontinence:** A sling for the bladder is formed by a suture attachment of vaginal wall to the abdominal wall. In addition, a suture is run from the vagina to a bone anchor placed in the pubic bone.

- **Transvaginal endoscopic bladder neck suspension for treatment of stress incontinence:** Endoscopic surgical suturing of the vaginal epithelium and the pubocervical fascia at the bladder neck level on both sides of the urethra. Two supporting sutures are run from the vagina to an anchor placed in the pubic bone on each side.

In a laparoscopic anterior urethropexy, the physician treats stress incontinence in the male or female patient. The physician makes a 1 cm incision just below the umbilicus through which a fiberoptic laparoscope is inserted. A second incision is made on the left or right side of the abdomen and a second instrument is passed into the abdomen. The physician then manipulates the tools so that the pelvic organs can be observed through the laparoscope. The bladder is suspended by placing several sutures through the tissue surrounding the urethra and into support structures. The sutures are pulled tight so that the urethra is elevated and moved forward. The instruments are removed and incisions are closed with sutures.

The physician may also perform a vesicourethropexy or urethropexy via an open approach. The physician makes a small horizontal incision in the abdomen above the symphysis pubis, which is the midline junction of the pubic bones at the front. The bladder is suspended by placing several sutures through the tissue surrounding the urethra and into the vaginal wall. The sutures are pulled tight so that the tissues are tacked to the symphysis pubis and the urethra is moved forward. The incision is closed by suturing.

In the Stamey procedure, the physician surgically suspends the bladder neck by suturing surrounding tissue to the fibrous membranes (fascia) of the abdomen in a female patient. After inserting a catheter through the urethra to visualize the bladder neck, the physician makes an incision in the vagina, extending it upward toward the base of the bladder. On both sides of the vesical neck, the physician passes a needle through a small incision in the skin above the pubic bone down through the vaginal incision. The physician threads the needle in the vagina and pulls the needle back through the suprapubic incision. Dacron tubing may be threaded onto the sutures to provide extra periurethral support. The physician repeats this process, using an endoscope to ensure proper placement of the suspending sutures. After placing sutures on both sides of the bladder neck, the physician uses moderate upward traction to tighten the bladder neck. The physician inserts a drain tube, bringing it out through a stab incision in the skin, and performs layered closure.

Coding Clarification
Use 59.79 to report a Tudor "rabbit ear" urethropexy, which is an anterior urethropexy.

The Stamey procedure is coded 59.79 but the Stamey test is assigned 59.8.

Documentation Tip
The Stamey procedure may also be documented as a Raz or Modified Pereyra procedure.

Review the documentation for specific information regarding the procedure prior to final code selection in order to avoid improper use of the "not otherwise specified" code and to ensure accurate code assignment.

Coding Guidance
AHA: 1Q, '00, 14, 15, 19; 2Q, '01, 20

59.8   Ureteral catheterization

Description
The physician inserts a catheter or stent through the renal pelvis into the ureter for drainage of urine and/or an injection. The physician usually inserts a long, thin needle with a removable probe in the skin of the back. The physician advances the needle toward the renal pelvis and into the ureter. When urine flows back through the needle, the physician

55-59

advances a catheter over the needle. The physician removes the needle and leaves the catheter in place for drainage and/or injection.

In an alternate technique, the physician percutaneously removes an internally dwelling ureteral stent through the renal pelvis in one example. With the patient under conscious sedation, a long, thin needle is advanced into the renal calyx under imaging guidance and the position is confirmed with contrast and fluoroscopy. A guidewire is threaded over the needle into the renal pelvis, the needle is removed, and a sheath is placed over the guidewire. A snare device is then threaded through the sheath into position. The indwelling stent is grasped and pulled out partially through the sheath until the proximal end is outside the ureter. A guidewire is threaded through the stent, which is then guided completely out. In some cases, the physician replaces the indwelling ureteral stent after removal of the old stent. The guidewire is left in place, the length of the old stent is noted, and the replacement stent is advanced into the ureter until the distal end is in the bladder and the distal loop is deployed. Stent position is confirmed with the proximal loop in the renal pelvis. The instruments are removed.

Coding Clarification
In some cases, a two-step procedure may be performed: a ureteral catheterization with manipulation of a ureteral stone back to the renal pelvis followed by percutaneous nephrostomy with stone fragmentation or extracorporeal shock wave lithotripsy of kidney, ureter, and/or bladder.

Code 59.8 is used to report drainage of a kidney by catheter, insertion of a ureteral stent, and ureterovesical orifice dilation.

Assign 59.8 for the insertion of a double J catheter or stent into the renal pelvis.

Code 59.8 is not used to report ureteral catheterization for transurethral removal of a calculus or clot from the ureter and renal pelvis (56.0) or retrograde pyelogram (87.74).

Code in addition any ureterotomy (56.2) performed.

Documentation Tip
Ureteral catheterization procedures are performed using a variety of surgical techniques and approaches ranging from open surgery to less invasive procedures, such as laparoscopy, percutaneous techniques, or transurethrally via cystoscopy.

Review the documentation for specific information regarding the procedure prior to final code selection in order to ensure accurate code assignment.

Coding Guidance
   AHA: S-O, '86, 10; 1Q, '89, 1; 3Q, '00, 7; 2Q, '03, 11; 2Q, '05, 12

59.9   Other operations on urinary system

Description
Subcategory 59.9 codes are used to report procedures of the urinary system that are not more precisely described by other codes in category 59.

Coding Clarification
To report nonoperative removal of a therapeutic device, see 97.61-97.69.

Documentation Tip
Review the documentation for specific information regarding the procedure prior to final code selection in order to ensure accurate code assignment.

59.91   Excision of perirenal or perivesical tissue

Description
The physician performs cryosurgical ablation of one or more renal mass lesions. The physician performs a laparotomy. Dissection is carried down to the kidney. Intraoperative ultrasound may be used to identify the lesion. Special cryosurgical probes are inserted into the kidney lesion. The cryosurgical probe delivers cryogen, a coolant, at subfreezing temperatures to freeze the lesion. The renal tissue is slowly thawed. A minimum of two cycles of freezing and thawing are performed. This is repeated for each lesion. When all lesions have been treated, the incision is closed with layered sutures.

The physician excises a cyst on the kidney or in the surrounding renal tissue. To access the kidney, the physician makes an incision in the skin of the flank, cuts the muscles, fat, and fibrous membranes (fascia) overlying the kidney, and sometimes removes a portion of the twelfth rib. After clearing away the fatty tissue surrounding the kidney, the physician excises the cyst from the renal surface. The physician destroys tiny vessels bordering the cyst with high-frequency electric current (fulguration) to minimize the need for sutures. If the cyst requires a deep excision, the physician usually sutures the renal tissue. The physician inserts a drain tube, bringing it out through a separate stab incision in the skin, and performs layered closure.

Coding Clarification
A biopsy of perirenal or perivesical tissue is reported with 59.21.

59.92   Other operations on perirenal or perivesical tissue

Description
The physician drains urine that has passed out of the urethra (extravasation) into the perineal tissue.

● New Code   ▲ Revised Code   ▶◀ Revised Text   © 2010 Ingenix

The physician makes an incision through the skin over the site. The incision is carried to the extravasation for drainage. Following drainage, the incision is closed with sutures.

59.93   Replacement of ureterostomy tube

Description
The physician changes a ureterostomy tube or an externally accessible ureteral stent via an ileal conduit. To remove the existing tube, the physician takes out the sutures securing the tube to the skin. The physician inserts a guidewire through the tube and passes the tube back over the guidewire. The physician passes a new tube over the guidewire, removes the guidewire, and sutures the tube to the skin. To change an externally accessible ureteral stent via an ileal conduit, a guidewire is inserted through the ileal conduit. An ileal conduit is an isolated loop of ileum to which the ureter has been anastomosed at one end with the opposite end exiting through the skin and attached to an ostomy bag. The existing stent is retrieved and a new stent is placed. The guidewire is removed.

Coding Clarification
Code 59.93 is used to report change of a ureterostomy tube or reinsertion of a ureterostomy tube.

Code 59.93 excludes nonoperative removal of a ureterostomy tube (97.62).

59.94   Replacement of cystostomy tube

Description
The physician changes a cystostomy tube. To remove the existing tube, the physician removes the sutures securing the tube to the skin. In some cases, the physician inserts a guidewire through the tube and passes the tube back over the guidewire. The physician passes a new tube over the guidewire, removes the guidewire, and sutures the tube to the skin. Occasionally, complications such as infection, inflammation, hemorrhage, constriction, or dilation may arise.

Coding Clarification
This code is not used to report nonoperative removal of a cystostomy tube; see 97.63.

59.95   Ultrasonic fragmentation of urinary stones

Description
The physician uses ultrasound to smash a calculus. The physician examines the urinary collecting system with a cystourethroscope passed through the urethra and bladder to remove a foreign body. The physician inserts an instrument that generates shock waves through the cystourethroscope. The physician crushes the calculus in the bladder (litholapaxy) and washes out the fragments through a catheter. Post-shockwave fragments too large to be easily suctioned may require manual crushing.

Coding Clarification
This code does not include percutaneous nephrostomy with fragmentation (55.04) or shockwave disintegration (98.51).

Assign 59.95 for ultrasonic or hydraulic shock fragmentation of a urinary stone(s). An additional code should be assigned for the approach used.

Coding Guidance
   AHA: S-0, '86, 11; 1Q, '89, 1

59.99   Other operations on urinary system

Description
Code 59.99 is used to report urinary system procedures that are not more precisely described by other codes in this chapter.

Coding Clarification
This code does not include instillation of medication into the urinary tract (96.49) or irrigation of the urinary tract (96.45-96.48).

Removal of an infected pubovaginal sling is assigned code 59.99 as a procedure code.

Documentation Tip
Review the documentation for specific information regarding the procedure prior to final code selection in order to ensure accurate code assignment.

Coding Guidance
   AHA: 2Q, '08, 14

60-64

Operations on the Male Genital Organs

The ICD-9-CM classification system for operations performed on the male reproductive system is divided into categories of procedures according to sites as follows:

- Operations on Prostate and Seminal Vesicles (60)
- Operations on Scrotum and Tunica Vaginalis (61)
- Operations on Testes (62)
- Operations on Spermatic Cord, Epididymis and Vas Deferens (63)
- Operations on Penis (64)

Coding Clarification
Many of the subcategories in this portion of the classification system require a fourth digit for further specificity with regard to type and/or site of the operation performed.

Operations classifiable to these procedures trigger Medicare Code Edit (MCE) 5, which is used to detect inconsistencies between the patient's sex and the procedure performed. Per these edits, procedures classified to this chapter are reportable only for male patients.

Documentation Tip
Documentation in the operative report must support code selection.

60   Operations on prostate and seminal vesicles

Description
The prostate is normally a walnut-sized gland situated just below the male urinary bladder. The main function of the prostate is to store and secrete seminal fluid (produced in part by the seminal vesicles) and spermatozoa, which combines to form semen. The seminal vesicles are ducted glands that transport seminal fluid through the vas deferens to the prostate gland. The involuntary (smooth)

muscles of the prostate contract to expel semen during ejaculation.

Category 60 provides codes for diagnostic and therapeutic procedures on the prostate and seminal vesicles including incisions, excisions, destruction, biopsy, resections, repairs, dilation, and other procedures.

Coding Clarification
Code also any application or administration of adhesion barrier substance (99.77).

Category 60 includes operations on periprostatic tissue.

Category 60 excludes prostate procedures associated with radical cystectomy (57.71).

60.0   Incision of prostate

Description
This procedure code describes an incision into the prostate, for removal of calculus, drainage of abscess, or other indication. Surgical approach and technique may vary, including:

- **Transurethral:** Through a cystourethroscope, the physician incises the prostate gland. Specimens may be removed through the endoscope. The prostate may be repaired or a drainage device sutured in place. The endoscope is removed upon completion of the procedure. The bladder is catheterized for the immediate postoperative period.

- **Open (incisional):** The physician makes an incision through the skin of the perineum and tissues are dissected to expose the prostate. The prostate is identified and an incision is performed to remove tissue, drain abscess, remove calculus, or other reason. Bleeding is controlled and the dissected tissues and skin incision are closed in layers by suturing.

Coding Clarification
Code 60.0 excludes incision and drainage of periprostatic tissue (60.81).

60-64

60.1   Diagnostic procedures on prostate and seminal vesicles

60.11   Closed (percutaneous) (needle) biopsy of prostate

Description
The physician obtains tissue from the prostate for analysis by needle or punch biopsy through one or more of three approaches. The biopsy needle is passed into the suspect area of the prostate by puncturing through skin of the perineum (the area between the base of the scrotum and the anus), by advancing the needle into the rectum by guidance with the index finger and puncturing through the rectal mucosa, or by advancing a biopsy instrument through the urethra. The biopsy needle is inserted into the prostate guided by an index finger or by ultrasound and the needle biopsy sheath is advanced over the needle and twisted to shear off the enclosed sample. The needle is withdrawn, containing the sample. This may be repeated two or more times to assure adequate sampling and the puncture site is bandaged.

Documentation Tip:
Procedures classifiable to this code may be documented as closed biopsy by the following approach or type:

- Transrectal
- Transurethral
- Punch

60.12   Open biopsy of prostate

Description
The physician obtains tissue from the prostate for analysis by direct incisional sampling. An incision is made and the tissues dissected to expose the prostate. The prostate is identified and an excision is performed to remove tissue for analysis. Bleeding is controlled and the dissected tissues and skin incision are closed in layers by suturing.

60.13   Closed (percutaneous) biopsy of seminal vesicles

Description
The physician obtains tissue from the seminal vesicles for analysis by closed (non-incisional) biopsy. The biopsy needle may be passed into the seminal vesicle by advancing the needle into the rectum by guidance with the index finger and puncturing through the rectal mucosa. The biopsy

needle is inserted into the seminal vesicle guided by an index finger or by ultrasound and the needle biopsy sheath is advanced over the needle and twisted to shear off the enclosed sample. The needle is withdrawn, containing the sample.

60.14   Open biopsy of seminal vesicles

Description
The physician obtains tissue from the seminal vesicle for analysis by direct incisional sampling. An incision is made and the tissues dissected to expose the seminal vesicle. The seminal vesicle is identified and an excision is performed to remove tissue for analysis. Bleeding is controlled and the dissected tissues and skin incision are closed in layers by suturing.

60.15   Biopsy of periprostatic tissue

Description
The physician obtains tissue from the tissue surrounding the prostate for analysis by direct incisional sampling. An incision is made and the tissues dissected to expose the area to be biopsied. The tissue or lesion is identified and an excision is performed to remove tissue for analysis. Bleeding is controlled and the dissected tissues and skin incision are closed in layers by suturing.

60.18   Other diagnostic procedures on prostate and periprostatic tissue

Description
This code describes other diagnostic procedures on prostate and periprostatic tissue not classifiable elsewhere in subcategory 60.1 as an open or closed biopsy.

Coding Clarification
Code 60.18 excludes diagnostic procedures classifiable to Chapter 16 Miscellaneous diagnostic and therapeutic procedures (87-99).

60.19   Other diagnostic procedures on seminal vesicles

Description
This code describes other diagnostic procedures on the seminal vesicles not classifiable elsewhere in subcategory 60.1 as an open or closed biopsy.

Coding Clarification
Code 60.19 excludes diagnostic procedures classifiable to Chapter 16 Miscellaneous diagnostic and therapeutic procedures (87-99).

60-64

● New Code   ▲ Revised Code   ▶◀ Revised Text   © 2010 Ingenix

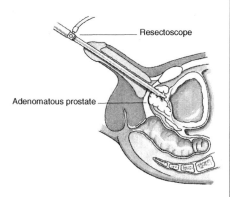

Resectoscope

Adenomatous prostate

60.2   Transurethral prostatectomy

Coding Clarification
Multiple, minimally-invasive therapeutic procedures for the treatment of benign prostatic hypertrophy are available as alternatives to more conventional methods of transurethral resection (TURP). These therapies include:

*   CSA—cryosurgical ablation (60.62)
*   TULIP—transurethral laser-guided prostatectomy (60.21)
*   TUMT—transurethral microwave thermotherapy (60.96)
*   TUNA—transurethral needle ablation (60.97)

Subcategory 60.2 excludes local excision of a lesion of the prostate (60.61).

Coding Guidance
AHA: 3Q, '92, 13; 2Q,'94, 9

60.21   Transurethral (ultrasound) guided laser induced prostatectomy (TULIP)

Description
The physician uses a laser to ablate the prostate through an endoscope inserted through the urethra. Dilation of the urethra may be necessary to permit endoscope insertion. The entire prostate is treated. To accomplish this, vasectomy, meatotomy, cystourethroscopy, and internal urethrotomy may be necessary. Once the laser treatment is complete, a urinary catheter is inserted and the incision is closed in layers.

Coding Scenario
A 67-year-old male presented to the outpatient surgery suite with a history of urinary retention. Diagnostic exam and testing confirmed the presence of an enlarged, obstructing prostate gland. Previous outpatient biopsy ruled out adenocarcinoma, but was diagnostic for benign prostatic hypertrophy. The patient underwent an ultrasound-guided transurethral laser vaporization of the prostate.

Code Assignment:

600.01   Hypertrophy (benign) of prostate with urinary obstruction and other lower urinary tract symptoms (LUTS)
788.20   Retention of urine, unspecified
60.21   Transurethral (ultrasound) guided laser induced prostatectomy (TULIP)

Coding Guidance
AHA: 4Q, '95, 71

60.29   Other transurethral prostatectomy

Description
The physician performs transurethral destruction or excision of the prostate. The physician inserts an endoscope in the penile urethra. Prior to endoscope placement, the urethra may need to be dilated to allow instrument passage. After the endoscope is passed, instrumentation is inserted in the urethra and the diseased prostate is treated with electrovaporization (TEVAP), sharp excision or curette, or other technique. The treated prostate is examined for evidence of bleeding, which may be controlled with electrocoagulation. The endoscope and instruments are removed. A urinary catheter is inserted into the bladder and left in place postoperatively.

Documentation Tip
Procedures classifiable to 60.29 may be documented as transurethral prostate:

*   Excision
*   Electrovaporization (TEVAP)
*   Enucleation
*   Resection (TURP)

Coding Guidance
AHA: 3Q, '97, 3

60.3   Suprapubic prostatectomy

Description
The physician performs resection of the prostate through an incision in the abdomen above the pubic arch.

60.4   Retropubic prostatectomy

Description
Retropubic prostatectomy is the removal of the prostate using an abdominal approach with direct cutting into the prostatic capsule. The physician removes the prostate gland through an incision made in the lower abdomen just above the pubic area. In preparation for removal of the prostate, the caliber (internal diameter) of the urethra is measured and if it is not adequate the opening of the urethra is enlarged (meatotomy) and the diameter of the penile urethra is enlarged with an instrument

60-64

(internal urethrotomy) and a catheter is passed into the urethra into the bladder. Through the lower abdominal incision, the urinary bladder is exposed and opened by an incision in the region just above the bladder neck. During the dissection to expose the bladder a vasectomy may be performed. The bladder mucosa over the prostate is removed by excision to expose the prostate. The gland is removed by "shelling it out" by blunt dissection with the surgeon's index finger. The bladder outlet and the bladder wall are revised and bleeding controlled by packing with rolls of gauze, by ligation, or cautery of bleeding vessels. A second catheter is placed and left in the bladder through the incision in the lower abdomen. A rubber drain is placed in the space between the pubic bone and the bladder and brought out through a separate stab wound. The dissected tissues and the skin incision are closed in layers by suturing.

Coding Clarification
Codes 60.3 and 60.4 exclude local excision of a lesion of the prostate (60.61) and prostatectomy specified as radical (60.5).

Documentation Tip
Procedures classifiable to 60.3 may be documented as a transvesical prostatectomy.

60.5   Radical prostatectomy

Description
This procedure code describes radical prostatectomy by any approach.

In a perineal approach, the physician performs a radical prostatectomy through an incision made in the skin between the base of the scrotum and the anus. If the internal diameter of the urethra is not adequate, the opening of the urethra is enlarged (meatotomy) and the diameter of the penile urethra is enlarged with an instrument (internal urethrotomy). A curved instrument (Lowery Tractor) is advanced into the urethra to the prostate to aid in the dissection. Through the perineal incision and with manipulation of the tractor, the tissues are dissected to expose the prostate. The curved tractor instrument in the urethra is replaced with a straight tractor. The entire gland is removed along with the seminal vesicles and the vas deferens. The bladder outlet is revised and bleeding controlled by ligation or cautery. Local lymph nodes may also be removed for analysis. A Foley catheter is placed and left in the bladder. A rubber drain may be placed in the site of the operative wound and brought out through a separate stab wound. The dissected tissues and the skin incision are closed in layers by suturing.

In a retropubic approach, the physician performs a radical prostatectomy (removal of the prostate gland) through an incision made in the lower abdomen just above the pubic area. In preparation for removal of the prostate, a catheter is passed into the urethra into the bladder. Through a lower abdominal incision, with or without care to spare the nerves in the area, the urinary bladder is exposed and displaced backwards to enter the space behind the pubic bone and expose the area of the prostate. The gland with the capsule intact, the seminal vesicles, and the portions of the vas deferens in the area are removed by freeing the prostate by blunt dissection and by transecting the urethra and cutting through the bladder outlet. The urinary catheter is brought into the operative site and used to create traction for the dissection. A second catheter is place in the bladder after the first one is removed along with the prostate. The transected urethra is repaired by suturing to the newly created bladder outlet. A rubber drain is placed in the space between the pubic bone and the bladder and brought out through a separate stab wound. The dissected tissues and the skin incision are closed in layers by suturing.

Coding Clarification
Radical prostatectomy is the removal of the prostate, epididymis, and vas ampullae. A prostatovesicul-ectomy is the removal of the prostate and epididymis.

Code 60.5 excludes (radical) cystoprostatectomy, which is the excision and removal of the prostate and bladder (57.71).

Coding Guidance
AHA: 3Q, '93, 12

60.6   Other prostatectomy

60.61   Local excision of lesion of prostate

Description
The physician excises a lesion from the prostate, either through the rectal mucosa or by advancing a transurethral instrument to facilitate excision of tissue. If the lesion is excised by open approach, an incision is made and the tissues dissected to expose the prostate. The lesion is identified and an excision is performed. Bleeding is controlled and the dissected tissues and skin incision are closed in layers by suturing.

Coding Clarification
Code 60.61 excludes local excision of a prostate lesion for biopsy (60.11-60.12) and laser interstitial thermal therapy (LITT) of lesions of the prostate under guidance (17.69).

60-64

60.62   Perineal prostatectomy

Description
The physician performs an excision of prostate tissue through an incision in the space between the scrotum and anus.

In a perineal approach, the physician performs a prostatectomy (removal of the prostate gland) through an incision made in the perineum. The caliber (internal diameter) of the urethra is measured and if it is not adequate, the opening of the urethra is enlarged (meatotomy) and the diameter of the penile urethra is enlarged with an instrument (internal urethrotomy). A curved instrument (Lowery Tractor) is advanced into the urethra to the prostate to help identify the structures and aid in the dissection. Through the perineal incision and with manipulation of the tractor, the tissues are dissected to expose the prostate. The curved tractor instrument in the urethra is replaced with a straight tractor. A portion of the prostate or the entire gland is removed with care to preserve the seminal vesicles. The operation is "subtotal" because the seminal vesicles remain intact. The bladder outlet is revised and the vas deferens is ligated and may be partially removed (vasectomy). Bleeding is controlled by ligation or cautery. A Foley catheter is placed in the bladder. A rubber drain may be placed in the site of the operative wound and brought out through a separate stab wound. The dissected tissues and the skin incision are closed in layers by suturing.

In a cryoprostatectomy, the physician performs cryosurgical ablation of the prostate with ultrasonic guidance for interstitial cryosurgical probe placement. The physician places a suprapubic catheter into the bladder through a stab incision just above the pubic hairline. Next, the physician inserts a warming catheter through the urethra and into the bladder. The scrotum is elevated out of the operative field using a gauze sling. An ultrasound probe is inserted into the rectum to monitor the freezing process, and to view in real-time the probe placement during the procedure. Under ultrasonic guidance, the surgeon inserts three to eight needles into the perineum and advances the needles into the prostate. The surgeon advances a guidewire into each needle to facilitate instrumentation. The skin is incised and a dilator is inserted over each guidewire to dilate the channels. Saline is injected to aid visibility of the ultrasound, the guidewire is removed, and a cryoprobe (3 mm diameter) is inserted through each dilator for direct contact with the prostate tissue. The cryoprobes, which deliver super-cooled liquid nitrogen or argon gas (both inert materials) to the prostate, are turned on at -70°C. Up to five cryoprobes can be running simultaneously at any one time. The five cryoprobes are turned on,

taking the temperature down to -190°C, while the warming catheter guards against freezing the ureter. If the prostate thaws, the probes may be re-positioned, and a second freeze may be performed. Once the prostate gland is completely frozen (resembling an ice ball) and all of the visible prostate tissue is destroyed, the surgeon removes the probes and applies pressure to the perineum to prevent hematoma formation. The punctures are sutured shut and the urethral warming catheter is removed.

Coding Clarification
Code 60.62 excludes local excision of a lesion of the prostate (60.61).

Documentation Tip
Procedures classifiable to 60.62 may be documented as prostate:

- Cryoablation
- Cryosurgery
- Cryoprostatectomy
- Radical cryosurgical ablation of prostate (RCSA)

Coding Guidance
AHA: 4Q, '95, 71

60.69   Other prostatectomy

Description
This code describes other prostatectomy procedures not classifiable elsewhere in category 60.

Coding Clarification
This procedure code should not be assigned if the medical record contains sufficient information to facilitate coding at a higher level of specificity.

Documentation Tip
If the documentation is ambiguous or unclear, the physician should be queried.

60.7   Operations on seminal vesicles

60.71   Percutaneous aspiration of seminal vesicle

Description
The physician obtains a specimen from the seminal vesicles by aspiration. An aspiration may be performed by advancing a needle into the rectum by guidance with the index finger and puncturing through the rectal mucosa. The needle is inserted into the seminal vesicle guided by an index finger or by ultrasound and a sheath is advanced over the needle. The aspirate is obtained in the needle and the needle is withdrawn.

Coding Clarification
Code 60.71 excludes aspiration for closed (needle) biopsy (60.13).

60–64

60.72   Incision of seminal vesicle

Description
The physician incises a seminal vesicle. The seminal vesicle is approached through an incision in the lower abdomen or an incision in the perineum (area between the base of the scrotum and the anus). In the abdominal method, the physician retracts the bladder forward toward the pubic bone to expose the back of the bladder where the seminal vesicles are positioned, or the surgeon cuts through the front and back walls to gain access to the gland. The operative wounds are closed in layers by suturing.

60.73   Excision of seminal vesicle

Description
This procedure code describes excision of the seminal vesicle or other associated lesion. Surgical technique may vary, including:

- **Open excision and removal of seminal vesicle:** The physician removes one of the seminal vesicles, the paired glands that lie behind the urinary bladder and produce a fluid that is mixed with semen from the testis. Through an incision in the lower abdomen or an incision in the perineum (area between the base of the scrotum and the anus), the seminal vesicle is approached. If the abdominal method is used, the surgeon retracts the bladder forward toward the pubic bone to expose the back of the bladder where the seminal vesicles are positioned or the surgeon cuts through the front and back walls to gain access to the glands. The surgeon dissects the gland free of its attachments and clips it at its joint with the ejaculatory duct and removes it. The operative wounds are closed in layers by suturing.

- **Excision of Mullerian duct cyst:** The physician excises a Mullerian duct cyst, a remnant of the prenatal development of the seminal vesicle. The seminal vesicles are paired glands that lie behind the urinary bladder and produce a fluid that is mixed with the semen from the testis. Through an incision in the lower abdomen or an incision in the perineum (area between the base of the scrotum and the anus), the seminal vesicle is approached. If the abdominal method is used, the surgeon retracts the bladder forward toward the pubic bone to expose the back of the bladder where the seminal vesicles are positioned or the surgeon cuts through the front and back walls to gain access to the glands. The surgeon dissects the cyst free of its attachments and clips it at the attachment to the seminal vesicle and removes it. The operative wounds are closed in layers by suturing.

Coding Clarification
Code 60.73 excludes excision for biopsy of the seminal vesicle (60.13-60.14) and prostatovesiculectomy (60.5).

60.79   Other operations on seminal vesicles

Description
This procedure code reports other operations on the seminal vesicles not classifiable elsewhere in category 60.

Coding Clarification
This procedure should not be assigned if the medical record contains sufficient information to facilitate coding at a higher level of specificity.

Documentation Tip
If the documentation is ambiguous or unclear, the physician should be queried.

60.8   Incision or excision of periprostatic tissue

60.81   Incision of periprostatic tissue

Description
The physician performs diagnostic or therapeutic cutting or puncturing of the tissue surrounding the prostate. The physician makes an incision into the tissue surrounding the prostate for drainage of an abscess or other reason. An incision is made and the periprostatic tissues are dissected to expose the area to be treated. The physician performs a precision incision or puncture. Bleeding is controlled and the skin incision is closed in layers by suturing.

60.82   Excision of periprostatic tissue

Description
The physician cuts and removes the tissue surrounding the prostate. The physician makes an incision into the tissue surrounding the prostate and sharply excises and removes a lesion or other tissue. An incision is made and the periprostatic tissues are dissected to expose the lesion or tissue to be excised. The physician performs a sharp excision and sutures or cauterizes the defect, if necessary. Bleeding is controlled and the skin incision is closed in layers by suturing.

60.9   Other operations on prostate

60.91   Percutaneous aspiration of prostate

Description
The physician obtains a fluid sample from the prostate for analysis by percutaneous needle aspiration. The needle is passed into the suspect area of the prostate with radiological guidance. Fluid is aspirated and withdrawn through the needle. If the approach to the prostate puncture is through the perineum, the puncture site is bandaged.

 ● New Code   ▲ Revised Code   ▶◀ Revised Text   © 2010 Ingenix

Coding Clarification
Code 60.91 excludes aspiration via needle biopsy of the prostate (60.11).

60.92   Injection into prostate

Description
This procedure code reports a locally acting medication or substance injected into the prostate by a radiologically-guided needle.

60.93   Repair of prostate

Description
This code describes other repair operation of the prostate not classifiable elsewhere in category 60.

Coding Clarification
This procedure code should not be assigned if the medical record contains sufficient information to facilitate coding at a higher level of specificity.

Documentation Tip
If the documentation is ambiguous or unclear, the physician should be queried.

60.94   Control of (postoperative) hemorrhage of prostate

Description
This code describes control of hemorrhage of the prostate, postoperative or other. Surgical technique and approach may vary, including:

* **Transurethral fulguration:** The physician inserts an endoscope in the urethra of the male patient and uses fulguration to control postoperative bleeding occurring after the global period has passed for the original surgery.

* **Laser vaporization or coagulation:** The physician uses a laser to coagulate or vaporize the prostate through an endoscope inserted through the urethra. Dilation of the urethra may be necessary to permit endoscope insertion. The entire prostate may be treated. To accomplish this, vasectomy, meatotomy, cystourethroscopy, and internal urethrotomy may be necessary. Once the laser treatment is complete, a urinary catheter is inserted and the incision is closed in layers.

60.95   Transurethral balloon dilation of the prostatic urethra

Description
The physician enlarges the diameter of the urethra that passes through the prostate by inflating a balloon catheter inside the urethra. The physician may first pass instruments through the urethra to prepare the way for the balloon catheter. The balloon portion of the catheter is positioned in the urethra surrounded by the prostate and gently inflated to enlarge the passageway by stretching the urethra and compressing the surrounding tissues. The inflation may be repeated several times until adequate dilation of the prostatic urethra is achieved. The scope and balloon catheter are removed.

Coding Guidance
    AHA: 4Q, '91, 23

60.96   Transurethral destruction of prostate tissue by microwave thermotherapy

60.97   Other transurethral destruction of prostate tissue by other thermotherapy

Description
The physician performs transurethral destruction of prostate tissue by microwave thermotherapy (60.96) or other thermotherapy (60.97). The urethra may need to be dilated to allow instrument passage. The physician inserts an endoscope in the penile urethra. After the endoscope is passed, a microwave thermotherapy, radiotherapy, or other stylet is inserted in the urethra and the diseased prostate is treated with electromagnetic or other radiation. The treated prostate is examined for evidence of bleeding, which may be controlled with electrocoagulation. The endoscope and instruments are removed. A urinary catheter is inserted into the bladder and left in place postoperatively.

In an alternate procedure (60.97), the physician performs transurethral destruction of prostate tissue by water-induced thermotherapy (WIT) using a topical urethral anesthetic. A catheter with a balloon tip is inserted through the penis to the prostatic urethra. The catheter shaft is insulated to protect the urethra. The other end of the catheter is connected to a console that heats water. Hot water (40 degrees centigrade) is circulated through the balloon for 45 minutes. The conductive heat transmitted by the balloon (generated by the hot water) to a specific area destroys (necrotizes) some of the prostatic tissue, effectively reducing the size of the prostate and relieving symptoms of urinary obstruction. At the end of the procedure, the balloon catheter is removed and a urinary catheter is left in place.

Coding Clarification
Codes 60.96 (TUMT) and 60.97 (includes TUNA) describe therapies that provide minimally-invasive alternatives to transurethral prostate resection (TURP). Both therapies utilize a sylet or needle placed through the urethra to deliver heat energy to destroy prostate tissue.

This procedure lists multiple exclusions for specific prostatectomy procedures classifiable elsewhere in category 60.

60-64

Coding Guidance
AHA: 4Q, '00, 67

60.99 Other operations on prostate

Description
This code describes other repair prostate procedures not classifiable elsewhere in category 60.

Coding Clarification
This procedure code should not be assigned if the medical record contains sufficient information to facilitate coding at a higher level of specificity.

Code 60.99 excludes prostatic massage (99.94).

Documentation Tip
If the documentation is ambiguous or unclear, the physician should be queried.

Coding Guidance
AHA: 3Q, '90, 12

---

61 Operations on scrotum and tunica vaginalis

Description
The scrotum is a sac-like structure of the male genitalia that contains the testicles. The main function of the scrotum is to encase the testes outside of the body, facilitating a slightly cooler, more beneficial temperature for the storage of sperm. The tunica vaginalis consists of a multi-layered, protective serous membrane covering the testes. Male reproductive diseases and disorders such as hernia, hydrocele, infection, injury, and disorders may necessitate surgical intervention.

Category 61 provides codes for diagnostic and therapeutic procedures on the scrotum and tunica vaginalis, including incisions, excisions, destruction, biopsy, repairs, and other procedures.

61.0 Incision and drainage of scrotum and tunica vaginalis

Description
The physician drains a collection of blood or an abscess within the scrotum. The testes may be held firmly with the scrotal skin stretched tightly over the testis and the epididymis positioned away from the site. An incision is made through the skin of the scrotum. The underlying tissues are incised and dissected to expose the site to be drained. The testis may be stabilized by two sutures as an incision is made. If the incision is for drainage of an abscess or a hematoma, fluid is expressed. Packing or a rubber drain may be placed to promote drainage. The incisions are usually not closed by suturing.

61.1 Diagnostic procedures on scrotum and tunica vaginalis

61.11 Biopsy of scrotum or tunica vaginalis

Description
The physician removes a biopsy sample of skin, subcutaneous tissue, and/or mucous membrane of the scrotum or tunica vaginalis for microscopic examination. Some normal tissue adjacent to the diseased tissue is also removed for comparison purposes. The excision site may be closed simply or may be allowed to granulate without closure.

61.19 Other diagnostic procedures on scrotum and tunica vaginalis

Description
This code describes other diagnostic procedures on the scrotum and tunica vaginalis not specified as biopsy.

Coding Clarification
This procedure should not be assigned if the medical record contains sufficient information to facilitate coding at a higher level of specificity.

Documentation Tip
If the documentation is ambiguous or unclear, the physician should be queried.

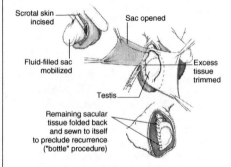

Scrotal skin incised — Sac opened — Fluid-filled sac mobilized — Excess tissue trimmed — Testis — Remaining sacular tissue folded back and sewn to itself to preclude recurrence ("bottle" procedure)

61.2 Excision of hydrocele (of tunica vaginalis)

Description
The physician performs excision of a tunica vaginalis hydrocele, which is removal of fluid collected in the serous membrane of the testes. Surgical technique may vary, including:

- **Excision of hydrocele:** A hydrocele is a sac of fluid in the tunica vaginalis or along the spermatic cord. The physician treats a hydrocele by removing it. After injecting an area with local anesthetic and using aseptic techniques, the physician makes an incision in the scrotum or in the inguinal area. Care is taken to keep the hydrocele intact while it is dissected free of its attachments to the testis and other structures. The sac is opened,

● New Code　　　▲ Revised Code　　　►◄ Revised Text　　　© 2010 Ingenix

drained, and partially excised leaving a remnant of tissue. The remaining tissue is swung back behind the epididymis and the spermatic cord and closed by suturing the edges together. The testis is anchored to the inside of the scrotum with three sutures to prevent later torsion or twisting of the testis. A rubber drain may be left in the scrotum and the incision is closed in layers by suturing.

- **Repair of bottle type hydrocele:** The physician treats a hydrocele by removing the abnormal fluid filled sac in the scrotum or in the inguinal canal. After injecting an area with local anesthetic and using aseptic techniques, the physician makes an incision in the scrotum or in the inguinal area. Care is taken to keep the hydrocele intact while it is dissected free of its attachments to the testis and other structures. The sac is opened high along its front surface and the testis is pushed up through the sac and out through the incision. This inverts the hydrocele sac, which is tacked by suturing to the spermatic cord structures behind the testis. The testis is returned to the scrotum and is anchored to the inside of the scrotum with three sutures to prevent later torsion or twisting of the testis. A rubber drain may be left in the scrotum and the incision is closed in layers by suturing.

Coding Clarification
Code 61.2 excludes percutaneous aspiration of a hydrocele (61.91).

61.3   Excision or destruction of lesion or tissue of scrotum

Description
This procedure code describes the excision, destruction, fulguration, or reduction of a lesion or tissue of the scrotum. Surgical technique may vary, depending on the nature of the diagnosis and extent of disease, including:

- **Excision:** The physician excises a lesion of the scrotum. After administering a local anesthetic, the physician makes a full-thickness incision through the dermis with a scalpel, usually in an elliptical shape around and under the lesion, and removes it. The physician may suture the wound simply.

- **Destruction:** The physician destroys a lesion of the scrotum. Destruction may be accomplished by using a laser or electrocautery to burn the lesion, cryotherapy to freeze the lesion, chemicals to destroy the lesion, or surgical curettement to remove the lesion.

Coding Clarification
Code 61.3 excludes excision for biopsy (61.11) or fistulectomy (61.42).

61.4   Repair of scrotum and tunica vaginalis

61.41   Suture of laceration of scrotum and tunica vaginalis

Description
The physician sutures a laceration of the scrotum or tunica vaginalis. A local anesthetic is injected around the laceration and the wound is cleansed, explored, and often irrigated with a saline solution. Tissues may be dissected free. The physician performs suture repair of the scrotum and/or tunica vaginalis wound. A drain may be placed. The incision is closed with layered sutures.

61.42   Repair of scrotal fistula

61.49   Other repair of scrotum and tunica vaginalis

Description
The physician repairs defects and other abnormalities of the scrotum by excision and repair (e.g., fistula 61.42) or the creation and suturing of simple scrotal skin flaps. Reconstruction (61.49) is a complex repair whereby the physician uses free skin grafts, mesh grafts, and/or the extensive use of rotational pedicle grafts from adjacent skin. Drains may be placed. Upon adequate repair of the defect, the incision is closed in layers.

61.9   Other operations on scrotum and tunica vaginalis

61.91   Percutaneous aspiration of tunica vaginalis

Description
A hydrocele is a sac of fluid in the tunica vaginalis or along the spermatic cord. The physician treats a hydrocele by aspirating the fluid. After injecting a small area with local anesthetic, the physician inserts a needle on an aspirating syringe into the fluid filled hydrocele sac and withdraws the fluid into the syringe. After the aspiration and with the needle still in place, the sac may be injected with sclerosing medication to prevent accumulation of new fluid by stimulating scarring and hardening of the empty sac.

61.92   Excision of lesion of tunica vaginalis other than hydrocele

Description
The physician excises a lesion or tissue other than a hydrocele from the tunica vaginalis. The physician makes an incision overlying the lesion and dissects skin and subcutaneous tissues to the tunica vaginalis. The lesion is identified, dissected free,

60–64

excised, and removed. The defect is repaired. Drains may be placed. The incision is closed in layers.

Coding Clarification
Code 61.92 includes excision of a hematocele, which is removal of blood collected in the tunica vaginalis.

61.99   Other operations on scrotum and tunica vaginalis

Description
This procedure code includes other operations on the scrotum and tunica vaginalis not classifiable elsewhere in category 61.

Coding Clarification
This procedure should not be assigned if the medical record contains sufficient information to facilitate coding at a higher level of specificity.

Documentation Tip
If the documentation is ambiguous or unclear, the physician should be queried.

---

62   Operations on testis

Description
The testes are a pair of male reproductive glands encased within the scrotal sac. The testicles play an important role in the male reproductive system as both reproductive organs that produce semen and endocrine organs that produce the male hormones, such as testosterone.

The testicles are sensitive to impact and injury, due to their location and position outside of the body, encased in the scrotum. Many diseases can have adverse effects on testicular function. Some of the most common conditions include:

*   Testicular tumors, including cancer
*   Torsion—painful twisting of the testicle or spermatic cord structure
*   Varicocele—varicose veins of the scrotum
*   Male infertility—conditions originating in the male that prohibit conception

Depending on the nature of the diagnosis, one or both testes may require surgical intervention. If removal of one or both testes is necessary, a prosthesis may be inserted to restore the appearance and feel of having both testicles.

Category 62 provides codes for diagnostic and therapeutic procedures on the testes, including biopsy, incisions, excisions, castration, repairs, and other procedures.

62.0   Incision of testis

Description
The physician performs a surgical incision into the testes for drainage or other reason. The testes may

be held firmly with the scrotal skin stretched tightly over the testis and the epididymis positioned away from the site. An incision is made through the skin of the scrotum. The underlying tissues are incised and dissected to expose the testis and the site to be incised or drained. The testis may be stabilized by two sutures as an incision is made into an abscess or hematoma and fluid is expressed. Packing or a rubber drain may be placed to promote drainage. The incisions are usually not closed by suturing.

62.1   Diagnostic procedures on testes

62.11   Closed (percutaneous) (needle) biopsy of testis

Description
The physician obtains a sample of testicular tissue by needle biopsy. While the testis is held firmly with the scrotal skin stretched tightly over the testis and the epididymis positioned away from the biopsy site, a biopsy needle is inserted into the testis at the area of concern. The needle biopsy sheath is advanced over the needle and twisted to shear off the enclosed sample and withdrawn with the sample enclosed. The scrotal wound may be closed by suturing.

62.12   Open biopsy of testis

Description
The physician obtains a sample of testicular tissue by direct incisional biopsy. The procedure is done under local or regional anesthesia. While the testis is held firmly with the scrotal skin stretched tightly over the testis and the epididymis positioned away from the biopsy site, a small incision is made through the skin of the scrotum. The underlying tissues are incised and dissected to expose the testis. The testis is stabilized by two sutures and an ellipse of tissue is removed between the two sutures. The incisions are closed by suturing.

62.19   Other diagnostic procedures on testes

Description
This code describes other diagnostic operation on the testes not classifiable as biopsy.

Coding Clarification
This procedure should not be assigned if the medical record contains sufficient information to facilitate coding at a higher level of specificity.

Documentation Tip
If the documentation is ambiguous or unclear, the physician should be queried.

62.2   Excision or destruction of testicular lesion

Description
The physician excises a lesion of the testis. The physician makes an inguinal incision, incising the skin and subcutaneous fat. The testicle is delivered

through the incision, the tunica vaginalis is opened, and the lesion is excised. The incision is closed with suture.

Coding Clarification
Code 62.2 excludes biopsy of testes (62.11-62.12).

Documentation Tip
Procedures classifiable to 62.2 may be documented as excision of:

- Appendix testes
- Cyst of Morgagni
- Hydatid of Morgagni

62.3   Unilateral orchiectomy

Description
An incision is made in one side of the scrotum and the tissues are separated to expose the spermatic cord. The spermatic cord is opened and the individual bundles making up the cord are cross-clamped, cut, and secured with nonabsorbable suture material. The testis is removed through the scrotal incision. If the patient so chooses, and if no contraindications are present, a prosthetic testis is inserted into the scrotum before the wound is closed in layers by suturing. An alternative method uses an incision in the groin. The testis is pulled through the incision after cutting and tying the cord in a fashion similar to the scrotal approach.

62.4   Bilateral orchiectomy

Description
The physician removes both testes.

Coding Clarification
Code also any synchronous lymph node dissection (40.3, 40.5).

Documentation Tip
Procedures classifiable to subcategory 62.4 may be documented as:

- Male castration
- Radical bilateral orchiectomy (with epididymectomy)—removal of both testes and structures that store sperm

62.41   Removal of both testes at same operative episode

62.42   Removal of remaining testis

Description
These procedure codes describe excision and removal of both testes in the same operative episode (62.41) or an excision of a solitary testicle (62.42). Surgical approach and technique may vary, including:

- **Simple:** The physician makes an incision in one side of the scrotum and the tissues are separated to expose the spermatic cord. The spermatic cord is opened and the individual bundles making up the cord are cross-clamped, cut, and secured with nonabsorbable suture material. The testis is removed through the scrotal incision. If the patient so chooses, and if no contraindications are present, a prosthetic testis is inserted into the scrotum before the wound is closed in layers by suturing. An alternative method uses an incision in the groin. The testis is pulled through the incision after cutting and tying the cord in a fashion similar to the scrotal approach.

- **Radical:** The physician performs a radical orchiectomy by removing the contents of the scrotum. An incision is made in the inguinal area from the pubic bone toward the lateral pelvic bone. The incision is made deep into the tissues and the spermatic cord is dissected free and cross-clamped. The testes and all associated structures are pushed up from the scrotum into the incision and removed. Packing is placed in the empty scrotum. When the spermatic cord is opened and the individual bundles making up the cord are cross-clamped, cut, and secured with nonabsorbable suture material, care is taken to avoid important nerves and vessels in the area. The packing is removed and bleeding controlled. Prosthetic testes may be placed in the scrotum before the incision is closed in layers by suturing. This procedure results in complete removal of the testis.

- **Laparoscopic:** The physician removes one or both testicles, which may be undescended, injured, or diseased using a laparoscope. The physician places a trocar at the umbilicus into the abdominal or retroperitoneal space and insufflates the abdominal cavity. The physician places a laparoscope through the umbilical incision and additional trocars are placed into the abdomen. The testis and all its associated structures are pushed up from the scrotum or freed from their undescended intraabdominal location and removed through the abdominal or retroperitoneal space via the trocar port. Packing may be placed in the empty scrotum. Care is taken to avoid important nerves and vessels in the area. A prosthetic testis may be placed in the scrotum before the incision is closed in layers by suturing. The trocars are removed and the incisions are closed with sutures.

60-64

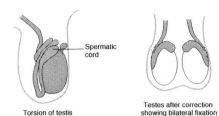

Torsion of testis

Testes after correction showing bilateral fixation

62.5   Orchiopexy

Description
This physician performs surgical fixation of the testes or testicle in the scrotum. Surgical technique may vary, including:

- **Inguinal or scrotal approach:** The physician makes an incision in the scrotum or the inguinal area from the pubic bone to the upper lateral pelvic area in the skin crease made by the thigh and the lower abdomen. If the orchiopexy is performed to treat an undescended testicle, the physician searches for a testis that failed to descend into the scrotum during development. The tissues are separated by dissection to find the testis in the inguinal canal area. The spermatic cord is mobilized to allow positioning of the testis in the scrotum. In the scrotum, a small pouch is created for the testis where the testis is sutured in place to prevent retraction back into the inguinal canal. If there is a concomitant hernia it is often repaired at the same time through the same incision. The hernia present in the inguinal canal is repaired by folding and suturing of tissues to strengthen the abdominal wall and correct the weakness responsible for the hernia. The incision is closed in layers by suturing.

- **Abdominal approach:** The physician makes an incision in the inguinal area from the pubic bone to the upper lateral pelvic area in the skin fold made by the thigh and the lower abdomen. If the orchiopexy is being performed to treat an undescended testicle, the physician searches the abdominal cavity for a testis that failed to descend into the scrotum during development. The tissues are separated by dissection and the incision is extended into the abdominal cavity to find the testis in the abdominal area. The tissues are separated by dissection to find the testis in the area. At this point several surgical options are available. The one chosen will depend on the mobility of the testis and how far it can be brought down through the inguinal canal and into the scrotum. The procedure may take two stages approximately six to 12 months apart. Eventually, the spermatic cord is

mobilized sufficiently to allow positioning of the testis in the scrotum. In the scrotum a small pouch is created for the testis where the testis is sutured in place to prevent retraction back into the inguinal canal or into the abdominal cavity. The incision is closed in layers by suturing.

- **Laparoscopic approach:** The physician performs an orchiopexy with the assistance of a fiberoptic laparoscope. A paraumbilical port is created by placing a trocar at the level of the umbilicus. The abdominal wall is insufflated. The laparoscope is placed through the umbilical port and additional trocars are placed into the abdominal cavity. The physician uses the laparoscope fitted with a fiberoptic camera and/or an operating instrument to search the abdominal cavity for undescended testes. The physician may have several surgical options depending on the mobility of the testis and how far it can be brought down through the inguinal canal and into the scrotum. The procedure may take two stages approximately three to 12 months apart. The spermatic cord is mobilized sufficiently to allow positioning of the testis in the scrotum, which often occurs during the first and perhaps only operative session. A small pouch is created for the testis where the testis is sutured in place to prevent retraction back into the inguinal canal or into the abdominal cavity. The small abdominal incisions are closed by staple or suture in the usual fashion.

Coding Clarification
This procedure may be performed as a staged procedure, in two stages performed approximately three to 12 months apart.

Documentation Tip:
Procedures classifiable code 62.5 may be documented as:

- Mobilization and replacement of testes in scrotum
- Orchiopexy with detorsion of testes
- Torek (-Bevan) operation
- Transplantation and fixation of testes

62.6   Repair of testes

Coding Clarification
Subcategory 62.6 excludes reduction of torsion (63.52).

62.61   Suture of laceration of testis

Description
The physician repairs injury (laceration or traumatic rupture) to the testis that occurs as the result of a blunt or penetrating injury. Often a laceration is present in the scrotum and the testis is explored and

● New Code   ▲ Revised Code   ►◄ Revised Text   © 2010 Ingenix

60-64

repaired through the open wound. Otherwise, an incision is made in the scrotum to expose the testis. Any devitalized testicular tissue is removed by sharp dissection and the thick tough fibrous tissue encasing the testis is closed by suturing. The scrotum is closed in layers by suturing. Often a rubber drain is placed to prevent the accumulation of fluid and blood in the scrotum.

62.69   Other repair of testis

Description
This procedure code describes other repair of the testes not specified as a suture of laceration.

Coding Clarification
This procedure should not be assigned if the medical record contains sufficient information to facilitate coding at a higher level of specificity.

Documentation Tip
If the documentation is ambiguous or unclear, the physician should be queried.

62.7   Insertion of testicular prosthesis

Description
For cosmetic reasons, the physician places an artificial testis in the scrotum of a patient. After adequate local anesthesia, an incision is made in the inguinal area and the empty scrotal sac is dilated by passing a dissecting finger or a moist gauze sponge through the inguinal canal into the scrotum. A prosthetic testis is inserted into the scrotal sac and the neck of the scrotum is closed by suturing. The inguinal incision is closed in layers by suturing.

62.9   Other operations on testes

62.91   Aspiration of testis

Description
The physician performs a percutaneous aspiration procedure that uses a fine gauge needle (22 or 25 gauge) and a syringe to sample fluid from a cyst or remove clusters of cells from a solid mass. First, the skin is cleansed. If a lump can be felt, the radiologist or surgeon guides a needle into the area by palpating the lump. If the lump is non-palpable, the FNA procedure is performed under image guidance using fluoroscopy, ultrasound, or computed tomography (CT), with the patient positioned according to the area of concern. In fluoroscopic guidance, intermittent fluoroscopy guides the advancement of the needle. Ultrasonography-guided aspiration biopsy involves inserting an aspiration catheter needle device through the accessory channel port of the echoendoscope. The needle is placed into the area to be sampled under endoscopic ultrasonographic guidance. After the needle is placed into the region of the lesion, a vacuum is

created and multiple in and out needle motions are performed. Several needle insertions may be required to ensure that an adequate tissue sample is taken. CT image guidance allows computer-assisted targeting of the area to be sampled. At the completion of the procedure, the needle is withdrawn and a small bandage is placed over the area.

Coding Clarification
Code 62.91 excludes percutaneous biopsy of testis (62.11).

62.92   Injection of therapeutic substance into testis

Description
This procedure code describes a locally acting medication or substance injected into the testis, possibly with the assistance of radiological guidance.

62.99   Other operations on testes

Description
This procedure code reports other operations on testes not classifiable elsewhere in category 62.

Coding Clarification
This procedure should not be assigned if the medical record contains sufficient information to facilitate coding at a higher level of specificity.

Documentation Tip
If the documentation is ambiguous or unclear, the physician should be queried.

63   Operations on spermatic cord, epididymis and vas deferens

Description
The spermatic cord refers to a group of structures that extend from the abdomen through the inguinal canal to the testes. The spermatic cord is comprised of the vas deferens, blood and lymphatic vessels, and nerves. The vas deferens contains tubular excretory ducts that function primarily to contract and propel or convey sperm forward into the urethra. The epididymis is tubules connected to the vas deferens from the testes. The main function of the epididymis is to store sperm for reproduction.

Many diseases can have adverse effects on the components of the male reproductive system. The spermatic cord, epididymis, and vas deferens are vulnerable to herniation (displacement), torsion (twisting) infection, and injury. These conditions may have a significant impact on function and fertility. Depending on the nature of the diagnosis, surgical intervention is often necessary.

Category 63 provides codes for diagnostic and therapeutic procedures on the spermatic cord, epididymis, and vas deferens, including biopsy, incisions, excisions, ligation, repairs, and other procedures.

63.0 Diagnostic procedures on spermatic cord, epididymis, and vas deferens

63.01 Biopsy of spermatic cord, epididymis, or vas deferens

Description
The physician may obtain a sample of male reproductive tissues by needle or incisional biopsy. While the testis is held firmly with the scrotal skin stretched tightly over the testis and the underlying structures positioned to facilitate isolation of appropriate tissues, a biopsy needle may be inserted into the area of concern. If a needle biopsy is performed, the needle biopsy sheath is advanced over the needle and twisted to shear off the enclosed sample and withdrawn containing the sample. If an incisional (open) biopsy is performed, tissues are dissected free and the site to be biopsied is exposed. Tissue is excised for biopsy and bleeding is controlled. The scrotal wound may be closed by suturing.

63.09 Other diagnostic procedures on spermatic cord, epididymis, and vas deferens

Description
This code describes other diagnostic procedures on the spermatic cord, epididymis, and vas deferens not classifiable as biopsy.

Coding Clarification
This procedure code should not be assigned if the medical record contains sufficient information to facilitate coding at a higher level of specificity.

Code 63.09 excludes diagnostic procedures classifiable to Chapter 16 Miscellaneous diagnostic and therapeutic procedures (87-99).

Documentation Tip
If the documentation is ambiguous or unclear, the physician should be queried.

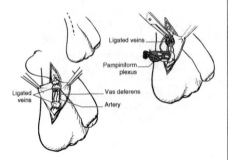

Ligated veins

Pampiniform plexus

Ligated veins

Vas deferens

Artery

63.1 Excision of varicocele and hydrocele of spermatic cord

Description
This procedure code reports excision of variocele and hydrocele of spermatic cord. Surgical technique may vary, including:

- **Open excision:** The physician treats a hydrocele of the spermatic cord by removing it from the spermatic cord above the testis in the scrotum or in the inguinal canal. After injecting the area with a local anesthetic, the physician makes an incision in the scrotum or in the inguinal area. The hydrocele is kept intact while it is freed of its attachments to the spermatic cord. The sac is opened, drained, and excised all the way to the internal inguinal ring in the upper groin area. The remaining tissues are repaired and closed by suturing. The testis is anchored to the inside of the scrotum with three sutures to prevent later torsion or twisting of the testis. A rubber drain may be placed in the scrotum and the incision closed in layers by suturing.

- **Laparoscopic excision:** The physician ligates (ties or binds with suture) the spermatic veins and/or excises a varicocele, which is an abnormal dilation of the veins of the spermatic cord in the scrotum. An umbilical port is created by placing a trocar at the level of the umbilicus. The abdominal wall is insufflated. The laparoscope is placed through the umbilical port and additional trocars are placed into the abdominal or pelvic cavity. The physician uses the laparoscope fitted with a fiberoptic camera and/or an operating instrument to explore and surgically ligate the spermatic veins to repair or remove the varicocele. The structures of the cord are dissected, the veins identified, and ligated with suture. The abdomen is deflated, the trocars removed, and the incisions are closed with sutures.

Documentation Tip:
Procedures classifiable to 63.1 may be documented as:

- High ligation of spermatic vein

- Hydrocelectomy of canal of Nuck

63.2 Excision of cyst of epididymis

Description
The physician removes a spermatocele, which is a small cyst filled with fluid and spermatozoa between the body of the testis and the epididymis. After adequate local anesthesia, an incision is made in the scrotum and the testis with its attached epididymis is brought out of the wound. The cyst is dissected free of the testis and excised. The involved area of

60-64

the epididymis is sutured to the underlying testis and the scrotal wound is closed by suturing. Alternately, the epididymis may be dissected free of all its attachments to the testis. The blood vessels involved are tied and cut and/or cauterized to control bleeding. The freed epididymis is removed, a rubber drain is placed in the scrotum, and the incision is closed by suturing.

63.3 Excision of other lesion or tissue of spermatic cord and epididymis

Description
The physician may remove a lesion of the spermatic cord or epididymis by direct incision. The procedure is done under local or regional anesthesia. While the testis is held firmly with the scrotal skin stretched tightly over the testis, a small incision is made through the skin of the scrotum. The underlying tissues are incised and dissected to expose the area lesion. The epididymis or spermatic cord may be stabilized by two sutures placed on each side of the lesion and an ellipse of tissue is removed from the epididymis or spermatic cord containing the lesion between the two sutures. The stabilizing sutures are tied across the excision site. The scrotal incision is closed by suturing.

Coding Clarification
Code 63.3 excludes excision for biopsy of the spermatic cord or epididymis (63.01).

63.4 Epididymectomy

Description
The physician removes the epididymis. After adequate local anesthesia, an incision is made in the scrotum and the testis with its attached epididymis is brought out of the wound. The epididymis is dissected free of all its attachments to the testis. The blood vessels involved are tied and cut and/or cauterized to control bleeding. The freed epididymis is removed, a rubber drain is left in the scrotum, and the incision is closed by suturing. If a bilateral epididymectomy is required, the procedure is repeated on the other site.

Coding Clarification
Code 63.4 excludes epididymectomy with synchronous orchiectomy (62.3-62.42).

63.5 Repair of spermatic cord and epididymis

63.51 Suture of laceration of spermatic cord and epididymis

Description
The physician repairs a laceration injury to the spermatic cord and epididymis. The wound may be repaired upon exploration of an open wound. Otherwise, an extension or incision is made in order

to remove any devitalized tissue and dissect the tissues to the site of laceration. The laceration is closed by suturing. Bleeding is controlled. A drain may be placed to prevent the accumulation of fluid and blood in the tissues. The wound is closed with layered sutures.

63.52 Reduction of torsion of testis or spermatic cord

Description
The physician corrects a twisted testes or spermatic cord. The physician makes an incision in the scrotum and exposes the twisted cord. The testis and/or spermatic cord is untwisted to restore blood flow to the organ. The incision is closed in layers by suturing.

Coding Clarification
Code 63.52 excludes reduction of torsion associated with orchiopexy (62.5).

63.53 Transplantation of spermatic cord

Description
The physician performs surgical grafting of spermatic cord tissues. The graft may be obtained from:

- A donor site in the patient's own body whereby the defective section of cord is replaced with a healthy section of cord
- Another person's (donor's) body
- Other donor species into the patient

63.59 Other repair of spermatic cord and epididymis

Description
This procedure code reports other spermatic cord or epididymis repair operations not classifiable elsewhere in subcategory 63.5 as suture, reduction of torsion, or transplantation.

Coding Clarification
This procedure code should not be assigned if the medical record contains sufficient information to facilitate coding at a higher level of specificity.

Documentation Tip
If the documentation is ambiguous or unclear, the physician should be queried.

63.6 Vasotomy

Description
The physician enters the vas deferens (the tube that carries spermatozoa from the testis) for the purpose of obtaining a sample of semen or testing the patency of the tubes. Under local anesthesia, an incision is made in the upper outer scrotum overlying the spermatic cord. The tissues are dissected to expose the vas deferens. The tube is entered by puncturing with a small needle and fluid samples removed or solution injected to check for

60-64

blockages. An alternate method involves the tube being cut open with a scalpel. A blunt needle is placed in the tube under direct vision and fluid samples removed or the tube checked for patency. If an incision is made in the tube, the tube must be repaired using microsurgical techniques before the scrotal incisions are closed in layers by suturing.

Documentation Tip
Code 63.6 includes vasostomy procedures; the surgical creation of an opening into the vas deferens.

63.7   Vasectomy and ligation of vas deferens

63.70   Male sterilization procedure, not otherwise specified

Description
This procedure code describes a male sterilization procedure not elsewhere classified in subcategory 63.7.

Coding Clarification
This procedure code should not be assigned if the medical record contains sufficient information to facilitate coding at a higher level of specificity.

Documentation Tip
If the documentation is ambiguous or unclear, the physician should be queried.

63.71   Ligation of vas deferens

Description
This code describes a ligation of the vas deferens. Surgical technique may vary.

The physician performs a ligation of the vas deferens (vasectomy) without cutting an incision in the skin. The procedure is done under local anesthesia. With thumb and index finger the surgeon grasps the spermatic cord beneath the skin, high in the scrotum near the inguinal area. The skin is pulled taught with the spermatic cord just underneath the skin. An instrument is pressed against the structures and activated sequentially. The instrument punctures the skin and cuts the spermatic cord, then clips the cord on each side of the cut area. The procedure may be repeated on the opposite side. The resulting puncture wounds are bandaged.

Documentation Tip
Procedures classifiable to 63.71 may be documented as:

- Crushing of vas deferens
- Division of vas deferens

63.72   Ligation of spermatic cord

Description
An incision is made in the pubic area and is carried down to the spermatic cord as it passes through the inguinal canal. The cord is brought up into the incision and the structures of the cord are dissected, ligated, crushed, clamped, or divided. The incision is closed in layers by suturing. The procedure may be repeated on the opposite side.

63.73   Vasectomy

Description
The physician grasps the upper scrotum near the inguinal area and holds the spermatic cord between the thumb and the index finger. The skin overlying the immobilized cord is injected with local anesthetic and an incision is made through the scrotal wall to expose the tubular structures. Another incision is made to expose the vas deferens (spermatic tube) and the tissues are dissected to free it from the adjacent vessels and supporting tissues. The isolated vas deferens is cut in two places and the intervening section of tube is removed. The cut ends of the vas deferens are cauterized and tied with suture material. The incisions are closed in layers by suturing. The procedure is usually repeated on the opposite side.

Coding Clarification
A vasectomy technique described as "no scalpel" vasectomy is a procedure that utilizes a single, tiny puncture (instead of an incision) through which the vas deferens is isolated and cauterized. "No scalpel" vasectomy is reported with 63.73.

Coding Guidance
   AHA: 2Q, '98, 13

63.8   Repair of vas deferens and epididymis

63.81   Suture of laceration of vas deferens and epididymis

Description
The physician repairs a laceration (injury) to the vas deferens and epididymis that occurs as a result of a blunt or penetrating injury. The wound is explored and may be repaired through the open wound, or by making an incision to extend the opening of the wound. Any devitalized tissue is removed by sharp dissection. The laceration of the internal structures of the epididymis or vas deferens is closed by suturing. Bleeding is controlled. The incision is closed in layers by suturing. The procedure is usually repeated on the opposite side. A drain may be placed to prevent the accumulation of fluid and blood in the associated tissues.

63.82   Reconstruction of surgically divided vas deferens

Description
The physician reverses a surgically created blockage or division in the vas deferens, the tube that carries

semen. After anesthesia, an incision is made in the scrotum. The testis with its attached epididymis and the vas deferens are brought out of the wound. Dye injection may be performed during the operation for optimal visualization. The vas deferens is transected in two places, one on each side of the affected area and the abnormal segment removed. The created cut ends are sutured together in one or two layers with care to align accurately the lumens of the tubes. The testis and associated structures are returned to the scrotum. A rubber drain is often placed in the scrotum and the incisions closed by suturing. The procedure is usually repeated on the opposite side.

63.83   Epididymovasostomy

Description
The physician treats obstruction of the flow of spermatozoa from the epididymis to vas deferens, the tube that carries the semen. After adequate anesthesia, an incision is made in the scrotum and the testis with its attached epididymis and the vas deferens is brought out of the wound. The vas deferens is transected and the selected area of the epididymis is opened and the appropriate tubule in the area is brought out of the surrounding tissues and transected. The cut ends of these two tubes are sutured together and the vas deferens is sutured to the epididymis. A rubber drain is often placed in the scrotum and the incision is closed by suturing. The procedure is usually repeated on the opposite side.

63.84   Removal of ligature from vas deferens

Description
The physician performs surgical removal of a previously placed ligature; a thread, cord or wire used to surgically occlude the vas deferens for reproductive sterilization.

63.85   Removal of valve from vas deferens

Description
The physician performs surgical removal of a valve from the vas deferens; a fold designed to prevent backward flow of material.

63.89   Other repair of vas deferens and epididymis

Description
This procedure code reports other repair of the vas deferens and epididymis not classifiable elsewhere in subcategory 63.8.

Coding Clarification
This procedure code should not be assigned if the medical record contains sufficient information to facilitate coding at a higher level of specificity.

Documentation Tip
If the documentation is ambiguous or unclear, the physician should be queried.

63.9   Other operations on spermatic cord, epididymis, and vas deferens

63.91   Aspiration of spermatocele

Description
The physician performs puncture of a cystic distention of the epididymis.

63.92   Epididymotomy

Description
The physician makes an incision in the scrotum. The procedure is done under local or regional anesthesia. While the testis is held firmly with the scrotal skin stretched tightly over the testis and the epididymis positioned just under the taught skin, a small incision is made through the skin of the scrotum. The underlying tissues are incised and dissected to expose the epididymis. An incision is made into the epididymis for exploration, drainage, or other reason. The incision is closed with simple suture. The scrotal incision is closed by suturing.

63.93   Incision of spermatic cord

Description
The physician performs surgical cutting into the spermatic cord (sperm storage structure).

63.94   Lysis of adhesions of spermatic cord

Description
The physician performs surgical division of adhesive scar tissues that constrict the spermatic cord.

63.95   Insertion of valve in vas deferens

Description
The physician performs surgical insertion or implantation of an artificial valve into the vas deferens.

63.99   Other operations on spermatic card, epididymis, and vas deferens

Description
This code includes other operations on the spermatic cord, epididymis, and vas deferens not classifiable elsewhere in category 63.

Coding Clarification
This procedure code should not be assigned if the medical record contains sufficient information to facilitate coding at a higher level of specificity.

Documentation Tip
If the documentation is ambiguous or unclear, the physician should be queried.

63-64

64   Operations on penis

Description

The penis is an external male reproductive and urinary organ that extends from the pubic area. The term penis originated as a Latin word that literally translates "tail." The human penis is comprised of three internal columns of tissue, two corpora cavernosa, and one corpus spongiosum, which are separated by a visible ridge on the underside of the penis called the raphe. The glans penis is located at the distal end of the corpus spongiosum. The glans is covered by a naturally occurring foreskin or prepuce that is attached to the underside of the penis by a fold of skin called the frenulum. The foreskin retracts to expose the glans penis. The external opening of the urethra is located at the tip of the glans penis, which functions as a passageway for urine and semen from the body. The penis is a soft tissue organ that relies on engorgement to produce an erectile state for copulatory purposes.

Penile disorders include a wide range of structural, functional, inflammatory, and infectious conditions, which include:

- Priapism—penile pain, or painful and prolonged erections

- Peyronie's disease—abnormal curve of the penis during erection

- Congenital malposition of the urethral opening (e.g., hypospadias, epispadias)

- Phimosis—condition in which the foreskin cannot be retracted to uncover the glans penis

- Balanitis—inflammation and edema of the glans penis

These conditions may have a significant impact on organ function and reproductive fertility. Depending on the nature of the diagnosis, surgical intervention is often necessary.

Category 64 provides codes for diagnostic and therapeutic procedures on the penis, including circumcision, incisions, excisions, repairs, and other procedures. Category 64 includes operations on:

- Corpora cavernosa

- Glans penis

- Prepuce

64.0   Circumcision

Description

The physician performs surgical removal of the penile foreskin. Surgical technique may vary.

After the administration of a local anesthetic by injection(s), the physician removes the foreskin of the penis by clamping the foreskin in a plastic device and trimming the excess protruding skin. A segment

of foreskin on the dorsal or the side of the penis is crushed with forceps. A cut is made through the crushed tissue with scissors, and the divided foreskin is fitted in a plastic bell-shaped clamp. The clamp crushes a ring of the foreskin and holds the skin edges together while the excess skin is trimmed from the top of the device. The clamp is left in place and simply falls off when healing has finished days later.

64.1   Diagnostic procedures on the penis

64.11   Biopsy of penis

Description

The physician performs biopsy of the penis. Surgical technique may vary:

- **Superficial:** The physician removes a portion of a skin lesion on the penis by punch biopsy or by excising a small portion of the lesion with scalpel or scissors. The resulting defect may require simple repair with sutures.

- **Deep tissues:** The physician removes a portion of a penile mass by deep punch biopsy or by making an incision in the penis and dissecting tissues to the deep mass and excising a portion of the lesion. The incision may be repaired with layered sutures.

64.19   Other diagnostic procedures on penis

Description

This code includes other diagnostic penile procedures not described as biopsy.

Coding Clarification

This procedure should not be assigned if the medical record contains sufficient information to facilitate coding at a higher level of specificity.

Documentation Tip

If the documentation is ambiguous or unclear, the physician should be queried.

64.2   Local excision or destruction of lesion of penis

Description

This procedure code describes an excision or destruction of a lesion of the penis. Surgical technique may include local application of a chemical, freezing, electrodesiccation, laser vaporization, or excision. Local anesthesia may be used for these procedures.

- **Electrodesiccation or chemical destruction:** The physician may treat skin lesions of the penis by local application of a chemical or local electrodesiccation to destroy the diseased tissue or organism. Using a cotton-tipped applicator soaked in the chemical or an electrodesiccator, the physician applies the treatment to the specific lesions only, taking care to avoid touching normal skin with the chemical or the electrodesiccator. Using either method, no tissue is removed and no closure is required.

- **Excision:** The physician excises lesions of the penis not removable by other methods. After adequate local anesthesia has been administered, the physician cuts out an elliptical piece of skin that includes the lesion and a rim of normal tissue. With a forceps or hemostat clamp, the physician grasps and elongates the involved skin containing the lesion, causing the tissue to tent. Using a scalpel or scissors, an ellipse of tissue containing the lesion is excised. The resulting defect is closed with sutures.

Coding Clarification
Code 64.2 excludes excision for a biopsy of the penis (64.11).

64.3   Amputation of penis

Description
The physician removes a portion or the entire penis due to disease or mutilating injury. The distal penis is enclosed in a rubber glove and a tourniquet is applied at the base of the penis. An incision is made completely around the penile shaft. The various structures of the penis are isolated and divided with care to leave enough of the urethra to form an opening for the passage of urine. The remaining tissues and skin are closed with layered sutures

64.4   Repair and plastic operation on penis

64.41   Suture of laceration of penis

Description
The physician sutures superficial lacerations of the penis. A local anesthetic is injected around the laceration and the wound is cleansed, explored, and often irrigated with a saline solution. The physician may perform a simple, one-layer repair of the epidermis, dermis, or subcutaneous tissues with sutures. For suture repair of more complex lacerations, deep subcutaneous or layered suturing techniques may be required. The physician may suture tissue layers under the skin with dissolvable sutures before suturing the skin.

64.42   Release of chordee

Description
The physician corrects downward displacement of the penis. To assist in planning the surgery, an artificial erection may be produced by placing a band around the base of the penis and injecting saline into the body of the penis. The area of deformity is

determined and by using a combination of incisions and excisions of abnormal fibrous tissue and sometimes normal tissue, the defect is corrected. Care is taken to dissect around nerves and blood vessels. Sometimes the urethra is dissected free of its position and retracted temporarily away from the operative site. The separate tissues of the penis are closed in layers with absorbable suture material. An artificial erection may again be produced to test and demonstrate the adequacy of the repair.

Coding Guidance
  AHA: 4Q, '96, 34

64.43   Construction of penis

64.44   Reconstruction of penis

Description
The physician performs construction (64.43) or reconstruction (64.44) of the penis. Depending on the indications for surgery, multiple surgical techniques are available. In general, penile construction or reconstruction procedures often use donor skin from other areas of the body such as the abdomen, forearm, or leg, which is then grafted to the pubic area. Surgical lengthening of the urethra is required to facilitate urination. Erection is accomplished by implanting a malleable rod or implanted pump device into the surgically created penis.

64.45   Replantation of penis

Description
The physician performs reattachment of an amputated or partially amputated penis. The physician may repair the injury using one or more plastic surgery techniques. The repair may require skin grafts, tissue grafts, urethral repair, extensive debridement, microsurgical repairs, or any combination.

64.49   Other repair of penis

Description
This code reports other penile repair operations not classifiable elsewhere in category 64.

Coding Clarification
This procedure code should not be assigned if the medical record contains sufficient information to facilitate coding at a higher level of specificity.

Code 64.49 excludes procedures specified as repair of epispadias or hypospadias (58.45).

Documentation Tip
If the documentation is ambiguous or unclear, the physician should be queried.

60-64

64.5 Operations for sex transformation, not elsewhere classified

Description

This code reports certain transgender surgeries not separately classifiable elsewhere. The process of gender transformation from one sex to another occurs over a period of time in a series of staged procedures and supplemental medical treatment.

- **Male to female:** In a series of staged procedures, the physician removes portions of the male genitalia and forms female external genitals. The penis is dissected and portions are removed with care to preserve vital nerves and vessels in order to fashion a clitoris-like structure. The urethral opening is moved to a position similar to that of a normal female. A vagina is made by dissecting and opening the perineum. This opening is lined using pedicle or split thickness grafts. Labia are created out of skin from the scrotum and adjacent tissue. A stent or obturator is usually left in place in the newly created vagina for three weeks or longer.

- **Female to male:** In a series of staged procedures, the physician forms a penis and scrotum using pedicle flap grafts and free skin grafts. Portions of the clitoris are used as well as the adjacent skin. Prostheses are often placed in the penis in order to have a sexually functional organ. Prosthetic testicles are fixed in the scrotum. The vagina is closed or removed.

64.9 Other operations on male genital organs

64.91 Dorsal or lateral slit of prepuce

Description

The prepuce is the fold of penile skin commonly called the foreskin. The physician makes a cut or slit in the prepuce to relieve a constriction that prevents the retraction of the foreskin back over the head of the penis. A segment of foreskin on the dorsal or the side of the penis is crushed with forceps. Using scissors, the physician makes a cut through the crushed tissue and sutures the divided skin to control bleeding.

64.92 Incision of penis

Description

The physician drains a deep abscess or hematoma (pocket of blood) by incising penile tissue. After instilling a local anesthesia, the physician makes an incision through the skin and deeper tissues into the abscessed cavity. The urethra and the main arteries and nerves are avoided. Often a drain is left in place to assure adequate drainage.

64.93 Division of penile adhesions

Description

The physician performs division of penile adhesions.

- **Post-circumcision adhesions:** The physician retracts the foreskin, releases the preputial post-circumcision adhesions, and cleanses the glans in a patient who is under general anesthesia. If retraction of the foreskin reveals a fibrous ring, the physician places two vertical incisions directly over the fibrous ring and the transversely running fibrous bands are divided to expose the underlying Bucks' fascia. With the foreskin retracted, the defect is closed horizontally with interrupted sutures.

- **Other adhesions:** The physician treats adhesions between the uncircumcised foreskin and the head of the penis that prevent the retraction of the foreskin. Adhesions are broken by stretching the foreskin back over the head of the penis onto the shaft or by inserting a clamp between the foreskin and the head of the penis and spreading the jaws of the clamp.

64.94 Fitting of external prosthesis of penis

Description

The physician performs fitting or adjustment of an artificial penis worn on the outside of the body.

64.95 Insertion or replacement of non-inflatable penile prosthesis

Description

The physician inserts a semi-rigid penile prosthesis, which is a hinged or malleable device. A transverse incision is made just above the penis over the pubic bone. With care to avoid important nerves and blood vessels, dissection is carried down to the erectile tissues at the base of the penis. Incisions are made in the thick fibrous membranes surrounding the two main erectile tissues to allow the insertion of dilators to create space for the prostheses. The incisions and tissues are closed by suturing. The operation can also be done in similar fashion using an incision just below the scrotum in the perineum to enter the erectile tissue or in the upper scrotum at the base of the penis.

64.96 Removal of internal prosthesis of penis

Description

The physician makes an incision using the same approach (i.e., penoscrotal or distal penile) as the original procedure to remove the non-inflatable or self-contained inflatable penile prosthesis in a patient who is under general anesthesia. An incision is made into the corpus cavernosum, the corporal tissue is dissected, and the prosthesis is removed from the corporal body. The wound is irrigated with antibiotics, and the corporotomy is closed by suture. The subcutaneous tissue is closed by suture and a dressing is applied to the incision. The bladder is emptied with a catheter.

64.97   Insertion or replacement of inflatable penile prosthesis

Description
The physician inserts an inflatable penile prosthesis made of three components: the reservoir, the pump, and two inflatable cylinders. A transverse incision is made at the base of the penis in the upper scrotum. With care to avoid the urethra and important nerves and blood vessels, dissection is carried down to the erectile tissues at the base of the penis. The thick fibrous membranes surrounding the two main erectile tissues are incised and dilators are inserted to create space for the prostheses. Two prosthetic devices are inserted into the two erectile tissue compartments down the length of the penis. A pouch is made in one side of the scrotum, and the pump mechanism and tubing are inserted into the space created. Using an index finger, the surgeon creates a tunnel from the pump to the space behind the pubic bone. The reservoir is placed behind the pubic bone with tubing running from it through the tunnel to the pump in the scrotum. The incisions and tissues are closed by suturing. The operation can also be done in similar fashion using an incision just below the scrotum in the perineum to enter the erectile tissue and in the area above the pubic bone to gain access to place the reservoir.

Coding Clarification
Code 64.97 excludes external prosthesis (64.94), insertion of non-inflatable prosthesis (64.95), or plastic repair operations classifiable to 64.43-64.49.

64.98   Other operations on penis

Description
This code includes other operations on the penis not classifiable elsewhere in category 64, such as:

- **Corpora cavernosa-corpus spongiosum shunt:** The physician creates a shunt for the diversion of blood from one region of the penis to an adjacent region. With a catheter in the urethra into the bladder, an incision is made in the side of the penis. Dissection is carried to the thick fibrous tissues surrounding one of the corpus cavernosum (erectile tissue) and to the corpus spongiosum, which is the erectile tissue around the urethra. Oval discs of the fibrous tissue are excised from the adjacent surfaces of these two structures. The excisional defects are sutured together creating a shunt (passageway) for the flow of blood from the engorged corpus cavernosum to the corpus spongiosum, thus relieving the erection. The tissues and the skin

are sutured closed. The procedure is sometimes repeated on the opposite side.

- **Corpora-saphenous shunt:** The physician creates a shunt for the diversion of blood from the penis to the femoral vein. An incision is made in the groin area of the thigh and the saphenous vein is cut and dissected free of its attachments creating a mobile segment about 10 cm long. A second incision is made at the base of the penis and the saphenous vein is tunneled through the subcutaneous tissues to the base of the penis. A 1 cm in diameter piece of the thick fibrous tissue of the corpus cavernosum (erectile tissue) is excised and the free end of the saphenous vein is sutured to the defect. The erection resolves as blood flows from the penis to the femoral vein through this saphenous vein segment. The incisions are closed by suturing. The procedure is sometimes repeated on the opposite side.

- **Irrigation of corpus cavernosum:** The corpora cavernosa are the spongy bodies of the penis, the dual columns of erectile tissue that form the back and sides of the penis. In conditions such as priapism, this spongy tissue may be in a state of persistent erection. The physician may treat priapism by irrigating the corpora cavernosa. After adequate local anesthesia, the physician passes a large bore needle into the body of the penis and aspirates a quantity of blood and irrigates the space with 20 to 30 ml of saline solution. This may be accompanied by injecting medication into the same region, repeating it several times to get the abnormal erection to resolve.

Coding Clarification
Code 64.98 excludes removal of foreign body, intraluminal (98.19), or without incision (98.24), and stretching of foreskin (99.95) procedures.

Documentation Tip
Code 64.98 includes a procedure that may be documented as arterialization of the deep dorsal vein of the penis. This procedure code describes a vascular shunt between the common femoral artery via a saphenous vein graft to the deep dorsal penile vein. This shunt procedure may be performed to treat arteriogenic impotence (impotence due to poor arterial blood supply to the penis).

Coding Guidance
   AHA: 3Q, '92, 9

64.99   Other operations on male genital organs

Description
This code reports other operations on male genital organs not classifiable elsewhere in category 64.

Coding Clarification
This procedure code should not be assigned if the medical record contains sufficient information to facilitate coding at a higher level of specificity.

Code 64.99 excludes collection of sperm for artificial insemination (99.96).

Documentation Tip
If the documentation is ambiguous or unclear, the physician should be queried.

60-64

65-71

Operations on the Female Genital Organs

The ICD-9-CM classification system for operations performed on the female genital organs is divided into categories of procedures according to site and type as follows:

- Operations on Ovary (65)
- Operations on Fallopian Tubes (66)
- Operations on Cervix (67)
- Other Excision and Incision of Uterus (68)
- Other Operations on Uterus and Supporting Structures (69)
- Operations on Vagina and Cul-de-sac (70)
- Operations on Vulva and Perineum (71)

65   Operations on ovary

Description
Category 65 provides codes for incisions, diagnostic procedures, excision or destruction of ovarian lesion or tissue, excisions, repairs, lysis of adhesions, and other operations on the ovary. Every subcategory, except the last for other operations on the ovary, has specific codes for use of a laparoscope. Review the documentation for operative approach to ensure correct code assignment.

Coding Clarification
For all procedures reported with codes from category 65, code also any application or administration of an adhesion barrier substance (99.77).

Documentation Tip
Surgical procedures on the ovaries and fallopian tubes are performed using a variety of surgical techniques and approaches ranging from open surgery to less invasive procedures such as laparoscopy.

An understanding of the following terms may aid in code selection:

- **Oophorotomy:** Incision into the ovary.
- **Salpingo-oophorotomy:** Incision into the ovary and fallopian tube.

- **Oophorectomy:** Surgical removal of one or both ovaries; also called ovariectomy or ovarian ablation.

65.0   Oophorotomy
Description
Subcategory 65.0 provides two codes to report oophorotomy or salpingo-oophorotomy. Fourth-digit specificity identifies approach.

65.01   Laparoscopic oophorotomy
Description
The physician makes a 1 cm incision in the umbilicus through which the abdomen is inflated and a fiberoptic laparoscope is inserted. A second incision is made directly below the umbilicus, just above the pubic hairline, through which a trocar can be passed into the abdominal cavity to deliver instruments. The physician manipulates the tools to view the pelvic organs through the laparoscope, and an incision into the ovary or the ovary and fallopian tubes is made. The instruments are removed and the incisions are sutured.

Coding Clarification
The following ovarian laparoscopic procedures are appropriately reported with 65.01:

- Aspiration
- Drainage
- Incision
- Oophorostomy

65.09   Other oophorectomy
Description
Code 65.09 is used to report oophorotomy procedures that are not more precisely described by other codes in category 65, such as those described here.

Through a small abdominal incision just above the pubic hairline or through a vaginal incision, the physician drains an abscess (infection) on the ovary. The abscess is drained, cleaned out, and irrigated with antibiotics. Temporary catheters and tubes are often left in place to help drainage.

The physician drains a cyst or cysts on one or both ovaries through an incision in the vagina or through a small incision just above the pubic hairline. A cyst is a sac containing fluid or semisolid material. The cyst is ruptured with a surgical instrument, electrocautery, or a laser, and the fluid is removed.

Documentation Tip
Review the documentation for specific information regarding the procedure prior to final code selection in order to ensure accurate code assignment.

65.1   Diagnostic procedures on ovaries

Description
The different types of diagnostic biopsy procedures performed on the ovaries are located under subcategory 65.1.

Coding Clarification
Biopsy procedures on the ovaries are performed using a variety of surgical techniques and approaches ranging from open surgery to less invasive procedures such as laparoscopy and aspiration techniques. Aspiration, biopsy, and drainage are performed percutaneously through an anterior abdominal approach or posterior transgluteal approach, a transabdominal route, or a transvaginal approach.

Documentation Tip
Review the documentation for specific information regarding the procedure prior to final code selection in order to ensure accurate code assignment.

65.11   Aspiration biopsy of ovary

Description
The physician uses transvaginal ultrasonographic guidance and a needle to aspirate a cystic pelvic mass for biopsy using the transvaginal route and an endoluminal transducer.

65.12   Other biopsy of ovary

Description
Code 65.12 is used to report other biopsy procedures of the ovaries that are not more precisely described by other codes in category 65.

For example, the physician takes a tissue sample from one or both ovaries for diagnosis. This procedure may be done through the vagina or abdominally through a small incision just above the pubic hairline.

Coding Clarification
Biopsy procedures on the ovaries are performed using a variety of surgical techniques and approaches ranging from open surgery to less

invasive procedures such as laparoscopy and aspiration techniques. Aspiration, biopsy, and drainage are performed percutaneously, through an anterior abdominal approach, a transabdominal route, or a transvaginal approach.

Documentation Tip
Review the documentation for specific information regarding the procedure prior to final code selection in order to ensure accurate code assignment.

65.13   Laparoscopic biopsy of ovary

Description
The physician makes a 1 cm incision in the umbilicus through which the abdomen is inflated and a fiberoptic laparoscope is inserted. Other incisions are also made through which trocars can be passed into the abdominal cavity to deliver instruments, a video camera, and, when needed, an additional light source. When biopsy of pelvic organs is performed, the physician may also insert an instrument through the vagina to grasp the cervix and pass another instrument through the cervix and into the uterus to manipulate the uterus. The biopsy is obtained by grasping a sample with a special biopsy forceps that is capable of biting off small pieces of tissue. When the procedure is complete, the laparoscope, instruments, and light source are removed and the incisions are closed with sutures.

Coding Clarification
Surgical procedures on the ovaries and fallopian tubes are performed using a variety of surgical techniques and approaches ranging from open surgery to less invasive procedures, such as laparoscopic or percutaneous techniques. Review the documentation for specific information regarding the procedure prior to final code selection in order to ensure accurate code assignment.

Coding Guidance
    AHA: 4Q, '96, 67

65.14   Other laparoscopic diagnostic procedures on ovaries

Description
Code 65.14 is used to report laparoscopic diagnostic procedures of the ovaries that are not more precisely described by other codes in category 65.

Documentation Tip
Surgical procedures on the ovaries and fallopian tubes are performed using a variety of surgical techniques and approaches ranging from open surgery to less invasive procedures, such as laparoscopic or percutaneous techniques. Review the documentation for specific information regarding the procedure prior to final code selection in order to ensure accurate code assignment.

● New Code   ▲ Revised Code   ▶◀ Revised Text   © 2010 Ingenix

65-71

65.19   Other diagnostic procedures on ovaries

Description
Code 65.19 is used to report non-laparoscopic diagnostic procedures of the ovaries that are not more precisely described by other codes in category 65. These diagnostic procedures may be performed percutaneously through an anterior abdominal approach or posterior transgluteal approach, a transabdominal route, or a transvaginal approach.

Coding Clarification
This code excludes microscopic examination of a specimen from the ovary; see 91.41-91.49.

Documentation Tip
Review the documentation for specific information regarding the procedure prior to final code selection in order to ensure accurate code assignment.

65.2   Local excision or destruction of ovarian lesion or tissue

Description
The different types of excision and destruction procedures performed on the ovaries are located under subcategory 65.2.

Coding Clarification
Surgical procedures on the ovaries and fallopian tubes are performed using a variety of surgical techniques and approaches ranging from open surgery to less invasive procedures, such as laparoscopic or percutaneous techniques. Review the documentation for specific information regarding the procedure prior to final code selection in order to ensure accurate code assignment.

65.21   Marsupialization of ovarian cyst

Description
The physician makes an incision in the skin over the cyst and carries it down through the cyst wall, which drains the fluid from the cyst. The physician sutures the lining of the cyst wall to the overlying skin to create a permanent drain site.

65.22   Wedge resection of ovary

Description
Through an abdominal incision just above the pubic hairline, the physician takes a pie-shaped section or half of one or both of the ovaries to reduce the size and then sutures the edges together.

Coding Clarification
Do not report 65.22 for a laparoscopic wedge resection of ovary; see 65.24.

Documentation Tip
Surgical procedures on the ovaries and fallopian tubes are performed using a variety of surgical techniques and approaches ranging from open surgery to less invasive procedures, such as

laparoscopic or percutaneous techniques. Review the documentation for specific information regarding the procedure prior to final code selection in order to ensure accurate code assignment.

65.23   Laparoscopic marsupialization of ovarian cyst

Description
The physician performs laparoscopic treatment of an ovarian cyst with the assistance of a fiberoptic laparoscope. The physician first inserts an instrument through the vagina to grasp the cervix and manipulate the uterus during surgery. Next, the physician makes a small incision just below the umbilicus through which a fiberoptic laparoscope is inserted. A second incision is made on the left or right side of the abdomen with additional instruments being placed through these incisions into the abdomen or pelvis. The physician manipulates the tools so that the pelvic organs can be observed, manipulated, and operated upon with the laparoscope. Once the cyst is identified with the laparoscope, a third incision is typically made to drain the fluid from the cyst. The physician sutures the lining of the cyst wall to the overlying skin to create a permanent drain site. The abdomen is deflated, the trocars removed, and the incisions are closed with sutures.

Coding Clarification
Do not report 65.23 for a non-laparoscopic marsupialization procedure on an ovarian cyst; see 65.21.

Documentation Tip
Surgical procedures on the ovaries and fallopian tubes are performed using a variety of surgical techniques and approaches ranging from open surgery to less invasive procedures, such as laparoscopic or percutaneous techniques. Review the documentation for specific information regarding the procedure prior to final code selection in order to ensure accurate code assignment.

65.24   Laparoscopic wedge resection of ovary

Description
The physician performs laparoscopic surgical removal of a pie-shaped section of one or both ovaries with the assistance of a fiberoptic laparoscope. The physician may first insert an instrument through the vagina to grasp the cervix and manipulate the uterus during surgery. Next, the physician makes a small incision just below the umbilicus through which a fiberoptic laparoscope is inserted. A second incision is made on the left or right side of the abdomen with additional instruments being placed through these incisions into the abdomen or pelvis. The physician then manipulates the tools so that the pelvic organs can be observed and manipulated. Removal of one or

both ovaries and the fallopian tubes can be performed with the laparoscope. The abdomen is then deflated, the trocars removed, and the incisions are closed with sutures.

Coding Clarification
Do not report 65.24 for a non-laparoscopic wedge resection of the ovary; see 65.22.

Documentation Tip
Surgical procedures on the ovaries and fallopian tubes are performed using a variety of surgical techniques and approaches ranging from open surgery to less invasive procedures, such as laparoscopic or percutaneous techniques. Review the documentation for specific information regarding the procedure prior to final code selection in order to ensure accurate code assignment.

65.25   Other laparoscopic local excision or destruction of ovary

Description
The physician performs laparoscopic electrical cautery destruction of an ovarian cyst with the assistance of a fiberoptic laparoscope. The physician may first insert an instrument through the vagina to grasp the cervix and manipulate the uterus during surgery. Next, the physician makes a small incision just below the umbilicus through which a fiberoptic laparoscope is inserted. A second incision is made on the left or right side of the abdomen with additional instruments being placed through these incisions into the abdomen or pelvis. The physician then manipulates the tools so that the pelvic organs can be observed, manipulated, and operated upon with the laparoscope. Once lesions are identified with the laparoscope, a third incision is typically made adjacent to the lesion through which an electric cautery tool, knife, or laser is inserted for lesion fulguration. The abdomen is then deflated, the trocars removed, and the incisions are closed with sutures.

Coding Clarification
Surgical procedures on the ovaries and fallopian tubes are performed using a variety of surgical techniques and approaches ranging from open surgery to less invasive procedures, such as laparoscopic or percutaneous techniques. Review the documentation for specific information regarding the procedure prior to final code selection in order to ensure accurate code assignment.

65.29   Other local excision or destruction of ovary

Description
Code 65.29 is used to report other excision or destruction procedures of the ovary that are not more precisely described by other codes in subcategory 65.2.

Coding Clarification
Surgical procedures on the ovaries and fallopian tubes are performed using a variety of surgical techniques and approaches ranging from open surgery to less invasive procedures, such as laparoscopic or percutaneous techniques.

Documentation Tip
Review the documentation for specific information regarding the procedure prior to final code selection in order to ensure accurate code assignment.

65.3   Unilateral oophorectomy

Description
The different types of unilateral oophorectomy procedures are located under subcategory 65.3.

Coding Clarification
When an oophorectomy or salpingo-oophorectomy is performed, the code choice is based on laterality in addition to the approach.

Use 65.31 (laparoscopic) or 65.39 for a unilateral removal of an ovary. However, if one ovary has already been removed, use 65.52 or 65.54 (laparoscopic) for the removal of a remaining ovary.

Use 65.41 (laparoscopic) or 65.49 for a unilateral salpingo-oophorectomy. However, if one ovary and tube have already been removed, use 65.62 or 65.64 (laparoscopic) for the removal of a remaining ovary and tube.

Documentation Tip
Surgical procedures on the ovaries and fallopian tubes are performed using a variety of surgical techniques and approaches ranging from open surgery to less invasive procedures, such as laparoscopic or percutaneous techniques. Review the documentation for specific information regarding the procedure prior to final code selection in order to ensure accurate code assignment.

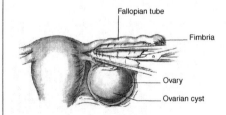

65.31   Laparoscopic unilateral oophorectomy

Description
Through a small abdominal incision just above the top of the pubic hairline, the physician removes part or all of one of the ovaries with the assistance of a fiberoptic laparoscope. After the ovaries are detached, they are removed though a small incision

● New Code   ▲ Revised Code   ▶◀ Revised Text   © 2010 Ingenix

at the top of the vagina. In some cases, the ovaries are cut into smaller sections and removed.

Coding Clarification
This procedure is also called an ovariectomy or ovarian ablation.

Documentation Tip
Surgical procedures on the ovaries and fallopian tubes are performed using a variety of surgical techniques and approaches ranging from open surgery to less invasive procedures, such as laparoscopic or percutaneous techniques. Review the documentation for specific information regarding the procedure prior to final code selection in order to ensure accurate code assignment.

65.39   Other unilateral oophorectomy

Description
Oophorectomy is usually done under general anesthesia. It is performed through the same type of incision, either vertical or horizontal, as an abdominal hysterectomy. After the incision is made, the abdominal muscles are pulled apart, not cut, so that the surgeon can see the ovaries. Then the ovaries, and often the fallopian tubes, are removed.

Coding Clarification
To report unilateral oophorectomy via a laparoscope, see 65.31.

Documentation Tip
Surgical procedures on the ovaries and fallopian tubes are performed using a variety of surgical techniques and approaches ranging from open surgery to less invasive procedures, such as laparoscopic or percutaneous techniques. Review the documentation for specific information regarding the procedure prior to final code selection in order to ensure accurate code assignment.

Coding Guidance
    AHA: 4Q, '96, 66

65.4   Unilateral salpingo-oophorectomy

Description
The different types of unilateral salpingo-oophorectomy procedures are located under this subcategory.

Coding Clarification
When an oophorectomy or salpingo-oophorectomy is performed, the code choice is based on laterality in addition to the approach.

Use 65.41 (laparoscopic) or 65.49 for a unilateral salpingo-oophorectomy. However, if one ovary and tube have already been removed, use 65.62 or 65.64 (laparoscopic) for the removal of a remaining ovary and tube.

Documentation Tip
Surgical procedures on the ovaries and fallopian tubes are performed using a variety of surgical techniques and approaches ranging from open surgery to less invasive procedures, such as laparoscopic or percutaneous techniques. Review the documentation for specific information regarding the procedure prior to final code selection in order to ensure accurate code assignment.

65.41   Laparoscopic unilateral salpingo-oophorectomy

Description
Through a small incision in the abdomen just above the pubic hairline, the physician removes part or all of the ovary and part or all of its fallopian tube on one side. The incision is closed by suturing.

In a more invasive procedure through a full abdominal incision extending from the top of the pubic hairline to the rib cage, the physician removes part or all of one or both ovaries depending on the extent of the malignancy. The physician takes a sampling of the lymph nodes surrounding the lower aorta within the pelvis and flushes the peritoneum, which is the lining of the abdominal cavity. The liquid is removed from the peritoneum to check for cancerous cells and multiple tissue samples are taken. The physician also examines and takes tissue samples of the diaphragm. The physician may elect to remove one or both fallopian tubes and the omentum. The abdominal incision is closed with layered suture.

Coding Clarification
Surgical procedures on the ovaries and fallopian tubes are performed using a variety of surgical techniques and approaches ranging from open surgery to less invasive procedures, such as laparoscopy and percutaneous techniques. Review the documentation for specific information regarding the procedure prior to final code selection in order to ensure accurate code assignment.

Coding Guidance
    AHA: 4Q, '96, 67

65.49   Other unilateral salpingo-oophorectomy

Description
The physician inserts a speculum into the vagina to view the cervix and perform amputation of the cervix. A tool is used to pull down the cervix. A scalpel is then used to divide the cervix from the uterus just after it enters the vagina. The physician removes the cervix through the vagina and stops the bleeding with cautery and sutures.

65-71

Coding Clarification
When an oophorectomy or salpingo-oophorectomy is performed, the code choice is based on laterality in addition to the approach.

Use 65.41 (laparoscopic) or 65.49 for a unilateral salpingo-oophorectomy. However, if one ovary and tube have already been removed, use 65.62 or 65.64 (laparoscopic) for the removal of a remaining ovary and tube.

Documentation Tip
Review the documentation for specific information regarding the procedure prior to final code selection in order to ensure accurate code assignment.

65.5   Bilateral oophorectomy

Description
The different types of bilateral salpingo-oophorectomy procedures are located under this subcategory.

Coding Clarification
When an oophorectomy or salpingo-oophorectomy is performed, the code choice is based on laterality in addition to the surgical approach.

Documentation Tip
Review the documentation for specific information regarding the procedure prior to final code selection in order to ensure accurate code assignment.

65.51   Other removal of both ovaries at same operative episode

Description
Code 65.51 is used to report other removal procedures of both ovaries that are not more precisely described by other codes in this subcategory.

Coding Clarification
Code 65.51 is used to report female castration procedures.

Do not use 65.51 to report this procedure when done laparoscopically; see 65.53.

Documentation Tip
When an oophorectomy or salpingo-oophorectomy is performed, the code choice is based on laterality in addition to the surgical approach. Review the documentation for specific information regarding the procedure prior to final code selection in order to ensure accurate code assignment.

65.52   Other removal of remaining ovary

Description
Code 65.52 is used to report other removal procedures of a solitary ovary that are not more precisely described by other codes in subcategory 65.5.

Coding Clarification
Do not use 65.52 to report the removal of a solitary ovary when performed laparoscopically; see 65.54.

Documentation Tip
Surgical procedures on the ovaries and fallopian tubes are performed using a variety of surgical techniques and approaches ranging from open surgery to less invasive procedures, such as laparoscopy and percutaneous techniques. Review the documentation for specific information regarding the procedure prior to final code selection in order to ensure accurate code assignment.

65.53   Laparoscopic removal of both ovaries at same operative episode

Description
The physician performs surgical laparoscopy to remove both ovaries. The patient is placed in the dorsal lithotomy position for the endoscopic portion. For the vaginal portion, the patient is positioned in stirrups. The physician inserts a speculum and attaches a uterine manipulator to the cervix. A Foley catheter is placed. A trocar is inserted periumbilically and the abdomen is insufflated with gas. Additional trocars are placed in the right and left lower quadrants. The round ligaments are ligated and incised. At this point, both of the ovaries are removed. The vagina is closed, and hemostasis is confirmed before the trocars are removed and the skin incisions are closed.

Coding Clarification
When an oophorectomy or salpingo-oophorectomy is performed, the code choice is based on laterality in addition to the surgical approach.

Documentation Tip
Review the documentation for specific information regarding the procedure prior to final code selection in order to ensure accurate code assignment.

65.54   Laparoscopic removal of remaining ovary

Description
Code 65.54 is used to report other laparoscopic removal procedures of a solitary ovary that are not more precisely described by other codes in subcategory 65.5.

Coding Clarification
Do not use 65.54 to report the removal of a solitary ovary when not performed with a laparoscope; see 65.52.

Documentation Tip
When an oophorectomy or salpingo-oophorectomy is performed, the code choice is based on laterality in addition to the surgical approach. Review the documentation for specific information regarding the procedure prior to final code selection in order to ensure accurate code assignment.

● New Code   ▲ Revised Code   ▶◀ Revised Text   © 2010 Ingenix

65.6   Bilateral salpingo-oophorectomy

Description

The different types of bilateral salpingo-oophorectomy procedures are located under subcategory 65.6.

Coding Clarification

When an oophorectomy or salpingo-oophorectomy is performed, the code choice is based on laterality in addition to the approach.

Use 65.41 (laparoscopic) or 65.49 for a unilateral salpingo-oophorectomy. However, if one ovary and tube have already been removed, use 65.62 or 65.64 (laparoscopic) for the removal of a remaining ovary and tube.

Documentation Tip

Surgical procedures on the ovaries and fallopian tubes are performed using a variety of surgical techniques and approaches ranging from open surgery to less invasive procedures, such as laparoscopy. Review the documentation for specific information regarding the procedure prior to final code selection in order to ensure accurate code assignment.

65.61   Other removal of both ovaries and tubes at same operative episode

Description

Code 65.61 is used to report other removal procedures of both ovaries and fallopian tubes that are not more precisely described by other codes in this subcategory. The physician performs surgical laparoscopy to remove both ovaries and fallopian tubes. The patient is placed in the dorsal lithotomy position for the endoscopic portion. For the vaginal portion, the patient is positioned in stirrups. The physician inserts a speculum and attaches a uterine manipulator to the cervix. A Foley catheter is placed. A trocar is inserted periumbilically and the abdomen is insufflated with gas. Additional trocars are placed in the right and left lower quadrants. The round ligaments are ligated and incised. At this point, the tubes and ovaries are removed. The vagina is closed, and hemostasis is confirmed before the trocars are removed and the skin incisions are closed.

Coding Clarification

Do not use 65.61 to report this procedure when done laparoscopically; see 65.53.

Documentation Tip

Surgical procedures on the ovaries and fallopian tubes are performed using a variety of surgical techniques and approaches ranging from open surgery to less invasive procedures, such as laparoscopy and percutaneous techniques. Review the documentation for specific information regarding the procedure prior to final code selection in order to ensure accurate code assignment.

Coding Guidance

AHA: 4Q, '96, 65

65.62   Other removal of remaining ovary and tube

Description

Through a full abdominal incision extending from the top of the pubic hairline to the rib cage, the physician removes part or all of one or both ovaries depending on the extent of the malignancy. The physician takes a sampling of the lymph nodes surrounding the lower aorta within the pelvis and flushes the peritoneum, which is the lining of the abdominal cavity. The physician removes one fallopian tube and ovary. The abdominal incision is closed with layered suture.

Coding Clarification

Code 65.62 is used to report other removal procedures of a solitary ovary and fallopian tube that are not more precisely described by other codes in subcategory 65.6.

Do not use 65.62 to report this procedure when done laparoscopically; see 65.54.

65.63   Laparoscopic removal of both ovaries and tubes at same operative episode

Description

The physician performs laparoscopic surgical removal of one or both ovaries and the accompanying fallopian tubes with the assistance of a fiberoptic laparoscope. The physician may first insert an instrument through the vagina to grasp the cervix and manipulate the uterus during surgery. Next, the physician makes a small incision just below the umbilicus through which a fiberoptic laparoscope is inserted. A second incision is made on the left or right side of the abdomen with additional instruments being placed through these incisions into the abdomen or pelvis. The physician then manipulates the tools so that the pelvic organs can be observed and manipulated. Removal of one or both ovaries and fallopian tubes can be performed with the laparoscope. The abdomen is then deflated, the trocars removed, and the incisions are closed with sutures.

Coding Clarification

Surgical procedures on the ovaries and fallopian tubes are performed using a variety of surgical techniques and approaches ranging from open surgery to less invasive procedures, such as laparoscopy and percutaneous techniques.

Documentation Tip

Review the documentation for specific information regarding the procedure prior to final code selection in order to ensure accurate code assignment.

65-71

Coding Guidance
> **AHA:** 4Q, '96, 68; 4Q, '06, 133, 134; ▶3Q, '09, 5◀

65.64   Laparoscopic removal of remaining ovary and tube

Description
The physician performs laparoscopic surgical removal of a solitary ovary and fallopian tube with the assistance of a fiberoptic laparoscope.

Coding Clarification
When an oophorectomy or salpingo-oophorectomy is performed, the code choice is based on laterality in addition to the approach.

Documentation Tip
Review the documentation for specific information regarding the procedure prior to final code selection in order to ensure accurate code assignment.

65.7   Repair of ovary

Description
The different types of repair procedures on the ovaries are located under subcategory 65.7. Surgical procedures on the ovaries and fallopian tubes are performed using a variety of surgical techniques and approaches ranging from open surgery to less invasive procedures, such as laparoscopy and percutaneous techniques.

Coding Clarification
Do not use subcategory 65.7 to report salpingo-oophorostomy; see 66.72.

Documentation Tip
Review the documentation for specific information regarding the procedure prior to final code selection in order to ensure accurate code assignment.

65.71   Other simple suture of ovary

Description
Code 65.71 is used to report other suturing procedures on the ovary that are not more precisely described by other codes in subcategory 65.7.

Coding Clarification
Do not use 65.71 to report suturing of an ovary that is performed using a laparoscope; see 65.74.

Documentation Tip
Surgical procedures on the ovaries and fallopian tubes are performed using a variety of surgical techniques and approaches ranging from open surgery to less invasive procedures, such as laparoscopy and percutaneous techniques. Review the documentation for specific information regarding the procedure prior to final code selection in order to ensure accurate code assignment.

65.72   Other reimplantation of ovary

Description
Code 65.72 is used to report other reimplantation procedures on the ovaries that are not more precisely described by other codes in subcategory 65.7. The physician performs a grafting procedure and repositioning of the ovary at the same site.

Coding Clarification
Do not use 65.72 to report reimplantation of an ovary that is performed using a laparoscope; see 65.75.

Documentation Tip
Surgical procedures on the ovaries and fallopian tubes are performed using a variety of surgical techniques and approaches ranging from open surgery to less invasive procedures, such as laparoscopy and percutaneous techniques. Review the documentation for specific information regarding the procedure prior to final code selection in order to ensure accurate code assignment.

65.73   Other salpingo-oophoroplasty

Description
Code 65.73 is used to report other salpingo-oophoroplasty procedures that are not more precisely described by other codes in subcategory 65.7.

Coding Clarification
An ovariostomy is performed to create a temporary fistula for the drainage of an ovarian cyst.

Surgical procedures on the ovaries and fallopian are coded based on laterality and the approach.

Do not use 65.73 to report other salpingo-oophorectomy procedures that are performed using a laparoscope; see 65.76.

Documentation Tip
Surgical procedures on the ovaries and fallopian tubes are performed using a variety of surgical techniques and approaches ranging from open surgery to less invasive procedures, such as laparoscopy and percutaneous techniques. Review the documentation for specific information regarding the procedure prior to final code selection in order to ensure accurate code assignment.

65.74   Laparoscopic simple suture of ovary

Description
Code 65.74 is used to report other suturing procedures on the ovaries that are not more precisely described by other codes in subcategory 65.7. The physician performs a simple suture procedure on an ovary.

Coding Clarification
Surgical procedures on the ovaries and fallopian
tubes are performed using a variety of surgical
techniques and approaches ranging from open
surgery to less invasive procedures, such as
laparoscopy and percutaneous techniques. Review
the documentation for specific information regarding
the procedure prior to final code selection in order to
ensure accurate code assignment.

65.75   Laparoscopic reimplantation of ovary

Description
Code 65.75 is used to report reimplantation
procedures on the ovaries performed
laparoscopically that are not more precisely
described by other codes in subcategory 65.7.

Coding Clarification
Surgical procedures on the ovaries and fallopian
tubes are performed using a variety of surgical
techniques and approaches ranging from open
surgery to less invasive procedures, such as
laparoscopy and percutaneous techniques. Review
the documentation for specific information regarding
the procedure prior to final code selection in order to
ensure accurate code assignment.

65.76   Laparoscopic salpingo-oophoroplasty

Description
Code 65.76 is used to report laparoscopic
salpingo-oophoroplasty procedures that are not
more precisely described by other codes in
subcategory 65.7.

Coding Clarification
Surgical procedures on the ovaries and fallopian
tubes are performed using a variety of surgical
techniques and approaches ranging from open
surgery to less invasive procedures, such as
laparoscopy and percutaneous techniques.

Documentation Tip
Review the documentation for specific information
regarding the procedure prior to final code selection
in order to ensure accurate code assignment.

65.79   Other repair of ovary

Description
The physician performs an oophoropexy by
laparotomy. A laparoscopic oophoropexy technique
involves placement of sutures through the
utero-ovarian ligaments and posterior uterus.

Coding Clarification
Surgical procedures on the ovaries and fallopian
tubes are performed using a variety of surgical
techniques and approaches ranging from open
surgery to less invasive procedures, such as
laparoscopy and percutaneous techniques.

Documentation Tip
Review the documentation for specific information
regarding the procedure prior to final code selection
in order to ensure accurate code assignment.

65.8   Lysis of adhesions of ovary and fallopian tube

Description
The different types of lysis of adhesion procedures
on the ovaries or fallopian tubes are located under
this subcategory.

Coding Clarification
Surgical procedures on the ovaries and fallopian
tubes are performed using a variety of surgical
techniques and approaches ranging from open
surgery to less invasive procedures, such as
laparoscopy and percutaneous techniques.

Documentation Tip
Review the documentation for specific information
regarding the procedure prior to final code selection
in order to ensure accurate code assignment.

65.81   Laparoscopic lysis of adhesions of ovary and fallopian tube

Description
The physician performs a laparoscopic surgical
cutting/releasing (lysis) of scar tissue (adhesions)
surrounding the ovaries and/or fallopian tubes with
the assistance of a fiberoptic laparoscope. The
physician may first insert an instrument through the
vagina to grasp the cervix and manipulate the uterus
during surgery. Next, the physician makes a small
incision just below the umbilicus through which a
fiberoptic laparoscope is inserted. A second incision
is made on the left or right side of the abdomen with
additional instruments being placed through these
incisions into the abdomen or pelvis. The physician
then manipulates the tools so that the pelvic organs
can be observed, manipulated, and lysis of
adhesions can be performed. The abdomen is then
deflated, the trocars removed, and the incisions
closed with sutures.

Coding Clarification
Surgical procedures on the ovaries and fallopian
tubes are performed using a variety of surgical
techniques and approaches ranging from open
surgery to less invasive procedures, such as
laparoscopy and percutaneous techniques.

When an oophorectomy or salpingo-oophorectomy is
performed, the code choice is based on laterality in
addition to the approach.

Documentation Tip
Review the documentation for specific information
regarding the procedure prior to final code selection
in order to ensure accurate code assignment.

65-71

Coding Guidance
AHA: 4Q, '96, 67

65.89   Other lysis of adhesions of ovary and fallopian tube

Description
The physician cuts free any fibrous tissue adhering to the ovaries or tubes through a small incision just above the pubic hairline.

Coding Clarification
Do not use 65.89 to report other lysis of adhesion procedures on the ovaries or fallopian tubes that are performed using a laparoscope; see 65.81.

Documentation Tip
Surgical procedures on the ovaries and fallopian tubes are performed using a variety of surgical techniques and approaches ranging from open surgery to less invasive procedures, such as laparoscopy and percutaneous techniques. Review the documentation for specific information regarding the procedure prior to final code selection in order to ensure accurate code assignment.

65.9   Other operations on ovary

Description
Other procedures on the ovaries that are not more precisely described by other codes in this category are located under subcategory 65.9.

Documentation Tip
Surgical procedures on the ovaries and fallopian tubes are performed using a variety of surgical techniques and approaches ranging from open surgery to less invasive procedures, such as laparoscopy and percutaneous techniques. Review the documentation for specific information regarding the procedure prior to final code selection in order to ensure accurate code assignment.

65.91   Aspiration of ovary

Description
The physician drains a cyst or cysts on one or both ovaries through an incision in the vagina or through a small incision just above the pubic hairline. The cyst is ruptured with a surgical instrument, electrocautery, or a laser, and the fluid is removed.

In an alternate procedure, the physician makes a 1 cm incision in the umbilicus through which the abdomen is inflated and a fiberoptic laparoscope is inserted. A second incision is made directly below the umbilicus, just above the pubic hairline, through which a trocar can be passed into the abdominal cavity to deliver instruments. The physician manipulates the tools to view the pelvic organs through the laparoscope. An additional incision may be needed for a second light source. Once the biopsy

site is viewed through the laparoscope, a 5 cm incision is made just above the site. Through this incision, the physician uses an aspirating probe to aspirate a cavity or cyst or to collect fluid for culture. The instruments are removed and the incisions are sutured.

Coding Clarification
Do not use 65.91 to report aspiration biopsy of the ovaries; see 65.11.

Documentation Tip
Aspiration, biopsy, and drainage procedures on the ovaries and fallopian tubes are performed percutaneously through an anterior abdominal approach or posterior transgluteal approach, a transabdominal route, or a transvaginal approach. Review the documentation for specific information regarding the procedure prior to final code selection in order to ensure accurate code assignment.

65.92   Transplantation of ovary

Description
High-dose chemotherapy and radiotherapy treatments for cancer may severely damage the ovaries. The process involves removing and freezing pieces of the patient's ovarian tissue prior to chemotherapy which is then transplanted back to help restore ovarian function after chemotherapy.

The cryopreservation of ovarian tissue begins with laparoscopy or mini-laparotomy. Usually only one ovary is removed to allow normal ovarian hormone production from the other ovary. The ovarian cortex is sliced and the tissue slices are cryopreserved until retransplantation of the ovarian tissue strips can be attempted. Ovarian tissue retransplantation in the abdomen near the fallopian tube allows natural ovulation and conception. The ovarian tissue begins to function again within several months of transplantation.

Coding Clarification
Do not use 65.92 to report reimplantation of an ovary; see 65.72 or 65.75.

65.93   Manual rupture of ovarian cyst

Description
The physician breaks up an ovarian cyst using a manual technique or blunt instruments. A cyst is a sac containing fluid or semisolid material. The physician drains a cyst or cysts on one or both ovaries through an incision in the vagina or through a small incision just above the pubic hairline. The cyst is ruptured with a surgical instrument, electrocautery, or a laser, and the fluid is removed.

Coding Clarification
Aspiration, biopsy, and drainage procedures on the ovaries and fallopian tubes are performed percutaneously through an anterior abdominal

65-71

approach or posterior transgluteal approach, a transabdominal route, or a transvaginal approach.

Documentation Tip
Review the documentation for specific information regarding the procedure prior to final code selection in order to ensure accurate code assignment.

65.94   Ovarian denervation
Description
The physician performs a destruction procedure on the nerve tracts to the ovary. The most common technique for denervation is by transection of the ovarian suspensory ligament in which the tissues over the ovarian suspensory ligament are excised. Partial denervation of the ovary can be accomplished by transection of the ovarian suspensory ligament or a sham operation. Denervation can also be achieved by freezing the ovarian vascular pedicle and suspensory ligament about 1 cm from the ovary.

Coding Clarification
Nerves to the ovary can be accessed along the arteries to the ovary or via the suspensory ligament. Review the documentation for specific information regarding the procedure and approach prior to final code selection in order to ensure accurate code assignment.

65.95   Release of torsion of ovary
Description
In ovarian torsion, which is considered to be rare, the ovary twists and cuts off blood supply. Ovarian torsion usually occurs unilaterally and in cases of an enlarged ovary creates a fulcrum, which the oviduct revolves around. Laparoscopy is performed to confirm the diagnosis and treatment consists of laparoscopic rotating of the twisted ovary and, in some cases, oophoropexy.

Coding Clarification
Ovarian torsion can involve just the ovary or both the ovary and the oviduct (i.e., adnexal torsion).

65.99   Other operations on ovary
Description
Code 65.99 is used to report other procedures of the ovary that are not more precisely described by other codes in this category, such as ovarian drilling. Ovarian drilling, done during laparoscopy, is a procedure in which a laser or electrosurgical needle punctures the ovary multiple times.

Coding Clarification
This treatment is often performed in women who have polycystic ovary syndrome.

Gamete intrafallopian transfer (GIFT) is the one step process of harvesting both ova and sperm, which are mixed and immediately transferred to the fallopian

tube. Fertilization then occurs in the natural environment of the fallopian tube. Assign 65.99 and 66.99 for this procedure.

Coding Guidance
   AHA: N-D, '86, 9

66   Operations on fallopian tubes
Description
A variety of procedures performed on the fallopian tubes are classified to category 66. They include such things as incision, diagnostic procedures, destruction or occlusion, excision, repair, and insufflation. Laterality is a factor in code selection in certain subcategories of 66. To ensure accurate code assignment, review the medical record for endoscopic approach and surgical technique along with determining laterality.

Coding Clarification
There are three subcategories (66.4, 66.5, and 66.6) for salpingectomy. Two of these require fourth digits: 66.5 and 66.6. Category 66.6 Other salpingectomy, includes codes for salpingectomy by cauterization, coagulation, electrocoagulation, and excision.

Assign 66.02 for removal of an ectopic pregnancy without salpingectomy.

Use 66.39 for bilateral partial salpingectomy for sterilization.

Use 66.52 for removal of a solitary fallopian tube.

Use 66.62 for a salpingectomy performed for the removal of a fallopian tube with removal of a tubal pregnancy. Assign an additional code for any synchronous oophorectomy.

Assign 66.79 for reanastomosis of fallopian tubes following tubal ligation.

Use 66.92 for unilateral destruction or occlusion of a fallopian tube. However, assign a code from the range 66.21-66.39 for destruction of a solitary fallopian tube.

Assign 66.99 for removal of a tubal pregnancy by "squeezing" it out of the end of the fallopian tube.

Gamete intrafallopian transfer (GIFT) is the one step process of harvesting both ova and sperm, which are mixed and immediately transferred to the fallopian tube. Fertilization then occurs in the natural environment of the fallopian tube. Assign 65.99 and 66.99 for this procedure.

66.0   Salpingotomy
Coding Clarification
An understanding of the following terms may aid in code selection:

- **Salpingotomy:** Surgical opening of a blocked fallopian tube.

- **Salpingostomy:** Surgical incision of a fallopian tube frequently performed to remove an ectopic pregnancy.

- **Salpingoplasty:** Plastic surgery of the fallopian tubes. This reconstructive procedure on the fallopian tubes is frequently done to treat conditions that cause infertility.

Documentation Tip
Laterality is a factor in code selection in certain subcategories of 66. To ensure accurate code assignment, review the medical record for endoscopic approach and surgical technique, along with determining laterality.

66.01   Salpingotomy

Description
Usually two operating trocars are inserted through lateral suprapubic incisions. In salpingotomy with suturing procedures, a suprapubic ancillary puncture site is used. The physician makes an incision for linear salpingotomy using a needle cautery or knife electrode and an irrigation and suction tube is introduced through the salpingotomy incision. All clots and trophoblastic tissues are aspirated. In most cases, aspiration removes the product of conception entirely. In other cases, saline solution is injected under high pressure or grasping forceps are used to separate the trophoblast from the tubal wall.

The physician treats a tubal ectopic pregnancy by removing the embryo from the tube. Through an incision in the lower abdomen, the physician explores the pelvic cavity, inspects the gestation site for bleeding, and removes all products of conception, clots, and free blood. If the embryo is implanted in the fallopian tube, the physician makes an incision to remove the embryo. The pelvis is lavaged with saline solution and the incision is closed with sutures.

Alternately, the physician may treat an ectopic pregnancy by laparoscopy without salpingectomy and/or oophorectomy. The physician inserts an instrument through the vagina to grasp the cervix while passing another instrument through the cervix and into the uterus to manipulate the uterus. Next, the physician makes a 1 cm incision in the umbilicus through which the abdomen is inflated and a fiberoptic laparoscope is inserted. A second incision is made on the left or right side of the abdomen. After locating the site of gestation, another small incision is made above the site. Instruments are passed into the abdomen through the incisions. The physician removes the ectopic pregnancy by

making an incision in the tube. The abdominal incisions are closed with sutures.

Coding Clarification
Laterality is a factor in code selection in certain subcategories of operations on the fallopian tubes.

Documentation Tip
To ensure accurate code assignment, review the medical record for endoscopic approach and surgical technique, along with determining laterality.

66.02   Salpingostomy

Description
Through a small incision just above the pubic hairline, the physician creates a new opening in the fallopian tube where the fimbrial end has been closed by inflammation, infection, or injury. The procedure is generally performed microsurgically in order to do an accurate repair.

In an alternate procedure, the physician performs laparoscopic surgical restoration of the patency of the uterine tube damaged typically by infection, tumor, or endometriosis. The physician may first insert an instrument through the vagina to grasp the cervix and manipulate the uterus during surgery. Next, the physician makes a small incision just below the umbilicus through which a fiberoptic laparoscope is inserted. A second incision is made on the left or right side of the abdomen with additional instruments being placed through these incisions into the abdomen or pelvis. The physician then manipulates the tools so that the pelvic organs can be observed, manipulated, and operated upon with the laparoscope. A third incision is typically made adjacent to the fallopian tubes. The physician performs surgical restoration of the fallopian tube (salpingostomy) using instruments placed through the abdomen and pelvic trocars. The abdomen is deflated, the trocars removed, and the incisions are closed with sutures.

Coding Clarification
Assign 66.02 for removal of an ectopic pregnancy without salpingectomy.

Documentation Tip
To ensure accurate code assignment, review the medical record for endoscopic approach and surgical technique, along with determining laterality.

66.1   Diagnostic procedures on fallopian tubes

Description
The different types of diagnostic procedures performed on the fallopian tubes are located under subcategory 66.1.

Coding Clarification
Laterality is a factor in code selection in certain subcategories of 66.

● New Code   ▲ Revised Code   ►◄ Revised Text   © 2010 Ingenix

Documentation Tip
To ensure accurate code assignment, review the medical record for endoscopic approach and surgical technique, along with determining laterality.

66.11   Biopsy of fallopian tube

Description
The physician makes a 1 cm incision in the umbilicus through which the abdomen is inflated and a fiberoptic laparoscope is inserted. Other incisions are also made through which trocars can be passed into the abdominal cavity to deliver instruments, a video camera, and when needed an additional light source. The physician manipulates the tools so that the pelvic organs, peritoneum, abdomen, and omentum can be viewed through the laparoscope and/or video monitor. Biopsy from the fallopian tube is obtained by grasping a sample with a special biopsy forceps that is capable of "biting off" small pieces of tissue. When the procedure is complete, the laparoscope, instruments, and light source are removed and the incisions are closed with sutures. The physician may also insert an instrument through the vagina to grasp the cervix and pass another instrument through the cervix and into the uterus to manipulate the uterus.

Coding Clarification
To ensure accurate code assignment, review the medical record for endoscopic approach and surgical technique, along with determining laterality.

66.19   Other diagnostic procedures on fallopian tubes

Description
Code 66.19 is used to report other diagnostic procedures of the fallopian tubes that are not more precisely described by other codes in subcategory 66.1.

Coding Clarification
Do not assign 66.19 to report microscopic examination of a specimen from fallopian tubes (91.41-91.49), radiography of fallopian tubes (87.82-87.83, 87.85), or a Rubin's test (66.8).

Documentation Tip
To ensure accurate code assignment, review the medical record for endoscopic approach and surgical technique, along with determining laterality. Review the documentation for specific information regarding the procedure prior to final code selection in order to ensure accurate code assignment.

66.2   Bilateral endoscopic destruction or occlusion of fallopian tubes

Description
This subcategory includes bilateral endoscopic destruction or occlusion of fallopian tubes by culdoscopy, endoscopy, hysteroscopy, laparoscopy, peritoneoscopy, and endoscopic destruction of a solitary fallopian tube.

Coding Clarification
Fourth-digit subclassifications report bilateral endoscopic destruction or occlusion of fallopian tubes by approach. An understanding of the following terms may aid in code selection:

- **Culdoscopy:** Endoscopic insertion through the posterior structure of the vagina.
- **Hysteroscopy:** Endoscopic insertion through the uterus.
- **Laparoscopy:** Endoscopic insertion through the abdomen.
- **Peritoneoscopy:** Endoscopic insertion through the abdominal serous membrane cavity.

Documentation Tip
To ensure accurate code assignment, review the medical record for endoscopic approach and surgical technique, along with determining laterality.

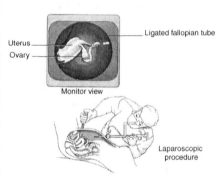

Uterus
Ovary
Ligated fallopian tube
Monitor view

Laparoscopic procedure

66.21   Bilateral endoscopic ligation and crushing of fallopian tubes

66.22   Bilateral endoscopic ligation and division of fallopian tubes

Description
The physician performs laparoscopic electrical cautery destruction of an oviduct (the uterine tube), with complete cutting through the fallopian tubes (transection), with the assistance of a fiberoptic laparoscope. The physician first inserts an instrument through the vagina to grasp the cervix and manipulate the uterus during surgery. Next, the physician makes a small incision just below the umbilicus through which a fiberoptic laparoscope is inserted. A second incision is made on the left or right side of the abdomen with additional instruments being placed through these incisions into the abdomen or pelvis. The physician manipulates the tools so that the pelvic organs can be observed, manipulated, and operated upon with the laparoscope. A third incision is typically made

65-71

adjacent to the fallopian tubes. The physician may cut the tubes and fulgurate or burn the ends. Additionally, the physician transects (cuts through) the fallopian tubes. The abdomen is deflated, the trocars removed, and the incisions are closed with sutures.

Coding Clarification
To ensure accurate code assignment, review the medical record for endoscopic approach and surgical technique, along with determining laterality.

Documentation Tip
Review the documentation for specific information regarding the procedure prior to final code selection in order to ensure accurate code assignment.

66.29   Other bilateral endoscopic destruction or occlusion of fallopian tubes

Description
Code 66.29 is used to report other bilateral endoscopic destruction or occlusion procedures on the fallopian tubes that are not more precisely described by other codes in subcategory 66.2.

Coding Clarification
To ensure accurate code assignment, review the medical record for endoscopic approach and surgical technique, along with determining laterality.

Documentation Tip
Review the documentation for specific information regarding the procedure prior to final code selection in order to ensure accurate code assignment.

66.3   Other bilateral destruction or occlusion of fallopian tubes

Description
Subcategory 66.3 includes codes for other ligation, crushing, division, destruction, and occlusion procedures on the fallopian tubes.

Coding Clarification
To ensure accurate code assignment, review the medical record for endoscopic approach and surgical technique, along with determining laterality.

66.31   Other bilateral ligation and crushing of fallopian tubes

Description
The physician ties off the fallopian tube or removes a portion of it on one side or both. The procedure may be done through the vagina or through a small incision just above the pubic hairline.

Coding Clarification
Subcategory 66.3 includes destruction procedures of a solitary fallopian tube.

To report endoscopic destruction or occlusion of the fallopian tubes, see 66.21-66.29.

Laterality is a factor in code selection in certain subcategories of 66.

Documentation Tip
To ensure accurate code assignment, review the medical record for endoscopic approach and surgical technique, along with determining laterality.

66.32   Other bilateral ligation and division of fallopian tubes

Description
The physician ties off the fallopian tube or removes a portion of it on one side or both. The procedure may be done through the vagina or through a small incision just above the pubic hairline. It is frequently performed vaginally during the same hospital stay as the delivery of a baby or at the time of a cesarean section or during intraabdominal surgery.

Coding Clarification
An excision of a ligated portion of the fallopian tubes is also known as a Pomeroy operation. A Pomeroy sterilization technique involves the ligation of a loop of fallopian tube and subsequent resection of the tied loop.

Documentation Tip
To ensure accurate code assignment, review the medical record for endoscopic approach and surgical technique, along with determining laterality.

66.39   Other bilateral destruction or occlusion of fallopian tubes

Description
The physician blocks one or both of the fallopian tubes with a band, clip, or Falope ring. The physician may elect to do the procedure through the vagina or through a small incision just above the pubic hairline.

Coding Clarification
Code 66.39 is used to report other female sterilization procedures that are not more precisely described by other codes in subcategory 66.3. This code is also reported when the documentation does not further specify the destruction or occlusion procedure.

To ensure accurate code assignment, review the medical record for endoscopic approach and surgical technique, along with determining laterality.

Documentation Tip
Review the documentation for specific information regarding the procedure prior to final code selection in order to avoid improper use of the "not otherwise specified" code and to ensure accurate code assignment.

● New Code   ▲ Revised Code   ▶◀ Revised Text   © 2010 Ingenix

66.4   Total unilateral salpingectomy

Description
Through a small incision in the lower abdomen just above the pubic hairline, the physician removes all of the fallopian tube on one side. The incision is closed by suturing.

Coding Clarification
There are three subcategories (66.4, 66.5, and 66.6) for salpingectomy. Two of these require fourth digits: 66.5 and 66.6. Category 66.6 Other salpingectomy, includes codes for salpingectomy by cauterization, coagulation, electrocoagulation, and excision.

Laterality is a factor in code selection in certain subcategories of operations on the fallopian tubes. To ensure accurate code assignment, review the medical record for endoscopic approach and surgical technique, along with determining laterality.

Documentation Tip
Review the documentation for specific information regarding the procedure prior to final code selection in order to ensure accurate code assignment.

66.5   Total bilateral salpingectomy

Description
Subcategory 66.5 provides two subclassification codes to report a total, or complete, bilateral salpingectomy.

Coding Clarification
Laterality is a factor in code selection in certain subcategories of operations on the fallopian tubes. To ensure accurate code assignment, review the medical record for endoscopic approach and surgical technique, along with determining laterality.

To report bilateral partial salpingectomy for sterilization, see 66.39. To report that with oophorectomy, see 65.61-65.64.

There are three subcategories (66.4, 66.5, and 66.6) for salpingectomy. Two of these require fourth digits: 66.5 and 66.6. Category 66.6 Other salpingectomy, includes codes for salpingectomy by cauterization, coagulation, electrocoagulation, and excision.

66.51   Removal of both fallopian tubes at same operative episode

Description
The physician performs a laparoscopic surgical removal of both fallopian tubes at the same time as another pelvic procedure. The physician may first insert an instrument through the vagina to grasp the cervix and manipulate the uterus during surgery. Next, the physician makes a small incision just below the umbilicus through which a fiberoptic laparoscope is inserted. A second incision is made on the left or right side of the abdomen with additional instruments being placed through these incisions into the abdomen or pelvis. The physician manipulates the tools so that the pelvic organs can be observed, manipulated, and removal of both fallopian tubes can be performed with the laparoscope. The abdomen is then deflated, the trocars removed, and the incisions are closed with sutures.

66.52   Removal of remaining fallopian tube

Description
Through a small incision in the lower abdomen just above the pubic hairline, the physician removes part or all of a solitary fallopian tube. The incision is closed by suturing.

Coding Clarification
Use 66.52 for removal of a solitary fallopian tube.

Use 66.62 if a salpingectomy is performed for removal of a fallopian tube with removal of a tubal pregnancy. Assign an additional code for any synchronous oophorectomy.

66.6   Other salpingectomy

Description
Category 66.6 Other salpingectomy, includes codes for salpingectomy by cauterization, coagulation, electrocoagulation, and excision.

Coding Clarification
There are three subcategories (66.4, 66.5, and 66.6) for salpingectomy. Two of these require fourth digits: 66.5 and 66.6.

To report fistulectomy, use 66.73.

66.61   Excision or destruction of lesion of fallopian tube

Description
The physician removes or destroys tumors, lesions, or cysts from the fallopian tubes. In an open procedure, the physician makes a large incision extending from just above the pubic hairline to the rib cage. The growths are removed using a laser, electrical cautery, or a scalpel. The incision is then closed by suturing.

In a less invasive procedure, the physician performs laparoscopic electrical cautery destruction of a lesion with the assistance of a fiberoptic laparoscope. The physician may first insert an instrument through the vagina to grasp the cervix and manipulate the uterus during surgery. Next, the physician makes a small incision just below the umbilicus through which a fiberoptic laparoscope is inserted. A second incision is made on the left or right side of the abdomen with additional instruments being placed through these incisions into the abdomen or pelvis. The physician then manipulates the tools so that the pelvic organs can

65-71

be observed, manipulated, and operated upon with the laparoscope. Once the lesions are identified with the laparoscope, a third incision is typically made adjacent to the lesion through which an electric cautery tool, knife, or laser is inserted for lesion fulguration. The abdomen is deflated, the trocars removed, and the incisions are closed with sutures.

Coding Clarification
To report biopsy of the fallopian tube, use 66.11.

66.62   Salpingectomy with removal of tubal pregnancy

Description
The physician treats an ectopic pregnancy by laparoscopy with salpingectomy and/or oophorectomy. The physician inserts an instrument through the vagina to grasp the cervix while passing another instrument through the cervix and into the uterus to manipulate the uterus. Next, the physician makes a 1 cm incision in the umbilicus through which the abdomen is inflated and a fiberoptic laparoscope is inserted. A second incision is made on the left or right side of the abdomen. After locating the site of the gestation, another small incision is made above the site. Instruments are passed into the abdomen through the incisions. The physician removes the tube and/or ovary containing the embryo and closes the abdominal incisions with sutures.

Coding Clarification
Also code any synchronous oophorectomy (65.31, 65.39) performed at the same operative session.

Coding Guidance
    AHA: S-O, '85, 14; 3Q, '95, 15

66.63   Bilateral partial salpingectomy, not otherwise specified

Description
Through a small incision in the lower abdomen just above the pubic hairline, the physician removes part of the fallopian tube on both sides. The incision is closed by suturing.

Coding Clarification
Code 66.63 is used to report bilateral partial salpingectomy procedures when the documentation does not further specify the procedure.

Documentation Tip
Review the documentation for specific information regarding the procedure prior to final code selection in order to avoid improper use of the "not otherwise specified" code and to ensure accurate code assignment.

66.69   Other partial salpingectomy

Description
Code 66.69 is used to report other bilateral partial salpingectomy procedures that are not more precisely described by other codes in subcategory 66.6.

Coding Clarification
Laterality is a factor in code selection in certain subcategories of 66. Surgical procedures on the fallopian tubes are performed using a variety of surgical techniques and approaches. In order to ensure accurate code assignment, it will be necessary to review the medical record documentation for endoscopic approach and surgical technique, along with determining laterality.

Documentation Tip
Review the documentation for specific information regarding the procedure prior to final code selection in order to avoid improper use of the "not otherwise specified" code and to ensure accurate code assignment.

66.7   Repair of fallopian tube

Description
The different types of repair procedures performed on the fallopian tubes, such as suturing, are located under subcategory 66.7.

Coding Clarification
Laterality is a factor in code selection in certain subcategories of 66.

Surgical procedures on the fallopian tubes are performed using a variety of surgical techniques and approaches. To ensure accurate code assignment, review the medical record for approach and surgical technique, along with determining laterality.

66.71   Simple suture of fallopian tube

Description
Through a small incision just above the pubic hairline, the physician closes an opening in the fallopian tube or sutures the clean edges together. The procedure is generally performed using a microsurgical technique.

Coding Clarification
Laterality is a factor in code selection in certain subcategories of 66.

Documentation Tip
Surgical procedures on the fallopian tubes are performed using a variety of surgical techniques and approaches. In order to ensure accurate code assignment, it will be necessary to review the medical record documentation for approach and surgical technique, along with determining laterality.

● New Code   ▲ Revised Code   ▶◀ Revised Text   © 2010 Ingenix

66.72   Salpingo-oophorostomy

Description
Through a small incision just above the pubic hairline, the physician creates a new opening in the fallopian tube where the fimbrial end has been closed by inflammation, infection, or injury. The procedure is generally performed microsurgically in order to do an accurate repair.

Coding Clarification
Surgical formation of a temporary fistula to drain an ovarian cyst is also called oophorostomy.

66.73   Salpingo-salpingostomy

Description
Through a small incision just above the pubic hairline, the physician excises the closed or blocked portion of the tube and sutures the clean edges together. The procedure is generally performed microsurgically in order to do an accurate repair.

Coding Clarification
Laterality is a factor in code selection in certain subcategories of 66 for operations on the fallopian tubes.

Surgical procedures on the fallopian tubes are performed using a variety of surgical techniques and approaches.

Documentation Tip
To ensure accurate code assignment, review the medical record for approach and surgical technique, along with determining laterality.

66.74   Salpingo-uterostomy

Description
Through a small incision just above the pubic hairline, the physician removes a blocked portion of the tube near its junction with the uterus and reimplants the tube into the uterus in the same place.

66.79   Other repair of fallopian tube

Description
Code 66.79 is used to report other repair procedures of the fallopian tubes that are not more precisely described by other codes in subcategory 66.7, including:

- Repair of the fallopian tube with an implanted graft.
- Reopening of divided fallopian tube or reconnection of a severed fallopian tube to restore patency.
- Plastic reconstruction of a fallopian tube defect (salpingoplasty).

Coding Clarification
Surgical procedures on the fallopian tubes are performed using a variety of surgical techniques and approaches. To ensure accurate code assignment, review the medical record for approach and surgical technique, along with determining laterality.

Coding Guidance
    AHA: 2Q, '95, 10

66.8   Insufflation of fallopian tube

Description
Insufflation involves the forceful blowing of gas or liquid into fallopian tubes. The physician introduces a catheter into the cervix and then takes it up into the uterus and through the fallopian tube. The catheter must be made of a material that will show up on x-ray film so that any blockages or abnormalities in the tube can be seen. The physician may elect to inject liquid radiographic contrast material into the endometrial cavity with mild pressure to force the material into the tubes. The shadow of this material on x-ray film permits examination of the uterus and tubes for any abnormalities or blockages.

Coding Clarification
Insufflation of the fallopian tube can be accomplished with air, dye, gas, or saline.

Use this code to report a Rubin's test, which involves introduction of carbon dioxide gas into fallopian tubes.

Do no use 66.8 to report insufflation of a therapeutic agent (66.95) or when performed for hysterosalpingography (87.82-87.83).

66.9   Other operations on fallopian tubes

Description
Codes in subcategory 66.9 are used to report other procedures of the fallopian tubes that are not more precisely described by other codes in category 66.

Coding Clarification
Laterality is a factor in code selection in certain subcategories of 66.

Surgical procedures on the fallopian tubes are performed using a variety of surgical techniques and approaches.

In order to ensure accurate code assignment, it will be necessary to review the medical record documentation for approach and surgical technique, along with determining laterality.

Documentation Tip
Review the documentation for specific information regarding the procedure prior to final code selection in order to ensure accurate code assignment.

65-71

66.91   Aspiration of fallopian tube

Description
The physician makes a 1 cm incision in the umbilicus through which the abdomen is inflated and a fiberoptic laparoscope is inserted. A second incision is made directly below the umbilicus, just above the pubic hairline, through which a trocar can be passed into the abdominal cavity to deliver instruments. The physician manipulates the tools to view the pelvic organs through the laparoscope. An additional incision may be needed for a second light source. Once the biopsy site is viewed through the laparoscope, a 5 cm incision is made just above the site. Through this incision, the physician uses an aspirating probe to aspirate a cavity or cyst or to collect fluid for culture. The instruments are removed and the incisions are sutured.

66.92   Unilateral destruction or occlusion of fallopian tube

Description
The physician blocks one of the fallopian tubes with a band, clip, or Falope ring. The physician may elect to do the procedure through the vagina or through a small incision just above the pubic hairline.

Coding Clarification
Code 66.92 is not used to report unilateral destruction or occlusion of a solitary fallopian tube; see 66.21-66.39.

Documentation Tip
Laterality is a factor in code selection in certain subcategories of 66.

Surgical procedures on the fallopian tubes are performed using a variety of surgical techniques and approaches. In order to ensure accurate code assignment, it will be necessary to review the medical record documentation for approach and surgical technique, along with determining laterality.

66.93   Implantation or replacement of prosthesis of fallopian tube

Description
The different types of fallopian tube prosthetic devices have two different functions. One device is designed to maintain the patency (openness) of the fallopian tube and is used after reconstructive surgery. The other type is Filshie clips, used to prevent pregnancy and sterilize women.

A fallopian tube prosthesis is inserted in the fallopian tubes after vaginoplasty or other reconstruction of the vagina to keep them open. A Teflon prosthesis is implanted into the uterine cornua and fixed subcutaneously in the abdominal wall. An alternate device is a self-expanding spindle made from tubular metal mesh that is implanted in a single fallopian tube using a female sterilization

procedure involving fallopian tube catheterization under fluoroscopic guidance and implantation of a prosthesis.

Coding Clarification
Laterality is a factor in code selection in certain subcategories of 66.

Documentation Tip
Surgical procedures on the fallopian tubes are performed using a variety of surgical techniques and approaches. To ensure accurate code assignment, review the medical record for approach and surgical technique, along with determining laterality.

66.94   Removal of prosthesis of fallopian tube

Description
The physician performs a procedure similar to a female sterilization procedure for the removal of an implanted fallopian tube prosthesis device, which was implanted in a single fallopian tube using fallopian tube catheterization under fluoroscopic guidance.

Coding Clarification
The different types of fallopian tube prosthesis devices have two main functions. One device is designed to maintain the patency (openness) of the fallopian tube and is typically used after reconstructive surgery. The other type is Filshie clips, used to prevent pregnancy and sterilize women.

Documentation Tip
Surgical procedures on the fallopian tubes are performed using a variety of surgical techniques and approaches. To ensure accurate code assignment, review the medical record for approach and surgical technique, along with determining laterality.

66.95   Insufflation of therapeutic agent into fallopian tubes

Description
The physician injects a liquid medication or saline solution into the uterine cavity and fallopian tubes. Insufflation involves the forceful blowing of gas or liquid into fallopian tubes. The physician introduces a catheter into the cervix and takes it up into the uterus and through the fallopian tube. The catheter must be made of a material that will show up on x-ray film so that any blockages or abnormalities in the tube can be seen. The physician may elect to inject liquid radiographic contrast material into the endometrial cavity with mild pressure to force the material into the tubes. The shadow of this material on x-ray film permits examination of the uterus and tubes for any abnormalities or blockages.

Coding Clarification
Insufflation of the fallopian tube can be accomplished with air, dye, gas, or saline.

● New Code   ▲ Revised Code   ▶◀ Revised Text   © 2010 Ingenix

65-71

This procedure is frequently performed during surgery, open or laparoscopic, to verify patency of tubes.

Do no use 66.95 when performed for hysterosalpingography (87.82-87.83).

66.96   Dilation of fallopian tube

Description
A common treatment for fallopian tube obstruction involves a surgical procedure through a laparoscope or a more invasive laparotomy. One procedure involves the use of a balloon catheter that is inserted into the fallopian tube on one side of the obstruction, which is then advanced through the obstruction to a location distally of the obstruction. The balloon is inflated and drawn through the lumen to achieve a progressive dilation along the length of the lumen and through the obstruction.

Coding Clarification
Laterality is a factor in code selection in certain subcategories of 66.

Documentation Tip
Surgical procedures on the fallopian tubes are performed using a variety of surgical techniques and approaches. To ensure accurate code assignment, review the medical record for approach and surgical technique, along with determining laterality.

66.97   Burying of fimbriae in uterine wall

Description
The fimbria is a fringe of tissue near the ovary leading to the fallopian tube. When ovulation occurs, hormones activate the fimbriae and the cilia of the fimbriae sweep the ovum into the fallopian tube.

The physician surgically implants the fringed edges of a fallopian tube into the uterine wall.

Documentation Tip
Surgical procedures on the fallopian tubes are performed using a variety of surgical techniques and approaches. To ensure accurate code assignment, review the medical record for approach and surgical technique, along with determining laterality.

66.99   Other operations on fallopian tubes

Description
Code 66.99 is used to report procedures of the fallopian tubes that are not more precisely described by other codes in subcategory 66.9, as in the following example.

The physician treats a tubal ectopic pregnancy by removing the embryo from the tube. Through an incision in the lower abdomen, the physician explores the pelvic cavity, inspects the gestation site for bleeding, and removes all products of conception,

clots, and free blood. If the embryo is implanted in the fallopian tube, the physician may do one of the following: manually remove the embryo from the tube, make an incision to remove the embryo, or excise the section of the tube containing the embryo. The pelvis is lavaged with saline solution and the incision is closed with sutures.

Coding Clarification
Do not use 66.99 to report lysis of adhesions of the ovary and fallopian tube; see 65.81 and 65.89.

Documentation Tip
Surgical procedures on the fallopian tubes are performed using a variety of surgical techniques and approaches. To ensure accurate code assignment, review the medical record for approach and surgical technique, along with determining laterality.

Coding Scenario
A physician treats a patient with a tubal pregnancy using diagnostic laparoscopy, exploratory laparotomy, and removal of the tubal pregnancy by squeezing the fimbria manually.

  Code Assignment:

  633.10 Tubal pregnancy without intrauterine
          pregnancy
  66.99   Other operations on fallopian tubes

Coding Guidance
  AHA: 2Q, '94, 11

---

67   Operations on cervix

Description
Many of the 14 codes under category 67 classify a variety of excisions. The other procedures include dilation and repair.

Coding Clarification
For all procedures reported by codes from category 67, code also any application or administration of an adhesion barrier substance (99.77).

A loop electrosurgical excision procedure (LEEP) is the surgical excision and simultaneous cautery of a lesion of the cervix using a thin wire through which an electrical current is delivered.

A large loop excision of the transformation zone (LLETZ) is the conization or total excision of the cervix utilizing an electrosurgical technique.

Assign 67.39 for destruction of a cervical lesion by laser.

Documentation Tip
Surgical procedures on the cervix are performed using a variety of surgical techniques and approaches including cryosurgery, laser, and electrosurgical techniques.

65-71

To ensure accurate code assignment, review the medical record to determine the approach and surgical technique.

67.0   Dilation of cervical canal

Description
The physician inserts a speculum into the vagina to view the cervix. A tool is used to grasp the cervix and pull it down. A dilator or series of dilators is then inserted into the endocervix and passed up through the cervical canal.

Coding Clarification
Use 67.0 for dilation of the cervical canal but not for dilation and curettage (D&C). Choose a code from range 69.01–69.09 for D&C. In addition, dilation for induction of labor is classified to 73.1.

Documentation Tip
Surgical procedures on the cervix are performed using a variety of surgical techniques and approaches including cryosurgery, laser, and electrosurgical techniques.

To ensure accurate code assignment, review the medical record to determine the approach and surgical technique.

67.1   Diagnostic procedures on cervix

Description
Diagnostic procedures on the cervix are performed using a variety of techniques and approaches. The different types of cervical biopsies include:

- **Punch biopsy:** Removal of a small piece of tissue from the cervix. Multiple punch biopsies may be performed on different areas of the cervix.

- **Cone biopsy or conization:** Laser or scalpel utilized to remove a cone-shaped piece of tissue from the cervix.

- **Endocervical curettage (ECC):** Curette is used to scrape the endocervical lining.

- Other biopsy procedures used to obtain cervical cells include loop electrosurgical excision procedure (LEEP), colposcopy, and Pap smear.

Documentation Tip
To ensure accurate code assignment, review the medical record to determine the approach and surgical technique.

67.11   Endocervical biopsy

Description
The physician views the cervix through a colposcope, which is a binocular microscope used for direct visualization of the vagina, ectocervix, and endocervix. A biopsy instrument is inserted in the vagina and used to take one or more small biopsies of the cervix. For endocervical curettage, a small curette is passed into the endocervical canal, which is the passage between the external cervical os and the uterine cavity. The specimen is obtained by scraping in the canal with the curette. The instruments are removed.

Coding Clarification
Code 67.11 is not used to report conization of the cervix; see 67.2.

Various different types of cervical biopsies include:

- **Punch biopsy:** Removal of a small piece of tissue from the cervix. Multiple punch biopsies may be performed on different areas of the cervix.

- **Cone biopsy or conization:** Laser or scalpel utilized to remove a cone-shaped piece of tissue from the cervix.

- **Endocervical curettage (ECC):** Curette is used to scrape the endocervical lining.

- Other biopsy procedures used to obtain cervical cells include loop electrosurgical excision procedure (LEEP), colposcopy, and Pap smear.

Documentation Tip
Surgical procedures on the cervix are performed using a variety of surgical techniques and approaches including cryosurgery, laser, and electrosurgical techniques.

To ensure accurate code assignment, review the medical record to determine the approach and surgical technique.

67.12   Other cervical biopsy

Description
The physician inserts a speculum into the vagina to view the cervix. A small cut is made in the cervix and biopsy forceps are used to remove a piece or multiple pieces of tissue. A small curette is used to scrape tissue from the endocervix, which is the region of the opening of the cervix into the uterine cavity.

In an alternate technique, the physician views the cervix, including the upper/adjacent portion of the vagina, through a colposcope, which is a binocular microscope used for direct visualization of the vagina, ectocervix, and endocervix. A biopsy instrument is inserted in the vagina and used to take one or more small biopsies of the cervix. The physician takes a biopsy of the cervix.

Coding Clarification
Code 67.12 is not used to report conization of the cervix; see 67.2.

Use 67.12 to report a punch biopsy of the cervix that is not further specified in the documentation.

Various different types of cervical biopsies include:

● New Code   ▲ Revised Code   ▶◀ Revised Text   © 2010 Ingenix

- **Punch biopsy:** Removal of a small piece of tissue from the cervix. Multiple punch biopsies may be performed on different areas of the cervix.
- **Cone biopsy or conization:** Laser or scalpel utilized to remove a cone-shaped piece of tissue from the cervix.
- **Endocervical curettage (ECC):** Curette is used to scrape the endocervical lining.

Other biopsy procedures used to obtain cervical cells include loop electrosurgical excision procedure (LEEP), colposcopy, and Pap smear.

Documentation Tip
Surgical procedures on the cervix are performed using a variety of surgical techniques and approaches.

To ensure accurate code assignment, review the medical record to determine the approach and surgical technique.

67.19   Other diagnostic procedures on cervix

Description
Code 67.19 is used to report other diagnostic procedures of the cervix that are not more precisely described by other codes in subcategory 67.1.

Coding Clarification
To report microscopic examination of a specimen from the cervix, see 91.41-91.49.

Documentation Tip
Review the documentation for specific information regarding the procedure prior to final code selection in order to ensure accurate code assignment.

67.2   Conization of cervix

Description
Cone biopsy, or conization, involves the use of a laser or scalpel to remove a cone-shaped piece of tissue from the cervix. The physician removes a cone-shaped section from the distal cervix so that cervical function is preserved. The physician inserts a speculum into the vagina to view and fully expose the cervix. In most cases, local anesthesia is administered. Using a scalpel or laser instrument, a cone or slice of tissue is cut from the end of the cervix with the axis of the cone parallel to the axis of the cervix. Bleeding may be stopped by electric current. The cervix may need to be dilated and a curette used directly after conization to scrape tissue that is to be taken from farther up inside the uterus. The physician also may need to place interrupted figure-of-eight sutures to incorporate the bleeding site if direct cautery does not achieve hemostasis. The speculum is removed.

Coding Clarification
Assign 67.2 for conization of the cervix; however, if the conization was by cryosurgery, use 67.33 and if by electrosurgery, assign 67.32.

LEEP cone biopsy is coded 67.32.

Documentation Tip
Surgical procedures on the cervix are performed using a variety of surgical techniques and approaches. To ensure accurate code assignment, review the medical record to determine the approach and surgical technique.

67.3   Other excision or destruction of lesion or tissue of cervix

Description
The different types of excision and destruction procedures performed on the cervix that are not more precisely described by other codes are located under subcategory 67.3, such as electroconization of cervix, loop electrosurgical excision procedure (LEEP), and large loop excision of the transformation zone (LLETZ).

Coding Clarification
Cryosurgery describes destruction of a lesion of the uterine neck by applying intense heat.

Electroconization is an electrocautery excision of a multilayer cone-shaped section from the uterine neck.

A **loop electrosurgical excision procedure (LEEP)** is the surgical excision and simultaneous cautery of a lesion of the cervix using a thin wire through which an electrical current is delivered.

A **large loop excision of the transformation zone (LLETZ)** is the conization or total excision of the cervix utilizing the above described electrosurgical technique.

Documentation Tip
To ensure accurate code assignment, review the medical record to determine the approach and surgical technique.

67.31   Marsupialization of cervical cyst

Description
The physician makes an incision and sutures open a cyst in the neck of the uterus. The physician makes an incision in the skin over the cyst and carries it down through the cyst wall, which drains the fluid from the cyst. The physician sutures the lining of the cyst wall to the overlying skin to create a permanent drain site.

Using a laparoscopic technique, the physician makes a small incision just below the umbilicus through which a fiberoptic laparoscope is inserted. A second incision is made on the left or right side of the abdomen with additional instruments being placed through these incisions into the abdomen or pelvis. Once the cyst is identified with the laparoscope, a third incision is typically made to the drain the fluid from the cyst. The physician sutures the lining of the cyst wall to the overlying skin to create a permanent drain site. The abdomen is deflated, the trocars removed, and the incisions are closed with sutures.

67.32   Destruction of lesion of cervix by cauterization

Description
An excision of cervical tissue can be performed by the loop electrode excision procedure (LEEP). LEEP uses a hot cautery wire with an electrical cutting current running through it and the grounding pad connected to the patient's leg to cut tissue.

To perform a loop electrode conization of the cervix (LEEP), the physician inserts a speculum into the vagina to fully expose the cervix. For most cases, the appropriate local anesthesia is administered as opposed to forms of premedication. The electric grounding pad is placed and safety checks are run. The cutting current is set. Using a loop that encompasses the entire lesion, an excision of the ectocervix is done with every effort made to remove the entire lesion in one specimen. If the lesion is large and another pass is required, two equal specimens are removed and labeled for the axis of orientation. The same procedure is done again with a smaller loop if an endocervical excision is necessary. The bleeding vessels are cauterized, the vagina is inspected for any accidental injury, and the instruments are removed.

Coding Clarification
Electroconization of the cervix is an electrocautery excision of a multilayer, cone-shaped section from the uterine neck.

A loop electrosurgical excision procedure (LEEP) is the surgical excision and simultaneous cautery of a lesion of the cervix using a thin wire through which an electrical current is delivered.

A large loop excision of the transformation zone (LLETZ) is the conization or total excision of the cervix utilizing the above described electrosurgical technique.

Documentation Tip
Surgical procedures on the cervix are performed using a variety of surgical techniques and approaches. To ensure accurate code assignment, review the medical record to determine the approach and surgical technique.

Coding Guidance
    AHA: 1Q, '98, 3

67.33   Destruction of lesion of cervix by cryosurgery

Description
The physician inserts a speculum into the vagina to view the cervix. The outer layers of the cervix are destroyed by freezing using a liquid such as carbon dioxide, Freon, nitrous oxide, nitrogen, or a low temperature instrument. The outer layers of the cervix slough off.

Coding Clarification
Cryoconization of the cervix involves the excision by freezing of a multilayer, cone-shaped section of abnormal tissue in the uterine neck.

67.39   Other excision or destruction of lesion or tissue of cervix

Description
Code 67.39 is used to report excision or destruction procedures of the cervix that are not more precisely described by other codes in subcategory 67.3.

Coding Clarification
To report microscopic examination of a specimen from the cervix, see 91.41-91.49.

Assign 67.39 for destruction of a cervical lesion by laser.

Do not assign 67.39 to report biopsy of the cervix (67.11-67.12), cervical fistulectomy (67.62), or conization of the cervix (67.2).

Documentation Tip
Review the documentation for specific information regarding the procedure to determine the approach and surgical technique prior to final code selection in order to ensure accurate code assignment.

67.4   Amputation of cervix

Description
The physician makes an incision horizontally just within the pubic hairline. The physician removes the cervical stump, which is the part of the cervix left after the supracervical uterus has been removed. The incision is closed by suturing. In an alternate procedure, the physician removes the cervical stump and repairs the muscular floor of the pelvis where the cervix rests using suture plication. This involves folding the tissues on top of each other and suturing. The incision is sutured.

Coding Clarification
Use 76.4 to report cervicectomy with synchronous colporrhaphy or the excision of the lower uterine neck with suturing of the vaginal stump.

Documentation Tip
Surgical procedures on the cervix are performed using a variety of surgical techniques and approaches. To ensure accurate code assignment, review the medical record to determine the approach and surgical technique.

● New Code   ▲ Revised Code   ►◄ Revised Text   © 2010 Ingenix

67.5   Repair of internal cervical os

Description
The physician repairs a cervical opening defect using a variety of surgical techniques, including cerclage of isthmus uteri, McDonald operation, Shirodkar operation, and transvaginal cerclage.

Documentation Tip
Surgical procedures on the cervix are performed using a variety of surgical techniques and approaches. To ensure accurate code assignment, review the medical record to determine the approach and surgical technique.

Coding Guidance
  AHA: 3Q, '00, 11; 4Q, '01, 63

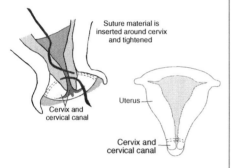

Suture material is inserted around cervix and tightened

Uterus

Cervix and cervical canal

Cervix and cervical canal

67.51   Transabdominal cerclage of cervix

Description
The physician inserts a speculum into the vagina to view the cervix. Heavy suture material or wire is threaded around the cervix and pulled tight to make the opening smaller.

Documentation Tip
Surgical procedures on the cervix are performed using a variety of surgical techniques and approaches. To ensure accurate code assignment, review the medical record to determine the approach and surgical technique.

67.59   Other repair of cervical os

Description
Code 67.59 is used to report other repair procedures of the internal cervical os that are not more precisely described by other codes in subcategory 67.5. Examples include cerclage of isthmus uteri, McDonald operation, Shirodkar operation, and transvaginal cerclage.

Coding Clarification
Do not assign 67.59 for a laparoscopically assisted supracervical hysterectomy [LASH] (68.31) or a transabdominal cerclage of cervix (67.51).

Cerclage of isthmus uteri is the placement of an encircling suture between the neck and body of the uterus.

Shirodkar operation is the placement of purse-string sutures in the internal cervical opening.

Documentation Tip
Review the documentation for specific information regarding the procedure prior to final code selection in order to ensure accurate code assignment.

Coding Guidance
  AHA: 4Q, '08, 83

67.6   Other repair of cervix

Description
Subcategory 67.6 codes include repair procedures of the cervix that are not more precisely described by other codes in category 67.

Coding Clarification
Do not assign subcategory 67.6 for repair of a current obstetric laceration; see 75.51.

Documentation Tip
Surgical procedures on the cervix are performed using a variety of surgical techniques and approaches. To ensure accurate code assignment, review the medical record to determine the approach and surgical technique.

67.61   Suture of laceration of cervix

Description
The physician inserts a speculum into the vagina to view the cervix. The physician performs plastic suture repair of a laceration or wound on the cervix. A plastic repair can also encompass excising scar tissue or tightening an incompetent cervix.

67.62   Repair of fistula of cervix

Description
The physician performs closure of a fistula in the lower uterus. Transabdominal and transvaginal surgical approaches are commonly chosen, although the site of the fistula dictates the surgical approach. The physician uses an abdominal, suprapubic, or transperitoneal transvesical approach for repair. The procedure can also be performed extraperitoneally. After excising the fistula, the physician sutures the clean percutaneous tissues together to create a smooth surface.

Coding Clarification
A cervicosigmoidal fistulectomy is the excision of an abnormal passage between the uterine neck and torsion of the large intestine.

Code 67.62 is not used to report fistulectomy: cervicovesical (57.84), ureterocervical (56.84), or vesicocervicovaginal (57.84).

65-71

Documentation Tip

Surgical procedures on the cervix are performed using a variety of surgical techniques and approaches. To ensure accurate code assignment, review the medical record to determine the approach and surgical technique.

67.69   Other repair of cervix

Description

Code 67.69 is used to report repair procedures of the cervix that are not more precisely described by other codes in category 67, such as the repair of an old obstetric cervical laceration.

Documentation Tip

Review the documentation for specific information regarding the procedure prior to final code selection in order to ensure accurate code assignment.

---

68   Other incision and excision of uterus

Description

Included under category 68 are incisions, diagnostic procedures, and excisions performed on the uterus and supporting structures. Seven of the 10 subcategories classify hysterectomies. The codes for biopsies found under subcategory 68.1 are subdivided according to open or closed and site (i.e., uterus or uterine ligaments).

Coding Clarification

Use additional codes for any removal of tubes and ovaries in conjunction with a hysterectomy.

Use additional codes for any lymph gland dissection in conjunction with radical hysterectomy.

Assign 68.23 for endometrial rollerball ablation.

Assign 68.51 and 65.63 for laparoscopically assisted vaginal hysterectomy with bilateral laparoscopic salpingo-oophorectomy.

A pelvic evisceration, code 68.8, involves the removal of ovaries, tubes, uterus, vagina, bladder, and urethra, as well as any excision of the sigmoid colon and rectum. Any synchronous colostomy, lymph gland dissection, or urinary diversion is coded separately.

Also code any application or administration of an adhesion barrier substance (99.77).

Documentation Tip

Different codes are available when the physician documents a hysterectomy. Check the operative report to determine if the hysterectomy was abdominal or vaginal and the extent of removal.

68.0   Hysterotomy

Description

Code 68.0 reports an incision into the uterus performed for exploration, foreign body removal, or for the removal of a hydatidiform mole.

The physician removes a hydatidiform mole through an incision in the abdominal wall and uterus. The surgery is similar to a cesarean section but the abdominal and uterine incisions are smaller. First, the lower abdominal wall is opened with a vertical or horizontal incision, and the uterus is entered through the lower uterine segment. The physician removes the hydatidiform mole and may also remove any remaining membranes and placenta from the uterine cavity. Curettage of the uterine cavity may also be performed. The abdominal and uterine incisions are closed by suturing.

Coding Clarification

Use 68.0 to report hysterotomy with removal of a hydatidiform mole.

Do not use this code to report hysterotomy for termination of a pregnancy (74.91).

68.1   Diagnostic procedures on uterus and supporting structures

Description

Subcategory 68.1 reports various types of diagnostic biopsy procedures performed on the uterus and supporting structures.

Coding Clarification

Biopsy procedures on the uterus are performed using a variety of surgical techniques and approaches ranging from open surgery to less invasive procedures such as laparoscopy and aspiration techniques. Aspiration, biopsy, and drainage can be performed percutaneously through an anterior abdominal approach, a transabdominal route, or a transvaginal approach.

Documentation Tip

To ensure accurate code assignment, review the medical record to determine the approach and surgical technique employed.

68.11   Digital examination of uterus

Description

The physician performs a manual examination of the uterus.

Coding Clarification

For a pelvic examination, see 89.26.

For a postpartal manual exploration of the uterine cavity, see 75.7.

● New Code   ▲ Revised Code   ►◄ Revised Text   © 2010 Ingenix

68.12   Hysteroscopy

Description
The physician performs a diagnostic inspection of the uterus using a hysteroscope. The physician advances the hysteroscope through the vagina and into the cervical os to gain entry into the uterine cavity. The physician inspects the uterine cavity with the fiberoptic scope for diagnostic purposes.

Coding Clarification
For hysteroscopy with biopsy, see 68.16.

Documentation Tip
To ensure accurate code assignment, review the medical record to determine the approach and surgical technique employed.

68.13   Open biopsy of uterus

Description
In an open procedure, the physician takes sample tissue from the uterus through an incision in the vagina. This procedure may also be performed through a small abdominal incision just above the pubic hairline.

Coding Clarification
For closed biopsy of the uterus, see 68.16.

Documentation Tip
Biopsy procedures on the uterus are performed using a variety of surgical techniques and approaches ranging from open surgery to less invasive procedures such as laparoscopy and aspiration techniques.

To ensure accurate code assignment, review the medical record to determine the approach and surgical technique employed.

68.14   Open biopsy of uterine ligaments

Description
Biopsy procedures on the uterus and supporting structures are performed using a variety of surgical approaches. This procedure may be done through the vagina or abdominally through a small incision just above the pubic hairline.

In an open procedure, using a vaginal approach, the physician takes sample tissue from the uterine ligaments through an incision in the vagina or using an abdominal approach through a small abdominal incision just above the pubic hairline.

Coding Clarification
For closed biopsy of the uterine ligaments, see 68.15.

Documentation Tip
To ensure accurate code assignment, review the medical record to determine the approach and surgical technique employed.

68.15   Closed biopsy of uterine ligaments

Description
The physician performs a diagnostic inspection of the uterus using a hysteroscope. The physician advances the hysteroscope through the vagina and into the cervical os to gain entry into the uterine cavity. The physician inspects the uterine cavity with the fiberoptic scope and removes a tissue sample of the uterine ligament.

Coding Clarification
Assign 68.15 for endoscopic (laparoscopy) biopsy of the uterine adnexa, except ovary and fallopian tube.

68.16   Closed biopsy of uterus

Description
The physician inserts a speculum into the vagina to view the cervix. A tool is used to grasp the cervix and pull it down. The physician places a curette in the endocervical canal and passes it into the uterus. The entire endometrial lining of the uterus is thoroughly scraped on all sides to obtain tissue for diagnosis or to remove unhealthy tissue. Biopsy may also be taken from the endocervix, without cervical dilation.

The physician performs a diagnostic inspection of the uterus using a hysteroscope and takes a uterine biopsy. The physician advances the hysteroscope through the vagina and into the cervical os to gain entry into the uterine cavity. The physician inspects the uterine cavity with the fiberoptic scope and removes a sample of the uterine lining or a growth (polypectomy) within the uterus and may perform a cervical dilation and uterine curettage scraping to take a complete sampling of the uterine lining.

Coding Clarification
Use 68.16 for endoscopic (laparoscopy) (hysteroscopy) biopsy of the uterus.

For open biopsy of the uterus, see 68.13.

Documentation Tip
Biopsy procedures on the uterus are performed using a variety of surgical techniques and approaches ranging from open surgery to less invasive procedures such as laparoscopy and aspiration techniques.

68.19   Other diagnostic procedures on uterus and supporting structures

Description
Code 68.19 is used to report other diagnostic procedures of the uterus and supporting structures that are not more precisely described by other codes in this subcategory.

Coding Clarification
Do not use 68.19 to report a diagnostic aspiration curettage (69.59), dilation and curettage (69.09),

© 2010 Ingenix   ● New Code   ▲ Revised Code   ▶◀ Revised Text   **541**

65-71

microscopic examination of specimen from uterus (91.41-91.49), or pelvic examination (89.26).

Code 68.19 is also not used to report radioisotope scans of the placenta (92.17) or uterus (92.19), ultrasonography of the uterus (88.78-88.79), or x-ray of the uterus (87.81-87.89).

Documentation Tip
Review the documentation for specific information regarding the procedure prior to final code selection in order to ensure accurate code assignment.

68.2   Excision or destruction of lesion or tissue of uterus

Description
The different types of excision and destruction procedures performed on the uterus are located under category 68.2.

Documentation Tip
To ensure accurate code assignment, review the medical record to determine the approach and surgical technique employed.

68.21   Division of endometrial synechiae

Description
The physician removes scar tissue (adhesions) from within the uterus using a fiberoptic hysteroscope. The physician advances the hysteroscope through the vagina and into the cervical os to gain entry into the uterine cavity. The physician inspects the uterine cavity with the fiberoptic scope and removes or divides adhesions (fibrous scar tissue) that are artificially connecting the walls of the uterus.

Documentation Tip
To ensure accurate code assignment, review the medical record to determine the approach and surgical technique employed.

68.22   Incision or excision of congenital septum of uterus

Description
The physician removes tissue abnormally dividing the intrauterine cavity using a fiberoptic hysteroscope. The physician advances the hysteroscope through the vagina and into the cervical os to gain entry into the uterine cavity. The physician inspects the uterine cavity with the fiberoptic scope and resects an intrauterine septum (tissue creating an abnormal partition in the uterus).

68.23   Endometrial ablation

Description
Ablation destroys a thin layer of the lining of the uterus and can be accomplished using a variety of techniques such as electrical, laser, cryoablation, and thermal. The rollerball or loop applies an electric

current to the surface as it is pulled across the lining. This current destroys the lining. A laser device burns the lining using a high-intensity light beam. The laser reaches the lining of the uterus through the hysteroscope. The laser then destroys the lining of the uterus. With thermal ablation, a device or fluid is inserted into the uterus. Heat and energy are applied to increase the temperature and destroy the lining.

Some endometrial ablation procedures are performed using a hysteroscope, a device inserted through the vagina for a visual examination, and ablation instruments can be inserted through the opening. For example, the physician surgically removes (ablates) the inner lining of the uterus with the assistance of a fiberoptic hysteroscope. The physician advances the hysteroscope through the vagina and into the cervical os to gain entry into the uterine cavity. The physician inspects the uterine cavity with the fiberoptic scope and ablates the endometrium by various methods, such as resection, electrosurgical ablation, or thermoablation.

Coding Clarification
Removal or destruction of uterine lining is usually accomplished by electrocautery or loop electrosurgical excision procedure (LEEP). LEEP is the surgical excision and simultaneous cautery of tissue using a thin wire through which an electrical current is delivered.

Use 68.23 to report dilation and curettage and hysteroscopic endometrial ablation.

Coding Scenario
The physician performs endometrial cryoablation using ultrasound guidance. The physician inserts a speculum for visualization of the cervix. A numbing block is placed in the cervix. A thin cryoablation device is inserted through the cervix into the uterus. The cryoablation device freezes targeted uterine endometrial tissue. The instrument is withdrawn following completion of the procedure.

Code Assignment:

68.23   Endometrial ablation

Coding Guidance
AHA: 4Q, '96, 68

68.29   Other excision or destruction of lesion of uterus

Description
Code 68.29 reports various forms of excision or destruction of uterine lesions, including focused ultrasound ablation. Focused ultrasound ablation is a noninvasive surgical technique that uses thermal ablation to destroy uterine leiomyomata. In focused ultrasound ablation, the ultrasound beam penetrates through soft tissues causing localized

high temperatures for a few seconds at the targeted site, in this case the uterine leiomyomata. This produces thermocoagulation and necrosis of the uterine leiomyomata without damage to overlaying and surrounding tissues. Magnetic resonance (MR) guidance is used in conjunction with focused ultrasound ablation to provide more precise target definition. Since certain MR parameters are also temperature sensitive, MR guidance also allows estimation of optimal thermal doses to the uterine leiomyomata and detection of relatively small temperature elevations in surrounding tissues thereby preventing any irreversible damage to surrounding tissues.

Coding Clarification

Code 68.29 is used to report a uterine myomectomy.

For biopsy of the uterus, see 68.13. For uterine fistulectomy, see 69.42.

Documentation Tip

Surgical procedures on the uterus are performed using a variety of surgical techniques and approaches ranging from open surgery to less invasive procedures, such as laparoscopy and percutaneous techniques. Review the documentation for specific information regarding the procedure prior to final code selection in order to ensure accurate code assignment.

Coding Guidance

AHA: 1Q, '96, 14; 3Q, '06, 18

68.3   Subtotal abdominal hysterectomy

Description

The physician performs a subtotal hysterectomy, which is also called partial or supracervical hysterectomy, in which the upper part of the uterus is removed but the cervix is left in place. Through a horizontal incision just within the pubic hairline, the physician removes the uterus above the cervix and may elect to remove one or both of the ovaries and one or both of the fallopian tubes (salpingo-oophorectomy). The supporting pedicles containing the tubes, ligaments, and arteries are clamped and cut free. The uterus is cut free from the cervix leaving the cervix still attached to the vagina. The abdominal incision is then closed by suturing.

Coding Clarification

A hysterectomy is the surgical removal of the uterus. The different types of hysterectomy include:

- **Hysterectomy with bilateral oophorectomy:** Removal of one or both ovaries, and sometimes the fallopian tubes, along with the uterus.

- **Radical hysterectomy:** Removal of the uterus, cervix, the top portion of the vagina, most of the tissue that surrounds the cervix in the pelvic cavity, and may include the removal of the pelvic lymph nodes.

- **Supracervical hysterectomy:** Partial or subtotal hysterectomy that involves the removal of the body of the uterus leaving the cervix intact.

- **Total hysterectomy:** Removal of the entire uterus, including the fundus and the cervix, but not the ovaries. This is the most common type of hysterectomy.

There are also different surgical techniques used to perform a hysterectomy including:

- **Abdominal hysterectomy:** Uterus is removed through the abdomen via a surgical incision. The incision can be made vertically, from the navel down to the pubic bone, or horizontally, along the top of the pubic hairline.

- **Laparoscope-assisted vaginal hysterectomy:** Vaginal hysterectomy performed with a laparoscope. Thin tubes are inserted through tiny incisions in the abdomen near the navel. The uterus is then removed in sections through the laparoscope tube or through the vagina.

- **Total hysterectomy:** Removal of the entire uterus, including the fundus and the cervix, but not the ovaries. This is the most common type of hysterectomy.

68.31   Laparoscopic supracervical hysterectomy [LSH]

Description

Supracervical hysterectomy, or a partial or subtotal hysterectomy, involves the removal of the body of the uterus leaving the cervix intact. The physician performs a hysterectomy using a laparoscope. The patient is placed is the dorsal lithotomy position. A trocar is inserted periumbilically and the abdomen is insufflated with gas. Additional trocars are placed in the right and left lower quadrants. An intraabdominal and pelvic survey is done. Attention is paid to limiting blood loss. The physician incises the uterus down through the myometrium. The uterine wall defects are then sutured laparoscopically, the trocars are removed, and the wounds are closed.

Coding Clarification

Assign 68.31 to report a classic infrafascial SEMM hysterectomy (CISH) or a laparoscopically assisted supracervical hysterectomy (LASH).

SEMM version of the supracervical hysterectomy is also called the classic infrafascial Semm hysterectomy (CISH).

Laparoscopically-assisted vaginal hysterectomy (LAVH) is a hysterectomy performed through an incision at the naval and vagina.

65-71

Laparoscopic supra hysterectomy (LSH) uses a laparoscopic procedure to remove the uterus while preserving the cervix.

Coding Guidance
> **AHA:** 4Q, '03, 98-99

68.39 Other and unspecified subtotal abdominal hysterectomy

Description
Code 68.39 is used to report subtotal abdominal hysterectomy procedures that are not more precisely described by other codes in subcategory 68.3. This code is also reported when the documentation does not further specify the hysterectomy procedure.

Coding Clarification
Assign 68.39 for a supracervical hysterectomy not specified as laparoscopic.

Do not use 68.39 to report a classic infrafascial SEMM hysterectomy (CISH) (68.31) or a laparoscopic supracervical hysterectomy (LSH) (68.31).

Different codes are available when the physician documents a hysterectomy. Check the operative report to determine if the hysterectomy was abdominal or vaginal and the extent of removal. The different types of hysterectomy include:

- **Hysterectomy with bilateral oophorectomy:** Removal of one or both ovaries, and sometimes the fallopian tubes, along with the uterus.

- **Radical hysterectomy:** Removal of the uterus, cervix, the top portion of the vagina, most of the tissue that surrounds the cervix in the pelvic cavity, and may include the removal of the pelvic lymph nodes.

- **Supracervical hysterectomy:** Partial or subtotal hysterectomy that involves the removal of the body of the uterus leaving the cervix intact.

- **Total hysterectomy:** Removal of the entire uterus, including the fundus and the cervix, but not the ovaries. This is the most common type of hysterectomy.

There are also different surgical techniques used to perform a hysterectomy including:

- **Abdominal hysterectomy:** Uterus is removed through the abdomen via a surgical incision. The incision can be made vertically, from the navel down to the pubic bone, or horizontally, along the top of the pubic hairline.

- **Laparoscope-assisted vaginal hysterectomy:** Vaginal hysterectomy performed with a laparoscope. Thin tubes are inserted through tiny incisions in the abdomen near the navel. The uterus is then removed in sections through the laparoscope tube or through the vagina.

- **Total hysterectomy:** Removal of the entire uterus, including the fundus and the cervix, but not the ovaries. This is the most common type of hysterectomy.

Documentation Tip
A SEMM version of a supracervical hysterectomy is also termed the classic infrafascial Semm hysterectomy (CISH).

Review the documentation for specific information regarding the procedure prior to final code selection in order to avoid improper use of the "not otherwise specified" code and to ensure accurate code assignment.

Coding Guidance
> **AHA:** 4Q, '03, 98

68.4 Total abdominal hysterectomy

Description
In abdominal hysterectomy, the doctor makes an incision through the skin and tissue in the lower abdomen to reach the uterus. The incision may be vertical or horizontal.

Coding Clarification
Code also any synchronous removal of tubes and ovaries performed using 65.31-65.64.

Do not assign 68.39 to report laparoscopic total abdominal hysterectomy (68.41) or radical abdominal hysterectomy, any approach (68.61-68.69).

Coding Guidance
> **AHA:** 4Q, '06, 130; 4Q, '96, 65

68.41 Laparoscopic total abdominal hysterectomy

Description
A total laparoscopic hysterectomy is done through small incisions in the abdomen using a laparoscope. The uterus is removed in small pieces through these incisions. In an open abdominal hysterectomy, the uterus is removed through the abdomen via a surgical incision about 6 to 8 inches long. The main surgical incision can be made vertically, from the navel to the pubic bone, or horizontally, along the top of the pubic hairline.

Coding Clarification
Different codes are available when the physician documents a hysterectomy. Check the operative report to determine if the hysterectomy was abdominal or vaginal and the extent of removal. The different types of hysterectomy include:

- **Hysterectomy with bilateral oophorectomy:** Removal of one or both ovaries, and sometimes the fallopian tubes, along with the uterus.

- **Radical hysterectomy:** Removal of the uterus, cervix, the top portion of the vagina, most of the

● New Code   ▲ Revised Code   ▶◀ Revised Text   © 2010 Ingenix

tissue that surrounds the cervix in the pelvic cavity, and may include the removal of the pelvic lymph nodes.

- **Supracervical hysterectomy:** Partial or subtotal hysterectomy that involves the removal of the body of the uterus leaving the cervix intact.

- **Total hysterectomy:** Removal of the entire uterus, including the fundus and the cervix, but not the ovaries. This is the most common type of hysterectomy.

- There are also different surgical techniques used to perform a hysterectomy including:

- **Abdominal hysterectomy:** Uterus is removed through the abdomen via a surgical incision. The incision can be made vertically, from the navel down to the pubic bone, or horizontally, along the top of the pubic hairline.

- **Laparoscope-assisted vaginal hysterectomy:** Vaginal hysterectomy performed with a laparoscope. Thin tubes are inserted through tiny incisions in the abdomen near the navel. The uterus is then removed in sections through the laparoscope tube or through the vagina.

- **Total hysterectomy:** Removal of the entire uterus, including the fundus and the cervix, but not the ovaries. This is the most common type of hysterectomy.

Coding Guidance
AHA: 4Q, '06, 133; ▶3Q, '09, 5◀

Coding Scenario
▶A 47-year-old female is admitted for a laparoscopic TAHBSO. The patient elected to have this surgery because both of her biological sisters and mother have all been diagnosed with ovarian cancer. Documentation shows that a malignancy was subsequently found in the body of the patient's uterus.

Code Assignment:

V50.42	Prophylactic ovary removal, 182.0 Malignant neoplasm of corpus uteri, except isthmus
V50.49	Prophylactic organ removal, other and V16.41 Family history of malignant neoplasm, Ovary
68.41	Laparoscopic total abdominal hysterectomy
65.63	Laparoscopic removal of both ovaries and tubes at the same operative episode◀

68.49 Other and unspecified total abdominal hysterectomy

Description
Code 68.49 is used to report other subtotal abdominal hysterectomy procedures that are not more precisely described by other codes in this subcategory.

Coding Clarification
Assign code 68.49 for an extended hysterectomy.

Documentation Tip
Different codes are available when the physician documents a hysterectomy and there are also different surgical techniques used to perform a hysterectomy. Check the operative report to determine if the hysterectomy was abdominal or vaginal and the extent of removal.

Coding Guidance
AHA: 4Q, '06, 130

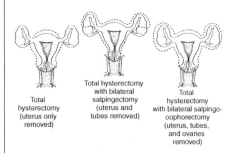

Total hysterectomy (uterus only removed)

Total hysterectomy with bilateral salpingectomy (uterus and tubes removed)

Total hysterectomy with bilateral salpingo-oophorectomy (uterus, tubes, and ovaries removed)

68.5 Vaginal hysterectomy

Description
Vaginal hysterectomy is the complete excision of the uterus using a vaginal approach in which the physician removes the uterus through the vaginal opening.

Coding Clarification
Code also any synchronous removal of tubes and ovaries (65.31-65.64), repair of cystocele or rectocele (70.50-70.52), or repair of pelvic floor (70.79).

Documentation Tip
Different codes are available when the physician documents a hysterectomy. Check the operative report to determine if the hysterectomy was abdominal or vaginal and the extent of removal. The different types of hysterectomy surgical techniques include:

- **Abdominal hysterectomy:** Uterus is removed through the abdomen via a surgical incision. The incision can be made vertically, from the navel down to the pubic bone, or horizontally, along the top of the pubic hairline.

- **Laparoscope-assisted vaginal hysterectomy:** Vaginal hysterectomy performed with a laparoscope. Thin tubes are inserted through tiny incisions in the abdomen near the navel. The uterus is then removed in sections through the laparoscope tube or through the vagina.

- **Total hysterectomy:** Removal of the entire uterus, including the fundus and the cervix, but not the ovaries. This is the most common type of hysterectomy.

65-71

68.51   Laparoscopically assisted vaginal hysterectomy (LAVH)

Description

The physician performs surgical laparoscopy with vaginal hysterectomy. The laparoscope is used to perform the initial operative portion of the hysterectomy. The patient is placed in dorsal lithotomy position for the endoscopic portion. For the vaginal portion, the patient is positioned in stirrups. A trocar is inserted periumbilically and the abdomen is insufflated with gas. Additional trocars are placed in the right and left lower quadrants. An intraabdominal and pelvic survey is done and any adhesions are lysed. The round ligaments are ligated and incised. Starting on the left round ligament, the vesicouterine peritoneal fold is incised and the peritoneal vessels are dissected and desiccated. The physician continues the incision across the lower uterine segment to the round ligament on the other side and dissects the bladder off the uterus and cervix. Staples are inserted through one port on the side to be stapled or a bipolar coagulation unit is inserted for electrocautery. At this point, if tubes and/or ovaries are to be removed (in a separately reportable procedure), the infundibulopelvic ligament is ligated lateral to the ovary. If not, the ligation is done medial to the ovary. Staple-ligation or electrodesiccation of the uterine vasculature is accomplished on both sides, followed by that of the cardinal ligaments. An anterior colpotomy incision is made to enter the vagina and the vaginal portion of the procedure is begun. The vaginal hysterectomy proceeds through a posterior cul-de-sac incision. The uterus is removed, the vagina is closed, and hemostasis is confirmed before the trocars are removed and the skin incisions are closed.

Documentation Tip

Different codes are available when the physician documents a hysterectomy. Check the operative report to determine if the hysterectomy was abdominal or vaginal and the extent of removal. The different types of hysterectomy surgical techniques include:

- **Abdominal hysterectomy:** Uterus is removed through the abdomen via a surgical incision. The incision can be made vertically, from the navel down to the pubic bone, or horizontally, along the top of the pubic hairline.

- **Laparoscope-assisted vaginal hysterectomy:** Vaginal hysterectomy performed with a laparoscope. Thin tubes are inserted through tiny incisions in the abdomen near the navel. The uterus is then removed in sections through the laparoscope tube or through the vagina.

- **Total hysterectomy:** Removal of the entire uterus, including the fundus and the cervix, but

not the ovaries. This is the most common type of hysterectomy.

Coding Guidance

AHA: 4Q, '96, 68

68.59   Other and unspecified vaginal hysterectomy

Description

Code 68.59 is used to report vaginal hysterectomy procedures that are not more precisely described by other codes in subcategory 68.5. This code is also reported when the documentation does not further specify the procedure.

Coding Clarification

Do not use 68.59 to report laparoscopically assisted vaginal hysterectomy (68.51) or radical vaginal hysterectomy (68.71-68.79).

Documentation Tip

Review the documentation for specific information regarding the procedure prior to final code selection in order to avoid improper use of the "not otherwise specified" code and to ensure accurate code assignment.

Different codes are available when the physician documents a hysterectomy. Check the operative report to determine if the hysterectomy was abdominal or vaginal and the extent of the removal.

68.6   Radical abdominal hysterectomy

Description

The physician excises the uterus, loose connective tissue, and smooth muscle around the uterus and vagina using an abdominal approach. The different types of hysterectomy include:

- **Hysterectomy with bilateral oophorectomy:** Removal of one or both ovaries, and sometimes the fallopian tubes, along with the uterus.

- **Radical hysterectomy:** Removal of the uterus, cervix, the top portion of the vagina, most of the tissue that surrounds the cervix in the pelvic cavity, and may include the removal of the pelvic lymph nodes.

- **Supracervical hysterectomy:** Partial or subtotal hysterectomy that involves the removal of the body of the uterus leaving the cervix intact.

- **Total hysterectomy:** Removal of the entire uterus, including the fundus and the cervix, but not the ovaries. This is the most common type of hysterectomy.

Coding Clarification

Code also any synchronous lymph gland dissection (40.3, 40.5) or removal of tubes and ovaries (65.31-65.64) performed at the same operative session.

● New Code   ▲ Revised Code   ▶◀ Revised Text   © 2010 Ingenix

To report pelvic evisceration, see 68.8.

Documentation Tip

Different codes are available when the physician documents a hysterectomy. Check the operative report to determine if the hysterectomy was abdominal or vaginal and the extent of removal. The different surgical techniques used to perform a hysterectomy include:

- **Abdominal hysterectomy:** Uterus is removed through the abdomen via a surgical incision. The incision can be made vertically, from the navel down to the pubic bone, or horizontally, along the top of the pubic hairline.
- **Laparoscope-assisted vaginal hysterectomy:** Vaginal hysterectomy performed with a laparoscope. Thin tubes are inserted through tiny incisions in the abdomen near the navel. The uterus is then removed in sections through the laparoscope tube or through the vagina.
- **Total hysterectomy:** Removal of the entire uterus, including the fundus and the cervix, but not the ovaries. This is the most common type of hysterectomy.

Coding Guidance

AHA: 4Q, '06, 130-134

68.61   Laparoscopic radical abdominal hysterectomy

Description

Radical hysterectomy consists of the removal of the uterus, cervix, top portion of the vagina, most of the tissue that surrounds the cervix in the pelvic cavity, and may include the removal of the pelvic lymph nodes. The physician performs a laparoscopic hysterectomy, bilateral total pelvic lymphadenectomy, and para-aortic lymph node sampling, and may remove all or portions of the fallopian tubes and ovaries. The patient is placed is the dorsal lithotomy position. After the insertion of a speculum in the vagina, the physician grasps the cervix with an instrument to manipulate the uterus during the surgery. A trocar is inserted periumbilically and the abdomen is insufflated with gas. Additional trocars are placed in the right and left lower quadrants. The uterus is dissected free from the bladder and surrounding tissue and its body with the cervix is dissected from the vagina. Alternately, the vagina may also be excised. Coagulation is achieved with the aid of electrocautery instruments. Some vessels may be ligated. The uterus is morcellized and removed using endoscopic tools. One or both ovaries and/or one or both fallopian tubes are removed in similar fashion. The physician removes the pelvic lymph nodes on both sides and takes samples or biopsies of the para-aortic lymph nodes. Once the excisions are complete, the abdominal cavity is deflated and instruments and trocars removed. The fascia and skin of the abdomen and vagina are closed with sutures.

Coding Clarification

Assign 68.61 to report a laparoscopic modified radical hysterectomy or a total laparoscopic radical hysterectomy (TLRH).

Code in addition the laparoscopic removal of both ovaries and tubes at same operative episode (65.63) if bilateral salpingo-oophorectomy is performed.

Code in addition the laparoscopic lysis of peritoneal adhesions (54.51) and/or laparoscopic lysis of perirenal or periureteral adhesions (59.03), if performed.

Coding Guidance

AHA: 4Q, '06, 130, 134

Documentation Tip

Different codes are available when the physician documents a hysterectomy. Check the operative report to determine if the hysterectomy was abdominal or vaginal and the extent of removal.

68.69   Other and unspecified radical abdominal hysterectomy

Description

Code 68.69 is used to report radical abdominal hysterectomy procedures that are not more precisely described by other codes in subcategory 68.6. This code is also reported when the documentation does not further specify the procedure. The different types of hysterectomy include:

- **Hysterectomy with bilateral oophorectomy:** Removal of one or both ovaries, and sometimes the fallopian tubes, along with the uterus.
- **Radical hysterectomy:** Removal of the uterus, cervix, the top portion of the vagina, most of the tissue that surrounds the cervix in the pelvic cavity, and may include the removal of the pelvic lymph nodes.
- **Supracervical hysterectomy:** Partial or subtotal hysterectomy that involves the removal of the body of the uterus leaving the cervix intact.
- **Total hysterectomy:** Removal of the entire uterus, including the fundus and the cervix, but not the ovaries. This is the most common type of hysterectomy.

Coding Clarification

Use 68.69 to report a modified radical hysterectomy or a Wertheim's operation.

Do not assign 68.69 to report laparoscopic total abdominal hysterectomy (68.41) or laparoscopic radical abdominal hysterectomy (68.61).

65-71

Documentation Tip
Different codes are available when the physician documents a hysterectomy. Check the operative report to determine if the hysterectomy was abdominal or vaginal and the extent of removal.

Review the documentation for specific information regarding the procedure prior to final code selection in order to avoid improper use of the "not otherwise specified" code and to ensure accurate code assignment.

Coding Guidance
  AHA: 4Q, '06, 130

68.7   Radical vaginal hysterectomy

Description
Radical hysterectomy consists of the removal of the uterus, cervix, the top portion of the vagina, most of the tissue that surrounds the cervix in the pelvic cavity, and may include the removal of the pelvic lymph nodes.

Coding Clarification
Code also any synchronous lymph gland dissection (40.3, 40.5) or removal of tubes and ovaries (65.31-65.64).

Do not assign subcategory 68.7 to report an abdominal hysterectomy, any approach (68.31-68.39, 68.41-68.49, 68.61-68.69, 68.9).

Documentation Tip
Different codes are available when the physician documents a hysterectomy. Check the operative report to determine if the hysterectomy was abdominal or vaginal and the extent of removal.

Coding Guidance
  AHA: 4Q, '06, 130-134

68.71   Laparoscopic radical vaginal hysterectomy [LRVH]

Description
The physician performs a laparoscopic hysterectomy, bilateral total pelvic lymphadenectomy, and para-aortic lymph node sampling, and may remove all or portions of the fallopian tubes and ovaries. The patient is placed is the dorsal lithotomy position. After the insertion of a speculum in the vagina, the physician grasps the cervix with an instrument to manipulate the uterus during the surgery. A trocar is inserted periumbilically and the abdomen is insufflated with gas. Additional trocars are placed in the right and left lower quadrants. The uterus is dissected free from the bladder and surrounding tissue and its body with the cervix is dissected from the vagina. Alternately, the vagina may also be excised. Coagulation is achieved with the aid of electrocautery instruments. Some vessels may be ligated. The uterus is morcellized and removed using

endoscopic tools. One or both ovaries and/or one or both fallopian tubes are removed in similar fashion. The physician removes the pelvic lymph nodes on both sides and takes samples or biopsies of the para-aortic lymph nodes. Once the excisions are complete, the abdominal cavity is deflated and instruments and trocars removed. The fascia and skin of the abdomen and vagina are closed with sutures.

Coding Clarification
Different codes are available when the physician documents a hysterectomy. Check the operative report to determine if the hysterectomy was abdominal or vaginal and the extent of removal. The different types of hysterectomy include:

• **Hysterectomy with bilateral oophorectomy:** Removal of one or both ovaries, and sometimes the fallopian tubes, along with the uterus.

• **Radical hysterectomy:** Removal of the uterus, cervix, the top portion of the vagina, most of the tissue that surrounds the cervix in the pelvic cavity, and may include the removal of the pelvic lymph nodes.

• **Supracervical hysterectomy:** Partial or subtotal hysterectomy that involves the removal of the body of the uterus leaving the cervix intact.

• **Total hysterectomy:** Removal of the entire uterus, including the fundus and the cervix, but not the ovaries. This is the most common type of hysterectomy.

Documentation Tip
Different codes are available when the physician documents a hysterectomy. Check the operative report to determine if the hysterectomy was abdominal or vaginal and the extent of removal.

Coding Guidance
  AHA: 4Q, '06, 130

68.79   Other and unspecified radical vaginal hysterectomy

Description
Code 68.79 is used to report other radical vaginal hysterectomy procedures that are not more precisely described by other codes in this subcategory such as hysterocolpectomy or a Schauta operation. This code is also reported when the documentation does not further specify the procedure.

Coding Clarification
Different codes are available when the physician documents a hysterectomy. Check the operative report to determine if the hysterectomy was abdominal or vaginal and the extent of removal. The different types of hysterectomy include:

● New Code   ▲ Revised Code   ►◄ Revised Text   © 2010 Ingenix

65-71

- **Hysterectomy with bilateral oophorectomy:** Removal of one or both ovaries, and sometimes the fallopian tubes, along with the uterus.

- **Radical hysterectomy:** Removal of the uterus, cervix, the top portion of the vagina, most of the tissue that surrounds the cervix in the pelvic cavity, and may include the removal of the pelvic lymph nodes.

- **Supracervical hysterectomy:** Partial or subtotal hysterectomy that involves the removal of the body of the uterus leaving the cervix intact.

- **Total hysterectomy:** Removal of the entire uterus, including the fundus and the cervix, but not the ovaries. This is the most common type of hysterectomy.

Documentation Tip
Different codes are available when the physician documents a hysterectomy. Check the operative report to determine if the hysterectomy was abdominal or vaginal and the extent of removal.

Coding Guidance
AHA: 4Q, '06, 130

68.8   Pelvic evisceration

Description
Through a horizontal incision just within the pubic hairline, the physician removes all of the organs and adjacent structures of the pelvis including the cervix, uterus, and all or part of the vagina. The supporting pedicles containing the tubes, ligaments, and arteries are clamped and cut free and the uterus, cervix, and all or part of the vagina are removed. The physician may remove one or both of the ovaries and one or both of the fallopian tubes (salpingo-oophorectomy). The physician removes the bladder and diverts urine flow by transplanting the ureters to the skin or colon. The rectum and part of the colon may be removed and an artificial abdominal opening in the skin surface is created for waste (colostomy). The abdominal incision is closed by suturing.

In an alternate technique, the physician removes pelvic organs, with or without a colostomy, including ovaries, tubes, uterus, vagina, bladder, and urethra due to cancer. The physician makes an abdominal incision. The distal colon and rectum are mobilized and divided proximal and distal to the segment of interest. The pelvic organs are dissected free of surrounding structures and removed. The colon and rectum may be reapproximated or the proximal end of the colon may be brought out through a separate incision on the abdominal wall as a colostomy and the remaining rectum closed with staples or sutures. The initial incision is closed.

Coding Clarification
Code also any synchronous colostomy (46.10-46.13), lymph gland dissection (40.3, 40.5), or urinary diversion (56.51-56.79).

Documentation Tip
Surgical procedures on the pelvic organs are performed using a variety of surgical techniques and approaches ranging from open surgery to less invasive procedures, such as laparoscopy, percutaneous techniques, or transurethrally. Review the documentation for specific information regarding the procedure prior to final code selection in order to ensure accurate code assignment.

68.9   Other and unspecified hysterectomy

Description
Code 68.9 is used to report hysterectomy procedures that are not more precisely described by other codes in category 68. This code is also reported when the documentation does not further specify the procedure.

Coding Clarification
Do not assign 68.9 to report abdominal hysterectomy, any approach (68.31-68.39, 68.41-68.49, 68.61-68.69) or vaginal hysterectomy, any approach (68.51-68.59, 68.71-68.79).

Documentation Tip
Different codes are available when the physician documents a hysterectomy. Check the operative report to determine if the hysterectomy was abdominal or vaginal and the extent of removal.

69   Other operations on uterus and supporting structures

Description
Category 69 includes operations other than incisions and excisions classified to category 68. These types of procedures include D&C, repairs, aspiration curettage, and other operations on the uterus and supporting structures.

Coding Clarification
For all procedures reported with a code from category 69, code also any application or administration of an adhesion barrier substance (99.77).

Subcategories for D&C (69.0) and aspiration curettage (69.5) include codes for the procedure performed for termination of pregnancy, following delivery or abortion, or for diagnostic purposes. Look for this documentation in the medical record to assist in proper code selection.

Use 69.02 for a D&C performed for a missed abortion.

65-71

Assign 69.09 for a D&C performed for a blighted ovum.

Do not use the codes under subcategory 69.4 Uterine repair, if the repair is a current obstetric laceration; see 75.50–75.52 for obstetrical procedures.

Use 69.59 for cervical dilation with both suction and sharp curette.

69.0   Dilation and curettage of uterus

Description
The dilation and curettage procedure is known as a D&C and consists of enlarging and scraping the lining of the uterus. D&C is usually a diagnostic procedure but can also be performed as therapeutic procedure, for example to diagnose or treat abnormal uterine bleeding.

Coding Clarification
Subcategories for D&C (69.0) and aspiration curettage (69.5) include codes for the procedure performed for termination of pregnancy, following delivery or abortion, or for diagnostic purposes. Look for this documentation in the medical record to assist in proper code selection.

Use 69.02 and not 69.01 for a D&C that was performed for a missed abortion.

Assign 69.09 for a D&C performed for a blighted ovum.

To report aspiration curettage of the uterus, see 69.51-69.59.

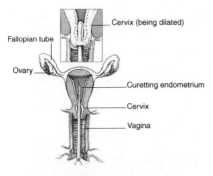

Cervix (being dilated)
Fallopian tube
Ovary
Curetting endometrium
Cervix
Vagina

69.01   Dilation and curettage for termination of pregnancy

Description
The physician performs the termination of a pregnancy by dilation and curettage (D&C) and uses a sharp instrument to remove tissue from inside the uterus. After dilating the cervical canal with a small probe, the physician passes a curette into the uterus. The curette is used to scrape the lining of the uterus and remove the tissue in the uterus.

Coding Clarification
Subcategories for D&C (69.0) and aspiration curettage (69.5) include codes for the procedure performed for termination of pregnancy, following delivery or abortion, or for diagnostic purposes. Look for this documentation in the medical record to assist in proper code selection.

Use 69.02 and not 69.01 for a D&C that was performed for a missed abortion.

Assign 69.09 for a D&C performed for a blighted ovum.

Coding Guidance
    AHA: 1Q, '98, 4

69.02   Dilation and curettage following delivery or abortion

Description
The physician removes the products of conception remaining after an incomplete spontaneous abortion in any trimester. To evacuate the uterus, the physician performs a dilation and suction curettage. The physician inserts a speculum into the vagina to view the cervix. A tenaculum is used to grasp the cervix, pull it down, and exert traction. If the cervix is not sufficiently dilated, a dilator is inserted into the endocervix and up through the cervical canal to enlarge the opening. The physician places a cannula in the endocervical canal and passes it into the uterus. The suction machine is then activated and the uterine contents are evacuated by rotation of the cannula. After suction curettage, a sharp curette may be used to gently scrape the uterus to ensure that it is empty.

In missed abortion, the fetus remains in the uterus four to eight weeks following its death. Ultrasonography may be needed to determine the size of the fetus prior to the procedure. The physician inserts a speculum into the vagina to view the cervix. A tenaculum is used to grasp the cervix, pull it down, and exert traction. A dilator is then inserted into the endocervix and up through the cervical canal to enlarge the opening. The physician places a cannula in the endocervical canal and passes it into the uterus. The suction machine is then activated and the uterine contents are evacuated by rotation of the cannula. After suction curettage, a sharp curette may be used to gently scrape the uterus to ensure that it is empty.

Coding Clarification
Subcategories for D&C (69.0) and aspiration curettage (69.5) include codes for the procedure performed for termination of pregnancy, following delivery or abortion, or for diagnostic purposes. Look for this documentation in the medical record to assist in proper code selection.

● New Code   ▲ Revised Code   ▶◀ Revised Text   © 2010 Ingenix

Use 69.02 for a D&C that was performed for a missed abortion.

Assign 69.09 for a D&C performed for a blighted ovum.

Coding Guidance
AHA: 3Q, '93, 6

69.09   Other dilation and curettage of uterus

Description
The physician performs a diagnostic D&C. The physician inserts a speculum into the vagina to view the cervix. A tenaculum is used to grasp the cervix and holds it in place. The cervix is dilated with a series of tapered rods of increasing widths that are inserted into the cervical opening (the OS). A curette is passed through the uterus and used to scrape the uterine walls. This loosens pieces of the lining, which are removed and sent to a lab for microscopic examination. Another method of obtaining a sample of the uterine lining is by applying suction through a narrow tube.

Coding Clarification
Subcategories for D&C (69.0) and aspiration curettage (69.5) include codes for the procedure performed for termination of pregnancy, following delivery or abortion, or for diagnostic purposes. Look for this documentation in the medical record to assist in proper code selection.

Use 69.02 for a D&C that was performed for a missed abortion.

Assign 69.09 for a D&C performed for a blighted ovum.

Coding Guidance
AHA: 1Q, '98, 4

69.1   Excision or destruction of lesion or tissue of uterus and supporting structures

Description
Subcategory 69.1 contains one code to report excision or destruction procedures of the uterus and supporting structures (other than a biopsy of a uterine ligament) that are not more precisely described by other codes in category 69.

Documentation Tip
Review the documentation for specific information regarding the procedure prior to final code selection in order to ensure accurate code assignment.

69.19   Other excision or destruction of uterus and supporting structures

Description
The physician performs a laparoscopic electrical cautery destruction of uterine tissue or a uterine lesion with the assistance of a fiberoptic laparoscope. The physician may first insert an

instrument through the vagina to grasp the cervix and manipulate the uterus during surgery. Next, the physician makes a small incision just below the umbilicus through which a fiberoptic laparoscope is inserted. A second incision is made on the left or right side of the abdomen with additional instruments being placed through these incisions into the abdomen or pelvis. The physician manipulates the tools so that the pelvic organs can be observed, manipulated, and operated upon with the laparoscope. Once lesions are identified with the laparoscope, a third incision is typically made adjacent to the lesion through which an electric cautery tool, knife, or laser is inserted for lesion fulguration. The abdomen is deflated, the trocars removed, and the incisions are closed with sutures.

In an alternate procedure, the physician removes or destroys tumors, cysts, or endometriomas (displaced endometrial tissue) located inside or just outside the peritoneal lining of the abdominal cavity. The physician makes a large incision extending from just above the pubic hairline to the rib cage. The growths are removed using a laser, electrical cautery, or a scalpel. The incision is closed by suturing.

Coding Clarification
To report a biopsy of a uterine ligament, see 68.14.

69.2   Repair of uterine supporting structures

Description
The different types of repair procedures performed on the supporting structures of the uterus are located under subcategory 69.2.

69.21   Interposition operation of uterine supporting structures

Description
The physician plicates the stretched broad ligaments that suspend the uterus, bringing it back into place. Plication shortens the ligament by folding and tacking it. The physician may elect to plicate the round and sacrouterine ligaments as well. A portion of the presacral sympathetic nerve is removed or destroyed to alleviate pelvic pain. The procedure may be done through a small abdominal incision or through the vagina.

Coding Clarification
A Watkins procedure is a repositioning or realignment of the bladder and uterus in which the bladder is separated from the anterior wall of the uterus and the uterus is positioned to support the bladder. This procedure is also called an interposition.

69.22   Other uterine suspension

Description
Code 69.22 is used to report other repair procedures on the uterus and supporting structures that are not

more precisely described by other codes in this subcategory.

Coding Clarification
Assign 69.22 to report:

- **Hysteropexy:** Fixation or anchoring of uterus.
- **Manchester operation:** Fixation or anchoring of uterus with supportive banding tissue of uterine neck and vagina.
- **Plication of uterine ligament:** Creation of tucks in suppurative uterine banding tissue.

Documentation Tip
Review the documentation for specific information regarding the procedure prior to final code selection in order to ensure accurate code assignment.

69.23   Vaginal repair of chronic inversion of uterus

Description
The physician performs a procedure for repositioning of an inverted uterus via vaginal approach or through a small incision in the lower abdomen. This often is an extensive procedure that involves removing abnormal tissues, rearranging the uterine walls, and suturing.

69.29   Other repair of uterus and supporting structures

Description
Code 69.29 is used to report repair procedures on the uterus and supporting structures that are not more precisely described by other codes in subcategory 69.2.

Documentation Tip
Review the documentation for specific information regarding the procedure prior to final code selection in order to ensure accurate code assignment.

69.3   Paracervical uterine denervation

Description
The physician performs a destruction procedure on the paracervical nerve tracts to the uterus. Different methods of surgical interruption of nerve pathways are used including uterosacral transection, in which the nerve fibers to the uterus are cut. Paracervical uterine denervation usually consists of amputation of the uterosacral ligaments. Presacral neurectomy involves transection of the superior hypogastric plexus at the level of the sacrum. Presacral neurectomy offers an alternative with the ability to perform presacral neurectomy endoscopically rather than by laparotomy. A vaginal approach to interrupt the uterosacral ligaments is an alternative to presacral neurectomy, which may require a laparotomy.

One technique of paracervical uterine denervation is a laparoscopic transection of the area at the back of the cervix deep enough to interrupt the lowest portions of the uterosacral ligaments at their point of insertion into the cervix and vaginal apex. A standard, three-puncture technique is employed using an umbilical trocar and two lateral suprapubic accessory trocars. Using the CO2 or contact laser, cautery, and/or scissors, the ligaments are interrupted at their insertion into the cervix, using an axial motion from medial to lateral.

Coding Clarification
Different methods of surgical interruption of nerve pathways are used including uterosacral transection by laser uterine nerve ablation-LUNA, laser neurectomy, uterosacral ligation, paracervical uterine denervation, uterosacral nerve resection, and presacral neurectomy.

Paracervical block (PCB) is routinely used in obstetrics and during curettage procedures; patients receive Xylocaine for paracervical block just before the procedure.

Documentation Tip
Review the documentation for specific information regarding the procedure and approach prior to final code selection in order to ensure accurate code assignment.

69.4   Uterine repair

Description
Codes in subcategory 69.4 are used to report uterine repair procedures that are not more precisely described by other codes in category 69.

Coding Clarification
Do not use subcategory 69.4 to report repair of current obstetric laceration (75.50-75.52).

Documentation Tip
Review the documentation for specific information regarding the procedure prior to final code selection in order to ensure accurate code assignment.

69.41   Suture of laceration of uterus

Description
The physician repairs a uterus that is lacerated or ruptured during pregnancy. A large incision is made in the abdomen and the uterus is sutured in multiple layers. The abdominal incision is then closed with sutures.

69.42   Closure of fistula of uterus

Description
The physician performs a closure of a fistula in the uterus. Transabdominal, transvaginal, suprapubic, and transperitoneal transvesical are commonly chosen surgical approaches; however, the site of the fistula dictates the surgical approach. The procedure can also be performed extraperitoneally. After excising the fistula, the physician sutures the clean percutaneous tissues together to create a smooth surface.

● New Code   ▲ Revised Code   ▶◀ Revised Text   © 2010 Ingenix

Coding Clarification

Do not use 69.42 to report uterovesical fistulectomy; see 57.84.

69.49   Other repair of uterus

Description

Code 69.49 is used to report uterine repair procedures that are not more precisely described by other codes in subcategory 69.4. The physician repairs a lacerated or ruptured uterus by suturing. A large incision is made in the abdomen and the uterus is sutured in multiple layers. The abdominal incision is then closed.

In an alternate technique, the physician performs plastic repair of a malformed uterus through a small incision in the lower abdomen. This often is an extensive procedure that involves removing abnormal tissues, rearranging the uterine walls, and suturing.

Coding Clarification

Assign 69.49 to report the repair of an old obstetric laceration of the uterus.

Documentation Tip

Review the documentation for specific information regarding the procedure prior to final code selection in order to ensure accurate code assignment.

69.5   Aspiration curettage of uterus

Description

Subcategory 69.5 includes codes for the procedure performed for termination of pregnancy, following delivery or abortion, and other indications. Look for this documentation in the medical record to assist in proper code selection.

Coding Clarification

Do not use subcategory 69.5 to report menstrual extraction; see 69.6.

69.51   Aspiration curettage of uterus for termination of pregnancy

Description

The physician terminates a pregnancy by dilation and evacuation (D&E). Because D&E requires wider cervical dilation than curettage, the physician may dilate the cervix with a laminaria several hours to several days before the procedure. At the time of the procedure, the physician inserts a speculum into the vagina to view the cervix. A tenaculum is used to grasp the cervix, pull it down, and exert traction. The physician places a cannula in the dilated endocervical canal and passes it into the uterus. The suction machine is activated and the uterine contents are evacuated by rotation of the cannula. For pregnancies through 16 weeks, the cannula will usually evacuate the pregnancy. For later pregnancies, the cannula is used to drain amniotic fluid and to draw tissue into the lower uterus for extraction by forceps. In either case, a sharp curette may be used to gently scrape the uterus to ensure that it is empty.

Coding Clarification

Subcategories for D&C (69.0) and aspiration curettage (69.5) include codes for the procedure performed for termination of pregnancy, following delivery or abortion, and other indications. Look for this documentation in the medical record to assist in proper code selection.

Documentation Tip

Code 69.51 is used to report a therapeutic abortion when the documentation does not further specify the procedure. Review the documentation for specific information regarding the procedure prior to final code selection in order to avoid improper use of the "not otherwise specified" code.

69.52   Aspiration curettage following delivery or abortion

Description

The physician scrapes the endometrial lining of the uterus following childbirth. The physician passes a curette through the cervix and endocervical canal, and into the uterus. Due to the large, soft postpartum uterus that is especially susceptible to perforation, a large blunt curette, also known as a "banjo" curette, is preferable to the suction curette. The physician gently scrapes the endometrial lining of the uterus to control bleeding, treat obstetric lacerations, or remove any remaining placental tissue.

69.59   Other aspiration curettage of uterus

Description

The physician performs an endometrial ablation, using heat without hysteroscopic guidance. The physician inserts a soft, flexible balloon attached to a thin catheter into the vagina through the cervix and into the uterus. The balloon is inflated with a sterile fluid, which expands to fit the size and shape of the patient's uterus. The fluid in the balloon is heated to 87°C or 188°F and maintained for eight to nine minutes while the uterine lining is treated. When the treatment cycle is complete, all the fluid is withdrawn from the balloon and the catheter is removed.

Coding Guidance

AHA: 1Q, '98, 7

69.6   Menstrual extraction or regulation

Description

The physician induces menstruation by low pressure suction. Menstrual extraction is performed as a surgical abortion technique or a menstrual hygiene procedure, in which uterine contents are removed through the cervix via manual suction and a cannula to terminate unwanted pregnancy or an entire menstrual period. It is almost identical to manual vacuum aspiration.

69.7   Insertion of intrauterine contraceptive device

Description
The physician inserts a speculum into the vagina to visualize the cervix. A tool is used to gently pull down the cervix; then it is dilated. An intrauterine device (IUD), any of a variety of shapes (coil, loop, T, 7), is guided into the uterus through an insertion tube. To remove a previously placed IUD, any of a variety of shapes (coil, loop, T, 7), from the uterus, a speculum is inserted into the vagina to visualize the cervix. The cervix is then dilated and a device is used to grasp and remove the IUD.

69.9   Other operations on uterus, cervix, and supporting structures

Description
The different types of procedures on the uterus, cervix, and supporting structures are included in subcategory 69.9.

Coding Clarification
Do not use subcategory 69.9 to report obstetric dilation or incision of the cervix; see 73.1 and 73.93.

69.91   Insertion of therapeutic device into uterus

Description
Preoperative radiation may be prescribed for patients who have endometrial cancer with major cervical involvement that precludes initial hysterectomy. Vaginal brachytherapy is administered using low-dose rate (LDR) or high-dose rate (HDR) radiotherapy. The upper half to two-thirds of the vagina is treated. HDR vaginal brachytherapy is delivered using intracavitary vaginal insertion with a Fletcher applicator, consisting of a uterine tandem and vaginal cylinders. HDR treatments require multiple insertions, generally with one insertion done every week for three to six weeks. Hospitalization is not required and each insertion takes only a brief amount of time. LDR treatments are delivered once but do require hospitalization for two to three days. Hysterectomy follows in four to six weeks.

Coding Clarification
Do not use 69.91 to report insertion of an intrauterine contraceptive device (69.7), laminaria (69.93), or obstetric insertion of bag, bougie, or pack (73.1).

69.92   Artificial insemination

Description
In one technique, the physician performs artificial insemination by injecting semen into the endocervical canal after inserting the blunt tip of a plastic syringe to the external os (opening) of the cervix. Sometimes a cervical cap is used to keep the semen in and around the cervix for eight to 16 hours. In an alternate technique, the physician dilates the cervix and inserts a long flexible tube into the cavity of the uterus. Semen is injected into the uterus by a syringe connected to the tube.

69.93   Insertion of laminaria

Description
Laminaria is a sea kelp and one variety, L. digitata, is dried and used to dilate the cervix for induction of labor. The laminaria is placed in the cervical os and allowed to work for about six to 12 hours.

Coding Guidance
AHA: ▶2Q, '10, 7◀

69.94   Manual replacement of inverted uterus

Description
To manually restore an inverted uterus, the patient is placed in the dorsal recumbent position. The physician grasps the inverted uterus and pushes it through the cervix toward the umbilicus to its normal anatomic position.

Coding Clarification
To report manual replacement of an inverted uterus in the immediate postpartal period, see 75.94.

69.95   Incision of cervix

Description
The physician makes an incision in the cervix.

Coding Clarification
A cervicotomy is an incision of the cervix uteri.

To report an incision of the cervix to assist delivery, see 73.93.

69.96   Removal of cerclage material from cervix

Description
The physician removes a ring inserted to restore uterine neck competency. The physician removes a cervical cerclage, a suture that had been placed to hold the cervix closed. A cerclage is most often placed when a cervix dilates too early during pregnancy and risks a miscarriage. The physician severs the sutures and removes them. This code includes anesthesia other than local.

● New Code   ▲ Revised Code   ▶◀ Revised Text   © 2010 Ingenix

69.97   Removal of other penetrating foreign body from cervix

Description
The physician surgically removes a foreign body with the assistance of a fiberoptic hysteroscope. The physician advances the hysteroscope through the vagina and sometimes into the cervical os. The physician inspects the cervix with the fiberoptic scope and removes a foreign body.

Coding Clarification
To report removal of an intraluminal foreign body from the cervix, see 98.16.

69.98   Other operations on supporting structures of uterus

Description
The physician plicates stretched uterine broad ligaments, bringing the uterus back into place. Plication shortens the ligament by folding and tacking it. The physician may elect to plicate the round and sacrouterine ligaments as well. This procedure may be done through a small abdominal incision or through an incision in the vagina.

Coding Clarification
Do not assign 69.98 to report biopsy of the uterine ligament; see 68.14.

Assign 69.98 to report procedures of the supporting structures of the uterus that are not more precisely described by other codes in subcategory 69.9.

Documentation Tip
Review the documentation for specific information regarding the procedure prior to final code selection in order to ensure accurate code assignment.

69.99   Other operations on cervix and uterus

Description
Code 69.99 is used to report procedures on the cervix and uterus that are not more precisely described by other codes in subcategory 69.9.

Coding Clarification
Do not assign 69.99 for removal of a foreign body (98.16), intrauterine contraceptive device (97.71), obstetric bag, bougie, or pack (97.72), or packing (97.72).

Documentation Tip
Review the documentation for specific information regarding the procedure prior to final code selection in order to ensure accurate code assignment.

70   Operations on vagina and cul-de-sac

Description
The different types of procedures (e.g., culdocentesis, incision, diagnostic procedures, excision, repair) performed on the vagina and cul-de-sac are classified under category 70. With more than one site represented under this category, site specificity occurs though the use of fourth digits. If a fistula is repaired, determine the site. There are numerous codes available depending on fistula location.

Coding Clarification
The cul-de-sac is also called the rectouterine pouch, which is a small pouch in the lower abdominal cavity formed by a fold in the peritoneum (cul-de-sac), also known as the cul-de-sac of Douglas.

70.0   Culdocentesis

Description
Culdocentesis is the aspiration of fluid in the peritoneum through the wall of the vagina that involves the insertion of a needle into the upper vaginal vault encircling the cervix to withdraw fluid. Through a speculum inserted in the vagina, the physician grasps the posterior lip of the cervix with a toothed instrument called a tenaculum. The cervix is lifted up exposing the posterior vaginal pouch and deep back wall of the vagina. A long needle attached to a syringe is inserted through the exposed vaginal wall and the posterior pelvic cavity is entered. Fluid is then aspirated through the needle into the syringe.

Coding Guidance
  AHA: 2Q, '90, 26

70.1   Incision of vagina and cul-de-sac

Description
The different types of procedures (e.g., culdocentesis, incision, diagnostic procedures, excision, repair) performed on the vagina and cul-de-sac are classified under category 70. With more than one site represented under this category, site specificity occurs though the use of fourth digits.

70.11   Hymenotomy

Description
The physician performs a hymenotomy. A hymen is a membrane that partially or wholly occludes the vaginal opening. Following local injection of an anesthetic, the physician incises the hymenal membrane with a stellate (star-shaped) incision. This procedure is sometimes preceded by aspiration of the intact membrane with a needle and syringe.

70.12   Culdotomy

Description
A culdotomy is a cut or needle puncture through the vagina into a small pouch in the lower abdominal cavity formed by a fold in the peritoneum (cul-de-sac), also known as the cul-de-sac of Douglas. Through a speculum inserted in the

65-71

vagina, the physician grasps the posterior lip of the cervix with a toothed instrument called a tenaculum. The cervix is lifted, exposing the posterior vaginal pouch. An incision is made through the back wall of the vagina into the posterior pelvic cavity. Through this opening, the pelvic cavity can be explored using instruments. After exploration, the physician closes the incision with absorbable sutures.

70.13   Lysis of intraluminal adhesions of vagina

Description
Using a colposcope, which is a binocular microscope used for direct visualization of the vagina and cervix, the physician identifies a lesion(s) in and/or around the vagina. The physician destroys the abnormal tissue by chemosurgery, electrosurgery, laser surgery, or cryotherapy.

70.14   Other vaginotomy

Description
The physician incises and drains a vaginal hematoma. The patient is placed in a dorsolithotomy position. The physician inserts a sterile speculum into the vagina. The hematoma is visualized and incised. The blood and clot are drained from the hematoma. Electrocautery or suture is used to control bleeding. When needed, a Hemovac drain is placed. The vagina is irrigated, and the area of hematoma is sponged with dressings. When hemostasis is achieved, the speculum is removed. Hemovac drains may be placed if the hematoma bed is still oozing.

Coding Clarification
Assign code 70.14 to report:

- Division of vaginal septum: Incision into partition of vaginal walls.

- Drainage of hematoma of vaginal cuff: Incision into vaginal tissue to drain collected blood.

70.2   Diagnostic procedures on vagina and cul-de-sac

Description
The different types of diagnostic procedures performed on the vagina and cul-de-sac are located under subcategory 70.2.

Coding Clarification
The cul-de-sac is also called the rectouterine pouch, which is a small pouch in the lower abdominal cavity formed by a fold in the peritoneum (cul-de-sac), also known as the cul-de-sac of Douglas.

70.21   Vaginoscopy

Description
The physician performs a colposcopy of the entire vagina and cervix, if present. The patient is placed in

the lithotomy position and a speculum is inserted into the vagina. The vagina is inspected through the colposcope, a kind of binocular microscope used for direct visualization of the vagina and cervix, to look for discharge, inflammation, ulceration, or any lesions. The cervix is then exposed, cleansed, and inspected for any ulceration or lesions. Acetic acid may be applied to help enhance visualization of the columnar villi and any lesions.

70.22   Culdoscopy

Description
Culdoscopy is a surgical technique that places a port 5 to 12 mm in size in the vagina and into the pelvic cavity to visualize and operate. This can be done with local, regional, or general anesthesia. Culdoscopy uses a rigid type of scope for visualization. The patient is placed in the lithotomy position or in a knee-chest position for this operation. Most cases require gas distention for visualization. The physician introduces an endoscope or culdoscope through the end of the vagina into the cul-de-sac. The cul-de-sac is also called the rectouterine pouch (cul-de-sac of Douglas), which is an extension of the peritoneal cavity between the rectum and back wall of the uterus.

Coding Clarification
Flexible culdoscopy uses 5 mm or smaller ports than in culdoscopy. A flexible type of telescope allows different views by curving the angles of the flexible scope.

Culdoscopy is commonly used as a diagnostic tool for infertility or pelvic pain, and used in surgeries like tubal ligation, ovarian cyst, lysis of adhesions, or biopsy of endometriosis.

70.23   Biopsy of cul-de-sac

Description
The physician takes a sample of vaginal mucosa from the rectouterine pouch for examination. After injecting a local anesthetic into the suspect area, the physician obtains a sample with a skin punch or sharp scalpel.

Coding Clarification
The cul-de-sac is also called the rectouterine pouch, which is a small pouch in the lower abdominal cavity formed by a fold in the peritoneum (cul-de-sac), also known as the cul-de-sac of Douglas.

70.24   Vaginal biopsy

Description
The physician takes a sample of vaginal mucosa for examination. After injecting a local anesthetic into the suspect area, the physician obtains a sample with a skin punch or sharp scalpel.

● New Code   ▲ Revised Code   ▶◀ Revised Text   © 2010 Ingenix

Documentation Tip

Surgical procedures on the vagina are performed using a variety of surgical techniques and approaches including cryosurgery, laser, and electrosurgical techniques. To ensure accurate code assignment, review the medical record to determine the approach and surgical technique.

70.29 Other diagnostic procedures on vagina and cul-de-sac

Description

The physician performs a manual examination of the vagina including the cervix, uterus, tubes, and ovaries. During the examination, the patient is under a general anesthesia because of the patient's inability to tolerate the procedure while awake.

Coding Clarification

A small pouch in the lower abdominal cavity formed by a fold in the peritoneum (cul-de-sac), is also known as the cul-de-sac of Douglas.

Documentation Tip

Surgical procedures on the vagina are performed using a variety of surgical techniques and approaches including cryosurgery, laser, and electrosurgical techniques. To ensure accurate code assignment, review the medical record to determine the approach and surgical technique.

70.3 Local excision or destruction of vagina and cul-de-sac

Description

Subcategory 70.3 codes describe various excision and destruction procedures on the vagina and cul-de-sac.

70.31 Hymenectomy

Description

A hymen is a membrane that partially or wholly occludes the vaginal opening. Following local injection of an anesthetic, the physician excises a portion of the hymenal membrane. Using a scalpel or scissors, the membrane is removed at its junction with the opening of the vagina. The cut margins of the vaginal mucosa are sutured with fine, absorbable material.

Documentation Tip

Surgical procedures on the vagina are performed using a variety of surgical techniques and approaches including cryosurgery, laser, and electrosurgical techniques. To ensure accurate code assignment, review the medical record to determine the approach and surgical technique.

70.32 Excision or destruction of lesion of cul-de-sac

Description

Using a colposcope, which is a binocular microscope used for direct visualization of the vagina and cervix, the physician identifies a lesion(s) in the vagina. The physician destroys the abnormal tissue by chemosurgery, electrosurgery, laser surgery, or cryotherapy.

Coding Clarification

Assign 70.32 to report endometrectomy of the cul-de-sac.

Do not assign 70.32 to report a biopsy of the cul-de-sac (70.23).

The cul-de-sac of Douglas is a small pouch in the lower abdominal cavity formed by a fold in the peritoneum (cul-de-sac).

Documentation Tip

Surgical procedures on the vagina are performed using a variety of surgical techniques and approaches including cryosurgery, laser, and electrosurgical techniques. To ensure accurate code assignment, review the medical record to determine the approach and surgical technique.

70.33 Excision or destruction of lesion of vagina

Description

Using a colposcope, which is a binocular microscope used for direct visualization of the vagina and cervix, the physician identifies a lesion(s) in and/or around the vagina. The physician destroys the abnormal tissue by chemosurgery, electrosurgery, laser surgery, or cryotherapy.

Coding Clarification

Do not assign 70.33 to report a biopsy of the vagina (70.24) or vaginal fistulectomy (70.72-70.75).

Documentation Tip

Surgical procedures on the vagina are performed using a variety of surgical techniques and approaches including cryosurgery, laser, and electrosurgical techniques. To ensure accurate code assignment, review the medical record to determine the approach and surgical technique.

70.4 Obliteration and total excision of vagina

Description

The physician performs complete removal of the vaginal wall. This is sometimes preceded by injection of medication to constrict blood vessels to control bleeding. The vagina is everted. An incision circumscribes the hymen, and the vagina is marked into four quadrants. Each quadrant of the vaginal wall is removed by sharp and blunt dissection. In one method, the physician removes surrounding diseased and/or damaged tissue. In another method, the physician removes surrounding

65-71

diseased and/or damaged tissue, in addition to removing the pelvic lymph nodes, and performs biopsy of the lymph nodes to check for the extent of disease. The remaining support tissues are inverted and sutured in place obliterating the space formerly occupied by the vagina. The perineum is closed over the former vaginal opening.

Coding Clarification
Assign 70.4 to report a vaginectomy or a removal of the vagina.

Do not assign 70.4 to report obliteration of the vaginal vault (70.8).

Documentation Tip
Surgical procedures on the vagina are performed using a variety of surgical techniques and approaches including cryosurgery, laser, and electrosurgical techniques. To ensure accurate code assignment, review the medical record to determine the approach and surgical technique.

70.5   Repair of cystocele and rectocele

Description
Subcategory 70.5 provides various subclassification codes to report pelvic prolapse repair procedures, including those involving various grafts and prosthesis materials such as autologous, allogenic, xenogenic, and synthetic materials (such as polypropylene, polyester mesh, Marlex, and Prolene) to repair the vaginal wall and pelvic tissues.

Coding Clarification
Instructional notes in this subcategory direct the coder to assign an additional code for the biological substance (70.94) or synthetic substance (70.95) used, if known.

To report repair of cystocele and rectocele with graft or prosthesis, use code 70.53.

Use code 70.54 to report repair of cystocele with graft or prosthesis.

70.50   Repair of cystocele and rectocele

Description
The physician repairs both a cystocele and rectocele by colporrhaphy. Colporrhaphy involves plastic repair of the vagina and the fibrous tissue separating the bladder, vagina, and rectum. A cystocele is a herniation of the bladder through its support tissues causing the anterior vaginal wall to bulge downward. A rectocele is a protrusion of part of the rectum through its support tissues causing the posterior vaginal wall to bulge. Using a combined vaginal approach and a posterior midline incision that includes the perineum and posterior vaginal wall, the physician dissects the tissues between the

bladder, urethra, vagina, and rectum. The specific tissue weaknesses are repaired and strengthened using tissue transfer techniques and layered and plication suturing. The physician may also repair a urethrocele, which is a prolapse of the urethra, and perform a perineorrhaphy, which is plastic repair of the perineum, including midline approximation of the levator and perineal muscles. The incisions are closed with sutures.

70.51   Repair of cystocele

Description
The physician repairs a cystocele, which is a herniation of the bladder through its support tissues and against the anterior vaginal wall causing it to bulge downward. The physician may also repair a urethrocele, which is a prolapse of the urethra. An incision is made from the apex of the vagina to within 1 cm of the urethral meatus. Plication sutures are placed along the urethral course from the meatus to the bladder neck. A suture is placed through the pubourethral ligament to the posterior symphysis pubis on each side of the urethra. The sutures are tied (ligated) and the posterior urethra is pulled upward to a retropubic position. If a cystocele is repaired, mattress sutures are placed in the mobilized paravesical tissue. The vaginal mucosa is closed.

Coding Guidance
AHA: N-D, '84, 20

70.52   Repair of rectocele

Description
The physician repairs a rectocele by colporrhaphy. A rectocele is a protrusion of part of the rectum through its supporting tissues against the vagina causing a bulging in the vagina. Colporrhaphy involves a plastic repair of the vagina and the fibrous tissue separating the vagina and rectum. The physician makes a posterior midline incision that includes the perineum and posterior vaginal wall. In order to strengthen the area, the rectovaginal fascia is plicated by folding and tacking, and it is closed with layered sutures. The physician may also perform a perineorrhaphy, which is plastic repair of the perineum, including midline approximation of the levator and perineal muscles. Excess fascia in the posterior vaginal wall is excised. The incisions are closed with sutures.

Coding Clarification
Do not report a staples transanal rectal resection (STARR procedure) with this code; see 48.74.

Coding Guidance
AHA: 1Q, '06, 12

● New Code   ▲ Revised Code   ▶◀ Revised Text   © 2010 Ingenix

70.53   Repair of cystocele and rectocele with graft or prosthesis

Description
Two curved needles are inserted through a midline incision in the posterior vaginal wall. A graft connector is attached to the needle and the needle is withdrawn through the skin incision. The graft is fixed at the apex and trimmed appropriately and the skin and vaginal incisions are closed.

Coding Clarification
Instructional notes in this subcategory direct the coder to assign an additional code for the biological substance (70.94) or synthetic substance (70.95) used, if known.

Subcategory 70.5 includes codes to identify pelvic repair procedures utilizing grafts or prostheses. The different types of grafts and prostheses used for gynecological surgery are autologous, allogenic, xenogenic, and synthetic (such as polypropylene, polyester mesh, Marlex, and Prolene).

Documentation Tip
A cystocele is a herniation of the bladder through its support tissues causing the anterior vaginal wall to bulge downward.

A rectocele is a protrusion of part of the rectum through its support tissues causing the posterior vaginal wall to bulge.

Coding Guidance
    AHA: 4Q, '07, 114-115

70.54   Repair of cystocele with graft or prosthesis

Description
Anterior vaginal colporrhaphy with prosthetic reinforcement is commonly used in treatment of cystoceles. Colporrhaphy can be performed prior to mesh placement and the prosthesis is introduced after routine colporrhaphy and anchored to the vaginal apex and levator fascia.

Coding Clarification
Instructional notes in this subcategory direct the coder to assign an additional code for the biological substance (70.94) or synthetic substance (70.95) used, if known.

Subcategory 70.5 includes codes to identify pelvic repair procedures utilizing grafts or prostheses. The different types of grafts and prostheses used for gynecological surgery are autologous, allogenic, xenogenic, and synthetic (such as polypropylene, polyester mesh, Marlex, and Prolene).

Documentation Tip
A cystocele is a herniation of the bladder through its support tissues causing the anterior vaginal wall to bulge downward.

A rectocele is a protrusion of part of the rectum through its support tissues causing the posterior vaginal wall to bulge.

Coding Guidance
    AHA: 4Q, '07, 114-115

70.55   Repair of rectocele with graft or prosthesis

Description
Polypropylene mesh is used for augmentation of a cystocele and rectocele. Needles are inserted through the transobturator space or ischiorectal fascia, based on anterior or posterior mesh placement. A mesh is then attached to the needles. The needles are withdrawn and tension secures the mesh to the anterior or posterior wall support.

Coding Clarification
Instructional notes in this subcategory direct the coder to assign an additional code for the biological substance (70.94) or synthetic substance (70.95) used, if known.

Subcategory 70.5 includes codes to identify pelvic repair procedures utilizing grafts or prostheses. The different types of grafts and prostheses used for gynecological surgery are autologous, allogenic, xenogenic, and synthetic (such as polypropylene, polyester mesh, Marlex, and Prolene).

Documentation Tip
A cystocele is a herniation of the bladder through its support tissues causing the anterior vaginal wall to bulge downward.

A rectocele is a protrusion of part of the rectum through its support tissues causing the posterior vaginal wall to bulge.

Coding Guidance
    AHA: 4Q, '07, 114-115

70.6   Vaginal construction and reconstruction

Description
Subcategory 70.6 provides codes to report pelvic prolapse repair procedures, including those involving various grafts and prosthesis materials such as autologous, allogenic, xenogenic, and synthetic materials (such as polypropylene, polyester mesh, Marlex, and Prolene) to repair the vaginal wall and pelvic tissues.

Documentation Tip
A cystocele is a herniation of the bladder through its support tissues causing the anterior vaginal wall to bulge downward.

A rectocele is a protrusion of part of the rectum through its support tissues causing the posterior vaginal wall to bulge.

65-71

70.61   Vaginal construction

Description
For construction of an artificial vagina without graft, the physician develops a vagina by a program of perineal pressure using progressively longer and wider firm obturators. Pressure is applied to the soft area between the urethra and rectum with an obturator. Over several months of consistent, daily use by the patient, a sexually functional vagina can be created. In one technique, the physician creates or enlarges the vagina using one or more skin grafts. Through a midline episiotomy incision, the physician creates a space between the urethra and rectum. Using split thickness or full thickness skin grafts, the space is lined and the vagina created. An obturator or mold is inserted into the vagina and a catheter is passed into the bladder and left for several days. The full thickness skin donor sites are closed using plastic surgical techniques. The split thickness sites are dressed with medicated gauze.

Coding Clarification
Instructional notes in this subcategory direct the coder to assign an additional code for the biological substance (70.94) or synthetic substance (70.95) used, if known.

Coding Guidance
AHA: 3Q, '06, 18

70.62   Vaginal reconstruction

Description
The physician uses various plastic surgical techniques to correct a small, underdeveloped vagina due to the overproduction of male hormones from the adrenal glands. The physician constructs a larger and more functional vagina using carefully placed incisions and skin grafts.

Coding Clarification
Instructional notes in this subcategory direct the coder to assign an additional code for the biological substance (70.94) or synthetic substance (70.95) used, if known.

Coding Guidance
AHA: N-D, '84, 20

70.63   Vaginal construction with graft or prosthesis

Description
In one technique, the physician creates or enlarges the vagina using one or more grafts. Through a midline episiotomy incision, the physician creates a space between the urethra and rectum. Using split-thickness or full-thickness skin grafts, the space is lined and the vagina created. An obturator or mold is inserted into the vagina and a catheter is passed into the bladder and left for several days. The full-thickness skin donor sites are closed using plastic surgical techniques. The split-thickness sites are dressed with medicated gauze.

Coding Clarification
Subcategory 70.6 includes codes to identify pelvic repair procedures utilizing grafts or prostheses. The different types of grafts and prostheses used for gynecological surgery are autologous, allogenic, xenogenic, and synthetic (such as polypropylene, polyester mesh, Marlex, and Prolene).

Instructional notes in this subcategory direct the coder to assign an additional code for the biological substance (70.94) or synthetic substance (70.95) used, if known.

Code 70.63 excludes vaginal construction (70.61).

Coding Guidance
AHA: 4Q, '07, 114-115

70.64   Vaginal reconstruction with graft or prosthesis

Description
The physician uses various plastic surgical techniques to correct a small, underdeveloped vagina due to the overproduction of male hormones from the adrenal glands. The physician constructs a larger and more functional vagina using carefully placed incisions and skin grafts.

Coding Clarification
Subcategory 70.6 includes codes to identify pelvic repair procedures utilizing grafts or prostheses. The different types of grafts and prostheses used for gynecological surgery are autologous, allogenic, xenogenic, and synthetic (such as polypropylene, polyester mesh, Marlex, and Prolene).

Instructional notes in this subcategory direct the coder to assign an additional code for the biological substance (70.94) or synthetic substance (70.95) used, if known.

Code 70.64 excludes vaginal reconstruction (70.62).

Coding Guidance
AHA: 4Q, '07, 114-115

70.7   Other repair of vagina

Description
The different types of repair procedures performed on the vagina that are not more precisely described by other codes are located under subcategory 70.7.

Coding Clarification
Do not assign 70.7 to report the lysis of intraluminal adhesions (70.13), repair of current obstetric laceration (75.69), or that associated with cervical amputation (67.4).

● New Code   ▲ Revised Code   ►◄ Revised Text   © 2010 Ingenix

70.71   Suture of laceration of vagina

Description
The physician inserts a speculum into the vagina and identifies the extent of the vaginal laceration or wound. Usually a local anesthetic is used; however, some instances may require general anesthesia. The wound is closed with absorbable sutures. In some cases after the speculum is removed, the perineal laceration is closed in layers with sutures. The physician repairs lacerations of the vagina. In a layered closure procedure, a local anesthetic is injected around the laceration and the wound is thoroughly cleansed, explored, and often irrigated with a saline solution. Due to deeper or more complex lacerations, deep subcutaneous or layered suturing techniques are required. The physician sutures tissue layers under the skin with dissolvable sutures before suturing the skin.

Coding Guidance
> **AHA:** N-D, '84, 20

70.72   Repair of colovaginal fistula

Description
The physician repairs a fistula (abnormal opening), between the last section of the large intestine and vagina using laparotomy and excision of the fistulous tract.

Coding Clarification
Treatment of a colovaginal fistula depends upon the location of the fistula and the etiology. A high-level fistula in the vagina requires a transabdominal approach but lower-level fistulas may be treated in a variety of ways including a transvaginal, perineal, transanal, or transsphincteric approach.
Laparotomy for segmental colonic resection is the accepted treatment; although a transvaginal closure of the fistula can also be performed.

70.73   Repair of rectovaginal fistula

Description
The physician repairs a rectovaginal fistula or sinus by pouch advancement using a transperineal or combined transperineal and transabdominal approach. An ileoanal pouch is created as a place for the storage of stool in patients that have had their large intestines removed due to disease. The pouch is connected to the anus, allowing the patient to have a bowel movement through the anus rather than needing a colostomy bag. If a drainage tract (fistula or sinus) erodes from an ileoanal pouch to the perineal area or into the vagina, it can be repaired by dissecting the tract from its external origin, the skin of the perineum or the lining of the vagina, to its source at the ileoanal pouch, and then closing the tissues. In one method, the tract is dissected (removed) and then closed starting in the perineal area. In another technique, the tract is dissected (removed) using an approach that combines dissection starting in the perineal area moving toward the pouch along with an incision in the lower abdominal wall that allows access to the ileoanal pouch internally. In both cases, any damage done to the pouch is repaired (pouch advancement).

70.74   Repair of other vaginoenteric fistula

Description
The physician corrects an abnormal opening between the vagina and intestine (other than mid or last sections.) The physician repairs a vaginoenteric fistula or sinus by pouch advancement using a transperineal or combined transperineal and transabdominal approach. An ileoanal pouch is created as a place for the storage of stool in patients that have had their large intestines removed due to disease. The pouch is connected to the anus, allowing the patient to have a bowel movement through the anus rather than needing a colostomy bag. If a drainage tract (fistula or sinus) erodes from an ileoanal pouch to the perineal area or into the vagina, it can be repaired by dissecting the tract from its external origin, the skin of the perineum or the lining of the vagina, to its source at the ileoanal pouch, and then closing the tissues. In one method, the tract is dissected (removed) and then closed starting in the perineal area. In an alternate technique, the tract is dissected (removed) using an approach that combines dissection starting in the perineal area moving toward the pouch along with an incision in the lower abdominal wall that allows access to the ileoanal pouch internally. In both cases, any damage done to the pouch is repaired (pouch advancement).

70.75   Repair of other fistula of vagina

Description
Code 70.75 is used to report other fistula repair procedures of the vagina that are not more precisely described by other codes in this subcategory.

Coding Clarification
Do not assign 70.75 to report any of the following fistula repairs: rectovesicovaginal (57.83), ureterovaginal (56.84), urethrovaginal (58.43), uterovaginal (69.42), vesicocervicovaginal (57.84), vesicosigmoidovaginal (57.83), vesicoureterovaginal (56.84), or vesicovaginal (57.84).

Documentation Tip
Review the documentation for specific information regarding the procedure prior to final code selection in order to ensure accurate code assignment.

70.76   Hymenorrhaphy

Description

A hymen is a membrane that partially or wholly occludes the vaginal opening. Following local injection of an anesthetic, the physician excises a portion of the hymenal membrane. Using a scalpel or scissors, the membrane is removed at its junction with the opening of the vagina. The cut margins of the vaginal mucosa are sutured with fine, absorbable material.

70.77   Vaginal suspension and fixation

Description

The physician performs a laparoscopic colpopexy and suspends, or reattaches, the apex of the vagina to the uterosacral ligaments to correct a uterovaginal prolapse and restore the vaginal apex back to its normal anatomic position, often post-hysterectomy. Through small stab incisions in the abdomen, a fiberoptic laparoscope and trocars are inserted into the abdominal/pelvic space. The bowel is mobilized or moved out of the way to provide a better view and easier access to the uterosacral ligaments. A vaginal probe is placed for manipulation and to help ensure the cul-de-sac is properly closed. The peritoneum is incised over the vaginal apex. After the vaginal vault is elevated back into its normal position, and the cul-de-sac is obliterated, a suture is placed through the base of the right uterosacral ligament and then through the apex of the vagina, securing it posteriorly to the top of the rectovaginal fascia and anteriorly to the pubocervical fascia (to a dermal or mesh graft, if placed) and tied down. Four total sutures are used to elevate the vagina, this being done twice through each ligament and the vaginal apex on each side.

70.78   Vaginal suspension and fixation with graft or prosthesis

Description

The physician makes a midline incision in the anterior vaginal wall and the vaginal mucosa is dissected up to apex. Two helical needles are inserted through obturator foramen on the patient's sides and exits through the vaginal incision. Two more needles are inserted through obturator foramen inferior to helical needles, exiting through the vaginal incision toward the apex. The graft connector is attached to the needle, the needle is withdrawn through the skin incision, and the graft is positioned to lay flat underneath the bladder. Final graft tensioning is done, the graft is trimmed at skin level, and the skin and vaginal incisions are closed.

Coding Clarification

Instructional notes in this subcategory direct the coder to assign an additional code for the biological substance (70.94) or synthetic substance (70.95) used, if known.

Coding Guidance

AHA: 4Q, '07, 114-115

70.79   Other repair of vagina

Description

Code 70.79 is used to report repair procedures of the vagina that are not more precisely described by other codes in subcategory 70.7.

Coding Clarification

Assign 70.79 to report colpoperineoplasty or repair of an old obstetric laceration of the vagina.

Documentation Tip

Review the documentation for specific information regarding the procedure prior to final code selection in order to ensure accurate code assignment.

70.8   Obliteration of vaginal vault

Description

Under a local or general anesthesia, the physician grasps the deepest portion of the vaginal vault and everts the vagina. Two large flaps of vaginal wall are removed from opposite sides of the prolapsed vagina. The vaginal walls are sutured to one another and this structure is inverted back inside the body. The former vaginal opening is closed with sutures obliterating the vagina and preventing uterine prolapse.

Coding Clarification

Assign 70.8 to report a LeFort operation that consists of uniting or sewing together the anterior and posterior vaginal walls at the middle line to repair uterine prolapse.

70.9   Other operations on vagina and cul-de-sac

Description

Codes in subcategory 70.9 are used to report procedures of the vagina and cul-de-sac that are not more precisely described by other codes in category 70.

Coding Clarification

Instructional notes following some of the codes in this subcategory direct the coder to first code the following procedures when done with graft or prosthesis:

- Other operations on cul-de-sac (70.93)
- Repair of cystocele (70.54)
- Repair of cystocele and rectocele (70.53)
- Repair of rectocele (70.55)
- Vaginal construction (70.63)
- Vaginal reconstruction (70.64)
- Vaginal suspension and fixation (70.78)

65-71

● New Code   ▲ Revised Code   ▶◀ Revised Text   © 2010 Ingenix

The cul-de-sac is also called the rectouterine pouch, which is a small pouch in the lower abdominal cavity formed by a fold in the peritoneum (cul-de-sac), also known as the cul-de-sac of Douglas.

Documentation Tip
Review the documentation for specific information regarding the procedure prior to final code selection in order to ensure accurate code assignment.

70.91 Other operations on vagina

Description
The physician revises or removes a previously placed prosthetic vaginal graft. The patient is placed in the lithotomy position and a speculum is inserted. The physician visualizes the neovagina. The apex of the vagina is accessed with deep retractors. Dissection is carried out to reach the affected graft material. Depending upon the type of complication (i.e., stricture or infection), the vaginal graft may be completely or partially excised to remove eroding mesh, or revisions may be made in the graft and surrounding tissue. The vaginal epithelial layers and pelvic fascia are rearranged or reapproximated and closed. Vaginal packing is put in place.

Coding Clarification
Do not assign 70.91 to report the insertion of a diaphragm (96.17), mold (96.15), pack (96.14), pessary (96.18), or suppository (96.49).

Do not assign 70.91 for removal of a diaphragm (97.73), foreign body (98.17), pack (97.75), or pessary (97.74)

Do not report 70.91 for replacement of a diaphragm (97.24), pack (97.26), pessary (97.25), vaginal dilation (96.16), or vaginal douche (96.44).

70.92 Other operations on cul-de-sac

Description
Code 70.92 is used to report procedures of the cul-de-sac that are not more precisely described by other codes in subcategory 70.9.

Coding Clarification
Assign 70.92 to report an obliteration of the cul-de-sac.

Assign 70.92 to report repair of a vaginal enterocele, which is the elimination of a herniated cavity within a pouch between the last part of large intestine and posterior uterus.

The cul-de-sac is also called the rectouterine pouch, which is a small pouch in the lower abdominal cavity formed by a fold in the peritoneum (cul-de-sac), also known as the cul-de-sac of Douglas.

Documentation Tip
Review the documentation for specific information regarding the procedure prior to final code selection in order to ensure accurate code assignment.

Coding Guidance
AHA: 4Q, '94, 54

70.93 Other operations on cul-de-sac with graft or prosthesis

Description
Code 70.93 is used to report procedures of the cul-de-sac using a graft or prosthesis that are not more precisely described by other codes in subcategory 70.9, such as the repair of a vaginal enterocele with graft or prosthesis.

Coding Clarification
The cul-de-sac is also called the rectouterine pouch, which is a small pouch in the lower abdominal cavity formed by a fold in the peritoneum (cul-de-sac), also known as the cul-de-sac of Douglas.

Various grafts and prosthesis materials that are currently being used include autologous, allogenic, xenogenic, and synthetic materials (such as polypropylene, polyester mesh, Marlex, and Prolene).

Documentation Tip
Review the documentation for specific information regarding the procedure prior to final code selection in order to ensure accurate code assignment.

Coding Guidance
AHA: 4Q, '07, 114-115

70.94 Other operations on vagina and cul-de-sac, insertion of biological graft

Description
This code reports the insertion of a biological graft, including allogenic, autologous, or xenogenic materials or substances, as well as allograft, autograft, and heterograft.

Coding Clarification
First code the following procedures when done with graft or prosthesis:

- Other operations on cul-de-sac (70.93)
- Repair of cystocele (70.54)
- Repair of cystocele and rectocele (70.53)
- Repair of rectocele (70.55)
- Vaginal construction (70.63)
- Vaginal reconstruction (70.64)
- Vaginal suspension and fixation (70.78)

Documentation Tip
Review the documentation for specific information regarding the procedure prior to final code selection in order to ensure accurate code assignment.

65-71

Coding Guidance
AHA: 4Q, '07, 116

70.95   Other operations on vagina and cul-de-sac, insertion of synthetic graft or prosthesis

Description
This code reports the insertion of synthetic grafts or prostheses, including artificial tissue.

Coding Clarification
Instructional notes in this subcategory direct the coder to first code the following procedures when done with graft or prosthesis:

- Other operations on cul-de-sac (70.93)
- Repair of cystocele (70.54)
- Repair of cystocele and rectocele (70.53)
- Repair of rectocele (70.55)
- Vaginal construction (70.63)
- Vaginal reconstruction (70.64)
- Vaginal suspension and fixation (70.78)

Documentation Tip
Review the documentation for specific information regarding the procedure prior to final code selection in order to ensure accurate code assignment.

Coding Guidance
AHA: 4Q, '07, 116

---

71   Operations on vulva and perineum

Description
Included under category 71 are operations such as incisions, diagnostic procedures, excision, and repair performed on the vulva and perineum. Procedures on the Bartholin's gland are included under subcategory 71.2.

Coding Clarification
There are three codes for vulvectomy: 71.5, 71.61, and 71.62. Use 71.5 when the physician indicates a radical vulvectomy was done. Any synchronous lymph gland dissection is coded in addition. Assign 71.61 for a unilateral vulvectomy and 71.62 for a bilateral vulvectomy.

Code also any application or administration of an adhesion barrier substance (99.77).

71.0   Incision of vulva and perineum

Description
Subcategory 71.0 provides two codes for the reporting of lysis or other incision of the vulva and perineum.

Coding Clarification
Code also any application or administration of an adhesion barrier substance (99.77).

71.01   Lysis of vulvar adhesions

Description
The labia majora and minora are the greater and lesser folds of skin on the pudendum on either side of the vagina. The physician separates the labia majora from the labia minora, which are fused by fibrous bands of scar tissue. Using a blunt instrument and/or scissors, the labia are separated by breaking or cutting the fibrous tissue. The procedure is accomplished using general or local anesthesia.

Coding Clarification
Code also any application or administration of an adhesion barrier substance (99.77)

71.09   Other incision of vulva and perineum

Description
The vulva includes the labia majora, labia minora, mons pubis, bulb of the vestibule, vestibule of the vagina, greater and lesser vestibular glands, and vaginal orifice. The perineum is the area between the vulva and the anus. The physician makes an incision into the abscess at its softest point and drains the purulent contents. The cavity of the abscess is flushed and often packed with medicated gauze to facilitate drainage.

Coding Clarification
Assign 71.09 for enlargement of introitus that is not further specified in the documentation.

For removal of a foreign body without an incision, see 98.23.

71.1   Diagnostic procedures on vulva

Description
The different types of diagnostic procedures performed on the vulva are located under subcategory 71.1.

Coding Clarification
Surgical procedures on the vulva are performed using a variety of surgical techniques and approaches. Review the documentation for specific information regarding the procedure prior to final code selection in order to ensure accurate code assignment.

Code also any application or administration of an adhesion barrier substance (99.77).

71.11   Biopsy of vulva

Description
The vulva includes the labia majora, labia minora, mons pubis, bulb of the vestibule, vestibule of the vagina, greater and lesser vestibular glands, and vaginal orifice. The perineum is the area between the vulva and the anus. The physician removes a sample of tissue from the vulva or perineum. After injecting

a local anesthetic around the suspect tissue, the physician obtains a sample using a skin punch or sharp scalpel. A clip or suture can be used to control bleeding if pressure is not successful.

Coding Clarification
Biopsy procedures on the vulva are performed using a variety of surgical techniques and approaches. Review the documentation for specific information regarding the procedure prior to final code selection in order to ensure accurate code assignment

71.19   Other diagnostic procedures on vulva
Description
The physician performs a colposcopy of the vulva, the external genitalia region of the female that includes the labia, clitoris, mons pubis, vaginal vestibule, bulb and glands, and the vaginal orifice. The patient is placed in the lithotomy position and the vulva is inspected through the colposcope, a kind of binocular microscope also used for direct visualization of the vagina and cervix. The bright light of the colposcope is directed so as to inspect the vulva and perianal area for any lesions or ulceration.

Coding Clarification
Diagnostic procedures on the vulva are performed using a variety of surgical techniques and approaches. Review the documentation for specific information regarding the procedure prior to final code selection in order to ensure accurate code assignment

71.2   Operations on Bartholin's gland
Description
The different types of procedures performed on the Bartholin's gland are located under subcategory 71.2.

Coding Clarification
Bartholin's gland is at the end of the bulb of the vestibule of the vagina and is connected by a duct to the mucosa at the opening of the vagina.

Code also any application or administration of an adhesion barrier substance (99.77).

71.21   Percutaneous aspiration of Bartholin's gland (cyst)
Description
The physician performs a puncture aspiration of an abscess, hematoma, bulla, or cyst. The palpable collection of fluid is located subcutaneously. The physician cleanses the overlying skin and introduces a large bore needle on a syringe into the fluid space. The fluid is aspirated into the syringe, decompressing the fluid space. A pressure dressing may be placed over the site.

Coding Clarification
Bartholin's gland is at the end of the bulb of the vestibule of the vagina and is connected by a duct to the mucosa at the opening of the vagina.

71.22   Incision of Bartholin's gland (cyst)
Description
The physician incises and drains a Bartholin's gland abscess. The physician makes an incision just inside the opening of the vagina through the mucosal surface into the cavity of the abscess to flush and drain it. A small wick or catheter may be left in the cavity to facilitate drainage.

Coding Clarification
Bartholin's gland is at the end of the bulb of the vestibule of the vagina and is connected by a duct to the mucosa at the opening of the vagina.

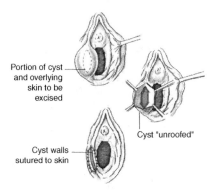

Portion of cyst and overlying skin to be excised

Cyst "unroofed"

Cyst walls sutured to skin

71.23   Marsupialization of Bartholin's gland (cyst)
Description
The physician treats a Bartholin's gland cyst with marsupialization. The physician makes an elliptical excision over the center of the Bartholin's gland cyst and drains it. The lining of the cyst is everted and approximated to the vaginal mucosa with sutures creating a pouch. Marsupialization prevents recurrent cysts and infections.

Coding Clarification
Bartholin's gland is at the end of the bulb of the vestibule of the vagina and is connected by a duct to the mucosa at the opening of the vagina.

Marsupialization of the Bartholin's gland is an incision and suturing opening of a cyst in Bartholin's gland.

71.24   Excision or other destruction of Bartholin's gland (cyst)
Description
The physician removes a cystic Bartholin's gland, which lies at the tail end of the bulb of the vestibular opening just inside of the vagina. The physician

---

---

makes an incision through the vaginal mucosa. The cyst is isolated through the vaginal incision by dissecting the deeper fatty tissues and is excised. The remaining cavity and skin are closed in layers using absorbable material.

Coding Clarification
The Bartholin's gland lies at the tail end of the bulb of the vestibular opening just inside of the vagina.

71.29 Other operations on Bartholin's gland

Description
Code 71.29 is used to report procedures on the Bartholin's gland that are not more precisely described by other codes in subcategory 71.2.

Documentation Tip
Review the documentation for specific information regarding the procedure prior to final code selection in order to ensure accurate code assignment.

71.3 Other local excision or destruction of vulva and perineum

Description
Code 71.3 is used to report local excision or destruction procedures on the vulva and perineum that are not more precisely described by other codes in category 71.

Coding Clarification
Assign 71.3 to report division of Skene's gland.

Do no assign 71.4 to report biopsy of vulva (71.11) or vulvar fistulectomy (71.72).

Laser vaporization of lesion of vulva or perineum is assigned code 71.3.

Documentation Tip
Review the documentation for specific information regarding the procedure prior to final code selection in order to ensure accurate code assignment.

Coding Guidelines
AHA: 4Q, '07, 91

71.4 Operations on clitoris

Description
The physician reduces the size of an enlarged clitoris, which has been masculinized by the production of male hormones from an abnormal adrenal gland. A portion of the body of the clitoris is resected with care to ensure preservation of vital nerves and blood vessels to the glans of the clitoris. The incisions are closed using plastic surgical techniques.

Coding Clarification
Assign code 71.4 to report:

- Amputation of clitoris: Removal of clitoris.
- Clitoridotomy: Incision into clitoris.

- Female circumcision: Incision of skin fold over clitoris.

71.5 Radical vulvectomy

Description
The physician removes the vulva to treat malignancy. A complete radical vulvectomy includes the removal of a large, deep segment of skin and tissue from the following structures: abdomen and groin, labia majora, labia minora, clitoris, mons veneris, and terminal portions of the urethra, vagina, and other vulvar organs. Deep tissue from more than 80 percent of the vulva is excised. Through incisions in the lower abdomen, thighs, and vulvar area, the physician removes skin, subcutaneous fatty tissue, and deeper tissues. Also included in the en bloc removal of tissue are portions of the saphenous veins and ligaments and the target lesion. The resulting large and disfiguring defect is usually closed in multiple layers using separately reported plastic surgical techniques, which may include pedicle flaps or free skin grafts. Subcutaneous rubber drains may be used, and vaginal gauze packing may be placed in the vagina.

Coding Clarification
Code also any synchronous lymph gland dissection (40.3, 40.5).

Documentation Tip
A radical vulvectomy is the removal of more than 80 percent of deep tissue from the vulva, including tissue of abdomen, groin, labia minora, labia majora, clitoris, mons veneris, and terminal portions of the urethra, vagina and other vulvar organs.

71.6 Other vulvectomy

Description
Code 71.6 is used to report other vulvectomy procedures that are not more precisely described by other codes in this subcategory.

Documentation Tip
Review the documentation for specific information regarding the procedure prior to final code selection in order to ensure accurate code assignment.

71.61 Unilateral vulvectomy

Description
The physician removes part, or all, of the vulva to treat premalignant or malignant lesions. A simple complete vulvectomy includes removal of all of the labia majora, labia minora, and clitoris, while a simple, partial vulvectomy may include removal of part or all of the labia majora and labia minora on one side and the clitoris. The physician examines the lower genital tract and the perianal skin with a colposcope. In one method, a wide semi-elliptical incision that contains the diseased area is made. In

● New Code   ▲ Revised Code   ▶◀ Revised Text   © 2010 Ingenix

65-71

an alternate technique, two wide elliptical incisions encompassing the entire vulvar area are made. One elliptical incision extends from well above the clitoris around both labia majora to a point just in front of the anus. The second elliptical incision starts at a point between the clitoris and the opening of the urethra and is carried around both sides of the opening of the vagina. The underlying subcutaneous fatty tissue is removed along with the large portion of excised skin. Vessels are clamped and tied off with sutures or are electrocoagulated to control bleeding. The considerable defect is usually closed in layers using separately reportable plastic techniques. Vaginal gauze packing may be placed in the vagina.

Documentation Tip
Review the documentation for specific information regarding the procedure prior to final code selection in order to ensure accurate code assignment.

Coding Guidance
   AHA: 2Q, '06, 19

71.62   Bilateral vulvectomy

Description
The physician removes part, or all, of the vulva to treat premalignant or malignant lesions. A simple complete vulvectomy includes removal of all of the labia majora, labia minora, and clitoris, while a simple, partial vulvectomy may include removal of part or all of the labia majora and labia minora on one side and the clitoris. The physician examines the lower genital tract and the perianal skin with a colposcope. Two wide elliptical incisions encompassing the entire vulvar area are made. One elliptical incision extends from well above the clitoris around both labia majora to a point just in front of the anus. The second elliptical incision starts at a point between the clitoris and the opening of the urethra and is carried around both sides of the opening of the vagina. The underlying subcutaneous fatty tissue is removed along with the large portion of excised skin. Vessels are clamped and tied off with sutures or are electrocoagulated to control bleeding. The considerable defect is usually closed in layers using separately reportable plastic techniques. Vaginal gauze packing may be placed in the vagina.

Coding Clarification
Code 71.62 is used to report vulvectomy procedures that are not more precisely described in the documentation.

71.7   Repair of vulva and perineum

Description
Subcategory 71.7 is assigned to report other repair procedures of the vulva and perineum that are not more precisely described in the documentation.

Coding Clarification
To report the repair of a current obstetric laceration use 75.69.

Documentation Tip
Review the documentation for specific information regarding the procedure prior to final code selection in order to ensure accurate code assignment.

71.71   Suture of laceration of vulva or perineum

Description
A local anesthetic is injected around the laceration and the wound is thoroughly cleansed, explored, and often irrigated with a saline solution. The physician performs a simple, one-layer repair of the epidermis, dermis, or subcutaneous tissues with sutures. In other cases, due to deeper or more complex lacerations, layered suturing techniques are required.

The physician repairs lacerations of the vulva or perineum using a layered closure. A local anesthetic is injected around the laceration and the wound is thoroughly cleansed, explored, and often irrigated with a saline solution. The physician sutures tissue layers under the skin with dissolvable sutures before suturing the skin.

71.72   Repair of fistula of vulva or perineum

Description
The physician repairs a fistula or sinus by pouch advancement using a transperineal or combined transperineal and transabdominal approach. An ileoanal pouch is created as a place for the storage of stool in patients that have had their large intestines removed due to disease. The pouch is connected to the anus, allowing the patient to have a bowel movement through the anus rather than needing a colostomy bag. If a drainage tract (fistula or sinus) erodes from an ileoanal pouch to the perineal area or into the vagina, it can be repaired by dissecting the tract from its external origin, the skin of the perineum or the lining of the vagina, to its source at the ileoanal pouch, and then closing the tissues. In one method, the tract is dissected (removed) and then closed starting in the perineal area. In an alternate method, the tract is dissected (removed) using an approach that combines dissection starting in the perineal area moving toward the pouch along with an incision in the lower abdominal wall that allows access to the ileoanal pouch internally. In both cases, any damage done to the pouch is repaired (pouch advancement).

Coding Clarification
Do not assign 71.72 to report repair of a fistula: urethroperineal (58.43), urethroperineovesical, (57.84), or vaginoperineal (70.75).

65-71

71.79   Other repair of vulva and perineum

Description

With upward traction on the vagina, the physician makes an incision from the lower vaginal opening to a point just in front of the anus. The underlying weakened tissues are dissected and repaired and tightened by suturing. This restores strength to the pelvic floor, closes tissue defects, and improves function of the perineal muscles.

Coding Clarification

Assign code 71.79 to report a repair of an old obstetric laceration of vulva or perineum.

Coding Guidance

    AHA: 1Q, '97, 9

71.8   Other operations on vulva

Description

Code 71.8 is used to report other procedures of the vulva that are not more precisely described by other codes in this subcategory.

Coding Clarification

Do not assign 71.8 to report removal of a foreign body without incision (98.23), packing (97.75), replacement of packing (97.26).

Documentation Tip

Review the documentation for specific information regarding the procedure prior to final code selection in order to ensure accurate code assignment.

71.9   Other operations on female genital organs

Description

Code 71.9 is used to report procedures of the female genital organs that are not more precisely described by other codes in category 71.

Documentation Tip

Review the documentation for specific information regarding the procedure prior to final code selection in order to ensure accurate code assignment.

Coding Guidance

    AHA: 1Q, '03, 13; 4Q, '04, 90

65-71

72-75

Obstetrical Procedures

The ICD-9-CM classification system for obstetrical operations is divided into categories of procedures according to sites as follows:

- Forceps, Vacuum and Breech Delivery (72)
- Other Procedures Inducing or Assisting Delivery (73)
- Cesarean Section and Removal of Fetus (74)
- Other Obstetric Operations (75)

Coding Clarification
Many of the subcategories in this portion of the classification system require a fourth digit for further specificity with regard to type of operation performed.

Operations classifiable to these procedures trigger Medicare Code Edit (MCE) 5, which is used to detect inconsistencies between the patient's sex and the procedure performed, and MCE 4, which is used to detect inconsistencies between the patient's age and the procedure performed. Per these edits, procedures classified to this chapter are reportable only for pregnant female patients in the reproductive stage of life, between 12 to 55 years of age.

Chapter 13 procedure codes are assigned only on the maternal record, never on the newborn record; and only during the episode of care for delivery, not on subsequent postpartum visits or admissions.

In accordance with the Uniform Hospital Discharge Data Set (UHDDS) guidelines, When more than one procedure is reported, the principal procedure should be identified by the one that relates to the principal diagnosis.

Documentation Tip
Documentation in the operative report or delivery record must support code selection.

72   Forceps, vacuum, and breech delivery

Description
Routine prenatal examinations assist in planning and preparing for the best possible method of delivery. The ability to identify certain conditions prior to labor and delivery greatly reduces complications associated with birth trauma of the mother and baby. However, surprises do occur. Unforeseen events, insufficient prenatal care, and other situations may arise during the labor and birth process that require specialized intervention, such as:

- Malposition of fetus
- Obstructed labor
- Maternal fatigue
- Failed uterine contractions (e.g., uterine inertia)
- Complications related to anesthetics, sedation, or other iatrogenic causes

Category 72 provides codes for obstetrical procedures performed due to complications of delivery such as malposition (breech presentation, malrotation) and certain types of obstruction requiring forceps or vacuum extraction.

The physician delivers an infant and placenta through the uterus and vagina. An assisted delivery may include the use of forceps or vacuum extraction to expel the fetus where maternal efforts alone may fail. The procedures listed in category 72 often require the administration of some type of anesthesia, whether epidural, spinal, or other.

Coding Clarification
Forceps are generally specialized, spoon-like paired instruments designed to aid the delivery of the infant by applying traction to the head of the fetus. Forceps are commonly used when the baby is in the lower portion of the birth canal (vaginal vault), which may be described as low or low outlet forceps application. Due to the risk to the mother and baby associated with the application of mid or high forceps, they are rarely used and have been largely replaced by vacuum extraction or cesarean delivery.

72.0   Low forceps operation

Description
The physician assists a vaginal delivery by the application of forceps instrumentation to the head of the fetus after it has descended into the lower portion of the vagina.

72.1   Low forceps operation with episiotomy

Description
The physician assists a vaginal delivery by the application of forceps instrumentation to the head of the fetus after it has descended into the lower portion of the vagina. To widen the external vaginal opening, the physician makes an incision in the perineum. This incision (episiotomy) may be performed to prevent obstetric trauma (tearing of the perineum) or to extend a perineal tear with a smooth incision, which is more easily repaired than a spontaneous perineal laceration. After the infant is delivered, the incision is sutured and repaired.

72.2   Mid forceps operation

Description
The physician assists a vaginal delivery by the application of forceps instrumentation to the head of the fetus after it has descended into the middle portion of the vagina.

72.21   Mid forceps operation with episiotomy

Description
The physician assists a vaginal delivery by the application of forceps instrumentation to the head of the fetus after it has descended into the middle portion of the vagina. To widen the external vaginal opening, the physician makes an incision in the perineum. This incision (episiotomy) may be performed to prevent obstetric trauma (tearing of the perineum) or to extend a perineal tear with a smooth incision, which is more easily repaired than a spontaneous perineal laceration. After the infant is delivered, the incision is sutured and repaired.

72.29   Other mid forceps operation

Description
The physician assists a vaginal delivery by the application of forceps instrumentation to the head of the fetus after it has descended into the middle portion of the vagina. However, due to the risk to the mother and baby associated with the application of mid forceps, they are rarely used and have been largely replaced by vacuum extraction or cesarean delivery.

72.3   High forceps operation

72.31   High forceps operation with episiotomy

72.39   Other high forceps operation

Description
The physician assists a vaginal delivery by application of forceps instrumentation to the head of the fetus before it has descended into the middle portion of the vagina by placing the instrumentation high in the vaginal vault. Due to the risk to the mother and baby associated with the application of mid forceps, they are rarely used and have been largely replaced by either vacuum extraction or cesarean delivery. Code 72.31 describes a high forceps procedure with episiotomy (a surgical incision into the perineum to widen the external vaginal opening). Code 72.39 describes a high forceps procedure without associated episiotomy.

72.4   Forceps rotation of fetal head

Description
This procedure involves a corrective rotation of a malposition of the fetal head (position other than occiput anterior) using forceps instrumentation. Technique may vary, depending on the nature of the malposition.

Coding Clarification
Code also any associated forceps extraction (72.0-72.39).

Documentation Tip
Procedures classifiable to 72.4 may be documented as:

• DeLee maneuver

• Key-in-lock rotation

• Kielland rotation

• Scanzoni's maneuver

72.5   Breech extraction

Description
Breech is the malposition of the fetus whereby the buttocks and/or the feet are the presenting parts. Although most breech presentations are delivered by cesarean section, vaginal delivery may occur. Technique may vary depending on the type of breech presentation, associated instrumentation necessary, and other factors.

An anesthesiologist and pediatrician should be present for delivery if possible. The physician may leave the fetal membranes intact as long as possible to assure adequate dilation and prevent umbilical cord prolapse. An episiotomy may be performed to widen the birth canal outlet and prevent dystocia. Specialized maneuvers may be performed to facilitate delivery of the legs, but no traction should be applied until the fetal umbilicus is past the perineum. Maternal pushing efforts should be coordinated with gentle downward and outward traction (assisted by wrapping the hips of the infant in a dry towel) until the shoulders are visible. Transfundal pressure from above should be exerted by an assistant to keep the fetal head flexed. Upon visualization of the scapula, a series of maneuvers may be required to deliver the arms and then the fetal head. Forceps may be used to maintain the

● New Code   ▲ Revised Code   ▶◀ Revised Text   © 2010 Ingenix

head in a flexed position, and minimize traction and hyperextension on the neck.

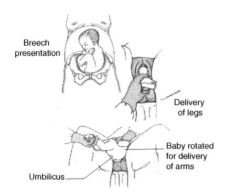

Breech presentation

Delivery of legs

Baby rotated for delivery of arms

Umbilicus

72.51 Partial breech extraction with forceps to aftercoming head

Description
The physician applies gentle traction to assist in delivery of a partial breech fetus, rotating its body as needed to deliver the shoulders, arms, and head.

72.52 Other partial breech extraction

72.53 Total breech extraction with forceps to aftercoming head

Description
The physician applies gentle traction and maneuvers the breech infant during the entire delivery process.

72.54 Other total breech extraction

72.6 Forceps application to aftercoming head

Coding Clarification
Code 72.6 excludes partial (72.51) or total (72.53) breech extraction procedures with application of forceps to the aftercoming head. Do not report 72.6 in addition to these procedures.

Documentation Tip
Procedures classifiable to 72.6 may be documented as Piper forceps operation.

72.7 Vacuum extraction

Description
The physician uses a vacuum assist device for certain labor complications, such as fetal distress, poor maternal pushing efforts, or failure to progress in the second stage of labor. In vacuum extraction, a plastic cup is inserted into the vagina and applied to the baby's head. The cup is generally placed as far posteriorly as possible in order to maintain flexion of the fetal head and avoid traction over the anterior

fontanel. The physician places the fingers of one hand against the suction cup and grasps the handle of the instrument with the other hand. Once vacuum is applied, the cup should not be twisted. Suction keeps the cup in place and the doctor provides gentle traction, pulling the baby through the birth canal by a handle attached to the cup. Traction may be coordinated with maternal contractions, whereby the traction is repeated with each contraction until the head is crowned. Once the head is delivered, suction is released and the cup is removed. This procedure may be performed with episiotomy (surgical incision of the perineum to widen the outlet of the vagina).

72.71 Vacuum extraction with episiotomy

72.79 Other vacuum extraction

Documentation Tip
Vacuum extraction may also be documented as Malstöm's extraction.

Coding Clarification
If vacuum extraction is used to assist in delivering the fetus during a cesarean section, assign code 72.79 in addition to the code for the cesarean section (category 74). Vacuum extraction is not routinely used in cesarean section operations and should be reported.

Coding Guidance
   AHA: 2Q, '06, 5

72.8 Other specified instrumental delivery

72.9 Unspecified instrumental delivery

Description
These procedure codes describe other (72.8) and unspecified (72.9) instrumental delivery not classifiable elsewhere in category 72.

Coding Clarification
This procedure code should not be assigned if the medical record contains sufficient information to facilitate coding at a higher level of specificity.

Documentation Tip
If the documentation is ambiguous or unclear, the physician should be queried.

73   Other procedures inducing or assisting delivery

Description
Category 73 provides codes for obstetrical procedures to induce or assist delivery such as rupture of membranes, medical or surgical induction, version, episiotomy, manual assistance, and other procedures.

© 2010 Ingenix   ● New Code   ▲ Revised Code   ▶◀ Revised Text

72-75

73.0   Artificial rupture of membranes

Description
Artificial rupture of the membranes is surgical rupture of the amniotic membrane (surgically "breaking the waters") performed to induce (73.01) or accelerate (73.09) labor or for other indications. The physician inserts an amniohook through the cervix, which opens or breaks the amniotic sac.

73.01   Induction of labor by artificial rupture of membranes

Coding Clarification
Code 73.01 includes surgical induction of labor by amniotomy. If amniotomy is performed at the time of delivery, see 73.09.

Coding Guidance
AHA: 3Q, '00, 5

73.09   Other artificial rupture of membranes

Coding Clarification
Code 73.09 includes artificial rupture.

Code 73.01 should be reported for induction of labor by artificial rupture of membranes in addition to the appropriate code(s) for the delivery and associated procedures, regardless of whether there is mention of indication. Code 73.01 should be reported to describe induction of labor even if the labor and delivery are without complication. Diagnosis code 650 Normal delivery does not preclude the use of procedure code 73.01 since the induction may be performed as part of a normal delivery and does not necessarily indicate the presence of a complication.

Coding Guidance
AHA: 3Q, '00, 5

73.1   Other surgical induction of labor

Description
This procedure code reports surgical induction of labor by methods not specified as amniotomy. Surgical technique may vary. The physician may insert a cervical dilator or other surgical device into the endocervix to stimulate and dilate the cervical canal. Alternately, the physician may inject a substance such as oxytocin into the amnion or strip the amniotic membrane to induce labor.

Coding Clarification
Code 73.1 excludes abortive procedures such as injection for abortion (75.0) and insertion of suppository for abortion (96.49).

73.2   Internal and combined version and extraction

Description
Version may be described as the manual corrective repositioning of the fetus in order to facilitate optimal presentation for delivery. Version procedures

are classified as external (73.91), internal, or combined:

- **External:** Rotation or manipulation of the fetus by applying precise, directed pressure through the abdominal wall of the mother.
- **Internal:** Rotation or manipulation of the fetus by inserting the hand or fingers through the dilated cervix.
- **Combined (also bimanual):** Repositioning by rotation of the fetus utilizing both internal and external manipulations (through the cervix and by exerting directed abdominal wall pressure).

73.21   Internal and combined version without extraction

Description
The physician performs corrective rotation or repositioning of the fetus without subsequent extraction (delivery) of the fetus during the same operative episode.

73.22   Internal and combined version with extraction

Description
The physician performs corrective rotation or repositioning of the fetus with subsequent extraction (delivery) of the fetus during the same operative episode.

73.3   Failed forceps

Description
This procedure involves the application of forceps, without successful delivery of the fetus.

Documentation Tip
Code 73.3 should be reported when a trial of forceps or application of forceps without delivery or failed forceps is documented in the medical record. Although in this instance the forceps do not facilitate delivery of the fetus, reporting this code accounts for the application and use of the instrumentation, with the associated resource utilization and risks involved.

73.4   Medical induction of labor

Description
The physician induces labor by administration of medications to initiate dilation of the cervix and uterine contractions. Route of administration may vary according to the type of medication.

The physician inserts a small tablet or suppository in the vagina up against the cervix, which melts in response to the body's temperature once in place, and releases the medication that softens and thins the cervix. After the medication is administered, the patient may start to have gentle labor contractions.

● New Code   ▲ Revised Code   ►◄ Revised Text   © 2010 Ingenix

Alternately, the physician orders and supervises the administration of a drug such as oxytocin (Pitocin). Although a woman's body makes oxytocin naturally, the synthetic form may be injected or infused intravenously, which strengthens the intensity of uterine contractions to induce labor.

Coding Guidance
AHA: ▶2Q, '10, 7◀

73.5   Manually assisted delivery
Description
The physician uses his hands to assist in the spontaneous delivery of an infant from the birth canal.

73.51   Manual rotation of fetal head
Description
The physician uses his hands to rotate the head of the fetus to assist in delivery.

73.59   Other manually assisted delivery
Description
The physician assists in the spontaneous delivery of an infant through the uterus and vagina, by application of hands to support the infant, and provide gentle traction when necessary, without the need of instrumentation such as forceps or vacuum extraction.

Coding Clarification
If an episiotomy is performed, report 73.6 in addition to 73.59.

Do not report 73.59 with delivery by vacuum extraction (72.71-72.79), forceps application (72.0-72.4, 72.6), or breech delivery (72.51-72.54).

Coding Scenario
A patient is admitted at 40 weeks gestation for elective induction of labor by artificial rupture of membranes (AROM). Labor progressed without complications. Spontaneous manually assisted delivery was complicated by second degree perineal tears, with subsequent suture repair.

Code Assignment:

664.11	Second-degree perineal laceration (complicating delivery)
V27.0	Single liveborn
73.59	Other manually assisted delivery
75.69	Repair of other current obstetric laceration
73.01	Induction of labor by artificial rupture of membranes

Coding Guidance
AHA: 4Q, '98, 76

73.6   Episiotomy
Description
An episiotomy is surgical incision through the perineum to enlarge the vaginal outlet to facilitate delivery of the infant (childbirth). Under local anesthesia, the physician performs a sharp incision at the midline of the perineum or at an angle from the posterior end of the vulva. The incision may extend into the perineum soft tissues (first degree), the perineal or pelvic muscles (second degree), into the anal sphincter (fourth degree), or into the anal or rectal mucosa (fourth degree). The incision is sutured closed after delivery.

Coding Clarification
Episiotomy is no longer recommended as a routine practice. An instructional note was added to code the episiotomy if performed.

All episiotomies are reported with 73.6, regardless of the degree of incision specified.

An extension of episiotomy (second incision to further open the previously performed episiotomy) is included in 73.6.

An episiotomy that extends spontaneously (not by surgical incision) is considered as spontaneous laceration or tear. Subsequent repair of spontaneous birth trauma lacerations of the perineum are classified to 75.69.

Episiotomy associated with the following procedures is not reported with 73.6, but by the method of delivery as specified, with episiotomy:

- Episiotomy with forceps delivery (72.1, 72.21, 72.31)
- Episiotomy with vacuum extraction (72.71)

Episiotomy procedures should not be confused with spontaneous perineal lacerations or tears that result from trauma due to the birthing process (75.69). Surgical incisions documented as episiotomy procedures are classified to 73.6 Episiotomy.

Also report the code for any episiotomy (73.6) performed in addition to a repair of other current obstetric laceration.

Documentation Tip
Procedures classifiable to 73.6 may be documented as:

- Episioproctotomy
- Episiotomy with episiorrhaphy

Coding Guidance
   AHA: 1Q, '92, 10; 4Q, '08, 192

73.8   Operations on fetus to facilitate delivery

Description
This procedure code describes a wide range of procedures not otherwise classifiable to category 73, performed to facilitate delivery of a fetus.

Documentation Tip
Procedures classifiable to 73.8 may be documented as:

* Clavicotomy—surgical fracture of the clavicle
* Destruction of fetus
* Needling of hydrocephalic head—cephalocentesis (drainage of excess fluid from head of fetus to facilitate passage for delivery)

73.9   Other operations assisting delivery

73.91   External version to assist delivery

Description
The physician turns the fetus from a breech presenting position to a cephalic presenting position. External cephalic version is performed by manipulating the fetus from the outside of the abdominal wall. The physician places both hands on the patient's abdomen and locates each pole of the fetus by palpation. The fetus is shifted so that the breech or rear end of the fetus is moved upward and the head downward. The physician may elect to use tocolytic drug therapy to suppress uterine contractions during the manipulation.

73.92   Replacement of prolapsed umbilical cord

Description
The physician replaces or repositions the umbilical cord so as to relieve compression. A prolapsed cord is an emergent condition that occurs when the umbilical cord displaces into the birth canal. The displacement creates a compression whereby oxygen and blood supply is impaired, which can be fatal to the baby. If the amniotic sac has not broken, the physician may manually reposition the cord to relieve compression. If the patient is dilated and in labor, the delivery may be hastened to relieve cord compression and maintain viability of the fetus.

73.93   Incision of cervix to assist delivery

Description
The physician performs an incision of the cervix to assist in delivery of the fetus, which may be performed in cases of cervical dilation arrest or failure. Surgical technique may vary.

For Dührssen's incisions, the physician makes three surgical incisions into an incompletely dilated cervix at approximately the 2, 6, and 10 o'clock positions, to precipitate delivery of the fetus.

73.94   Pubiotomy to assist delivery

Description
The physician performs surgical division or cutting of the pubic bone at the symphysis pubis (where the pelvic bones fuse together) to widen the size of the pelvic outlet to permit delivery of the baby.

Documentation Tip
Procedures classifiable to this code may be documented as:

* Gigli's operation
* Symphysiotomy
* Pelviotomy

73.99   Other operations to assist delivery

Description
This procedure code reports other operations assisting delivery not classifiable elsewhere in category 73.

Coding Clarification
Code 73.99 excludes cervical dilation or other means to induce labor classifiable to 73.1.

Also excluded from 73.99 is the removal of cerclage material (69.96).

This procedure code should not be assigned if the medical record contains sufficient information to facilitate coding at a higher level of specificity.

Documentation Tip
If the documentation is ambiguous or unclear, the physician should be queried.

74   Cesarean section and removal of fetus

Description
Category 74 procedures describe cesarean section (c-section) procedures in which a surgical incision is made through the mother's abdomen and uterus to deliver the baby. Cesarean sections are usually performed when the mother or infant is at risk, or when a vaginal delivery is otherwise contraindicated, such as:

* Cephalopelvic disproportion
* Failure of labor to progress
* Complicating medical conditions or diseases
* Labor complications or trauma
* Fetal distress

● New Code   ▲ Revised Code   ▶◀ Revised Text   © 2010 Ingenix

Under spinal or other anesthesia, the abdomen is prepped with antiseptic solution. The physician most commonly makes a small, horizontal incision in the skin above the pubic bone (low transverse incision). The physician dissects the underlying tissue to the uterus. The abdominal muscles are separated and spread to expose the contents of the pelvis. Upon visualization of the uterus, a horizontal incision is usually made in the lower uterine section (low transverse incision). However, the physician may elect to perform a vertical or "classical" incision depending on the nature of the uterus or pregnancy at the time of cesarean section. The physician manually removes the baby from the uterine incision. If the uterus has ruptured, the physician removes the baby from the peritoneal or extraperitoneal cavity. In such cases, the physician may perform an associated and separately reportable emergency hysterectomy. The baby may be placed on the mother's abdomen directly, or passed to a pediatrician or nurse for examination. The physician removes the placenta and closes the abdominal incision in layers with sutures and staples.

Coding Clarification
For procedures classifiable to category 74, code also any synchronous:

- Hysterectomy (68.3-68.4, 68.6, 68.8)
- Myomectomy (68.29)
- Sterilization (66.31-66.39, 66.63)

74.0   Classical cesarean section

Description
The physician performs surgical delivery of a baby through a vertical incision into the uterus.

74.1   Low cervical cesarean section

Description
The physician performs surgical delivery of a baby through a transverse incision into the lower segment of the uterus.

Coding Guidance
    AHA: 1Q, '01, 11

74.2   Extraperitoneal cesarean section

Description
The extraperitoneal approach for cesarean section delivery was utilized in the early 1900s as a means to avoid peritonitis complications associated with surgical childbirth. This approach was further refined over the next few decades until the advent of penicillin essentially eliminated the need for this specific technique.

74.3   Removal of extratubal ectopic pregnancy

Description
The physician removes an embryo or fetus implanted in the abdomen. The fertilized ovum may have implanted directly in the abdomen (primary) or it may have implanted after escaping from the tube through a rupture or through the fimbriated end (secondary). After making an abdominal incision, the physician surgically removes the fetus from the abdomen. The membranes are also removed and the cord is ligated near the placenta. The placenta is usually not removed unless attached to the fallopian tube, ovary, or uterine broad ligament. Abdominal lavage may also be indicated. The abdominal incision is closed with sutures. Although this procedure is rare, it can be done any time during gestation, even at or near term.

Coding Clarification
Code 74.3 includes procedures described as removal of ectopic abdominal pregnancy or removal of fetus from peritoneal or peritoneal cavity following uterine or tubal rupture.

Code 74.3 excludes removal of extratubal ectopic pregnancy by salpingostomy (66.02), salpingotomy (66.01), or with synchronous salpingectomy (66.62).

Coding Guidance
    AHA: 1Q, '89, 11; 2Q, '90, 25

74.4   Cesarean section of other specified type

Description
The physician performs a cesarean section of other specified type, not classifiable elsewhere within category 74.

Coding Clarification
This procedure code should not be assigned if the medical record contains sufficient information to facilitate coding at a higher level of specificity.

Documentation Tip
Procedures classifiable to code 74.4 may be documented as:

- Peritoneal exclusion cesarean section
- Transperitoneal cesarean section NOS
- Vaginal cesarean section

74.9   Cesarean section of unspecified type

74.91   Hysterotomy to terminate pregnancy

Documentation Tip
The physician performs a therapeutic abortion through an incision in the abdominal wall and uterus. The surgery is similar to a cesarean section but the abdominal and uterine incisions are smaller. The lower abdominal wall is opened with a vertical or horizontal incision and the uterus is entered

72-75

through the lower uterine segment. The physician removes the embryo or fetus and may also remove any remaining membranes and placenta from the uterine cavity. Curettage of the uterine cavity may also be performed. The abdominal and uterine incisions are closed by suturing.

74.99   Other cesarean section of unspecified type

Description
The physician performs a cesarean section of other or unspecified type, not classifiable elsewhere in category 74.

Coding Clarification
This procedure code should not be assigned if the medical record contains sufficient information to facilitate coding at a higher level of specificity.

Documentation Tip
If the documentation is ambiguous or unclear, the physician should be queried.

Procedures classifiable to code 74.99 may be documented as:

- Cesarean section NOS
- Obstetrical abdominouterotomy
- Obstetrical hysterotomy

Coding Scenario
A 38-year-old female presented for medical induction of labor due to maternal hypertension (pre-eclampsia). Three trials of prostaglandin fail to produce contractions of adequate strength and duration. On the third day of admission, Pitocin induction is attempted. Due to maternal exhaustion at the trials of labor, the decision is made to rupture membranes to force labor to full progression. At rupture, the amount of fluid was consistent with polyhydramnios. During labor, epidural was discontinued due to interference with pushing efforts. High forceps, low (outlet) forceps, and vacuum assistance were tried to no avail. Despite favorable prenatal cephalopelvic measurements, the patient was determined to be in obstructed labor due to disproportion. After 3½ hours of pushing efforts with assistance and resultant maternal exhaustion, the decision was made to deliver by emergency cesarean section. The patient delivered a term liveborn female infant by low transverse cesarean section (LTCS). The infant sustained pulmonary collapse and significant craniofacial hematoma due to birth trauma, with resultant jaundice.

Code Assignment:

74.1   Low cervical cesarean section
73.3   Failed forceps
73.09   Other artificial rupture of membranes (AROM)

75   Other obstetric operations

Description
Category 75 describes other obstetric operations not classifiable elsewhere in Chapter 13. These procedures include:

- Procedures performed during pregnancy for diagnostic or therapeutic purposes, including intrauterine procedures and procedures on the fetus.

- Therapeutic procedures performed after delivery of the baby, such as repair, hemorrhage control, uterine exploration, and placenta removal.

- Treatment of other obstetrical complications.

- Other obstetrical procedures.

75.0   Intra-amniotic injection for abortion

Description
This procedure involves the termination of a pregnancy by intra-amniotic injection. Technique may vary.

The physician terminates a pregnancy by inducing labor with amniocentesis and intra-amniotic injections. This method is usually used after the first trimester (13 weeks or more). The physician inserts an amniocentesis needle into the abdomen to obtain a free flow of clear amniotic fluid. A hypertonic solution is administered by gravity drip. The hypertonic solution results in fetal death and labor usually results. The fetus and placenta are delivered through the vagina.

Coding Clarification
Code 75.0 excludes insertion of prostaglandin suppository for abortion (96.49).

Documentation Tip
Procedures classifiable to 75.0 may be documented as:

- Injection of prostaglandin or saline for abortion
- Termination of pregnancy by intrauterine injection

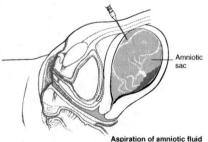

Aspiration of amniotic fluid

● New Code   ▲ Revised Code   ►◄ Revised Text   © 2010 Ingenix

75.1   Diagnostic amniocentesis

Description

The physician aspirates fluid from the amniotic sac for diagnostic purposes. Using ultrasonic guidance, the physician inserts an amniocentesis needle through the abdominal wall into the interior of the pregnant uterus and directly into the amniotic sac to collect amniotic fluid for analysis.

75.2   Intrauterine transfusion

Description

The physician performs a blood transfusion to a fetus. The physician uses ultrasound guidance to locate the umbilical vein. A needle is directed through the abdominal wall into the amniotic cavity. The umbilical vein is pierced and fetal blood is exchanged with transfused blood. The needle is withdrawn and the fetus is observed by ultrasound imaging.

Coding Clarification

Code also any hysterotomy (uterine incision) approach (68.0).

Documentation Tip

Procedures classifiable to 75.2 may be documented as:

- Exchange transfusion in utero
- Insertion of catheter into abdomen of fetus for transfusion

75.3   Other intrauterine operations on fetus and amnion

Coding Clarification

Code also any hysterotomy approach (68.0).

75.31   Amnioscopy

Coding Clarification

An understanding of the following terms may aid in code selection:

- **Amnioscopy:** Prenatal examination of the fetus and amniotic fluid by insertion of an endoscope through the cervix. Amnioscopy is performed during the first trimester of pregnancy.

- **Fetoscopy:** Prenatal examination of the fetus by insertion of an endoscope inside the uterus and amniotic cavity. Fetoscopy is performed after the first trimester of pregnancy after the amniotic membrane has fused to the uterine wall.

Documentation Tip

Procedures classifiable to 75.31 may also be documented as laparoamnioscopy.

Coding Guidance

AHA: 3Q, '06, 16-17

75.32   Fetal EKG (scalp)

Description

The physician attaches an electrode directly to the presenting fetus' scalp via the cervix. The electrocardiographic impulses are transmitted to a cardiotachometer, which converts the fetal electrocardiographic pattern into recorded electronic impulses. A catheter is inserted through the dilated cervix into the amniotic sac to measure and record the intervals between contractions. The procedure is supervised during labor until delivery. The recordings are analyzed and accompanied by an interpretive report.

75.33   Fetal blood sampling and biopsy

Description

This procedure code describes diagnostic sampling of blood or tissue from the fetus for analysis to rule out or confirm certain suspected chromosomal and genetic disorders or other conditions. Due to the ongoing advances in maternal-fetal medicine, procedural approach and techniques may vary.

The physician uses ultrasound guidance to sample fetal blood or tissue for diagnostic purposes. A fine needle is passed through the mother's uterus to collect tissue or blood samples. Blood is aspirated into a tube. The tube and needle are withdrawn, and the mother and fetus are monitored for complications.

Coding Clarification

Fetal blood sampling involves the withdrawal of blood via precision needle placement from the baby's umbilical cord or other fetal blood vessel for analysis.

Fetal skin, muscle, or liver biopsy involves a fetoscopic (endoscopic examination of the fetus) approach to obtain a sample of skin, muscle, or other tissue from the fetus via an endoscopic needle for analysis.

75.34   Other fetal monitoring

Description

This code describes other diagnostic fetal monitoring examinations and procedures.

The physician evaluates fetal response to induced contractions in the mother. The physician applies external fetal monitors to the maternal abdominal wall. Pitocin is given intravenously to the mother to cause uterine contractions. The fetal heart rate and uterine contractions are monitored and recorded for 20 minutes to determine the effect of contractions on

72-75

the fetus. This procedure is usually performed during the third trimester.

Alternatively, the physician evaluates fetal heart rate response to its own activity. The patient reports fetal movements as an external monitor records fetal heart rate changes. The procedure is noninvasive and takes 20 to 40 minutes to perform. If the fetus is not active, an acoustic device may be used to stimulate activity.

Coding Clarification
Code 75.34 excludes fetal pulse oximetry (75.38).

Documentation Tip
Procedures classifiable to 75.34 may be documented as:

• Antepartum fetal nonstress test

• Fetal monitoring, not otherwise specified

75.35   Other diagnostic procedures on fetus and amnion

Description
This code includes other diagnostic procedures on the fetus and amnion not classifiable elsewhere in category 75.

For cordocentesis, the physician removes blood from the fetal umbilical cord for diagnostic purposes. Using separately reportable ultrasonic guidance, the physician inserts an amniocentesis needle through the abdominal wall into the cavity of the pregnant uterus and into the umbilical vessels to obtain fetal blood. This may be accomplished with a transplacental or transamniotic approach.

For chorionic villous sampling, the physician samples tissue from the placenta for diagnostic purposes. This procedure uses ultrasonic guidance and can be done by any one of three methods. In the transcervical method, the physician inserts a catheter through the cervix and into the uterine cavity toward the placental site. A sample of the placenta (chorionic villus) is aspirated to obtain placental cells for analysis for chromosomal abnormalities. The procedure may also be performed transvaginally or transabdominally.

Coding Clarification
Code 75.35 excludes amniocentesis (75.1) and diagnostic procedures on gravid uterus and placenta classifiable to Chapter 16 Miscellaneous diagnostic and therapeutic procedures (87-99).

Coding Guidance
    AHA: 3Q, '06, 16-17

75.36   Correction of fetal defect

Description
This procedure code classifies a range of corrective procedures on the fetus not elsewhere classifiable in category 75.

Coding Clarification
Surgery performed on a fetus is reported as an obstetric encounter. Invasive in utero surgeries are reported on the mother's inpatient medical record with the appropriate diagnosis code from category 655 Known or suspected fetal abnormalities affecting management of the mother, to identify the fetal condition. It is inappropriate to assign a perinatal diagnosis from Chapter 15 Conditions in the perinatal period to describe the condition necessitating the in vitro procedure.

Coding Guidance
    AHA: 4Q, '06, 12

75.37   Amnioinfusion

Description
Amnioinfusion is the instillation of saline or antibiotics into the uterine cavity (antepartum or during labor) to replace amniotic fluid or treat infection. The physician infuses the amniotic sac with fluid. Amnioinfusion may be performed transcervically or transabdominally. This may be done as a prophylactic measure for the fetus or to enhance sonographic imaging. An amniocentesis needle is placed through the mother's abdomen and advanced between extremities of the fetus under separately reportable ultrasound guidance. Normal sterile saline is infused into the uterus until the fetal anatomy is adequately visualized. The needle is removed and a detailed ultrasound is carried out.

Coding Clarification
Code also any injection of an antibiotic associated with this procedure (99.21).

Coding Guidance
    AHA: 4Q, '98, 76

75.38   Fetal pulse oximetry

Description
A sensor is inserted through the birth canal after a cervical dilation of greater than 2 cm has been achieved and the amniotic membrane is ruptured. The sensor is positioned to rest against the fetal cheek, forehead, or temple. An infrared beam of light aimed at the fetal skin is reflected back through the sensor for analysis. The percentage of oxygen saturation is recorded and displayed on a monitor.

Documentation Tip
Procedures classifiable to 75.38 may be documented as:

* Transcervical fetal oxygen saturation monitoring

* Transcervical fetal SpO2 monitoring

Coding Guidance
   AHA: 4Q, '01, 64

75.4   Manual removal of retained placenta

Description
The physician removes a retained placenta following delivery of the fetus after separation of the placenta from its intrauterine attachment. The physician places abdominal pressure just above the symphysis to elevate the uterus into the abdomen and prevent inversion of the uterus. This also helps move the placenta downward into the vagina. The umbilical cord is very gently pulled to help guide the placenta out of the birth canal. If the placenta cannot be removed by this technique or there is brisk bleeding, manual removal of the placenta may be indicated. Manual removal requires adequate analgesia or anesthesia. It is accomplished by grasping the fundus of the uterus with a hand on the abdomen. The other hand, wearing an elbow-length glove, is passed through the vagina into the uterus to separate the placenta and remove it.

Coding Clarification
Code 75.4 excludes aspiration curettage (69.52) or dilatation and curettage (69.02).

Coding Guidance
   AHA: 3Q, '06, 11

75.5   Repair of current obstetric laceration of uterus

Description
Procedures classified to subcategory 75.5 describe repair of spontaneous traumatic lacerations or tears of the uterus or cervix that occur as complications of the delivery process. These procedures are classified according to anatomic site as follows:

75.50   Repair of current obstetric laceration of uterus, not otherwise specified

75.51   Repair of current obstetric laceration of cervix

75.52   Repair of current obstetric laceration of corpus uteri

Description
These procedure codes describe a repair of a traumatic obstetric wound of the uterus or cervix. Surgical approach and technique may vary, depending on the site, nature, and severity of the wound. The physician may insert a speculum into the vagina to view the cervix or uterus, or perform the repair via an open incision. The physician performs a plastic suture repair of a laceration or wound. If an incision is required to access the wound, it is closed in sutures and/or stapled layers.

Coding Clarification
Code 75.50 is a nonspecific procedure that should not be assigned to report a procedure occurring during an inpatient hospital admission if the medical record contains sufficient information to facilitate coding at a higher level of specificity. The site of laceration repair should be documented.

Documentation Tip
If the documentation is ambiguous or unclear, the physician should be queried.

Coding Guidance
   AHA: 2Q, '08, 8

75.6   Repair of other current obstetric laceration

Description
Procedures classified to subcategory 75.6 describe repair of spontaneous traumatic lacerations or tears of the lower urinary tract organs, rectum or anus, and perineum or external genitalia that occur as complications of the delivery process. These procedures are classified according to anatomic site.

Coding Clarification
Coding guidance instructs that an episiotomy that extends spontaneously is to be considered a laceration. Coders are instructed to report repair of the extension and laceration to the appropriate code under category 75.6 Repair of other current obstetric laceration, (codes 75.61–75.69). In order to accurately reflect clinical practice and allow proper tracking of episiotomies that extend spontaneously, an instructional note was added directing the coder to also code the episiotomy, if performed (73.6).

Coding Guidance
   AHA: 1Q, '92, 11

75.61   Repair of current obstetric laceration of bladder and urethra

Description
The physician sutures a wound, injury, or rupture in the bladder. To access the bladder, urethra, and ureters, the physician makes an incision in the skin of the abdomen and cuts the corresponding muscles, fat, and fibrous membranes (fascia). To provide support during healing, the physician may insert a catheter through the urethra. The physician inserts a drain tube and performs layered closure.

The physician repairs a urethral wound or injury, including the skin or complicated wounds requiring more than a layered closure. This procedure includes debridement of cuts (lacerations) or tears

72-75

(avulsion). Suturing of the urethra is done in layers to prevent later complications and fistula formations.

75.62 Repair of current obstetric laceration of rectum and sphincter ani

Description
The physician repairs an obstetrical laceration of the rectum or anus. Depending on the site and severity of the wound, the physician may make an abdominal incision, or may suture and repair the wound through the anus or rectum. The wound injury is explored and repaired with sutures.

75.69 Repair of other current obstetric laceration

Description
The physician sutures and repairs vaginal, perineal, or other spontaneous tears or lacerations associated with delivery.

Coding Clarification
Code 75.69 excludes repair of a routine episiotomy (73.6).

Documentation Tip
Procedures classifiable to 75.69 may be documented as:

- Episioperineorrhaphy
- Secondary repair of episiotomy
- Repair of pelvic floor, perineum, vagina, or vulva

Coding Guidance
　　AHA: 4Q, '07, 125; 4Q, '08, 192

75.7 Manual exploration of uterine cavity, postpartum

Description
The physician performs postpartum manual exploration of the uterine cavity after delivery. This procedure may be performed to assess whether the entire placenta has been delivered or whether portions of the placenta are retained, causing complications such as hemorrhage. The physician empties the uterus and removes the retained placental fragments with a gloved hand. The physician passes a gloved hand into the shape of a cone and carefully inserts the hand through the cervix into the lower uterine segment. The other hand is placed on the abdomen at the uterine fundus. The physician may remove clots. The uterine cavity is gently explored for the presence of defects or rupture.

75.8 Obstetric tamponade of uterus or vagina

Description
This code describes the insertion of a device used to control hemorrhage. The type, manufacturer, and

technique may vary. However, some tamponades (e.g., Sengstaken-Blakemore tube) have an open tip to permit drainage and are similar to a Foley catheter with a balloon that is inflated to provide pressure to the site of bleeding. Once hemostasis has been achieved, the balloon is deflated and the tamponade removed.

Coding Clarification
Code 75.8 excludes antepartum tamponade (73.1).

75.9 Other obstetric operations

75.91 Evacuation of obstetrical incisional hematoma of perineum

Description
The physician incises and drains a perineal hematoma occurring as a result of a complication of an obstetrical incision (episiotomy) performed to assist in delivery. The patient is placed in a dorsolithotomy position. The hematoma is visualized and incised. Blood and clots are drained from the hematoma. Electrocautery or suture is used to control bleeding. When needed, a Hemovac drain is placed. The perineum is irrigated and the area of hematoma is dressed.

Coding Clarification
Evacuation of an obstetrical hematoma of the vagina or vulva is reported with 75.92.

Documentation Tip
Procedures classifiable to 75.91 may be documented as evacuation of hematoma of episiotomy or perineorrhaphy.

75.92 Evacuation of other hematoma of vulva or vagina

Description
The physician incises and drains a vaginal hematoma in an obstetrical or postpartum patient. The patient is placed in a dorsolithotomy position. The physician inserts a speculum into the vagina. The hematoma is visualized and incised. Blood and clots are drained from the hematoma. Electrocautery or suture is used to control bleeding. When needed, a Hemovac drain is placed. The vagina is irrigated and the area of hematoma is sponged with dressings. When hemostasis is achieved, the speculum is removed.

Coding Clarification
Evacuation of an obstetrical hematoma of the perineum is reported with 75.91.

75.93 Surgical correction of inverted uterus

Description
This code reports surgical correction of inverted uterus. Surgical approach and technique may vary.

Under general anesthesia, the physician makes a midline vertical incision from the pubic line to the umbilicus to the fascia. The fascia is incised and the abdominal muscles are separated. The peritoneum is opened and the bladder is retracted. The cervix is dilated digitally. A tenaculum is inserted through the cervix and the inverted fundus is grasped. Continuous gentle traction is applied to the uterine fundus, and a manual correction may be attempted. If the traction fails, the cervical ring may be incised and traction repeated. Upon successful correction, the abdomen is closed in layers.

Coding Clarification
Code 75.93 excludes vaginal repair of chronic inversion of the uterus (69.23).

75.94   Manual replacement of inverted uterus

Description
Wearing sterile gloves, the physician grasps the uterus and pushes it through the cervix toward the umbilicus to its normal position, using the other hand to support the uterus.

75.99   Other obstetric operations

Description
This procedure code includes other obstetrical operations not classifiable elsewhere in category 75.

Coding Clarification
This procedure code should not be assigned if the medical record contains sufficient information to facilitate coding at a higher level of specificity.

Documentation Tip
If the documentation is ambiguous or unclear, the physician should be queried.

Coding Guidance
   AHA: 3Q, '06, 16-17

72-75

76-84

Operations on the Musculoskeletal System

2011 Changes

Multiple changes were made to subcategories 81.0 Spinal fusion and 81.3 Refusion of spine, including code title and inclusion term revisions, to allow for further specification of anatomic site of procedure and surgical technique. Instructional notes were added for clarification.

New code 81.88 reports a surgical alternative to conventional total shoulder replacement, mainly for patients who suffer rotator cuff arthropathy. Inclusion, exclusion, and code title revisions were made to codes 81.83, 81.80, and 81.97 to accommodate this change in shoulder arthroplasty classification.

New code 84.94 reports a rigid plate sternal fixation system consisting of implanted plates and screws that can significantly reduce the incidence of sternal wound dehiscence and subsequent deep sternal wound infections (DSWI) in certain cardiothoracic surgery patients. An exclusion term was added for this new procedure to subcategory 78.5 Internal fixation of bone without fracture reduction.

Code title and exclusion term revisions were made to code 83.21 Open biopsy of soft tissue, to differentiate between closed biopsy of skin and subcutaneous tissue (86.11).

The ICD-9-CM classification system for operations performed on the musculoskeletal system is divided into categories of procedures according to site and type as follows:

- Operations on Facial Bones and Joints (76)
- Incision, Excision, and Division of Other Bones (77)
- Other Operations on Bones, Except Facial Bones (78)
- Reduction of Fracture and Dislocation (79)
- Incision and Excision of Joint Structures (80)
- Repair and Plastic Operations on Joint Structures (81)

- Operations on Muscle, Tendon, and Fascia of Hand (82)
- Operations on Muscle, Tendon, Fascia, and Bursa Except Hand (83)
- Other Operations on Musculoskeletal System (84)

76   Operations on facial bones and joints

Description
Category 76 provides codes for incisions, diagnostic procedures, excisions, repairs, fracture reductions, and other operations on the facial bones and joints. This category, however, does not include the accessory sinuses, nasal bones, or skull.

Subcategory 76.6 Other facial bone repair and orthognathic surgery, requires a fourth digit to identify the type and site of the procedure. Subcategory 76.7 Reduction of facial fracture, also requires a fourth digit to describe the site of the fracture and whether the treatment involved open or closed reduction. The care of a nasal bone fracture is classified elsewhere.

Coding Clarification
Use 76.19 for arthroscopy of the temporomandibular joint.

When any synchronous bone graft (76.91) or synthetic implant (76.92) is used, an additional code is necessary.

Do not assign category 76 codes to report procedures of the accessory sinuses (22.00-22.9), nasal bones (21.00-21.99), and skull (01.01-02.99).

76.0   Incision of facial bone without division

76.01   Sequestrectomy of facial bone

Description
The physician removes a portion of dead bone that has separated from healthy bone as a result of injury or disease.

The physician removes infected or dead bone tissue from the mandible. This procedure can be performed intraorally through the mucosa or extraorally through a skin incision. If only a small amount of bone is affected, the physician may saucerize the area by grinding the dead bone away with drills or osteotomes. Healthy bone and the continuity of the mandible are left intact. Antibiotic-impregnated acrylic beads may be implanted into the surgical site to stop infection after the removal of bone. These beads are removed at a later time. Extensive bone removal in large sections or blocks may require a separate bone harvesting/grafting procedure to repair continuity defects. The incisions are closed simply.

The physician removes dead or infected bone from other facial bones. A transoral incision in the maxillary buccal vestibule is the most frequent approach. Facial incisions would only be used for large lesions or for additional surgical access. The physician reflects the overlying mucosa, exposing the dead bone. Drills, saws, and osteotomes are used to remove the bone. The transoral incisions are closed in a single layer. Any cutaneous incision is closed in layers.

Coding Clarification
Sequestrum is a piece of dead bone that has become separated from the healthy bone as a result of necrosis from injury or disease.

Sequestrectomy is the surgical removal of a sequestrum.

Video-assisted thoracoscopic surgery is frequently performed for pulmonary sequestration. Early resection obviates the risk of infection. Elective ligation of the aberrant artery is a safe alternative to the use of stapling devices or clips. Cosmetic results are excellent.

76.09   Other incision of facial bone

Description
Code 76.09 is used to report other incisional procedures on the facial bones that are not more precisely described by other codes in subcategory 76.0, such as reopening of an osteotomy site of the facial bone.

Coding Clarification
To report osteotomy associated with orthognathic surgery, see 76.61-76.69.

Do not use 76.09 to report removal of an internal fixation device; see 76.97.

Documentation Tip
In order to ensure accurate code assignment and avoid improper use of a nonspecific code, review the documentation for specific information regarding the procedure prior to final code selection.

76.1   Diagnostic procedures on facial bones and joints

Coding Clarification
Diagnostic procedures on the facial bones and joints are performed using a variety of surgical techniques. Biopsy procedures are also performed using a variety of surgical techniques and approaches ranging from open surgery to less invasive procedures such as aspiration to biopsy performed percutaneously.

Documentation Tip
To ensure accurate code assignment, it will be necessary to review the medical record documentation for approach and surgical technique.

76.11   Biopsy of facial bone

Description
The physician performs an open biopsy on bone to confirm a suspected growth, disease, or infection. With the patient under general anesthesia, and placed in the appropriate position, the physician makes an incision overlying the biopsy site and carries it down through the tissue to the level of the bone being biopsied. A piece of bone tissue is removed and sent for examination. The wound is sutured closed and the patient is moved to the recovery area.

Coding Clarification
Biopsy procedures are performed using a variety of surgical techniques and approaches ranging from open surgery to less invasive procedures such as aspiration to biopsy performed percutaneously.

Documentation Tip
To ensure accurate code assignment, it will be necessary to review the medical record documentation for approach and surgical technique.

76.19   Other diagnostic procedures on facial bones and joints

Description
The physician inserts an arthroscope into the temporomandibular joint to examine the joint space(s). The physician may lavage or wash the joint. The physician makes a 0.5 cm vertical incision anterior to the contour of the ear. The arthroscope is inserted into the joint through the incision. A needle is placed into the joint in front of the arthroscope to allow the saline from the arthroscope to flow out of the joint. An instrument may also be inserted through the arthroscope for biopsy of the synovium (lining of the joint). The arthroscope and outflow needle are removed and the incision is closed with simple sutures.

● New Code   ▲ Revised Code   ▶◀ Revised Text   © 2010 Ingenix

Coding Clarification
Code 76.19 does not include a contrast arthrogram of temporomandibular joint (87.13) or other x-ray (87.11-87.12, 87.14-87.16).

Coding Guidance
>   **AHA:** N-D, '87, 12

76.2 Local excision or destruction of lesion of facial bone

Description
In one procedure, the physician removes a cyst or benign tumor from the maxilla (upper jaw) or the zygoma (arched cheekbone) by enucleation and/or curettage, not requiring osteotomy. Using an intraoral approach, the physician incises and reflects a mucosal flap of tissue inside the mouth overlying the tumor. In an extraoral approach, the physician approaches the defect through an external skin incision. The tumor is identified and removed from the maxilla or zygoma by scraping with a curette or by cutting the tumor out in such a way as to leave it intact and remove it whole. The mucosal flap is then sutured primarily or the subcutaneous tissues and skin incisions on the face are closed with layered sutures.

Coding Clarification
Do not assign 76.2 to report biopsy of a facial bone (76.11) or excision of an odontogenic lesion (24.4).

Other procedures that may be appropriately reported with 76.2 include:

* Debridement of open fracture of facial bone
* Exostosis of facial bone
* Excision of jaw bone lesion
* Excision of a lingual or mandibular torus

76.3 Partial ostectomy of facial bone

Description
The physician performs a partial ostectomy by removing a 2 mm thick fragment of the bone. The ostectomy enhances vascular supply to promote healing of the soft tissues. The incision is repaired in multiple layers with sutures, staples, and/or Steri-strips.

In one technique, the physician removes infected or dead bone tissue from the mandible. This procedure can be performed intraorally through the mucosa or extraorally through a skin incision. If only a small amount of bone is affected, the physician may saucerize the area by grinding the dead bone away with drills or osteotomes. Healthy bone and the continuity of the mandible are left intact. Antibiotic-impregnated acrylic beads may be implanted into the surgical site to stop infection after the removal of bone. These beads are removed at a later time.

Coding Clarification
Extensive bone removal in large sections or blocks may require a separate bone harvesting/grafting procedure to repair continuity defects.

76.31 Partial mandibulectomy

Description
The physician performs a hemimandibulectomy, or the resection of one half of the mandible, by intraoral or extraoral osteotomy. For the intraoral approach, the physician incises and reflects a mucosal flap of tissue inside the mouth overlying the tumor to reach the bone. In an extraoral approach, the physician approaches the defect through an external skin incision and dissects down through the tissue layers to reach the tumor. The tumor is identified and removed along with overlying bone by cutting into the mandible using a drill or osteotome. Additional bone removal from the mandible is done to excise the tumor fully. With large tumors, the surgical wounds may be packed and sutured or reconstructive procedures such as harvesting of bone for grafting may be needed, depending on the size of the surgical wound. The mucosal flap is then sutured primarily or the subcutaneous tissues and skin incisions on the face are closed with layered sutures.

Coding Clarification
Do not assign 76.31 to report partial mandibulectomy associated with temporomandibular arthroplasty (76.5).

Hemimandibulectomy is excision of one half of the lower jawbone.

Coding Guidance
>   **AHA:** 2Q, '05, 8

76.39 Partial ostectomy of other facial bone

Description
Code 76.39 is used to report other partial ostectomy procedures on the facial bones that are not more precisely described by other codes in subcategory 76.3, such as the partial excision of a facial bone other than the lower jawbone.

Coding Clarification
Assign 76.39 to report a hemimaxillectomy with a bone graft or prosthesis.

Hemimaxillectomy is the excision of one side of the upper jawbone and restoration with bone graft or prosthesis.

Documentation Tip
Review the documentation for specific information regarding the procedure prior to final code selection in order to ensure accurate code assignment.

Coding Guidance
    AHA: J-F, '87, 14

76.4   Excision and reconstruction of facial bones

76.41   Total mandibulectomy with synchronous reconstruction

Description
The physician removes a malignant tumor from the mandible in a radical resection using an intraoral and/or extraoral approach to reach the site of the tumor. The tumor and surrounding tissues are removed. Resection or removal of a part, or all, of the mandible is performed. Immediate reconstruction with bone grafts, tissue rearrangement, flaps, or prosthetic devices is performed. The skin incisions are closed with layered sutures.

Coding Scenario
Using an intraoral approach, the physician placed metal implants into the bone of the maxilla or mandible. Precision holes were drilled in the bone and implants were placed. The mucosa was sutured over the top of the implant and the incisions were then closed simply.

    Code Assignment:

    76.41   Total mandibulectomy with synchronous
            reconstruction

76.42   Other total mandibulectomy

Description
Code 76.42 is used to report other total mandibulectomy procedures that are not more precisely described by other codes in subcategory 76.4. An intraoral and/or extraoral approach can be used to reach the site and removal of the entire mandible is performed. Immediate or delayed reconstruction with bone grafts, tissue rearrangement, flaps, or prosthetic devices is sometimes required.

Documentation Tip
Review the documentation for specific information regarding the procedure prior to final code selection in order to ensure accurate code assignment.

76.43   Other reconstruction of mandible

Description
In one reconstruction technique, the physician places a metal framework between the mucosa and the bone of the maxilla or mandible. The metal framework has posts that extend vertically and protrude through the mucosa into the mouth. The posts are used to retain an upper denture in the maxilla or lower denture in the mandible when teeth are missing. Intraoral surgery is performed in one or two sessions. The physician makes an incision along the crest of the edentulous area (without teeth) and exposes as much of the bone as possible.

If performed in two sessions, the physician makes impressions of the exposed bone and sutures the mucosa closed. The impression is used to make models for custom framework. At the second surgical session, the physician removes the sutures and again exposes the bone. The metal framework, with the attached posts, is placed on the bone. The mucosa and periosteum are sutured over the framework and around the protruding posts. Scarring, which occurs with healing, keeps the framework in place.

If performed in one session, a CT scan is used to make a plastic model of the mandible or maxilla from which the framework and posts are fabricated. A single surgical session is used to insert the framework as described above. Incisions are closed simply with sutures.

Coding Clarification
Do not assign 76.43 to report genioplasty (76.67-76.68) or reconstruction with synchronous total mandibulectomy (76.41).

Coding Guidance
    AHA: 2Q, '03, 13

76.44   Total ostectomy of other facial bone with synchronous reconstruction

Description
The physician performs total excision of a facial bone with reconstruction during the same operative session. This procedure can be performed intraorally through the mucosa or extraorally through a skin incision. A transoral incision in the maxillary buccal vestibule is the most frequent approach used to remove dead or infected bone from facial bones. The physician reflects the overlying mucosa, exposing the dead bone. Drills, saws, and osteotomes are used to remove the bone. The transoral incisions are closed in a single layer. Any cutaneous incision is closed in multiple layers. If only a small amount of bone is affected, the physician may saucerize the area by grinding the dead bone away with drills or osteotomes. Healthy bone and the continuity of the mandible are left intact. Antibiotic-impregnated acrylic beads may be implanted into the surgical site to stop infection after the removal of bone. These beads are removed at a later time.

Coding Clarification
Facial incisions are typically used for large lesions or for additional surgical access.

● New Code   ▲ Revised Code   ▶◀ Revised Text   © 2010 Ingenix

Extensive bone removal in large sections or blocks may require a separate bone harvesting/grafting procedure to repair continuity defects.

Coding Guidance
AHA: 3Q, '93, 6

76.45   Other total ostectomy of other facial bone

Description
Code 76.45 is used to report other ostectomy procedures on the facial bones that are not more precisely described by other codes in subcategory 76.4.

In one example, with the patient under anesthesia, the physician makes a horizontal cut through the maxillary sinuses and nasal septum through an intraoral incision, and into the pterygoid fissure. Surgical instruments are used to complete the separation of the maxilla from the skull base. The maxilla is down-fractured to mobilize it and can be moved into the proper predetermined position. If segmental surgery in the maxilla was necessary, the mobilized segments are held in position by a template secured to the upper teeth. Maxillary malpositioning is corrected and the maxilla is wired to the mandible, which is positioned as a whole unit. Rigid fixation of the maxilla is achieved with miniplates or intermaxillary wires. The operative site is irrigated with antibiotic solution and the oral mucosa is closed as needed.

Documentation Tip
Review the documentation for specific information regarding the procedure prior to final code selection in order to ensure accurate code assignment.

76.46   Other reconstruction of other facial bone

Description
The physician performs reconstructive surgery of the forehead and the supraorbital rims of both eyes to correct skeletal deformities of the cranium. With the patient under anesthesia, the physician uses any of a variety of incisions about the eyes, forehead, and scalp to gain access to these bones. The soft tissues are dissected as needed to expose the bones. Osteotomies of the bones are performed in multiple places to facilitate manipulating the bones into the desired position. The bones are shaped as needed. Pins, wires, plates, and screws are used to hold the bones and graft in rigid reduction. The wounds are irrigated and closed in layers.

Coding Clarification
The physician utilizes autografts, harvested from the patient's hip, rib, or skull, allografts, or synthetic prosthetic material to augment the reconstruction.

Do not assign 76.46 to report other reconstruction of the facial bone performed with synchronous total ostectomy (76.44).

76.5   Temporomandibular arthroplasty

Description
The physician repairs or reconstructs the temporomandibular joint using arthroscopic surgery with lysis and lavage. An incision is made through the skin anterior to the contour of the ear or within the ear. The tissues are dissected and the joint is exposed. Once the joint is exposed, a variety of repairs may be performed. In one example, the physician repairs or reconstructs the temporomandibular joint with a donor graft. Donor tissue (allograft material) is used to replace the articular disc or other parts of the joint. The incisions are closed directly.

Coding Clarification
The physician utilizes autografts, harvested from the patient's hip, rib, or skull, allografts, or synthetic prosthetic material to augment the reconstruction.

Coding Guidance
AHA: 4Q, '99, 20

76.6   Other facial bone repair and orthognathic surgery

Coding Clarification
Instructional notes indicate any synchronous bone graft (76.91) or synthetic implant (76.92) performed should also be coded.

Do no assign 76.6 to report reconstruction of facial bones (76.41-76.46).

76.61   Closed osteoplasty (osteotomy) of mandibular ramus

Description
The physician may excise a cyst or benign tumor from the mandible (lower jaw) by intraoral osteotomy or by extraoral osteotomy and partial mandibulectomy. For the intraoral approach, the physician incises and reflects a mucosal flap of tissue inside the mouth overlying the tumor to reach the bone. In an extraoral approach, the physician approaches the defect through an external skin incision and dissects down through the tissue layers to reach the tumor. The tumor is identified and removed along with overlying bone by cutting into the mandible using a drill or osteotome. Additional bone removal from the mandible may be needed to excise the tumor fully. With large tumors, the surgical wounds may be packed and sutured or reconstructive procedures such as harvesting of bone for grafting may be needed, depending on the size of the surgical wound. The mucosal flap is then sutured primarily or the subcutaneous tissues and

76-84

skin incisions on the face are closed with layered sutures.

In an alternate procedure, the physician reconstructs the mandibular ramus to lengthen, set back, or rotate the mandible. Using an intraoral approach, the physician makes an incision overlying the external oblique ridge, through the mucosa near the second mandibular molars. The mandibular ramus is then exposed by reflecting the tissue from both sides of the ramus. Drills, saws, and/or osteotomes are used to cut the mandible along the inside, top, and outside surfaces of the bone, but not completely through. The physician uses osteotomes and/or other instruments to pry the mandible apart along the bone cuts in a sagittal plane. Once separated, the physician moves the mandible into the desired position and holds the bone in reduction using wires. In some cases, no rigid internal fixation devices are used and in others, screws or plates are placed in or on the bone. The physician may also make small 0.5 cm skin incisions near the mandibular angle, through which instruments place the plates or screws. The mucosal and skin incisions are then sutured closed.

Coding Clarification
▶Closed osteoplasty (76.61) may be differentiated from open osteoplasty (76.62) by surgical approach whereby the lower jawbone projection is reshaped and restored through a closed surgical field approach, a limited keyhole incision.◀

To report a mandibular osteoplasty that is not further specified in the documentation, see 76.64.

With large mandibular tumors, the surgical wounds may be packed and sutured or reconstructive procedures such as harvesting of bone for grafting may be needed, depending on the size of the surgical wound.

Documentation Tip
Gigli saw osteotomy is a plastic repair procedure using a flexible wire with saw teeth.

76.62   Open osteoplasty (osteotomy) of mandibular ramus

Description
The physician places an implant or a graft onto the chin to augment or enlarge it. Various materials can be used, including tissue grafted from the patient's own body or taken from a tissue bank. Prosthetic devices may also be used. This procedure is most commonly performed from an intraoral approach. The physician makes an incision in the mandibular labial vestibule inside the lower lip. The mucosa is then reflected from the chin and the implanted material placed between the mucosa and the bone. A skin incision may also be made under the chin. The implant may be secured to the bone using wires or

screws or may be left to be held in place by the surrounding tissue. The mucosa is then sutured simply.

Coding Clarification
To report a mandibular osteoplasty that is not further specified in the documentation, see 76.64.

With large mandibular tumors, the surgical wounds may be packed and sutured or reconstructive procedures such as harvesting of bone for grafting may be needed, depending on the size of the surgical wound.

Documentation Tip
Gigli saw osteotomy is a plastic repair procedure using a flexible wire with saw teeth.

76.63   Osteoplasty (osteotomy) of body of mandible

Description
The physician performs a vertical ramus osteotomy, which is an osteotomy of the posterior ramus of the lower jaw or mandible in the vertical dimension, which can be performed intraorally or extraorally, to reposition the mandible.

Coding Clarification
Do not assign 76.63 to report a mandibular osteoplasty that is not further specified in the documentation; see 76.64.

76.64   Other orthognathic surgery on mandible

Description
Orthognathic surgery involves surgical repositioning of the maxilla, mandible, and the dentoalveolar segments to restore facial balance. The physician performs an osteotomy on a segment of the mandible to correct a localized deformity. The teeth are moved within a segment or block of bone. Using an intraoral approach, the physician makes an incision in the mucosa to expose the segment of bone to be moved. Drills, saws, and/or osteotomes are used to cut a section of the alveolar bone. These cuts do not extend entirely through the mandible, but include only a segment above the inferior border. The segment is moved into the desired position and held in reduction with wires, screws, or plates. The segment may also be held in place by a preformed acrylic interocclusal splint. The mucosa is then sutured simply.

Coding Clarification
Assign 76.64 to report a mandibular osteoplasty NOS and segmental or subapical osteotomy.

Code 76.64 is assigned to report other orthognathic mandibular procedures that are not more precisely described by other codes in this subcategory. This code is also reported when the documentation does not further specify the procedure.

● New Code   ▲ Revised Code   ▶◀ Revised Text   © 2010 Ingenix

Documentation Tip
Review the documentation for specific information regarding the procedure prior to final code selection in order to avoid improper use of the "not otherwise specified" code and to ensure accurate code assignment.

Coding Guidance
　　AHA: 2Q, '04, 9, 10

76.65　Segmental osteoplasty (osteotomy) of maxilla

Description
The physician performs an osteotomy on a segment of the maxilla to correct a localized deformity. The teeth are moved within a segment or block of bone. Using a circumvestibular incision, the physician exposes the segment of bone to be moved. Drills, saws, and/or osteotomes are used to cut a section of the alveolar bone. These cuts do not extend entirely through the maxilla, but include only a segment. The segment is moved into the desired position and held in reduction with wires, screws, or plates. The segment may also be held in place by a preformed acrylic interocclusal splint. The mucosa is then sutured simply and intermaxillary fixation may or may not be placed.

Coding Clarification
Assign 76.65 to report a maxillary osteoplasty that is not further specified in the documentation.

76.66　Total osteoplasty [osteotomy] of maxilla

Description
The physician augments the facial bones with implanted grafts or prosthetic devices, altering the contours of the face. The physician may use an intraoral approach or other incisions to access the operative site. The tissue is dissected, exposing the bone for augmentation. A bone graft, prosthetic implants, or donor bone is grafted onto the facial bone to contour the face. The implant is secured to the bone using screws, wires, or plates. The mucosa is then sutured simply.

Coding Clarification
A bone graft can be taken from another part of the body, such as the hip, rib, or skull. Other materials such as prosthetic implants or donor bone may also be used.

76.67　Reduction genioplasty

Description
Genioplasty is plastic surgery of the chin and reduction involves removal of bone and other tissues to reduce size. The physician removes protrusions of excess or misshaped facial bone to reduce the contours of the face. The physician may use an intraoral approach or other incisions to access the operative site. The tissue is dissected, exposing the bone for reduction. A reciprocation saw or drill is used to cut and remove the bone, reducing its contours. The mucosal incision is sutured simply.

Coding Clarification
Assign 76.67 to report a reduction mentoplasty that involves the reduction of a protruding chin or lower jawbone.

76.68　Augmentation genioplasty

Description
Genioplasty is plastic surgery on the chin and augmentation involves the addition of bone or other tissue by graft or implant to increase size. The physician places an implant or a graft onto the chin to augment or enlarge it. Various materials can be used, including tissue grafted from the patient's own body or taken from a tissue bank. Prosthetic devices may also be used. This procedure is most commonly performed from an intraoral approach. The physician makes an incision in the mandibular labial vestibule inside the lower lip. The mucosa is then reflected from the chin and the implanted material placed between the mucosa and the bone. A skin incision may also be made under the chin. The implant may be secured to the bone using wires or screws or may be left to be held in place by the surrounding tissue. The mucosa is then sutured simply.

Coding Clarification
Code 76.68 is used to report mentoplasty with graft or implant that is not further specified by the procedural documentation.

76.69　Other facial bone repair

Description
Code 76.69 is assigned to report other repair procedures on the facial bones that are not more precisely described by other codes in subcategory 76.6.

Coding Clarification
Assign 76.69 to report osteoplasty procedures on facial bones that are not further specified in the documentation.

76.7　Reduction of facial fracture

Coding Clarification
Subcategory 76.7 includes internal fixation.

Also code any synchronous bone graft (76.91) or synthetic implant (76.92) procedures performed.

To report reduction of fractured nasal bones, see 21.71-21.72.

76-84

76.70 Reduction of facial fracture, not otherwise specified

Description
Code76.70 is assigned when the documentation does not further specify the facial fracture reduction procedure.

Coding Clarification
Subcategory 76.7 includes internal fixation.

Code also any synchronous bone graft (76.91) or synthetic implant (76.92) procedures performed.

To report fracture reduction procedures of nasal bones, see 21.71-21.72.

Documentation Tip
Review the documentation for specific information regarding the procedure prior to final code selection in order to avoid improper use of the "not otherwise specified" code and to ensure accurate code assignment.

76.71 Closed reduction of malar and zygomatic fracture

Description
The physician percutaneously reduces a fracture of the malar or cheek area, including the zygomatic arch. A stab incision is made through the skin overlying the fracture area. Without soft tissue dissection, an instrument (e.g., bone hook, Carroll-Girard screw) is inserted and then used to lift, manipulate, and reduce the fracture. The stab incision is closed in a single layer.

Coding Clarification
Subcategory 76.7 includes internal fixation.

Code also any synchronous bone graft (76.91) or synthetic implant (76.92) procedures performed.

To report fracture reduction procedures of nasal bones, see 21.71-21.72.

76.72 Open reduction of malar and zygomatic fracture

Description
The physician reduces a depressed fracture of the zygomatic arch through an indirect approach. No internal fixation is used. A facial incision (e.g., Gillies approach) is made in the scalp extending beneath the temporalis fascia. An instrument is inserted through the incision, following underneath the fascia, and taken to the middle surface of the zygomatic arch. The instrument is swept along the arch upwardly and outwardly to reduce the fracture back into proper position. A transoral incision (e.g., Keen approach) may also be used, made in the posterior buccal sulcus. An elevator instrument is inserted through the incision and taken to the medial surface of the zygomatic arch, avoiding damage to branches of the facial nerve passing

beside the arch. The arch is then lifted laterally to its correct anatomic position. The facial incision is closed in layers. The transoral incision is closed in a single layer.

Coding Clarification
Code also any synchronous bone graft (76.91) or synthetic implant (76.92) procedures performed.

To report fracture reduction procedures of nasal bones, see 21.71-21.72.

76.73 Closed reduction of maxillary fracture

Description
The physician stabilizes and repairs a fracture of the maxillary alveolar bone without making incisions. The physician moves the fractured bone into the desired position manually. The fracture is stabilized by wiring both the involved teeth and adjacent stable teeth to an arch bar. Another technique utilizes dental composite bonding of both involved and stable teeth to a heavy, stainless steel wire. A customized acrylic splint may be used to stabilize the teeth. Intermaxillary fixation may also be applied.

Coding Clarification
Subcategory 76.7 includes internal fixation.

Code also any synchronous bone graft (76.91) or synthetic implant (76.92) procedures performed.

To report fracture reduction procedures of nasal bones, see 21.71-21.72.

76.74 Open reduction of maxillary fracture

Description
The physician uses open treatment to reposition and stabilize a maxillary fracture (LeFort I type). Transoral incisions are made in the maxillary buccal (cheek) vestibule to expose the maxillary fracture. The fracture is repositioned and stabilized with plates, screws, and/or wires. The transoral mucosal incision is closed in a single layer. A customized acrylic palatal splint may be wired to the maxillary teeth to stabilize the palatal fracture. Intermaxillary fixation may be applied.

Coding Clarification
Subcategory 76.7 includes internal fixation.

Code also any synchronous bone graft (76.91) or synthetic implant (76.92) procedures performed.

To report fracture reduction procedures of nasal bones, see 21.71-21.72.

76.75 Closed reduction of mandibular fracture

Description
The physician treats a mandibular fracture percutaneously by applying external fixation. The physician makes 0.5 cm stab incisions in the skin at

● New Code   ▲ Revised Code   ▶◀ Revised Text   © 2010 Ingenix

several points near the inferior border of the mandible on both sides of the fracture. Without soft tissue dissection, holes are drilled and threaded rods or pins are screwed into the holes and then used to manipulate and reduce the fracture. A metal or acrylic bar is connected to the protruding posts in a horizontal fashion, stabilizing the fracture.

Coding Clarification
Subcategory 76.7 includes internal fixation.

Code also any synchronous bone graft (76.91) or synthetic implant (76.92) procedures performed.

To report fracture reduction procedures of nasal bones, see 21.71-21.72.

76.76   Open reduction of mandibular fracture

Description
The physician treats a mandibular fracture through incisions and by applying external fixation. An intraoral approach may be used or a skin incision may be made overlying the area. The tissue is dissected to the bone and the fracture is exposed and repositioned directly. The fracture may also be approached through traumatic lacerations. Once the fracture is moved to the desired position, the physician makes 0.5 cm incisions in the skin at several points near the inferior border of the mandible on both sides of the fracture. Holes are drilled into the mandible and threaded rods or pins are screwed into the holes. A metal or acrylic bar is connected to the protruding posts in a horizontal fashion, stabilizing the fracture. Intermaxillary fixation may be placed.

Coding Clarification
Subcategory 76.7 includes internal fixation.

Code also any synchronous bone graft (76.91) or synthetic implant (76.92) procedures performed.

76.77   Open reduction of alveolar fracture

Description
The physician stabilizes and reduces a fracture of the mandibular or maxillary alveolar bone from an incisional access site. Intraoral incisions are made in the buccal vestibule to expose the fracture. The physician moves the fractured bone into the desired position manually. The fracture is stabilized by wiring both the involved teeth and adjacent stable teeth to an arch bar. A customized acrylic splint may be used to stabilize the teeth. The fractured alveolar bone may be reduced by wires, plates, and/or screws. Intermaxillary fixation may also be applied. The intraoral incision is closed in a single layer.

Coding Clarification
Subcategory 76.7 includes internal fixation.

Code also any synchronous bone graft (76.91) or synthetic implant (76.92) procedures performed.

To report fracture reduction procedures of nasal bones, see 21.71-21.72.

76.78   Other closed reduction of facial fracture

Description
Code 76.78 reports other closed facial fracture reduction procedures that are not more precisely described by other codes in subcategory 76.7. One example is a closed reduction of non-displaced or minimally displaced fracture of the orbital rims or walls that can be identified on x-ray. No incisions are necessary. The physician may realign the fractured bones by using manual manipulation or with bone hooks and Carroll-Girard screws. The realigned bones are stable and no internal fixation is necessary.

Documentation Tip
Review the documentation for specific information regarding the procedure prior to final code selection in order to ensure accurate code assignment.

76.79   Other open reduction of facial fracture

Description
Code 76.79 reports other closed reduction procedures of facial fracture that are not more precisely described by other codes in subcategory 76.7, such as an open reduction of the orbit rim or a wall fracture.

Coding Clarification
Subcategory 76.7 includes internal fixation.

Code also any synchronous bone graft (76.91) or synthetic implant (76.92) procedures performed.

To report open fracture reduction procedures of nasal bones, see 21.71.

76.9   Other operations on facial bones and joints

Coding Clarification
Subcategory 76.9 includes other procedures on the facial bones and joints that are not more precisely described by other codes in subcategory 76. Different types of facial bone grafting procedures are performed using a variety of surgical techniques and materials such as bone bank or heterogenous graft to facial bone or alloplastic implant.

76.91   Bone graft to facial bone

Description
Bone grafts offer physicians excellent building blocks when repairing skeletal problems. The physician makes an incision overlying the rib, ilium, fibula, or other site from which the autograft will be harvested. Fascia and muscles are incised and retracted. A knife, chisel, cutter, or saw may be used to obtain the bone graft, which will be prepared as needed for implantation. Cancellous bone chips may

76-84

be obtained as well. The incision is closed with sutures. In some cases, the graft is small; in others, the graft is larger than a dowel or a button.

Coding Clarification
Different types of facial bone grafting procedures are performed using a variety of surgical techniques and materials, such as bone bank or heterogenous graft to facial bone or alloplastic implant. Review the documentation for specific information regarding the procedure prior to final code selection in order to ensure accurate code assignment.

76.92   Insertion of synthetic implant in facial bone

Description
The physician uses prosthetic material to augment the body or angle of the mandible. The physician may use an intraoral approach or may make skin incisions extraorally below the body or angle of the mandible. The physician dissects tissues away and the bone of the body or angle is exposed. A synthetic material is placed on the mandible to augment the contours. The material is secured with screws or wires. The incisions are sutured simply.

Coding Clarification
Different types of facial bone grafting procedures are performed using a variety of surgical techniques and materials, such as bone bank or heterogenous graft to facial bone or alloplastic implant. Use 76.92 to report an alloplastic implant to facial bone.

76.93   Closed reduction of temporomandibular dislocation

Description
The physician repositions a dislocation of the temporomandibular joint. No incisions are made and no intermaxillary fixation is used. The physician corrects the dislocation manually to rearticulate the joint. In a more complicated dislocation that may be recurrent and require immobilization, the physician corrects the dislocation manually to rearticulate the joint. Intermaxillary fixation is then applied. The physician wires arch bars to the upper and lower dental arches with individual wire ligatures around the teeth or uses other wiring and splinting techniques and the jaws are wired together.

Coding Clarification
Different types of facial bone grafting procedures are performed using a variety of surgical techniques and materials, such as bone bank or heterogenous graft to facial bone or alloplastic implant. Review the documentation for specific information regarding the procedure prior to final code selection in order to ensure accurate code assignment.

76.94   Open reduction of temporomandibular dislocation

Description
The physician surgically repositions a dislocation of the temporomandibular joint. The physician exposes the joint by making an incision anterior to the contour of the ear or through the ear. Tissues are dissected to expose the joint. The condyle and disc are then moved into normal position using instruments. The ligaments may be repaired. The incision is then closed with layered sutures.

Coding Clarification
Different types of facial bone grafting procedures are performed using a variety of surgical techniques and materials, such as bone bank or heterogenous graft to facial bone or alloplastic implant. Review the documentation for specific information regarding the procedure prior to final code selection in order to ensure accurate code assignment.

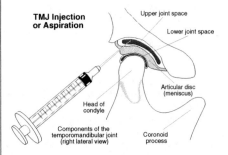

TMJ Injection or Aspiration

Upper joint space

Lower joint space

Articular disc (meniscus)

Head of condyle

Components of the temporomandibular joint (right lateral view)

Coronoid process

76.95   Other manipulation of temporomandibular joint

Description
The physician repositions a dislocation of the temporomandibular joint. No incisions are made and no intermaxillary fixation is used. The physician corrects the dislocation manually to rearticulate the joint.

Coding Clarification
Use 76.95 to report other manipulation procedures on the temporomandibular joint that are not more precisely described by other codes in subcategory 76.9.

76.96   Injection of therapeutic substance into temporomandibular joint

Description
After administering a local anesthetic, the physician inserts a needle through the skin and into a joint or bursa. A fluid may be injected for lavage or drug therapy. The needle is withdrawn and pressure is applied to stop any bleeding.

Coding Clarification
Joint or bursa injection or aspiration procedures can be performed on:

- Small joints such as the fingers or toes
- Intermediate joints including the wrist, elbow, ankle, olecranon bursa, or temporomandibular or acromioclavicular area
- Major joints including the shoulder, hip, knee joint, or subacromial bursa

76.97 Removal of internal fixation device from facial bone

Description
The physician makes a small incision overlying the site of the implant and removes the implant by pulling or unscrewing it. The incision is closed with sutures and/or Steri-strips. In some cases, deep dissection is carried down to visualize the implant, which is usually below the muscle level and within bone. The physician uses instruments to remove the implant from the bone. The incision is repaired in multiple layers using sutures, staples, and/or Steri-strips.

Coding Clarification
Do not assign 76.97 to report the removal of dental wiring (97.33) or an external mandibular fixation device NEC (97.36).

76.99 Other operations on facial bones and joints

Description
Code 76.99 is used to report other procedures on facial bones and joints that are not more precisely described by other codes in this chapter. This code is also reported when the documentation does not further specify the procedure.

Documentation Tip
Review the documentation for specific information regarding the procedure prior to final code selection in order to avoid improper use of an unspecified code and to ensure accurate code assignment.

---

77 Incision, excision, and division of other bones

Description
Use category 77 for incisions, excisions, and divisions of other bones. This category does not include the accessory sinuses, ear ossicles, facial bones, joint structures, mastoid, nasal bones, or skull. Each subcategory requires a fourth digit, 0–9, except for subcategory 77.5, to identify the site where the procedure was performed. Subcategory 77.5 Excision and repair of bunion and other toe deformities, also requires a fourth digit. Do not assign subcategory 77.6 Local excision of lesion or tissue of bone, for a debridement of a compound fracture, see 79.60–79.69. Use 77.65 for a core

decompression of the hip. In this procedure, a reaming device is introduced into the neck and head of the femur to remove a cored column of bone.

Coding Clarification
Each subcategory, except for 77.5, requires fourth digit 0 to 9 to identify the site where the procedure was performed. The following fourth-digit subclassification is for use with appropriate categories in section 77 to identify the site:

0   unspecified site
1   scapula, clavicle, and thorax [ribs and sternum]
2   humerus
3   radius and ulna
4   carpals and metacarpals
5   femur
6   patella
7   tibia and fibula
8   tarsals and metatarsals
9   other (pelvic bones, phalanges, vertebrae)

Codes in this category do not include laminectomy for decompression (03.09) or operations on accessory sinuses (22.00-22.9), ear ossicles (19.0-19.55), facial bones (76.01-76.99), joint structures (80.00-81.99), mastoid (19.9-20.99), nasal bones (21.00-21.99), and skull (01.01-02.99).

Documentation Tip
Similar to other sections of the procedure classification, the patient's diagnosis plays a role in code selection for subcategory 77.5 Excision and repair of bunion and other toe deformities. If the medical record documentation does not state the condition utilized in the procedural descriptor, it will be necessary to choose another code.

77.0 Sequestrectomy

Description
The physician removes infected portions of the bone due to a bone abscess or osteomyelitis. This infection often leaves open sinus tracts in the bone that require removal. An incision is made over the infected part of the bone and the underlying soft tissues are divided to expose the bone. The joint capsule may be incised if necessary. The periosteum is reflected back and the infected portion of bone is removed and irrigated. The excavation of bone may excise a crater-like piece, leave a small saucer-like shelf depression in the bone, or may remove a portion of the shaft (diaphysis) of a long bone. If a significant portion of bone is removed, the physician may choose to use bone graft material to fill the cavity left in the bone. The periosteum is closed over the bone, the soft tissues are sutured closed, and a soft dressing is applied.

76-84

Coding Clarification

Subcategory 77.0 requires a fourth digit, 0–9, to identify the site where the procedure was performed. The following fourth-digit subclassification is for use to identify the site.

0   unspecified site
1   scapula, clavicle, and thorax [ribs and sternum]
2   humerus
3   radius and ulna
4   carpals and metacarpals
5   femur
6   patella
7   tibia and fibula
8   tarsals and metatarsals
9   other (pelvic bones, phalanges, vertebrae)

Coding Scenario

The physician made an incision overlying the sequestered area of bone in the clavicle. Once the skin and soft tissues were reflected back, a small window was cut into the bone to gain access to the sequestrum, a necrosed piece of bone separated from sound bone. All purulent material and scarred or necrotic tissue was removed. The remaining space was filled with surrounding soft tissues or free tissue transfer. The area was irrigated and an antibiotic solution was used to prevent further infection. The wound was closed loosely over drains. The arm was positioned in a sling and protected to prevent fracture of the clavicle.

Code Assignment:

77.01 Sequestrectomy of the scapula, clavicle, and thorax [ribs and sternum]

77.1   Other incision of bone without division

Description

The physician makes an incision into bone (e.g., to drain an infected bursa). The physician incises the bone cortex of infected bone in the forearm and/or wrist to treat an abscess or osteomyelitis. The physician makes an incision over the affected area. Dissection is carried down through the soft tissues to expose the bone. The periosteum is split and reflected back from the bone overlying the infected area. A curette may be used to scrape away the abscess or infected portion down to healthy bony tissue or drill holes may be made through the cortex into the medullary canal in a window outline around the infected or abscessed bone. The area is drained and debrided of infected bony and soft tissue. The physician then irrigates the area with antibiotic solution, the periosteum is closed over the bone, and the soft tissues are sutured closed; or the wound is packed and left open, allowing the area to drain.

Secondary closure is performed approximately three weeks later. Dressings are changed daily. A splint may be applied to limit wrist motion.

Coding Clarification

Assign codes from subcategory 77.1 to report reopening of an osteotomy site.

Subcategory 77.1 codes are not assigned to report aspiration of bone marrow (41.31, 41.91) or removal of an internal fixation device (78.60-78.69).

Subcategory 77.1 requires a fourth digit, 0–9, to identify the site where the procedure was performed. The following fourth-digit subclassification is for use to identify the site:

0   unspecified site
1   scapula, clavicle, and thorax [ribs and sternum]
2   humerus
3   radius and ulna
4   carpals and metacarpals
5   femur
6   patella
7   tibia and fibula
8   tarsals and metatarsals
9   other (pelvic bones, phalanges, vertebrae)

77.2   Wedge osteotomy

Description

The physician performs an osteotomy, which is removal of a wedge-shaped piece of bone. The physician makes an incision in the skin overlying the affected area. Tissue is dissected down to the bone. Using a surgical saw or other sharp instrument, the physician cuts through the bone. Surgical screws, a metal plate, or wires may secure the cut bone in the correct position. The wound is irrigated and the skin is closed in layers.

Coding Clarification

Use 77.51 to report wedge osteotomy for hallux valgus.

Subcategory 77.2 requires a fourth digit, 0–9, to identify the site where the procedure was performed. The following fourth-digit subclassification is for use to identify the site:

0   unspecified site
1   scapula, clavicle, and thorax [ribs and sternum]
2   humerus
3   radius and ulna
4   carpals and metacarpals
5   femur
6   patella
7   tibia and fibula

8   tarsals and metatarsals

9   other (pelvic bones, phalanges, vertebrae))

Osteotomy for Kyphotic Spine

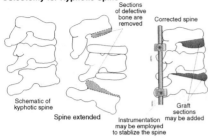

Sections of defective bone are removed

Corrected spine

Schematic of kyphotic spine

Spine extended

Instrumentation may be employed to stablize the spine

Graft sections may be added

77.3   Other division of bone

Description

The physician performs an osteotomy (bone cut) of a bone that is not healing or has healed in an unacceptable position. The physician makes an incision in the skin overlying the affected area. Tissue is dissected down to the bone. Using a surgical saw or other sharp instrument, the physician cuts through the bone. Surgical screws, a metal plate, or wires may secure the cut bone in the correct position. The physician harvests a bone graft from the patient through a separate incision. The physician then repairs the surgically created graft donor site. The graft is placed in the clavicle. Surgical screws, plates, or other hardware secure the bone graft. The incision is closed in multiple layers.

Coding Clarification

Use subcategory 77.3 to report osteoarthrotomy.

Subcategory 77.3 is not used to report clavicotomy of fetus (73.8), laminotomy or incision of vertebra (03.01-03.09), or pubiotomy to assist delivery (73.94).

Sternotomy performed incidental to a thoracic operation is not reported separately.

Coding Clarification

Subcategory 77.3 requires a fourth digit, 0-9, to identify the site where the procedure was performed. The following fourth-digit subclassification is for use to identify the site:

0   unspecified site

1   scapula, clavicle, and thorax [ribs and sternum]

2   humerus

3   radius and ulna

4   carpals and metacarpals

5   femur

6   patella

7   tibia and fibula

8   tarsals and metatarsals

9   other (pelvic bones, phalanges, vertebrae)

77.4   Biopsy of bone

Description

The physician usually performs a biopsy on bone to confirm a suspected growth, disease, or infection. The physician normally uses local anesthesia; however, general anesthesia may be used. The physician places a large needle into the spinous process or other superficial bone to obtain the sample. For sampling a deeper lying bone, such as a vertebra, an exploring needle is passed through a larger needle to the desired depth and a piece of tissue is removed for testing. Radiographs are sometimes used to confirm the placement of the needle.

Coding Clarification

Subcategory 77.4 requires a fourth digit, 0-9, to identify the site where the procedure was performed. The following fourth-digit subclassification is for use to identify the site:

0   unspecified site

1   scapula, clavicle, and thorax [ribs and sternum]

2   humerus

3   radius and ulna

4   carpals and metacarpals

5   femur

6   patella

7   tibia and fibula

8   tarsals and metatarsals

9   other (pelvic bones, phalanges, vertebrae)

Documentation Tip

Different approaches are taken for vertebral biopsies, based on differing levels of vertebrae. The top three cervical vertebrae are approached from a pharyngeal or anterior approach. The lower four cervical vertebrae are approached from a lateral direction. Thoracic and lumbar vertebras are approached from behind and to the right to avoid major arteries.

Review the documentation for specific information regarding the procedure prior to final code selection in order to ensure accurate code assignment.

Coding Guidance

AHA: 2Q, '98, 12; 3Q, '06, 13

76-84

77.5 Excision and repair of bunion and other toe deformities

Description
The physician corrects a hallux rigidus deformity and performs a cheilectomy. Hallux rigidus is a condition caused by degenerative (DJD) arthritic changes at the first metatarsophalangeal joint. The condition causes pain, limited range of motion, and dorsiflexion. In the context of this procedure, a cheilectomy refers to excision of part of the lip of the first metatarsophalangeal joint. The podiatrist makes a dorsal incision over the first metatarsophalangeal joint. The extensor hallucis longus tendon is retracted and the joint capsule is entered. Osteophytes and part of the metatarsal head are excised. Bony irregularities may be removed using a chisel, and edges smoothed with a rasp. When adequate dorsiflexion (60-80 degrees) is obtained, the capsule is closed, the tendon is returned to its correct anatomical position, and the skin is closed with sutures.

Coding Clarification
Subcategory 77.5 requires fourth-digit specificity to identify the type of procedure performed.

A bunion, or bunion deformity, is an enlargement of the joint at the base of the big toe comprised of bone and soft tissue that causes pain to the first metatarsal head.

A bunionectomy is the surgical removal of a bunion.

77.51 Bunionectomy with soft tissue correction and osteotomy of the first metatarsal

Description
The physician makes an incision to remove a big toe bony prominence and performs reconstruction with soft tissue. Surgical treatment consists of removing bone from the first metatarsal head. Some cases require cutting and relocation of the joint.

Coding Clarification
A bunion, or bunion deformity, is an enlargement of the joint at the base of the big toe comprised of bone and soft tissue that causes pain to the first metatarsal head.

A bunionectomy is the surgical removal of a bunion.

77.52 Bunionectomy with soft tissue correction and arthrodesis

Description
The physician removes a big toe bony prominence and performs a reconstruction with soft tissue and joint fixation. In one technique, the physician treats a bunion of the foot using a Lapidus-type procedure in which the joint between the first metatarsal bone and first cuneiform bone is fused. The physician makes an incision in the skin between the first and

second toes on the top of the foot. The incision is extended deep to the first metatarsophalangeal joint. The physician releases the contracted structures of the lateral joint. A second incision is then made in the top of the foot over the first metatarsocuneiform joint. The joint capsule is exposed and opened. The articular cartilage of the joint is removed. The ends of the bones are fashioned so they fit intimately together. The joint and bones of the big toe are then manipulated into alignment. Fixation devices are needed to fuse the metatarsal and cuneiform bones. Prior to closing the incisions, the sesamoid bones are examined and removed as needed. The wounds are irrigated and closed in layers.

Coding Clarification
A bunion, or bunion deformity, is an enlargement of the joint at the base of the big toe comprised of bone and soft tissue that typically causes pain at the first metatarsal head.

A bunionectomy is the surgical removal of a bunion.

Coding Scenario
The physician fused the joint between the great toe and the first metatarsal bone. A longitudinal incision was made on the dorsal surface of the first toe. It was deepened through the subcutaneous tissue and fascia to the first metatarsophalangeal joint. The nerves and tendons were retracted. A capsulotomy was performed. The physician made parallel cuts of the metatarsal with a saw or osteotome. The two cuts were placed together in the desired alignment and position. Fixation devices hold the bones in position. The wound was irrigated and closed in layers.

Code Assignment:

77.52   Bunionectomy with soft tissue correction and arthrodesis

77.53 Other bunionectomy with soft tissue correction

Description
The physician treats a bunion of the foot with tendon transplants. The physician makes an incision over the top of the foot between the first and second toes. The incision is carried deep to the metatarsophalangeal joint. The extensor tendon of the big toe is identified and cut to restore the toe to its correct alignment. The extensor tendon is then reattached (transplanted) to the head of the metatarsal bone. Other tendons may also be cut and reattached until correct anatomical alignment is achieved. Any contracted structures are released as needed. The sesamoid bones are examined and removed as necessary. A second incision is typically made over the inside of the big toe. This incision is carried deep to the bony eminence, or bunion, which is surgically removed. The proximal phalanx and

● New Code   ▲ Revised Code   ▶◀ Revised Text   © 2010 Ingenix

metatarsal bone are fused. The incisions are thoroughly irrigated and closed in layers.

Coding Clarification
Code 77.53 is assigned when the procedure is not more precisely described by other codes in this subcategory. This code is also reported when the documentation does not further specify the bunion procedure.

Documentation Tip
Review the documentation for specific information regarding the procedure prior to final code selection in order to avoid improper use of the "not otherwise specified" code.

77.54   Excision or correction of bunionette

Description
The physician performs a resection with osteotomy of the fifth metatarsal head including imbrication of the capsule, by exposing the joint. The physician makes a lateral incision over the distal third of the fifth metatarsal bone to expose the metatarsal head. An osteotome is used to remove the lateral extension of the bone (bunionette). The cut is made along the shaft of the bone. The wound is irrigated and the soft tissues are sutured. Soft dressing is applied and weight bearing is allowed as tolerated.

Coding Clarification
A bunion is an enlargement of the joint at the base of the big toe comprised of bone and soft tissue. A bunionette is the same condition but on the outside of the foot at the base of the little toe. A bunionette is also called tailor's bunion.

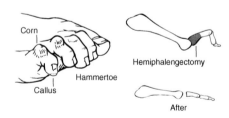

77.56   Repair of hammer toe

Description
The physician repairs a claw-like toe defect using joint fusion or partial removal of the toe via a traction technique. The physician makes an elliptical incision over the proximal interphalangeal joint 5 to 6 mm wide. A portion of the extensor tendon and joint capsule under the skin is removed. The collateral ligaments are cut to allow the toe to be flexed to 90 degrees. The head and neck of the

proximal phalanx are removed with a small power blade saw and the ends of the bones are smoothed. The toe is checked for ROM and the extensor tendon is reattached and the incision is closed with sutures.

Coding Clarification
Hammertoe describes an abnormal flexion posture of the proximal interphalangeal joint of one of the lesser toes.

Use 77.56 to report fusion repair, phalangectomy (partial), or filleting of a hammer toe.

77.57   Repair of claw toe

Description
The physician repairs a claw-like toe defect by joint fusion, partial removal of toe, joint capsule incision, or lengthening of fibrous muscle attachment. The physician performs a Jones type procedure. The physician fuses the interphalangeal joint of the great toe and transfers the extensor hallucis longus tendon from its insertion on the phalanges to the first metatarsal bone. An incision is made on the dorsal aspect of the great toe and distal first metatarsal. It is continued deep to the extensor hallucis longus tendon. The physician fuses the interphalangeal joint. Fixation devices hold the fusion in place for healing. The neck of the first metatarsal bone is identified dorsally. The extensor hallucis longus tendon is identified dorsally. The extensor hallucis longus tendon is attached to the metatarsal using any of a variety of fixation devices. The incision is irrigated and closed in layers.

Coding Clarification
Surgical procedures to correct toe defects and deformities are performed using a variety of surgical techniques and approaches, such as fusion, phalangectomy (partial), capsulotomy, and tendon lengthening techniques. Review the documentation for specific information regarding the procedure prior to final code selection in order to ensure accurate code assignment.

77.58   Other excision, fusion, and repair of toes

Description
An elliptical shaped incision is made in the skin under the fifth toe. The soft tissues are reflected back to expose the underlying structures. The proximal phalanx is removed leaving a space between the base of the metatarsal and the distal phalanx. The deep tissues and skin incisions are closed with sutures.

Coding Clarification
Use 77.58 to report a cockup toe repair, an overlapping toe repair, or other repair with the use of prosthetic materials.

76-84

77.59   Other bunionectomy

Description
Code 77.59 reports other bunionectomy procedures that are not more precisely described by other codes in subcategory 77.5, such as resection of the hallux valgus joint with insertion of a prosthesis.

77.6   Local excision of lesion or tissue of bone

Description
A bone cyst or benign tumor is removed. The physician makes an incision in the area overlying the cyst or tumor. The skin and underlying soft tissues are reflected back to expose the periosteum, which is separated from the bone. Curettes or osteotomes are used to scrape or cut the lesion from the bone. Once the benign tumor or cyst is removed and healthy bone tissue is present, the periosteum is repositioned and the incision is repaired in multiple layers. If the bone defect created requires a graft for repair, the physician obtains the necessary size bone graft from a separate donor site on the patient (usually the iliac crest) and packs it into the site where the tumor or bone cyst was removed or uses a bone bank allograft.

Coding Clarification
Do not assign subcategory 77.6 codes to report a biopsy of a bone (77.40-77.49) or debridement of a compound fracture (79.60-79.69).

Subcategory 77.6 requires a fourth digit, 0–9, to identify the site where the procedure was performed. The following fourth-digit subclassification is for use to identify the site:

0   unspecified site
1   scapula, clavicle, and thorax [ribs and sternum]
2   humerus
3   radius and ulna
4   carpals and metacarpals
5   femur
6   patella
7   tibia and fibula
8   tarsals and metatarsals
9   other (pelvic bones, phalanges, vertebrae)

Coding Guidance
AHA: S-O, '85, 4; 1Q, '99, 8; 2Q, '00, 18; 3Q, '01, 9; 1Q, '02, 3; 4Q, '04, 128; 1Q, '08, 4

77.7   Excision of bone for graft

Description
Bone grafts offer physicians excellent building blocks when repairing skeletal problems. The physician makes an incision overlying the rib, ilium, fibula, or other site from which the autograft will be harvested. Fascia and muscles are incised and retracted. A knife, chisel, cutter, or saw may be used to obtain the bone graft, which will be prepared as needed for implantation. Cancellous bone chips may be obtained, as well. The incision is closed with sutures.

Coding Clarification
A bone graft can be taken from another part of the body, such as the hip, rib, or skull. In some cases, the graft is larger than a dowel or a button. Other materials may also be used such as prosthetic implants or donor bone.

Subcategory 77.7 requires a fourth digit, 0–9, to identify the site where the procedure was performed. The following fourth-digit subclassification is for use to identify the site:

0   unspecified site
1   scapula, clavicle, and thorax [ribs and sternum]
2   humerus
3   radius and ulna
4   carpals and metacarpals
5   femur
6   patella
7   tibia and fibula
8   tarsals and metatarsals
9   other (pelvic bones, phalanges, vertebrae)

Coding Guidance
AHA: 4Q, '99, 11, 13; 2Q, '00, 12, 13; 2Q, '07, 6; 1Q, '08, 5; 4Q, '99, 11, 13; 2Q, '00, 12, 13; 2Q, '02, 16; 4Q, '02, 107, 109-110; 2Q, '03, 13; 3Q, '03, 19; 2Q, '07, 5; 1Q, '08, 5

77.8   Other partial ostectomy

Description
Assign subcategory 77.8 for other partial ostectomy procedures that are not more precisely described by other codes in category 77, such as condylectomy.

For example, the physician performs a partial excision of the talus or calcaneus, a tarsal or metatarsal bone, or the phalanx of a toe to remove infected bone or bony prominence. An incision is made over the affected part of the foot, ankle, heel, or toe and the underlying soft tissues are divided to expose the bone. The periosteum is reflected and the infected portion of bone is removed and irrigated. The excavation of bone may excise a crater-like piece, leave a small saucer-like shelf depression in the bone, or may remove a portion of the shaft (diaphysis) of a long bone. If a significant portion of bone is removed, the physician may use bone graft material to fill the cavity left in the bone. The periosteum is closed over the bone, the soft tissues are sutured closed, and a soft dressing is applied. A short leg cast may be applied to keep the foot and ankle in position.

● New Code   ▲ Revised Code   ►◄ Revised Text   © 2010 Ingenix

Coding Clarification

Subcategory 77.8 requires a fourth digit, 0–9, to identify the site where the procedure was performed. The following fourth-digit subclassification is for use to identify the site:

0   unspecified site
1   scapula, clavicle, and thorax [ribs and sternum]
2   humerus
3   radius and ulna
4   carpals and metacarpals
5   femur
6   patella
7   tibia and fibula
8   tarsals and metatarsals
9   other (pelvic bones, phalanges, vertebrae)

Do not assign codes from subcategory 77.8 to report the following procedures:

- Amputation (84.00-84.19, 84.91)
- Arthrectomy (80.90-80.99)
- Excision of bone ends associated with arthrodesis (81.00-81.39) or arthroplasty (81.40-81.59, 81.71-81.85)
- Excision of cartilage (80.5-80.6, 80.80-80.99)
- Excision of head of femur with synchronous replacement (00.70-00.73, 81.51-81.53)
- Hemilaminectomy (03.01-03.09)
- Laminectomy (03.01-03.09)
- Ostectomy for hallux valgus (77.51-77.59)
- Partial amputation of the finger (84.01), thumb (84.02), or toe (84.11)

Resection of ribs incidental to thoracic operation is not separately reported.

Partial ostectomy that is performed incidentally to another operation is also not separately reportable.

Coding Guidance

AHA: 2Q, '02, 8

77.9   Total ostectomy

Description

In one example, excision of the femoral head and/or neck is performed on patients with severe hip dysplasia or pain such as that from DJD or subluxation. The femoral neck ostectomy involves cutting the femoral head off and removing it. An incision is made at the level of the deformity and a small line is cut longitudinally in the shaft of the femur. The femoral head and a portion of the femoral neck are removed so that bone-to-bone contact does not occur. Fibrous scar tissue forms around the end of the bone as the muscles, ligaments, and tendons hold the bone in place and the remaining joint space

fills with fibrous scar tissue that acts as padding between the hip and the femur. This procedure eliminates the bone-on-bone contact between the femur and acetabulum.

Coding Clarification

Subcategory 77.9 requires a fourth digit, 0–9, to identify the site where the procedure was performed. The following fourth-digit subclassification is for use to identify the site:

0   unspecified site
1   scapula, clavicle, and thorax [ribs and sternum]
2   humerus
3   radius and ulna
4   carpals and metacarpals
5   femur
6   patella
7   tibia and fibula
8   tarsals and metatarsals
9   other (pelvic bones, phalanges, vertebrae)

Do not assign subcategory 77.9 for amputation of a limb (84.00-84.19, 84.91).

Do not report ostectomy that is incidental to other operation.

Coding Scenario

A physician performed a femoral head and neck ostectomy on a patient to treat hip pain secondary to an extensive acetabular carcinoma.

Code Assignment:

77.95   Total ostectomy of femur

78   Other operations on bones, except facial bones

Description

The codes under category 78 classify bone grafts, application of external fixation device, limb shortening and limb lengthening procedures, other repair of plastic operations on bone, internal fixation of bone without fracture reduction, removal of implanted devices from bone, and other operations. For each of the subcategories, except the two for limb shortening and limb lengthening procedures, assign a fourth digit from 0–9 for the site where the operation occurred. Subcategories 78.2 and 78.3 also require fourth digits but are limited to 0, 2–5, and 7–9. The following fourth-digit subclassification is for use with categories in section 78 to identify the site.

0   unspecified site
1   scapula, clavicle, and thorax [ribs and sternum]
2   humerus

76-84

3   radius and ulna
4   carpals and metacarpals
5   femur
6   patella
7   tibia and fibula
8   tarsals and metatarsals
9   other (pelvic bones, phalanges of foot and hand, vertebrae)

Coding Clarification
Category 78 should not be used for operations on the accessory sinuses (22.00-22.9), facial bones (76.01-76.99), joint structures (80.00-81.99), nasal bones (21.00-21.99), or skull (01.01-02.99).

78.0 Bone graft

Description
Bone grafts offer physicians excellent building blocks when repairing skeletal problems. A bone graft can be taken from another part of the body, such as the hip, rib, or skull. A bone bank graft (autogenous, heterogenous) or other materials such as prosthetic implants or donor bone may also be used.

For example, the physician makes an incision overlying the rib, ilium, fibula, or other site from which the autograft will be harvested. Fascia and muscles are incised and retracted. A knife, chisel, cutter, or saw may be used to obtain the bone graft, which will be prepared as needed for implantation. Cancellous bone chips may be obtained, as well. The incision is closed with sutures. In some cases, the graft is larger than a dowel or a button.

Coding Clarification
The following fourth-digit subclassification is required to identify the site:

0   unspecified site
1   scapula, clavicle, and thorax [ribs and sternum]
2   humerus
3   radius and ulna
4   carpals and metacarpals
5   femur
6   patella
7   tibia and fibula
8   tarsals and metatarsals
9   other (pelvic bones, phalanges of foot and hand, vertebrae)

Assign a code for excision of bone for graft (77.70–77.79) in addition to the code for the bone graft, 78.0x.

Use 78.0x for autograft of bone and 41.01 for autograft of bone marrow.

Use 78.0x for placement of interpore bone substitute at the fracture site.

Do not assign subcategory 78.0 for a bone graft for bone lengthening (78.30-78.39) or when performed with debridement of bone graft site or removal of sclerosed, fibrous, or necrotic bone or tissue.

Also assign a code for any excision of bone for graft (77.70-77.79).

Coding Scenario
The physician made an incision overlying a bone cyst in the wrist. The skin and underlying soft tissues were reflected back to expose the periosteum, which was separated from the bone. Curettes or osteotomes were used to scrape or cut the lesion from the bone. Once the cyst was removed and healthy bone tissue was present, the periosteum was repositioned and the incision was repaired in multiple layers.

Code Assignment:

733.20   Cyst of bone, unspecified
78.04   Bone graft of carpals and metacarpals

Coding Guidance
AHA: 1Q, '91, 3; 3Q, '94, 10; 2Q, '98, 12; 2Q, '02, 11

78.1   Application of external fixator device

Description
The physician applies an external fixation system to help a fracture or joint injury heal. This procedure is performed in addition to a coded treatment of fracture or joint injury unless listed as part of the basic procedure. This procedure involves the use of an external fixator to stabilize an injury such as a simple fracture. One or more pins or wires may by used. Small stab incisions are made in the skin and a drill is used to make a hole into the bone. Each pin or wire is inserted into the bone through the drill holes and secured to an external fixation device. This holds the fracture or joint in a stable position.

Coding Clarification
The following fourth-digit subclassification is required to identify the site:

0   unspecified site
1   scapula, clavicle, and thorax [ribs and sternum]
2   humerus
3   radius and ulna
4   carpals and metacarpals
5   femur
6   patella
7   tibia and fibula
8   tarsals and metatarsals
9   other (pelvic bones, phalanges of foot and hand, vertebrae)

Assign subcategory 78.1 for fixator procedures with insertion of pins/wires/screws into bone.

● New Code   ▲ Revised Code   ►◄ Revised Text   © 2010 Ingenix

76-84

Uniplane fixation or multiplane fixation may be applied.

Code also any type of fixator device, if known (84.71-84.73).

Do not assign 78.1 for other immobilization, pressure, and attention to wound (93.51-93.59).

Coding Guidance
AHA: 2Q, '94, 4; 4Q, 05, 129

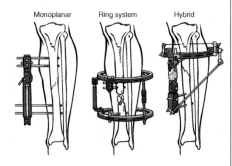

Monoplanar   Ring system   Hybrid

78.2   Limb shortening procedures

Description
In one procedure, the physician performs osteoplasty of the humerus for shortening or lengthening. An incision is made through the skin, fascia, and muscle in the upper arm over the humeral shaft. Vessels and nerves are exposed and retracted. Dissection continues to expose the shaft of the humerus. An osteotomy is made at the determined point on the humerus. The physician removes a wedge of bone. To shorten the humeral shaft, a plate is attached to the distal segment with screws. Reduction forceps are used to hold and compress the osteotomy while the plate is attached to the proximal fragment with screws. To lengthen the bone, the segments are retracted, usually 2 to 3 mm, and fixed at that distance with plates and screws. X-rays are used to check rotational alignment of the segments. Drain tubes are inserted, the incision is repaired in multiple layers with sutures, staples, and/or Steri-strips, and the arm is immobilized.

Coding Clarification
Subcategory 78.2 reports epiphyseal stapling, open epiphysiodesis, and percutaneous epiphysiodesis.

Subcategories 78.2 and 78.3 also require fourth digits but are limited to 0, 2-5, and 7-9:

0   unspecified site

1   scapula, clavicle, and thorax [ribs and sternum]
2   humerus
3   radius and ulna
4   carpals and metacarpals
5   femur
6   patella
7   tibia and fibula
8   tarsals and metatarsals
9   other (pelvic bones, phalanges of foot and hand, vertebrae)

78.3   Limb lengthening procedures

Description
Codes from this subcategory report limb lengthening procedures of various sites.

Femoral shortening or lengthening techniques equalize leg lengths or treat malunions of the femur. In some cases, both lengthening and shortening are performed. For femoral lengthening, two puncture wounds are made laterally in the distal and proximal femur. Two holes at each end are drilled in the bone, and a screw is inserted in each drill hole. The physician makes a lateral longitudinal incision 6 to 8 cm long to expose the femur. At the osteotomy site, an oscillating saw cuts through the femur. The Wagner distraction apparatus is then attached to the two sets of screws, so that the apparatus is 1 to 2 cm lateral to the thigh. The incision is repaired in multiple layers. The device is then distracted up to 5 to 6 mm immediately. The apparatus is operated by a knob. Lengthening is about 1.5 mm or 1 cm per week. When the appearance of the femur is normal and the medullary has been reestablished, the plate and screws are removed.

Coding Clarification
Subcategories 78.2 and 78.3 also require fourth digits but are limited to 0, 2-5, and 7-9:

0   unspecified site
2   humerus
3   radius and ulna
4   carpals and metacarpals
5   femur
7   tibia and fibula
8   tarsals and metatarsals
9   other (pelvic bones, phalanges of foot and hand, vertebrae)

Subcategory 78.3 reports bone graft procedures with or without internal fixation devices or osteotomy and distraction technique with or without corticotomy/osteotomy.

Code also any application of an external fixation device (78.10-78.19).

76-84

78.4 Other repair or plastic operations on bone

Description

Subcategory 78.4 reports plastic or malunion or nonunion fracture repair procedures on bone that are not more precisely described by other codes in category 78.

Coding Clarification

The following fourth-digit subclassification is required to identify the site:

0   unspecified site
1   scapula, clavicle, and thorax [ribs and sternum]
2   humerus
3   radius and ulna
4   carpals and metacarpals
5   femur
6   patella
7   tibia and fibula
8   tarsals and metatarsals
9   other (pelvic bones, phalanges of foot and hand, vertebrae)

Code 78.4x does not include application of external fixation device (78.10-78.19), limb lengthening procedures (78.30-78.39), limb shortening procedures (78.20-78.29), osteotomy (77.3), reconstruction of thumb (82.61-82.69), repair of pectus deformity (34.74), or repair with bone graft (78.00-78.09).

Coding Guidance

AHA: 4Q, '88, 11; 3Q, '91, 20; 4Q, '88, 11; 3Q, '91, 20; 1Q, '97, 5; 4Q, '99, 22; 2Q, '02, 14, 15, 16; 3Q, '02, 12; 3Q, '04, 9

78.5 Internal fixation of bone without fracture reduction

Description

In one example, the physician repairs a nonunion or malunion of the humerus without using a graft or with an iliac or other autograft. The physician exposes the nonunion or malunion of the humerus by making a 10 to 15 cm longitudinal incision through the skin, fascia, and muscle over the fracture site. With a reciprocating saw, the bone is divided through the nonunion. The fragments are aligned. A compression plate is centered over the fracture and screws are inserted. In some cases, a bone graft is needed to help heal the fracture due to bone loss. Autogenous iliac bone is typically used, but proximal tibia grafts may also be used. Both require a separate incision and wound closure of the harvest site. The physician uses an osteotome to harvest strips of bone, which are then placed around the ends of the humeral fracture in addition to the compression plate for internal fixation. The incision

is repaired in multiple layers with sutures, staples, and/or Steri-strips. The limb is immobilized.

Coding Clarification

The following fourth-digit subclassification is required to identify the site:

0   unspecified site
1   scapula, clavicle, and thorax [ribs and sternum]
2   humerus
3   radius and ulna
4   carpals and metacarpals
5   femur
6   patella
7   tibia and fibula
8   tarsals and metatarsals
9   other (pelvic bones, phalanges of foot and hand, vertebrae)

Assign subcategory 78.5 for internal fixation of bone (prophylactic), reinsertion of internal fixation device, or revision of displaced or broken fixation device.

Do not assign subcategory 78.5 for arthroplasty and arthrodesis (81.00-81.85), bone graft (78.00-78.09), limb shortening procedures (78.20-78.29), ▶insertion of sternal fixation device with rigid plates (84.94),◀ or when performed for fracture reduction (79.10-79.19, 79.30-79.59).

Documentation Tip

▶Internal fixation procedures include those specified as prophylactic cephalomedullary trochanteric nail fixation and intramedullary nail fixation.◀

Coding Guidance

AHA: 2Q, '94, 4; 2Q, '99, 11; 4Q, '99, 13; 2Q, '03, 15; 3Q, 04, 6; ▶2Q, '10, 6◀

78.6 Removal of implanted device from bone

Description

Various types of procedures are performed to remove implanted devices from bone. The physician makes an incision overlying the site of the implant. Deep dissection is carried down to visualize the implant, which is usually below the muscle level and within bone. The physician uses instruments to remove the implant from the bone. The incision is repaired in multiple layers using sutures, staples, and/or Steri-strips. In some cases, the physician removes the external fixation frame and pulls pins out manually while the patient is under anesthesia. In other cases, the physician uses instruments to remove the implant from the bone.

Coding Clarification

The following fourth-digit subclassification is required to identify the site:

0   unspecified site

76-84

1   scapula, clavicle, and thorax [ribs and sternum]
2   humerus
3   radius and ulna
4   carpals and metacarpals
5   femur
6   patella
7   tibia and fibula
8   tarsals and metatarsals
9   other (pelvic bones, phalanges of foot and hand, vertebrae)

Assign subcategory 78.6 for removal of pedicle screw(s) used in spinal fusion, external fixator device (invasive), internal fixation device, bone growth stimulator (invasive), or an internal limb lengthening device.

Do not assign subcategory 78.6 for removal of a cast, splint, and traction device (Kirschner wire) (Steinmann pin) (97.88) or removal of skull tongs or a halo traction device (02.95). This subcategory also excludes the removal of a posterior spinal motion preservation device (facet replacement, pedicle-based dynamic stabilization, interspinous process) (80.09).

Coding Guidance
AHA: 1Q, '00, 15; 2Q, '00, 18; 4Q, '02, 110; 2Q, '03, 14

78.7   Osteoclasis

Description
The physician performs a surgical breaking or rebreaking of a bone to correct a deformity (e.g., to repair a nonunion or malunion of the femur). The physician makes a lateral incision to expose the femur. If there is no distortion of the intramedullary canal, intramedullary nailing is performed for fixation of the nonunion. If failed internal fixation is present, the physician removes the plates and screws. If there is malalignment of the medullary canal, a compression plate and screws are used for repair. If there is a loss of bone, the physician harvests bone with an osteotome from the iliac crest or from the femur itself and closes the surgically created donor site. Copious amounts of bone are placed around the nonunion site. The incision is repaired in multiple layers and a temporary drain is applied.

Coding Clarification
The following fourth-digit subclassification is required to identify the site:

0   unspecified site
1   scapula, clavicle, and thorax [ribs and sternum]
2   humerus
3   radius and ulna
4   carpals and metacarpals

5   femur
6   patella
7   tibia and fibula
8   tarsals and metatarsals
9   other (pelvic bones, phalanges of foot and hand, vertebrae)

Osteoclasis occurs during normal growth of bone or as part of healing at a fracture site.

78.8   Diagnostic procedures on bone, not elsewhere classified

Description
Codes in subcategory 78.8 are used to report diagnostic procedures on bones that are not more precisely described by other codes in category 78. Codes from this subcategory are also reported when the documentation does not further specify the diagnostic procedure.

Coding Clarification
The following fourth-digit subclassification is required to identify the site:

0   unspecified site
1   scapula, clavicle, and thorax [ribs and sternum]
2   humerus
3   radius and ulna
4   carpals and metacarpals
5   femur
6   patella
7   tibia and fibula
8   tarsals and metatarsals
9   other (pelvic bones, phalanges of foot and hand, vertebrae)

Do not assign subcategory 78.8 for biopsy of bone (77.40-77.49), magnetic resonance imaging (88.94), microscopic examination of specimen from bone (91.51-91.59), radioisotope scan (92.14), skeletal x-ray (87.21-87.29, 87.43, 88.21-88.33), or thermography (88.83).

Documentation Tip
Review the documentation for specific information regarding the procedure prior to final code selection in order to avoid improper use of the "not otherwise specified" code and to ensure accurate code assignment.

78.9   Insertion of bone growth stimulator

Description
Electrical bone growth stimulation involves the use of a device that uses an electric current to stimulate the growth of bone tissue. These devices are used for the treatment of many orthopedic conditions such as fracture non-unions, bone fusion procedures, and other conditions where bone growth is abnormal.

76-84

The device is implanted surgically into the bone at the area requiring treatment. One type of implanted device uses a wire coil that is wrapped around the bone site.

Coding Clarification
The following fourth-digit subclassification is required to identify the site:

0   unspecified site
1   scapula, clavicle, and thorax [ribs and sternum]
2   humerus
3   radius and ulna
4   carpals and metacarpals
5   femur
6   patella
7   tibia and fibula
8   tarsals and metatarsals
9   other (pelvic bones, phalanges of foot and hand, vertebrae)

Current treatment includes invasive, semi-invasive, and non-invasive electrical bone growth stimulation devices. The different types of electrical bone growth stimulation devices include:

- **Direct current electrical stimulation (DCES)**, which applies an electrical current directly to the treatment area.

- **Pulsing electromagnetic fields (PEMF)**, which create an electrical field to stimulate bone growth; these devices may be implanted or worn externally.

- **Capacitively coupled electric energy (CCEE) devices**, which are worn externally and create an electrical field around the area requiring treatment. CCEE devices are commonly used for spine treatments and consist of adhesive electrodes attached to the skin. A battery and control unit is attached by wires and worn on a belt or in a pocket.

Codes from subcategory 78.9 are not assigned to report non-invasive (transcutaneous) (surface) stimulator (99.86).

Assign codes from this subcategory to report insertion of a bone stimulator (electrical) to aid bone healing, osteogenic electrodes for bone growth stimulation, or totally implanted device (invasive).

79   Reduction of fracture and dislocation

Description
The 10 subcategories under category 79 include codes for fracture and dislocation treatment. Reduction is the restoring of displaced bone segments to their normal position. Closed reduction means that the fracture site is not surgically opened

(exposed to the external environment and directly visualized). Open treatment is used when the fracture is surgically opened (exposed to the external environment). In this instance, the fracture (bone ends) is visualized, and internal fixation may be used. Internal fixation is a method of stabilization, not reduction. Internal fixation may be performed in conjunction with open or closed reduction techniques.

Skin traction applies force (longitudinal) to a limb using felt or strapping applied directly to the skin only. Skeletal traction uses force (distracting or traction force) on a limb or segment through a wire, pin, screw, or clamp that penetrates the bone. Skeletal traction is often initially necessary when an open procedure cannot be performed.

External fixation is based on the principle of "load transference." Forces normally transmitted through the fracture site are bypassed through the external fixator frame and pin/bone interface at an early stage of treatment. When the fracture is stable or healed, all forces are borne by the bone; the external fixation is then no longer needed and can be safely removed.

Internal fixation is the stabilization of a fracture involving pins, wires, screws, plates, and intramedullary nails. Internal fixation can be accomplished percutaneously or by incision.

Included with procedures classified to category 79 is any application of a cast or splint or reduction with insertion of a traction device such as Kirschner wire or Steinmann pin. Any external fixation device application is coded in addition. However, external fixation devices alone for immobilization of fracture, internal fixation without reduction of fracture, or traction alone for reduction of fracture are coded elsewhere.

As in other categories in this chapter, fourth digits are required to identify the treatment site. In addition, the choice of codes is dependent on the type of reduction, open or closed, and in the case of fracture reduction whether internal fixation was involved.

The following fourth-digit subclassification is for use with appropriate categories in section 79 to identify the site:

0   unspecified site
1   scapula, clavicle, and thorax [ribs and sternum]
2   humerus
3   radius and ulna
4   carpals and metacarpals
5   femur
6   patella
7   tibia and fibula

8   tarsals and metatarsals
9   other (pelvic bones, phalanges of foot and hand, vertebrae)

Coding Clarification
Use the code for closed reduction with internal fixation when the reduction is performed prior to making an incision for the internal fixation.

In the case of an open reduction of a fracture with internal and external skeletal fixation, assign two codes, one from subcategory 79.3x and one from subcategory 78.1x.

If an open fracture site requires debridement, see 79.6x.

Use 79.75 for closed reduction of a dislocated hip prosthesis.

Also code any application of an external fixator device (78.10-78.19), and the type of fixator device, if known (84.71-84.73).

To report external fixation alone for immobilization of fracture, see 93.51-93.56, 93.59. To report internal fixation without reduction of fracture, see 78.50-78.59.

Do not assign codes from this category to report operations on facial bones (76.70-76.79), nasal bones (21.71-21.72), orbit (76.78-76.79), skull (02.02), vertebrae (03.53); or to report removal of a cast or splint (97.88), replacement of a cast or splint (97.11-97.14), or traction alone for reduction of fracture (93.41-93.46).

Coding Guidance
AHA: 4Q, '88, 11; 3Q, '89, 17; 2Q, '94, 3

79.0   Closed reduction of fracture without internal fixation

Description
Codes in this subcategory report a closed fracture reduction without the use of internal fixation, as in the following example:

The physician treats a stable, non-displaced proximal humeral fracture with manipulative realignment without incision or internal fixation. The physician manipulates (pushes, pulls, or moves) the upper arm in the shoulder area to align the fractured pieces. The physician uses a combination of traction and counter traction with manual manipulation of the fracture. Serial x-rays may be necessary while the manipulation is performed to confirm alignment. A brace, splint, or cast may be applied to hold the bones in the correct position until they are healed.

Coding Clarification
Do not assign codes from this subcategory when performed for separation of epiphysis; see 79.40-79.49.

As in other categories in this chapter, fourth digits are required to identify the treatment site. In addition, the choice of codes is dependent on the type of reduction, open or closed, and in the case of fracture reduction whether internal fixation was involved.

The following fourth-digit subclassification is for use subcategory 79.0 to identify the site:

0   unspecified site
1   scapula, clavicle, and thorax [ribs and sternum]
2   humerus
3   radius and ulna
4   carpals and metacarpals
5   femur
6   patella
7   tibia and fibula
8   tarsals and metatarsals
9   other (pelvic bones, phalanges of foot and hand, vertebrae)

Coding Guidance
AHA: 4Q, '88, 11; 3Q, '89, 16; 2Q, '94, 3

79.1   Closed reduction of fracture with internal fixation

Description
The physician performs a manipulative realignment of a fracture with internal fixation but without incision. As an example, with the patient in a supine (face up) position, the physician inserts two to three pins through the skin and into the iliac crest on both right and left sides. The pins are directed at specific angles. The physician attaches pin holders to each ring and curved ring segments to pin holders. The physician uses the rings to gently reduce (reposition) an unstable pelvic fracture or dislocation, if needed. Frame clamps are then attached to the rings and tightened down to secure fixation. The frame is left in place for approximately eight to 12 weeks.

Coding Clarification
Use subcategory 79.1 for closed reduction with internal fixation when the reduction is performed prior to making an incision for the internal fixation.

Do not assign codes from this subcategory when performed for separation of epiphysis; see 79.40-79.49.

As in other categories in this chapter, fourth digits are required to identify the treatment site. In addition, the choice of codes is dependent on the type of reduction, open or closed, and in the case of

76-84

fracture reduction whether internal fixation was involved.

The following fourth-digit subclassification is for use with subcategory 79.1 to identify the site:

0   unspecified site
1   scapula, clavicle, and thorax [ribs and sternum]
2   humerus
3   radius and ulna
4   carpals and metacarpals
5   femur
6   patella
7   tibia and fibula
8   tarsals and metatarsals
9   other (pelvic bones, phalanges of foot and hand, vertebrae)

Coding Guidance
   AHA: 1Q, '93, 27; 4Q, '93, 35; 2Q, '94, 4

79.2   Open reduction of fracture without internal fixation

Description
Codes contained in this subcategory report open reduction of fracture (ORIF) without the use of internal fixation, as in the following example:

The physician performs open treatment of a proximal humeral (surgical or anatomical neck) fracture. An incision is made anteromedially extending posteriorly along the acromion to the lateral half of the spine of the scapula. The deltoid is detached from the exposed portion of the spine of the scapula. The deltoid is reflected down to expose the joint capsule and the humerus. The fractured portion of the proximal humerus (surgical or anatomical neck) is identified and the fracture is aligned. If the tuberosity is involved, it is repaired. External or internal fixation may be used to stabilize the fracture site. Once the fracture is stabilized, the wound is irrigated. The deltoid is repositioned and sutured in place. The skin is sutured and the wound is covered with a soft dressing. The arm is positioned in a sling and movement is restricted to allow for proper healing.

Coding Clarification
Do not assign codes in subcategory 79.2 when performed for separation of epiphysis (79.50-79.59).

As in other categories in this chapter, fourth digits are required to identify the treatment site. In addition, the choice of codes is dependent on the type of reduction, open or closed, and in the case of fracture reduction whether internal fixation was involved.

The following fourth-digit subclassification is for use with subcategory 79.3 to identify the site:

0   unspecified site
1   scapula, clavicle, and thorax [ribs and sternum]
2   humerus
3   radius and ulna
4   carpals and metacarpals
5   femur
6   patella
7   tibia and fibula
8   tarsals and metatarsals
9   other (pelvic bones, phalanges of foot and hand, vertebrae)

Coding Guidance
   AHA: 2Q, '94, 3

79.3   Open reduction of fracture with internal fixation

Description
The physician performs an open realignment of a fracture with an incision and internal fixation. In one example, the physician performs open treatment of a proximal humeral (surgical or anatomical neck) fracture. An incision is made anteromedially extending posteriorly along the acromion to the lateral half of the spine of the scapula. The deltoid is detached from the exposed portion of the spine of the scapula. The deltoid is reflected down to expose the joint capsule and the humerus. The fractured portion of the proximal humerus (surgical or anatomical neck) is identified and the fracture is aligned. If the tuberosity is involved, it is repaired. External or internal fixation may be used to stabilize the fracture site. Once the fracture is stabilized, the wound is irrigated. The deltoid is repositioned and sutured in place. The skin is sutured and the wound is covered with a soft dressing. The arm is positioned in a sling and movement is restricted to allow for proper healing.

Coding Clarification
Use the code for closed reduction with internal fixation when the reduction is performed prior to making an incision for the internal fixation.

In the case of an open reduction of a fracture with internal and external skeletal fixation, assign two codes: one from subcategory 79.3x and one from subcategory 78.1x.

Do not assign 79.3 subcategory codes when performed for separation of epiphysis (79.50-79.59).

As in other categories in this chapter, fourth digits are required to identify the treatment site. In addition, the choice of codes is dependent on the type of reduction, open or closed, and in the case of fracture reduction whether internal fixation was involved.

The following fourth-digit subclassification is for use with subcategory 79.3 to identify the site:

0   unspecified site
1   scapula, clavicle, and thorax [ribs and sternum]
2   humerus
3   radius and ulna
4   carpals and metacarpals
5   femur
6   patella
7   tibia and fibula
8   tarsals and metatarsals
9   other (pelvic bones, phalanges of foot and hand, vertebrae)

Coding Guidance
AHA: 4Q, '93, 35; 2Q, '94, 3; 3Q, '94, 10; 2Q, '98, 12

79.4   Closed reduction of separated epiphysis
Description
The physician performs a manipulative reduction of an expanded joint end of a long bone to normal position without making an incision. This can be done with or without internal fixation.

For example, the physician treats a Colles fracture, or a fracture of the distal radius with dorsal displacement. If good alignment and correct angulation of the distal radial articular surface is present, the physician immobilizes the wrist and forearm in a cast or splint until the fracture or epiphyseal separation is stable. If manipulation is required to reduce an unstable and/or displaced fracture or epiphyseal separation, analgesia or sedation may be necessary to achieve reduction. The physician uses a combination of longitudinal distraction of the fracture and manipulation of the distal fragment to achieve reduction. The wrist and forearm are placed in a cast or splint until the fracture or epiphyseal separation is stable.

Coding Clarification
As in other categories in this chapter, fourth digits are required to identify the treatment site. In addition, the choice of codes is dependent on the type of reduction, open or closed, and in the case of fracture reduction, whether internal fixation was involved.

The following fourth-digit subclassification is appropriate for use with subcategory 79.4:

0   unspecified site
1   scapula, clavicle, and thorax [ribs and sternum]
2   humerus
5   femur
6   patella

9   other (pelvic bones, phalanges of foot and hand, vertebrae)

79.5   Open reduction of separated epiphysis
Description
The physician performs an open reduction with or without internal fixation, as in the following example:

The physician makes a 7.5 cm longitudinal incision along the anterolateral aspect of the distal forearm. The physician exposes the fracture by dissecting between the planes of muscles and tendons of the lateral wrist area while protecting the median nerve. The pronator quadratus muscle is severed from the radius. The physician reduces the fracture or separation. A small T-plate is fixed to the proximal fragment with one or two screws. Usually no screw is inserted through the distal part of the plate since it acts as a buttress and helps hold the fracture in reduction. Direct visualization and x-rays are used to confirm correct reduction and restoration of the joint surface. The pronator quadratus is replaced at its origin on the radius. The incision is repaired in layers using sutures, staples, and/or Steri-strips. The arm is immobilized in a cast.

Coding Clarification
As in other categories in this chapter, fourth digits are required to identify the treatment site. In addition, the choice of codes is dependent on the type of reduction, open or closed, and in the case of fracture reduction, whether internal fixation was involved.

The following fourth-digit subclassification is appropriate for use with subcategory 79.5:

0   unspecified site
1   scapula, clavicle, and thorax [ribs and sternum]
2   humerus
5   femur
6   patella
9   other (pelvic bones, phalanges of foot and hand, vertebrae)

79.6   Debridement of open fracture site
Description
The physician surgically removes foreign matter and contaminated or devitalized skin and other tissue in and around the site of a fracture or dislocation. This debridement is done in preparation for treating the fracture. Debridement reported with this service includes prolonged cleansing of the wound; removal of all foreign or dead tissue material using forceps, scissors, scalpel, or other instruments; exploration of all injured soft tissue including tendons, ligaments, and nerves; as well as irrigation of all

76-84

layers of tissue. Contamination of a wound by foreign matter is usually associated with open fractures, although this type of debridement may be performed with open or closed fractures and/or dislocations and is done to reduce swelling and bleeding, and to leave behind viable tissue.

Coding Clarification

A debridement performed on an open fracture site is assigned to 79.60-79.69.

Do not assign 86.22 when debridement of an open fracture site is performed because the debridement of the skin and subcutaneous tissue is an integral part of the fracture debridement procedure and should not be coded separately.

As in other categories in this chapter, fourth digits are required to identify the treatment site. In addition, the choice of codes is dependent on the type of reduction, open or closed, and in the case of fracture reduction, whether internal fixation was involved.

The following fourth-digit subclassification is for use with subcategory 79.6:

0   unspecified site
1   scapula, clavicle, and thorax [ribs and sternum]
2   humerus
3   radius and ulna
4   carpals and metacarpals
5   femur
6   patella
7   tibia and fibula
8   tarsals and metatarsals
9   other (pelvic bones, phalanges of foot and hand, vertebrae)

Coding Guidance

AHA: 3Q, '89, 16; 3Q, '95, 12

79.7   Closed reduction of dislocation

Description

The physician performs a manipulative reduction of a displaced joint without an incision, with or without external traction. The physician treats an interphalangeal joint dislocation using manipulation; anesthesia may be used if necessary. The physician determines the dislocated position of the bone and uses external manipulation to relocate the bone.

In another example, the physician performs closed reduction of a shoulder dislocation with surgical or anatomical neck fracture. With the patient positioned prone and the arm hanging toward the floor, manual distraction is attempted. If not successful, the physician may hang a five-pound weight from the arm in an attempt to reduce the

shoulder into place. Once shoulder reduction is obtained, a neurovascular examination is performed and treatment of the humeral surgical or anatomical neck fracture is addressed. The arm is immobilized for three to six weeks.

Coding Clarification

Do not assign 79.7 subcategory codes to report closed reduction of dislocation of temporomandibular joint (76.93).

As in other categories in this chapter, fourth digits are required to identify the treatment site.

The following fourth-digit subclassification is for use with subcategory 79.7 to identify the site of the closed reduction:

0   unspecified site
1   shoulder
2   elbow
3   wrist
4   hand and finger
5   hip
6   knee
7   ankle
8   foot and toe
9   other specified sites

Coding Guidance

AHA: N-D, '86, 7

79.8   Open reduction of dislocation

Description

The physician performs reduction of a displaced joint via an incision, with or without internal and external fixation. In one example, the physician openly treats a periarticular fracture (distal humerus and proximal ulna and/or proximal radius) and/or dislocation of the elbow. The physician may make more than one incision depending on the extent of the fractures and/or dislocation. If there is a dislocation, it is reduced (realigned) first. The fractures are then reduced and secured with plates, screws, pins, wires, or a combination of these. The physician may place a pin through the olecranon for skeletal traction in a patient with multiple injuries to temporarily stabilize the fracture and/or dislocation. If joint surface congruity cannot be restored, the physician performs a total elbow arthroplasty. For elbow arthroplasty, the physician makes a straight, midline, posterior incision. The ulnar nerve is identified and retracted for protection. The triceps mechanism is elevated from the olecranon. The collateral ligaments are preserved. A portion of the olecranon is cut and removed to allow implantation of the ulnar stem. The distal humerus is then prepared by removing cancellous bone with a curette. The physician uses a rasp to open and contour the humeral and ulnar medullary canals for

76-84

insertion of the prosthetic stems. Cement is inserted into the ulnar and humeral medullary canals with a cement gun or syringe. The elbow is flexed and the prosthesis is inserted into the humeral and ulnar medullary canals at the same time. The elbow joint is fully extended while the cement hardens. The triceps mechanism is sutured back to fascia. The ulnar nerve is positioned anterior to the elbow. Arthroplasty may be performed in conjunction with some internal fixation for fracture reduction and stabilization.

Coding Clarification
As in other categories in this chapter, fourth digits are required to identify the treatment site.

The following fourth-digit subclassification is for use with subcategory 79.7 to identify the site of the open reduction:

0   unspecified site
1   shoulder
2   elbow
3   wrist
4   hand and finger
5   hip
6   knee
7   ankle
8   foot and toe
9   other specified sites

79.9   Unspecified operation on bone injury

Description
Codes in subcategory 79.9 are used to report bone injury procedures that are not more precisely described by other codes in category 79. Codes from this subcategory are also reported when the documentation does not further specify the procedure.

Coding Clarification
As in other categories in this chapter, fourth digits are required to identify the treatment site. In addition, the choice of codes is dependent on the type of reduction, open or closed, and in the case of fracture reduction, whether internal fixation was involved.

The following fourth-digit subclassification is for use with subcategory 79.9:

0   unspecified site
1   scapula, clavicle, and thorax [ribs and sternum]
2   humerus
3   radius and ulna
4   carpals and metacarpals
5   femur
6   patella
7   tibia and fibula

8   tarsals and metatarsals
9   other (pelvic bones, phalanges of foot and hand, vertebrae)

Documentation Tip
Review the documentation for specific information regarding the procedure prior to final code selection in order to avoid improper use of the "not otherwise specified" code and to ensure accurate code assignment.

80   Incision and excision of joint structures

Description
Category 80 includes codes for operations on the capsule of the joint, cartilage (except the ear, nose, or temporomandibular joint), condyle, ligament, meniscus, and synovial membrane. Included under category 80 is the code for excision of intervertebral disk and disk fragments. This code is not site specific (i.e., it is used for any level of the vertebral column: cervical, thoracic, or lumbar). However, if any concomitant decompression of the spinal nerve root at a different level than the excision site is performed or a concurrent spinal fusion is completed, these procedures require the use of additional codes.

Coding Clarification
Subcategory 80.0 includes the removal of posterior spinal motion preservation devices such as facet replacement devices, pedicle-based dynamic stabilization devices, and interspinous process devices (80.09).

Only when laminotomy, laminectomy, or foraminotomy is performed at a different vertebral level than the excision of an intervertebral disc, it is appropriate to assign both codes: one for the laminotomy, laminectomy, or foraminotomy and one for the excision.

Assign two codes for the two staged cartilage transplantation: 80.6 for the harvesting of the cartilage (first stage) and 81.47 for the transplantation of the cells (second stage).

Assign 80.59 for a percutaneous suction or percutaneous automated diskectomy.

Osteochondral autograft transfer system (OATS) is a two-step procedure that involves excision of the semilunar cartilage of the knee: 80.6 for harvesting the graft material for autografting to the talus and 81.49.

Use only 80.6 for an arthroscopic meniscectomy.

Assign codes in this category to report operations on the capsule of a joint, cartilage, condyle, ligament, meniscus, and synovial membrane.

76-84

Do not assign codes in this category to report operations on the cartilage of the ear (18.01-18.9), nose (21.00-21.99), or temporomandibular joint (76.01-76.99).

The following fourth-digit subclassification is for use with appropriate categories in section 80 to identify the site:

0   unspecified site
1   shoulder
2   elbow
3   wrist
4   hand and finger
5   hip
6   knee
7   ankle
8   foot and toe
9   other specified sites (spine)

Coding Guidance
  AHA: 2Q, '91, 18

80.0   Arthrotomy for removal of prosthesis without replacement, unspecified side

Description
The physician makes an incision overlying the site of the implant to remove a prosthesis. An incision is made over the joint to be exposed. The soft tissues are dissected away and the joint capsule is exposed and incised. The prosthesis is removed and the joint space is debrided of all cement, abscesses, and necrotic tissue; any infection or abnormal fluid is drained. The wound is irrigated with antibiotic solution. The physician may leave the wound packed open with daily dressing changes to allow for further drainage and secondary healing by granulation. If the incision is repaired, drain tubes may be inserted and the incision is repaired in multiple layers with sutures, staples, and/or Steri-strips. A splint may be applied to limit shoulder motion.

Coding Clarification
▶Subcategory 80.0 codes are *not* assigned if a new prosthesis is inserted to replace the prosthesis being removed.◀ Subcategory 80.0 includes the removal of a posterior spinal motion preservation (dynamic stabilization, facet replacement, and interspinous process) device(s).

Subcategory 80.0 excludes the removal of pedicle screws used in spinal fusion (78.69).

Code also any insertion of a (cement) (joint) spacer (84.56) or removal of a (cement) (joint) spacer (84.57).

The following fourth-digit subclassification is for use with subcategory 80.0:

0   unspecified site

1   shoulder
2   elbow
3   wrist
4   hand and finger
5   hip
6   knee
7   ankle
8   foot and toe
9   other specified sites (spine)

A Girdlestone operation involves removing the femoral head without any replacement. When a Girdlestone operation is performed to remove an infected hip prosthesis, assign code 80.05.

Coding Guidance
  AHA: 2Q, '97, 10; 2Q, '08, 4, 5; ▶4Q, '09, 148-149◀

80.1   Other arthrotomy

Description
In one example, the physician performs an arthrotomy on the elbow that includes exploration, drainage, or removal of any foreign body. A longitudinal incision is made over the part of the elbow to be exposed (e.g., the anterior, posterior, medial, or lateral aspect). The soft tissues are dissected away and the joint capsule is exposed and incised. The joint is explored, any necrotic tissue is removed, and infection or abnormal fluid is drained. If a foreign body is present (e.g., bullet, nail, gravel), it is exposed and removed. The wound is irrigated with antibiotic solution. The physician may leave the wound packed open with daily dressing changes to allow for further drainage and secondary healing by granulation. If the incision is repaired, drain tubes may be inserted and the incision is repaired in multiple layers with sutures, staples, and/or Steri-strips. A splint may be applied to limit elbow motion.

Coding Clarification
Report subcategory 80.1 for arthrostomy or other incision or creation of opening into joint; other than to remove a prosthesis.

Do not assign subcategory 80.1 for arthrography (88.32), arthroscopy (80.20-80.29), injection of a drug (81.92), or when used as the operative approach.

The following fourth-digit subclassification is for use with subcategory 80.1:

0   unspecified site
1   shoulder
2   elbow
3   wrist
4   hand and finger
5   hip
6   knee

● New Code   ▲ Revised Code   ▶◀ Revised Text   © 2010 Ingenix

7   ankle
8   foot and toe
9   other specified sites (spine)

Coding Guidance
AHA: 3Q, '06, 22-23

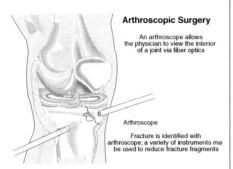

Arthroscopic Surgery

An arthroscope allows
the physician to view the interior
of a joint via fiber optics

Arthroscope

Fracture is identified with
arthroscope; a variety of instruments may
be used to reduce fracture fragments

80.2   Arthroscopy

Description
The physician performs a diagnostic arthroscopy
and examines all parts of a joint with the
arthroscope. Any loose bodies (e.g., small pieces of
cartilage from chondral injuries) or foreign bodies
are removed by identifying them through the
arthroscope and using another portal incision to
remove the object. In some cases, the physician uses
the arthroscope to examine the joint and
debridement is performed on proliferative cartilage,
a degenerative joint, or frayed articular cartilage. The
physician uses instruments through the arthroscope
to cut and remove inflamed and proliferated
synovium and to clean and smooth the articular
joint surfaces. The portal incisions are closed with
sutures or Steri-strips.

Coding Clarification
The following fourth-digit subclassification is for use
with subcategory 80.2:

0   unspecified site
1   shoulder
2   elbow
3   wrist
4   hand and finger
5   hip
6   knee
7   ankle
8   foot and toe
9   other specified sites (spine)

The five most commonly used portals are the lateral,
anterolateral, anteromedial, posterolateral, and
straight positions.

Coding Scenario
The physician made 1 cm portal incisions to insert
the arthroscope into the elbow joint space. The

physician placed the arthroscope into the elbow joint
and examined the humeral-ulnar and radial-ulnar
joints. The elbow was flexed and extended, and
pronated and supinated to allow visualization and
examination of all joint spaces and surfaces.

Code Assignment:

80.22   Arthroscopy (elbow)

Coding Guidance
AHA: 1Q, '93, 23; 3Q, '93, 5

80.3   Biopsy of joint structure

Description
The physician performs an arthrotomy of a joint with
a biopsy. An incision is made over the joint to be
incised. The soft tissues are dissected away and the
joint capsule is exposed and incised. A tissue sample
is removed for biopsy and the wound is irrigated.
The incision is closed in multiple layers with
sutures, staples, and/or Steri-strips.

Coding Clarification
Assign subcategory 80.3 to report aspiration biopsy
of a joint.

The following fourth-digit subclassification is for use
with subcategory 80.3:

0   unspecified site
1   shoulder
2   elbow
3   wrist
4   hand and finger
5   hip
6   knee
7   ankle
8   foot and toe
9   other specified sites (spine)

Coding Guidance
AHA: 3Q, '05, 13-14

80.4   Division of joint capsule, ligament, or cartilage

Description
This procedure is often performed in an effort to
correct club foot deformity. A medial incision is
made on the inner ankle to expose the underlying
tissues. The skin and tendons are reflected back to
expose the joint capsule of the talonavicular joint.
The joint capsule is cut by sharp dissection to
release the deformity of the mid foot. Several
releases can be made from this approach. A
particular order is followed in order to obtain the
appropriate amount of release. The incision is closed
with sutures and a cast is applied.

When posterior, medial, and subtalar soft tissue
contractures are released to correct severe clubfoot
deformity, the patient is placed supine and a

76-84

posteromedial skin incision is made. The tibialis posterior, flexor digitorum longus, and flexor hallucis longus are identified and mobilized. The contracted tendons are lengthened. The talonavicular and talotibial joint capsules are incised. The joint capsules are cut by sharp dissection to release the deformity. Bones are then placed in correct alignment and secured with a single Kirschner wire.

Coding Clarification
Subcategory 80.4 reports excision or destruction of the intervertebral disc, Goldner clubfoot release, Heyman-Herndon (-Strong) correction of metatarsus varus, and release of adherent or constrictive joint capsule ligament.

Do not assign subcategory 80.4 for symphysiotomy to assist delivery (73.94), when performed for carpal tunnel syndrome (04.43), or tarsal tunnel syndrome (04.44).

Prior to the creation of 84.60-84.69 these procedures were reported with 80.51 Excision of intervertebral disc. However, 80.51 only describes the removal of the intervertebral disc and does not include the replacement of the disc with a prosthesis.

The following fourth-digit subclassification is for use with subcategory 80.4:

    0   unspecified site
    1   shoulder
    2   elbow
    3   wrist
    4   hand and finger
    5   hip
    6   knee
    7   ankle
    8   foot and toe
    9   other specified sites (spine)

Coding Scenario
The surgeon performs an anterior spinal release on a patient with scoliosis.

    Code Assignment:

    737.30 Scoliosis
    80.49   Division of joint capsule, ligament, or
            cartilage; other specified sites

Coding Guidance
AHA: 2Q, '02, 16

80.5   Excision, destruction and other repair of intervertebral disc

Coding Clarification
Included under subcategory 80.5 is the code for excision of intervertebral disk and disk fragments. This code is not site specific (i.e., it is used for any level of the vertebral column: cervical, thoracic, or lumbar). However, if any concomitant decompression

of the spinal nerve root at a different level than the excision site is performed or a concurrent spinal fusion completed, these procedures require the use of additional codes.

Do not assign subcategory 80.5 for laminectomy for exploration of the intraspinal canal (03.09), laminotomy for decompression of the spinal nerve root only (03.09), when performed for insertion of (non-fusion) a spinal disc replacement device (84.60-84.69), or with corpectomy (vertebral) (80.99).

Prior to the creation of 84.60-84.69, these procedures were reported with 80.51. However, 80.51 describes the removal of the intervertebral disc and does not include the replacement of the disc with a prosthesis.

80.50   Excision or destruction of intervertebral disc, unspecified

Description
Code 80.50 is used to report excision and destruction procedures of intervertebral discs that are not more precisely described by other codes in subcategory 80.5. This code is also reported when the documentation does not further specify the excision or destruction procedure.

Documentation Tip
Review the documentation for specific information regarding the procedure prior to final code selection in order to avoid improper use of the unspecified code and to ensure accurate code assignment.

80.51   Excision of intervertebral disc

Description
The physician performs a diskectomy to remove an intervertebral disc by laminotomy or hemilaminectomy with decompression of the spinal nerve root at the same level. Through a posterior (back) approach, a midline incision is made overlying the vertebrae. The incision is carried down through the tissue to the paravertebral muscles, which are retracted. The ligamentum flavum, which attaches the lamina from one vertebra to the lamina of another, may be partially or completely removed. Part of the lamina is removed on one side to allow access to the spinal cord. If a disc has ruptured, fragments or the part of the disc compressing the nerves are removed. A partial removal of a facet (facetectomy) or removal of bone around the foramen (foraminotomy) may also be performed to relieve pressure on the nerve. When decompression is complete, a free-fat graft may be placed to protect the nerve root. If the ligamentum flavum was not removed, it is placed over the fat graft. Paravertebral muscles are repositioned and the tissue is closed in layers.

● New Code   ▲ Revised Code   ▶◀ Revised Text   © 2010 Ingenix

76-84

Note that lumbar approaches may be performed using an open approach as described above or an endoscopically assisted approach. In an endoscopically assisted approach, a small guide probe is inserted under fluoroscopic guidance. Using magnified video as well as fluoroscopic guidance, the endoscope is manipulated through the foramen and into the spinal canal. Once the guide probe has been advanced to the surgical site, a slightly larger tube is manipulated over the guide probe. Surgical instruments are advanced through the hollow center of the tube. Herniated disc fragments are removed and the disc is reconfigured to eliminate pressure on the nerve root(s). The endoscope is withdrawn. The incision is sutured or simply dressed with an adhesive bandage.

Coding Clarification
Code also any concurrent spinal fusion (81.00-81.08).

Code 80.51 requires an additional code for any concomitant decompression of the spinal nerve root at a different level from the excision site.

Do not assign 80.51 for intervertebral chemonucleolysis (80.52), laminectomy for exploration of the intraspinal canal (03.09), laminotomy for decompression of the spinal nerve root only (03.09), that for insertion of a (non-fusion) spinal disc replacement device (84.60-84.69), or that with corpectomy (vertebral) (80.99).

Coding Guidance
AHA: S-O, '86, 12; 2Q, '90, 27; 2Q, '95, 9; 1Q, '96, 7; 3Q, '03, 12; 4Q, '04, 133; 1Q, '06, 12; 1Q, '07, 9; 1Q, '08, 4; 2Q, '08, 14; 2Q, '09, 4-5

80.52 Intervertebral chemonucleolysis

Description
This procedure introduces a corrective chemical enzyme into a herniated disc. The patient is placed in a spinal tap position on the left side. In a separately reported procedure, an x-ray verifies location of the disc. Once the disc is located, local anesthesia is injected and a small stab wound is made. A spinal needle is inserted with additional monitoring of placement and injection of anesthesia. Without puncturing the dura, the physician inserts the needle into the disc. This procedure can be performed with one or two needles. A separately reportable saline acceptance test is performed to verify correct placement. Discography is performed with an opaque substance to verify location of the herniated disc. A reparative enzyme is injected. The needles are removed and the wound is dressed.

Coding Clarification
Code 80.52 is assigned to report the destruction of an intervertebral disc via an injection of enzyme or the injection of a proteolytic enzyme into intervertebral space such as chymopapain.

Do not assign 80.52 for the injection of an anesthetic substance (03.91) or injection of other substances (03.92).

80.53 Repair of the anulus fibrosus with graft or prosthesis

80.54 Other and unspecified repair of the anulus fibrosus

Description
An intervertebral disc consists of three components: the anulus fibrosus, nucleus pulposus, and cartilaginous endplates. The anulus fibrosus is a ring of cartilage and fibrous tissue surrounding the nucleus pulposus of the intervertebral disc. When the annulus fibrosus is compromised, the nucleus pulposus is prone to herniation. Following discectomy surgery to remove a herniated disc of the spine, a hole is left in the anulus. These codes are used to report the repair of the anulus fibrosus by various techniques such as graft, prosthesis, or other devices.

Coding Clarification
Code 80.54 is used to report microsurgical suture repair without fascial autograft or percutaneous repair of the anulus fibrosus. Code 80.53 reports repair of the anulus fibrosus with graft or prosthesis including microsurgical suture repair with fascial autograft, soft tissue reapproximation repair with tension bands, and surgical mesh repair.

Also code any application or administration of adhesion barrier substance performed (99.77), intervertebral discectomy (80.51) if performed, and locally harvested fascia for the graft (83.43).

Coding Scenario
The physician repairs a defect in a vertebral disc after a lumbar discectomy for degenerative disc disease. Sutures are fastened to the vertebral disc and a mesh device is positioned adjacent to the defect. Tension is applied to the sutures, which are then attached to hold the mesh adjacent the defect.

Code Assignment:

722.52 Degeneration of lumbar or lumbosacral intervertebral disc
80.53 Repair of the anulus fibrosus with graft or prosthesis

Coding Guidance
AHA: 4Q, '08, 183-184

80.59   Other destruction of intervertebral disc

Description
A procedure that corrects a bulge in an intervertebral disc is commonly referred to as percutaneous discectomy, and may be accomplished by several techniques, including non-automated (manual), automated, or laser. For all techniques, the patient is placed in a spinal tap position on the left side. A C-arm x-ray verifies placement of the needle in the disc. Once the disc is located, local anesthesia is injected and a small stab wound is made. A spinal needle is inserted with additional monitoring of placement and injection of anesthesia. Using a manual technique, the physician inserts one or two needles into the disc without puncturing the dura. The patient is placed on pure oxygen and the nucleus pulposus is suctioned out until the desired decompression is accomplished. The needle(s) is removed and the wound dressed. The automated technique makes use of a probe that can simultaneously dissect the disc and suck it into the probe. Laser discectomy accomplishes the decompression by vaporizing the protruding disc.

Coding Clarification
Code 80.59 is used to report intervertebral disc destruction procedures that are not more precisely described by other codes in subcategory 80.5, such as destruction by laser. This code is also reported when the documentation does not further specify the destruction procedure.

Documentation Tip
Review the documentation for specific information regarding the procedure prior to final code selection in order to avoid improper use of the "not otherwise specified" code and to ensure accurate code assignment.

Coding Guidance
   AHA: 3Q, '02, 10

80.6   Excision of semilunar cartilage of knee

Description
The physician makes an incision along the anteromedial or anterolateral aspect of the knee, depending on which cartilage is torn. Dissection is carried down to the cartilage. The patella is shifted to the side and the knee joint exposed. The torn cartilage is removed and the roughened edges are smoothed. A partial synovectomy and release or excision (partial or total) of plica may be performed. Plica is a fold, pleat, band, or shelf of synovial tissue (e.g., transverse suprapatellar, medial suprapatellar, mediopatellar, and infrapatellar). Debridement of the chondral surface of the patella may be performed as well. A temporary drain may be applied. The incision is repaired in layers with sutures, staples, and/or Steri-strips.

For an arthroscopic meniscectomy, the physician makes 1 cm long portal incisions on either side of the patellar tendon for arthroscopic access into the knee joint. Once the meniscal tear is identified, additional portal incisions may be made to provide easier access to the area. There may be a tear on both the medial and lateral meniscus or on only the medial or lateral meniscus. The procedure is the same for medial or lateral meniscal tears. Angled scissors, a motorized cutter, or punch forceps remove torn fragments. The remaining intact meniscus is trimmed and contoured. A temporary drain may be applied and the incisions closed with sutures and Steri-strips.

Coding Clarification
Osteochondral autograft transfer system (OATS) is a two-step procedure that involves excision of the semilunar cartilage of the knee: 80.6 for harvesting the graft material for autografting to the talus and 81.49. Assign both codes to fully describe OATS.

Assign two codes for the two-staged cartilage transplantation: 80.6 for the harvesting of the cartilage (first stage) and 81.47 for the transplantation of the cells (second stage).

Use only 80.6 for an arthroscopic meniscectomy.

Coding Guidance
   AHA: 1Q, '93, 23; 2Q, '96, 3; 3Q, '00, 4; 2Q, '03, 18

80.7   Synovectomy

Description
When the physician performs an arthroscopic synovectomy, 1 cm long portal incisions are made on either side of the patellar tendon for arthroscopic access into the joint. Proliferative, diseased synovium is removed with a motorized, suction, cutting resector. If the plica located along the medial side of the patella is inflamed, it may require removal. Removal is accomplished by dividing and excising the plica. For a more extensive synovectomy, up to six portal incisions may be made to access all of the involved compartments of the knee. A temporary drain may be applied and incisions are closed with sutures and Steri-strips.

Coding Clarification
Assign subcategory 80.7 for excision of an inner membrane of a joint capsule and complete or partial resection of a synovial membrane.

Do not assign subcategory 80.7 for excision of a Baker's cyst (83.39).

The following fourth-digit subclassification is for use with subcategory 80.7:

   0   unspecified site
   1   shoulder
   2   elbow

● New Code   ▲ Revised Code   ►◄ Revised Text   © 2010 Ingenix

3 wrist
4 hand and finger
5 hip
6 knee
7 ankle
8 foot and toe
9 other specified sites (spine)

80.8 Other local excision or destruction of lesion of joint

Description
A bone cyst or benign tumor of the radius or ulna, excluding the head, neck, or olecranon process, is removed. The physician makes an incision in the forearm overlying the cyst or tumor. The skin and underlying soft tissues are reflected to expose the periosteum, which is separated from the bone. Curettes or osteotomes are used to scrape or cut the lesion from the bone. Once the benign tumor or cyst is removed and healthy bone tissue is present, the periosteum is repositioned and the incision is repaired in layers. If the bone defect created requires a graft for repair, the physician obtains the necessary size bone graft from a separate donor site on the patient and packs it into the site where the tumor or bone cyst was removed or uses a bone bank allograft.

Coding Clarification
The following fourth-digit subclassification is for use with subcategory 80.8:

0 unspecified site
1 shoulder
2 elbow
3 wrist
4 hand and finger
5 hip
6 knee
7 ankle
8 foot and toe
9 other specified sites (spine)

Coding Guidance
AHA: 1Q, '08, 7

80.9 Other excision of joint

Description
Physicians perform vertebral corpectomy with diskectomy with correction of spinal cord or nerve root compression for fractures or tumors of the vertebrae. The body of the vertebra may be partially or completely resected. The lateral extracavitary approach is done with a midline incision made in the area of the fractured segment and inferiorly curved out to the lateral plane. The paraspinous muscles are exposed, lifted off the spinous processes, then divided and lifted off the ribs. The targeted vertebral body is identified. The corresponding ribs are dissected from the intercostal muscles and the pleura and resected in one piece from the posterior curve to the costovertebral connection. The appropriate transverse process and part of the facet and pedicle are removed with a drill from the lateral aspect. The dura and the vertebral body are now exposed from the dorsolateral view. Further posterior and lateral access to the vertebral body is gained by gently retracting the nerve root and surrounding structures. The central portion of the vertebral body is removed with a drill, exposing more area, and any bone fragments or tumor masses are carefully removed away from the spinal cord or nerve roots. Curettes and rongeurs are used to remove disc material. At this point, any necessary fusion, intervertebral reconstruction, or grafting is undertaken and reported separately. Cartilage is scraped, bone is decorticated, and an arthrodesis or reconstruction is accomplished by tapping bone graft material into the vertebral endplates. A drain is placed and closure is done in layers.

Coding Clarification
Use 80.99 for a vertebral corpectomy.

A diskectomy is inherent to the corpectomy and therefore is included in the code assignment for the corpectomy.

Do no assign subcategory 80.9 to report cheilectomy of joint (77.80-77.89) or excision of bone ends (77.80-77.89).

The following fourth-digit subclassification is for use with subcategory 80.8:

0 unspecified site
1 shoulder
2 elbow
3 wrist
4 hand and finger
5 hip
6 knee
7 ankle
8 foot and toe
9 other specified sites (spine)

Coding Guidance
AHA: 1Q, '07, 20

81 Repair and plastic operations on joint structures

Description
Included under category 81 are codes for arthrodesis, arthroplasty, and other operations on joint structures. The first three subcategories, 81.0, 81.1, and 81.2, classify arthrodesis and include any

76-84

bone graft and internal fixation when done in conjunction with the fusion. Refusions are coded to category 81.3 based on the level of refusion (fifth-digit subclassification) and include correction of pseudoarthrosis of the spine. In the case of an arthroplasty (81.4, 81.5, 81.7, and 81.8), any external traction or fixation, graft of bone or cartilage, or internal fixation device or prosthesis is included in the repair codes. Review the operative report for the site of the spinal fusion and technique used (e.g., anterior, posterior). Correct code assignment is dependent on this information.

Coding Clarification

When a physician removes the lamina (laminectomy and hemilaminectomy) and performs foraminotomies in conjunction with a spinal fusion, both procedures are considered a part of the operative approach and not coded separately.

For arthroplasties, determine if the surgeon performed a total or partial replacement and whether it was an initial or revision procedure, as the ICD-9-CM system provides different codes depending on documentation.

The code for the revision of joint replacement of the upper extremity is not listed with the other codes for initial joint replacement of the specific site.

When the classification does not differentiate between a unilateral and bilateral procedure and significant uses of resources are used to achieve the bilateral procedures, record the procedure code twice.

81.0   Spinal fusion

Description

Subcategory 81.0 classifies procedures for immobilization of the spinal column. Spinal fusion, also known as arthrodesis, fuses together two or more vertebrae with screw fixation and, in some cases, bone grafting. Spinal arthrodesis may be performed to treat conditions such as degenerative, traumatic, or congenital lesions; herniated disks; or to stabilize fractures or dislocations of the spine. Codes identify whether a fusion or refusion was performed, the spinal level where the procedure was performed (cervical, thoracic, lumbar, or sacral), the approach (anterior, posterior, lateral transverse) ▶or technique,◀ and the number of vertebrae fused or refused.

Spinal fusion is accomplished using a variety of surgical techniques including:

- Anterior interbody fusion—excising the disc and cartilage end plates and inserting a bone graft between two vertebrae.
- Posterolateral fusion and lateral fusion—decorticating and bone grafting the

zygapophysial joint, pars interarticularis, and transverse process.

- Posterior fusion—decorticating and bone grafting neural arches between the right and left zygapophysial joints.
- One-level fusion—fuses together two vertebral bones and one disc.
- Two-level fusion—fuses three vertebral bones with two discs.

Coding Clarification

▶The anterior column can be fused using an anterior, lateral, or posterior technique.

A posterior column fusion can be performed using a posterior, posterolateral, or lateral transverse technique. Subcategory 81.0 includes arthrodesis of spine with bone graft internal fixation.◀

Also assign codes for any insertion of interbody spinal fusion device (84.51), insertion of recombinant bone morphogenetic protein (84.52), or any synchronous excision of locally harvested bone for graft (77.00-77.79).

Remember to code the total number of vertebrae fused (81.62-81.64).

Subcategory 81.0 excludes corrections of pseudarthrosis of spine (81.30-81.39) and refusion of spine (81.30-81.39).

Coding Guidance

AHA: 4Q, '03, 99

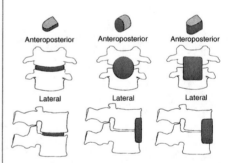

81.00   Spinal fusion, not otherwise specified

Description

Code 81.00 is assigned when the documentation does not further specify the fusion procedure. This code is also used to report spinal fusion procedures that are not more precisely described by other codes in subcategory 81.0.

Coding Clarification

Spinal fusion is accomplished using a variety of surgical techniques. Codes identify whether a fusion or refusion was performed, the spinal level where the procedure was performed (cervical, thoracic, lumbar or sacral), and the approach (anterior, posterior, lateral transverse), as well as the number of vertebrae fused or refused. Review the documentation for specific information regarding the procedure prior to final code selection in order to ensure accurate code assignment.

81.01   Atlas-axis spinal fusion

Description
The physician performs spinal arthrodesis using an anterior, transoral, or posterior technique. Skull tong traction is applied. The physician may incise the back of the throat, but most often enters from the outside of the neck, left of the throat, to reach the C1-C2 (atlas-axis) vertebrae. The patient is placed in a Stryker frame with a previously applied halo vest. The physician makes an incision from the occiput to the fourth or fifth vertebra and exposes the posterior arch of the atlas (C1) and laminae of the axis (C2) and removes all soft tissue from bony surfaces. The upper arch of C1 is exposed and a wire loop is brought from upward under the arch of the atlas and sutured. The physician passes the free ends through the loop, grasping the arch of C1. A graft taken from the iliac crest or other donor bone is placed against the lamina of the C2 and the arch of C1 beneath the wire. The physician then passes one end of the wire through the spinous process of C2 and twists it securely into place. The retractors are removed and the incision is closed over a drain.

Coding Clarification
Code 81.01 is assigned to report craniocervical fusion, C1-C2 fusion, or occiput C2 fusion using an anterior, transoral, or posterior technique.

Documentation Tip
Spinal fusion is accomplished using a variety of surgical techniques. Codes identify whether a fusion or refusion was performed, the spinal level where the procedure was performed (cervical, thoracic, lumbar or sacral), and the approach (anterior, posterior, lateral transverse), as well as the number of vertebrae fused or refused. Review the documentation for specific information regarding the procedure prior to final code selection in order to ensure accurate code assignment.

▲ 81.02   Other cervical fusion of the anterior column, anterior technique

Description
The physician uses an anterior approach to reach the damaged vertebrae. An incision is made through the neck, avoiding the esophagus, trachea, and thyroid. Retractors separate the intervertebral muscles. A drill is inserted in the affected vertebrae and the location is confirmed by x-ray. The physician incises a trough in the front of the

vertebrae with a drill or saw. The physician cleans out the intervertebral disk spaces with a rongeur and removes the cartilaginous plates above and below the vertebrae to be fused. The physician obtains and packs separately reportable grafts of iliac or other donor bone into the spaces and trims them. Traction is gradually decreased to maintain the graft in its bed. The fascia is sutured. A drain is placed and the incision is sutured.

Coding Clarification
Assign 81.02 to report arthrodesis of C2 level or below using an anterior (interbody) or anterolateral technique.

Documentation Tip
Spinal fusion is accomplished using a variety of surgical techniques. Codes identify whether a fusion or refusion was performed, the spinal level where the procedure was performed (cervical, thoracic, lumbar or sacral), and the approach (anterior, posterior, lateral transverse), as well as the number of vertebrae fused or refused. Review the documentation for specific information regarding the procedure prior to final code selection in order to ensure accurate code assignment.

Coding Guidance
  AHA: 1Q, '96, 7; 1Q, '01, 6; 4Q, '03, 101

▲ 81.03   Other cervical fusion of the posterior column, posterior technique

Description
The physician performs spinal arthrodesis using a posterior technique. The physician makes an incision overlying the vertebrae and separates the fascia and the supraspinous ligaments in line with the incision. The physician prepares the vertebrae and lifts ligaments and muscles out of the way. A chisel elevator is used to strip away the capsules of the lateral articulations and the articular cartilage and cortical bone is excised. Separately reportable chips are cut from the fossa below the lateral articulations and from the laminae, or fragments of the spinous process are taken and then used to fill the interlaminal space and the gap left by the articular cartilage removal. Additional bone grafts are taken from the ilium or other donor bone and are used to join the laminae. The periosteum, ligaments, and paravertebral muscles are sutured to secure the bone grafting. The skin and subcutaneous tissues are closed with sutures, as well.

Coding Clarification
Code 81.03 is assigned to report arthrodesis of C2 level or below using a posterior or posterolateral technique.

Documentation Tip
Spinal fusion is accomplished using a variety of surgical techniques. Codes identify whether a fusion

76-84

or refusion was performed, the spinal level where the procedure was performed (cervical, thoracic, lumbar, or sacral), and the approach (anterior, posterior, lateral transverse), as well as the number of vertebrae fused or refused. Review the documentation for specific information regarding the procedure prior to final code selection in order to ensure accurate code assignment.

▲ 81.04 Dorsal and dorsolumbar fusion of the anterior column, anterior technique

Description
Spinal arthrodesis, or fusion, to correct a spinal deformity is performed using an anterior approach. In the case of affected thoracolumbar vertebrae, the dissection is carried out through the abdominal muscles to the tenth rib, which is resected to allow access to the vertebrae in back. Dissection continues until the vertebral bodies are exposed. The physician cleans out the intervertebral disk spaces and removes the cartilaginous plates above and below the vertebrae to be fused. The physician obtains and packs separately reportable grafts of iliac or other donor bone into the spaces. Separately reportable instrumentation may be affixed to the spine. A drainage tube may be placed and the surgical wound is sutured closed. A cast may or may not be applied to stabilize the spine.

Coding Clarification
Code 81.04 is assigned to report arthrodesis of the thoracic or thoracolumbar region using an anterior (interbody), extracavitary or anterolateral technique.

Documentation Tip
Spinal fusion is accomplished using a variety of surgical techniques. Codes identify whether a fusion or refusion was performed, the spinal level where the procedure was performed (cervical, thoracic, lumbar, or sacral), and the approach (anterior, posterior, lateral transverse), as well as the number of vertebrae fused or refused. Review the documentation for specific information regarding the procedure prior to final code selection in order to ensure accurate code assignment.

Coding Guidance
    AHA: 3Q, '03, 19

▲ 81.05 Dorsal and dorsolumbar fusion of the posterior column, posterior technique

Description
The physician performs arthrodesis of the thoracic or thoracolumbar spine using a posterior approach. The physician makes an incision overlying the vertebrae and separates the fascia and the supraspinous ligaments in line with the incision. The physician prepares the vertebrae and lifts ligaments and muscles out of the way. A chisel

elevator is used to strip away the capsules of the lateral articulations and the articular cartilage and cortical bone is excised. Chips are cut from the fossa below the lateral articulations and from the laminae, or fragments of the spinous process are taken and then used to fill the interlaminal space and the gap left by the articular cartilage removal. Additional bone grafts are taken from the ilium or other donor bone and are used to join the laminae. The periosteum, ligaments, and paravertebral muscles are sutured to secure the bone grafting. The skin and subcutaneous tissues are closed with sutures, as well.

Coding Clarification
Code 81.05 reports arthrodesis of the thoracic or thoracolumbar region using a posterior or posterolateral technique.

Documentation Tip
Spinal fusion is accomplished using a variety of surgical techniques. Codes identify whether a fusion or refusion was performed, the spinal level where the procedure was performed (cervical, thoracic, lumbar, or sacral), and the approach (anterior, posterior, lateral transverse), as well as the number of vertebrae fused or refused. Review the documentation for specific information regarding the procedure prior to final code selection in order to ensure accurate code assignment.

Coding Guidance
    AHA: 4Q, '99, 11; 2Q, '02, 16

▲ 81.06 Lumbar and lumbosacral fusion of the anterior column, anterior technique

Description
The physician uses an anterior approach to reach the damaged vertebrae. The physician makes an incision overlying the vertebrae and separates the fascia and the supraspinous ligaments in line with the incision. The physician prepares the vertebrae and lifts ligaments and muscles out of the way. A chisel elevator is used to strip away the capsules of the lateral articulations and the articular cartilage and cortical bone is excised. Chips are cut from the fossa below the lateral articulations and from the laminae, or fragments of the spinous process are taken and then used to fill the interlaminal space and the gap left by the articular cartilage removal. Additional bone grafts are taken from the ilium or other donor bone and are used to join the laminae. The periosteum, ligaments, and paravertebral muscles are sutured to secure the bone grafting. The skin and subcutaneous tissues are closed with sutures, as well.

Coding Clarification
▶Code 81.06 includes the following surgical techniques (approach):

 ● New Code   ▲ Revised Code   ▶◀ Revised Text   © 2010 Ingenix

- Anterior or anterolateral
- Direct lateral interbody fusion (DLIF)
- Extreme lateral interbody fusion (XLIF™)
- Retroperitoneal
- Transperitoneal◄

Documentation Tip

Spinal fusion is accomplished using a variety of surgical techniques. Codes identify whether a fusion or refusion was performed, the spinal level where the procedure was performed (cervical, thoracic, lumbar, or sacral), and the approach (anterior, posterior, lateral transverse), as well as the number of vertebrae fused or refused. Review the documentation for specific information regarding the procedure prior to final code selection in order to ensure accurate code assignment.

Coding Guidance

AHA: 4Q, '99, 11; 4Q, '02, 107; 4Q, '05, 122; 2Q, '08, 14

▲ 81.07 Lumbar and lumbosacral fusion of the posterior column, posterior technique

Description

A lumbosacral spinal arthrodesis, or fusion, is done using a lateral transverse process technique. The physician makes an incision overlying the vertebrae and separates the fascia and the supraspinous ligaments in line with the incision. The physician prepares the vertebrae and lifts ligaments and muscles out of the way. A chisel elevator is used to strip away the capsules of the lateral articulations and the articular cartilage and cortical bone is excised. Separately reportable chips are cut from the fossa below the lateral articulations and from the laminae, or fragments of the spinous process are taken and then used to fill the interlaminal space and the gap left by the articular cartilage removal. Additional bone grafts are taken from the ilium or other donor bone and are used to join the laminae. The periosteum, ligaments, and paravertebral muscles are sutured to secure the bone grafting. The skin and subcutaneous tissues are closed with sutures, as well.

Coding Clarification

►Code 81.07 includes the following surgical techniques (approach):

- Posterior or posteriolateral technique
- Facet fusion
- Transverse process technique◄

Documentation Tip

Spinal fusion is accomplished using a variety of surgical techniques. Codes identify whether a fusion or refusion was performed, the spinal level where the procedure was performed (cervical, thoracic, lumbar, or sacral), and the approach (anterior, posterior, lateral transverse), as well as the number of vertebrae fused or refused. Review the documentation for specific information regarding the procedure prior to final code selection in order to ensure accurate code assignment.

Coding Guidance

AHA: 4Q, '02, 108; 2Q, '09, 4

▲ 81.08 Lumbar and lumbosacral fusion of the anterior column, posterior technique

Description

Lumbosacral spinal arthrodesis, or fusion, may be done using a posterior technique. The physician makes an incision overlying the lumbar vertebrae and separates the fascia and the supraspinous ligaments in line with the incision. The physician prepares the vertebrae and lifts ligaments and muscles out of the way. A chisel elevator is used to strip away the capsules of the lateral articulations and the articular cartilage and cortical bone is excised. Chips are cut from the fossa below the lateral articulations and from the laminae, or fragments of the spinous process are taken and then used to fill the interlaminal space and the gap left by the articular cartilage removal. Part of the lamina may be removed on one side and/or part of the disk may be removed to facilitate preparation of the interspace for fusion. Additional bone grafts are taken from the ilium or other donor bone and are used to bridge the laminae. The periosteum, ligaments, and paravertebral muscles are sutured to secure the bone grafting. The skin and subcutaneous tissues are closed with sutures as well.

In an alternate procedure, spinal arthrodesis, or fusion, is done to correct a spinal deformity. The patient is placed prone. A midline posterior incision is made overlying the affected vertebrae. The fascia and the paravertebral muscles are incised and retracted. The physician uses a curette and rongeur to clean interspinous ligaments. One of several techniques may be used. In one, the spinous processes are split and removed and a curette is used to cut into the lateral articulations. Thin pieces of separately reportable iliac or other donor bone graft are placed in these slots. Grafts are obtained, prepared, and packed on both sides of the spinal curve, with more bone chips on the concave sides. Separately reportable instrumentation may be affixed to the spine. The incision is closed with layered sutures. A cast may or may not be applied to stabilize the spine.

Coding Clarification

►Code 81.08 includes the following surgical techniques (approach):

- Axial lumbar interbody fusion (AxiaLIF)
- Posterior lumbar interbody fusion (PLIF)

76-84

- Transforaminal lumbar interbody fusion (TLIF)◄

OptiMesh system used in interbody posterior spinal fusion is a mesh pouch filled with morcellized bone graft that is inserted into the disc space once the disc is removed. The use of OptiMesh is included in the code 81.08; no additional code is reported for OptiMesh.

Coding Scenario

►A patient presents with severe lumbar degenerative disc disease at L3-L4. After being placed under general anesthesia and having the proper monitoring devices applied, the patient underwent an axial lumbar interbody fusion (AxiaLIF) with discectomy, application of intervertebral biomechanical spacers, and bone morphogenetic protein. Lateral fluoroscopic imaging demonstrated that the instrumentation was in good position and the patient's alignment was stable.

Code Assignment:

722.52	Degeneration of lumbar or lumbosacral intervertebral disc
81.08	Lumbar and lumbosacral fusion of the anterior column, posterior technique
80.51	Excision of intervertebral disc
84.51	Insertion of interbody fusion device
84.52	Insertion of recombinant bone morphogenetic protein
81.62	Fusion or refusion of 2-3 vertebrae◄

Documentation Tip

Spinal fusion is accomplished using a variety of surgical techniques. Codes identify whether a fusion or refusion was performed, the spinal level where the procedure was performed (cervical, thoracic, lumbar, or sacral), and the approach (anterior, posterior, lateral transverse), as well as the number of vertebrae fused or refused. Review the documentation for specific information regarding the procedure prior to final code selection in order to ensure accurate code assignment.

Coding Guidance

AHA: 2Q, '95, 9; 4Q, '99, 13; 2Q, '00, 12, 13; 4Q, '02, 107, 109; 4Q, '05, 122, 123; 1Q, '06, 12, 13; 1Q, '08, 5; 2Q, '09, 5

81.1   Arthrodesis and arthroereisis of foot and ankle

Coding Clarification

Subcategory 81.1 classifies arthrodesis procedures of the foot and ankle. The procedures in this subcategory include any bone graft and internal fixation when done in conjunction with the fusion.

Arthrodesis, or fusion, is accomplished using a variety of surgical techniques. Review the operative report for specific information regarding the site of

the fusion and technique used in order to ensure accurate code assignment.

81.11   Ankle fusion

Description

The physician fuses several joints in and around the ankle. It can be performed in one operation or in two separate surgeries. In either case, the physician makes at least one incision around the ankle. Incisions are continued deep to the ankle mortise itself and to the following joints: the talocalcaneal, the talonavicular, and the calcaneocuboid. The capsule of each joint is opened, explored, and debrided. Osteotomies are performed so that viable bone is available on each side of the joints. The physician utilizes a variety of internal fixation devices such as pins, wires, plates, or screws to connect the bones together across each joint. This allows the bones to fuse together as they heal. Because of the extensive nature of the surgery, and the time required for healing, the surgery is frequently performed in two stages. Incisions are irrigated and closed as usual. A cast is applied until the fusion is solidly healed.

Coding Clarification

Assign 81.11 to report a tibiotalar fusion.

Ankle fusion, or arthrodesis, is accomplished using a variety of surgical techniques; review the documentation for specific information regarding the procedure prior to final code selection in order to ensure accurate code assignment.

81.12   Triple arthrodesis

Description

The physician fuses the talonavicular, the calcaneocuboid, and the subtalar (talocalcaneal) joints. The physician makes incisions on each side of the foot. These are carried deep to the joints. Tendons are reflected and protected. Each joint is identified. Soft tissues are debrided. The capsules are opened and the joints visualized. Surgical Curettes are used to remove the articular cartilage of the joints one at a time so that viable bone is exposed. The physician uses any of a variety of surgical fixation devices including screws, plates, or wires to connect the bones of each individual joint together. The incisions are irrigated and closed in layers. A cast is applied and continued until all three joints are solidly fused.

Coding Clarification

A triple arthrodesis fuses the talus to the calcaneus and calcaneus to cuboid and navicular.

Arthrodesis, or fusion, is accomplished using a variety of surgical techniques. Review the operative report for specific information regarding the site of the fusion and technique used in order to ensure accurate code assignment.

● New Code   ▲ Revised Code   ►◄ Revised Text   © 2010 Ingenix

81.13 Subtalar fusion

Description
The physician fuses the subtalar (talocalcaneal) joint. An incision is made over the lateral ankle and foot. The physician extends this incision deep to the subtalar joint. Tendons and nerves are retracted and protected. Soft tissues are debrided. The joint capsule is incised and the joint is debrided as necessary. Surgical instruments including curettes are utilized to remove the articular cartilage of the joint. Fixation devices such as screws, pins, or wires are employed to maintain fixation of the talus. The incision is closed in layers. A cast is typically applied.

Coding Clarification
Do not assign 81.13 to report arthroereisis (81.18).

Arthrodesis, or fusion, is accomplished using a variety of surgical techniques. Review the operative report for specific information regarding the site of the fusion and technique used in order to ensure accurate code assignment.

81.14 Midtarsal fusion

Description
The physician fuses one of the midtarsal or tarsometatarsal joints of the foot. X-rays are used to determine the particular joint to be fused. The physician makes an incision in the skin directly overlying the joint. Tendons and nerves are retracted and a capsulotomy is performed. The physician removes the articular cartilage of the bones on both sides of the joint. The bony surfaces are fashioned for a close fit. Any of a variety of fixation devices are used to hold the bones in proper alignment. The wound is irrigated and debrided. The incision is closed in layers.

Coding Clarification
Arthrodesis, or fusion, is accomplished using a variety of surgical techniques. Review the operative report for specific information regarding the site of the fusion and technique used in order to ensure accurate code assignment.

81.15 Tarsometatarsal fusion

Description
The physician performs surgery on the foot in which more than one of the midtarsal or tarsometatarsal joints are fused. The physician makes one or more incisions over the dorsal aspect of the foot in the skin overlying the affected joints. The incisions are continued deep through the subcutaneous tissue. Nerves and tendons are retracted. The physician identifies the specific problem joints of the tarsals and metatarsals, performing capsulotomies. The joints are entered, explored, and debrided. The physician utilizes any of a variety of friction devices to hold each joint in its fused position. The wounds are irrigated and closed in layers.

In an alternate procedure, the physician performs surgery on the foot in which more than one of the midtarsal or tarsometatarsal joints are fused. The metatarsals are also osteotomized to correct for a flat foot deformity. The physician makes one or more incisions in the dorsal skin of the foot overlying the affected joints and metatarsals. The incisions are continued deep to the particular joints. Nerves and tendons are retracted. The shafts of the metatarsals that will undergo osteotomy are isolated and debrided. The physician performs capsulotomy on each joint to be fused. The metatarsals are cut and realigned in a plantar flexion position to correct flatfoot deformity. The joints, debrided of their articular cartilage, are fashioned for a close fit. The physician utilizes any of a variety of fixation devices such as wires, plates, pins, or screws to hold the metatarsal and the joints in alignment. The incisions are irrigated and closed in layers.

Coding Clarification
Arthrodesis, or fusion, is accomplished using a variety of surgical techniques. Review the operative report for specific information regarding the site of the fusion and technique used in order to ensure accurate code assignment.

81.16 Metatarsophalangeal fusion

Description
The physician fuses the joint between the great toe and the first metatarsal bone. A longitudinal incision is made on the dorsal surface of the first toe. It is deepened through the subcutaneous tissue and fascia to the first metatarsophalangeal joint. The nerves and tendons are retracted. A capsulotomy is performed. The physician makes parallel cuts of the metatarsal with a saw or osteotome. The two cuts are placed together in the desired alignment and position. Fixation devices hold the bones in position. The wound is irrigated and closed in layers.

Coding Clarification
Arthrodesis, or fusion, is accomplished using a variety of surgical techniques. Review the operative report for specific information regarding the site of the fusion and technique used in order to ensure accurate code assignment.

81.17 Other fusion of foot

Description
Code 81.17 is used to report other arthrodesis procedures of the foot that are not more precisely described by other codes in subcategory 81.1.

Coding Clarification
Arthrodesis, or fusion, is accomplished using a variety of surgical techniques. Review the operative report for specific information regarding the site of the fusion and technique used in order to ensure accurate code assignment.

76-84

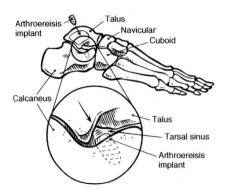

Arthroereisis implant — Talus — Navicular — Cuboid

Calcaneus

Talus — Tarsal sinus — Arthroereisis implant

81.18   Subtalar joint arthroereisis

Description
Subtalar arthroereisis is also referred to as arthrorisis. The physician inserts an endoprosthesis implant between the talus and the calcaneus to limit excessive movement of the subtalar joint. This subtalar implant acts as a spacer to permit normal subtalar joint motion while preventing pronation and displacement of the talus.

In one example, the physician performs surgery on the foot in which more than one of the midtarsal or tarsometatarsal joints are fused. The physician makes one or more incisions over the dorsal aspect of the foot in the skin overlying the affected joints. The incisions are continued deep through the subcutaneous tissue. Nerves and tendons are retracted. The physician identifies the specific problem joints of the tarsals and metatarsals, performing capsulotomies. The joints are entered, explored, and debrided. The physician utilizes any of a variety of friction devices to hold each joint in its fused position. The wounds are irrigated and closed in layers.

In another example, the metatarsals are also osteotomized to correct for a flat foot deformity. The physician makes one or more incisions in the dorsal skin of the foot overlying the affected joints and metatarsals. The incisions are continued deep to the particular joints. Nerves and tendons are retracted. The shafts of the metatarsals that will undergo osteotomy are isolated and debrided. The physician performs capsulotomy on each joint to be fused. The metatarsals are cut and realigned in a plantar flexion position to correct flatfoot deformity. The joints, debrided of their articular cartilage, are fashioned for a close fit. The physician utilizes any of a variety of fixation devices such as wires, plates, pins, or screws to hold the metatarsal and the joints in alignment. The incisions are irrigated and closed in layers.

Coding Clarification
Subtalar arthroereisis and subtalar arthrodesis are significantly different procedures and are not interchangeable. Review the operative report for specific information regarding the site and technique used in order to ensure accurate code assignment.

Coding Guidance
AHA: 4Q, '05, 124

81.2   Arthrodesis of other joint

Coding Clarification
Subcategory 81.2 classifies arthrodesis procedures such as excision of bone ends and compression. These subcategory codes include any bone graft and internal fixation done in conjunction with the fusion. As in other categories in this chapter, fourth digits specify the treatment site. Subcategory 81.2 includes fourth-digit subclassifications that identify the joint on which the procedure was performed.

81.20   Arthrodesis of unspecified joint

Description
Code 81.20 is used to report arthrodesis procedures when the joint treated is not identified in the documentation.

Documentation Tip
Review the documentation for specific information regarding the procedure prior to final code selection in order to avoid improper use of the "not otherwise specified" code and to ensure accurate code assignment.

81.21   Arthrodesis of hip

Description
To perform an intraarticular arthrodesis, the physician makes an anterior iliofemoral incision. The sartorius and rectus femoris muscles are then detached from their origins. The iliopsoas is reflected from the front of the hip joint. The physician dislocates the hip anteriorly. Cartilage is removed from the femoral head and acetabulum down to bleeding cancellous bone. The physician then packs the space between the surfaces of the femoral head and acetabulum with cancellous autogenous bone grafts. The physician may use compression screws to increase the stability of the fusion. The sartorius and rectus femoris muscles are reattached. The screws are placed through the femoral head and into the supraacetabular area of the ilium. The incision is repaired in multiple layers with suction drains. The limb may be placed in a single spica cast or in balanced suspension.

In some cases, the physician harvests a bone graft from the patient's iliac wing and crest and closes the surgically created graft donor site. The graft is positioned so it spans the anterior aspect of the hip from the pubic ramus to the femoral neck. The graft is secured with cancellous lag screws. A subtrochanteric osteotomy (bone cut) is made just below the lesser trochanter. The sartorius and rectus femoris muscles are reattached and the iliopsoas muscle is repositioned. The incision is repaired in multiple layers with suction drains. A one and one-half spica cast is applied.

Coding Clarification
An example of the position in which the hip may be fused is 30 degrees of flexion, 0 to 5 degrees of adduction, and 10 degrees of external rotation.

81.22   Arthrodesis of knee

Description
The physician makes a long incision along the inside of the patella. The patella is reflected laterally to expose the knee joint. Bone cuts are made to flatten out the joint surfaces of the femur and tibia. A U-shaped groove is made on the underneath side of the patella and a corresponding one on the femur. The patella is placed into the femoral groove and secured with screws. The physician makes an incision overlying the iliac crest, harvests a graft, and closes the surgically created graft donor site. The bone graft is placed between the joint surfaces. An external fixator compresses the joint surfaces. The knee is typically fused in 10 to 15 degrees of flexion. The incision is closed with sutures, staples, and/or Steri-strips.

Coding Clarification
Subcategory 81.2 includes any bone graft and internal fixation done in conjunction with the fusion.

Fourth-digit subclassifications specify the treatment site. Review the operative report for specific information regarding the site and technique used in order to ensure accurate code assignment.

81.23   Arthrodesis of shoulder

Description
The physician performs arthrodesis of the glenohumeral joint. The shoulder is positioned in what is considered the most functional position, slightly abducted to the side with forward elevation. A dorsolateral semicircular incision is made across the glenohumeral joint and carried distally at the midpoint. The articular cartilage is removed from the head of the humerus (ball) and the glenoid cavity (socket). The head is split and a wedge of bone is removed. This wedge is where the acromion will rest when the arm is positioned in abduction. At this point, bone grafting or plate fixation may be added to the procedure to stabilize the glenohumeral joint. If a plate is used, a second procedure will be needed to remove the hardware. Cast application or external

fixation may be used in a number of ways. In some cases, an autogenous graft is used.

Coding Clarification
Subcategory 81.2 includes any bone graft and internal fixation done in conjunction with the fusion.

Fourth-digit subclassifications specify the treatment site. Review the operative report for specific information regarding the site and technique used in order to ensure accurate code assignment.

81.24   Arthrodesis of elbow

Description
The physician performs an arthrodesis of the elbow joint by making a posterior longitudinal or posterolateral incision. The triceps tendon is split and released from the olecranon. The joint capsule is incised to expose the radial head and neck and the radial head is excised. A posterior and anterior synovectomy is performed. The physician trims the olecranon into a triangular shape with a saw. A triangular hole is created through the lower end of the humerus and the olecranon is inserted through this triangular hole. The physician places a bone screw obliquely through the humerus and into the ulna. The triceps tendon is repaired with sutures. The physician repairs the incision in layers and the elbow is immobilized in a long arm cast.

Coding Clarification
Subcategory 81.2 includes any bone graft and internal fixation done in conjunction with the fusion.

Fourth-digit subclassifications specify the treatment site. Review the operative report for specific information regarding the site and technique used in order to ensure accurate code assignment.

81.25   Carporadial fusion

Description
The physician performs fusion of the wrist joint. The radiocarpal joint, or wrist joint, is the joint between the distal end of the radius and its articular disk, and a row of carpal bones. The physician exposes the wrist through a dorsal, longitudinal incision. A dorsal tenosynovectomy is performed, and the wrist capsule is elevated exposing the radiocarpal joint. The physician excises the distal ulna and performs a synovectomy of the radiocarpal joint. The radial collateral ligament is released from the radial styloid. The cartilage and sclerotic bond is removed from the distal radius and proximal carpal row. Using an awl, the physician makes a channel in the medullary canal of the radius, through which a Steinman pin is used for internal fixation. The pin is drilled through the carpus to exit between the second and third, or between the third and fourth metacarpal, depending on alignment between the carpus and the radius. One or two small staples, or an obliquely-placed

Kirschner, may be used to provide additional fixation on the radiocarpal joint. The position of the wrist can be varied only five to 10 degrees by adjusting the direction of the pin as it is driven into the radius. A drain is placed in the subcutaneous and prior to skin closure. A milky compression dressing is applied, and the wrist is splinted in the desired position of fusion.

Coding Clarification
Subcategory 81.2 includes any bone graft and internal fixation done in conjunction with the fusion.

Fourth-digit subclassifications specify the treatment site. Review the operative report for specific information regarding the site and technique used in order to ensure accurate code assignment.

81.26   Metacarpocarpal fusion

Description
The physician performs fusion of the wrist joint, including the radiocarpal, intercarpal and/or carpometacarpal joints. The physician exposes the wrist through a dorsal, longitudinal incision. A dorsal tenosynovectomy is performed, and the wrist capsule is elevated exposing the radiocarpal joint. The physician excises the distal ulna and performs a synovectomy of the radiocarpal joint. The radial collateral ligament is released from the radial styloid. The cartilage and sclerotic bond is removed from the distal radius and proximal carpal row. Using an awl, the physician makes a channel in the medullary canal of the radius, through which a Steinman pin is used for internal fixation. The pin is drilled through the carpus to exit between the second and third, or between the third and fourth metacarpal, depending on alignment between the carpus and the radius. One or two small staples, or an obliquely-placed Kirschner, may be used to provide additional fixation on the radiocarpal joint. A drain is placed in the subcutaneous and prior to skin closure. A milky compression dressing is applied, and the wrist is splinted in the desired position of fusion.

Coding Clarification
Subcategory 81.2 includes any bone graft and internal fixation done in conjunction with the fusion.

Fourth-digit subclassifications specify the treatment site. Review the operative report for specific information regarding the site and technique used in order to ensure accurate code assignment.

81.27   Metacarpophalangeal fusion

Description
The physician fuses a metacarpophalangeal joint. Internal or external fixation may be used. The physician incises the overlying skin and dissects to the metacarpophalangeal joint. The physician may use a wire to stabilize the joint until fusion is

complete. In some cases an autograft is obtained and used. Bone is harvested from the distal radius or iliac crest and interposed between the two bones to prevent movement. The operative incision is closed in sutured layers and the hand is splinted.

Coding Clarification
Subcategory 81.2 includes any bone graft and internal fixation done in conjunction with the fusion.

Fourth-digit subclassifications specify the treatment site. Review the operative report for specific information regarding the site and technique used in order to ensure accurate code assignment.

81.28   Interphalangeal fusion

Description
The physician fuses an interphalangeal joint. Internal or external fixation may be used. The physician incises the overlying skin and dissects to the interphalangeal joint. The physician may use a wire to stabilize the joint until fusion is complete. A graft may be harvested from the distal radius or iliac crest and interposed between the bones to prevent movement. The operative incision is closed in sutured layers and the hand is splinted.

Coding Clarification
Use 81.28 to report fixation of a finger joint (finger capsulodesis).

Subcategory 81.2 includes any bone graft and internal fixation done in conjunction with the fusion.

Fourth-digit subclassifications specify the treatment site. Review the operative report for specific information regarding the site and technique used in order to ensure accurate code assignment.

81.29   Arthrodesis of other specified joint

Description
Code 81.29 is assigned to report arthrodesis procedures that are not more precisely described by other codes in subcategory 81.2. This code is also reported when the documentation does not further specify the site of the procedure performed.

Coding Clarification
Subcategory 81.2 includes any bone graft and internal fixation done in conjunction with the fusion.

Review the operative report for specific information regarding the site and technique used in order to ensure accurate code assignment.

81.3   Refusion of spine

Description
Spinal fusion codes identify whether a fusion or refusion was performed, the spinal level where the procedure was performed (cervical, thoracic, lumbar, or sacral), and the approach ▶or technique◀

● New Code   ▲ Revised Code   ▶◀ Revised Text   © 2010 Ingenix

(anterior, posterior, lateral transverse), as well as the number of vertebrae fused or refused. Refusions are coded to category 81.3 based on the level of refusion (fourth-digit subclassification). These codes include arthrodesis of spine with bone graft, internal fixation, and correction of pseudoarthrosis of spine.

Coding Clarification
▶The anterior column can be re-fused using an anterior, lateral, or posterior technique.

A posterior column refusion can be performed using a posterior, posterolateral, or lateral transverse technique.◀

Also assign a code for any synchronous excision of a harvested bone for graft (77.70-77.79).

Also code any insertion of interbody spinal fusion devices (84.51) or insertion of recombinant bone morphogenetic protein (84.52).

Remember to also code the total number of vertebrae fused (81.62-81.64).

360 degree spinal fusions are coded based on the type of fusion performed (81.06, 81.08, 81.36, and 81.38).

Coding Guidance
AHA: 4Q, '01, 64; 4Q, '03, 99

81.30   Refusion of spine, not otherwise specified

Description
Code 81.30 is assigned when the documentation does not further specify the refusion procedure. This code is also used to report spinal fusion procedures that are not more precisely described by other codes in subcategory 81.3.

Coding Clarification
Spinal fusion is accomplished using a variety of surgical techniques. To ensure accurate code assignment, review the documentation for specific information regarding whether a fusion or refusion was performed, the spinal level where the procedure was performed (cervical, thoracic, lumbar, or sacral), and the approach (anterior, posterior, lateral, transverse), as well as the number of vertebrae fused or refused.

Documentation Tip
Review the documentation for specific information regarding the procedure prior to final code selection in order to avoid improper use of the "not otherwise specified" code.

81.31   Refusion of Atlas-axis spine

Description
The physician performs spinal arthrodesis using an anterior, transoral, or posterior technique. Skull tong traction is applied. The physician may incise the back of the throat, but most often enters from the outside of the neck, left of the throat to reach the C1-C2 (atlas-axis) vertebrae. The patient is placed in a Stryker frame with a previously applied halo vest. The physician makes an incision from the occiput to the fourth or fifth vertebra and exposes the posterior arch of the atlas (C1) and laminae of the axis (C2) and removes all soft tissue from bony surfaces. The upper arch of C1 is exposed and a wire loop is brought from below upward under the arch of the atlas and sutured. The physician passes the free ends through the loop, grasping the arch of C1. A graft taken from the iliac crest or other donor bone is placed against the lamina of the C2 and the arch of C1 beneath the wire. The physician then passes one end of the wire through the spinous process of C2 and twists it securely into place. The retractors are removed and the incision is closed over a drain.

Coding Clarification
Spinal fusion is accomplished using a variety of surgical techniques. Review the operative report for the site of the spinal fusion and technique used (e.g., anterior, posterior). Correct code assignment is dependent on this information.

Code 81.31 reports craniocervical fusion, C1-C2 fusion, and occiput C2 fusion.

▲ 81.32   Refusion of other cervical spine, anterior column, anterior technique

Description
The physician uses an anterior approach to reach the damaged vertebrae. An incision is made through the neck, avoiding the esophagus, trachea, and thyroid. Retractors separate the intervertebral muscles. A drill is inserted in the affected vertebrae and the location is confirmed by separately reportable x-ray. The physician incises a trough in the front of the vertebrae with a drill or saw. The physician cleans out the intervertebral disk spaces with a rongeur and removes the cartilaginous plates above and below the vertebrae to be fused. The physician obtains and packs separately reportable grafts of iliac or other donor bone into the spaces and trims them. Traction is gradually decreased to maintain the graft in its bed. The fascia is sutured. A drain is placed and the incision is sutured.

Coding Clarification
Code 81.32 reports arthrodesis of C2 level or below using an anterior interbody or anterolateral technique.

Documentation Tip
Spinal fusion is accomplished using a variety of surgical techniques. Review the operative report for the site of the spinal fusion and technique used (e.g., anterior, posterior) prior to final code selection in order to ensure accurate code assignment.

76-84

▲ 81.33 Refusion of other cervical spine, posterior column, posterior technique

Description
The physician performs spinal arthrodesis using a posterior technique. The physician makes an incision overlying the vertebrae and separates the fascia and the supraspinous ligaments in line with the incision. The physician prepares the vertebrae and lifts ligaments and muscles out of the way. A chisel elevator is used to strip away the capsules of the lateral articulations and the articular cartilage and cortical bone is excised. Separately reportable chips are cut from the fossa below the lateral articulations and from the laminae, or fragments of the spinous process are taken and then used to fill the interlaminal space and the gap left by the articular cartilage removal. Additional bone grafts are taken from the ilium or other donor bone and are used to join the laminae. The periosteum, ligaments, and paravertebral muscles are sutured to secure the bone grafting. The skin and subcutaneous tissues are closed with sutures, as well.

Coding Clarification
Spinal fusion is accomplished using a variety of surgical techniques. Code 81.33 reports arthrodesis of C2 level or below using a posterior or posterolateral technique.

Documentation Tip
Review the operative report for the site of the spinal fusion and technique used (e.g., anterior, posterior) prior to final code selection in order to ensure accurate code assignment.

▲ 81.34 Refusion of dorsal and dorsolumbar spine, anterior column anterior technique

Description
Spinal arthrodesis, or fusion, to correct a spinal deformity is performed using an anterior approach. In the case of affected thoracolumbar vertebrae, the dissection is carried out through the abdominal muscles to the tenth rib, which is resected to allow access to the vertebrae in back. Dissection continues until the vertebral bodies are exposed. The physician cleans out the intervertebral disk spaces and removes the cartilaginous plates above and below the vertebrae to be fused. The physician obtains and packs separately reportable grafts of iliac or other donor bone into the spaces. Separately reportable instrumentation may be affixed to the spine. A drainage tube may be placed and the surgical wound is sutured closed. A cast may or may not be applied to stabilize the spine.

Coding Clarification
Spinal arthrodesis may be performed using a variety of surgical techniques. Code 81.34 reports arthrodesis of the thoracic or thoracolumbar region

using an anterior interbody or anterolateral or extracavitary technique.

Documentation Tip
Review the operative report for the site of the spinal fusion and technique used (e.g., anterior, posterior) prior to final code selection in order to ensure accurate code assignment.

▲ 81.35 Refusion of dorsal and dorsolumbar spine, posterior column, posterior technique

Description
The physician performs arthrodesis of the thoracic or thoracolumbar spine using a posterior approach. The physician makes an incision overlying the vertebrae and separates the fascia and the supraspinous ligaments in line with the incision. The physician prepares the vertebrae and lifts ligaments and muscles out of the way. A chisel elevator is used to strip away the capsules of the lateral articulations and the articular cartilage and cortical bone is excised. Separately reportable chips are cut from the fossa below the lateral articulations and from the laminae, or fragments of the spinous process are taken and then used to fill the interlaminal space and the gap left by the articular cartilage removal. Additional bone grafts are taken from the ilium or other donor bone and are used to join the laminae. The periosteum, ligaments, and paravertebral muscles are sutured to secure the bone grafting. The skin and subcutaneous tissues are closed with sutures, as well.

Coding Clarification
Spinal fusion is accomplished using a variety of surgical techniques. Code 81.35 reports arthrodesis of the thoracic or thoracolumbar region using posterior (interbody) or posterolateral technique.

Documentation Tip
Review the operative report for the site of the spinal fusion and technique used (e.g., anterior, posterior) prior to final code selection in order to ensure accurate code assignment.

▲ 81.36 Refusion of lumbar and lumbosacral spine, anterior column, anterior technique

Description
The physician uses an anterior approach to reach the damaged vertebrae. The physician makes an incision overlying the vertebrae and separates the fascia and the supraspinous ligaments in line with the incision. The physician prepares the vertebrae and lifts ligaments and muscles out of the way. A chisel elevator is used to strip away the capsules of the lateral articulations and the articular cartilage and cortical bone is excised. Separately reportable chips are cut from the fossa below the lateral articulations and from the laminae, or fragments of

● New Code ▲ Revised Code ▶◀ Revised Text © 2010 Ingenix

the spinous process are taken and then used to fill the interlaminal space and the gap left by the articular cartilage removal. Additional bone grafts are taken from the ilium or other donor bone and are used to join the laminae. The periosteum, ligaments, and paravertebral muscles are sutured to secure the bone grafting. The skin and subcutaneous tissues are closed with sutures, as well.

Coding Clarification

Spinal fusion is accomplished using a variety of surgical techniques, including:

- Anterior or anterolateral
- Direct lateral interbody fusion (DLIF)™
- Extreme lateral interbody fusion (XLIF™)
- Retroperitoneal
- Transperitoneal

Code 81.36 reports refusion of an anterior lumbar interbody fusion (ALIF). ALIF is an interbody fusion of the anterior and middle columns of the spine that is performed laparoscopically or through an anterior incision.

Documentation Tip

Review the operative report for the site of the spinal fusion and technique used (e.g., anterior, posterior) prior to final code selection in order to ensure accurate code assignment.

Coding Guidance

AHA: 4Q, '05, 122-123

▲ 81.37 Refusion of lumbar and lumbosacral spine, posterior column, posterior technique

Description

A lumbosacral spinal arthrodesis, or fusion, is done using a lateral transverse process technique. The physician makes an incision overlying the vertebrae and separates the fascia and the supraspinous ligaments in line with the incision. The physician prepares the vertebrae and lifts ligaments and muscles out of the way. A chisel elevator is used to strip away the capsules of the lateral articulations and the articular cartilage and cortical bone is excised. chips are cut from the fossa below the lateral articulations and from the laminae, or fragments of the spinous process are taken and then used to fill the interlaminal space and the gap left by the articular cartilage removal. Additional bone grafts are taken from the ilium or other donor bone and are used to join the laminae. The periosteum, ligaments, and paravertebral muscles are sutured to secure the bone grafting. The skin and subcutaneous tissues are closed with sutures, as well.

Coding Clarification

Spinal fusion is accomplished using a variety of surgical techniques, including:

- Posterior or posteriolateral technique
- Facet fusion
- Transverse process technique

Documentation Tip

Refusions are coded based on the level of refusion (fourth-digit subclassification).

Review the operative report for the site of the spinal fusion and technique used (e.g., anterior, posterior) prior to final code selection in order to ensure accurate code assignment.

81.38 Refusion of lumbar and lumbosacral spine, anterior column, posterior technique

Description

Lumbosacral spinal arthrodesis, or fusion, may be done using a posterior technique. The physician makes an incision overlying the lumbar vertebrae and separates the fascia and the supraspinous ligaments in line with the incision. The physician prepares the vertebrae and lifts ligaments and muscles out of the way. A chisel elevator is used to strip away the capsules of the lateral articulations and the articular cartilage and cortical bone is excised. Chips are cut from the fossa below the lateral articulations and from the laminae, or fragments of the spinous process are taken and then used to fill the interlaminal space and the gap left by the articular cartilage removal. Part of the lamina may be removed on one side and/or part of the disk may be removed to facilitate preparation of the interspace for fusion. Additional bone grafts are taken from the ilium or other donor bone and are used to bridge the laminae. The periosteum, ligaments, and paravertebral muscles are sutured to secure the bone grafting. The skin and subcutaneous tissues are closed with sutures as well.

In an alternate procedure, spinal arthrodesis, or fusion, is done to correct a spinal deformity. The patient is placed prone. A midline posterior incision is made overlying the affected vertebrae. The fascia and the paravertebral muscles are incised and retracted. The physician uses a curette and rongeur to clean interspinous ligaments. One of several techniques may be used. In one, the spinous processes are split and removed and a curette is used to cut into the lateral articulations. Thin pieces of separately reportable iliac or other donor bone graft are placed in these slots. Grafts are obtained, prepared, and packed on both sides of the spinal curve, with more bone chips on the concave sides. Separately reportable instrumentation may be affixed to the spine. The incision is closed with

76-84

layered sutures. A cast may or may not be applied to stabilize the spine.

Coding Clarification
Spinal fusion is accomplished using a variety of surgical techniques. Code 81.38 reports arthrodesis of the lumbar or lumbosacral region using a posterior (interbody) or posterolateral technique.

Code 81.38 reports posterior lumbar interbody fusion (PLIF), which involves an anterior and middle column fusion using a posterior approach, transforaminal lumbar interbody fusion (TLIF), which involves a transverse lateral interbody fusion, and axial lumbar interbody fusion (AxiaLIF), all using a posterior approach.

A 360-degree spinal fusion is coded based on the type of fusion performed (81.06, 81.08, 81.36, and 81.38).

Documentation Tip
Review the operative report for the site of the spinal fusion and technique used (e.g., anterior, posterior) prior to final code selection in order to ensure accurate code assignment.

Coding Guidance
AHA: 4Q, '02, 110; 4Q, '05, 122-123

81.39   Refusion of spine, not elsewhere classified

Description
Spinal arthrodesis, or fusion, may be performed to treat conditions such as degenerative, traumatic, or congenital lesions; herniated disks; or to stabilize fractures or dislocations of the spine. Spinal fusion is accomplished using a variety of surgical techniques. Code 81.39 is used to report spinal refusion procedures that are not more precisely described by other codes in subcategory 81.3.

Coding Clarification
Spinal fusion is accomplished using a variety of surgical techniques. Refusions are coded based on the level of refusion (fourth-digit subclassification).

Documentation Tip
Review the operative report for the site of the spinal fusion and technique used (e.g., anterior, posterior) prior to final code selection in order to ensure accurate code assignment.

81.4   Other repair of joint of lower extremity

Coding Clarification
Review the operative report for the site of the spinal fusion and technique used (e.g., anterior, posterior). Correct code assignment is dependent on this information.

For arthroplasties, determine if the surgeon performed a total or partial replacement and whether it was an initial or revision procedure, as the ICD-9-CM system provides different codes depending on the documentation.

Assign two codes for the two-staged cartilage transplantation: 80.6 for the harvesting of the cartilage (first stage) and 81.47 for the transplantation of the cells (second stage).

Osteochondral autograft transfer system (OATS) is a two-step procedure that involves excision of the semilunar cartilage of the knee (80.6) and harvesting the graft material for autografting to the talus (81.49). Assign both codes to fully describe OATS.

Any external traction or fixation, graft of bone or cartilage, or internal fixation device or prosthesis is included in an arthroplasty.

Use 81.45 for the Losee procedure (i.e., the reconstruction of the cruciate ligament[s] for stabilization of knee joint[s]).

Only one code, 81.47, is used for an arthroscopy with arthroscopic abrasion chondroplasty, synovectomy, and excision of plica.

Coding Guidance
AHA: S-O, '85, 4

81.40   Repair of hip, not elsewhere classified

Description
Code 81.40 is assigned to report other hip repair procedures that are not more precisely described by other codes in subcategory 81.4, such as acetabuloplasty, which redirects the inclination of the acetabular roof by an osteotomy of the ilium. The Pemberton acetabuloplasty is described as follows:

The patient is placed in a supine (face up) position. Using an anterior iliofemoral approach, the physician carries dissection down to expose the hip joint capsule and sciatic notch. The capsule is incised. Using a curved osteotome, a bone cut is made through the lateral cortex of the ilium. Another cut is made through the medial cortex of the ilium. After completing the osteotomy, a wide, curved osteotome is inserted into the front part of the osteotomy and used to lever the distal fragment distally, until the front edges are 2.5 to 3 cm apart. A wedge of bone is then resected (excised) from the iliac crest and placed in the initial osteotomy made earlier in the ilium. The wedge is driven firmly into place. If necessary, the graft may be secured with two pins. The hip is then reduced (repositioned) and the capsule is tightened with sutures. The incision is repaired in multiple layers. A spica cast is applied from the nipple line to the toes on the affected side and to above the knee on the opposite side. The cast is worn for approximately three months.

Documentation Tip
Review the documentation for specific information regarding the procedure prior to final code selection in order to ensure accurate code assignment.

81.42   Five-in-one repair of knee

Description
A five-in-one knee repair consists of a medial meniscectomy, medial collateral ligament repair, vastus medialis advancement, semitendinosus advancement, and pes anserinus transfer. The knee joint is made up of bone, cartilage, ligaments, tendons, and muscles. The thigh muscles, or quadriceps, include the rectus femoris, vastus medialis, vastus medialis obliquus, vastus intermedius, and vastus lateralis. The meniscus is made up of cartilage that cushions the joint and provides a smooth surface for motion and rotation of the knee joint. The knee has two menisci, located on either side, that cushion the knee joint to facilitate weight bearing and joint movement. The medial collateral ligament (MCL) and lateral collateral ligament (LCL) control the side to side motion of the knee. The anterior cruciate ligament (ACL) in the center of the knee and the posterior cruciate ligament (PCL) control the forward and back motion of the knee.

Coding Clarification
Surgical procedures on the knees are performed using a variety of surgical techniques and approaches. The physician may also use the arthroscope for all or part of the procedure. To ensure accurate code assignment, it will be necessary to review the medical record documentation for information regarding the approach and surgical technique, along with determining the bones, cartilage, ligaments, tendons, or muscles treated.

81.43   Triad knee repair

Description
A triad knee repair consists of a medial meniscectomy with repair of the anterior cruciate ligament and the medial collateral ligament. The "triad" refers to three structures of the knee: the medial collateral ligament, anterior cruciate ligament, and the medial meniscus. For a primary collateral repair, the physician makes an incision on the lateral or medial aspect of the knee, depending on which ligament is torn (medial collateral or lateral collateral). Sutures may be used to tie the torn ends together. If the attachment of the ligament to the bone is torn away, a screw may be used for fixation. For a cruciate ligament primary repair, an incision is made to gain access into the knee joint (the physician may use the arthroscope for part of the procedure). Screws and/or sutures are used to reattach the torn end to

the bone. Incisions are closed with sutures, staples, and/or Steri-strips. A temporary drain may be applied.

Coding Clarification
The O'Donoghue triad is used to describe an ACL, MCL, and meniscus injury and repair procedure. O'Donoghue's triad of ACL, MCL, and medial meniscus injuries is associated with the mechanism of valgus in external rotation, or the "clipping" injury.

Documentation Tip
Surgical procedures on the knees are performed using a variety of surgical techniques and approaches. The physician may also use the arthroscope for all or part of the procedure. To ensure accurate code assignment, it will be necessary to review the medical record documentation for information regarding the approach and surgical technique, along with determining the bones, cartilage, ligaments, tendons, or muscles treated.

Coding Scenario
The physician performed an osteotomy of the tibia to correct lateral rotation for a patient with a history of a twisting injury accompanied by a pop and tearing sensation and a subsequent effusion. The procedure involved a posterior cruciate ligament repair through a mid-line approach in which a portion of bone was removed from the anteromedial surface and transverse cuts were made to allow rotation.

Code Assignment:

81.43   Triad knee repair

81.44   Patellar stabilization

Description
The physician performs stabilization of the patella using a lateral ligament transposition to stabilize the patella. The knee joint consists of the tibiofemoral and patellofemoral joints. The patella, or knee cap, is a triangular bone within the tendon of the quadriceps muscles that connects with the top of the thighbone (femoral trochlea). Various different surgical procedures are used to treat patellar instability including a lateral release, medial plication, and the Roux-Goldthwait patellar tendon transposition. In one example, an anteromedial incision is made parallel to the quadriceps tendon and the patella. Dissection is carried down to the vastus medialis muscle/tendon to the site where it attaches to the patella. An incision is made along the vastus medialis tendon parallel to the patella. The tendon is overlapped and sutured, pulling the patella more medially and allowing for improved patellar alignment. Tissue layers are closed with sutures. The incision is closed with sutures and Steri-strips.

76-84

In an alternate procedure, an incision is made on the anteromedial aspect of the knee beginning above the patella and ending 1.3 cm below the tibial tuberosity. The area where the patellar tendon inserts into the tibial tuberosity is resected, including a thin piece of bone 1.3 cm square. The patellar tendon is pulled medially and distally on the tibia and a site is selected for reattachment. At the site, an "I" shaped incision is made and the patellar tendon is secured here temporarily with sutures. Next, the insertion of the vastus medialis muscle is transformed laterally and distally and sutured in place. After the alignment of the patella has been checked, the patellar tendon is anchored into the tibia with a staple. The incision is closed with sutures, staples, or Steri-strips.

Patellectomy is removal of the patella. A transverse, U-shaped incision is made over the anterior aspect of the knee just below the patella. The skin edges are retracted, and the incision is carried through the quadriceps expansion at the level of the distal third of the patella. The patella is excised from the capsule, quadriceps, and patellar tendons. The proximal part of the capsule and quadriceps tendon are taken medially and distally so that they overlap the distal part of the capsule by 1.3 cm and are sutured in place. The insertion of the vastus medialis is freed and transferred distally and laterally. Incisions are closed in layers with sutures.

Coding Clarification
Code 81.44 reports a Roux-Goldthwait operation for recurrent dislocation of the patella.

Documentation Tip
Surgical procedures on the knees are performed using a variety of surgical techniques and approaches. The physician may also use the arthroscope for all or part of the procedure. To ensure accurate code assignment, it will be necessary to review the medical record documentation for information regarding the approach and surgical technique, along with determining the bones, cartilage, ligaments, tendons, or muscles treated.

81.45 Other repair of the cruciate ligaments

Description
Code 81.45 is assigned to report other repair procedures of the cruciate ligaments that are not more precisely described by other codes in subcategory 81.4, such as arthroscopically aided anterior cruciate ligament repair/augmentation or reconstruction. In one example, the physician makes a portal incision 1 cm long on either side of the inferior patella for arthroscopic access into the knee joint. If the ligament is intact but torn away from its bony attachment, the physician may reattach the

ligament with a screw. If the ligament is nonfunctional, it is removed with the arthroscope. For an anterior cruciate ligament reconstruction, a 5 to 12 cm incision is made on the anterior lower patella and upper tibia. A tunnel is drilled through the tibia into the knee joint. A second tunnel is drilled from inside the knee joint, through the femur. With the aid of the arthroscope for visualization, a new ligament graft is placed in the tibial tunnel and positioned inside the knee joint. The bony ends of the ligament are placed in the tibial and femoral tunnels. The ligament is secured with interference screws in both tunnels. For a posterior cruciate ligament reconstruction, an additional 3 to 5 cm incision is made along the medial aspect of the knee joint to allow for proper location of the femoral tunnel. Incisions are closed with staples or Steri-strips. A temporary drain may be inserted.

Coding Clarification
Use 81.45 for the Losee procedure, which is reconstruction of the cruciate ligament for stabilization of the knee joint.

The knee joint is made up of bone, cartilage, ligaments, tendons, and muscles. The anterior cruciate ligament (ACL) is in the center of the knee and the posterior cruciate ligament (PCL) control the forward and backward motion of the knee.

Documentation Tip
Surgical procedures on the knees are performed using a variety of surgical techniques and approaches. The physician may also use the arthroscope for all or part of the procedure. To ensure accurate code assignment, it will be necessary to review the medical record documentation for information regarding the approach and surgical technique, along with determining the bones, cartilage, ligaments, tendons, or muscles treated.

Coding Guidance
AHA: M-A, '87, 12

81.46 Other repair of the collateral ligaments

Description
Code 81.46 is assigned to report other repair procedures of the collateral ligaments that are not more precisely described by other codes in subcategory 81.4. For a primary collateral repair, the physician makes an incision on the lateral or medial aspect of the knee, depending on which ligament is torn (medial collateral or lateral collateral). Sutures may be used to tie the torn ends together. If the attachment of the ligament to the bone is torn away, a screw may be used for fixation. Incisions are closed with sutures, staples, and/or Steri-strips. A temporary drain may be applied.

● New Code ▲ Revised Code ▶◀ Revised Text © 2010 Ingenix

Coding Clarification
The knee joint is made up of bone, cartilage, ligaments, tendons, and muscles. The medial collateral ligament (MCL) and lateral collateral ligament (LCL) control the side to side motion of the knee.

Documentation Tip
Surgical procedures on the knees are performed using a variety of surgical techniques and approaches. The physician may use the arthroscope for all or part of the procedure. To ensure accurate code assignment, it will be necessary to review the medical record documentation for information regarding the approach and surgical technique, along with determining the bones, cartilage, ligaments, tendons, or muscles treated.

81.47   Other repair of knee

Description
Code 81.47 is used to report other repair procedures of the knee that are not more precisely described by other codes in subcategory 81.4, such as arthroscopic abrasion chondroplasty in which the physician makes 1 cm long portal incisions on either side of the patellar tendon for arthroscopic access into the knee joint. Lesions of the articular cartilage are identified by the arthroscope and the use of a probe. Additional portal incisions may be made to provide better access to the lesions. Debridement of the unstable or fragmented cartilage is accomplished with a motorized suction cutter. The cartilage is smoothed down to the layer of subchondral bone, which promotes bleeding and regeneration of cartilage. Any loose bodies are removed. The physician may also drill holes into the subchondral bone or create tiny fractures (microfractures) to further promote cartilage regeneration. The joint is thoroughly flushed. A temporary drain may be applied. Incisions are closed with sutures and Steri-strips.

Coding Clarification
Assign two codes for a two-staged cartilage transplantation: 80.6 for the harvesting of the cartilage (first stage) and 81.47 for the transplantation of the cells (second stage).

Only one code, 81.47, is used for an arthroscopy with arthroscopic abrasion chondroplasty, synovectomy, and excision of plica.

Code 81.47 reports arthroplasty using a UniSpacer(TM) knee system. The UniSpacer(TM) is a unicompartmental device inserted to cushion and stabilize the knee that does not require fixation.

Documentation Tip
Surgical procedures on the knees are performed using a variety of surgical techniques and approaches. The physician may use the arthroscope

for all or part of the procedure. To ensure accurate code assignment, it will be necessary to review the medical record documentation for information regarding the approach and surgical technique, along with determining the bones, cartilage, ligaments, tendons, or muscles treated.

Coding Guidance
    AHA: 3Q, '93, 5; 1Q, '96, 3; 1Q, '00, 12, 13; 2Q, '03, 18

81.49   Other repair of ankle

Description
Code 81.49 is used to report other repair procedures of the ankle that are not more precisely described by other codes in subcategory 81.4. For example, the physician performs arthroplasty to correct joint problems caused by arthritis. Three portal incisions are made at the front and sides of the ankle. Joint surfaces are smoothed and scar tissues are removed from the joint. If excessive damage is noted or a loose component must be revised, the physician replaces damaged parts of the ankle with a prosthesis.

Documentation Tip
Surgical procedures on the ankles are performed using a variety of surgical techniques and approaches.

Review the documentation for specific information regarding the procedure prior to final code selection in order to ensure accurate code assignment.

Coding Guidance
    AHA: 3Q, '00, 4; 2Q, '01, 15

81.5   Joint replacement of lower extremity

Coding Clarification
Category 81.5 includes arthroplasty of a lower extremity with external traction or fixation, graft of bone chips or cartilage, an internal fixation device or prosthesis, and removal of a cement spacer.

Removal of a prior prosthesis is considered integral to the procedure and, as such, is not coded separately.

Documentation Tip
For arthroplasties, it is necessary to determine if the surgeon performed a total or partial replacement and whether it was an initial or revision procedure as the ICD-9-CM system provides different codes depending on the documentation.

Coding Guidance
    AHA: S-O, '85, 4; 4Q, '09, 149

81.51   Total hip replacement

Description
The physician performs a total reconstruction of the hip with replacement of both the femoral head and

acetabulum by prosthesis. To repair both surfaces of the hip joint with a prosthesis, the physician makes an incision along the posterior aspect of the hip with the patient in a lateral decubitus (lying on the side) position. The short external rotator muscles are released by incision from their insertion on the femur, exposing the joint capsule. The physician incises the capsule. The hip is then dislocated posteriorly. The physician resects (excises) the femoral head with a reciprocating saw. The physician removes any osteophytes around the rim of the acetabulum with an osteotome. The acetabulum is then reamed out with a power reamer, exposing both subchondral and cancellous bone. The acetabular component is inserted. The femoral canal is then prepared using either a hand or power reamer. The excised femoral head is measured with a caliper to determine the appropriate size for replacement. The physician prepares the femoral shaft by enlarging the canal with a rasp. The physician then selects the type of stem to be used. The stem is secured into the femoral shaft. The stem is inserted and pounded into place with an impactor. The physician then reduces (repositions) the femoral stem prosthesis. The physician may augment the area with an autograft or allograft. The graft may be harvested from the resected (excised) femoral head. Donor bone (allograft) may be used instead. The physician places the bone graft into the canal and/or acetabulum. The hip is reduced (repositioned). The external rotator muscles are reattached. The incision is repaired in multiple layers with suction drains.

Coding Clarification
Code also any type of bearing surface materials used in the prosthetic hip implants, if known (00.74-00.77).

Code 81.51 includes arthroplasty of the lower extremity with external traction or fixation, graft of bone chips or cartilage, an internal fixation device or prosthesis, and removal of a cement spacer.

Documentation Tip
For arthroplasties, it is necessary to determine if the surgeon performed a total or partial replacement and whether it was an initial or revision procedure as the ICD-9-CM system provides different codes depending on the documentation.

Coding Guidance
AHA: 2Q, '91, 18; 4Q, '04, 113; 2Q, '09, 11

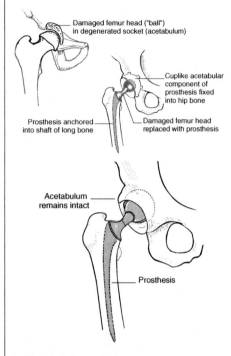

Damaged femur head ("ball") in degenerated socket (acetabulum)

Cuplike acetabular component of prosthesis fixed into hip bone

Prosthesis anchored into shaft of long bone

Damaged femur head replaced with prosthesis

Acetabulum remains intact

Prosthesis

81.52   Partial hip replacement

Description
The physician performs a repair of a single surface of a hip joint with a prosthesis. The physician makes a posterolateral incision over the hip with the patient in a lateral decubitus position (lying on the side). The fascia lata is incised and the muscles around the hip joint are retracted to visualize the capsule. The physician then incises the capsule, exposing the femoral neck. The femoral neck is resected (excised) with a reciprocating saw. The excised femoral head is measured with a caliper to determine the appropriate size for replacement. The physician prepares the femoral shaft by enlarging the canal with a rasp. The physician then selects the type of stem to be used. The stem is secured into the femoral shaft. The stem is inserted and pounded into place with an impactor. The physician then reduces (repositions) the femoral stem prosthesis. Hip motion and stability are evaluated. The capsule is then closed and the incision repaired in multiple layers.

In another example, the physician directly exposes the femoral fracture for treatment. The patient is placed in a supine (face up) position or slightly rolled up onto the other side. A 15 cm incision is made over the lateral hip. The fascia lata is split and the vastus lateralis muscle is detached from the femur. The physician then exposes the femoral neck and head. A small periosteal elevator or Kirschner wire is used to reduce (reposition) the fracture. The physician

76-84

● New Code   ▲ Revised Code   ▶◀ Revised Text   © 2010 Ingenix

places guide pins through the bone and across the fracture. The guide pins help determine correct screw length. The physician may use cannulated screws or compression hip screws and a plate to achieve internal fixation. In some cases due to the risk of subsequent non-union or avascular necrosis, the physician may replace the femoral head with a femoral prosthesis. The femoral canal is reamed out. A prosthesis of the proper size and length is then selected and inserted into the femoral canal. The physician then reduces the prosthesis into the acetabulum. The incision is repaired in multiple layers with sutures, staples, and/or Steri-strips.

Coding Clarification
Use 81.52 for a bipolar endoprosthesis.

Code also any type of bearing surface materials used in the prosthetic hip implants, if known (00.74-00.77).

Code 81.52 includes external traction or fixation, graft of bone chips or cartilage, and internal fixation device or prosthesis.

Coding Guidance
AHA: 2Q, '91, 18

81.53   Revision of hip replacement, not otherwise specified

Description
Total hip replacement is replacement of both the femoral head and acetabulum. This code is assigned to report revision of a hip replacement when the components replaced (acetabular, femoral or both) are not specified.

When the physician performs a conversion of a previous hip surgery to total hip replacement, the physician may access the area through the previous hip surgery incision, extending it to allow adequate exposure of the hip joint. Muscles are reflected as well. The physician removes any hardware (internal fixation). The physician incises the capsule. The hip is then dislocated. The physician resects (excises) the femoral head with a reciprocating saw. Next, the acetabulum is prepared. The physician removes any osteophytes around the rim of the acetabulum with an osteotome. The acetabulum is reamed out with a power reamer, exposing both subchondral and cancellous bone. The acetabular component is inserted. The femoral canal is then prepared using a hand or power reamer. The excised femoral head is measured with a caliper to determine the appropriate size for replacement. The physician prepares the femoral shaft by enlarging the canal with a rasp. The physician then selects the type of stem to be used. The stem is secured into the femoral shaft. The stem is inserted and pounded into place with an impactor. The physician then reduces (repositions) the femoral stem prosthesis. The

physician may augment the area with an autograft or allograft. The graft may be harvested from the resected femoral head (autograft). Donor bone (allograft) may be used instead. The hip is reduced (repositioned). Any reflected muscles are reattached. The incision is then repaired in multiple layers with suction drains.

Coding Clarification
Also code any removal of a cement joint spacer (84.57) and the type of bearing surface materials used in the prosthetic hip implants, if known (00.74-00.77).

Do not assign 81.53 for revision of a hip replacement when the components are specified (00.70-00.73).

Coding Guidance
AHA: 4Q '05, 125; 4Q, '06, 120

81.54   Total knee replacement

Description
The physician replaces severely damaged or worn cartilage of the knee joint. This code is assigned to report repair of a knee joint with prosthetic implant in one compartment (unicompartmental, or hemijoint), two compartments (bicompartmental), or three (tricompartmental) compartments. Code 81.54 also reports partial knee replacement.

A midline incision is made over the knee. Dissection is carried down to expose the knee joint. The physician may release soft tissues and/or ligaments in order to correct deformities and improve range of motion. The physician uses a cutting-alignment jig placed on the upper tibia to remove the tibial joint surface (both medial and lateral compartments) by making a bone cut. A cutting-alignment jig is also used on the femoral condyles to make the appropriate bone cut. Depending on the integrity of the joint surface of the patella, the physician may also make a bone cut to remove damaged cartilage. If the joint surface is healthy, it is left intact. Peg holes are usually made, and the components of the prosthesis are placed into position on the tibia, femur, and, if needed, the patella. The components are secured with glue and/or bone screws. The incision is repaired in multiple layers with sutures, staples, and/or Steri-strips.

Coding Clarification
When the classification does not differentiate between a unilateral and bilateral procedure and significant resources are used to perform the bilateral procedures, report the procedure code twice.

The knee joint is made up of bone, cartilage, ligaments, tendons, and muscles. The thigh muscles, or quadriceps, include the rectus femoris, vastus medialis, vastus medialis obliquus, vastus

76-84

intermedius, and vastus lateralis. The meniscus is made up of gelatinous cartilage that cushions the joint and provides a smooth surface for motion and rotation of the knee joint. The knee has two menisci, located on either side, that cushion the knee joint to facilitate weight bearing and joint movement. The medial collateral ligament (MCL) and lateral collateral ligament (LCL) control the side to side motion of the knee. The anterior cruciate ligament (ACL) in the center of the knee and the posterior cruciate ligament (PCL) control the forward and backward motion of the knee.

Documentation Tip
Surgical procedures on the knees are performed using a variety of surgical techniques and approaches. The physician may use the arthroscope for all or part of the procedure. To ensure accurate code assignment, it will be necessary to review the medical record documentation for information regarding the approach and surgical technique, along with determining the bones, cartilage, ligaments, tendons, or muscles treated.

Code 81.54 includes external traction or fixation, graft of bone chips or cartilage, and an internal fixation device or prosthesis.

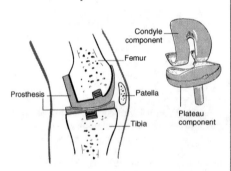

81.55 Revision of knee replacement, not otherwise specified

Description
Code 81.55 is used to report other revision procedures of knee replacements that are not more precisely described by other codes in subcategory 81.5. Knee replacement revision may include replacing one component of a prosthetic implant or all of the components (femoral, patellar or tibial). This code is also reported when the documentation does not further specify the revision procedure.

Typically, when the physician performs a revision of a total knee arthroplasty, previous skin incisions are incorporated to expose the knee. One or both (femoral and tibial) components are removed as determined by the physician. In order to remove the components, an osteotome or saw may be used to

loosen the cement or bone so that the prosthesis can be topped out with a mallet. If any cement is present, it is removed in order to protect and preserve as much bone as possible. Bone cuts are made to accommodate the new prosthesis. If significant bone defects are present on the femur, tibia, or both, a bone graft may be needed. An allograft (donor bone) may be packed into the defect. The components of the new prosthesis are placed into position and may be cemented for fixation. The femoral and entire tibial components are revised in some cases. The incision is repaired with sutures, staples, and/or Steri-strips.

Coding Clarification
Codes 00.80, 00.81, 00.82, 00.83, and 00.84 should be used to report the specific components replaced in knee replacement revision surgery. If the specific component is not documented, assign 81.55.

Use 84.57 for any synchronous removal of cement or joint spacer performed.

When the classification does not differentiate between a unilateral and bilateral procedure and significant resources are used to perform the bilateral procedures, report the procedure code twice.

Documentation Tip
Surgical procedures on the knees are performed using a variety of surgical techniques and approaches. The physician may use the arthroscope for all or part of the procedure. To ensure accurate code assignment, it will be necessary to review the medical record documentation for information regarding the approach and surgical technique, along with determining the bones, cartilage, ligaments, tendons, or muscles treated.

Coding Guidance
  AHA: 2Q, '97, 10; 4Q, '05, 113

81.56 Total ankle replacement
Description
The physician performs arthroplasty to correct joint problems caused by arthritis. Three portal incisions are made at the front and sides of the ankle. Joint surfaces are smoothed and scar tissues are removed from the joint. If a loose component must be revised or if excessive damage is noted, the physician replaces damaged parts of the ankle with a prosthesis.

Coding Clarification
When the classification does not differentiate between a unilateral and bilateral procedure and significant resources are used to perform the bilateral procedures, report the procedure code twice.

76-84

Code 81.56 includes external traction or fixation, graft of bone chips or cartilage, and an internal fixation device or prosthesis.

81.57   Replacement of joint of foot and toe

Description
There are 28 bones and more than 30 joints in the foot. Ligaments hold the bones and joints in place. Foot joints include the ankle or tibiotalar joint, the subtalar or talocalcaneal joint, the talonavicular joint, the calcaneocuboid joint, the metatarsocuneiform joint in the midfoot, and the great toe or first metatarsophalangeal joint.

The physician performs arthrodesis and replacement arthroplasty of the first metatarsophalangeal (MTP) joint with a great toe implant to treat advanced degenerative changes in the first MTP joint. Arthroplasty of the first metatarsophalangeal joint with an artificial implant is a common procedure performed. Various materials have been used in first metatarsophalangeal joint replacement, such as ceramic, silicone, or titanium-based prostheses.

Coding Clarification
Code 81.57 includes external traction or fixation, graft of bone chips or cartilage, and an internal fixation device or prosthesis.

Documentation Tip
Surgical procedures on the foot and toes are performed using a variety of surgical techniques and approaches. To ensure accurate code assignment, it will be necessary to review the medical record documentation for information regarding the approach and surgical technique, along with determining the bones or joints treated.

81.59   Revision of joint replacement of lower extremity, not elsewhere classified

Description
Code 81.59 is assigned to report other joint replacement revision procedures of the lower extremity that are not more precisely described by other codes in subcategory 81.5. For example, when the physician performs arthroplasty, three portal incisions are made at the front and sides of the ankle. Joint surfaces are smoothed and scar tissues are removed from the joint. If excessive damage is noted, the physician replaces damaged parts of the ankle with a prosthesis; in other cases a loose component must be revised.

Coding Clarification
Surgical procedures on the foot and toes are performed using a variety of surgical techniques and approaches. To ensure accurate code assignment, it will be necessary to review the medical record

documentation for information regarding the approach and surgical technique, along with determining the bones or joints treated.

Code 81.59 includes external traction or fixation, graft of bone chips or cartilage, and an internal fixation device or prosthesis.

81.6   Other procedures on spine

Description
The spine consists of vertebrae with cushioning discs between them. The vertebral spine consists of 25 vertebrae in the following order and number:

- Cervical: C1 (atlas), C2 (axis), C3, C4, C5, C6, C7

- Thoracic or dorsal: T1, T2, T3, T4, T5, T6, T7, T8, T9, T10, T11, T12

- Lumbar and sacral: L1, L2, L3, L4, L5, S1

Spinal fusion, also known as arthrodesis, fuses together two or more vertebrae with screw fixation and, in some cases, bone grafting. Spinal arthrodesis may be performed to treat conditions such as degenerative, traumatic, or congenital lesions; herniated disks; or to stabilize fractures or dislocations of the spine. Codes identify whether a fusion or refusion was performed, the spinal level where the procedure was performed (cervical, thoracic, lumbar, or sacral), the approach (anterior, posterior, lateral, transverse), and the number of vertebrae fused or refused.

Spinal fusion is accomplished using a variety of surgical techniques including:

- Anterior interbody fusion—excising the disc and cartilage end plates and inserting a bone graft between two vertebrae.

- Posterolateral fusion and lateral fusion—decorticating and bone grafting the zygapophysial joint, pars interarticularis, and transverse process.

- Posterior fusion—decorticating and bone grafting of neural arches between the right and left zygapophysial joints.

- One-level fusion—fuses together two vertebral bones and one disc.

- Two-level fusion—fuses three vertebral bones with two discs.

Coding Clarification
Assign one code from series 81.62-81.64 to report the total number of vertebrae fused.

Assign codes to report the level and approach of the fusion or refusion (81.00-81.08, 81.30-81.39).

Coding Guidance
    AHA: 4Q, '03, 99

76-84

81.62   Fusion or refusion of 2-3 vertebrae

Description

Spinal arthrodesis, or fusion, is performed on two to three vertebrae. An anterior approach is used. In the case of affected thoracolumbar vertebrae, the dissection is carried out through the abdominal muscles to the tenth rib, which is resected to allow access to the vertebrae in back. Dissection continues until the vertebral bodies are exposed. The physician cleans out the intervertebral disc spaces and removes the cartilaginous plates above and below the vertebrae to be fused. The physician obtains and packs separately reportable grafts of iliac or other donor bone into the spaces. Separately reportable instrumentation may be affixed to the spine. A drainage tube may be placed and the surgical wound is sutured closed. A cast may be applied to stabilize the spine.

Coding Clarification

Assign one code from series 81.62-81.64 to report the total number of vertebrae fused.

Documentation Tip

Spinal fusion is accomplished using a variety of surgical techniques. To ensure accurate code assignment, review the documentation for specific information regarding whether a fusion or refusion was performed, the spinal level where the procedure was performed (cervical, thoracic, lumbar, sacral), the approach (anterior, posterior, lateral, transverse), and the number of vertebrae fused or refused.

Coding Guidance

> **AHA:** 4Q, '03, 99; 4Q, '05, 123; 1Q, '06, 12, 13;1Q, '07, 20; 1Q, '08, 5; 2Q, '08, 14

81.63   Fusion or refusion of 4-8 vertebrae

Description

Spinal arthrodesis or fusion on four to eight vertebrae is done using a posterior approach. The patient is placed prone. A midline posterior incision is made overlying the affected vertebrae. The fascia and the paravertebral muscles are incised and retracted. The physician uses a curette and rongeur to clean interspinous ligaments. One of several techniques may be used. In one, the spinous processes are split and removed and a curette is used to cut into the lateral articulations. Thin pieces of separately reportable iliac or other donor bone graft are placed in these slots. Grafts are obtained, prepared, and packed on both sides of the spinal curve, with more bone chips on the concave sides. Separately reportable instrumentation may be affixed to the spine. The incision is closed with layered sutures. A cast may be applied to stabilize the spine.

Coding Clarification

Assign one code from series 81.62-81.64 to report the total number of vertebrae fused.

Documentation Tip

Spinal fusion is accomplished using a variety of surgical techniques. To ensure accurate code assignment, review the documentation for specific information regarding whether a fusion or refusion was performed, the spinal level where the procedure was performed (cervical, thoracic, lumbar, sacral), the approach (anterior, posterior, lateral, transverse), and the number of vertebrae fused or refused.

Coding Guidance

> **AHA:** 4Q, '03, 99-101

81.64   Fusion or refusion of 9 or more vertebrae

Description

Spinal arthrodesis or fusion on nine or more vertebrae is performed for conditions such as herniated discs; degenerative, traumatic, or congenital lesions; or to stabilize fractures or dislocations of the spine. The physician makes an incision overlying the lumbar vertebrae and separates the fascia and the supraspinous ligaments in line with the incision. The physician prepares the vertebrae and lifts ligaments and muscles out of the way. A chisel elevator is used to strip away the capsules of the lateral articulations and the articular cartilage and cortical bone is excised. Separately reportable chips are cut from the fossa below the lateral articulations and from the laminae, or fragments of the spinous process are taken and used to fill the interlaminal space and the gap left by the articular cartilage removal. Part of the lamina may be removed on one side and/or part of the disc may be removed to facilitate preparation of the interspace for fusion. Additional bone grafts are taken from the ilium or other donor bone and are used to bridge the laminae. The periosteum, ligaments, and paravertebral muscles are sutured to secure the bone grafting. The skin and subcutaneous tissues are closed with sutures as well.

Coding Clarification

Assign one code from series 81.62-81.64 to report the total number of vertebrae fused.

Documentation Tip

Spinal fusion is accomplished using a variety of surgical techniques. To ensure accurate code assignment, review the documentation for specific information regarding whether a fusion or refusion was performed, the spinal level where the procedure was performed (cervical, thoracic, lumbar, sacral), the approach (anterior, posterior, lateral, transverse), and the number of vertebrae fused or refused.

Coding Guidance

> **AHA:** 4Q, '03, 99-101

● New Code   ▲ Revised Code   ►◄ Revised Text   © 2010 Ingenix

81.65   Percutaneous vertebroplasty

Description
Vertebroplasty is a minimally invasive surgical procedure for treating vertebral compression fractures, which involves a cement-like material injected into the collapsed bone to stabilize the fracture. The physician inserts a trocar into the vertebral bone and a cement mixture is injected.

Percutaneous vertebroplasty is performed by a one- or two-sided injection of a vertebral body. A local anesthetic is administered. In a separately reportable procedure, the radiologist uses imaging techniques, such as CT scanning and fluoroscopy, to guide percutaneous placement of the needle during the procedure and to monitor the injection procedure. Sterile biomaterial such as methyl methacrylate is injected from one side or both sides into the damaged vertebral body and acts as a bone cement to reinforce the fractured or collapsed vertebra. The procedure does not restore the original shape to the vertebra, but it does stabilize the bone, preventing further fracture or collapse. Following the procedure, the patient may experience significant, almost immediate, pain relief.

Coding Clarification
Vertebroplasty and vertebral augmentation are percutaneous procedures performed to treat fractured or diseased vertebrae using cement or other fillers. Conventional vertebroplasty is a single-step procedure in which bone cement is percutaneously injected into the vertebrae under imaging guidance. Vertebral augmentation is a two-step procedure using a variety of techniques and devices to mechanically augment vertebral body height followed by injection of the cement filler.

Code 81.65 excludes kyphoplasty (81.66). Kyphoplasty is vertebroplasty with an additional step of inserting an inflatable balloon into the vertebra.

Bone void fillers are used in certain procedures on the spine extremities and pelvis to fill gaps that are surgically created or the result of trauma or disease processes. Autologous bone grafts harvested from the patient's iliac crest have typically been used to fill bony voids; however, synthetic products have been developed to fill bony voids. Bone void fillers include acrylic cement, calcium based fillers, and polymethylmethacrylate (PMMA).

A variation of a percutaneous vertebroplasty in which no cavity is created prior to injection of bone void filler is called the ARCUATE ™ XP procedure. A special mechanical device cuts an arc within the vertebral body to allow for the dispersion of injected bone cement.

Coding Guidance
AHA: 2Q, '08, 15

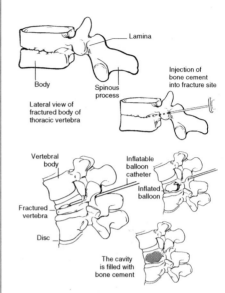

81.66   Percutaneous vertebral augmentation

Description
Kyphoplasty involves insertion of an inflatable balloon, bone tamps, or other device under fluoroscopic guidance to create a cavity and the cavity is filled with a cement-like material to further stabilize the bone.

The physician performs a percutaneous kyphoplasty, a modification of the percutaneous vertebroplasty, to reduce the pain associated with osteoporotic vertebral compression fractures. This procedure has the added advantage of restoring vertebral body. The procedure is performed under separately reported x-ray. The patient is placed in a prone, slightly flexed position. A 5 to 7 mm incision is made and small cannulas are inserted into the vertebral body from both sides. Balloon catheters, called tamps, are inserted into the vertebra and inflated. The tamps create a void in the soft trabecular bone and restore vertebral alignment. The balloon is removed and bone cement is injected into the cavity.

Coding Clarification
Vertebral augmentation is a two-step procedure using a variety of techniques and devices to mechanically augment vertebral body height followed by injection of the cement filler. Conventional vertebroplasty is a single-step procedure in which bone cement, or polymethylmethacrylate (PMMA), is percutaneously injected into the vertebrae under imaging guidance.

76-84

Code 81.66 excludes vertebroplasty (81.65). Kyphoplasty is vertebroplasty with an additional step of inserting an inflatable balloon into the vertebra.

Bone void fillers are used in certain procedures on the spine, extremities, and pelvis to fill gaps that are surgically created or the result of trauma or disease processes. Autologous bone grafts harvested from the patient's iliac crest have typically been used to fill bony voids; however, synthetic products have been developed to fill bony voids. Bone void fillers include acrylic cement, calcium based fillers, and polymethylmethacrylate (PMMA).

Documentation Tip
To ensure accurate code assignment, carefully review the medical record documentation for specific information regarding the procedure performed. Both conventional vertebroplasty and vertebral augmentation are percutaneous procedures performed to treat fractured or diseased vertebrae using cement or other fillers.

Procedures classifiable to code 81.66 may be documented with the following terminology:

- Arcuplasty
- Kyphoplasty
- Skyphoplasty
- Spineoplasty

Coding Guidance
AHA: 3Q, '06, 13; 1Q, '07, 5, 7

81.7   Arthroplasty and repair of hand, fingers, and wrist

Description
Subcategory 81.7 describes plastic surgery on the hand, fingers, and wrist joints. In the case of an arthroplasty, any external traction or fixation, graft of bone or cartilage, or internal fixation device or prosthesis is included in the repair codes. Review the operative report for the site and technique used (e.g., anterior, posterior). Correct code assignment is dependent on this information.

Coding Clarification
For arthroplasties, it is necessary to determine if the surgeon performed a total or partial replacement and whether it was an initial or revision procedure, as the ICD-9-CM system provides different codes depending on the documentation.

Subcategory 81.7 excludes operations on the muscle, tendon, and fascia of the hand (82.01-82.99).

81.71   Arthroplasty of metacarpophalangeal and interphalangeal joint with implant

Description
The physician performs an arthroplasty on the metacarpophalangeal joint. The physician incises the overlying the skin and dissects to the MP joint. If performing an arthroplasty on the interphalangeal joint, the physician dissects to the I-P joint. In this case, a prosthetic joint is used to replace the diseased joint.

81.72   Arthroplasty of metacarpophalangeal and interphalangeal joint without implant

Description
When performing an arthroplasty on the metacarpophalangeal joint, the physician incises the overlying the skin and dissects to the MP joint. If performing an arthroplasty on the interphalangeal joint, the physician dissects to the I-P joint. In this code, the joint is reconstructed using neighboring tissue rather than a prosthetic implant.

Coding Clarification
For arthroplasties, determine if the surgeon performed a total or partial replacement and whether it was an initial or revision procedure as the ICD-9-CM system provides different codes depending on documentation.

Coding Guidance
AHA: 1Q, '93, 28; 3Q, '93, 8

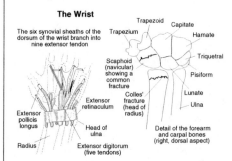

The Wrist

The six synovial sheaths of the dorsum of the wrist branch into nine extensor tendon

Trapezoid
Capitate
Trapezium
Hamate
Scaphoid (naviular) showing a common fracture
Triquetral
Pisiform
Colles' fracture (head of radius)
Lunate
Extensor retinaculum
Ulna
Extensor pollicis longus
Head of ulna
Detail of the forearm and carpal bones (right, dorsal aspect)
Radius
Extensor digitorum (five tendons)

81.73   Total wrist replacement

Description
The physician performs a total wrist arthroplasty. The physician makes a straight, dorsal, longitudinal incision centered over the wrist from the middle of the third metacarpal proximally. The skin and subcutaneous tissues are elevated off the underlying fascia and retinaculum. The retinaculum over the fourth dorsal compartment is incised longitudinally and elevated. The extensor pollicis longus is freed and retracted radically. A longitudinal incision is made in the capsule overlying the distal radius. Ulnarly, a capsular periosteal flap is elevated

● New Code   ▲ Revised Code   ▶◀ Revised Text   © 2010 Ingenix

through the dorsal radioulnar ligaments. Radially, the subperiosteal dissection continues to the radial styloid beneath the first dorsal compartment. The distal radius is excised, as is the distal ulna if it is dislocated or severely involved. A cut, made to match the shape of the prosthesis of choice, is made through the hamate, capitate, trapezoid, and distal scaphotrapezoid area. The carpus is removed. The medullary canal of the radius is reamed. A fine awl is used to penetrate the base of the capitate and the shaft of the third metacarpal. The medullary canal of this bone is reamed. If using a double-stemmed component, an additional canal is prepared in the second metacarpal. The component is inserted into the canals. Appropriate short canals are prepared in the carpal bases. The metallic components are inserted. The prosthetic polyethylene ball is placed on the trunnion and motion is tested. When desired motion is achieved, cement is mixed and injected into the medullary canals. The capsular-periosteal tissues are repaired over the prosthesis. The extensor retinaculum may be used to reinforce the capsule. The skin is closed over a deep and a superficial suction drain.

Coding Clarification
For arthroplasties, determine if the surgeon performed a total or partial replacement and whether it was an initial or revision procedure as the ICD-9-CM system provides different codes depending on documentation.

81.74 Arthroplasty of carpocarpal or carpometacarpal joint with implant

Description
The physician performs an interposition arthroplasty of the carpometacarpal joint. The physician makes a zig-zag incision over the proximal one third of the first metacarpal and extends it along the first wrist extensor compartment. The metacarpal joint is vertically incised to release the capsule from the base of the metacarpal. The joint is completely dislocated to expose the metacarpal end. The physician resects the metacarpal based perpendicular to its long axis. The base is shaped to allow the insertion of a Swanson great toe prosthesis. The medullary canal of the metacarpal is reamed to accept the prosthetic stem. The stem is inserted and the base of the prosthesis is seated on the flat surface of the trapezium bone. A Kirschner wire is inserted through the first metacarpal and into the carpus to ensure alignment. The capsule and the wounds are sutured closed.

Coding Clarification
For arthroplasties, determine if the surgeon performed a total or partial replacement and whether it was an initial or revision procedure as the

ICD-9-CM system provides different codes depending on documentation.

81.75 Arthroplasty of carpocarpal or carpometacarpal joint without implant

Description
An incision is made over the joint to be exposed. The soft tissues are dissected away and the joint capsule is exposed and incised. The metacarpal joint is vertically incised to release the capsule from the base of the metacarpal. The joint is completely dislocated to expose the metacarpal end. The physician resects the metacarpal based perpendicular to its long axis. A Kirschner wire is inserted through the first metacarpal and into the carpus to ensure alignment. The capsule and the wounds are sutured closed.

Coding Clarification
For arthroplasties, determine if the surgeon performed a total or partial replacement and whether it was an initial or revision procedure as the ICD-9-CM system provides different codes depending on documentation.

Coding Guidance
AHA: 3Q, '93, 8

81.79 Other repair of hand, fingers, and wrist

Description
Code 81.79 is used to report other repair procedures of the hands, fingers, and wrists that are not more precisely described by other codes in subcategory 81.7. For example, the physician performs an arthroplasty with prosthetic replacement of the trapezium. The physician makes a straight, longitudinal cut from the middle of the thumb metacarpal to the radial styloid. The capsule is split longitudinally from the metacarpal to the scaphoid. The capsule and periosteum are elevated off the trapezium. The radial portion of the trapezoid is removed. The base of the first metacarpal is squared off. A triangular hole is made in the base of the metacarpal, and the canal is made to accept the implant stem. The size of the implant should be slightly smaller than a tight fit. The capsule is repaired and reinforced by suturing slips of the abductor pollicis and flexor carpi radialis muscles to the capsule. A K-wire is placed through the implant and into the trapezoid or capitate to stabilize the position for six weeks. The skin is closed, leaving the wire protruding through incision, and a bulky dressing is applied to keep the thumb abducted.

Documentation Tip
Review the documentation for specific information regarding the procedure prior to final code selection in order to ensure accurate code assignment.

81.8   Arthroplasty and repair of shoulder and elbow

Description
Subcategory 81.8 describes arthroplasty repairs of the shoulder and elbow. This subcategory includes arthroplasty of an upper limb with external traction or fixation, graft of bone or cartilage, and an internal fixation device or prosthesis.

Coding Clarification
For arthroplasties, determine if the surgeon performed a total or partial replacement and whether it was an initial or revision procedure as the ICD-9-CM system provides different codes depending on documentation.

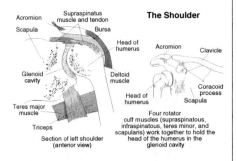

The Shoulder

Acromion
Suprapinatus muscle and tendon
Scapula
Bursa
Head of humerus
Acromion
Clavicle
Glenoid cavity
Deltoid muscle
Coracoid process
Head of humerus
Scapula
Teres major muscle
Triceps
Four rotator cuff muscles (supraspinatous, infraspinatous, teres minor, and scapularis) work together to hold the head of the humerus in the glenoid cavity
Section of left shoulder (anterior view)

▲ 81.80   Other total shoulder replacement

Description
A total shoulder replacement is done for the glenohumeral joint. A long curved incision is made from the superior aspect of the acromion along the deltopectoral interval to the deltoid insertion. The deltoid is retracted laterally and pectoralis medially. The fascia between the pectoralis and the clavicle is divided and the subacromial space is freed with a gloved finger or periosteal elevator. The coracoacromial ligament is freed and often an acromioplasty is performed to allow for freedom of movement after surgery. The subscapularis tendon is tagged and removed from the capsule. The anterior joint capsule is divided and the glenohumeral joint is dislocated by further external rotation and extension of the arm. The joint is explored and all loose bodies are removed. The humeral head is removed with a reciprocating saw or osteotome. In addition, a prosthetic device is placed proximally at the glenoid to articulate with the prosthetic humeral head. Prior to placement of the humeral prosthesis, the joint is opened to fully expose the glenoid surface. The surface cartilage of the glenoid is removed. A power drill is used to cut a slot into the glenoid the exact size of the holding device of the glenoid component. Small curettes are used to remove cancellous bone from the base of the coracoid bone. With a bur, articular cartilage is removed from the surface of the glenoid. A trial glenoid component is used to properly prepare the

bone and fit the prosthesis. Once the glenoid preparation is complete, the glenoid vault is drilled and filled with polymethylmethacrylate (bone cement). The glenoid component is pushed into place and held until the cement is cured. Prior to final insertion of the humeral component, an anterior acromioplasty and acromioclavicular arthroplasty are performed, if necessary. If large rotator cuff tears are found, they are repaired at this time. The joint is brought through a full range of motion and fully irrigated. The subscapularis tendon is repaired to stabilize the joint; however, the joint capsule is not usually resutured. Drains are placed and the deltopectoral interval is sutured closed. The arm is placed in a sling and swathe.

Coding Clarification
Surgical procedures on the shoulder and elbow are performed using a variety of surgical approaches and techniques, including open and arthroscopic methods. For arthroplasties, determine if the surgeon performed a total or partial replacement and whether it was an initial or revision procedure as the ICD-9-CM system provides different codes depending on documentation.

▶Code 81.80 excludes reverse total shoulder replacement (81.88).◀

Documentation Tip
To ensure accurate code assignment, review the medical record documentation for approach and surgical technique.

Coding Guidance
   AHA: 2Q, '08, 5

81.81   Partial shoulder replacement

Description
A partial acromioplasty or acromionectomy, with or without coracoacromial ligament release, is done. This procedure is also commonly performed during repair to the rotator cuff in an effort to increase the space below the acromion where the cuff tendons traverse toward their insertion on the humerus. An incision is made overlying the area. Dissection is carried down to the acromion. Acromioplasty involves the division of the acromioclavicular ligament followed by the use of a burr to cut away the under surface of the acromion. During acromionectomy, the distal portion of the acromion is removed. The coracoacromial ligament, a wide, strong band spanning between the acromion and the coracoid process of the scapula, may also be released. The joint is irrigated and the incisions are closed with sutures or Steri-strips.

In an alternate procedure, the physician performs open treatment of a proximal humeral (surgical or anatomical neck) fracture. An incision is made anteromedially extending posteriorly along the

76-84

acromion to the lateral half of the spine of the scapula. The deltoid is detached from the exposed portion of the spine of the scapula. The deltoid is reflected down to expose the joint capsule and the humerus. The fractured portion of the proximal humerus (surgical or anatomical neck) is identified and the fracture is aligned. If the tuberosity is involved, it is repaired. External or internal fixation may be used to stabilize the fracture site. Once the fracture is stabilized, the wound is irrigated. The deltoid is repositioned and sutured in place. The skin is sutured and the wound is covered with a soft dressing. The arm is positioned in a sling and movement is restricted to allow for proper healing.

Coding Clarification
Surgical procedures on the shoulder and elbow are performed using a variety of surgical approaches and techniques, including open and arthroscopic methods. For arthroplasties, determine if the surgeon performed a total or partial replacement and whether it was an initial or revision procedure as the ICD-9-CM system provides different codes depending on documentation.

Documentation Tip
To ensure accurate code assignment, review the medical record documentation for approach and surgical technique.

81.82   Repair of recurrent dislocation of shoulder

Description
The most common approach to reconstruct a complete rotator cuff avulsion tear of the shoulder is an anterior approach through an incision over the acromioclavicular joint. If the infraspinatus is to be shifted, a second incision is made along the scapular spine posteriorly, detaching a portion of the posterior deltoid if necessary. The margins of the tear are freshened and a non-absorbable suture closes the longitudinal portion of the tear. A portion of the articular cartilage on the under side of the humeral head is removed. The raw edges of the torn tendon are brought into contact with raw bone and the ends of the sutures are passed through holes drilled through the greater tuberosity and tied over its lateral aspect. The physician performs an acromioplasty. Acromioplasty involves the division of the acromioclavicular ligament followed by the use of a burr to cut away the under surface of the acromion. During acromionectomy, the entire distal portion of the acromion is removed. Once the reconstruction is complete, the incision is closed and the arm may be positioned in an abduction splint or pillow for protection.

Coding Clarification
Open surgical treatment, particularly the Bankart procedure, is frequently performed for treatment of recurrent shoulder dislocation and instability.

Coding Scenario
The physician repaired recurrent shoulder joint dislocations by making a long incision and cutting through the deltoid muscle and suturing the joint capsule to the detached labrum tissues. The torn ligaments are reattached to the proper place in the shoulder joint.

   Code Assignment:

   81.82   Repair of recurrent dislocation of shoulder

Coding Guidance
   AHA: 3Q, '95, 15

81.83   Other repair of shoulder

Description
Code 81.83 is used to report other repair procedures of the shoulder that are not more precisely described by other codes in subcategory 81.8.

Coding Clarification
▶Assign code 81.83 to report shoulder procedures documented as capsular shift reconstruction or superior glenoid labrum lesion (SLAP) repair.◀

Coding Guidance
   AHA: 3Q, '93, 5; 2Q, '00, 14; 4Q, '01, 51; 1Q, '02, 9

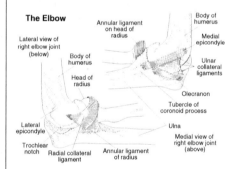

81.84   Total elbow replacement

Description
The physician openly treats a periarticular fracture (distal humerus and proximal ulna and/or proximal radius) and/or dislocation of the elbow. The physician may make more than one incision depending on the extent of the fractures and/or dislocation. If there is a dislocation, it is reduced (realigned) first. The fractures are then reduced and secured with plates, screws, pins, wires, or a combination of these. The physician may place a pin through the olecranon for skeletal traction in a patient with multiple injuries to temporarily stabilize the fracture and/or dislocation. If joint surface congruity cannot be restored, the physician performs a total elbow arthroplasty. For elbow

76-84

arthroplasty, the physician makes a straight, midline, posterior incision. The ulnar nerve is identified and retracted for protection. The triceps mechanism is elevated from the olecranon. The collateral ligaments are preserved. A portion of the olecranon is cut and removed to allow implantation of the ulnar stem. The distal humerus is then prepared by removing cancellous bone with a curette. The physician uses a rasp to open and contour the humeral and ulnar medullary canals for insertion of the prosthetic stems. Cement is inserted into the ulnar and humeral medullary canals with a cement gun or syringe. The elbow is flexed and the prosthesis is inserted into the humeral and ulnar medullary canals at the same time. The elbow joint is fully extended while the cement hardens. The triceps mechanism is sutured back to fascia. The ulnar nerve is positioned anterior to the elbow. Arthroplasty may be performed in conjunction with some internal fixation for fracture reduction and stabilization.

Coding Clarification

Surgical procedures on the shoulder and elbow are performed using a variety of surgical approaches and techniques, including open and arthroscopic methods. For arthroplasties, determine if the surgeon performed a total or partial replacement and whether it was an initial or revision procedure as the ICD-9-CM system provides different codes depending on documentation. Code 81.84 also reports partial elbow replacement.

To ensure accurate code assignment, review the medical record documentation for approach and surgical technique.

81.85   Other repair of elbow

Description

Code 81.85 is used to report other repair procedures of the elbow that are not more precisely described by other codes in subcategory 81.8.

Coding Clarification

Surgical procedures on the shoulder and elbow are performed using a variety of surgical approaches and techniques, including open and arthroscopic methods. For arthroplasties, determine if the surgeon performed a total or partial replacement and whether it was an initial or revision procedure as the ICD-9-CM system provides different codes depending on documentation.

Documentation Tip

To ensure accurate code assignment, review the medical record documentation for approach and surgical technique.

● 81.88   Reverse total shoulder replacement

Description

▶Reverse total shoulder replacement is an alternative procedure for patients with certain diagnoses who cannot be treated effectively with conventional total shoulder replacement, the most common of which includes rotator cuff arthropathy. Other indications include certain complex humeral head fracture and advanced glenohumeral pathology. Since the reverse procedure may not restore full function, it is commonly performed for patients 65 to 70 years of age to relieve pain and restore basic function. In a reverse total shoulder replacement, the ball is placed on the glenoid and the socket is placed on top of the humerus; this is the reverse position from conventional shoulder replacement, hence "reverse shoulder replacement." The deltoid muscle is employed to compensate for otherwise irreparable rotator cuff damage. The reverse shoulder prosthesis provides a fixed fulcrum for the shoulder joint, allowing the arm to be raised overhead. This configuration adds stability, enabling the deltoid muscle to elevate the shoulder. In some cases, transfer of nearby muscles and tendons such as the latissimus dorsi is also performed to help restore rotation and ensure stability of the joint postoperatively. Five or more implants are typically used: a baseplate screwed into a glenosphere, a metallic stem and neck implanted into the humerus that rests on a polyethylene liner or cup insert, with a spacer inserted for proper joint tensioning.◀

Coding Clarification

▶Joint capsule division, tendon release, and debridement of rotator cuff tissue and bone are integral components of the reverse total shoulder replacement procedure and should not be reported separately.

Conversion of prior (failed) total shoulder replacement (arthroplasty) to reverse total shoulder replacement is excluded from this procedure as a revision arthroplasty classified to code 81.97.◀

Coding Scenario

▶A 72-year-old woman presents for repair of degenerative rotator cuff arthropathy with a complete rupture of the rotator cuff by reverse total shoulder replacement of the right shoulder.

Code Assignment:

727.61   Complete rupture of rotator cuff
726.10   Disorders of bursae and tendons in shoulder region, unspecified
81.88   Reverse total shoulder replacement◀

81.9   Other operations on joint structures

Description
Subcategory 81.9 includes diagnostic procedures on joint structures such as arthrocentesis, injections into joints or ligaments, suturing, and revisions of joint replacements.

81.91   Arthrocentesis

Description
Joint aspiration involves the insertion of a needle to withdraw fluid from a small joint, (e.g., fingers or toes), an intermediate joint (e.g., wrist, elbow, ankle, olecranon bursa, or temporomandibular or acromioclavicular), or a major joint (e.g., shoulder, hip, knee joint, or subacromial bursa). After administering a local anesthetic, the physician inserts a needle through the skin and into a joint. A fluid sample may be removed from the joint or a fluid may be injected for lavage or drug therapy. The needle is withdrawn and pressure is applied to stop any bleeding.

Coding Clarification
Do not assign 81.91 to report arthrocentesis for arthrography (88.32), biopsy of joint structure (80.30-80.39), or for injection of drug (81.92).

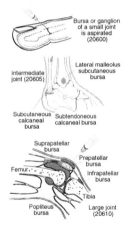

81.92   Injection of therapeutic substance into joint or ligament

Description
The physician injects the sacroiliac joint, the articulation between the sacrum and ilium in the pelvis. The physician draws contrast, an anesthetic, and/or a steroid into a syringe. Through a posterior approach, a needle (syringe attached) is inserted into the sacroiliac joint. The physician pushes on the syringe to deliver its content into the joint. The needle is withdrawn. CT or fluoroscopic guidance may be used to guide the sacroiliac injection.

In an alternate procedure, the physician injects a therapeutic agent into a tendon sheath, ligament, or aponeurosis such as the plantar fascia. The physician identifies the injection site by palpation or radiographs (reported separately) and marks the injection site. The needle is inserted and the medicine is injected. After withdrawing the needle, the patient is monitored for reactions to the therapeutic agent.

Coding Guidance
AHA: 3Q, '89, 16; 2Q, '00, 14

81.93   Suture of capsule or ligament of upper extremity

Description
The surgical approach for a capsulorrhaphy of the glenohumeral joint for any type of multidirectional instability may differ from case to case because the incision is determined by the side with the most significant instability. An arthroscopic examination of the shoulder is usually performed first to fully determine the extent of damage to the joint and the appropriate surgical approach. An anterior H-plasty is commonly used to tighten the capsule. In some cases, both medial and lateral capsular incisions may be required to provide sufficient capsular tension.

In an arthroscopic capsulorrhaphy, the patient is positioned side-lying with the arm suspended using a weight and a pulley system. An anesthetic is administered. Two to four small poke hole incisions are made around the shoulder joint to allow access to all areas of the shoulder joint. A sterile solution is pumped through one of these incisions and into the joint to expand the joint for better visualization and to cleanse the joint. The arthroscope is inserted through a hole allowing the physician to perform a diagnostic arthroscopic exam by visualizing the shoulder joint. The coricoid process is identified and the tendon of the biceps (short head) is at times incised distal to coricoid for exposure. The anterior capsule is visualized through a small transverse incision of the subscapularis tendon which is tagged for identification and removed from its attachment on the capsule. The quality and laxity of the capsule are assessed and the joint is explored for damage to the labrum or glenoid. The joint is irrigated to remove any loose bodies. If there is no other abnormal laxity, the capsule is advance superiorly and attached to the labrum with sutures. An appropriate amount of slack is taken up to provide stability within the joint. Once the capsule is reattached, the subscapularis tendon is reapproximated but not tightened and repaired. A long acting local anesthetic may be injected into the joint to help with post-operative pain. The joint is irrigated and suture or Steri-strip closes the

76-84

incisions. The area is covered with a sterile dressing and a sling or shoulder immobilizer is applied.

Coding Clarification
Do not assign 81.93 for suturing associated with arthroplasty (81.71-81.75, 81.80-81.81, 81.84).

81.94   Suture of capsule or ligament of ankle and foot

Description
The collateral ligament is a two-part ligament that stabilizes the medial side of the ankle. The physician makes a curved incision across the inside of the ankle. The skin is reflected to expose the torn ligament. Holes are drilled diagonally across the talus and two non-absorbable sutures are placed through these holes and the ligament. A similar procedure is performed to attach the ligament to the medial malleolus, which requires the placement of a screw through the fibula to the tibia. The wound is closed and dressed. The leg is immobilized in a long leg cast with the knee flexed 30-45 degrees for four weeks followed by a walking cast for four weeks.

Secondary repair of the collateral ligament of the ankle may be done sometime after an injury or following a previous surgical repair. There are several techniques, including Watson-Jones, Evan, and Chrisman-Snook. In a Watson-Jones repair, an ankle incision is made and the peroneus brevis tendon divided and mobilized. It is then passed through drill holes in the talus and fibular malleolus to reconstruct both the calcaneofibular and anterior talofibular ligaments (lateral collateral ligament). An Evans procedure involves mobilizing the peroneus brevis tendon and passing it through a drill hole in the lateral fibular malleolus to reconstruct the collateral ligament. A Chrisman-Snook procedure involves dividing the peroneus brevis tendon and using it in the repair of the collateral ligament.

Coding Clarification
Do not assign 81.94 for suturing associated with arthroplasty (81.56-81.59).

81.95   Suture of capsule or ligament of other lower extremity

Description
For a primary collateral repair, the physician makes an incision on the lateral or medial aspect of the knee, depending on which ligament is torn (medial collateral or lateral collateral). Sutures may be used to tie the torn ends together. If the attachment of the ligament to the bone is torn away, a screw may be used for fixation. For a cruciate ligament primary repair, an incision is made to gain access into the knee joint (the physician may use the arthroscope for part of the procedure). Screws and/or sutures are used to reattach the torn end to the bone. Both collateral and cruciate ligaments are repaired in

some cases. Incisions are closed with sutures, staples, and/or Steri-strips. A temporary drain may be applied.

Coding Clarification
Do not assign 81.95 for suturing associated with arthroplasty (81.51-81.55, 81.59).

81.96   Other repair of joint

Description
Code 81.96 is used to report other joint repair procedures that are not more precisely described by other codes in subcategory 81.9, such as when the physician amputates the arm through the humerus bone and places a surgical implant in the arm.

The physician makes an incision in a circular fashion around the arm distal to the level of the planned amputation of the humerus. The vessels and nerves are identified, divided, and ligated. The humerus bone is divided in two, completing the amputation. The physician spares the skin, soft tissue, and muscle needed to close the amputation incision. Any of a variety of implants, such as rods, are utilized to maintain the length of the arm or to replace a portion of the amputated humerus. Fixation devices are used. The incision is irrigated. Retained muscle flaps are closed over exposed bone. The wound is closed in layers and a soft dressing is applied.

Documentation Tip
Review the documentation for specific information regarding the procedure prior to final code selection in order to ensure accurate code assignment.

81.97   Revision of joint replacement of upper extremity

Description
The physician performs a partial or total revision of an upper extremity joint replacement including removal of the previous joint component and cemented components. For example, when a hemiarthroplasty is performed on the glenohumeral joint, a long curved incision is made from the superior aspect of the acromion along the deltopectoral interval to the deltoid insertion. The deltoid is retracted laterally and the pectoralis medially. The fascia between the pectoralis and the clavicle is divided and the subacromial space is freed with a gloved finger or periosteal elevator. The coracoacromial ligament is freed and often an acromioplasty is performed to allow for freedom of movement after surgery. The subscapularis tendon is tagged and removed from the capsule. The anterior joint capsule is divided and the glenohumeral joint is dislocated by further external rotation and extension of the arm. The joint is explored and all loose bodies are removed. The

76-84

● New Code   ▲ Revised Code   ►◄ Revised Text   © 2010 Ingenix

humeral head is removed with a reciprocating saw or osteotome. A prosthesis is placed along the proximal humerus as a guide for proper inclination of the osteotomy. A horizontal cut (osteotomy) is made as previously determined and a large curette is used to open the medullary canal for placement of the stem of the prosthesis. The canal is enlarged with a reamer to the appropriate size. The prosthesis is positioned in proper rotational alignment to articulate with the glenoid. Any remaining osteophytes (bone spurs) are removed. The joint is irrigated thoroughly. The prosthesis is reduced into the glenoid and the subscapularis tendon is sutured in place with multiple interrupted non-absorbable sutures with the shoulder in neutral position. The deltopectoral interval is closed loosely over drainage tubes. The arm is placed in a sling and swathe bandage.

A total shoulder replacement can also be performed for the glenohumeral joint. A long curved incision is made from the superior aspect of the acromion along the deltopectoral interval to the deltoid insertion. The deltoid is retracted laterally and pectoralis medially. The fascia between the pectoralis and the clavicle is divided and the subacromial space is freed with a gloved finger or periosteal elevator. The coracoacromial ligament is freed and often an acromioplasty is performed to allow for freedom of movement after surgery. The subscapularis tendon is tagged and removed from the capsule. The anterior joint capsule is divided and the glenohumeral joint is dislocated by further external rotation and extension of the arm. The joint is explored and all loose bodies are removed. The humeral head is removed with a reciprocating saw or osteotome. In addition, a prosthetic device is placed proximally at the glenoid to articulate with the prosthetic humeral head. Prior to placement of the humeral prosthesis, the joint is opened to fully expose the glenoid surface. The surface cartilage of the glenoid is removed. A power drill is used to cut a slot into the glenoid the exact size of the holding device of the glenoid component. Small curettes are used to remove cancellous bone from the base of the coracoid bone. With a bur, articular cartilage is removed from the surface of the glenoid. A trial glenoid component is used to properly prepare the bone and fit the prosthesis. Once the glenoid preparation is complete, the glenoid vault is drilled and filled with polymethylmethacrylate (bone cement). The glenoid component is pushed into place and held until the cement is cured. Prior to final insertion of the humeral component, an anterior acromioplasty and acromioclavicular arthroplasty are performed, if necessary. If large rotator cuff tears are found, they are repaired at this time. The joint is brought through a full range of motion and fully irrigated. The subscapularis tendon

is repaired to stabilize the joint; however, the joint capsule is not usually resutured. Drains are placed and the deltopectoral interval is sutured closed. The arm is placed in a sling and swathe.

Coding Clarification
Code 81.97 reports a partial or total revision of joint replacement of an upper extremity and includes removal of a cement spacer.

▶Code 81.97 includes revision of arthroplasty of the shoulder, as well as a conversion of a prior failed total shoulder replacement to reverse total shoulder replacement.◀

Coding Guidance
   AHA: 1Q, '04, 12

81.98   Other diagnostic procedures on joint structures

Description
Code 81.98 is used to report other diagnostic procedures of the joint structures that are not more precisely described by other codes in subcategory 81.9.

Coding Clarification
Code 81.98 does not include arthroscopy (80.20-80.29), biopsy of joint structure (80.30-80.39), microscopic examination of specimen from a joint (91.51-91.59), thermography (88.83), or x-ray (87.21-87.29, 88.21-88.33).

Documentation Tip
Review the documentation for specific information regarding the procedure prior to final code selection in order to ensure accurate code assignment.

81.99   Other operations on joint structures

Description
Code 81.99 is used to report other procedures on joint structures that are not more precisely described by other codes in subcategory 81.9.

Documentation Tip
Review the documentation for specific information regarding the procedure prior to final code selection in order to ensure accurate code assignment.

Coding Guidance
   AHA: 4Q, '05, 124

---

82   Operations on muscle, tendon, and fascia of hand

Description
Category 82 classifies incision, division, excision, suture, transplantation, reconstruction, plastic, and other procedures on the muscle, tendon, fascia, and bursa. Operations on the aponeurosis synovial membrane or tendon sheath are also included in this category. To choose the correct code for suture,

review the documentation for evidence of delayed suturing because different codes exist if this is stated in the medical record.

Coding Clarification
Coding the removal of foreign bodies from subcutaneous tissue is determined by whether an incision was necessary and the depth of the foreign body. Removal without incision is coded as 98.20–98.29. Removal of a foreign body from only subcutaneous tissue with an incision is coded 86.05, and incisional removal of a foreign body from the soft tissue (i.e., muscle, tendon, fascia, and bursa) is coded as 82.09 (hand) or 83.09 (other sites).

Use 82.79 for both stages of a two-stage tendon graft procedure on the hand where first the surgeon excises the tendon and inserts a plastic rod and then the plastic rod is removed and a tendon graft is inserted.

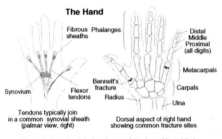

The Hand

Fibrous sheaths

Phalanges

Distal
Middle
Proximal
(all digits)

Metacarpals

Synovium

Bennett's fracture

Flexor tendons

Radius

Carpals

Ulna

Tendons typically join in a common synovial sheath (palmar view, right)

Dorsal aspect of right hand showing common fracture sites

The major muscles of the hand are on the palmar side and their flexor tendons arise in the forearm and extend to the fingertips. Numerous fascial compartments exist in the palm

82.0   Incision of muscle, tendon, fascia, and bursa of hand

Description
Subcategory 82.0 includes incisional procedures of the muscle, tendon, fascia or bursa of the hand.

82.01   Exploration of tendon sheath of hand

Description
The physician makes an incision into the skin and dissects to the hand's muscle or sheath to explore its accompanying supportive, connective tissue, bands, and sacs. The physician incises the skin above the affected sheath and dissects to the tendon sheath. The area is explored, any necrotic tissue is removed, and infection or abnormal fluid is drained. An irrigation catheter may be placed and the wound is irrigated for up to 48 hours. The incision may be closed in sutured layers if clean or packed if contaminated by the object.

Coding Clarification
Use 82.01 for removal of rice bodies in the tendon sheath of the hand.

This code does not include division of a tendon (82.11).

82.02   Myotomy of hand

Description
In myotomy of the hand, the physician makes an incision into hand muscle and dissects the muscles. The physician incises the skin and dissects to the muscle or sheath. The incision may be closed if clean or packed if contaminated by the object.

Coding Clarification
Tenontomyotomy, or myotenotomy, involves incision through the tendon of a hand muscle, with partial or total division of the muscle itself.

If myotomy is performed for division of a hand muscle, see 82.19.

82.03   Bursotomy of hand

Description
The physician drains a palmar bursa or multiple bursas located on the ulnar or radial side of the palm. The physician incises the skin over the bursa and dissects to the bursa. The bursa is lanced and irrigated with a catheter. The catheter is removed and the incision is sutured in layers.

Coding Clarification
A bursa is a small fibrous sac filled with synovial fluid located between the bone and muscles, skin, or tendons. Bursal inflammation, or bursitis due to infection, is treated with bursotomy or bursectomy.

A bursotomy involves an incision through the wall of a bursa.

A bursectomy entails the surgical removal of a bursa.

82.04   Incision and drainage of palmar or thenar space

Description
To drain fluid located in a tendon sheath in the palm, the physician incises the skin above the affected sheath and dissects to the tendon sheath. The sheath is lanced and drained.

The physician uses a transverse approach or oblique incision across the palm to access the midpalmar space. After evacuation and irrigation, the incision is closed using layered sutures. An irrigation catheter may be placed and the wound is irrigated for up to 48 hours.

Coding Clarification
Various surgical approaches are used in procedures of the hand. For example, a transverse approach or oblique incision across the palm can be used to access the midpalmar space. To access the thenar space, a dorsal longitudinal incision perpendicular

to the web may be used, a palmar incision parallel to the thenar crease may be used, or a combination of the two. Review the documentation for specific information regarding the procedure prior to final code selection in order to ensure accurate code assignment.

82.09   Other incision of soft tissue of hand

Description
The physician makes an incision through skin directly over an abscessed area. The abscess cavity is explored, debrided, and drained. For a deep or complicated abscess procedure, the physician may evaluate the underlying muscle, fascia, and/or bone. Depending on the appearance of the area, the physician may remove dead bone and/or place a drain or packing after copious irrigation of the area.

Coding Clarification
Coding the removal of foreign bodies from subcutaneous tissue is determined by whether an incision was necessary and the depth of the foreign body. Removal without incision is coded as 98.20–98.29. Removal of a foreign body from only subcutaneous tissue with an incision is coded 86.05, and incisional removal of a foreign body from the soft tissue (i.e., muscle, tendon, fascia, and bursa) is coded as 82.09 (hand) or 83.09 (other sites).

Code 82.09 reports an incision of the soft tissue of the hand for removal of a foreign body; do not assign this code to report incision of the skin and subcutaneous tissue alone (86.01-86.09).

Coding Guidance
AHA: N-D, '87, 10

82.1   Division of muscle, tendon, and fascia of hand

Description
Subcategory 82.1 includes codes for fasciotomy, tenotomy, tenontomyotomy, or myotenotomy, which involves an incision through the tendon of a hand muscle, with partial or total division of the muscle itself. A tenotomy is the surgical division of a tendon usually done to treat congenital or acquired shortening of a muscle. A fasciotomy involves an incision through a fascia. Excisional procedures of the hand are accomplished using a variety of surgical techniques. A careful review of the operative report for specific information regarding the site and technique used is necessary prior to final code selection in order to ensure accurate code assignment.

Coding Clarification
A Dupuytren's contracture is a shortening of the palmar fascia resulting in flexion deformity of a finger.

82.11   Tenotomy of hand

Description
A tenotomy is the surgical division of a tendon usually done to treat congenital or acquired shortening of a muscle. In a percutaneous tenotomy, the tendon is severed through the subcutaneous tissue. In an alternate procedure, the physician incises a flexor tendon by incising the overlying skin and dissects to the flexor tendon. The tendon is incised. The incision is sutured in layers.

Coding Clarification
Tenontomyotomy, or myotenotomy, involves incision through the tendon of a hand muscle, with partial or total division of the muscle itself.

A fasciotomy involves an incision through a fascia.

Documentation Tip
Excisional procedures of the hand are accomplished using a variety of surgical techniques. A careful review of the operative report for specific information regarding the site and technique used is necessary prior to final code selection in order to ensure accurate code assignment.

82.12   Fasciotomy of hand

Description
A fasciotomy involves an incision through a fascia. The physician incises the palmar fascia to release a Dupuytren's contracture. In one technique, the physician makes a stab wound through the subcutaneous tissue to the palmar fascia, which is incised. In an alternate technique, the subcutaneous tissue is incised and retracted to expose the palmar fascia. The palmar fascia is incised to relieve tension and allow the hand to extend correctly. The operative wound is sutured in layers.

Coding Clarification
A tenotomy is the surgical division of a tendon usually done to treat congenital or acquired shortening of a muscle.

Tenontomyotomy, or myotenotomy, involves incision through the tendon of a hand muscle, with partial or total division of the muscle itself.

A Dupuytren's contracture is a shortening of the palmar fascia resulting in flexion deformity of a finger.

82.19   Other division of soft tissue of hand

Description
A division of a muscle of the hand is performed to release the intrinsic muscles of the hand to restore intrinsic function. The physician incises the overlying skin and dissects to the contracted muscle. The intrinsic muscle is incised to release contracture. The operative incision is closed in sutured layers. When reporting this procedure,

76-84

indicate which intrinsic muscle was released (interossei or lumbricals). In an alternate procedure, the physician incises the overlying skin and dissects to the thenar muscle. Scarred muscle tissue is incised to release contracture. The operative incision is closed in sutured layers.

Coding Clarification
Code 82.19 is used to report other division procedures of the soft tissue of the hand that are not more precisely described by other codes in this subcategory.

Documentation Tip
Excisional procedures of the hand are accomplished using a variety of surgical techniques. A careful review of the operative report for specific information regarding the site and technique used is necessary prior to final code selection in order to ensure accurate code assignment.

82.2   Excision of lesion of muscle, tendon, and fascia of hand

Description
Subcategory 82.2 includes procedures in which the physician excises a lesion of the muscle, tendon, or fascia in the hand.

Coding Clarification
Excisional procedures of the hand are accomplished using a variety of surgical techniques. A careful review of the operative report for specific information regarding the site and technique used is necessary in order to ensure accurate code assignment.

82.21   Excision of lesion of tendon sheath of hand

Description
The physician excises a lesion of the tendon sheath or joint capsule in the hand or finger, such as a cyst or ganglion. The physician incises the overlying skin and dissects to locate the affected area. The lesion, cyst, or ganglion is identified and excised from the tendon sheath or joint capsule. The operative incision is closed in sutured layers.

In a commonly performed excision, the physician removes a ganglion from the wrist. An incision is made overlying the ganglion. The tissues are dissected around the ganglion, freeing it from surrounding tissue. Scar tissue may be removed. The physician may dissect deep within the wrist joint in order to excise the entire ganglion. The ganglion is then removed. The joint or muscle tissue may be repaired. The physician irrigates the wound with antibiotic solution and closes the wound in layers.

A radical excision is removal of all diseased and/or inflamed tissue and may include removal of a portion of surrounding normal tissue. The physician excises the bursa, synovia of the wrist, or forearm tendon sheaths of the flexors and extensors. A

longitudinal incision over the volar aspect of the distal forearm and wrist is made. Dissection is carried down to expose the flexor tendons of the wrist. The physician excises the bursa and any inflamed and hypertrophied tissues from around the tendons. The tendons are left intact, allowing them to glide better during wrist movement. The physician may perform a transposition of the dorsal retinaculum if enough tissue is removed from the wrist extensors. A transposition makes a smooth gliding surface no longer present between the extensor tendons and carpal bones of the wrist. The dorsal retinaculum is incised in the mid-line, tucked underneath the extensor tendons, and closed with sutures. The incisions are repaired in multiple layers with sutures, staples, and/or Steri-strips. The wrist may be placed in a splint.

Coding Clarification
Code 82.21 reports a ganglionectomy of the tendon sheath of the wrist.

Excisional procedures of the hand are accomplished using a variety of surgical techniques. A careful review of the operative report for specific information regarding the site and technique used is necessary in order to ensure accurate code assignment.

82.22   Excision of lesion of muscle of hand

Description
The physician removes a tumor or vascular malformation from the soft tissue of the hand or finger that is located within the muscle. With the proper anesthesia administered, the physician makes an incision in the skin overlying the mass and dissects down to the tumor or malformation. The extent of the tumor is identified and a dissection is undertaken all the way around the tumor. The blood vessels are ligated and the defective tissue of the vascular malformation is excised. A portion of neighboring soft tissue may also be removed to ensure adequate removal of all tumor tissue. A drain may be inserted, and the incision is repaired in multiple layers of sutures, staples, or Steri-strips.

Coding Clarification
Excisional procedures of the hand are accomplished using a variety of surgical techniques. A careful review of the operative report for specific information regarding the site and technique used is necessary in order to ensure accurate code assignment.

82.29   Excision of other lesion of soft tissue of hand

Description
The physician removes a tumor or vascular malformation from the soft tissue of the hand or finger that is located in the subcutaneous tissue, or in the deep soft tissue below the fascial plane. The physician removes a malignant soft tissue tumor

● New Code   ▲ Revised Code   ▶◀ Revised Text   © 2010 Ingenix

from the hand or finger. An incision is made over the tumor and dissection is carried down to expose it. The tumor and any adjacent tissue that may be affected by the spread of the neoplasm are excised. Large resections may be needed. The type and stage of the lesion will determine the extent of the tumor margin resection area. Muscle or fascia may need to be repaired and drains may be placed. The surgical wound is then repaired by intermediate or complex closure, adjacent tissue transfer, or graft.

Coding Clarification

Excisional procedures of the hand are accomplished using a variety of surgical techniques. A careful review of the operative report for specific information regarding the site and technique used is necessary in order to ensure accurate code assignment.

Do not assign this code to report excision of a lesion of the skin and subcutaneous tissue (86.21-86.3).

82.3   Other excision of soft tissue of hand

Description

Excisional procedures of the hand are accomplished using a variety of surgical techniques. Review the operative report for specific information regarding the site and technique used in order to ensure accurate code assignment.

Coding Clarification

Report any skin graft performed (86.61-86.62, 86.73).

Subcategory 82.3 is not assigned to report excision of skin and subcutaneous tissue; see 86.21-86.3.

Documentation Tip

Excisional procedures on the soft tissue of the hand are accomplished using a variety of surgical techniques. A careful review of the operative report for specific information regarding the site and technique used is necessary prior to final code selection in order to ensure accurate code assignment.

82.31   Bursectomy of hand

Description

The physician treats septic bursitis with surgical drainage and removal of the infected bursa sac. The physician excises the bursa by making a longitudinal incision and dissecting down to expose the bursa, the fluid filled sac that lubricates the joint against friction. The bursa is excised. The surrounding tissue is examined for any sign of infection. The wound is irrigated and the incision is repaired in layers with sutures, staples, and/or Steri-strips. The area is covered with a sterile dressing.

Coding Clarification

A bursa is a small fibrous sac filled with synovial fluid located between the bone and muscles, skin, or tendons. Bursal inflammation, or bursitis due to infection, is treated with bursotomy with incision and drainage, or bursectomy to surgically remove the infected bursa.

A bursotomy involves an incision through the wall of a bursa.

A bursectomy entails the surgical removal of a bursa.

82.32   Excision of tendon of hand for graft

Description

The physician performs a resection and excision of fibrous tissue connecting bone to the hand muscle for grafting. To excise an extensor tendon in a finger or hand, the physician incises the overlying skin and dissects to the tendon. The tendon is freed. The proximal and distal ends are severed and the tendon is removed. The incision is closed.

Coding Clarification

Excisional procedures of the hand are accomplished using a variety of surgical techniques. A careful review of the operative report for specific information regarding the site and technique used is necessary in order to ensure accurate code assignment.

82.33   Other tenonectomy of hand

Description

Code 82.33 is assigned to report other tenonectomy procedures of the hand that are not more precisely described by other codes in this subcategory. Excisional procedures of the hand are accomplished using a variety of surgical techniques. A careful review of the operative report for specific information regarding the site and technique used is necessary in order to ensure accurate code assignment.

Coding Clarification

A tenonectomy involves the removal of fibrous bands connecting muscle to bone of the hand.

A tenosynovectomy of the hand involves the excision of fibrous band connecting muscle and bone of hand and removal of coverings.

Do not assign 82.33 for excision of a lesion of a tendon (82.29) or sheath (82.21).

Documentation Tip

Excisional procedures of the hand are accomplished using a variety of surgical techniques. A careful review of the operative report for specific information regarding the site and technique used is necessary prior to final code selection in order to ensure accurate code assignment.

82.34   Excision of muscle or fascia of hand for graft

Description
The physician performs a resection and excision of a muscle or fascia of the hand for grafting. An incision is made over the site and dissection exposes it. The physician makes an incision over the fascia in order to obtain the needed tissue. Muscle, myocutaneous or fasciocutaneous, may be excised. Drains may be placed. The surgical wound is repaired by intermediate or complex closure.

Coding Clarification
Excisional procedures of the hand are accomplished using a variety of surgical techniques. Review the operative report for specific information regarding the site and technique used in order to ensure accurate code assignment.

82.35   Other fasciectomy of hand

Description
The physician excises fibrous connective tissue of the hand, other than for grafting or removing lesion. In one example, the physician removes the palmar fascia. The physician incises the overlying skin and subcutaneous tissue. The palmar fascia is exposed and resected. Tendon sheaths are freed. The incision is sutured in layers if possible. Z-plasties are performed or skin grafts are obtained to close the wound if necessary. In some cases, the palmar fascia is removed and in others, part of the palmar fascia is removed and flexor tendons at proximal interphalangeal joints are released.

Coding Clarification
A flexor tendon sheath is a tube, or sheath, that covers the palm-side tendons of the fingers and hand.

Do not assign 82.35 for excision of a lesion of the fascia (82.29).

Coding Scenario
The physician performed surgical release for Dupuytren's contracture, which involves excision of fibrous connective tissue to correct flexion of fingers. The diseased tissue attached to the skin, palm, and fingers, so the physician severed the cords of tissue under the skin and removed the diseased tissue.

Code Assignment:

728.6   Contracture of palmar fascia
82.35   Other fasciectomy of hand

82.36   Other myectomy of hand

Description
The physician surgically removes necrotic skin, underlying tissue, and muscle of the hand. The physician uses a scalpel to excise the affected tissue into the muscle layer. The dissection is continued until viable, bleeding tissue is encountered.

Depending on wound size, closure may be immediate or delayed. The wound may be packed open with gauze and require immediate or delayed reconstruction.

Coding Clarification
Code 82.36 reports other myomectomy procedures of the hand that are not more precisely described by other codes in subcategory 82.3.

Do not assign this code for excision of a lesion of the muscle (82.22).

82.39   Other excision of soft tissue of hand

Description
Code 82.39 is used to report other excision procedures of the soft tissue of the hand that are not more precisely described by other codes in subcategory 82.3.

Coding Clarification
Do not assign 82.39 for excision of the skin (86.21-86.3) or excision of a soft tissue lesion (82.29).

When multiple layers are debrided at a single site, assign a code for the deepest layer of debridement.

Documentation Tip
Review the documentation for specific information regarding the procedure prior to final code selection in order to ensure accurate code assignment.

82.4   Suture of muscle, tendon, and fascia of hand

Coding Clarification
To choose the correct code for suture in subcategory 82.4, review the documentation for evidence of delayed suturing because different codes exist if this is stated in the medical record.

82.41   Suture of tendon sheath of hand

Description
The physician sutures a tendon sheath of the hand at the subcutaneous level. The physician incises the overlying skin through the subcutaneous tissue. The tendon sheath is closed with sutures. The operative incision is closed in sutured layers.

Coding Clarification
To choose the correct code for suture, review the documentation for evidence of delayed suturing because different codes exist if this is stated in the medical record.

82.42   Delayed suture of flexor tendon of hand

Description
The physician repairs or advances a single flexor tendon, a fibrous band, between flexor muscle and bone following initial repair. The physician incises the skin overlying the medial phalanx and dissects

● New Code   ▲ Revised Code   ▶◀ Revised Text   © 2010 Ingenix

to the tendon. The tendon is repaired with sutures or advanced and sutured to improve joint function. If a graft is needed for secondary repair, it is obtained from the palmaris longus tendon or from the foot. The incision is sutured in layers.

Coding Clarification
Primary repair is done immediately after injury and secondary repair is done sometime after the incident of injury or following a previous surgical repair.

To choose the correct code for suture, review the documentation for evidence of delayed suturing because different codes exist if this is stated in the medical record.

82.43   Delayed suture of other tendon of hand

Description
The physician repairs or advances a single extensor tendon located in the finger, other than the flexor tendon. The physician incises the skin overlying the tendon. The tendon is repaired with sutures or advanced to improve joint function. Primary repair is done immediately after injury. Secondary repair is done sometime after the incident of injury or following a previous surgical repair. If a graft is needed for secondary repair, it is obtained from the palmaris longus tendon or from the foot. The incision is sutured in layers.

Coding Clarification
Primary repair is done immediately after injury and secondary repair is done sometime after the incident of injury or following a previous surgical repair.

To choose the correct code for suture, review the documentation for evidence of delayed suturing because different codes exist if this is stated in the medical record.

82.44   Other suture of flexor tendon of hand

Description
In a procedure that is not more precisely described by the other codes in subcategory 82.4, the physician repairs a single flexor tendon, a fibrous band between flexor muscle and bone. The physician incises the skin overlying the proximal or distal phalanx and dissects to the tendon. The tendon is repaired with sutures or advanced and sutured to improve joint function. The incision is sutured in layers. The incision is sutured in layers.

Coding Clarification
To choose the correct code for suture, review the documentation for evidence of delayed suturing because different codes exist if this is stated in the medical record.

To report a delayed suture of flexor tendon of hand, see 82.42.

82.45   Other suture of other tendon of hand

Description
Code 82.45 is used to report other suture procedures on the tendons of the hand other than the flexor tendon that are not more precisely described by other codes in subcategory 82.4. This code is also reported when the documentation does not further specify the tendon or the procedure.

Coding Clarification
To choose the correct code for suture, review the documentation for evidence of delayed suturing because different codes exist if this is stated in the medical record.

Assign 82.43 for delayed suture of other tendon of hand.

82.46   Suture of muscle or fascia of hand

Description
The physician repairs the intrinsic muscles of the hand to restore intrinsic function. The physician incises the overlying skin and dissects to the damaged muscle. The integrity of the tendons and muscles are tested. Defects are corrected to restore function. The incision is sutured in layers. When reporting this procedure, indicate which intrinsic muscle was repaired (interossei or lumbricales). Report each muscle separately.

Coding Clarification
To choose the correct code for suture, review the documentation for evidence of delayed suturing because different codes exist if this is stated in the medical record.

82.5   Transplantation of muscle and tendon of hand

Description
Subcategory 82.5 reports transplantation procedures of muscles and tendons of the hand.

Coding Guidance
    AHA: 1Q, '93, 28

82.51   Advancement of tendon of hand

Description
The physician performs a detachment of fibrous connective muscle band and bone with reattachment at advanced point of hand. In one example, the physician advances a single extensor tendon located in the finger. The physician incises the skin overlying the tendon. The tendon is repaired with sutures or advanced to improve joint function. Primary repair is done immediately after injury. Secondary repair is done sometime after the incident of injury or following a previous surgical repair. If a graft is needed for secondary repair, it is obtained from the palmaris longus tendon or from the foot. The incision is sutured in layers.

82.52   Recession of tendon of hand

Description
The physician performs a tendon recession involving a detachment of a fibrous band of muscle and bone with reattachment at drawn-back point of hand. The physician transfers or transplants a tendon; a free tendon graft may be used if necessary. The physician incises the overlying skin and dissects to the tendon to be moved. The tendon is freed, transferred and sutured into place. The operative incision is closed in sutured layers.

Coding Clarification
If a free tendon graft is used, it is typically obtained from the palmaris longus tendon or from the foot.

82.53   Reattachment of tendon of hand

Description
The physician repairs the distal insertion of an extensor tendon (mallet finger), using a graft if necessary. The physician incises the overlying skin and dissects to the damaged tendon. The tendon is repaired with sutures to improve joint function. If a graft is needed for repair, it is obtained from the palmaris longus tendon or from the foot. The operative incision is closed in sutured layers.

Coding Clarification
Primary repair is done immediately after injury. Secondary repair is done sometime after the incident of injury or following a previous surgical repair.

82.54   Reattachment of muscle of hand

Description
The physician makes an incision overlying the muscle that has detached from its insertion point. The muscle is reattached and the fascia repaired as well. Screws and/or sutures may be used to reattach the torn end to the bone. The incision is then repaired in multiple layers with sutures, staples, and/or Steri-strips.

Coding Clarification
Primary repair is done immediately after injury. Secondary repair is done sometime after the incident of injury or following a previous surgical repair.

82.55   Other change in muscle or tendon length of hand

Description
The physician lengthens an extensor tendon in a hand or a finger. The physician incises the overlying skin and dissects to the tendon. The physician performs step cuts to lengthen the tendon. The operative incision is closed in sutured layers. Report each tendon separately.

In another example, the physician shortens a flexor tendon in the hand or finger. The physician incises

the overlying skin and dissects to the tendon. The physician removes a section of the tendon and sutures the ends back together, shortening the tendon. The operative incision is closed in sutured layers. Report each tendon separately.

Coding Clarification
Procedures of the hand are accomplished using a variety of surgical techniques, including microvascular transfer techniques. Review the operative report for specific information regarding the site and technique used in order to ensure accurate code assignment.

82.56   Other hand tendon transfer or transplantation

Description
The physician transfers or transplants a tendon. A free tendon graft may be used if necessary. The physician incises the overlying skin and dissects to the tendon to be moved. The tendon is freed, transferred and sutured into place. If a free tendon graft is used, it is obtained from the palmaris longus tendon or from the foot. The operative incision is closed in sutured layers. A free graft is used for transfer or transplant of a carpometacarpal or dorsum of hand tendon.

Coding Clarification
Do not assign 82.56 for pollicization of thumb (82.61) or transfer of a finger other than the thumb (82.81).

Documentation Tip
Tendon transfer procedures of the hand are accomplished using a variety of surgical techniques, including microvascular transfer techniques. Review the operative report for specific information regarding the site and technique used in order to ensure accurate code assignment.

Coding Guidance
AHA: 4Q, '98, 40; 2Q, '99, 10

82.57   Other hand tendon transposition

Description
The physician transfers or transplants a tendon. A free tendon graft may be used if necessary. The physician incises the overlying skin and dissects to the tendon to be moved. The tendon is freed, transferred and sutured into place. If a free tendon graft is used, it is obtained from the palmaris longus tendon or from the foot. The operative incision is closed in sutured layers.

Coding Clarification
Tendon transfer procedures of the hand are accomplished using a variety of surgical techniques, including microvascular transfer techniques. Review the operative report for specific information

regarding the site and technique used in order to ensure accurate code assignment.

Coding Guidance
AHA: 1Q, '93, 28; 3Q, '93, 8

82.58   Other hand muscle transfer or transplantation
Description
Code 82.58 is used to report other transfer or transplant procedures of the hand muscle that are not more precisely described by other codes in subcategory 82.5.

Coding Clarification
Muscle transfer procedures of the hand are accomplished using a variety of surgical techniques, including microvascular transfer techniques. Review the operative report for specific information regarding the site and technique used in order to ensure accurate code assignment.

82.59   Other hand muscle transposition
Description
Code 82.59 is used to report other muscle transposition procedures of the hand that are not more precisely described by other codes in subcategory 82.5.

Documentation Tip
Review the documentation for specific information regarding the procedure prior to final code selection in order to ensure accurate code assignment.

82.6   Reconstruction of thumb
Description
Reconstruction procedures on the thumb, such as digital transfer and grafting, are described in subcategory 82.6. Coders are instructed to also assign a code to report any amputation performed for digital transfer (84.01, 84.11).

82.61   Pollicization operation carrying over nerves and blood supply
Description
Pollicization involves the reconstruction of the thumb, often using another digit such as the index finger or the great toe. The physician replaces all or part of a thumb with the index finger. The extent of an index finger used is determined by the size of the defect. The physician harvests the index finger with its tendons, blood vessels, and nerves intact and transfers the digit to the thenar eminence. If the thenar eminence must be created, the physician will transfer the index metacarpal along with the digit. If the index metacarpal is not needed, it is removed to provide space for function. The tendons are sutured to the new digit to provide abduction function. The skin is reapproximated and closed in sutured layers.

82.69   Other reconstruction of thumb
Description
The physician performs this procedure to provide functional thumb reconstruction in cases of traumatic thumb amputation and congenital absence of the thumb. Two surgical teams are employed: one at the hand and the other at the foot. One physician makes a linear incision over the dorsal aspect of the foot, traveling from proximal to distal, aiming toward the great toe. This incision stops at the base of the toe and a circular incision is made around the toe. The medial and lateral dorsal foot flaps are raised. The first dorsal metatarsal artery (FDMA) and deep peroneal nerve (DPN) are identified and exposed proximally to the dorsalis pedis artery (DPA). The portion of the DPA that passes to the plantar side of the foot is ligated. On the plantar surface, the flexor hallucis longus (FHL) is identified along with the plantar digital nerves and arteries on either side. The physician dissects into the web space between the great and second toes where the first plantar metatarsal artery (FPMA) is divided, as are vessels to the second toe. The DPN is split and the fibers to the great toe are divided. On the plantar surface, the digital nerves are divided. The FHL is divided through a separate incision in the midfoot, and is pulled into the distal wound. The tourniquet is released and adequate circulation is confirmed. The great toe is perfused for 20 minutes prior to completion of the dissection and transfer to the hand. The second surgical team begins preparing the hand soon after toe dissection begins. The physicians on this team make a radially based palmar thumb skin flap. The dorsal incision extends into the wrist area where the cephalic vein, superficial radial nerve, dorsal dominant branch of the radial artery, and extensor tendons are identified. A transverse incision is made over the volar wrist to allow identification of the flexor pollicis longus (FPL). The thumb metacarpal or phalanx is cut squarely at a right angle to two vertically placed interosseous compression wires and longitudinally placed K-wire, which helps hold the digit in extension. Extensor tendon and flexor tendon repairs are performed. The abductor and adductor tendons are repaired to the extensor mechanism. The vascular repairs are completed using standard microvascular techniques. The superficial radial nerve and DPN are joined dorsally, and the digital nerve repairs are completed volarly. The skin is closed with drains. If a skin graft is necessary, it is placed dorsally over the area of the dorsal veins. The donor site is closed by removal of the metatarsal condyles and suturing of the volar plate and sesamoids to the distal metatarsal.

76-84

Coding Clarification

Assign 82.69 for bone to thumb grafts or skin (pedicle) to thumb grafts such as a "cocked-hat procedure" involving a skin flap and bone.

82.7 Plastic operation on hand with graft or implant

Description

Subcategory 82.7 includes plastic procedures on the hand involving grafts or implants.

82.71 Tendon pulley reconstruction on hand

Description

The physician reconstructs a tendon pulley. The physician incises the overlying skin and dissects to the damaged pulley located in the A1 position or the distal interphalangeal joint position. In some cases, the tendon pulley is reconstructed using neighboring tissue; in others, the physician obtains a fascial graft for reconstruction. A tendon prosthesis can also be used for reconstruction.

Coding Clarification

Code 82.71 reports reconstruction for opponensplasty.

82.72 Plastic operation on hand with graft of muscle or fascia

Description

The physician implants a free muscle or myocutaneous flap with microvascular anastomosis. With the patient under general anesthesia, the physician prepares and irrigates the wound. The muscle or myocutaneous flap is removed from the donor site and prepared. The physician inserts the flap and uses half-mattress sutures to secure the section. Using microscopy, the physician joins the vessels, uniting the flap tissue to the site. Before all are joined, the physician may inject fluorescein dye in the vascular system and check the area for fluorescence under an ultraviolet light. Adjustments and corrections to the vascular connections are made and the physician sutures the skin. A light dressing is applied and, in many cases, the flap is splinted to help prevent shrinkage. The donor site is sutured and covered with a light dressing.

82.79 Plastic operation on hand with other graft or implant

Description

The physician excises a flexor tendon in a finger or hand and implants a synthetic rod for delayed tendon graft. The physician incises the overlying skin and dissects to the tendon. The tendon is freed. The proximal and distal ends are severed and the tendon is removed. The physician implants a synthetic rod so the surrounding tissue will form a natural tube for a tendon graft. The operative

incision is closed. This code is reported once for each rod that is implanted.

Coding Guidance

AHA: J-F, '87, 6

82.8 Other plastic operations on hand

82.81 Transfer of finger, except thumb

Description

The physician sometimes uses this procedure in cases of traumatic thumb amputation or congenital absence. Two surgical teams are used to complete the transfer. The first team makes a linear incision over the dorsal aspect of the foot, lateral to the dorsalis pedis artery (DPA), traveling from proximal to distal, aiming toward the second toe. Depending on the joint used, the physician may save skin for a graft. The physician harvests two veins in the foot, the dorsalis pedis and metatarsal arteries, the deep peroneal nerve branch, and the extensor tendon to the second toe, and performs an osteotomy at the joint needed. Digital nerves are harvested from the plantar surface. The second team prepares for the toe by making an incision over the wrists where the cephalic vein, superficial radial nerve, dorsal dominant branch of the radial artery, and the flexor pollicis longus (FPL). The thumb metacarpal or phalanx is cut squarely at a right angle to its long axis after appropriate measurement. If the toe is being transferred to a different finger position, the vein, superficial nerve, digital artery, and extensor tendon are all dissected. To attach the toes to the needed position, the physician affixes the bones by crossed Kirschner wires. The flexor muscles are attached to those of the toe. The digital nerves are repaired, and the palmar wounds are closed. The extensor tendons are attached, followed by the approximation of the dorsal sensory nerves, followed by vascular anastomoses. Incisions are closed using sutures.

Coding Clarification

Do not assign 82.81 for pollicization of thumb (82.61).

Coding Guidance

AHA: 2Q, '05, 7

82.82 Repair of cleft hand

Description

The physician repairs a cleft hand. A cleft hand is a malformation where the division between the fingers extends into the metacarpus. The middle digits may be absent and remaining digits are abnormally large. The physician incises the overlying skin and dissects to the deformity. The tissues are brought together with sutures, and the tendons are approximated to produce tensor and extensor function. Following

76-84

correction of the metacarpus, the skin is reapproximated, reduced, and closed in sutured layers.

Coding Clarification
Code 82.82 reports correction of a fissure defect of the hand.

82.83   Repair of macrodactyly

Description
The physician corrects macrodactylia. The physician incises and retracts the skin to expose the underlying tissue. Reduction is accomplished by removing excess connective tissue and bone if necessary. The tissues are reanastomosed and secured with sutures. The operative incisions are closed in sutured layers.

Coding Clarification
This procedure is performed to reduce the size of abnormally large fingers.

82.84   Repair of mallet finger

Description
The physician repairs the distal insertion of an extensor tendon (mallet finger), using a graft if necessary. In one technique, the physician repairs the distal insertion extensor tendon without incising the skin. The physician uses a splint to pin the finger in an extended position. If extensive damage occurred during injury, pins may be used to stabilize the joint.

In an alternate technique, the physician incises the overlying skin and dissects to the damaged tendon. The tendon is repaired with sutures to improve joint function. If a graft is needed for repair, it is obtained from the palmaris longus tendon or from the foot. The operative incision is closed in sutured layers. Primary repair is done immediately after injury. Secondary repair is done sometime after the incident of injury or following a previous surgical repair.

Coding Clarification
Assign this code for repair of a flexed little finger.

Mallet finger, also known as baseball finger, involves a partial or complete avulsion of the extensor from the base of the distal phalanx.

82.85   Other tenodesis of hand

Description
The physician performs a tenodesis at the wrist. In one example, the physician exposes the flexor tendons of the fingers at the wrist level. The terminal phalangeal flexors to be fixated (usually all four) are identified in the depths of the wound. A window is made in the anterior surface of the distal radius proximal to the wrist. A similar second window is made more proximally. A criss-cross type of suture

is passed through all four flexor digitorum profundi tendons side-by-side. The tendons are transected proximal to this suture. The tendons are then drawn into the more distal window in the radius, through the medullary canal, out the proximal window, and sutured back to themselves. The tension on the tenodesis is adjusted so that with the wrist in extension, the fingers naturally flex into the palm, closing the hand as desired. Tenodesis of the finger flexors can give an enhanced natural grip action using wrist extension for those with impaired control of movement. All open soft tissues are sutured in layers. The wrist is immobilized in five to 10 degrees of extension with the metacarpophalangeal joints flexed and the interphalangeal joints extended. In an alternate technique, the extensors of the fingers are fixated to bone at the wrist.

Coding Clarification
Code 82.85 is used to report tendon fixation of a hand that is not more precisely described by other codes in subcategory 82.8. This code is also reported when the documentation does not further specify the tendon fixation procedure.

Documentation Tip
Review the documentation for specific information regarding the procedure prior to final code selection in order to avoid improper use of the "not otherwise specified" code and to ensure accurate code assignment.

82.86   Other tenoplasty of hand

Description
The physician repairs or advances a single flexor tendon located in "no man's land." "No man's land" is located between the A1 pulley and the insertion of the superficialis tendon. The physician incises the skin overlying the medial phalanx and dissects to the tendon. The tendon is repaired with sutures or advanced and sutured to improve joint function. Primary repair is done immediately after injury. Secondary repair is done sometime after the incident of injury or following a previous surgical repair. If a graft is needed for secondary repair, it is obtained from the palmaris longus tendon or from the foot. The operative incision is closed in sutured layers.

Coding Clarification
Code 82.86 reports myotenoplasty of the hand, which is plastic repair of muscle and fibrous band connecting muscle to bone.

82.89   Other plastic operations on hand

Description
Code 82.89 is used to report other plastic procedures of the hand that are not more precisely described by other codes in subcategory 82.8, such as plication of fascia, folding and suturing of the

76-84

tissues, or the Krukenberg procedure, a forearm amputation.

The physician longitudinally splits the stump into radial and ulnar rays by making a dorsal, longitudinal incision toward the ulnar aspect of the forearm. Also, a volar, longitudinal incision is made toward the radial aspect of the forearm. The muscles left or transferred to the radial side of the forearm are the radial wrist extensors and flexors, the flexors of the index and long fingers, the index and long finger extensors, the pronator teres, the palmaris longus, and the brachioradialis. The remaining muscles are left or inserted on the ulnar side of the forearm. On occasion, some muscles need resection to reduce bulk, but the pronator teres must be preserved. The interosseous membrane is freed along its ulnar border. Skin closure is performed, ensuring the tactile skin is placed over the contact surfaces between the radius and ulna.

Coding Clarification
Do not assign 82.89 for plastic operations on the hand with a graft or implant (82.71-82.79).

82.9   Other operations on muscle, tendon, and fascia of hand

Description
Subcategory 82.9 includes other operations on muscle, tendon, and fascia of the hand that are not more precisely described by other codes in category 82. To report diagnostic procedures on soft tissue of hand, see 83.21-83.29.

82.91   Lysis of adhesions of hand

Description
The physician surgically frees adhesions of fascia, muscle, and tendon of hand. The physician removes scar tissue to release a flexor tendon in a finger or the palm. The physician incises the overlying tissue and dissects to the affected tendon. The scar tissue is debrided and removed, freeing the tendon. The operative incision is closed in sutured layers.

Coding Clarification
Do not assign 82.91 for decompression of carpal tunnel (04.43) or lysis of adhesions by stretching or manipulation only (93.26).

82.92   Aspiration of bursa of hand

Description
After administering a local anesthetic, the physician inserts a needle through the skin and into a joint or bursa. A fluid sample may be removed from the joint or a fluid may be injected for lavage or drug therapy. The needle is withdrawn and pressure is applied to stop any bleeding.

Coding Clarification
A bursa is a small fibrous sac filled with synovial fluid located between the bone and muscles, skin, or tendons. Bursal inflammation is treated with bursotomy or bursectomy.

A bursotomy involves an incision through the wall of a bursa.

A bursectomy entails the surgical removal of a bursa.

82.93   Aspiration of other soft tissue of hand

Description
After administering a local anesthetic, the physician inserts a needle through the skin and into the soft tissue of the hand. A fluid sample is removed. The needle is withdrawn and pressure is applied to stop any bleeding.

Coding Clarification
To report aspiration of the skin and subcutaneous tissue, see 86.01.

82.94   Injection of therapeutic substance into bursa of hand

Description
After administering a local anesthetic, the physician inserts a needle through the skin and into a bursa. A therapeutic substance is injected for drug therapy. The needle is withdrawn and pressure is applied to stop any bleeding.

82.95   Injection of therapeutic substance into tendon of hand

Description
The physician injects a therapeutic agent into a single tendon sheath, or ligament, aponeurosis such as the plantar fascia or into a single tendon origin/insertion site. The physician identifies the injection site by palpation or radiographs and marks the injection site. The needle is inserted and the medicine is injected. After withdrawing the needle, the patient is monitored for reactions to the therapeutic agent.

82.96   Other injection of locally-acting therapeutic substance into soft tissue of hand

Description
The physician draws an anesthetic into a syringe and administers an injection of local anesthetic. The needle is withdrawn and pressure is applied to stop any bleeding.

Coding Clarification
Do not assign 82.96 for a subcutaneous or intramuscular injection; see 99.11-99.29.

● New Code   ▲ Revised Code   ▶◀ Revised Text   © 2010 Ingenix

82.99 Other operations on muscle, tendon, and fascia of hand

Description
Code 82.99 is used to report other procedures of the muscle, tendon, or fascia of the hand that are not more precisely described by other codes in subcategory 82.9.

Documentation Tip
Review the documentation for specific information regarding the procedure prior to final code selection in order to ensure accurate code assignment.

83 Operations on muscle, tendon, fascia, and bursa, except hand

Description
Category 83 classifies incision, division, excision, suture, transplantation, reconstruction, plastic repair, and other procedures on the muscle, tendon, fascia, and bursa. It also includes operations on aponeurosis, synovial membrane of bursa, and tendon sheaths.

Coding Clarification
To choose the correct code for suture, review the documentation for evidence of delayed suturing. Different codes exist if this is stated in the medical record.

Category 83 excludes operations on the diaphragm (34.81-34.89), hand (82.01-82.99), and eye muscles (15.01-15.9).

83.0 Incision of muscle, tendon, fascia, and bursa

Description
Subcategory 83.0 includes incisional procedures of the muscle, tendon, fascia, or bursa of sites other than the hand.

83.01 Exploration of tendon sheath

Description
The physician incises the site and dissects down to the muscle or sheath. Exploration of the site is done. The wound is closed in sutured layers.

Coding Clarification
Code 83.01 is assigned to report the removal of rice bodies from a tendon sheath other than that of the hand. Rice bodies are small, often calcified loose bodies called such because of their similarity to grains of white rice. They are commonly associated with rheumatoid arthritis (RA) and inflammatory arthritis.

83.02 Myotomy

Description
The hyoid bone is a small, C-shaped bone in the neck above the Adam's apple, or thyroid cartilage,

with muscles of the tongue and throat attached to it. Hyoid myotomy and suspension is done to open the oro-hypopharyngeal airway for correcting breathing in sleep apnea. It involves repositioning and fixating the hyoid bone to improve the airway. A submental incision is made to expose the hyoid bone in the neck. The muscles below the hyoid are transected and separated to expose a small, isolated, mid-portion of the hyoid bone. Strips of fascia lata (bands of fibrous tissue), nonresorbable suture, or other strong materials are wrapped around the body of the hyoid and used to pull it forward and secure it to the inferior mandibular border. An alternative method pulls the hyoid downward to the voice box cartilage for thyrohyoid suspension and secures it there.

Coding Clarification
To report a cricopharyngeal myotomy, see 29.31.

Coding Guidance
AHA: 2Q, '89, 18; 4Q, '08, 135

83.03 Bursotomy

Description
The physician makes an incision overlying the site of the bursa. Dissection is carried through the deep subcutaneous tissues and continued into the fascia or muscle to expose the bursa. The incision may be extended if the mass is larger than expected. When the infected bursa is identified, it is incised and the contents are drained. The area is irrigated and the incision is repaired in layers with sutures, staples, and/or Steri-strips; closed with drains in place; or simply left open to further facilitate drainage of infection.

Coding Clarification
A bursa is a small fibrous sac filled with synovial fluid located between the bone and muscles, skin, or tendons. Bursal inflammation, or bursitis due to infection, is treated with bursotomy or bursectomy.

A bursotomy involves an incision through the wall of a bursa.

A bursectomy entails the surgical removal of a bursa.

Assign 83.03 for removal of a calcareous deposit of bursa.

Do not assign 83.03 for percutaneous aspiration of a bursa (83.94).

83.09 Other incision of soft tissue

Description
The physician removes a foreign body from the soft tissue including muscle, tendon, fascia, and bursa. The physician makes an incision through skin directly over an abscessed area. The abscess cavity

is explored, debrided, and drained. For a deep or complicated abscess procedure, the physician may evaluate the underlying muscle, fascia, and/or bone. Depending on the appearance of the area, the physician may remove dead bone and/or place a drain or packing after copious irrigation of the area.

Coding Clarification
Coding the removal of foreign bodies for subcutaneous tissue is determined by whether an incision was necessary and the depth of the foreign body. Removal without incision is coded with 98.20–98.29. Removal of a foreign body from subcutaneous tissue only with incision is coded 86.05, and incisional removal of a foreign body from the soft tissue (i.e., muscle, tendon, fascia, and bursa) is coded as 82.09 (hand) or 83.09 (other sites).

Code 83.09 may be reported for procedures described as incision and drainage for a closed internal degloving injury. Internal degloving is detachment of subcutaneous tissue from the underlying fascia, which creates a cavity filled with hematoma and liquified fat.

To report incision of skin and subcutaneous tissue alone, see 86.01-86.09.

Coding Guidance
AHA: 1Q, '09, 10

83.1   Division of muscle, tendon, and fascia

Description
Subcategory 83.1 includes division procedures of the fascia, tendon or muscle, tenotomy, tendon release, and transection.

Coding Clarification
Division of fascia involves an incision to separate fibrous connective tissue.

Division of the iliotibial band is an incision to separate fibrous band connecting tibial bone to muscle in flank.

Fascia stripping consists of an incision and lengthwise separation of fibrous connective tissue.

Release of Volkmann's contracture by fasciotomy is a divisional incision of connective tissue to correct defects in flexion of finger(s).

Aponeurotomy involves the incision and separation of fibrous cords attaching a muscle to bone to aid movement.

Division of tendon, or separation of fibrous band connecting muscle to bone, is performed for tendon release. Tendon transection involves an incision across width of fibrous bands between muscle and bone.

83.11   Achillotenotomy

Description
The physician performs a percutaneous tenotomy of the Achilles tendon. The physician infiltrates the skin and Achilles tendon with a local anesthetic about 1 cm above the insertion into the calcaneus. A knife blade or tenotome held vertically is inserted through the skin and subcutaneous tissue into the Achilles tendon. The blade is turned medially and laterally and swept back forth, creating a nick in the tendon, until the foot can be dorsiflexed at the ankle. Pressure is applied over the incision for about five minutes. A dressing and long leg cast are applied with the ankle in 10 degree dorsiflexion and the knee in maximal extension.

Coding Clarification
This procedure is performed with local anesthesia most often; however, general anesthesia is sometimes required.

83.12   Adductor tenotomy of hip

Description
The physician makes a small incision approximately 0.5 inches long over the origin of the adductor muscles. Dissection is carried down to the adductor tendon. The physician uses a small blade to release (free by incision) the tendon. The incision is then repaired in layers with sutures and Steri-strips. A spica cast is applied for three to four weeks to keep the hip in abduction.

83.13   Other tenotomy

Description
This procedure may be performed if closed manipulation under anesthesia is unsuccessful to gain adequate motion of the shoulder. An incision along the anterior deltoid and pectoral region is made and the skin is reflected back to expose the underlying muscles. The subscapularis tendon is removed from the glenoid rim of the scapula. The physician may also release portions of the pectoral muscle fibers to gain further motion of the shoulder. The incision is closed with sutures and the arm is passively placed in abduction. In some cases, a tenotomy is performed on multiple tendons through the same incision.

Coding Clarification
Code 83.13 reports aponeurotomy, division of tendon, tendon release, tendon transection, and tenotomy for thoracic outlet decompression.

83.14   Fasciotomy

Description
The physician performs a lateral or medial fasciotomy. Fasciotomy may also be termed as a percutaneous release for tennis elbow. The more

76-84

common problem is located on the lateral epicondyle. The physician makes a 1.5 to 2.5 cm incision anterior to the epicondyle. The common tendon origin of the extensors is exposed on the lateral elbow (or flexors on the medial side if this is where the incision was made). The physician uses a scalpel to free the tendinous origin of the common extensors or flexors from the epicondyle. The skin is closed with sutures and/or Steri-strips. The elbow is placed in a sling.

Coding Clarification
Use 83.14 for both open and endoscopic fasciotomies, as ICD-9-CM does not provide different codes depending on approach.

Coding Guidance
AHA: 3Q, '98, 8; 4Q, '06, 102

83.19   Other division of soft tissue

Description
The physician performs a surgical procedure where the scalenus anticus muscle is divided, usually for the purpose of treating thoracic outlet syndrome. With the patient under anesthesia, the physician makes an incision overlying the scalene muscle. This incision is carried deep to the muscle. The muscle is exposed and identified. A discission of the muscle is performed in line of the fibers. This relieves the pressure on the neurovascular structures. The wound is thoroughly irrigated and closed in layers.

Coding Clarification
Code 83.19 is assigned to report division of muscle for muscle release, myotomy for thoracic outlet decompression, and scalenotomy, which is the division of the anterior scalene muscle.

83.2   Diagnostic procedures on muscle, tendon, fascia, and bursa, including that of hand

Description
Subcategory 83.2 includes biopsy procedures and other diagnostic procedures of the muscle, tendon, fascia, or bursa, including that of the hand, that are not more precisely described by other codes in category 83.

Documentation Tip
Review the documentation for specific information regarding the procedure prior to final code selection in order to ensure accurate code assignment.

▲ 83.21   Open biopsy of soft tissue

Description
Code 83.21 reports the biopsy of soft tissues of various sites. For example, the physician performs a biopsy of the soft tissues of the neck or thorax. With proper anesthesia administered, the physician

identifies the mass through palpation and x-ray (reported separately), if needed. An incision is made over the site and dissection is taken down to the subcutaneous fat or further into the fascia or muscle to reach the lesion. A portion of the tissue mass is excised and submitted for pathology. The area is irrigated and the incision is closed with layered sutures.

In an alternate procedure, the physician performs a biopsy of the soft tissues of the leg or ankle area. With proper anesthesia administered, an incision is made over the biopsy area. Dissection is carried down within the superficial soft tissue layers in some cases, usually the subcutaneous fat to the uppermost fascial layer. In other cases, dissection is taken down deep within the soft tissue, such as into the fascial layer or within the muscle. A portion of the tissue is excised and submitted for pathology. The area is irrigated and the incision is closed with layered sutures, staples, or Steri-strips.

Coding Clarification
Do not assign subcategory 83.2 for biopsy of the chest wall (34.23) or closed biopsy of skin and subcutaneous tissue (86.11).

83.29   Other diagnostic procedures on muscle, tendon, fascia, and bursa, including that of hand

Description
This code is used to report other diagnostic procedures of the muscle, tendon, fascia, and bursa, including that of hand, that are not more precisely described by other codes in subcategory 83.2. For example, the physician inserts an interstitial fluid pressure monitoring device into a muscle compartment using a wick catheter, needle, or other method. The physician checks the monitoring device for escalation of pressure, which indicates developing compartment syndrome and tissue ischemia. Once the data has been gathered, the catheter or needle is removed.

Coding Clarification
Code 83.29 should not be used to report microscopic examination of a specimen (91.51-91.-59), soft tissue x-ray (87.09, 87.38-87.39, 88.09, 88.35, 88.37), or thermography of muscle (88.84).

83.3   Excision of lesion of muscle, tendon, fascia, and bursa

Description
Subcategory 83.3 includes lesion excisions of muscle, tendon, fascia, and bursa.

Coding Clarification
To report biopsy of soft tissue, see 83.21.

76-84

83.31   Excision of lesion of tendon sheath

Description
The physician makes an incision overlying the affected tendon. Dissection is carried down to expose the affected tendon. The lesion is then excised or shelled out, leaving normal tissue intact. If incised, the tendon sheath is closed. The incision is repaired in multiple layers with sutures, staples, and/or Steri-strips.

Coding Clarification
Use 83.31 to report excision of a ganglion of a tendon sheath except of the hand.

83.32   Excision of lesion of muscle

Description
The physician removes a tumor from within the muscle. With the proper anesthesia administered, the physician makes an incision in the skin overlying the mass and dissects down to the tumor. The extent of the tumor is identified and a dissection is undertaken all the way around the tumor. A portion of neighboring soft tissue may also be removed to ensure adequate removal of all tumor tissue. A drain may be inserted and the incision is repaired with multiple layers of sutures, staples, or Steri-strips.

Coding Clarification
Code 83.32 reports excision of heterotopic bone or muscle and excision of myositis ossificans (bony deposits in muscle).

This code is also used to report excision of scar tissue for release of Volkmann's contracture or contracture caused by scarred muscle tissue that interferes with finger flexion.

83.39   Excision of lesion of other soft tissue

Description
The physician removes a soft tissue tumor from the face or scalp, not involving bone. An incision is made over the tumor and dissection is carried down to expose it. The tumor and any adjacent tissue that may be affected by the spread of the neoplasm are excised. Large resections may be needed. The type and stage of the lesion will determine the extent of the tumor margin resection area. Muscle or fascia may need to be repaired and drains may be placed. The surgical wound is then repaired by intermediate or complex closure, adjacent tissue transfer, or graft.

Coding Clarification
For debridement of soft tissue or excision of a Baker's cyst, see 83.39.

Do not assign 83.39 for bursectomy (83.5), excision of a lesion of skin and subcutaneous tissue (86.3), or synovectomy (80.70-80.79).

In order to code excisional debridements of sites deeper than subcutaneous tissue that are not

included in the index or tabular listing, coders should look up excision or destruction of lesions of that site.

Coding Guidance
AHA: 2Q, '97, 6; 2Q, '05, 3

83.4   Other excision of muscle, tendon, and fascia

Description
Subcategory 83.4 includes excisional procedures of muscle tendon and fascia, tenonectomy, myotomy, and scalenectomy.

83.41   Excision of tendon for graft

Description
The physician decides on a donor site and makes a cut down to the desired tendon. The tendon is severed and one end held with a hemostat. Dissection is then carried to the muscular origin and the tendon is removed. A pressure dressing is applied.

83.42   Other tenonectomy

Description
The long tendon of the biceps is resected or transplanted. The long head of the biceps tendon is an important stabilizer of the humeral head. When the proximal end of the tendon is detached from the glenoid, it is rolled or knotted, sutured, and inserted through a keyhole-shaped opening in the cortex of the humerus in the floor of the bicipital groove. This is performed through a longitudinal incision at the anterior aspect of the shoulder. Once proper fixation is obtained, the incision is closed and the arm is supported in a sling. Active elbow flexion and shoulder elevation are limited until proper fixation and healing are complete.

Coding Clarification
Use 83.42 to report excision of an aponeurosis, tendon sheath, and tenosynovectomy.

83.43   Excision of muscle or fascia for graft

Description
Fascia lata is a thick band of connective tissue lying underneath the skin of the thigh. To obtain a portion to use for a graft, the physician incises skin and subcutaneous tissue, and elevates the flap off the fascia lata. The amount of connective tissue is then acquired by incising and elevating the fascia of the thigh musculature. A small strip or patch may be obtained in this manner. The wound is closed primarily.

In an alternate technique, the physician harvests fascia lata by making a small incision over the lateral aspect of the lower thigh. A stripper instrument is advanced upward underneath the fascia as the physician maintains downward pressure on the cut end of fascia lata. Once the desired graft length is obtained, the cutting mechanism on the stripper is used to release the fascia from above. The stripper and graft are then removed together and the wound is sutured. A compressive dressing is also applied.

Coding Clarification
Fascia lata, a thick band of connective tissue underneath the skin of the thigh, is also called the external investing fascia.

83.44   Other fasciectomy
Description
When the foot's connective tissue, called the fascia, becomes irritated or inflamed, pain can result. Prior to surgery, a tourniquet is applied to the ankle. The physician makes a longitudinal incision inside the heel and the fat that has filled the wound is separated with a key elevator. The medial third of the plantar fascia is identified using right angle retractors under direct vision. The medial third of the plantar fascia is incised and a 1 cm segment is removed. The tourniquet is released and the skin closed with nonabsorbable sutures. A dressing and a removable walking boot are applied. The sutures are removed in about three weeks and weightbearing is increased; though the radical procedure increases the postoperative recovery period.

Coding Clarification
Assign 83.44 for excision of fascia other than for graft.

83.45   Other myectomy
Description
Scalenectomy is the removal of thoracic scalene muscle tissue. Using an incision above the clavicle, the physician performs a scalenectomy to remove the scalene muscles that are causing compression on the brachial plexus nerves.

Coding Clarification
This code is assigned for debridement of muscle when the documentation does not further specify the procedure.

Scalene muscles are a group of muscles located under the trapezius muscles in the neck and shoulders extending from the cervical vertebrae to the first and second ribs. The scalene muscles attach to the first rib. Scalenectomy is the removal of thoracic scalene muscle tissue.

Coding Guidance
   AHA: 1Q, '99, 8

83.49   Other excision of soft tissue
Description
The physician removes a tumor from the soft tissue of the foot that is located in the subcutaneous tissue, in the deep soft tissue, or below the fascial plane. With the proper anesthesia administered, the physician makes an incision in the skin overlying the mass and dissects down to the tumor. The extent of the tumor is identified and a dissection is undertaken all the way around the tumor. A portion of neighboring soft tissue may also be removed to ensure adequate removal of all tumor tissue. A drain may be inserted and the incision is repaired with layers of sutures, staples, or Steri-strips.

Coding Clarification
Code 83.49 is used to report other soft tissue excision procedures that are not more precisely described by other codes in subcategory 83.4.

83.5   Bursectomy
Description
A bursa is a small fibrous sac filled with synovial fluid located between the bone and muscles, skin, or tendons. The physician makes an incision over the area, debrides granulation tissue, and the bursa is excised.

Coding Clarification
Bursal inflammation or bursitis due to infection is treated with bursotomy or bursectomy.

• A bursotomy involves an incision through the wall of a bursa.

• A bursectomy entails the surgical removal of a bursa.

Coding Guidance
   AHA: 2Q, '99, 11

83.6   Suture of muscle, tendon, and fascia
Description
Subcategory 83.6 includes suture procedures on the muscle, tendon, and fascia.

83.61   Suture of tendon sheath
Description
If the tendon has ruptured, surgery may be required to repair the ruptured tendon. An incision is made from the upper portion of the patella extending to a point just medial to the lower part of the tibial tuberosity. The patellar tendon is exposed, and all scar tissue removed. The ruptured ends of the tendon are then debrided. Sutures are passed through the ruptured ends to bring them together. A fascia lata graft may be used for reinforcement of the suture line by being incorporated in both ends of the ruptures in a figure eight fashion. The semitendinosus tendon is then looped through the

76-84

drill holes and sewn back onto itself at the tibial tubercle. The incision is closed with sutures and staples or Steri-strips.

Coding Clarification

Another technique for reinforcement is to sever the semitendinosus tendon, and then make transverse drill holes through the distal third of the patella and transversely through the tibial tuberosity.

Primary repair is done immediately after injury and secondary repair is done sometime after the incident of injury or following a previous surgical repair. To choose the correct code for suture, review the documentation for evidence of delayed suturing because different codes exist if this is stated in the medical record.

83.62   Delayed suture of tendon

Description

The skin is reflected and the ends of the tendon are exposed and cleaned for easier attachment. The ends are brought together and sutured. The wound is closed and a soft dressing is applied.

Coding Clarification

Primary repair is done immediately after injury and secondary repair is done sometime after the incident of injury or following a previous surgical repair. To choose the correct code for suture, review the documentation for evidence of delayed suturing because different codes exist if this is stated in the medical record.

83.63   Rotator cuff repair

Description

The physician repairs a ruptured rotator cuff in an open procedure. A longitudinal incision is made along the anterior portion of the shoulder and the skin is reflected. The deltoid fibers and the underlying tissues are divided. The coracoacromial ligament is divided and the supraspinatus tendon is detached by a transverse incision along the greater tuberosity. The distal frayed edges of the tendon are removed. A trench is chiseled into the humeral bone along the level of the anatomical neck of the humerus. The supraspinatus tendon flap is buried in it. The flap is fixed with sutures tied to the tendon and passed through holes drilled in the bone. The repair is completed with side-to-side sutures of the supraspinatus to the adjacent subscapularis and infraspinatus tendons. The incision is closed and a soft dressing is applied. Protected motion in a specific progression of exercises is followed.

The physician may also perform a surgical arthroscopy of the shoulder to repair a torn rotator cuff. The patient is positioned side-lying with the arm suspended. Small poke hole incisions are made around the shoulder through which the arthroscopic instruments are inserted. A solution is pumped through one of these incisions to cleanse and expand the joint for better visualization. The physician first performs a diagnostic arthroscopic exam to assess the joint. A limited bursectomy may be performed with a subacromial decompression in which the undersurface of the anterolateral acromion is cleared of soft tissue, if necessary. A small skin incision may be made laterally incorporating one of the portholes to facilitate the arthroscopic repair. The deltoid muscle is split from its acromion attachment about 5 cm and the tendon edge is debrided and mobilized. A transverse bony trough 3 to 4 mm is made and tunnels are drilled through the bone trough to the lateral cortex of the greater tuberosity. The tendon edge is brought into the trough with permanent sutures and anchor sutures are placed. Sutures are placed into the bone and brought through the tendon. A hemostat is placed on the cuff to retract the tendon and take tension off the sutures. The anchor sutures are tied down, followed by the sutures to the bony trough. The free ends of the sutures are passed through the tunnels and tied over a bony bridge. The longitudinal portions of the tear are closed with absorbable suture and a range of motion check is done on the arm. The deltoid splits, subcutaneous tissue, and skin are closed and the arm is placed in a sling to maintain abduction.

Coding Clarification

The rotator cuff, which encapsulates the shoulder, is formed by four rotator muscles (supraspinatus, infraspinatus, teres minor, and scapularis) that hold the head of the humerus in place.

Coding Guidance

AHA: 2Q, '93, 8; 1Q, '06, 6

83.64   Other suture of tendon

Description

The physician repairs a ruptured Achilles tendon. An incision is made overlying the tendon. The physician extends the incision through the tissues to the tendon. The physician identifies the tear and debrides any rough edges. The physician harvests a fascial graft from the patient through a separate incision. The physician then repairs the surgically created graft donor site. The graft is then incorporated into the repair of the tendon and secured to the area with fixation (e.g., screw). The tendon is then repaired, typically with a heavy nonabsorbable suture. The wound is irrigated with antibiotic solution, then closed in multiple layers. A cast, splint, or brace may be applied.

Coding Clarification

Code 83.64 is assigned to report achillorrhaphy (suture of fibrous band connecting Achilles tendon to heel bone) and aponeurorrhaphy (suture of fibrous cords connecting muscle to bone).

Do not assign 83.64 for delayed suture of a tendon (83.62).

Documentation Tip
Primary repair is done immediately after injury and secondary repair is done sometime after the incident of injury or following a previous surgical repair. To choose the correct code for suture, review the documentation for evidence of delayed suturing because different codes exist if this is stated in the medical record.

83.65   Other suture of muscle or fascia

Description
The physician makes an incision over the site of injury. Dissection is carried down to the ruptured muscle. The torn ends are debrided so that healthy muscle tissue can be accurately opposed. Nonabsorbable sutures are placed close together around the circumference of the muscle. The repair may be reinforced by using strips of fascia lata tissue. The physician makes an incision over the fascia lata in order to obtain the needed tissue. The fascia lata strips are then interwoven with sutures around the ruptured muscle. Incisions are repaired with sutures and staples or Steri-strips.

Coding Clarification
Code 83.65 is assigned to report repair of diastasis recti.

Primary repair is done immediately after injury and secondary repair is done sometime after the incident of injury or following a previous surgical repair. To choose the correct code for suture, review the documentation for evidence of delayed suturing because different codes exist if this is stated in the medical record.

83.7   Reconstruction of muscle and tendon

Description
Subcategory 83.7 contains codes to report reconstruction procedures on muscles and tendons such as advancement, recession, transfers, or transplants. Tendon transfer procedures of the hand are accomplished using a variety of surgical techniques, including microvascular transfer techniques.

Coding Clarification
Do not assign subcategory 83.7 for reconstruction of muscle and tendon associated with arthroplasty.

83.71   Advancement of tendon

Description
The tendon is advanced to improve joint function. The physician incises the skin overlying the tendon,

detaching fibrous cord between muscle and bone, and reattaches it at advanced point. The incision is sutured in layers.

Coding Clarification
Tendon transfer procedures of the hand are accomplished using a variety of surgical techniques, including microvascular transfer techniques. Review the operative report for specific information regarding the site and technique used in order to ensure accurate code assignment.

83.72   Recession of tendon

Description
The physician performs a tendon recession involving a detachment of a fibrous band of muscle and bone with reattachment at drawn-back point. The physician transfers or transplants a tendon; a free tendon graft may be used if necessary. The physician incises the overlying skin and dissects to the tendon to be moved. The tendon is freed, transferred and sutured into place. The operative incision is closed in sutured layers.

Coding Clarification
Tendon transfer procedures of the hand are accomplished using a variety of surgical techniques, including microvascular transfer techniques. Review the operative report for specific information regarding the site and technique used in order to ensure accurate code assignment.

83.73   Reattachment of tendon

Description
The physician repairs the distal insertion of a tendon, using a graft if necessary. The physician incises the overlying skin and dissects to the damaged tendon. The tendon is repaired with sutures to improve joint function. The operative incision is closed in sutured layers.

83.74   Reattachment of muscle

Description
The physician makes an incision overlying the muscle that has detached from its insertion point. The muscle is reattached and the fascia repaired as well. Screws and/or sutures may be used to reattach the torn end to the bone. The incision is then repaired in multiple layers with sutures, staples, and/or Steri-strips.

Coding Clarification
Tendon transfer procedures of the hand are accomplished using a variety of surgical techniques, including microvascular transfer techniques. Review the operative report for specific information regarding the site and technique used in order to ensure accurate code assignment.

76-84

83.75 Tendon transfer or transplantation

Description
The physician transfers or transplants a tendon; a free tendon graft may be used if necessary. The physician incises the overlying skin and dissects to the tendon to be moved. The tendon is freed, transferred and sutured into place. The operative incision is closed in sutured layers.

Coding Clarification
Tendon transfer procedures of the hand are accomplished using a variety of surgical techniques, including microvascular transfer techniques. Review the operative report for specific information regarding the site and technique used in order to ensure accurate code assignment.

83.76 Other tendon transposition

Description
Code 83.76 is used to report other tendon transposition procedures that are not more precisely described by other codes in this subcategory.

Coding Clarification
Tendon transfer procedures of the hand are accomplished using a variety of surgical techniques, including microvascular transfer techniques. Review the operative report for specific information regarding the site and technique used in order to ensure accurate code assignment.

83.77 Muscle transfer or transplantation

Description
Code 83.77 is used to report other transfer or transplant procedures of the muscle that are not more precisely described by other codes in this subcategory. An example is transfer of the latissimus dorsi muscle. This transfer restores active elbow flexion by transferring the origin and belly of the latissimus dorsi to the arm and anchoring the origin near the radial head. The patient is placed side lying with the affected side up. An incision is made starting at the loin and extending up to the axilla and then distally along the medial aspect of the arm to the anterior elbow. The physician cuts free the origin of the latissimus dorsi. The muscle itself is cut free from the underlying abdominal muscles. The origin of the latissimus dorsi muscle is sutured to the biceps tendon and the periosteal tissues about the radial tuberosity. The incision is repaired in multiple layers with sutures, staples, and/or Steri-strips.

Coding Scenario
The physician performed a release of Volkmann's contracture by muscle transplantation.

Code Assignment:

83.77   Muscle transfer or transplantation

Documentation Tip
Muscle transfer procedures of the hand are accomplished using a variety of surgical techniques, including microvascular transfer techniques. Review the operative report for specific information regarding the site and technique used in order to ensure accurate code assignment.

83.79 Other muscle transposition

Description
Code 83.79 is used to report other plastic procedures of the muscle, tendon, and fascia that are not more precisely described by other codes in subcategory 83.7.

Documentation Tip
Review the documentation for specific information regarding the procedure prior to final code selection in order to ensure accurate code assignment.

83.8 Other plastic operations on muscle, tendon, and fascia

Description
Subcategory 83.8 includes codes to report plastic achillotenotomy, tendon and fascia plication, tenoplasty, tenodesis, quadricepsplasty, myotenoplasty, and tendon fixation.

Coding Clarification
Do not assign codes from subcategory 83.8 for plastic operations on muscle, tendon, and fascia associated with arthroplasty.

83.81 Tendon graft

Description
The lateral collateral ligament (LCL) of the elbow is reconstructed with a tendon graft. The LCL is the ligament along the outer aspect of the elbow that connects the distal end of the humerus to the proximal end of the ulna. It provides lateral stability to the joint and injury to the LCL can lead to elbow dislocation. Anterior-posterior and lateral x-rays of the elbow are taken and reported separately. The physician administers a local anesthetic block, makes an incision, and dissects to the damaged lateral collateral ligament. The palmaris longus tendon is usually used for the graft. The physician makes a transverse proximal wrist crease incision directly over the tendon, divides it, and holds it taut. A second transverse incision is made about 8 cm above the first incision on the forearm to again identify the tendon. The graft segment is divided and withdrawn. Alternatively, a tendon stripper can be used. The tendon is grafted to the lateral collateral ligament to restore functionality. The wound is closed and a dressing applied. The hand and wrist may be put in a plaster cast, splint, or bandage, depending on which tendons were involved.

Coding Clarification

Tendon grafting procedures are accomplished using a variety of surgical techniques, including microvascular techniques. Review the operative report for specific information regarding the site and technique used in order to ensure accurate code assignment.

83.82   Graft of muscle or fascia

Description

The physician repairs a defect area using a muscle, muscle and skin, or a fascia and skin flap. The physician rotates the prepared flap from the donor area to the site needing repair, suturing the flap in place. The donor area is closed primarily with sutures.

Coding Clarification

If a skin graft or flap is used to repair the donor site, it is considered an additional procedure and is reported separately.

▶Venous and arterial anastomoses inherent to muscle graft procedures are not separately reported.

If a muscle flap graft fails, it should be reported as documented—regardless of the subsequent viability of the graft.◀

Coding Guidance

AHA: 3Q, '01, 9; ▶1Q, '10, 7◀

83.83   Tendon pulley reconstruction on muscle, tendon, and fascia

Description

The physician reconstructs a tendon pulley. The physician incises the overlying skin and dissects to the damaged pulley located in the A1 position or the distal interphalangeal joint position. In some cases, the tendon pulley is reconstructed using neighboring tissue; while in other cases, the physician obtains a fascial graft for reconstruction.

Coding Clarification

Assign 83.83 when the physician performs a reconstruction of fibrous cord between muscle and bone at a site other than the hand.

83.84   Release of clubfoot, not elsewhere classified

Description

This procedure is often performed in an effort to correct club foot deformity. A medial incision is made on the inner ankle to expose the underlying tissues. The skin and tendons are reflected to expose the joint capsule of the talonavicular joint. The joint capsule is cut by sharp dissection to release the deformity of the mid foot. Several releases can be made from this approach. A particular order is followed in order to obtain the appropriate amount of release. The incision is closed with sutures and a

cast is applied. In some cases tendon lengthening is also performed and in others, posterior, medial, and subtalar soft tissue contractures are released to correct severe clubfoot deformity. The patient is placed supine and a posteromedial skin incision is made. The tibialis posterior, flexor digitorum longus, and flexor hallucis longus are identified and mobilized. The contracted tendons are lengthened. The talonavicular and talotibial joint capsules are incised. The joint capsules are cut by sharp dissection to release the deformity. Bones are placed in correct alignment and secured with a single Kirschner wire.

Coding Clarification

Use 83.84 for the release of clubfoot that is not more precisely described by other codes in this subcategory.

Coding Scenario

For treatment of club foot, the physician performed an Evans operation by posteromedial release with a wedge resection and fusion of the calcaneocuboid joint.

> Code Assignment:
>
> 754.70   Talipes, unspecified
>
> 83.84   Release of clubfoot, not elsewhere classified

83.85   Other change in muscle or tendon length

Description

The physician performs an arthrotomy on the ankle for posterior capsular release, with Achilles tendon lengthening by making an incision along the Achilles tendon and retracting the muscles to expose the posterior ankle capsule. The capsule is incised to increase dorsiflexion. If the Achilles tendon is lengthened, the physician notches the tendon at the medial and lateral aspects to release contracture. The wound is sutured in layers.

Coding Clarification

Assign 83.85 when the physician performs a plastic achillotenotomy to increase heel cord length or tendon plication, which is a surgical folding of a tendon.

83.66

Description

The physician corrects a shortened or fibrotic quadriceps muscle. An anterior longitudinal incision is made from the upper one third of the thigh to the lower part of the patella. Deep fascia is divided and the rectus femoris muscle is separated from the vastus medialis and lateralis muscles. The vastus intermedius muscle is excised because it is usually scarred and is binding the posterior surface of the rectus femoris and patella to the femur. If the vastus medialis and lateralis muscles are badly scarred,

76-84

subcutaneous tissue and fat are interposed between them and the rectus. If these muscles are relatively normal, they are sutured to the rectus at the lower one third of the thigh. Layers and incisions are closed with sutures, staples, or Steri-strips.

Coding Clarification
Code 83.86 is assigned to report Bennett or Thompson type quadricepsplasties.

Autologous fascia and muscle are often used for grafting in a musculoplasty procedure.

83.87   Other plastic operations on muscle

Description
The physician makes an incision over the site of injury. Dissection is carried down to the ruptured muscle. The torn ends are debrided so that healthy muscle tissue can be accurately opposed. Nonabsorbable sutures are placed close together around the circumference of the muscle. In some cases, the repair may be reinforced by using strips of fascia lata tissue. The physician makes an incision over the fascia lata in order to obtain the needed tissue. The fascia lata strips are interwoven with sutures around the ruptured muscle. Incisions are repaired with sutures, staples, or Steri-strips.

Coding Clarification
Autologous fascia and muscle are often used for grafting in a musculoplasty procedure.

Coding Guidance
    AHA: 1Q, '97, 9

83.88   Other plastic operations on tendon

Description
A Seddon-Brookes type upper arm tenoplasty with muscle transfer restores elbow flexion by prolonging the tendon of the pectoralis major muscle with the long head of the biceps brachii. The physician makes an incision from the deltopectoral groove to the midportion of the upper arm. The pectoralis major tendon is exposed through dissection, detached from its insertion, and mobilized from the chest wall toward the clavicle. The tendon of the long head of the biceps is exposed and severed from its origin and withdrawn into the wound. The long head of the biceps is dissected from the short head. An L-shaped incision is made over the anterior aspect of the elbow. The long head of the biceps is divided and freed distally to its attachment on the radius. The biceps tendon and muscle are withdrawn through the distal L-shaped incision. Through the proximal incision, the tendon and muscle belly of the long head of the biceps is passed through two slits in the tendon of the pectoralis major and looped on itself so that its proximal tendon is brought into the distal L-shaped incision. The end of the proximal tendon is sutured through a slit in the distal tendon and the

tendon of the pectoralis major is sutured to the long head of the biceps at their junction. The incisions are repaired in layers using sutures, staples, and/or Steri-strips. A posterior plaster splint is applied with the elbow in flexion.

Coding Clarification
Code 83.88 is used to report other plastic procedures on tendons that are not more precisely described by other codes in this subcategory, including myotenoplasty, tendon fixation, tenodesis, or tenoplasty.

83.89   Other plastic operations on fascia

Description
The physician repairs a fascial defect of the leg. The physician incises the skin overlying the defect. If underlying muscles are herniated through the fascial defect, they are pulled to their correct anatomical position and secured with sutures. The wound is sutured in layers.

Coding Clarification
Code 83.89 is used to report other plastic procedures on fascia that are not more precisely described by other codes in this subcategory, including fascial lengthening, fascioplasty, and plication of fascia.

83.9   Other operations on muscle, tendon, fascia, and bursa

Description
Subcategory 83.9 includes codes to report other procedures of muscle, tendon, fascia, and bursa, such as lysis of adhesions; aspirations and injections; and implantation, insertion, placement, or replacement of skeletal muscle stimulators and electrodes.

Coding Clarification
Codes in subcategory 83.9 are not used to report nonoperative manipulation (93.25-93.29) or stretching (93.27-93.29) of muscles and tendons.

83.91   Lysis of adhesions of muscle, tendon, fascia, and bursa

Description
The physician performs a separation of fibrous structures from muscle, connective tissues, bands and sacs. The procedure can be performed on a single tendon or multiple tendons, requiring separate incisions, may be freed from tightened or adhesed tendon sheaths. In one example, the physician corrects a tightened or adhesed tendon sheath in the leg or ankle by making a longitudinal incision over the restricted tendon. Skin is retracted and scar tissue is removed. The physician dissects the tendon with a sharp instrument to free it from

● New Code   ▲ Revised Code   ▶◀ Revised Text   © 2010 Ingenix

the bone. The wound is sutured and dressed with compression bandages.

Coding Clarification
Code 83.91 is not assigned when the procedure is done for tarsal tunnel syndrome (04.44).

83.92 Insertion or replacement of skeletal muscle stimulator

Description
The physician implants, inserts, places, or replaces skeletal muscle electrodes or a stimulator. In one procedure, the physician creates a pocket for the electrical stimulator in the fascia of the muscle and inserts an electrode.

Coding Clarification
Any synchronous tendon transfer performed with the insertion of the muscle stimulator should also be coded.

Coding Guidance
AHA: 2Q, '99, 10

83.93 Removal of skeletal muscle stimulator

Description
The physician makes an incision overlying the site of the implant. Dissection is carried down to visualize the implant and the physician uses instruments to remove the implant. The incision is repaired in layers using sutures, staples, and/or Steri-strips.

83.94 Aspiration of bursa

Description
After administering a local anesthetic, the physician inserts a needle through the skin and into a bursa and fluid is withdrawn. The needle is withdrawn and pressure is applied to stop any bleeding. In an alternate procedure, the physician drains a bursa using an incision. The bursa is lanced and irrigated with a catheter. The catheter is removed and the incision is sutured in layers.

Coding Clarification
A bursa is a small fibrous sac filled with synovial fluid located between the bone and muscles, skin, or tendons. Bursal inflammation, or bursitis due to infection, is treated with bursotomy or bursectomy.

83.95 Aspiration of other soft tissue

Description
After administering a local anesthetic, the physician inserts a needle through the skin and into the soft tissue. A fluid sample is removed. The needle is withdrawn and pressure is applied to stop any bleeding.

Coding Clarification
Do not assign 83.95 for aspiration of skin and subcutaneous tissue (86.01).

Code 83.95 is used to report other aspiration procedures of soft tissue that are not more precisely described by other codes in this category.

83.96 Injection of therapeutic substance into bursa

Description
After administering a local anesthetic, the physician inserts a needle through the skin and into a bursa. A fluid is injected for lavage or drug therapy. The needle is withdrawn and pressure is applied to stop any bleeding.

Coding Clarification
Corticosteroid injections, such as methylprednisolone, are a common treatment for acute or chronic bursa inflammation.

83.97 Injection of therapeutic substance into tendon

Description
The physician injects a therapeutic agent into a tendon. The physician identifies the injection site by palpation or radiographs and marks the injection site. The needle is inserted and the medicine is injected. After withdrawing the needle, the patient is monitored for reactions to the therapeutic agent.

83.98 Injection of locally acting therapeutic substance into other soft tissue

Description
In one example, a physician injects a canal or passage leading to an abscess (sinus tract), with a therapeutic agent such as Betadine, to act as a chemical irritant or antibiotic to clear the infection in an abscess or a cyst. In an alternate procedure, the physician injects a sinus tract with a radiopaque agent to determine the existence, nature, or size of an abscess or a cyst.

Coding Clarification
Do no assign 83.98 for subcutaneous or intramuscular injection (99.11-99.29).

83.99 Other operations on muscle, tendon, fascia, and bursa

Description
Code 83.99 is used to report other procedures of the muscle, tendon, fascia, or bursa that are not more precisely described by other codes in category 83, such as suture of bursa to repair a partial-thickness, bursal-surface tear of a tendon.

Coding Clarification
Surgical procedures on the muscle, tendon, fascia, and bursa are performed using a variety of surgical techniques and approaches. Review the documentation for specific information regarding the procedure prior to final code selection in order to ensure accurate code assignment.

76-84

84 Other procedures on musculoskeletal system

Description

Category 84 includes upper and lower limb amputation, extremity reattachment, revision of amputation stump, implantation or fitting of prosthetic limb device, and other operations. The site is important to code choice for all of these procedures.

Coding Clarification

Disarticulation is amputation at the joint.

If the physician performs an amputation at a higher anatomical site than the previous amputation, code the site where the current amputation occurred. Do not assign the code for revision or reamputation of stump.

Revision of an amputation stump includes debridement or trimming and secondary closure of the site. For revision of an amputation stump, see 84.3.

Following amputation of the limb, post-surgical or "early" dressings are applied to the surgical stump, sometimes during the same operative session. These early applications are designed to compress and prepare the distal tissues in anticipation of fitting a test socket and later a permanent socket. Early applications may be known as immediate post-surgical fittings (IPSF).

A prosthesis must be fitted to the patient individually and the surgical incision site must heal before fitting can begin. Fitting a prosthetic limb device involves assessment and preparation of the stump, modifying the fit using stump socks or socket liners, and training in the use of the prosthetic device. A major consideration for prosthetists is the constantly changing size and shape of the residual limb, or stump, which is the attachment site for a prosthesis.

84.0 Amputation of upper limb

Description

Subcategory 84.0 reports amputations of fingers, hand, wrist, forearm, elbow, or humerus and interthoracoscapular amputation. The thumb is a commonly performed individual digit amputation. When more than one finger is amputated, adjunct surgical procedures are often performed to reconstruct muscles to help restore functionality. A metacarpal amputation is amputation of the whole hand leaving the wrist intact. Plastic sockets may be used to serve as wrists after the removal of the hand at the wrist joint (wrist disarticulation). Elbow

disarticulation involves the removal of the forearm at the elbow, which creates a stump that can hold weight. Shoulder disarticulation and forequarter amputations entail the removal of the entire arm.

Coding Clarification

The primary difference among the amputation procedure codes is the site of the amputation.

For revision of an amputation stump, see 84.3.

Documentation Tip

An understanding of the following terms may aid in code selection:

- **Closed flap amputation:** Sewing a created skin flap over the stump end of the upper limb.

- **Disarticulation of shoulder:** Amputation of the arm through a shoulder joint.

- **Interthoracoscapular amputation:** Removal of the upper arm, shoulder bone, and collarbone.

- **Kineplastic amputation:** Amputation and preparation of the stump of the upper limb to permit movement.

- **Open or guillotine amputation:** Straight incision across upper limb; used when primary closure is contraindicated.

84.00 Upper limb amputation, not otherwise specified

Description

Code 84.00 is used to report upper limb amputation procedures that are not more precisely described by other codes in subcategory 84.0, including closed flap amputation, kineplastic amputation, and revision or reconstruction of a traumatic amputation to enable closure. This code is also reported when the documentation does not further specify the procedure.

Coding Clarification

The primary difference among the amputation procedure codes is the site of the amputation.

A closed flap amputation consists of sewing a created skin flap over the stump end of the upper limb.

A kineplastic amputation involves amputation and preparation of the stump of the upper limb to permit movement.

Open or guillotine amputation uses a straight incision across the upper limb.

Documentation Tip

Review the documentation for specific information regarding the procedure prior to final code selection in order to avoid improper use of the "not otherwise specified" code and to ensure accurate code assignment.

● New Code ▲ Revised Code ▶◀ Revised Text © 2010 Ingenix

84.01   Amputation and disarticulation of finger

Description
The physician amputates a metacarpal bone. An interosseous transfer may be performed. The physician incises the overlying skin and dissects to the defective metacarpal bone. The bone is freed of all muscular and vascular attachments and removed, using a saw if necessary. Tissues that are no longer necessary for anatomical function are removed. Interossei muscles may be transferred to adjacent metacarpals to retain intrinsic muscle function. Soft tissue structures are returned to anatomic position; the skin is reapproximated, reduced and closed in sutured layers.

Coding Clarification
Code 84.01 is not used to report ligation of supernumerary finger (86.26).

84.02   Amputation and disarticulation of thumb

Description
The thumb is a commonly performed individual digit amputation in which the physician amputates a thumb, primary or secondary to injury. Neurectomies are performed. The overlying skin is incised and the tissues are dissected to the bone. The bone is removed, using a saw if necessary. The vessels and nerves are ligated using microsurgical techniques. In some cases, the wound is skin is approximated, reduced, and closed in sutured layers; other times, local advancement flaps are necessary for closure.

Coding Clarification
Primary amputation is removal of the digit following an acute injury or infection.

Secondary amputation is removal of the digit after conservative methods to preserve the digit have failed.

84.03   Amputation through hand

Description
The physician performs an amputation through carpals. The physician makes circumferential incisions around each digit excluding the thumb. These incisions are carried out at the mid-proximophalangeal level. The extensor digitorum communis of each digit (also the extensor indicis proprius of the index and the extensor digiti minimi of the little) are transected at the metacarpal bases. Individually, each metacarpal bone is transected and elevated from its soft tissue bed. The lumbar cals and dorsal interossei are sectioned. Identified blood vessels are ligated. Nerves are ligated and transected. The flexor tendons are transected and allowed to retract in the palm. The volar plate, ligaments, and palmar fascia at this level are all cut and amputated digits are removed. The

open periosteal tubes are closed. The soft tissue flaps are drawn over the end of the stump, and interrupted sutures are used. A soft dressing is applied.

Coding Clarification
Secondary closure or scar revision and a re-amputation all use a similar technique. Review the documentation for specific information regarding the procedure prior to final code selection in order to ensure accurate code assignment.

84.04   Disarticulation of wrist

Description
The physician disarticulates (amputates) the hand from the forearm through the wrist. The physician makes a long, palmar flap and a short, dorsal flap at a level distal to the radioulnar joint. These flaps are pulled back proximally and all veins are ligated. The physician cuts the superficial branch of the radial nerve and the dorsal sensory branch of the ulnar nerve. The lateral and medial antebrachial cutaneous nerves are cut. The radial and ulnar blood vessels are severed proximate to the wrist. The median nerve is cut while traction is applied. The flexor and extensor tendons are pulled distally and cut. The physician makes a transverse, dorsal incision of the dorsal radiocarpal ligament to view the radiocarpal joint. Circumferential dissection of the radiocarpal capsular and ligamentous attachments are carried out. The amputated specimen is removed. The styloid processes are rounded off, and the skin flaps are closed in two layers of subcutaneous tissue and skin. A soft dressing is applied distal to proximal.

Coding Clarification
Secondary closure or scar revision and a re-amputation all use a similar technique. Review the documentation for specific information regarding the procedure prior to final code selection in order to ensure accurate code assignment.

84.05   Amputation through forearm

Description
In below-elbow amputations, the physician cuts the soft tissue flaps distal to the intended level of bone amputation. The physician dissects the superficial veins and cuts them at the level of the amputation. Cutaneous nerves are cut proximal to the level of the amputation. The dorsal and volar antebrachial fascia is cut, and, depending on the level of amputation, either the tendons or muscle bellies are divided after the radial and ulnar vessels are severed. Muscle bellies are incised just distal to the planned level of bony resection. Nerves are cut through a separate incision, and brought under the muscle. The anterior and posterior interosseous vessels should be ligated or coagulated with

76-84

electrocautery. An incision in the periosteum is carried out sharply and circumferentially. The bone is transected at the desired level at this time and the specimen is removed. The bone ends are smoothed with a rasp. Closure is accomplished after hemostasis is obtained following tourniquet release. The skin flaps can be fashioned, and subcutaneous tissue and skin are closed in separate layers. A drain is sometimes placed. The stump is dressed and wrapped with an elastic bandage applied more firmly distally than proximally.

Coding Clarification
Code 84.05 is used to report forearm amputation.

84.06 Disarticulation of elbow

Description
Elbow disarticulation or amputation is the removal of the whole forearm at the elbow. For elbow disarticulation, an artificial elbow joint is needed and typically flat metal hinges are used to construct the elbow joint.

Coding Clarification
Disarticulation of the elbow is amputation of the forearm through the elbow joint.

84.07 Amputation through humerus

Description
The physician amputates the arm through the humerus. The physician makes an incision distal to the intended level of bone section, and fashions anterior and posterior skin flaps. The brachial artery and vein are identified, double ligated, and divided just proximal to the level of bone section. Nerves are also divided proximal to the site to ensure retraction to the end of the stump. Muscles are sectioned slightly distal to the stump. The humerus is divided and the end is smoothed. The triceps muscle is flapped over the end of the bone and sutured into the anterior fascia. The wound is closed over a drain tube with suction and the fascia and skin flaps are closed.

84.08 Disarticulation of shoulder

Description
The physician disarticulates the shoulder. Shoulder disarticulation is the removal of the entire arm through the shoulder joint leaving a length of bone for a prosthetic device. The physician incises the skin overlying the shoulder. The rotator cuff is incised, freeing the arm of ligamentous and muscular attachments. The arm is removed and the wound is closed in sutured layers.

Coding Clarification
Secondary closure or scar revision and a re-amputation all use a similar technique. Review the documentation for specific information regarding the procedure prior to final code selection in order to ensure accurate code assignment.

84.09 Interthoracoscapular amputation

Description
The physician preforms a forequarter interthoracoscapular amputation. The physician incises the skin overlying the shoulder and dissects the disease-free soft tissue away from the bone to create a skin flap to cover the wound. The clavicle is disarticulated from the sternum and the chest wall is freed from muscular attachments to the arm. The quarter section is removed and the wound is closed in sutured layers. If enough disease-free tissue is not available for primary closure, the wound is packed closed with gauze.

Coding Clarification
Interthoracoscapular or forequarter amputation involves the removal of the upper arm, shoulder bone, and collarbone.

84.1 Amputation of lower limb

Description
Subcategory 84.1 reports amputations of foot, toes, ankle, knee, or hip. The primary difference among the amputation procedure codes is the site of the amputation. Toe amputations are a common treatment for frostbite. Ankle disarticulation is an amputation of the entire ankle. Hip disarticulation involves removing the entire leg bone. A below-knee amputation is an amputation below the knee but above the ankle and an above-knee amputation is an amputation in the thigh.

Coding Clarification
The primary difference among the amputation procedure codes is the site of the amputation.

If the surgeon performs an amputation at a higher anatomical site than the previous amputation, code the site where the current amputation occurred. Do not assign the code for revision or reamputation of stump.

Disarticulation is the amputation at the joint.

Revision of an amputation stump includes debridement or trimming and secondary closure of the site. To report revision of an amputation stump, see 84.3.

84.10 Lower limb amputation, not otherwise specified

Description
Code 84.10 is used to report lower limb amputation procedures that are not more precisely described by other codes in this subcategory, including closed flap amputation, kineplastic amputation, and revision or reconstruction of a traumatic amputation to enable

closure. This code is also reported when the documentation does not further specify the lower limb site or the procedure.

Coding Clarification
The primary difference among the amputation procedure codes is the site of the amputation.

Documentation Tip
Review the documentation for specific information regarding the procedure prior to final code selection in order to avoid improper use of the "not otherwise specified" code and to ensure accurate code assignment.

84.11   Amputation of toe

Description
Surgical removal of the toe(s), or amputation, is commonly performed in severe cases of frostbite and gangrene. The physician performs an amputation of a toe at the metatarsophalangeal joint. An incision is made over and around the affected toe where the toe joins the foot. The physician continues the incision deep to the metatarsophalangeal joint. The capsule is identified and a capsulotomy is performed. The proximal phalanx bone is disarticulated from the metatarsal bone. The joint is debrided. The tendon and soft tissues are excised for closure and skin coverage. The toe is excised free from the foot. The wound is irrigated and closed in layers. A dressing and firm-soled shoe are applied.

Coding Clarification
Code 84.11 is used for disarticulation of toe.

Do not assign 84.11 to report ligation of a supernumerary toe (86.26).

Coding Scenario
The physician performed a Ray amputation of a foot, which involves disarticulation of the metatarsal head of the toe extending across the forefoot, just proximal to the metatarsophalangeal crease.

    Code Assignment:

    84.11   Amputation of toe

Coding Guidance
AHA: 4Q, '99, 19; 2Q, '05, 7

84.12   Amputation through foot

Description
The physician amputates the foot across the transmetatarsal region or the midtarsal region. The physician makes the incision so that skin flaps are made dorsally and plantarly. The skin is refracted and the dissection is carried down through the soft tissue. The tendons are severed and allowed to retract. The dorsal and plantar ligaments of the calcaneocuboid and talonavicular joints are released so that the foot can be removed. The physician may

also perform a percutaneous Achilles to prevent flexion contracture. Skin flaps are closed and a soft compression dressing is applied.

In an alternate procedure, the physician performs an amputation of a metatarsal bone and its attached toe. An incision is made dorsally over the involved metatarsal and toe. This is carried deep to the tarsometatarsal joint. The joint and capsule are identified. A capsulotomy is performed and the metatarsal is disarticulated from the other toes. The incision is continued around the toe itself. Tendons are retracted or removed as indicated. The metatarsal bone and the toe are completely dissected free from the foot and removed. The wound is irrigated and debrided. It is closed in layers. A dressing and a cast or a brace are applied.

Coding Clarification
Amputation procedures on the foot are performed using different surgical techniques and approaches:

- **Amputation of forefoot:** Removal of foot in front of the joint between toes and body of foot.

- **Chopart's amputation:** Removal of foot with retention of heel, ankle, and other associated ankle bones.

- **Midtarsal amputation:** Amputation of foot through tarsals.

- **Transmetatarsal amputation:** Amputation of foot through metatarsals.

Documentation Tip
To ensure accurate code assignment, review the medical record documentation for approach and surgical technique.

Coding Guidance
AHA: 4Q, '99, 19

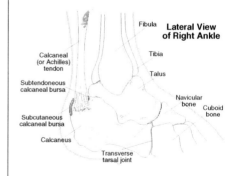

Lateral View of Right Ankle

Fibula
Tibia
Talus
Calcaneal (or Achilles) tendon
Subtendoneous calcaneal bursa
Navicular bone
Cuboid bone
Subcutaneous calcaneal bursa
Calcaneus
Transverse tarsal joint

84.13   Disarticulation of ankle

Description
The physician performs an amputation of the ankle directly through the joint with removal of the foot. An incision is made overlying the ankle joint. The incision is carried around the ankle and deep to the

76-84

joint. The tissues are dissected and the major arteries, veins, and nerves are identified then individually ligated. The ankle joint is opened through an arthrotomy incision and the foot is dislocated from the ankle joint and removed. Tissue is debrided as necessary. Muscles and tendons are attached to the remaining tibia and fibula bones as appropriate. The wound is thoroughly irrigated with antibiotic solution and may be closed in layers. If infection is present, the incision is temporarily left open to drain. A soft dressing, cast, or splint may be applied.

Coding Clarification
Ankle disarticulation is the removal of the foot through the ankle bone.

84.14   Amputation of ankle through malleoli of tibia and fibula

Description
The physician performs an amputation of the foot near the ankle while leaving much of the soft tissue of the heel intact. The physician makes a long incision in the skin overlying the ankle at about the level of the medial and lateral malleoli. The incision is carried deep to the ankle joint. The talus bone is removed from the joint and the incision is carried to the heel bone (calcaneus). The soft tissues of the bottom of the heel are kept with the leg. The skin on the bottom of the foot is cut to complete the amputation of the foot. The major arteries, veins, and nerves are identified and ligated. The wound is thoroughly irrigated with antibiotic solution and may be closed in layers. If infection of the foot is present, this operation is performed in two stages. The amputation is performed and then later the soft tissues and skin are repaired and closed. A soft dressing is applied.

84.15   Other amputation below knee

Description
The physician performs an amputation of the leg below the knee. The physician makes an incision in the skin of the leg at the level where the amputation is to take place. The incision is carried completely around the leg. The tissue is dissected down to the bones. The large arteries, veins, and nerves are identified and tied off prior to being cut. Tissue is further debrided as needed. The tibia and fibula are identified. The physician surgically cuts the bones, completing the amputation. The wound is thoroughly irrigated and then closed in layers, including the skin. A soft dressing is placed over the stump.

An alternate amputation of the leg through tibia and fibula is an open or guillotine amputation. The physician places a pneumatic tourniquet on the thigh. The limb is measured for optimal stump

length and marks are made to facilitate skin flap preparation. Progressive incisions are made through soft tissues, and nerves and vessels are ligated. The tibia and fibula are bisected with a circular saw, rounded, and smoothed. The calf muscles are brought forward over the ends of the tibia and fibula and attached to the connective tissue on the front of the stump. The tourniquet is released and bleeding points are electrocoagulated. A drainage tube is placed deep in the muscle flap and the skin flaps are closed and sutured. A soft dressing is applied, followed by a rigid dressing in preparation for prosthetic devices fabrication.

Coding Clarification
This code is used to report amputation of a leg through tibia and fibula that is not more precisely described by other codes in subcategory 84.1. This code is also reported when the documentation does not further specify the BKA procedure.

84.16   Disarticulation of knee

Description
The physician performs disarticulation at the knee, which is a disjoining but not removal of bone above the knee. Equal anterior and posterior incisions are made around the knee. The patellar tendon is sectioned close to where it attaches to the tibial tubercle. The tendons surrounding the knee are divided from their insertions on the tibia. The same is done with the cruciate ligaments. Arteries and veins are ligated and nerves are divided. The patella is removed. A saw is used to remove the femoral condyles 1.5 cm above the level of the knee joint. The patellar tendon is pulled into the intercondylar notch and sutured to the remaining portions of the cruciate ligaments. The hamstring tendons are then sutured to the patellar tendon. A temporary drain is placed in the knee joint and the incision is closed in multiple layers.

Coding Clarification
Assign 84.16 for amputations with the following procedure names: Batch, Spitler, and McFaddin amputation, Mazet or S.P. Roger's amputation.

84.17   Amputation above knee

Description
The physician makes incisions so that equal anterior and posterior flaps are fashioned. Dissection is carried down to the femur. Arteries and veins are doubly ligated and transected. The sciatic nerve is divided. A Gigli saw is then used to section the femur and bevel the cut ends. The anterior and posterior myofascial flaps are sutured together and secured to the lower end of the femur through drill holes. Incisions are closed in layers and a temporary drain is applied. For fitting (27591) an immediate postoperative prosthesis (IPOP), a rigid dressing is

applied at the time of amputation. A sterile, closed-end stump sock is placed over the dressings. Felt pads are used over bony prominences to evenly distribute the pressure. An elastic, plaster cast is applied over the amputation site. A belt suspension apparatus may be incorporated into the cast. If immediate weight bearing is planned, an end-plate is wrapped into the lower portion of the cast to allow attachment of a temporary prosthesis.

Coding Clarification
Use 84.17 for conversion of a below-knee amputation into above-knee amputation and supracondylar above-knee amputation.

Coding Guidance
AHA: 3Q, '03, 14; 1Q, '05, 16

Anterior View of Knee

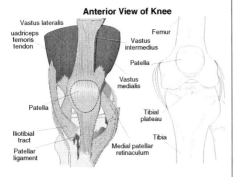

84.18   Disarticulation of hip

Description
The physician makes an anterior racquet-shaped incision beginning at the anterosuperior iliac spine and curving distally and medially. The incision extends to a point on the medial aspect of the thigh, 5 cm below the origin of the adductor muscles. The femoral artery and vein are ligated. The femoral nerve is divided. The physician continues the incision around the posterior aspect of the thigh to 5 cm below the ischial tuberosity and then laterally to the base of the greater trochanter. All muscles around the hip are detached. The physician then detaches the gluteal muscles, reflecting the muscle mass proximally for later use as a flap. The sciatic nerve is ligated and separated. The physician incises the hip joint capsule and ligamentum teres to complete the disarticulation. The gluteal flap is then brought around the wound and sutured. The physician places a drain in the inferior part of the incision. The edges of skin are closed with nonabsorbable sutures.

Coding Clarification
Hip disarticulation is the removal of a leg through the hip joint.

84.19   Abdominopelvic amputation

Description
The patient is placed in a lateral (on the side) position with the operative side up. There are three parts to this procedure including, anterior, perineal, and posterior. Each part requires a separate incision for exposure, dissection, and development of skin flaps. The physician separates the nerves and ligates the vessels. Vessels are ligated anteriorly and posteriorly; the sciatic nerve is cut high and tied. The pelvic ring, extending from the symphysis pubis to the attachment of the ilium to the sacrum, is sectioned and removed. Some muscle is retained, such as the gluteus maximus part of the skin flaps. The flaps are then closed with interrupted sutures over drains. The drains are removed in 48 to 72 hours.

Coding Clarification
Hemipelvectomy is the removal of the leg and lateral pelvis.

84.2   Reattachment of extremity

Description
The different types of extremity reattachment procedures are located under this subcategory. The primary difference among these procedure codes is the extremity involved.

Coding Guidance
AHA: 1Q, '95, 8

84.21   Thumb reattachment

Description
The physician reattaches the thumb that has been completely severed from the hand at the attachment of the thumb to the hand itself. With the patient under anesthesia, the physician identifies severed structures, including nerves, blood vessels, tendons, and bones. Dead tissue is debrided and the wound is thoroughly irrigated. Each tissue is systematically reattached using sutures, wires, plates, or other devices. Skin is joined in layers with sutures.

In an alternate procedure, the physician reattaches a thumb that has been completely severed from the hand at a point distal to where the thumb attaches to the hand. With the patient under anesthesia, the physician carefully identifies severed tissues, including nerves, blood vessels, tendons, and bones. Dead tissue is debrided and the wound is thoroughly irrigated. Each tissue is systematically reattached using sutures, wires, plates, or other devices. Skin is joined in layers with sutures.

76-84

84.22   Finger reattachment

Description
The physician reattaches one of the four fingers, excluding the thumb, which has been completely severed from the hand at or near its articulation with its specific metacarpal bone. With the patient under anesthesia, the physician identifies the nerves, tendons, blood vessels, and bones. Dead tissue is debrided and the wound is irrigated thoroughly. Each tissue is systematically reattached using sutures, wires, plates, or other devices. Skin is joined and sutured closed.

In an alternate procedure, the physician reattaches one of the four fingers, excluding the thumb, which has been completely severed from the hand at a level between the fingertip and the attachment of the finger to the hand itself. With the patient under anesthesia, the physician identifies severed structures, including nerves, blood vessels, tendons, and bones. Dead tissue is debrided and the wound is thoroughly irrigated. Each tissue is systematically reattached using sutures, wires, plates, or other devices. Skin is joined in layers with sutures.

Coding Clarification
Different types of extremity reattachment procedures are located under this subcategory. The primary difference among the procedure codes is the extremity involved.

84.23   Forearm, wrist, or hand reattachment

Description
The physician reattaches a severed forearm at a level between the wrist and the elbow. With the patient under anesthesia, the physician identifies each structure that has been cut or separated. The nerves, blood vessels, tendons, and bone are each reattached using sutures, wires, plates, or other fixation devices. Dead tissue is debrided. The skin is joined and closed with sutures after thorough cleaning and irrigation.

In an alternate procedure, the physician reattaches a hand that has been completely severed from the forearm between the wrist and the fingers. With the patient under anesthesia, the physician identifies the nerves, blood vessels, tendons, and bones. Each structure is reattached in a systematic fashion with debridement of dead tissue. Sutures, wires, plates, or other devices may be used. Copious irrigation is required. The overlying soft tissues and skin are joined with sutures in layers.

84.24   Upper arm reattachment

Description
The physician replants an arm following a complete amputation. The physician reattaches the upper extremity at a level between the elbow and shoulder.

With the patient under anesthesia, the physician identifies the severed neurovascular structures, muscles, bone, and tendons. Each tissue is systematically reattached using sutures, wires, plates, or other fixation devices. Dead tissue is debrided. The skin is joined and closed with sutures after thorough cleaning and irrigation.

Coding Clarification
Use 84.24 for reattachment of the arm when the documentation does not further specify the procedure.

84.25   Toe reattachment

Description
The physician reattaches one of the four fingers, excluding the thumb, which has been completely severed from the hand at or near its articulation with its specific metacarpal bone. With the patient under anesthesia, the physician identifies the nerves, tendons, blood vessels, and bones. Dead tissue is debrided and the wound is irrigated thoroughly. Each tissue is systematically reattached using sutures, wires, plates, or other devices. Skin is joined and sutured closed.

The physician reattaches one of the four fingers, excluding the thumb, which has been completely severed from the hand at a level between the fingertip and the attachment of the finger to the hand itself. With the patient under anesthesia, the physician identifies severed structures, including nerves, blood vessels, tendons, and bones. Dead tissue is debrided and the wound is thoroughly irrigated. Each tissue is systematically reattached using sutures, wires, plates, or other devices. Skin is joined in layers with sutures.

84.26   Foot reattachment

Description
The physician reattaches a foot that has been completely amputated at or near the ankle. With the patient under anesthesia, the physician carefully identifies severed structures, including blood vessels, nerves, tendons, and bones. Dead tissue is debrided and the wound is thoroughly irrigated. Each tissue is reattached using sutures, wires, plates, pins, or other devices. Skin is joined in layers with sutures.

84.27   Lower leg or ankle reattachment

Description
This code is used to report lower leg or ankle reattachment procedures that are not more precisely described by other codes in subcategory 84.2. This code is also reported when the documentation does not further specify the procedure.

● New Code   ▲ Revised Code   ►◄ Revised Text   © 2010 Ingenix

84.28   Thigh reattachment

Description
Surgical reattachment of a thigh muscle is
performed using a longitudinal incision. The rectus
femoris muscle is mobilized and scar tissue is
excised. The muscle was reattached by direct suture
repair.

Coding Scenario
During a game, a soccer player felt a tearing in his
right thigh and subsequently developed severe
bruising, swelling, and a painful lump in his thigh
during muscle contraction. Surgical reattachment
was performed.

Code Assignment:

84.28   Thigh reattachment

84.29   Other reattachment of extremity

Description
Code 84.29 is used to report other extremity
reattachment procedures that are not more precisely
described by other codes in subcategory 84.2.

Documentation Tip
Review the documentation for specific information
regarding the procedure prior to final code selection
in order to ensure accurate code assignment.

84.3   Revision of amputation stump

Description
After the stump has granulated or healed by scar,
the physician performs secondary closure or scar
revision. This procedure will usually be performed
two to three weeks or more after the initial open
amputation was completed. Additional bone is
sectioned, usually at a more proximal or higher level.
Skin flaps are fashioned and pulled down over the
stump and closed with nonabsorbable sutures. A
temporary drain or suction tubes are used as well.

Coding Clarification
Use 84.3 for reamputation, secondary closure, or
trimming of an amputation stump.

Do not assign 84.3 for revision of a current
traumatic amputation or revision by further
amputation of a current injury (84.00-84.19, 84.91).

Coding Guidance
AHA: 4Q, '88, 12; 2Q, '98, 15; 4Q, '99, 15

84.4   Implantation or fitting of prosthetic limb device

Description
Prostheses are artificial devices used to replace a
body part. Prostheses include artificial limbs,
hearing aids, false teeth and eyes, pacemakers, and
plastic heart valves. Due to advances in medical
technology, myoelectric arms have been developed,

which are electronically operated by impulses from
body muscles.

A major consideration for prosthetists is the
constantly changing size and shape of the residual
limb, or stump, which is the attachment site for a
prosthesis. The prosthesis must be fitted to the
patient individually and the surgical incision site
must heal before fitting for the prosthesis can begin.

Fitting a prosthetic limb device involves assessment
and preparation of the stump and modifying the fit
using stump socks or socket liners and training in
the use of the prosthetic device.

Following amputation of the limb, post-surgical or
early dressings are applied to the surgical stump,
sometimes during the same operative session, to
compress and prepare the tissues in anticipation of
fitting a test socket and later a permanent socket. In
some instances, a plaster cast or other rigid dressing
is hand molded to the residual limb as the
amputation session is completed. In other instances,
the initial dressing is applied up to several days
following surgery. In some cases, removable casts or
caps are devised. These devices may be removed and
reapplied several times.

Coding Clarification
Centers for Medicare and Medicaid Services (CMS)
requires a functional level determination with
certificates of medical necessity for prostheses.

84.40   Implantation or fitting of prosthetic limb device, not otherwise specified

Description
Code 84.40 is used to report implantation or fitting
of a prosthetic limb device when the documentation
does not further specify the procedure performed.
This code is also reported when the procedure
performed is not more precisely described by other
codes in this subcategory.

Coding Clarification
The prosthesis must be fitted to the patient
individually and the surgical incision site must heal
before fitting for the prosthesis can begin. A major
consideration for prosthetists is the constantly
changing size and shape of the residual limb, or
stump, which is the attachment site for a prosthesis.

84.41   Fitting of prosthesis of upper arm and shoulder

Description
Fitting a prosthetic limb device involves assessment
and preparation of the stump, modifying the fit
using stump socks or socket liners, and training in
the use of the prosthetic device. In this procedure,
the physician fits the patient for an upper arm or
shoulder prosthetic device. The patient's skin
integrity, edema, and surgical wound healing also

76-84

need to be assessed when determining the choice of materials used.

Coding Clarification
The prosthesis must be fitted to the patient individually and the surgical incision site must heal before fitting for the prosthesis can begin. A major consideration for prosthetists is the constantly changing size and shape of the residual limb, or stump, which is the attachment site for a prosthesis.

84.42   Fitting of prosthesis of lower arm and hand

Description
Fitting a prosthetic limb device involves assessment and preparation of the stump, modifying the fit using stump socks or socket liners, and training in the use of the prosthetic device. The provider fits the patient for a lower arm or hand prosthetic device. This includes assessment for the appropriate type of prosthetic device. The patient's skin integrity, edema, and surgical wound healing also need to be assessed when determining the choice of materials used. The clinician may perform an assessment of the suitability and benefits of acquiring any assistive technology device or equipment that will help restore, augment, or compensate for existing functional ability in the patient.

Coding Clarification
The prosthesis must be fitted to the patient individually and the surgical incision site must heal before fitting for the prosthesis can begin. A major consideration for prosthetists is the constantly changing size and shape of the residual limb, or stump, which is the attachment site for a prosthesis.

84.43   Fitting of prosthesis of arm, not otherwise specified

Description
Code 84.43 is assigned to report fitting of a prosthetic arm device when the documentation does not further specify the procedure performed. Fitting a prosthetic limb device involves assessment and preparation of the stump, modifying the fit using stump socks or socket liners, and training in the use of the prosthetic device. This code is also reported when the procedure performed is not more precisely described by other codes in subcategory 84.4.

84.44   Implantation of prosthetic device of arm

Description
Removal of the proximal portion of the humerus is often performed for aggressive benign lesions and low-grade malignancies. The physician amputates the arm through the humerus bone and places a surgical implant in the arm. The physician makes an incision in a circular fashion around the arm distal to the level of the planned amputation of the

humerus. The vessels and nerves are identified, divided, and ligated. The humerus bone is divided in two, completing the amputation. The physician spares the skin, soft tissue, and muscle needed to close the amputation incision. Any of a variety of implants, such as rods, are utilized to maintain the length of the arm or to replace a portion of the amputated humerus. Fixation devices are used. The incision is irrigated. Retained muscle flaps are closed over exposed bone. The wound is closed in layers and a soft dressing is applied.

Coding Clarification
Cineplasty is an outdated procedure performed for upper arm amputation to create a muscle motor that acts on an inserted pin to provide the energy for prosthetic action or movement.

Contraction of the muscle causes displacement of the tunnel and the pin and provides the motor energy for prosthetic action. This has been replaced by technological advances that use myoelectrical sensors attached to the skin.

84.45   Fitting of prosthesis above knee

Description
The physician makes incisions so that equal anterior and posterior flaps are fashioned. Dissection is carried down to the femur. Arteries and veins are doubly ligated and transected. The sciatic nerve is divided. A Gigli saw is used to section the femur and bevel the cut ends. The anterior and posterior myofascial flaps are sutured together and secured to the lower end of the femur through drill holes. Incisions are closed in layers and a temporary drain is applied. For fitting an immediate postoperative prosthesis (IPOP), a rigid dressing is applied at the time of amputation. A closed-end stump sock is placed over the dressings. Felt pads are used over bony prominences to evenly distribute the pressure. An elastic, plaster cast is applied over the amputation site. A belt suspension apparatus may be incorporated into the cast. If immediate weight bearing is planned, an end-plate is wrapped into the lower portion of the cast to allow attachment of a temporary prosthesis.

Coding Clarification
Fitting a prosthetic limb device involves assessment and preparation of the stump, modifying the fit using stump socks or socket liners, and training in the use of the prosthetic device.

84.46   Fitting of prosthesis below knee

Description
This code reports early fittings following below-the-knee amputation or disarticulation at the knee joint. A major consideration for prosthetists is the constantly changing size and shape of the

residual limb, or stump, which is the attachment site for a prosthesis. Following amputation of the limb, post-surgical or "early" dressings are applied to the surgical stump, sometimes during the same operative session. These early applications are designed to compress and prepare the distal tissues in anticipation of fitting a test socket and later a permanent socket. Early applications may be known as immediate post-surgical fittings (IPSF). The accepted plan for most lower limb amputations is to transition the patient as quickly as possible to use of a prosthesis. This minimizes muscle atrophy and limb weakness seen in longer convalescences. In some instances, a plaster cast or other rigid dressing is hand molded to the residual limb as the amputation session is completed. In other instances, the initial dressing is applied up to several days following surgery. As swelling diminishes and also to access the surgical closure, the dressing must be periodically changed out. These early dressings may be fitted to interface with test prosthetic devices.

Coding Clarification
Fitting a prosthetic limb device involves assessment and preparation of the stump, modifying the fit using stump socks or socket liners, and training in the use of the prosthetic device.

84.47 Fitting of prosthesis of leg, not otherwise specified
Description
Fitting a prosthetic limb device involves assessment and preparation of the stump, modifying the fit using stump socks or socket liners, and training in the use of the prosthetic device.

The clinician fits the patient in the use of an orthotic device for the leg or performs an assessment of the suitability and benefits of acquiring any assistive technology device or equipment that will help restore, augment, or compensate for existing functional ability in the patient. This includes assessment as to type of prosthesis when appropriate.

Coding Clarification
Code 84.47 is used to report fitting of a prosthetic leg device when the documentation does not further specify the procedure. This code is also reported when the procedure performed is not more precisely described by other codes in subcategory 84.4.

The major components of a lower extremity prosthesis are the socket, a sock or gel liner, a suspension system, an articulating joint (if needed), a pylon, and a terminal device, which is typically a foot.

84.48 Implantation of prosthetic device of leg
Description
Code 84.48 is used to report prosthetic leg device implantation that is not more precisely described by other codes in subcategory 84.4. This code is also reported when the documentation does not further specify the procedure.

Coding Clarification
The components of a lower extremity prosthesis include the socket, a sock or gel liner, a suspension system, an articulating joint (if needed), a pylon, and a terminal device, which is typically a foot.

84.5 Implantation of other musculoskeletal devices and substances
Description
Subcategory 84.5 includes codes to report insertion of an interbody fusion cage, synthetic cages or spacers, threaded bone dowels, and bone void fillers such as acrylic cement, polymethylmethacrylate (PMMA), and calcium based bone void filler.

Coding Clarification
Subcategory 84.5 should not be assigned for insertion of a (non-fusion) spinal disc replacement device (84.60-84.69).

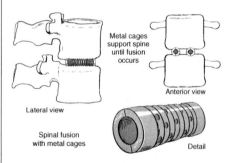

Metal cages support spine until fusion occurs

Anterior view

Lateral view

Spinal fusion with metal cages

Detail

84.51 Insertion of interbody spinal fusion device
Description
This code describes the procedures used to surgically implant devices used in spinal fixation, such as wires, screws, cables, plates, or rods. The patient is placed in the position dictated by the failure. The physician makes a midline incision overlying the damaged section. The fascia, paravertebral muscles, and ligaments are retracted. A number of reparative techniques may be used, depending on the device and site. The physician closes the muscles, fascia, and skin with layered sutures.

Coding Clarification
For insertion of an intervertebral spinal fusion device (i.e., cages, synthetic spacers [PEEK, metal, etc.], or

threaded bone dowels), the hospital would report ICD-9 code 84.51.

Also code spinal fusion (81.00-81.08) or refusion of spine (81.30-81.39); however, insertion of bone graft is included in the spinal fusion procedure and not reported separately.

Coding Guidance
AHA: 4Q, '02, 108-110; 1Q, '04, 21; 4Q, '05, 123; 2Q, '08, 14; 2Q, '09, 5

84.52   Insertion of recombinant bone morphogenetic protein

Description
Code 84.52 reports surgical implantation of bone morphogenetic proteins (BMP) and recombinant BMP (rhBMP) to induce new bone growth formation. BMPs are being tested for use in promoting bone growth in spinal fusions, delayed unions, and nonunions of fractured bones. BMP is surgically implanted. Clinical applications include delayed unions and nonunions, fractures, and in place of a bone graft in spinal fusions. It is applied with an absorbable collagen sponge, coral, ceramic, and other carriers, or in an interbody fusion device that is then implanted at the fusion site.

Coding Clarification
Code also the primary procedure performed such as fracture repair (79.00-79.99), spinal fusion (81.00-81.08), and spinal refusion (81.30-81.39).

Coding Guidance
AHA: 2Q, '09, 4-5

84.53   Implantation of internal limb lengthening device with kinetic distraction

Description
Kinetic distraction is a method used to stimulate osteogenesis, or the development of new bone, between bone segments that are surgically severed and then progressively pulled apart. The connective tissue that surrounds bones fills the gap with newly created bone.

In one example, the physician performs osteoplasty of the humerus for shortening or lengthening. An incision is made through the skin, fascia, and muscle in the upper arm over the humeral shaft. Vessels and nerves are exposed and retracted. Dissection continues to expose the shaft of the humerus. An osteotomy is made at the determined point on the humerus. The physician removes a wedge of bone. To shorten the humeral shaft, a plate is attached to the distal segment with screws. Reduction forceps are used to hold and compress the osteotomy while the plate is attached to the proximal fragment with screws. To lengthen the bone, the segments are retracted, usually 2 to 3 mm, and fixed

at that distance with plates and screws. X-rays are used to check rotational alignment of the segments. Drain tubes are inserted, the incision is repaired in layers with sutures, staples, and/or Steri-strips, and the arm is immobilized.

Coding Clarification
Code also any limb lengthening procedure (78.30-78.39).

Specific codes exist to report internal limb lengthening device with kinetic distraction (84.53) vs. other internal limb-lengthening devices (84.54).

84.54   Implantation of other internal limb lengthening device

Description
Code 84.54 is used to report implantation of an internal limb lengthening device that is not more precisely described by other codes in this subcategory. This code is also reported when the documentation does not further specify the procedure. Femoral shortening or lengthening techniques equalize leg lengths or treat malunions of the femur. For femoral lengthening, two puncture wounds are made laterally in the distal and proximal femur. Two holes at each end are drilled in the bone, and a screw is inserted in each drill hole. The physician makes a lateral longitudinal incision 6 to 8 cm long to expose the femur. At the osteotomy site, an oscillating saw cuts through the femur. The Wagner distraction apparatus is then attached to the two sets of screws, so that the apparatus is 1 to 2 cm lateral to the thigh. The incision is repaired in multiple layers. The device is then distracted up to 5 to 6 mm immediately. The apparatus is operated by a knob. Lengthening is about 1.5 mm or 1 cm per week. When the appearance of the femur is normal and the medullary has been reestablished, the plate and screws are removed.

Coding Clarification
Report any limb lengthening procedure (78.30-78.39) performed.

84.55   Insertion of bone void filler

Description
The physician performs a preventative nailing, plating, pinning, or wiring of the clavicle to the coracoid process in order to gain better fixation and prevent further dislocation of the acromioclavicular joint. Access to the joint is obtained through a lateral incision over the acromion process. The skin and soft tissues are reflected back. The screw or other fixation device of choice is positioned and may be checked by separately reportable x-ray. The procedure may or may not be accomplished with the use of methylmethacrylate, which can be injected into a weak or defective bone area and then hardens

to act like bone cement. The incision is closed with sutures and movement is restricted for four to six weeks. The hardware is removed when stability is determined.

Coding Clarification

Bone void fillers are used in certain procedures to fill gaps that are surgically created or the result of trauma and disease processes. Autologous bone grafts harvested from the patient's iliac crest have typically been used to fill bony voids; however, synthetic products have been developed to fill bony voids. Bone void fillers include acrylic cement, calcium based fillers, and polymethylmethacrylate (PMMA).

Do not assign 84.55 for insertion of bone void filler associated with percantaneous vertebral augmentation (81.66) or that with percutaneous vertebroplasty (81.65).

Coding Guidance
AHA: 4Q, '04, 128

84.56   Insertion or replacement of (cement) spacer
Description
After the physician removes an existing prosthetic device, a cement spacer is inserted to maintain the space until the prosthetic device is replaced. The physician accesses the prosthesis through the previous surgery incision. A spacer of methylmethacrylate formed into a cube shape may be inserted into the space. The spacer prevents the soft tissues from compressing the joint space. The spacer is secured until another prosthetic device is inserted. Drains may be placed. The wound may be left open for healing or the incision is repaired in multiple layers.

Coding Clarification
Code 84.56 reports insertion or replacement of a joint (methylmethacrylate) spacer.

A cement spacer is not inserted during the same operative session as a joint replacement prosthesis; this is typically done in a two-stage procedure.

Do not assign code 84.56 for the implantation of antibiotic impregnated cement during a hip revision or replacement.

Coding Scenario
Using a posterior approach, the physician performed a nonfusion implantation of an interspinous process decompressive (IPD) device between the spinous processes to limit extension.

Code Assignment:

84.56   Insertion of (cement) spacer

Coding Guidance
AHA: 4Q, '05, 124; 2Q, '08, 4

84.57   Removal or replacement of (cement) spacer
Description
The patient is placed in a lateral decubitus position (lying on the side). The physician may access the prosthesis through the previous hip surgery incision. Any scar tissue is resected. The physician exposes and incises the hip joint capsule. The hip is then manually dislocated. Methylmethacrylate (cement) is removed from the upper portion of the stem. The physician removes the stem with forceful blows. The physician removes any cement. The physician may make a bone window in the femoral cortex to remove additional cement. If there is bony ingrowth, flexible osteotomes may be used to remove the bone, allowing further stem retraction. The physician removes cement from the border of the implant with chisels and gouges. Any remaining loose cement is removed with a large curette or other instrument. Drains may be placed. The wound may be left open for healing or the incision is repaired in multiple layers.

Coding Clarification
Code 84.57 reports removal of a joint (methylmethacrylate) spacer.

Coding Guidance
AHA: 4Q, '05, 113, 124-125; 2Q, '08, 4, 5

84.59   Insertion of other spinal devices
Description
This code describes the procedures performed to insert various devices used in spinal fixation. These devices act as a spacer between the spinous processes to provide posterior stabilization, with or without surgical decompression, while retaining motion. In general, the physician makes a midline incision overlying the damaged section. The fascia, paravertebral muscles, and ligaments are retracted. The physician closes the muscles, fascia, and skin with layered sutures. A number of reparative techniques may be used, depending on the device and site.

Internal spinal fixation by wiring the spinous processes, also called Drummond wiring, is done with wires attached to a button that gives the needed purchase at the base of the spinous process and has a hole in its surface for the wire coming from the opposite direction to pass through. The spine is exposed in the standard manner and a hook is used to grasp the upper and lower pedicle of the selected fusion levels. Using an awl or a clamp, the physician makes a hole in the base of each involved spinous process and passes two button wire implants in opposite directions through the bony hole, making sure that each wire also passes through the hole in the opposite button, and pulls the buttons snugly to the base of the spinous process. The buttons are tamped into place. In some cases, only one button

76-84

wire is passed from the convex to the concave side. A contoured distraction rod is inserted into the open loops of the wire implants and the hooks at the top and bottom and secured. Distraction is applied for correction, which is maintained by tightening the wires. Further distraction may be applied to the rod and a clamp placed to prevent loss of the correction. The laminae and transverse processes lateral to the buttons may be decorticated before closure of the wound.

In another example, segmental instrumentation is placed with fixation not only at either end but also at the levels inbetween. The physician makes a midline incision in the skin, fascia, and paravertebral muscles over the affected vertebrae. Multiple hooks or screws are introduced into the vertebral pedicles where fixation is needed. Dual rods, such as Harrington distraction and compression rods, are anchored to the screws or hooks. Distraction is the force that produces kyphosis and compression corrects kyphosis, the abnormal hunchback curvature of the spine. To achieve correction, the compression assembly is tightened in place before distraction is applied and secured in position. The wound is closed with layered sutures. The Harrington rod instrumentation techniques are being replaced by three-dimensional correction techniques where rods can be bent along the entire length and applied at any level, in rotation, with distraction and compression applied between segments.

Coding Clarification

Several types of the interspinous devices reported with 84.59 are currently in use, such as the Dynesys stabilization device, the X-Stop® Interspinous Process Decompression (IPD ®) and the Wallis® Stabilization System; others are currently in development. These devices act as a spacer between the spinous processes to provide posterior stabilization, with or without surgical decompression, while retaining motion.

Coding Scenario

A patient with a herniated L4 disk causing lumbar spinal stenosis undergoes an excision of the herniated disk and a non-fusion posterior spinal stabilization procedure using the Dynesys® Spinal System.

    Code Assignment:

    722.10 Displacement of thoracic or lumbar
            intervertebral disc without myelopathy,
            Lumbar intervertebral disc without
            myelopathy
    80.51   Excision of intervertebral disc
    84.59   Insertion of other spinal devices

Coding Guidance
AHA: 1Q, '07, 9, 10

84.6   Replacement of spinal disc

Description
Subcategory 84.6 includes non-fusion arthroplasty of the spine with insertion of an artificial disc prosthesis. Spinal disc prostheses are used to restore disc height. The prostheses can replace the disc nucleus (partial disc prosthesis) or the entire disc (total disc prosthesis). This technology provides a minimally invasive substitute for spinal fusion or arthrodesis. Specific codes included in this subcategory differentiate between partial and total spinal disc prosthesis and revision procedures. For example, partial disc prosthesis of the cervical spine (84.61) and the lumbosacral spine (84.64) vs. codes for total disc prosthesis insertion of the cervical spine (84.62) and the lumbosacral spine (84.65). Specific codes are also included for the revision or replacement of artificial disc prosthesis of the cervical spine (84.66) and lumbosacral spine (84.68); however, these revision codes do not distinguish between partial or total disc prostheses.

Coding Clarification
Codes may distinguish between partial or total spinal disc prosthesis:

*   A partial spinal disc prosthesis, or nucleus prosthesis, is designed to replace only the nucleus pulposus or the soft, gelatinous center of a spinal disc. A nucleus prosthesis restores function by restoring proper load transfer from one vertebra to the next.

*   A total disc prosthesis is used to replace all the component structures of a disc (the nucleus pulposus, the annulus fibrosis, and the vertebral end plates) to restore disc motion, stiffness, and stability.

Documentation Tip
Codes included in this subcategory differentiate between partial and total spinal disc prosthesis and revision procedures. Different approaches are used for vertebral procedures based on differing levels of vertebrae. The top three cervical vertebrae are approached from a pharyngeal or anterior approach. The lower four cervical vertebrae are approached from a lateral direction. Thoracic and lumbar vertebrae are approached from behind and to the right to avoid major arteries. A careful review of the operative report for specific information regarding the site and technique used is necessary prior to final code selection in order to ensure accurate code assignment.

84.60   Insertion of spinal disc prosthesis, not otherwise specified

Description
Code 84.60 is used to report insertion of a spinal disc prosthesis when the documentation does not

● New Code   ▲ Revised Code   ▶◀ Revised Text   © 2010 Ingenix

further specify the site or procedure. This code is also reported for a spinal disc prosthesis that is not more precisely described by other codes in subcategory 84.6.

Coding Clarification
Diskectomy (discectomy) is included in 84.60.

Documentation Tip
Specific codes are included in this subcategory that differentiate between partial and total spinal disc prosthesis and revision or replacement procedures. Different approaches are used for vertebral procedures based on different levels of vertebrae. A careful review of the operative report for specific information regarding the site and technique used is necessary prior to final code selection in order to ensure accurate code assignment.

84.61 Insertion of partial spinal disc prosthesis, cervical

Description
A partial disc excision is performed to achieve increased flexion, extension, rotation, and bending of the affected vertebral segment. The physician approaches the cervical vertebrae by making an incision through the neck, avoiding the esophagus, trachea, and thyroid. Retractors separate the intervertebral muscles. The area is explored and debrided. Stiffness decreases as the amount of nuclear material removed increases. When the procedure is complete, the fascia and vertebral muscles are repaired and returned to their anatomical positions. The wound is closed.

Coding Clarification
Assign 84.61 for insertion of a cervical nuclear replacement device, partial cervical artificial disc prosthesis, and replacement of a nuclear disc (nucleus pulposus) in the cervical spine.

Diskectomy (discectomy) is included in 84.61.

Codes included in this subcategory differentiate between partial and total spinal disc prosthesis and revision procedures. Review the documentation for specific information regarding the procedure prior to final code selection in order to ensure appropriate code assignment.

84.62 Insertion of total spinal disc prosthesis, cervical

Description
The physician uses an anterior approach to reach damaged cervical vertebrae by making an incision through the neck, avoiding the esophagus, trachea, and thyroid. Retractors separate the intervertebral muscles. The affected intervertebral disc location is confirmed by separately reportable x-ray. The physician cleans out the intervertebral disk space

with a rongeur, removing the cartilaginous material to be replaced in preparation for inserting the implant. One type of implant for total disc replacement has two endplates made of a metal alloy and a convex weight-bearing surface made of ultra high molecular weight polyethylene. The endplates are inserted in a collapsed form and seated into the vertebral bodies above and below the interspace. Minimal distraction is applied to open the intervertebral space and the polyethylene disc material is snap-fit into the lower endplate. With the disc assembly complete, the wound is closed and a drain may be placed.

Coding Clarification
Use 84.62 for replacement of a cervical spinal disc that is not further specified in the documentation.

Diskectomy (discectomy) is included in 84.62.

84.63 Insertion of spinal disc prosthesis, thoracic

Description
Different approaches are taken for vertebral procedures based on the different levels of vertebrae. Thoracic and lumbar vertebrae are approached from behind and to the right to avoid major arteries.

This procedure is performed to replace a vertebral body or partial vertebral body resected due to destruction by disease, trauma, or other processes. Once the vertebral body has been removed, a hole is cored out of the vertebral bodies above and below the removed vertebrae to secure a biomechanical device (ceramic block, metal/synthetic cage, threaded bone dowel, methylmethacrylate). The physician selects the biomechanical device best suited to the location and type of deformity being corrected. For example, to correct a deformity caused by a malignancy, the physician may elect to inject methylmethacrylate into the area and allow it to dry to replace the excised vertebral body. Screws, wires, or plates may be used to secure the device. Muscles are allowed to fall back into place and the wound is closed over a drain with layered sutures.

Coding Clarification
Codes included in subcategory 84.6 differentiate between partial and total spinal disc prosthesis; however, the code for thoracic spinal disc prosthesis (84.63) does not differentiate between partial or total spinal disc prosthesis.

Diskectomy (discectomy) is included in 84.63.

84.64 Insertion of partial spinal disc prosthesis, lumbosacral

Description
A partial disc excision is performed to achieve increased flexion, extension, rotation, and bending of the affected vertebral segment. The physician uses

an anterior approach to reach the damaged lumbar vertebrae by making an incision through the abdomen. Retractors separate the intervertebral muscles. The affected intervertebral disc location is confirmed by separately reportable x-ray. The physician cleans out the intervertebral disk space with a rongeur, removing the cartilaginous material to be replaced in preparation for inserting the implant.

Coding Clarification
Use 84.64 for insertion of a lumbosacral nuclear replacement device, partial cervical artificial disc prosthesis, and replacement of nuclear disc (nucleus pulposus) in the cervical spine.

Diskectomy (discectomy) is included in 84.64.

Documentation Tip
Codes included in this subcategory differentiate between partial and total spinal disc prosthesis and revision procedures. Different approaches are used for vertebral procedures based on differing levels of vertebrae. The top three cervical vertebrae are approached from a pharyngeal or anterior approach. The lower four cervical vertebrae are approached from a lateral direction. Thoracic and lumbar vertebrae are approached from behind and to the right to avoid major arteries. A careful review of the operative report for specific information regarding the site and technique used is necessary prior to final code selection in order to ensure accurate code assignment.

84.65   Insertion of total spinal disc prosthesis, lumbosacral

Description
Total disc arthroplasty is done to replace a severely damaged or diseased intervertebral disc, most often caused by degenerative disc disease. The physician uses an anterior approach to reach the damaged lumbar vertebrae by making an incision through the abdomen. Some implants require only minimal access, approximately 7 cm long, for a mini-retroperitoneal approach. Retractors separate the intervertebral muscles. The affected intervertebral disc location is confirmed by separately reportable x-ray. The physician cleans out the intervertebral disk space with a rongeur, removing the cartilaginous material to be replaced in preparation for inserting the implant. One type of implant for total disc replacement has two endplates made of a metal alloy and a convex weight-bearing surface made of ultra high molecular weight polyethylene. The endplates are inserted in a collapsed form and seated into the vertebral bodies above and below the interspace. Minimal distraction is applied to open the intervertebral space and the polyethylene disc material is snap-fit into the lower

endplate. With the disc assembly complete, the wound is closed and a drain may be placed.

Coding Clarification
Use 84.65 for replacement of a lumbar spinal disc that is not further specified in the documentation.

Diskectomy (discectomy) is included in 84.65.

Coding Guidance
   AHA: 4Q, '04, 133

84.66   Revision or replacement of artificial spinal disc prosthesis, cervical

Description
The physician revises an artificial disc prosthesis placed during a previous disc arthroplasty. The physician approaches the cervical vertebrae by making an incision through the neck, avoiding the esophagus, trachea, and thyroid. The lumbar vertebrae are approached by making an incision through the abdomen. Retractors separate the intervertebral muscles. The implant is located, the area is explored, and any adhesions are freed. The prosthesis may be partially replaced or adjusted during the exploration. When the revision is complete, the fascia and vertebral muscles are repaired and returned to their anatomical positions. The incision is closed.

Coding Clarification
Use 84.66 for removal of a partial or total cervical spinal disc prosthesis with synchronous insertion of new spinal disc prosthesis, and repair of a previously inserted cervical spinal disc prosthesis.

Codes included in this subcategory differentiate between partial and total spinal disc prosthesis and revision procedures. Review the documentation for specific information regarding the procedure prior to final code selection in order to ensure appropriate code assignment.

84.67   Revision or replacement of artificial spinal disc prosthesis, thoracic

Description
The physician revises an artificial disc prosthesis placed during a previous disc arthroplasty. The physician approaches the cervical vertebrae by making an incision through the neck, avoiding the esophagus, trachea, and thyroid. The lumbar vertebrae are approached by making an incision through the abdomen. Retractors separate the intervertebral muscles. The implant is located, the area is explored, and any adhesions are freed. The prosthesis may be partially replaced or adjusted during the exploration. When the revision is complete, the fascia and vertebral muscles are repaired and returned to their anatomical positions. The incision is closed.

Coding Clarification
Use 84.67 for removal of a partial or total thoracic spinal disc prosthesis with synchronous insertion of a new spinal disc prosthesis and repair of a previously inserted thoracic spinal disc prosthesis.

84.68 Revision or replacement of artificial spinal disc prosthesis, lumbosacral

Description
The physician removes an artificial disc prosthesis placed during a previous disc arthroplasty. The physician approaches the cervical vertebrae by making an incision through the neck, avoiding the esophagus, trachea, and thyroid. The lumbar vertebrae are approached by making an incision through the abdomen. Retractors separate the intervertebral muscles. The implant is located and any adhesions are freed. Distraction is applied to open the intervertebral space and the implant is removed. The area is explored and debrided. When the procedure is complete, the fascia and vertebral muscles are repaired and returned to their anatomical positions. The wound is closed.

Coding Clarification
Use 84.68 for replacement or revision of a partial or total lumbosacral spinal disc prosthesis with synchronous insertion of a new spinal disc prosthesis, and repair of a previously inserted lumbosacral spinal disc prosthesis.

84.69 Revision or replacement of artificial spinal disc prosthesis, not otherwise specified

Description
The physician performs replacement or revision of a partial or total spinal disc prosthesis with synchronous insertion of new spinal disc prosthesis, and repair of a previously inserted spinal disc prosthesis that is not further specified in the documentation.

84.7 Adjunct codes for external fixator devices

Coding Clarification
When assigning codes from subcategory 84.7, remember to also code any primary procedure performed, such as application of an external fixator device (78.10, 78.12-78.13, 78.15, 78.17-78.19) or reduction of a fracture and dislocation (79.00-79.89).

Coding Guidance
  AHA: 4Q, '05, 127-129

84.71 Application of external fixator device, monoplanar system

Description
The physician applies an external fixation system to help a fracture or joint injury heal. Monoplanar

instrumentation provides percutaneous neutralization, compression, and/or distraction of bone in a single plane by applying force within that plane. This procedure involves the use of an external fixator to stabilize an injury such as a simple fracture. One or more pins or wires may by used. Small stab incisions are made in the skin and a drill is used to make a hole into the bone. Each pin or wire is inserted into the bone through the drill holes and secured to an external fixation device. This holds the fracture or joint in a stable position.

Coding Clarification
This procedure is performed in addition to a coded treatment of fracture or joint injury unless listed as part of the basic procedure.

Do not assign 84.71 for other hybrid device or system (84.73) or a ring device or system (84.72).

Coding Guidance
  AHA: 4Q, '05, 129

84.72 Application of external fixator device, ring system

Description
The physician applies an external fixation system to help a fracture or joint injury heal. Ring system instrumentation provides percutaneous neutralization, compression, and/or distraction of bone through 360 degrees of force application. This procedure involves the use of an external fixator to stabilize an injury such as a simple fracture. One or more pins or wires may by used. Small stab incisions are made in the skin and a drill is used to make a hole into the bone. Each pin or wire is inserted into the bone through the drill holes and secured to an external fixation device. This holds the fracture or joint in a stable position.

Coding Clarification
This procedure is performed in addition to a coded treatment of fracture or joint injury unless listed as part of the basic procedure.

Ring systems include Ilizarov type or Sheffield type.

Do not assign 84.72 for a monoplanar device or system (84.71) or other hybrid device or system (84.73).

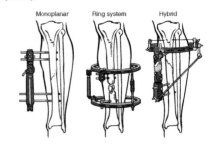

Monoplanar   Ring system   Hybrid

76-84

84.73   Application of hybrid external fixator device

Description
The physician applies an external fixation system to help a fracture or joint injury heal. Hybrid external fixator instrumentation provides percutaneous neutralization, compression, and/or distraction of bone by applying multiple external forces using monoplanar and ring device combinations. This procedure involves the use of an external fixator to stabilize an injury such as a simple fracture. One or more pins or wires may be used. Small stab incisions are made in the skin and a drill is used to make a hole into the bone. Each pin or wire is inserted into the bone through the drill holes and secured to an external fixation device. This holds the fracture or joint in a stable position.

Coding Clarification
This procedure is performed in addition to treatment of a fracture or joint injury unless listed as part of the basic procedure.

Do not assign 84.73 for a monoplanar device or system when used alone (84.71) or a ring device or system when used alone (84.72).

84.8   Insertion, replacement and revision of posterior spinal motion preservation device(s)

Description
Subcategory 84.8 describes various motion preservation technologies that are currently in use. These technologies enable spinal stabilization without the restrictions created by fusion. Motion preservation technologies include interspinous process devices, pedicle screw dynamic stabilization systems, facet replacement systems, intervertebral disc replacements, and disc repair systems. Interspinous process, pedicle screw dynamic stabilization, and facet replacement devices are inserted in the posterior column of the lumbar spine. Interspinous process devices that act as spacers between the vertebral bodies may also provide decompression. Pedicle screw stabilization systems provide posterior stabilization forces and facet replacement systems replace facet joints, both without loss of motion.

Coding Clarification
The initial insertion of pedicle screws with spinal fusion is not separately reported. Any facetectomy (partial, total) performed at the same level synchronously is included in the procedure; however, any synchronous surgical decompression (foraminotomy, laminectomy, laminotomy) (03.09) should be coded.

Do not use this code to report removal of pedicle screws used in spinal fusion (78.69), replacement of pedicle screws used in spinal fusion (78.59), revision of an interspinous process device(s) (84.81), revision

of a pedicle-based dynamic stabilization device(s) (84.83), fusion of spine (81.00-81.08, 81.30-81.39), insertion of an artificial disc prosthesis (84.60-84.69), or insertion of an interbody spinal fusion device (84.51).

Coding Guidance
   AHA: 4Q, '07, 116-120

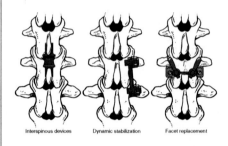

Interspinous devices   Dynamic stabilization   Facet replacement

84.80   Insertion or replacement of interspinous process device(s)

Description
Code 84.80 describes recent advances in motion preservation technology. This technology enables spinal stabilization without the restrictions in motion that are created by spinal fusion. Motion preservation technologies include interspinous process devices, pedicle screw dynamic stabilization systems, facet replacement systems, intervertebral disc replacements, and disc repair systems. Interspinous process, pedicle screw dynamic stabilization, and facet replacement devices are inserted in the posterior column of the lumbar spine. Interspinous process devices act as spacers between the vertebral bodies, and may also provide decompression. Pedicle screw stabilization systems provide posterior stabilization forces and facet replacement systems replace facet joints, both without loss of motion.

Coding Clarification
Interspinous process decompression devices are also known as interspinous process distraction devices.

Do not report this code for insertion or replacement of a facet replacement device (84.84) or insertion or replacement of a pedicle-based dynamic stabilization device (84.82).

Coding Guidance
   AHA: 4Q, '07, 116-120

84.81   Revision of interspinous process device(s)

Description
The physician repairs a previously inserted interspinous process device(s). Motion preservation technology enables spinal stabilization without the

● New Code   ▲ Revised Code   ▶◀ Revised Text   © 2010 Ingenix

76-84

restrictions in motion created by spinal fusion. Interspinous process devices are inserted in the posterior column of the lumbar spine and act as spacers between the vertebral bodies, and may also provide decompression.

Coding Clarification
Motion preservation technologies include interspinous process devices, pedicle screw dynamic stabilization systems, facet replacement systems, intervertebral disc replacements, and disc repair systems.

Do not use this code for revision of a facet replacement device(s) (84.85) or revision of a pedicle-based dynamic stabilization device (84.83).

84.82 Insertion or replacement of pedicle-based dynamic stabilization device(s)

Description
Code 84.82 describes procedures involving motion preservation technology. This technology enables spinal stabilization without the restrictions in motion that are created by spinal fusion. Pedicle screw dynamic stabilization devices are inserted in the posterior column of the lumbar spine. Pedicle screw stabilization systems provide posterior stabilization without loss of motion.

Coding Clarification
Motion preservation technologies include interspinous process devices, pedicle screw dynamic stabilization systems, facet replacement systems, intervertebral disc replacements, and disc repair systems.

The initial insertion of pedicle screws with spinal fusion is not separately reported.

Any facetectomy (partial, total) performed at the same level synchronously is included in the procedure; however, any synchronous surgical decompression (foraminotomy, laminectomy, laminotomy) (03.09) should be coded.

Do not assign 84.82 for insertion or replacement of a facet replacement device(s) (84.84), insertion or replacement of an interspinous process device(s) (84.80), or replacement of pedicle screws used in spinal fusion (78.59).

84.83 Revision of pedicle-based dynamic stabilization device(s)

Description
The physician repairs a previously inserted pedicle-based dynamic stabilization device(s). Motion preservation technology enables spinal stabilization without the restrictions in motion created by spinal fusion. Pedicle screw dynamic stabilization devices are inserted in the posterior column of the lumbar

spine. Pedicle screw stabilization systems provide posterior stabilization without loss of motion.

Coding Clarification
Motion preservation technologies include interspinous process devices, pedicle screw dynamic stabilization systems, facet replacement systems, intervertebral disc replacements, and disc repair systems.

The initial insertion of pedicle screws with spinal fusion is not separately reported.

Do not report this code for removal of pedicle screws used in spinal fusion (78.69), replacement of pedicle screws used in spinal fusion (78.59), revision of facet replacement device(s) (84.85), or revision of interspinous process device(s) (84.81).

Any facetectomy (partial, total) synchronously performed at the same level is included in the procedure; however, any synchronous surgical decompression (foraminotomy, laminectomy, laminotomy) (03.09) should be coded.

84.84 Insertion or replacement of facet replacement device(s)

Description
The paravertebral facet joint consists of the bony surfaces between the vertebrae that articulate with each other. Facet replacement devices are inserted in the posterior column of the lumbar spine. The device replaces all or a portion of a facet joint on a vertebral body. The physician removes, by partial resection, a posterior vertebral component, or facet and inserts a facet prosthesis. The patient is placed prone and an incision is made overlying the affected vertebra and taken down to the level of the fascia. The fascia is incised and the paravertebral muscles are retracted. The physician removes the affected facet. Paravertebral muscles are repositioned and the tissue and skin are closed with layered sutures.

Coding Clarification
Motion preservation technology enables spinal stabilization without the restrictions in motion that are created by spinal fusion. Motion preservation technologies include interspinous process devices, pedicle screw dynamic stabilization systems, facet replacement systems, intervertebral disc replacements, and disc repair systems.

The initial insertion of pedicle screws with spinal fusion is not separately reported.

Do not assign 84.84 for insertion or replacement of an interspinous process device(s) (84.80), insertion or replacement of a pedicle-based dynamic stabilization device(s) (84.82), or replacement of pedicle screws used in spinal fusion (78.59).

76-84

Coding Guidance
AHA: 4Q, '07, 120

84.85   Revision of facet replacement device(s)

Description
The physician repairs a previously inserted facet replacement device(s). The paravertebral facet joint consists of the bony surfaces between the vertebrae that articulate with each other. Facet replacement devices are inserted in the posterior column of the lumbar spine. The device replaces all or a portion of a facet joint on a vertebral body.

Coding Clarification
Do not report this code for removal of pedicle screws used in spinal fusion (78.69), replacement of pedicle screws used in spinal fusion (78.59), revision of an interspinous process device(s) (84.81), or revision of a pedicle-based dynamic stabilization device(s) (84.83).

Motion preservation technology enables spinal stabilization without the restrictions in motion that are created by spinal fusion. Motion preservation technologies include interspinous process devices, pedicle screw dynamic stabilization systems, facet replacement systems, intervertebral disc replacements, and disc repair systems.

84.9   Other operations on musculoskeletal system

Description
Subcategory 84.9 includes codes assigned to report procedures that are not more precisely described by other codes in this chapter. This code is also reported when the documentation does not further specify the amputation procedure.

Coding Clarification
To report nonoperative manipulation, see 93.25-93.29.

84.91   Amputation, not otherwise specified

Description
Code 84.91 is assigned to report amputation procedures on the musculoskeletal system that are not more precisely described by other codes in this subcategory or in other categories in this chapter. This code is also reported when the documentation does not further specify the amputation procedure.

Documentation Tip
Review the documentation for specific information regarding the procedure prior to final code selection in order to ensure accurate code assignment.

84.92   Separation of equal conjoined twins

Description
There are two basic categories of conjoined twins: symmetrical (or equal) conjoined twins and asymmetrical (unequal) twins in which an incomplete twin is joined to a fully developed twin. Surgery to separate conjoined twins varies based on the point of attachment and which internal organs or structures are shared. Frequently, conjoined twins are fused at the thorax or abdomen; however, the union may also be at the head. Twins with cranial fusion who share brain function are usually not separable. In some cases, the twins have conjoined hearts, necessitating a heart transplant.

Coding Clarification
Assign 84.93 if the documentation does not further specify the conjoined twins or the separation procedure.

An asymmetrical or unequal conjoined twin may also be termed a parasitic twin. The undeveloped twin is described as parasitic, rather than conjoined, because it is not completely formed or it is entirely dependent on the body functions of the complete twin.

Thoracopagus conjoined twins' bodies are fused at the thorax.

Diplopagus conjoined twins are joined equally with near complete body, only sharing a few organs.

Parapagus conjoined twins are joined with a lateral union of the lower half.

84.93   Separation of unequal conjoined twins

Description
There are two basic categories of conjoined twins: symmetrical or equal conjoined twins and asymmetrical (unequal) twins in which an incomplete twin is joined to a fully developed twin. Surgery to separate conjoined twins varies based on the point of attachment and which internal organs or structures are shared. Frequently, conjoined twins are fused at the thorax or abdomen; however, the union may also be at the head. Twins with cranial fusion who share brain function are usually not separable. In some cases, the twins have conjoined hearts, necessitating a heart transplant.

Coding Clarification
Assign 84.93 when the documentation does not further specify the separation procedure.

An asymmetrical or unequal conjoined twin may also be termed a parasitic twin. The undeveloped twin is described as parasitic, rather than conjoined, because it is not completely formed or it is entirely dependent on the body functions of the complete twin.

Thoracopagus conjoined twins' bodies are fused at the thorax.

Diplopagus conjoined twins are joined equally with near complete body, only sharing a few organs.

● New Code   ▲ Revised Code   ▶◀ Revised Text   © 2010 Ingenix

Parapagus conjoined twins are joined with a lateral union of the lower half.

● 84.94 Insertion of sternal fixation device with rigid plates

Description
▶Rigid plate fixation of the sternum, in contrast to conventional sternal wire fixation, can significantly reduce the incidence of sternal wound dehiscence and subsequent deep sternal wound infections (DSWI) in certain cardiothoracic surgery patients. Risk factors for SD and DSWI include obesity, diabetes mellitus, COPD, renal failure, chronic steroid use, and tobacco abuse. The Synthes Titanium Sternal Fixation System (TSFS) is a rigid plate fixation system that consists of implanted plates and screws for sternal closure and reconstruction. The system provides rigid fixation using locking plate technology that functions like an "external fixator" but is applied internally to the sternum to close the chest cavity and secure the operative sternal wound. The plates reattach the surgically bisected sternum, and screws secure the plates to the sternum and the ribs. A unique code for reporting rigid plate fixation has been created in response to the U.S. Department of Health and Human Services action plan to prevent health care-associated infections, whereby CMS designated DSWI as a hospital-acquired condition (HAC).

This new code assists ongoing data tracking and quality measures associated with SD and DSWI prevention.◀

Coding Clarification
▶Previously, this procedure was classified to code 78.51. New code 84.94 excludes insertion of sternal fixation device for internal fixation of fracture (79.39).◀

Coding Scenario
▶A patient with steroid-dependent chronic obstructive asthma presents for a three-vessel native coronary artery bypass graft. The Synthes Titanium Sternal Fixation System was implanted for closure of the chest cavity by rigid plate fixation of the sternum.

Code Assignment:

414.01 Coronary atherosclerosis of native coronary artery
493.20 Chronic obstructive asthma
V58.65 Long term (current) use of steroids
36.13 Aortocoronary bypass of three coronary arteries
39.61 Cardiopulmonary bypass
84.94 Insertion of sternal fixation device with rigid plates◀

84.99 Other operations on musculoskeletal system

Description
Code 84.99 is used to report other procedures on the musculoskeletal system that are not more precisely described by other codes in this chapter.

Documentation Tip
Review the documentation for specific information regarding the procedure prior to final code selection in order to ensure accurate code assignment.

76-84

85-86

Operations on the Integumentary System

2011 Changes

Three new codes have been added to describe certain fat graft procedures. Previously, ICD-9-CM did not provide specific codes for harvesting or placing fat grafts used in reconstructive surgery. New code 85.55 reports extraction of fat for autologous graft, fat transplantation or transfer, micro-fat grafting, and injection of fat graft of breast whereas new code 86.87 reports fat-grafting procedures of skin and subcutaneous tissues of other anatomic sites. New code 86.90 specifically identifies extraction of fat for graft or banking. Excludes notes have been added and revised to procedures in this section to parallel the code changes.

Other changes include a code title revision to code 86.11 Closed biopsy of skin and subcutaneous tissue, and the addition of exclusion terms to neurostimulator codes 86.94–86.98 to differentiate these procedures from cranial neurostimulator procedures classifiable to code 01.20.

The ICD-9-CM classification system for operations performed on the integumentary system is divided into two categories of procedures as follows:

- Operations on the Breast (85)
- Operations on Skin and Subcutaneous Tissue (86)

Coding Clarification
Many of the subcategories in this portion of the classification system require a fourth digit for further specificity with regard to type and/or site of the operation performed.

Documentation Tip
Documentation in the operative report must support code selection.

85 Operations on the breast

Description
The female breast is a complex organ that produces first colostrum and then milk for the nourishment of an infant. The onset of this process, known as lactation, may occur during pregnancy or post-delivery due to the complex hormonal changes that occur as an infant develops and a mother prepares to give birth. The glandular, fatty, and fibrous tissues that comprise the breast are located above the pectoral muscles of the chest wall, and attach to the chest wall by connective ligaments known as Cooper's ligaments. The amount of fatty tissue within the breast varies widely, but its main function is to support and protect the glandular, milk-producing structures.

Breast tissue normally swells during the menstrual cycle due to changes in the body's levels of estrogen and progesterone. This may cause the breasts to be temporarily painful, tender, or lumpy. Patients with fibrocystic breasts experience more severe responses to these hormonal changes. At menopause (usually occurring between mid 40s to mid 50s), a woman's body stops producing estrogen and progesterone, and the breasts undergo changes in response to the hormonal shifts. Historically, breast cancer was thought to be associated with perimenopausal and postmenopausal hormone changes. However, increased incidences of breast cancer in younger women are challenging that assumption.

Category 85 provides diagnostic and therapeutic procedures including incisions, excisions, mastectomy, mammoplasty (repairs), and other operations.

Coding Clarification
Codes in category 85 include operations on male or female breast tissue, skin, and subcutaneous tissue, as well as operations on previous mastectomy sites.

85.0 Mastotomy

Description
This procedure involves an incision into the breast. Surgical technique may vary, depending on the indications for procedure:

- **Incision, drainage, or exploration:** The physician makes an incision in the skin of the breast over the site of an abscess or suspicious tissue for exploration or drainage. The infected cavity is accessed and specimens for culture are taken before the cavity is irrigated with warm saline solution. Bleeding vessels may be tied or cauterized. If no abscess or suspicious tissue is found, the wound is closed with sutures. In the case of an abscess, the wound is usually loosely packed with gauze to promote free drainage rather than being closed with sutures.

- **Insertion of catheter:** A balloon catheter for interstitial radiotherapy treatment may be placed in the breast following partial mastectomy. Catheter placement is often performed in a separate encounter, following the neoplasm excision surgery. A small incision is first made and the uninflated balloon catheter is guided into position under radiological imaging. After correct placement is determined, the balloon is inflated with saline to fit snugly into the lumpectomy cavity and the breast is bandaged. The catheter remains until radiotherapy treatment sessions are complete.

Coding Clarification
Code 85.0 excludes aspiration of breast (85.91) and incision for removal of implant (85.94).

Coding Guidance
AHA: 2Q, '90, 27; 1Q, '04, 3

85.1   Diagnostic procedures on breast

85.11   Closed (percutaneous) (needle) biopsy of breast

Description
The physician inserts a large gauge needle through the skin of the breast and into the suspect breast tissue. The needle is removed along with a core of breast tissue. Pressure is applied to the puncture site to stop any bleeding.

Coding Clarification
A mammotome biopsy is excision of breast tissue using a needle inserted through a small incision, followed by a full cut circle of tissue surrounding the core biopsy to obtain multiple contiguous directional sampling for definitive diagnosis and staging of cancer.

Coding Guidance
AHA: 3Q, '89, 17; 2Q, '00, 10

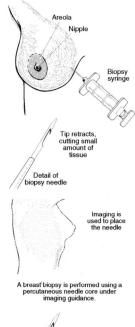

Areola
Nipple

Biopsy syringe

Tip retracts, cutting small amount of tissue

Detail of biopsy needle

Imaging is used to place the needle

A breast biopsy is performed using a percutaneous needle core under imaging guidance.

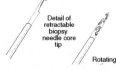

Detail of retractable biopsy needle core tip

Rotating

85.12   Open biopsy of breast

Description
The physician removes tissue for biopsy. The physician makes an incision in the skin of the breast near the site of the suspect mass. The mass is identified and a sample of the lesion is removed. This specimen is often examined immediately. If the lesion is benign, the incision is repaired with layered closure. If malignant, the incision may be closed pending a separate, more extensive surgical session, or a more extensive surgery may occur immediately, in which case this code would not be reported.

Coding Guidance
AHA: M-A, '86, 11; 3Q, '89, 17

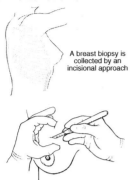

A breast biopsy is collected by an incisional approach

85.19   Other diagnostic procedures on breast

Description
The physician performs other diagnostic operations on the breast, not classifiable as biopsy.

Coding Clarification
This code should not be assigned if the medical record contains sufficient information to facilitate coding at a higher level of specificity.

Code 85.19 lists multiple exclusions for procedures classifiable to chapter 16 Miscellaneous diagnostic and therapeutic procedures (87-99).

Documentation Tip
If the documentation is ambiguous or unclear, the physician should be queried.

85.2   Excision or destruction of breast tissue

Description
This subcategory lists specific excision or destruction operations on breast tissue including local excision, resection, subtotal mastectomy, and other procedures.

Coding Clarification
This subcategory excludes excision or destruction breast procedures specified as mastectomy (85.41-85.48) or reduction mammoplasty (85.31-85.32).

85.20   Excision or destruction of breast tissue, not otherwise specified

Description
The physician performs an excision or destruction of breast tissue of unspecified type, site, or technique.

Coding Clarification
Code 85.20 is not used to report laser interstitial thermal therapy (LITT) of tissue of the breast under guidance (17.69). This code should not be assigned if

the medical record contains sufficient information to facilitate coding at a higher level of specificity.

Documentation Tip
If the documentation is ambiguous or unclear, the physician should be queried.

85.21   Local excision of lesion of breast

Description
The physician excises and removes a lesion in the breast. After administering a local or other anesthetic, the physician makes a full-thickness incision through the skin, usually in an elliptical shape around and under the lesion. The lesion and a margin of normal tissue are removed. The skin incision may be closed with simple or layered sutures, depending on the site and complexity of the lesion.

Coding Clarification
Code 85.21 excludes excision for biopsy of breast (85.11-85.12), in which a portion of a lesion is excised for tissue analysis.

Code 85.21 should be reported for excisional biopsy procedures in which the entire breast lesion is excised and removed.

Documentation Tip
Procedures classifiable to 85.21 may be documented as:

• Lumpectomy

• Removal of an area of fibrosis from breast

A procedure specified as a lumpectomy should be classified according to the extent of the procedure performed, such as:

• Local excision of a lump, mass, or lesion (85.21)

• Lumpectomy by quadrant resection (85.22)

• Lumpectomy by partial mastectomy (85.23)

Coding Guidance
   AHA: S-O, '85, 12; M-A, '86, 11; 3Q, '89, 17; 2Q, '90, 27

85.22   Resection of quadrant of breast

Description
The physician excises a breast tumor and a margin of normal tissue. The physician performs a quadrant mastectomy by making an incision through the skin and fascia over a section of breast tissue that contains the breast malignancy. The physician clamps the lymphatic and blood vessels. The physician excises the mass along with a quadrant-sized section or margin of healthy tissue. A drainage tube may be placed through a separate stab incision to enhance drainage from the wound or lymphatic system. The incision is repaired with layered closure and a dressing is applied.

85-86

85.23   Subtotal mastectomy

Description
The physician performs a partial mastectomy by making an incision through the skin and fascia over a breast malignancy and clamping any lymphatic and blood vessels. The physician excises the mass along with a section of healthy tissue. A drainage tube may be placed through a separate stab incision to enhance drainage from the wound or lymphatic system. The incision is repaired with layered closure and a dressing is applied.

Coding Clarification
Code 85.23 excludes quadrant resection of a breast (85.22).

Documentation Tip
This procedure may also be documented as a segmental mastectomy.

Coding Guidance
AHA: 2Q, '92, 7

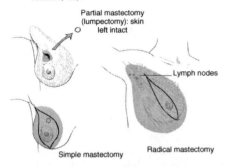

Partial mastectomy (lumpectomy): skin left intact

Lymph nodes

Simple mastectomy

Radical mastectomy

85.24   Excision of ectopic breast tissue

Description
The physician excises an anomalous portion of breast tissue (e.g., accessory nipple). After administering a local anesthetic, the physician makes a full-thickness incision through the dermis with a scalpel, usually in an elliptical shape around and under the anomalous tissue, and removes it. Depending on the size and amount of tissue resected, the physician may suture the wound simply, perform a layered closure, or a separately reportable complex repair, if required. Bleeding vessels are controlled with electrocautery or ligated with sutures. A drain may be inserted into the wound. The incision is sutured in layered closure and a light pressure dressing is applied.

85.25   Excision of nipple

Description
The physician makes an incision in the skin around the areola. The nipple is dissected free and removed. Bleeding vessels are controlled with electrocautery or ligated with sutures. A drain may be inserted into

the wound. The incision is sutured in layered closure and a light pressure dressing is applied.

Coding Clarification
Code 85.25 excludes excision of an accessory nipple (85.24).

85.3   Reduction mammoplasty and subcutaneous mammectomy

Description
This subcategory classifies reduction mammoplasty and subcutaneous mammectomy—as unilateral (one) or bilateral (both) breast procedure.

Coding Guidance
AHA: 4Q, '95, 79, 80

85.31   Unilateral reduction mammoplasty

85.32   Bilateral reduction mammoplasty

Description
These procedure codes describe reduction mammoplasty of the breast, unilateral (85.31) or bilateral (85.32). A mammoplasty is reconstructive surgery to alter the size and appearance or otherwise repair the breast. Surgical technique may vary, including:

- **Mastectomy for gynecomastia:** Gynecomastia is a condition of abnormal enlargement of breast tissue in a male patient. The physician makes a circular incision in the skin of the breast at the edge of the areola or in the inframammary fold. Extraneous fat and breast tissue are dissected from the pectoral fascia and removed. Bleeding vessels are ligated with sutures or cauterized. The incision is sutured in layered closure and a dressing is applied.

- **Reduction mammoplasty:** The physician reduces the size of the breast, removing wedges of skin and breast tissue from a female patient. The physician makes a circular skin incision above the nipple, in the position to which the nipple will be elevated. Another skin incision is made around the circumference of the nipple. Two incisions are made from the circular cut above the nipple to the fold beneath the breast, one on either side of the nipple, creating a keyhole shaped skin and breast incision. Wedges of skin and breast tissue are removed until the desired size is achieved. Bleeding vessels may be ligated or cauterized. The physician elevates the nipple and its pedicle of subcutaneous tissue to its new position and sutures the nipple pedicle with layered closure. The remaining incision is repaired with layered closure.

85-86

85.33   Unilateral subcutaneous mammectomy with synchronous implant

85.34   Other unilateral subcutaneous mammectomy

85.35   Bilateral subcutaneous mammectomy with synchronous implant

85.36   Other bilateral subcutaneous mammectomy

Description
These codes describe subcutaneous mammectomy operations in which the mammary tissue underlying the skin is removed, but the skin and nipple is left intact. These procedures may be performed on one breast (85.33-85.34) or both breasts (85.35-85.36) during the operative episode. Following the removal of subcutaneous breast tissue, a prosthesis may be inserted to restore the appearance of the breast (85.33, 85.35).

To perform a subcutaneous mastectomy, the physician makes an incision in the inframammary crease. The breast is dissected from the pectoral fascia and from the skin. The breast tissue is removed, but the skin and pectoral fascia remain. The physician may ligate any bleeding vessels. The nipple and areola may be examined by a pathologist and retained if free of disease. If no prosthesis is to be inserted, a closed wound suction catheter may be inserted. The wound is closed and a light pressure dressing is applied. If an implant is inserted, the physician dissects the breast tissue and muscle layer free from the chest wall to accommodate a prosthesis. As an alternative, the prosthesis may also be positioned between the muscle and the existing breast tissue or skin. The incision is repaired with layered closure.

85.4   Mastectomy

Description
The physician surgically removes the breast. This subcategory lists mastectomy procedures classified as unilateral (one breast) or bilateral (both breasts) or according to type as simple, extended, radical, or specific variations of these procedures.

85.41   Unilateral simple mastectomy

85.42   Bilateral simple mastectomy

Description
The physician removes all subcutaneous breast tissue, with or without nipple and skin. The physician performs a simple, complete mastectomy. The physician makes an elliptical incision around the breast that includes the tail of Spence, the extension of mammary tissue into the axillary region. The breast tissue is dissected from the pectoral fascia and sternum. The breast tissue is

removed, along with a portion of skin, including the nipple. In a modification of the simple mastectomy, skin and nipple may be spared, but all subcutaneous breast tissue is removed. The physician ligates any bleeding vessels. A closed wound drainage catheter may be inserted and the edges of skin are approximated, sutured, and a dressing is applied.

Coding Clarification
A simple mastectomy involves surgical excision and removal of the entire breast with axillary lymph nodes and vessels remaining intact.

85.43   Unilateral extended simple mastectomy

85.44   Bilateral extended simple mastectomy

Description
The physician makes an elliptical incision that includes the nipple and the tail of Spence, the extension of mammary tissue into the axillary region. The breast tissue and skin are dissected from the pectoral fascia and removed from the pectoral muscle. The pectoralis minor muscle may also be resected to facilitate the axillary dissection, but the pectoralis major muscle is left intact. Bleeding vessels are ligated or electrocauterized. The breast tissue and axillary tissue, including lymph nodes, are removed en bloc and the wound is irrigated. Adequate skin is usually available for primary closure. Patients with insufficient skin for coverage may require skin grafts or myocutaneous flaps. A closed wound suction catheter may be inserted. The wound is closed and a pressure dressing is applied.

Coding Clarification
An extended simple mastectomy involves surgical excision and removal of the entire breast and a few regional axillary lymph nodes.

Documentation Tip
Procedures classifiable to 85.43 may be documented as:

• Extended simple mastectomy NOS

• Modified radical mastectomy

• Simple mastectomy with excision of regional lymph nodes

Coding Guidance
    AHA: 2Q, '91, 21; 3Q, '91, 24; 2Q, '92, 7

85.45   Unilateral radical mastectomy

85.46   Bilateral radical mastectomy

Description
The physician makes an elliptical incision that includes the nipple and the tail of Spence, the extension of mammary tissue into the axillary region. The breast, along with the overlying skin, the

pectoralis major and minor muscles, and the lymph nodes in the axilla, are removed as a single specimen. Bleeding vessels are ligated or electrocauterized. In large-breasted patients, adequate skin may be available for primary closure. Patients with insufficient skin for coverage may require skin grafts or myocutaneous flaps. If no prosthesis is to be inserted, a closed wound suction catheter may be inserted. The wound is closed and a pressure dressing is applied.

Coding Clarification
A radical mastectomy involves surgical excision and removal of one breast, regional lymph nodes, chest muscle, and adjacent tissue.

Coding Guidance
AHA: 2Q, '91, 21

85.47   Unilateral extended radical mastectomy

85.48   Bilateral extended radical mastectomy

Description
The physician performs a radical mastectomy. The physician makes an elliptical incision that includes the nipple and the tail of Spence, the extension of mammary tissue into the axillary region. The breast, along with the overlying skin, the pectoralis major and minor muscles, and the lymph nodes in the axilla and middle chest are removed as a single specimen. Bleeding vessels are ligated or electrocauterized. In large-breasted patients, adequate skin may be available for primary closure. Patients with insufficient skin for coverage may require skin grafts or myocutaneous flaps. If no prosthesis is to be inserted, a closed wound suction catheter may be inserted. The wound is closed and a pressure dressing is applied.

Coding Clarification
An extended radical mastectomy involves surgical excision and removal of one breast, regional and middle chest lymph nodes, chest muscle, and adjacent tissue.

85.5   Augmentation mammoplasty

Description
The physician performs plastic surgery to increase the breast size.

Coding Clarification
Subcategory 85.5 excludes augmentation mammoplasty associated with subcutaneous mammectomy (85.33, 85.35).

Coding Guidance
AHA: 4Q, '95, 76, 80; 3Q, '97, 12

85.50   Augmentation mammoplasty, not otherwise specified

Description
This procedure code reports an augmentation mammoplasty of unspecified type, laterality, or technique.

The physician may increase the size of the breast without using a prosthesis or implant by rearranging existing fat and mammary tissue of the patient. The physician makes a skin incision in the fold beneath the breast or in a circular cut around the areola. This skin is cut away from the breast tissue and the breast tissue is rearranged. The physician may excise redundant skin to augment the breast's appearance. The incisions are repaired with layered closure.

Coding Clarification
This code should not be assigned if the medical record contains sufficient information to facilitate coding at a higher level of specificity.

Documentation Tip
If the documentation is ambiguous or unclear, the physician should be queried.

85.51   Unilateral injection into breast for augmentation

85.52   Bilateral injection into breast for augmentation

Description
These codes describe the unilateral (85.51) or bilateral (85.52) enlargement of the breast by injection of silicone, fat, or other substances into the breast for cosmetic reasons. Augmentation by direct injection into the tissues of the breast was performed during the 1950s and 1960s prior to the availability of prosthetic implants. Injection augmentation is no longer utilized, as many women suffered complications such as painful granulomas and hardening of the breasts, often requiring mastectomy.

Today, certain prosthetic implants and tissue expanders enable the injection of saline into a prosthesis or expander device, to allow for gradual enlargement of the breast, or to make size and symmetry adjustments.

Coding Clarification
Codes 85.51 and 85.52 include injection of saline into a breast tissue expander.

►Codes 85.51 and 85.52 exclude injection of fat graft of breast (85.55).◄

Coding Guidance
AHA: 3Q, '97, 13

85.53   Unilateral breast implant

85.54   Bilateral breast implant

Description
The physician increases the size of the breast by inserting a prosthesis or implant. The physician makes an incision in the fold under the breast and dissects the breast tissue and muscle layer free from the chest wall to accommodate a prosthesis positioned under the muscle. As an alternative, the prosthesis may also be positioned between the muscle and the existing breast tissue or skin. The incision is repaired with layered closure.

● **85.55   Fat graft to breast**

Description
▶Fat grafting is a technique in which prepared autologous fat cells are injected to correct soft tissue defects. Fat grafts are commonly used in reconstructive procedures, particularly in the breast following lumpectomy and as an adjunctive procedure with postmastectomy reconstruction. Fat is harvested by liposuction from elsewhere on the patient's body, typically an unobtrusive area such as the abdomen, flanks, or thighs. The lipoaspirate is centrifuged and filtered to concentrate the number of fat cells. Fat graft enrichment with adipose progenitor cells (a.k.a., adipose-derived regenerative stem cells) may be added to the fat graft to reduce the incidence of ischemia complications. Fat grafts are most commonly placed by injection technique, whereby the graft material is loaded into a syringe or cannula and evenly placed into the defect to achieve cosmetically optimal contour and texture. Fat grafting may be performed as an adjunct to a primary procedure or as a solo procedure. Total operative time depends on the size, nature, and anatomic site of the defect.◀

Coding Clarification
▶Code 85.55 includes extraction of fat for autologous graft, fat transplantation or transfer, micro-fat grafting, injection of fat graft of breast, and fat graft to breast with or without use of enriched graft.

A breast fat graft procedure with synchronous breast reconstruction is excluded from new code 85.55 and

is instead reported with a code from the range 85.70–85.79.

Extraction or harvesting of fat for future use is reported with new code 86.90.◀

Coding Scenario
▶A postmastectomy patient presents for fat graft to right breast to cosmetically correct surgical disproportion and achieve optimal symmetry. Fat was harvested by liposuction technique from the patient's thigh and injected via cannula. The lipoaspirate graft was fanned during placement and manually smoothed to achieve cosmesis.

Code Assignment:

612.1   Disproportion of reconstructed breast
85.55   Fat graft to breast◀

85.6   Mastopexy

Description
The physician performs a breast lift, or mastopexy, relocating the nipple and areola to a higher position and removing excess skin below the nipple and above the lower breast crease. The physician makes a skin incision above the nipple, in the location to which the nipple will be elevated. Another skin incision is made around the circumference of the nipple. Two skin incisions are made from the circular cut above the nipple to the fold beneath the breast, one on either side of the nipple, forming a keyhole shaped skin incision. This skin is cut away from the breast tissue and removed. The physician elevates the breast to its new position and closes the incision, excising any redundant skin in the fold beneath the breast. The incision is repaired with layered closure.

85.7   Total reconstruction of breast

Description
Breast reconstruction involves creating a breast mound that is similar in size, shape, contour, and position to the opposite breast. Subcategory 85.7 includes codes that report the different types of breast reconstruction after mastectomy. Reconstructive techniques vary in complexity and resources used and include implant, latissimus flap, pedicled transverse rectus abdominis musculocutaneous (TRAM) flap, and free TRAM flap.

85–86

85.70   Total reconstruction of breast, not otherwise specified

85.71   Latissimus dorsi myocutaneous flap

85.72   Transverse rectus abdominis myocutaneous (TRAM) flap, pedicled

85.73   Transverse rectus abdominis myocutaneous (TRAM) flap, free

85.74   Deep inferior epigastric artery perforator (DIEP) flap, free

85.75   Superficial inferior epigastric artery (SIEA) flap, free

85.76   Gluteal artery perforator (GAP) flap, free

85.79   Other total reconstruction of breast

Description
There are many types of breast reconstruction including implants, TRAM, Latissimus Dorsi, GAP, and DIEP flaps. In autologous breast reconstruction, the patient's own muscle, fat, and skin are used to create a new breast. In the DIEP flap, no muscle is taken, but the muscle is dissected and preserved. No muscle or overlying muscle fascia is used in DIEP breast reconstructions, the vessels with the overlying flesh are removed and the muscle is left in place. This is in contrast to the TRAM flap which relies on circulation supplied by the muscles and the perforators, so rectus muscle is used along with the overlying rectus fascia from the abdomen.

The physician may reconstruct the breast by raising a flap from the abdomen, using abdominal skin and fatty tissues and rectus abdominis vasculature. The rectus abdominus muscle and skin/fat pad is passed under the upper abdominal skin to the chest wall and molded into a new breast.

The physician may cut a skin island flap on the lower abdominal wall. A superior skin and fat flap is elevated off the rectus abdominis muscle. A transverse incision is made in the rectus sheath and the muscle is divided and elevated, keeping the superior epigastric arteries intact for blood supply. Once the muscle is elevated, the physician makes an incision through the chest skin. This is also elevated, creating a pocket for the muscle flap. A connecting tunnel is made between the elevated chest skin and the inferiorly positioned flap. The flap is passed superiorly under the tunnel of tissue, placed into its new position, and sutured, after contouring a breast. The abdominal wall is closed by reapproximating the remaining anterior rectus muscle to the remaining lateral muscle and sheath. Skin edges are brought

together and sutured in layers. Suction drains are also placed.

Coding Clarification
The TRAM flap is the most frequent procedure performed for autologous breast reconstruction.

In a pedicled TRAM, the flap of muscle, fat and skin is dissected free and rotated through a subcutaneous tunnel into the mastectomy defect where it is shaped into the form of a breast and sutured in place. In the free TRAM technique the flap and the inferior vascular pedicle are dissected free and detached; the flap is then brought to mastectomy site and the deep inferior epigastric vessels are reconnected to vessels in the chest.

The free TRAM and SIEP/DIEP flaps involve microsurgical transplant of an abdominal flap composed of fat, while a Gluteal Artery Perforator (GAP) flap involves microvascular transplant of buttock flap.

The latissimus flap technique is an example of a pedicled flap in which the flap is rotated to a new location while it remains attached to its original blood supply. The physician raises the latissimis dorsi muscle of the back along with the overlying skin and fat then transfers them to the anterior chest wall. This technique is most commonly used in combination with an implant.

Assign code 85.70 to report perforator flap, free reconstruction of the breast.

Documentation Tip
This procedure may be documented as TRAM flap reconstruction of the breast.

Coding Scenario
A female patient who is status post mastectomy for breast carcinoma undergoes a breast reconstruction procedure. The physician excises skin and fatty tissue from the abdominal wall. Transplantation of the flap to the mastectomy site is accomplished by completely detaching the blood supply and then reattaching it to recipient vessels using microvascular surgery. The deep inferior epigastric artery is used to supply circulation to the flap. The physician adjusts the flap for the most aesthetic appearance and secures it with sutures to the chest wall, adjacent muscles, and skin.

Code Assignment:

V51.0   Encounter for breast reconstruction following mastectomy

V45.71   Acquired absence of breast

V10.3   Personal history of malignant neoplasm, breast

85.74   Deep inferior epigastric artery perforator (DIEP) flap, free

● New Code   ▲ Revised Code   ▶◀ Revised Text   © 2010 Ingenix

85.8   Other repair and plastic operations on breast

Coding Clarification
Subcategory 82.8 excludes breast repair and plastic operations for:

* Augmentation (85.50-85.54)
* Reconstruction (85.70-85.76, 85.79)
* Reduction (85.31-85.32)

Coding Guidance
   AHA: 4Q, '95, 77

85.81   Suture of laceration of breast

Description
The physician sutures a laceration of the breast. A local anesthetic is injected around the laceration and the wound is cleansed, explored, and often irrigated with a saline solution. The physician performs a simple or more complex repair with sutures, as required by the severity of the wound. For complex wounds, deep subcutaneous or layered suturing techniques are required. The physician sutures tissue layers under the skin with dissolvable sutures before suturing the skin.

85.82   Split-thickness graft to breast

Description
The physician takes a dermal autograft from one area of the body and grafts it to an area needing repair. This procedure is performed when direct wound closure or adjacent tissue transfer is not possible. A dermal skin graft is harvested by first raising a split-thickness skin graft 0.010 to 0.015 inches in depth with a dermatome, but not removing it. The dermatome is adjusted to remove the desired graft and a second pass is made over the newly created donor site at that depth to remove a dermal layer autograft. The dermal autograft is sutured or stapled onto the recipient area on the breast.

85.83   Full-thickness graft to breast

Description
The physician harvests a full thickness skin graft with a scalpel from one area of the body and grafts it to an area needing repair. A full-thickness skin graft consists of both the superficial and deeper layers of skin (epidermis and dermis). The resulting surgical wound at the donor site is closed by lifting the remaining skin edges and placing sutures to close directly. Fat is removed from the graft, which is sutured onto the recipient bed to cover a defect of the breast.

Coding Guidance
   AHA: 4Q, '95, 77

85.84   Pedicle graft to breast

Description
The physician forms a pedicle flap. A defect is being covered by elevation of a flap of skin and subcutaneous tissue. The flap is rotated into a nearby but not immediately adjacent defect. Often this flap will be transferred through a tunnel underneath the skin and sutured into its new position. The donor site is closed directly.

Coding Guidance
   AHA: 4Q, '95, 77

85.85   Muscle flap graft to breast

Description
The physician performs breast reconstruction with a latissimus dorsi flap. The physician transfers skin and muscle from the patient's back to the breast area to correct defects created from a previous modified radical or radical mastectomy. The physician makes a skin incision in the back and dissects a portion of the latissimus muscle and the overlying skin from surrounding structures. The muscle-skin flap remains attached to a main artery. In preparation for the transfer, a mastectomy scar may be excised. The muscle flap is rotated to the front of the chest through a tunnel under the armpit so that it extends through to the mastectomy incision. The incision in the back is repaired with layered closure. The physician adjusts the flap for the most aesthetic appearance and secures it with sutures to the chest wall, adjacent muscles, and skin. The incision is repaired with sutures.

Coding Guidance
   AHA: 4Q, '95, 77

85.86   Transposition of nipple

Description
The physician relocates a nipple to a new (usually higher) position on the chest. It may be performed as part of a breast reduction surgery or other plastic repair. The physician often preserves the blood supply to the nipple by creating a pedicle flap graft. Surgical technique may vary. Final positioning of the nipple depends on the individual aesthetics of the breast.

Coding Guidance
   AHA: 4Q, '95, 78

85.87   Other repair or reconstruction of nipple

Description
This procedure code includes other repair or reconstruction of the nipple not classifiable

elsewhere in subcategory 85.8. Surgical technique may vary.

The nipple and areola are reconstructed. The physician excises graft skin, usually from the inner thigh, behind the ear, or a section excised from the patient's existing areola. The donor site is repaired with sutures. To create a new nipple, the physician excises the lower section of tissue from the patient's existing nipple or removes tissue from the ear or labia. This donor site is repaired with sutures. A thin, circular layer of surface skin is removed from the breast at the site of the graft. The areola skin graft is positioned and sutured to the breast and the nipple graft is sutured to a small, circular incision in the areola's center.

Inverted nipples are corrected by making two or more radial incisions in the areola and elevating the inverted nipple into an everted position. Ductal channels and fibrous bands may be transected to accomplish this. Tissue may be removed. The nipple is secured with sutures and incisions in the areola are closed.

Coding Guidance
AHA: 4Q, '95, 78

85.89   Other mammoplasty
Description
This code describes other repair or plastic operation on the breast not classifiable elsewhere in subcategory 85.8.

Coding Clarification
This code should not be assigned if the medical record contains sufficient information to facilitate coding at a higher level of specificity.

Documentation Tip
If the documentation is ambiguous or unclear, the physician should be queried.

85.9   Other operations on the breast
Description
This subcategory lists breast operations not classifiable elsewhere in category 85, including aspiration, injection, and implant or tissue expander removal and revision.

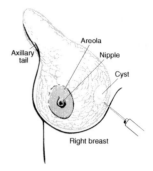

A breast cyst is punctured and needle aspirated

85.91   Aspiration of breast
Description
The physician punctures with a syringe needle the skin of the breast overlying a cyst or other lesion. The needle is inserted into the lesion and fluid is evacuated into the syringe. If the lesion is a cyst, the size of the cyst may be reduced by this procedure. The physician withdraws the needle and applies pressure to the puncture wound to stop the bleeding.

Coding Clarification
Code 85.91 excludes aspiration biopsy of the breast (85.11).

85.92   Injection of therapeutic agent into breast
Description
The physician performs an injection procedure. A needle is inserted into the duct, lesion, or other tissue of the breast. A therapeutic drug or medication is injected into the breast. The needle or cannula is removed once the injection has been completed.

Coding Clarification
Code 85.92 excludes injection of augmentation of breast (85.51-85.52, 85.55).

85.93   Revision of implant of breast
Description
Revision is often performed on a reconstructed breast to correct a problem with asymmetry. The physician makes an incision in the breast skin along the areola or at the fold under the breast or in prior surgical incisions. Tissue therein may be rearranged or secured with sutures to revise the shape of the reconstructed breast. An existing breast prosthesis may be replaced with a prosthesis of a different configuration. Excess skin or tissue from the reconstructed breast may be removed. Once the breast has been revised to its desired shape, the physician repairs the incision with layered closure.

 ● New Code   ▲ Revised Code   ▶◀ Revised Text   © 2010 Ingenix

Coding Guidance
AHA: 4Q, '95, 76; 2Q, '98, 14

85.94 Removal of implant of breast

Description
A breast implant or prosthesis that is still intact is removed. The physician makes an incision in the fold under the breast, around the nipple, or at the site of an existing mastectomy incision and dissects muscle, fat, and breast tissue from the existing implant. The intact implant is removed. Any infection is irrigated. The physician repairs the incision with layered closure.

Coding Guidance
AHA: 3Q, '92, 4; 2Q, '98, 14

85.95 Insertion of breast tissue expander

Description
The physician makes an incision in the skin of a patient who has undergone a mastectomy. A pocket is created using an existing chest wall muscle and an expandable implant is placed into it at the site of the mastectomy. In some cases, the implant's button-shaped portal may be brought out through the skin so it is accessible by needle. Usually, the portal remains beneath the surface of the skin. The physician injects saline into the access portal to expand the implant until it has stretched the surrounding tissue to a size slightly larger than the patient's existing breast. In some cases, the expander remains a permanent prosthesis and small amount of fluid is aspirated until it duplicates the size of the existing breast. In other cases, a second surgery (reported separately) excises the implant and replaces it with a permanent breast prosthesis.

85.96 Removal of breast tissue expander (s)

Description
The physician removes a subcutaneous tissue expander. Initially, the tissue expander is deflated. The physician uses a scalpel to make an incision. Blunt dissection is used to remove the tissue expander. A surgical drain may be placed in the wound. The incision is closed with sutures.

Coding Guidance
AHA: 4Q, '95, 77; 2Q, '00, 18

85.99 Other operations on the breast

Description
This code includes other operations on the breast not classifiable elsewhere in category 85.

Coding Clarification
This code should not be assigned if the medical record contains sufficient information to facilitate coding at a higher level of specificity.

Documentation Tip
If the documentation is ambiguous or unclear, the physician should be queried.

86 Operations on skin and subcutaneous tissue

Description
The skin is composed of two main layers: the epidermis and the dermis. The epidermis is the outer layer of the skin. The dermis is the inner layer that is composed of connective tissue, lymph structures, nerves, blood vessels, glands, and hair follicles. The dermis is attached to underlying structures by connective subcutaneous tissues that support, nourish, insulate, and cushion the skin.

The main functions of the skin include providing a protective barrier, facilitating temperature regulation, sensation, and secretion. In addition to protecting the body against infection, injury, and other harmful exposures, the skin also assists in the synthesis of certain nutrients, such as vitamin D. The integumentary system responds to internal or environmental stimuli that elicit autonomic nervous system responses. For example, temperature regulation is achieved through the skin by dilation or constriction of the blood vessels in response to environmental stimuli. Similarly, skin sensation occurs as a result of millions of microscopic nerve endings that act as receptors for pain, touch, temperature, and pressure. Nerve impulses are sent to the cerebral cortex of the brain in response to stimulation of these nerve endings, and the necessary response is triggered.

The skin produces excretions such as sweat and sebum, which are produced by millions of sudoriferous (sweat) and sebaceous (oil) glands within the dermis. These secretions perform functions vital to maintaining the health of the skin and body by eliminating waste and providing a protective and lubricated barrier.

Skin diseases and conditions may be due to external causes such as infectious organisms or exposures to irritants. However, many conditions that require surgical intervention may be secondary to other systemic diseases, genetic predisposition, or compromised states of health that result in an increased vulnerability of the skin.

Category 86 provides diagnostic and therapeutic skin procedures including incisions, excisions, implantations, grafts, repairs, and other operations.

Coding Clarification
Codes in category 86 include operations on the integumentary accessory organs and structures such as:

85-86

- Hair follicles
- Nails
- Sebaceous glands
- Sudoriferous glands
- subcutaneous fatty tissue
- Male perineum
- Superficial fossae

Multiple exclusions are listed in category 86. These exclusions apply to procedures on the skin classifiable to other specific anatomic sites, such as a previous mastectomy site (85.0-85.99), skin of the eyelid (08.01-08.99), and female perineum (71.01-71.9).

86.0   Incision of skin and subcutaneous tissue

Description
This subcategory describes incisional procedures on the skin, whereby a surgical cut is made into the dermis for diagnostic or therapeutic purposes. These procedures include aspirations, injections, implantations, and other procedures.

86.01   Aspiration of skin and subcutaneous tissue

Description
The physician performs puncture aspiration of an abscess, hematoma, seroma, bulla, or cyst of the nail, skin, or subcutaneous tissue. A palpable collection of fluid may be located subcutaneously. The physician cleanses the overlying skin and introduces a large bore needle on a syringe into the fluid space. The fluid is aspirated into the syringe, decompressing the fluid space. A pressure dressing may be placed over the site.

Coding Guidance
   AHA: 3Q, '89, 16

86.02   Injection or tattooing of skin lesion or defect

Description
This procedure involves injection or tattooing of a skin lesion or defect, which may include adding pigment or color to the skin (tattooing) or insertion or injection of filling material. Procedure technique may vary, depending on the indication, including:

- **Tattooing:** The physician introduces insoluble opaque pigment into color defects of the skin. A marking pen is used first to outline the area to be tattooed. The dye is injected into the skin with a pneumatic tattooing instrument to create an artificially pigmented area that approximates the appearance of normal skin tissue.

- **Other intradermal injection:** The physician uses an injectable dermal implant to correct small soft tissue deformities. This technique is used to treat facial wrinkles, post-surgical

defects, and acne scars. The injectable filling material can be autologous fat, synthetic surgical compound, or a commercially produced collagen preparation. The physician uses a syringe to inject the selected material into the dermis of the skin. The injection will augment the dermal layer and alleviate the soft tissue depression.

86.03   Incision of pilonidal sinus or cyst

Description
Pilonidal cysts are entrapped epithelial tissue located in the sacrococcygeal region above the buttocks. These cysts may produce fluid or exudate into the cystic lining and are usually associated with ingrown hair. An incision is made to allow drainage of cystic fluid or exudate. Curettage is performed to remove the cystic epithelial lining. The wound heals secondarily relying on local wound care.

Coding Clarification
Code 86.03 excludes marsupialization of a pilonidal cyst (86.21).

86.04   Other incision with drainage of skin and subcutaneous tissue

Description
The physician makes a small incision through the skin overlying an abscess, cyst, or other lesion for incision and drainage. The lesion is opened with a surgical instrument, allowing the contents to drain. The lesion may be curetted and irrigated. The physician leaves the surgical wound open to allow for continued drainage.

Coding Clarification
Code 86.04 excludes drainage of:

- Fascial compartments of mouth (27.0)
- Palmar or thenar space (82.04)
- Pilonidal sinus or cyst (86.03)

Coding Guidance
   AHA: 4Q, '04, 76; 1Q, '09, 11

86.05   Incision with removal of foreign body or device from skin and subcutaneous tissue

Description
The physician removes a foreign body that may be traumatically embedded or surgically implanted in the subcutaneous tissue. The physician makes a simple incision in the skin overlying the foreign body. The foreign body is retrieved using hemostats or forceps, or dissected free and removed. The skin may be sutured or allowed to heal secondarily.

In an alternate procedure, the physician revises or removes a peripheral or gastric neurostimulator pulse generator or receiver with or without replacement. The placement incision is reopened

● New Code   ▲ Revised Code   ▶◀ Revised Text   © 2010 Ingenix

and tissues are dissected to the transmitter pocket. If the procedure is performed because the device is malfunctioning, the unit is checked and repairs made or a new unit is inserted. If the device is no longer required, it is removed. The incision is closed in layered sutures.

Coding Clarification
Code 86.05 excludes removal of foreign body without incision (98.20-98.29).

Documentation Tip
Procedures classifiable to 86.05 may be documented as:

- Removal of loop recorder
- Removal of neurostimulator pulse generator
- Removal of tissue expander from skin or soft tissue other than breast tissue

Coding Guidance
AHA: N-D, '86, 9; N-D, '87, 10; 2Q, '96, 15

86.06   Insertion of totally implantable infusion pump

Description
The physician inserts an implantable infusion pump. Surgical technique may vary, depending on the site of the infusion and the patient's diagnosis:

- **Intra-arterial:** Implantable infusion pumps are self-contained devices that are surgically implanted, usually via laparotomy. The physician may perform an upper abdominal incision to expose the hepatic artery. The physician punctures the hepatic artery with a large needle and passes a guidewire via the needle into the punctured artery. The physician removes the needle while leaving the guidewire in place. The physician slides the infusion catheter over the guidewire into the arterial lumen. The physician secures the catheter with suture and closes the abdominal wound around the proximal end of the infusion catheter. The physician may use the catheter to administer chemotherapeutic medication.

- **Intrathecal:** This procedure is performed to allow medication (e.g., cancer chemotherapy, pain management drugs) to be placed into a subcutaneous reservoir for intrathecal (spinal) or epidural drug infusion. The physician makes a midline incision overlying the placement site. The reservoir is placed in the subcutaneous tissues and attached to a previously placed catheter. Layered sutures are used to close the incision.

Coding Guidance
AHA: 4Q, '90, 14; 2Q, '99, 4

86.07   Insertion of totally implantable vascular access device (VAD)

Description
The physician inserts a totally implantable vascular access device (TIVAD) in which the catheter system is fully implanted under the skin. Central venous access is obtained through skin puncture with a special needle. Totally implantable vascular devices facilitate safe and comfortable access for infusion of long-term or permanent therapies such as chemotherapy, antibiotics, or hemodialysis.

For insertion of a subcutaneous port, the site over the access vein is injected with local anesthesia and punctured with a needle. A guidewire is inserted. The central venous catheter is placed over the guidewire and fed through the vein in the arm into the superior vena cava. The port may be placed in the chest in a subcutaneous pocket created through an incision in the chest wall, or placed in the arm through a small incision just above or halfway between the elbow crease and the shoulder on the inside of the arm. The port is attached to the catheter and checked. Ultrasound guidance may be used to gain venous access and/or fluoroscopy to check the positioning of the catheter tip. The catheter and port are secured into position and incisions are closed and dressed.

Coding Clarification
Code 86.07 excludes insertion of a totally implantable infusion pump (86.06).

Documentation Tip
Procedures classifiable to 86.07 may be documented as:

- Port-a-cath
- Perm-a-cath
- Hemo-cath
- Subcutaneous port
- Hickman catheter
- Broviac catheter

A vascular access device (VAD) is a general term that describes the insertion of a venous or arterial catheter system. Many different types of VADs are available, and not all are classified the same. Code 86.07 describes a completely embedded device that is anchored into the subcutaneous tissue, with no portion brought out above the surface of the skin. Other devices that may be documented as VADs, but are classified elsewhere include:

- Arterial line (38.91)
- Central line (38.93)
- PICC line, peripherally inserted central venous catheter (38.93)
- Peripheral IV (not reported)

Coding Scenario

A 48-year-old male with metastatic adenocarcinoma of the lung presented to the outpatient surgery suite for placement of a chemotherapy access port. The patient was prepped, draped and anesthetized for the procedure. A port was introduced through the external jugular vein into the superior vena cava and tied into place. It was tunneled subcutaneously into the anterior chest wall. The port was connected to a port-a-cath device, which was anchored into the pectoralis. The incision was closed in layers.

Code Assignment:

162.9   Malignant neoplasm of bronchus and lung, unspecified

86.07   Insertion of totally implantable vascular access device (VAD)

Coding Guidance
AHA: 2Q, '94, 11; 1Q, '96, 3; 1Q, '01, 13

86.09   Other incision of skin and subcutaneous tissue

Description
This code describes other incisional procedures on the skin and subcutaneous tissues. Surgical technique may vary in accordance with the diagnosis or other indication for procedure, including:

- **Repositioning of central venous catheter (with incision):** A previously placed central venous catheter needs to be repositioned. It is possible for catheter position to change significantly after the procedure is completed. Catheter position change and tip migration occur most often with subclavian venous access, in women and obese patients, owing to the fact that the soft tissues of the chest wall move inferiorly with standing and often cause the catheter to get pulled back. When a catheter tip is incorrectly placed, it can increase the risks of thrombosis, fibrin sheath formation, perforation of the vein, and even arrhythmias. Fluoroscopy is used to check the positioning of the catheter tip and guide it to its correct position. Local anesthesia is given and the sutures securing the cuff of the catheter may be freed from the skin. The catheter is partially withdrawn and a sheath may be placed over the catheter at the existing venous access site. A guidewire is inserted through the catheter and advanced. The central venous catheter is maneuvered back into correct position and monitored with fluoroscopy to view correct placement of the tip.

- **Escharotomy:** The physician performs an escharotomy. Eschar is a leathery slough produced by thermal burns. The physician makes an incision through the area of eschar and undermines it. With adequate incision of the eschar, the physician achieves release of movement for the underlying tissue.

- **Exploration of penetrating traumatic wound, extremity:** The physician explores a penetrating wound to identify damaged structures. Nerve, organ, and blood vessel integrity is assessed. The wound may be sharply enlarged to help assess the damage. The wound is closed (if clean) or packed open if contaminated by the penetrating body.

Coding Clarification
Code 86.09 lists multiple exclusions. Procedures specified as revision of cardiac pacemaker or AICD device pockets are classified to 37.79. Other incisional procedures of specific sites such as the mouth or face may be more appropriately classified elsewhere.

This code should not be assigned if the medical record contains sufficient information to facilitate coding at a higher level of specificity.

Documentation Tip
If the documentation is ambiguous or unclear, the physician should be queried.

Procedures classifiable to 86.09 may be documented as:

- Creation of subcutaneous pocket for thalamic stimulator pulse generator, new site
- Relocation of subcutaneous pocket, NEC
- Reopening of subcutaneous pocket for device revision without replacement
- Undercutting of hair follicle
- Exploration of sinus tract, skin
- Exploration of superficial fossa

Coding Guidance
AHA: N-D, '84, 6; N-D, '86, 1; 3Q, '89, 17; 4Q, '97, 57; 4Q, '99, 21

86.1   Diagnostic procedures on skin and subcutaneous tissue

▲ 86.11   Closed biopsy of skin and subcutaneous tissue

Description
The physician sharply removes a biopsy sample of skin, subcutaneous tissue, and/or mucous membrane by excision for analysis. Some normal tissue adjacent to the diseased tissue may also be removed for comparison purposes.

Code 86.11 reports a closed, percutaneous or needle biopsy of the skin and subcutaneous tissue. Biopsy of soft tissue via open incision is reported with code 83.21 Open biopsy of soft tissue.

Coding Guidance
AHA: 4Q, '08, 99

86.19   Other diagnostic procedures on skin and subcutaneous tissue

Description
This code describes other diagnostic procedures on the skin and subcutaneous tissue not specified as biopsy.

Coding Clarification
This code should not be assigned if the medical record contains sufficient information to facilitate coding at a higher level of specificity.

Documentation Tip
If the documentation is ambiguous or unclear, the physician should be queried.

86.2   Excision or destruction of lesion or tissue of skin and subcutaneous tissue

Description
This subcategory classifies multiple specific types of procedures in which skin or subcutaneous tissue is excised and removed or otherwise destroyed. Numerous surgical techniques exist to treat specific types of integumentary diseases and disorders. Codes in this section are subclassified according to type of lesion, site of lesion, and surgical technique employed.

86.21   Excision of pilonidal cyst or sinus

Description
The physician may use a scalpel to completely excise the cyst and sinus tract tissue. The wound may be sutured in a single layer. The wound may be sutured in several layers, or the wound may be left open to heal by granulation.

Coding Clarification
Code 86.21 excludes incision of a pilonidal cyst or sinus (86.03).

An understanding of the following terms may aid in code selection:

- **Marsupialization of cyst:** Incision of cyst with suturing of the edges of the cyst to the skin to allow for continuous drainage.

- **Pilonidal cyst:** Hair-containing cyst or sinus in the tissues of the sacrococcygeal area; often drains through an opening at the postanal dimple.

86.22   Excisional debridement of wound, infection, or burn

Description
The physician surgically removes devitalized or necrotic skin. The physician uses a scalpel or dermatome to remove a superficial layer of affected skin. The epidermal layer is removed with the underlying dermis remaining intact. The partial thickness of skin is excised until viable, bleeding tissue is encountered. A topical antibiotic is placed on the wound. A gauze dressing or an occlusive dressing may be placed over the surgical site.

Coding Clarification
Code 86.22 lists multiple exclusions for debridement of other specific anatomic sites or conditions, such as:

- Abdominal wall (wound) (54.3)
- Bone (77.60-77.69)
- Muscle (83.45) or hand muscle (82.36)
- Nail bed or nail fold (86.27)
- Nonexcisional debridement (86.28)
- Open fracture site (79.60-79.69)
- Pedicle or flap graft (86.75)

Documentation Tip
The use of a sharp instrument does not necessarily indicate an excisional debridement. The physician must document that excisional debridement was carried out.

Coding Guidance
AHA: N-D, '86, 1; 4Q, '88, 5; 3Q, '89, 16; 3Q, '91,18; 2Q, '92, 17; 1Q, '99, 8; 2Q, '00, 9; 3Q, '02, 23; 2Q, '06, 11; 3Q, '08, 8

86.23   Removal of nail, nailbed, or nail fold

Description
The physician excises all or part of a fingernail or toenail. The physician may bluntly dissect the nail plate away from the nail bed. The germ matrix may be excised or destroyed using electrocautery. Bleeding is stopped with electrocautery and the wound is dressed.

86.24   Chemosurgery of skin

Description
The physician applies chemicals to peel away or destroy skin tissue. Surgical technique and the chemical utilized may vary, depending on the nature and type of lesion, including:

- **Chemical peel of skin:** The physician performs a chemical peel of the epidermal or dermal layers of the skin. The physician uses chemical agents, such as glycolic acid or phenol, to remove fine wrinkles or areas of abnormal pigmentation.

- **Chemical destruction of granulation tissue:** The physician destroys a form of exuberant or excessive healing tissue known as granulation tissue or proud flesh. The physician destroys the tissue by applying chemicals such as silver nitrate.

- **Mohs micrographic destruction of skin:** The physician performs chemosurgery using Mohs micrographic technique. The physician places a chemical agent on the lesion prior to excision. This chemical acts as a tissue fixative. The lesion is excised via serial tangential cuts, allowing the physician to more closely assess wound margins and the extent of the defect being excised.

86.25   Dermabrasion

Description
The physician performs dermabrasion for conditions such as acne scarring, fine wrinkling, rhytids, and general keratosis. The physician uses a powered rotary instrument to sand down or smooth scarred or wrinkled areas. The physician lowers raised lesions or thins thickened tissue to regenerate skin with a smoother appearance.

Coding Clarification
Dermabrasion may be performed with the assistance of laser technology.

Code 86.25 excludes dermabrasion of a wound to remove embedded debris (86.28).

86.26   Ligation of dermal appendage

Description
The physician ties a suture around the neck of skin appendage or skin tag to remove the growth of excess skin.

86.27   Debridement of nail, nail bed, or nail fold

Description
The physician debrides fingernails or toenails, including tops and exposed undersides, by any method. The cleaning is performed manually with cleaning solutions, abrasive materials, and tools. The nails are shortened and shaped.

Coding Clarification
Code 86.27 excludes the removal of a nail, nail bed, or nail fold by excision (86.23).

86.28   Nonexcisional debridement of wound, infection, or burn

Description
The physician removes damaged skin by methods other than sharp excision. The physician applies dressing materials and removes nonviable or nonadherent tissue from a burn or other wound. Devitalized tissue or tissue that is contaminated by bacteria, foreign material, slough, or granulation is removed by non-excisional methods such as pressurized irrigation, brushing, water scalpel, or scrubbing. The wound is cleansed and a dressing is applied.

Coding Clarification
Maggot therapy is considered nonexcisional debridement and is reported with 86.28.

Code 86.28 also correctly reports debridement using a VersaJet debrider ▶regardless of the depth of tissue treated.◀

▶Code 86.28 includes debridement by the Arobella Qoustic (ultrasonic-assisted) Wound Therapy System. If excisional debridement is performed in addition to this device, report the excisional debridement separately.◀

Coding Guidance
AHA: N-D, '86, 1; 4Q, '88, 5; 3Q, '89, 16; 3Q, '91,18; 2Q, '92, 17; 1Q, '99, 8; 2Q, '00, 9; 3Q, '02, 23; 2Q, '06, 11; ▶3Q, 09, 13; 2Q, '10, 11◀

86.3   Other local excision or destruction of lesion or tissue of skin and subcutaneous tissue

Description
The physician destroys or excises lesions under local or other anesthesia, using a laser, electrosurgery, cryosurgery, chemical treatment, or surgical curettement. Surgical technique may vary, depending on the nature and size of the lesion, including:

- **Excision skin lesion:** The physician excises a skin lesion, including the margin of normal tissue, for analysis or other therapeutic reasons. After administering a local anesthetic, the physician makes an incision through the dermis with a scalpel, usually in an elliptical shape around and under the lesion, and removes it. The physician may suture the wound simply. If the lesion is large or complicated, an adjacent tissue transfer (z-plasty) may be required.

- **Laser destruction of psoriasis lesions:** The physician uses a fiberoptic handpiece to deliver short pulses from a 308-nm UV-B laser for the treatment of psoriatic skin lesions. Prior to the start of treatment, the optimal dose is determined by exposing uninvolved skin to the minimal effective amount of UV-B. Once this dose is established, mineral oil is applied on the lesion to enhance penetration and reduce scattering. The physician uses the fiberoptic handpiece to irradiate the lesions by using a "painting" motion. The treatment is usually painless and does not require anesthesia.

Coding Clarification
Code 86.3 excludes excision or destruction of skin described as:

- Adipectomy (86.83)
- Biopsy of skin (86.11)
- Wide or radical excision of skin (86.4)
- Z-plasty without excision (86.84)

● New Code   ▲ Revised Code   ▶◀ Revised Text   © 2010 Ingenix

Code 86.3 reports excision or destruction of skin tissue not classifiable to subcategory 86.2. Subcategory 86.2 lists specific types of skin excision or destruction procedures, or procedures performed on specific anatomic sites or for specific indications/diagnoses.

Documentation Tip
Procedures classifiable to 86.3 may be documented as destruction of skin by/with:

- Cauterization
- Cryosurgery
- Fulguration
- Laser
- With z-plasty
- Photothermolysis

Coding Scenario
A 46-year-old male presented for excision of a subcutaneous fibroadenoma of the upper arm with local rotation flap closure. Under local anesthesia, an elliptical incision was made through the dermis with a scalpel circumferentially around and under the lesion. The lesion and a margin of normal adjacent tissue were removed in toto. The defect was closed by rotating and advancing a flap of adjacent tissue and suturing into place with layered sutures.

Code Assignment:

215.2	Other benign neoplasm of connective and other soft tissue, upper limb
86.3	Other local excision or destruction of skin and subcutaneous tissue
86.74	Attachment of pedicle or flap graft to other site

Coding Guidance
AHA: 4Q, '88, 7; 1Q, '89, 12; 3Q, '89, 18; 2Q, '90, 27; 1Q, '96, 15

86.4 Radical excision of skin lesion

Description
The physician makes a wide excision to remove a large skin lesion, including a margin of normal tissue that may leave a large defect. After administering the anesthetic, the physician makes an incision through the dermis with a scalpel, usually in an elliptical shape around and under the lesion, and removes it. Wide and radical excision may include dissection and removal of adjacent soft tissue of other structure. Closure is usually complex; adjacent tissue transfer or other skin graft may be required.

Coding Clarification
Code also any lymph node dissection (40.3-40.5).

Documentation Tip
Procedures classifiable to 86.4 include those described as wide excision of skin lesion.

Coding Guidance
AHA: ▶4Q, '09, 74◀

86.5 Suture or other closure of skin and subcutaneous tissue

86.51 Replantation of scalp

Description
The physician performs complex, layered suturing of torn, crushed, or deeply lacerated scalp tissue. The physician debrides the wound by removing foreign material or damaged tissue. Irrigation of the wound is performed and antimicrobial solutions are used to decontaminate and cleanse the wound. The physician may trim skin margins with a scalpel or scissors to allow for proper closure. The wound is closed in layers. Stents or retention sutures may also be used in complex repair of a wound.

86.59 Closure of skin and subcutaneous tissue of other sites

Description
The physician sutures lacerations of the skin and subcutaneous tissue. Anesthetic is injected around the laceration and the wound is cleansed, explored, and often irrigated with a saline solution. The physician performs a repair of the epidermis, dermis, or subcutaneous tissues with sutures, staples, or adhesives as necessary to achieve optimal closure and facilitate healing.

Coding Clarification
Code 86.59 excludes application of adhesive strips (omit code—do not report).

Code 86.59 includes closure of skin and subcutaneous tissue with:

- Adhesives
- Staples
- Sutures

Coding Guidance
AHA: 4Q, '99, 23

86.6 Free skin graft

Description
The physician transplants skin to another site.

Coding Clarification
This subcategory includes excision of skin for autogenous graft; skin taken from one area of the patient and transplanted to another area.

This subcategory excludes free skin grafts performed as part of procedures classifiable elsewhere, such as construction and reconstruction of:

- Penis (64.43-64.44)
- Trachea (31.75)
- Vagina (70.61-70.62)

86.60   Free skin graft, not otherwise specified

Description
This code describes other free skin graft procedures, not specifically classifiable elsewhere in subcategory 86.6.

Coding Clarification
This code is a nonspecific procedure that should not be assigned for hospital inpatient admissions if the medical record contains sufficient information to facilitate coding at a higher level of specificity.

Documentation Tip
If the documentation is ambiguous or unclear, the physician should be queried.

86.61   Full-thickness skin graft to hand

Description
The physician harvests a full-thickness skin graft with a scalpel from one area of the body and grafts it to a defect on the hand. A full-thickness skin graft consists of both the superficial and deeper layers of skin (epidermis and dermis). The resulting surgical wound at the donor site is closed by lifting the remaining skin edges and placing sutures for direct closure. Fat is removed from the graft, which is sutured onto the recipient bed to cover a defect of the hand.

Coding Clarification
Code 86.61 excludes heterograft (86.65) or homograft (86.66); grafts from other species or other human donor.

86.62   Other skin graft to hand

Description
The physician takes a split-thickness skin or other autograft from one area of the body and grafts it to a defect on the hand. This procedure is performed when direct wound closure or adjacent tissue transfer is not possible. The physician harvests a split-thickness skin graft with a dermatome. The epidermis or top layer of skin is taken, along with a small portion of the dermis or bottom layer of the skin. This graft is sutured or stapled onto the recipient area on the hand.

Coding Clarification
Code 86.62 excludes heterograft (86.65) or homograft (86.66); grafts from other species or other human donor.

86.63   Full-thickness skin graft to other sites

Description
The physician harvests a full-thickness skin graft with a scalpel from one area of the body and grafts it to an area needing repair. A full-thickness skin graft consists of both the superficial and deeper layers of skin (epidermis and dermis). The resulting surgical wound at the donor site is closed by lifting the remaining skin edges and placing sutures to close directly. Fat is removed from the graft, which is sutured onto the recipient bed to cover the defect.

Coding Clarification
Code 86.63 excludes heterograft (86.65) or homograft (86.66); grafts from other species or other human donor.

86.64   Hair transplant

Description
The physician performs hair transplantation. Surgical technique may vary. In general, a donor area is selected, usually the back and sides of the head that contain healthy, abundant hair follicles. Section(s) of tissue are removed from the donor area and dissected under an operating microscope into individual hair follicle units for micro-grafting. The prepared grafts are then strategically placed into bald or thinning areas of the scalp.

Coding Clarification
Code 86.64 excludes hair follicle transplant to eyebrow or eyelash (08.63).

86.65   Heterograft to skin

Description
The physician applies a xenograft to cover a wound on the patient. Xenograft dermal (skin) tissue is harvested from a non-human species (usually porcine) and is used to cover a skin defect in humans. The physician covers the recipient site with this temporary resurfacing material to maintain viability of the tissue underneath the wound until a future transplant of appropriate skin graft material can be done. This procedure is often performed on burn patients when autografting is not feasible.

Coding Clarification
Code 86.65 excludes application of porcine dressing only (93.57).

Coding Guidance
   AHA: 3Q, '02, 23

86.66   Homograft to skin

Description
The physician applies a skin homograft or allograft for temporary wound closure to a wound. A skin allograft is used as a temporary measure to close the wound and provide a barrier against infection and

fluid loss, reduce pain, and promote healing of underlying tissues until a permanent graft can be applied. The allograft is obtained from the skin bank and fashioned to fit the size and contours of the previously prepared wound bed on the trunk, arms, or legs. The skin allograft is placed over the wound and sutured or stapled into place.

86.67   Dermal regenerative graft

Description
The physician replaces the dermis and epidermal layer of skin by cultured or regenerated autologous tissue; used to treat full-thickness or deep partial-thickness burns. Surgical technique and graft materials may vary, including:

- **Acellular dermal autograft:** The physician applies an acellular dermal allograft to a wound of the trunk, arms, or legs. An acellular dermal allograft is a chemically treated, cadaver-harvested allograft that has been processed to remove all epidermal antigenic cellular components, rendering the graft immunologically inert while preserving the dermal matrix. The dermal allograft is fashioned to fit the size and contours of the previously prepared wound bed, once healthy viable tissue has been exposed. The graft is placed over the wound and sutured or stapled into place. In a separately reportable procedure, the dermal allograft is covered with a local skin flap or a split-thickness autograft. The wound is dressed.

- **Tissue cultured allogenic skin substitute:** The physician applies a tissue cultured allogeneic skin substitute to a wound. The skin substitute is fenestrated, placed onto the wound site, and secured with interrupted sutures. Using this type of graft requires only minimal site preparation and debridement, which are not reported separately. Allogeneic skin substitutes may be temporary or permanent. Temporary skin substitutes are used on fresh, partial thickness wounds and are left until healed. Temporary skin substitutes have an outer epidermal barrier made of a thin silicon film and an inner dermal layer of human-derived fibroblast products, such as collagen, fibronectin, and glycosaminoglycan, or collagen bonded onto nylon filament weave. The dermal layer provides an adherent protective dressing that supports infiltration and proliferation of new matrix cells in normal tissue alignment. Permanent skin substitutes have a bioactive dermal layer, composed of a collagen and fibroblast or collagen and glycosaminoglycan matrix that incorporates itself with neodermis growth or biodegrades as neodermis is formed. The outer, epidermal layer

may also be biologic, derived from human epidermis (e.g., neonatal male foreskin) or a thin silicone elastomer, which is later replaced with epidermal autografts.

Coding Clarification
Code 86.67 excludes heterograft (86.65) or homograft (86.66); grafts from other species or other human donor.

Documentation Tip
Procedures classifiable to 86.67 may be documented as:

- Artificial skin, NOS
- Creation of neodermis
- Decellularized allodermis
- Integumentary matrix implants
- Prosthetic implant of dermal layer of skin
- Regenerate dermal layer of skin
- Cultured epidermal autograft (CEA)

Coding Guidance
    AHA: 3Q, '06, 19; 4Q, '98, 76, 79

86.69   Other skin graft to other sites

Description
This procedure code includes other skin grafts to other sites not classifiable elsewhere in subcategory 86.6.

Coding Clarification
This code should not be assigned if the medical record contains sufficient information to facilitate coding at a higher level of specificity.

Documentation Tip
If the documentation is ambiguous or unclear, the physician should be queried.

Coding Guidance
    AHA: 4Q, '99, 15; ▶1Q, '10, 7◀

86.7   Pedicle grafts or flaps

Description
A full-thickness skin and subcutaneous tissue is partially attached to the body by a narrow strip of tissue so that it retains its blood supply. The unattached portion is sutured to the defect.

Coding Clarification
Subcategory 86.7 excludes construction or reconstruction of:

- Penis (64.43-64.44)
- Trachea (31.75)
- Vagina (70.61-70.62)

The procedures in this subcategory are classified according to the stages of the skin graft operation or when specific anatomic sites are involved, as:

85-86

- Cutting and preparation of graft (86.71)
- Advancement of pedicle graft (86.72)
- Attachment of pedicle or flap graft to hand (86.73)
- Attachment of pedicle or flap to other sites (86.74)
- Revision of previous pedicle flap or graft procedure (86.75)

86.70   Pedicle or flap graft, not otherwise specified

Description
This code describes a pedicle or flap graft not otherwise classifiable elsewhere in subcategory 86.7.

Coding Clarification
This is a non-specific code that should not be assigned for inpatient hospital admissions if the medical record contains sufficient information to facilitate coding at a higher level of specificity.

Documentation Tip
If the documentation is ambiguous or unclear, the physician should be queried.

86.71   Cutting and preparation of pedicle grafts or flaps

Description
The physician forms a direct or tubed pedicle flap to reconstruct traumatic defects. A pedicle flap of full-thickness skin and subcutaneous tissue that retains its supporting blood vessels is developed in the donor area. A tubed pedicle flap maintains two vascular ends and the cut edges of the raised flap are sutured together to form a tube. The flap may be rotated or transferred to the defect area and sutured to the recipient bed in layers. The physician closes the harvest region in layers or covers it with a split-thickness skin graft. Repairs to the donor area using skin grafts or flaps are reported separately. Other exposed regions, including portions of the pedicle, may also be covered with a split-thickness skin graft. Once the recipient site has healed, a second surgery will detach the pedicle and return the unused flap to its anatomic location.

Coding Clarification
Code 86.71 excludes pollicization or digital transfer (82.61, 82.81) and revision of pedicle (86.75).

Documentation Tip
Procedures classifiable to 86.71 may be documented as:

- Elevation of pedicle—separation of tissue implanted from its bed
- Pedicle flap design and raising—planning and elevation of tissue to be implanted
- Partial cutting of pedicle or tube

- Pedicle delay—elevation and preparation of tissue still attached to vascular bed; delayed implant

Coding Guidance
AHA: 4Q, '01, 66

86.72   Advancement of pedicle graft

Description
A previously placed pedicle flap has been in position long enough to receive a good blood supply from the recipient area. As an intermediate step, the physician releases the flap from its donor attachment and moves it to a new location. This same tissue may be moved further along the body in a similar manner at a later date. This is known as walking the flap or walk up procedure.

Coding Guidance
AHA: 3Q, '99, 9, 10

86.73   Attachment of pedicle or flap graft to hand

86.74   Attachment of pedicle or flap graft to other sites

Description
These procedures describe the attachment of a pedicle or flap graft to the hand (86.73) or other sites (86.74). Surgical technique may vary, depending on the type of graft utilized and indications for procedure, including:

- **Flap graft:** The physician transfers or rearranges adjacent tissue to repair traumatic or surgical wounds of the scalp, arms, and/or legs. This includes, but is not limited to, such rearrangement procedures as Z-plasty, W-plasty, ZY-plasty, or tissue transfers such as rotational or advancement flaps.

- **Pedicle graft:** The physician forms a direct or tubed pedicle flap to reconstruct traumatic defects. A pedicle flap of full-thickness skin and subcutaneous tissue that retains its supporting blood vessels is developed in the donor area. A tubed pedicle flap maintains two vascular ends and the cut edges of the raised flap are sutured together to form a tube. The flap may be rotated or transferred to the defect area and sutured to the recipient bed in layers. The physician closes the harvest region in layers or covers it with a split-thickness skin graft. Repairs to the donor area using skin grafts or flaps are reported separately. Other exposed regions, including portions of the pedicle, may also be covered with a split-thickness skin graft. Once the recipient site has healed, a second surgery will detach the pedicle and return the unused flap to its anatomic location.

● New Code   ▲ Revised Code   ▶◀ Revised Text   © 2010 Ingenix

Documentation Tip

Procedures classifiable to 86.74 may be documented as:

- Advanced flap—sliding tissue implant into new position

- Double pedicle flap—implant connected to two vascular beds

- Rotating flap—implant rotated along a curved incision

- Sliding flap—sliding implant to site

- Tube graft—double tissue implant to form tube with base connected to original site

86.75   Revision of pedicle or flap graft

Description
The physician revises a prior pedicle or flap graft, including debridement or defatting of the graft. Surgical technique may vary, depending on the revision required.

86.8   Other repair and reconstruction of skin and subcutaneous tissue

86.81   Repair for facial weakness

Description
The physician harvests a graft for facial nerve paralysis. The physician removes connective tissue (fascia) from a predetermined location of the body (often fascia lata from the leg). This graft is transplanted to the face and sutured into place underneath the skin in order to partially suspend or reanimate previously paralyzed areas of the face. Surgical technique may vary. A free muscle graft, a free muscle flap by microsurgical technique, or a regional muscle transfer may be performed.

86.82   Facial rhytidectomy

Description
The physician performs rhytidectomy, or face lift procedures. To tighten and lift certain areas of the face, specific surgical techniques may vary, including:

- **Forehead:** The physician performs a rhytidectomy of the forehead. The physician excises a portion of skin in order to eliminate wrinkles in the forehead. Most commonly an incision is made in the hairline and a subcutaneous dissection is carried down to the level of the eyebrow. The excess skin is removed and the forehead is elevated and sutured into the new position. Incisions are repaired in layers. If the rhytidectomy is done to reduce glabellar frown lines, the vertical furrows in the forehead area between the eyebrows, the corrugator and procerus muscles may be debulked before incisions in the eyebrows are closed.

- **Neck:** The physician performs a rhytidectomy of the neck. The physician makes an incision usually in front of the ear. Tension is increased in the facial muscles by freeing the superficial musculoaponeurotic system (SMAS) (facial muscles are interlinked by the SMAS). The physician trims and tightens the SMAS by securing it with sutures to tissues in front of the ear. An additional incision below the chin is necessary to correct the platysma muscle. The physician makes an incision through the platysma muscle, creating a flap, which is moved up and back. The muscle is tightened, trimmed, and secured with layered sutures. The skin incisions are closed with layered sutures.

- **Cheek/chin/neck:** The physician makes an incision in a crease or wrinkle of the cheek, chin, or neck to perform a rhytidectomy. Tension is increased by removing excess skin and fat. An additional incision in front of the ear may be necessary. Tension is increased in the facial muscles by freeing the superficial musculoaponeurotic system (SMAS) (facial muscles are interlinked by the SMAS). The physician trims and tightens the SMAS by securing it with sutures to tissues in front of the ear.

Coding Clarification
Code 86.82 excludes rhytidectomy of the eyelid (08.86-08.87).

86.83   Size reduction plastic operation

Description
The physician reduces tissue size whereby excess fatty tissue is removed from specific areas of the body for aesthetic purposes. Surgical technique may vary, including:

- **Lipectomy:** The physician removes excessive skin and subcutaneous tissue (including lipectomy). To reduce pendulous abdomen, the physician makes an incision traversing the abdomen below the belly button in a horizontal fashion. Excessive skin and subcutaneous tissue are elevated off the abdominal wall and excess tissue and fat are excised. The flaps are brought together and sutured in at least three layers. The physician may also suture the rectus abdominis muscles together in the midline to reinforce the area. The physician may remove excess skin and subcutaneous tissue on the thigh, leg, hip, buttock, arm, submental fat pad (inferior to the chin), or other area in a similar fashion.

- **Liposuction:** A liposuction cannula is inserted through a regional incision and the physician moves the cannula through the fat deposits, creating tunnels and removing excess deposits. The incisions are closed simply.

Coding Clarification
Code 86.83 excludes size reduction or plastic operations on the breast (85.31-85.32) ▶and liposuction to harvest the fat graft (86.90).◀

Coding Guidance
AHA: 2Q, '06, 10

86.84   Relaxation of scar or web contracture of skin
Description
The physician transfers or rearranges adjacent tissue to repair and release a scar or contracture of the skin. Surgical technique may vary.

Z-plasty is a surgical repositioning of a scar to ease discomfort associated with contracture and improve aesthetics. Under local anesthesia, the scar is excised and surgical incisions are made on each side, creating small triangular flaps of skin. The flaps are rearranged to cover the wound at a different angle, resulting in a "Z" pattern.

86.85   Correction of syndactyly
Description
The physician repairs a syndactyly (web finger) using skin flaps and grafts. The physician incises the skin of the web for digital release and the underlying tissues are freed. The repair may be accomplished with skin flaps from the incision area, or the physician may obtain grafts to provide skin coverage. Complex syndactyly repair may involve the phalangeal bones and fingernails. When possible, the bones are separated. Bone grafts are obtained when necessary for reconstruction. When reconstruction is complete, the skin is reapproximated and sutured in layers.

86.86   Onychoplasty
Description
The physician repairs a damaged nail bed. The physician removes the damaged and surrounding nail from the nail bed. The nail bed is sutured into correct position. Bleeding is controlled through electrocautery and the wound is dressed. The physician may repair a damaged nail bed using a skin graft. The physician cleans the nail bed and prepares it for the graft. The graft is obtained and sutured into place. Hemostasis is achieved and a dressing is applied.

● 86.87   Fat graft of skin and subcutaneous tissue
Description
▶Fat grafting is a technique in which prepared autologous fat cells are injected to correct soft tissue defects. Fat grafts are commonly used in cosmetic procedures, such as augmenting lips and filling in facial wrinkles. Fat grafts are also used in certain plastic reconstructive procedures. Fat is harvested by liposuction from elsewhere on the patient's body, typically an unobtrusive area such as the abdomen, flanks, or thighs. The lipoaspirate is centrifuged and filtered to concentrate the number of fat cells. Fat graft enrichment with adipose progenitor cells (a.k.a., adipose-derived regenerative stem cells) may be added to the fat graft to reduce the incidence of ischemia complications. Fat grafts are most commonly placed by injection technique, whereby the graft material is loaded into a syringe or cannula and evenly placed into the defect to achieve cosmetically optimal contour and texture. Fat grafting may be performed as an adjunct to a primary procedure or as a solo procedure. Total operative time depends on the size, nature, and anatomic site of the defect.◀

Coding Clarification
▶Code 86.87 includes extraction of fat for autologous graft of skin and subcutaneous tissue, with or without the use of enriched graft.

Code 86.87 excludes fat graft procedures to the breast (85.55).

Extraction or harvesting of fat for future use is reported with new code 86.90◀

86.89   Other repair and reconstruction of skin and subcutaneous tissue
Description
This code describes other repair or reconstructive procedures not classifiable elsewhere in subcategory 86.8.

Coding Clarification
This code should not be assigned if the medical record contains sufficient information to facilitate coding at a higher level of specificity.

Code 86.89 excludes mentoplasty (76.67-76.68); plastic repair or correction of deformities or defects of the chin.

Documentation Tip
If the documentation is ambiguous or unclear, the physician should be queried.

Coding Guidance
AHA: 2Q, '92, 17; 2Q '93, 11; 2Q, '98, 20; 1Q, '00, 26, 4Q, '02, 107

86.9 Other operations on skin and subcutaneous tissue

● 86.90 Extraction of fat for graft or banking

Description
▶This code reports the harvest of fat for extraction of cells for future use (e.g., liposuction), including fat harvesting or banking procedures. Fat grafting is a technique in which prepared autologous fat cells are injected to correct soft tissue defects. Fat is harvested by liposuction from elsewhere on the patient's body, typically an unobtrusive area such as the abdomen, flanks, or thighs. The lipoaspirate is centrifuged and filtered to concentrate the number of fat cells. Fat graft enrichment with adipose progenitor cells (a.k.a., adipose-derived regenerative stem cells) may be added to the fat graft to reduce the incidence of ischemia complications. Fat graft placement procedures to either the breast (85.55) or other skin and subcutaneous tissue (86.87) are separately reported.◀

Coding Clarification
▶Previously, ICD-9-CM did not provide specific codes for harvesting of fat for graft or banking. Extraction of fat with synchronous graft procedures during the same operative episode are reported with code 85.55 or 86.87, as appropriate.◀

86.91 Excision of skin for graft

Description
The physician harvests skin (keratinocytes and dermal tissue) for a skin graft. The donor site is first injected with epinephrine solution to control blood loss and aid the skin harvesting technique. Skin is harvested by taking a split-thickness graft with a dermatome, and the donor site is dressed. This code reports only the skin harvesting to be used for skin grafting.

Coding Clarification
Code 86.91 excludes excision of skin for graft at the same operative episode as the placement of an autogenous skin graft (86.60-86.69).

86.92 Electrolysis and other epilation of skin

Description
The physician uses electrolysis to remove hair. This code is used to report a 30-minute session. The physician inserts the electroneedle into the hair follicle and applies electrical current, killing the follicle. The electroneedle is removed.

Coding Clarification
Code 86.92 excludes epilation of the eyelid (08.91-08.93).

86.93 Insertion of tissue expander

Description
The physician uses a tissue expander to stretch skin and soft tissue prior to definitive reconstruction on tissue other than breast. These expanders are balloon-type devices that stretch the skin and enhance epithelial and collagen expansion and reduce or eliminate the need for skin grafts during reconstruction. The physician makes an incision into the skin. The subcutaneous layer is identified. Blunt dissection is used to separate the skin and subcutaneous layers. The tissue expander is placed into the prepared site. The wound is sutured. The expander is inflated. During the post-operative visits, greater volume is placed into the expander stretching the skin. The expander remains in place until the final reconstruction is performed.

Coding Clarification
Code 86.93 excludes insertion of tissue expander of breast (85.95).

86.94 Insertion or replacement of single array neurostimulator pulse generator, not specified as rechargeable

86.95 Insertion or replacement of dual array neurostimulator pulse generator, not specified as rechargeable

86.96 Insertion or replacement of other neurostimulator pulse generator

86.97 Insertion or replacement of single array rechargeable neurostimulator pulse generator

86.98 Insertion or replacement of dual array rechargeable neurostimulator pulse generator

Description
Codes 86.94-86.98 describe the insertion or replacement of neurostimulator pulse generator devices into the skin or subcutaneous (soft tissue) pocket. This section of codes classifies neurostimulator pulse generator insertion by type of device. These codes apply to neurostimulator pulse generator devices described as:

- Intracranial
- Spinal
- Peripheral

Within this section of codes, these devices are further classified as:

- Single array (86.94, 86.97)—a single generator with one lead
  - rechargeable (86.97)
  - not specified as rechargeable (86.94)

85-86

- Dual array (86.95, 86.98)—a single generator with a single tunnel and two leads to stimulate two different areas
  - rechargeable (86.98)
  - not specified as rechargeable (86.95)
- Other (86.96)

Neurostimulator systems consist of a battery-operated generator inserted into a subcutaneous pocket connected to an electrode (lead) situated at the target organ via a subcutaneous tunnel. Codes 86.94-86.98 require that an additional code be reported for synchronous insertion of leads, if applicable:

- 02.93 Implantation or replacement of intracranial neurostimulator lead(s)
- 03.93 Implantation or replacement of spinal neurostimulator lead(s)
- 04.92 Implantation or replacement of peripheral neurostimulator lead(s)

Intracranial neurostimulator devices are implanted into the brain for deep brain stimulation (DBS) to control tremors in patients diagnosed with essential tremor, epilepsy, or Parkinson's disease. The pulses interrupt the thalamic signals that play a role in causing the tremor. The physician inserts or replaces a cranial neurostimulator pulse generator or receiver into a subcutaneous pocket. The physician selects a location site, usually the infraclavicular area, and incises the skin. Using blunt dissection, the physician creates a pocket for the generator or receiver. The unit is connected to a previously positioned single electrode array. After ensuring that the device is functioning, the generator or receiver is sutured into place within its subcutaneous pocket.

Spinal cord neurostimulator devices block pain conduction pathways to the brain. They are used to treat chronic, intractable pain due to disease or trauma, including spinal cord injuries. The physician inserts or replaces a spinal neurostimulator pulse generator or receiver into a subcutaneous pocket. Placing a spinal neurostimulator is often done to treat cases of intractable pain. The physician selects a location site, usually the abdominal area, and incises the skin. Using blunt dissection, the physician creates a pocket for the generator or receiver. The unit is connected to a previously placed electrode, which is separately implanted and normally positioned in a dural/epidural pocket over the spinal cord of the affected vertebral area. After ensuring that the device is functioning, the generator or receiver is sutured into place within its subcutaneous pocket.

Peripheral neurostimulator devices may be implanted to stimulate motor nerves in cases of muscle paralysis to prevent atrophy or sensory

nerves to decrease pain sensation along the nerve distribution or to assist in bladder control. The physician inserts or replaces a peripheral or gastric neurostimulator pulse generator or receiver into a subcutaneous pocket. Peripheral neurostimulators are used to transmit electrical impulses to nerves outside of the brain or spinal cord, such as the sacral nerve to help the bladder muscles contract and treat cases of urinary incontinence or retention, or for pain relief. Gastric neurostimulators transmit electrical impulses in the same way, to treat nausea and vomiting in patients with gastroparesis. The physician selects a location site, usually the abdominal area, and incises the skin. Using blunt dissection, the physician creates a pocket for the generator or receiver. The unit is connected to a previously placed electrode, which is separately implanted to stimulate the target nerve. After ensuring that the device is functioning, the generator or receiver is sutured into place within its subcutaneous pocket.

The physician revises or removes a peripheral or gastric neurostimulator pulse generator or receiver with or without replacement. The placement incision is reopened and tissues are dissected to the transmitter pocket. If the procedure is performed because the device is malfunctioning, the unit is checked and repairs made or a new unit is inserted. The incision is closed in layered sutures.

Coding Clarification
▶Codes 86.94–86.98 exclude cranial implantation or replacement of neurostimulator pulse generator, or RNS™ systems (01.20) without a subcutaneous pocket procedural component.◀

Coding Guidance
AHA: 4Q, '04, 135; 4Q, '05, 130; 2Q, '06, 5-6; 2Q, '07, 8

86.99 Other operations on skin and subcutaneous tissue

Description
This procedure code reports other operations on skin and subcutaneous tissue not classifiable elsewhere in category 86.

Coding Clarification
This code should not be assigned if the medical record contains sufficient information to facilitate coding at a higher level of specificity.

Code 86.99 excludes procedures classifiable to Chapter 16 Miscellaneous diagnostic and therapeutic procedures (87-99).

Documentation Tip
If the documentation is ambiguous or unclear, the physician should be queried.

Coding Guidance
AHA: N-D, '86, 1; 4Q, '97, 57

87-99

Miscellaneous Diagnostic and Therapeutic Procedures

2011 Changes

Changes to this section for 2011 include a revision of code titles 88.59 Intraoperative coronary fluorescence vascular angiography and 99.14 Injection or infusion of immunoglobulin. Also, an inclusion term was added to code 99.14.

The ICD-9-CM classification system for miscellaneous diagnostic and therapeutic procedures is divided into categories of procedures according to type as follows:

- Diagnostic radiology (87)
- Other Diagnostic Radiology and Related Techniques (88)
- Interview, Evaluation, Consultation and Examination (89)
- Microscopic Examination—I (90)
- Microscopic Examination—II (91)
- Nuclear Medicine (92)
- Physical Therapy, Respiratory Therapy, Rehabilitation, and Related Procedures (93)
- Procedures Related to the Psyche (94)
- Ophthalmologic and Otologic Diagnosis and Treatment (95)
- Nonoperative Intubation and Irrigation (96)
- Replacement and Removal of Therapeutic Appliances (97)
- Nonoperative Removal of Foreign Body or Calculus (98)
- Other Nonoperative Procedure (99)

Categories 87 and 88 provide codes for diagnostic radiological procedures and other related techniques of specific sites. There are subcategories for soft tissue, contrast, computerized axial tomography, ultrasound, magnetic resonance imaging, and other types of imaging. All require the assignment of a fourth digit.

87 Diagnostic radiology

Description
This category classifies radiological procedures that serve to identify characteristics of disease processes through the use of various forms of x-ray technology. Subcategories 87.1-87.9 classify these procedures by anatomic site. Within each subcategory, specific diagnostic radiology techniques may be separately classified to identify specific technologies.

87.0 Soft tissue x-ray of face, head, and neck

Coding Clarification
This subcategory excludes angiography (88.40-88.68).

87.01 Pneumoencephalogram

Description
The physician performs a radiographic exam of cerebral ventricles and subarachnoid spaces with injection of air or gas for contrast.

87.02 Other contrast radiogram of brain and skull

Description
This procedure involves an injection procedure followed by radiological studies of specific sites, including:

- **Pneumocisternogram:** A radiographic study using fluoroscopy is performed on the posterior fossa when a lesion is suspected. Contrast medium, usually barium sulfate, may be used to enhance visibility and is instilled in the patient through a lumbar area puncture into the subarachnoid space. The radiologist takes a series of pictures by sending an x-ray beam through the body, using fluoroscopy to view the enhanced structure on a television camera. The patient is angled from an erect position through a recumbent position with the body tilted so as to maintain feet higher than the head to help the flow of contrast into the study area.

- **Cisternography/posterior fossa myelogram:** The physician performs a spinal puncture in the high cervical region (C1-C2) or at the base of the skull in the cisterna magna (cerebellomedullary cistern). For lateral cervical puncture, the physician uses a paramedian approach. For cisternal punctures, the needle is placed at the base of the skull and contrast is injected for diagnostic study.

87.03 Computerized axial tomography of head

Description
Computed tomography directs multiple narrow beams of x-rays around the body structure being studied and uses computer imaging to produce thin cross-sectional views of various layers (or slices) of the body. It is useful for the evaluation of trauma, tumor, and foreign bodies as CT is able to visualize soft tissue as well as bones. Patients are required to remain motionless during the study and sedation may need to be administered as well as a contrast medium for image enhancement. This code reports an exam of the head or brain.

Coding Guidance
AHA: 3Q, '99, 7; 3Q, '05, 12

87.04 Other tomography of head

Description
This procedure code reports other tomography of the head, not specified as computerized axial tomography (87.03).

Coding Clarification
This code should not be assigned if the medical record contains sufficient information to facilitate coding at a higher level of specificity.

Documentation Tip
If the documentation is ambiguous or unclear, the physician should be queried.

87.05 Contrast dacryocystogram

Description
Dacryocystography is the radiographic evaluation of the lacrimal system to localize the site of an obstruction. One cc of a water-soluble contrast medium is injected through the lower canaliculus and x-rays of the excretory system are obtained. The physician supervises the procedure and interprets and reports the findings

Documentation Tip
Procedures classifiable to 87.05 may be documented as:

- Contrast radiogram of nasolacrimal ducts [nasopharynx is 87.06]
- Radiographic lacrimal flow study

87.06 Contrast radiogram of nasopharynx

Description
A radiologic examination is performed to visualize the pharynx, which serves as passage for both food and air, and larynx, or the organ of voice. Films are typically taken to show soft tissues of the neck. The films are often taken while the patient inhales or makes phonetic sounds. The key element of this code is that it includes x-ray fluoroscopy and/or magnification technique in addition to the radiologic exam.

87.07 Contrast laryngogram

Description
A radiographic contrast study is performed of the larynx, or organ of voice. Iodized oil is given in conjunction with the examination via tubing, which allows oil to drip down the patient's throat at the radiologist's discretion. The radiologist, via x-ray fluoroscopy, simultaneously watches the image amplified and displayed on a TV monitor. Rapid film sequencing must be used to record the image, which may be studied and interpreted by the radiologist.

87.08 Cervical lymphangiogram

Description
This procedure is a radiographic contrast study of the cervical (neck) lymphatic structures. Vital blue dye is injected into the subcutaneous tissues for outlining of skin lymphatics. As soon as the lymphatic vessels are visualized by their blue color, the radiologist makes a small longitudinal incision over the area. Exposure of the lymph vessel is accomplished, the vessel is made taut, and it is cannulated with a 27 or 30 gauge needle with a fine catheter attached. A small amount of dye is injected to ensure correct placement, and the needle is advanced 2 to 3 mm into the vessel. The needle and catheter are secured. Dye is injected with a 10 cc syringe. X-rays are made and repeated 24 hours later. The physician removes the needle and closes the incision with sutures.

87.09 Other soft tissue x-ray of face, head, and neck

Description
The technologist uses x-rays to obtain soft tissue images of the patient's neck rather than bone. The radiologist obtains two views, typically front to back (AP), and side to side (lateral). This procedure is performed to visualize abnormal air patterns or suspected foreign bodies or obstructions within the throat or neck.

Coding Clarification
Code 87.09 includes non-contrast x-ray of:

- Adenoid
- Larynx

- Nasolacrimal duct
- Nasopharynx
- Salivary gland
- Thyroid region
- Uvula

Code 87.09 excludes x-ray study of the eye (95.14).

87.1   Other x-ray of face, head, and neck

Coding Clarification
This subcategory excludes angiography
(88.40-88.86).

87.11   Full-mouth x-ray of teeth

Description
Films are taken of the mouth to show teeth and/or
surrounding bone. In dental radiography, the film
may be placed inside or outside the mouth. This
code describes imaging of a full mouth exam.

87.12   Other dental x-ray

Description
Code 87.12 describes other dental x-rays. Technique
and scope may vary, depending on the reason for the
exam, including:

- **Orthodontic cephalogram:** A lateral or frontal
  x-ray projection is taken to examine the skull,
  jaw, and related tooth positions. The machine
  holds the patient's head in the same position
  each time so that a series of cephalograms can
  be directly compared for growth and
  development over time.

- **Orthopantogram:** A panoramic radiographic
  study is performed on the mandibular arch and
  its supporting structures. A single image is
  produced of the mandible for diagnostic
  purposes. The physician evaluates trauma,
  third molar, and other unique disease
  conditions. Tooth development and anomalies
  may also be studied.

Coding Clarification
Code 87.12 includes:

- Orthodontic cephalogram or cephalometrics
- Panorex examination of mandible
- Root canal x-ray

87.13   Temporomandibular contrast arthrogram

Description
A radiographic contrast study is performed on the
temporomandibular joint. A contrast material is
injected into the joint spaces, followed by x-ray
examination of the joint. This allows the physician to
see the position of the structures not normally seen
on conventional x-rays.

87.14   Contrast radiogram of orbit

Description
Radiological examination of the orbits is useful in
the evaluation of trauma, tumors, or foreign bodies.
After positioning the patient, the radiologist obtains
a minimum of four x-ray views of the orbits.
Standard methods include posteroanterior (PA)
exposures from two different positions, lateral views,
optic canal projections, and oblique views of each
side for comparison. The physician supervises the
procedure and interprets and reports the findings.

87.15   Contrast dacryocystogram

Description
This procedure involves contrast radiogram of the
sinus. Technique and extent of exam may vary,
including:

- **Less than 3 views:** Films are taken of the
  paranasal sinuses in one or two views. Although
  there are several sinus projections, each serving
  a specific purpose, many of them are used only
  when required to visualize a specific lesion.
  Typically, but not necessarily, this code would
  call for a side to side (lateral) view and a back to
  front (PA) view, depending on the specific sinus
  in question. The projections are routinely taken
  with the patient in an erect position to
  demonstrate presence or absence of fluid.

- **Complete exam:** Films are taken of the
  paranasal sinuses for a complete study, with a
  minimum of three views. There are several
  sinus projections used when required to
  visualize a specific lesion. Projections routinely
  taken consist of four to five standard views of
  the skull, which adequately demonstrate all of
  the paranasal sinuses on a majority of patients.
  Specific exams may be included to test a
  particular sinus, e.g., frontal sinus, maxillary
  sinus, and sphenoid or ethmoid sinuses. These
  projections are routinely taken with the patient
  in an erect position to demonstrate presence or
  absence of fluid.

87.16   Other x-ray of facial bones

Description:
X-rays of the facial bones are obtained to determine
an injury, fracture, or neoplasm. After positioning
the patient, a complete series of x-rays of the facial
bones, with a minimum of three views may be
obtained. The physician supervises the procedure
and interprets and reports the findings.

Coding Clarification
Code 87.16 includes x-ray of:

- Frontal area
- Mandible

- Maxilla
- Nasal sinuses
- Nose
- Orbit
- Supraorbital area
- Symphysis menti
- Zygomaticomaxillary complex

87.17   Other x-ray of skull

Description
Films are taken of the skull bones. In some studies, three or less views are taken, or a complete exam with a four view minimum may be performed. The most common projections for routine skull series are AP axial (front to back), lateral, and PA axial (back to front). X-rays may be taken with the patient placed erect, prone, or supine and either code may include stereoradiography, which is a technique that produces three-dimensional images.

Coding Clarification
Code 87.17 includes:

- Lateral projection—side to side view of head
- Sagittal projection—view of body in plane running midline from front to back
- Tangential projection—views from adjacent skull surfaces

87.2   Contrast myelogram

87.21   Contrast myelogram

Description
In myelography, a radiographic study using fluoroscopy is performed on the spinal cord and nerve root branches when a lesion is suspected. A nonionic water-soluble radiopaque contrast media is used to enhance visibility and is instilled in the patient through a lumbar or cervical area puncture into the subarachnoid space. The radiologist takes a series of pictures by sending an x-ray beam through the body, using fluoroscopy to view the enhanced structure on a television camera. The patient is angled from an erect position through a recumbent position with the body tilted so as to maintain feet higher than the head to help the flow of contrast into the study area.

Coding Clarification
Contrast myelogram is a radiographic exam of the space between the middle and outer spinal cord coverings after injection of contrast.

87.22   Other x-ray of cervical spine

87.23   Other x-ray of thoracic spine

87.24   Other x-ray of lumbosacral spine

87.29   Other x-ray of spine

Description
A radiologic examination of the spine is performed that includes a minimum of two views a minimum of four views or a complete study. The complete study includes films taken in oblique (angled) positions and in flexion and/or extension positioning.

Coding Clarification
Code 87.24 includes sacrococcygeal x-ray.

Assign 87.29 to report spinal x-ray NOS.

87.3   Soft tissue x-ray of thorax

Coding Clarification
Subcategory 87.3 excludes angiocardiography (88.50-88.58) and angiography (88.40-88.68).

87.31   Endotracheal bronchogram

Description
The physician injects contrast material for a bronchography into the trachea, just below the voice box. The physician palpates the laryngeal structures and identifies the tracheal rings. The physician inserts a needle into the trachea. After verifying placement, the physician injects the contrast material for a bronchography. The physician views the airway using a bronchoscope introduced through the nasal or oral cavity, using local anesthesia of the patient's airway. The physician uses the views obtained through the bronchoscope to identify the bronchial segment to be studied. The physician may use fluoroscopy (x-ray) to assist with navigation of the bronchoscope tip. The physician passes a needle or catheter through a channel in the bronchoscope into the bronchial segment and injects the contrast material for bronchography. The bronchoscope is removed.

Coding Clarification
An endotracheal bronchogram is a radiographic exam of lung, main branch, with contrast introduced through the windpipe.

87.32   Other contrast bronchogram

Description
This procedure code reports a bronchogram performed by approach other than endotracheal. The physician injects contrast material for a bronchography into the trachea, just below the voice box. The physician palpates the laryngeal structures and identifies the tracheal rings. The physician inserts a needle into the trachea. After verifying

placement, the physician injects the contrast material for a bronchography (reported separately).

Coding Clarification
Code 87.32 includes transcricoid bronchogram, which is a radiographic exam of lung, main branch, with contrast introduced through cartilage of the neck.

87.33   Mediastinal pneumogram

Coding Clarification
A mediastinal pneumogram is a radiographic exam of the cavity containing the heart, esophagus, and adjacent structures.

87.34   Intrathoracic lymphangiogram

Description
The physician may inject vital blue into the subcutaneous tissues to outline the lymphatics. As soon as the lymphatic vessels are visualized by their blue color, the radiologist makes a small longitudinal incision over the area. Exposure of the lymph vessel is accomplished, the vessel is made taut, and it is cannulated with a 27 or 30 gauge needle with a fine catheter attached. A small amount of dye may be injected to ensure correct placement, and the needle is advanced 2 to 3 mm into the vessel. The needle and catheter are secured. Dye may be injected with a 10 cc syringe. X-rays are made and repeated 24 hours later. The physician removes the needle and closes the incision with sutures.

Coding Clarification
Code 87.34 includes contrast radiogram of the lymphatic vessels within the chest.

87.35   Contrast radiogram of mammary ducts

Description
The physician performs an injection procedure for mammary ductogram or galactogram. A needle and cannula are inserted into the duct of the breast. Contrast medium is introduced into the breast duct for the radiographic visualization. A dissecting microscope may be used to aid in placing the cannula. The needle and cannula are removed when the study is complete.

87.36   Xerography of breast

Description
The physician performs a radiographic exam of the breast via selenium-coated plates.

87.37   Other mammography

Description
Mammography is a radiographic technique used to diagnose breast cysts or tumors in women with symptoms of breast disease or to detect them before

they are palpable in women who are asymptomatic. Mammography is done using a different type of x-ray than is used for routine exams that do not penetrate tissue as easily. The breast is compressed firmly between two planes and pictures are taken. This spreads the tissue and allows for a lower x-ray dose.

Coding Guidance
   AHA: N-D, '87, 1; 3Q, '89, 17; 2Q, ' 90, 28

87.38   Sinogram of chest wall

Description
An injection of radiopaque material is made directly into a sinus tract of the chest wall (an abnormal canal or passage) or through a previously placed catheter, to determine the existence, nature, or size of an abscess or fistula (an abnormal tube-like passage from a normal body cavity to a free surface or to another body cavity).

Coding Clarification
Code 87.38 includes fistulogram of chest wall, which is a radiographic exam of an abnormal opening in the chest.

87.39   Other soft tissue x-ray of chest wall

Description
This procedure code describes other soft tissue x-ray of the chest wall not classifiable as a sonogram (87.38).

Coding Clarification
This code should not be assigned if the medical record contains sufficient information to facilitate coding at a higher level of specificity.

Documentation Tip
If the documentation is ambiguous or unclear, the physician should be queried.

87.4   Other x-ray of thorax

Coding Clarification
This subcategory excludes angiocardiography (88.50-88.58) and angiography (88.40-88.68).

87.41   Computerized axial tomography of thorax

Description
Computed tomography directs multiple narrow beams of x-rays around the body structure being studied and uses computer imaging to produce thin cross-sectional views of various layers (or slices) of the body. It is useful for the evaluation of trauma, tumor, and foreign bodies as CT is able to visualize soft tissue as well as bones. Patients are required to remain motionless during the study and sedation may need to be administered as well as a contrast medium for image enhancement. These codes report an exam of the thorax. Techniques may vary. This exam may be performed with contrast or performed

first without contrast and again following the injection of contrast.

Coding Clarification
Assign code 87.41 to report CAT scan of the heart.

Documentation Tip
Procedures classifiable to 87.41 may be documented as a thoracic:

- C.A.T. scan
- Crystal linea scan of x-ray beam
- Electronic subtraction
- Photoelectric response
- Tomography with use of computer, x-rays, and camera

87.42   Other tomography of thorax

Description
This code describes tomography of thorax, not specified as computer axial tomography (87.41). Techniques and extent of testing may vary, including:

- **Cardiac tomogram:** Computed tomography directs multiple narrow beams of x-rays around the body structure being studied and uses computer imaging to produce thin cross-sectional views of various layers (or slices) of the body. It is useful for the evaluation of calcium deposits on the coronary tree. Patients are required to remain motionless during the study. This code reports the CT of the heart and computerized image post-processing that focuses upon evidence of calcium deposits in the coronary tree. High levels of calcium deposits in the heart triple a person's likelihood of suffering an adverse coronary event (e.g., myocardial infarct, cardiac arrest, etc.).

- **Cardiac tomogram with gating and 3D imaging:** Computed tomography (CT) of a heart with congenital anomalies, first without contrast followed by contrast, including cardiac gating and 3D image post-processing is performed to evaluate cardiac structure and morphology. CT directs multiple, thin beams of x-rays at the body and uses computer imaging to produce thin cross-sectional views of various layers of the body. It is useful in the evaluation of soft tissue. Because patients are required to be motionless during CT, this creates issues when producing CT images of the heart, which is continually moving rhythmically. In a cardiac gating technique, the patient is undergoing CT while attached to ECG leads. CT image acquisition is triggered by the ECG, allowing for coordination of imaging with periods of movement and rest within the heart.

Coding Clarification
Code 87.42 includes cardiac tomogram.

87.43   X-ray of ribs, sternum, and clavicle

Description
This procedure code describes radiological examination of the ribs, sternum and clavicle for injury or abnormality. Technique and extent of examination may vary, including:

- **Rib x-ray:** Films may be taken unilaterally of the affected side of the ribs with two views in AP (front to back) or PA (back to front) views, or of the affected side of the ribs for a minimum of three views, including the posterior ribs. Films may be taken bilaterally of the ribs for three views of the ribcage, with the patient placed supine and the x-ray directed at the thorax midpoint, above or below the xiphoid process. A minimum of four films may be taken bilaterally of the ribcage, including the posterior ribs, with the patient placed supine for AP and PA views and the x-ray directed at the thorax midpoint, above or below the xiphoid process.

- **Sternum/sternoclavicular:** Films are taken of the sternum with a minimum of two views from an anterior oblique and lateral position. Films are taken of the sternoclavicular joint or joints with a minimum of three views from posteroanterior and oblique projections.

Coding Clarification
Code 87.43 includes examination for cervical rib or fracture.

87.44   Routine chest x-ray, so described

Description
Chest x rays include radiographic views of the lungs, heart, small portions of the gastrointestinal tract, thyroid gland and thoracic skeletal structures by utilizing a form of radiation that can penetrate the body and produce an image on an x ray film. Routine chest x-rays consists of two views; frontal and lateral. The frontal view may also be referred to as posterior-anterior or PA. The patient is usually positioned standing, particularly when studying collection of fluid in the lungs. The chest x ray can be an important tool in the diagnosis of disease or trauma, to evaluate a patient's progress to medical treatment and to assist in the correct placement of chest tubes or catheters.

Coding Clarification
Code 87.44 includes x-ray of chest NOS.

87.49   Other chest x-ray

Description
This code includes other chest x-ray not classifiable elsewhere in subcategory 87.4. Technique and

extent of exam may vary. In one example, radiographs are taken of the patient's chest. This code reports special views, but does not specify number of films allowed. Specific examples may include Bucky studies and/or lateral decubitus studies, wherein the patient is prone or supine and the x-ray beam is directed through the side of the chest. This lateral projection shows change in position of fluid and reveals areas that are obscured by the fluid in standard, upright projections.

Coding Clarification
This code should not be assigned if the medical record contains sufficient information to facilitate coding at a higher level of specificity.

Code 87.49 includes x-ray of:

- Bronchus NOS
- Diaphragm NOS
- Heart NOS
- Lung NOS
- Mediastinum NOS
- Trachea NOS

Documentation Tip
If the documentation is ambiguous or unclear, the physician should be queried.

87.5   Biliary tract x-ray

Description
This subcategory classifies biliary tract x-rays, including studies specified as performed by percutaneous or intravenous techniques, also intraoperative and other exams.

87.51   Percutaneous hepatic cholangiogram

Description
The physician performs a radiographic exam of the bile tract of the gallbladder; with needle injection of contrast into the bile duct of liver. In percutaneous cholangiography, a radiographic medium is injected into the common bile duct for diagnostic purposes. The physician inserts a needle between the ribs into the lumen of the common bile duct and checks positioning by aspiration.

Coding Guidance
AHA: N-D, '87, 1; 2Q, '90, 28

87.52   Intravenous cholangiogram

Description
The physician injects a concentrated iodine-containing dye intravenously into the blood. The dye is then removed from blood by the liver which excretes it into the bile. As it is secreted into bile it provides a radio-opaque image of the bile ducts, including any gallstones that may be within

them. The gallbladder may not be visualized by IVC since the iodine-containing bile may bypass the gallbladder and empty directly into the small intestine.

87.53   Intraoperative cholangiogram

Description
In intraoperative cholangiography, the common bile duct is directly injected with radiopaque material. The surgeon removes the gallbladder. Stones appear as radiolucent shadows. Gallstones, tumors, or strictures cause partial or total obstruction of the flow of dye into the duodenum.

Coding Guidance
AHA: 4Q, '88, 7; 3Q, '89, 18; 2Q, '90, 28; 1Q, '96, 12

87.54   Other cholangiogram

Description
This code reports other cholangiogram, not specified as percutaneous, intravenous, or intraoperative.

Postoperative cholangiography is performed through an existing catheter and is used to detect retained common bile duct stones after the gallbladder has been removed, and to demonstrate good flow of bile contrast into the duodenum. Radiopaque dye is injected through a T-tube, which is a device inserted into the biliary duct and brought out through the abdominal wall after bile duct exploration and removal of the gallbladder. It allows for drainage of the bile duct and for introduction of contrast medium for postoperative radiological study of the bile duct.

87.59   Other biliary tract x-ray

Description
This code includes other biliary tract x-rays not classifiable elsewhere in subcategory 87.5.

Oral cholecystography provides radiographic visualization of the gallbladder after the oral ingestion of a radiopaque, iodinated dye that comes in the form of pills. Adequate visualization of the gallbladder requires concentration of this dye within the gallbladder. On x-ray film, the biliary calculi (gallstones) are visualized as radiolucent shadows within a dye-filled gallbladder. Gallbladder polyps and tumors occasionally also can be seen as filling defects.

Coding Clarification
This code should not be assigned if the medical record contains sufficient information to facilitate coding at a higher level of specificity.

Documentation Tip
If the documentation is ambiguous or unclear, the physician should be queried.

87.6   Other x-ray of digestive system

87.61   Barium swallow

Description
A radiologic exam is made of the upper gastrointestinal tract using fluoroscopy with a contrast material, known as barium swallow or barium "milkshake." This exam aids in diagnosing neoplasms, ulcers, obstructions, hiatal hernias and enteritis. The patient is strapped to the table and swallows the barium while standing upright. Throughout the exam, the table is tilted at various angles for differing views from the fluoroscope. For the small intestine follow-through, several hours must elapse before the contrast medium reaches the point of study in the intestine. All codes may be performed with or without glucagon, which relaxes smooth muscle found in the GI tract and inhibits the muscle motility, thereby making better quality of images.

87.62   Upper GI series

Description
Films are taken of the upper gastrointestinal tract in an anterior oblique or lateral view. Breath is held during the film taking for either view positioning. This radiological exam helps diagnose neoplasms, ulcers, obstructions, and other diseases. The series may be performed with or without delayed films and with or without a general x-ray of the mid-abdominal section.

87.63   Small bowel series

Description
This exam includes a radiologic exam of the small intestine in addition to the upper GI tract and multiple films taken in a series. The patient is face down for the small intestine films. The patient holds his or her breath during film taking.

87.64   Lower GI series

Description
This procedure involves a large bowel serial examination. Technique may vary.

A radiological exam of the large intestine is carried out after the administration of a barium enema to instill contrast into the colon. Fluoroscopy and x-rays are used to observe the image as the contrast fills the colon. This test helps to diagnose cancer, colitis, and other diseases. After the patient has emptied the colon, more films are taken. A general x-ray of the abdomen may also be performed.

In an alternate procedure, a radiological exam of the colon is carried out. The morning of the exam, a rectal bisacodyl suppository is given. One mg of glucagon may be administered through IV. Glucagon relaxes smooth muscle found in the GI tract and inhibits muscle motility, thereby making better quality of images. The rectal tip of the enema kit is inserted and a high-density barium suspension (85% w/v) is administered undiluted. The colon is distended with air and the barium, which coats the colon walls and acts as a contrast agent to enable the physician to identify any abnormalities. Fluoroscopy is used to take images of the colon walls and acts as a contrast agent to enable the physician to identify any abnormalities.

87.65   Other x-ray of intestine

Description
This procedure code includes other x-ray of the intestine not classifiable elsewhere in subcategory 87.6.

Coding Clarification
This code should not be assigned if the medical record contains sufficient information to facilitate coding at a higher level of specificity.

Documentation Tip
If the documentation is ambiguous or unclear, the physician should be queried.

87.66   Contrast pancreatogram

Description
This procedure code describes the radiological imaging obtained when the physician injects contrast through the pancreatic ducts—usually performed as part of an endoscopic retrograde cholangiopancreatography (ERCP). The physician passes the endoscope through the patient's oropharynx, esophagus, stomach, and into the small intestine. A smaller subscope is inserted through the sphincter of Oddi into the system of ducts that drain the pancreas. Contrast is injected through the catheter and images are obtained, often to test the patency of the ducts and assess for biliary obstruction or disease.

87.69   Other digestive tract x-ray

Description
This procedure code reports other digestive tract x-ray, not classifiable elsewhere in subcategory 87.6.

Coding Clarification
This code should not be assigned if the medical record contains sufficient information to facilitate coding at a higher level of specificity.

Documentation Tip
If the documentation is ambiguous or unclear, the physician should be queried.

● New Code   ▲ Revised Code   ▶◀ Revised Text   © 2010 Ingenix

87.7 X-ray of urinary system

Coding Clarification

This subcategory excludes angiography of renal vessels (88.45, 88.65).

87.71 Computerized axial tomography of kidney

Description

Computed tomography directs multiple thin beams of x-rays at the body structure being studied and uses computer imaging to produce thin cross-sectional views of various layers (or slices) of the body. It is useful for the evaluation of trauma, tumor, and foreign bodies as CT is able to visualize soft tissue as well as bones. Patients are required to remain motionless during the study and sedation may need to be administered as well as a contrast medium for image enhancement. These codes report an exam of the kidney.

87.72 Other nephrotomogram

Description

This procedure code describes other nephrotomogram not specified as computerized axial tomography (87.71). Technique may vary.

Radiographic imaging of the kidneys and ureters is done immediately following an infused intravenous drip or a rapid bolus injection of contrast agent. A front to back film of the abdomen is taken after contrast administration. Nephrotomography involves the use of x-rays taken onto film moving opposite the beams to yield a single plane shadowless image. This can be used to check the patency of a nephrostomy tube.

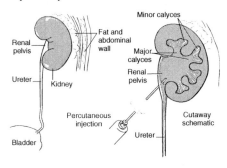

87.73 Intravenous pyelogram

Description

Radiographic imaging of the kidneys and ureters is done before and after the administration of an intravenous contrast material to identify abnormalities of the kidneys and urinary tract. Abdominal films are obtained and contrast medium is injected into a vein. Radiographs are again obtained while the contrast material is being excreted. This is also known as intravenous pyelography or IVP. This procedure may be done with or without a general abdominal x-ray, or with or without tomography, x-rays taken onto film moving opposite to the beams to yield a single plane shadowless image.

Documentation Tip:

This procedure may be documented as diuretic infusion pyelogram.

87.74 Retrograde pyelogram

Description

Radiographic imaging of the kidneys and ureters is done following retrograde (against the normal flow) administration of a radiopaque contrast material, usually barium sulfate. A catheter is passed into the bladder and on through a ureter into the kidney. The contrast material is injected through the catheter or tube. Films are taken to show the flow of contrast as it moves through the urethra and into the upper urinary tract. This may be performed with a general x-ray of the abdomen.

87.75 Percutaneous pyelogram

Description

A radiographic exam of the urinary tract is performed with injection or instillation of a contrast medium. This test is done to follow the normal flow of urine through the tract (antegrade) and may identify obstructions, abnormalities in the urinary tract, or assess function following surgery. Contrast medium is introduced percutaneously with a needle or though an existing tube, catheter, or stoma. For percutaneous needle injection, the skin is anesthetized and the needle inserted under fluoroscopic guidance into a calyx of the kidney. Contrast medium is injected and radiographs are taken.

87.76 Retrograde cystourethrogram

Description

A radiographic exam of the urethra and bladder is performed using contrast material to diagnose strictures, obstructions and abnormalities, or as postoperative functional assessments. It is most often performed on males. A balloon catheter is threaded into the urethra and the balloon is inflated. Fluoroscopy is used to aid in injecting the contrast medium through the catheter. Films are taken to show the flow of contrast as it moves retrograde (against the normal flow) through the urethra and into certain parts of the bladder. The bladder is next drained and more images may be taken of the urethra.

87.77 Other cystogram

Description
For a cystogram, a radiographic exam of the bladder with a minimum of three views is performed using contrast material to diagnose rupture, injury, or stress incontinence. A catheter is inserted into the bladder and contrast medium is instilled using mild pressure injection. The catheter is clamped after the contrast medium has filled the bladder and the bladder is fully expanded. Films are taken to observe any medium that is outside the bladder. The bladder is next drained and more films may be taken to look for other evidence of rupture following the flow of contrast outside the bladder.

Coding Clarification
This procedure code includes other cystogram not classifiable elsewhere in subcategory 87.7. Technique may vary.

87.78 Ileal conduitogram

Description
A radiographic exam of the urinary tract is performed with injection or instillation of a contrast medium. Contrast medium is introduced percutaneously with a needle or though an existing tube, catheter, or stoma. This test is done to follow the normal flow of urine through the tract (antegrade) and may identify obstructions, abnormalities in the urinary tract, or assess function following surgery. Contrast medium is injected and radiographs are taken.

Coding Guidance
AHA: M-J, '87, 11; ▶2Q, '10, 6◀

87.79 Other x-ray of the urinary system

Description
This procedure code reports other x-ray of the urinary system, not classifiable elsewhere in subcategory 87.79.

Coding Clarification
This code should not be assigned if the medical record contains sufficient information to facilitate coding at a higher level of specificity.

Documentation Tip
This procedure may also be documented as a KUB (kidney, ureter and bladder) x-ray.

87.8 X-ray of female genital organs

Description
This subcategory classifies diagnostic radiological procedures of the female genital organs; therefore, these codes are acceptable only for female patients.

87.81 X-ray of gravid uterus

Description
Although most abnormalities of the female pelvis or gravid uterus can be suspected by using clinical measurements, x-ray can assist in determining adequacy of the pelvic bony structures for a normal vaginal delivery or identify other abnormalities. However, radiographic imaging is not used often in modern obstetrics because of the risks associated with radiation.

Documentation Tip
This procedure may be documented as intrauterine cephalometry by x-ray.

87.82 Gas contrast hysterosalpingogram

Description
The physician performs a radiographic exam of the uterus and fallopian tubes with gas contrast.

87.83 Opaque dye contrast hysterosalpingogram

87.84 Percutaneous hysterogram

Description
In hysterosalpingography, the uterine cavity and fallopian tubes are visualized radiographically after the injection of contrast material through the cervix. Uterine tumors, intrauterine adhesions, and developmental anomalies can be seen. Tubal obstruction caused by internal scarring, tumor, or kinking also can be detected. A small catheter is introduced into the cervical opening and a saline solution (for saline infusion sonohysterography [SIS]) or liquid radiographic contrast material (for hysterosalpingography) is injected into the endometrial cavity with mild pressure to force the material into the fallopian tubes. The shadow of the contrast material appears on separately reported x-ray films, permitting examination of the uterus and fallopian tubes for any abnormalities or blockages. When sonohysterography is performed, a thin catheter is inserted into the uterus and one to two teaspoons of saline solution is injected into the uterine cavity. When sonohysterography is performed, a thin catheter is inserted into the uterus and one to two teaspoons of saline solution is injected into the uterine cavity. A fluid enhanced endovaginal ultrasound may be performed with the saline solution acting as a contrast medium to view any abnormal anatomic findings in the uterus.

87.85 Other x-ray of fallopian tubes and uterus

Description
The physician introduces a catheter into the cervix, and takes it into the uterus and through the fallopian tube. The catheter must be made of a material that will show on x-ray film so that any

blockages or abnormalities in the tube can be seen. The physician injects contrast material into the endometrial cavity with mild pressure to force the material into the tubes. The shadow of this material on separately reported x-ray film permits examination of the uterus and tubes for any abnormalities or blockages.

87.89   Other x-ray of female genital organs

Description
This code includes other female genital organ x-ray, not classifiable elsewhere in subcategory 87.8.

Coding Clarification
This code should not be assigned if the medical record contains sufficient information to facilitate coding at a higher level of specificity.

Documentation Tip
If the documentation is ambiguous or unclear, the physician should be queried.

87.9   X-ray of male genital organs

Description
This subcategory classifies diagnostic radiological procedures of the male genital organs. Therefore, these codes are acceptable only for male patients.

87.91   Contrast seminal vesiculogram

Description
The physician enters the vas deferens (the tube that carries spermatozoa from the testis) for purpose of testing the patency of the spermatozoa collecting system. For vesiculography the vas deferens is delivered through an incision in the scrotum, which is cleared of its coverings so that a neat incision into its lumen, preferably in long axis is made. About 5 c.c. of lipiodol is introduced through a blunted hypodermic needle and radiographs taken.

87.92   Other x-ray of prostate and seminal vesicles

87.93   Contrast epididymogram

87.94   Contrast vasogram

87.95   Other x-ray of epididymis and vas deferens

Description
The physician enters the vas deferens (the tube that carries spermatozoa from the testis) for purpose of testing the patency of the spermatozoa collecting system. A radiographic exam is done to determine obstruction in the epididymis, seminal vesicle duct, or vas deferens. Methylene blue is injected into the vas to test for obstruction of the ejaculatory duct. If

during cystoscopy, dye is seen, the ducts are patent and vesiculography may be obtained to further determine obstruction. The vas is approached through an incision in the scrotum. The testis is freed and the vas separated. After a catheter is threaded into the vas, saline or lactated Ringers are instilled to determine patency or blockage. Flow resistance may require more formal vasography, with water-soluble contrast media instilled through a ureteral catheter fed to the seminal vesicles through a dilated vas. Epididymography requires taking images of the coiled tube connecting the testis to the vas deferens.

Coding Clarification
This procedure includes diagnostic radiography of the male reproductive system by injection of contrast media. Technique and extent of exam may vary.

87.99   Other x-ray of male genital organs

Description
This code classifies other x-ray of the male genital organs not classifiable elsewhere in subcategory 87.9

Coding Clarification
This code should not be assigned if the medical record contains sufficient information to facilitate coding at a higher level of specificity.

Documentation Tip
If the documentation is ambiguous or unclear, the physician should be queried.

88   Other diagnostic radiology and related techniques

Description
This category classifies radiological procedures that serve to identify characteristics of disease processes through the use of various forms of x-ray technology. Subcategories 88.0-88.9 classify these procedures by anatomic site or as other x-ray. Within each subcategory particular diagnostic radiology techniques may be subclassified to identify specific technologies.

Coding Clarification
Use a code from the range 88.40-88.49 for digital subtraction angiography.

Do not assign a separate code for an ergonovine provocation test when done with a coronary arteriogram.

Assign 88.71 for diagnostic ultrasound of the carotid arteries. Use this code also for a transcranial Doppler with carotid duplex scans.

88.0   Soft tissue x-ray of abdomen

88.01   Computerized axial tomography of abdomen

Description
Computed tomography (C.A.T.) directs multiple thin beams of x-rays at the body structure being studied and uses computer imaging to produce thin cross-sectional views of various layers (or slices) of the body. It is useful for the evaluation of trauma, tumor, and foreign bodies as CT is able to visualize soft tissue as well as bones. Patients are required to remain motionless during the study and sedation may need to be administered as well as a contrast medium for image enhancement. These codes report an exam of the abdomen

Coding Clarification
Code 88.01 excludes C.A.T. scan of kidney (87.71)

Coding Guidance
AHA: 2Q, '98, 13

88.02   Other abdomen tomography

Description
This procedure code includes other abdominal tomography not described as computerized axial tomography.

Coding Clarification
Code 88.02 excludes nephrotomogram (87.72).

Tomography is an x-ray that produces a cross-section image of a solid object by specific planes.

88.03   Sinogram of abdominal wall

Description
The physician performs a radiographic exam of an abnormal abdominal passage. An injection of radiopaque material is made directly into a sinus tract (a canal or passage leading to an abscess) or through a previously placed catheter, to determine the existence, nature, or size of an abscess or fistula (an abnormal tube-like passage from a normal body cavity to a free surface or to another body cavity).

Documentation Tip
This procedure may also be documented as a fistulogram of the abdominal wall.

88.04   Abdominal lymphangiogram

Description
The physician performs a radiographic exam of abdominal lymphatic vessels with contrast. Vital blue dye is injected into the subcutaneous tissues for outlining of skin lymphatics. As soon as the lymphatic vessels are visualized by their blue color, the physician makes a small incision to gain access. The lymph vessel is cannulated with a needle and a fine catheter is attached. A small amount of dye is injected to ensure correct placement and the needle is advanced a few millimeters into the vessel. The needle and catheter are secured and dye is injected with a syringe. X-ray images are recorded.

88.09   Other soft tissue x-ray of abdominal wall

Description
Films are taken of the abdominal cavity in one view from front to back. Because an abdominal x-ray usually precedes another diagnostic imaging procedure, it is not coded separately unless performed as a separately identifiable examination.

Coding Clarification
This code describes other abdominal wall soft tissue x-ray, not classifiable elsewhere in subcategory 88.0. Technique and extent of procedure may vary.

88.1   Other x-ray of abdomen

Description
This subcategory classifies other abdominal x-rays, not classifiable to soft tissue x-ray (88.0x). Procedures in this subcategory are subclassified by a fourth digit, which indicates the anatomic site of study as:

- Pelvic
- Peritoneal
- Retroperitoneal
- Other

Fourth-digit subclassifications in category 88.1 also serve to specify the technique utilized (e.g., opaque dye contrast, gas contrast, etc.).

88.11   Pelvic opaque dye contrast radiography

88.12   Pelvic gas contrast radiography

88.13   Other peritoneal pneumogram

Description
A radiographic exam is done on the peritoneal cavity to define the pattern of air in the cavity after injection of air or contrast. The physician inserts a needle or catheter in to the peritoneal cavity and injects air (gas) or contrast as a diagnostic procedure. X-rays are taken. The needle or catheter is removed.

88.14   Retroperitoneal fistulogram

Description
An injection of radiopaque material is made directly into a sinus tract (a canal or passage leading to an abscess) or through a previously placed catheter, to determine the existence, nature, or size of an abscess or fistula (an abnormal tube-like passage from a normal body cavity to a free surface or to another body cavity).

● New Code   ▲ Revised Code   ▶◀ Revised Text   © 2010 Ingenix

88.15   Retroperitoneal pneumogram

Description
A radiographic exam is done on the retroperitoneal space to define the pattern of air in the cavity after injection of air or contrast. The physician inserts a needle or catheter in to the retroperitoneal space and injects air (gas) or contrast as a diagnostic procedure. X-rays are taken. The needle or catheter is removed.

88.16   Other retroperitoneal x-ray

Description
This procedure code includes other retroperitoneal x-ray not classifiable elsewhere in subcategory 88.1.

Coding Clarification
This code should not be assigned if the medical record contains sufficient information to facilitate coding at a higher level of specificity.

Documentation Tip
If the documentation is ambiguous or unclear, the physician should be queried.

88.19   Other x-ray of abdomen

Description
This procedure code reports other abdominal x-ray not classifiable elsewhere in subcategory 88.1. In one example, films are taken of the abdominal cavity in one view from front to back. Because an abdominal x-ray usually precedes another diagnostic imaging procedure, it is not coded separately unless performed as a separately identifiable examination.

Coding Clarification
This code should not be assigned if the medical record contains sufficient information to facilitate coding at a higher level of specificity.

Documentation Tip
If the documentation is ambiguous or unclear, the physician should be queried.

Coding Guidance
   AHA: 3Q, '99, 9

88.2   Skeletal x-ray of extremities and pelvis

Description
This subcategory describes skeletal s-rays of the extremities and pelvis.

Coding Clarification
Subcategory 88.2 excludes contrast radiogram of joint (88.32).

88.21   Skeletal x-ray of shoulder and upper arm

Description
Films are taken of the shoulder and upper arm. The patient is supine with the arm extended to a 90 degree angle from the body and externally rotated while the head is turned to face opposite the affected side.

88.22   Skeletal x-ray of elbow and forearm

Description
A radiologic examination of the elbow joint is made. Films of the elbow may be taken in the AP position with the hand supinated, oblique positioning with the hand pronated and/or externally rotated, and in the lateral position with the wrist lateral and the elbow flexed at 90 degrees.

88.23   Skeletal x-ray of wrist and hand

Description
A radiologic examination of the wrist is made in either in posteroanterior, oblique, or lateral views. Alternately, a radiologic exam of the hand is made with films being taken in the PA (posteroanterior), internal or external oblique, or lateral positions

88.24   Skeletal x-ray of upper limb, not otherwise specified

Description
Code 88.24 describes a radiologic exam of the upper limb that is not more specifically described by codes 88.21-88.23.

88.25   Pelvimetry

Description
Although most abnormalities of the female pelvis can be suspected by using clinical measurements, x-ray pelvimetry is the most accurate means of determining adequacy of the pelvic bony structures for a normal vaginal delivery. With pelvimetry, comparison is made with the capacity of the pelvis to the size of the infant's head, in order to discover any disproportion. However, radiographic pelvimetry is not used often in modern obstetrics because of the risks associated with radiation.

88.26   Other skeletal x-ray of pelvis and hip

Description
One or two views are taken of the pelvis. The most common view is from front to back (AP) with the patient lying supine with feet inverted 15 degrees to overcome the anteversion (or rotation) of the femoral necks. The pelvic girdle, femoral head, neck, trochanters, and upper femurs may also be shown.

One or more films are taken of the hip. For a front to back (AP) view, the patient is placed supine with the toes on the affected side inverted. For a frogleg view, the affected hip is flexed with the knee bent.

88.27 Skeletal x-ray of thigh, knee, and lower leg

Description
This procedure involves skeletal x-ray of the lower limb, which may be performed in sections, such as:

- **X-ray of femur:** Two films only are taken of the femur, or thigh bone, the longest and largest in the body. In the front to back or lateral views, the x-ray beam is aimed at the midshaft. For the AP (front to back) view, the patient is supine with the foot turned inward a few degrees. For a lateral view, the patient is placed laterally with the knee flexed and the affected side down.

- **X-ray of knee:** The patient is positioned for the desired view(s) of the knee and x-ray films are taken. Films may include one or two views, three views or a complete exam of the knee with a minimum of four views.

- **X-ray of tibia and fibula:** At a minimum, two films of the lower leg bones are usually taken. The physician interprets and reports the findings.

88.28 Skeletal x-ray of ankle and foot

Description
Two films may be taken of the ankle, or a complete radiologic exam with three or more films. The physician interprets and reports the findings.

88.29 Skeletal x-ray of lower limb, not otherwise specified

Description
This procedure code includes other skeletal x-ray of the lower limb, not classifiable elsewhere in subcategory 88.2.

Coding Clarification
This code should not be assigned if the medical record contains sufficient information to facilitate coding at a higher level of specificity.

Documentation Tip
If the documentation is ambiguous or unclear, the physician should be queried.

88.3 Other x-ray

Description
This subcategory lists other x-ray procedures not classifiable elsewhere in category 88.

88.31 Skeletal series

Description
This procedure involves a radiological exam of the total skeleton. Technique may vary, depending on the type of exam and indications, including:

- **Bone length studies (orthoroentgenogram):** Bone length studies accurately measure the length of the long bones in the skeleton. Typically, four film exposures are performed during a scanogram, as it is usually called. Views of the hip, leg, knee, and ankle are usually taken. However, there is no number or type of views specified for this code.

- **Osseous survey, axial and appendicular skeleton:** A radiologic exam is performed in which the axial (head and trunk) and appendicular (extremities) skeleton is surveyed for evidence of metastatic disease. It may also be performed on children to identify current and/or old healed fractures in the case of suspected child abuse. This procedure is rarely performed for metastatic disease, having been replaced by nuclear bone scanning, which is more precise method of study for diagnosing metastases.

88.32 Contrast arthrogram

Description
This procedure is a diagnostic imaging procedure of a joint structure using radiopaque contrast injection.

The synovial joint of the shoulder is visualized internally through arthrography, the direct injection of air and/or contrast material into the joint for radiological examination. Local anesthesia in injected into the joint followed by the contrast material and/or air. A series of images are taken and interpreted. Fluoroscopic films and guidance for needle localization is included. Arthrography helps diagnose conditions of cartilage abnormalities, arthritis and bursitis, rotator cuff tear, and frozen joint. AP (front to back) views are taken with the affected arm rotated externally and internally and with the arm in a neutral, flexed position lying over the abdomen.

Coding Clarification
Code 88.32 excludes arthrography of the temporomandibular joint (87.13).

88.33 Other skeletal x-ray

Description
This code reports other skeletal x-ray not classifiable elsewhere in category 88.

Coding Clarification
This code should not be assigned if the medical record contains sufficient information to facilitate coding at a higher level of specificity.

Code 88.33 lists multiple exclusions. Skeletal x-ray procedures of the following anatomic sties are appropriately classified elsewhere:

- Extremities and pelvis (88.21-88.29)

- Face, head, and neck (87.11-87.17)

● New Code ▲ Revised Code ▶◀ Revised Text © 2010 Ingenix

- Spine (87.21-87.29)
- Thorax (87.43)

Documentation Tip
If the documentation is ambiguous or unclear, the physician should be queried.

88.34 Lymphangiogram of upper limb

Description
Vital blue dye is injected into the subcutaneous tissues for outlining of skin lymphatics. As soon as the lymphatic vessels are visualized by their blue color, the physician makes a small incision to gain access. The lymph vessel is cannulated with a needle and a fine catheter is attached. A small amount of dye is injected to ensure correct placement and the needle is advanced a few millimeters into the vessel. The needle and catheter are secured and dye is injected with a syringe. X-rays are made. This code reports lymphangiography of an upper extremity.

88.35 Other soft tissue x-ray of upper limb

Description
This code includes other soft tissue x-ray of the upper limb not classifiable elsewhere in category 88.

Coding Clarification
X-rays described as "skeletal" are more appropriately classified elsewhere, by type and site.

This code should not be assigned if the medical record contains sufficient information to facilitate coding at a higher level of specificity.

Documentation Tip
If the documentation is ambiguous or unclear, the physician should be queried.

88.36 Lymphangiogram of lower limb

Description
Vital blue dye is injected into the subcutaneous tissues for outlining of skin lymphatics. As soon as the lymphatic vessels are visualized by their blue color, the physician makes a small incision to gain access. The lymph vessel is cannulated with a needle and a fine catheter is attached. A small amount of dye is injected to ensure correct placement and the needle is advanced a few millimeters into the vessel. The needle and catheter are secured and dye is injected with a syringe. X-rays are made. This code reports lymphangiography of a lower extremity.

88.37 Other soft tissue x-ray of lower limb

Description
Code 88.37 inlcudes other soft tissue x-ray of the lower limb not classifiable elsewhere in category 88.

Coding Clarification
X-rays described as "skeletal" are more appropriately classified elsewhere, by type and site.

Code 88.37 excludes femoral angiography (88.48, 88.66).

This code should not be assigned if the medical record contains sufficient information to facilitate coding at a higher level of specificity.

Documentation Tip
If the documentation is ambiguous or unclear, the physician should be queried.

88.38 Other computerized axial tomography

Description
This procedure code describes other computerized axial tomography (C.A.T. scan) procedure not classifiable elsewhere in categories 88 or 87.

Coding Clarification
This code should not be assigned if the medical record contains sufficient information to facilitate coding at a higher level of specificity.

Code 88.38 excludes C.A.T. scans of the following specific anatomic sites:

- Abdomen (88.01)
- Head (87.03)
- Heart (87.41)
- Kidney (87.71)
- Thorax (87.41)

Documentation Tip
If the documentation is ambiguous or unclear, the physician should be queried.

Coding Guidance
　　AHA: 3Q, '05, 13-14

88.39 X-ray, other and unspecified

Description
This procedure code reports other and unspecified x-ray procedures not classifiable elsewhere in categories 88 or 87.

Coding Clarification
This code should not be assigned if the medical record contains sufficient information to facilitate coding at a higher level of specificity.

Documentation Tip
If the documentation is ambiguous or unclear, the physician should be queried.

88.4 Arteriography using contrast material

Description
This subcategory classifies arteriography by injection of a radiopaque contrast. Fourth-digit

subclassifications within this category identify the site of study, not the site of injection.

Coding Clarification
Use a code from the range 88.40–88.49 for digital subtraction angiography.

Subcategory 88.4 includes:

- Angiography of arteries
- Arterial puncture for injection of contrast material
- Radiography of arteries (by fluoroscopy)
- Retrograde arteriography

Subcategory 88.4 excludes arteriography using:

- Radioisotopes or radionuclides (92.01-92.19)
- Ultrasound (88.71-88.79)
- Fluorescein angiography of eye (95.12)

Coding Guidance
AHA: N-D, '85, 14

88.40 Arteriography using contrast material, unspecified site

Description
This code describes contrast arteriography of unspecified site.

Coding Clarification
This code should not be assigned if the medical record contains sufficient information to facilitate coding at a higher level of specificity.

Documentation Tip
If the documentation is ambiguous or unclear, the physician should be queried.

88.41 Arteriography of cerebral arteries

Description
The injection site (usually in the leg) is prepped and anesthetized. The access artery is punctured, and a needle is inserted into the artery. A long flexible catheter is inserted through the needle into the artery. The catheter is threaded through the large, main vessels of the abdomen and chest until it is placed into the arteries of neck selected for study. Contrast is injected into the selected vessels, and the x-ray images are recorded, and the needle and catheter are removed.

Documentation Tip:
Angiography classifiable to 88.41 may be documented as:

- Basilar artery
- Carotid (internal)
- Posterior cerebral circulation
- Vertebral artery

Coding Guidance
AHA: 1Q, '97, 3; 1Q, '99, 7; 1Q, '00, 16

88.42 Aortography

Description
The access area is prepped and anesthetized. A vascular access catheter is inserted through a small incision in upper extremity or groin artery. The catheter is guided by fluoroscopic imaging and threaded into the aorta. When the catheter is in place, dye is injected to make the aorta visible. X-ray images are recorded, and the needle and catheter are removed.

Coding Clarification
Code 88.42 includes arteriography of aorta and aortic arch.

Coding Guidance
AHA: 1Q, '99, 7; ▶2Q, '10, 9◀

88.43 Arteriography of pulmonary arteries

Description
The access area is prepped and anesthetized. A vascular access catheter is inserted through a small incision, usually a vein in the groin. The catheter is guided by fluoroscopic imaging and threaded through the aorta and cardiac chambers to the pulmonary artery. When the catheter is in place, dye is injected into the pulmonary arteries. X-ray images are recorded, and the needle and catheter are removed.

88.44 Arteriography of other intrathoracic vessels

Description
The access area is prepped and anesthetized. A vascular access catheter is inserted through a small incision, usually a vessel in the groin or upper extremity. The catheter is guided by fluoroscopic imaging and threaded through to the selected intra thoracic blood vessel. When the catheter is in place, dye is injected. X-ray images are recorded, and the needle and catheter are removed.

Coding Clarification
Code 88.44 excludes angiocardiography (88.50-88.58) and coronary arteriography (88.55-88.57).

88.45 Arteriography of renal arteries

Description
The access area is prepped and anesthetized. A vascular access catheter is inserted through a small incision, usually an artery in the groin region. The catheter is guided by fluoroscopic imaging and threaded through the pelvic vessels and the aorta to renal artery. When the catheter is in place, dye is

injected. X-ray images are recorded, and the needle and catheter are removed.

88.46   Arteriography of placenta

Description
The physician takes a radiographic image of the vessels of the placenta after injection of radiopaque contrast.

88.47   Arteriography of other intraabdominal arteries

Description
The access area is prepped and anesthetized. A vascular access catheter is inserted through a small incision, usually an artery in the groin. The catheter is guided by fluoroscopic imaging and threaded through to the selected intra abdominal blood vessel. When the catheter is in place, dye is injected. X-ray images are recorded, and the needle and catheter are removed.

Coding Guidance
AHA: N-D, '87, 4; 1Q, '00, 18

88.48   Arteriography of femoral and other lower extremity arteries

Description
A local anesthetic is applied over an access artery; usually the femoral artery. The artery is percutaneously punctured with a needle and a guidewire is fed through the artery to the point of study. A catheter is threaded over the guidewire until it, too, reaches the point of study and the guidewire is removed. Contrast medium is injected through the catheter and a series of x-rays or fluoroscopic images taken to visualize the vessels and evaluate any abnormalities. The catheter is removed and pressure applied to the site.

Coding Guidance
AHA: 2Q, '89, 17; 2Q, '96, 6; 1Q, '03, 17; 3Q, '03, 10; 2Q, '06, 23

88.49   Arteriography of other specified sites

Description
This code reports arteriography of other specified site not classifiable elsewhere in subcategory 88.4.

Coding Clarification
This code should not be assigned if the medical record contains sufficient information to facilitate coding at a higher level of specificity.

Documentation Tip
If the documentation is ambiguous or unclear, the physician should be queried.

Coding Guidance
AHA: ▶2Q, '10, 9◀

88.5   Angiocardiography using contrast material

Description
This subcategory classifies diagnostic radiological imaging of the vasculature of the heart by injection of a radiopaque contrast. Fourth-digit subclassifications within this category identify the specific anatomic site of study.

Coding Clarification
This subcategory includes arterial puncture and catheterization for injection of contrast media, cineangiocardiography, and selective angiocardiography.

Code also synchronous cardiac catheterization (37.21-37.23).

This subcategory excludes angiography of pulmonary vessels (88.43, 88.62).

Coding Guidance
AHA: 3Q, '08, 18

88.50   Angiocardiography, not otherwise specified

Description
This code describes contrast coronary angiocardiography, without further specification to the anatomic site of study.

Coding Clarification
This code should not be assigned if the medical record contains sufficient information to facilitate coding at a higher level of specificity.

Documentation Tip
If the documentation is ambiguous or unclear, the physician should be queried.

88.51   Angiocardiography of venae cavae

Description
A local anesthetic is applied over a distal vein (typically antecubital, internal jugular, subclavian, or femoral) and the vein is percutaneously punctured with a needle. A guidewire is fed through the vein to the inferior vena cava and the superior vena cava. The physician may slide an introducer sheath over the guidewire into the venous lumen before inserting a catheter. The catheter is inserted into the vein and threaded over the guidewire to the inferior or superior vena cava. The guidewire is removed. Contrast medium is injected and a series of x-rays performed to visualize and evaluate any abnormalities. In venography, contrast medium is injected into the catheter that has traveled to an area upstream of the site under investigation.

Documentation Tip
This procedure may also be documented as:

*   Inferior vena cavography
*   Phlebography of vena cava (inferior) (superior)

88.52   Angiocardiography of right heart structures

Description
The physician injects dye through a previously placed and separately reportable catheter threaded through a central line. This procedure includes injecting dye into the right ventricle or atrium to evaluate function with fluoroscopy. The catheter is removed and pressure applied to the wound. Any required repositioning of catheters or use of automatic power injectors is included in this procedure.

Coding Clarification
Code 88.52 includes angiocardiography of:

*   Pulmonary valve

*   Right atrium

*   Right ventricle (outflow tract)

Code 88.52 excludes that combined with left heart angiocardiography (88.54) and intraoperative fluorescence vascular angiography (88.59).

Coding Guidance
    AHA: 1Q, '07, 16

88.53   Angiocardiography of left heart structures

Description
The physician injects dye through a previously placed and separately reportable catheter threaded through a central line. This procedure includes injecting dye into the left ventricle or atrium to evaluate function with fluoroscopy. The catheter is removed and pressure applied to the wound. Any required repositioning of catheters or use of automatic power injectors is included in this procedure.

Coding Clarification
Code 88.53 includes angiocardiography of:

*   Aortic valve

*   Left atrium

*   Left ventricle (outflow tract)

Code 88.53 excludes that combined with right heart angiocardiography (88.54) and intraoperative fluorescence vascular angiography (88.59).

Coding Guidance
    AHA: 4Q, '88, 4; 1Q, '00, 20; 3Q, '05, 14; 4Q, '05, 71; 1Q, '07, 11, 17

88.54   Combined right and left heart angiocardiography

Description
The physician injects dye through a previously placed and separately reportable catheter threaded through a central line. This code applies to injecting dye into the right ventricle or atrium and the left ventricle or atrium to evaluate function with

fluoroscopy. The catheter is removed and pressure applied to the wound. Any required repositioning of catheters or use of automatic power injectors is included in this procedure.

88.55   Coronary arteriography using single catheter

88.56   Coronary arteriography using two catheters

Description
A diagnostic angiography is the x-ray visualization of the heart and blood vessels after the introduction of a radiopaque contrast medium. Technique and extent of exam may vary. The physician may employ Sones technique, utilizing a single catheter (88.55) or Judkins, Abrams or Ricketts technique utilizing two catheters (88.56) Testing for patient hypersensitivity to the iodine content of the medium is advised before the radiopaque substance is used. The physician injects the contrast medium into a catheter inserted into a peripheral artery and threaded through the vessel to the visceral site. This code reports imaging and injection procedures of the coronary arteries.

Coding Clarification
Code 88.56 includes angiocardiography described as:

*   Coronary arteriography by Sones technique

*   Direct selective coronary arteriography using a single catheter

Coding Guidance
    AHA: 4Q, '88, 4; 1Q, '00, 20; 3Q, '02, 20; 2Q, '06, 25-26; 3Q, '06, 8

88.57   Other and unspecified coronary arteriography

Description
This procedure code includes other an unspecified coronary arteriography not classifiable elsewhere in subcategory 88.5.

Coding Clarification
This code should not be assigned if the medical record contains sufficient information to facilitate coding at a higher level of specificity.

Documentation Tip
If the documentation is ambiguous or unclear, the physician should be queried.

Coding Guidance
    AHA: 1Q, '00, 21; 2Q, '05, 17; 3Q, '05, 14; 4Q, '05, 71; 2Q, '06, 25; 1Q, '07, 15

88.58   Negative-contrast cardiac roentgenography

Coding Clarification
Roentgenography is defined as photographic images using x-ray technology.

● New Code   ▲ Revised Code   ▶◀ Revised Text   © 2010 Ingenix

Code 88.58 includes cardiac roentgenography with injection of carbon dioxide.

▲ 88.59   Intra-operative coronary fluorescence vascular angiography

Description
SPY intraoperative fluorescence vascular angiography (or SPY angiography) is an imaging technology used to test cardiac graft patency and technical adequacy at the time of coronary artery bypass grafting (CABG). The SPY images are generated from the fluorescence excitation of indocyanine green (IC-Green™) dye that is injected into the bloodstream via an existing central venous catheter, or into the cardiopulmonary bypass circuit. The IC-Green™ rapidly binds to plasma proteins in blood when injected into the bloodstream and is confined to the intravascular compartment. This imaging sequence is repeated for each graft placed during the CABG procedure. Images can readily be obtained regardless of whether the patient is operated upon with a conventional cardiopulmonary bypass supported approach or done as an off pump coronary artery bypass (OPCAB) procedure. Prior to closing the chest, a final image of the grafts encompassing the proximal anastomoses is typically performed. This image evaluates all of the grafts with the heart in its normal anatomic position. The same visual assessment described above is conducted, to confirm that the bypass grafts are not kinked, twisted or stretched in their natural anatomic position. If there are no abnormalities noted and the image indicates a technically adequate result, the surgeon confirms that the assessment process is complete.

Coding Clarification
Code 88.59 includes:

- Intraoperative laser arteriogram (SPY)
- SPY arteriogram
- SPY arteriography

▶Code 88.59 excludes intra-operative noncoronary fluorescence vascular angiography (IFVA), which is assigned code 17.71.◀

Coding Scenario
A patient was admitted for coronary artery bypass grafting (CABG). During the procedure, the physician used intraoperative fluorescence vascular angiography first to locate the vessel and again after the bypass graft to assess the quality of the anastomosis and graft patency. The physician performed a final image prior to closing the chest to evaluate all of the grafts with the heart in its normal anatomic position.

Code Assignment:

36.11   Aortocoronary bypass of one coronary artery

88.59   Intraoperative fluorescence vascular angiography using SPY technique
39.61   Extracorporeal circulation auxiliary to open heart surgery

Coding Guidance
AHA: 4Q, 07, 121

88.6   Phlebography

Description
This subcategory classifies phlebography by injection of a radiopaque contrast. Fourth-digit subclassifications within this category identify the site of study, not the site of injection.

Coding Clarification
Phlebography is electromagnetic wave photography of veins with contrast.

Subcategory 88.6 includes:

- Angiography of veins
- Radiography of veins (by fluoroscopy)
- Retrograde phlebography
- Venipuncture for injection of contrast material
- Venography using contrast material

Subcategory 88.6 excludes:

- Angiography using radioisotopes or radionuclides (92.01-92.19) or ultrasound (88.71-88.79)
- Fluorescein angiography of eye (95.12)

88.60   Phlebography using contrast material, unspecified site

88.61   Phlebography of veins of head and neck using contrast material

88.62   Phlebography of pulmonary veins using contrast material

88.63   Phlebography of other intrathoracic veins using contrast material

88.64   Phlebography of the portal venous system using contrast material

88.65   Phlebography of other intraabdominal veins using contrast material

88.66   Phlebography of femoral and other lower extremity veins using contrast material

88.67   Phlebography of other specified sites using contrast material

Description
A local anesthetic is applied over the site where the catheter is to be introduced and the access vein is

percutaneously punctured with a needle. A guidewire is inserted and advanced through the vein until it reaches the desired location in the venous system for imaging. A catheter is threaded over the guidewire to the selected point and the wire is removed. Non-ionic diluted contrast medium is injected over approximately 30 seconds through the catheter that has traveled to an area upstream of the site under investigation. Images are acquired.

Coding Guidance
AHA: 2Q, '06, 23; 3Q, '08, 18

88.68   Impedance phlebography

Description
This procedure is a test used to measure blood volume in the lower leg. A pneumatic cuff is placed around the thigh and inflated to sufficient pressure to cut off venous flow but not arterial flow. This pressure causes the venous blood pressure to rise until it equals the pressure under the cuff. The cuff is released, resulting in a rapid venous runoff and a return to the resting blood volume. The presence of venous thrombosis will alter the normal response in a highly characteristic way, causing a delay in venous emptying after the release of the tourniquet.

Coding Clarification
Impedance phlebography is a non-invasive medical test that measures blood volume changes, which may assist in diagnosis of venous thrombosis.

88.7   Diagnostic ultrasound

Description
This subcategory classifies diagnostic imaging by ultrasound technology. Fourth-digit subclassifications within this subcategory identify the anatomic site of study.

Coding Clarification
A diagnostic ultrasound is a graphic recording of anatomical structures via high frequency, sound-wave imaging and computer graphics.

Subcategory 88.7 includes:

- Echography
- Non-invasive ultrasound
- Ultrasonic angiography
- Ultrasonography

Subcategory 88.7 excludes:

- Intravascular imaging (adjunctive) (IVUS) (00.21-00.29)
- Therapeutic ultrasound (00.01-00.09)

88.71	Diagnostic ultrasound of head and neck
88.72	Diagnostic ultrasound of heart
88.73	Diagnostic ultrasound of other sites of thorax
88.74	Diagnostic ultrasound of digestive system
88.75	Diagnostic ultrasound of urinary system
88.76	Diagnostic ultrasound of abdomen and retroperitoneum
88.77	Diagnostic ultrasound of peripheral vascular system
88.78	Diagnostic ultrasound of gravid uterus

88.79   Other diagnostic ultrasound

Description
Diagnostic ultrasound is an imaging technique bouncing sound waves far above the level of human perception through interior body structures. The sound waves pass through different densities of tissue and reflect back to a receiving unit at varying speeds. The unit converts the waves to electrical pulses that are immediately displayed in picture form on screen. Real time scanning displays structure images and movement with time.

Coding Guidance
AHA: 1Q, '92, 11; 1Q, '02, 10; 4Q, '08, 125; ▶2Q, '10, 7◀

88.8   Thermography

Description
This subcategory reports thermography procedures. Thermography is infrared photography to determine various body temperatures. Fourth-digit subclassifications within this subcategory identify the anatomic site of study.

88.81	Cerebral thermography
88.82	Ocular thermography
88.83	Bone thermography
88.84	Muscle thermography
88.85	Breast thermography
88.86	Blood vessel thermography
88.89	Thermography of other sites

Description
A thermogram is a method of recording the body's heat differentials, often in relation to blood flow. In

most cases, this technique is performed with a camera called a thermograph, which identifies hot and cold by color-coding the image.

88.9   Other diagnostic imaging

Description
This subcategory includes other diagnostic imaging procedures including magnetic resonance imaging (MRI) and bone mineral density studies. Fourth-digit subclassifications within this subcategory identify the anatomic site of study for MRI procedures and present additional coding options not classifiable elsewhere in category 88.

88.90   Diagnostic imaging, not elsewhere classified

Description
This procedure code reports diagnostic imaging procedures not classifiable elsewhere in category 88.

Coding Clarification
This code should not be assigned if the medical record contains sufficient information to facilitate coding at a higher level of specificity.

Documentation Tip
If the documentation is ambiguous or unclear, the physician should be queried.

Coding Guidance
   AHA: 2Q, '06, 25-26

88.91   Magnetic resonance imaging of brain and brain stem

88.92   Magnetic resonance imaging of chest and myocardium for evaluation of hilar and mediastinal lymphadenopathy

88.93   Magnetic resonance imaging of spinal canal

88.94   Magnetic resonance imaging of musculoskeletal structures

88.95   Magnetic resonance imaging of pelvis, prostate, and bladder

88.96   Other intraoperative magnetic resonance imaging

88.97   Magnetic resonance imaging of other and unspecified sites

Description
Magnetic resonance imaging (MRI) is a radiation-free, noninvasive, technique to produce high quality sectional images of the inside of the body in multiple planes. MRI uses the natural magnetic properties of the hydrogen atoms in our bodies that emit radiofrequency signals when exposed to radio waves within a strong

electro-magnetic field. These signals are processed and converted by the computer into high-resolution, three-dimensional, tomographic images. Patients with metallic or electronic implants or foreign bodies cannot be exposed to MRI. The patient must remain still while lying on a motorized table within the large, circular MRI tunnel. A sedative may be administered as well as contrast material for image enhancement.

Coding Clarification
Codes 88.91-88.97 exclude laser interstitial thermal therapy (LITT) under guidance for lesions or tissue of the brain (17.61), breast (17.69), lung (17.69), prostate (17.69), and other unspecified sites (17.69).

Coding Guidance
   AHA: 4Q, '02, 111; ▶2Q, '10, 13◀

88.98   Bone mineral density studies

Description
This procedure code classifies bone mineral density studies. Technique may vary, including:

- **Dual photon absorptiometry:** An x-ray density study is performed to measure the patient's bone mass. Bone mineral density is evaluated as a screening test for osteoporosis, to evaluate diseases of bone, and to review the responses of bone disease to treatment. Densities can be measured at the wrist, radius, hip, pelvis, spine, or heel. Dual energy x-ray absorptiometry (DEXA) is a two-dimensional projection system that involves two x-ray beams with different levels of energy being pulsed alternately. The results are given in two scores reported as standard deviations from bone density of a person 30 years of age, which is the age of peak bone mass.

- **Quantitative computed tomography (CT) studies:** A CT density study is performed to measure the patient's bone mass. Bone mineral density is evaluated as a screening test for osteoporosis, to evaluate diseases of bone, and to review the responses of bone disease to treatment. Densities can be measured at the wrist, hip, spine, or calcaneus. The studies assess bone mass or density associated with such diseases as osteoporosis, osteomalacia, and renal osteodystrophy. This particular bone density study uses computerized tomography (CT) for the imaging modality. CT directs multiple, narrow beams of x-rays around the body structure being studied and uses computer imaging to produce thin cross-sectional views of various layers (or slices) of the body.

- **Radiographic densitometry:** Bone mineral density studies are used to evaluate diseases of bone and/or the responses of bone disease to treatment. Densities are measured at the wrist, hip, spine, or calcaneus. The studies assess bone mass or density associated with such diseases as osteoporosis, osteomalacia, and renal osteodystrophy. Photodensitometry, or radiographic absorptiometry, provides a quantitative measurement of the bone mineral density of the cortical bone (outer layer) by taking two radiographs with direct exposure film at different settings. This procedure is done to monitor for gross bone changes as occurs with osteoporosis.

- **Single photon absorptiometry:** Single photon absorptiometry is a noninvasive technique to measure the absorption of the monochromatic photon beam by bone material. The painless study device is placed directly on the patient and uses a small amount of radionuclide to measure the bone mass absorption efficiency of the energy used. This provides a quantitative measurement of the bone mineral density of cortical bone in diseases like osteoporosis and can be used to assess an individual's response to treatment at different intervals.

89 Interview, evaluation, consultation, and examination

Description
This category includes a number of different types of procedures including diagnostic interview and evaluation, consultations, anatomic and physiologic measurements and manual examinations, nonoperative cardiac and vascular diagnostic tests, circulatory monitoring, general physical examination, and autopsy.

89.0 Diagnostic interview, consultation, and evaluation

Coding Clarification
Subcategory 89.0 excludes psychiatric diagnostic interview (94.11-94.19).

89.01 Interview and evaluation, described as brief

Description
This procedure code reports a diagnostic interview or evaluation for the purpose of obtaining patient history and assessing characteristics including signs and symptoms in order to identify disease processes and determine course of treatment. This code classifies such diagnostic interviews and evaluations described as brief or abbreviated.

89.02 Interview and evaluation, described as limited

Description
This procedure code involves a diagnostic interview or evaluation for the purpose of obtaining patient history and assessing characteristics including signs and symptoms in order to identify disease processes and determine course of treatment. This code classifies such diagnostic interviews and evaluations described as interval or limited.

89.03 Interview and evaluation, described as comprehensive

Description
This procedure code describes a diagnostic interview or evaluation for the purpose of obtaining patient history and assessing characteristics including signs and symptoms in order to identify disease processes and determine course of treatment. This code classifies such diagnostic interviews and evaluations described as comprehensive, including history or evaluation of a new sign, symptom or problem necessitating investigation.

89.04 Other interview and evaluation

89.05 Diagnostic interview and evaluation, not otherwise specified

Description
These procedures are diagnostic interviews or evaluations for the purpose of obtaining patient history and assessing characteristics including signs and symptoms in order to identify disease processes and determine course of treatment. These codes classify such diagnostic interviews and evaluations which are not specifically quantifiable as brief, limited or comprehensive (89.05) and those which are not classifiable elsewhere in subcategory 89.0 (89.04).

89.06 Consultation, described as limited

Description
This procedure is an interview or evaluation for the purpose of providing an opinion or other information which assists a physician in identifying disease and determination of the course of treatment. This code classifies such consultation interviews and evaluations described as limited or of a single organ system.

89.07 Consultation, described as comprehensive

Description
This procedure code describes an interview or evaluation for the purpose of providing an opinion or other information which assists a physician in identifying disease and determination of the course of treatment. This code classifies such consultation

interviews and evaluations described as comprehensive.

89.08   Other consultation

89.09   Consultation, not otherwise specified

Description

These codes describe an interview or evaluation for the purpose of providing an opinion or other information which assists a physician in identifying disease and determination of the course of treatment. These codes classify such consultation interviews and evaluations which are not specifically quantifiable as limited or comprehensive (89.09) and those which are not classifiable elsewhere in subcategory 89.0 (89.08).

89.1   Anatomic and physiologic measurements and manual examinations — nervous system and sense organs

Coding Clarification

Subcategory 89.1 excludes:

- Ear examination (95.41-95.49)

- Eye examination (95.01-95.26)

- The listed procedures when done as part of a general physical examination (89.7)

89.10   Intracarotid amobarbital test

Description

The physician places sensors on a patient's head in an electroencephalogram (EEG) to measure and record the brain's electrical activity. Amobarbital is injected into the internal carotid artery to induce hemiparalysis in order to determine the hemisphere that controls speech and language or memory. Test stimuli will be presented to the patient while he/she is hemiparetic. Approximately 10 minutes after the initial anesthetic injection, recall and recognition of presented material will be assessed.

Documentation Tip

Procedures classifiable to this code may be documented as Wada activation test, which is used to evaluate function of the brain hemispheres.

89.11   Tonometry

Description

This procedure is a test that measures pressure or tension. Although some pressure and tension measurements may be obtained by other means, ICD-9-CM currently assumes tonometry of an ocular site.

In a healthy eye's anterior chamber, aqueous humor is continually drained and renewed to maintain a constant overall pressure. Increased pressure from this fluid causes glaucoma and can lead to

blindness. Serial tonometry involves multiple pressure checks over the course of a day to monitor significant peaks and acute elevations in intraocular pressure within a 24-hour period (diurnal curve). Different tonography testing equipment and techniques may be used. In Goldmann's applanation tonometry, or the blue-light glaucoma-screening test, the patient is given a drop of fluorescein staining dye and anesthetic. The forehead and chin are supported on a headrest. A slit lamp is positioned until the tonometer probe just touches the cornea and the physician can view a limbal glow, or blue light circle. This applanation method measures the force required to flatten a certain area of the cornea, which is dependent upon the pressure in the eye. The force per area is converted to the intraocular pressure measurement. A portable TonoPen is a device that gives an instant digital measurement when touched to the eye.

89.12   Nasal function study

Description

Nasal function studies are performed for analyzing nasal resistance during breathing. In rhinomanometry, the physician uses a tubular probe to generate and transmit an audible sound signal into the patient's nasal cavity through an anatomically fitted nosepiece. A microphone picks up the sound from the nasal cavity and the data is analyzed by computer to determine area distance in the nasal cavity.

89.13   Neurologic examination

Description

This procedure involves an examination of the neurological system with recording of anatomic and physiologic neurological findings. A wide scope of specific neurological diagnostic examinations may be classifiable to this general code including those that may incorporate questions and answers or objective recordings of measurable physical signs. A neurological examination may include several components or focus on specific components, such as:

- Mental status

- Cranial nerves

- Motor system

- Sensory system

- Deep tendon reflexes

- Coordination and the cerebellum

- Gait

89.14   Electroencephalogram

When reporting intraoperative anesthetic effect monitoring and titration (IAEMT), the official index indicates that two codes must be reported: code 00.94 Intraoperative neurophysiologic monitoring, and 89.14. The most common IAEMT system is the BIS Monitoring System.

89.15   Other nonoperative neurologic function tests

Description
Sensors are placed on a patient's head in an electroencephalogram (EEG) to measure and record the brain's electrical activity. Brain waves are captured on paper or electronic medium for study. This code applies to checking a patient for brain activity and determining whether the patient is brain dead. This involves evaluation by isoelectric encephalogram for a minimum of 30 minutes with no EEG change in response to sound or pain.

Coding Clarification
Code 89.14 excludes EEG with polysomnogram (89.17).

Codes 89.14 and 89.15 describe nonoperative (non-invasive) diagnostic neurological function tests.

Coding Guidance
    AHA: N-D, '84, 6; J-F, '87, 16; 2Q, '91, 14; 3Q, '95, 5; 3Q, '05, 12

89.16   Transillumination of newborn skull

Description
This procedure is a non-invasive diagnostic examination of the newborn skull in which a light is shined against the head to verify normal anatomy or identify suspected deformities or anomalous conditions such as hydrocephalus.

89.17   Polysomnogram

Description
Physiological parameters of a patient asleep in a lab setting are monitored for at least six hours for polysomnography studies. In contrast to sleep studies, polysomnography details measurements such as sleep staging with electroencephalogram (EEG), electro-oculogram, and submental electromyogram. Polysomnography may include measurements of respiration, reparatory effort, airflow, oximetry, ventilation, heart rate, oxygen saturation, muscle activity, vital signs, and snoring. A physician interprets the results.

89.18   Other sleep disorder function tests

Description
This code reports other sleep disorder function tests not described as polysomnography (89.17).

In a multiple sleep latency test (MSLT), a nap study is conducted in a series of five, 20-minute periods scheduled two hours apart. It is often performed the morning after an overnight sleep study. Electrodes

are applied to record brainwave activity (EEG), heart rate and rhythm (EKG) and other data including muscle activity and eye movements. The patient is monitored for approximately 20 minutes every two hours. A physician interprets the results.

89.19   Video and radio-telemetered electroencephalographic monitoring

Description
This procedure involves monitoring of brain waves and patterns by 12-line tracings and video or radio telemetry EEG recordings are obtained. The patient stays in a special hospital unit for at least 24 hours, where a continuous study can be performed. Seizure medication may be temporarily stopped during this test to allow for event recording of abnormal brain activity.

Coding Guidance
    AHA: 2Q, '90, 27; 1Q, '92, 17

89.2   Anatomic and physiologic measurements and manual examinations — genitourinary system

Coding Clarification
Subcategory 89.2 excludes the listed procedures when done as part of a general physical examination (89.7)

There is no single code for urodynamics. Determine the type of urodynamic study to select a code from subcategory 89.2.

Coding Guidance
    AHA: 1Q, '90, 27

89.21   Urinary manometry

Description
The physician connects an indwelling ureteral catheter or existing ureterostomy to a manometer line to measure pressure and flow in the kidneys and ureters. The physician connects a ureteral catheter or ureterostomy to a manometer line filled with fluid. The physician inserts a bladder catheter that may be irrigated. The physician measures intrarenal and/or extra renal pressure. After discontinuing perfusion of fluid, the physician aspirates residual fluid from the kidney and disconnects the manometer line. The physician may remove the ureteral catheter or ureterostomy tube (if applicable) and dress the wound.

Coding Clarification
Code 89.21 includes manometry through:

*   Indwelling ureteral catheter
*   Nephrostomy
*   Pyelostomy
*   Ureterostomy

● New Code   ▲ Revised Code   ▶◀ Revised Text   © 2010 Ingenix

89.22 Cystometrogram

Description
The physician inserts a pressure catheter into the bladder and connects it to a manometer line filed with fluid to measure pressure and flow in the lower urinary tract. During a more extensive exam, the physician inserts an electronic microtip pressure-transducer catheter into the bladder and connects it to electronic equipment to measure pressure and flow in the lower urinary tract.

89.23 Urethral sphincter electromyogram

Description
The physician places a pad in the urethral sphincter and measures the electrical activity with the bladder filled and during emptying.

89.24 Uroflowmetry (UFR)

Description
For simple uroflowmetry, the physician assesses the rate of emptying the bladder by stopwatch, recording the volume of urine per time. For complex uroflowmetry, the physician assesses the rate of emptying of the bladder by electronic equipment, recording the volume of urine per time.

89.25 Urethral pressure profile (UPP)

Description
The physician measures urethral pressure by pulling a transducer through the urethra and noting the pressure change.

89.26 Gynecological examination

Description
The physician performs a manual examination of the vagina including the cervix, uterus, tubes, and ovaries. The physician palpates (feels the organs from outside the body) the pelvic organs by pressing on the lower abdomen, checking for proper position of the uterus and any areas of tenderness, pain or other abnormality. The physician will perform a manual examination of the vagina and may palpate the internal organs with one hand pressing on the abdomen. The patient is then positioned with knees flexed and feet elevated in holders called stirrups. A speculum is inserted trans-vaginally to open and widen the vagina and visualize the cervix. A plastic spatula and a small brush are inserted to collect a sample of cells from the cervix (Pap smear). A sample of fluid may be collected from the vagina. The specimens are sent to the laboratory for microscopic analysis to rule out the presence of abnormal cells or infection. A digital rectal examination may also be performed as part of the examination.

Coding Clarification
Code 89.26 is acceptable for female patients only. It triggers MCE edit 5, which is used to detect inconsistencies between the patient's sex and the procedure.

Documentation Tip
This procedure may be documented as a (female) pelvic examination.

89.29 Other nonoperative genitourinary system measurements

Description
This procedure code includes other nonoperative (non-incisional) measurements of the genitourinary system not classifiable elsewhere in subcategory 89.2.

Coding Clarification
This code should not be assigned if the medical record contains sufficient information to facilitate coding at a higher level of specificity.

Documentation Tip
If the documentation is ambiguous or unclear, the physician should be queried.

Coding Guidance
AHA: N-D, '84, 6

89.3 Other anatomic and physiologic measurements and manual examinations

Description
This subcategory classifies other anatomic and physiologic measurements and manual examinations not classifiable elsewhere in category 89.

Coding Clarification
Subcategory 89.2 excludes the listed procedures when done as part of a general physical examination (89.7)

89.31 Dental examination

Description
This code reports a general dental examination. The dentist or physician assesses the health of the mouth by examining the teeth and supportive soft tissues. Medical and dental histories are obtained. The extent of examination depends on the general health of patient and indications for exam. Components of a dental examination may include:

- Visual inspection—observing the teeth and oral cavity to check for decay, lesions, infection or other abnormality.

- Periodontal screening—gentle probing of gums to assess health.

- Occlusion—assessment of the patient's bite (how the teeth close together).

Coding Clarification
A dental examination performed in a dentist office often includes separately reportable diagnostic x-rays and dental cleaning.

89.32   Esophageal manometry

Description
The physician inserts a tube with sensors into the patient's nose or mouth and down into the stomach to perform an esophageal motility study. The muscles of the esophagus and/or the gastroesophageal junction, which propel food and water into the stomach, are studied to measure the pressure of the contraction waves and diagnose abnormalities in the esophageal muscle that affect swallowing. The tube is slowly withdrawn and stopped at different points along the esophagus. The patient is directed to swallow a little amount of water at each stopping point and the contraction wave pressure and swallowing action are measured and graphed.

Documentation Tip
This procedure may also be documented as an esophageal motility study.

Coding Guidance
   AHA: 3Q, '96, 13

89.33   Digital examination of enterostomy stoma

Description
The physician or provider checks the stoma site and the stoma's function by digital examination with gloved finger. The examination includes assessment of patency of stoma and assessment of peri-stomal health to rule out infection, obstruction or other complication.

89.34   Digital examination of rectum

Description
The physician performs a diagnostic digital rectal exam. The physician examines the external perineal area. A gloved finger is inserted through the anus and the rectum is palpated for the presence of masses or other abnormality. In the male patient, the prostate is palpated and assessed for enlargement or masses.

89.35   Transillumination of nasal sinuses

Description
This procedure involves visualization of the nasal sinuses by shining a light against the sinus to assess the health status of the sinus cavity. Normal sinuses glow when trans-illuminated. Diseased or obstructed nasal do not glow.

89.36   Manual examination of breast

Description
Code 89.36 reports a clinical breast examination performed by a health professional. The physician examines the breast, and axilla for changes in breast size, asymmetry, skin changes, and other abnormalities. The physician will palpate each breast and the axillary area to check for painful areas or abnormal lumps and palpate the nipple to check for abnormal discharge.

89.37   Vital capacity determination

Description
This procedure measures the largest volume of air a patient can expire from his lungs. The patient amount of air inhaled and exhaled is measured and calculated with body size to determine the capacity of the lungs. This test is important for determining the threshold of capacity needed for vitality in patients with compromised respiration. For men, this is typically four to five liters; for women, this is normally three to four liters.

89.38   Other nonoperative respiratory measurements

Description
This procedure code reports other respiratory measurements, including plethysmography.

Pulmonary function testing is performed in a pulmonary lab using helium, nitrogen open circuit, or another method to check lung functions to include residual capacity or residual volume, the volume of air remaining in the lung after a patient exhales. The physician interprets results. This code applies to measuring the resistance to airflow using oscillatory or plethysmographic methods.

Coding Clarification
There are different types of plethysmography. Coding is dependent on its purpose or use and not by the type of instrument or technology used. Body and thoracic impedance plethysmography are coded 89.38, while oculoplethysmography, venous occlusion, segmental, and peripheral vascular plethysmography are coded 89.58.

Coding Guidance
   AHA: S-O, '87, 6

89.39   Other nonoperative measurements and examinations

Description
This code describes other nonoperative testing and measurement procedures not classifiable elsewhere in category 89, including:

*   **Urea breath test, C-14:** The urea breath test is a noninvasive method of diagnosing a Helicobacter pylori infection of the stomach. The

● New Code   ▲ Revised Code   ▶◀ Revised Text   © 2010 Ingenix

patient swallows a pill or drinks a solution containing the chemical urea, labeled with the radioactive isotope C-14. The bacteria will produce an enzyme that breaks down the urea into ammonia and carbon dioxide gas, if they are present. The gas contains the tagged carbon and is quickly absorbed into the bloodstream and expelled in the breath. Breath samples are taken six, 12, and 20 minutes after swallowing the pill. Urease activity produced by the bacteria, when present, will be made manifest in the breath samples collected by the presence of exhaled tagged carbon molecules. Analysis is done using a scintillation counter in a nuclear medicine or radiology department.

- **Gastric analysis test:** The physician performs a gastric analysis test, also known as a Hollander Test, to determine the acidity of stomach secretions, the effectiveness of a vagotomy, or the possibility or ulcer recurrence. The physician inserts a tube through the patient's nose or mouth and down into the stomach. Gastric contents are suctioned out for collection to determine basal acid output (BAO). Insulin, or other gastric secretion stimulant, such as histamine, pentagastrin, calcium, or secretin, is given to the patient. Blood glucose is monitored while continued collection of gastric contents is done. Following sample collection, gastric contents undergo volume, pH, acid concentration, and volume measurements. BAO is calculated in mmol of acid secreted/hour and compared to the stimulant induced peak acid output.

- **Gastric motility study:** The physician inserts a tube with sensors into the patient's nose or mouth and down into the stomach to perform a gastric motility study. The muscles of the stomach and the gastroduodenal junction, which propel food and water into the first part of the small intestines, are studied to measure the pressure of the contraction waves and diagnose abnormalities in the muscle that affect digestion. Sensors on the tube measure the amount of pressure generated by the stomach muscles as food is moved into the small intestine. The tighter the muscles contract around the tube, the greater pressure that is sensed. The data is recorded for computer analysis.

Coding Clarification
Code 89.39 excludes:

- Body measurement (93.07)
- Cardiac tests (89.41-89.69)
- Fundus photography (95.11)
- Limb length measurement (93.06)

Coding Guidance
AHA: N-D, '84, 6; 1Q, '94, 18; 3Q, '96, 12; 3Q, '00, 9; 2Q, '01, 9

89.4   Cardiac stress test, pacemaker and defibrillator checks

89.41   Cardiovascular stress test using treadmill
Description
A continuous recording of electrical activity of the heart is acquired by an assistant supervised by a physician while the patient is exercising on a treadmill and/or given medicines. The stress on the heart during the test is monitored.

Coding Guidance
AHA: 1Q, '88, 11

89.42   Masters' two-step stress test
Description
The physician performs a diagnostic test that measures the pulse and blood pressure in evaluating cardiac capacity.

Coding Guidance
AHA: 1Q, '88, 11

89.43   Cardiovascular stress test using bicycle ergometer
Description
A continuous recording of electrical activity of the heart is acquired by an assistant supervised by a physician while the patient is exercising on a bicycle and/or given medicines. The stress on the heart during the test is monitored.

Coding Guidance
AHA: 1Q, '88, 11

89.44   Other cardiovascular stress test
Description
Radionuclide, which will adhere to the patient's red blood cells, is injected intravenously for cardiac blood pool imaging. Multiple images of the heart, synchronized with the electrocardiographic RR interval (ECG gated), are taken several minutes later, after the radionuclide has spread through the blood pool. These images are computer synthesized and data is generated to produce a video display of cardiac wall motion, calculation of left ventricular ejection fractions, and images based on computer manipulation of the data received.

89.45   Artificial pacemaker rate check
Coding Guidance
AHA: 1Q, '02, 3

89.46   Artificial pacemaker artifact wave form check

89.47   Artificial pacemaker electrode impedance check

89.48   Artificial pacemaker voltage or amperage threshold check

Description
Patients with previously implanted pacemakers require periodic analysis of pacemaker function. These codes apply to routine or problem-focused electronic pacemaker testing of the component parts as specified in the code description. Routine interrogation includes an electrocardiogram, tests, and physician's interpretation of the tests.

Coding Clarification
Code 89.45 excludes:

- Catheter based invasive electrophysiologic testing (37.26)

- Non-invasive programmed electrical stimulation (NIPS) (arrhythmia induction) (37.20)

89.49   Automatic implantable cardioverter/defibrillator (AICD) check

Description
Patients with previously implanted or wearable cardio-defibrillators require periodic analysis of their function. This code applies to routine electronic analysis of a cardioverter-defibrillator. This code includes interrogation, evaluation of pulse generator status, evaluation of programmable parameters at rest and during activity, using electrocardiographic recording and interpretation of recordings at rest and during exercise, and the analysis of event markers and device response. This code does not include reprogramming.

Coding Clarification
Code 89.49 excludes:

- Catheter based invasive electrophysiologic testing (37.26)

- Non-invasive programmed electrical stimulation (NIPS) (arrhythmia induction) (37.20)

Coding Guidance
AHA: 4Q, '04, 136

89.5   Other nonoperative cardiac and vascular diagnostic procedures

Coding Clarification
Subcategory 89.5 excludes fetal EKG (75.32).

89.50   Ambulatory cardiac monitoring

Description
This procedure describe ambulatory cardiac monitoring procedures incorporating several

possible techniques and components in order to evaluate the patient's ambient heart rhythm over a period of time, such as a 24 hour cycle. The physician instructs the patient in the use of the electrocardiographic (ECG) recorder (also known as a Holter monitor). A technician places ECG leads on the patient's chest and the patient wears the recorder for 24 hours. The patient returns the device and the recorded heart rhythm is played back into digital format by a technician. The technician uses visual superimposition scanning to classify different ECG waveforms and to generate a report. The generated report describes the overall rhythm and significant arrhythmias. Rhythm strips are also generated. The physician reviews these data and provides the final interpretation in a report.

Coding Guidance
AHA: 4Q, '91, 23; 4Q, '99, 21

89.51   Rhythm electrocardiogram

Description
One to three electrodes placed on a patient's chest are used to record electrical activity of the heart. The physician interprets the report.

89.52   Electrocardiogram

Description
Twelve electrodes are placed on a patient's chest to record the electrical activity of the heart. A physician interprets the findings.

Coding Clarification
Electrocardiography mapping is classified to 89.52.

Coding Guidance
AHA: S-O, '87, 6; 1Q, '88, 11

89.53   Vectorcardiogram (with ECG)

Description
A vectorcardiogram is a graphic representation of the magnitude and direction of the electrical currents of the heart's action in the form of a vector loop.

89.54   Electrographic monitoring

Description
The patient is connected to telemetry equipment that monitors heart activity. These measuring, recording, and transmitting devices also produce a data log that is used by the physician to monitor and diagnose the patient's condition. Medical telemetry devices monitor a patient's vital signs and other parameters and transmit this information to a remote location where they are displayed, recorded, and analyzed. A medical telemetry unit (e.g., cardiac care telemetry unit or step-down unit) is designed to provide continuous heart monitoring for patients who are at risk for abnormal heart activity.

● New Code   ▲ Revised Code   ▶◀ Revised Text   © 2010 Ingenix

Coding Clarification
Code 89.54 excludes:

- Ambulatory cardiac monitoring
- Electrographic monitoring during surgery—omit code

Documentation Tip
This procedure may also be documented as telemetry.

89.55   Phonocardiogram with ECG lead

Description
The phonogram allows detection of sounds and murmurs not audible by stethoscope, and provides a record of their occurrence, enabling the physician to quantify the sounds.

89.56   Carotid pulse tracing with ECG lead

Description
A graphic record is taken of the rhythmic expansion and contraction of the major arteries on each side of the neck.

Coding Clarification
Code 89.54 excludes oculoplethysmography (89.58).

89.57   Apexcardiogram (with ECG lead)

Description
A recording is taken of the pattern of relaxation and contraction of the heart muscle, including the rate and filling measurements.

Coding Clarification
Apexcardiogram assists in early detection of heart disease and hypertension. It is also utilized to provide information regarding the progression of cardiovascular disease.

Coding Guidance
AHA: J-F, '87, 16

89.58   Plethysmogram

Description
In a penile plethysmography, the physician measures the physiological potential of the penis to attain and maintain an erection using plethysmography. The volume change of the penis is measured in response to external stimuli.

In a plethysmogram, plethysmography measures and records changes in the volume of a body part in response to variations in the amount of blood passing through or contained in that body part. Total body plethysmography uses a chamber enclosing the body and is used primarily to assess respiratory function.

Coding Clarification:
Code 89.58 excludes plethysmography (for):

- Measurement of respiratory
- Function (89.38)
- Thoracic impedance (89.38)

Coding Guidance
AHA: S-O, '87, 7

89.59   Other nonoperative cardiac and vascular measurements

Description
This code describes other nonoperative cardiovascular measurement procedures not classifiable elsewhere in subcategory 89.5.

Tilt table test:
In a tilt table test, the patient's susceptibility to neurocardiogenic syncope is evaluated. The physician secures the patient to the tilt table and attaches ECG leads to the chest. The physician also attaches an intermittent blood pressure monitor. The physician tilts the table, with the patient on it, and monitors the patient's symptoms, heart rhythm, and blood pressure. The physician may infuse medication, such as isoproterenol, through a standard intravenous catheter and repeat the tilt test.

Coding Clarification
▶Code 89.59 includes intracoronary acetylcholine challenge test.◀

Coding Guidance
AHA: 2Q, '92, 12; 3Q, '03, 23; 3Q, '05, 21; ▶2Q, '10, 11◀

89.6   Circulatory monitoring

Coding Clarification
Subcategory 89.6 excludes:

- Electrocardiographic monitoring during surgery—omit code
- Implantation or replacement of subcutaneous device for intracardiac hemodynamic monitoring (00.57)
- Insertion or replacement of implantable pressure sensor (lead) for intracardiac hemodynamic monitoring (00.56)

Do not report code 89.61 for the following procedures classifiable elsewhere:

- Intra-aneurysm sac pressure monitoring (intraoperative) (00.58)
- Intravascular pressure measurement of intrathoracic arteries (00.67)
- Intravascular pressure measurement of peripheral arteries (00.68)

Use 89.61–89.69 for circulatory monitoring and pressure recording. A severely ill patient may have a wedge-pressure recording with a balloon-tip catheter

(89.64) and pulmonary arterial pressure monitoring (89.63) at the bedside. This is considered hemodynamic monitoring and not a diagnostic catheterization.

Coding Guidance
AHA: M-J, '87, 11

89.60   Continuous intra-arterial blood gas monitoring

Description
This procedure uses a system composed of intra-arterial sensors, a monitor and a calibrator. The sensor measures on pH, pCO_2, pO_2, temperature, bicarbonate, base excess and oxygen saturation levels. It is inserted through an arterial catheter into the selected artery, usually a peripheral radial or femoral artery. For neonatal patients, the umbilical artery is selected for catheterization. Continuous recordings are obtained. The recordings are displayed on a monitor.

Coding Guidance
AHA: 4Q, '02, 111

89.61   Systemic arterial pressure monitoring

Description
The physician accesses an artery such as the ulnar or radial artery to insert a cannula (a tube-shaped portal). The physician inserts a needle through the skin to puncture the artery and inserts a cannula. The physician may make an incision in the skin overlying the artery and dissect the surrounding tissue to access it. The artery is sometimes nicked with a thin-bladed scalpel before the physician inserts the cannula. This cannula acts as a portal for arterial pressure monitoring. The cannula is connected to a sterile liquid interface and an electronic pressure transducer. Arterial pressure is constantly monitored beat-by-beat, and pressure readings are recorded and graphically displayed.Once the procedure is complete, the cannula is removed. In an open procedure, the opening in the artery may be sutured and the incision repaired with a layered closure. Pressure is applied to the puncture if a percutaneous approach is used.

89.62   Central venous pressure monitoring

Description
This procedure involves monitoring of venous pressure through a sensor introduced through an intravenous catheter. CVP monitoring provides an accurate measurement of the changes in the pressure of the blood returning to the heart. The physician inserts a venous catheter into an upper extremity or subclavian vein and advances it just superior to the right atrium of the heart. Positioning is verified by x-ray. The catheter is attached to

monitoring systems that record and display the data. Venous pressure is detected by the sensor at the tip of the catheter which travels through the fluid-filled catheter to the transducer where it is transformed into a signal that is recorded by the CVP recording unit. Once the procedure is complete, the catheter is removed.

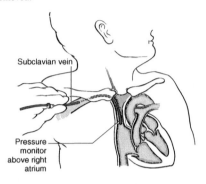

Subclavian vein

Pressure monitor above right atrium

89.63   Pulmonary artery pressure monitoring

89.64   Pulmonary artery wedge monitoring

Description
Pulmonary artery pressure monitoring is done via a catheter. The physician threads a catheter to the right heart through a central intravenous line often inserted up the femoral vein to take blood samples, pressure and electrical recordings, and/or other tests. This code applies to the insertion of a flow directed catheter, such as the Swan-Ganz (89.64) device, used for measuring pressure and related parameters.

Coding Clarification
Codes 89.63 and 89.64 include the introduction of an access catheter (such as Swan-Ganz) to the pulmonary artery via the heart ventricle. The catheterization facilitates measuring and monitoring of pulmonary arterial pressure. The measurement and monitoring function also assists in determination of cardiac output.

89.65   Measurement of systemic arterial blood gases

89.66   Measurement of mixed venous blood gases

Description
This code describes the measurement of systemic blood gases. Measurement may require swan-Ganz catheterizations in order to obtain adequate blood samples. Blood gases are usually requested to evaluate disturbances of acid-base balance, which may be caused by respiratory or metabolic disorders. Any combination of pH, pCO_2, pO_2, CO_2, and HCO_3, including calculated O_2 saturation may be obtained. O_2 saturation may performed by direct

measurement. Method is selective electrode, potentiometry, or spectrophotometry (O2 saturation).

Coding Clarification
Code 89.65 excludes continuous intra-arterial blood gas monitoring (89.60)

89.67 Monitoring of cardiac output by oxygen consumption technique

Description
The physician indirectly measures cardiac output through blood volume flow over pulmonary capillaries. This determines oxygen absorption by measurement of arterial oxygen content vs. venous oxygen content.

89.68 Monitoring of cardiac output by other technique

Description
This procedure code reports cardiac output monitoring by other techniques not classifiable elsewhere in subcategory 89.6.

Indicator dilution studies use a technique based on the principle that the volume of a fluid within a container can be determined by adding a known quantity of an indicator to the fluid and measuring the concentration of the indicator after it has completely mixed with the fluid. A time-concentration curve arises and the area of the inscribed curve is calculated. The physician threads a catheter through a central line leading to the heart and dye, such as nontoxic, water-soluble indocyanine green, or a thermal indicator, usually iced saline, is injected. In the thermodilution method, cardiac output is measured by a computer using an equation that incorporates body temperature, injection volume and temperature, time, and other calculated ratios over a denominator of the integral of the change in blood temperature during the cold injection, reflected by the area of the inscribed curve. Cardiac output is measured and recorded.

89.69 Monitoring of coronary blood flow

Description
This procedure involves monitoring of coronary blood flow not classifiable as output or by other technique specified elsewhere in subcategory 89.6.

Coding Clarification
Code 89.69 includes monitoring of coronary blood flow by coincidence counting technique

89.7 General physical examination

Description
This code describes a general physical examination. The extent and focus of the examination may vary, depending on the patient's age and state of health. A physical examination may involve an evaluation of the patient's concurrent medical care and history. The patient will review any recent constitutional symptoms, which may consist of weigh loss or gain, fever, fatigue or other complaints. The physician will take an inventory of the health status of the body systems through a series of questions and perform body system-specific examinations in order to identify if any significant signs and symptoms of health problems exist. For example, the physician may perform a cardiovascular system examination during which the patient's current blood pressure and pulse are noted and by listening to the patient's hearth through a stethoscope. This may be followed by a respiratory system exam in which the physician reviews the patient's respiratory rate and listens to the patient's breath sounds through a stethoscope. During the course of the complete examination, the physician may identify signs or symptoms that require further testing, and determine the course of treatment necessary. Upon completion of the examination, the physician records the patient's state of health and any significant findings.

89.8 Autopsy

Description
This code reports the examination of a body after death. The body is dissected. The organs and tissues (excluding the brain and central nervous system) are systematically examined and described. This is usually done to determine the cause of death, to improve diagnosis and treatment of diseases, or to benefit family members in cases of heritable illnesses.

90 Microscopic examination - I

Description
This category classifies an examination of a specimen (a sample of tissue or fluid) for laboratory of analysis. The type of analysis performed may vary depending on the patient's clinical presentation, suspected conditions and differential diagnoses. The third-digit classification designates the body system, organ or tissues from which the specimen was obtained:

90.0   **Microscopic examination of specimen from nervous system and of spinal fluid**

90.1   **Microscopic examination of specimen from endocrine gland, not elsewhere classified**

90.2   **Microscopic examination of specimen from eye**

90.3   **Microscopic examination of specimen from ear, nose, throat, and larynx**

90.4   **Microscopic examination of specimen from trachea, bronchus, pleura, lung, and other thoracic specimen, and of sputum**

90.5   **Microscopic examination of blood**

90.6   **Microscopic examination of specimen from spleen and of bone marrow**

90.7   **Microscopic examination of specimen from lymph node and of lymph**

90.8   **Microscopic examination of specimen from upper gastrointestinal tract and of vomitus**

90.9   **Microscopic examination of specimen from lower gastrointestinal tract and of stool**

Description
The fourth-digit subclassification [1-6, 9] designates the type of examination performed.

1 Bacterial smear
Several methods and techniques may be utilized for analysis of the presence of bacteria, several of which overlap other fourth digit subclassifications, including:

- **Concentration (any type), for infectious agents:** Concentration may also be referred to as thick smear preparation. The source samples are treated to concentrate the presence of suspect organisms, usually through sedimentation or flotation. There are two common methods of concentration for ova and parasite exams: formalin concentration and zinc sulfate flotation. The two most common concentration methods for AFB stains or cultures are the N-acetyl-L cysteine method and the Zephiran-trisodium phosphate method.

- **Smear, wet mount for infectious agents (e.g., saline, India ink, KOH preps):** This test may be requested as a KOH prep. A wet mount is prepared from a primary source to detect bacteria. Motility of organisms is visible on wet mounts and the addition of a simple stain, such as iodine, India ink, or simple dyes, may aid detection of bacteria and other infectious

organisms. An interpretation of findings is included.

- **Smear, Gram or Giemsa stain for bacteria:** Any smear done on a primary source (e.g., sputum, CSF, etc.) to identify bacteria, other infectious organisms and cell types. An interpretation of findings is provided. Bacteria, WBCs, and epithelial cells may be estimated in quantity with an interpretation as to the possibility of contamination by normal flora. A gram stain may be the most commonly performed smear of this type.

2 Culture
A culture is performed to identify or rule out microscopic organisms as the cause of illness or infection. Cultures may be described as with presumptive identification or definitive identification of microorganisms. Presumptive identification may be defined as identification of a microorganism colony by growth on selective media. Definitive identification may be defined as identification of the genus or species of microorganism. Methodology and specimen source may vary, including:

- **Culture, presumptive, pathogenic organisms:** This is a presumptive screening culture for one or more pathogenic organisms. The methodology is by culture and the culture should be identified by type (e.g., anaerobic, aerobic) and specimen source (e.g., pleural, peritoneal, bronchial aspirates). If a specific organism is suspected, the person ordering the test will typically use common names, such as strep screen, staph screen, etc., to specify the organism for screening. Presumptive identification includes gram staining as well as up to three tests, such as a catalase, oxidase, or urease test. Screenings included in this code are nonmotile, catalase-positive, gram-positive rod bacteria.

- **Culture, bacterial; quantitative, anaerobic:** The most common name for this procedure is anaerobic culture. Presumptive identification of anaerobic pathogens or microorganisms in the sample is by means of identifying colony morphology. The test includes gram staining and subculturing to selective media for the detection of bacterial growth. There are several automated systems that detect the presence of bacteria using colorimetric, radiometric, or spectrophotometric means. This culture test detects the presence of anaerobic bacteria in a body site or source, except blood, urine, or stool, and identifies the micro-organism(s), but not to the specific level of genus or species requiring additional testing, such as slide cultures. The isolate(s) identified is quantified in growth numbers. Tissues, fluids, and aspirations, except from blood, urine, or stool samples, are collected in anaerobic vials or with anaerobic transport swabs and transported immediately. Anaerobic bacteria are sensitive to oxygen and cold.

- **Culture, bacterial; blood, aerobic:** Samples for bacterial blood culture are drawn by venipuncture and usually consist of a set of bottles, an aerobic and an anaerobic bottle. Drawing at least two sets of cultures increases the effectiveness of the test. This code includes anaerobic culture along with aerobic, if appropriate. Presumptive identification of aerobic pathogens or microorganisms in the blood sample is by means of identifying colony morphology. The test includes gram staining and subculturing to selective media for the detection of bacterial growth. There are several automated systems that detect the presence of bacteria using colorimetric, radiometric, or spectrophotometric means. The purpose of blood culture tests is to detect the presence of aerobic and anaerobic bacteria in blood and to identify the bacteria, but not to the specific level of genus or species requiring additional testing, such as slide cultures.

3 Culture and sensitivity

This subclassification describes a microscopic culture exam. A culture is performed to identify or rule out microscopic organisms as the cause of illness or infection. Some common types of culture methodologies are described above under fourth-digit subclassification 2. Sensitivity describes a test that determines which medicine (e.g., antibiotic) should be used to best treat the illness or infection. Methodology and specimen source may vary, including:

- **Susceptibility studies, antimicrobial agent; agar dilution method:** A susceptibility study is performed to determine the susceptibility of a bacterium to an antibiotic. The methodology is agar diffusion (the E test is a method of agar diffusion). The specific antibiotics could be chosen and limited. The test is reported per antibiotic tested. The agar dilution is reported as minimum inhibitory concentration (MIC), which is a method of measuring the exact amount of antibiotic needed to inhibit an organism.

- **Susceptibility studies, antimicrobial agent; disk method:** This is commonly called a Kirby-Bauer or Bauer-Kirby sensitivity test. It is a sensitivity test to determine the susceptibility of a bacterium to an antibiotic. The methodology is disk diffusion and results are reported as sensitive, intermediate, or resistant. As many as 12 antibiotic disks may be used per

plate and the procedure is billed per plate not per antibiotic disk.

- **Susceptibility studies, antimicrobial agent; mycobacteria, proportion method:** Mycobacterium susceptibility test is a procedure done only on mycobacterium (e.g., M. tuberculosis, M. marinum, etc.). Proportion method is used and involves testing of a panel of antibiotics used only for the treatment of mycobacterium. Results are given as sensitive or resistant.

4 Parasitology

This subclassification describes a laboratory examination that is used to identify or rule out the presence of parasitic organisms that infect humans. Parasites may be defined as organisms that derive food or shelter from another organism or host organism. Methodology and specimen source may vary, including:

- **Smear, special stain for or parasites (e.g., malaria, coccidia, microsporidia):** This is a stain to look for inclusion bodies or parasites (e.g., malaria inside red cells). Its use to detect herpes has been outdated by amplification and immunological methods. An interpretation is included.

- **Ova and parasite smears:** Common names for this procedure are ova and parasite exam, or O & P. Stool is collected in a clean, leak-proof container (when processed within one hour) or the specimen is added to formalin or fixative (both available in commercial kits). The methodology of an ova and parasite exam for stools includes a direct smear, and smear of concentrated material, such as formalin concentration technique or zinc flotation method. Identification is by observing parasites with the aid of a microscope.

- **Smear, wet mount for infectious agents:** This test may be requested as a KOH prep. A wet mount is prepared from a primary source to detect bacteria, fungi, or ova and parasites. Motility of organisms is visible on wet mounts and the addition of a simple stain, such as iodine, India ink, or simple dyes, may aid detection of parasites.

- **Concentration (any type), for infectious agents:** Concentration may also be referred to as thick smear preparation. The source samples are treated to concentrate the presence of suspect organisms, usually through sedimentation or flotation. There are two common methods of concentration for ova and parasite exams: formalin concentration and zinc sulfate flotation. The two most common concentration methods for AFB stains or cultures are the N-acetyl-L cysteine method and the Zephiran-trisodium phosphate method.

5 Toxicology

This subclassification describes a laboratory test that is used to identify or rule out the presence of toxins (i.e., harmful substances, poisons) in the body. An extensive array of chemistry examinations, assays and screenings are available to test for the presence of suspected toxins. Methodology and specimen source may vary, including:

- **Toxin or antitoxin assay, tissue culture (e.g., Clostridium difficile toxin):** This procedure is a toxin assay for diagnosis of toxin producing organisms, such as Clostridium difficile, E. coli 0157, enterotoxigenic E. coli, and Vibrio cholerae. Stool is collected for testing. Filtrates of the stool are inoculated into cell cultures and observed for CPE (cytopathic effect) microscopically. Confirmation of toxin production may be done by toxin neutralization. Different cell cultures are used to test for different toxins, so organism must be specified.

- **Silica assay:** Silica is a naturally occurring and common mineral found in sands, clays, and quartz deposits. Exposure is commonly by inhalation of dusts during rock mining and certain manufacturing. Deposition on the eyes and mucosal surfaces may also be a pathway of exposure. Most commonly, however, phagocytic cells may distribute the silica along lymph channels once the particles are inhaled and collect in lung alveoli. Long-term exposure is linked to numerous illnesses, including silicosis. But testing methods for silica in the system seem unclear in the literature.

- **Chlorinated hydrocarbons, screen:** Chlorinated hydrocarbons are contained in solvents and are absorbed cutaneously and by inhalation. While they vary in toxicity, all are CNS depressants and can cause liver and kidney damage with prolonged exposure. This test is used to screen for toxic levels. Levels of one or more of the following substances are screened: carbon tetrachloride, chloroform, dichloromethane, trichloroethylene, and tetrachloroethylene. Testing methods include gas chromatography flame ionization detection (GC-FID) and gas chromatography electron capture detector (GC-ECD). Colorimetry measurement of metabolites may also be used but is nonspecific.

- **Quantitative heavy metal (e.g., arsenic, barium, beryllium, bismuth, antimony, mercury):** This test may be requested as a toxic metal or poisonous metal quantitation. Blood specimen is obtained by venipuncture. A 24-hour urine specimen is required. The patient flushes the first urine of the day and discards it. All urine for the next 24-hours is collected and refrigerated. Method is atomic absorption spectrometry (AAS), colorimetry, or neutron activation analysis (NAA). This test measures (quantifies) of the amount of each single metal present. Each metal quantified is reported separately.

6 Cell block and Papanicolaou smear

This subclassification describes a laboratory test that is used to identify or rule out the presence abnormal cells in the body. Certain abnormal cell formations can indicate the presence of neoplasm (tumor) or other disease. Methodology and specimen source may vary, including:

- **Cytopathology smears, fluid washings or brushings, except cervical or vaginal:** These tests have many different names, depending on the type of specimen obtained for analysis (e.g., bronchial cytology, esophageal cytology, etc.). Specimen is obtained by separately reportable washing or brushing procedure. Cytopathology evaluation of smear specimens, including alcohol fixed, Papanicolaou, direct smear with 95 percent ethanol, or liquid fixative; filter method and cytopathology evaluation of specimen using both smear and filtration techniques. Depending on the type of specimen and the reason for the pathology examination, different stains may be required to highlight or outline cells for identification.

- **Cytopathology, Papanicolaou smear, cervical or vaginal (the Bethesda system):** These tests may be identified as a cervical smear, Pap smear, or vaginal cytology. Specimen collection is by scraping or brushing the cervix or endocervix, or aspiration of vaginal fluid. Method is microscopy examination of a spray or liquid coated smear. The physician may use the Bethesda System of evaluating and describing cervical/vaginal cytopathology slides.

9 Other microscopic examination

This subclassification describes other microscopic examinations not classifiable elsewhere in category 90.

Coding Clarification

This code should not be assigned if the medical record contains sufficient information to facilitate coding at a higher level of specificity.

Documentation Tip

If the documentation is ambiguous or unclear, the physician should be queried.

91   Microscopic examination - II

Description

This category describes an examination of a specimen (a sample of tissue or fluid) for laboratory of analysis. The type of analysis performed may vary depending on the patient's clinical presentation, suspected conditions and differential diagnoses. The third-digit classification designates the body system, organ or tissues from which the specimen was obtained:

91.0   **Microscopic examination of specimen from liver, biliary tract, and pancreas**

91.1   **Microscopic examination of peritoneal and retroperitoneal specimen**

91.2   **Microscopic examination of specimen from kidney, ureter, perirenal and periureteral tissue**

91.3   **Microscopic examination of specimen from bladder, urethra, prostate, seminal vesicle, perivesical tissue, and of urine and semen**

91.4   **Microscopic examination of specimen from female genital tract**

91.5   **Microscopic examination of specimen from musculoskeletal system and of joint fluid**

91.6   **Microscopic examination of specimen from skin and other integument**

91.7   **Microscopic examination of specimen from operative wound**

91.8   **Microscopic examination of specimen from other site**

91.9   **Microscopic examination of specimen from unspecified site**

Description

The fourth-digit subclassification designates the type of examination performed. See fourth-digit descriptions as listed under category 90.

Coding Clarification

Subcategory 91.6 excludes mucous membrane sites—code to the organ. To report examination of a specimen from an operative wound, use codes 91.71–91.79.

92   Nuclear medicine

Description

Category 92 classifies nuclear medicine procedures. Nuclear medicine utilizes the nuclear properties of

matter to obtain specialized medical images and deliver certain therapies by the use of radioactive substances, such as radioisotopes or radiopharmaceuticals. For diagnostic imaging, these substances are administered to the patient and the radiation emitted is measured by a specialized camera or probe. Nuclear imaging is distinct from other imaging techniques because of the ability to display not only anatomic characteristics, but physiological function. Therapeutic nuclear medicine often utilizes radioactive substances to provide palliative pain relief or treat disease.

Category 92 provides codes for radioisotope scans and function studies, therapeutic nuclear medicine, and stereotactic radiosurgery. Subcategories 92.0 and 92.1 are diagnostic in nature, and choice of fourth digit is based on the anatomic site. Subcategories 92.2 and 92.3 are therapeutic in nature and list codes according to the type of procedure performed or techniques utilized.

Documentation Tip

Procedures classifiable to category 92 that utilize a scintillation camera to record images may be documented as scintiscan, scintillography, or scintiphotography procedures.

92.0   **Radioisotope scan and function study**

92.01   **Thyroid scan and radioisotope function studies**

Description

- **Uptake exam:** The uptake test is a measure of thyroid function to determine how much iodine the thyroid will take up and is expressed as the percentage of the administered radioiodine present in the thyroid gland at a given time after administration. A standard count must be taken of the Iodide-123 capsule before giving it to the patient by using an uptake probe, a sodium iodide counter within a lead shield. For a single, two-hour uptake exam, the neck is extended with the patient supine and the probe placed over the gland. A background count is also taken over the thigh by placing a probe over one leg. Net counts are obtained by subtracting background counts.

- **Function study:** The thyroid imaging scan is performed for anatomical size and physiological evaluation. A radioactive tracer that will focus in the thyroid, such as an Iodide-123 capsule or a 99m-technietium injection is administered. The physician palpates the patient's neck and outlines areas to be marked. With the patient supine, the neck is extended and the head immobilized. Images are scanned by a scintillation or gamma camera that detects the radiation from the tracer in the target tissue. Thyroid carcinoma functions much less than normal thyroid tissue and appears as a cold lesion with little or no accumulation of the radioiodine.

Documentation Tip

Procedures classifiable to 92.01 may be documented as:

* Iodine-131 uptake
* Protein-bound iodine
* Radio-iodine uptake

92.02   Liver scan and radioisotope function study

Description

* **Scan:** Radiolabeled sulphur colloid is the most commonly used radiopharmaceutical for diagnostic nuclear imaging of the liver because it is taken up by the reticuloendothelial cells. The radioisotope is injected into a peripheral vein and extracted by the liver. For imaging done with a vascular flow test, red blood cells are labeled to image the blood flow. A scintillation or gamma camera takes images of the liver on computer screen or film by detecting the gamma radiation from the radiopharmaceutical in the tissue and the blood as it flows through the liver. This helps characterize lesions or tumors and determine vascular complications in the liver. Impaired blood flow and reticuloendothelial function can show up as patchy colloid uptake in the liver with preferential bone marrow and spleen uptake.

* **Function study:** Special radiolabeled aminoacetic acids that are rapidly cleared by hepatocytes and excreted in the bile are used in a nuclear liver function study. The radiotracer is injected into a peripheral vein and followed by serial imaging with a scintillation, or gamma camera, on computer screen or film by detecting the gamma radiation from the radiopharmaceutical in the liver and throughout the biliary tract as it is expelled. Biliary function scanning is used in diagnosing acute cholecystitis, cholestasis, obstructions, leaks, biliary-enteric fistulas, and cysts.

92.03   Renal scan and radioisotope function study

Description

* **Imaging and function study:** Diagnostic nuclear medicine uses small amounts of gamma-emitting radioactive materials, or tracers, to determine a structural cause of the medical problem in the kidney. For kidney imaging, a radionuclide such as 99mTc-DMSA is chosen because it will travel to the kidney and remain in the functional tissue there. It is injected into the patient and a scintillation or

gamma camera takes planar images of the kidney on computer screen or film by detecting the gamma radiation from the radiopharmaceutical in the renal tissue as it "scintillates" or gives off energy in a flash of light when coming in contact with the camera's detector. If a vascular flow test is performed, the radionuclide will follow the blood as it flows through the kidney and also identify any obstruction in the collecting system to determine the rate at which the kidney's are filtering. It is injected into the patient the scintillation or gamma camera takes planar images of the study area on computer screen or film by detecting the gamma radiation from the radiopharmaceutical as it flows through the kidney.

* **Non-imaging function study:** A non-imaging radioisotopic study of kidney function requires a radioisotope that is cleared from the body only by the glomerular filtration action of the kidneys. Measuring the glomerular filtration rate (GFR) is the best assessment of total renal function. The radioisotope is injected and blood samples are taken at two, three, and four hours for radioactive concentration counts. The filtration rate of the kidneys is proportional to the clearance rate of the radioisotope from the blood and is calculated using this information together with the distribution volume. The GFR can also be calculated by using urine collections but this method has more intrinsic complications than blood sampling.

92.04   Gastrointestinal scan and radioisotope function study

Description

This procedure code reports gastrointestinal scans and functions studies. Anatomic site of exam and technique may vary, including:

* **Schilling test:** The Schilling test checks for vitamin B12 deficiency. The patient swallows a capsule that contains radioactive vitamin B12 and an hour later is given an injection of vitamin B12 that is not radioactively labeled. All urine excreted in the following 24 hours is collected and checked for radioactive B12 which will be present if it was absorbed. If the first test shows that it was not absorbed, the same test is done again except that this time the patient also takes a capsule containing intrinsic factor. If there is now radioactive vitamin B12 in the urine, an intrinsic factor deficiency is likely the cause of the vitamin B12 deficiency.

* **Gastric mucosal imaging:** Radiolabeled pertechnetate is administered intravenously for a nuclear imaging study of gastric mucosa,

● New Code   ▲ Revised Code   ▶◀ Revised Text   © 2010 Ingenix

especially in children. A scintillation, or gamma camera, scans a wide vision field from the xiphoid to the symphysis pubis and takes planar images by detecting the gamma radiation from the radiopharmaceutical. Gastric mucosa surfaces of the stomach will selectively collect and secrete the pertechnetate. Gastric mucosa in an ectopic site, such as Meckel's diverticulum, will accumulate the radiotracer the same as in the stomach, and allow visualization of the ectopic area as long as there is sufficient mucosa to focally concentrate the tracer.

- **Esophageal motility imaging:** Diagnostic nuclear medicine uses small amounts of gamma-emitting radioactive materials, or tracers, to determine the cause of the medical problem based on the function, or chemistry, of the organ or tissue. For esophageal motility imaging, a radioactive sulfur colloid in water is administered orally and followed by a scintillation, or gamma camera, that takes planar images by detecting the gamma radiation from the radiopharmaceutical as it gives off energy while being swallowed down the esophagus. This test is done to diagnose motility and neurodegenerative disorders, reverse peristalsis, and dysphagia.

- **Intestinal imaging:** Intestine imaging done with nuclear scintigraphy involves injecting the patient with radioactive sodium pertechnetate. With the patient supine, the scintillation, or gamma camera, scans a wide field of view covering the abdominal area and takes images on camera or film by detecting the gamma radiation from the radioactive tracer introduced into the patient. Structural abnormalities, such as ectopic gastric mucosa, diverticula, or twisting of the bowel causing obstruction may be detected and localized. Gastric mucosa surfaces in an ectopic site will selectively collect and secrete the pertechnetate. Patients suspected of Meckel's diverticulum are given a medication to increase gastric uptake of the pertechnetate. When scanning for inflammatory disorders of the bowel, such as Crohn's disease and ulcerative colitis, autologous radiolabeled white blood cells, which focus at inflammation sites, are used as the radiotracer for imaging purposes.

92.05   Cardiovascular and hematopoietic scan and radioisotope function study

Description
This code includes a wide array of radioisotope scans and function studies of cardiovascular and hematopoietic (blood forming) anatomic sites.

Anatomic site of exam and technique utilize may vary, including:

- **SPECT (single photon emission computed tomographic), myocardial:** For tomographic myocardial perfusion imaging, the patient receives an intravenous injection of a radionuclide, usually thallium or technetium-99m, which will localize only in nonischemic tissue. Tomographic SPECT (single photon emission computed tomographic) images of the heart are taken immediately to identify areas of perfusion vs. infarction. SPECT imaging differs from planar imaging by using a single or multiple-head camera that rotates around the patient to give three-dimensional tomographic imaging of the heart displayed in thin slices. In the nonstress version of the procedure, radionuclide is injected and images are taken without stress induction. If the test is to be done at a stress condition, it is induced with the standard treadmill exercise test or pharmacologically with the infusion of a vasodilator. Multiple studies may be done at rest and/or stress with a second injection of radionuclide given again in the redistribution and/or resting phase just prior to resting images being taken. These codes also include attenuation correction (AC), which provides a more accurate diagnostic image for diagnosing defects or infarcted areas by raising the importance of radioactivity distribution counts arising from certain areas. For instance, counts from the anterior wall may be reduced or impeded by the presence of the breast.

- **Myocardial imaging, positron emission tomography (PET):** The cardiac muscle is imaged using data received from positron-emitting radionuclides administered to the patient. The collision of the positrons emitted by the radionuclide with the negatively-charged electrons normally present in tissue is computer synthesized to produce an image, usually in color. This image will show the presence or absence of ischemic or fibrotic cardiac tissue and allow evaluation of metabolic functioning of cardiac tissue.

- **Non-tomographic:** For planar myocardial perfusion imaging, stress is induced with the standard treadmill exercise test or pharmacologically with the infusion of a vasodilator, if the test is to be done at stress conditions. The patient receives an intravenous injection of a radionuclide, usually thallium or technetium-99m, which will localize only in nonischemic tissue. Planar images of the heart are scanned immediately with a gamma camera that detects the radiation in the heart tissue to identify areas of infarction. In the nonstress version of the procedure, radionuclide is injected and images taken without stress induction. A single study may be performed, at rest or stress. Multiple procedures may be performed at rest and/or at stress with a second injection of radionuclide given again in the redistribution or resting phase just prior to resting images being taken.

- **Bone marrow imaging:** Radiolabeled sulphur colloid is the most commonly used radiopharmaceutical for bone marrow imaging. The radiotracer is injected into the patient and images are obtained after a two or three-hour delay for optimal evaluation. A scintillation or gamma camera takes planar images of the study area on computer screen or film by detecting the gamma radiation from the radionuclide that has traveled to the bone marrow as it "scintillates" or gives off energy in a flash of light when coming in contact with the camera's detector. The bone marrow scan provides information about the distribution of functioning bone marrow and any irregular pattern of marrow tissue expansion occurring in different clinical states such as malignancy or infection.

Coding Clarification
Code 92.05 includes the following anatomic sites or types:

- Bone marrow
- Cardiac output
- Circulation time
- Radionuclide cardiac ventriculogram
- Spleen

Coding Guidance
AHA: 1Q, '88, 11; 2Q, '92, 7

92.09   Other radioisotope function studies
Description
This procedure code includes other radioisotope function studies not classifiable elsewhere in subcategory 92.0.

Coding Clarification
This code should not be assigned if the medical record contains sufficient information to facilitate coding at a higher level of specificity.

Documentation Tip
If the documentation is ambiguous or unclear, the physician should be queried.

92.1   Other radioisotope scan

92.11   Cerebral scan
Description
This procedure involves a radioisotope scan of the brain. Technique may vary, including:

- **Brain imaging, limited procedure:** Diagnostic nuclear medicine uses small amounts of gamma-emitting radioactive materials, or tracers, to determine the cause of the medical problem based on the function, or chemistry, of the organ or tissue. The organ, tissue, or bone under study determines the type of radioactive material used and how it is administered to the patient. In a static test, the radionuclide travels to the intended organ and in a vascular flow test, the radionuclide labels red blood cells and therefore goes wherever the blood flows. A scintillation or gamma camera takes images of the study area on computer screen or film by detecting the gamma radiation from the radiopharmaceutical in the tissue and blood as it flows through the study area. This helps characterize lesions or tumors and determine vascular complications in an organ.

- **Brain imaging, tomographic (SPECT):** Tomographic SPECT (single photon emission computed tomography) imaging permits an in-depth evaluation of the complex anatomy and functional activity of the brain by introducing a radionuclide and detecting the distribution of gamma radiation emitted from the radiopharmaceutical introduced into the brain tissue. SPECT images differ from the usual planar scans of the gamma camera by rotating a single or multiple-head camera mounted on a gantry around the patient to give three-dimensional computer reconstructed views of cross-sectional slices of the brain.

- **Brain imaging, positron emission tomography (PET):** PET produces thin slice images of the body that can be reassembled into three-dimensional representations by detecting positron-emitting radionuclides from a radiopharmaceutical introduced into the body. These radionuclides must be produced in a cyclotron or generator that can bombard chemicals with neutrons to produce unstable, short-lived radioisotopes, such as carbon-11, nitrogen-13, and oxygen-15. These can be readily incorporated into common and important, biological body compounds for administration. Data from the imaging yields metabolic or biochemical function information depending on the type of molecule tagged. In PET imaging of the brain with metabolic evaluation, the radionuclide in injected

● New Code   ▲ Revised Code   ▶◀ Revised Text   © 2010 Ingenix

intravenously and carried to the brain where the scanner detects the radioactivity as the compound accumulates in different regions of the brain. By using specifically tagged compounds, information on glucose, oxygen, or drug metabolism in the brain is obtained.

92.12   Scan of other sites of head

Description
This procedure code reports radioisotope scan of other sites of the head, except the brain (92.11). Anatomic site and technique may vary, including:

- **Salivary gland imaging:** Diagnostic nuclear medicine uses small amounts of gamma-emitting radioactive materials, or tracers, to determine the cause of the medical problem based on the function, or chemistry, of the organ or tissue. In a static test, the radionuclide travels to the intended organ. For salivary gland imaging, the patient is injected with a low-level radiotracer and immediately imaged with a scintillation or gamma camera that takes planar images of the salivary, or parotid, gland by detecting the gamma radiation from the radiopharmaceutical in the body tissue. Imaging may be performed by serial imaging and another set for comparison is taken after the patient has been given lemon candy to stimulate the salivary glands.

- **Cerebrospinal fluid flow, imaging, cisternography:** Diagnostic nuclear medicine uses small amounts of gamma-emitting radioactive materials, or tracers, to determine the cause of the medical problem based on the function, or chemistry, of the organ or tissue. Cisternography is done to determine if there is any abnormal cerebral spinal fluid flow occurring in or around the brain. A lumbar puncture is necessary to inject the radiotracer into the lower spinal canal region. A scintillation or gamma camera takes planar images of the study area on computer screen or film by detecting the gamma radiation from the radiopharmaceutical in the body tissue as it "scintillates" or gives off energy when coming in contact with the camera's detector. Cisternography is a multiple-day procedure requiring 6-hour, 24-hour, and 48-hour scan sessions.

- **Cerebrospinal fluid flow, imaging, tomographic SPECT:** Tomographic SPECT (single photon emission computed tomography) imaging permits an in-depth evaluation of complex anatomy or functional activity in the body by injecting a radionuclide and detecting the distribution of gamma radiation emitted from the radiopharmaceutical introduced into

the body tissues being studied. Cerebrospinal fluid (CSF) flow imaging will detect any abnormalities or injury occurring in the normal pathways of CSF. A lumbar puncture is necessary to inject the radiotracer into the lower spinal canal region. SPECT images differ from the usual planar scans of the gamma camera by rotating a single or multiple-head camera mounted on a gantry around the patient to give three-dimensional, computer-reconstructed views of cross-sectional slices of the body.

Coding Clarification
Code 92.12 excludes other radioisotope scan of the eye (95.16).

92.13   Parathyroid scan

Description
Parathyroid imaging is a diagnostic tool for localizing parathyroid adenomas and hyperplastic glands by using dual radiotracer imaging and obtaining two sets of pictures. Thallium-210, which is taken up by the thyroid gland, is injected and the patient is placed supine with the neck extended and the camera centered over the neck. 60-second images are taken from 5 to 20 minutes following the injection. 99m-technetium is also injected and thyroid images taken from 5 to 10 minutes after injection. The images are normalized to each other and the technetium images are subtracted, distinguishing normal tissue from the parathyroid tissue. A thyroid image may be obtained 16 to 24 hours after oral administration of Iodine-123 and subtracted from thallium images to yield a more optimal subtraction image due to a better thyroid-to-background ratio.

92.14   Bone scan

Description
This procedure involves a radioisotope scan of bone. Technique and type of exam may vary, including:

- **Bone and/or joint imaging:** Various radiopharmaceutical agents are used for diagnostic nuclear imaging of bones and/or joints. Gallium, a calcium analogue, is the radiopharmaceutical of choice when scanning for an inflammatory process because it accumulates in areas of bone mineral turnover, such as fractures, and localizes to infected or inflamed areas like inflammatory arthritis. Combining gallium with radiolabeled white blood cells, which also localize at infection sites, enables the physician to obtain a greater degree of diagnostic specificity for certain conditions. Radioactive diphosphonates are used for bony metastatic disease screening. A camera scans the area of study and detects the gamma radiation from the radiotracer introduced into the patient to detect and localize the disease process.

- **Bone and/or joint imaging; tomographic SPECT:** Tomographic SPECT (single photon emission computed tomography) imaging permits an in-depth evaluation of complex anatomy within body structures such as the bones and joints by introducing a radionuclide and detecting the distribution of gamma radiation emitted from the radiotracer with a single or multiple-head camera mounted on a gantry to rotate around the patient. SPECT images give three-dimensional computer reconstructed views of cross-sectional slices of the body. Gallium, a calcium analogue, is the radiopharmaceutical of choice when scanning for an inflammatory process in the bones or joints because it accumulates in areas of bone mineral turnover, such as fractures, and localizes to infected or inflamed areas like inflammatory arthritis. Combining gallium with radiolabeled white blood cells, (which also localize at infection sites) enables the physician to obtain a greater degree of diagnostic specificity for certain conditions. Radioactive diphosphonates are used for bony metastatic disease screening.

- **Bone density (bone mineral content) study, absorptiometry:** Single and dual photon absorptiometry are both noninvasive techniques to measure the absorption of the mono or dichromatic photon beam by bone material. The painless study device is placed directly on the patient and uses a small amount of radionuclide to measure the bone mass absorption efficiency of the energy used. This provides a quantitative measurement of the bone mineral density of cortical bone in diseases like osteoporosis and can be used to assess an individual's response to treatment at different intervals.

92.15   Pulmonary scan

Description
This procedure involves a radioisotope scan of the lung. Technique, type, and extent of exam may vary, including:

- **Pulmonary perfusion imaging, particulate:** Nuclear pulmonary perfusion imaging uses a venous injection of radioactive macroaggregated albumin particles which are too large to pass through the pulmonary capillary bed and accumulate there as they are strained out. A scintillation or gamma camera takes planar images on computer screen or film by detecting the gamma radiation from the radiopharmaceutical in the lungs as it "scintillates" or gives off energy in a flash of light

when coming in contact with the camera's detector. Localization of the radioactive particles is proportional to the blood flow and thereby maps lung perfusion. Standard perfusion imaging usually consists of 8 planar images from different projections with the posterior oblique views being most important since they image the lower lobes, the most common site for pulmonary embolism.

- **Pulmonary perfusion imaging, particulate, with ventilation:** Ventilation and perfusion imaging of the lungs is used to detect pulmonary embolism and the percentage of total perfusion and ventilation attributable to each lung. Perfusion imaging is done after a venous injection of radioactive macroaggregated albumin is given to the patient. The albumin particles are too large to pass through the pulmonary capillary bed and accumulate there as they are strained out. This localization of particles is proportional to the blood flow and thereby maps lung perfusion. A nuclear ventilation image is obtained to complement the perfusion image. For a single breath image, a posterior view of the thorax is taken as the patient inhales radiolabeled Xenon gas in a single breath and holds it as long as possible. This image obtained from the gamma camera that detects the radioactivity from the gas in the lungs will show well-ventilated areas having uniform activity and poorly ventilated areas with decreased or absent radioactivity. For ventilation images, a series of single or multiple projection views, comparable to the perfusion views, are taken after the patient has inhaled a radiolabeled aerosol. The radioactivity stays in the area where it was deposited long enough to take images. If there is no obstruction, consistent appearance and disappearance of the radioactive gas in the air spaces of the lungs is shown.

92.16   Scan of lymphatic system

Description
Diagnostic nuclear lymphatic and lymph node imaging is a tool for studying diseases involving nodal tissue and evaluating lymphatic transport. The patient is placed in a supine position and radioactive antimony sulfide colloid is injected according to the lymph node to be visualized. For axillary and apical lymph nodes, for example, the injection is into the medial two interdigital webs of the hand and imaging is done two to four hours later. For the internal mammary lymph nodes, the injection is into the posterior rectus sheath below the rib cage and imaging is dependent upon the study. For the iliopelvic nodes, injection is into the perianal region with the patient in a knee to chest

position. A scintillation or gamma camera takes planar images of the study area on computer screen or film by detecting the gamma radiation from the radiopharmaceutical in the lymphatic tissue as it "scintillates" or gives off energy when coming in contact with the camera's detector.

92.17   Placental scan

Description
This procedure involves a placental scan by instillation of radioisotope. Placental scanning is typically performed utilizing ultrasound technology, which carries less risk to the fetus. Radioisotopes are contraindicated in pregnancy.

In studies, one indication of a placental scan has been to localize the placenta using indium-113m (In-113m) to aid in the management of cases of antepartum bleeding. One millicurie of In-113m is mixed with the threshold volume of the patient's plasma and is then reinjected into the patient. After ten minutes, a photoscan of the abdomen is taken. In-113m is felt by some researchers to be advantageous over other radioisotopes in this procedure due to its rapid decay, shorter half-life, and higher photon output, yet a reduced amount of absorbed radiation from an initially small dose injected.

92.18   Total body scan

Description
Gallium, a calcium analogue, is the radiopharmaceutical of choice when scanning for an inflammatory process because it localizes to infected areas by attaching to plasma proteins found at infection sites and accumulating in areas of bone mineral turnover, such as fractures and inflammatory arthritis. Gallium is often combined with radiolabeled white blood cells, which also accumulate at infection sites but not at areas of increased bone replenishing, to augment accuracy in inflammatory localization. After administration of the specialized radiotracer, a camera, called a scintillation or gamma camera, takes planar images of the study area on computer screen or film by detecting the gamma radiation from the radiopharmaceutical in the body tissue as it "scintillates" or gives off energy when coming in contact with the camera's detector. This code describes a total body scan.

92.19   Scan of other site

Description
This code describes a radioisotope scan not otherwise classifiable to subcategory 92.1.

Coding Clarification
This code should not be assigned if the medical record contains sufficient information to facilitate coding at a higher level of specificity.

Documentation Tip
If the documentation is ambiguous or unclear, the physician should be queried.

92.2   Therapeutic radiology and nuclear medicine

Description
External radiation treatment delivery involves the delivery of a beam of radioactive electromagnetic energy from a treatment machine distanced from the treatment area. External radiation is very often delivered by linear accelerator which can deliver x-rays (photons) or electrons to a targeted area. Cobalt teletherapy units and cesium teletherapy units are also used to direct gamma rays from a distance to the targeted area. Photons can target deeper lying tumor tissue, while electrons are used for the maximum dose of radiation near the skin surface, making the method suitable to treat skin, superficial lesions, and shallow tumor volumes where underlying tissues need to be protected.

Internal radiation treatment delivery involves the infusion, injection or instillation of radioisotopes, by intravenous method or into a body cavity or other anatomic site. Radioactive material is encapsulated for intracavitary or interstitial implantation or prepared in liquid solutions for instillation or oral administration.

Radiation treatment delivery codes are dependent upon type of radiation therapy and method of delivery

Coding Clarification
Subcategory 92.2 excludes radiotherapy for:

*   Ablation of pituitary gland (07.64-07.69)
*   Destruction of chorioretinal lesion (14.26-14.27)

Coding Guidance
   AHA: 3Q, '92, 5; 4Q, '05, 117-118

92.20   Infusion of liquid brachytherapy radioisotope

Description
The physician infuses a radioactive solution to kill cancerous cells. Brachytherapy is the application of radioactive isotopes for internal radiation. This procedure specifically describes the infusion of liquid brachytherapy radioisotope into a body cavity. Radioactive material is prepared in solutions for intracavitary infusion or oral administration. For this brachytherapy procedure, the physician infuses a radioactive substance (e.g., Iodine-125) into a body cavity.

For example, a liquid form of Iodine-125 (Iotrex) may be delivered by a separately reportable balloon-tipped catheter delivery system directly into a malignant brain tumor cavity after surgical removal of the tumor. The Iotrex is instilled through the catheter into the balloon, which remains in situ for three to seven days, irradiating the tumor cavity and surrounding tissues. This allows for a precise delivery of high dose radiation and minimizes damage to healthy brain tissue. Upon completion of therapy, the Iotrex is removed from the balloon catheter, and the catheter is removed from the treatment site.

Coding Clarification
Procedures classifiable to 92.20 include:

- I-125 radioisotope
- Intracavitary brachytherapy
- Removal of radioisotope

92.21   Superficial radiation

Description
This procedure code reports external radiation specified as superficial or contact radiation therapy, with a dosage of up to 150 KVP. This type of radiation therapy causes less scarring and yields more favorable aesthetic (cosmetic) results than the traditional surgical approach. A low energy radiation beam which only penetrates the top surface layer of the skin, avoiding deep tissue, is applied to the lesion. Alternately, the physician may perform a surface application by placing the radioactive source sealed in a small holder against a tumor. However, dosage, technique and anatomic site of treatment may vary.

Coding Clarification
Code 92.21 includes contact radiation (up to 150 KVP).

92.22   Orthovoltage radiation

Description
In this procedure, orthovoltage radiation is used to treat shallow tumor volumes where underlying tissues need to be protected. Orthovoltage radiation therapy may be used to treat superficial skin lesions.

Coding Clarification
Code 92.22 includes deep radiation (200-300 KVP).

92.23   Radioisotopic teleradiotherapy

Description
This procedure involves the use of certain radioisotope radioactive substances to conduct external radiation therapy (teleradiotherapy). A radioisotope may be defined as a specific group of unstable elements that release radiation as they break down. Specific isotopes are effective in treating

certain types of tumors. Cobalt teletherapy units and cesium teletherapy units may be used to direct gamma rays from a distance to the targeted area. For example, when Cobalt-60 breaks down at a molecular level, it releases gamma radiation which is effective in the treatment of certain tumors when delivered by external beam radiation. However, due to advances in radiation oncology many cobalt gamma ray systems have been replaced with linear accelerators, which are more effective at destroying some tumors.

Coding Clarification
Code 92.23 includes radioisotopic teleradiotherapy using:

- Cobalt-60
- Iodine-125
- Radioactive cesium

92.24   Teleradiotherapy using protons

92.25   Teleradiotherapy using electrons

Description
External radiation is very often delivered by linear accelerator which can deliver high energy radiation to a targeted area. Radiation therapy damages the DNA of the tumor cells by directing a focused beam of photon or electron waves or particles to the tumor. This disrupts the renders the cell's ability to divide and reproduce, either destroying or effectively shrinking the tumor. Photons can target deeper lying tumor tissue, while electrons are used for the maximum dose of radiation near the skin surface.

Coding Clarification
Code 92.24 includes teleradiotherapy using photons specified as:

- Megavoltage NOS
- Supervoltage NOS
- Use of Betatron or linear accelerator

Code 92.25 includes teleradiotherapy using beta particles.

Code 92.25 excludes intraoperative electron radiation therapy (92.41).

92.26   Teleradiotherapy of other particulate radiation

Description
This procedure describes radiation therapy specified as teleradiation or particulate radiation therapy. Dosage, technique, and anatomic site of treatment may vary, including:

- **High energy neutron radiation treatment:** External beam radiotherapy is radiation delivered from a distant source outside the body and directed at the patient's cancer site. High-energy neutron radiotherapy destroys the cells ability to divide and grow by damaging the cells through nuclear interactions, which decreases the damaged cells chances of repairing themselves. Since high-energy neutron radiotherapy works in the absence of oxygen, unlike conventional radiation therapy, it is used to treat larger tumors and is particularly effective in treating inoperable salivary gland tumors, bone cancers, and certain types of advanced malignancies of the pancreas, bladder, lung, prostate, and uterus. Due to the high potency of neutron radiation, the required dose is much less than with conventional radiotherapy, and a full course may be delivered in 10 to 12 treatments rather than the usual 30 to 40.

- **Proton radiation treatment:** Protons are positively charged particles that are particularly beneficial in treating malignancies and other neoplastic abnormalities near sensitive structures such as the optic nerve and spinal cord. Proton beam treatment delivers higher doses of radiation to tumors than photon beams and at the same time does not exceed radiation tolerance of normal, healthy tissue next to the targeted area. Because of the physical properties of the positively-charged protons, they stop short just at the target and do not deposit a dose beyond that boundary, making proton beam treatment advantageous for deep seated and solid tumors in any body site.

92.27   Implantation or insertion of radioactive elements

Description
This procedure code reports the implantation or insertion of a radiation source within a cavity (intracavitary) or tissue (interstitial), to deliver precision therapy to a treatment area. Radioactive elements (seeds) may be implanted by surgical incision or inserted through a catheter or endoscope. The delivery device may be placed on a previous encounter, and the patient admitted for radiotherapy at a later date. However, endoscopic placement of a radiation source may be performed during one encounter. For example, a lung tumor may be treated by bronchoscopic placement of a radioactive seeds.

Coding Clarification
Code also incision of site.

Code 92.27 excludes infusion of liquid brachytherapy radioisotope (92.20).

Code 92.27 includes radiation therapy for treatment of coronary artery stent narrowing or occlusion. This procedure may be described as catheter-based

intravascular radiation therapy. Upon angioplasty, a ribbon of radioactive seeds or a radioactive stent is inserted across the lesion to prevent re-stenosis.

Coding Guidance
AHA: 1Q, '88, 4; 3Q, '94, 11; 1Q, '00, 11, 12; Q, '04, 3-4

92.28   Injection or instillation of radioisotopes

Description
The physician injects or instills a radioactive solution to kill cancerous cells. Brachytherapy is the application of radioactive isotopes for internal radiation. Radioactive materials or solutions may be prepared in solutions for intravenous or other route of instillation or injection. This type of brachytherapy may be referred to as unsealed internal radiation therapy.

Coding Clarification
Injection is the act of forcing a liquid substance into the body, usually by means of a syringe.

Instillation is the act of forcing a liquid substance into the body, usually by means of a syringe.

Code 92.28 includes:

- Injection or infusion of radioimmunoconjugate
- Intracavitary injection or instillation
- Intravenous injection or instillation
- Iodine-131 [I-131] tositumomab
- Radioimmunotherapy
- Ytrium-90 [Y-90] ibritumomab tiuxetan

Code 92.28 excludes infusion of liquid brachytherapy radioisotope (92.20).

Code 92.28 includes radioimmunotherapy, a method of radiation treatment that targets radiation to the tumor using monoclonal antibodies (MAbs). Monoclonal antibodies bind specifically to cancer cell-antigens and induce an immunological response against the cancer cell. This enhances patient's immune response to act against cell growth factors and stop cancer cell growth.

92.29   Other radiotherapeutic procedure

Description
This code reports other radiotherapy not classifiable elsewhere in subcategory 92.2.

Coding Clarification
This code should not be assigned if the medical record contains sufficient information to facilitate coding at a higher level of specificity.

Documentation Tip
If the documentation is ambiguous or unclear, the physician should be queried.

92.3 Stereotactic radiosurgery

Coding Clarification
Code also stereotactic head frame application (93.59).

This subcategory excludes stereotactic biopsy procedures.

Fourth-digit subclassifications describe the type of radiation therapy provided.

Coding Guidance
AHA: 4Q, '95, 70; 4Q, '98, 79

92.30 Stereotactic radiosurgery, not otherwise specified

92.31 Single source photon radiosurgery

92.32 Multi-source photon radiosurgery

Coding Guidance
AHA: 4Q, '04, 113

92.33 Particulate radiosurgery

92.39 Stereotactic radiosurgery, not elsewhere classified

Description
Prior to imaging and radiation treatment, a stereotactic head frame is applied to immobilize the head and enable accurate, precision delivery. Using stereotactic techniques, a precise 3-dimensional location of the brain lesion is identified using CT, MRI, or angiogram. The physician uses the coordinates obtained from the images to focus gamma ray or proton beam energy onto the lesion, thereby destroying it. This is a non-invasive procedure that does not require incision of the scalp or drilling into the skull.

92.4 Intra-operative radiation procedures

92.41 Intra-operative electron radiation therapy

Description
These procedures involve an intensive radiation treatment administered during surgery by a specialized, light-weight, self-shielded linear accelerator designed for use in the operative room (OR). This mobile device enables radiation treatment to be administered at the time of surgery, directly to the tumor or post-resection tumor bed. IOERT applies precision electron radiation beams to highly-focused anatomic sites, protecting the normal surrounding tissues from exposure. Utilization of this mobile unit also solves the logistical problems that arise when patients are transported from the OR to radiation treatment at a separate location. Providing therapy in the sterile surgical environment

also reduces the risk of infection and other post-surgical complications. Performance of this procedure requires specific equipment and the presence of a surgeon and radiation oncologist to verify the margins and determine the depth and scope of treatment. The average time for completion of this procedure is 2-3 minutes. However, the total time may exceed 30-40 minutes depending on the complexity of treatment and number of treatment sites.

Coding Clarification
Code 92.41 identifies the intraoperative radiation therapy as electron-based.

Coding Scenario
A patient was admitted for surgical removal and treatment of a malignant pancreatic tumor. Immediately after tumor resection was completed, the radiation oncologist delivered a specialized high dose of focal radiation directly to the tumor bed while normal tissues were protected.

Code Assignment:

157.9	Malignant neoplasm of pancreas, part unspecified
52.22	Other excision or destruction of lesion or tissue of pancreas or pancreatic duct
92.41	Intra Operative Radiation Therapy

Coding Guidance
AHA: 4Q, '07, 122

---

93 Physical therapy, respiratory therapy, rehabilitation, and related procedures

Description
Category 93 classifies both diagnostic and therapeutic procedures. Subcategory 93.0 lists diagnostic evaluations used to evaluate the patient's status and establish treatment plan for therapy. Category 93 classifies therapeutic physical, speech, occupational, respiratory, and other rehabilitative procedures. Subcategories 93.0–93.3 classify different types of physical therapy evaluation and treatments. Subcategory 93.4 is used for skeletal and other types of traction. For other types of immobilization, such as the application of a neck support or pressure dressing, see subcategory 93.5. To code osteopathic manipulation treatment, ICD-9-CM lists 7 codes under subcategory 93.6. Codes for rehabilitation are found under subcategories 93.7 and 93.8. The final subcategory classifies respiratory therapy. It will be necessary to review the medical record for information on the specific type of procedure in order to choose the most appropriate code from this group of subcategories.

93.0   Diagnostic physical therapy

Description

Physical therapy is a health care specialty utilizes specially trained practitioners and personnel to treat disorders of the musculoskeletal system and physical movement associated with disease, injury or other illness. Physical therapy includes a diagnostic assessment which enables the development of a treatment strategy and patient goals. Modalities of treatment may vary, depending on the patient's needs and abilities.

Coding Guidance

   AHA: N-D, '86, 7

93.01   Functional evaluation

Description

The health care provider examines the patient/client. This includes taking a comprehensive history, systems review, and tests and measures. Tests and measures may include but are not limited to tests of range of motion, motor function, muscle performance, joint integrity and neuromuscular status. The physical therapist formulates an assessment, prognosis, and notes an anticipated intervention.

93.02   Orthotic evaluation

93.03   Prosthetic evaluation

Description

The health care provider examines the patient/client. Tests and measures include evaluation and review of prosthetic or orthotic devices. Various movements required for activities of daily living are examined. Dexterity, range of movement, and other elements may also be studied to evaluate the performance and function of the devices. The PT formulates an assessment, prognosis, and notes an anticipated intervention.

93.04   Manual testing of muscle function

Description

Muscles or muscle groups of the body are tested for strength and function.

Coding Guidance

   AHA: J-F, '87, 16

93.05   Range of motion testing

Description

Testing determines active and passive range of motion the joint structures of the body. This code applies to manually testing the range of motion to joints such as the major and minor joints of the extremities or spine for flexibility and comfort. Testing determines active and passive range of

motion for extremities and joints. This procedure includes diagnostic manipulation to determine range of motion.

Coding Clarification

In the situation of manipulation of a joint, determine the purpose for which the manipulation is done as this influences the code choice. For example, use 93.05 for the diagnostic manipulation of the knee such as to determine range of motion.

Coding Guidance

   AHA: J-F, '87, 16

93.06   Measurement of limb length

Description

This procedure code reports limb measurement. Technique may vary, however leg length may be measured by direct or indirect method. Direct limb measurement is taken from the anterior superior iliac spine (ASIS) to the medial malleolus. Indirect measurement involves palpation of the iliac crests in a standing position. The level of the hands indicates the limb length discrepancy. Blocks are then placed under the short leg until the hands are equal. The blocks are then measured and the discrepancy is calculated. The procedure may be repeated with the anterior and posterior iliac spine.

93.07   Body measurement

Description

This procedure uses body measurement to assist in diagnosis and establishment of treatment plans. This procedure includes body measurement such as abdominal girth and head circumference. Abdominal girth is the measurement of the distance around the abdomen at a specific point, usually at the level of the belly button (navel). Head circumference is measured by positioning a tape measure so that its edge follows the hair line around the head and nape of the neck.

93.08   Electromyography

Description

Electromyography is a medical technique used for evaluating and recording physiologic properties of muscles at rest and while contracting. Technique and anatomic site of evaluation may vary.

Needle electromyography (EMG) records the electrical properties of muscle using an oscilloscope. Recordings, which may be amplified and heard through a loudspeaker, are made during needle insertion, with the muscle at rest, and during contraction. This procedure uses a single fiber electrode to obtain additional information on specific muscles, including quantitative measurement of jitter, blocking, and/or fiber density.

Coding Clarification
Code 93.08 excludes:

- Eye EMG (95.25)

- That with polysomnogram (89.17)

- Urethral sphincter EMG (89.23)

Coding Clarification:
Kinetic studies are classified in accordance with the type of kinetic study documented in the medical record. It may be appropriate to assign a code from category 93 or 89 such as neurological function test (89.15) or electromyography (93.08).

Coding Guidance
> **AHA:** J-F, '87, 16

93.09   Other diagnostic physical therapy procedure

Description
This code describes other diagnostic physical therapy procedures not classifiable elsewhere in subcategory 93.0

Coding Clarification
This code should not be assigned if the medical record contains sufficient information to facilitate coding at a higher level of specificity.

Documentation Tip
If the documentation is ambiguous or unclear, the physician should be queried.

93.1   Physical therapy exercises

Description
This subclassification includes processes used to restore motion to a joint.

Coding Guidance
> **AHA:** N-D, '86, 7; J-F, '87, 16

93.11   Assisting exercise

93.12   Other active musculoskeletal exercise

93.13   Resistive exercise

93.14   Training in joint movements

93.15   Mobilization of spine

93.16   Mobilization of other joints

93.17   Other passive musculoskeletal exercise

93.18   Breathing exercise

93.19   Exercise, not elsewhere classified

Description
The health care provider uses dynamic therapeutic activities designed to achieve improved functional

performance and ease of movement (mobilization).The physical therapist uses these codes to report the unique manual treatments used to influence joint, musculoskeletal and physiological function. Several modalities exist and multiple anatomic sites may be treated.

Coding Clarification
Code 93.11 excludes assisted exercise in pool (93.31).

Code 93.16 excludes manipulation of the temporomandibular joint (76.95).

93.2   Other physical therapy musculoskeletal manipulation

Coding Guidance
> **AHA:** N-D, '86, 7

93.21   Manual and mechanical traction

Description
The health care provider applies sustained or intermittent mechanical traction to the body by the application of manual or mechanical forces which serve to relieve pain and increase tissue flexibility.

Coding Clarification
Code 93.21 excludes:

- Skeletal traction (93.43-93.44)

- Skin traction (93.45-93.46)

- Spinal traction (93.41-93.42)

93.22   Ambulation and gait training

Description
The health care provider instructs the patient in specific activities that will facilitate ambulation and stair climbing with or without an assistive device. Proper sequencing and safety instructions are included when appropriate.

93.23   Fitting of orthotic device

93.24   Training in use of prosthetic or orthotic device

Description
The health care provider fits or trains the patient in the use of an orthotic or prosthetic device for one or more body parts. This includes assessment as to type of orthotic when appropriate. This does not include fabrication time, if appropriate, or cost of materials.

93.25   Forced extension of limb

93.26   Manual rupture of joint adhesions

93.27   Stretching of muscle or tendon

93.28   Stretching of fascia

Description
The health care provider uses dynamic therapeutic activities designed to achieve improved functional performance and ease of movement (mobilization).The physical therapist uses these codes to report the unique manual treatments used to influence joint, musculoskeletal and physiological function. Several modalities exist and multiple anatomic sites may be treated. These codes include forcible mobilization to rupture joint adhesions (93.26) or to stretch muscles and tendons (93.27) or fascia (93.28).

93.29   Other forcible correction of musculoskeletal deformity

Description
This procedure code includes other physical therapy therapeutic procedures not classifiable elsewhere in subcategories 93.1 or 93.2.

Coding Clarification
This code should not be assigned if the medical record contains sufficient information to facilitate coding at a higher level of specificity.

Code 93.29 includes manipulation for correction of certain joint contractures.

Documentation Tip
If the documentation is ambiguous or unclear, the physician should be queried.

Coding Guidance
 AHA: N-D, '85, 11

93.3   Other physical therapy therapeutic procedures

Description
This subcategory lists a variety of physical therapy therapeutic procedures not classifiable elsewhere in subcategories 93.1 or 93.2. Several treatment modalities exist and multiple anatomic sites may be treated.

93.31   Assisted exercise in pool

Description
The health care provider directs or performs therapeutic exercises with the patient in an aquatic environment. Aquatic, or pool therapy, uses the physical properties of water (i.e., buoyancy, warmth, viscosity, hydrostatic pressure) to assist in patient

treatment. The water provides buoyancy and resistance, which allows for muscle strengthening with decreased joint stress, making it is easier and less painful to perform exercises.

93.32   Whirlpool treatment

Description
The health care provider uses a whirlpool to provide superficial heat in an environment that facilitates tissue debridement, wound cleaning, and/or exercise. The clinician decides the appropriate water temperature and provides safety instruction.

93.33   Other hydrotherapy

Description
Hubbard tank is used when it is necessary to immerse the full body into water. Care of wounds and burns may require use of the Hubbard tank to facilitate tissue cleansing and debridement.

93.34   Diathermy

Description
The health care provider uses diathermy or microwave as a form of superficial heat for one or more body areas. After application and safety instructions have been provided, the clinician supervises the treatment.

93.35   Other heat therapy

Description
The health care provider uses a paraffin bath to apply superficial heat to a hand or foot. The part is repeatedly dipped into the paraffin forming a glove. Use of paraffin facilitates treatment of arthritis and other conditions that cause limitations in joint flexibility.

In an alternate treatment, the health care provider applies heat (dry or moist) or cold to one or more body parts with appropriate padding to prevent skin irritation. The patient is given necessary safety instructions.

Coding Clarification
Code 93.35 includes:

*   Acupuncture with smoldering moxa

*   Hot packs

*   Hyperthermia NEC

*   Infrared irradiation

*   Moxibustion

*   Paraffin bath

Code 93.35 excludes hyperthermia for treatment of cancer (99.85).

93.36 Cardiac retraining

Description
The health care provider instigates a cardiac rehabilitation regimen following myocardial infarction or coronary bypass graft procedure.

93.37 Prenatal training

Description
This code describes training for natural childbirth.

93.38 Combined physical therapy without mention of the components

Coding Clarification
The use of this code would be inappropriate for reporting an inpatient procedure since it is a nonspecific code. If the medical record does not contain sufficient information for identification of the involved services, the health care provider should be queried.

93.39 Other physical therapy

Description
Code 93.39 may be used to report application of a TENS unit (a nerve stimulation device commonly used to relieve pain).

Coding Guidance
   AHA: 3Q, '91, 15; 3Q, '97, 12; 4Q, '03, 105-106, 108-110; 2Q, '05, 6

93.4 Skeletal traction and other traction

Description
This subcategory lists a skeletal traction and other traction procedures. Several types of traction treatment modalities exist and multiple anatomic sites may be treated. Traction may be defined as the act of drawing or pulling, associated with forces applied to the body to stretch or separate certain anatomic sites or parts. Traction may be used in treatment of fractures, spinal disorders and other musculoskeletal or joint maladies to relive pain and immobility.

93.41 Spinal traction using skull device

Description
The physician applies a device to the head to exert pulling force on the spine.

Coding Clarification
Code 93.41 includes traction using:

- Caliper tongs
- Crutchfield tongs
- Halo device
- Vinke tongs

Code 93.41 excludes insertion of tongs or halo traction device (02.94).

Coding Guidance
   AHA: 2Q, '94, 3; 3Q, '96, 14; 3Q, '01, 8

93.42 Other spinal traction

Description
The health care provider applies sustained or intermittent mechanical traction to the cervical and/or lumbar spine. The mechanical force produces distraction between the vertebrae thereby relieving pain and increasing tissue flexibility.

Coding Clarification
Code 93.42 includes Cotrel's traction.

Code 93.42 excludes cervical collar (93.52).

93.43 Intermittent skeletal traction

Description
This code describes starting and stopping the application of traction at specific intervals of time to facilitate gradual therapeutic healing.

93.44 Other skeletal traction

Documentation Tip
Traction procedures classifiable to 93.44 may be documented as:

- Bryant's
- Dunlop's
- Lyman Smith
- Russell's

93.45 Thomas' splint traction

Description
The physician places a ring around the thigh, attached to rods running the length of the leg, for therapeutic purposes.

93.46 Other skin traction of limbs

Coding Clarification
Code 93.46 includes:

- Adhesive tape traction
- Boot traction
- Buck's traction
- Gallows traction

93.5 Other immobilization, pressure, and attention to wound

Coding Clarification
Subcategory 93.5 excludes external fixator device (84.71-84.73) and wound cleansing (96.58-96.59).

Report separately any documented wound treatment such as excisional (86.22) or non-excisional (86.28) wound debridement.

● New Code   ▲ Revised Code   ►◄ Revised Text   © 2010 Ingenix

93.51 Application of plaster jacket

Description

- **Halo body cast:** The physician constructs this body cast to provide a foundation for a halo in which the cervical spine must be stabilized. This involves use of a torso body cast to which the halo is attached. Casting material is applied tightly, beginning at the pelvis and extending up the torso to the upper chest. Extenders from the halo (which is already inserted around the head) can be attached to the body cast. This holds the halo very securely. An alternative is to use a prefabricated torso/chest brace that is placed on the upper torso. The previously applied halo is attached.

- **Risser jacket:** The physician applies a Risser jacket, a method of correction for a scoliotic curve. The physician places the patient face up on a canvas strap tied to a rectangular frame. A stockinette is stretched over the patient from the head to the knees. A metallic half-circle carrying a moveable jack with a metal plate to be directed toward the apex of the angulation of the ribs is suspended beneath the frame. The rib angulation area is protected by a heave piece of felt covered with a contoured square piece of plaster that rests on the plate. The jack is turned so that it presses the plate in a direction on the rib angulation that corrects the scoliotic curvature. A second jack may be applied to correct a double primary curve or a secondary lumbar curve. The cast is applied in sections while traction is applied to the head with a hatter and the pelvis with a pelvic belt attached to the plaster girdle. The casting begins with a well-molded neck and shoulder section and finishes with incorporating the trunk.

- **Turnbuckle jacket:** The physician applies a turnbuckle jacket to treat scoliotic curves. The physician places the patient face up on a horizontal canvas strap attached to a rectangular frame. Traction is applied by pulling distally on the pelvis on the convex side of the scoliotic curve and the head is pulled toward the concave side. All bony prominences are padded well and two or three layers of felt are placed under the proposed location of the anterior hinge. A body cast is applied extending from the neck to above the knee on the convex side of the curve. Metal hinges are placed in the front and back of the cast toward the convex side of the curve. The cast is allowed to dry for three to five days, cut at the level of the hinges on the concave side forward and back to the hinges. Turnbuckle lugs are inserted into these cuts. A turnbuckle is attached to these edges. From the opposite side of the cast, the physician

removes a large elliptical window between the hinges. The turnbuckle is turned each morning. When x-rays (reported separately) indicate the hinges are on the convex side of the curve, no further correction may be obtained by traction. The sides of the cast are reinforced with plaster and wood strips. The turnbuckle and lugs are removed. A large window is cut in the cast over the area of fusion.

Coding Clarification

Code 93.51 excludes Minerva jacket (93.52).

93.52 Application of neck support

Coding Clarification

Code 93.52 includes application of:

- Cervical collar

- Minerva jacket

- Molded neck support

93.53 Application of other cast

Description

This procedure code describes the application of other cast not classifiable elsewhere in subcategory 93.5.

Coding Clarification

This code should not be assigned if the medical record contains sufficient information to facilitate coding at a higher level of specificity.

Documentation Tip

If the documentation is ambiguous or unclear, the physician should be queried.

93.54 Application of splint

Description

This code reports the application of a rigid device used to stabilize and prevent motion of a joint structure or fractured bones. Anatomic site of application and type of splint device may vary, including:

- **Short arm splint:** The physician applies a splint from the forearm to the hand. A short arm splint is used to immobilize the wrist. Cotton padding is applied from midforearm to the midpalm region. Plaster strips or fiberglass splint material are applied along the palm side of the hand, extending to midforearm, maintain the wrist in the desired position. An Ace wrap is applied by the physician to hold the splint material in position.

- **Short leg splint:** The physician applies a short leg splint from calf to foot. A short leg splint is used to immobilize the ankle. The physician wraps cotton bandaging from just below the knee to the toes. Plaster strips or fiberglass splinting material are applied to the posterior of the calf, around the heel, and along the bottom of the foot to the toes. The splint material is allowed to dry. The splint is secured into place with an Ace wrap.

Coding Clarification
Code 93.54 includes plaster and tray splint.

Code 93.54 excludes periodontal splint (24.7).

93.55   Dental wiring

Description
The physician treats conditions other than fractures, such as temporomandibular dislocations, by applying intermaxillary fixation (wiring the jaws together) for immobilization. No incisions are made with this technique; however, the physician may have already surgically reduced the dislocation. The physician may wire arch bars to the teeth or use other wiring techniques to provide the interdental fixation. For edentulous patients (without teeth), dentures or custom made acrylic splints are wired to the jaws. The jaws are wired together.

Coding Clarification
Code 93.55 excludes wiring for orthodontia (24.7).

93.56   Application of pressure dressing

Coding Clarification
Code 93.56 includes application of:

*   Gibney bandage
*   Robert Jones' bandage
*   Shanz dressing

93.57   Application of other wound dressing

Coding Clarification
Code 93.57 includes application of OASIS wound dressing.

Coding Guidance
   AHA: 3Q, '02, 23

93.58   Application of pressure trousers

Coding Clarification
Code 93.58 includes application of:

*   Pressure trousers
*   Anti-shock trousers
*   MAST trousers
*   Vasopneumatic device

Coding Guidance
   AHA: 3Q, '96, 13

93.59   Other immobilization, pressure, and attention to wound

Description
This code describes application of other immobilization or pressure devices or attention to wound procedures not classifiable elsewhere in subcategory 93.5. Anatomic site of application and type of device or treatment may vary, including:

*   **Application of stereotactic frame:** The physician applies a stereotactic frame to stabilize an injured cervical spine for radiography, a stretch test, surgery, or spinal realignment. The physician places the patient supine with the head supported just over the end of the table. The physician applies Betadine solution with sponges to the ears. The physician separates or removes hair 1 cm above the ears slightly posterior to the midlateral line. A local anesthetic is injected into the areas selected for pin insertion. Tongs are held in the appropriate position while both skull pins are inserted simultaneously, keeping the tongs equidistant from the skull on either side. The pins are advanced until the indicator button on one pin protrudes 2 mm to 3 mm. Lock nuts are applied and the pins are checked every two to three hours for proper tightness.

*   **Strapping, lower extremity or hip:** The physician or medical professional uses tape to strap a lower extremity. Taping of the hip for immobilization is rarely used because of the hip muscles' superior strength to that of the tape. A spica taping procedure may be used to hold analgesic packs in place and to offer mild support to injured joint or muscle. The patient stands with all weight on the unaffected leg. Six inch Ace wrap is usually used. The end of the wrap begins slightly above the affected area of the leg and encircles the leg, crossing the starting point. For hip injuries, when the starting end is reached the roll is taken completely around the waist and fixed firmly above the iliac crest. The wrap is carried around the thigh at groin level and up again around the waist. The end is secured with tape.

Coding Clarification
Code 93.59 includes:

*   Elastic stockings
*   Electronic gaiter
*   Intermittent pressure device
*   Oxygenation of wound (hyperbaric)
*   Stereotactic head frame application
*   Strapping (non-traction)
*   Velpeau dressing

● New Code   ▲ Revised Code   ▶◀ Revised Text   © 2010 Ingenix

- High-voltage stimulation for healing of decubitus ulcer

Coding Guidance
AHA: 1Q, '89, 12; 1Q, '91, 11; 1Q, '99, 12, 13; 3Q, '99, 7

93.6   Osteopathic manipulative treatment

Description
This category describes osteopathic manipulative treatment (OMT), which is a method of therapy that employs the use of the hands to diagnose, treat, and prevent illness or injury. The physician, who is a specially trained Doctor of Osteopathic Medicine (D.O.), uses the hands to move muscles and joints using techniques including stretching, gentle pressure, and resistance to ease pain, promote healing, and increase mobility.

Terms used to describe specific forces of osteopathic manipulative therapies include:

- Velocity—speed of motion, swiftness.
- Amplitude—magnitude, breadth or range.
- Isotonic—involving muscular contraction in which the muscle remains under relatively constant tension while its length changes.
- Isometric—involving muscular contraction in which tension increases while length remains constant.

OMT includes isolating and reducing tensions and malalignments in the soft tissues, bones, and joints. OMT techniques vary depending on the nature of the presenting problem and focus of therapy, counterstrain, cranial, muscle energy, myofascial release (MFR), and high velocity-low amplitude (HVLA) thrust, among others.

93.61   Osteopathic manipulative treatment for general mobilization

Description
As tolerated by the patient, the physician gently and repeatedly forces the joint to the point of resistance, reducing the restrictive barrier to improve range motion.

93.62   Osteopathic manipulative treatment using high-velocity, low-amplitude forces

Description
The physician slowly eases the joint in the direction of resistance. At the point of resistance, the physician pulls gently against the restraint while applying a quick force to affect a "pop" in the joint, resulting in immediate increased range and freedom of motion.

93.63   Osteopathic manipulative treatment using low-velocity, high-amplitude forces

Description
The physician may engage the restrictive barrier repeatedly to produce an increased freedom of motion.

93.64   Osteopathic manipulative treatment using isotonic, isometric forces

Description
The physician conducts manipulations utilizing the force of muscle contractions in a specific way to release pain in an affected area and increase range of motion. Isometric manipulations consist of the force applied by the physician on a particular muscle or muscle group, which is equal to the force exerted by the patient. Isotonic manipulations consist of a force applied by the physician on a particular muscle or muscle group, which is less than the force exerted by the patient.

93.65   Osteopathic manipulative treatment using indirect forces

Description
The physician treats pain, tissue or malalignments by exerting pressure or tension on opposing parts to causing an indirect release. Technique may vary.

In a facilitated positional release (FPR), the physician provides myofascial treatment. The body is placed into a neutral position, diminishing tissue and joint tension in all planes. A force such as compression or torsion may be added. This provides therapeutic results without direct manipulation of the affected region.

93.66   Osteopathic manipulative treatment to move tissue fluids

Description
This procedure involves manipulations in which the impact of pressure induces therapeutic changes on lymphatic flow.

93.67   Other specified osteopathic manipulative treatment

Description
This procedure code describes other OMT treatment not classifiable elsewhere in subcategory 93.6.

Coding Clarification
This code should not be assigned if the medical record contains sufficient information to facilitate coding at a higher level of specificity.

Documentation Tip
If the documentation is ambiguous or unclear, the physician should be queried.

93.7 Speech and reading rehabilitation and rehabilitation of the blind

93.71 Dyslexia training

93.72 Dysphasia training

Description
Under direction of a physician, the patient undergoes developmental programs such as speech therapy, sign language, or lip reading instruction or hearing rehabilitation. In auditory processing disorders, the patient (usually a child) cannot process the information heard due to lack of integration between the ears and the brain, even though hearing may be normal. Central auditory processing disorder (CAPD) is often confused with or functions as an underlying factor to a number of learning disabilities.

Coding Clarification
Dysphasia training (93.72) involves training patients with speech impairments to coordinate and arrange words in the proper order.

93.73 Esophageal speech training

Description
A voice prosthetic device, such as an amplifier, is used to augment speech for a patient with complete or partial speech loss. This code includes evaluating the patient for use of and/or fitting the device often by a speech therapist or physician.

Coding Clarification
Esophageal speech training (93.73) is speech training after removal of the voice box; sound is produced by the vibration of an air column in the esophagus against the contracting ring-like musculature closing of the windpipe.

93.74 Speech defect training

93.75 Other speech training and therapy

Description
The physician takes a history of the patient, including speech and language development, hearing loss, and physical and mental development. A physical examination is performed. Hearing tests and speech/language evaluations are performed. Assessment of deficits and a plan for the patient are made. These plans may involve speech therapy, hearing aids, etc. In auditory processing disorders, the patient (usually children) cannot process the information heard due to lack of integration between the ears and the brain, even though hearing may be normal. Central auditory processing disorder (CAPD) is often confused with or functions as an underlying factor to a number of learning disabilities. Under direction of a physician, the patient undergoes

developmental programs such as speech therapy, sign language, or lip reading instruction or hearing rehabilitation. In auditory processing disorders, the patient (usually a child) cannot process the information heard due to lack of integration between the ears and the brain, even though hearing may be normal. Central auditory processing disorder (CAPD) is often confused with or functions as an underlying factor to a number of learning disabilities.

Coding Guidance
    AHA: 3Q, '97, 12; 4Q, '97, 36; 4Q, '03, 105, 109

93.76 Training in use of lead dog for the blind

93.77 Training in braille or moon

93.78 Other rehabilitation for the blind

Description
These procedures involve specific modalities of training for the blind to assist in activities of daily living. Therapies and training vary depending on the type of vision loss, the extent of vision loss, progression of blindness and the patient's needs and any other health concerns. Specific skills include the use of devices such as a cane, reading machine or learning Braille. Training may also include the assistance of a guide dog, which includes proper canine care and handling.

93.8 Other rehabilitation therapy

Description
This subcategory lists other rehabilitation therapy procedures not classifiable elsewhere in category 93. Rehabilitation is a system of therapeutic medicine that assists a patient in regaining strength, relearning skills or adjusting to life after a serious illness or injury. The type of therapy a patient needs and the goals of therapy vary depending on the nature of illness or injury suffered and the deficits or impairments that remain.

93.81 Recreational therapy

Description
This procedure code includes therapeutic recreation and leisure activities to improve the physical, emotional, cognitive and social functioning of patients suffering from illness, disability or other challenges. Goals and objectives are individualized to patient needs to provide the development of lifetime leisure skills.

Coding Clarification
Code 93.81 includes:

*   Diversional therapy
*   Play therapy

Code 93.81 excludes play psychotherapy (94.36).

93.82   Educational therapy

Description

This procedure involves therapeutic intervention to assist a patient with learning difficulties. The goals of educational therapy often include improving the learning process, developing learning strategies and restoration of self esteem. Educational therapy differs from tutoring by focusing on attention and focus, visual and auditory processing and memory skills, whereby tutoring mainly focuses on remediation of academic skills. The patient's challenges are identified through an evaluation process, and therapy plan is developed.

Coding Clarification

Code 93.82 includes:

- Education of bed-bound children

- Special schooling for the handicapped

93.83   Occupational therapy

Description

This procedure code describes rehabilitative treatment that assists patients to develop or achieve independence in their lives. Health conditions such as injuries, debilitating disease, disabilities, post-surgical status, fracture and other problems can benefit from occupational therapy. Treatments is tailored to the patient's individual needs, which may include improving the patient's ability to perform daily activities, assistance with adaptation or provision and training in the use of specialized equipment.

Coding Clarification

Code 93.83 excludes training in activities of daily living for the blind (93.78).

Coding Guidance

AHA: 3Q, '97, 12; 4Q, '03, 105-106, 108, 110; 2Q, '05, 6

93.84   Music therapy

Description

This procedure code includes rehabilitative treatment which uses music to accomplish individualized goals to improve motor skills, cognitive development, self-awareness and other enhancements. The therapist designs music sessions for individuals or groups based on their needs and preferences. Music therapy may include making music, writing songs, listening to music or imagery and learning through music.

93.85   Vocational rehabilitation

Description

This procedure involves an employment program for patients with disabilities or certain health-related challenges. An assessment is performed to identify the patient's strengths, skills, needs capabilities and preferences. Specialized programs and services may be available for patients with specific disabilities such as visual impairment or blindness.

Coding Clarification

Code 93.85 includes:

- Sheltered employment

- Vocational assessment, retraining or training

93.89   Rehabilitation, not elsewhere classified

Description

This code reports rehabilitation not classified elsewhere in subcategory 93.8.

Coding Clarification

This code should not be assigned if the medical record contains sufficient information to facilitate coding at a higher level of specificity.

Documentation Tip

If the documentation is ambiguous or unclear, the physician should be queried.

Coding Guidance

AHA: 2Q, '05, 06

93.9   Respiratory therapy

Coding Clarification

Subcategory 93.9 excludes insertion of airway (96.01-96.05); other continuous invasive (through endotracheal term tube or tracheostomy) mechanical ventilation is reported with codes 96.70-96.72.

93.90   Non-invasive mechanical ventilation

Description

A mechanical ventilator is applied with a mask over the nose and mouth or through a tube placed into the trachea for patients requiring help breathing due to a lung disorder. Intermittent positive pressure breathing uses positive pressure during the inspiration phase of breathing. This code applies to initial evaluation or application of continuous positive airway pressure for ventilation assistance with positive pressure during inspiration and exhalation.

Coding Clarification

A CPAP is defined as a noninvasive ventilation support system that augments the ability to breathe spontaneously without the insertion of an endotracheal tube or tracheostomy.

Code 93.90 includes:

- BiPAP without (delivery through) endotracheal tube or tracheostomy

- CPAP without (delivery through) endotracheal tube or tracheostomy

- Mechanical ventilation NOS

- Non-invasive PPV
- NPPV
- Mechanical ventilation delivered by non-invasive interface (e.g., face mask, nasal mask, nasal pillow, oral mouthpiece, oronasal mask)

When a patient is admitted on noninvasive mechanical ventilation and subsequently requires invasive mechanical ventilation, both types of mechanical ventilation should be coded.

Code 93.90 excludes invasive (through endotracheal tube or tracheostomy) continuous mechanical ventilation (96.70–96.72).

Coding Guidance
AHA: 1Q, '08, 8-9; 4Q, '91, 21; 3Q, '98, 14; 1Q, '02, 12, 13; 3Q, '04, 3; 1Q, '08, 8-9; 4Q, '08, 187-189

93.91   Intermittent positive pressure breathing (IPPB)
Description
A pressurized or nonpressurized inhalation treatment is applied for an acute obstruction of the airway, preventing the patient from taking in sufficient air on his or her own, or for sputum induction for diagnostic purposes. This is done with an aerosol generator, nebulizer, metered dose inhaler or intermittent positive pressure breathing (IPPB) device.

Coding Guidance
AHA: 4Q, '91, 21

93.93   Nonmechanical methods of resuscitation
Description
This procedure involves cardiopulmonary resuscitation by non-mechanical means. Cardiopulmonary arrest occurs when the patient's heart and lungs suddenly stop. In a clinical setting, cardiopulmonary resuscitation, the attempt at restarting the heart and lungs, is usually directed by a health care provider who is certified in Advanced Cardiac Life Support (ACLS). The patient's lungs are ventilated by mouth-to-mouth breathing or by a bag and mask. The patient's circulation is assisted using external chest compression.

Coding Clarification
Code 93.93 includes:

- Artificial respiration
- Manual resuscitation
- Mouth-to-mouth resuscitation

Coding Guidance
AHA: 2Q, '03. 17

93.94   Respiratory medication administered by nebulizer
Description
This procedure code reports administration of medication by mist or nebulizer therapy. A demonstration may be performed for the patient on how to use an aerosol generator, nebulizer, metered dose inhaler or other associated device. The patient's utilization is evaluated.

93.95   Hyperbaric oxygenation
Description
This procedure involves oxygen therapy delivered by a specialized pressure chamber that allows high levels of oxygen exposure to the organs and tissues of the body. The oxygen concentration inside the chamber is typically two times greater than normal atmospheric concentrations. Exposure to concentrated oxygen has proven effective treating conditions such as non-healing wounds, burns and infections.

Coding Clarification
Code 93.95 excludes oxygenation of wound (93.59) and SuperSaturated oxygen therapy (00.49).

93.96   Other oxygen enrichment
Description
This code describes the therapeutic administration of oxygen. Method of delivery may vary depending on the patient's individual circumstances. Oxygen therapy increases the supply of oxygen to the lungs, increasing the availability of oxygen to the body tissues.

Coding Clarification
Code 93.96 includes:

- Catalytic oxygen therapy
- Cytoreductive effect
- Oxygenators
- Oxygen therapy

Code 93.96 excludes oxygenation of wound (93.59) and SuperSaturated oxygen therapy (00.49).

93.97   Decompression chamber
Description
This procedure involves a specialized pressurized vessel used to allow deep sea divers and other underwater workers a safe, staged decompression process to prevent life-threatening decompression sickness and other diving disorders. A decompression chamber allows readjustment to normal atmospheric pressure after resurfacing from a dive, rather than making the necessary decompression stops while still underwater. The pressure inside the chamber neutralizes excess

nitrogen in the patient's bloodstream derived from rapid ascent ("the bends").

93.98 Other control of atmospheric pressure and composition

Description
This procedure code includes other atmospheric pressure and composition control procedures not classifiable elsewhere in subcategory 93.9.

Coding Clarification
This code should not be assigned if the medical record contains sufficient information to facilitate coding at a higher level of specificity.

Code 93.98 includes antigen-free air conditioning and Helium therapy.

Code 93.98 excludes inhaled nitric oxide therapy (INO) (00.12).

Documentation Tip
If the documentation is ambiguous or unclear, the physician should be queried.

Coding Guidance
  AHA: 1Q, '02, 14

93.99 Other respiratory therapy

Description
This code reports other respiratory therapeutic procedures not classifiable elsewhere in subcategory 93.9.

Coding Clarification
This code should not be assigned if the medical record contains sufficient information to facilitate coding at a higher level of specificity.

Code 93.99 includes continuous negative pressure ventilation (CNP) and postural drainage.

Documentation Tip
If the documentation is ambiguous or unclear, the physician should be queried.

Coding Guidance
  AHA: 4Q, '91, 22; 3Q, '99, 11; 4Q, '03, 108

94 Procedures related to the psyche

Description
A variety of procedures related to the psyche are classified to category 94. They include psychologic evaluation, testing, interviews, consultations, somatotherapy, psychotherapy, counseling, and alcohol and drug rehabilitation and detoxification. Individual psychotherapy has it is own subcategory, 94.3, as do referrals of psychologic rehabilitation, subcategory 94.5.

94.0 Psychologic evaluation and testing

Description
Psychology may be defined in general terms as the study of mental processes and behavior, and the treatment of associated mental health problems. Psychological treatment includes diagnostic patient evaluation and testing and the development of treatment plans, counseling, and therapies. A psychologist is not a physician, but is a licensed mental health professional that has a doctoral degree (e.g., PhD, PsyD, EdD) in counseling, industrial, education or clinical psychology. Patients that require medical care for mental health disease are treated by a psychiatric physician.

94.01 Administration of intelligence test

Description
This procedure code describes intelligence test procedures, during which a series of tasks or questions are presented to the person being tested, and the responses are graded according to a set of guidelines or references. The test results are compiled and compared to those of a similar population. Many types of tests are available, the most common of which are the Stanford-Binet Intelligence Scale and the Wechsler Intelligence Scales. Intelligence tests typically test for several types of mental processes such as spatial thinking, language processing, cognitive ability, comprehension, perception recall and reasoning. Many tests are revised on a regular basis to remove gender, racial and other biases.

94.02 Administration of psychologic test

Description
This code reports psychological testing procedures, during with a series of tasks or questions are presented to the person being tested, and the responses are graded according to a set of guidelines or references. The test results are compiled and compared to those of a similar population. There are many categories and types of psychological tests available. Tests may attempt to analyze and rate such categories as achievement and aptitude, memory functioning neuropsychological tests, occupational testing, personality traits and other factors.

94.03 Character analysis

Description
This procedure involves character testing procedures, during which a series of tasks or questions are presented to the person being tested, and the responses are graded according to a set of guidelines or references. The test results are compiled and compared to those of a similar population. Character testing may be used to assist

in conflict resolution, counseling and other therapies.

94.08   Other psychologic evaluation and testing

94.09   Psychologic mental status determination, not otherwise specified

Description
These codes report other testing procedures (94.08) not classifiable elsewhere in subcategory 94.0 and unspecified psychological or mental status determinations (94.09). In general, the physician or psychologist administers and interprets the results of intellectual and psychological testing. The testing in written, oral, computer, or combined formats measures personality, emotions, intellectual functioning, and psychopathology.

Coding Clarification
These codes should not be assigned if the medical record contains sufficient information to facilitate coding at a higher level of specificity.

Documentation Tip
If the documentation is ambiguous or unclear, the physician should be queried.

94.1   Psychiatric interviews, consultations, and evaluations

Description
Psychiatry may be defined in general terms as the study of mental health illness, and the associated medical treatment of mental health disease. Psychiatric treatment includes a medical evaluation and supervision of medical or other counseling and therapies. A psychiatrist is a physician, a doctor of medicine (M.D.) or osteopathy (D.O.) who is licensed and certified to treat medical illness. There are multiple psychiatric subspecialties that treat specific patient populations such as children, the elderly, or those suffering from addiction. Patients that do not require medical care for mental or behavioral health problems may be treated by a psychologist.

94.11   Psychiatric mental status determination

Description
The physician interviews the patient in an initial diagnostic examination, which includes taking the patient's history and assessing his/her mental status, as well as disposition. The psychiatrist may spend time communicating with family, friends, coworkers, or other sources as part of this examination and may even perform the diagnostic interview on the patient through other informative sources. Laboratory or other medical studies and their interpretation are also included. The physician may perform a psychiatric diagnostic examination on the patient using interactive methods of

interviewing. This is most often the method used with individuals who are too young or incapable of developing expressive communication skills, or individuals who have lost that ability. This type of diagnostic interview is often done with children. Toys, physical aids, and non-verbal interaction and interpretation skills are employed to gain communication with a patient not capable of engaging with the clinician by using adult language skills.

Coding Clarification
Code 94.11 includes:

- Clinical psychiatric mental status determination
- Evaluation for criminal responsibility
- Evaluation for testamentary capacity
- Medicolegal mental status determination
- Mental status determination NOS

94.12   Routine psychiatric visit, not otherwise specified

94.13   Psychiatric commitment evaluation

94.19   Other psychiatric interview and evaluation

Description
Commitment interviews (94.13) focus on the voluntary or involuntary admission for psychiatric treatment in an inpatient or outpatient psychiatric program. Psychiatric services may be provided during a routine or other psychiatric visit, (94.12, 94.19) which may include managing the patient's medications, including the patient's current use of the medicines, a medical review of the benefits and treatment progression, management of side effects, and review or change of prescription. However, medical management services may be pharmacologically focused, involving only minimal medical psychotherapy.

94.2   Psychiatric somatotherapy

Description
The physician performs biological treatment of mental disorders, employing chemical or physical methods.

94.21   Narcoanalysis

Description
A hypnotic drug known as Amytal or sodium amobarbital is infused into the patient via an intravenous drip for psychiatric diagnostic or psychotherapeutic treatment purposes. Amytal is a hypnotic sedative used for diagnosing dissociative disorders and to treat trauma victims by accessing repressed memories, emotions, or events to facilitate

healing. This is often used after other measures have failed and/or when gaining a definitive diagnosis is medically essential. A sodium Amytal interview is often conducted in an inpatient setting, to monitor the effects of the drug. The patient is in a hypnotic state, where memories, as the patient perceives them, are more confidently reviewed. These interviews are often videotaped for later discussion.

94.22   Lithium therapy

Description
This procedure involves the supervised dosage and administration of Lithium for the treatment of bipolar disorders as a mood stabilizer to control the depression and mania. Lithium carries a high risk of overdose and toxicity. The required dosage is only slightly less than the toxic level, requiring the patient to be closely monitored during treatment.

94.23   Neuroleptic therapy

Description
This procedure code reports the supervised dosage and administration of neuroleptic medications (e.g., haloperidol, fluphenazine) which are potent antipsychotic agents. These medications carry a high risk or overdose and toxicity. A rare, but potentially fatal condition, neuroleptic malignant syndrome may occur in patients with an adverse reaction to neuroleptic medication.

94.24   Chemical shock therapy

Description
This procedure involves the use of certain chemical agents to treat psychiatric conditions such as schizophrenia, depression or bipolar disorders. In the late 1920's and 1930's, Insulin, Metrazol and other medications were used to induce seizure and coma as a form of shock therapy. Due to the associated health risks, these treatments have long since been replaced by neuroleptic medications and electroconvulsive therapies.

94.25   Other psychiatric drug therapy

Description
This code includes other psychiatric drug therapy not classifiable elsewhere in subcategory 94.2.

Coding Clarification
This code should not be assigned if the medical record contains sufficient information to facilitate coding at a higher level of specificity.

Documentation Tip
If the documentation is ambiguous or unclear, the physician should be queried.

Coding Guidance
AHA: S-O, '86, 4

94.26   Subconvulsive electroshock therapy

94.27   Other electroshock therapy

Description
The treating clinician initiates a seizure using electroconvulsive therapy (ECT), most often to combat chronic or profound depression, especially psychotic or intractable manic forms and used for people who cannot take antidepressants. The clinician anesthetizes the patient with a barbiturate and a muscle relaxant. Electrodes are placed on the patient's temples and/or forehead and a measured electrical dose is applied for about a second to commence the seizure, typically lasting 30 seconds to a minute. EEG and EKG monitors follow the seizure activity and heart rhythm while the patient sleeps through the therapy. The patient awakens a few minutes later.

94.29   Other psychiatric somatotherapy

Description
This procedure code reports other psychiatric somatotherapy not classifiable elsewhere in subcategory 94.2.

Coding Clarification
This code should not be assigned if the medical record contains sufficient information to facilitate coding at a higher level of specificity.

Documentation Tip
If the documentation is ambiguous or unclear, the physician should be queried.

94.3   Individual psychotherapy

Description
Psychotherapy may be defined as a general term for the treatment of mental or emotional illness by various interpersonal or relational psychological methods to facilitate dialogue, communications and behavior change techniques designed to improve the well-being and mental health of the patient. Psychotherapy may be used in conjunction with drug therapy, electroconvulsive therapy or other treatments. Psychotherapy type and technique may vary depending on the needs of the patient.

94.31   Psychoanalysis

Description
The therapist performs psychoanalysis by utilizing methods of intense observation and analytical skills to investigate the patient's past experiences, unconscious motivations, and internal conflicts, as well as contributing medical conditions, to discover how these pilot the patient's current behavior and emotions. The psychiatrist seeks to produce change in maladapted behavior. Psychoanalysis includes reviewing medical notes and making clinical setting

arrangements, assisting the patient in further self-awareness, working through barriers, understanding self-observations, and modifying mental behavior and status while continuing to elicit more information and personal exploration. This code also includes follow-up work of documentation, content review, and peer consultation.

94.32   Hypnotherapy

Description
Hypnosis is used as a modality for psychotherapy. The therapist induces an altered state of consciousness, or focused attention, in the patient. While patients are in this relaxed state of heightened awareness and suggestibility, they can experience changes in the way they feel, think, and behave in response to suggestions directed to them by the hypnotherapist. This modality for psychiatric services helps the therapist to achieve an alteration in the patient's thought and behavior patterns.

94.33   Behavior therapy

94.34   Individual therapy for psychosexual dysfunction

94.35   Crisis intervention

Description
The therapist provides individual psychotherapy in an office or outpatient facility using supportive interactions, suggestion, persuasion, reality discussions, re-education, behavior modification techniques, reassurance, and the occasional aid of medication. These interactions are done with the goal of gaining further insight and affecting behavior change or support through understanding. Technique and type of therapy may vary in accordance with the patient's circumstances. Behavior therapy (94.33) may employ a variety of techniques to assist patients in overcoming destructive behaviors. Crisis therapy (94.35) provides supportive therapy to assist a patient in overcoming assault, violence or other trauma. Psychosexual therapy (94.34) focuses on assisting the in improving intimacy issues and psychological attitudes towards sex arising from sexual dysfunction.

Coding Clarification
Code 94.33 includes psychotherapeutic techniques specified as:

*   Aversion therapy
*   Behavior modification
*   Desensitization therapy
*   Extinction therapy
*   Relaxation training

*   Token economy

94.36   Play psychotherapy

Description
The therapist provides interactive psychiatric services in an office or outpatient facility for therapeutic purposes. The interactive method is most often used with individuals who are too young, or incapable, of developing expressive communication skills, or individuals who have lost that ability. This type of psychotherapy is often done with children. Toys, physical aids, and non-verbal play and interaction, including the use of interpreter skills, are employed to gain communication with a patient not capable of engaging with the clinician by using adult language skills.

94.37   Exploratory verbal psychotherapy

Description
The therapist provides interactive conversation to explore underlying unconscious patterns which may be influencing the patient's life. This method seeks to determine the underlying cause(s) for fear, self-judgment, or self-attack which may contribute to the patient's choices and patterns of behavior. Through a process of mutual collaboration, these causal factors are identified to facilitate healthier relationships and behaviors.

94.38   Supportive verbal psychotherapy

Description
The therapist facilitates psychotherapeutic services that focus on strengthening the patient's defenses or providing encouragement and advice to sustain the patient through crisis periods, stressful situations, or other life changes.

94.39   Other individual psychotherapy

Description
Code 94.39 includes other psychotherapy not classifiable elsewhere in subcategory 94.3. Technique may vary.

The treating clinician gives individual psychophysiological therapy by utilizing biofeedback training together with psychotherapy to modify behavior. The clinician prepares the patient with sensors that read and display skin temperature, blood pressure, muscle tension, or brain wave activity. The patient is taught how certain thought processes, stimuli, and actions affect these physiological responses. The treating clinician works with the patient to learn to recognize and manipulate these responses, to control maladapted physiological functions, through relaxation and awareness techniques. Psychotherapy is also rendered using supportive interactions, suggestion, persuasion,

● New Code   ▲ Revised Code   ►◄ Revised Text   © 2010 Ingenix

reality discussions, re-education, behavior modification techniques, reassurance, and the occasional aid of medication. Individual psychophysiological therapy is performed face to face with the patient.

94.4 Other psychotherapy and counseling

94.41 Group therapy for psychosexual dysfunction

Description
The psychiatric treatment provider conducts psychosexual dysfunction psychotherapy for a group of several patients with a similar diagnosis in one session. Emotional and rational cognitive interactions between individual persons in the group are facilitated and observed. Personal dynamics of any individual patient may be discussed within the group setting. Processes that help patients move toward emotional healing and modification of thought and behavior are use.

94.42 Family therapy

Description
- **Single family group:** The therapist provides family psychotherapy in a setting where the care provider meets with the patient's family without the patient present. The family is part of the patient evaluation and treatment process. Family dynamics as they relate to the patient's mental status and behavior are a main focus of the sessions. Attention is also given to the impact the patient's condition has on the family, with therapy aimed at improving the interaction between the patient and family members.

- **Multiple family groups:** The therapist provides multiple family group psychotherapy by meeting with several patients' families together. This is usually done in cases involving similar issues and often in settings of group homes, drug treatment facilities, or hospital rehabilitation centers. The session may focus on the issues of the patient's hospitalization or substance abuse problems. Attention is also given to the impact the patient's condition has on the family. This code is reported once for each family group present.

94.43 Psychodrama

Description
This procedure involves drama therapy that explores emotional problems through role-playing in a group setting. Patients (clients) examine relationships or

shared problems by interacting with a structured group and assuming roles. Techniques such as role reversal, mirror, stream of consciousness and monologues may be utilized.

94.44 Other group therapy

Description
The psychiatric treatment provider conducts psychotherapy for a group of several patients in one session. Group dynamics are explored. Emotional and rational cognitive interactions between individual persons in the group are facilitated and observed. Personal dynamics of any individual patient may be discussed within the group setting. Processes that help patients move toward emotional healing and modification of thought and behavior are used, such as facilitating improved interpersonal exchanges, group support, and reminiscing. The group may be composed of patients with separate and distinct maladaptive disorders or persons sharing some facet of a disorder.

94.45 Drug addiction counseling

94.46 Alcoholism counseling

Description
This procedure involves addiction counseling, which is a form of "talk therapy" used during the rehabilitation phase of drug or alcohol rehabilitation therapy. Normally, detoxification should have previously occurred to assure that the patient is lucid enough to communicate, comprehend and make decisions effectively. Goals of addiction counseling include identification of negative influences, recognition of one's cycle of addition and identification of methods and techniques to assume positive changes.

94.49 Other counseling

Description
This code reports other modalities of psychotherapy and counseling that are not more specifically described by other codes in subcategory 94.4.

Coding Clarification
This code should not be assigned if the medical record contains sufficient information to facilitate coding at a higher level of specificity.

Documentation Tip
If the documentation is ambiguous or unclear, the physician should be queried.

94.5   Referral for psychologic rehabilitation

94.51   Referral for psychotherapy

94.52   Referral for psychiatric aftercare

94.53   Referral for alcoholism rehabilitation

94.54   Referral for drug addiction rehabilitation

94.55   Referral for vocational rehabilitation

94.59   Referral for other psychologic rehabilitation

Description
Subcategory 94.5 lists referrals for specific types of psychological rehabilitation to provide the patient with continued support from one phase of treatment or therapy to another. Referrals for such therapy are often made by a patient's physician or other licensed health care practitioner as required by each state. The clinician, social workers, and other personnel may work as a team with the patient and the patient's insurance company or other payer to assure that the referral process proceeds smoothly. Referral and admission requirements vary depending on the type of facility, program, and state requirements.

94.6   Alcohol and drug rehabilitation and detoxification

Coding Guidance
    AHA: 2Q, '91, 12

94.61   Alcohol rehabilitation

Description
A program is designed to restore social and physical functioning, free of the dependence of alcohol.

94.62   Alcohol detoxification

Description
A patient is treated for physical symptoms during withdrawal from alcohol dependence.

94.63   Alcohol rehabilitation and detoxification

Description
A program is designed to treat the physical symptoms during withdrawal from alcohol dependence and restore social and physical functioning, free of the dependence of alcohol.

94.64   Drug rehabilitation

Description
A program is designed to restore social and physical functioning, free of the dependence of drugs.

94.65   Drug detoxification

Description
A patient is treated for physical symptoms during withdrawal from drug dependence.

94.66   Drug rehabilitation and detoxification

Description
A program is designed to treat the physical symptoms during withdrawal from drug dependence and then restore social and physical functioning, free of the dependence of drugs.

94.67   Combined alcohol and drug rehabilitation

94.68   Combined alcohol and drug detoxification

94.69   Combined alcohol and drug rehabilitation and detoxification

Description
These codes involve the medical (detoxification) and therapeutic process (rehabilitation) designed to treat dependency addictive drugs and alcohol. The detoxification process involves cessation of use and prevention of withdrawal symptoms, which treats the patient's physical addition. The rehabilitation process focuses on the psychological components of addictive behaviors by providing psychotherapeutic counseling and support strategies for the patient.

95   Ophthalmologic and otologic diagnosis and treatment

Description
Eye and ear examinations and tests are grouped together under category 95. Individual subcategories are available for general eye examinations, 95.0, Examinations of form and structure of the eye, 95.1, Objective functional tests of the eye, 95.2, Special vision services, 95.3, and nonoperative procedures related to hearing, 95.4. A fourth-digit assignment is required for all subcategories to describe the specific type of study or test performed.

95.0   General and subjective eye examination

95.01   Limited eye examination

95.02   Comprehensive eye examination

95.03   Extended ophthalmologic work-up

Description
The physician performs a visual system examination and reviews the patient's medical history. Gross visual fields and basic sensorimotor examinations may be performed, including biomicroscopy, examination with cycloplegia (temporary

immobilization of the ciliary body) or mydriasis (the dilation of pupils), and tonometry. Other examination techniques such as retinoscopy, keratometry, slit lamp viewing, tear testing, corneal staining, corneal sensitivity, fundus examination, and exophthalmometry may also be employed when initiation of diagnostic or treatment is dependent upon the examining techniques. The examiner determines the prescription required for the patient's eyeglasses or contact lenses by evaluating the effectiveness of a series of lenses through which the patient is asked to view an eye chart. This is usually accomplished with a refractor, a device that contains a range of lens powers that can be quickly changed, allowing the patient to compare various combinations when viewing the eye chart. A prescription is issued; no fitting for eyeglasses or contact lenses occurs at this time.

Coding Clarification
A limited eye examination (95.01) includes an eye examination with prescription of spectacles.

A comprehensive eye examination (95.02) includes an eye examination covering all aspects of the visual system.

An extended ophthalmologic work-up (95.03) includes an examination for glaucoma, neuro-ophthalmology, or retinal disease.

95.04   Eye examination under anesthesia
Description
The physician performs an eye exam and evaluation under general anesthesia. The patient may have significant injury or cannot otherwise tolerate the examination while conscious. This exam may include manipulation of the globe to establishing the passive range of motion or another manipulation to help in diagnosing the condition.

Coding Clarification
Code also the type of examination.

95.05   Visual field study
Description
A visual field test measures the extent of the field of vision as an eye fixates straight ahead, with standard illumination. Any peripheral vision loss or blind spots are documented. The blind spots are plotted on visual field charts. Examination may include a tangent screen, Autoplot, arc perimeter, or a single stimulus level automated test, such as Octopus 3 or 7.

- **Tangent screen:** A tangent screen is a black screen made of felt mounted on the wall that has meridians, blind spot, and degrees from fixation stitched into it. Fixation is the direction

of gaze that allows the object's visual image to fall on the central fovea of the retina—the area of most acute vision. With one eye occluded and full distance correction worn, white spots are introduced and the patient is tested at one and/or two meters. The points are transferred from screen to a chart.

- **Goldmann perimeter:** The Goldmann perimeter may be used with at least two isopters plotted. An isopter is the outer margins of a visual field within which any particular object or stimulus should be seen. A hollow white spherical bowl device is positioned a set distance from the patient and luminous targets that differ in size and intensity are projected onto standardized background illumination, statically or kinetically. The stimulus check is usually static, not moving, when testing inside 30 degrees. This method can test the full limit of peripheral vision and uses internationally standardized testing conditions with fixation always monitored. Fixation is the direction of gaze that allows the object's visual image to fall on the central fovea of the retina—the area of most acute vision.

95.06   Color vision study
Description
This test describes an extended color vision examination involving an anomaloscope or equivalent, which is an instrument used to diagnose abnormalities of color perception in which one-half of a field of color is matched by mixing two other colors.

95.07   Dark adaptation study
Description
This exam tests the function of the two photoreceptors: the rods and the cones. Rods are most sensitive in dim illumination and are responsible for night vision. The cones are more sensitive in bright luminations and are responsible for day vision. The eye to be tested is exposed to a bright light and the room is darkened. At 30-second intervals, the light is increased and the effect of the stimulus on the retina is measured by a Goldmann-Weekers machine.

95.09   Eye examination, not otherwise specified
Description
This procedure code reports an eye examination or vision check, not otherwise specified.

Coding Clarification
This code should not be assigned if the medical record contains sufficient information to facilitate coding at a higher level of specificity.

Documentation Tip
If the documentation is ambiguous or unclear, the physician should be queried.

95.1   Examinations of form and structure of eye

95.11   Fundus photography
Description
The physician or technician aligns the fundus camera, which is attached to an ophthalmoscope, along the patient's optical axis after the patient's pupil has been dilated. The 35 mm camera is, in effect, a large ophthalmoscope that allows viewing of the retina and a light flash system for producing color photographs of the retina. Both eyes are photographed. The results are interpreted by the physician.

95.12   Fluorescein angiography or angioscopy of eye
Description
This procedure is for detection of abnormalities of retinal blood vessels. The patient's eyes are dilated. The angioscopy begins when a small amount of fluorescein dye is injected into the arm. The dye is transported to the eye through the blood vessels. As the dye traverses the retinal vessels, the retina is viewed through the ophthalmoscope using filters that enhance the fluorescence of the eye.

95.13   Ultrasound study of eye
Description
This procedure involves diagnostic ophthalmic ultrasound. Technique may vary, including:

* **A-scan:** A-scan is a one-dimensional measurement procedure using high-frequency sound waves introduced into the eye in a straight line by a transducer placed on the eye. As the waves reflect off the eye tissue, they are picked up by the same transducer, converted to electrical pulses, and displayed on screen. The resulting single-dimensional image is composed of vertical spikes that vary according to the tissue density. Quantitative A-scan only is applied for this code. Quantitative A-scan provides information about a lesion's tissue structure, and reflective/sound absorptive properties.

* **B-scan:** B-scan utilizes sound waves in a two-dimensional scanning procedure to display a two-dimensional image of the internal ocular structures. A transducer placed on the eye sends high-frequency sound waves into the eye, which reflect back to a receiver, are converted into electrical pulses, and displayed on screen. B-scan can locate structures in the eye that may be obscured by cataract, hemorrhages, or opacities and provides information as to a lesion's shape, mobility, insertion, or relationship to neighboring structures. Diagnostic B-scan is applied for this code with or without superimposed non-quantitative A-scan. Superimposed non-quantitative A-scan may be topographical and can give more precise measurements along one parallel sound beam, and identify the borders or maximum height of the tumor.

95.14   X-ray study of eye
Description
X-rays of the eyes are obtained to determine the location of a foreign body in the eye. After positioning the patient, a one- or two-view x-ray is obtained. Transparent objects such as glass may not be good candidates for x-ray visualization. The physician supervises the procedure and interprets and reports the findings.

95.15   Ocular motility study
Description
The examiner utilizes a series of vertical and horizontal prism bars or individual handheld prisms to measure ocular deviation in a sensorimotor examination. Ocular deviations, such as strabismus, are seen when the eyes position themselves to each other on axes different from what is needed. Ocular deviations can occur in the horizontal or vertical plane. The eyes may move in toward each other (convergent) or away from each other (divergent). One eye (monocular) or both eyes (binocular) may be affected. The deviation may be observed to be the same no matter what direction the eyes are looking (concomitant) or to vary depending on where the eyes are looking (nonconcomitant). These deviations can be caused by ocular muscle anomalies, trauma or disease, or neuromuscular damage. The patient is asked to focus on a distant or near object in varying locations. An occluder may be alternately used to cover one eye while testing the other. Multiple measurements are taken and interpreted and a report is prepared.

95.16   P32 and other tracer studies of eye
Description
A tracer study is the introduction of substance into the eye that provides a means by which certain substances or structures can be identified or followed, (e.g., radioactive tracer exam with uptake).

95.2   Objective functional tests of eye

Coding Clarification
Code 95.2 excludes functional test with polysomnogram (89.17)

● New Code   ▲ Revised Code   ►◄ Revised Text   © 2010 Ingenix

95.21   Electroretinogram (ERG)

Description
A normal retina has a predictable electrical response to light. To determine if the retina is damaged, the physician places an ocular fitted contact lens electrode on the patient's eye and another electrode on the forehead so that the retina's electrical responses to external stimuli can be recorded under light-adapted conditions. This procedure, often abbreviated ERG, is repeated in dark-adapted conditions. The ERG waves are analyzed by the physician.

95.22   Electro-oculogram (EOG)

Description
A normal retina has a predictable electrical response to light. The EOG records metabolic changes in the retinal pigment epithelium by evaluating the retina's response to light. The physician or technician places electrodes on the skin around the eye so that eye movements of both eyes can be recorded separately or together. The EOG is often used in cases where the electroretinography isn't sensitive enough to pick up macular degeneration. The physician interprets the results of the test.

95.23   Visual evoked potential (VEP)

Description
The physician measures and records evoked visual responses of body and senses.

95.24   Electronystagmogram (ENG)

Description
The physician monitors brain waves to record induced and spontaneous eye movements.

95.25   Electromyogram of eye (EMG)

Description
The physician or technician applies concentric needle electrodes to the patient's extraocular muscles to record muscle actions. This procedure is mostly applied for research into eye movement.

95.26   Tonography, provocative tests, and other glaucoma testing

Description
This procedure code describes tonography and other provocative tests. Technique may vary, including:

- **Tonography; recording indentation tonometer method or perilimbal suction method:** In a healthy eye's anterior chamber, aqueous humor is continually drained and renewed to maintain a constant overall pressure. Increased pressure from this fluid causes glaucoma and can lead to blindness. Indentation tonometry is a method of measuring and recording intraocular pressure. This technique uses an instrument such as a flat or weighted plunger centered within a footplate or a probe. When the probe/footplate is placed on the cornea, the plunger force required to cause a lateral movement (indentation change) or displacement of the plunger on the flattened area of the cornea is measured based on the instrument weight used or the calibrated displacement sensitivity of the plunger. The measurements convert to the intraocular pressure within the eye. The findings are recorded on a scaled strip of paper or digitally. Interpretation and report are included.

- **Tonography with water provocation:** In a healthy eye's anterior chamber, aqueous humor is continually drained and renewed to maintain a constant overall pressure. Increased pressure from this fluid causes glaucoma and can lead to blindness. In tonographic water provocation testing, the patient drinks one quart of water after fasting and the intraocular pressure changes are measured and recorded using a tonometric device. Tonography indirectly measures the intraocular pressure by determining the amount of force required to cause an indentation or displacement on the eye. This force is relational to the resistance, hence pressure, within the eye.

- **Provocative tests for glaucoma, without tonography:** In a healthy eye's anterior chamber, aqueous humor is continually drained and renewed to maintain a constant overall pressure. Increased pressure from this fluid causes glaucoma and can lead to blindness. In a provocative test for glaucoma, the patient is given drops to dilate the pupil, or may also be placed in a dark room, to cause the iris to fall forward in an attempt to close off the drainage angle. When the angle closes, pressure in the eye is measured for the increase in intraocular pressure since the fluid cannot drain. Increases at 10 mmHg or above are said to be indicative of risk for angle-closure glaucoma. The physician interprets the results and prepares a report. These tests are not commonly performed today and should be coded with care.

95.3   Special vision services

95.31   Fitting and dispensing of spectacles

Description
The physician or technician measures the patient's anatomical facial characteristics, records the laboratory specifications, and performs the final adjustment of the spectacles to the visual axes and anatomical topography. Adjustments may be made

to the ear or nosepieces or plastic frames may be heated and bent to better fit the patient, who has natural or artificial intraocular lenses.

95.32   Prescription, fitting, and dispensing of contact lens

Description
Using a keratometer, the technician determines the patient's corneal curvatures. The lenses are fitted for power, size, curvature, flexibility, and lens type. The fitting includes instruction and training of the wearer and incidental revision of the lens during the training period.

95.33   Dispensing of other low vision aids

Description
This procedure involves the dispensing of other low vision aids not classifiable elsewhere in subcategory 95.3 as spectacles (95.31) or contact lenses (95.32).

Coding Clarification
This code should not be assigned if the medical record contains sufficient information to facilitate coding at a higher level of specificity.

Documentation Tip
If the documentation is ambiguous or unclear, the physician should be queried.

95.34   Ocular prosthetics

Description
The physician fabricates a custom orbital prosthesis for the orbit of the eye for the purpose of protecting surrounding structures while surgery is performed or for the healing of facial and skull injuries. The physician identifies the extent of the patient's injuries or disease to determine the exact nature of the required prosthesis. Impressions of the orbit of the eye are taken and used to make models. A custom prosthesis for the particular patient is made from the models. Alternately, the physician modifies an ocular implant that has been created elsewhere. The modifications may include the addition of screws or other prosthetic appendages to alter the shape of the prosthesis so that it better fits the patient's eye. The physician may drill holes to accommodate the screws.

95.35   Orthoptic training

Description
The physician prescribes exercises to correct ocular problems, most frequently caused by ocular muscle imbalances. The patient is trained to perform these therapeutic exercises to improve vision by gaining the proper binocular cooperation of the eyes one with the other, such as when one eye's vision and movement is neglected to avoid seeing double. These exercises frequently include repetitive tasks with

prisms, color cards, or rods and moving objects progressively closer or further away in different planes.

95.36   Ophthalmologic counseling and instruction

Description
This procedure includes ophthalmologic verbal counseling and instruction, including counseling in adaptation to visual loss and use of low vision aids.

95.4   Nonoperative procedures related to hearing

95.41   Audiometry

Description
This procedure code describes audiometry examinations, which is the measurement of hearing. Often physicians or technicians can diagnose a cause of hearing loss through tests using an audiometer or other instrumentation. Many causes of hearing loss have characteristic threshold curves. Several types of audiometry test exist, including:

- **Pure tone audiometry (threshold):** In pure tone audiometry, earphones are placed and the patient is asked to respond to tones of different pitches (frequencies) and intensities. The threshold, which is the lowest intensity of the tone that the patient can hear 50 percent of the time, is recorded for a number of frequencies on each ear. Bone thresholds are obtained in a similar manner except a bone oscillator is used on the mastoid or forehead to conduct the sound instead of tones through earphones. The air and bone thresholds are compared to differentiate between conductive, sensorineural, or mixed hearing losses.

- **Bekesy audiometry:** Bekesy audiometry is a complex and rarely used diagnostic test. A special audiometer is used to deliver pulsing and continuous tones to the patient through earphones. The patient makes an audiogram by pushing and relaxing a button to indicate whether or not the tone was heard at changing intensity levels. Audiograms may be used as a screening tool to determine hearing thresholds. Tracings may be analyzed and categorized into several different hearing patterns.

- **Comprehensive audiometry:** In comprehensive audiometry, earphones are placed and the patient is asked to respond to tones of different pitches (frequencies) and intensities. The threshold, which is the lowest intensity of the tone that the patient can hear 50 percent of the time, is recorded for a number of frequencies on each ear. Bone thresholds are obtained in a similar manner except a bone oscillator is used on the mastoid or forehead to conduct the sound instead of tones through earphones. The

● New Code   ▲ Revised Code   ▶◀ Revised Text   © 2010 Ingenix

air and bone thresholds are compared to differentiate between conductive, sensorineural, or mixed hearing losses. With the earphones in place, the patient is also asked to repeat bisyllabic (spondee) words. The softest level at which the patient can correctly repeat 50 percent of the spondee words is called the speech reception threshold. The threshold is recorded for each ear. The word discrimination score is the percentage of spondee words that a patient can repeat correctly at a given intensity level above his or her speech reception threshold. This is also measured for each ear.

95.42 Clinical test of hearing

Description
In a filtered speech test, the patient is presented monosyllabic words, which are low pass filtered, allowing only the parts of each word below a certain frequency (pitch) to be presented. A score is given on the number of correct responses. This test is most commonly used to identify central auditory dysfunction.

95.43 Audiological evaluation

Description
The physician takes a history of the patient, including speech and language development, hearing loss, and physical and mental development. A physical examination is performed. Hearing tests and speech/language evaluations are performed. Assessment of deficits and a plan for the patient are made. These plans may involve speech therapy, hearing aids, etc. In auditory processing disorders, the patient (usually children) cannot process the information heard due to lack of integration between the ears and the brain, even though hearing may be normal. Central auditory processing disorder (CAPD) is often confused with or functions as an underlying factor to a number of learning disabilities.

95.44 Clinical vestibular function tests

Description
This procedure code classifies vestibular function tests. Nystagmus is uncontrolled rapid movement of the eyeball in a horizontal, vertical, or rotary motion. It can be a symptom of a disturbance in the patient's vestibular system and can be induced to measure the difference between the patient's right and left vestibular functions. Technique may vary, including:

- **Caloric/thermal vestibular test:** Each ear is separately irrigated with cold water and warm water to create nystagmus in the patient. The physician or audiologist observes the patient to

detect any difference between the reaction of the right side and the left side. Four irrigations occur: a warm and cold irrigation for both the right and the left ear.

- **Spontaneous nystagmus test:** The patient's eyes are observed for spontaneous nystagmus as the patient is asked to look straight ahead, 30 degrees to 45 degrees to the right, and 30 degrees to 45 degrees to the left.

- **Positional nystagmus test:** A positional nystagmus test measures whether the eyes can maintain a static position when the head is in different position, which helps in documenting and quantifying patient complaints of dizziness in certain positions. The test also may be performed as a diagnostic tool to determine if an abnormality is associated with the central nervous system or the peripheral nervous system. The patient is placed in a variety of positions including supine with head extended dorsally, left and right, and sitting in an attempt to induce nystagmus. This is done with the patient's eye open so that eye movements can be observed directly. No recording electrodes are used to record the nystagmus.

95.45 Rotation tests

Description
Nystagmus is uncontrolled rapid movement of the eyeball in a horizontal, vertical, or rotary motion. It can be a symptom of a disturbance in the patient's vestibular system and can be induced to measure the difference between the patient's right and left vestibular functions. The patient is seated in a rotary chair with the head bent forward 30 degrees. ENG electrodes are placed to measure nystagmus while the chair is rotated with the patient's eyes closed. A recording is made and studied to determine an abnormal labyrinthine response on one side or the other.

95.46 Other auditory and vestibular function tests

Description
This procedure code includes other auditory and vestibular function tests not classifiable elsewhere in subcategory 95.4.

Coding Clarification
This code should not be assigned if the medical record contains sufficient information to facilitate coding at a higher level of specificity.

Documentation Tip
If the documentation is ambiguous or unclear, the physician should be queried.

95.47   Hearing examination, not otherwise specified

Description
This procedure code reports a hearing examination, not otherwise specified in the medical record documentation.

Coding Clarification
This code should not be assigned if the medical record contains sufficient information to facilitate coding at a higher level of specificity.

Documentation Tip
If the documentation is ambiguous or unclear, the physician should be queried.

95.48   Fitting of hearing aid

Description
This procedure code includes other nonoperative auditory procedures.

A diagnostic analysis of a cochlear implant, including programming, is done post-operatively to fit the previously placed external devices, connect to the implant, and program the stimulator. Cochlear implants are equipped with software that allows for different programming specific to the patient's daily activities. Threshold levels, volume, pulse widths, live-voice speech adjustments, input dynamic range, and frequency shaping templates are evaluated and set according to individual needs.

Coding Clarification
Code 95.48 excludes implantation of an electromagnetic hearing device (20.95).

Coding Guidance
  AHA: 4Q, '89, 5

95.49   Other nonoperative procedures related to hearing

Description
This code reports nonoperative hearing-related procedures that are not more appropriately described by other codes in subcategory 95.4, including adjustment of the external components of a cochlear prosthetic device, battery replacement and hearing aid check, and deaf training.

The audiologist inspects the hearing aid and checks the battery. The aid is cleaned and the power and clarity are checked using a special stethoscope, which attaches to the hearing aid.

Under direction of a physician, the patient undergoes developmental programs such as lip reading instruction or hearing rehabilitation. In auditory processing disorders, the patient (usually a child) cannot process the information heard due to lack of integration between the ears and the brain, even though hearing may be normal. Central auditory processing disorder (CAPD) is often confused with or functions as an underlying factor to a number of learning disabilities.

96   Nonoperative intubation and irrigation

Description
Category 96 classifies nonoperative intubation and irrigation procedures. Third and fourth-digit subclassifications describe the site and type of procedure.

96.0   Nonoperative intubation of gastrointestinal and respiratory tracts

96.01   Insertion of nasopharyngeal airway

Description
This procedure code describes the nonoperative insertion of a tube into the nostril to crate a passage between the nose and nasopharynx. This intubation may facilitate suctioning of secretions in special care environments, and may serve as an alternate airway during surgical procedures or when the airway is otherwise obstructed (e.g., trauma).

Documentation Tip
Certain types of oropharyngeal airway tubes may be documented as "trumpets".

96.02   Insertion of oropharyngeal airway

Description
This procedure is the nonoperative insertion of a curved piece of plastic over the tongue that to create an air passage way between the mouth and the posterior pharyngeal wall. This tube can assist in keeping the epiglottis or tongue from obstructing the flow of air, such as occurs in anesthetized or unconscious patients.

96.03   Insertion of esophageal obturator airway

Description
This procedure involves a nonoperative device which generally consists of an occlusive balloon and a tube that is used to maintain an airway in unconscious patients to facilitate resuscitation. The balloon component or inflatable cuff is inflated to blockade the esophagus, preventing air from entering the stomach and gastric contents from entering the lungs during breathing cycle.

96.04   Insertion of endotracheal tube

Description
The physician places an endotracheal tube to provide air passage in emergency situations. The patient is ventilated with a mask and bag and positioned by extending the neck anteriorly and the head posteriorly. The physician places the

● New Code   ▲ Revised Code   ►◄ Revised Text   © 2010 Ingenix

laryngoscope into the patient's mouth and advances the blade toward the epiglottis until the vocal cords are visible. An endotracheal tube is inserted between the vocal cords and advanced to the proper position. The cuff of the endotracheal tube is inflated.

Coding Guidance
AHA: 2Q, '05, 19; 3Q, '05, 10; 4Q, '05, 88; 2Q, '06, 8; 1Q, '07, 11; 2Q, '09, 11

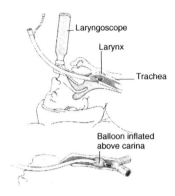

Laryngoscope

Larynx

Trachea

Balloon inflated above carina

96.05   Other intubation of respiratory tract

Description
This procedure code reports other nonoperative intubation of respiratory tract not classifiable elsewhere in subcategory 96.0.

Coding Clarification
This code should not be assigned if the medical record contains sufficient information to facilitate coding at a higher level of specificity.

Code 96.05 excludes endoscopic insertion or replacement of a bronchial device or substance (33.71, 33.79).

Documentation Tip
If the documentation is ambiguous or unclear, the physician should be queried.

Coding Guidance
AHA: 1Q, '97, 14

96.06   Insertion of Sengstaken tube

Description
The physician inserts a multi-lumen tube into the esophagus through which a balloon is passed for the tamponade of bleeding esophageal varices. The balloon is inflated to exert pressure on the varices to stop bleeding. The balloon is left inflated so coagulation can occur before the physician proceeds with definitive treatment.

96.07   Insertion of other (naso-)gastric tube

Description
The physician places a naso- or orogastric tube. The patient is placed in an upright position. The physician checks the nostrils for obstruction and selects the nostril for tube insertion. The physician may swab the nostril and spray the oropharynx with medication to numb the nasal passage and suppress the gag reflex. Next, the physician lubricates the tube, elevates the tip of the nose, and introduces the nasogastric tube into the nostril. The tube is advanced and the position of the tube is checked using fluoroscopy to ensure it is aligned to enter the oropharynx. As the patient swallows, the physician advances the tube through the pharynx, esophagus, and into the stomach. Air is injected into the tube (at the nose) while the physician listens with a stethoscope positioned at the stomach for the air to come out of the tube. Gastric contents are aspirated. These precautions are performed to ensure the tube is positioned in the stomach. The nasogastric tube is taped to the nostril. If the tube is fitted with a balloon (at the end of the tube in the stomach), it is inflated to hold the tube in place.

Coding Guidance
AHA: 4Q, '08, 187-190

96.08   Insertion of (naso-) intestinal tube

Description
A long, Miller-Abbott gastrointestinal tube with a mercury-filled balloon at the bottom is introduced, usually nasally, and used to clear gastrointestinal strictures. The patient is seated lower than the person performing the procedure and the dilator is placed in the posterior pharynx. The patient swallows and the tube and balloon are carried into the small intestine. The balloon is inflated and withdrawn until resistance is encountered. The balloon is partially deflated, withdrawn a little more and re-inflated. This process is repeated several times to achieve dilation of the stricture. This procedure may be done without fluoroscopy or with fluoroscopy by instilling a diluted contrast into the balloon.

96.09   Insertion of rectal tube

Description
This procedure involves the nonoperative insertion of a tube into the rectum for diagnostic or therapeutic purposes.

96.1   Other nonoperative insertion

Coding Clarification
Subcategory 96.1 excludes nasolacrimal intubation (09.44)

96.11 Packing of external auditory canal

Description
The external auditory canal (EAC) is packed with absorbable packing, after surgery or other indication, to allow minimal drainage, facilitate healing and in some cases, to prevent stenosis. EAC packing may include non absorbable materials (gauze), which may require general anesthesia for optimal removal.

96.14 Vaginal packing

Description
The physician pushes gauze packing into the vagina to put pressure on bleeding that is not related to childbirth or pregnancy. The packing may be coated with a chemical to make the blood clot and stop hemorrhaging.

96.15 Insertion of vaginal mold

Description
A vaginal mold device is inserted into a vaginal opening to facilitate opening, usually after surgical treatment for congenital anomalies such vaginal atresia or agenesis. The mold is retained in place for a period of time postoperatively to prevent closure complications.

96.16 Other vaginal dilation

Description
The physician enlarges the vagina by using a set of progressively longer and wider vaginal obturator dilators. The physician inserts the vaginal dilators sequentially from smaller to larger with firm and gentle pressure. The patient may be anesthetized for this procedure.

96.17 Insertion of vaginal diaphragm

Description
The physician fits a diaphragm or cervical cap and provides instructions for use. A diaphragm is a device that acts as a mechanical barrier between the vagina and the cervical canal. Cervical caps are larger, cup-like diaphragms placed over the cervix and held in place by suction. Either device can be used to prevent pregnancy.

96.18 Insertion of other vaginal pessary

Description
The physician fits a pessary to a patient, provides instructions for its use, and inserts it into the vagina. A pessary is a prosthesis that comes in different shapes and styles and is used to support the uterus, cervical stump, or hernias of the pelvic floor. The pessary selection and fitting will depend on the patient's symptoms and anatomy.

96.19 Rectal packing

Description
The physician places an absorbable gauze packing into the rectum post-surgically or after other treatment. The packing may be coated with a chemical to facilitate clotting and prevent bleeding.

96.2 Nonoperative dilation and manipulation

96.21 Dilation of frontonasal duct

Description
This procedure code describes dilation of the frontonasal duct; a tubular opening in the wall of the nasal cavity that extends from the frontal sinus to the ethmoid bone. Dilation may be accomplished with a balloon-tipped catheter or other expandable device.

96.22 Dilation of rectum

Description
The physician dilates the rectum or rectal stricture. This procedure may require anesthesia. The physician performs dilation of a rectum or area of stricture digitally (with gloved fingers) or with a dilating instrument.

96.23 Dilation of anal sphincter

Description
The physician dilates the anal sphincter. This procedure may require anesthesia. The physician performs dilation of the anal sphincter digitally (with gloved fingers) or with a dilating instrument.

96.24 Dilation and manipulation of enterostomy stoma

Description
The physician widens or enlarges a previously placed enterostomy stoma in the event of narrowing, stricture, stoma or other obstructive complication to achieve patency. This procedure may require anesthesia. The physician dilates the enterostomy opening digitally (with gloved fingers) or with a dilating instrument.

96.25 Therapeutic distention of bladder

Description
Code 96.25 describes a therapeutic dilation of the urinary bladder, often with a water-inflated balloon-type device or water pressure. Dilation of the bladder may be indicated for patients with atrophy, stenosis, fibrosis or other bladder diseases and anomalies which result in limited urinary capacity and frequent urination.

96.26   Manual reduction of rectal prolapse

Description
The physician reduces a rectal prolapse (procidentia) to a patient under general anesthesia. The physician performs a manual reduction of an incarcerated rectal prolapse by pushing the prolapsed segment into the anus.

96.27   Manual reduction of hernia

Description
The physician positions the patient appropriately depending on the type of hernia and forces the herniation back through the fascial defect by pressing the hernia back into the body cavity.

96.28   Manual reduction of enterostomy prolapse

Description
The physician positions the patient appropriately depending on site of the stoma and forces the herniation back through the stoma by pressing the herniated portion of bowel back through the enterostomy opening into the body cavity.

Coding Guidance
    AHA: N-D, '87, 11

96.29   Reduction of intussusception of alimentary tract

Description
This procedure involves the non-surgical reduction of a bowel that collapses into itself, similar to the closing of a telescope. Multiple non-surgical methods are available.

An enema of air or barium contrast is administered to reduce an intussusception or obstruction. An intussusception is a section of bowel that has slipped into another loop of bowel and can cause necrosis of the tissue, perforation and infection, even death. With the patient in position, the air or contrast is instilled into the colon through the anus to reduce the intussusception, straighten the bowel back to normal position and clear any intraluminal obstruction.

Coding Clarification
Code 96.29 includes intussusception reduction with:

- Fluoroscopy
- Ionizing radiation enema
- Ultrasonography guidance
- Hydrostatic reduction
- Pneumatic reduction

Code 96.29 excludes intraabdominal manipulation of intestine, not otherwise specified. (46.80)

Coding Guidance
    AHA: 4Q, '98, 82

96.3   Nonoperative alimentary tract irrigation, cleaning, and local instillation

96.31   Gastric cooling

Description
The physician reduces internal temperature by cooling lavage of the stomach.

Documentation Tip
This procedure may also be documented as gastric hypothermia.

96.32   Gastric freezing

Description
This procedure is a formerly popular treatment for chronic peptic ulcer whereby the affected area was frozen by super-cooled fluid introduced into the stomach via a balloon catheter. This treatment was thought to reduce or eliminate production of stomach acid by freezing of the secretory cells. It is no longer considered an effective ulcer treatment.

96.33   Gastric lavage

Description
The physician performs gastric lavage, also known as stomach pumping. This code applies to evacuating stomach contents for therapeutic treatment, such as for ingested poisons or decompression for intestinal obstruction. A nasogastric or orogastric tube is inserted down into the patient's stomach and the stomach's contents are suctioned out with the aid of an irrigating fluid, such as saline. The physician removes the tube.

96.34   Other irrigation of (naso-)gastric tube

Description
This procedure code reports other irrigation of previously placed nasogastric tube, which may be performed for clearing of secretions and to ensure patency of the tube, as well as to wash or irrigate the stomach.

96.35   Gastric gavage

Description
Gastric gavage is forced tubal feeding into the stomach.

96.36   Irrigation of gastrostomy or enterostomy

Description
This procedure describes a washing or cleansing of previously placed gastrostomy or enterostomy by introducing a stream of sterile saline or other fluid into the stoma through a tube or catheter.

96.37   Proctoclysis

Description

Large amounts of fluid are slowly introduced into the lower large intestine.

96.38   Removal of impacted feces

Description

This procedure entails the removal of impacted feces by flushing or other manual methods.

Abnormalities in the rectal emptying can lead to disorders of defecation and severe cases of impaction. Pulsed Irrigation Evacuation (PIE) of fecal impaction is an automated enema that is also used for bowel management of chronic constipation patients without voluntary bowel control (e.g., quadriplegics, paraplegics, and spina bifida). The PIE system consists of a speculum, tubing, a disposable collection container, and an electrical unit that delivers positive and negative air pressure through the tubing. During the procedure, small pulses of warm tap water are delivered into the rectum, serving to rehydrate feces and promote peristalsis.

96.39   Other transanal enema

Description

This code describes irrigation of the rectum, to remove retained (non-impacted) feces. Rectal irrigation (enema) may be performed as preparation for surgical procedure or other indication.

96.4   Nonoperative irrigation, cleaning, and local instillation of other digestive and genitourinary organs

Description

This subcategory classifies the following nonoperative digestive and genitourinary system procedures:

*   **Irrigation**—a form of washing or cleansing by a stream of sterile saline, water, or other fluid.

*   **Instillation (local)**—to slowly infuse, impart, or pour in a liquid substance into or through a limited area (e.g., body cavity or stoma) drop by drop.

Irrigation and instillation procedures are classified within this category according to anatomic site. The fourth-digit subclassification describes the specific post-surgical site or body cavity:

96.41   Irrigation of cholecystostomy and other biliary tube

96.42   Irrigation of pancreatic tube

96.43   Digestive tract instillation, except gastric gavage

96.44   Vaginal douche

96.45   Irrigation of nephrostomy and pyelostomy

96.46   Irrigation of ureterostomy and ureteral catheter

96.47   Irrigation of cystostomy

96.48   Irrigation of other indwelling urinary catheter

96.49   Other genitourinary instillation

Coding Guidance

   AHA: 1Q, '01, 5

Description

Irrigation and instillation procedures are often performed to cleanse a body cavity or surgically created opening. This procedure may be in the interest of maintaining hygiene, to prevent infection or to deliver a (usually diluted) medicinal or therapeutic substance.

Coding Clarification

Code 96.49 includes insertion of prostaglandin suppository.

96.5   Other nonoperative irrigation and cleaning

Description

This subcategory classifies nonoperative irrigation and cleansing procedures not classifiable to digestive or genitourinary sites (96.4). Irrigation may be defined as a form of washing or cleansing by a stream of sterile saline, water, or other fluid.

Irrigation and instillation procedures are classified within this category according to anatomic site. The fourth-digit subclassification describes the specific site, purpose, or device.

96.51   Irrigation of eye

Coding Clarification

Code 96.51 excludes irrigation with removal of foreign body (98.21).

96.52   Irrigation of ear

Coding Clarification

Code 96.52 includes irrigation with removal of cerumen (ear wax).

96.53   Irrigation of nasal passages

96.54   Dental scaling, polishing, and debridement

Coding Clarification
Code 96.54 includes plaque removal and other prophylactic (preventative) dental cleansing.

96.55   Tracheostomy toilette

96.56   Other lavage of bronchus and trachea

Coding Clarification
Code 96.56 excludes diagnostic bronchioalveolar lavage (BAL) (33.24) and whole lung lavage (33.99).

Coding Guidance
   AHA: 3Q, '02, 18

96.57   Irrigation of vascular catheter

Coding Guidance
   AHA: 3Q, '93, 5

96.58   Irrigation of wound catheter

96.59   Other irrigation of wound

Coding Guidance
   AHA: S-O, '85, 7

Description
Irrigation and cleansing procedures are often performed to cleanse a body cavity, a surgically created opening, device, wound or other body site. This procedure may be in the interest of maintaining health and hygiene, to prevent infection, to ensure patency of a device (e.g., catheter or stoma) or to deliver a (usually diluted) medicinal or therapeutic substance.

96.6   Enteral infusion of concentrated nutritional substances

Description
This procedure involves the infusion of a concentrated nutritional substance (food substitute) into the patient's stomach or other gastrointestinal site via a previously placed feeding tube. Route and method of administration may vary. This procedure is performed to provide nutritional support to patients who are not able to take food by mouth, due to post-surgical states, health status or other circumstances.

96.7   Other continuous invasive mechanical ventilation

Coding Clarification
This subcategory includes:

- BiPAP delivered through endotracheal tube or tracheostomy (invasive interface)

- CPAP delivered through endotracheal tube or tracheostomy (invasive interface)
- Invasive positive pressure ventilation [IPPV]
- Mechanical ventilation through invasive interface

Coding Clarification
This subcategory excludes:

- Non-invasive bi-level positive airway pressure (BiPAP) (93.90)
- Non-invasive continuous negative pressure ventilation (CNP) (iron lung) (cuirass) (93.99)
- Continuous positive airway pressure (CPAP) (93.90)
- Intermittent positive pressure breathing (IPPB) (93.91)
- Non-invasive positive pressure (NIPPV) (93.90)
- That by face mask (93.90-93.99)
- That by nasal cannula (93.90-93.99)
- That by nasal catheter (93.90-93.99)

When using a code from subcategory 96.7, assign an additional code for any associated endotracheal tube insertion (96.04) and/or tracheostomy (31.1–31.29).

The number of hours must be calculated in order to assign the fourth digit to subcategory 96.7. To calculate the number of hours of continuous mechanical ventilation during a hospitalization, begin the count from the start of the (endotracheal) intubation. The duration ends with (endotracheal) extubation. If a patient is intubated prior to admission, begin counting the duration from the time of the admission. If a patient is transferred (discharged) while intubated, the duration would end at the time of transfer (discharge).

For patients who begin on (endotracheal) intubation and subsequently have a tracheostomy performed for mechanical ventilation, the duration begins with the (endotracheal) intubation and ends when the mechanical ventilation is turned off (after the weaning period).

For a tracheostomy, to calculate the number of hours of continuous mechanical ventilation during a hospitalization, begin counting the duration when mechanical ventilation is started. The duration ends when the mechanical ventilator is turned off (after the weaning period).

If a patient has received a tracheostomy prior to admission and is on mechanical ventilation at the time of admission, begin counting the duration from the time of the admission. If a patient is transferred (discharged) while still on mechanical ventilation via tracheostomy, the duration would end at the time of transfer (discharge).

Coding Guidance
   AHA: 4Q, '91, 16, 18, 21; 2Q, '92, 13; 3Q, '04, 3

96.70   Continuous invasive mechanical ventilation of unspecified duration

96.71   Continuous invasive mechanical ventilation for less than 96 consecutive hours

Coding Guidance
   AHA: 1Q, '01, 6; 1Q, '02, 12; 2Q, '02, 19; 3Q, '04, 11; 3Q, '05, 10; 3Q, '07, 7

96.72   Continuous invasive mechanical ventilation for 96 consecutive hours or more

Description
Codes 96.70-96.72 describe procedures in which the patient's breathing is replaced or augmented by means of a mechanical device when the patient cannot breathe independently. There are several types and methods of continuous mechanical ventilation. The physician determines the type of ventilatory support depending upon the needs of the patient. In general, continuous mechanical ventilation requires oral or nasal placement of an endotracheal tube or tracheostomy (artificial opening in the trachea), as access for the ventilatory support machine. Ventilation is weaned slowly, as clinical and physiological criteria are met. This ensures that the patient can gradually build respiratory efforts and breathing independence as strength is regained.

Coding Guidance
   AHA: 1Q, '04, 23; 2Q, '05, 19; 4Q, '08, 187-190; 2Q, '09, 11

97   Replacement and removal of therapeutic appliances

Description
Category 97 provides codes for nonoperative replacement and removal of various therapeutic medical or post-surgical appliances from specific anatomic sites. Codes from category 97 should not be used to report the nonoperative removal of foreign bodies, which is correctly reported with the appropriate code from category 98.

97.0   Nonoperative replacement of gastrointestinal appliance

Description
Procedures listed under subcategory 97.0 describe the nonoperative replacement of a previously placed tube, stent, or enterostomy device. A patient may require insertion of a tube into a body cavity when bodily intake or output is nonfunctional or otherwise

contraindicated. A stent is a tubular device deployed to maintain patency of a tubular organ or tissue of the body. An enterostomy is a surgically created opening from the bowel to the exterior of the body to facilitate enteral (tube) feeding or removal of waste products when a patient's digestive pathways are nonfunctional due to postsurgical status or other disease. Occasionally, these supportive mechanical devices and appliances may fail, breakdown, obstruct, or otherwise necessitate replacement. These codes describe procedures in which a pre-existing device is replaced without the need for surgical intervention.

97.01   Replacement of (naso-)gastric or esophagostomy tube

97.02   Replacement of gastrostomy tube

Coding Guidance
   AHA: 1Q, '97, 11

97.03   Replacement of tube or enterostomy device of small intestine

Coding Guidance
   AHA: 1Q, '03, 10

97.04   Replacement of tube or enterostomy device of large intestine

97.05   Replacement of stent (tube) in biliary or pancreatic duct

Coding Guidance
   AHA: 2Q, '99, 13

97.1   Nonoperative replacement of musculoskeletal and integumentary system appliance

Description
Procedures listed under subcategory 97.1 describe the nonoperative replacement of a previously placed cast, immobilization, or wound healing device. A patient may require casting or other immobilization to facilitate healing of musculoskeletal injuries such as fracture, dislocation, sprain and strain. Casting and immobilization may also be previously placed at the time of surgical intervention, and require replacement at a later date. Similarly, traumatic or operative wounds may require drainage tubes and catheters, packing or other healing dressings and devices that require replacement at a later date to maintain hygiene and prevent opportunistic infection or other complications. These codes describe procedures in which a pre-existing device or appliance is replaced without the need for surgical intervention.

● New Code   ▲ Revised Code   ▶◀ Revised Text   © 2010 Ingenix

97.11	**Replacement of cast on upper limb**
97.12	**Replacement of cast on lower limb**
97.13	**Replacement of other cast**
97.14	**Replacement of other device for musculoskeletal immobilization**
97.15	**Replacement of wound catheter**
97.16	**Replacement of wound packing or drain**
97.2	**Therapeutic radiology and nuclear medicine**

Description
Procedures listed under subcategory 97.2 describe the nonoperative replacement of a previously placed packing, tube, drain, or other appliance. Traumatic or operative wounds may require drainage tubes and catheters, packing, or other healing dressings and devices that require replacement at a later date to maintain hygiene and prevent opportunistic infection or other complications. Similarly, devices such as a diaphragm or pessary, which are placed for therapeutic or preventative purposes, require replacement to maintain health and hygiene. These codes describe procedures in which a pre-existing device or appliance is replaced without the need for surgical intervention.

97.21	**Replacement of nasal packing**
97.22	**Replacement of dental packing**
97.23	**Replacement of tracheostomy tube**

Coding Guidance
AHA: N-D, '87, 11

97.24	**Replacement and refitting of vaginal diaphragm**
97.25	**Replacement of other vaginal pessary**
97.26	**Replacement of vaginal or vulvar packing or drain**
97.29	**Other nonoperative replacements**

Coding Guidance
AHA: 3Q, '98, 12; 3Q, '99, 9

Coding Clarification
Code 97.29 may be used to report non-surgical replacement of a Tenckhoff catheter. Non-surgical removal (without replacement) of a Tenckhoff catheter may be reported with 97.82.

97.3	**Nonoperative removal of therapeutic device from head and neck**

Description
Procedures listed under subcategory 97.3 describe the nonoperative removal of a previously packing, fixation, or other therapeutic device from the head and neck. Prosthetics replace damaged anatomy or body parts that are removed due to trauma or disease in order to maintain function or aesthetics. A patient may require insertion of a tube into a cavity or organ when bodily intake or output is compromised or as a supportive measure when an organ or process is nonfunctional or otherwise compromised. Wiring other fixation devices serve to keep structural anatomy such as connective tissues, bones and teeth in correct alignment after surgical treatment or other intervention. Sutures serve to close traumatic or operative wounds, prevent infection, and facilitate healing. Upon healing or for other reasons these devices may need to be removed. These codes describe procedures in which a pre-existing device is removed without the need for surgical intervention.

97.31	**Removal of eye prosthesis**
97.32	**Removal of nasal packing**
97.33	**Removal of dental wiring**
97.34	**Removal of dental packing**
97.35	**Removal of dental prosthesis**
97.36	**Removal of other external mandibular fixation device**
97.37	**Removal of tracheostomy tube**
97.38	**Removal of sutures from head and neck**
97.39	**Removal of other therapeutic device from head and neck**
97.4	**Nonoperative removal of therapeutic device from thorax**

Description
Procedures listed under subcategory 97.4 describe the nonoperative removal of previously placed sutures, drain or other appliance from the thorax. In this context, the thorax may be defined as the chest cavities, or vital organs located in the chest. Traumatic or operative wounds may require drainage tubes and catheters, packing or other healing dressings and devices that require removal at a later date, either to treat opportunistic infection or other complications or because they are no longer needed. Similarly, sutures serve to close traumatic

or operative wounds, prevent infection and facilitate healing. Certain types of sutures require nonoperative removal after the wound has been healed. These codes describe procedures in which a pre-existing device or appliance is removed without the need for surgical intervention.

97.41 Removal of thoracotomy tube or pleural cavity drain

Coding Guidance
AHA: 1Q, '99, 10

97.42 Removal of mediastinal drain

97.43 Removal of sutures from thorax

97.44 Nonoperative removal of heart assist system

Coding Clarification
Code 97.44 includes:

• Explantation (removal) of circulatory assist device

• Explantation (removal) of percutaneous

• External heart assist device

• Removal of extrinsic heart assist device

• Removal of pVAD

• Removal of percutaneous heart assist device

Coding Guidance
AHA: 4Q, '01, 65

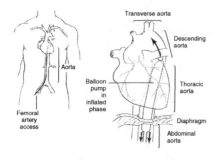

97.49 Removal of other device from thorax

Description
Code 97.49 may be used to report non-surgical removal of a Hickman catheter from the subclavian vein.

Coding Clarification
Code 97.49 excludes the endoscopic removal of a bronchial device(s) or substances (33.78).

Coding Guidance
AHA: N-D, ' 86, 9

97.5 Nonoperative removal of therapeutic device from digestive system

Description
Procedures listed under subcategory 97.5 describe the nonoperative removal of previously placed drains, tubes, or other appliance from the digestive system. Traumatic or operative wounds may require drainage tubes and catheters, packing or other healing dressings and devices that require removal at a later date, either to treat opportunistic infection or other complications or because they are no longer needed. A patient may require insertion of a tube into a cavity or organ when bodily intake or output is compromised or as a supportive measure when an organ or process is non-functional or otherwise compromised. A stent is a tubular device deployed to maintain patency of a tubular organ or tissue of the body. These codes describe procedures in which a pre-existing device or appliance is removed without the need for surgical intervention.

97.51 Removal of gastrostomy tube

97.52 Removal of tube from small intestine

97.53 Removal of tube from large intestine or appendix

97.54 Removal of cholecystostomy tube

97.55 Removal of T-tube, other bile duct tube, or liver tube

Coding Guidance
AHA: 1Q, '01, 8

97.56 Removal of pancreatic tube or drain

97.59 Removal of other device from digestive system

Coding Clarification
Subcategory 97.5 classifies nonoperative removal of therapeutic device from the digestive system, such as tubes, drains, catheters, and certain stents. Subcategory 97.0 classifies nonoperative replacement of gastrointestinal appliances such as enterostomy stomas and tubes and certain stents.

Note that 97.05 reports replacement of a biliary stent or tube, while 97.55 reports the removal (without replacement) of biliary duct stent or tube.

97.6 Nonoperative removal of therapeutic device from urinary system

Description
Procedures listed under subcategory 97.6 describe the nonoperative removal of previously placed drains, catheters, tubes, or other appliances from the urinary system. A patient may require insertion

of a tube into a cavity or organ when bodily intake or output is compromised or as a supportive measure when an organ or process is non-functional or otherwise compromised. A stent is a tubular device deployed to maintain patency of a tubular organ or tissue of the body. These codes describe procedures in which a pre-existing device or appliance is removed without the need for surgical intervention.

97.61   Removal of pyelostomy and nephrostomy tube

Description
The physician performs non-surgical removal of tubes from the lower part of the kidney.

97.62   Removal of ureterostomy tube and ureteral catheter

97.63   Removal of cystostomy tube

97.64   Removal of other urinary drainage device

Coding Clarification
Code 97.64 includes removal of indwelling urinary catheter.

97.65   Removal of urethral stent

97.69   Removal of other device from urinary system

97.7   Nonoperative removal of therapeutic device from genital system

Description
Procedures listed under subcategory 97.7 describe the nonoperative removal of previously placed drains, catheters, tubes, or other appliances from the genital system. Traumatic or operative wounds may require drainage tubes and catheters, packing or other healing dressings and devices that require removal at a later date, either to treat opportunistic infection or other complications or because they are no longer needed. Similarly, devices such as a diaphragm or pessary, which are placed for therapeutic or preventative purposes, may require removal to maintain health and hygiene. A patient may require insertion of a tube into a cavity or organ when bodily intake or output is compromised or as a supportive measure when an organ or process is non-functional or otherwise compromised. These

codes describe procedures in which a pre-existing device or appliance is removed without the need for surgical intervention.

97.71   Removal of intrauterine contraceptive device

97.72   Removal of intrauterine pack

97.73   Removal of vaginal diaphragm

97.74   Removal of other vaginal pessary

97.75   Removal of vaginal or vulvar packing

97.79   Removal of other device from genital tract

97.8   Other nonoperative removal of therapeutic device

Description
Codes in subcategory 97.8 describe the nonoperative removal of previously placed drains, catheters, tubes, or other appliances from anatomic sites not classified elsewhere in category 97. Traumatic or operative wounds may require sutures, drainage tubes, and catheters, packing, or other healing dressings and devices that require removal at a later date, either to treat opportunistic infection or other complications or because they are no longer needed. Similarly, immobilization devices such as casts, braces, or splints require removal after healing has occurred. These codes describe procedures in which a pre-existing device or appliance is removed without the need for surgical intervention.

97.81   Removal of retroperitoneal drainage device

97.82   Removal of peritoneal drainage device

Coding Clarification
Code 97.82 may be reported for removal of a permanent peritoneal cannula without incision of the peritoneum.

Code 97.82 may be reported for the non-surgical removal (without replacement) of a Tenckhoff catheter. Replacement of a Tenckhoff catheter is reported with 97.29.

Coding Guidance
  AHA: S-O, '86, 12; 2Q, '90, 28

97.83 Removal of abdominal wall sutures

97.84 Removal of sutures from trunk, not elsewhere classified

97.85 Removal of packing from trunk, not elsewhere classified

97.86 Removal of other device from abdomen

97.87 Removal of other device from trunk

97.88 Removal of external immobilization device

97.89 Removal of other therapeutic device

98 Nonoperative removal of foreign body or calculus

Description
Category 98 provides codes for nonoperative removal of a foreign body or calculus (naturally occurring calcification or stone). In general, third-digit classifications describe the body system involved, and the fourth-digit subclassifications describe the specific location of the foreign body or calculus. However, subcategory 98.5 specifically lists disintegration of stones of the certain urinary and digestive sites by extracorporeal induced shockwaves.

Codes from category 97 Replacement and removal of therapeutic appliances, should not be used to report the nonoperative removal of foreign bodies or calculi, which are correctly reported with the appropriate code from category 98.

98.0 Removal of intraluminal foreign body from digestive system without incision

Description
Subcategory 98.0 lists procedures that describe the retrieval of a foreign body from the digestive system that are contained within a tubular structure or organ (intraluminal), not requiring incision.

Coding Clarification
Subcategory 98.0 excludes removal of therapeutic device (97.51-97.59).

98.01 Removal of intraluminal foreign body from mouth without incision

98.02 Removal of intraluminal foreign body from esophagus without incision

98.03 Removal of intraluminal foreign body from stomach and small intestine without incision

98.04 Removal of intraluminal foreign body from large intestine without incision

98.05 Removal of intraluminal foreign body from rectum and anus without incision

Description
These procedures describe nonoperative, nonincisional removal of a foreign body from the digestive system. If the foreign body is visible through an orifice such as the mouth or anus, the physician may simply grasp the object with an instrument and remove it. Any wound sustained in the removal of the foreign body may necessitate closure. The physician may use an endoscope to examine the digestive tract to locate and remove a foreign body. Upper gastrointestinal endoscopy may used to retrieve a foreign body of the esophagus, stomach, and small bowel by passing the scope through the oral cavity. A large bowel endoscopy, (e.g., colonoscopy, sigmoidoscopy, proctoscopy, anoscopy) may be used to retrieve a foreign body of the colon, rectum, or anus by passing the scope through the anal sphincter. Once the foreign body is located, it may be suctioned, or grasped with forceps and retracted through the endoscope.

98.1 Removal of intraluminal foreign body from other sites without incision

Description
Subcategory 98.1 lists procedures that describe the retrieval of a foreign body from anatomic sites other than the digestive system that are contained within a tubular structure or organ (intraluminal), not requiring incision.

Coding Clarification
Subcategory 98.1 excludes removal of a therapeutic device (97.31-97.49, 97.61-97.89).

● New Code   ▲ Revised Code   ►◄ Revised Text   © 2010 Ingenix

98.11   Removal of intraluminal foreign body from ear without incision

98.12   Removal of intraluminal foreign body from nose without incision

98.13   Removal of intraluminal foreign body from pharynx without incision

98.14   Removal of intraluminal foreign body from larynx without incision

98.15   Removal of intraluminal foreign body from trachea and bronchus without incision

Coding Clarification
Code 98.15 excludes the endoscopic removal of a bronchial device(s) or substances (33.78).

98.16   Removal of intraluminal foreign body from uterus without incision

Coding Clarification
Code 98.16 excludes removal of an intrauterine contraceptive device (97.71).

98.17   Removal of intraluminal foreign body from vagina without incision

98.18   Removal of intraluminal foreign body from artificial stoma without incision

98.19   Removal of intraluminal foreign body from urethra without incision

Description
These procedures describe nonoperative, nonincisional removal of a foreign body from anatomic sites other than the digestive system. If the foreign body is visible through an orifice such as the ear, nose, or vagina, the physician may simply grasp the object with an instrument and remove it. Any wound sustained in the removal of the foreign body may necessitate closure. The physician may use an endoscope to examine the organ or tract to locate and remove a foreign body. Bronchoscopy may used to retrieve a foreign body of the trachea and bronchus by passing the scope through the oral cavity and airway. A hysteroscope may be used to retrieve a foreign body of uterus or cervix by passing the scope through vagina. Once the foreign body has been located either by direct visualization or endoscopic assistance, it may be suctioned, or grasped with forceps and retracted directly, or through the endoscope.

98.2   Removal of other foreign body without incision

Description
Subcategory 98.2 lists procedures that describe the removal of a foreign body from superficial anatomic sites, not requiring incision.

The physician identifies a foreign body, embedded in superficial tissues of the eyes, skin or mucous membranes. Without incision, the physician isolates the object. The object may need to be grasped firmly with forceps or other instrumentation. The object is removed with care to avoid damaging tissues. The wound may be closed if clean or packed if contaminated by the object.

If the foreign body is located in the superficial eye or eyelid, the physician picks the foreign body from the conjunctiva, cornea or eyelid with a q-tip or the side of the beveled edge of a needle. A slit lamp may be used when removing any embedded foreign body. After the removal, the physician may apply a broad spectrum antibiotic and a moderate pressure patch over the closed lid for 24 to 48 hours.

Coding Clarification
Subcategory 98.2 excludes removal of an intraluminal foreign body (98.01-98.19).

98.20   Removal of foreign body, not otherwise specified

98.21   Removal of superficial foreign body from eye without incision

98.22   Removal of other foreign body without incision from head and neck

Coding Clarification
Code 98.22 includes removal of an embedded foreign body from the eyelid or conjunctiva without incision.

98.23   Removal of foreign body from vulva without incision

98.24   Removal of foreign body from scrotum or penis without incision

98.25   Removal of other foreign body without incision from trunk except scrotum, penis, or vulva

98.26   Removal of foreign body from hand without incision

Coding Guidance
     AHA: N-D, '87, 10

98.27   Removal of foreign body without incision from upper limb, except hand

98.28   Removal of foreign body from foot without incision

98.29   Removal of foreign body without incision from lower limb, except foot
>   AHA: ▶2Q, '10, 4, 6, 14◀

98.5   Extracorporeal shockwave lithotripsy (ESWL)

Coding Clarification
Subcategory 98.5 includes:

- Lithotriptor tank procedure

- Disintegration of stones by extracorporeal induced shockwaves

- That with insertion of stent

98.51   Extracorporeal shockwave lithotripsy (ESWL) of the kidney, ureter and/or bladder

Coding Guidance
>   AHA: 1Q, '89, 2; 4Q, '95, 73

98.52   Extracorporeal shockwave lithotripsy (ESWL) of the gallbladder and/or bile duct

98.59   Extracorporeal shockwave lithotripsy (ESWL) of other sites

Description
The physician pulverizes a kidney stone (renal calculus), gallbladder stone or calculus of other sites by directing shock waves through a liquid medium. Two different methods are currently available to accomplish this procedure. The physician first uses radiological guidance to determine the location and size of the calculus. In the first method, the patient is immersed in a liquid medium (degassed, deionized water) with shock waves directed through the liquid to the stone. In the second method, the one most often used, the patient is placed on a treatment table. A series of shock waves are directed through a water-cushion, or bellow that is placed against the patient's body at the location of the stone. Each shock wave is directed to the stone for only a fraction of a second, and the procedure generally takes from 30 to 50 minutes. The treatment table is equipped with video x-ray so the physician can view the pulverization process. Over several days or weeks, the tiny stone fragments pass harmlessly though the patient's system and are discharged during urination, digestion or other process, depending on the site of the stone.

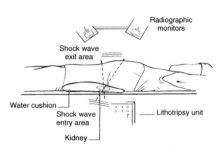

Extracorporeal Shock Wave Lithotripsy

---

99   Other nonoperative procedures

Description
Category 99 contains numerous nonoperative procedures including transfusions, injections, or infusions of therapeutic or prophylactic substances, prophylactic vaccination and inoculation against certain diseases, conversion of cardiac rhythm, therapeutic apheresis, and miscellaneous procedures not classified elsewhere.

99.0   Transfusion of blood and blood components

Description
These procedures describe blood transfusions whereby blood or blood-derived products are transferred from one person (donor) to another. Transfusions may be used to replace blood lost during surgery or trauma or to treat certain medical conditions, such as those in which the patient's body does not make enough of a specific blood component, resulting in an anemic disease. In general, the physician or clinician transfuses blood or blood components by establishing venous access with a sterile needle and catheter through which blood products are infused into the recipient patient's circulatory system.

Coding Clarification
Use an additional code for transfusion done through a catheter or by cut-down (38.92-38.94).

99.00   Perioperative autologous transfusion of whole blood or blood components

Coding Guidance
>   AHA: 4Q, '95, 69

99.01   Exchange transfusion

Description
Repetitive withdrawal of blood is performed, replaced by donor blood.

Coding Guidance
>   AHA: 2Q, '89, 15

● New Code   ▲ Revised Code   ▶◀ Revised Text   © 2010 Ingenix

99.02 Transfusion of previously collected autologous blood

Description
A transfusion is performed with the patient's own previously withdrawn and stored blood.

Coding Guidance
AHA: J-A, '85, 16; 1Q, '90, 10; 4Q, '95, 69

99.03 Other transfusion of whole blood

Coding Clarification
Code 99.03 is assigned to report blood transfusion that is not otherwise specified and hemodilution replacement.

99.04 Transfusion of packed cells

99.05 Transfusion of platelets

Coding Clarification
The use of this code would be appropriate for reporting transfusion of thrombocytes.

99.06 Transfusion of coagulation factors

Coding Clarification
Transfusion of antihemophilic factor is reported with 99.06.

99.07 Transfusion of other serum

Coding Clarification
Code 99.07 is used to report transfusion of plasma. Do not assign this code to report injection [transfusion] of:

- Antivenin (99.16)
- Gamma globulin (99.14).

99.08 Transfusion of blood expander

Coding Clarification
Code 99.08 is assigned for transfusion of Dextran.

99.09 Transfusion of other substance

Coding Clarification
Code 99.09 describes transfusion of other substances such as blood surrogate or granulocytes.

99.1 Injection or infusion of therapeutic or prophylactic substance

Description
Subcategory 99.1 lists procedures that describe injection or infusion of a therapeutic (to treat illness) or prophylactic (preventive) substance. The physician or an assistant under direct physician supervision administers a therapeutic or prophylactic substance by subcutaneous or intramuscular injection or intravenous route under sterile technique.

Coding Clarification
Subcategory 99.1 includes injection or infusion acting locally or systemically which is given:

- Hypodermically (subcutaneously; subq)—under the skin
- Intramuscularly (IM)—into the muscle
- Intravenously (IV)—into the vein

99.10 Injection or infusion of thrombolytic agent

Description
A thrombolytic agent is a substance that dissolves a thrombus, a localized clot formation that impairs circulation.

Coding Clarification
Code 99.10 excludes circulating (systemically-acting) anticoagulants and similar substances such as:

- Aspirin—omit code
- GP IIb/IIIa platelet inhibitors (99.20)
- Heparin (99.19)
- SuperSaturated oxygen therapy (00.49)
- Warfarin—omit code

Documentation Tip
Thrombolytics classifiable to 99.10 may be documented as:

- Alteplase
- Anistreplase
- Reteplase
- Streptokinase
- Tenecteplase
- Tissue plasminogen activator (TPA)
- Urokinase

Coding Guidance
AHA: 4Q, '98, 83; 2Q, '01, 7-9, 23; 4Q, '05, 101-103

99.11 Injection of Rh immune globulin

Coding Clarification
Code 99.11 includes injection of:

- Anti-D (Rhesus) globulin
- RhoGAM

99.12 Immunization for allergy

Documentation Tip
Procedures classifiable to 99.12 may be documented as desensitization.

99.13   Immunization for autoimmune disease

▲ 99.14   Injection or infusion of immunoglobulin

Documentation Tip
▶Procedures classifiable to 99.14 may be
documented as injection of immune sera, or gamma
globulin.◀

**99.15   Parenteral infusion of concentrated nutritional
substances**

Documentation Tip
Procedures classifiable to 99.15 may be documented
as:

* Hyperalimentation
* Total parenteral nutrition [TPN]
* Peripheral parenteral nutrition [PPN]

Coding Guidance
   AHA: 4Q, '03, 104

99.16   Injection of antidote

Documentation Tip
Procedures classifiable to 99.16 may be documented
as injection of:

* Antivenin
* Heavy metal antagonist

99.17   Injection of insulin

99.18   Injection or infusion of electrolytes

99.19   Injection of anticoagulant

**99.2   Injection or infusion of other therapeutic or
prophylactic substance**

Description
Subcategory 99.2 lists procedures that describe
injection or infusion of other therapeutic (to treat
illness) or prophylactic (preventive) substances not
classifiable to subcategory 99.1. The physician or an
assistant under direct physician supervision
administers a therapeutic or prophylactic substance
by subcutaneous or intramuscular injection or
intravenous route under sterile technique.

Coding Clarification
Subcategory 99.2 includes injection or infusion
acting locally or systemically which is given:

* Hypodermically (subcutaneously; subq)—under
  the skin
* Intramuscularly (IM)—into the muscle
* Intravenously (IV)—into the vein

Use an additional code for injection into the following
sites separately classifiable elsewhere:

* Breast (85.92)
* Bursa (82.94, 83.96)
* Intraperitoneal (cavity) (54.97)
* Intrathecal (03.92)
* Joint (76.96, 81.92)
* Kidney (55.96)
* Liver (50.94)
* Orbit (16.91)
* Other sites
* Perfusion: NOS (39.97)
* Intestine (46.95, 46.96)
* Kidney (55.95)
* Liver (50.93)
* Total body (39.96)

99.20   Injection or infusion of platelet inhibitor

Coding Clarification
Code 99.20 excludes:

* Infusion of heparin (99.19)
* Injection or infusion of a thrombolytic agent
  (99.10)

Documentation Tip
Procedures classifiable to 99.20 may be documented
as:

* Glycoprotein IIb/IIIa inhibitor
* GP IIb-IIIa inhibitor or GP IIb/IIIa inhibitor

Coding Guidance
   AHA: 4Q, '98, 85; 4Q, '02, 114; 2Q, '04, 3

99.21   Injection of antibiotic

Coding Clarification
Code 99.21 excludes injection or infusion of
oxazolidinone class of antibiotics (00.14).

Coding Guidance
   AHA: M-A, '87, 9; 2Q, '90, 24; 4Q, '98, 76

99.22   Injection of other anti-infective

Coding Clarification
Code 99.22 excludes injection or infusion of
oxazolidinone class of antibiotics (00.14).

99.23   Injection of steroid

Coding Clarification
Code 99.23 includes injection of cortisone and
subdermal implantation of progesterone.

Coding Guidance
   AHA: S-O, '85, 7; 3Q, '92, 9; 3Q, '96, 7; 1Q, '99, 8; 3Q,
   '00, 15

● New Code   ▲ Revised Code   ▶◀ Revised Text   © 2010 Ingenix

99.24   Injection of other hormone

Coding Guidance
   AHA: 1Q, '06, 9

99.25   Injection or infusion of cancer chemotherapeutic substance

Description
The physician or supervised assistant prepares and administers a chemotherapeutic medication to combat malignant neoplasms or microorganisms. This code describes intravenous (IV) infusions through catheter tubing or drug administered using push technique. Medication may also be injected directly into the lesion, under the skin (subcutaneous), or into a muscle (intramuscular), often in the arm or leg.

Coding Clarification
An additional code should be assigned for disruption of the blood brain barrier, if performed (BBBD) (00.19).

Code 99.25 includes:

*   Chemoembolization
*   Injection or infusion of antineoplastic agent

Code 99.25 excludes:

*   Immunotherapy, antineoplastic (00.15, 99.28)
*   Implantation of chemotherapeutic agent (00.10)
*   Injection of radioisotope (92.28)
*   Injection or infusion of biological response modifier (BRM) as an anti-neoplastic agent (99.28)
*   Intravenous infusion of clofarabine (17.70)

Coding Scenario
A patient with a metastatic brain tumor was taken to the interventional radiology suite. After an infusion of Mannitol into the carotid artery, chemotherapy was infused into the same artery.

   Code Assignment:

   191.9   Malignant neoplasm of brain, unspecified site
   00.19   Disruption of blood brain barrier via infusion [BBBD]
   99.25   Chemotherapy

Coding Guidance
   AHA: N-D, '86, 11; 1Q, '88, 8; 1Q, '92, 12; 2Q, '92, 7; 4Q, '95, 67; 3Q, '96, 11; 1Q, '98, 6; 1Q, '99, 4; 4Q, '02, 93; 2Q, ' 03, 6, 16; 4Q, '07, 104; 4Q, '08, 82; 4Q, '09, 79

99.26   Injection of tranquilizer

99.27   Iontophoresis

Description
The physician introduces soluble salts into tissues via electric current.

99.28   Injection or infusion of other therapeutic or prophylactic substance

Coding Clarification
Code 99.28 includes:

*   Immunotherapy, antineoplastic
*   Infusion of cintredekin besudotox
*   Interleukin therapy
*   Low-dose interleukin-2 (IL-2) therapy
*   Tumor vaccine

Code 99.28 excludes:

*   High-dose infusion interleukin-2 (IL-2) (00.15)
*   SuperSaturated oxygen therapy (00.49)

Coding Guidance
   AHA: 4Q, '94, 51; 2Q, '98, 10; 2Q, '99, 8; 4Q, '03, 92

99.29   Injection or infusion of other therapeutic or prophylactic substance

Coding Clarification
▶Code 99.29 includes percutaneous uterine artery embolization performed using embospheres or spherical embolics.◀

Code 99.29 excludes the infusion of a blood brain barrier disruption substance (00.19).

Code 99.29 lists multiple exclusions classifiable to specific type, site, or substance. This code should not be assigned if the medical record contains sufficient information to facilitate coding at a higher level of specificity.

Documentation Tip
If the documentation is ambiguous or unclear, the physician should be queried.

Coding Guidance
   AHA: N-D, '87, 4; S-O, '87, 11; 1Q, '88, 9; 2Q, '89, 17; 2Q, '90, 23; 4Q, '90, 14; 2Q, '95, 12; 4Q, '95, 67; 1Q, '97, 3; 2Q, '97, 11; 1Q, '98, 6; 2Q, '98, 17, 18, 23, 24; 4Q, '98, 83; 3Q, '99, 21; 4Q, '99, 17; 1Q, '00, 8, 18, 23; 2Q, '00, 14; 1Q, '01, 15; 3Q, '02, 19, 24; 2Q, '03, 10; ▶1Q, '10, 21; 2Q, '10, 5, 7, 14◀

99.3   Prophylactic vaccination and inoculation against certain bacterial diseases

Description
This subcategory describes prophylactic vaccination and inoculation against specific diseases caused by bacterial microorganisms. A physician, nurse, or medical assistant administers an injectable (percutaneous, intradermal, subcutaneous, or intramuscular) immunization to the patient. The vaccine may consist of a single vaccine or a combination vaccine/toxoid in one immunization administration (e.g., diphtheria, pertussis, and tetanus toxoids are in a single DPT immunization).

99.31   Vaccination against cholera

99.32   Vaccination against typhoid and paratyphoid fever

99.33   Vaccination against tuberculosis

99.34   Vaccination against plague

99.35   Vaccination against tularemia

99.36   Administration of diphtheria toxoid

99.37   Vaccination against pertussis

99.38   Administration of tetanus toxoid

99.39   Administration of diphtheria-tetanus-pertussis, combined

99.4   Prophylactic vaccination and inoculation against certain viral diseases

Description
This subcategory describes prophylactic vaccination and inoculation against specific diseases caused by viral microorganisms. A physician, nurse, or medical assistant administers an injectable (percutaneous, intradermal, subcutaneous, or intramuscular) immunization to the patient. The vaccine may consist of a single vaccine or a combination vaccine/toxoid in one immunization administration (e.g., measles, mumps and rubella are in a single MMR immunization).

99.41   Administration of poliomyelitis vaccine

99.42   Vaccination against smallpox

99.43   Vaccination against yellow fever

99.44   Vaccination against rabies

99.45   Vaccination against measles

99.46   Vaccination against mumps

99.47   Vaccination against rubella

99.48   Administration of measles-mumps-rubella vaccine

99.5   Other vaccination and inoculation

Description
This subcategory describes other vaccination and inoculation not classifiable elsewhere in category 99. Vaccines, inoculations and antitoxins classifiable to this category are specifically classified according to the type of organism.

99.51   Prophylactic vaccination against the common cold

99.52   Prophylactic vaccination against influenza

99.53   Prophylactic vaccination against arthropod-borne viral encephalitis

99.54   Prophylactic vaccination against other arthropod-borne viral diseases

99.55   Prophylactic administration of vaccine against other diseases

Coding Clarification
Code 99.55 includes vaccination against:

- Anthrax
- Brucellosis
- Rocky Mountain spotted fever
- Staphylococcus
- Streptococcus
- Typhus

Coding Guidance
   AHA: 1Q, '94, 10; 2Q, '00, 9

99.56   Administration of tetanus antitoxin

99.57   Administration of botulism antitoxin

99.58   Administration of other antitoxins

Coding Clarification
Code 99.55 includes administration of:

- Diphtheria antitoxin
- Gas gangrene antitoxin
- Scarlet fever antitoxin

99.59   Other vaccination and inoculation

Coding Clarification
Code 99.59 excludes injection of:

- Gamma globulin (99.14)
- Rh immune globulin (99.11)
- Immunization for allergy (99.12) or autoimmune disease (99.13)

99.6   Conversion of cardiac rhythm

Description
The physician corrects cardiac rhythm.

Coding Clarification
This subcategory excludes open chest cardiac:

- Electric stimulation (37.91)
- Massage (37.91)

● New Code   ▲ Revised Code   ▶◀ Revised Text   © 2010 Ingenix

Coding Guidance
AHA: 3Q, '93, 13

99.60 Cardiopulmonary resuscitation, not otherwise specified

Description
The physician performs application of electric shock to the upper heart chamber to restore normal heart rhythm.

Coding Guidance
AHA: 1Q, '94, 16

99.61 Atrial cardioversion

99.62 Other electric countershock of heart

Description
The physician may administer an electronic shock to the patient's chest to regulate heartbeats considered dangerously irregular. The physician may use a defibrillator machine and place two paddles on the patient's chest and/or back. A measured electric shock is delivered through the chest to the heart to convert the heartbeat to a regular rhythm.

Coding Clarification
Code 99.62 includes:

• Cardioversion specified NOS or external

• Conversion to sinus rhythm

• Defibrillation

• External electrode stimulation

99.63 Closed chest cardiac massage

Description
Alternating manual pressure is applied over the breastbone to restore normal heart rhythm.

99.64 Carotid sinus stimulation

Description
Interventional stimulation is performed of a tiny bundle of nerves ("pressure sensors") located near the carotid sinus, which results in increased parasympathetic (vagal) response decreasing heart rate and blood pressure.

99.69 Other conversion of cardiac rhythm

Description
This procedure code reports other conversion of cardiac rhythm not classifiable elsewhere in subcategory 99.6.

Coding Clarification
This code should not be assigned if the medical record contains sufficient information to facilitate coding at a higher level of specificity.

Documentation Tip
If the documentation is ambiguous or unclear, the physician should be queried.

Coding Guidance
AHA: 4Q, '88, 11

99.7 Therapeutic apheresis or other injection, administration, or infusion of other therapeutic or prophylactic substance

99.71 Therapeutic plasmapheresis

99.72 Therapeutic leukopheresis

99.73 Therapeutic erythrocytapheresis

Coding Guidance
AHA: 1Q, '94, 20

99.74 Therapeutic plateletpheresis

Description
Therapeutic apheresis is the removal of some specific circulating blood component, cells or plasma solute, which is directly responsible for a disease process. Cells and plasma components may also be mobilized from other tissue storage during apheresis, such the from the spleen and lymph nodes, for enhanced clearance of the undesired element. The patient is prepared much the same as giving a regular blood donation. Whole blood is drawn out of one arm and into an instrument called a separator, which uses a microprocessing technique to draw the blood, anticoagulate it, and separate the component to be removed by centrifugal spinning, filtration, or column adsorption with the help of computerized calibration. The cells to be removed are collected while the remainder of the blood is recombined and returned to the patient through a tube and needle in the other arm. Code 99.71 describes removal of plasma, 99.72 white blood cell isolation and removal (leukapheresis or lymphocytapheresis), 99.73 red blood cell removal, and 99.74 for removal of platelets.

99.75 Administration of neuroprotective agent

Description
A neuroprotective agent (e.g., nimodipine) is applied to minimize ischemic injury by inhibiting toxic neurotransmitters, blocking free ions, removing free radicals, and causing vasodilation.

Coding Clarification
This code describes the administration of neuroprotective agents, such as nimodipine, that work directly on the nerve cells to minimize ischemic injury caused by strokes.

Coding Guidance
AHA: 4Q, '00, 68

99.76   Extracorporeal immunoadsorption

Description
Apheresis for plasma with extracorporeal immunoadsorption and reinfusion of the patient's plasma is done using Protein A columns to specifically remove circulating immune complexes. Therapeutic apheresis is the removal of some specific circulating blood component, cells or plasma solute, which is directly responsible for a disease process. Cells and plasma components may also be mobilized from other tissue storage during apheresis, such the from the spleen and lymph nodes, for enhanced clearance of the undesired element. The patient is prepared much the same as giving a regular blood donation. Whole blood is drawn out of one arm and into an instrument called a separator, which uses a microprocessing technique to draw the blood, anticoagulate it, and separate the component to be removed by centrifugal spinning, filtration, or column adsorption with the help of computerized calibration. The cells to be removed are collected while the remainder of the blood is recombined and returned to the patient through a tube and needle in the other arm. This code describes isolation of antibodies from plasma.

Coding Guidance
AHA: 4Q, '02, 112

99.77   Application or administration of adhesion barrier substance

Description
The physician applies a temporary bioresorbable membrane prior to closure of an abdominal surgical wound. This substance is designed to reduce the formation of postoperative adhesions. The body absorbs the barrier substance during the healing process.

Coding Guidance
AHA: 4Q, '02, 113; ▶1Q, '10, 11◀

99.78   Aquapheresis

99.79   Other therapeutic apheresis

Description
Therapeutic apheresis is the removal of some specific circulating blood component, cells or plasma solute, which is directly responsible for a disease process. Cells and plasma components may also be mobilized from other tissue storage during apheresis, such the from the spleen and lymph nodes, for enhanced clearance of the undesired element. The patient is prepared much the same as giving a regular blood donation. Whole blood is drawn out of one arm and into an instrument called a separator, which uses a microprocessing technique to draw the blood, anticoagulate it, and separate the component to be removed by centrifugal spinning, filtration, or column adsorption with the help of computerized calibration. The cells to be removed are collected while the remainder of the blood is recombined and returned to the patient through a tube and needle in the other arm. Code 99.78 describes removal of water from plasma. Code 99.79 describes other apheresis, such as the isolation of stem cells for harvesting.

Coding Clarification
Code 99.78 includes:

* Plasma water removal
* Ultrafiltration (for water removal)

Code 99.78 excludes:

* Hemodiafiltration (39.95)
* Hemodialysis (39.95)
* Therapeutic plasmapheresis (99.71)

Coding Guidance
AHA: 4Q, '97, 55; 1Q, '05, 16; 1Q, '06, 12, 13; 3Q, '08, 19

99.8   Miscellaneous physical procedures

99.81   Hypothermia (central) (local)

Description
The physician lowers the temperature of part or all of a patient's body to facilitate surgery requiring the suppression of the patient's metabolism. This is accomplished by infusion of cold fluids, ice packs, or other methods.

Coding Clarification
Code 99.81 excludes:

* Gastric cooling (96.31)
* Gastric freezing (96.32)
* That incidental to open heart surgery (39.62)

99.82   Ultraviolet light therapy

Description
The physician treats disease with ultraviolet light rays of various concentrations.

99.83   Other phototherapy

Description
The physician treats disease with light rays of various concentrations.

Coding Clarification:
Code 99.83 includes phototherapy of the newborn.

Code 99.83 excludes extracorporeal photochemotherapy (99.88) and photocoagulation of retinal lesion (14.23-14.25, 14.33-14.35, 14.53-14.55).

Coding Guidance
AHA: 2Q, '89, 15

99.84   Isolation

Description
This code describes the quarantine of an individual for the protection of others due to the presence of contagious disease or for the protection of the patient due to vulnerability caused by immunocompromised states.

Coding Clarification:
Code 99.84 includes:

- Isolation after contact with infectious disease
- Protection of individual from his surroundings
- Protection of surroundings from individual
- Hyperthermia for treatment of cancer

99.85   Hyperthermia for treatment of cancer

Description
Hyperthermia (adjunct therapy) is induced by microwave, ultrasound, low energy radio frequency, probes (interstitial), or other means for the treatment of cancer. Hyperthermia uses heat in an attempt to speed cell metabolism. This is performed to increase potential cell destruction in the treatment of a malignancy by making tumors more susceptible to the therapy. The heat can be generated by a variety of sources, including microwave, ultrasound and radio frequency conduction. Hyperthermia may be externally generated, superficial (i.e., heating to a depth of 4 cm or less) or deep (i.e., heating to depths greater than 4 cm). Alternately, heat generated by interstitial probes acting like small antennae or microwave radiators placed directly into the tumor area or into a body cavity.

Coding Clarification
Code also any concurrent chemotherapy or radiation therapy.

Coding Guidance
AHA: 3Q, '89, 17 3Q, '96, 11

99.86   Non-invasive placement of bone growth stimulator

Description
The physician performs electrical stimulation of bone. The physician places electrodes over the skin surface along the region of a fracture or defect and administers a low voltage current. This is a non-surgical technique used to stimulate bone healing.

Coding Clarification
Code 99.86 includes transcutaneous (surface) placement of pads or patches for stimulation to aid bone healing.

Code 99.86 excludes insertion of invasive or semi-invasive bone growth stimulators (device) (percutaneous electrodes) (78.90-78.99).

99.88   Therapeutic photopheresis

Description
The physician draws a patient's blood and exposes the blood to light to eliminate destructive elements. The physician establishes venous access or attaches the machine to an existing central venous catheter line. The blood is removed and cycled through the pheresis machine where it is exposed to therapeutic wavelengths of light. The conditioned blood is returned to the patient through a catheter and a needle inserted in the vein.

Coding Clarification
Code 99.88 excludes:

- Other phototherapy (99.83)
- Ultraviolet light therapy (99.82)

Documentation Tip
Procedures classifiable to 99.88 may be documented as:

- Extracorporeal photochemotherapy
- Extracorporeal photopheresis

Coding Guidance
AHA: 2Q, '99, 7

99.9   Other miscellaneous procedures

Description
This subcategory classifies other miscellaneous procedures not classifiable elsewhere in category 99.

99.91   Acupuncture for anesthesia

99.92   Other acupuncture

Description
The health care provider applies acupuncture therapy by inserting one or more fine needles into the patient as dictated by acupuncture meridians for the relief of pain or anesthesia. The needles are twirled or manipulated by hand to generate therapeutic stimulation. Electrical stimulation may be employed with this procedure.

99.93   Rectal massage (for levator spasm)

Description
This procedure involves a therapeutic manual rubbing or manipulation of the muscles supporting the rectum to relieve pain, spasm or other symptoms.

99.94   Prostatic massage

Description
This procedure is a therapeutic compression or manipulation of the prostate gland to stimulate the prostate gland in order to relieve congestion of seminal fluids.

99.95   Stretching of foreskin

Description
The physician treats adhesions between the uncircumcised foreskin and the head of the penis that prevent the retraction of the foreskin. Adhesions are broken by stretching the foreskin back over the head of the penis onto the shaft or by inserting a clamp between the foreskin and the head of the penis and spreading the jaws of the clamp.

99.96   Collection of sperm for artificial insemination

Description
This procedure code describes the collection of sperm for artificial insemination. The physician may utilize an electrovibratory device to stimulate ejaculation. The electrostimulator probe is placed in the rectum and positioned adjacent to the prostate gland and a current of electricity is passed into the region of the prostate, seminal vesicles and the vas deferens. The stimulation excites the nerves of the area, causing ejaculation. The semen is collected and used for artificial insemination.

99.97   Fitting of denture

Description
This procedure involves the evaluation and adjustment of dental prosthesis to ensure adequate fit, function and aesthetics. Improperly fitting dentures may result in increased pain, wear, irritation and infection that can result in progression of periodontal disease.

99.98   Extraction of milk from lactating breast

Description
This procedure describes the manual or mechanical extraction of breast milk to prevent engorgement or to encourage the production of breast milk to assure adequate supply for a nursing infant.

99.99   Other miscellaneous procedures

Description
This procedure code reports other miscellaneous procedures not classifiable elsewhere in category 99.

In leech therapy, leeches are applied to treat a wide range of medical disorders, such as to remove blood (phlebotomize) from patients suffering from certain blood disorders, to remove devitalized tissue from a wound, or to relieve circulatory congestion. Leeches are reported to release both anesthetic and anticoagulant natural substances that facilitate healing and provide a degree of pain relief.

Coding Clarification
This code should not be assigned if the medical record contains sufficient information to facilitate coding at a higher level of specificity.

Documentation Tip
If the documentation is ambiguous or unclear, the physician should be queried.